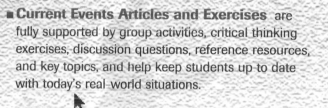

■ **Current Events Articles and Exercises** are fully supported by group activities, critical thinking exercises, discussion questions, reference resources, and key topics, and help keep students up to date with today's real-world situations.

■ **Interactive Study Guide** online self-assessments offers multiple-choice, true/false, and essay questions for every chapter. Graded by our server, these quizzes provide students with immediate feedback, including additional help and page references linked to the text. Results for these activities, as well as the online quizzes and exams, can be sent to as many as four e-mail addresses.

■ **Internet Exercises** are based on links to relevant Web sites.

■ **Syllabus Manager,** an easy-to-use program that allows faculty to create online custom syllabi hosted on Prentice Hall servers. Syllabus Manager provides instructors with an easy, step-by-step process to create and revise syllabi, with direct links into Companion Web sites and other online content. Changes you make to your syllabus are immediately available to your students at their next login. Your students need only know the Web address for the Companion Web site, and the password you've assigned to your syllabus, and they may log on to your syllabus during any study session.

For more information, please visit the on-line demo located at **www.prenhall.com/demo.**

PRINCIPLES OF MARKETING

PRINCIPLES OF MARKETING

NINTH EDITION

PHILIP KOTLER
Northwestern University

GARY ARMSTRONG
University of North Carolina

Prentice
Hall

Upper Saddle River, NJ 07458

Acquisitions Editor: Whitney Blake
Assistant Editor: Anthony Palmiotto
Managing Editor (Editorial): Bruce Kaplan
Editor-in-Chief: Jim Boyd
Marketing Manager: Shannon Moore
Managing Editor (Production): John Roberts
Permissions Coordinator: Suzanne Grappi
Production Manager: Arnold Vila
Associate Director, Manufacturing: Vincent Scelta
Design Manager: Patricia Smythe
Interior Design: Karen Quigley
Photo Research Supervisor: Elisabeth Boyd
Image Permission Supervisor: Kay Dellosa
Photo Researchers: Melinda Alexander, Teri Stratford, Diane Austin
Cover Design: Blair Brown
Cover Illustration: Salem Krieger
Composition: Carlisle Communications

Credits and acknowledgments for materials borrowed from other sources and reproduced, with
permission, in this textbook appear on page C-1.

Library of Congress Cataloging-in-Publication Data
Kotler, Philip.
   Principles of marketing / Philip Kotler, Gary Armstrong.—9th ed.
    p. cm.
   Includes bibliographical references and index.
   ISBN 0-13-026312-5 (hardcover)
   1. Marketing. I. Armstrong, Gary. II. Title.
  HF5415 .K636 2001
  658.8—dc21   00-027875

Printed in the United States of America
10 9 8 7 6 5 4 3 2
ISBN 0-13-026312-5

ABOUT THE
AUTHORS

As a team, Philip Kotler and Gary Armstrong provide a blend of skills uniquely suited to writing an introductory marketing text. Professor Kotler is one of the world's leading authorities on marketing. Professor Armstrong is an award-winning teacher of undergraduate business students. Together they make the complex world of marketing practical, approachable, and enjoyable.

PHILIP KOTLER is the S. C. Johnson & Son Distinguished Professor of International Marketing at the Kellogg Graduate School of Management, Northwestern University. He received his master's degree at the University of Chicago and his Ph.D. at M.I.T., both in economics. Dr. Kotler is author of *Marketing Management: Analysis, Planning, Implementation, and Control* (Prentice Hall), now in its tenth edition and the most widely used marketing textbook in graduate schools of business. He has authored several successful books and has written over 100 articles for leading journals. He is the only three-time winner of the coveted Alpha Kappa Psi award for the best annual article in the *Journal of Marketing*. Dr. Kotler's numerous major honors include the Paul D. Converse Award given by the American Marketing Association to honor "outstanding contributions to science in marketing" and the Stuart Henderson Britt Award as Marketer of the Year. He was named the first recipient of two major awards: the Distinguished Marketing Educator of the Year Award given by the American Marketing Association and the Philip Kotler Award for Excellence in Health Care Marketing presented by the Academy for Health Care Services Marketing. He has also received the Charles Coolidge Parlin Award which each year honors an outstanding leader in the field of marketing. In 1995, he received the Marketing Educator of the Year Award from Sales and Marketing Executives International. Dr. Kotler has served as chairman of the College on Marketing of the Institute of Management Sciences (TIMS) and a director of the American Marketing Association. He has received honorary doctorate degrees from DePaul University, the University of Zurich, and the Athens University of Economics and Business. He has consulted with many major U.S. and foreign companies on marketing strategy.

GARY ARMSTRONG is Crist W. Blackwell Distinguished Professor of Undergraduate Education in the Kenan-Flagler Business School at the University of North Carolina at Chapel Hill. He holds undergraduate and masters degrees in business from Wayne State University in Detroit, and he received his Ph.D. in marketing from Northwestern University. Dr. Armstrong has contributed numerous articles to leading business journals. As a consultant and researcher, he has worked with many companies on marketing research, sales management, and marketing strategy. But Professor Armstrong's first love is teaching. His Blackwell Distinguished Professorship is the only permanent endowed professorship for distinguished undergraduate teaching at the University of North Carolina at Chapel Hill. He has been very active in the teaching and administration of Kenan-Flagler's undergraduate program. His recent administrative posts include Chair of the Marketing Faculty, Associate Director of the Undergraduate Business Program, Director of the Business Honors Program, and others. He works closely with business student groups and has received several campus-wide and Business School teaching awards. He is the only repeat recipient of the school's highly regarded Award for Excellence in Undergraduate Teaching, which he won for the third time in 1993.

BRIEF
CONTENTS

UNDERSTANDING MARKETING AND THE MARKETING PROCESS 3

DEVELOPING MARKETING OPPORTUNITIES AND STRATEGIES 129

DEVELOPING THE MARKETING MIX 289

MANAGING MARKETING 665

CONTENTS

III DEVELOPING THE MARKETING MIX 289

Contents

Preface

This new edition is more than just words on a page.

It is an entryway.

A jumping off point.

A place to begin the journey.

Phil and Gary realized the folly of trying to lay down a staid marketing gospel. Because the changes are not finished. The revolution is still happening. They realized that what they were seeing across the globe was so exciting that they had to do more than just write about it: they had to show students, get them involved, get them to participate.

HOW DID THEY DO THIS?

Phil and Gary take you on a World Tour. A series of videos profile innovative companies and marketing campaigns from Berlin to Hong Kong. These videos work with the text to bring the new world of marketing to life. In a CD-ROM, students use their experiences with the videos to make decisions in this new marketing environment. The result — a student better prepared for new marketing challenges.

KEY CHANGES

Key changes

The authors did not solely rely on an innovative new supplements package. They re-thought and re-wrote the text from top to bottom. The most important change is, of course, the emphasis and expanded coverage of the revolutionary new marketing technologies. Not only is an entire chapter devoted to the burgeoning use of the Internet, but each chapter provides fresh new material on everything from virtual reality displays to e-commerce databases. Plus, **Internet Connections** at the end of each chapter provide exercises to reinforce the chapter's highlights.

INTERNET CONNECTIONS 45

ONLINE MARKETING

Online marketing can bring benefits to customers that other channels cannot. A good example is online music stores, where customers can listen to clips of selected tracks before buying a CD. Other online benefits are ease of communication with customers and adaptability to marketplace changes. Visit CDNow (www.cdnow.com) and look up three CDs of your choosing. For each CD, record below the total number of tracks on that CD and the number of tracks that CDNow will let you sample.

CD Title	Total Tracks	Tracks Available to Sample

Kotler & Armstrong, Principles of Marketing, 9e

At the same time, Phil and Gary keep their readers abreast of the most current thinking on customer management, assessing customer value, brand equity and value positioning. There is an even greater emphasis on using actual companies to bring concepts to life for students. Each **company case** in this new edition is new or completely revised.

Let's look at the text changes in more detail. The ninth edition of **Principles of Marketing** retains all of the elements that have made the text a worldwide leader for almost two decades, but has been thoroughly revised around the major marketing theme of the coming millennium: connectedness.

It offers **important ne**

↖ **thinking and expanded**

Connecting with customers: connecting more selectively, more directly, and for life:

- **Relationship marketing**—finding, keeping, and growing profitable customers and capturing customer lifetime value by building value-laden customer relationships.

- **Delivering superior customer value, satisfaction, and quality**—attracting, keeping, and cultivating customers by developing market-centered strategies and "taking care of the customer." Integrated chapter-by-chapter coverage accompanies a full chapter on developing customer value, satisfaction, and relationships.

The following reproduces a sample textbook page:

34   Part 3 Developing Marketing Mix

MARKETING HIGHLIGHT 17-3

PERMISSION-BASED MARKETING: CLICK HERE FOR OUR PITCH

Companies that send marketing pitches via e-mail walk a fine and dangerous line. One false move—such as sending e-mail to a customer who didn't request it—can quickly damage a company's reputation. Yet, more and more companies are now walking that fine line, and for good reason. Done right, an e-mail campaign can build profitable customer relationships at a fraction of the cost of a "d-mail" (direct-mail) campaign.

E-mail marketing offers several real benefits. The Internet gives marketers immediate access to millions of customers and prospects. Studies show that 80 percent of Internet users respond to e-mail within 36 hours, compared with a 2 percent response rate for the average direct-mail campaign. Also, compared to other forms of online promotion, e-mail is usually a hands-down winner. Consider the "click-through" rate. A click-through occurs whenever a user follows links—whether they are provided through a site's ad banners or e-mail—to a company's home page or sales site. The average click-through rate for ad banners has dropped to less than 1 percent whereas click-through rates for e-mail are running around 80 percent. Then there's cost. Paper, printing, and postage are expensive and getting more so every year. In contrast, e-mail costs almost nothing to produce and send. For example, Microsoft used to spend approximately $70 million a year on paper-driven campaigns. Now, the software giant sends out 20 million pieces of e-mail every month at a significant savings over the costs of paper-based campaigns.

There is a catch, though. In order to achieve stellar click-throughs and to get recipients to respond quickly—or even at all—marketers must follow the cardinal rule of e-mail marketing: Get the consumer's permission. In fact, Seth Godin, a pioneer of direct marketing on the Web and CEO of Yoyodyne Entertainment Inc. (recently acquired by Yahoo!), has even come up with a term—"permission-based marketing"—to define the new e-mail marketing model. According to Godin, whose company specializes in developing Web-based marketing relationships for its clients, consumers are wary of unwanted marketing pitches. Permission-based marketing provides the perfect remedy by using the interactivity of the Internet to let consumers have a say in what is sent to them. Godin compares permission-based marketing to dating; if a company conducts itself well in its first contact with consumers, it will build up trust that encourages them to open up to subsequent offers.

One company that has been successful in using permission-based e-mail marketing campaigns is Iomega Corporation, which markets computer storage devices such as the popular Zip drive. Iomega always starts its e-mail campaigns with its base of registered customers. From this select list, it mails only to those who have given Iomega permission to send them e-mail. By targeting customers who actively agree to receive e-mail, companies can increase their chances of getting a

---

🔵 **INTEGRATED DIRECT MARKETING**

Integrated direct marketing
Direct-marketing campaigns that use multiple vehicles and multiple stages to improve response rates and profits.

Too often, a company's individual direct-marketing efforts are not well integrated with one another or with other elements of its marketing and promotion mixes. For example, a firm's media advertising may be handled by the advertising department working with a traditional advertising agency. Meanwhile, its direct-mail and catalog business efforts may be handled by direct-marketing specialists while its Web site is developed and operated by an outside Internet firm.

Within a given direct-marketing campaign, too many companies use only a "one-shot" effort to reach and sell a prospect or a single vehicle in multiple stages to trigger purchases. For example, a magazine publisher might send a series of four direct-mail notices to a household to get a subscriber to renew before giving up. A more powerful approach is **integrated direct marketing**, which involves using carefully coordinated multiple-media, multiple-stage campaigns. Such campaigns

---

• **Connecting technologies**—employing the Internet and other information, computer, communications, and transportation technologies to connect directly with customers and to shape marketing offers tailored to their needs. This edition offers integrated chapter-by-chapter coverage, plus a full chapter on Direct and Online Marketing.

Connecting with the world around us

coverage on:

Connecting with marketing partners:
connecting *inside* and *outside* the company to jointly bring more value to customers:

- **The company value chain**—connecting *inside* the company to create cross-functional, customer-focused teamwork and integrated action.

- **Value-delivery networks**—connecting with partners *outside* the company to create effective supply-chains.

ONLINE MARKETING AND ELECTRONIC COMMERCE

Online marketing
Marketing conducted through interactive online computer systems, which link consumers with sellers electronically.

Commercial online services
Services that offer online information and marketing services to subscribers who pay a monthly fee, such as America Online, CompuServe, and Prodigy.

Internet
The vast and burgeoning global web of computer networks with no central management or ownership.

World Wide Web (the Web)
The user-friendly Internet access standard.

Online marketing is conducted through interactive online computer systems, which link consumers with sellers electronically. There are two types of online marketing channels: commercial online services and the Internet.

Commercial online services offer online information and marketing services to subscribers who pay a monthly fee. The best known online service provider is giant America Online, which has more than 19 million subscribers. Microsoft Network (MSN) and Prodigy trail far behind AOL with 2.48 million and 1 million subscribers, respectively.[33] These online services provide subscribers with information (news, libraries, education, travel, sports, reference), entertainment (fun and games), shopping services, dialogue opportunities (bulletin boards, forums, chat boxes), and e-mail.

After growing rapidly through the mid-1990s, the commercial online services have now been overtaken by the **Internet** as the primary online marketing channel. In fact, all of the online service firms now offer Internet access as a primary service. The Internet is a vast and burgeoning global web of computer networks. It evolved from a network created by the Defense Department during the 1960s, initially to link government labs, contractors, and military installations. Today, this huge, public computer network links computer users of all types all around the world. Anyone with a PC, a modem, and the right software can browse the Internet to obtain or share information on almost any subject and to interact with other users.[34]

Internet usage surged with the development of the user-friendly **World Wide Web** (the Web) and Web browser software such as Netscape Navigator and Microsoft Internet Explorer. Today, even novices can surf the Internet and experience fully integrated text, graphics, images, and sound. Users can send e-mail, exchange views, shop for products, and access news, food recipes, art, and business information. The Internet itself is free, although individual users usually must pay a commercial access provider to be hooked up to it.

Commercial online services: Leader America Online has more than 19 million subscribers who pay a monthly fee for its information and marketing services.

The direct-marketing industry is addressing issues of ethics and public policy. For example, the Direct Marketing Association (DMA)—the largest association for businesses interested in interactive and database marketing with more than 4,600 member companies—recently developed its "Privacy Promise to American Consumers." This initiative, an effort to build consumer confidence in shopping direct, requires that all DMA members adhere to a carefully developed set of consumer privacy rules. The Privacy Promise requires that members notify customers when any personal information is rented, sold, or exchanged with others. Members must also honor consumer requests not to receive mail, telephone, or other solicitations again.

Direct marketers know that, left unattended, such problems will lead to increasingly negative consumer attitudes, lower response rates, and calls for more restrictive state and federal legislation. More importantly, most direct marketers want the same things that consumers want: honest and well-designed marketing offers targeted only toward consumers who will appreciate and respond to them. Direct marketing is just too expensive to waste on consumers who don't want it.

The DMA recently developed its "Privacy Promise to American Consumers," which attempts to build consumer confidence by requiring that all DMA members adhere to certain carefully developed consumer privacy rules.

Connecting with the world around us:

- **Global marketing**—connecting globally with customers and marketing partners. The ninth edition offers integrated chapter-by-chapter coverage plus a full chapter focusing on global marketing considerations.

- **Marketing ethics, environmentalism, and social responsibility**—reexamining connections with social values and responsibilities. This edition offers integrated chapter-by-chapter coverage including a chapter on social responsibility and marketing ethics.

- **Broadened connections**—the increasing adoption of marketing by nonprofit and government organizations.

KEY FEATURES

Phil and Gary guide students through this New World of marketing.

DIRECT AND ONLINE MARKETING: THE NEW MARKETING MODEL

CHAPTER 17

When 19-year-old Michael Dell began selling personal computers out of his college dorm room in 1984, few would have bet on his chances for success. In those days, most computer makers sold their PCs through an extensive network of all-powerful distributors and resellers. Even as the fledgling Dell Computer Corporation began to grow, competitors and industry insiders scoffed at the concept of mail-order computer marketing. PC buyers, they contended, needed the kind of advice and hand-holding that only full-service channels could provide.

Yet young Michael Dell has proved the skeptics wrong—way wrong. In little more than a decade and a half, he has turned his dorm-room mail-order business into a burgeoning, $12 billion computer empire. Dell Computer is now the world's largest direct marketer of computer systems, the number-two PC maker, and the world's fastest-growing computer manufacturer. Over the past three years, Dell's sales have increased at an average of 53 percent per year, twice as fast as any competitor and five times the industry average. Profits have skyrocketed 89 percent per year. Since 1990, Dell's stock has risen an incredible 29,600 percent! Direct buyers now account for nearly a third of all PC sales, and Dell's

once-skeptical competitors are now scrambling to build their own direct-marketing systems.

What's the secret to Dell's stunning success? Anyone at Dell can tell you without hesitation: It's the company's radically different business model—the *Direct model*. "We have a tremendously clear business model," says Michael Dell, the 34-year-old founder. "There's no confusion about what the value proposition is, what the company offers, and why it's great for customers. That's a very simple thing, but it has tremendous power and appeal." It also garners tremendous success for the company.

Dell's direct-marketing approach delivers greater customer value through an unbeatable combination of product customization, low prices, fast delivery, and award-winning customer service. A customer can talk by phone with a Dell representative on Monday morning; order a fully customized, state-of-the-art PC to suit his or her special needs; and have the machine delivered to his or her doorstep by Wednesday—all at a price that's 10 to 15 percent below competitors' prices for a comparably performing PC. Dell backs its products with high-quality service and support. As a result, Dell consistently ranks among the industry leaders in product reliability and service,

CHAPTER-OPENING EXAMPLES

Each chapter starts with a dramatic marketing story that introduces the chapter material and arouses student interest.

CHAPTER-OPENING OBJECTIVES

Each chapter begins with learning objectives that preview the flow of concepts in the chapter.

MARKETING HIGHLIGHTS

Additional examples and important information are featured in Marketing Highlight exhibits throughout the text.

KEY TERMS

Key terms are highlighted within the text, clearly defined in the margins of the pages on which they appear, and listed at the end of each chapter.

INTERNET CONNECTION EXERCISES

Each chapter ends with a carefully designed Internet exercise that demonstrates the power of the Web as a marketing tool.

---

36   Part 3   Developing Marketing Mix

MARKETING HIGHLIGHT 17.4

AMERICAN STANDARD'S INTEGRATED DIRECT MARKETING: ANYTHING BUT STANDARD

You probably haven't thought much about your bathroom—it's not something that most of us get all that inspired about. But as it turns out, you probably have a relationship with your bathroom unlike that with any other room in your house. It's where you start and end your day, primp and preen and admire yourself, escape from the rigors of everyday life, and do some of your best thinking. The marketers at American Standard, the plumbing fixtures giant, understand this often-overlooked but special little room. A few years back they set out upon a mission to help people design bathrooms worthy of their finest moments.

Working with its ad agency, Carmichael Lynch, American Standard created a wonderfully warm and highly effective but not-so-standard integrated marketing campaign. The campaign, called "We want you to love your bathroom," targeted men and women aged 25 to 54 from households planning to remodel bathrooms or replace fixtures. The campaign employed a carefully integrated mix of brand-image and direct-response media ads, direct

mailings, and personal contacts to create a customer database, generate sales leads, gently coax customers into its retail showroom, and build sales and market share.

The campaign begins with a series of humorous, soft-sell brand-image ads in home and shelter magazines such as *Home, House Beautiful,* and *Country Living,* which reach a high percentage of readers undertaking remodeling projects. Featuring simple but artistic shots of ordinary bathroom fixtures and scenes, the ads positioned American Standard as a company that understands the special relationships we have with our bathroom. For example, one ad showed a white toilet and a partially unwound roll of toilet paper, artfully arranged in a corner against plain blue-gray walls. "We're not in this business for the glory," proclaimed the headline. "Designing a toilet or sink may not be as glamorous as, say, designing a Maserati. But to us, it's every bit as important. After all, more people will be sitting on our seats than theirs."

Another ad showed the feet of a man standing on a white tile bathroom floor wearing his goofy-looking

floppy-eared dog slippers. "The rest of the world thinks you're a genius," noted the ad. But "after a long day of being brilliant, witty, and charming, it's nice just to be comfortable. The right bathroom understands. And accepts you unconditionally." Each simple but engaging ad included a toll-free phone number and urged readers to call for a free guidebook "overflowing with products, ideas, and inspiration."

Whereas the brand-image ads positioned American Standard and its products, when it came to generating inquiries, the real workhorses were the one-third-page, couponlike direct-response ads that ran in the same magazines. One such ad noted, "You will spend seven years of your life in the bathroom. You will need a good book." Readers could obtain the free guidebook by mailing in the coupon or calling the toll-free number listed in the ad. Consumers who responded found that they'd taken the first step in a carefully orchestrated relationship-building venture. First, they received the entertaining, highly informative, picture-filled 30-page guidebook *We Want You to Love Your Bathroom,* along

creates product awareness and stimulates inquiries. The company immediately sends direct mail to those who inquire. Within a few days, the company follows up with a phone call seeking an order. Some prospects will order by phone; others might request a face-to-face sales call. In such a campaign, the marketer seeks to improve response rates and profits by adding media and stages that contribute more to additional sales than to additional costs (see Marketing Highlight 17.4).

PUBLIC POLICY AND ETHICAL ISSUES IN DIRECT MARKETING

Direct marketers and their customers usually enjoy mutually rewarding relationships. Occasionally, however, a darker side emerges. The aggressive and sometimes

CHAPTER-ENDING SUMMARIES

At the end of each chapter, summaries are provided for each chapter objective to reinforce main points and concepts.

CONNECTING WITH THE CONCEPTS DISCUSSION AND APPLICATIONS QUESTIONS

Each chapter contains a set of discussion questions and application exercises covering major chapter concepts.

COMPANY CASES

Company Cases for class or written discussion are provided at the end of each chapter, with integrative comprehensive cases following each major part of the text. These cases challenge students to apply marketing principles to companies in real situations.

VIDEO CASES

A full selection of written video cases accompanies the ninth edition, supported by exciting and original videos developed for Principles of Marketing. The videos and cases help to bring key marketing concepts and issues to life in the classroom.

APPENDIXES

Three appendixes, "Measuring and Forecasting Demand," "Marketing Arithmetic," and "Careers in Marketing," provide additional, practical information for students.

GLOSSARY

At the end of the book, an extensive glossary provides quick reference to the key terms found in the book.

INDEXES

Subject, company, and author indexes reference all information and examples in the book.

"Your Companions in this
New World of Market

A hallmark of this edition is the World Marketing Tour videos and accompanying
Phil and Gary are your guides from Berlin to Hong Kong and from London to Los A

CELEBRITY MARKETING
LOS ANGELES

PRODUCTS & SERVICES
YMCA INTERNATIONAL IN LONDON

PLACEMENT
ERICSSON IN STOCKHOLM

CONSUMER BEHAVIOR
WARNER BROTHERS IN HONG KONG

NOT-FOR PROFIT MARKETING
YMCA INTERNATIONAL IN HONG KONG

STRATEGY & PLANNING
GERMAN GOVERNMENT IN BERLIN

INTERNET MARKETING
BLAIR WITCH PROJECT IN LOS ANGELES

THE MARKETING ENVIRONMENT
UNITED STATES MILITARY ACADEMY IN WEST POINT, NY

The Kotler and Armstrong World Tour CD-ROM extends the video cases and brings students into the New World of marketing. Students make decisions based on marketing challenges around the globe. Extensive questions and feedback mechanisms test student mastery of key concepts. Additional study guides help students review material.

Prentice Hall

Kotler & Armstrong,
Principles of Marketing, 9e

PASSPORT

United States
of America

DON'T LEAVE HOME WITHOUT THESE

A successful marketing course requires more than a well–written book. Connecting in today's classroom requires a dedicated teacher and a fully-integrated teaching system.

Principles of Marketing, Ninth edition, is supported by an extensive teaching package:

INSTRUCTORS' MANUAL

Contains chapter objectives, chapter overviews, and complete teaching outlines, lecture notes for each chapter. Outlines incorporate key terms, figures, and PowerPoint slides. The manual also includes answers to all end-of-chapter questions and comments on the company and comprehensive cases.

TEST ITEM FILE

Comprised of over 2000 questions (100 per chapter) in a variety of formats, including multiple choice, true/false, and essay. Questions are rated by difficulty and linked by page reference to the text. The Test Item File is also produced in an electronic format. (Prentice Hall Custom Test)

COLOR TRANSPARENCIES

Available as acetates or PowerPoint slides. Includes key terms, important figures, and chapter concepts. Improvements: use of company examples provides jumping-off points for class discussion; slides are geared towards helping students learn; more slides per chapter.

INSTRUCTOR RESOURCE CD-ROM:

This all-in-one multimedia product is an invaluable asset for professors who prefer to work with electronic

files rather than traditional print supplements. This single CD-ROM contains the Instructor's Manual, the complete set of PowerPoint slides, the Test Item File, and the Prentice Hall Test Manager program.

ADVERTISING TRANSPARENCIES

A collection of over 70 color transparencies featuring advertisements that illustrate various marketing concepts. Also includes an expanded table of contents, which points out the marketing terms or ideas exhibited in each advertisement.

FACULTY ACTIVITIES AND CLASSROOM TEACHING STRATEGIES (F.A.C.T.S.) GUIDE

Created to help instructors energize students and promote discussion through projects, ideas, and Internet experiences, this supplement makes use of active learning practices to make time in the classroom interesting and memorable for students. Includes, for each textbook chapter, a section titled "Barriers to Effective Learning," which alerts the instructor to potential learning obstacles and difficult lessons.

THE INTERNET: A NEW MARKETING TOOL 2001

A practical and updated guide to marketing on the Internet, providing both an application of the marketing principles explained in the textbook and a look at some companies that use them. Authors Raymond Frost and Judy Strauss developed pedagogy that requires students to search for answers and observe marketing methods of on-line companies.

MARKETING PLAN PRO

(available for $10 with every student textbook) This new software is totally interactive, featuring ten sample marketing plans, excellent help, customizable charts and professional-looking color print-outs. The plan wizards enable you to easily customize your marketing plan to fit your marketing needs. You then follow the clearly outlined steps - define, plan, budget, forecast, track and measure - to progress from strategy to implementation. Click to print, and your text, spreadsheet and charts come together to create a powerful marketing plan.

myPHLIP

PRENTICE HALL *(Learning on the Internet Partnership)*

Welcome to myPHLIP—
your personal guide to the free online resources
for your book!

Featuring one click access to all of the new
resources created by our award-winning team of
educators, myPHLIP provides a **personalized
view** of the great new resources available:

 myPHLIP pages—your personal access
page unites all your myPHLIP texts.

 Notes—add personal notes to our resources
for personal reminders and references.

 Messages—instructors can send messages to
individual students, or all students linked to
your course.

 Student Resources—add premium PHLIP
resources for your students to view and
download (such as our PowerPoints™, videos,
and spreadsheets).

 Business Headlines—provides links to
articles in today's business news!

Search—search all PHLIP resources for
relevant articles and exercises.

Instructor's Manual—myPHLIP Instructor
Manual provides tips and suggestions from our
PHLIP faculty for integrating PHLIP resources
into your course.

Combined with the resources you have trusted
throughout the years to provide you with the best
business resources available:

In the News—New current events articles are
added throughout the year. Each article is
summarized by our teams of expert professors, and fully supported by exercises,
activities, and instructor materials.

On-Line Study Guide—Results from the
automatically graded questions for every
chapter provide immediate feedback for students that can be e-mailed to the instructor.

Research Area—Your own personal resource
library includes tutorials, descriptive links
to virtual libraries, and a wealth of search
engines and resources.

Internet Resources—Links to discipline-
specific sites, including preview information
that allows you to review site information
before you view the site, ensuring you visit
the best available business resources found
by our learning community.

FOR THE PROFESSOR

- **Teaching Resources** include resources
  contributed by professors throughout the
  world, including teaching tips, techniques,
  academic papers, and sample syllabi

- **Talk to the Team**, a moderated faculty
  chat room.

- **On-line faculty support**

FOR THE STUDENT

- **Talk to the Tutor**, virtual office hours that
  allow students to post questions from any
  supported discipline and receive responses
  from the dedicated PHLIP/CW
  faculty team.

- **Writing Resource Center**, an on-line
  writing center that provides links to on-line
  directories, thesauruses, writing tutors, style
  and grammar guides, and additional tools.

- **Career Center**, helps access career
  information, view sample resumes, even apply
  for jobs on-line.

- **Study Tips**, an area for students to learn
  to develop better study skills.

WEB*CT*

Now you have the freedom to personalize your own on-line course materials! Prentice Hall Business Publishing provides the content and support you need to create and manage your own on-line course materials in WebCT. With quality materials and the best support package available, we make it easy for you to use WebCT's course management tools.

WebCT is a Course Management System with robust course management tools, includes page tracking, progress tracking, class and student management, grade book, communication, calendar, reporting tools, and more.

The Principles of Marketing, 9e Online Course provides:

Customizable Content:
Use Prentice Hall materials created by professors for professors and their students. Our development team:
- checks course material and tests for accuracy;
- clears permissions for content and images;
- edits material for consistency with the supported title.

Some examples of content created for each course include:
- **Lecture Notes** containing additional exercises, discussion questions, lecture notes, and graphics created to reinforce concepts in the book.

Instructional Design:
- **Readiness Assessment Quizzes** allow students to pre-test their understanding of chapter material.
- **Discussion Questions** are built into the lectures to encourage interpersonal relationships by asking students to discuss questions in the conference or chat rooms.

- **In-Line Exercises**, built into the lecture materials, serve as pedagogical speedbumps, requiring students to stop and make sure they understand the material.

- **Tests and Quizzes** created for each chapter give instructors hundreds of questions to select and customize for every chapter.

Support:
Prentice Hall Business Publishing provides the best support package available for a WebCT course.

- Business Publishing print instructor manual
- course-specific on-line instructor manual
- course-specific on-line student manual
- Gold Level Technical Support hotline
- Technology Enhanced Teaching course created by our WebCT team of professors and instructional designers, this course provides a background of instructional design and teaching tips for teaching an online course

Solutions

BLACKBOARD

Easy to use. Blackboard's simple templates and tools make it easy to create, manage, and use online course materials

Course Management Tools

Include progress tracking, class and student management, grade book, communication, assignments, and reporting tools.

Communication Tools

Blackboard offers Communication Tools such as the Virtual Classroom (chat rooms, whiteboard, slides), document sharing, and bulletin boards.

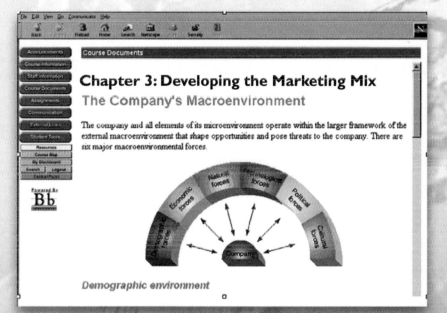

Testing

Testing programs include the ability for the Instructor create on-line quizzes and tests, and automatically grade and track results.

Design Tools

Blackboard's design tools and pre-set designs help you customize your course.

Content

Prentice Hall content is available for each course, including additional course material, exercises, and tests.

Service

- Online Instructor and Student Manuals
- Downloadable Instructor and Student Manuals
- Online Tutorials
- CD Tutorials
- On-site Training

ACKNOWLEDGMENTS

No book is the work only of its authors. We owe much to the pioneers of marketing who first identified its major issues and developed its concepts and techniques. Our thanks also go to our colleagues at the J. L. Kellogg Graduate School of Management, Northwestern University, and at the Kenan–Flagler Business School, University of North Carolina at Chapel Hill, for ideas and suggestions. We owe special thanks to Lew Brown and Martha McEnally, both of the University of North Carolina, Greensboro, for their valuable work in preparing high-quality company cases and video cases. Other portions of the supplements package were prepared by John R. Brooks Jr., Houston Baptist University; Kellye Brooks, Houston Baptist University; Judy Strauss, University of Nevada–Reno; Raymond Frost, Ohio University; R. Nicholas Gerlich, West Texas A&M University; Thomas Paczkowski, Cayuga Community College; and Christina Sergott, University of Nevada–Reno. Finally, we thank Eva Chang for her insights concerning figures and illustrations and Betsey Christian for her able editing assistance.

Many reviewers at other colleges provided valuable comments and suggestions. We are indebted to the following colleagues:

Sang T. Choe	University of Southern Indiana
Mark Alpert	University of Texas at Austin
Patricia M. Manninen	North Shore Community College
Martin Meyers	University of Wisconsin–Stevens Point
Andrew Yap	Florida International University
Irvin A. Zaenglein	Northern Michigan University

We would like to thank the many colleagues who reviewed previous editions of this book:

Martin St. John	Westmoreland County Community College
Preyas Desai	Purdue University
Carl Obermiller	Seattle University
Richard Leventhal	Metropolitan State College–Denver
Allan L. Appell	San Francisco State University
John Stovall	University of Illinois–Chicago
Jeff Streiter	SUNY Brockport
H. Lee Meadow	Northern Illinois University
Alan T. Shao	University of North Carolina–Charlotte
David M. Nemi	Niagra County Community College
J. Ford Laumer, Jr.	Auburn University
Donna Tillman	California State Polytechnic University

In this Internet environment on college campuses, we have benefited enormously from student comments and suggestions sent to us through the book's PHLIP Web site. Some of these students identified themselves, and some did not. To all of them, we owe a debt of gratitude.

We also owe a great deal to the people at Prentice Hall who helped develop this book. Bruce Kaplan, Managing Editor, provided gentle encouragement, insightful feedback, and constant support. Marketing Editor Whitney Blake ably managed the many facets of this complex revision project. We also owe much thanks to Managing Editor John Roberts, who helped shepherd the project smoothly through production. Additional thanks go to Marketing Manager Shannon Moore, Assistant Editor Anthony

Palmiotto, Design Manager Pat Smythe, Media Project Manager Cindy Harford, and Production Manager Arnold Vila.

Finally, we owe many thanks to our families—Kathy, KC, and Mandy Armstrong, and Nancy, Amy, Melissa, and Jessica Kotler—for their constant support and encouragement. To them, we dedicate this book.

Philip Kotler
Gary Armstrong

After studying this chapter, you should be able to
1. define what marketing is and discuss its core concepts
2. explain the relationships between customer value, satisfaction, and quality
3. define marketing management and understand how marketers manage demand and build profitable customer relationships
4. compare the five marketing management philosophies
5. analyze the major challenges facing marketers heading into the new millennium

MARKETING IN A CHANGING WORLD: CREATING CUSTOMER VALUE AND SATISFACTION

The "swoosh"—it's everywhere! Just for fun, try counting the swooshes whenever you pick up the sports pages or watch a pickup basketball game or tune into a televised golf match. Nike has built the ubiquitous swoosh (which represents the wing of Nike, the Greek goddess of victory) into one of the best-known brand symbols on the planet.

The power of its brand and logo speaks loudly of Nike's superb marketing skills. The company's strategy of building superior products around popular athletes and its classic "Just do it!" ad campaign have forever changed the face of sports marketing. Nike spends hundreds of millions of dollars each year on big-name endorsements, splashy promotional events, and lots of attention-getting ads. Over the years, Nike has associated itself with some of the biggest names in sports. No matter what your sport, chances are good that one of your favorite athletes wears the Nike swoosh.

Nike knows, however, that good marketing is more than promotional hype and promises—it means consistently delivering real value to customers. Nike's initial success resulted from the technical superiority of its running and basketball shoes, pitched to serious athletes who were frustrated by the lack of innovation in athletic equipment. To this day, Nike leads the industry in product development and innovation.

Nike gives its customers more than just good athletic gear. As the company notes on its Web page (www.nike.com), "Nike has always known the truth—it's not so much the shoes but where they take you." Beyond shoes, apparel, and equipment, Nike markets a way of life, a sports culture, a "just do it" attitude. Phil Knight, Nike's founder and chief executive, says, "Basically, our culture and our style is to be a rebel." The company was built on a genuine passion for sports, a maverick disregard for convention, hard work, and serious sports performance. Ask anyone at Nike and that person will tell you: Nike is athletes, athletes are sports, *Nike is sports*.

Nike seems to care as much about its customers' lives as their bodies. It doesn't just promote sales, it promotes *sports* for the benefit of all. For example, a recent series of "Nike: Just do it" ads provided strong support to women's sports and the many benefits of sports participation for girls and young women. Nike also invests in a wide range of lesser known sports, even though they provide less lucrative marketing opportunities. Such actions establish Nike as not just a producer of good athletic gear but also as a good and caring company.

Taking care of customers has paid off handsomely for Nike. Over the decade ending in 1997,

Nike's revenues grew at an incredible annual rate of 21 percent; annual return to investors averaged 47 percent. Nike flat-out dominates the world's athletic footwear market. It currently captures an eye-popping 47 percent share of the U.S. market—twice that of its nearest competitor, Reebok—and a 27 percent share internationally. Nike moved aggressively into new product categories, sports, and regions of the world. In only a few years, Nike's sports apparel business grew explosively to account for nearly a quarter of Nike's $9.5 billion in yearly sales. And Nike slapped its familiar swoosh logo on everything from sunglasses and soccer balls to batting gloves and hockey sticks. It invaded a dozen new sports, including baseball, golf, ice and street hockey, in-line skating, wall climbing, and hiking.

In 1998, however, Nike stumbled and its sales slipped. Many factors contributed to the company's sales woes. The "brown shoe" craze for hiking and outdoor styles such as Timberland's ate into the athletic sneaker business. Competition improved: A revitalized Adidas saw its U.S. sales surge as Nike's sales declined. To make matters worse, college students on many campuses protested against Nike for its alleged exploitation of child labor in Asia and its commercialization of sports.

But Nike's biggest obstacle may be its own incredible success—it may have overswooshed America. The brand now appears to be suffering from big-brand backlash, and the swoosh is becoming too common to be cool. According to one analyst, "When Tiger Woods made his debut in Nike gear, there were so many logos on him that he looked as if he'd got caught in an embroidering machine." A Nike executive admits, "There has been a little bit of backlash about the number of swooshes that are out there." Moreover, with sales of more than $9 billion, Nike has moved from maverick to mainstream. Today, rooting for Nike is like rooting for Microsoft.

To address these problems, Nike returned to the basics—focusing on innovation, developing new product lines, creating subbrands (such as the Michael Jordan line with its "jumping man" logo), and deemphasizing the swoosh. For example, recent advertising focuses once again on product performance and concludes with the Nike script logo name—not a swoosh in sight. The sports giant is also trimming its costs, including substantial cuts in its formerly lavish advertising budget. These moves appear to be working, and Nike's profits and stock price are once again on the rise.

Nike is also entering new markets aggressively, especially overseas markets. Nike sales outside the United States now represent about 38 percent of total sales. However, to dominate globally as it does in the United States, Nike must dominate in soccer, the world's most popular sport. The multibillion-dollar world soccer market currently accounts for only 3 percent of its sales. Now, soccer is Nike's top priority. In typical fashion, Nike has set World Cup 2002 as its deadline for becoming the world's number-one supplier of soccer footwear, apparel, and equipment.

Elbowing its way to the top by 2002 won't be easy. World soccer has long been dominated by Adidas, which claims an 80 percent global market share in soccer gear. Nike will have to build in just a few years what Adidas has built over the past 50. Employing classic in-your-face marketing tactics, Nike is spending hundreds of millions of dollars in an all-out assault on competitors. Nike's open-wallet spending has dazzled the soccer world, and its vast resources are rapidly changing the economics of the game. For example, it paid a record-setting $200 million over 10 years to snatch sponsorship of the World Cup champion Brazil national team from Umbro. Similarly, it paid $130 million for sponsorship of the U.S. soccer team.

Competitors can hope that Nike's slump will continue, but few are counting on it. Most can only sit back and marvel at Nike's marketing prowess. One market analyst comments, "Nike remains one of the great American brands, as well known around the world as Coke or McDonald's." Says Fila's advertising vice president, "They are so formidable, no matter how well we may execute something, our voice will never be as loud as theirs." As for soccer, the president of Puma North America sees Nike's tactics as heavy-handed but has little doubt that Nike's superb marketing will prevail. He states flatly, "Nike will control the soccer world."

Still, winning in worldwide soccer, or in anything else Nike does, will take more than just writing fat checks. To stay on top, Nike will have to deliver worldwide the same kind of quality, innovation, and value that built the brand so powerfully in the United States. It will have to earn respect on a country-by-country basis and become a part of the cultural fabric of each new market. No longer the rebellious, anti-establishment upstart, huge Nike must continually reassess its relationships with customers. Says Knight, "Now that we've [grown so large], there's a fine line between being a rebel and being a bully. [To our customers,] we have to be beautiful as well as big."[1]

Today's successful companies at all levels have one thing in common: Like Nike they are strongly customer focused and heavily committed to marketing. These companies share an absolute dedication to understanding and satisfying the needs of customers in well-defined target markets. They motivate everyone in the organization to produce superior value for their customers, leading to high levels of customer satisfaction. As Bernie Marcus of Home Depot asserts, "All of our people understand what the Holy Grail is. It's not the bottom line. It's an almost blind, passionate commitment to taking care of customers."

WHAT IS MARKETING?

Marketing, more than any other business function, deals with customers. Understanding, creating, communicating, and delivering customer value and satisfaction are at the very heart of modern marketing thinking and practice. Although we will explore more detailed definitions of marketing later in this chapter, perhaps the simplest definition is this one: *Marketing is the delivery of customer satisfaction at a profit.* The twofold goal of marketing is to attract new customers by promising superior value and to keep current customers by delivering satisfaction.

Wal-Mart has become the world's largest retailer by delivering on its promise, "Always low prices—always." FedEx dominates the U.S. small-package freight industry by consistently making good on its promise of fast, reliable small-package delivery. Ritz-Carlton promises and delivers truly "memorable experiences" for its hotel guests. Coca-Cola, long the world's leading soft drink, delivers on the simple but enduring promise, "Always Coca-Cola"—always thirst-quenching, always good with food, always cool, always a part of your life. These and other highly successful companies know that if they take care of their customers, market share and profits will follow.

Sound marketing is critical to the success of every organization—large or small, for-profit or not-for-profit, domestic or global. Large for-profit firms such as Microsoft, Sony, FedEx, Wal-Mart, IBM, and Marriott use marketing. But so do not-for-profit organizations such as colleges, hospitals, museums, symphony orchestras, and even churches. Moreover, marketing is practiced not only in the United States but also in the rest of the world. Most countries in North and South America, Western Europe, and Asia have well-developed marketing systems. Even in Eastern Europe and other parts of the world where marketing has long had a bad name, dramatic political and social changes have created new opportunities for marketing. Business and government leaders in most of these nations are eager to learn everything they can about modern marketing practices.

You already know a lot about marketing—it's all around you. You see the results of marketing in the abundance of products in your nearby shopping mall. You see marketing in the advertisements that fill your TV, spice up your magazines, stuff your mailbox, or enliven your Internet pages. At home, at school, where you work, and where you play, you are exposed to marketing in almost everything you do. Yet, there is much more to marketing than meets the consumer's casual eye. Behind it all is a massive network of people and activities competing for your attention and purchasing dollars.

This book will give you a more complete and formal introduction to the basic concepts and practices of today's marketing. In this chapter, we begin by defining marketing and its core concepts, describing the major philosophies of marketing thinking and practice, and discussing some of the major new challenges that marketers face as we whirl into the new millennium.

Marketing Defined

What does the term *marketing* mean? Many people think of marketing only as selling and advertising. It is no wonder—every day we are bombarded with television commercials, newspaper ads, direct-mail campaigns, Internet pitches, and sales calls. However, selling and advertising are only the tip of the marketing iceberg. Although they are important, they are only two of many marketing functions and are often not the most important ones.

Today, marketing must be understood not in the old sense of making a sale—"telling and selling"—but in the new sense of *satisfying customer needs.* Selling occurs only after a product is produced. By contrast, marketing starts long before a company has a product. Marketing is the homework that managers undertake to assess needs, measure their extent and intensity, and determine whether a profitable opportunity exists. Marketing continues throughout the product's life, trying to find new customers and keep current customers by improving product appeal and performance, learning from product sales results, and managing repeat performance. If the marketer does a good job of understanding consumer needs, develops products that provide superior value, and prices, distributes, and promotes them effectively, these products will sell very easily. Thus, selling and advertising are only part of a larger "marketing mix"—a set of marketing tools that work together to affect the marketplace.

Marketing
A social and managerial process whereby individuals and groups obtain what they need and want through creating and exchanging products and value with others.

We define **marketing** as a social and managerial process whereby individuals and groups obtain what they need and want through creating and exchanging products and value with others.[2] To explain this definition, we will examine the following important terms: *needs, wants,* and *demands; products* and *services; value, satisfaction,* and *quality; exchange, transactions,* and *relationships;* and *markets.* Figure 1.1 shows that these core marketing concepts are linked, with each concept building on the one before it.

Needs, Wants, and Demands

Need
A state of felt deprivation.

The most basic concept underlying marketing is that of human needs. Human **needs** are states of felt deprivation. They include basic *physical* needs for food, cloth-

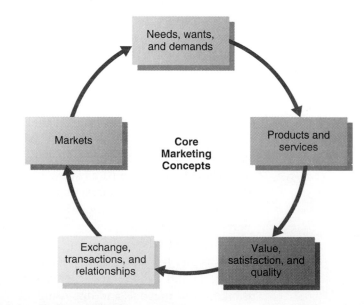

FIGURE I.I Core marketing concepts

ing, warmth, and safety; *social* needs for belonging and affection; and *individual* needs for knowledge and self-expression. These needs were not invented by marketers; they are a basic part of the human makeup.

Want
The form taken by a human need as shaped by culture and individual personality.

Wants are the form human needs take as they are shaped by culture and individual personality. An American *needs* food but *wants* a hamburger, French fries, and a soft drink. A person in Mauritius *needs* food but *wants* a mango, rice, lentils, and beans. Wants are shaped by one's society and are described in terms of objects that will satisfy needs.

People have almost unlimited wants but limited resources. Thus, they want to choose products that provide the most value and satisfaction for their money. When backed by buying power, wants become **demands.** Consumers view products as bundles of benefits and choose products that give them the best bundle for their money. A Honda Civic means basic transportation, affordable price, and fuel economy; a Lexus means comfort, luxury, and status. Given their wants and resources, people demand products with the benefits that add up to the most satisfaction.

Demands
Human wants that are backed by buying power.

Outstanding marketing companies go to great lengths to learn about and understand their customers' needs, wants, and demands. They conduct consumer research about consumer likes and dislikes. They analyze customer inquiry, warranty, and service data. They observe customers using their own and competing products and train salespeople to be on the lookout for unfulfilled customer needs.

In these outstanding companies, people at all levels—including top management—stay close to customers. For example, top executives from Wal-Mart spend two days each week visiting stores and mingling with customers. At Disney World, at least once in his or her career, each manager spends a day touring the park in a Mickey, Minnie, Goofy, or other character costume. Moreover, all Disney World managers spend a week each year on the front line—taking tickets, selling popcorn, or loading and unloading rides. At AT&T, CEO C. Michael Armstrong often visits one of the company's customer service centers, dons a headset, and fields orders to get a better sense of the problems and frustrations that AT&T business customers face.[3] At Marriott, to stay in touch with customers, Chairman of the Board and President Bill Marriott personally reads some 10 percent of the 8,000 letters and 2 percent of the 750,000 guest comment cards submitted by customers each year. Understanding customer needs, wants, and demands in detail provides important input for designing marketing strategies (see Marketing Highlight 1.1).

Products and Services

Product
Anything that can be offered to a market for attention, acquisition, use, or consumption that might satisfy a want or need. It includes physical objects, services, persons, places, organizations, and ideas.

People satisfy their needs and wants with products and services. A **product** is anything that can be offered to a market to satisfy a need or want. The concept of *product* is not limited to physical objects—anything capable of satisfying a need can be called a product. In addition to tangible goods, products include **services,** which are activities or benefits offered for sale that are essentially intangible and do not result in the ownership of anything. Examples include banking, airline, hotel, tax preparation, and home repair services.

Service
Any activity or benefit that one party can offer to another that is essentially intangible and does not result in the ownership of anything.

More broadly defined, products also include other entities such as *experiences, persons, places, organizations, information,* and *ideas.* For example, by orchestrating several services and goods, companies can create, stage, and market experiences. Disneyland is an experience; so is a visit to Nikeworld or Barnes & Noble. In fact, as products and services increasingly become commodities, experiences have emerged for many firms as the next step in differentiating the company's offer. In recent years, for example, a rash of theme stores and restaurants have burst onto the scene offering much more than just merchandise or food:

MARKETING HIGHLIGHT 1.1

NO ONE KNOWS BETTER THAN MOM, RIGHT?

No one knows better than Mom, right? But does she know how much underwear you own? Jockey International does. Or the number of ice cubes you put in a glass? Coca-Cola knows that one. Or how about which pretzels you usually eat first, the broken ones or the whole ones? Try asking Frito-Lay. Big companies know the whats, wheres, hows, and whens of their consumers' needs, wants, and demands. They figure out all sorts of things about us that we don't even know ourselves. To marketers, this isn't trivial pursuit—knowing all about customer needs is the cornerstone of effective marketing. Most companies research us in detail and amass mountains of facts.

Coke knows that we put 3.2 ice cubes in a glass, see 69 of its commercials every year, and prefer cans to pop out of vending machines at a temperature of 35 degrees. One million of us drink Coke with breakfast every day. Each new day brings piles of fresh research reports detailing our buying habits and preferences. Did you know that 38 percent of Americans would rather have a tooth pulled than take their car to a dealership for repairs? We each spend $20 a year on flowers; Arkansas has the lowest consumption of peanut butter in the United States; 51 percent of all males put their left pants leg on first, whereas 65 percent of women start with the right leg; and if you send a husband and a wife to the store separately to buy beer, there is a 90 percent chance they will return with different brands.

Nothing about our behavior is sacred. Procter & Gamble once conducted a study to find out whether most of us fold or crumple our toilet paper; another study showed that 68 percent of consumers prefer their toilet

★ Stores such as Niketown, Cabella's, and Recreational Equipment Incorporated draw consumers in by offering fun activities, fascinating displays, and promotional events (sometimes labeled "shoppertainment" or "entertailing"). At theme restaurants such as the Hard Rock Cafe, Planet Hollywood, or the House of Blues, the food is just a prop for what's known as "eatertainment." [One] entrepreneur in Israel has entered the experience economy with the opening of Cafe Ke'ilu, which roughly translates as "Cafe Make Believe." Manager Nir Caspi told a reporter that people come to cafes to be seen and to meet people, not for the food; Cafe Ke'ilu pursues that observation to its logical conclusion. The establishment serves its customers empty plates and mugs and charges guests $3 during the week and $6 on weekends for the social experience.[4]

Thus, the term *product* includes much more than just physical goods or services. Consumers decide which events to experience, which entertainers to watch on television, which places to visit on vacation, which organizations to support through contributions, and which ideas to adopt. To the consumer, these are all products. If at times the term *product* does not seem to fit, we could substitute other terms such as *satisfier, resource,* or *marketing offer.*

Many sellers make the mistake of paying more attention to the specific products they offer than to the benefits produced by these products. They see themselves as selling a product rather than providing a solution to a need. A manufacturer of drill bits may think that the customer needs a drill bit, but what the customer *really* needs is a hole. These sellers may suffer from "marketing myopia"—they are so taken with their products that they focus only on existing wants and lose sight of underlying customer needs.[5] They forget that a product is only a tool to solve a consumer problem. These sellers will have trouble if a new product comes along that serves the customer's need better or less expensively. The customer with the same *need* will *want* the new product.

paper to unwind over the spool rather than under. Abbott Laboratories figured out that one in four of us has "problem" dandruff, and Kimberly-Clark, which makes Kleenex, has calculated that the average person blows his or her nose 256 times a year.

It's not that Americans are all that easy to figure out. A few years ago, Campbell Soup gave up trying to learn our opinions about the ideal-size meatball after a series of tests showed that we prefer one so big it wouldn't fit in the can.

Hoover hooked up timers and other equipment to vacuum cleaners in people's homes and learned that we spend about 35 minutes each week vacuuming, sucking up about 8 pounds of dust each year and using 6 bags to do so. Banks know that we write about 24 checks a month, and pharmaceutical companies know that all of us together take 52 million aspirins and 30 million sleeping pills a year. In fact, almost everything we swallow is closely monitored by someone. Each year, we consume 156 hamburgers, 95 hot dogs, 283 eggs, 5 pounds of yogurt, 9 pounds of cereal, 2 pounds of peanut butter, and 46 quarts of popcorn. We spend 90 minutes a day preparing our food and 40 minutes a day munching it. As a nation, we down $650 million of antacid a year to help digest the food we eat.

Of all businesses, however, the prize for research thoroughness may go to toothpaste makers. Among other things, they know that our favorite toothbrush color is blue and that only 37 percent of us are using one that's more than six months old. About 47 percent of us put water on our brush before we apply the paste, 15 percent put water on after the paste, 24 percent do both, and 14 percent don't wet the brush at all.

Thus, most big marketing companies have answers to all the what, where, when, and how questions about their consumer demand. Seemingly trivial facts add up quickly and provide important input for designing marketing strategies. But to influence demand, marketers need the answer to one more question: Beyond knowing the whats and wherefores of demand, they need to know the *whys*—what *causes* us to want the things we buy? That's a much harder question to answer.

Sources: John Koten, "You Aren't Paranoid If You Feel Someone Eyes You Constantly," *Wall Street Journal*, March 29, 1985, pp. 1, 22; and "Offbeat Marketing," *Sales & Marketing Management*, January 1990, p. 35.

Value, Satisfaction, and Quality

Consumers usually face a broad array of products and services that might satisfy a given need. How do they choose among these many products and services? Consumers make buying choices based on their perceptions of the value that various products and services deliver.

Customer value

The difference between the values the customer gains from owning and using a product and the costs of obtaining the product.

Customer value is the difference between the values the customer gains from owning and using a product and the costs of obtaining the product. For example, FedEx customers gain a number of benefits. The most obvious are fast and reliable package delivery. However, when using FedEx, customers also may receive some status and image values. Using FedEx usually makes both the package sender and the receiver feel more important. When deciding whether to send a package via FedEx, customers will weigh these and other values against the money, effort, and psychic costs of using the service. Moreover, they will compare the value of using FedEx against the value of using other shippers—UPS, Airborne, the U.S. Postal Service—and select the one that gives them the greatest delivered value.

Customers often do not judge product values and costs accurately or objectively. They act on *perceived* value. For example, does FedEx really provide faster, more reliable delivery? If so, is this better service worth the higher prices FedEx charges? The U.S. Postal Service argues that its express service is comparable, and its prices are much lower. However, judging by market share, most consumers perceive otherwise. FedEx dominates with more than a 45 percent share of the U.S. express-delivery market, compared with the U.S. Postal Service's 8 percent. The Postal Service's challenge is to change these customer value perceptions.[6]

Customer satisfaction

The extent to which a product's perceived performance matches a buyer's expectations. If the product's performance falls short of expectations, the buyer is dissatisfied. If performance matches or exceeds expectations, the buyer is satisfied or delighted.

Customer satisfaction depends on a product's perceived performance in delivering value relative to a buyer's expectations. If the product's performance falls

Products do not have to be physical objects. Here the product is an idea: Smoking bothers others.

short of the customer's expectations, the buyer is dissatisfied. If performance matches expectations, the buyer is satisfied. If performance exceeds expectations, the buyer is delighted. Outstanding marketing companies go out of their way to keep their customers satisfied. Satisfied customers make repeat purchases, and they tell others about their good experiences with the product. The key is to match customer expectations with company performance. Smart companies aim to *delight* customers by promising only what they can deliver, then delivering *more* than they promise.[7]

Customer satisfaction is closely linked to quality. In recent years, many companies have adopted **total quality management (TQM)** programs, designed to constantly improve the quality of their products, services, and marketing processes. Quality has a direct impact on product performance and hence on customer satisfaction.

In the narrowest sense, quality can be defined as "freedom from defects." But most customer-centered companies go beyond this narrow definition of quality. Instead, they define quality in terms of customer satisfaction. For example, the vice president of quality at Motorola, a company that pioneered total quality efforts in

Total quality management (TQM)

Programs designed to constantly improve the quality of products, services, and marketing processes.

the United States, says that "Quality has to do something for the customer. . . . Our definition of a defect is 'if the customer doesn't like it, it's a defect.' "[8] Similarly, the American Society for Quality Control defines *quality* as the totality of features and characteristics of a product or service that bear on its ability to *satisfy customer needs.* These customer-focused definitions suggest that a company has achieved total quality only when its products or services meet or exceed customer expectations. Thus, the fundamental aim of today's *total quality* movement has become *total customer satisfaction.* Quality begins with customer needs and ends with customer satisfaction. We will examine customer satisfaction, value, and quality more fully in chapter 18.

Exchange, Transactions, and Relationships

Marketing occurs when people decide to satisfy needs and wants through exchange. **Exchange** is the act of obtaining a desired object from someone by offering something in return. Exchange is only one of many ways that people can obtain a desired object. For example, hungry people could find food by hunting, fishing, or gathering fruit. They could beg for food or take food from someone else. Or they could offer money, another good, or a service in return for food.

Exchange
The act of obtaining a desired object from someone by offering something in return.

As a means of satisfying needs, exchange has much in its favor. People do not have to prey on others or depend on donations, nor must they possess the skills to produce every necessity for themselves. They can concentrate on making things that they are good at making and trade them for needed items made by others. Thus, exchange allows a society to produce much more than it would with any alternative system.

Whereas exchange is the core concept of marketing, a transaction, in turn, is marketing's unit of measurement. A **transaction** consists of a trade of values between two parties: One party gives X to another party and gets Y in return. For example, you pay Sears $350 for a television set. This is a classic *monetary transaction,* but not all transactions involve money. In a *barter transaction,* you might trade your old refrigerator in return for a neighbor's secondhand television set.

Transaction
A trade between two parties that involves at least two things of value, agreed upon conditions, a time of agreement, and a place of agreement.

In the broadest sense, the marketer tries to bring about a response to some offer. The response may be more than simply buying or trading goods and services. A political candidate, for instance, wants votes, a church wants membership, and a social action group wants idea acceptance. Marketing consists of actions taken to obtain a desired response from a target audience toward some product, service, idea, or other object.

Relationship marketing
The process of creating, maintaining, and enhancing strong, value-laden relationships with customers and other stakeholders.

Transaction marketing is part of the larger idea of **relationship marketing.** Beyond creating short-term transactions, marketers need to build long-term relationships with valued customers, distributors, dealers, and suppliers. They want to build strong economic and social connections by promising and consistently delivering high-quality products, good service, and fair prices. Increasingly, marketing is shifting from trying to maximize the profit on each individual transaction to building mutually beneficial relationships with consumers and other parties. In fact, ultimately, a company wants to build a unique company asset called a *marketing network.* A marketing network consists of the company and all its supporting stakeholders: customers, employees, suppliers, distributors, retailers, ad agencies, and others with whom it has built mutually profitable business relationships. Increasingly, competition is not between companies but rather between whole networks, with the prize going to the company that has built the better network. The operating principle is simple: Build a good network of relationships with key stakeholders and profits will follow.[9]

*Relationship marketing:
Saturn builds lasting relationships with customers. Many
dealers post "pinups" of customers in their service areas to
help employees place customer
faces with cars. "Hey you is
not exactly the most endearing
greeting, especially to someone
who took the time to shop at
your place and who spent
hard-earned money on one of
your cars."*

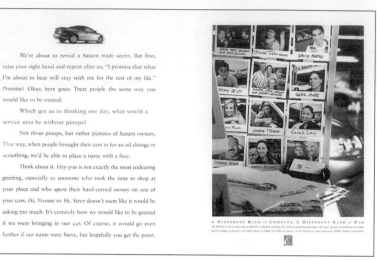

Market
The set of all actual and
potential buyers of a product or
service.

Markets

The concepts of exchange and relationships lead to the concept of a market. A **market** is the set of actual and potential buyers of a product. These buyers share a particular need or want that can be satisfied through exchanges and relationships. Thus, the size of a market depends on the number of people who exhibit the need, have resources to engage in exchange, and are willing to offer these resources in exchange for what they want.

Originally the term *market* stood for the place where buyers and sellers gathered to exchange their goods, such as a village square. Economists use the term *market* to refer to a collection of buyers and sellers who transact in a particular product class, as in the housing market or the grain market. Marketers, however, see the sellers as constituting an industry and the buyers as constituting a market. The relationship between the *industry* and the *market* is shown in Figure 1.2. Sellers and the buyers are connected by four flows. The sellers send products, services, and communications to the market; in return, they receive money and information. The inner loop shows an exchange of money for goods; the outer loop shows an exchange of information.

Modern economies operate on the principle of division of labor, whereby each person specializes in producing something, receives payment, and buys needed things with this money. Thus, modern economies abound in markets. Producers go to resource markets (raw material markets, labor markets, money markets), buy resources, turn them into goods and services, and sell them to intermediaries, who sell them to consumers. The consumers sell their labor, for which they receive income to pay for the goods and services that they buy. The government is another market that plays several roles. It buys goods from resource, producer, and intermediary markets; it pays them; it taxes these markets (including consumer markets); and

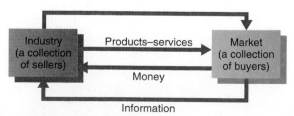

FIGURE 1.2   A simple marketing system

it returns needed public services. Thus, each nation's economy and the whole world economy consist of complex, interacting sets of markets that are linked through exchange processes.

Marketers are keenly interested in markets. Their goal is to understand the needs and wants of specific markets and to select the markets that they can serve best. In turn, they can develop products and services that will create value and satisfaction for customers in these markets, resulting in sales and profits for the company.

Marketing

The concept of markets finally brings us full circle to the concept of marketing. Marketing means managing markets to bring about exchanges and relationships for the purpose of creating value and satisfying needs and wants. Thus, we return to our definition of marketing as a process by which individuals and groups obtain what they need and want by creating and exchanging products and value with others.

Exchange processes involve work. Sellers must search for buyers, identify their needs, design good products and services, set prices for them, promote them, and store and deliver them. Activities such as product development, research, communication, distribution, pricing, and service are core marketing activities. Although we normally think of marketing as being carried on by sellers, buyers also carry on marketing activities. Consumers do marketing when they search for the goods they need at prices they can afford. Company purchasing agents do marketing when they track down sellers and bargain for good terms.

Figure 1.3 shows the main elements in a modern marketing system. In the usual situation, marketing involves serving a market of end users in the face of competitors. The company and the competitors send their respective products and messages to consumers either directly or through marketing intermediaries to the end users. All of the actors in the system are affected by major environmental forces (demographic, economic, physical, technological, political–legal, social–cultural).

Each party in the system adds value for the next level. Thus, a company's success depends not only on its own actions but also on how well the entire system serves the needs of final consumers. Wal-Mart cannot fulfill its promise of low prices unless its suppliers provide merchandise at low costs. Ford cannot deliver high quality to car buyers unless its dealers provide outstanding service.

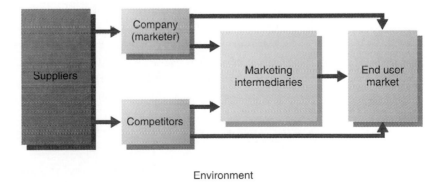

Environment

FIGURE 1.3 Main actors and forces in a modern marketing system

MARKETING MANAGEMENT

Marketing management
The analysis, planning, implementation, and control of programs designed to create, build, and maintain beneficial exchanges with target buyers for the purpose of achieving organizational objectives.

We define **marketing management** as the analysis, planning, implementation, and control of programs designed to create, build, and maintain beneficial exchanges with target buyers for the purpose of achieving organizational objectives. Thus, marketing management involves managing demand, which in turn involves managing customer relationships.

Demand Management

Some people think of marketing management as finding enough customers for the company's current output but this view is too limited. The organization has a desired level of demand for its products. At any point in time, there may be no demand, adequate demand, irregular demand, or too much demand, and marketing management must find ways to deal with these different demand states. Marketing management is concerned not only with finding and increasing demand but also with changing or even reducing it.

Demarketing
Marketing to reduce demand temporarily or permanently; the aim is not to destroy demand, but only to reduce or shift it.

For example, the Golden Gate Bridge sometimes carries an unsafe level of traffic, and Yosemite National Park is badly overcrowded in the summer. Power companies sometimes have trouble meeting demand during peak usage periods. In these and other cases of excess demand, **demarketing** may be required to reduce demand temporarily or permanently. The aim of demarketing is not to destroy demand but only to reduce or shift it.[10] Thus, marketing management seeks to affect the level, timing, and nature of demand in a way that helps the organization achieve its objectives. Simply put, marketing management is *demand management*.

Building Profitable Customer Relationships

Managing demand means managing customers. A company's demand comes from two groups: new customers and repeat customers. Traditionally, marketers have focused on *attracting* new customers and creating *transactions* with them. In today's marketing environment, however, changing demographic, economic, and competitive factors mean that there are fewer new customers to go around. The costs of attracting new customers are rising. Thus, although finding new customers remains very important, the emphasis is shifting toward *retaining* profitable customers and building lasting *relationships* with them.

Companies have also discovered that losing a customer means losing not just a single sale but also a lifetime's worth of purchases and referrals. For example, the *customer lifetime value* of a Taco Bell customer exceeds $12,000. For Lexus, one satisfied customer is worth $600,000 in lifetime purchases. Thus, working to keep profitable customers makes good economic sense.[11] The key to customer retention is superior customer value and satisfaction. With this in mind, many companies are going to extremes to keep their customers satisfied. (See Marketing Highlight 1.2.)

Marketing Management Practice

All kinds of organizations use marketing, and they practice it in widely varying ways. Many large firms apply standard marketing practices in a formalized way. However, other companies use marketing in a less formal and orderly fashion. A recent book, *Radical Marketing,* praises companies such as Harley-Davidson, Virgin

Atlantic Airways, and Boston Beer for succeeding by breaking many of the rules of marketing.[12] Instead of commissioning expensive marketing research, spending huge sums on mass advertising, and operating large marketing departments, these companies stretched their limited resources, lived close to their customers, and created more satisfying solutions to customer needs. They formed buyer's clubs, used creative public relations, and focused on delivering high product quality and winning long-term customer loyalty. It seems that not all marketing must follow in the footsteps of marketing giants such as Procter & Gamble.

In fact, marketing practice often passes through three stages: entrepreneurial marketing, formulated marketing, and intrepreneurial marketing.

★ *Entrepreneurial marketing:* Most companies are started by individuals who live by their wits. They visualize an opportunity and knock on every door to gain attention. Jim Koch, founder of Boston Beer Company, whose Samuel Adams beer has become a top-selling "craft" beer, started out in 1984 carrying bottles of Samuel Adams beer from bar to bar to persuade bartenders to carry it. He would coax them into adding Samuel Adams beer to their menus. For 10 years, he couldn't afford advertising; he sold his beer through direct selling and grassroots public relations. Today, however, his business pulls in $210 million, making it the leader in the craft beer market.

★ *Formulated marketing:* As small companies achieve success, they inevitably move toward more formulated marketing. Boston Beer recently opted to spend more than $15 million on television advertising in selected markets. The company now employs more than 175 salespeople and has a marketing department that carries out market research. Although Boston Beer is far less sophisticated than its archcompetitor, Anheuser-Busch, it has adopted some of the tools used in professionally run marketing companies.

★ *Intrepreneurial marketing:* Many large and mature companies get stuck in formulated marketing, poring over the latest Nielsen numbers, scanning market research reports, and trying to fine-tune dealer relations and advertising messages. These companies sometimes lose the marketing creativity and passion that they had at the start. They now need to reestablish within their companies the entrepreneurial spirit and actions that made them successful in the first place. They need to encourage more initiative and "intrepreneurship" at the local level. Their brand and product managers need to get out of the office, start living with their customers, and visualize new and creative ways to add value to their customers' lives.

The bottom line is that effective marketing can take many forms. There will be a constant tension between the formulated side of marketing and the creative side. It is easier to learn the formulated side of marketing, which will occupy most of our attention in this book. But we will also see how real marketing creativity and passion operate in many companies—whether small or large, new or mature—to build and retain success in the marketplace.

MARKETING MANAGEMENT PHILOSOPHIES

We describe marketing management as carrying out tasks to achieve desired exchanges with target markets. What *philosophy* should guide these marketing efforts? What weight should be given to the interests of the organization, customers, and society? Very often these interests conflict.

MARKETING HIGHLIGHT
1.2

CUSTOMER RELATIONSHIPS: KEEPING CUSTOMERS SATISFIED

Some companies go to extremes to coddle their customers. Consider the following examples:

• An L.L. Bean customer says he lost all his fishing equipment—and nearly his life—when a raft he bought from the company leaked and forced him to swim to shore. He recovered the raft and sent it to the company along with a letter asking

for a new raft and $700 to cover the fishing equipment he says he lost. He gets both.

• An American Express cardholder fails to pay more than $5,000 of his September bill. He explains that during the summer he'd purchased expensive rugs in Turkey. When he got home, appraisals showed that the rugs were worth half of what he'd

paid. Rather than asking suspicious questions or demanding payment, the American Express representative notes the dispute, asks for a letter summarizing the appraisers' estimates, and offers to help solve the problem. Until the conflict is resolved, American Express doesn't ask for payment.

• Under the sultry summer sun, a Southwest Airlines flight attendant pulls shut the door and the Boeing 737 pushes away. Meanwhile, a ticketholder, sweat streaming from her face, races down the jetway, only to find that she's arrived too late. However, the Southwest pilot spies the anguished passenger and returns to the gate to pick her up. Says Southwest's executive vice president for customers, "It broke every rule in the book, but we congratulated the pilot on a job well done."

• A frustrated home owner faces a difficult and potentially costly home plumbing repair. He visits the nearby Home Depot store, prowls the aisles, and picks up an armful of parts and supplies— $67.00 worth in all—that he thinks he'll need to do the job. However, before he gets to the checkout

Delighted customers come back again and again. American Express loves to tell stories about how its people have rescued customers from disasters ranging from civil wars to earthquakes, no matter what the cost.

There are five alternative concepts under which organizations conduct their marketing activities: the *production, product, selling, marketing,* and *societal marketing* concepts.

The Production Concept

Production concept
The philosophy that consumers will favor products that are available and highly affordable and that management should therefore focus on improving production and distribution efficiency.

The **production concept** holds that consumers will favor products that are available and highly affordable. Therefore, management should focus on improving production and distribution efficiency. This concept is one of the oldest philosophies that guides sellers.

The production concept is still a useful philosophy in two types of situations. The first occurs when the demand for a product exceeds the supply. Here, management should look for ways to increase production. The second situation occurs counter, a Home Depot salesperson heads him off. After some coaxing, the salesperson finally convinces the do-it-yourselfer that there's a simpler solution to his repair problem. The cost: $5.99 and a lot less trouble.

- A Nordstrom salesclerk stops a customer in the store and asks if the shoes she's wearing had been bought there. When the customer says yes, the clerk insists on replacing them on the spot because "they have not worn as well as they should." In another case, a salesclerk gives a customer a refund on a tire—Nordstrom doesn't carry tires, but the store prides itself on a no-questions-asked return policy.

From a dollars-and-cents point of view, these examples sound like a crazy way to do business. How can you make money by giving away your products, providing free extra services, talking your customers into paying less, or letting customers get away without paying their bills on time? Yet studies show that going to such extremes to keep customers happy, although costly, goes hand in hand with good financial performance. Satisfied customers come back again and again. Thus, in today's highly competitive marketplace, companies can well afford to lose money on one transaction if it helps to cement a profitable long-term customer relationship.

Keeping customers satisfied involves more than simply opening a complaint department, smiling a lot, and being nice. Companies that do the best job of taking care of customers set high customer service standards and often make seemingly outlandish efforts to achieve them. At these companies, exceptional value and service are more than a set of policies or actions—they are a companywide attitude, an important part of the overall company culture.

American Express loves to tell stories about how its people have rescued customers from disasters ranging from civil wars to earthquakes, no matter what the cost. The company gives cash rewards of up to $1,000 to "Great Performers," such as Barbara Weber, who moved mountains of U.S. State Department and Treasury Department bureaucracy to refund $980 in stolen traveler's checks to a customer stranded in Cuba. Four Seasons Hotels, long known for its outstanding service, tells its employees the story of Ron Dyment, a doorman in Toronto, who forgot to load a departing guest's briefcase into his taxi. The doorman called the guest, a lawyer in Washington, D.C., and learned that he desperately needed the briefcase for a meeting the following morning. Without first asking for approval from management, Dyment hopped on a plane and returned the briefcase. The company named Dyment Employee of the Year. Similarly, the Nordstrom department store chain thrives on stories about its service heroics, such as employees dropping off orders at customers' homes or warming up cars while customers spend a little more time shopping. There's even a story about a man whose wife, a loyal Nordstrom customer, died with her Nordstrom account $1,000 in arrears. Not only did Nordstrom settle the account, it also sent flowers to the funeral.

There's no simple formula for taking care of customers, but neither is it a mystery. According to the president of L.L. Bean, "A lot of people have fancy things to say about customer service . . . but it's just a day-in, day-out, ongoing, neverending, unremitting, persevering, compassionate type of activity." For the companies that do it well, it's also very rewarding.

Sources: Bill Kelley, "Five Companies That Do It Right—and Make It Pay," *Sales & Marketing Management,* April 1988, pp. 57–64; Patricia Sellers, "Companies That Serve You Best," *Fortune,* May 31, 1993, pp. 74–88; Rahul Jacob, "Why Some Customers Are More Equal Than Others," *Fortune,* September 19, 1994, pp. 215–24; Brian Silverman, "Shopping for Loyal Customers," *Sales & Marketing Management,* March 1995, pp. 96–97; and Howard E. Butz Jr. and Leonard Goodstein, "Measuring Customer Value: Gaining the Strategic Advantage," *Organizational Dynamics,* Winter 1996, pp. 63–77.

when the product's cost is too high and improved productivity is needed to bring it down. For example, Henry Ford's whole philosophy was to perfect the production of the Model T so that its cost could be reduced and more people could afford it. He joked about offering people a car of any color as long as it was black.

For many years, Texas Instruments (TI) followed a philosophy of increased production and lower costs in order to bring down prices. It won a major share of the American handheld calculator market using this approach. However, companies operating under a production philosophy run a major risk of focusing too narrowly on their own operations. For example, when TI used this strategy in the digital watch market, it failed. Although TI's watches were priced low, customers did not find them very attractive. In its drive to bring down prices, TI lost sight of something else that its customers wanted—namely, affordable, *attractive* digital watches.

The Product Concept

Product concept
The idea that consumers will favor products that offer the most quality, performance, and features and that the organization should therefore devote its energy to making continuous product improvements. A detailed version of the new-product idea stated in meaningful consumer terms.

Another major concept guiding sellers, the **product concept,** holds that consumers will favor products that offer the most in quality, performance, and innovative features. Thus, an organization should devote energy to making continuous product improvements. Some manufacturers believe that if they can build a better mousetrap, the world will beat a path to their door.[13] But they are often rudely shocked. Buyers may well be looking for a better solution to a mouse problem but not necessarily for a better mousetrap. The solution might be a chemical spray, an exterminating service, or something that works better than a mousetrap. Furthermore, a better mousetrap will not sell unless the manufacturer designs, packages, and prices it attractively; places it in convenient distribution channels; brings it to the attention of people who need it; and convinces buyers that it is a better product.

The product concept also can lead to marketing myopia. For instance, railroad management once thought that users wanted *trains* rather than *transportation* and overlooked the growing challenge of airlines, buses, trucks, and automobiles. Many colleges have assumed that high school graduates want a liberal arts education and thus have overlooked the increasing challenge of vocational schools.

The Selling Concept

Selling concept
The idea that consumers will not buy enough of the organization's products unless the organization undertakes a large-scale selling and promotion effort.

Many organizations follow the **selling concept,** which holds that consumers will not buy enough of the organization's products unless it undertakes a large-scale selling and promotion effort. The concept is typically practiced with unsought goods—those that buyers do not normally think of buying, such as encyclopedias or insurance. These industries must be good at tracking down prospects and selling them on product benefits.

Most firms practice the selling concept when they have overcapacity. Their aim is to sell what they make rather than make what the market wants. Such marketing carries high risks. It focuses on creating sales transactions rather than on building long-term, profitable relationships with customers. It assumes that customers who are coaxed into buying the product will like it. Or, if they don't like it, they will possibly forget their disappointment and buy it again later. These are usually poor assumptions to make about buyers. Most studies show that dissatisfied customers do not buy again. Worse yet, whereas the average satisfied customer tells three others about good experiences, the average dissatisfied customer tells ten others about his or her bad experiences.[14]

The Marketing Concept

Marketing concept
The marketing management philosophy that holds that achieving organizational goals depends on determining the needs and wants of target markets and delivering the desired satisfactions more effectively and efficiently than competitors do.

The **marketing concept** holds that achieving organizational goals depends on determining the needs and wants of target markets and delivering the desired satisfactions more effectively and efficiently than competitors do. The marketing concept has been stated in colorful ways, such as "We make it happen for you" (Marriott); "To fly, to serve" (British Airways); "We're not satisfied until you are" (GE); and "Let us exceed your expectations" (Celebrity Cruise Lines).

The selling concept and the marketing concept are sometimes confused. Figure 1.4 compares the two concepts. The selling concept takes an *inside-out* perspective. It starts with the factory, focuses on the company's existing products, and calls for heavy selling and promotion to obtain profitable sales. It focuses primarily on customer conquest—getting short-term sales with little concern about who buys or why.

FIGURE 1.4   The selling and marketing concepts contrasted

In contrast, the marketing concept takes an *outside-in* perspective. As Herb Kelleher, Southwest Airlines's colorful CEO, puts it, "We don't have a Marketing Department; we have a Customer Department." The marketing concept starts with a well-defined market, focuses on customer needs, coordinates all the marketing activities affecting customers, and makes profits by creating long-term customer relationships based on customer value and satisfaction. Thus, under the marketing concept, customer focus and value are the *paths* to sales and profits. In the words of one Ford executive, "If we're not customer driven, our cars won't be either."

Many successful and well-known companies have adopted the marketing concept. Procter & Gamble, Disney, Wal-Mart, Marriott, Nordstrom, Dell Computer, and Southwest Airlines follow it faithfully. The goal is to build customer satisfaction into the very fabric of the firm. L.L. Bean, the highly successful catalog retailer, was founded on the marketing concept. In 1912, in his first circulars, L.L. Bean included the following notice: "I do not consider a sale complete until goods are worn out and the customer still is satisfied. We will thank anyone to return goods that are not perfectly satisfactory   Above all things we wish to avoid having a dissatisfied customer."

Today, L.L. Bean dedicates itself to giving "perfect satisfaction in every way." To inspire its employees to practice the marketing concept, L.L. Bean has for decades displayed posters around its offices that proclaim the following:

> What is a customer? A customer is the most important person ever in this company—in person or by mail. A customer is not dependent on us, we are dependent on him. A customer is not an interruption of our work, he is the purpose of it. We are not doing a favor by serving him, he is doing us a favor by giving us the opportunity to do so. A customer is not someone to argue or match wits with—nobody ever won an argument with a customer. A customer is a person who brings us his wants—it is our job to handle them profitably to him and to ourselves.

In contrast, many companies claim to practice the marketing concept but do not. They have the *forms* of marketing, such as a marketing vice president, product managers, marketing plans, and marketing research, but this does not mean that they are market-focused and customer-driven companies. The question is whether they are finely tuned to changing customer needs and competitor strategies. Formerly great companies—General Motors, Sears, Zenith—all lost substantial market share because they failed to adjust their marketing strategies to the changing marketplace.

Implementing the marketing concept often means more than simply responding to customers' stated desires and obvious needs. *Customer-driven* companies research

The marketing concept: L.L. Bean and its reps dedicate themselves to delivering the promise first spelled out in a 1916 L.L. Bean circular and still practiced today.

Notice

I do not consider a sale complete until goods are worn out and the customer is still satisfied. We will thank anyone to return goods that are not perfectly satisfactory.

Should the person reading this notice know of anyone who is not satisfied with our goods, I will consider it a favor to be notified.

Above all things we wish to avoid having a dissatisfied customer.

current customers to learn about their desires, gather new product and service ideas, and test proposed product improvements. Such customer-driven marketing usually works well when a clear need exists and when customers know what they want. In many cases, however, customers *don't* know what they want or even what is possible. Such situations call for *customer-driving* marketing—understanding customer needs even better than customers themselves do, and creating products and services that will meet existing and latent needs now and in the future.

> Customers are notoriously lacking in foresight. Ten or 15 years ago, how many of us were asking for cellular telephones, fax machines, and copiers at home, 24-hour discount brokerage accounts, multivalve automobile engines, compact disk players, cars with onboard navigation systems, handheld global satellite positioning receivers, MTV, or the Home Shopping Network? As Akio Morita, Sony's visionary leader puts it: "Our plan is to lead the public with new products rather than ask them what kinds of products they want. The public does not know what is possible, but we do. So instead of doing a lot of market research, we refine our thinking on a product and its use and try to create a market for it by educating and communicating with the public."[15]

Several years of hard work are needed to turn a sales-oriented company into a marketing-oriented company. Customer satisfaction is no longer a fad. As one marketing analyst notes, "It's becoming a way of life in corporate America . . . as embedded into corporate cultures as information technology and strategic planning."[16]

The Societal Marketing Concept

Societal marketing concept
The idea that the organization should determine the needs, wants, and interests of target markets and deliver the desired satisfactions more effectively and efficiently than do competitors in a way that maintains or improves the consumer's and society's well being.

The **societal marketing concept** holds that the organization should determine the needs, wants, and interests of target markets. It should then deliver superior value to customers in a way that maintains or improves the consumer's *and the society's* well being. The societal marketing concept is the newest of the five marketing management philosophies.

The societal marketing concept questions whether the pure marketing concept is adequate in an age of environmental problems, resource shortages, rapid popula-

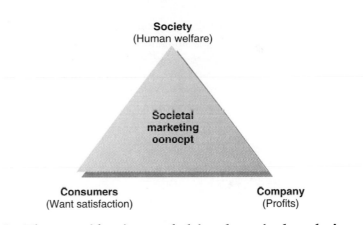

FIGURE 1.5   Three considerations underlying the societal marketing concept

tion growth, worldwide economic problems, and neglected social services. It asks if the firm that senses, serves, and satisfies individual wants is always doing what's best for consumers and society in the long run. According to the societal marketing concept, the pure marketing concept overlooks possible conflicts between consumer *short-run wants* and consumer *long-run welfare.*

Consider the fast-food industry. Most people see today's giant fast-food chains as offering tasty and convenient food at reasonable prices. Yet many consumer and environmental groups have voiced concerns. Critics point out that hamburgers, fried chicken, French fries, and most other foods sold by fast-food restaurants are high in fat and salt. The products are wrapped in convenient packaging, but this leads to waste and pollution. Thus, in satisfying consumer wants, the highly successful fast-food chains may be harming consumer health and causing environmental problems.

Such concerns and conflicts led to the societal marketing concept. As Figure 1.5 shows, the societal marketing concept calls on marketers to balance three considerations in setting their marketing policies: company profits, consumer wants, *and* society's interests. Originally, most companies based their marketing decisions largely on short-run company profit. Eventually, they began to recognize the long-run importance of satisfying consumer wants, and the marketing concept emerged. Now many companies are beginning to think of society's interests when making their marketing decisions.

One such company is Johnson & Johnson, rated each year in a *Fortune* magazine poll as one of America's most admired companies, especially for its community and environmental responsibility. Johnson & Johnson's concern for societal interests is summarized in a company document called "Our Credo," which stresses honesty, integrity, and putting people before profits. Under this credo, Johnson & Johnson would rather take a big loss than ship a bad batch of one of its products. The company supports many community and employee programs that benefit its consumers and workers and the environment. Johnson & Johnson's chief executive puts it this way: "If we keep trying to do what's right, at the end of the day we believe the marketplace will reward us."[17]

The company backs these words with actions. Consider the tragic tampering case in which eight people died from swallowing cyanide-laced capsules of Tylenol, a Johnson & Johnson brand. Although Johnson & Johnson believed that the pills had been altered in only a few stores, not in the factory, it quickly recalled all of its product. The recall cost the company $240 million in earnings. In the long run, however, the company's swift recall of Tylenol strengthened consumer confidence and loyalty, and Tylenol remains the nation's leading brand of pain reliever. In this and

Johnson & Johnson's concern for society is summarized in its credo and in the company's actions over the years. Says one executive, "It's just plain good business."

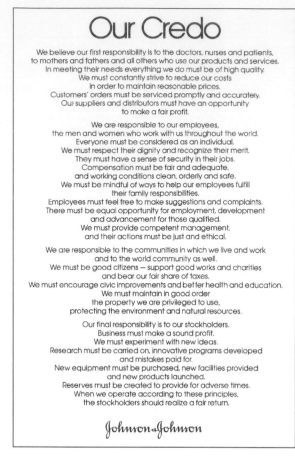

other cases, Johnson & Johnson management has found that doing what's right benefits both consumers and the company. Says the chief executive, "The Credo should not be viewed as some kind of social welfare program . . . it's just plain good business."[18] Thus, over the years, Johnson & Johnson's dedication to consumers and community service has made it one of America's most admired companies *and* one of the most profitable.

MARKETING CHALLENGES IN THE NEW "CONNECTED" MILLENNIUM

As the world spins into the first decade of the twenty-first century, dramatic changes are occurring in the marketing arena. Richard Love of Hewlett-Packard observes, "The pace of change is so rapid that the ability to change has now become a competitive advantage." Yogi Berra, the legendary New York Yankees catcher, summed it up more simply when he said, "The future ain't what it used to be." Technological advances, rapid globalization, and continuing social and economic shifts—all are causing profound changes in the marketplace. As the marketplace changes, so must those who serve it.

The major marketing developments today can be summed up in a single theme: *connectedness.* Now, more than ever before, we are all connected to each other and to things near and far in the world around us. Moreover, we are connecting in new and different ways. Where it once took weeks or months to travel across the United States, we can now travel around the globe in only hours or days. Where it once took days or even weeks to receive news about important world events, we now see

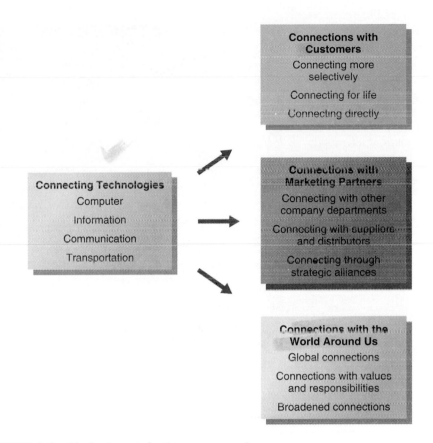

Connections with Customers

Connecting more selectively

Connecting for life

Connecting directly

Connecting Technologies

Computer

Information

Communication

Transportation

Connections with Marketing Partners

Connecting with other company departments

Connecting with suppliers and distributors

Connecting through strategic alliances

Connections with the World Around Us

Global connections

Connections with values and responsibilities

Broadened connections

FIGURE 1.6   Today's marketing connections

them as they are occurring through live satellite broadcasts. Where it once took days or weeks to correspond with others in distant places, they are now only moments away by phone or the Internet.

In this section, we examine the major trends and forces that are changing the marketing landscape and challenging marketing strategy in this new, connected millennium. As shown in Figure 1.6 and discussed in the following pages, sweeping changes in connecting technologies are causing marketers to redefine how they connect with the marketplace—with their customers, with marketing partners inside and outside the company, and with the world around them. We first look at the dramatic changes that are occurring in the connecting technologies. Then, we examine how these changes are affecting marketing connections.

Technologies for Connecting

The major force behind the new connectedness is technology. Explosive advances in computer, telecommunications, information, transportation, and other connecting technologies has had a major impact on the way companies bring value to their customers. The technology boom has created exciting new ways to learn about and track customers, create products and services tailored to meet customer needs, distribute products more efficiently and effectively, and communicate with customers in large groups or one-to-one. For example, through videoconferencing, marketing researchers at a company's headquarters in New York can look in on focus groups in Chicago or Paris without ever stepping onto a plane. With only a few clicks of a mouse button, a direct marketer can tap into online data services to learn anything from what car you drive to what you read to what flavor of ice cream you prefer.

Explosive advances in connecting technologies have created exciting new ways to learn about customers and to create tailored products, distribute them more effectively, and communicate with customers in large groups or one-to-one.

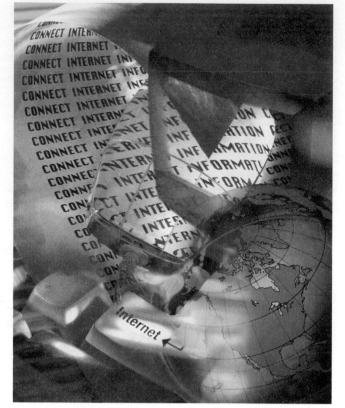

Using today's vastly more powerful computers, marketers create detailed databases and use them to target individual customers with offers designed to meet their specific needs and buying patterns. With a new wave of communication and advertising tools—ranging from cell phones, fax machines, and CD-ROM to interactive TV and video kiosks at airports and shopping malls—marketers can zero in on selected customers with carefully targeted messages. Through electronic commerce, customers can design, order, and pay for products and services without ever leaving home. Then, through the marvels of express delivery, they can receive their purchases in less than 24 hours.

From virtual reality displays that test new products to online virtual stores that sell them, the boom in computer, information, telecommunication, and transportation technology is affecting every aspect of marketing. Consider the rapidly changing face of personal selling. Many companies now equip their salespeople with the latest sales automation tools, including the capacity to develop individualized multimedia presentations and to develop customized market offerings and contracts. Many buyers now prefer to meet salespeople on their computer screens rather than in the office. An increasing amount of personal selling is occurring through videoconferences or live Internet presentations, where buyers and sellers can interact across great distances without the time, costs, or delays of travel.

The Internet

Internet (or the Net)
The vast and burgeoning global web of computer networks with no central management or ownership.

Perhaps the most dramatic new technology driving the connected age is the **Internet.** The Internet is a vast and burgeoning global web of computer networks with no central management or ownership. It was created during the late 1960s by the U.S. Department of Defense, initially to link government labs, contractors, and military installations. Today, the Internet links computer users of all types around the world. Anyone with a PC, a modem, and the right software—or a TV with a set-top "Web box"—can browse the Internet to obtain or share information on almost any subject and to interact with other users.

The Internet has been hailed as the technology behind a new model for doing business. It allows anytime, anywhere connections to information, entertainment, and communication. Companies are using the Internet to build closer relationships with customers and marketing partners and to sell and distribute their products more efficiently and effectively. They are rapidly converting from "snail mail" and the telephone to the *Internet* (connecting with customers), *intranets* (connecting with others in the company), and *extranets* (connecting with strategic marketing partners, suppliers, and dealers). Beyond competing in traditional *marketplaces,* they now have access to exciting new *marketspaces.*

Internet usage surged in the early 1990s with the development of the user-friendly World Wide Web. The U.S. Internet population grew from only 6 million households in 1994 to more than 40 million today; it will grow to a projected 60 million households by the year 2003. The Internet is truly a worldwide phenomenon. Forrester Research projects that U.S. Internet purchasing will grow from only about $21.5 billion in 1995 to more than $1.4 trillion in 2003.[19] Notes one analyst, "In just [a few short years], the Net has gone from a playground for nerds into a vast communications and trading center where . . . people swap information and do deals around the world. . . . More than 400,000 companies have hung www.single.com atop their digital doorways with the notion that being anywhere on the Net means selling virtually everywhere."[20]

Companies of all types are now attempting to snare new customers on the Web. Many traditional "brick-and-mortar" companies have now ventured online in an effort to snare new customers and build stronger customer relationships. For example

★ Car makers such as Toyota (www.Toyota.com) use the Internet to develop relationships with owners as well as to sell cars. Its site offers product information, dealer services and locations, leasing information, and much more. For example, visitors to the site can view any of seven lifestyle magazines—*alt.Terrain, A Man's Life, Women's Web Weekly, Sportzine, Living Arts, Living Home,* and *Car Culture*—designed to appeal to Toyota's well-educated, above-average-income target audience.

★ Sports fans can cozy up with Nike by logging onto www.nike.com, where they can check out the latest Nike products, explore the company's history, or download their favorite athlete's stats. Through its Web page, in addition to its mass-media presence, Nike relates with customers in a more personal, one-to-one way.

The Internet has also spawned an entirely new breed of companies—the so-called "dot coms"—which operate *only* online. For example

★ Fast-growing eToys is quickly becoming an indispensable ally to time-starved parents looking for a fast and convenient way to buy toys for their children. The three-year-old Web-only retailer pioneered in selling everything from teddy bears to Barbies online. Now the site offers more than 100,000 toys, books, software, videos, and other kid items. Twenty-four hours a day, seven days a week, shoppers can click onto eToys (www.eToys.com), search for a specific item or browse one of several categories, drop their selections into a virtual shopping cart, pay for them with a credit card, and have them delivered within a day or two by express shipping. The eToys Web site also offers recommendations by age groups, a gift registry, a bestsellers list, and features on the latest children's products. Is the site successful? After only three years, eToys has won some 600,000 customers and almost $30 million of their purchases. "There is tremendous

Companies of all types are now snaring new customers on the Web, including an entirely new breed of companies—the so-called "dot coms," such as eToys—which operate only online.

competition," says eToys CEO Toby Lenk. "The difference is we are just kids and we are just the Web."[21]

It seems that almost every business—from garage-based start-ups to established giants such as IBM, GE, Marriott Hotels, JCPenney, and American Airlines—is setting up shop on the Internet. All are racing to explore and exploit the Web's marketing possibilities. However, for all its potential, the Internet does have drawbacks. Despite growing use of the Web for shopping, in a recent survey 54 percent of Web users said that they were not likely to use the Internet for online purchases ever in the future. Although the value of a Web site is difficult to measure, the actuality is that few companies have made much money from their Internet efforts.[22]

Thus, changes in connecting technologies are providing exciting new opportunities for marketers. We now look at the ways these changes are affecting how companies connect with their customers, marketing partners, and the world around us (see Figure 1.6).

Connections with Customers

The most profound new developments in marketing involve the ways in which today's companies are connecting with their customers. Yesterday's companies focused on mass marketing to all comers at arm's length. Today's companies are selecting their customers more carefully and building more lasting and direct relationships with these carefully targeted customers.

Connecting with More Carefully Selected Customers

Few firms today still practice true mass marketing—selling in a standardized way to any customer who comes along. Today, most marketers are realizing that they don't want to connect with just *any* customers. Instead, most are targeting fewer, potentially more profitable customers.

The United States—in fact, the world—has become more of a "salad bowl" of diverse ethnic, cultural, social, and locational groups. Although these diverse groups have mixed together, they maintain diversity by keeping and valuing important differences. Moreover, customers themselves are connecting in new ways to form specific "consumer communities," in which buyers connect with each other by common interests, situations, and activities.

Greater diversity and these new consumer connections have meant greater market fragmentation. In response, most firms have moved from mass marketing to segmented marketing, in which they target carefully chosen submarkets or even individual buyers. "One-to-one marketing" has become the order of the day for some marketers. They build extensive customer databases containing rich information on individual customer preferences and purchases. Then, they mine these databases to gain segment and customer insights by which they can "mass-customize" their offerings to deliver greater value to individual buyers.

At the same time that companies are finding imaginative new ways to deliver more value *to* customers, they are also beginning to assess carefully the value *of* customers to the firm. They want to connect only with customers that they can serve *profitably*. Once they identify profitable customers, firms can create attractive offers and special handling to capture these customers and earn their loyalty. The banking industry has led the way in assessing customer profitability. After decades of casting a wide net to lure as many customers as possible, many banks are now mining their vast databases to identify winning customers and weed out losing ones. Take First Union as an example:

> Fielding phone calls at First Union's huge customer service center [in Charlotte, NC], Amy Hathcock is surrounded by reminders to deliver the personal touch. Televisions hang from the ceiling so she can glance at the Weather Channel to see if her latest caller just came in from the rain; a bumper sticker in her cubicle encourages, "Practice random kindness and senseless acts of beauty." But when it comes to answering yes or no to a customer who wants a lower credit-card interest rate or to escape the bank's $28 bounced-check fee, there is nothing random about it. The service all depends on the color of a tiny square—green, yellow, or red—that pops up on Ms. Hathcock's computer screen next to the customer's name. For customers who get a red pop-up, Ms. Hathcock rarely budges; these are the ones whose accounts lose money for the bank. Green means the customers generate hefty profits for First Union and should be granted waivers. Yellow is for in-between customers: There's a chance to negotiate. The bank's computer system, called "Einstein," takes just 15 seconds to pull up the ranking on a customer, using a formula that calculates [customer value based on the account's] minimum balances, account activity, branch visits, and other variables. "Everyone isn't all the same anymore," says Steven G. Boehm, general manager of First Union's customer-information center.[23]

Connecting for a Customer's Lifetime

At the same time that companies are being more selective about which customers they choose to serve, they are serving those they choose in a deeper, more lasting way. In the past, many companies have focused on finding *new customers* for their products and closing *sales* with them. In recent years, this focus has shifted toward keeping *current customers* and building lasting *relationships* based on superior customer satisfaction and value. Increasingly, the goal is shifting from making a profit on each sale to making long-term profits by managing the lifetime value of a customer.

In turn, as businesses do a better and better job of keeping old customers, competitors find it increasingly difficult to acquire new customers. As a result, marketers now spend less time figuring out how to increase "share of market" and more time trying to grow "share of customer." They offer greater variety to current customers and train employees to cross-sell and up-sell in order to market more products and services to existing customers. For example, Amazon.com began as an online bookseller, but now offers music, videos, gifts, toys, consumer electronics, home improvement items, and even an online auction as well, increasing per-customer sales. In addition, based on each customer's purchase history, the company recommends related books, CDs, or videos that might be of interest. In this way, Amazon.com captures a greater share of each customer's leisure and entertainment budget.

Connecting Directly

Today, beyond connecting more deeply, many companies are also taking advantage of new technologies that let them connect more *directly* with their customers. In fact, direct marketing is booming. Virtually all products are now available without going to a store—by telephone, mail-order catalogs, kiosks, and electronic commerce. For example, customers surfing the Internet can view pictures of almost any product, read the specs, shop among online vendors for the best prices and terms, speak with online vendors' shopping consultants, and even place and pay for their orders—all with only a few mouse clicks. Business-to-business purchasing over the Internet has increased even faster than online consumer buying. Business purchasing agents routinely shop on the Web for items ranging from standard office supplies to high-priced, high-tech computer equipment.

Some companies sell *only* via direct channels—firms such as Dell Computer, Lands' End, 1-800-Flowers, and Amazon.com, to name only a few. Other companies use direct connections as a supplement to their other communications and distribution channels. For example, Procter & Gamble sells Pampers disposable diapers through retailers, supported by millions of dollars of mass-media advertising. However, P&G uses its www.Pampers.com Web site to build relationships with young parents by providing information and advice on everything from diapering to baby care and child development. Similarly, you can't buy crayons from the Crayola Web site (www.crayola.com). However, you can find out how to remove crayon marks from your prize carpeting or freshly painted walls.

Direct marketing is redefining the buyer's role in connecting with sellers. Instead of being the targets of a company's one-way marketing efforts, customers have now become active participants in shaping the marketing offer and process. Many companies now let customers design their own desired products online. For example, shoppers at the Lands' End site (www.LandsEnd.com) can build a "personal model" with their own hair color, height, and shape. They then visit an online

Share of customer: To capture a greater share of customers' leisure and entertainment budget, Amazon.com recommends books, CDs, videos, gifts, and home improvement items based on customers' purchase histories.

dressing room, where they can try clothes on the model to see how they would look in them. The site also gives buyers tips on how best to dress given their individual body styles.

Some marketers have hailed direct marketing as the "marketing model of the next millennium." They envision a day when all buying and selling will involve direct connections between companies and their customers. Others, although agreeing that direct marketing will play a growing and important role, see it as just one more way to approach the marketplace. We will examine the exploding world of direct marketing in more detail in chapter 8.

Connections with Marketing Partners

In these ever more connected times, major changes are occurring in how marketers connect with others inside and outside the company to jointly bring greater value to customers.

Connecting Inside the Company

Traditionally, marketers have played the role of intermediary, charged with understanding customer needs and representing the customer to different company departments, which then acted upon these needs. The old thinking was that marketing is done only by marketing, sales, and customer support people. However, in today's connected world, every functional area can interact with customers, especially electronically. Marketing no longer has sole ownership of customer interactions. The new thinking is that every employee must be customer focused. David Packard, cofounder of Hewlett-Packard, wisely said: "Marketing is far too important to be left only to the marketing department."[24]

Today's forward-looking companies are reorganizing their operations to align them better with customer needs. Rather than letting each department pursue its own objectives, firms are linking all departments in the cause of creating customer value. Rather than assigning only sales and marketing people to customers, they are forming cross-functional customer teams. For example, Procter & Gamble assigns "customer development teams" to each of its major retailer accounts. These teams—consisting of sales and marketing people, operations and logistics specialists, market and financial analysts, and others—coordinate the efforts of many P&G departments toward serving the retailer and helping it to be more successful.

Connecting with Outside Partners

Rapid changes are also occurring in how marketers connect with their suppliers, channel partners, and even competitors. Most companies today are networked companies, relying heavily on partnerships with other firms.

Supply Chain Management.   Marketing channels consist of distributors, retailers, and others who connect the company to its buyers. The *supply chain* describes a longer channel, stretching from raw materials to components to final products that are carried to final buyers. For example, the supply chain for personal computers consists of suppliers of computer chips and other components, the computer manufacturer, and the distributors, retailers, and others who sell the computers to businesses and final customers. Each member of the supply chain creates and captures only a portion of the total value generated by the supply chain.

Through *supply chain management,* many companies today are strengthening their connections with partners all along the supply chain. They know that their fortunes rest not only on how well they perform but also on how well their entire supply chain performs against competitors' supply chains. Rather than treating suppliers as vendors and distributors as customers, it treats both as partners in delivering value to consumers. For example, Wal-Mart works with suppliers like Procter & Gamble, Rubbermaid, and Black & Decker to streamline logistics and reduce joint distribution costs, resulting in lower prices to consumers. Saturn, on the one hand, works closely with carefully selected suppliers to improve quality and operations efficiency. On the other hand, it works with its franchise dealers to provide top-grade sales and service support that will bring customers in the door and keep them coming back.

Strategic Alliances.   Beyond managing the supply chain, today's companies are also discovering that they need *strategic* partners if they hope to be effective. In the new global environment, with greater competition from more and more products and choices, going it alone is going out of style. *Strategic alliances* are booming across the entire spectrum of industries and services. A recent study found that one in every four dollars earned by the top 1,000 U.S. companies flows from alliances, double the rate in the early 1990s.[25] As Jim Kelly, CEO at UPS puts it, "the old adage 'If you can't beat 'em, join 'em,' is being replaced by 'Join 'em and you can't be beat.' " Notes another analyst

> [Think about] how Home Depot and other large retailers operate behind the scenes. They might sell do-it-yourself to consumers, but their own business proposition is do-it-together. Increasingly, enlightened companies are forming strategic alliances with customers, suppliers, and other venture partners. . . . They are replacing go-it-alone strategies with reliance on partnering. . . . Do-it-together means leveraging the strengths of a business partner to create more value and build more sales than either company could do alone. . . . Large companies often count on technological breakthroughs from tiny focused partners who, in turn, need large partners to reach international markets and build credibility. Every search for ways to build sales should include a search for partners who can help reach that goal faster.[26]

Many strategic alliances take the form of *marketing alliances.* These may be *product* or *service alliances* in which one company licenses another to produce its product, or two companies jointly market their complementary products. For instance, Apple Computer joined with Digital Vax to codesign, comanufacture, and comarket a new product. Through *promotional alliances,* one company agrees to join in a promotion for another company's product or service. For example, McDonald's teamed up with Ty to offer an incredibly successful Beanie Babies promotion for its value meals. Companies may form *logistics alliance*s in which one company offers distribution services for another company's product. Abbott Laboratories warehouses and delivers all of 3M's medical and surgical products to hospitals across the United States. Finally, one or more companies may join in special *pricing alliances,* as when hotel and rental car companies join forces to offer mutual price discounts.

Companies need to give careful thought to finding partners who might complement their strengths and offset their weaknesses. Well-managed alliances can have a huge impact on sales and profits. Corning, the $5-billion-a-year glass and ceramics maker, is renowned for making partnerships. It has derived half of its profits from joint ventures that apply its glass technology to various products in many countries, and even defines itself as a "network of organizations." That network includes German and Korean electronics giants, Seimens and Samsung, and Mexico's biggest glassmaker, Vitro. Another good example is AT&T and Sovintel, a Russian telephone company. The two joined forces to offer high-speed ISDN services for digitized voice, data, and video communication between the two countries. By joining together, the two telecommunications companies can offer new services for more business customers than either could do alone.[27]

Connections with the World Around Us

Beyond redefining their relationships with customers and partners, marketers are taking a fresh look at the ways in which they connect with the broader world around them. Here we look at trends toward increasing globalization, more concern for social environmental responsibility, and greater use of marketing by nonprofit and public-sector organizations.

Global Connections

In an increasingly smaller world, many marketers are now connected *globally* with their customers and marketing partners. The world economy has undergone radical change during the past two decades. Geographical and cultural distances have shrunk with the advent of jet planes, fax machines, global computer and telephone hookups, world television satellite broadcasts, and other technical advances. This has allowed companies to greatly expand their geographical market coverage, purchasing, and manufacturing. The result is a vastly more complex marketing environment for both companies and consumers.

Today, almost every company, large or small, is touched in some way by global competition—from the neighborhood florist that buys its flowers from Mexican nurseries to the U.S. electronics manufacturer that competes in its home markets with giant Japanese rivals; from the fledgling Internet retailer that finds itself receiving orders from all over the world to the large American consumer goods producer that introduces new products into emerging markets abroad.

American firms have been challenged at home by the skillful marketing of European and Asian multinationals. Companies such as Toyota, Seimens, Nestlé, Sony, and Samsung have often outperformed their U.S. competitors in American markets. Similarly, U.S. companies in a wide range of industries have found new opportunities abroad. Coca-Cola, General Motors, Exxon, IBM, General Electric, DuPont, Motorola, and dozens of other American companies have developed truly global operations, making and selling their products worldwide. Marketing Highlight 1.3 provides just one of countless examples of U.S. companies taking advantage of global marketing opportunities.

Today, companies are not only trying to sell more of their locally produced goods in international markets, they also are buying more components and supplies abroad. For example, Bill Blass, one of America's top fashion designers, may choose cloth woven from Australian wool with designs printed in Italy. He will design a dress and fax the drawing to a Hong Kong agent, who will place the order with a Chinese factory. Finished dresses will be air-freighted to New York, where they will be redistributed to department and specialty stores around the country.

Thus, managers in countries around the world are increasingly taking a global, not just local, view of the company's industry, competitors, and opportunities. They are asking: What is global marketing? How does it differ from domestic marketing? How do global competitors and forces affect our business? To what extent should we "go global"? Many companies are forming strategic alliances with foreign companies, even competitors, who serve as suppliers or marketing partners. Winning companies in the future may well be those that have built the best global networks.

MARKETING HIGHLIGHT
1 . 3

GOING GLOBAL: COCA-COLA DOMINATES

Coca-Cola is certainly no stranger to global marketing. Long the world's leading soft drink maker, the company now sells its brands in more than 200 countries. In fact, in recent years, as its domestic markets have lost their fizz, Coca-Cola has revved up every aspect of its global marketing. The result: near world dominance of the soft drink market.

The great "global cola wars" between Coca-Cola and rival Pepsi have become decidedly one-sided. In the 1990s, while Pepsi's sales volume rose just 2 percent, Coke Classic consumption increased by more than 30 percent. Since the early 1980s, soft drink consumption has grown at a rate of 3 percent annually both domestically and internationally; during that same period, Coke's volume has grown 5 percent and 7 percent, respectively.

Coca-Cola's international prowess has played a major role in its dominance. In fact, Coca-Cola earns over 70 percent of its profits abroad. Whereas in the United States Coca-Cola captures a 44 percent market share versus Pepsi's 31 percent, it outsells Pepsi 3 to 1 overseas and boasts 4 of the world's 5 leading soft drink brands: Coca-Cola, Diet Coke, Sprite, and Fanta. Coca-Cola has handed Pepsi a number of crushing international setbacks. As a result, Pepsi has recently experienced flat or declining international soda sales. During the same period, Coca-Cola has reported strong growth in Latin America and grew a stunning 29 percent in China, 17 percent in India, and 16 percent in the Philippines.

Pepsi is now retrenching its efforts abroad by focusing on emerging markets—China, India, and Indonesia—where Coke is growing but does not yet dominate. Together,

Coca-Cola dominates the global soft-drink market, selling its products in more than 200 countries.

Connections with Our Values and Social Responsibilities

Marketers are reexamining their connections with social values and responsibilities and with the very Earth that sustains us. As the worldwide consumerism and environmentalism movements mature, today's marketers are being called upon to take greater responsibility for the social and environmental impact of their actions. Corporate ethics and social responsibility have become hot topics in almost every business arena, from the corporate boardroom to the business school classroom. And few companies can ignore the renewed and very demanding environmental movement.

The social responsibility and environmental movements will place even stricter demands on companies in the future. Some companies resist these movements, these three emerging markets boast 2.4 billion people, nearly half the world's total population. With their young populations, exploding incomes, and underdeveloped soft drink demand, they represent prime potential for Coca-Cola and Pepsi. For example, China's 1.2 billion consumers drink an average of only 5 servings of soda per year, compared with 343 in the United States, creating heady opportunities for growth. Indonesia, with 200 million people, nearly all of whom are Muslims forbidden to consume alcohol, is what one top Coca-Cola executive calls a "soft drink paradise."

But even in these emerging markets, Pepsi will find the going rough in the face of Coca-Cola's international marketing savvy and heavy investment. For instance, by the turn of the century, Coca-Cola will have spent almost $2 billion building state-of-the-art Asian bottling plants and distribution systems. And Coca-Cola possesses proven marketing prowess. It carefully tailors its ads and other marketing efforts for each local market. For example, its Chinese New Year television ad featured a dragon in a holiday parade, adorned from head to tail with red Coke cans. The spot concluded, "For many centuries, the color red has been the color for good luck and prosperity. Who are we to argue with ancient wisdom?" In India, Coca-Cola aggressively cultivates a local image. It claimed official sponsorship for World Cup cricket, a favorite national sport, and used Indian cricket fans rather than actors to promote Coke products. Coca-Cola markets effectively to both retailers and imbibers. Observes one Coke watcher, "The company hosts massive gatherings of up to 15,000 retailers to showcase everything from the latest coolers and refrigerators, which Coke has for loan, to advertising displays. And its salespeople go house-to-house in their quest for new customers. In New Delhi alone, workers handed out more than 100,000 free bottles of Coke and Fanta last year."

Nothing better illustrates Coca-Cola's surging global power than the explosive growth of Sprite. Sprite's advertising uniformly targets the world's young people with the tag line "Image is nothing. Thirst is everything. Obey your thirst." The campaign taps into the rebellious side of teenagers and into their need to form individual identities. According to Sprite's director of brand marketing, "The meaning of [Sprite] and what we stand for is exactly the same globally. Teens tell us it's incredibly relevant in nearly every market we go into." However, as always, Coca-Cola tailors its message to local consumers. In China, for example, the campaign has a softer edge: "You can't be irreverent in China, because it's not acceptable in that society. It's all about being relevant [to the specific audience]," notes the marketer. As a result of such smart targeting and powerful positioning, Sprite's worldwide sales have surged 35 percent in the past three years, making it the world's number-four soft drink brand.

Coca-Cola's success as a global power has made it one of the most enduringly profitable companies in history. As one observer states, "Coke will remain the 800 pound gorilla in the soft drink business for the foreseeable future." How profitable has Coca-Cola been over the decades? Incredibly, a single share of Coca-Cola stock purchased for $40 in 1919 would be worth $4,847,000 today.

Sources: Quotes from Mark L. Clifford and Nicole Harris, "Coke Pours into Asia," *Business Week,* October 28, 1996, pp. 72–77; Mark Gleason, "Sprite Is Riding Global Ad Effort to No. 4 Status," *Advertising Age,* November 18, 1996, p. 30; and Scott Reeves, "Pepsi's Fizz," *Barron's,* January 12, 1998, p. 15. Also see Larry Light, "The Pepsi Regeneration," *Business Week,* March 22, 1999, p. 44; Rick Wise, "Why Things Go Better at Coke," *The Journal of Business Strategy,* January–February 1999, pp. 15–19; and Patricia Sellers, "Crunch Time for Coke," *Fortune,* July 19, 1999, pp. 72–78.

budging only when forced by legislation or consumer outcries. More forward-looking companies, however, readily accept their responsibilities to the world around them. They view socially responsible actions as an opportunity to do well by doing good—to profit by serving the best long-run interests of their customers and communities. Some companies—such as Ben & Jerry's, Saturn, The Body Shop, and others—are practicing "caring capitalism" and distinguishing themselves by being more civic-minded and caring. They are building social responsibility and action into their company value and mission statements. For example, Ben & Jerry's mission statement challenges all employees, from top management to ice cream scoopers in each store, to include concern for individual and community welfare in their day-to-day decisions.[28]

Broadening Connections

More and more different kinds of organizations are using marketing to connect with customers and other important constituencies. In the past, marketing has been most widely applied in the for-profit business sector. In recent years, however, marketing also has become a major component in the strategies of many nonprofit organizations, such as colleges, hospitals, museums, symphony orchestras, and even churches. Consider the following examples:

★ Siskin Hospital, a rehabilitation facility in the southeastern United States, has developed a marketing Web site—www.siskinrehab.org. The purpose of the site is to position the hospital as a leader in the rehabilitation field. It provides information and education to the hospital's 14 distinct target audiences, ranging from current and potential patients to health care professionals, hospital staff, job seekers, and the general public. Visitors to the Web site can browse through an online newsletter to learn more about physical rehabilitation and Suskin's programs; review case histories of past patients and their successes; ask questions of the hospital's doctors, nurses, and therapists; and link to other information sources on the Web or in the hospital's "Patient's Library." Siskin regularly markets the Web site through events, specialty advertising items with the imprinted Web site address, and high-impact, direct-mail pieces sent to key prospective users. How has the effort paid off? The site receives more than 400 hits per day and averages 10 to 15 inquiries weekly from potential employees or individuals seeking information on specific rehabilitation-related conditions or treatment programs.[29]

★ At the Sausalito Presbyterian Church, an affluent congregation just across the Golden Gate Bridge from San Francisco, worshipers who'd rather watch football or go to the beach on Sunday morning do church on Saturday evening, at a rock and gospel music service called "Saturday Night Alive." What's particularly revealing about this gathering is the way it's advertised on the church's Web site, www.SausalitoPresbyterian.com. Saturday night worship, it seems, is very user-friendly. "Following the service," the Web page reads, "there is plenty of time to go to dinner, the movies, attend a party or other activities." It's a small but significant disclaimer, revealing how worship must now be marketed as just another diversion in the busy lives of folks in northern California. Church leaders across the nation are using computerized demographic studies and other sophisticated marketing techniques to fill their pews. "Mainline churches don't have to die," says church marketing consultant Richard Southern. "Anyone can learn these marketing and outreach techniques. You don't have to change your theology or your political stance." Southern encourages "an essential . . . shift in the way church is done," putting the needs of potential "customers" before the needs of the institutional church. "Baby boomers think of churches like they think of supermarkets," Southern observes. "They want options, choices, and convenience. Imagine if Safeway was only open one hour a week, had only one product, and didn't explain it in English."[30]

Similarly, many private colleges, facing declining enrollments and rising costs, are using marketing to compete for students and funds. They are defining target markets, improving their communication and promotion, and responding better to student needs and wants. Many performing arts groups—even the Lyric Opera Company of Chicago, which has seasonal sellouts—face huge operating deficits that they must cover by more aggressive donor marketing. Finally, many long-standing nonprofit organizations—the YMCA, the Salvation Army, the Girl Scouts—have lost members and are now modernizing their missions and "products" to attract more members and donors.[31]

Even government agencies have shown an increased interest in marketing. For example, the U.S. Army has a marketing plan to attract recruits, and various government agencies are now designing *social marketing campaigns* to encourage energy

Siskin Hospital's marketing Web site provides information and education to the 14 distinct target audiences, positioning the hospital as a leader in the rehabilitation field

conservation and concern for the environment or to discourage smoking, excessive drinking, and drug use. Even the once-stodgy U.S. Postal Service has developed innovative marketing to sell commemorative stamps, promote its priority mail services against those of its competitors, and lift its image. It has invested heavily in its "Fly Like an Eagle" image advertising campaign. Roxanne Symko, the USPS's manager of advertising and promotion, comments, "We want to position ourselves in a new light, as innovative and looking forward."[32]

Thus, it seems that every type of organization can connect through marketing. The continued growth of nonprofit and public-sector marketing presents new and exciting challenges for marketing managers.

The New Connected World of Marketing

So, today, smart marketers of all kinds are taking advantage of new opportunities for connecting with their customers, their marketing partners, and the world around them. Table 1.1 compares the old marketing thinking to the new. The old marketing thinking saw marketing as little more than selling or advertising. It viewed marketing as customer acquisition rather than customer care. It emphasized trying to make a profit on each sale rather than trying to profit by managing customer lifetime value. It also concerned itself with trying to sell products rather than to understand, create, communicate, and deliver real value to customers.

Fortunately, this old marketing thinking is now giving way to newer ways of thinking. Today's smart marketing companies are improving their customer knowledge and customer connections. They are targeting profitable customers, then finding innovative ways to capture and keep these customers. They are forming more direct connections with customers and building lasting customer relationships. They are using more targeted media and integrating their marketing communications to deliver meaningful and consistent messages through every customer contact. They are employing more technologies such as videoconferencing, sales automation software, and the Internet, intranets, and extranets. They see their suppliers and distributors as partners, not adversaries. In sum, they are forming new kinds of connections for delivering superior value to their customers.

TABLE 1.1 MARKETING CONNECTIONS IN TRANSITION

The Old Marketing Thinking	The New Marketing Thinking
Connections with Customers	
Be sales and product centered	Be market and customer centered
Practice mass marketing	Target selected market segments or individuals
Focus on products and sales	Focus on customer satisfaction and value
Make sales to customers	Develop customer relationships
Get new customers	Keep old customers
Grow share of market	Grow share of customer
Serve any customer	Serve profitable customers, "fire" losing ones
Communicate through mass media	Connect with customers directly
Make standardized products	Develop customized products
Connections with Marketing Partners	
Leave customer satisfaction and value to sales and marketing	Enlist all departments in the cause of customer satisfaction and value
Go it alone	Partner with other firms
Connections with the World Around Us	
Market locally	Market locally *and* globally
Assume profit responsibility	Assume social and environmental responsibility
Market for profits	Market for nonprofits
Conduct commerce in market*places*	Conduct e-commerce in market*spaces*

We will explore all of these developments in more detail in future pages. For now, we must recognize that marketing will continue to change dramatically as we move into the twenty-first century. The new millennium offers many exciting opportunities for forward-thinking marketers.

REVIEW OF CONCEPT CONNECTIONS

Today's successful companies—whether large or small, for-profit or nonprofit, domestic or global—share a strong customer focus and a heavy commitment to marketing. Many people think of marketing as only selling or advertising. But marketing combines many activities—marketing research, product development, distribution, pricing, advertising, personal selling, and others—designed to sense, serve, and satisfy consumer needs while meeting the organization's goals. Marketing seeks to attract new customers by promising superior value and to keep current customers by delivering satisfaction.

Marketing operates within a dynamic global environment. Rapid changes can quickly make yesterday's winning strategies obsolete. Marketers face many new challenges and opportunities. To be successful, companies will have to be strongly market focused.

1. Define what marketing is and discuss its core concepts.
Marketing is a social and managerial process whereby individuals and groups obtain what they need and want through creating and exchanging products and value with others. The core concepts of marketing are *needs, wants,* and *demands; products* and *services; value, satisfaction,* and *quality; exchange, transactions,* and *relationships;* and *markets. Wants* are

the form assumed by human needs when shaped by culture and individual personality. When backed by buying power, wants become *demands.* People satisfy their needs, wants, and demands with products and services. A *product* is anything that can be offered to a market to satisfy a need or want. Products also include *services* and other entities such as *experiences, persons, places, organizations, information,* and *ideas.*

2. Explain the relationships between customer value, satisfaction, and quality.
In deciding which products and services to buy, consumers rely on their perception of relative value. *Customer value* is the difference between the values the customer gains from owning and using a product and the costs of obtaining and using the product. *Customer satisfaction* depends on a product's perceived performance in delivering value relative to a buyer's expectations. Customer satisfaction is closely linked to *quality,* leading many companies to adopt *total quality management (TQM)* practices. Marketing occurs when people satisfy their needs and wants through *exchange.* Beyond creating short-term exchanges, marketers need to build long-term relationships with valued customers, distributors, dealers, and suppliers.

3. Define marketing management and examine how marketers manage demand and build profitable customer relationships.

Marketing management is the analysis, planning, implementation, and control of programs designed to create, build, and maintain beneficial exchanges with target buyers for the purpose of achieving organizational objectives. It involves more than simply finding enough customers for the company's current output. Marketing is at times also concerned with changing or even reducing demand. Managing demand means managing customers. Beyond designing strategies to *attract* new customers and create *transactions* with them, today's companies are focusing on *retaining* current customers and building lasting relationships through offering superior customer value and satisfaction.

4. Compare the five marketing management philosophies.

Marketing management can be guided by five different philosophies. The *production concept* holds that consumers favor products that are available and highly affordable; management's task is to improve production efficiency and bring down prices. The *product concept* holds that consumers favor products that offer the most in quality, performance, and innovative features; thus, little promotional effort is required. The *selling concept* holds that consumers will not buy enough of the organization's products unless it undertakes a large-scale selling and promotion effort. The *marketing concept* holds that achieving organizational goals depends on determining the needs and wants of target markets and delivering the desired satisfactions more effectively and efficiently than competitors do. The *societal marketing concept* holds that generating customer satisfaction *and* long-run societal well-being are the keys to achieving both the company's goals and its responsibilities.

5. Analyze the major challenges for future marketers.

Dramatic changes in the marketplace are creating many marketing opportunities and challenges. Major marketing developments can be summed up in a single theme: *connections*. The explosive growth in connecting technologies—computer, telecommunications, information, and transportation technologies—has created exciting new ways for marketers to learn about and serve consumers, in large groups or one-to-one. Marketers are rapidly redefining how they connect with their customers, with their marketing partners, and with the world around them. They are choosing their customers more carefully and developing closer, more lasting, and more direct connections with them. Realizing that going it alone is going out of style, they are connecting more closely with other company departments and with other firms in an integrated effort to bring more value to customers. They are taking a fresh look at the ways in which they connect with the broader world, resulting in increased globalization, growing attention to social and environmental responsibilities, and greater use of marketing by nonprofit and public-sector organizations. The new, connected millennium offers exciting possibilities for forward-thinking marketers.

KEY TERMS

Customer satisfaction
Customer value
Demands
Demarketing
Exchange
Internet
Market

Marketing
Marketing concept
Marketing management
Needs
Product
Product concept
Production concept

Relationship marketing
Selling concept
Service
Societal marketing concept
Total quality management (TQM)
Transaction
Wants

ISSUES FOR DISCUSSION

The delivery of customer satisfaction at a profit.

1. Answer the question, "What is marketing?"
2. Discuss the concept of customer value and its importance to successful marketing. How are customer value and relationship marketing linked? *A perception, feeling*
3. Marketing can be practiced in many ways. Discuss the three stages through which marketing practice often passes. Identify each stage, describe the stage's characteristics, and provide an example of a company in that stage.
4. What is the single biggest difference between the marketing concept and the production, product, and selling

concepts? Which concepts are easier to adopt in the short run? Which concept offers the best chances of long-run success? Why?

5. Select a company that makes a product that consumers want but which may run contrary to society's best interests (for example, tobacco, liquor, or environmentally harmful products). Considering the company's profit goals, discuss the ways in which it might resolve the conflicts that arise between satisfying individual wants and guarding societal welfare.

INSIDE-out v.s. outside-in

6. As we enter the new millennium, major marketing developments are summed up by a single theme: *connectedness*. List and discuss three important connections made possible by the connecting technologies (such as computer, information, and transportation technologies). Give examples of companies taking advantages of such connections.

p.23 *Yahoo, etrade, ebay*

7. Perhaps the most dramatic new technology driving the connected age is the Internet. Why is this true? Provide examples that demonstrate how marketers can use the Internet to (a) reach new customers, (b) form new distribution channels, and (c) meet or beat competition.

CONNECT THE WORLD w/o BORDER

MARKETING APPLICATIONS

1. Companies can apply the marketing concept on their Web sites by including features that are important to customers and prospects. At the least, Web users want to know about product benefits and where they can buy products. However, sites that give users something beyond product descriptions create additional customer value and build long-term relationships. Many sites target specific customer segments by focusing on language, age, gender, or technical understanding. Finally, an important sign of customer orientation is having an e-mail address that is easy to remember, use, and communicate to the consumer. Evaluate the following Web site based on its apparent attention to the marketing concept: www.apple.com.
   a. What is the most important customer benefit stressed at this site?
   b. What new products did you find? Which one(s) did you find most interesting?
   c. To what extent does this site apply the marketing concept? Explain.
   d. Should anything be added to the site? Explain.
   e. How does Apple attempt to build relationships with Web site visitors? What "connections" is Apple attempting to make?

2. Few companies do as much to apply the societal marketing concept as Ben & Jerry's Ice Cream (see www.benjerry.com). The company's two founders have made a strong and sincere commitment to a wide range of ecological and social causes. In addition, the company often takes a light-hearted approach to what others perceive to be serious business matters, such as the annual shareholder's meeting. At Ben & Jerry's, this meeting might well take the form of large picnic or rock concert at which the annual report is sung to the tune of a popular song rather than just being read in a boring way.
   a. Visit the Ben & Jerry's Web site. What impresses you most? What marketing efforts are evident?
   b. What social and ecological causes does the company support?
   c. What values are communicated by the company? Do these values appear to help or hinder its marketing efforts? Its profitability?
   d. How does the company attempt to build relationships or "connections" with its customers?
   e. If you were a competitor seeking to expand market share, what vulnerabilities do you see in Ben & Jerry's that could be exploited? Write a brief plan for doing this.

INTERNET CONNECTIONS

THE MARKETING CONCEPT

Web sites can demonstrate the marketing concept by exhibiting a company's special features to customers and prospects. Many sites target customer segments by language, gender, and age, providing slightly different content for each target. In general, Web users want to know about product benefits. However, sites that give surfers something of interest beyond product descriptions create additional value. The most attractive site advantages tend to be interactive in nature. For example, e-mail and surveys allow for customer feedback; intelligent agents can find the right product for the customer's needs; and retail locators tell the customer where she can buy the product that she needs. Complete the following chart to indicate which benefits are supported on the Web sites of three athletic shoe companies. Then decide which firm is the most customer oriented.

FOR DISCUSSION

1. Of the benefits listed in the chart, which three do you think are the most important? Why?
2. Overall, which site best embodies the marketing concept? Why?
3. Suggest one or more customer benefits not listed in the chart, that the best site contains.
4. Based on your analysis of Nike's site, are they interested in relationship marketing? Support your answer.

Benefit	Nike www.nike.com	Reebok www.reebok.com	New Balance www.newbalance.com
Retail locator	***	**	**
Nonproduct information	*	***	**
Multiple languages	✗	***	****
Multiple targets: Gender	⊘ ⊘ *Both*	*female/male*	—
Multiple targets: Age	*none*	*none*	*kids → adult*
Multiple targets: Different sports	*basketball, football*	*tennis, running ...*	*many, yes*
Customer feedback	✗	**	**
Intelligent agents	**	**	***
Fun to surf?	***	**	

tech   *tech*

SAVVY SITES

Which are the best sites on the Web? Check out the following sites to see what the experts think:

★ MediaMetrix (www.mediametrix.com) measures surfing behavior in their panel of Internet users and releases listings of top ranked sites according to number of visitors.

★ NetMarketing (www.netb2b.com) reviews and rates the top 200 Web sites in the business-to-business market.

★ Webnet Web Ratings (www.webratings.net) is a nonprofit organization that rates submitted Web sites on a 1-to-5 scale based on content, navigation of site, appearance, and ease of reading.

NOTES

1. Quotes from Bill Saporito, "Can Nike Get Unstuck?" *Time,* March 30, 1998, pp. 48–53; Jolie Solomon, "When Cool Goes Cold," *Newsweek,* March 30, 1998, pp. 36–37; and Jerry Edgerton, "Can Nike Still Play Above the Rim?" *Money,* May 1999, p. 48. Also see Linda Himelstein, "The Swoosh Heard 'Round the World," *Business Week,* May 12, 1997, p. 76; Patricia Sellers, "Four Reasons Nike's Not Cool," *Fortune,* March 30, 1998, pp. 26–27; "Thanks, Mike: Phil Knight on Michael Jordan's Retirement," Nike press release, www.nikebiz.com, January 13, 1999; Nike's Web page at www.nike.com, November, 1999; and Louise Lee, "Can Nike Still Do It?" *Business Week,* February 21, 2000, pp. 121–128.

2. Here are some other definitions: "*Marketing* is the performance of business activities that direct the flow goods and services from producer to consumer or user." "*Marketing* is getting the right goods to the right people at the right place at the right time at the right price with the right communication and promotion." "*Marketing* is the creation of a standard of living." The American Marketing Association offers this definition: "*Marketing* is the process of planning and executing the conception, pricing, promotion, and distributing of ideas, goods, and services to create exchanges that satisfy individual and organizational objectives."

3. Andrew Kupfer, "AT&T Gets Lucky," *Fortune,* November 9, 1998, pp. 108–10.

4. See B. Joseph Pine II and James Gilmore, "Welcome to the Experience Economy," *Harvard Business Review,* July–August 1998, p. 99. Also see Philip Kotler, *Marketing Management: Analysis, Planning, Implementation, and Control,* 10th ed. (Upper Saddle River, NJ: Prentice Hall, 2000), pp. 3–5.

5. See Theodore Levitt's classic article, "Marketing Myopia," *Harvard Business Review,* July–August 1960, pp. 45–56. For more recent discussions, see Dhananjayan Kashyap, "Marketing Myopia Revisited A Look Through the 'Colored Glass of a Client,'" *Marketing and Research Today,* August 1996, pp. 197–201; Colin Grant, "Theodore Levitt's Marketing Myopia," *Journal of Business Ethics,* February 1999, pp. 397–406; and Jeffrey M. O'Brien, "Drums in the Jungle," *MC Technology Marketing Intelligence,* March 1999, pp. 22–30.

6. See Andy Cohen, "Federal Express," *Sales & Marketing Management,* November 1996, p. 50. For good discussions of defining and measuring customer value, see Howard E. Butz Jr. and Leonard D. Goodstein, "Measuring Customer Value: Gaining Strategic Advantage," *Organizational Dynamics,* Winter 1996, pp. 63–77; Robert B. Woodruff, "Customer Value: The Next Source of Competitive Advantage," *Journal of the Academy of Marketing Science,* Spring 1997, pp. 139–53; James C. Anderson and James A. Narus, "Business Marketing: Understand What Customers Value," *Harvard Business Review,* November–December 1998, pp. 53–61; and W. Chan Kim and Renee Mauborgne, "Creating New Market Space," *Harvard Business Review,* January–February 1999, pp. 83–93.

7. For more on customer satisfaction, see Jaclyn Fierman, "Americans Can't Get No Satisfaction," *Fortune,* December 11, 1995, p. 186; Richard A. Spreng, Scott B. MacKenzie, and Richard W. Olshavsky, "A Reexamination of the Determinants of Customer Satisfaction," *Journal of Marketing,* July 1996, pp. 15–32; Thomas A. Stewart, "A Satisfied Customer Isn't Enough," *Fortune,* July 21, 1997, pp. 112–13; and Subhash Sharma, Ronald W. Niedrich, and Greg Dobbins, "A Framework for Monitoring Customer Satisfaction," *Industrial Marketing Management,* May 1999, pp. 231–43.

8. Lois Therrien, "Motorola and NEC: Going for Glory," *Business Week,* special issue on quality, 1991, pp. 60–61. For more on quality, see Roland T. Rust, Anthony J. Zahorik, and Timothy L. Keiningham, "Return on Quality (ROQ): Making Service Quality Financially Accountable," *Journal of Marketing,* April 1995, pp. 58–70; Iris Mohr-Jackson, "Managing a Total Quality Orientation: Factors Affecting Customer Satisfaction," *Industrial Marketing Management,* March 1998, pp. 109–25; Melissa Larson, "Whatever Happened to TQM?" *Quality,* June 1999, pp. 32–35; and Zhu Zhiwei and Larry Scheuermann, "A Comparison of Quality Programs: Total Quality Management and ISO 9000," *Total Quality Management,* March 1999, pp. 291–95.

9. See James C. Anderson, Hakan Hakansson, and Jan Johanson, "Dyadic Business Relationships Within a Business Network Context," *Journal of Marketing,* October 15, 1994, pp. 1–15. For more discussion of relationship marketing, see Thomas W. Gruen, "Relationship Marketing: The Route to Marketing Efficiency and Effectiveness," *Business Horizons,* November–December 1997, pp. 32–38; and John V. Petrof, "Relationship Marketing: The Emperor in Used Clothes," *Business Horizons,* March–April 1998, pp. 79–82.

10. For more discussion on demand states, see Kotler, *Marketing Management: Analysis, Planning, Implementation, and Control,* chap. 1.

11. For more on assessing customer value, see Gordon A. Wyner, "Customer Valuation: Linking Behavior and Economics," *Marketing Research,* Summer 1996, pp. 36–38; Gordon A. Wyner, "Which Customers Will Be Valuable in the Future?" *Marketing Research,* Fall 1996, pp. 44–46; Bill Stoneman, "Banking on Customers," *American Demographics,* February 1997, pp. 37–41; Paul D. Berger, "Customer Lifetime Value: Marketing Models and Applications," *Journal of Interactive Marketing,* Winter 1998, pp. 17–30; and Libby Estell, "This Call Center Accelerates Sales," *Sales & Marketing Management,* February 1999, p. 72.

12. Sam Hill and Glenn Rifkin, *Radical Marketing* (New York: HarperBusiness, 1999).

13. Ralph Waldo Emerson offered this advice: "If a man . . . makes a better mousetrap . . . the world will beat a path to his door." Several companies, however, have built better mousetraps yet failed. One was a laser mousetrap costing $1,500. Contrary to popular assumptions, people do not automatically learn about new products, believe product claims, or willingly pay higher prices.

14. Barry Farber and Joyce Wycoff, "Customer Service: Evolution and Revolution," *Sales & Marketing Management,* May 1991, p. 47. Also see Jaclyn Fierman, "Americans Can't Get No Satisfaction," *Fortune,* December 11, 1995, pp. 186–94.

15. Gary Hamel and C. K. Prahalad, "Seeing the Future First," *Fortune,* September 5, 1994, pp. 64–70. Also see Philip Kotler, *Kotler on Marketing* (New York: Free Press, 1999), pp. 20–24.

16. Howard Schlossberg, "Customer Satisfaction: Not a Fad, but a Way of Life," *Marketing News,* June 10, 1991, p. 18. Also see Bernard J. Jaworski and Ajay K. Kohli, "Market Orientation: Antecedents and Consequences," *Journal of Marketing,* July 1993, pp. 53–70; and E. K. Valentin, "The Marketing Concept and the Conceptualization of Market Strategy," *Journal of Marketing Theory and Practice,* Fall 1996, pp. 16–27.

17. See "Leaders of the Most Admired," *Fortune,* January 29, 1990, pp. 40–54; and Thomas A. Stewart, "America's Most Admired Companies," *Fortune,* March 2, 1998, pp. 70–82.

18. "Leaders of the Most Admired," p. 54.

19. Internet usage and buying statistics provided by Forrester Research, August 1999.

20. Robert D. Hof, "The 'Click Here' Economy," *Business Week,* June 22, 1998, pp. 122–28.

21. Patricia Sellers, "Inside the First E-Christmas," *Fortune,* February 1, 1999, pp. 70–73; Nanette Byrnes and Paul C. Judge, "Internet Anxiety," *Business Week,* June 28, 1999, pp. 79–88; Heather Green, "The Great Yuletide Shakeout," *Business Week,* November 1, 1999, p. Eb22.

22. Wallys W. Conhaim, "E-Commerce," *Link-Up,* March–April 1998, pp. 8–10.

23. Rick Brooks, "Unequal Treatment: Alienating Customers Isn't Always a Bad Idea, Many Firms Discover," *Wall Street Journal,* January 7, 1999, p. A1. Also see Erika Rasmusson, "Wanted: Profitable Customers," *Sales & Marketing Management,* May 1999, pp. 28–34.

24. Philip Kotler, *Kotler on Marketing* (New York: Free Press, 1999), p. 20.

25. Thor Valdmanis, "Alliances Gain Favor over Risky Mergers," *USA Today,* February 4, 1999, p. 3B.

26. Rosabeth Moss Kanter, "Why Collaborate?" *Executive Excellence,* April 1999, p. 8.

27. Ibid.; and Kotler, *Marketing Management: Analysis, Planning, Implementation, and Control,* p. 82. For more on strategic alliances, see Peter Lorange and Johan Roos, *Strategic Alliances: Formation, Implementation and Evolution* (Cambridge, MA: Blackwell, 1992); Jordan D. Lewis, *Partnerships for Profit: Structuring and Managing Strategic Alliances* (New York: Free Press, 1990); and Gabor Gari, "Leveraging the Rewards of Strategic Alliances," *The Journal of Business Strategy,* April 1999, pp. 40–43.

28. See Ben & Jerry's full mission statement online at www.benjerry.com. For more reading on environmentalism, see William S. Stavropoulos, "Environmentalism's Third Wave," *Executive Speeches,* August–September 1996, pp. 28–30; Stuart L. Hart,

"Beyond Greening: Strategies for a Sustainable World," *Harvard Business Review*, January–February 1997, pp. 67–76; and Michael Lounsbury, "From Heresy to Dogma: An Institutional History of Corporate Environmentalism," *Administrative Science Quarterly*, March 1999, pp. 193–95. For more on marketing and social responsibility, see Daniel Kadlec, "The New World of Giving," *Time*, May 5, 1997, pp. 62–64; Heather Salerno, "From Selling Cars to Building Playgrounds," *Washington Post*, June 9, 1997, p. F11; and "Can Doing Good Be Good for Business?" *Fortune*, February 2, 1998, pp. 148G–48J.

29. Thomas G. Widmer and C. David Shepherd, "Developing a Hospital Web Site as a Marketing Tool: A Case Study," *Marketing Health Services*, Spring 1999, pp. 32–33.

30. Richard Cimino and Don Lattin, "Choosing My Religion," *American Demographics*, April 1999, pp. 60–65.

31. For other examples, and for a good review of nonprofit marketing, see Philip Kotler and Alan R. Andreasen, *Strategic Marketing for Nonprofit Organizations*, 5th ed. (Upper Saddle River, NJ: Prentice Hall, 1996); Philip Kotler and Karen Fox, *Strategic Marketing for Educational Institutions* (Upper Saddle River, NJ: Prentice Hall, 1995); Norman Shawchuck, Philip Kotler, Bruce Wren, and Gustave Rath, *Marketing for Congregations: Choosing to Serve People More Effectively* (Nashville, TN: Abingdon Press, 1993); William P. Ryan, "The New Landscape for Nonprofits," *Harvard Business Review*, January–February 1999, pp. 127–36; Denise Nitterhouse, "Nonprofit and Social Marketing," *Nonprofit Management and Leadership*, Spring 1999, pp. 323–28; and Diane Bradley, "Uncle Sam Wants You . . . to Have Fun," *Business Week*, February 21, 2000, pp. 98–101.

32. Ira Teinowitz, "Postal Service Tries Image of Innovation," *Advertising Age*, October 1998, p. 6.

COMPANY CASE

Priceline.com: Changing Business in the New Millennium?

Creating value for customers means not only making better products and services but also helping consumers obtain those product and services easily. If you wanted a new shirt in the year 1701, you might have had it custom-made by your mother, grandmother, sister, or, if you had the money, a tailor. In 1801, you might have bought it at a draper's, a specialty store that sold clothes and a few other dry goods. By 1901, you could have purchased the shirt off the rack in one of the big new department stores, such as Wannamaker's. In 1959, you'd have visited the new retailing institution of the day—the shopping center. In 1979, it was the discount store; and in 1990, the warehouse store. In 2001, going full circle, consumers may well be ordering custom-made shirts again, this time over the Internet.

The industrial revolution created more goods more cheaply, but it also required a new means of selling all those goods. As product assortments swelled, retailers realized that the expanded assortments couldn't all be sold in limited-line shops. Thus developed the department store, where consumers could find many different types of goods under one roof. Shopping became easier through the aggregation of goods, and stores provided many services, such as credit and delivery of large goods. They carried merchandise across multiple price ranges with the best goods several floors above and real bargains in the basement. Social needs were accommodated through lunch and tea rooms, where weary shoppers could rest their feet and recuperate before continuing to shop.

As more and more goods poured onto the market, no single store could accommodate them. Stores began to group together in central shopping districts or shopping centers to give consumers more choice. As competition for consumer dollars increased, some retailers began offering lower prices to attract shoppers away from department stores with their high overheads. Early discount stores reduced their services, even to the point of eliminating sales clerks, locating in low-rent locations, and operating in spartan facilities. Eventually some of these discounters would follow the department store idea of aggregating product assortments into larger stores such as warehouse stores.

Throughout this retailing evolution, aggregation and convenience seem to have been the guiding principles. Make it easier for consumers to shop by providing them with more goods in one location. Today, a prime example of these principles is the massive Mall of America in Minneapolis, which features more than 10 department stores, 400 specialty shops, dozens of eating facilities, and even a theme park—all under one roof. Even low-priced discounters have followed the aggregation principle. Category killers such as such as Office Depot or Home Depot offer deep assortments of goods in their product categories.

Aggregation and convenience also seem to be keywords for retailing in the beginning of the new millennium. Can you imagine a brick-and-mortar bookstore large enough to hold the entire inventory of Amazon.com? How about a flea market the size of eBay.com, or a shopping center with as many vendors as America Online or Yahoo!? The Internet offers almost unlimited shopping possibilities, all from the comfort of your own home, whenever it's convenient for you, from anywhere around the globe.

From the department store to the Internet, the underlying business model is the same. A marketing intermediary (Wannamaker's, Wal-Mart, Amazon.com) assembles an assortment of many items, often from far-flung and numerous sources, and makes them conveniently available to consumers in a single location. Consumers examine the merchandise, look at the price, and make a purchase decision. Sometimes they can even have shopping assistants (or "bots" in the case of Internet shopping) do the search and comparison for them.

Some Internet merchants adjust this model a little. Online auction sites, such as those of eBay.com and Amazon.com, use dynamic pricing by allowing consumers to bid on items. However, most of the goods offered at auction are unique items, such as collectibles, rather than regular merchandise.

Priceline.com is building on the success of these online auction sites. At the Priceline Web site, consumers can bid on nonunique items, such airline tickets, mortgages, hotel rooms, autos, groceries, and now even telephone time. Priceline lets consumers specify the goods they want and the price they are willing to pay, then determines whether one of its suppliers will accept that bid. Although much heralded as a new business model benefiting consumers, a closer examination suggests that Priceline's operation benefits sellers as much as or more than it benefits consumers.

In the airline industry, for example, where unsold seats are perishable, an airline would always prefer to sell the seats even at rock-bottom prices than to leave them empty. So the airlines tell Priceline what prices they will accept for these seats and specify conditions. For example, if you want to fly from Chicago to Miami, you log on to Priceline, give dates, departure and destination cities, a price bid, and a credit card number. If your bid matches an airline price, Priceline completes the sale. However, you have no control over flight times or on which airline you fly, and frequently you may find yourself flying through smaller airports and making more plane changes. What's more, if the airline accepts your bid, you cannot refuse to buy the ticket. Thus, under the Priceline model, consumers have become commodities, willing to fly whenever and on whatever routes the airlines select.

Selling space in hotels through Priceline is essentially a demand collection system. Consumers indicate where they want to go and what they want to pay, giving the hotels a picture of their daily demand. Consumers can specify the area of a city in which they wish to stay but not the specific hotel. The same holds true for mortgages and cars—consumers cannot specify the specific lender or dealer. Similarly, groceries purchased through Priceline must be picked up in a participating store. The consumer must still walk the aisles and when checking out must separate the bid items from those purchased at the regular price.

Even Priceline CEO Jay Walker admits that Priceline isn't going to help consumers find fantastic low rates. "We are not a discount ticket warehouse. We're the place to go when you can't find a published fare you can live with. The bottom line is that Priceline.com works best if you want to fly soon and face only the highest-price tickets, because you'll likely land the usual 21-day advance purchase fare." In such cases, it might well be worth giving up control over airlines, flight times, and routes.

Another Internet company, NexTag.com, follows a somewhat different model. Using NexTag, consumers can bid on computers, electronics, books, software, and movies. In each product category, would-be buyers get a list of sellers and their suggested prices. Once a consumer makes a bid, NexTag lets merchants compete for the business. The consumer gets to pick the merchant and even drive prices down. However, consumers need to do their homework before going online. To get a good deal, they need to check manufacturers' and retailers' regular prices and allow for some profit margin. Otherwise, there's no reason for the seller to accept their bid.

If they can't get rock-bottom prices on the Web, will people want to buy groceries and telephone time over the Internet? Even if they get a penny-per-minute reduction on a long-distance call, that's still a savings of only 60 cents an hour. Is it worth your time and effort to get a 2-cent reduction on a can of peas? Two cents on fifty items amounts to only a $1 reduction at the store, and you must spend time making bids and waiting for acknowledgment of them. Thus, many analysts believe that low-priced items such as groceries and telephone calls are not suitable for Internet selling. For the time being, traditional sellers of low-priced items appear to be safe from Internet competition.

Further, the impact of dynamic pricing on the Internet may not be to lower prices significantly. Even with the lower prices offered by Internet sellers such as Amazon.com, price savings must be weighed against waiting for goods, the lack of personal assistance, and the want of an active shopping experience. Thus, the main benefit of such Internet shopping may simply be to make larger assortments of goods available than local retailers can.

QUESTIONS

1. How does the Internet illustrate the marketing concept in action?
2. Explain how department stores, shopping centers, discounters, and warehouse stores created value for consumers.
3. How do Internet sellers such as Priceline.com, NexTag.com, and Amazon.com create value for con-

sumers? Contrast this value creation with that of traditional retailers in question 2.

4. How does the Internet create value for goods and service producers?

5. Can a company like Priceline.com sell low-priced items such as groceries and telephone calls?

6. How does a firm like Priceline.com exemplify the new model for connecting with customers as explained in the chapter?

Sources: "Going, Going, Gone," *Business Week,* April 12, 1999, p. 30; "Let the Buyer Be in Control," *Business Week,* November 8, 1999, p. 100; "Priceline Fills Hotel Demand Niche," *Lodging Hospitality,* August 1999, p. 69; Katherine T. Beddingfield, "Airfare Roulette," *U.S. News & World Report,* April 27, 1998, p. 75; Peter Elkind, "The Hype Is Big, Really Big," *Fortune,* September 6, 1999, p. 193; Louis Lavelle, "New Internet Service Allows Savvy Car Buyers to Name Their Price," *Knight-Ridder/Tribune Business News,* July 14, 1998; Nick Wingfield, "New Battlefield for Priceline Is Diapers, Tuna," *Wall Street Journal,* September 24, 1999, pp. B1, B4.

After studying this chapter, you should be able to
1. explain companywide strategic planning and its four steps
2. discuss how to design business portfolios and growth strategies
3. explain functional planning strategies and assess marketing's role in strategic planning
4. describe the marketing process and the forces that influence it
5. list the marketing management functions, including the elements of a marketing plan

CHAPTER 2

STRATEGIC PLANNING AND THE MARKETING PROCESS

For more than 25 years, Intel has dominated the microprocessor market for personal computers. Its sales and profits have soared accordingly. In the little more than a dozen years since IBM introduced its first PCs based on Intel's 8088 microprocessor, the chip giant's sales have jumped more than twentyfold to over $25 billion. Its share of the microprocessor market now tops 90 percent, turning competitors such as Advanced Micro Devices (AMD) and Cyrix into little more than also-rans. During the past 10 years, with gross margins hovering at around 60 percent, Intel's average annual return has been an astounding 36 percent.

Intel's stunning success results from strong strategic planning and its relentless dedication to a simple marketing strategy: Provide the most value and satisfaction to customers through product leadership. Some companies deliver superior value through convenience and low prices; others by coddling their customers and tailoring products to meet the special needs of precisely defined market niches. In contrast, Intel's strong connection with consumers rests on delivering superior value by creating a continuous stream of leading-edge products. Then, it communicates its superior value directly to final buyers. The result is intense cus-

Don't just get onto the Internet, get into it.

tomer loyalty and preference, both from the computer and software producers who add ever more features that require increasingly brawny microprocessors and from final PC buyers who want their PCs to do ever more cool things.

Intel's microprocessors are true wonders of modern technology. Intel invests heavily to develop state-of-the-art products and bring them quickly to market—last year alone it spent a whopping $5 billion on R&D and capital spending. The result is a rapid succession of ever better chips that no competitor can match. For example, less than a decade ago, we marveled at Intel's i386 microprocessors, which contained one-quarter-million transistors and ran at clock speeds approaching 20 megahertz. However, Intel's next generation Pentium series microprocessors contained more than 5 million transistors and ran at speeds exceeding 450 megahertz. Its current Pentium III processor will soon break the 1 gigahertz (1,000 megahertz) mark. Incredibly, the Intel microprocessors of 2011 will pack a cool *billion* transistors and will blaze along at clock speeds of 10 gigahertz (or 10,000 megahertz).

In fact, Intel has innovated at such a torrid pace that its microprocessors have at times outpaced market needs and capabilities. For example, in the early 1990s, the industry's existing bus system—the internal network that directs the flow of electrons within a computer—served up data at a far slower rate than Intel's new Pentium could handle. Why should producers buy the faster chips if existing PC architecture couldn't take advantage of them? Instead of waiting for PC makers to act, Intel quickly designed a new bus called PCI and shared it with computer makers. The PCI became the standard bus on PCs, paving the way for Intel's faster chips.

Intel's growth depends on increasing the demand for microprocessors, which in turn depends on growth in PC applications and sales. Thus, moving into the new millennium, Intel has taken its marketing strategy a step further. Rather than sitting back and relying on others to create new market applications requiring its increasingly powerful microprocessors, it now develops such applications itself. According to one account, to ensure continued growth in the demand for its microprocessors, Intel has set out "to make the PC the central appliance in our lives. In [Intel's] vision, we will use PCs to watch TV, to play complex games on the Internet, to store and edit family photos, to manage the appliances in our homes, and to stay in regular video contact with our family, friends, and co-workers." Of course, at the heart of all of these applications will be the latest Intel-powered PC.

To realize this vision, Intel has invested heavily in market development. For example, it set up the Intel Architecture Labs (IAL), where 600 employees work to expand the market for all PC-related products, not just Intel products. One IAL project involves finding ways to help popularize Internet telephony, through which PC owners can make long-distance voice phone calls over the Internet. IAL helped develop better technology for making such calls, worked with the Internet industry to develop telephony standards, and gave away Intel software supporting the standard. Next, Intel will promote technologies and software for Internet videophones. It expects that PC makers will soon build these telephony functions into their products. The result: More people will buy new PCs containing powerful Intel microprocessors.

In recent years, Intel has also invested in dozens of small companies working on projects that might spark demand for the processing power that only Intel can supply. The company's widely varied investments include the Palace, which creates virtual Web communities; Citrix Systems, which makes software to link Internet users; biztravel.com, an online travel service; and CyberCash, which is developing an online payment system. Another Intel acquisition, OnLive! Technologies, is an Internet chat room program that offers online interactions through 3-D characters. "The next killer app," says the former head of Intel's Internet and Communications Group, "is use of the Internet for online [socializing]." He sees the day when individuals can use computers in their own homes to watch a ball game or movie as a group, making comments through their online 3-D characters as they watch. Again, such connections will require far more computing power than today's PCs afford, and new Intel chips will provide the needed power.

Intel's marketing strategy goes far beyond superior products and market development. In mid-1991, Intel began strengthening its direct connections with consumers by launching the "Intel Inside" advertising campaign. Traditionally, chip companies like Intel had marketed only to the manufacturers who buy chips directly. But as long as microprocessors remained anonymous little lumps hidden inside a user's computer, Intel remained at the mercy of the clone makers and other competitors. The groundbreaking "Intel Inside" campaign appeals directly to final computer buyers—Intel's customers' customers. Brand-awareness ads—such as those in the current "Bunny People" campaign—create brand personality and convince PC buyers that Intel microprocessors really are superior. Intel also subsidizes ads by PC manufacturers that include the "Intel Inside" logo. Over the years, the hundreds of millions of dollars invested in the "Intel Inside" campaign have created strong brand preference for Intel chips among final buyers. This, in turn, has made Intel's chips more attractive to computer manufacturers.

Looking ahead, Intel must plan its strategy carefully. Its continued torrid growth and industry dominance will depend on its ability to produce a steady flow of state-of-the-art chips for markets ranging from inexpensive home computers to high-end servers. It will have to create irresistible new applications that will lure new consumers into PC ownership and encourage current owners to trade up their machines. Intel's top executives don't foresee any slowing of the pace. Says Intel President Craig Barrett, "We picture ourselves going down the road at 120 miles an hour. Somewhere there's going to be a brick wall, . . . but our view is that it's better to run into the wall than to anticipate it and fall short."[1]

All companies must look ahead and develop long-term strategies to meet the changing conditions in their industries. Each company must find the game plan that makes the most sense given its specific situation, opportunities, objectives, and resources. The hard task of selecting an overall company strategy for long-run survival and growth is called *strategic planning*.

In this chapter, we look first at the organization's overall strategic planning. Next, we discuss marketing's role in the organization as it is defined by the overall strategic plan. Finally, we explain the marketing management process—the process that marketers undertake to carry out their role in the organization.

STRATEGIC PLANNING

Many companies operate without formal plans. In new companies, managers are sometimes so busy they have no time for planning. In small companies, managers sometimes think that only large corporations need formal planning. In mature companies, many managers argue that they have done well without formal planning and that therefore it cannot be too important. They may resist taking the time to prepare a written plan. They may argue that the marketplace changes too quickly for a plan to be useful, that it would end up collecting dust.

Granted, planning is not much fun, and it takes time away from doing. Yet companies must plan. As someone said, "If you fail to plan, you are planning to fail."[2] Formal planning can yield many benefits for all types of companies, large and small, new and mature.

The process of planning may be as important as the plans that emerge. Planning encourages management to think systematically about what has happened, what is happening, and what might happen. It forces the company to sharpen its objectives and policies, leads to better coordination of company efforts, and provides clearer performance standards for control. The argument that planning is less useful in a fast-changing environment makes little sense. In fact, the opposite is true: Sound planning helps the company to anticipate and respond quickly to changes, and to prepare better for sudden developments. Thus planning turns out to be an essential part of good management.

Strategic planning
The process of developing and maintaining a strategic fit between the organization's goals and capabilities and its changing marketing opportunities. It involves defining a clear company mission, setting supporting objectives, designing a sound business portfolio, and coordinating functional strategies.

Companies usually prepare annual plans, long-range plans, and strategic plans. The annual and long-range plans deal with the company's current businesses and how to keep them going. In contrast, the strategic plan involves adapting the firm to take advantage of opportunities in its constantly changing environment. We define **strategic planning** as the process of developing and maintaining a strategic fit between the organization's goals and capabilities and its changing marketing opportunities.

Strategic planning sets the stage for the rest of the planning in the firm. It relies on defining a clear company mission, setting supporting company objectives, designing a sound business portfolio, and coordinating functional strategies (see Figure 2.1). At the corporate level, the company first defines its overall purpose and

FIGURE 2.1   Steps in strategic planning

mission. This mission then is turned into detailed supporting objectives that guide the whole company. Next, headquarters decides what portfolio of businesses and products is best for the company and how much support to give each one. In turn, each business and product unit must develop detailed marketing and other departmental plans that support the companywide plan. Thus, marketing planning occurs at the business unit, product, and market levels. It supports company strategic planning with more detailed planning for specific marketing opportunities.[3]

Defining the Company's Business and Mission

An organization exists to accomplish something. At first, it has a clear purpose or mission, but over time its mission may become unclear as the organization grows, adds new products and markets, or faces new conditions in the environment. When management senses that the organization is drifting, it must renew

Company mission: 3M does more than just make adhesives, scientific equipment, health care, and communications products. It solves people's problems by putting innovation to work for them.

its search for purpose. It is time to ask: What is our business? Who is the customer? What do consumers value? What should our business be? These simple-sounding questions are among the most difficult the company will ever have to answer. Successful companies continuously raise these questions and answer them carefully and completely.

Mission statement
A statement of the organization's purpose—what it wants to accomplish in the larger environment.

Many organizations develop formal mission statements that answer these questions. A **mission statement** is a statement of the organization's purpose—what it wants to accomplish in the larger environment. A clear mission statement acts as an "invisible hand" that guides people in the organization.

Traditionally companies have defined their businesses in product terms ("We manufacture furniture") or in technological terms ("We are a chemical-processing firm"). But mission statements should be *market oriented* (see Marketing Highlight 2.1). Products and technologies eventually become outdated, but basic market needs may last forever. A market-oriented mission statement defines the business in terms of satisfying basic customer needs. For example, AT&T is in the communications business, not the telephone business. 3M does more than just make adhesives, scientific equipment, and health care products. It solves people's problems by putting innovation to work for them. Southwest Airlines sees itself as providing not just air travel but total customer service. Its mission: "The mission of Southwest Airlines is dedication to the highest quality of customer service delivered with a sense of warmth, friendliness, individual pride, and company spirit." Likewise, Amazon.com's mission isn't simply to sell books, CDs, videos, toys, and consumer electronics. Instead, it wants to "transform Internet buying into the fastest, easiest, and most enjoyable shopping experience possible—to be the place where you can find and discover anything you want to buy online."[4] Table 2.1 provides several other examples of product-oriented versus market-oriented business definitions.

TABLE 2.1 MARKET-ORIENTED BUSINESS DEFINITIONS

Company	Product-Oriented Definition	Market-Oriented Definition
Revlon	We make cosmetics.	We sell lifestyle and self-expression; success and status; memories, hopes, and dreams.
Disney	We run theme parks.	We create fantasies—a place where America still works the way it's supposed to.
Wal-Mart	We run discount stores.	We deliver value through low prices to Middle Americans.
Xerox	We make copying, fax, and other office machines.	We make businesses more productive by helping them scan, store, retrieve, revise, distribute, print, and publish documents.
O. M. Scott	We sell grass seed and fertilizer.	We deliver green, healthy-looking yards.
Home Depot	We sell tools and home repair and improvement items.	We provide advice and solutions that transform ham-handed homeowners into Mr. and Mrs. Fixits.
Amazon.com	We sell books, videos, CDs, toys, consumer electronics, home improvement items, and other products.	We make the Internet buying experience fast, easy, and enjoyable—we're the place where you can find and discover anything you want to buy online.
Ritz-Carlton Hotels	We rent rooms.	We create the Ritz-Carlton experience—one which enlivens the senses, instills well-being, and fulfills even the unexpressed wishes and needs of our guests.

MARKETING HIGHLIGHT
2.1

IBM: BIG BLUE DINOSAUR OR E-BUSINESS ANIMAL?

Only a decade ago, if you'd asked top managers at IBM what business they were in, they might well have answered, "We sell computer hardware and software." Laboring under a pretty bad case of marketing myopia, a heavily product-focused IBM lost sight of its customers' needs. As a result, as customer needs changed, IBM didn't, and its fortunes slipped accordingly. By the early 1990s, "Big Blue's" market

IBM defines its business as delivering solutions to customers' e-business problems. Nick Simicich, an IBM "ethical hacker" and "paid professional paranoid," helps protect customers' information systems against hackers.

share and stock price were falling rapidly.

Since those sadly blue days, however, IBM has undergone a remarkable transformation. The turnaround started in 1993, when new CEO Lou Gerstner brought a renewed customer focus to IBM. As one of his first acts, Gerstner asked all top IBM managers to meet face-to-face with important customers—what he called "bear-hugging customers"—and report back concerning their problems and priorities. Gerstner and his managers learned that corporate computing is getting more and more confusing for customers. In this new high-tech, connected age, companies must master a dizzying array of information technologies to serve not just their customers but also suppliers, distributors, and employees.

Gerstner realized that in this more complex computing world, customers are buying much more from IBM than just computer hardware and software. They are buying solutions to ever-more-bewildering information technology (IT) problems. This realization led to a fundamental redefinition of IBM's business. Now, if you ask almost any IBM manager to define the business, he or she will tell you, "we deliver *solutions* to customers' information technology problems."

The fact is that most customers don't really care whose hardware or

software they buy. For example, Pat Zilvitis, chief information officer at Gillette in Boston and a big IBM customer, claims that it's not IBM's PCs, servers, mainframes, or software that attracts him. "I often don't know if I need hardware or software or services, and I don't care," he says. What draws him to IBM is that Big Blue employs an unmatched breadth of products, people, and services to deliver an IT system that works. "I don't view IBM as a hardware vendor anymore," he says. "I think of them as an information technology [partner] that can help me in a number of different ways."

The new customer solutions focus has greatly promoted the role of services relative to hardware and software in the IBM mix. The company now offers an expanded set of IT consulting, total systems management, strategic outsourcing, and e-business services that can help customers with everything from assessing, planning, designing, implementing, and running their IT systems to bringing them up to speed on e-commerce. Some companies, such as Eastman Kodak and Hertz, have outsourced their entire IT systems to IBM. In such deals, IBM runs the whole IT show—the customer's IT employees work for IBM, and IBM owns the customer's computers, which it then manages.

Services are now IBM's hottest growth area, accounting for almost

Management should avoid making its mission too narrow or too broad. A pencil manufacturer that says it is in the communication equipment business is stating its mission too broadly. Missions should be *realistic*. Singapore Airlines would be deluding itself if it adopted the mission to become the world's largest airline. Missions should also be *specific*. Many mission statements are written for public relations purposes and lack specific, workable guidelines. The statement "We want to become the

30 percent of the company's more than $80 billion in sales and 39 percent of its profits. Analysts predict that services will generate almost half of IBM's revenues by 2003. As one IBM watcher comments, "IBM—International Business Machines—is becoming IBS, where 'S' is for services, software, and solutions."

Still, few people realize that IBM is the world's largest supplier of IT services. To help close this perceptual gap, IBM recently launched a $75 million global services ad campaign with the tag line "People Who Think. People Who Do. People Who Get It." To counter the out-of-date notion that IBM provides only computer hardware, the campaign profiles specific IBM people—the "strategists, problem solvers, implementers . . . who make sure that the solution you want is the solution you get." One ad showcases Nick Simicich, an IBM ethical hacker (unofficial title: "paid professional paranoid") who purposely invades customers' critical information systems to see if they're safe from more hostile hackers. Another features Patrick McMahon, who helped Prudential reengineer its sales processes, doubling the number of policies sold and raising commissions 153 percent in the pilot program. Patrick's mission: "To work with clients to ensure that IT solutions run smoothly and support their business objectives." According to an executive at IBM's advertising agency, the message is simple: "IBM has people who [can help you] excel in e-business and consulting, business recovery, and network systems management."

In this latest phase of its customer-solutions makeover, IBM is positioning itself as the "e-business solutions company." (It has coined *e-business* as a catch-all term for Internet, intranet, and e-commerce applications.) As more and more companies use the Internet as their primary connecting technology, e-business is growing explosively. IBM wants to be *the* company to turn to for e-business strategies and solutions.

In 1999, IBM has introduced 20 new e-business services, including customer relationship management, business intelligence, supply chain management, and business process management services. Big Blue claims to have 10,000 e-business customers. For some, this means little more than having IBM host their Web sites on one of its servers. For others, however, it means having IBM create and implement a totally new business–customer connection. For example, Federated Department Stores selected IBM to remake its rudimentary Macy's Web site into a full e-commerce enterprise. The results were dazzling. In only six months, IBM converted Macys.com from a site selling 5,000 products to one that now features 250,000 products, along with software "wizards" that help visitors find the products they seek. IBM now serves as consultant and hosts the site.

E-business appears to be an ideal setting for IBM's soup-to-nuts menu of IT solutions. Over one-quarter of IBM's revenues now come from e-business products and services. Moreover, IBM appears to be capturing the minds of e-business customers as well as their purchases. As a result of both its e-business deeds

and millions of dollars spent on worldwide advertising proclaiming its e-business prowess, IBM appears to own a major portion of the e-business position. In recent surveys, customers associated IBM with e-business seven times more than any of its competitors.

Thus, in a remarkably short time, IBM has transformed itself from a company that "sells computer hardware and software" to one that "delivers customer IT solutions." It's not the old IBM anymore and the marketplace has responded strongly. Over the past four years, IBM has experienced steady sales growth, rapidly improving profits, and a fivefold increase in its stock price. By defining itself in terms of the customer needs it serves rather than the products it sells, IBM has been transformed "from a big blue dinosaur to an e-business animal."

Sources: Quotes from David Kirkpatrick, "IBM: From Big Blue Dinosaur to E-Business Animal," *Fortune*, April 26, 1999, pp. 116–25; and Laura Loro, "IBM Touts Position as No. 1 in IT Services," *Advertising Age's Business Marketing*, April 1999, p. 41. Also see Bruce Caldwell, "IBM Defines a Concept While Redefining Itself," *Information Week*, July 6, 1998, pp. 74–75; Richard R. Rogoski, "Big Blue Focuses Initiative on Improving E-Commerce," *Triangle Business Journal*, January 22, 1999, p. 31; Bradley Johnson, "IBM Pushes the Limits of Business on the Internet," *Advertising Age*, May 3, 1999, pp. S2, S10; and Ira Sager, "Big Blue at Your Service," *Business Week*, June 21, 1999, pp. 130–32.

leading company in this industry by producing the highest-quality products with the best service at the lowest prices" sounds good, but it is full of generalities and contradictions. Celestial Seasonings' mission statement is very specific: "Our mission is to grow and dominate the U.S. specialty tea market by exceeding consumer expectations with: The best tasting, 100 percent natural hot and iced teas, packaged with Celestial art and philosophy, creating the most valued tea experience. . . ."[5]

Missions should fit the *market environment*. The Girl Scouts of America would not recruit successfully in today's environment with their former mission: "to prepare young girls for motherhood and wifely duties." The organization should base its mission on its *distinctive competencies*. McDonald's could probably enter the solar energy business, but that would not take advantage of its core competence—providing low-cost food and fast service to large groups of customers.

Finally, mission statements should be *motivating*. A company's mission should not be stated as making more sales or profits—profits are only a reward for undertaking a useful activity. A company's employees need to feel that their work is significant and that it contributes to people's lives. Contrast the missions of IBM and Microsoft. When IBM sales were $50 billion, then-President John Akers said that IBM's mission was to become a $100 billion company by the end of the century. Meanwhile, Microsoft's long-term mission has been IAYF—"information at your fingertips"—to put information at the fingertips of every person. Microsoft's mission is much more motivating than is IBM's.[6]

One study found that "visionary companies" set a purpose beyond making money. For example, Walt Disney Company's aim is "making people happy." But even though profits may not be part of these companies' mission statements, they are the inevitable result. The study showed that 18 visionary companies outperformed other companies in the stock market by more than 6 to 1 over the period from 1926 to 1990.[7]

Setting Company Objectives and Goals

The company's mission needs to be turned into detailed supporting objectives for each level of management. Each manager should have objectives and be responsible for reaching them. For example, Monsanto operates in many businesses, including agriculture, pharmaceuticals, and food products. The company defines its mission as one of helping to feed the world's exploding population while at the same time sustaining the environment. This mission leads to a hierarchy of objectives, including business objectives and marketing objectives. Monsanto's overall objective is to create environmentally better products and get them to market faster at lower costs.

Monsanto defines its mission as one of "food, health, hope"—of helping to feed the world's exploding population while at the same time sustaining the environment. This mission leads to specific business and marketing objectives.

Topic: Working Together

CARING ABOUT LIFE IS ONE OF OUR STRONGEST INSTINCTS.

MONSANTO
Food · Health · Hope

For its part, the agricultural division's objective is to increase agricultural productivity and reduce chemical pollution by researching new pest- and disease-resistant crops that produce higher yields without chemical spraying. But research is expensive and requires improved profits to plow back into research programs. So improving profits becomes another major business objective. Profits can be improved by increasing sales or reducing costs. Sales can be increased by improving the company's share of the U.S. market, by entering new foreign markets, or both. These goals then become the company's current marketing objectives.[8]

Marketing strategies must be developed to support these marketing objectives. To increase its U.S. market share, Monsanto might increase its product's availability and promotion. To enter new foreign markets, the company may cut prices and target large farms abroad. These are its broad marketing strategies. Each broad marketing strategy must then be defined in greater detail. For example, increasing the product's promotion may require more salespeople and more advertising; if so, both requirements will have to be spelled out. In this way, the firm's mission is translated into a set of objectives for the current period. The objectives should be as specific as possible. The objective to "increase our market share" is not as useful as the objective to "increase our market share to 15 percent by the end of the second year."

DESIGNING THE BUSINESS PORTFOLIO

Business portfolio
The collection of businesses and products that make up the company.

Guided by the company's mission statement and objectives, management now must plan its **business portfolio**—the collection of businesses and products that make up the company. The best business portfolio is the one that best fits the company's strengths and weaknesses to opportunities in the environment. The company must (1) analyze its *current* business portfolio and decide which businesses should receive more, less, or no investment, and (2) develop growth strategies for adding *new* products or businesses to the portfolio.[9]

Analyzing the Current Business Portfolio

Portfolio analysis
A tool by which management identifies and evaluates the various businesses that make up the company.

The major activity in strategic planning is business **portfolio analysis,** whereby management evaluates the businesses making up the company. The company will want to put strong resources into its more profitable businesses and phase down or drop its weaker ones. For example, in recent years, Dial Corporation has strengthened its portfolio by selling off its less attractive businesses: bus line (Greyhound), knitting supplies, meatpacking, and computer leasing businesses. At the same time, it invested more heavily in its consumer products (Dial soap, Armour Star meats, Purex laundry products, and others) and services (Premier Cruise Lines, Dobbs airport services).

Strategic business unit (SBU)
A unit of the company that has a separate mission and objectives and that can be planned independently from other company businesses. An SBU can be a company division, a product line within a division, or sometimes a single product or brand.

Management's first step is to identify the key businesses making up the company. These can be called the strategic business units. A **strategic business unit (SBU)** is a unit of the company that has a separate mission and objectives and that can be planned independently from other company businesses. An SBU can be a company division, a product line within a division, or sometimes a single product or brand.

The next step in business portfolio analysis calls for management to assess the attractiveness of its various SBUs and decide how much support each deserves. In some companies, this is done informally. Management looks at the company's collection of businesses or products and uses judgment to decide how much each SBU should contribute and receive. Other companies use formal portfolio-planning methods.

The purpose of strategic planning is to find ways in which the company can best use its strengths to take advantage of attractive opportunities in the environment. So most standard portfolio-analysis methods evaluate SBUs on two important dimensions—the attractiveness of the SBU's market or industry and the strength of the SBU's position in that market or industry. The best-known portfolio-planning method was developed by the Boston Consulting Group, a leading management consulting firm.

The Boston Consulting Group Approach

Growth-share matrix
A portfolio-planning method that evaluates a company's strategic business units in terms of their market growth rate and relative market share. SBUs are classified as stars, cash cows, question marks, or dogs.

Using the Boston Consulting Group (BCG) approach, a company classifies all its SBUs according to the **growth-share matrix** shown in Figure 2.2. On the vertical axis, *market growth rate* provides a measure of market attractiveness. On the horizontal axis, *relative market share* serves as a measure of company strength in the market. By dividing the growth-share matrix as indicated, four types of SBUs can be distinguished:

Stars: Stars are high-growth, high-share businesses or products. They often need heavy investment to finance their rapid growth. Eventually their growth will slow down, and they will turn into cash cows.

Cash cows: Cash cows are low-growth, high-share businesses or products. These established and successful SBUs need less investment to hold their market share. Thus, they produce a lot of cash that the company uses to pay its bills and to support other SBUs that need investment.

Question marks: Question marks are low-share business units in high-growth markets. They require a lot of cash to hold their share, let alone increase it. Management has to think hard about which question marks it should try to build into stars and which should be phased out.

Dogs: Dogs are low-growth, low-share businesses and products. They may generate enough cash to maintain themselves but do not promise to be large sources of cash.

The ten circles in the growth-share matrix represent a company's ten current SBUs. The company has two stars, two cash cows, three question marks, and three dogs. The areas of the circles are proportional to the SBU's dollar sales. This company is in fair shape, although not in good shape. It wants to invest in the more promising question marks to make them stars and to maintain the stars so that they will become cash cows as their markets mature. Fortunately, it has two good-sized cash cows whose income helps finance the company's question marks, stars, and

FIGURE 2.2   The BCG growth-share matrix

dogs. The company should take some decisive action concerning its dogs and its question marks. The picture would be worse if the company had no stars, if it had too many dogs, or if it had only one weak cash cow.

Once it has classified its SBUs, the company must determine what role each will play in the future. One of four strategies can be pursued for each SBU. The company can invest more in the business unit in order to *build* its share. Or it can invest just enough to *hold* the SBU's share at the current level. It can *harvest* the SBU, milking its short-term cash flow regardless of the long-term effect. Finally, the company can *divest* the SBU by selling it or phasing it out and using the resources elsewhere.

As time passes, SBUs change their positions in the growth–share matrix. Each SBU has a life cycle. Many SBUs start out as question marks and move into the star category if they succeed. They later become cash cows as market growth falls, then finally die off or turn into dogs toward the end of their life cycle. The company needs to add new products and units continuously so that some of them will become stars and, eventually, cash cows that will help finance other SBUs.

The General Electric Approach

General Electric introduced a comprehensive portfolio planning tool called a *strategic business-planning grid* (see Figure 2.3). Like the BCG approach, it uses a matrix with two dimensions—one representing industry attractiveness (the vertical axis) and one representing company strength in the industry (the horizontal axis). The best businesses are those located in highly attractive industries where the company has high business strength.

The GE approach considers many factors besides market growth rate as part of industry attractiveness. It uses an industry attractiveness index made up of market size, market growth rate, industry profit margin, amount of competition, seasonality and cyclicity of demand, and industry cost structure. Each of these factors is rated and combined in an index of industry attractiveness. For our purposes, an industry's attractiveness will be described as high, medium, or low. As an example, Kraft has identified numerous highly attractive industries—natural foods, specialty frozen foods, physical fitness products, and others. It has withdrawn from less attractive industries such as bulk oils and cardboard packaging.

For *business strength,* the GE approach again uses an index rather than a simple measure of relative market share. The business strength index includes factors such as the company's relative market share, price competitiveness, product quality, cus-

FIGURE 2.3   General Electric's strategic business–planning grid

tomer and market knowledge, sales effectiveness, and geographic advantages. These factors are rated and combined in an index of business strength, which can be described as strong, average, or weak. Thus, Kraft has substantial business strength in food and related industries but is relatively weak in the home appliances industry.

The grid is divided into three zones. The green cells at the upper left include the strong SBUs in which the company should invest and grow. The yellow diagonal cells contain SBUs that are medium in overall attractiveness. The company should maintain its level of investment in these SBUs. The three orange cells at the lower right indicate SBUs that are low in overall attractiveness. The company should give serious thought to harvesting or divesting these SBUs.

The circles represent four company SBUs; the areas of the circles are proportional to the relative sizes of the industries in which these SBUs compete. The pie slices within the circles represent each SBU's market share. Thus, circle A represents a company SBU with a 75 percent market share in a good-size, highly attractive industry in which the company has strong business strength. Circle B represents an SBU that has a 50 percent market share, but the industry is not very attractive. Circles C and D represent two other company SBUs in industries where the company has small market shares and not much business strength. Altogether, the company should build A, maintain B, and make some hard decisions about what to do with C and D.

Management would also plot the projected positions of the SBUs with and without changes in strategies. By comparing current and projected business grids, management can identify the major strategic issues and opportunities it faces.

Problems with Matrix Approaches

The BCG and other formal methods revolutionized strategic planning. However, such approaches have limitations. They can be difficult, time-consuming, and costly to implement. Management may find it difficult to define SBUs and measure market share and growth. In addition, these approaches focus on classifying *current* businesses but provide little advice for *future* planning. Management must still rely on its own judgment to set the business objectives for each SBU, to determine what resources each will be given, and to figure out which new businesses should be added.

Formal planning approaches can also lead the company to place too much emphasis on market-share growth or growth through entry into attractive new markets. Using these approaches, many companies plunged into unrelated and new high-growth businesses that they did not know how to manage—with very bad results. At the same time, these companies were often too quick to abandon, sell, or milk to death their healthy mature businesses. As a result, many companies that diversified too broadly in the past now are narrowing their focus and getting back to the basics of serving one or a few industries that they know best.

Despite such problems, and although many companies have dropped formal matrix methods in favor of more customized approaches that are better suited to their situations, most companies remain firmly committed to strategic planning. During the 1970s, many companies embraced high-level corporate strategy planning as a kind of magical path to growth and profits. By the 1980s, however, such strategic planning took a backseat to cost and efficiency concerns, as companies struggled to become more competitive through improved quality, restructuring, downsizing, and reengineering. Recently, strategic planning has made a strong comeback. However, unlike former strategic-planning efforts, which rested mostly in the hands of senior managers, today's strategic planning has been decentralized. Increasingly, companies are moving responsibility for strategic planning out of company headquarters and placing it in the hands of cross-functional teams of line and staff managers who are close to their markets. Some teams even include customers and suppliers in their strategic-planning processes.[10]

Such analysis is no cure-all for finding the best strategy. But it can help management to understand the company's overall situation, to see how each business or product contributes, to assign resources to its businesses, and to orient the company for future success. When used properly, strategic planning is just one important aspect of overall strategic management, a way of thinking about how to manage a business.

Developing Growth Strategies in the Age of Connectedness

Beyond evaluating current businesses, designing the business portfolio involves finding businesses and products the company should consider in the future. Companies need growth if they are to compete more effectively, satisfy their stakeholders, and attract top talent. "Growth is pure oxygen," states one executive. "It creates a vital, enthusiastic corporation where people see genuine opportunity. . . . In that way, growth is more than our single most important financial driver; it's an essential part of our corporate culture." At the same time, a firm must be careful not to make growth itself an objective. The company's objective must be "profitable growth."

Marketing has the main responsibility for achieving profitable growth for the company. Marketing must identify, evaluate, and select market opportunities and lay down strategies for capturing them. One useful device for identifying growth opportunities is the **product–market expansion grid,** shown in Figure 2.4.[11] We apply it here to Starbucks (see Marketing Highlight 2.2).

First, Starbucks management might consider whether the company can achieve deeper **market penetration**—making more sales to current customers without changing its products. It might add new stores in current market areas to make it easier for more customers to visit. Improvements in advertising, prices, service, menu selection, or store design might encourage customers to stop by more often or to buy more during each visit. For example, Starbucks recently began adapting its menu to local tastes around the country.

★ In the South, where customers tend to come later in the day and linger for a bit, [such tailoring] meant adding more appealing dessert offerings, as well as designing larger, more comfortable locations. [In Atlanta, Starbucks] opened bigger stores with such amenities as couches and outdoor tables, so that people would feel comfortable hanging out, especially in the evening. . . . "Building on its Atlanta experience, Starbucks is tailoring its stores to local tastes around the country. That's why you find café au lait as well as toasted items in New Orleans, neither of which is available elsewhere in the

---

Product–market expansion grid

A portfolio-planning tool for identifying company growth opportunities through market penetration, market development, product development, or diversification.

Market penetration

A strategy for company growth by increasing sales of current products to current market segments without changing the product.

	Existing products	New products
Existing markets	Market penetration	Product development
New markets	Market development	Diversification

FIGURE 2.4   Market opportunity identification through the product–market expansion grid

**MARKETING
HIGHLIGHT
2 . 2**

STARBUCKS COFFEE: WHERE THINGS ARE REALLY PERKING

Back in 1983, Howard Schultz hit on the idea of bringing a European-style coffeehouse to America. People needed to slow down, he believed—to "smell the coffee" and enjoy life a little more. The result was Starbucks, the coffeehouse chain that started the trend in America of enjoying coffee to its fullest. Starbucks doesn't sell just coffee, it sells an experience. Howard Behar, Starbucks's international president, says, "We're not in the business of filling bellies, we're in the business of filling souls."

Starbucks is now a powerhouse premium brand in a category where only cheaper commodity products existed just a decade ago. As the brand has perked, Starbucks's sales and profits have risen like steam off a mug of hot java. Nine million customers visit the company's more than 2,100 stores each week—10 percent of them drop by twice a day. During the past five years, Starbucks's total sales have grown at an average of over 34 percent annually; profits have grown at an incredible 68 percent a year.

Starbucks's success, however, has drawn a full litter of copycats, ranging from direct competitors such as Caribou Coffee to fast-food merchants. These days it seems that everyone is peddling its own brand of premium coffee. "Pull up to a Mobil gas station and the convenience store has certified organic coffee supplied by Green Mountain Coffee Co.," observes one analyst. "In the Pacific Northwest, McDonald's pours a blend from Seattle Coffee Co." To maintain its phenomenal growth in an increasingly overcaffeinated marketplace, Starbucks has brewed up an ambitious, multipronged growth strategy. Let's examine the key elements of this strategy:

- *More store growth:* Over 85 percent of Starbucks's sales comes from its stores. So, not surprisingly, Starbucks is in the thick of its biggest wave of store openings ever. It plans to open one new store a day, every day, for the next two years. Although it may seem

that there aren't many places left without a Starbucks, there's still plenty of room to expand. For example, Kansas City has only two Starbucks; the entire state of Indiana has only one; and the states of Alabama, Arkansas, Mississippi, and Tennessee have none at all. Even in crowded markets, such as New York City or San Francisco, the company seems unconcerned about store saturation. "Three years ago, when I said we were going to have 100 stores in New York, people thought it was crazy," says Schultz. "Well, now we have 70, and we're going to 200." He points to Vancouver, Canada, where competing Starbucks stores are located directly across the street from one another. Both stores generate more than $1 million in annual sales, each well above the sales of a typical Starbucks. One three-block stretch in Chicago contains six of the trendy coffee bars.

Beyond opening new shops, Starbucks is expanding each store's food offerings, testing everything from Krispy Kreme doughnuts in New York City to Fresh Fields gourmet sandwiches in Washington, DC. Currently, beverages account for 80 percent of Starbucks's sales. By offering more food, the company hopes to increase the average customer sales ticket while also boosting lunch and dinner traffic.

- *New retail channels:* The vast majority of coffee in America is bought in stores and sipped at home. To capture this demand, Starbucks is also pushing into America's supermarket aisles. However, rather than

To maintain its phenomenal growth, Starbucks's ambitious growth strategy includes going global. Here, in Beijing, a barista wields a "Mercury machine" to dispense jolts of java to curious customers.

going head-to-head with giants such as Procter & Gamble (Folgers) and Kraft (Maxwell House, Sanka), Starbucks struck a cobranding deal with Kraft. Under this deal, Starbucks will continue to roast and package its coffee while Kraft will market and distribute it. Both companies benefit: Starbucks gains quick entry into 25,000 U.S. supermarkets, supported by the marketing muscle of 3,500 Kraft salespeople. Kraft tops off its coffee line with the best-known premium brand and gains quick entry into the fast-growing premium coffee segment.

Beyond supermarkets, Starbucks has forged an impressive set of new ways to bring its brand to market. Some examples: Host Marriott operates Starbucks kiosks in more than 30 U.S. airports and several airlines serve Starbucks coffee to their passengers. Westin and Sheraton hotels offer packets of Starbucks brew in their rooms. Barnes & Noble serves Starbucks coffee in all of the 375 cafés in its bookstores, making it one of the nation's largest retailers of both books and specialty coffees. Starbucks also sells gourmet coffee, tea, gifts, and related goods through business and consumer catalogs. It recently opened its own Web site, Starbucks.com, where it sells coffee, tea, coffeemaking equipment, compact disks, gifts, and collectibles Starbucks customers' demographics are ideal for e-commerce—about 70 percent of customers are already on the Web and their typical household income approaches $75,000.

- *New products and store concepts:* Starbucks has partnered with several firms to extend its brand into new categories. For example, it joined with PepsiCo to stamp the Starbucks brand on bottled Frappuccino drinks. Starbucks ice cream, marketed in a joint venture with Breyer's, is now the leading brand of coffee ice

cream. Moreover, at the same time it is trying to squeeze more business out of its regular coffee shops, Starbucks is also examining new store concepts. In Seattle, it is testing Café Starbucks, a European-style family bistro with a menu featuring everything from huckleberry pancakes to oven-roasted seared sirloin and Mediterranean chicken breast on focaccia. Whereas Starbucks's traditional coffeehouses ring up about half their sales before 11 A.M., Café Starbucks is designed to generate sales evenly throughout the day. Starbucks is also testing Circadia in San Francisco—a kind of bohemian coffeehouse concept with tattered rugs, high-speed Internet access, and live music as well as coffee specialties.

- *International growth:* Finally, Starbucks is taking its American-brewed concept global, especially in Asia. Long lines are common at the more than 50 Japanese Starbucks stores, and the company plans to have at least 250 stores in Japan by the end of 2003. It is expanding rapidly in Taiwan, Malaysia, Singapore, and the Philippines, and this year the company opened its first three locations in China. Starbucks also operates 80 stores in the United Kingdom and plans to invade mainland Europe starting in mid-2000.

Although Starbucks's growth strategy so far has met with great success, some analysts express strong concerns. What's wrong with Starbucks's rapid expansion? Some critics worry that the company may be overextending the Starbucks brand name. "People pay up to $3.15 for a caffe latte because it's supposed to be a premium product," asserts one such critic. "When you see the Starbucks name on what an airline is pouring, you wonder." Others fear that, by pursuing such a broad-based growth strategy, Starbucks will stretch its resources too thin or lose its focus. According to one account:

"All this sounds properly ambitious and aggressive, but to some . . . it has an ominous ring. The late 1990s are littered with the wreckage of restaurant chains that expanded too fast for their market and eventually collapsed. Two years ago, Planet Hollywood, with high-profile backers like Bruce Willis and Arnold Schwarzeneger, was an investor darling. The stock hit $25 a share; today it trades for just over $1." Then there's Boston Market, the once high-flying chain that ended up declaring bankruptcy last year.

Others, however, remain true believers. Some even see similarities between Starbucks and a young McDonald's, which rode the humble hamburger to such incredible success. "The similar focus on one product, the overseas opportunities, the rapid emergence as the dominant player in a new niche," says Goldman Sachs analyst Steve Kent, "this all applies to Starbucks, too." Only time will tell whether Starbucks turns out to be the next McDonald's or the next Boston Market. It all depends how well the company manages growth. For now, things are really perking, but Starbucks has to be careful that it doesn't boil over.

Sources: Quotes from Nelson D. Schwartz, "Still Perking After All These Years," *Fortune,* May 24, 1999, pp. 203–10; Janice Matsumoto, "More than Mocha—Café Starbucks," *Restaurants and Institutions,* October 1, 1998, p. 21; and Kelly Barron, "The Cappuccino Conundrum," *Forbes,* February 22, 1999, pp. 54–55. Also see Mark Hamstra, "Starbucks' Pasqua Purchase Dovetails with Food-Café Tests," *Nation's Restaurant News,* January 4, 1999, pp. 3, 104; Richard Gibson, "Starbucks Plans a New Category in Cybercommerce," *Wall Street Journal,* April 26, 1999, p. B10; Eli Lehrer, "When Starbucks Takes over the World," *Insight on the News,* July 19, 1999, p. 4; information accessed online at www.starbucks.com, September 1999; and Louise Lee, "Now Starbucks Uses Its Bean," *Business Week,* February 14, 2000, pp. 92–94.

country. (Bagel sales in New Orleans tripled once Starbucks began toasting them.) Or why coffee cake is featured in the Northeast, where it's more popular.[12]

Basically, Starbucks would like to increase patronage by current customers and attract competitors' customers to Starbucks shops.

Market development
A strategy for company growth by identifying and developing new market segments for current company products.

Second, Starbucks management might consider possibilities for **market development**—identifying and developing new markets for its current products. For instance, managers could review new *demographic markets*—such as senior consumers or ethnic groups—to see if new groups could be encouraged to visit Starbucks coffee shops for the first time or to buy more from them. Managers also could review new *geographical markets*. Starbucks is now expanding swiftly into new U.S. markets, especially in the Southeast and Southwest. It is also developing its international markets, with stores popping up rapidly in Asia, Europe, and Australia.

Product development
A strategy for company growth by offering modified or new products to current market segments. Developing the product concept into a physical product in order to ensure that the product idea can be turned into a workable product.

Third, management could consider **product development**—offering modified or new products to current markets. For example, Starbucks is increasing its food offerings in an effort to bring customers into its stores during the lunch and dinner hours and to increase the amount of the average customer's sales ticket. The company is also partnering with other firms to sell coffee in supermarkets and to extend its brand to new products, such as coffee ice cream (with Breyer's) and bottled Frappuccino drinks (with PepsiCo).

Diversification
A strategy for company growth by starting up or acquiring businesses outside the company's current products and markets.

Fourth, Starbucks might consider **diversification.** It could start up or buy businesses outside of its current products and markets. For example, Starbucks is testing two new restaurant concepts—Café Starbucks and Circadia—in an effort to offer new formats to related but new markets. In a more extreme diversification, Starbucks might consider leveraging its strong brand name by making and marketing a line of branded casual clothing consistent with the "Starbucks experience." However, this would probably be unwise. Companies that diversify too broadly into unfamiliar products or industries can lose their market focus, something that some critics are already concerned about with Starbucks.

Planning Cross-Functional Strategies

The company's strategic plan establishes what kinds of businesses the company will be in and its objectives for each. Then, within each business unit more detailed planning must take place. The major functional departments in each unit—marketing, finance, accounting, purchasing, manufacturing, information systems, human resources, and others—must work together to accomplish strategic objectives.

Marketing's Role in Strategic Planning

There is much overlap between overall company strategy and marketing strategy. Marketing looks at consumer needs and the company's ability to satisfy them; these same factors guide the company's overall mission and objectives.

Marketing plays a key role in the company's strategic planning in several ways. First, marketing provides a guiding *philosophy*—the marketing concept—that suggests company strategy should revolve around serving the needs of important consumer groups. Second, marketing provides *inputs* to strategic planners by helping to identify attractive market opportunities and by assessing the firm's potential to take advantage of them. Finally, within individual business units, marketing designs *strategies* for reaching the unit's objectives. Once the unit's objectives are set, marketing's task is to carry them out profitably.

Marketing and the Other Business Functions

Marketers play an important role in delivering customer value and satisfaction. However, as we noted in chapter 1, marketing cannot do this alone. Because customer value and satisfaction are affected by the performance of other functions, *all* departments must work together to deliver superior value and satisfaction. Marketing plays an integrative role to help ensure that all departments work together toward this goal.

Cross-Functional Conflict

Each business function has a different view of which publics and activities are most important. Operations focuses on suppliers and production; finance is concerned with stockholders and sound investment; marketing emphasizes consumers and products, pricing, promotion, and distribution. Ideally, the different functions should work in harmony to produce value for consumers. But in practice, departmental relations are full of conflicts and misunderstandings. The marketing department takes the consumer's point of view. But when marketing tries to develop customer satisfaction, it often causes other departments to do a poorer job *in their terms.* Marketing department actions can increase purchasing costs, disrupt production schedules, increase inventories, and create budget headaches. Thus, the other departments may resist bending their efforts to the will of the marketing department.

Yet marketers must get all departments to "think consumer" and to put the consumer at the center of company activity. Customer satisfaction requires a total company, cross-functional effort to deliver superior value to target customers.

> ★ Creating value for buyers is much more than a "marketing function"; rather, [it's] analogous to a symphony orchestra in which the contribution of each subgroup is tailored and integrated by a conductor—with a synergistic effect. A seller must draw upon and integrate effectively . . . its entire human and other capital resources. . . . [Creating superior value for buyers] is the proper focus of the entire business and not merely of a single department in it.[13]

The DuPont "Adopt a Customer" program recognizes the importance of having people in all of its functions who are "close to the customer." For example, operators from DuPont's nylon spinning mills visit customer factories where DuPont nylon is transformed into swimsuits and other garments, talking to the customer's operators about quality and other problems they encounter with the nylon. Then, the DuPont operators represent their customers on the factory floor. If quality or delivery problems arise, the operators are more likely to see their adopted customers' point of view and to make decisions that will keep this customer happy.[14]

Jack Welch, General Electric's highly regarded CEO, tells his employees: "Companies can't give job security. Only customers can!" He emphasizes that all General Electric people, regardless of their department, have an impact on customer satisfaction and retention. His message: "If you are not thinking customer, you are not thinking."[15]

STRATEGIC PLANNING AND SMALL BUSINESSES

Many discussions of strategic planning focus on large corporations with many divisions and products. However, small businesses can also benefit from sound strategic planning. Whereas most small ventures start out with extensive business and marketing plans used to attract potential investors, strategic planning often falls by the wayside once the business gets going. Entrepreneurs and presidents of small companies are more likely to spend their time "putting out fires" than planning. But what does a small firm do when it finds that it has taken on too much debt, when its growth is exceeding production capacity, or when it's losing market share to a competitor with lower prices? Strategic planning can help small business managers to anticipate such situations and determine how to prevent or handle them.

King's Medical Company of Hudson, Ohio, provides an example of how one small company uses very simple strategic-planning tools to chart its course every three years. King's Medical owns and manages magnetic-resonance-imaging (MRI) equipment—million-dollar-plus machines that produce X-ray-type pictures. Several years ago, Dr. William Patton, Ph.D., then a consultant and the company's "planning guru," pointed to strategic planning as the key to his small company's very rapid growth and high profit margins. Patton claimed, "A lot of literature says there are three critical issues to a small company: cash flow, cash flow, cash flow. I agree those issues are critical, but so are three more: planning, planning, planning." King's Medical's planning process, which hinges on an assessment of the company, its place in the market, and its goals, includes the following steps.[16]

Small business strategic planning: King's Medical Company uses very simple strategic planning tools to chart its course.

1. Identify the major elements of the business environment in which the organization has operated over the past few years.
2. Describe the mission of the organization in terms of its nature and function for the next two years.
3. Explain the internal and external forces that will impact the mission of the organization.
4. Identify the basic driving force that will direct the organization in the future.
5. Develop a set of long-term objectives that will identify what the organization will become in the future.
6. Outline a general plan of action that defines the logistical, financial, and personnel factors needed to integrate the long-term objectives into the total organization.

Clearly, strategic planning is crucial to a small company's future. Thom Wellington, president of Wellington Environmental Consulting and Construction, Inc., says that it's important to do strategic planning at a site away from the office. An off-site location offers psychologically neutral ground where employees can be "much more candid," and it takes entrepreneurs away from the scene of the fires they spend so much time stamping out.[17]

THE MARKETING PROCESS

Marketing process
The process of (1) analyzing marketing opportunities, (2) selecting target markets, (3) developing the marketing mix, and (4) managing the marketing effort.

The strategic plan defines the company's overall mission and objectives. Within each business unit, marketing plays a role in helping to accomplish the overall strategic objectives. Marketing's role and activities in the organization are shown in Figure 2.5, which summarizes the entire **marketing process** and the forces influencing company marketing strategy.

Target consumers stand in the center. The goal is to build strong and profitable connections with these consumers. The company first identifies the total market, then divides it into smaller segments, selects the most promising segments, and focuses on serving and satisfying these segments. It designs a marketing mix made up of factors under its control—product, price, place, and promotion. To find the best marketing mix and put it into action, the company engages in marketing analysis, planning, implementation, and control. Through these activities, the company watches and adapts to the marketing environment. We will now look briefly at each element in the marketing process. In later chapters, we will discuss each element in more depth.

Connecting with Consumers

To succeed in today's competitive marketplace, companies must be customer centered, winning customers from competitors, then keeping and growing them by delivering greater value. But before it can satisfy consumers, a company must first understand their needs and wants. Thus, sound marketing requires a careful analysis of consumers. Companies know that they cannot connect profitably all consumers in a given market—at least not all consumers in the same way. There are too many different kinds of consumers with too many different kinds of needs. And some companies are in a better position to serve certain segments of the market. Thus, each company must divide up the total market, choose the best segments, and design strategies for profitably serving chosen segments better than its competitors

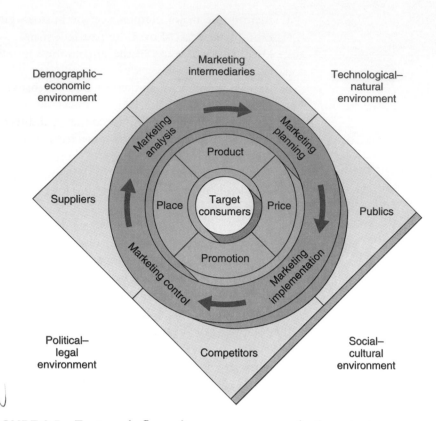

FIGURE 2.5   Factors influencing company marketing strategy

do. This process involves three steps: *market segmentation, market targeting,* and *market positioning.*

Market Segmentation

The market consists of many types of customers, products, and needs, and the marketer has to determine which segments offer the best opportunity for achieving company objectives. Consumers can be grouped and served in various ways based on geographic, demographic, psychographic, and behavioral factors. The process of dividing a market into distinct groups of buyers with different needs, characteristics, or behavior who might require separate products or marketing mixes is called **market segmentation.**

Every market has segments, but not all ways of segmenting a market are equally useful. For example, Tylenol would gain little by distinguishing between male and female users of pain relievers if both respond the same way to marketing efforts. A **market segment** consists of consumers who respond in a similar way to a given set of marketing efforts. In the car market, for example, consumers who choose the biggest, most comfortable car regardless of price make up one market segment. Another segment would be customers who care mainly about price and operating economy. It would be difficult to make one model of car that was the first choice of every consumer. Companies are wise to focus their efforts on meeting the distinct needs of one or more market segments.

Market Targeting

After a company has defined market segments, it can enter one or many segments of a given market. **Market targeting** involves evaluating each market segment's

Market segmentation
Dividing a market into distinct groups of buyers on the basis of needs, characteristics, or behavior who might require separate products or marketing mixes.

Market segment
A group of consumers who respond in a similar way to a given set of marketing efforts.

Market targeting
The process of evaluating each market segment's attractiveness and selecting one or more segments to enter.

attractiveness and selecting one or more segments to enter. A company should target segments in which it can profitably generate the greatest customer value and sustain it over time. A company with limited resources might decide to serve only one or a few special segments or "market niches." This strategy limits sales but can be very profitable. Or a company might choose to serve several related segments perhaps those with different kinds of customers but with the same basic wants. Or a large company might decide to offer a complete range of products to serve all market segments.

Most companies enter a new market by serving a single segment, and if this proves successful, they add segments. Large companies eventually seek full market coverage. They want to be the General Motors of their industry. GM says that it makes a car for every "person, purse, and personality." The leading company normally has different products designed to meet the special needs of each segment.

Market Positioning

After a company has decided which market segments to enter, it must decide what positions it wants to occupy in those segments. A product's *position* is the place the product occupies relative to competitors in consumers' minds. If a product is perceived to be exactly like another product on the market, consumers would have no reason to buy it.

Market positioning

Arranging for a product to occupy a clear, distinctive, and desirable place relative to competing products in the minds of target consumers.

Market positioning is arranging for a product to occupy a clear, distinctive, and desirable place relative to competing products in the minds of target consumers. Thus, marketers plan positions that distinguish their products from competing brands and give them the greatest strategic advantage in their target markets. For example, the Ford Taurus is "built to last"; Chevy Blazer is "like a rock." Saturn is "a different kind of company, different kind of car," and you can just "Imagine Yourself in a Mercury." Lexus avows "the relentless pursuit of excellence," Jaguar is positioned as "a blending of art and machine," and Mercedes is "engineered like no other car in the world." The luxurious Bentley promises "18 handcrafted feet of shameless luxury." Such deceptively simple statements form the backbone of a product's marketing strategy.

Positioning: Bentley promises "18 handcrafted feet of shameless luxury." Such deceptively simple statements form the backbone of a product's marketing strategy.

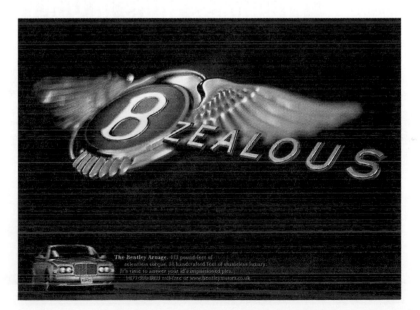

In positioning its product, the company first identifies possible competitive advantages on which to build the position. To gain competitive advantage, the company must offer greater value to chosen target segments, either by charging lower prices than competitors do or by offering more benefits to justify higher prices. But if the company positions the product as *offering* greater value, it must then *deliver* that greater value. Thus, effective positioning begins with actually *differentiating* the company's marketing offer so that it gives consumers more value than they are offered by the competition. Once the company has chosen a desired position, it must take strong steps to deliver and communicate that position to target consumers. The company's entire marketing program should support the chosen positioning strategy.

Marketing Strategies for Competitive Advantage

To be successful, the company must do a better job than its competitors of satisfying target consumers. Thus, marketing strategies must be geared to the needs of consumers and also to the strategies of competitors.

Designing competitive marketing strategies begins with thorough competitor analysis. The company constantly compares the value and customer satisfaction delivered by its products, prices, channels, and promotion with those of its close competitors. In this way it can discern areas of potential advantage and disadvantage. The company asks: Who are our competitors? What are their objectives and strategies? What are their strengths and weaknesses? How will they react to different competitive strategies we might use?

The competitive marketing strategy a company adopts depends on its industry position. A firm that dominates a market can adopt one or more of several *market leader* strategies. Well-known leaders include Coca-Cola (soft drinks), Microsoft (computer software), Caterpillar (large construction equipment), IBM (computers and information technology services), Wal-Mart (retailing), Boeing (aircraft), and America Online (Internet and online services). *Market challengers* are runner-up companies that aggressively attack competitors to get more market share. For example, Pepsi challenges Coke, Komatsu challenges Caterpillar, and MSN challenges

Nichers specialize along market, customer, product, or marketing-mix lines. For example, Arm & Hammer has a lock on the baking soda corner of most consumer goods categories.

America Online. The challenger might attack the market leader, other firms its own size, or smaller local and regional competitors.

Some runner-up firms will choose to follow rather than challenge the market leader. Firms using *market follower* strategies seek stable market shares and profits by following competitors' product offers, prices, and marketing programs. Smaller firms in a market, or even larger firms that lack established positions, often adopt *market nicher* strategies. They specialize in serving market niches that major competitors overlook or ignore. For example, Arm & Hammer has a lock on the baking soda corner of most consumer goods categories, including toothpaste, deodorizers, and others. Oshkosh Truck has found its niche as the world's largest producer of airport rescue trucks and front-loading concrete mixers. "Nichers" avoid direct confrontations with the majors by specializing along market, customer, product, or marketing mix lines. Through smart niching, smaller firms in an industry can be as profitable as their larger competitors. We will discuss competitive marketing strategies more fully in chapter 18.

Developing the Marketing Mix

Marketing mix
The set of controllable tactical marketing tools—product, price, place, and promotion—that the firm blends to produce the response it wants in the target market.

Once the company has decided on its overall competitive marketing strategy, it is ready to begin planning the details of the marketing mix, one of the major concepts in modern marketing. We define **marketing mix** as the set of controllable, tactical marketing tools that the firm blends to produce the response it wants in the target market. The marketing mix consists of everything the firm can do to influence the demand for its product. The many possibilities can be collected into four groups of variables known as the "four Ps": *product, price, place,* and *promotion.*[18] Figure 2.6 shows the particular marketing tools under each *P.*

Product means the goods and services combination the company offers to the target market. Thus, a Ford Taurus product consists of nuts and bolts, spark plugs, pistons, headlights, and thousands of other parts. Ford offers several Taurus styles and

FIGURE 2.6   The four Ps of the marketing mix

dozens of optional features. The car comes fully serviced and with a comprehensive warranty that is as much a part of the product as the tailpipe.

Price is the amount of money customers have to pay to obtain the product. Ford calculates suggested retail prices that its dealers might charge for each Taurus. But Ford dealers rarely charge the full sticker price. Instead, they negotiate the price with each customer, offering discounts, trade-in allowances, and credit terms to adjust for the current competitive situation and to bring the price into line with the buyer's perception of the car's value.

Place includes company activities that make the product available to target consumers. Ford maintains a large body of independently owned dealerships that sell the company's many different models. Ford selects its dealers carefully and supports them strongly. The dealers keep an inventory of Ford automobiles, demonstrate them to potential buyers, negotiate prices, close sales, and service the cars after the sale.

Promotion means activities that communicate the merits of the product and persuade target customers to buy it. Ford spends more than $1.2 billion each year on advertising to tell consumers about the company and its products. Dealership salespeople assist potential buyers and persuade them that Ford is the best car for them. Ford and its dealers offer special promotions—sales, cash rebates, low financing rates—as added purchase incentives.

An effective marketing program blends all of the marketing mix elements into a coordinated program designed to achieve the company's marketing objectives by delivering value to consumers. The marketing mix constitutes the company's tactical tool kit for establishing strong positioning in target markets.

Some critics feel that the four Ps may omit or underemphasize certain important activities. For example, they ask, "Where are services?" Just because they don't start with a P doesn't justify omitting them. The answer is that services, such as banking, airline, and retailing services, are products too. We might call them *service products.* "Where is packaging?" the critics might ask. Marketers would answer that they include packaging as just one of many product decisions. All said, as Figure 2.6 suggests, many marketing activities that might appear to be left out of the marketing mix are subsumed under one of the four Ps. The issue is not whether there should be four, six, or ten Ps so much as what framework is most helpful in designing marketing programs.

There is another concern, however, that is valid. It holds that the four Ps concept takes the seller's view of the market, not the buyer's view. From the buyer's viewpoint, in this age of connectedness, the four Ps might be better described as the four Cs:[19]

4Ps	4Cs
Product	Customer solution
Price	Customer cost
Place	Convenience
Promotion	Communication

Thus while marketers see themselves as selling a product, customers see themselves as buying value or a solution to their problem. Customers are interested in more than the price; they are interested in the total costs of obtaining, using, and disposing of a product. Customers want the product and service to be as conveniently available as possible. Finally, they want two-way communication. Marketers would do well to first think through the four Cs and then build the four Ps on that platform.

MANAGING THE MARKETING EFFORT

The company wants to design and put into action the marketing mix that will best achieve its objectives in its target markets. Figure 2.7 shows the relationship between the four marketing management functions—*analysis, planning, implementation,* and *control.* The company first develops overall strategic plans, then translates these companywide strategic plans into marketing and other plans for each division, product, and brand. Through implementation, the company turns the plans into actions. Control consists of measuring and evaluating the results of marketing activities and taking corrective action where needed. Finally, marketing analysis provides information and evaluations needed for all of the other marketing activities.

Marketing Analysis

Managing the marketing function begins with a complete analysis of the company's situation. The company must analyze its markets and marketing environment to find attractive opportunities and to avoid environmental threats. It must analyze company strengths and weaknesses as well as current and possible marketing actions to determine which opportunities it can best pursue. Marketing provides input to each of the other marketing management functions. We discuss marketing analysis more fully in chapter 4.

Marketing Planning

Through strategic planning, the company decides what it wants to do with each business unit. Marketing planning involves deciding on marketing strategies that will help the company attain its overall strategic objectives. A detailed marketing plan is needed for each business, product, or brand. What does a marketing plan look like? Our discussion focuses on product or brand plans.

Table 2.2 outlines the major sections of a typical product or brand plan. The plan begins with an executive summary, which quickly overviews major assessments, goals, and recommendations. The main section of the plan presents a detailed analysis of the current marketing situation as well as potential threats and

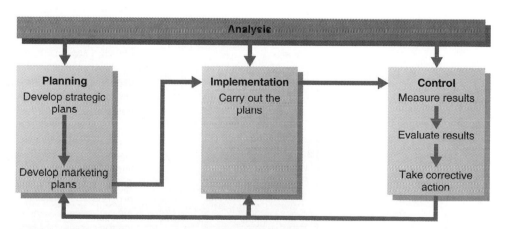

FIGURE 2.7   The relationship between analysis, planning, implementation, and control

TABLE 2.2   CONTENTS OF A MARKETING PLAN

Section	Purpose
Executive summary	Presents a brief summary of the main goals and recommendations of the plan for management review, helping top management to find the plan's major points quickly. A table of contents should follow the executive summary.
Current marketing situation	Describes the target market and company's position in it, including information about the market, product performance, competition, and distribution. This section includes: • A *market description* that defines the market and major segments, then reviews customer needs and factors in the marketing environment that may affect customer purchasing. • A *product review* that shows sales, prices, and gross margins of the major products in the product line. • A review of *competition,* which identifies major competitors and assesses their market positions and strategies for product quality, pricing, distribution, and promotion. • A review of *distribution,* which evaluates recent sales trends and other developments in major distribution channels.
Threats and opportunity analysis	Assesses major threats and opportunities that the product might face, helping management to anticipate important positive or negative developments that might have an impact on the firm and its strategies.
Objectives and issues	States the marketing objectives that the company would like to attain during the plan's term and discusses key issues that will affect their attainment. For example, if the goal is to achieve a 15 percent market share, this section looks at how this goal might be achieved.
Marketing strategy	Outlines the broad marketing logic by which the business unit hopes to achieve its marketing objectives and the specifics of target markets, positioning, and marketing expenditure levels. It outlines specific strategies for each marketing mix element and explains how each responds to the threats, opportunities, and critical issues spelled out earlier in the plan.
Action programs	Spells out how marketing strategies will be turned into specific action programs that answer the following questions: *What* will be done? *When* will it be done? *Who* is responsible for doing it? *How* much will it cost?
Budgets	Details a supporting marketing budget that is essentially a projected profit-and-loss statement. It shows expected revenues (forecasted number of units sold and the average net price) and expected costs (of production, distribution, and marketing). The difference is the projected profit. Once approved by higher management, the budget becomes the basis for materials buying, production scheduling, personnel planning, and marketing operations.
Controls	Outlines the control that will be used to monitor progress and allow higher management to review implementation results and spot products that are not meeting their goals.

Marketers must continually plan their analysis, implementation, and control activities.

opportunities. It next states major objectives for the brand and outlines the specifics of a marketing strategy for achieving them.

Marketing strategy
The marketing logic by which the business unit hopes to achieve its marketing objectives.

A **marketing strategy** is the marketing logic whereby the company hopes to achieve its marketing objectives. It consists of specific strategies for target markets, positioning, the marketing mix, and marketing expenditure levels. In this section, the planner explains how each strategy responds to the threats, opportunities, and critical issues spelled out earlier in the plan. Additional sections of the marketing plan lay out an action program for implementing the marketing strategy along with the details of a supporting *marketing budget*. The last section outlines the controls that will be used to monitor progress and take corrective action.[20]

Marketing Implementation

Marketing implementation
The process that turns marketing strategies and plans into marketing actions in order to accomplish strategic marketing objectives.

Planning good strategies is only a start toward successful marketing. A brilliant marketing strategy counts for little if the company fails to implement it properly. **Marketing implementation** is the process that turns marketing *plans* into marketing *actions* in order to accomplish strategic marketing objectives. Implementation involves day-to-day, month-to-month activities that effectively put the marketing plan to work. Whereas marketing planning addresses the *what* and *why* of marketing activities, implementation addresses the *who, where, when,* and *how*.

Many managers think that "doing things right" (implementation) is as important, or even more important, than "doing the right things" (strategy). The fact is that both are critical to success.[21] However, companies can gain competitive advantages through effective implementation. One firm can have essentially the same strategy as another yet win in the marketplace through faster or better execution. Still, implementation is difficult—it is often easier to think up good marketing strategies than it is to carry them out.

In an increasingly connected world, people at all levels of the marketing system must work together to implement marketing plans and strategies. At Black & Decker, for example, marketing implementation for the company's power tool products requires day-to-day decisions and actions by thousands of people both inside and outside the organization. Marketing managers make decisions about target segments, branding, packaging, pricing, promoting, and distributing. They connect with people elsewhere in the company to get support for their products and programs. They talk with engineering about product design, with manufacturing about production and inventory levels, and with finance about funding and cash flows. They also connect with outside people, such as advertising agencies to plan ad campaigns and the media to obtain publicity support. The sales force urges Home Depot, Wal-Mart, and other retailers to advertise Black & Decker products, provide ample shelf space, and use company displays.

Successful marketing implementation depends on how well the company blends its people, organizational structure, decision and reward systems, and company culture into a cohesive action program that supports its strategies. At all levels, the company must be staffed by people who have the needed skills, motivation, and personal characteristics. The company's formal organization structure plays an important role in implementing marketing strategy; so do its decision and reward systems. For example, if a company's compensation system rewards managers for short-run profit results, they will have little incentive to work toward long-run market-building objectives.

Finally, to be successfully implemented, the firm's marketing strategies must fit with its company culture, the system of values and beliefs shared by people in the organization. A study of America's most successful companies found that these companies have almost cultlike cultures built around strong, market-oriented missions. At companies such as Wal-Mart, Microsoft, Nordstrom, Citicorp, Procter & Gamble, Walt Disney, and Hewlett-Packard, "employees share such a strong vision that they know in their hearts what's right for their company."[22]

Marketing Department Organization

The company must design a marketing department that can carry out marketing strategies and plans. If the company is very small, one person might do all of the marketing work—research, selling, advertising, customer service, and other activities. As the company expands, a marketing department organization emerges to plan and carry out marketing activities. In large companies, this department contains many specialists. Thus, Black & Decker has product and market managers, sales managers and salespeople, market researchers, advertising experts, and other specialists.

Modern marketing departments can be arranged in several ways. The most common form of marketing organization is the *functional organization* in which different marketing activities are headed by a functional specialist—a sales manager, advertising manager, marketing research manager, customer service manager, new-product manager. A company that sells across the country or internationally often uses a *geographic organization* in which its sales and marketing people are assigned to specific countries, regions, and districts. Geographic organization allows salespeople to settle into a territory, get to know their customers, and work with a minimum of travel time and cost.

Companies with many, very different products or brands often create a *product management organization*. Using this approach, a product manager develops and implements a complete strategy and marketing program for a specific product or brand. Product management first appeared at Procter & Gamble in 1929. A new company soap, Camay, was not doing well, and a young P&G executive was assigned to give his exclusive attention to developing and promoting this product. He was successful, and the company soon added other product managers.[23] Since then, many firms, especially consumer products companies, have set up product management organizations. However, recent dramatic changes in the marketing environment have caused many companies to rethink the role of the product manager (see Marketing Highlight 2.3).

For companies that sell one product line to many different types of markets that have different needs and preferences, a *market management organization* might be best. A market management organization is similar to the product management organization. Market managers are responsible for developing marketing strategies and plans for their specific markets. This system's main advantage is that the company is organized around the needs of specific customer segments.

Large companies that produce many different products flowing into many different geographic and customer markets usually employ some *combination* of the functional, geographic, product, and market organization forms. This ensures that each function, product, and market receives its share of management attention. However, it can also add costly layers of management and reduce organizational flexibility. Still, the benefits of organizational specialization usually outweigh the drawbacks.[24]

Marketing Control

Marketing control

The process of measuring and evaluating the results of marketing strategies and plans and taking corrective action to ensure that marketing objectives are achieved.

Because many surprises occur during the implementation of marketing plans, the marketing department must practice constant marketing control. **Marketing control** involves evaluating the results of marketing strategies and plans and taking corrective action to ensure that objectives are attained. Figure 2.8 shows that implementation involves four steps. Management first sets specific marketing goals. It then measures its performance in the marketplace and evaluates the causes of any differences between expected and actual performance. Finally, management takes corrective action to close the gaps between its goals and its performance. This may require changing the action programs or even changing the goals.

Operating control involves checking ongoing performance against the annual plan and taking corrective action when necessary. Its purpose is to ensure that the company achieves the sales, profits, and other goals set out in its annual plan. It also involves determining the profitability of different products, territories, markets, and channels.

Strategic control involves looking at whether the company's basic strategies are well matched to its opportunities. Marketing strategies and programs can quickly become outdated, and each company should periodically reassess its overall

FIGURE 2.8 The control process

MARKETING
HIGHLIGHT
2 . 3

BRAND MANAGEMENT OR *CUSTOMER* MANAGEMENT?

Brand management has become a fixture in most consumer packaged-goods companies. Brand managers plan brand strategy and watch over their brands' profits. Working closely with advertising agencies, they create national advertising campaigns to build market share and consumer brand loyalty. The brand management system made sense in its earlier days, when the food companies were all-powerful, consumers were brand loyal, and national media could reach mass markets effectively. Recently, however, many companies have begun to question whether this system fits well with today's marketing realities.

Two major forces are causing companies to rethink brand management. First, consumers, markets, and marketing strategies have changed dramatically. Today's consumers face an ever-growing set of acceptable brands and never-ending price promotions. Moreover, the rapid growth of the Internet and other communication technologies has given consumers more control over their information and buying environments. As a result, customers are more knowledgeable and less brand loyal. Second, larger, more powerful, and better-informed retailers are now demanding more trade promotions in exchange for scarce shelf space. This leaves fewer dollars for national advertising, the brand manager's primary marketing tool. Retailers also want more customized "multibrand" promotions that are beyond the scope of any single brand manager.

To address these and other changes, many companies have adopted *category management* systems and *category teams*. Under this system, brand managers report to a category manager, who has total responsibility for an entire product line. For example, instead of having several cookie brand managers, Nabisco has three cookie category-management teams—one each for adult rich cookies, nutritional cookies, and children's cookies. Headed by a category manager, each category team includes several marketing people—brand managers, a sales-planning manager, and a marketing information specialist—who handle brand strategy, advertising, and sales promotion. Each team also includes specialists from finance, research and development, manufacturing, engineering, and distribution. Thus, category managers act as small business-people, with complete responsibility for an entire category and with a full complement of people to help them plan and implement category marketing strategies.

Category management offers many advantages. Rather than focusing on specific brands, category managers shape the company's entire category offering. This results in a more complete and coordinated category offer. Perhaps the most important benefit of category management is that it links up better with retailer category-buying systems, in which retailers have begun making their individual buyers responsible for working with all suppliers of a specific product category.

Marketing audit

A comprehensive, systematic, independent, and periodic examination of a company's environment, objectives, strategies, and activities to determine problem areas and opportunities and to recommend a plan of action to improve the company's marketing performance.

approach to the marketplace. A major tool for such strategic control is a **marketing audit.** The marketing audit is a comprehensive, systematic, independent, and periodic examination of a company's environment, objectives, strategies, and activities to determine problem areas and opportunities. The audit provides good input for a plan of action to improve the company's marketing performance.[25]

The marketing audit covers *all* major marketing areas of a business, not just a few trouble spots. It assesses the marketing environment, marketing strategy, marketing organization, marketing systems, marketing mix, and marketing productivity and profitability. The audit is normally conducted by an objective and experienced outside party. Table 2.3 shows the kinds of questions the marketing auditor might ask. The findings may come as a surprise—and sometimes as a shock—to management. Management then decides which actions make sense and how and when to implement them.

Still, the biggest problem with brand and category management systems is that they are product driven, not customer driven. Brand and category managers often concentrate so heavily on their brands that they lose sight of the marketplace. But today, more than ever, companies must start not with brands, but with the needs of the consumers and retailers that these brands serve. One industry expert observes, "When there were unique products, and fewer media and distribution channels, it was fairly easy for a company to make a great product, tell consumers about it, and get it to them. But, today, brand managers need to dig deeper—to let customer knowledge drive day-to-day decision making, to focus on the end goal of a loyal customer, not just the sale through the channel." In short, he adds, "customer management will come to drive brand management." In fact, some forward-thinking companies are now transforming their *brand* management organizations into *customer* management organizations.

Procter & Gamble, for example, is shifting toward a "market development organization." Under this new organization, marketing directors and brand managers in P&G's global marketing units are responsible for advertising, product development, packaging, and other efforts to build the company's brands. Meanwhile, dozens of brand managers are being assigned to one of eight geographically organized market development organizations (MDOs), where they find themselves spending more time managing customers than managing brands. Their new duties include working on "customer business teams," developing marketing programs with retailers, redesigning stores, creating marketing programs for special markets, and forging partnerships with other marketers.

P&G thinks that the new organization gives its managers a broader perspective and deeper customer focus. "You're out there looking at more cosmic marketing issues than just what your little brand might be in the life of that consumer," says a senior P&G marketing executive. The new organization also aligns the company better with its distribution partners. "They've looked out five years and realized there are going to be 20 retailers who make a huge difference in their business across all channels," observes an industry analyst. "If they're not aligned properly with those retailers, [the future] is going to look fairly bleak." Thus, the market development organization focuses attention not on the company's brands, but on how those brands can help P&G's retailing partners and final customers.

So brand management is changing, and these changes are much needed. Today's marketing environment calls for less brand focus and more customer focus. Colgate recently took a step in this direction. It moved from *brand management* (Colgate brand toothpaste) to *category management* (all Colgate-Palmolive toothpaste brands) to a new stage, *customer need management* (customers' oral health needs). This last stage finally gets the entire organization to focus on building long-term customer relationships based on fulfilling customer needs.

Sources: Quotes from Jack Neff, "P&G Redefines Brand Manager for MDO Days," *Advertising Age,* April 26, 1999, pp. 4, 50; and Doug Barton, "Customer vs. Brand Management," *Brandweek,* November 2, 1998, pp. 32–34. Also see "Death of the Brand Manager," *The Economist,* April 9, 1994, pp. 67–68; Alan J. Bergstrom, "Brand Management Poised for Change," *Marketing News,* July 7, 1997, p. 5; James Bell, "Brand Management for the Next Millennium," *The Journal of Business Strategy,* March–April 1998, p. 7; Peter Galuszka, "P&G: How New and Improved?" *Business Week,* June 21, 1999, p. 36; and Jack Neff, "The New Brand Management," *Advertising Age,* November 8, 1999, pp. S2, S18.

The Marketing Environment

Managing the marketing function would be hard enough if the marketer had to deal only with the controllable marketing mix variables. But the company operates in a complex marketing environment, consisting of uncontrollable forces to which the company must adapt. The environment produces both threats and opportunities. The company must carefully analyze its environment so that it can avoid the threats and take advantage of the opportunities.

The company's marketing environment includes forces close to the company that affect its ability to serve consumers, such as other company departments, channel members, suppliers, competitors, and publics. It also includes broader demographic and economic forces, political and legal forces, technological and ecological forces, and social and cultural forces. In order to connect effectively with

TABLE 2.3   MARKETING AUDIT QUESTIONS

Marketing Environment Audit

1. The *macroenvironment:* What major *demographic, economic, natural, technological, political,* and *cultural* trends pose threats and opportunities for this company?
2. The *task environment:*
   - *Markets and customers:* What is happening to marketing size, growth, geographic distribution, and profits? What are the major market segments? How do customers make their buying decisions? How do they rate the company on product quality, value, and service?
   - *Other factors* in the marketing system: Who are the company's major *competitors* and what are their strategies, strengths, and weaknesses? How are the company's *channels* performing? What trends are affecting *suppliers?* What key *publics* provide problems or opportunities?

Marketing Strategy Audit

1. *Business mission and marketing objectives:* Is the mission clearly defined and market oriented? Has the company set clear objectives to guide marketing planning and performance?
2. *Marketing strategy:* Does the company have a strong marketing strategy for achieving its objectives?
3. *Budgets:* Has the company budgeted sufficient resources to segments, products, territories, and marketing mix elements?

Marketing Organization Audit

1. *Formal structure:* Are marketing activities optimally structured along functional, product, market, and territory lines?
2. *Functional efficiency:* Do marketing and sales communicate effectively? Is marketing staff well trained, supervised, motivated, and evaluated?
3. *Cross-functional efficiency:* Do marketing people work well with people in operations, R&D, purchasing, human resources, information technology, and other nonmarketing areas?

Marketing Systems Audit

1. *Marketing information system:* Is the marketing intelligence system providing accurate and timely information? Is the company using marketing research effectively?
2. *Marketing planning system:* Does the company prepare annual, long-term, and strategic plans? Are they used?
3. *Marketing control system:* Are annual plan objectives being achieved? Does management periodically analyze product, market, and channel sales and profitability?
4. *New-product development:* Does the company have an effective new-product development process? Has the company succeeded with new products?

Marketing Productivity Audit

1. *Profitability analysis:* How profitable are the company's different products, markets, territories, and channels? Should the company enter, expand, or withdraw from any business segments?
2. *Cost-effectiveness analysis:* Do any marketing activities have excessive costs? How can costs be reduced?

Marketing Function Audit

1. *Products:* What are the company's product line objectives? Should some current products be phased out or new products be added? Would some products benefit from changes in quality, features, or style?
2. *Price:* Are the company's pricing policies and procedures appropriate? Are prices in line with customers' perceived value?
3. *Distribution:* What are the company's distribution objectives and strategies? Should existing channels be changed or new ones added?
4. *Promotion:* Does the company have well-developed *advertising, sales promotion,* and *public relations* programs? Is the *sales force* large enough and well trained, supervised, and motivated?

consumers, others in the company, external partners, and the world around them, marketers need to consider all of these forces when developing and positioning its offer to the target market. The marketing environment is discussed more fully in chapter 3.

REVIEW OF CONCEPT CONNECTIONS

Strategic planning sets the stage for the rest of the company's planning. Marketing contributes to strategic planning, and the overall plan defines marketing's role in the company. Although formal planning offers a variety of benefits to companies, not all companies use it or use it well. Although many discussions of strategic planning focus on large corporations, small business also can benefit greatly from sound strategic planning.

1. Explain companywide strategic planning and its four steps.

Strategic planning involves developing a strategy for long-run survival and growth. It consists of four steps: defining the company's mission, setting objectives and goals, designing a business portfolio, and developing functional plans. *Defining a clear company mission* begins with drafting a formal mission statement, which should be market oriented, realistic, motivating, and consistent with the market environment. The mission is then transformed into detailed *supporting goals and objectives* to guide the entire company. Based on those goals and objectives, headquarters designs a *business portfolio,* deciding which businesses and products should receive more or fewer resources. In turn, each business and product unit must develop detailed marketing plans in line with the companywide plan. Comprehensive and sound marketing plans support company strategic planning by detailing specific opportunities.

2. Discuss how to design business portfolios and develop growth strategies

Guided by the company's mission statement and objectives, management plans its *business portfolio,* or the collection of businesses and products that make up the company. To produce a business portfolio that best fits the company's strengths and weaknesses to opportunities in the environment, the company must analyze and adjust its *current* business portfolio and develop growth strategies for adding *new* products or businesses to the portfolio. The company might use a formal portfolio-planning method like the *BCG growth-share matrix.* But many companies are now designing more customized portfolio-planning approaches that better suit their unique situations. The *product–market expansion grid* suggests four possible growth paths: market penetration, market development, product development, and diversification.

3. Explain functional planning strategies and marketing's role in strategic planning.

Once strategic objectives have been defined, management within each business must prepare a set of *functional plans* that coordinates the activities of the marketing, finance, operations, and other departments. A company's success depends on how well each department performs its customer value-adding activities and on how well the departments work together to serve the customer. Each department has a different idea about which objectives and activities are most important. The marketing department stresses the consumer's point of view, whereas the operations department may be more concerned with reducing production costs. In order to best accomplish the firm's overall strategic objectives, marketing managers must understand other functional managers' points of view.

Marketing plays an important role throughout the strategic planning process. It provides *inputs* to strategic planning concerning attractive market possibilities, and marketing's customer focus serves as a *guiding philosophy* for planning. Marketers design *strategies* to help meet strategic objectives and prepare programs to carry them out profitably. Marketing also plays an integrative role to help ensure that departments work together toward the goal of delivering superior customer value and satisfaction.

4. Describe the marketing process and the forces that influence it.

The *marketing process* matches consumer needs with the company's capabilities and objectives. Consumers are at the center of the marketing process. The company divides the total market into smaller segments, selecting the segments it can best serve. It then designs a *marketing mix* to differentiate its marketing offer and position this offer in selected target segments. The marketing mix consists of product, price, place, and promotion decisions.

5. List the marketing management functions, including the elements of a marketing plan.

To find the best mix and put it into action, the company engages in marketing analysis, planning, implementation, and control. The main components of a *marketing plan* are the executive summary, current marketing situation, threats and opportunities, objectives and issues, marketing strategies, action programs, budgets, and controls. To plan good strategies is often easier than to carry them out. To be successful, companies must also be effective at *implementation*—turning marketing strategies into marketing actions.

Much of the responsibility for implementation goes to the company's marketing department. Modern marketing departments can be organized in one or a combination of ways: *functional marketing organization, geographic organization, product management organization,* or *market management organization.* Marketing organizations carry out *marketing control,* both operating control and strategic control. They use *marketing audits* to determine marketing opportunities and problems and to recommend short-run and long-run actions to improve overall marketing performance. Through these activities, the company watches and adapts to the marketing environment.

KEY TERMS

Business portfolio
Diversification
Growth-share matrix
Market development
Market penetration
Market positioning
Market segment

Market segmentation
Market targeting
Marketing audit
Marketing control
Marketing implementation
Marketing mix
Marketing process

Marketing strategy
Mission statement
Portfolio analysis
Product development
Product–market expansion grid
Strategic business unit (SBU)
Strategic planning

ISSUES FOR DISCUSSION

1. Define strategic planning. List and briefly review the four steps in the strategic planning process.
2. In a series of job interviews, you ask three recruiters to describe the missions of their companies. One says, "To make profits." Another says, "To create customers." The third says, "To fight world hunger." Analyze and discuss what these mission statements tell you about each of the companies. Which statement most closely matches the four criteria for all good mission statements?
3. An electronics manufacturer obtains the semiconductors it uses in production from a company-owned subsidiary that also sells to other manufacturers. The subsidiary is smaller and less profitable than are competing producers, and its growth rate has been below the industry average during the past five years. Into which cell of the BCG growth-share matrix does this strategic business unit fall? What should the parent company do with this SBU? Why?
4. Compare the General Electric strategic business-planning grid and the Boston Consulting Group approach. How do the industry attractiveness and business strength dimensions of the GE grid compare with the market growth rate and relative market share dimensions of the BCG grid? What other similarities and differences do you see? Where would an SBU located in the yellow zone of the GE grid most likely be located in the BCG grid? What strategy might this suggest for the SBU?
5. Beyond evaluating current businesses, designing the business portfolio involves finding businesses and products the company should consider in the future. Apply the product-market expansion grid to assess how one of the following companies might grow: (a) Dell Computer, (b) Kodak, (c) Levi Strauss, (d) E*Trade online investment services. Be sure that your answer covers all the cells in the grid.
6. Today's companies must be customer centered in order to win, keep, and grow customers. This involves careful market segmentation, targeting, and positioning. Briefly describe these three marketing process steps and apply them to AT&T, MCI, or Sprint in the long-distance communication market. Based on advertisements and other information, assess each company's targeting and position strategy.
7. Which competitive marketing strategy is best for a company depends on its industry position. Which of the four possible strategies discussed in the chapter would be best for each of the following firms? (a) The Harlem Globetrotters, (b) General Electric's small appliances division, (c) Fuji film, (d) Barnes&Noble.com.
8. What activities make up the implementation phase of marketing management? Is it better to have a good marketing strategy that is poorly implemented, or a mediocre strategy that is well implemented?

MARKETING APPLICATIONS

1. E-commerce is experiencing explosive growth. Many experts predict that it is the marketing model of the future. Thus many people are now asking, "How does one get started in becoming a cyberpreneur?" Some examples of successful cyberpreneurs include www.violet.com, www.800Flowers.com, and www.hotwired.com (*Wired* magazine). Assume that you wish to start a business on the Internet.
   a. How would you look for a promising opportunity?
   b. Select a specific opportunity. What makes this opportunity distinctive and promising?
   c. Describe your target market and how you would serve it differently than current businesses do.
   d. What marketing mix would you use for your business?
   e. Write a brief marketing plan (see Table 2.2) for this promising opportunity. After writing the plan, assess your chances for success in starting such a business.
2. For more than a decade, such notable companies as Nike, Reebok, Adidas, New Balance, Puma, and Converse have been fighting a no-holds-barred battle in what has come to be known as the Sneaker Wars. Visit these firms at their respective Web sites at www.nike.com, www.reebok.com, www.adidas.com, www.newbalance. com, www.puma.com, and www.converseshoes.com. As a future marketing strategist, answer the following questions:
   a. Which firm is the market leader? Which are market challengers, market followers, and market nicher? Explain.
   b. Critique the various Web sites. Do the sites match your assessments of industry positions? Why or why not?
   c. Assume the position of one the market challengers. Design a strategy for overtaking the market leader. Be specific in your suggestions.
   d. Assume the position of a market nicher and design a strategy for expanding your business without drawing attacks from your stronger rivals.
   e. Select a market nicher. How might this nicher improve its Web site? Be specific.

INTERNET CONNECTIONS

STRATEGIC PLANNING FOR ONLINE MARKETING

Online book selling is big business. The first successful online bookseller was Amazon.com, an exclusively online retailer. The company quickly established itself as the market leader. Attracted by the profit potential, Barnes & Noble, Borders, and others have followed suit. More recently Amazon has diversified into many other lines of business: music, video, electronics, toys, pharmaceuticals, and online auctions. Is this a good strategy for Amazon? To partially answer this question, conduct an analysis of the online toy industry. Complete the following table by first visiting www.bizrate.com to identify two of Amazon's toughest online toy store competitors in addition to eToys. Then review the BizRate comments and visit each competitor's site to finish the table.

	Amazon www.amazon.com	eToys www.etoys.com	Other competitor	Other competitor
Who rated site for BizRate?				
BizRate overall customer rating				
Products sold in addition to toys				
Market positioning*				
Competitive advantage*				
Competitive weakness*				

*infer from viewing site and ratings

FOR DISCUSSION

Analyze Amazon's strategy by answering the following questions.

1. How does Amazon compare to its competition in the toy industry?

2. What is Amazon's mission statement? You can guess at this by reading about the company at www.amazon.com.

3. Does the toy business fit with Amazon's mission? Why or why not?

4. Should Amazon be in the toy business? Justify your response.

5. Is there any synergy between Amazon's many product areas? If so, what is it?

6. Years ago Sears used to advertise that "Sears has everything!" Is Amazon becoming the Sears of the Internet? If so, is this a good strategy?

7. Does Amazon pursue different product strategies in its U.K. and German operations?

8. Based on what you have learned, do you think Amazon is pursuing the correct strategy? Why or why not?

SAVVY SITES

- CNET (www.news.com) focuses on the latest news in the Internet and computer industries.

- Liszt (www.liszt.com) provides links to over 90,000 mailing lists. A subscriber can read and discuss trends in just about any industry.

- American Demographics and Marketing Tools (www.demographics.com) both provide lots of information and identify marketing firms qualified to aid companies with strategic planning.

NOTES

1. Quotes from David Kirkpatrick, "Intel's Amazing Profit Machine," *Fortune,* February 17, 1997, pp. 60–72; and Damon Darlin, "Intel's Palace," *Forbes,* September 9, 1996, pp. 42–43. Also see Andy Reinhardt, "Pentium: The Next Generation," *Business Week,* May 12, 1997, pp. 42–43; "The Fortune 500 Largest Firms," *Fortune,* April 22, 1998, pp. F1–F2; Brent Schlender, "The New Man Inside Intel," *Fortune,* May 11, 1998, pp. 161–62; Lawrence M. Fisher, "Sales of High-End Chips Help Intel Beat Estimates," *New York Times,* January 13, 1999; and "Intel Breaks 1 GHz, Presents Pentium III," *Semiconductor International,* April 1999, p. 22.

2. See Philip Kotler, *Kotler on Marketing* (New York: Free Press, 1999), pp. 165–66.

3. For a more detailed discussion of corporate- and business-level strategic planning as they apply to marketing, see Philip Kotler, *Marketing Management: Analysis, Planning, Implementation, and Control,* 10th ed. (Upper Saddle River, NJ: Prentice Hall, 2000), chap. 3.

4. The preceding examples are from Romauld A. Stone, "Mission Statements Revisited," *SAM Advanced Management Journal,* Winter 1996, pp. 31–37; Rhymer Rigby, "Mission Statements," *Management Today,* March 1998, pp. 56–58; and "About Amazon.com," accessed online at www.amazon.com, September 1999.

5. Stone, "Mission Statements Revisited," p. 33.

6. See Bradley Johnson, "Bill Gates' Vision of Microsoft in Every Home," *Advertising Age,* December 19, 1994, pp. 14–15. For more on mission statements, see J.W. Graham and W. C. Havlick, *Mission Statements: A Guide to the Corporate and Nonprofit Sectors* (New York: Garland Publishing, 1994); P. Jones and L. Kahaner, *Say It and Live It: The 50 Corporate Mission Statements That Hit the Mark* (New York: Doubleday, 1995); Thomas A. Stewart, "A Refreshing Change: Vision Statements That Make Sense," *Fortune,* September 30, 1996, pp. 195–96; and Christopher K. Bart,

"Making Mission Statements Count," *CA Magazine,* March 1999, pp. 37–38.

7. Gilbert Fuchsberg, " 'Visioning' Mission Becomes Its Own Mission," *Wall Street Journal,* January 7, 1994, pp. B1, 3. Also see Sal Marino, "Where There Is No Visionary, Companies Falter," *Industry Week,* March 15, 1999, p. 20.

8. See Linda Grant, "Monsanto's Bet: There's Gold in Going Green," *Fortune,* April 14, 1997, pp. 116–18; Richard A. Melcher and Amy Barrett, "Fields of Genes," *Business Week,* April 12, 1999, p. 62; and David Stipp, "Is Monsanto's Biotech Worth Less Than a Hill of Beans?" *Fortune,* February 21, 2000, pp. 157–60.

9. For an interesting discussion of assessing the business portfolio, see John O. Whitney, "Strategic Renewal of Business Units," *Harvard Business Review,* July–August 1996, pp. 84–98.

10. See John A. Byrne, "Strategic Planning," *Business Week,* August 26, 1996, pp. 46–51; Pete Bogda, "Fifteen Years Later, the Return of 'Strategy,' " *Brandweek,* February 1997, p. 18; and Diane Sanchez, "Now That's Customer Focus," *Sales & Marketing Management,* April 1998, p. 24. Also see Nryan W. Barry, "A Beginner's Guide to Strategic Planning," *The Futurist,* April 1998, pp. 33–36; and Ian Wilson, "Strategic Planning for the Millennium: Resolving the Dilemma," *Long Range Planning,* August 1998, pp. 507–13.

11. H. Igor Ansoff, "Strategies for Diversification," *Harvard Business Review,* September–October 1957, pp. 113–24. Also see Kotler, *Kotler on Marketing,* pp. 46–48.

12. Nelson D. Schwartz, "Still Perking After All These Years," *Fortune,* May 24, 1999, pp. 203–10.

13. John C. Narver and Stanley F. Slater, "The Effect of a Market Orientation on Business Profitability," *Journal of Marketing,* October 1990, pp. 20–35.

14. See Brian Dumaine, "Creating a New Company Culture," *Fortune,* January 15, 1990, p. 128; and Howard E. Butz Jr. and

Leonard D. Goodstein, "Measuring Customer Value: Gaining Strategic Advantage," *Organizational Dynamics,* Winter 1996, pp. 63–77.

15. Kotler, *Kotler on Marketing,* pp. 20–22.

16. Leslie Brokaw, "The Secrets of Great Planning," *Inc.,* October 1992, p. 152; and Kotler, *Marketing Management: Analysis, Planning, Implementation, and Control,* chap. 3.

17. Bradford McKee, "Think Ahead, Set Goals, and Get Out of the Office," *Nation's Business,* May 1993, p. 10. For more on small business strategic planning, see Nancy Drozdow, "Tools for Strategy Development in Family Firms," *Sloan Management Review,* Fall 1997, pp. 75–88; and Wendy M. Beech, "In It for the Long Haul," *Black Enterprise,* March 1998, p. 25.

18. The four Ps classification was first suggested by E. Jerome McCarthy, *Basic Marketing: A Managerial Approach* (Homewood, IL: Irwin, 1960). For more discussion of this classification scheme, see Walter van Waterschoot and Christophe Van den Bulte, "The 4P Classification of the Marketing Mix Revisited," *Journal of Marketing,* October 1992, pp. 83–93; and Michael G. Harvey, Robert F. Lusch, and Branko Cavarkapo, "A Marketing Mix for the 21st Century," *Journal of Marketing Theory and Practice,* Fall 1996, pp. 1–15.

19. Robert Lauterborn, "New Marketing Litany: 4P's Passé; C-Words Take Over," *Advertising Age,* October 1, 1990, p. 26. Also see Kotler, *Marketing Management: Analysis, Planning, Implementation, and Control,* chap. 1, p. 16.

20. For more on marketing plans, see Jay Winchester, "What's the Plan?" *Sales & Marketing Management,* October 1997, pp. 73–78.

21. For a good discussion of gaining advantage through implementation effectiveness versus strategic differentiation, see Michael E. Porter, "What Is Strategy," *Harvard Business Review,* November–December 1996, pp. 61–78. Also see Charles H. Noble and Michael P. Mokwa, "Implementing Marketing Strategies: Developing and Testing a Managerial Theory," *Journal of Marketing,* October 1999, pp. 57–73.

22. Brian Dumaine, "Why Great Companies Last," *Business Week,* January 16, 1995, p. 129. See James C. Collins and Jerry I. Porras, *Built to Last: Successful Habits of Visionary Companies* (New York: HarperBusiness, 1995); Geoffrey Brewer, "Firing Line: What Separates Visionary Companies from All the Rest?" *Performance,* June 1995, pp. 12–17; and Rob Goffee and Gareth Jones, *The Character of a Corporation: How Your Company's Culture Can Make or Break Your Business* (New York: HarperBusiness, 1998).

23. Joseph Winski, "One Brand, One Manager," *Advertising Age,* August 20, 1987, p. 86. Also see Jack Neff, "P&G Redefines the Brand Manager," *Advertising Age,* October 13, 1997, pp. 1, 18; Alan J. Bergstrom, "Brand Management Poised for Change," *Marketing News,* July 7, 1997, p. 5; James Bell, "Brand Management for the Next Millennium," *The Journal of Business Strategy,* March–April 1998, p. 7; and Jack Neff, "The New Brand Management," *Advertising Age,* November 8, 1999, pp. S2, S18.

24. For more complete discussions of marketing organization approaches and issues, see Robert W. Ruekert, Orville C. Walker Jr., and Kenneth J. Roering, "The Organization of Marketing Activities: A Contingency Theory of Structure and Performance," *Journal of Marketing,* Winter 1985, pp. 13–25; Ravi S. Achrol, "Evolution of the Marketing Organization: New Forms for Turbulent Environments," *Journal of Marketing,* October 1991, pp. 77–93; and Geoffrey Brewer, "Love the Ones You're With," *Sales & Marketing Management,* February 1997, pp. 38–45.

25. For details, see Kotler, *Marketing Management: Analysis, Planning, Implementation, and Control,* chap. 20.

COMPANY CASE

2

Trap-Ease America: The Big Cheese of Mousetraps

One April morning, Martha House, president of Trap-Ease America, entered her office in Costa Mesa, California. She paused for a moment to contemplate the Ralph Waldo Emerson quote which she had framed and hung near her desk.

> If a man [can] . . . make a better mousetrap than his neighbor . . . the world will make a beaten path to his door.

Perhaps, she mused, Emerson knew something that she didn't. She *had* the better mousetrap—Trap-Ease—but the world didn't seem all that excited about it.

Martha had just returned from the National Hardware Show in Chicago. Standing in the trade show display booth for long hours and answering the same questions hundreds of times had been tiring. Yet, this show had excited her. Each year, National Hardware Show officials held a contest to select the best new product introduced at the show. Of the more than 300 new products introduced at that year's show, her mousetrap had won first place. Such notoriety was not new for the Trap-Ease mousetrap. *People* magazine had written about the mousetrap in an article, and numerous talk shows and trade publications had featured it. Despite all of this attention, however, the expected demand for the trap had not materialized. Martha hoped that this award might stimulate increased interest and sales.

A group of investors who had obtained worldwide rights to market the innovative mousetrap had formed Trap-Ease America in January. In return for marketing rights, the group agreed to pay the inventor and patent holder, a retired rancher, a royalty fee for each trap sold. The group then hired Martha to serve as president and to develop and manage the Trap-Ease America organization.

The Trap-Ease, a simple yet clever device, is manufactured by a plastics firm under contract with Trap-Ease America. It consists of a square, plastic tube measuring about 6 inches long and 1 1/2 inches square. The tube bends in the middle at a 30 degree angle, so that when the front part of the tube rests on a flat surface, the other end is elevated. The elevated end holds a removable cap into which the user places bait (cheese, dog food, or some other tidbit). A hinged door is attached to the front end of the tube. When the trap is "open," this door rests on two narrow "stilts" attached to the two bottom corners of the door.

The trap works with simple efficiency. A mouse, smelling the bait, enters the tube through the open end. As it walks up the angled bottom toward the bait, its weight makes the elevated end of the trap drop downward. This elevates the open end, allowing the hinged door to swing closed, trapping the mouse. Small teeth on the ends of the stilts catch in a groove on the bottom of the trap, locking the door closed. The mouse can be disposed of live, or it can be left alone for a few hours to suffocate in the trap.

Martha felt the trap had many advantages for the consumer when compared with traditional spring-loaded traps or poisons. Consumers can use it safely and easily with no risk of catching their fingers while loading it. It poses no injury or poisoning threat to children or pets. Furthermore, with Trap-Ease, consumers can avoid the unpleasant "mess" they encounter with the violent spring-loaded traps—it creates no "clean-up" problem. Finally, the consumer can reuse the trap or simply throw it away.

Martha's early research suggested that women are the best target market for the Trap-Ease. Men, it seems, are more willing to buy and use the traditional, spring-loaded trap. The targeted women, however, do not like the traditional trap. They often stay at home and take care of their children. Thus, they want a means of dealing with the mouse problem that avoids the unpleasantness and risks that the standard trap creates in the home.

To reach this target market, Martha decided to distribute Trap-Ease through national grocery, hardware, and drug chains such as Safeway, Kmart, Hechingers, and CB Drug. She sold the trap directly to these large retailers, avoiding any wholesalers or other intermediaries.

The traps sold in packages of two, with a suggested retail price of $2.49. Although this price made the Trap-Ease

about five to ten times more expensive than smaller, standard traps, consumers appeared to offer little initial price resistance. The manufacturing cost for the Trap-Ease, including freight and packaging costs, was about 31 cents per unit. The company paid an additional 8.2 cents per unit in royalty fees. Martha priced the traps to retailers at 99 cents per unit and estimated that, after sales and volume discounts, Trap-Ease would realize net revenues from retailers of 75 cents per unit.

To promote the product, Martha had budgeted approximately $60,000 for the first year. She planned to use $50,000 of this amount for travel costs to visit trade shows and to make sales calls on retailers. She would use the remaining $10,000 for advertising. So far, however, because the mousetrap had generated so much publicity, she had not felt that she needed to do much advertising. Still, she had placed advertising in *Good Housekeeping* and in other "home and shelter" magazines. Martha was the company's only "salesperson," but she intended to hire more salespeople soon.

Martha had initially forecasted Trap-Ease's first-year sales at five million units. Through April, however, the company had sold only several hundred thousand units. Martha wondered if most new products got off to such a slow start, or if she was doing something wrong. She had detected some problems although none seemed overly serious. For one, there had not been enough repeat buying. For another, she had noted that many of the retailers on whom she called kept their sample mousetraps on their desks as conversation pieces—she wanted the traps to be used and demonstrated. Martha wondered if consumers were also buying the traps as novelties rather than as solutions to their mouse problems.

Martha knew that the investor group believed that Trap-Ease America had a "once-in-a-lifetime chance" with its innovative mousetrap. She sensed the group's impatience. She had budgeted approximately $250,000 in administrative and fixed costs for the first year (not including marketing costs). To keep the investors happy, the company needed to sell enough traps to cover those costs and make a reasonable profit.

In these first few months, Martha had learned that marketing a new product is not an easy task. For example, one national retailer had placed a large order with instructions that the order was to be delivered to the loading dock at one of its warehouses between 1:00 and 3:00 P.M. on a specified day. When the truck delivering the order had arrived late, the retailer had refused to accept the shipment. The retailer had told Martha it would be a year before she got another chance. Perhaps, Martha thought, she should send the retailer and other customers a copy of Emerson's famous quote.

Questions

1. Martha and the Trap-Ease America investors feel they face a once-in-a-lifetime opportunity. What information

do they need to evaluate this opportunity? How do you think the group would write its mission statement? How would *you* write it?

2. Has Martha identified the best target market for Trap-Ease? What other market segments might the firm target?

3. How had the company positioned the Trap-Ease relative to the chosen target market? Could it position the product in other ways?

4. Describe the current marketing mix for Trap-Ease. Do you see any problems with this mix?

5. Who is Trap-Ease America's competition?

6. How would you change Trap-Ease's marketing strategy? What kinds of control procedures would you establish for this strategy?

After studying this chapter, you should be able to
1. describe the environmental forces that affect the company's ability to serve its customers
2. explain how changes in the demographic and economic environments affect marketing decisions
3. identify the major trends in the firm's natural and technological environments
4. explain the key changes in the political and cultural environments
5. discuss how companies can react to the marketing environment

THE MARKETING ENVIRONMENT

As we hurtle into the new millennium, social experts are busier than ever assessing the impact of a host of environmental forces on consumers and the marketers who serve them. "An old year turns into a new one," observes one such expert, "and the world itself, at least for a moment, seems to turn also. Images of death and rebirth, things ending and beginning, populate . . . and haunt the mind. Multiply this a thousand-fold, and you get 'millennial fever' . . . driving consumer behavior in all sorts of interesting ways."

Such millennial fever has hit the nation's baby boomers, the most commercially influential demographic group in history, especially hard. The oldest boomers, now in their fifties, are resisting the aging process with the vigor they once reserved for antiwar protests. Other factors are also at work. Today, people of all ages seem to feel a bit overworked, overstimulated, and overloaded. "Americans are overwhelmed . . . by the breathtaking onrush of the Information Age, with its high-speed modems, cell phones, and pagers," sug-

Lemon.

Lime.

gests the expert. "While we hail the benefits of the wired '90s, at the same time we are buffeted by the rapid pace of change."

The result of this "millennial fever" is a yearning to turn back the clock, to return to simpler times. This yearning has in turn produced a massive nostalgia wave. "We are creating a new culture, and we don't know what's going to happen," explains a noted futurist. "So we need some warm fuzzies from our past." Marketers of all kinds have responded to these nostalgia pangs by recreating products and images that help take consumers back to "the good old days." Examples are plentiful: Kellogg has revived old Corn Flakes packaging and car makers have created retro roadsters such as the Porsche Boxter. A Pepsi commercial rocks to the Rolling Stones's "Brown Sugar," James Brown's "I Feel Good" helps sell Senokot laxatives, and Janis Joplin's raspy voice crows, "Oh Lord, won't you buy me a Mercedes-Benz?" Disney developed an entire town—Celebration, Florida—to recreate the look and feel of 1940s neighborhoods. Heinz reintroduced its classic glass ketchup bottle, supported by nostalgic "Heinz was there" ads showing two 1950s-era boys eating hot dogs at a ballpark. Master marketer Coca-Cola resurrected the old red button logo and its heritage contour bottle. The current ad theme, "Always Coca-Cola," encapsulates both the past and the future. According to a Coca-Cola marketing executive, when the company introduced a plastic version of its famous contour bottle in 1994, sales grew by double digits in some markets.

Perhaps no company has more riding on the nostalgia wave than Volkswagen. The original Volkswagen Beetle first sputtered into America in 1949. With its simple, buglike design, no-frills engineering, and economical operation, the Beetle was the antithesis of Detroit's chrome-laden gas guzzlers. Although most owners would readily admit that their Beetles were underpowered, noisy, cramped, and freezing in the winter, they saw these as endearing qualities. Overriding these minor inconveniences, the Beetle was cheap to buy and own, dependable, easy to fix, fun to drive, and anything but flashy.

During the 1960s, as young baby boomers by the thousands were buying their first cars, demand exploded and the Beetle blossomed into an unlikely icon. Bursting with personality, the understated Bug came to personify an era of rebellion against conventions. It became the most popular car in American history, with sales peaking at 423,000 in 1968. By the late 1970s, however, the boomers had moved on, Bug mania had faded, and Volkswagen had dropped Beetle production for the United States. Still, more than 20 years later, the mere mention of these chugging oddities evokes smiles and strong emotions. Almost everyone over the age of 25, it seems, has a "feel-good" Beetle story to tell.

Now, in an attempt to surf the nostalgia wave, Volkswagen has introduced a New Beetle. Outwardly, the reborn Beetle resembles the original, tapping the strong emotions and memories of times gone by. Beneath the skin, however, the New Beetle is packed with modern features. According to an industry expert, "The Beetle comeback is . . . based on a combination of romance and reason—wrapping up modern

conveniences in an old-style package. Built into the dashboard is a bud vase perfect for a daisy plucked straight from the 1960s. But right next to it is a high-tech, multispeaker stereo—and options like power windows, cruise control, and a power sunroof make it a very different car than the rattly old Bug. The new version . . . comes with all the modern features car buyers demand, such as four air bags and power outlets for cell phones. But that's not why VW expects folks to buy it. With a familiar bubble shape that still makes people smile as it skitters by, the new Beetle offers a pull that is purely emotional."

Advertising for the New Beetle plays strongly on the nostalgia theme, while at the same time refreshing the old Beetle heritage. "If you sold your soul in the '80s," tweaks one ad, "here's your chance to buy it back." Other ads read, "Less flower, more power," and "Comes with wonderful new features. Like heat." Still another ad declares "0 to 60? Yes." The car's Web page (www3.vw.com/cars/newbeetle/main.html) summarizes: "The New Beetle has what any Beetle always had. Originality. Honesty. A point of view. It's an exhaustive and zealous rejection of banality. Isn't the world ready for that kind of car again?"

Volkswagen invested $560 million to bring the New Beetle to market. However, this investment appears to be paying big dividends. Demand quickly outstripped supply. Even before the first cars reached VW showrooms, dealers across the country had long waiting lists of people who'd paid for the car without ever seeing it, let alone driving it. One California dealer claimed that the New Beetle was such a traffic magnet that he had to remove it from his showroom floor every afternoon at 2 P.M. to discourage gawkers and let his salespeople work with serious prospects. The dealer encountered similar problems when he took to the streets in the new car. "You can't change lanes," said the dealer. "People drive up beside you to look."

Volkswagen's initial first-year sales projections of 50,000 New Beetles in North America proved pessimistic. After only nine months, the company had sold more than 64,000 of the new Bugs in the United States and Canada. The smart little car also garnered numerous distinguished awards, including *Motor Trend*'s 1999 Import Car of the Year, *Time* magazine's The Best of 1998 Design, *Business Week*'s

Best New Products, and 1999 North American Car of the Year, awarded by an independent panel of top journalists who cover the auto industry.

The New Beetle appears to be a cross-generational hit, appealing to more than the stereotyped core demographic target of Woodstock-recovered baby boomers. Even kids too young to remember the original Bug appear to love this new one. "It's like you have a rock star here and everybody wants an autograph," states a VW sales manager. "I've never seen a car that had such a wide range of interest, from 16-year-olds to 65-year-olds." One wait-listed customer confirms the car's broad appeal. "In 1967, my Dad got me a VW. I loved it. I'm sure the new one will take me back," says the customer. "I'm getting the New Beetle as a surprise for my daughter, but I'm sure I'm going to be stealing it from her all the time."

"Millennial fever" results from the convergence of a wide range of forces in the marketing environment—from technological, economic, and demographic forces to cultural, social, and political ones. Most trend analysts believe that the nostalgia craze will only grow as the baby boomers continue to age. If so, the New Beetle, so full of the past, has a very bright future. "The Beetle is not just empty nostalgia," says Gerald Celente, publisher of *Trend Journal*. "It is a practical car that is also tied closely to the emotions of a generation." Says another trend analyst, the New Beetle "is our romantic past, reinvented for our hectic here-and-now. Different, yet deeply familiar—a car for the times."[1]

Marketing environment
The actors and forces outside marketing that affect marketing management's ability to develop and maintain successful transactions with its target customers.

As noted in chapter 1, marketers operate in an increasingly connected world. Today's marketers must connect effectively with customers, others in the company, and external partners in the face of major environmental forces that buffet all of these actors. A company's **marketing environment** consists of the actors and forces outside marketing that affect marketing management's ability to develop and maintain successful relationships with its target customers. The marketing environment offers both opportunities and threats. Successful companies know the vital importance of constantly watching and adapting to the changing environment.

As we enter the new millennium, both consumers and marketers wonder what the future will bring. The environment continues to change at a rapid pace. For example, think about how you buy groceries today. How will your grocery buying change during the next few decades? What challenges will these changes present for marketers? Here's what two leading futurists envision for the year 2025.[2]

We won't be shopping in 21-aisle supermarkets in 2025, predicts Gary Wright, corporate demographer for Procter & Gamble in Cincinnati. The growth of e-commerce and the rapid speed of the Internet will lead to online ordering of lower priced, nonperishable products—everything from peanut butter to coffee filters. Retailers will become "bundlers," combining these orders into large packages of goods for each household and delivering them efficiently to their doorsteps. As a result, we'll see mergers between retailing and home-delivery giants—think Wal-MartExpress, a powerful combo of Wal-Mart and Federal Express. Consumers won't waste precious time searching for the best-priced bundle. Online information agents will do it for them, comparing prices among competitors.

Smart information agents also play a role in the world imagined by Ryan Mathews, futurist at First Matter LLC in Detroit. By 2025, computers will essentially be as smart as humans, he contends, and consumers will use them to exchange information with on-screen electronic agents that ferret out the best deals online. Thanks to embedded-chip technology in the pantry, products on a CHR (continuous household replenishment) list—like paper towels and pet food—will sense when they're running low and reorder themselves automatically. If the information agent finds a comparable but cheaper substitute for a CHR product, the item will be switched instantly.

Grocery shopping in 2025 will mean online ordering of everything from peanut butter to coffee filters. But it's already happening at Peapod.com, the nation's first and largest online grocery shopping and delivery service.

Microenvironment
The forces close to the company that affect its ability to serve its customers—the company, suppliers, marketing channel firms, customer markets, competitors, and publics.

Macroenvironment
The larger societal forces that affect the microenvironment—demographic, economic, natural, technological, political, and cultural forces.

Such pictures of the future give marketers plenty to think about. A company's marketers take the major responsibility for identifying and predicting significant changes in the environment. More than any other group in the company, marketers must be the trend trackers and opportunity seekers. Although every manager in an organization needs to observe the outside environment, marketers have two special aptitudes. They have disciplined methods—marketing intelligence and marketing research—for collecting information about the marketing environment. They also spend more time in the customer and competitor environment. By conducting systematic environmental scanning, marketers are able to revise and adapt marketing strategies to meet new challenges and opportunities in the marketplace.

The marketing environment is made up of a *microenvironment* and a *macroenvironment*. The **microenvironment** consists of the forces close to the company that affect its ability to serve its customers—the company, suppliers, marketing channel firms, customer markets, competitors, and publics. The **macroenvironment** consists of the larger societal forces that affect the microenvironment—demographic, economic, natural, technological, political, and cultural forces. We look first at the company's microenvironment.

THE COMPANY'S MICROENVIRONMENT

Marketing management's job is to attract and build relationships with customers by creating customer value and satisfaction. However, marketing managers cannot accomplish this task alone. Their success will depend on other actors in the company's microenvironment—other company departments, suppliers, marketing intermediaries, customers, competitors, and various publics, which combine to make up the company's value delivery system.

The Company

In designing marketing plans, marketing management takes other company groups into account—groups such as top management, finance, research and development (R&D), purchasing, manufacturing, and accounting. All these interrelated groups

FIGURE 3.1   The company's internal environment

form the internal environment (see Figure 3.1). Top management sets the company's mission, objectives, broad strategies, and policies. Marketing managers make decisions within the plans made by top management, and marketing plans must be approved by top management before they can be implemented.

Marketing managers must also work closely with other company departments. Finance is concerned with finding and using funds to carry out the marketing plan. The R&D department focuses on designing safe and attractive products. Purchasing worries about getting supplies and materials, whereas manufacturing is responsible for producing the desired quality and quantity of products. Accounting has to measure revenues and costs to help marketing know how well it is achieving its objectives. Together, all of these departments have an impact on the marketing department's plans and actions. Under the marketing concept, all of these functions must "think consumer," and they should work in harmony to provide superior customer value and satisfaction.

Suppliers

Suppliers are an important link in the company's overall customer value delivery system. They provide the resources needed by the company to produce its goods and services. Supplier problems can seriously affect marketing. Marketing managers must watch supply availability—supply shortages or delays, labor strikes, and other events can cost sales in the short run and damage customer satisfaction in the long run. Marketing managers also monitor the price trends of their key inputs. Rising supply costs may force price increases that can harm the company's sales volume.

Marketing Intermediaries

Marketing intermediaries
Firms that help the company to promote, sell, and distribute its goods to final buyers; they include resellers, physical distribution firms, marketing service agencies, and financial intermediaries.

Marketing intermediaries help the company to promote, sell, and distribute its goods to final buyers. They include *resellers, physical distribution firms, marketing services agencies,* and *financial intermediaries. Resellers* are distribution channel firms that help the company find customers or make sales to them. These include wholesalers and retailers, who buy and resell merchandise. Selecting and working with resellers is not easy. No longer do manufacturers have many small, independent resellers from which to choose. They now face large and growing reseller organizations. These organizations frequently have enough power to dictate terms or even shut the manufacturer out of large markets.

Physical distribution firms help the company to stock and move goods from their points of origin to their destinations. Working with warehouse and transportation firms, a company must determine the best ways to store and ship goods, balancing factors such as cost, delivery, speed, and safety. *Marketing services agencies* are the marketing research firms, advertising agencies, media firms, and marketing consulting firms that help the company target and promote its products to the right markets. When the company decides to use one of these agencies, it must choose carefully because these firms vary in creativity, quality, service, and price. *Financial intermediaries* include banks, credit companies, insurance companies, and other businesses that help finance transactions or insure against the risks associated with the buying and selling of goods. Most firms and customers depend on financial intermediaries to finance their transactions.

Like suppliers, marketing intermediaries form an important component of the company's overall value delivery system. In its quest to create satisfying customer relationships, the company must do more than just optimize its own performance. It must partner effectively with marketing intermediaries to optimize the performance of the entire system.

Thus, today's marketers recognize the importance of working with their intermediaries as partners rather than simply as channels through which they sell their products. For example, Coca-Cola recently signed a 10-year deal with Wendy's that will make Coke the exclusive soft drink provider to the fast-food chain, picking up more than 700 Wendy's franchises that were previously served by Pepsi. In the deal, Coca-Cola promised Wendy's much more that just its soft drinks. It pledged the powerful marketing support that comes along with an exclusive partnership with Coke.

★   [Along with the soft drinks,] Wendy's gets a cross-functional team of 50 Coke employees in various regions of the country who are now dedicated to "understanding the nuances of Wendy's business," says [a Wendy's executive]. Wendy's also will benefit from Coke dollars in joint marketing campaigns. "There are significant, big-time

Working with intermediaries as partners: Wendy's deal with Coca-Cola brought it much more that just soft drinks. It brought the powerful marketing support that comes with an exclusive partnership with Coke.

marketing sponsorships that they can bring to Wendy's, as they have to other chains," [adds the executive]. "That's huge." Bigger still is the staggering amount of consumer research that Coca-Cola provides its partners. [Coke] provides both analysis of syndicated information and access to Coke's own internal research aimed at "trying to understand consumers as they eat out." Coke goes to great lengths to understand beverage drinkers—and to make sure their partners can use those insights. . . . The company also has analyzed the demographics of every zip code in the country and used the information to create a software program called Solver. By answering questions about their target audience, franchise owners can determine which Coke brands are preferred by the clientele in their area. [Coca Cola] also has been studying the design of drive-through menu boards to better understand which layouts, fonts, letter sizes, colors, and visuals induce consumers to order more food and drink. Coke even aids its partners with research on issues that are not related to soft drink sales, such as hiring and retaining workers while unemployment is low.[3]

Customers

The company needs to study its customer markets closely. Figure 3.2 shows five types of customer markets. *Consumer markets* consist of individuals and households that buy goods and services for personal consumption. *Business markets* buy goods and services for further processing or for use in their production process, whereas *reseller markets* buy goods and services to resell at a profit. *Government markets* are made up of government agencies that buy goods and services to produce public services or transfer the goods and services to others who need them. Finally, *international markets* consist of these buyers in other countries, including consumers, producers, resellers, and governments. Each market type has special characteristics that call for careful study by the seller.

Competitors

The marketing concept states that to be successful, a company must provide greater customer value and satisfaction than its competitors do. Thus, marketers must do more than simply adapt to the needs of target consumers. They also must gain strategic advantage by positioning their offerings strongly against competitors' offerings in the minds of consumers.

No single competitive marketing strategy is best for all companies. Each firm should consider its own size and industry position compared to those of its competitors. Large firms with dominant positions in an industry can use certain

FIGURE 3.2   Types of customer markets

strategies that smaller firms cannot afford. But being large is not enough. There are winning strategies for large firms, but there are also losing ones. Small firms can develop strategies that give them better rates of return than large firms enjoy.

Publics

Public

Any group that has an actual or potential interest in or impact on an organization's ability to achieve its objectives.

The company's marketing environment also includes various publics. A **public** is any group that has an actual or potential interest in or impact on an organization's ability to achieve its objectives. Figure 3.3 shows seven types of publics.

★ *Financial publics* influence the company's ability to obtain funds. Banks, investment houses, and stockholders are the major financial publics.

★ *Media publics* carry news, features, and editorial opinion. They include newspapers, magazines, and radio and television stations.

★ *Government publics:* Management must take government developments into account. Marketers must often consult the company's lawyers on issues of product safety, truth in advertising, and other matters.

★ *Citizen action publics:* A company's marketing decisions may be questioned by consumer organizations, environmental groups, minority groups, and others. Its public relations department can help it stay in touch with consumer and citizen groups.

★ *Local publics* include neighborhood residents and community organizations. Large companies usually appoint a community relations officer to deal with the community, attend meetings, answer questions, and contribute to worthwhile causes.

★ *General public:* A company needs to be concerned about the general public's attitude toward its products and activities. The public's image of the company affects its buying.

★ *Internal publics* include workers, managers, volunteers, and the board of directors. Large companies use newsletters and other means to inform and motivate their internal publics. When employees feel good about their company, this positive attitude spills over to external publics.

A company can prepare marketing plans for these major publics as well as for its customer markets. Suppose the company wants a specific response from a particular public, such as goodwill, favorable word of mouth, or donations of time or money. The company would have to design an offer to this public that is attractive enough to produce the desired response.

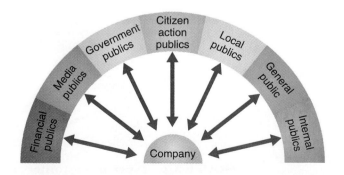

FIGURE 3.3   Types of publics

Publics: In this ad, Wal-Mart recognizes the importance of both its local and employee publics. Its Competitive Edge scholarship program "is just one of the reasons Wal-Mart associates (such as Maxine) in Mississippi, and all over the country, are proud to get involved in the communities they serve."

THE COMPANY'S MACROENVIRONMENT

The company and all of the other actors operate in a larger macroenvironment of forces that shape opportunities and pose threats to the company. Figure 3.4 shows the six major forces in the company's macroenvironment. In the remaining sections of this chapter, we examine these forces and show how they affect marketing plans.

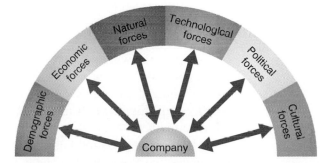

FIGURE 3.4   Major forces in the company's macroenvironment

MARKETING HIGHLIGHT 3.1

IF THE WORLD WERE A VILLAGE

Think for a few minutes about the world and your place in it. If we reduced the world to a village of 1,000 people representative of the world's population, this would be our reality:

- Our village would have 520 women and 480 men, 330 children and 60 people over age 65, 10 college graduates and 335 illiterate adults.

- We'd have 52 North Americans, 55 Russians, 84 Latin Americans, 95 Europeans, 124 Africans, and 584 Asians.

- Communication would be difficult: 165 of us would speak Mandarin, 86 English, 83 Hindi, 64 Spanish, 58 Russian, and 37 Arabic. The other half of us would speak one of more than 200 other languages.

- Among us we'd have 329 Christians, 178 Moslems, 132 Hindus, 62 Buddhists, 3 Jews, 167 nonreligious, 45 atheists, and 84 others.

- About one-third of our people would have access to clean, safe drinking water. About half of our children would be immunized against infections.

- The woodlands in our village would be decreasing rapidly and wasteland would be growing. Forty percent of the village's crop land, nourished by 83 percent of our fertilizer, would produce 72 percent of the food to feed its 270 well-fed owners. The remaining 60 percent of the land and 17 percent of the fertilizer would produce 28 percent of the food to feed the other 730 people. Five hundred people in the village would suffer from malnutrition.

- Only 200 of the 1,000 people would control 75 percent of our village's wealth. Another 200 would receive only 2 percent of the wealth. Seventy people would own cars. One would have a computer, and that computer probably would not be connected to the Internet.

Source: Taken from The World Village Project Web site, www.WorldVillage.org, March 2000.

Demographic Environment

Demography
The study of human populations in terms of size, density, location, age, gender, race, occupation, and other statistics.

Demography is the study of human populations in terms of size, density, location, age, gender, race, occupation, and other statistics. The demographic environment is of major interest to marketers because it involves people, and people make up markets.

The world population is growing at an explosive rate. It now totals more than 6 billion and will exceed 7.9 billion by the year 2025.[4] The explosive world population growth has major implications for business. A growing population means growing human needs to satisfy. Depending on purchasing power, it may also mean growing market opportunities. For example, to curb its skyrocketing population, the Chinese government has passed regulations limiting families to one child each. As a result, Chinese children are spoiled and fussed over as never before. Known in China as "little emperors," Chinese children are being showered with everything from candy to computers as a result of what's known as the "six-pocket syndrome." As many as six adults—including parents and two sets of doting grandparents—may be indulging the whims of each child. Parents in the average Beijing household now spend about 40 percent of their income on their cherished only child. This trend has encouraged toy companies such as Japan's Bandai Company (known for its Mighty Morphin Power Rangers), Denmark's Lego Group, and Mattel to enter the Chinese market.[5]

The world's large and highly diverse population poses both opportunities and challenges (see Marketing Highlight 3.1). Thus, marketers keep close track of demographic trends and developments in their markets, both at home and abroad. They track changing age and family structures, geographic population shifts, educational

FIGURE 3.5   Age distribution of the U.S. population

characteristics, and population diversity. Here, we discuss the most important demographic trends in the United States.

Changing Age Structure of the Population

The U.S. population stood at more than 273 million in 1999 and may reach 300 million by the year 2020.[6] The single most important demographic trend in the United States is the changing age structure of the population. As shown in Figure 3.5, the age distribution of the U.S. population is rapidly assuming an "hourglass" shape. Two very large age groups, the baby boomer generation and the baby boomlet generation, surround the smaller Generation Xers.

The Baby Boomers.   The post–World War II **baby boom** produced 78 million baby boomers born between 1946 and 1964. Since then, the baby boomers have become one of the most powerful forces shaping the marketing environment. The boomers have presented a moving target, creating new markets as they grew from infancy to their preadolescent, teenage, young adult, and now middle-age to mature years. Today's baby boomers account for about 30 percent of the population but earn more than half of all personal income.

Baby boomers cut across all walks of life. But marketers typically have paid the most attention to the smaller upper crust of the boomer generation—its more educated, mobile, and wealthy segments. These segments have gone by many names. In the 1980s, they were called "yuppies" (young urban professionals), "bumpies" (black upwardly mobile professionals) "yummies" (young upwardly mobile mommies), and "DINKs" (dual-income, no-kids couples). In the 1990s, however, yuppies and DINKs gave way to a new breed, with names such as "DEWKs" (dual earners with kids) and "MOBYs" (mother older, baby younger). Now, to the chagrin of many in this generation, they are acquiring such titles as "WOOFs" (well-off older folks) or even "GRUMPIES" (just what the name suggests).

The oldest boomers are now in their fifties; the youngest are in their mid-to-late thirties. Thus, the boomers have evolved from the "youthquake generation" to the "backache generation." They are also reaching their peak earning and spending years. Thus, they constitute a lucrative market for housing, furniture and appliances, healthful foods and beverages, physical fitness products, high-priced cars, convenience products, and travel and financial services.

Baby boom

The major increase in the annual birthrate following World War II and lasting until the early 1960s. The "baby boomers," now moving into middle age, are a prime target for marketers.

The maturing boomers are experiencing the pangs of midlife and rethinking the purpose and value of their work, responsibilities, and relationships. They are approaching life with a new stability and reasonableness in the way they live, think, eat, and spend. As they continue to age, they will create a large and important seniors market. By 2025, there will be 64 million baby boomers aged 61 to 79, a 90 percent increase in the size of this population from today.[7]

Generation X.   The baby boom was followed by a "birth dearth," creating another generation of 45 million people born between 1965 and 1976. Author Douglas Coupland calls them "Generation X," because they lie in the shadow of the boomers and lack obvious distinguishing characteristics. Others call them the "baby busters," "shadow generation," "twentysomethings," or "yiffies"—young, individualistic, freedom-minded few.

The GenXers are defined as much by their shared experiences as by their age. Increasing divorce rates and higher employment for their mothers made them the first generation of latchkey kids. Whereas the boomers created a sexual revolution, the GenXers have lived in the age of AIDS. Having grown up during times of recession and corporate downsizing, they have developed a more cautious economic outlook. As a result, the GenXers are a more skeptical bunch, cynical of frivolous marketing pitches that promise easy success. They buy lots of products, such as sweaters, boots, cosmetics, electronics, cars, fast food, beer, computers, and mountain bikes. However, their cynicism makes them more savvy shoppers, and their financial pressures make them more value conscious. They like lower prices and a more functional look. The GenXers respond to honesty in advertising, and they like irreverence and sass and ads that mock the traditional advertising approach. For example, recent Miller Brewing Company ads appealing to this group advised "It's time to embrace your inner idiot" and one features images of a frenetic, sloppy hot-dog-eating contest.

GenXers share new cultural concerns. They care about the environment and respond favorably to socially responsible companies. Although they seek success, they are less materialistic; they prize experience, not acquisition. They are cautious romantics who want a better quality of life and are more interested in job satisfaction than in sacrificing personal happiness and growth for promotion.

Once labeled as "The MTV generation: Net surfing, nihilistic [body-piercing slackers] whining about McJobs," the GenXers are now growing up and beginning to take over. They do surf the Internet more than other groups, but with serious intent. The GenXers are poised to displace the lifestyles, culture, and materialistic values of the baby boomers. They represent $125 billion in annual purchasing power. By the year 2010, they will have overtaken the baby boomers as a primary market for almost every product category. According to one analyst, "They are flocking to technology start-ups, founding small businesses, and even taking up causes—all in their own way. There are the next big thing. Boomers, beware!"[8]

The Echo Boomers.   Both the baby boomers and GenXers will one day be passing the reins to the latest demographic group, the **echo boomers** (or baby boomlet generation). Born between 1977 and 1994, these children of the baby boomers now number 72 million, dwarfing the GenXers and almost equal in size to the baby boomer segment. Ranging from preteens to twenties, the echo boomer generation is still forming its buying preferences and behaviors.

The baby boomlet has created large and growing kid and teens markets. Teens and preteens under 20 years of age spend $130 billion on their own and influence upward of $500 billion of their parents' spending.[9] After years of bust, markets for

Echo boomers
The generation born between 1977 and 1994, the children of the baby boomers now numbering 72 million.

In response to the echo boom, designers and retailers have created new lines and even stores devoted to children and teens. For example, upscale retailer Talbots opened its Talbots Kids & Babies stores.

children's toys and games, clothes, furniture, and food are enjoying a boom. For instance, Sony and other electronics firms are now offering products designed especially for children. In recent years, designers and retailers have created new lines, new products, and even new stores devoted to children and teens—Tommy Hilfiger, DKNY, Gap, Toys "R" Us, Guess, Talbots, Pottery Barn, and Eddie Bauer, to name just a few. A number of new media have appeared that cater specifically to this market: *Time, Sports Illustrated,* and *People* have all started new editions for kids and teens. Banks offer banking and investment services for kids, including investment camps. Major advertising agencies have even opened new divisions—such as Saatchi & Saatchi Advertising's Kid Connection division and Grey Advertising's 18 & Under division—that specialize in helping their clients shape their appeals for young audiences.[10]

Like the trailing edge of the Generation Xers ahead of them, one distinguishing characteristic of the echo boomers is their utter fluency and comfort with computer, digital, and Internet technology. For this reason, one analyst has christened them the Net-Gens (or N-Gens). He observes:

> What makes this generation different . . . is not just its demographic muscle, but it is the first to grow up surrounded by digital media. Computers and other digital technologies, such as digital cameras, are commonplace to N-Gen members. They work with them at home, in school, and they use them for entertainment. Increasingly these technologies are connected to the Internet. . . . Constantly surrounded by technology, today's kids are accustomed to its strong presence in their lives. [They] are so bathed in bits that they are no more intimidated by digital technology than a VCR or a toaster. And it is through their use of the digital media that N-Gen will develop and superimpose its culture on the rest of society. Boomers stand back. Already these kids are learning, playing, communicating, working, and creating communities very differently than did their parents. They are a force for social transformation.[11]

Generational Marketing.   Do marketers have to create separate products and marketing programs for each generation? Some experts caution that each generation spans decades of time and many socioeconomic levels. "These segments are so large they're meaningless as marketing targets," notes one such expert. "'Matures' range in age from 54 to 90; that isn't a target, it's a happening." Similarly, . . . "boomers span almost twenty years." He suggests that marketers should form more precise age-specific segments within each group.

Changing American family: The increase in the number of working women has spawned many business opportunities.

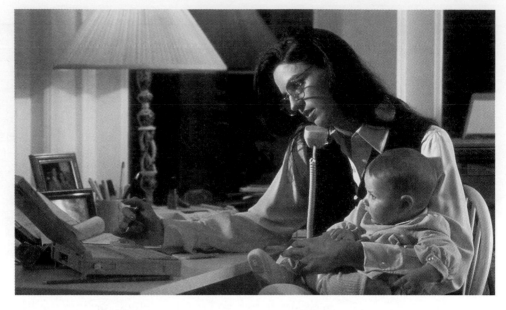

Others warn that marketers have to be careful about turning off one generation each time they craft a product or message that appeals effectively to another. "The idea is to try to be broadly inclusive and at the same time offer each generation something specifically designed for it. Tommy Hilfiger has big brand logos on his clothes for teenagers and little pocket polo logos on his shirts for baby boomers. It's a brand that has a more inclusive than exclusive strategy."[12]

The Changing American Family

The "traditional household" consists of a husband, wife, and children (and sometimes grandparents). Yet, the once American ideal of the two-child, two-car suburban family has lately been losing some of its luster. In fact, couples with children under 18 now make up only about 35 percent of all U.S. families.[13] In the United States today, one in eight households is "diverse" or "nontraditional" and includes single live-alones, adult live-togethers of one or both sexes, single-parent families, childless married couples, or empty nesters. More people are divorcing or separating, choosing not to marry, marrying later, or marrying without the intention to have children. Marketers must increasingly consider the special needs of nontraditional households, because they are now growing more rapidly than traditional households. Each group has a distinctive set of needs and buying habits. For example, people in the SSWD group (single, separated, widowed, divorced) need smaller apartments; inexpensive and smaller appliances, furniture, and furnishings; and food packaged in smaller sizes.

The number of working women has also increased greatly. This trend has spawned the child day care business and increased consumption of convenience foods and services, career-oriented women's clothing, financial services, and many other business opportunities. Here are two examples:

★ More and more workplaces and child care centers are installing monitoring setups such as "I See You" equipment from Simplex Knowledge in White Plains, New York. This system allows parents to see their children at different points throughout the day. Via still photos taken by a camera in the child care center and posted on a secure Web site on the Internet, working parents who long to spend more time with their young ones get reassuring glimpses throughout the day.[14]

⭐ Whereas shopping malls are in decline, there's been a boom in niche malls that cater to the needs of working women. Shops at Somerset Square in Glastonbury, Connecticut, is one such open-air shopping center. It features a customized retail mix of specialty shops, targeted promotions, and phone-in shopping in which shoppers phone ahead with sizes and color preferences while store employees perform a "wardrobing" service. Many of the stores also informally extend hours for working women who find time to shop only before or after work.[15]

Geographic Shifts in Population

This is a period of great migratory movements between and within countries. Americans, for example, are a mobile people with about 12 million U.S. households (more than one out of every ten) moving each year.[16] Over the past two decades, the U.S. population has shifted toward the Sunbelt states. The West and South have grown while the Midwest and Northeast states have lost population. Such population shifts interest marketers because people in different regions buy differently. For example, research shows that people in Seattle buy more toothbrushes per capita than people in any other U.S. city; people in Salt Lake City eat more candy bars; people from New Orleans use more ketchup; and people in Miami drink more prune juice.

Also, for more than a century, Americans have been moving from rural to metropolitan areas. In the 1950s, they made a massive exit from the cities to the suburbs. Today, the migration to the suburbs continues, and demographers are noting another shift that they call "the rural rebound." Nonmetropolitan counties that lost population to cities for most of this century are now attracting large numbers of urban refugees. More and more Americans are moving to "micropolitan areas," small cities located beyond congested metropolitan areas. These smaller micros offer many of the advantages of metro areas—jobs, restaurants, diversions, community organizations—but without the population crush, traffic jams, high crime rates, and high property taxes often associated with heavily urbanized areas.[17]

The shift in where people live has also caused a shift in where they work. For example, the migration toward micropolitan and rural areas has resulted in a rapid increase in the number of people who "telecommute"—work at home or in a remote office and conduct their business by phone, fax, modem, or the Internet. This trend, in turn, has created a booming SOHO (small office/home office) market. Nearly 40 million Americans are now working out of their homes with the help of electronic conveniences like personal computers, cell phones, fax machines, and handheld organizers. Many marketers are actively courting the home office segment of this lucrative SOHO market. One example is Kinko's Copy Centers:

⭐ Founded in the 1970s as a campus photocopying business, Kinko's is now reinventing itself as the well-appointed office outside the home. Where once there were copy machines, Kinko's 902 stores in this country and abroad now feature a uniform mixture of fax machines, ultrafast color printers, and networks of computers equipped with popular software programs and high-speed Internet connections. People can come to a Kinko's store to do all their office jobs: they can copy, send and receive faxes, use various programs on the computer, go on the Internet, order stationery and other printed supplies, and even teleconference. As more and more people join the work-at-home trend, Kinko's offers an escape from the isolation of the home office. The office-support chain is hoping to increase its share of industry revenue by getting people to spend more time—and hence, more money—at its stores. Besides adding state-of-the-art equipment, the company is talking to Starbucks about opening up coffee shops adjacent to some Kinko's. The lettering on the Kinko's door sums up the $1 billion company's new business model: "Your branch office/Open 24 hours."[18]

Geographic shifts: The shift in where people live has also caused a shift in where they work, creating a booming SOHO (small office/home office) market.

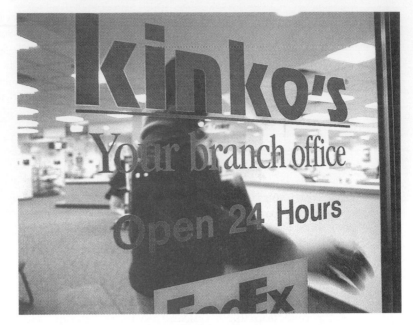

A Better-Educated and More White-Collar Population

The U.S. population is becoming better educated. For example, in 1996, 82 percent of the U.S. population over age 25 had completed high school and 24 percent had completed college, compared with 69 percent and 17 percent in 1980. The rising number of educated people will increase the demand for quality products, books, magazines, travel, personal computers, and Internet services. It suggests a decline in television viewing because college-educated consumers watch less TV than the population at large. The workforce also is becoming more white collar. Between 1950 and 1985, the proportion of white-collar workers rose from 41 percent to 54 percent, that of blue-collar workers declined from 47 percent to 33 percent, and that of service workers increased from 12 percent to 14 percent. These trends have continued into the new millennium.[19]

Increasing Diversity

Countries vary in their ethnic and racial makeup. At one extreme is Japan, where almost everyone is Japanese. At the other extreme is the United States, with people from virtually all nations. The United States has often been called a melting pot in which diverse groups from many nations and cultures have melted into a single, more homogenous whole. Instead, the United States seems to have become more of a "salad bowl" in which various groups have mixed together but have maintained their diversity by retaining and valuing important ethnic and cultural differences.

Marketers are facing increasingly diverse markets, both at home and abroad as their operations become more international in scope. In the United States alone, ethnic population growth is six times greater than the Caucasian growth rate, and ethnic consumers buy more than $600 billion of goods and services each year. The U.S. population is 72 percent white, with African Americans making up another 13 percent. The Hispanic population has grown rapidly and now stands at about 11 percent of the U.S. population. The U.S. Asian population also has grown rapidly in recent years and now totals about 3 percent of the population. The remaining 1 percent of the population is made up of Native Americans, Eskimos, and Aleuts. During the next half century, the proportions of both Hispanics and Asians will more than double. Moreover, there are nearly 25 million people living in the United States— over 9 percent of the population—who were born in another country.[20]

Many large companies, ranging from large retailers such as Sears and Wal-Mart to consumer products companies such as Levi-Strauss and Procter & Gamble, now target specially designed products and promotions to one or more of these groups. Miller beer, for example, created television ads for the Hispanic market shown exclusively on Spanish-speaking channels. Even within the Hispanic market, however, different consumers have diverse interests and beliefs depending on country of origin, length of time in the United States, geographic placement, and other factors. Thus, although Miller employs the same visual elements across the country, it alters background music and voice-overs to reflect differences between, for example, Cubans in New York City and Mexican Americans in Los Angeles.

Diversity goes beyond ethnic heritage. For example, there are more than 52 million disabled people in the United States—a market larger than African Americans or Hispanics—representing almost $800 million in annual spending power. People with mobility challenges are an ideal target market for companies such as Peapod (www.peapod.com), which teams up with large supermarket chains in many heavily populated areas to offer online grocery shopping and home delivery. They also represent a growing market for travel, sports, and other leisure-oriented products and services (see Marketing Highlight 3.2).[21]

Economic Environment

Markets require buying power as well as people. The **economic environment** consists of factors that affect consumer purchasing power and spending patterns. Nations vary greatly in their levels and distribution of income. Some countries have *subsistence economies*—they consume most of their own agricultural and industrial output. These countries offer few market opportunities. At the other extreme are *industrial economies,* which constitute rich markets for many different kinds of goods. Marketers must pay close attention to major trends and consumer spending patterns both across and within their world markets. Following are some of the major economic trends in the United States.

Changes in Income

During the 1980s—tabbed the "roaring eighties" by some—American consumers fell into a consumption frenzy, fueled by income growth, federal tax reductions, rapid increases in housing values, and a boom in borrowing. They bought and bought, seemingly without caution, amassing record levels of debt. "It was fashionable to describe yourself as 'born to shop.' When the going gets tough, it was said, the tough go shopping."[22]

During the 1990s, the baby boom generation moved into its prime wage-earning years, and the number of small families headed by dual-career couples continued to increase. Thus, many consumers continued to demand quality products and better service, and they were able to pay for them. However, the free spending and high expectations of the 1980s were dashed by the recession in the early 1990s. In fact, the 1990s became the decade of the "squeezed consumer." Along with rising incomes in some segments came increased financial burdens—repaying debts acquired during earlier spending splurges, facing increased household and family expenses, and saving for college tuition payments and retirement. These financially squeezed consumers sobered up, pulled back, and adjusted to their changing financial situations. They spent more carefully and sought greater value in the products and services they bought. *Value marketing* became the watchword for many marketers.

As we move into the 2000s, despite several years of strong economic performance, consumers continue to spend carefully. Hence, the trend toward value marketing continues. Rather than offering high quality at a high price, or lesser quality

Economic environment
Factors that affect consumer buying power and spending patterns.

MARKETING HIGHLIGHT
3.2

GOOD FUN: MARKETING RECREATION TO THE DISABLED

Julie Perez sees the difference when she goes to the Divi Hotels resort at Flamingo Beach on the Caribbean island of Bonaire. "It's famous for being totally accessible," she says. "The hotel brochures show the wheelchair access. The dive staff are trained and aware, and they really want to take disabled people diving. They're not afraid." Perez, 35, of Ventura, California, is an experienced scuba diver, a travel agent—and a quadriplegic. Before she had children, she made five trips a year to the Caribbean; these days, she gets there only once or twice a year.

People with disabilities are not only scuba diving, they are playing golf, riding horses, and whitewater rafting. They surf the Internet, work in their gardens, and read. Businesses are beginning to recognize the significance of this vast market of 52 million people who represent almost $800 billion in spending power. According to a report by Packaged Facts, a New York City research company, the figure will exceed $1 trillion by 2001. This spending power is likely to increase even more in the years ahead, as the wealthier, freer-spending baby boomers enter the "age of disabilities." As a result, new stores, services, products, and publications pop up all the time to serve the disabled.

The nonprofit American Association of People with Disabilities recently began publishing *Enable,* a bimonthly magazine that hopes to attract advertising from mainstream corporations. According to *Enable* CEO Sandy Watson, the magazine will "educate corporate America that these people exist. You have a target market." *Enable* features a Recreation and Leisure section that, in its inaugural issue last fall, offered features on wheelchair athletes playing basketball, tennis, and rugby ("The hit ain't real till you bend some steel"), a guide to accessible summer camps, and a primer on San Francisco for travelers with disabilities Similarly, the Canadian Abilities Foundation provides a Web site (Enable Link) and magazine (*Abilities*) targeting people with disabilities.

Many product and marketing efforts targeting the disabled have

People with disabilities present a large and growing market. The Canadian Abilities Foundation provides a Web site (EnableLink) and magazine (Abilities) targeting this segment.

been inspired by friends and relatives with disabilities. For example, Joe Montgomery, founder and president of Cannondale bicycles, has a son with cerebral palsy. The father saw a boy brimming with energy and determination, and a love of horseback riding, swimming, skiing, and karate. But he also saw a child limited by wheelchairs he labeled "technological dinosaurs." A lightbulb went on, and Montgomery recognized that Cannondale could take the famous design of its high-end bicycles and make lightweight racing wheelchairs. "The market for lightweight wheelchairs is roughly $400 million per year," says company spokesman Bill Teel. "We're hoping to grab 10 percent of that in the next few years." Cannondale's strong brand name from bicycles should give the company a running start. "We've been getting calls nonstop since we made the first announcement," says Teel.

As Cannondale enters a market traditionally controlled by makers of conventional wheelchairs, the company plans to play by a different set of rules. Instead of selling the racing chairs at specialized medical equipment shops, Cannondale will sell them in bike shops. The company figures that kids in wheelchairs want to shop at the same stores as their ambulatory peers. "Younger kids in wheelchairs don't want to be Jim Knaub," Teel says, referring to a five-time wheelchair winner of the Boston Marathon. "They aspire to be Michael Jordan."

Centex Life Solutions is going a slightly different route in its effort to create a mainstream shopping experience for those with special needs. Its stores aim to be big, bright, cheery, one-stop outlets where shoppers can find things "to make people's lives more enjoyable and help them stay in their homes longer," says Centex CEO Mike Albright. Although in many cases this means assistive devices such as lift chairs to carry people

upstairs and products for bedroom and bathroom safety, the stores also carry aromatherapy devices, treadmills with wider and longer bases, and more than 100 different styles of walking shoes. "We think we have the largest selection—4,000 pairs," says Albright. "That's a lot of shoes." He wants the stores to look more like a Sharper Image or Brookstone store than a medical-equipment supplier. In-store coffee shops will provide a place for people to relax.

Catalog shopping is convenient for everyone; those with mobility or other limitations are no exception. The adaptAbility Catalog from S&S Worldwide includes an extensive selection of "Leisure Time" products. These include large-face playing cards, automatic card shufflers, lightweight binoculars that double the size of television images, a pedal exerciser for use from a standard chair, and water dumbbells for low-impact water aerobics. Another S&S catalog features people in wheelchairs using special bowling ramps and bowling-ball pushers, taking shots on a minibasketball set, and playing beanbag horseshoes.

People in the field, whether in business or as advocates for those with disabilities, have one simple piece of advice for those wanting to tap the disabled market: Make your product as accessible as possible. "Don't design for a disability," says ProMatura Group's Margaret Wylde. "Strive for universal design. A well-designed product is a benefit for lots and lots of people." Universal design means "products designed for the widest number of people," says Mary Lester, associate director of the Alliance for Technology Access, a group that works to make sure people with disabilities have access to the latest and greatest technology.

If a computer is made with built-in options for scanning, or a more wrist-friendly keyboard, "it's a better product," Lester says. Anyone can

benefit. "A company can, if it spends time on design from top to bottom, from the packaging to plugging it into the wall, enhance and enlarge its market," says Wylde. For instance, says former alliance director Fred Fiedler, people with disabilities led the move to "having the on–off button in front of the computer, instead of in the back where no one can reach." Vibrating pagers are another innovation, spurred by the hearing-impaired but now popular with the general population. Oxo kitchen utensils have excellent grips, says Wylde, appealing not only to people with arthritis, but to anyone who prepares food. Its carrot peeler "looks neat, very stylish. Nothing about it says 'disability.'" She also praises Rubbermaid for adding a tab to the lip of its lids. "It's easier to use. Period," Wylde says.

By the same token, make advertising inclusive. "Ads that feature people with disabilities appeal to everyone," says the Packaged Facts report. "Able-bodied persons are not put off by seeing attractive people with disabilities in advertising." Advertisers should keep images positive. "People with disabilities are very sensitive to being portrayed as dependent, vulnerable, or as objects of pity," says Packaged Facts. "Already well aware of the difficulties they face, they like to see images of themselves overcoming these difficulties, transcending their limits, and living life as other people do."

Source: Adapted from Dan Frost, "The Fun Factor: Marketing Recreation to the Disabled," *American Demographics,* February 1998, pp. 54–58. Also see *Marketing to Americans with Disabilities,* Packaged Facts, New York, 1997; and Michelle Wirth Fellman, "Selling IT Goods to Disabled End-Users," *Marketing News,* March 15, 1999, pp. 1, 17.

at very low prices, marketers are looking for ways to offer today's more financially cautious buyers greater value—just the right combination of product quality and good service at a fair price.

Marketers should pay attention to *income distribution* as well as average income. Income distribution in the United States is still very skewed. At the top are *upper-class* consumers, whose spending patterns are not affected by current economic events and who are a major market for luxury goods. There is a comfortable *middle class* that is somewhat careful about its spending but can still afford the good life some of the time. The *working class* must stick close to the basics of food, clothing, and shelter and must try hard to save. Finally, the *underclass* (persons on welfare and many retirees) must count their pennies when making even the most basic purchases.

Over the past three decades, the rich have grown richer, the middle class has shrunk, and the poor have remained poor. In 1994, the top 5 percent of income-earning households in the United States captured over 21 percent of aggregate income, up from 16.6 percent in 1970. Meanwhile, the share of income captured by the bottom 20 percent of income-earning households decreased from 4.1 percent to 3.6 percent.[23] This distribution of income has created a two-tiered market. Many companies are aggressively targeting the affluent:

> Driven by the heavenward ascent of the Dow, low unemployment and inflation, and vast numbers of duel-income boomers in their prime earning years, . . . marketers have responded with a ceaseless array of pricey, upscale products aimed at satisfying wealthy Americans' appetite for "the very best": leather-lined SUVs as big as tanks, $1,300 sheets, restaurant-quality appliances, and vast cruise ships offering every form of luxurious coddling. . . . Huge increases in wealth among the very rich have fueled the sales of $17,500 Patek Philippe watches that are sold as family heirlooms (thus justifying the price tag), created the clamor for a $48,000 Lexus (options extra), and resulted in a two-year waiting list for $14,000 Hermes Kelly bags.[24]

Other companies are now tailoring their marketing offers to two different markets—the affluent and the less affluent. For example, Walt Disney Company markets two distinct Winnie-the-Pooh bears:

> The original line-drawn figure appears on fine china, pewter spoons, and pricey kids' stationery found in upscale specialty and department stores such as Nordstrom and Bloomingdale's. The plump, cartoonlike Pooh, clad in a red shirt and a goofy smile, adorns plastic key chains, polyester bed sheets, and animated videos. It sells in Wal-Mart stores and five-and-dime shops. Except at Disney's own stores, the two Poohs do not share the same retail shelf. [Thus, Disney offers both] upstairs and downstairs Poohs, hoping to land customers on both sides of the [income] divide.[25]

Changing Consumer Spending Patterns

Engel's laws
Differences noted over a century ago by Ernst Engel in how people shift their spending across food, housing, transportation, health care, and other goods and services categories as family income rises.

Table 3.1 shows the proportion of total expenditures made by U.S. households at different income levels for major categories of goods and services. Food, housing, and transportation use up most household income. However, consumers at different income levels have different spending patterns. Some of these differences were noted over a century ago by Ernst Engel, who studied how people shifted their spending as their income rose. He found that as family income rises, the percentage spent on food declines, the percentage spent on housing remains about constant (except for such utilities as gas, electricity, and public services, which decrease), and both the percentage spent on most other categories and that devoted to savings increase. **Engel's laws** generally have been supported by later studies.

TABLE 3.1 CONSUMER SPENDING AT DIFFERENT INCOME LEVELS			
	% of Spending at Different Income Levels		
Expenditure	**$10,000–15,000**	**$20,000–30,000**	**$70,000 and Over**
Food	16.4	15.6	11.6
Housing	35.9	31.3	29.5
Utilities	9.4	7.9	4.7
Clothing	5.4	5.5	5.2
Transportation	15.6	17.8	17.0
Health care	6.5	6.8	5.9
Entertainment	4.9	4.7	5.7
Tobacco	1.3	1.3	0.37
Contributions	2.1	3.2	4.7
Insurance	3.4	7.6	15.6

Source: Consumer Expenditure Survey, U.S. Department of Labor, Bureau of Labor Statistics, Bulletin 2462, September 1995, pp. 15–17. Also see Paula Mergenhagan, "What Can Minimum Wage Buy," *American Demographics*, January 1996, pp. 18–21.

Changes in major economic variables such as income, cost of living, interest rates, and savings and borrowing patterns have a large impact on the marketplace. Companies watch these variables by using economic forecasting. Businesses do not have to be wiped out by an economic downturn or caught short in a boom. With adequate warning, they can take advantage of changes in the economic environment.

Natural Environment

Natural environment
Natural resources that are needed as inputs by marketers or that are affected by marketing activities.

The **natural environment** involves the natural resources that are needed as inputs by marketers or that are affected by marketing activities. Environmental concerns have grown steadily during the past three decades. Some trend analysts labeled the 1990s as the "Earth Decade," claiming that the natural environment is the major worldwide issue facing business and the public. The Earth Day movement turned 30 in the year 2000. In many cities around the world, air and water pollution have reached dangerous levels. World concern continues to mount about the depletion of the earth's ozone layer and the resulting "greenhouse effect," a dangerous warming of the Earth. And many environmentalists fear that we soon will be buried in our own trash.

Marketers should be aware of several trends in the natural environment. The first involves growing *shortages of raw materials*. Air and water may seem to be infinite resources, but some groups see long-run dangers. Air pollution chokes many of the world's large cities and water shortages are already a big problem in some parts of the United States and the world. Renewable resources, such as forests and food, also have to be used wisely. Nonrenewable resources, such as oil, coal, and various minerals, pose a serious problem. Firms making products that require these scarce resources face large cost increases, even if the materials do remain available.

A second environmental trend is *increased pollution*. Industry will almost always damage the quality of the natural environment. Consider the disposal of chemical and nuclear wastes; the dangerous mercury levels in the ocean; the quantity of chemical pollutants in the soil and food supply; and the littering of the environment with nonbiodegradable bottles, plastics, and other packaging materials.

A third trend is *increased government intervention* in natural resource management. The governments of different countries vary in their concern and efforts to promote a clean environment. Some, like the German government, vigorously pursue environmental quality. Others, especially many poorer nations, do little about pollution, largely because they lack the needed funds or political will. Even the richer nations lack the vast funds and political accord needed to mount a worldwide environmental effort. The general hope is that companies around the world will accept more social responsibility, and that less expensive devices can be found to control and reduce pollution.

In the United States, the Environmental Protection Agency (EPA) was created in 1970 to set and enforce pollution standards and to conduct pollution research. In the future, companies doing business in the United States can expect strong controls from government and pressure groups. Instead of opposing regulation, marketers should help develop solutions to the material and energy problems facing the world.

Concern for the natural environment has spawned the so-called green movement. Today, enlightened companies go beyond what government regulations dictate. They are developing *environmentally sustainable* strategies and practices in an effort to create a world economy that the planet can support indefinitely. They are responding to consumer demands with ecologically safer products, recyclable or biodegradable packaging, better pollution controls, and more energy-efficient operations. 3M runs a Pollution Prevention Pays program that has led to a substantial reduction in pollution and costs. AT&T uses a special software package to choose the least harmful materials, cut hazardous waste, reduce energy use, and improve product recycling in its operations. McDonald's eliminated polystyrene cartons and now uses smaller, recyclable paper wrappings and napkins. IBM's AS/400e series of midrange business computers is more energy efficient, contains recycled content, and is designed to be disassembled for recycling. Dixon-Ticonderoga, the folks who developed the first pencil made in the United States, developed Prang crayons made from soybeans rather than paraffin wax, a by-product of oil drilling. Soybeans are a renewable resource and produce brighter, richer colors and a smoother texture. More and more, companies are recognizing the link between a healthy economy and a healthy ecology.[26]

Technological Environment

Technological environment
Forces that create new technologies, creating new product and market opportunities.

The **technological environment** is perhaps the most dramatic force now shaping our destiny. Technology has released such wonders as antibiotics, organ transplants, notebook computers, and the Internet. It also has released such horrors as nuclear missiles, chemical weapons, and assault rifles. It has released such mixed blessings as the automobile, television, and credit cards. Our attitude toward technology depends on whether we are more impressed with its wonders or its blunders.

The technological environment changes rapidly. Think of all of today's common products that were not available 100 years ago, or even 30 years ago. Abraham Lincoln did not know about automobiles, airplanes, radios, or the electric light. Woodrow Wilson did not know about television, aerosol cans, automatic dishwashers, room air conditioners, antibiotics, or computers. Franklin Delano Roosevelt did not know about xerography, synthetic detergents, tape recorders, birth control pills, or earth satellites. John F. Kennedy did not know about personal computers, compact disk players, VCRs, or the World Wide Web.

New technologies create new markets and opportunities. However, every new technology replaces an older technology. Transistors hurt the vacuum-tube industry, xerography hurt the carbon-paper business, the auto hurt the railroads, and compact disks hurt phonograph records. When old industries fought or ignored

Technological environment: Technology is perhaps the most dramatic force shaping the marketing environment. Here a Samburu warrior in northern Kenya makes a call on a cellular telephone.

new technologies, their businesses declined. Thus, marketers should watch the technological environment closely. Companies that do not keep up with technological change soon will find their products outdated. They will miss new product and market opportunities.

The United States leads the world in research and development spending.[27] Scientists today are researching a wide range of promising new products and services, ranging from practical solar energy, electric cars, and cancer cures to voice-controlled computers and genetically engineered food crops. Today's research usually is carried out by research teams rather than by lone inventors like Thomas Edison, Samuel Morse, or Alexander Graham Bell. Many companies are adding marketing people to R&D teams to try to obtain a stronger marketing orientation. Scientists also speculate on fantasy products, such as flying cars, three-dimensional televisions, and space colonies. The challenge in each case is not only technical but also commercial—to make *practical, affordable* versions of these products.

As products and technology become more complex, the public needs to know that these are safe. Thus, government agencies investigate and ban potentially unsafe products. In the United States, the Federal Food and Drug Administration has set up complex regulations for testing new drugs. The Consumer Product Safety Commission sets safety standards for consumer products and penalizes companies that fail to meet them. Such regulations have resulted in much higher research costs and in longer times between new-product ideas and their introduction. Marketers should be aware of these regulations when applying new technologies and developing new products.

Political environment

Laws, government agencies, and pressure groups that influence and limit various organizations and individuals in a given society.

Political Environment

Marketing decisions are strongly affected by developments in the political environment. The **political environment** consists of laws, government agencies, and pressure groups that influence and limit various organizations and individuals in a given society.

Legislation Regulating Business

Even the most liberal advocates of free-market economies agree that the system works best with at least some regulation. Well-conceived regulation can encourage competition and ensure fair markets for goods and services. Thus, governments develop *public policy* to guide commerce—sets of laws and regulations that limit business for the good of society as a whole. Almost every marketing activity is subject to a wide range of laws and regulations.

Increasing Legislation.   Legislation affecting business around the world has increased steadily over the years. The United States has many laws covering issues such as competition, fair trade practices, environmental protection, product safety, truth in advertising, packaging and labeling, pricing, and other important areas (see Table 3.2). The European Commission has been active in establishing a new framework of laws covering competitive behavior, product standards, product liability, and commercial transactions for the nations of the European Union. Several countries have gone farther than the United States in passing strong consumerism legislation. For example, Norway bans several forms of sales promotion—trading stamps, contests, premiums—as being inappropriate or unfair ways of promoting products. Thailand requires food processors selling national brands to market low-price brands also, so that low-income consumers can find economy brands on the shelves. In India, food companies must obtain special approval to launch brands that duplicate those already existing on the market, such as additional cola drinks or new brands of rice.

Understanding the public policy implications of a particular marketing activity is not a simple matter. For example, in the United States, there are many laws created at the national, state, and local levels, and these regulations often overlap. Aspirins sold in Dallas are governed both by federal labeling laws and by Texas state advertising laws. Moreover, regulations are constantly changing—what was allowed last year may now be prohibited, and what was prohibited may now be allowed. For example, with the demise of the Soviet bloc, ex-Soviet nations are rapidly passing laws to both regulate and promote an open-market economy. Marketers must work hard to keep up with changes in regulations and their interpretations.

Business legislation has been enacted for a number of reasons. The first is to *protect companies* from each other. Although business executives may praise competition, they sometimes try to neutralize it when it threatens them. So laws are passed to define and prevent unfair competition. In the United States, such laws are enforced by the Federal Trade Commission and the Antitrust Division of the Attorney General's office.

The second purpose of government regulation is to *protect consumers* from unfair business practices. Some firms, if left alone, would make shoddy products, tell lies in their advertising, and deceive consumers through their packaging and pricing. Unfair business practices have been defined and are enforced by various agencies.

The third purpose of government regulation is to *protect the interests of society* against unrestrained business behavior. Profitable business activity does not always create a better quality of life. Regulation arises to ensure that firms take responsibility for the social costs of their production or products.

Changing Government Agency Enforcement.   International marketers will encounter dozens, or even hundreds, of agencies set up to enforce trade policies and regulations. In the United States, Congress has established federal regulatory agencies such as the Federal Trade Commission, the Food and Drug Administration, the

TABLE 3.2   MAJOR U.S. LEGISLATION AFFECTING MARKETING

Legislation	Purpose
Sherman Antitrust Act (1890)	Prohibits monopolies and activities (price-fixing, predatory pricing) that restrain trade or competition in interstate commerce.
Federal Food and Drug Act (1906)	Forbids the manufacture or sale of adulterated or fraudulently labeled foods and drugs. Created the Food and Drug Administration.
Clayton Act (1914)	Supplements the Sherman Act by prohibiting certain types of price discrimination, exclusive dealing, and tying clauses (which require a dealer to take additional products in a seller's line).
Federal Trade Commission Act (1914)	Establishes a commission to monitor and remedy unfair trade methods.
Robinson–Patman Act (1936)	Amends Clayton Act to define price discrimination as unlawful. Empowers FTC to establish limits on quantity discounts, forbid some brokerage allowances, and prohibit promotional allowances except when made available on proportionately equal terms.
Wheeler–Lea Act (1938)	Makes deceptive, misleading, and unfair practices illegal regardless of injury to competition. Places advertising of food and drugs under FTC jurisdiction.
Lanham Trademark Act (1946)	Protects and regulates distinctive brand names and trademarks.
National Traffic and Safety Act (1958)	Provides for the creation of compulsory safety standards for automobiles and tires.
Fair Packaging and Labeling Act (1966)	Provides for the regulation of packaging and labeling of consumer goods. Requires that manufacturers state what the package contains, who made it, and how much it contains.
Child Protection Act (1966)	Bans sale of hazardous toys and articles. Sets standards for child-resistant packaging.
Federal Cigarette Labeling and Advertising Act (1967)	Requires that cigarette packages contain the following statement: "Warning: The Surgeon General Has Determined That Cigarette Smoking Is Dangerous to Your Health."
National Environmental Policy Act (1969)	Establishes a national policy on the environment. The 1970 Reorganization Plan establishes the Environmental Protection Agency.
Consumer Product Safety Act (1972)	Establishes the Consumer Product Safety Commission and authorizes it to set safety standards for consumer products as well as exact penalties for failure to uphold those standards.
Magnuson–Moss Warranty Act (1975)	Authorizes FTC to determine rules and regulations for consumer warranties and provides consumer access to redress, such as the "class-action" suit.
Children's Television Act (1990)	Limits number of commercials aired during children's programs.
Nutrition Labeling and Education Act (1990)	Requires that food product labels provide detailed nutritional information.
Telephone Consumer Protection Act (1991)	Establishes procedures to avoid unwanted telephone solicitations. Limits marketers' use of automatic telephone-dialing systems and artificial or prerecorded voices.

Interstate Commerce Commission, the Federal Communications Commission, the Federal Power Commission, the Civil Aeronautics Board, the Consumer Products Safety Commission, the Environmental Protection Agency, and the Office of Consumer Affairs. Because such government agencies have some discretion in enforcing the laws, they can have a major impact on a company's marketing performance. At times, the staffs of these agencies have appeared to be overly eager and unpredictable. Some of the agencies sometimes have been dominated by lawyers and economists who lacked a practical sense of how business and marketing work. In recent years, the Federal Trade Commission has added staff marketing experts, who can better understand complex business issues.

New laws and their enforcement will continue or increase. Business executives must watch these developments when planning their products and marketing programs. Marketers need to know about the major laws protecting competition, consumers, and society. They need to understand these laws at the local, state, national, and international levels.[28]

Increased Emphasis on Ethics and Socially Responsible Actions

Written regulations cannot possibly cover all potential marketing abuses, and existing laws are often difficult to enforce. However, beyond written laws and regulations, business is also governed by social codes and rules of professional ethics. Enlightened companies encourage their managers to look beyond what the regulatory system allows and simply "do the right thing." These socially responsible firms actively seek out ways to protect the long-run interests of their consumers and the environment.

The recent rash of business scandals and increased concerns about the environment have created fresh interest in the issues of ethics and social responsibility. Almost every aspect of marketing involves such issues. Unfortunately, because these issues usually involve conflicting interests, well-meaning people can honestly disagree about the right course of action in a given situation. Thus, many industrial and professional trade associations have suggested codes of ethics, and many companies now are developing policies and guidelines to deal with complex social responsibility issues.

The boom in e-commerce and Internet marketing has created a new set of social and ethical issues. Privacy issues are the primary concern. For example, Web site visitors often provide extensive personal information that might leave them open to abuse by unscrupulous marketers. Moreover, both Intel and Microsoft have been accused of covert, high-tech computer chip and software invasions of customers' personal computers to obtain information for marketing purposes.

Another cyberspace concern is that of access by vulnerable or unauthorized groups. For example, marketers of adult-oriented materials have found it difficult to restrict access by minors. In a more specific example, sellers using eBay.com, the online auction Web site, recently found themselves the victims of a 13-year-old boy who'd bid on and purchased more than $3 million worth of high-priced antiques and rare art works on the site. eBay has a strict policy against bidding by anyone under 18 but works largely on the honor system. Unfortunately, this honor system did little to prevent the teenager from taking a cyberspace joyride.[29]

Of course, cyberspace also has its own examples of more typical consumer abuses. For example, although America Online has been hugely successful and is the country's most popular online service provider, it has lost millions of dollars due to consumer complaints regarding unethical marketing tactics:

★ In 1998, America Online agreed to pay a $2.6 million penalty and revamp some of its business practices to settle deceptive-marketing complaints brought by 44 state attorneys general. In this instance, AOL failed to clearly notify consumers that the "50 free hours" in its online service's much-touted trial memberships must be used within a one-month period and that users would incur subscription fees after the first month. This was AOL's third settlement with state regulators in less than two years. Previous settlements dealt with the company's data network congestion in early 1997 (due to a move to flat rate pricing that gave the company more subscriptions than it had equipment to handle) and efforts in late 1996 to switch customers to a higher priced subscription plan. The three agreements not only cost the company $34 million in total, but created a barrage of negative publicity that AOL had to work hard to counter.[30]

Throughout the text, we present Marketing Highlight exhibits that summarize the main public policy and social responsibility issues surrounding major marketing decisions. These exhibits discuss the legal issues that marketers should understand and the common ethical and societal concerns that marketers face. In chapter 20, we discuss a broad range of societal marketing issues in greater depth.

Cultural Environment

Cultural environment
Institutions and other forces that affect society's basic values, perceptions, preferences, and behaviors.

The **cultural environment** is made up of institutions and other forces that affect a society's basic values, perceptions, preferences, and behaviors. People grow up in a particular society that shapes their basic beliefs and values. They absorb a world view that defines their relationships with others. The following cultural characteristics can affect marketing decision making.

Persistence of Cultural Values
People in a given society hold many beliefs and values. Their core beliefs and values have a high degree of persistence. For example, most Americans believe in working, getting married, giving to charity, and being honest. These beliefs shape more specific attitudes and behaviors found in everyday life. *Core* beliefs and values are passed on from parents to children and are reinforced by schools, churches, business, and government.

Secondary beliefs and values are more open to change. Believing in marriage is a core belief; believing that people should get married early in life is a secondary belief. Marketers have some chance of changing secondary values, but little chance of changing core values. For example, family-planning marketers could argue more effectively that people should get married later than that they should not get married at all.

Shifts in Secondary Cultural Values
Although core values are fairly persistent, cultural swings do take place. Consider the impact of popular music groups, movie personalities, and other celebrities on young people's hairstyling, clothing, and sexual norms. Marketers want to predict cultural shifts in order to spot new opportunities or threats. Several firms offer "futures" forecasts in this connection, such as the Yankelovich Monitor, Market Facts' BrainWaves Group, and the Trends Research Institute. The Yankelovich Monitor tracks 41 U.S. cultural values, such as "antibigness," "mysticism," "living for today," "away from possessions," and "sensuousness." Monitor describes the percentage of the population that shares the attitude as well as the percentage that goes against the trend.[31] For instance, the percentage of people who value physical fitness and well-being has risen steadily over the years. Such information helps marketers cater to trends with appropriate products and communication appeals.

The major cultural values of a society are expressed in people's views of themselves and others, as well as in their views of organizations, society, nature, and the universe.

People's Views of Themselves.   People vary in their emphasis on serving themselves versus serving others. Some people seek personal pleasure, wanting fun, change, and escape. Others seek self-realization through religion, recreation, or the avid pursuit of careers or other life goals. People use products, brands, and services as a means of self-expression, and they buy products and services that match their views of themselves.

In the 1980s, personal ambition and materialism increased dramatically, with significant marketing implications. In a "me society," people buy their "dream cars" and take their "dream vacations." They tended to spend to the limit on self-indulgent goods and services. Today, in contrast, people are adopting more conservative behaviors and ambitions. They are more cautious in their spending patterns and more value driven in their purchases. Moving into the new millennium, materialism, flashy spending, and self-indulgence have been replaced by more sensible spending, saving, family concerns, and helping others. The aging baby boomers are limiting their spending to products and services that improve their lives instead of boosting their images. This suggests a bright future for products and services that serve basic needs and provide real value rather than those relying on glitz and hype.

People's Views of Others.   Recently, observers have noted a shift from a me society to a "we society" in which more people want to be with and serve others. Notes one trend tracker, "People want to get out, especially those 48 million people working out of their home and feeling a little cooped-up [and] all those shut-ins who feel unfulfilled by the cyberstuff that was supposed to make them feel like never leaving home."[32] This trend suggests a greater demand for "social support" products and services that improve direct communication between people, such as health clubs and family vacations.

People's Views of Organizations.   People vary in their attitudes toward corporations, government agencies, trade unions, universities, and other organizations. By and large, people are willing to work for major organizations and expect them, in turn, to carry out society's work. The late 1980s saw a sharp decrease in confidence in and loyalty toward America's business and political organizations and institutions. In the workplace, there has been an overall decline in organizational loyalty. During the 1990s, waves of company downsizings bred cynicism and distrust. Many people today see work not as a source of satisfaction but as a required chore to earn money to enjoy their nonwork hours.

This trend suggests that organizations need to find new ways to win consumer and employee confidence. They need to review their advertising communications to make sure their messages are honest. Also, they need to review their various activities to make sure that they are being good corporate citizens. More companies are linking themselves to worthwhile causes, measuring their images with important publics, and using public relations to build more positive images (see Marketing Highlight 3.3).[33]

People's Views of Society.   People vary in their attitudes toward their society; patriots defend it, reformers want to change it, malcontents want to leave it. People's orientation to their society influences their consumption patterns, levels of savings, and attitudes toward the marketplace.

The past two decades have seen an increase in consumer patriotism. For example, one study showed that over 80 percent of those surveyed say, "Americans should always try to buy American"—up from 72 percent in 1972.[34] Many U.S. companies have responded with "made in America" themes and flag-waving promotions. For example, Black & Decker added a flaglike symbol to its tools. For the past several years, the American textile industry has blitzed consumers with its "Crafted with Pride in the USA" advertising campaign, insisting that "made in the USA" matters. In 1991, many companies used patriotic appeals and promotions to express their support of American troops in the Gulf War and to ride the wave of national pride and patriotism that followed.

People's Views of Nature.   People vary in their attitudes toward the natural world. Some feel ruled by it, others feel in harmony with it, and still others seek to master it. A long-term trend has been people's growing mastery over nature through technology and the belief that nature is bountiful. More recently, however, people have recognized that nature is finite and fragile, that it can be destroyed or spoiled by human activities.

Love of nature is leading to more camping, hiking, boating, fishing, and other outdoor activities. Business has responded by offering more products and services catering to these interests. Tour operators are offering more wilderness adventures, and retailers are offering more fitness gear and apparel. Food producers have found growing markets for "natural" products such as natural cereal, natural ice cream, and health foods. Marketing communicators are using appealing natural backgrounds in advertising their products.

People's Views of the Universe.   Finally, people vary in their beliefs about the origin of the universe and their place in it. Although most Americans practice religion, religious conviction and practice have been dropping off gradually through the years. Some futurists, however, have noted a renewed interest in spirituality, perhaps as a part of a broader search for a new inner purpose. People have been moving away from materialism and dog-eat-dog ambition to seek more permanent values—family, community, earth, faith—and a more certain grasp of right and wrong.

"Americans are on a spiritual journey," observes one expert, "increasingly concerned with the meaning of life and issues of the soul and spirit. The journey can encompass religion, but it is much more likely to take the form of . . . 'spiritual individualism.' " This new spiritualism affects consumers in everything from the television shows they watch and the books they read to the products and services they buy. "Since consumers don't park their beliefs and values on the bench outside the marketplace," adds the expert, "they are bringing this awareness to the brands they buy. Tapping into this heightened sensitivity presents a unique marketing opportunity for brands."[35]

RESPONDING TO THE MARKETING ENVIRONMENT

Someone once observed, "There are three kinds of companies: those who make things happen; those who watch things happen; and those who wonder what's happened."[36] Many companies view the marketing environment as an uncontrollable element to which they must adapt. They passively accept the marketing environment and do not try to change it. They analyze the environmental forces and design strategies that will help the company avoid the threats and take advantage of the opportunities the environment provides.

Other companies take an **environmental management perspective**.[37] Rather than simply watching and reacting, these firms take aggressive actions to affect the publics and forces in their marketing environment. Such companies hire lobbyists to influence legislation affecting their industries and stage media events

Environmental management perspective
A management perspective in which the firm takes aggressive actions to affect the publics and forces in its marketing environment rather than simply watching and reacting to them.

MARKETING HIGHLIGHT 3.3

CAUSE-RELATED MARKETING: DOING WELL BY DOING GOOD

These days, every product seems to be tied to some cause. Buy Purina cat food and help the American Association of Zoological Parks and Aquariums save endangered big cat species. Drink Tang and earn money for Mothers Against Drunk Driving. Drive a Dollar rental car and help support the Special Olympics. Or if you want to help the Leukemia Society of America, buy Helping Hand trash bags or toilet paper. Pay for these purchases with the right charge card and you can support a local cultural arts group or help fight cancer or heart disease.

Cause-related marketing has become one of the hottest forms of corporate giving. It lets companies "do well by doing good" by linking purchases of the company's products or services with fund-raising for worthwhile causes or charitable organizations. Cause-related marketing has grown rapidly since the early 1980s, when American Express offered to donate 1 cent to the restoration of the Statue of Liberty for each use of its charge card. American Express ended up having to contribute $1.7 million, but the cause-related campaign produced a 28 percent increase in card usage.

Companies now sponsor dozens of cause-related marketing campaigns each year. Many are backed by large budgets and a full complement of marketing activities. Here are other examples:

Johnson & Johnson teams with the Children's Hospital Medical Center and the National Safety Council to sponsor a cause-related marketing campaign to reduce preventable children's injuries, the leading killer of children. Some 43 other nonprofit groups, including the American Red Cross, National Parent Teachers Association, and the Boy and Girl Scouts of America, have helped to promote the campaign. The campaign offers consumers a free Safe Kids safety kit for children in exchange for proofs of purchase. Consumers can also buy a Child's Safety Video for $9.95. The video features a game-show format that makes learning about safety entertaining as well as educational. To promote the campaign, Johnson & Johnson has distributed almost 50 million advertising inserts in daily newspapers and developed a special information kit for retailers containing posters, floor displays, and other in-store promotion materials. Safe Kids Safety Tip Sheets and emergency phone stickers are also available as free consumer handouts.

Cause-related marketing: As part of its Breast Cancer Awareness Crusade, Avon sponsored a series of dramatic fundraising walks called the Avon Breast Cancer 3-Day. Proceeds support programs that provide low-income, minority, and older women with education and early cancer screening services.

to gain favorable press coverage. They run advertorials (ads expressing editorial points of view) to shape public opinion. They press lawsuits and file complaints with regulators to keep competitors in line, and they form contractual agreements to better control their distribution channels.

Often, companies can find positive ways to overcome seemingly uncontrollable environmental constraints. For example

Since 1993, American Express has joined with Share Our Strength (SOS), a hunger-relief organization, to sponsor its Charge Against Hunger program. Every time someone uses an American Express card between November 1 and December 31, the company donates 3 cents to SOS, up to a total of $5 million per year. In recent years, other corporations have "joined the charge," including Kmart, Melville Corporation, Calphalon, and the National Football League. For example, in 1994, Kmart donated 10 cents for every American Express card transaction at its stores between November 27 and the end of the year. The program has been highly successful. Over the past three years, American Express and its partners have donated more than $16 million to SOS. American Express has found that the program has increased card transactions, merchant card acceptance, and cardholder support.

Avon, the world's largest direct seller of cosmetics and beauty items, has for years sponsored programs aimed at raising national and global awareness of breast cancer, a problem afflicting its target audience—women. Avon's Breast Cancer Awareness Crusade in the United States raises money for programs that provide women—especially low-income, minority, and older women with education and early cancer screening services. The company sells products featuring a pink ribbon (the international symbol of breast cancer) through its 450,000 sales representatives, then donates proceeds to nonprofit and university-based programs. Avon publicizes these efforts in its bimonthly sales brochures to 15 million U.S. customers and on its Web site. In addition, the company's famous in-person sales force is fully briefed on the company's efforts, putting a familiar face

on the campaign. "The message in the United States and across all of the countries [where Avon does business] is the same: We're looking to position Avon as the company for women, whether that's the place to buy a product, to start your own business, where your health needs are addressed, [or] to function as an advocate on behalf of women's health," says Joanne Mazurki, Avon's director of global cause-related marketing.

Cause-related marketing has stirred some controversy. Critics are concerned that cause-related marketing might eventually undercut traditional "no-strings" corporate giving, as more and more companies grow to expect marketing benefits from their contributions. Critics also worry that cause-related marketing will cause a shift in corporate charitable support toward more visible, popular, and low-risk charities—those with more certain and substantial marketing appeal. For example, MasterCard's "Choose to Make a Difference" campaign raises money for six charities, each selected in part because of its popularity in a consumer poll. Finally, critics worry that cause-related marketing is more a strategy for selling than a strategy for giving, that "cause-related" marketing is really "cause-exploitative" marketing. Thus, companies using cause-related marketing might find themselves walking a fine line between increased sales and an improved image, and facing charges of exploitation.

However, if handled well, cause-related marketing can greatly benefit both the company and the cause. The company gains an effective marketing tool while building a more positive public image. One recent study found

that 61 percent of consumers believe that cause-related marketing should be a standard practice. Some 83 percent say they have a more positive image of a company that supports a cause they care about, and two-thirds say that if price and quality are equal, they are likely to switch to a civic-minded brand or retailer. Similarly, the charitable organization or cause gains greater visibility and important new sources of funding. This additional funding can be substantial. In total, such campaigns now contribute some $100 million annually to the coffers of charitable organizations, and surveys show that these cause-related contributions usually add to, rather than undercut, direct company contributions. Thus, when cause marketing works, everyone wins.

Sources: See Nancy Arnott, "Marketing with a Passion," *Sales & Marketing Management*, January 1994, pp. 64–71; Minette E. Drumwright, "Company Advertising with a Social Dimension: The Role of Noneconomic Criteria," *Journal of Marketing*, October 1996, pp. 71–87; Alan R. Andreason, "Profits of Nonprofits," *Harvard Business Review*, November–December 1996, pp. 47–59; Julie Garrett and Lisa Rochlin, "Cause Marketers Must Learn to Play by Rules," *Marketing News*, May 12, 1997, p. 4; Deborah J Webb and Lois A. Mohr, "A Typology of Consumer Responses to Cause-Related Marketing: From Skeptics to Socially Concerned," *Journal of Marketing & Public Policy*, Fall 1998, pp. 226–38; "Consumers Care About Causes," *Sales & Marketing Management*, June 1999, p. 74; Michelle Wirth Fellman, "Cause Marketing Takes a Strategic Turn," *Marketing News*, April 26, 1999, p. 4; and Jerry C. Welsh, "Good Cause, Good Business," *Harvard Business Review*, September–October 1999, pp. 21–24.

★ Cathay Pacific Airlines . . . determined that many travelers were avoiding Hong Kong because of lengthy delays at immigration. Rather than assuming that this was a problem they could not solve, Cathay's senior staff asked the Hong Kong government how to avoid these immigration delays. After lengthy discussions, the airline agreed to make an annual grant-in-aid to the government to hire more immigration inspectors—but these reinforcements would service primarily the Cathay Pacific gates. The reduced waiting period increased customer value and thus strengthened [Cathay's competitive advantage].[38]

MARKETING HIGHLIGHT
3.4

YOURCOMPANYSUCKS.COM

Richard Hatch is one of the few people in this world with a passion for both Harley-Davidson motorcycles and collecting dolls and cute little toys. One day in 1997, the tattooed, 210-pound Hatch got into a shouting match with an employee in his local Wal-Mart and was banned from the store. Hatch claims that his actions didn't warrant his ousting. He says he'd complained to store managers for months that employees were snapping up the best Hot Wheels and NASCAR collectible toy cars before they hit the shelves.

Environmental management: The best strategy for dealing with consumer hate sites is to address complaints directly. If a company solves my problem, why would I keep up the Web site?

Wal-Mart didn't budge and the angry Hatch retaliated. He hired a Web designer and created the Wal-Mart Sucks Web site (www.walmartsucks.com). In only a few years, according to one account, the Web site "sprouted beyond Hatch's wildest dreams of revenge. More than 1,500 customers have written in to attack rude store managers, complain about alleged insects in the aisles, offer shoplifting tips, and, from time to time, write romantic odes to cashiers." Hatch, who has amassed some 5,000 Beanie Babies, also had a dispute with employees at his local Toys "Я" Us store about similar complaints. He was banished from there as well. His response? You guessed it: another sucks.com Web site (www.toysrussucks.com).

An extreme event? Not anymore. As more and more well-intentioned grassroots organizations, consumer watchdog groups, or just plain angry consumers take their gripes to the Web, such "sucks.com" sites are becoming almost commonplace. A recent Yahoo! search for the words *hate* and *sucks* yielded 628 hits. The sites target some highly respected companies with some highly *dis*respectful labels: Microsucks; The I Hate McDonald's Page; Just Do Not Do It (Nike); America Offline; Untied Airlines: The Most Unfriendly Skies; The Unofficial BMW Lemon Site; and Allsnake: The Good Hands People? to name only a few. Some of these attack sites are little more than a nuisance. Others, however, can draw serious attention and create real headaches. "The same people who used to stand on [the] corner and rail against things to 20 people now can put up a Web site and rail in front of 2 million people," says William Comcowich, whose firm helps companies monitor what's said about them on the Internet.

How should companies react to these attack sites? The real quandary

Marketing management cannot always control environmental forces. In many cases, it must settle for simply watching and reacting to the environment. For example, a company would have little success trying to influence geographic population shifts, the economic environment, or major cultural values. But whenever possible, smart marketing managers will take a *proactive* rather than *reactive* approach to the marketing environment (see Marketing Highlight 3.4).

for targeted companies is figuring out how far they can go to protect their image without fueling the fire already raging at the sites. One point upon which all experts seem to agree: Don't try to retaliate in kind. "Avoid 'testosterosis'—or the urge to hit someone in the face because they are doing something you don't like," advises one consultant. "It's a free country, and the Web is completely unregulated. Don't get angry and think about doing foolish things."

Some companies have tried to silence the critics through lawsuits but few have succeeded. For example, Wal-Mart's attorneys threatened Hatch with legal action unless he shut down his Wal-Mart Sucks Web site. However, Hatch stood up to the $138 billion retailer, and Wal-Mart eventually backed down. As it turns out, a company has legal recourse only when the unauthorized use of its trademarks, brand names, or other intellectual property is apt to be confusing to the public. No reasonable person is likely to be confused that Wal-Mart maintains and supports a site tagged walmart sucks.com. Beyond the finer legal points, Wal-Mart also feared that a lawsuit would only draw more attention to the consumer hate site. An industry analyst comments: "Those who operate hate sites adore posting cease-and-desist letters they receive from corporate attorneys. Such letters also validate their fight for the cause, whatever they perceive that to be, and they can use

them to cast yet another negative spotlight on the company. They revel in the attention."

Given the difficulties of trying to sue consumer hate sites out of existence, some companies have tried other strategies. For example, most big companies now routinely buy up Web addresses for their firm names preceded by the words "Ihate" or followed by "sucks.com." In general, however, attempts to block, counterattack, or shut down consumer hate sites may be shortsighted. Such sites are often based on real consumer concerns. Hence, the best strategy might be to proactively monitor these sites and respond positively to the concerns they express.

Some targeted companies actively listen to concerns posted on hate sites and develop Web presentations to tell their own side of the story. For example, Nike is the target of at least eight different attack sites, mostly criticizing it for alleged unfair labor practices in Southeast Asia. In response, Nike commissioned an independent investigation of labor practices in its Indonesian factories and presented the results on its own Web site (www.Nikebiz.com/social/labor). Monitoring consumer hate sites can yield additional benefits. For example, some sites can actually provide the targeted company with useful information. Walmartsucks.com posts customers' ratings of local stores for cleanliness, prices, and customer service, information that would be costly for Wal-Mart to develop on its own.

According to James Alexander, president of EWatch, an Internet monitoring service, the best strategy for dealing with consumer hate sites is to address their complaints directly. "If a company solves my problem," he says, "why would I keep up the Web site?" Take Dunkin' Donuts, for example

After a disgruntled customer established dunkindonuts.org, an attack site that appeared on many Internet search engines ahead of the company's own Web page, the company contacted about 25 people who had written in with complaints and offered them coupons for free donuts. "If this was where customers were going to post their comments, we thought it was important for us to go ahead and address them," says spokesperson Jennifer Rosenberg. Now, the company is in negotiations to buy the site from its founder, 25-year-old David Felton, who says he'll sell because "they have been taking complaints and responding."

By proactively responding to a seemingly uncontrollable event in its environment, Dunkin' Donuts has been able to turn a negative into a positive. At Dunkin' Donuts, sucks.com is now all smiles.com.

Sources: Quotes and excerpts from Leslie Goff, "<YourCompanyNameHere>sucks.com," *Computerworld,* July 20, 1998, pp. 57–58; and Mike France, "A Site for Soreheads," *Business Week,* April 12, 1999, pp. 86–90.

REVIEW OF CONCEPT CONNECTIONS

Companies must constantly watch and adapt to the *marketing environment* in order to seek opportunities and ward off threats. The marketing environment comprises all the actors and forces influencing the company's ability to transact business effectively with its target market.

1. Describe the environmental forces that affect the company's ability to serve its customers.

The company's *microenvironment* consists of other actors close to the company that combine to form the company's value delivery system or that affect its ability to serve its customers. It includes the company's *internal environment*—its several departments and management levels—as it influences marketing decision making. *Marketing channel firms*—suppliers and marketing intermediaries, including resellers, physical distribution firms, marketing services agencies, and financial intermediaries—cooperate to create customer value. Five types of customer *markets* include consumer, producer, reseller, government, and international markets. *Competitors* vie with the company in an effort to serve customers better. Finally, various *publics* have an actual or potential interest in or impact on the company's ability to meet its objectives.

The *macroenvironment* consists of larger societal forces that affect the entire microenvironment. The six forces making up the company's macroenvironment include demographic, economic, natural, technological, political, and cultural forces. These forces shape opportunities and pose threats to the company.

2. Explain how changes in the demographic and economic environments affect marketing decisions.

Demography is the study of the characteristics of human populations. Today's *demographic environment* shows a changing age structure, shifting family profiles, geographic population shifts, a better-educated and more white-collar population, and increasing diversity. The *economic environment* consists of factors that affect buying power and patterns. The economic environment is characterized by lower real income and shifting consumer spending patterns. Today's squeezed consumers are seeking greater value—just the right combination of good quality and service at a fair price. The distribution of income also is shifting. The rich have grown richer, the middle class has shrunk, and the poor have remained poor, leading to a two-tiered market. Many companies now tailor their marketing offers to two different markets—the affluent and the less affluent.

3. Identify the major trends in the firm's natural and technological environments.

The *natural environment* shows three major trends: shortages of certain raw materials, higher pollution levels, and more government intervention in natural resource management. Environmental concerns create marketing opportunities for alert companies. The marketer should watch for four major trends in the *technological environment*: the rapid pace of technological change, high R&D budgets, the concentration by companies on minor product improvements, and increased government regulation. Companies that fail to keep up with technological change will miss out on new product and marketing opportunities.

4. Explain the key changes in the political and cultural environments.

The *political environment* consists of laws, agencies, and groups that influence or limit marketing actions. The political environment has undergone three changes that affect marketing worldwide: increasing legislation regulating business, strong government agency enforcement, and greater emphasis on ethics and socially responsible actions. The *cultural environment* is made up of institutions and forces that affect a society's values, perceptions, preferences, and behaviors. The environment shows long-term trends toward a we society, a return to cautious trust of institutions, increasing patriotism, greater appreciation for nature, a new spiritualism, and the search for more meaningful and enduring values.

5. Discuss how companies can react to the marketing environment.

Companies can passively accept the marketing environment as an uncontrollable element to which they must adapt, avoiding threats and taking advantage of opportunities as they arise. Or they can take an *environmental management perspective,* proactively working to change the environment rather than simply reacting to it. Whenever possible, companies should try to be proactive rather than reactive.

KEY TERMS

Baby boom
Cultural environment
Demography
Echo boomers
Economic environment
Engel's laws

Environmental management
    perspective
Macroenvironment
Marketing environment
Marketing intermediaries
Microenvironment

Natural environment
Political environment
Public
Technological environment

ISSUES FOR DISCUSSION

1. In the 1930s, President Franklin Roosevelt used his cigarette holder as a personal "trademark." Discuss how the cultural environment has changed. Would a president be seen smoking today? Considering the rash of recent court rulings and settlements concerning the tobacco industry, how might a cigarette manufacturer market its products differently in this new environment? What are the long-term prospects for the tobacco industry?

2. Define "millennial fever" and provide several examples. How can marketers apply this phenomenon in designing their marketing strategies? Will this fever pass, or is it a long-term phenomenon?

3. It has been said that the single most important demographic trend in the United States is the changing age structure of the population. Take three industries—automobiles, computers/software, and toys/games—and suggest specific strategies that would help these industries deal successfully with changing age patterns in the United States during the next decade. Be sure to address the opportunities presented by the echo boomers.

4. Americans are becoming more concerned about the natural environment. Explain how this trend would affect a company that markets (a) sandwich bags, (b) tires, (c) computers, and (d) electrical power. Suggest some effective responses to these concerns.

5. In 1999, hardly a day passed without an article describing potential "Y2K bug" difficulties (the inability of computers to deal with dates of 2000 and beyond). At the time, experts disagreed about how much confusion and damage this problem would cause for government, economy, and various businesses. What finally happened with the Y2K problem? Did you feel any affects personally? Give an example of a company that met the problem proactively rather than reactively.

6. Businesses are feeling increasing pressure to be more ethically and socially responsible. The latest area of concern involves the Internet and e-commerce. What are the key issues regarding online ethics and social responsibilities? How should online businesses respond to these issues? Give an example of an online marketer that is not behaving responsibly. What would you propose to correct this situation?

7. Suppose that you have been assigned the task of explaining the core cultural values of people in the United States to a foreign marketer who wishes to sell a new line of men's and women's clothing in this country. Identify at least six core values that you think that the foreign marketer would need to understand. Explain how the marketer might apply these values.

8. Assume that you are marketing manager for Home Depot and that your company has recently come under attack by Mr. Richard Hatch (see Marketing Highlight 3.4). Outline an action plan for proactively dealing with this situation.

MARKETING APPLICATIONS

1. Changes in the marketing environment mean that marketers must meet new consumer needs that may be very different from—even directly opposite to—those of the past. Mattel's Barbie dolls began as high-fashion playthings for young girls. In those days, Mattel assumed that most young girls would become homemakers and that high-fashion fantasy was an appropriate dream. Today, Mattel seeks a very different role and relationship with young women. Visit Mattel's Barbie Web site at www.barbie.com. See if you can track changes in the marketing environment by looking at how Mattel has modified Barbie.

   a. Make a list of the ways Barbie has changed to meet the evolving needs and expectations of young women. How do these modifications reflect female self-image, self-confidence, and life goals?

   b. Apply your list to other gender-related Web sites, such as www.women.com and www.ivillage.com. Do you see any similarities with respect to trends reflected in these sites?

   c. Using your list, construct a gender-sensitive marketing plan for a specific automobile brand that wishes to target young female drivers. How does your plan reflect what you have learned from the Barbie and other Web sites?

2. When Stanford University graduate students Jerry Yang and David Filo developed Yahoo!, they had little idea how far their revolutionary concept would go. Their original concept was to make "wasting time on the Internet" easier. Commercial applications came later. Today, more Internet users recognize the name Yahoo! than recognize Microsoft. One of the reasons for Yahoo!'s

popularity is its ability to focus on people's tastes rather than on just delivering information or access to every Web site possible. Yahoo! has become a full-blown package of information and services relating to health, real estate, finance, news, personalization, travel, and shopping. The major challenge now facing Yahoo! is how to convince corporate America that Yahoo! constitutes an effective advertising medium. Primary future challenges will come from America Online and Microsoft.

a. How will a portal site like Yahoo! affect a marketing company's technological environment?

b. Suppose you are marketing manager for a company that makes and sells consumer electronics products. After visiting Yahoo! at www.yahoo.com and competing sites, assess Yahoo! as an advertising medium for your product. What types of ads would you consider placing on such a site?

c. Given the rapid pace of change in the Internet environment, how do you think Yahoo! will fair in the future? Which environmental issues seem most critical to Yahoo!'s success? If you were the marketing manager of Yahoo!, what strategic alliances would you investigate?

 # INTERNET CONNECTIONS

IS "WORLD WIDE WEB" A MISNOMER?

In this chapter you learned the importance of technology, demographics, and other macroenvironmental factors for a company's marketing efforts. The Internet's rapid growth creates opportunities for companies to reach consumers all over the globe. But is the Web truly global, or are some geographic markets better than others for online product offerings? In this exercise, you'll explore five countries outside the United States to see which has the best potential for a firm wanting to sell music CDs online internationally. Locate information on Norway, Canada, India, Mexico, and Japan, and find as much information as possible to complete the table. Good sources for this exercise are listed in the Savvy Sites that follow, but you might also want to use a search engine to find information. *Hint:* The press releases at CyberAtlas are quite helpful.

	Norway	Canada	India	Mexico	Japan
Total population					
Number online					
Percent of population online					
Internet adoption growth rate					
Number who shop online					
Best demographic group for targeting					
Barriers to Internet adoption growth					

FOR DISCUSSION

1. Which country has the highest Internet penetration? The fastest growth rate?
2. Based on your research, what is the biggest barrier to Internet adoption outside the United States?
3. Which country has the best potential for selling music CDs online? Justify your selection.
4. What other key macroenvironmental factors would a firm have to consider before marketing to your selected country? Explain.
5. Based on your research, what advice do you have for a firm creating a Web site to sell CDs in your recommended country?

SAVVY SITES

- NUA Internet Surveys (www.nua.ie) contains lots of current statistics on Internet adoption in various countries.
- CyberAtlas (cyberatlas.internet.com) reprints published studies of Internet user demographics, geographics, and behavior for many countries.
- The U.S. Department of Commerce (www.stat-usa.gov) maintains an extensive database that includes statistics helpful to businesses, especially in the area of international trade.
- I-tools (www.iTools.com) helps you find "anything" on the Internet, including country population.

NOTES

1. Quotes from James R. Rosenfield, "Millennial Fever," *American Demographics,* December 1997, pp. 47–51; Keith Naughton and Bill Vlasic, "The Nostalgia Boom: Why the Old Is New Again," *Business Week,* March 23, 1998, pp. 58–64; and "New Beetles: Drivers Wanted," accessed online at www.vw.com/cars/new-beetle/main.html, August 11, 1998. Also see Greg Farrell, "Getting the Bugs Out," *Brandweek,* April 6, 1998, pp. 30–40; "Beetle Mania," *Adweek,* July 13, 1998, p. 24; "Volkswagen's New Beetle Selected 1999 North American Car of the Year," press release accessed online at www.vw.com, January 4, 1999; remarks by Jens Neumann at the 1999 North American International Auto Show, accessed online at www.vw.com, January 4, 1999; and Judann Pollack, "Heinz Waxes Nostalgic over Revived Glass Bottle," *Advertising Age,* May 3, 1999, p. 17.

2. Jennifer Lach, "Dateline America: May 1, 2025," *American Demographics,* May 1999, pp. 19–20.

3. Sarah Lorge, "The Coke Advantage," *Sales & Marketing Management,* December 1998, p. 17.

4. World POPClock, U.S. Census Bureau, www.census.gov, September 1999. This Web site provides continuously updated projections of the world population.

5. Sally D. Goll, "Marketing: China's (Only) Children Get the Royal Treatment," *Wall Street Journal,* February 8, 1995, pp. B1, B3; and Lorien Holland, "Baby Boom," *Far Eastern Economic Review,* June 24, 1999, p. 61.

6. See Diane Crispell, "Generations to 2025," *American Demographics,* January 1995, p. 4; and POPClock Projection, U.S. Census Bureau, www.census.gov, September 1999.

7. Lach, "Dateline America: May 1, 2025," p. 19.

8. Margot Hornblower, "Great X," *Time,* June 9, 1997, pp. 58–69. Also see Janus Dietz, "When Gen X Meets Aging Baby Boomers," *Marketing News,* May 10, 1999, p. 17.

9. See Philip Kotler, *Marketing Management: Analysis, Planning, Implementation, and Control,* 10th ed. (Upper Saddle River, NJ: Prentice Hall, 2000), p. 141.

10. See James U. McNeal, "Tapping the Three Kids' Markets," *American Demographics,* April 1998, pp. 37–40; Carolyn M. Edy, "Babies Mean Business," *American Demographics,* May 1999, pp. 46–47; and Jennifer Gilbert, "New Teen Obsession," *Advertising Age,* February 14, 2000, p. 38.

11. Accessed online from www.growingupdigital.com/FLecho.html, October 1999. Also see Douglas Tapscott, *Growing Up Digital: The Rise of the Net Generation* (New York: McGraw-Hill, 1999).

12. See J. Walker Smith and Ann Clurman, *Rocking the Ages* (New York: HarperBusiness, 1998); and Mercedes M. Cardona, "Hilfiger's New Apparel Lines Getting Individual Efforts," *Advertising Age,* February 8, 1999, p. 24.

13. See Diane Crispell, "Married Couples Endure," *American Demographics,* January 1998, p. 39; and www.census.gov/population/projections/nation/hh-fam/table5n.txt, accessed online, June 1999.

14. Sue Shellenbarger, " 'Child-Care Cams': Are They Good News for Working Parents?" *Wall Street Journal,* August 19, 1998, p. B11.

15. Kelly Shermach, "Niche Malls: Innovation for an Industry in Decline," *Marketing News,* February 26, 1996, p. 1.

16. Dan Fost, "Americans on the Move," *American Demographics,* Tools Supplement, January–February 1997, pp. 10–13.

17. See Kevin Heubusch, "Small Is Beautiful," *American Demographics,* January 1998, pp. 43–49; Brad Edmondson, "A New Era for Rural Americans," *American Demographics,* September 1997, pp. 30–31; and Kenneth M. Johnson and Calvin L. Beale, "The Rural Rebound," *The Wilson Quarterly,* Spring 1998, pp. 16–27.

18. Lauri J. Flynn, "Not Just a Copy Shop Any Longer, Kinko's Pushes Its Computer Services," *New York Times,* July 6, 1998, p. D12. Also see Carol Leonetti Dannhauser, "Who's in the Home Office," *American Demographics,* June 1999, pp. 50–56.

19. See Fabian Linden, "In the Rearview Mirror," *American Demographics,* April 1984, pp. 4–5; Peter Francese, "America at Mid-Decade," *American Demographics,* February 1995, pp. 23–29; Rebecca Piirto Heath, "The New Working Class," *American Demographics,* January 1998, pp. 51–55; and *Digest of Education Statistics 1997,* National Center for Education Statistics, January 1998, at http://nccs01.ed.gov/pubs/digest97.

20. See "A True Melting Pot," *Advertising Age,* February 17, 1997, p. S2; "Foreign-Born Diversity," *American Demographics,* July 1997, p. 33; Nancy Coltun Webster, "Multicultural," *Advertising Age,* November 17, 1997, pp. S1–S2; and "Diversity," *Advertising Age,* February 16, 1998, pp. S1, S14.

21. Dan Frost, "The Fun Factor: Marketing Recreation to the Disabled," *American Demographics,* February 1998, pp. 54–58; and Michelle Wirth Fellman, "Selling IT Goods to Disabled End-Users," *Marketing News,* March 15, 1999, pp. 1, 17.

22. James W. Hughes, "Understanding the Squeezed Consumer," *American Demographics,* July 1991, pp. 44–50. For more on consumer spending trends, see Cheryl Russell, "The New Consumer Paradigm," *American Demographics,* April 1999, pp. 50–58.

23. See U.S. Census Bureau, Income Inequity—Table 2, February 25, 1997, at www.census.gov/hes/income/incineq/p60tb2.html, John McManus, "Gap Analysis," *American Demographics,* July 1999, p. 6; and Frank Levy, "Rhetoric and Reality," *Harvard Business Review,* September–October 1999, pp. 163–71.

24. Debra Goldman, "Paradox of Pleasure," *American Demographics,* May 1999, pp. 50–53.

25. David Leonhardt, "Two-Tier Marketing," *Business Week,* March 17, 1997, pp. 82–90.

26. For more discussion, see the "Environmentalism" section in chap. 20. Also see Michael E. Porter and Claas van der Linde, "Green *and* Competitive: Ending the Stalemate," *Harvard Business Review,* September–October 1995, pp. 120–34; Stuart L. Hart, "Beyond Greening: Strategies for a Sustainable World," *Harvard Business Review,* January–February 1997, pp. 67–76; Jacquelyn Ottman, "Environment Winners Show Sustainable Strategies," *Marketing News,* April 27, 1998, p. 6; Lisa E. Phillips, "Green Attitude," *American Demographics,* April 1999, pp. 46–47; and Forest L. Reinhardt, "Bringing the Environment down to Earth," *Harvard Business Review,* July–August 1999, pp. 149–57.

27. See M. F. Wolff, "Real R&D Spending Increase Forecast for 1998," *Research Technology Management,* March–April, 1998, p. 6.

28. For a summary of U.S. legal developments in marketing, see Louis W. Stern and Thomas L. Eovaldi, *Legal Aspects of Marketing Strategy: Antitrust and Consumer Protection Issues* (Upper Saddle River, NJ: Prentice Hall, 1984); Robert J. Posch Jr., *The Complete Guide to Marketing and the Law* (Upper Saddle River, NJ: Prentice Hall, 1988); Robert J. Posch Jr., *The Complete Guide to Marketing and the Law, 1990 Cumulative Supplement* (Upper Saddle River, NJ: Prentice Hall, 1990); Dorothy Cohen, *Legal Issues in Marketing Decision Making* (Southwestern Publishing, 1994); and Theodore L. Banks, *Distribution Law: Antitrust Principles and Practice* (Aspen Publishers, 1998).

29. "13-Year-Old Bids over $3M for Items in eBay Auctions," *USA Today,* April 30, 1999, p. 10B.

30. Rajiv Chandrasekaran, "AOL Settles Marketing Complaints," *Washington Post,* May 29, 1998, p. F1.

31. For more on today's shifting values, see Chip Walker and Elissa Moses, "The Age of Self-Navigation," *American Demographics,* September 1996, pp. 36–42; and Paul H. Ray, "The Emerging Culture," *American Demographics,* February 1997, pp. 29–34.

32. See Cyndee Miller, "Trendspotters: 'Dark Ages' Ending; So Is Cocooning," *Marketing News,* February 3, 1997, pp. 1, 16.

33. Also see V. Kasturi Rangan, Sohel Karim, and Sheryl K. Sandberg, "Do Better at Doing Good," *Harvard Business Review,* May–June 1996, pp. 42–54; Julie Garrett and Lisa Rochlin, "Cause Marketers Must Learn to Play by Rules," *Marketing News,* May 12, 1997, p. 4; and Sarah Lorge, "Is Cause-Related Marketing Worth It?" *Sales & Marketing Management,* June 1998, p. 72.

34. Bill McDowell, "New DDB Needham Report: Consumers Want It All," *Advertising Age,* November 1996, pp. 32–33.

35. Myra Stark, "Celestial Season," *Brandweek,* November 16, 1998, pp. 25–26. Also see Jennifer Harrison, "Advertising Joins the Journal of the Soul," *American Demographics,* June 1997, pp. 22–28; David B. Wolfe, "The Psychological Center of Gravity," *American Demographics,* April 1998, pp. 16–19; and Richard Cimino and Don Lattin, "Choosing My Religion," *American Demographics,* April 1999, pp. 60–65.

36. Philip Kotler, *Kotler on Marketing* (New York: Free Press, 1999), p. 3.

37. See Carl P. Zeithaml and Valerie A. Zeithaml, "Environmental Management: Revising the Marketing Perspective," *Journal of Marketing,* Spring 1984, pp. 46–53.

38. Howard E. Butz Jr. and Leonard D. Goodstein, "Measuring Customer Value: Gaining the Strategic Advantage," *Organizational Dynamics,* Winter 1996, pp. 66–67.

COMPANY CASE

3

The Newest Avon Lady—Barbie!

SELLING TRADITION

"Ding-dong, Avon calling." With that simple advertising message over the past 112 years, Avon Products built a $4 billion worldwide beauty-products business. Founded in 1886, and incorporated as California Perfume Products in 1916, Avon deployed an army of women to sell its products. These "Avon ladies," 40 million of them over the company's history, met with friends and neighbors in their homes, showed products, took and delivered orders, and earned sales commissions. Through direct selling, Avon bypassed the battle for retail space and attention waged by its competitors in department stores, and later in discount drug stores and supermarkets. Direct selling also offered convenience for the customer, coupled with personal beauty-care advice from a friend.

Avon's plan worked well. Most members of its up to 500,000-member U.S. salesforce were homemakers who needed extra money, but did not want a full-time job outside the home. They developed client lists of friends and neighbors whom they called on from time to time. Customers could also call them between visits. Recruiting salespeople was easy, and a good salesperson could develop a loyal core of customers who made repeat purchases. Avon paid the salespeople a commission based on their sales, and a successful salesperson could earn an attractive income.

TIMES CHANGE

However, during the 1970s and 1980s, the environment changed. First, more women found that they needed to work outside the home. As a result, when Avon ladies rang the doorbell, often no one answered. Second, many Avon ladies decided that they needed more than part-time jobs, and Avon's annual salesforce turnover rates soared to more than 200 percent. Third, because of high salesforce turnover, many Avon customers wanting to see a salesperson could not find one. Fourth, more competitors, such as Amway, Mary Kay Cosmetics, and Tupperware, were competing for the pool of people interested in full- or part-time direct-selling jobs. Finally, in addition to all those factors, increasing mobility of the U.S. population meant that both customers and salespeople were moving. This made it difficult for salespeople to establish loyal, stable customer bases.

A NEW STRATEGY

To deal with these issues, in 1988 Avon Products tapped James E. Preston to serve as its chair and chief executive. Preston decided that Avon needed to overhaul its marketing strategy. First, he refocused the company on its core business—selling cosmetics, fragrances, and toiletries—and sold unrelated businesses. Next, he drastically cut prices on Avon products. Finally, he tried a new compensation program called "Leadership" that allowed sales representatives to earn up to 21 percent in bonuses based on the sales of new representatives they recruited. Such multilevel selling is common among direct-sales companies. However, by late 1991, Avon killed the program, arguing that it did not fit Avon's culture.

Preston believed that Avon had left as many as ten million former or potential customers stranded. These customers wanted to buy Avon products, but salesforce turnover meant that they did not know how to find a salesperson or order products. Fourteen percent of American women accounted for one-third of Avon's sales. Another 62 percent were fringe customers. These customers viewed Avon positively but did not buy regularly. Another 15 percent of American women were potentially receptive to Avon, but were not necessarily interested in dealing with a traditional Avon sales representative.

Thus, Preston decided to develop another program he called "Avon Select." The program featured a catalog and toll-free telephone number that allowed direct-mail selling. Avon's research revealed that its median customer was 45 years old and had an average household income of under $30,000. The catalog would reach younger, higher-income customers. Preston believed that, with a catalog, the company could cut the median customer age to 38 and increase average household income to more than $30,000. Avon supported the catalog program by kicking off a national advertising campaign that featured the slogan "Avon—The Smartest Shop in Town." To fund the advertising, the company cut sales commissions and incentives and laid off scores of executives.

As you might imagine, all these changes created lots of turmoil at Avon including three different heads of the U.S. operation in a short period. However, Preston vowed to keep pursuing changes. To keep customers, "change we did, change we must, and change we will," Preston asserted. To make good on his promise, he launched a $30 million ad campaign in 1994 with the theme, "Just Another Avon Lady." Market research showed that, despite all Avon's changes, consumers still thought of "Ding-dong" and the Avon lady when asked what they associated with the company. Observers wondered if the use of the term *lady* in the mid-1990s would cause negative reactions among many women. After all, even Avon had avoided using the term in advertising for 20 years.

Between 1992 and 1996, Avon's sales and profits rose slowly but steadily, driven primarily by sales in international markets. Then, in late 1997, Avon announced what might be its most radical change yet. It announced that it would soon test the idea of selling its products through *retail stores*. Although the company had been using retail stores in some foreign markets for years, this approach would be new to the U.S. market. Preston argued that no matter how great Avon's products were, many customers just weren't interested in buying from Avon ladies in a one-on-one situation. To pacify the company's 440,000 U.S. sales reps, Avon said it would consider giving them a share of the new business either through franchising or referrals from the stores. It also announced that it would cut its product line by 30 percent in order to put its marketing resources behind fewer products, pursue the creation of global brands out of several of its skin-care and cosmetics products, and standardize its promotion efforts using the same promotions for its products around the world.

GLOBAL REACH

The value of Avon's global reach and it 2.3 million sales representatives worldwide had not gone unnoticed by other firms wanting to crack international markets. Mattel, Inc. announced in 1997 that it would partner with Avon to allow its salespeople to begin selling its Barbie dolls. In a 1996 test, Avon sold $43 million worth of two versions of Barbie, including more than one million of one version in just two weeks. Andrea Jung, Avon's president of global marketing noted that, "Our powerful distribution channel combined with their powerful brand is a huge opportunity."

Companies like Mattel are attracted to direct salesforces like Avon's for several reasons. In international markets, the companies do not have to wait for retailers to build stores if they use a direct salesforce. Further, in many developing economies, being a direct sales rep may be the most attractive job for many women, thus making recruitment easy. However, there are problems. Turnover is often high and many sales representatives are not really committed to the company. Further, many don't have formal business training or basic skills needed to perform their duties.

Although Avon and Mattel limited distribution to the U.S. market initially, they planned to have Avon ladies selling Barbies in China as early as spring 1998. Mattel would introduce an "international Barbie," but she did not look Asian. In an earlier test in Japan, Mattel found that Asian girls preferred the standard American Barbie. Avon also planned to introduce a Barbie-branded line of toiletries and fragrances for girls in the U.S. and abroad.

However, in early 1998, the Chinese government threw a monkey wrench into Avon's plans. The government announced that it was banning direct sales throughout the country. Government officials were responding to news reports of bogus sales schemes in which salespeople duped unsuspecting customers into spending their savings on overpriced, inferior goods. Further, officials believed that the direct-selling companies used their sales meetings to start secret societies and sell smuggled or fake goods.

The ban prompted protests from the affected companies, like Avon, Mary Kay, and Amway, as well as the U.S. government. In addition, thousands of salespeople rioted in several Chinese cities, protesting the loss of their jobs. By mid-June 1998, however, Avon had successfully negotiated with the Chinese government to restart its business. Avon agreed to operate as a wholesaler, selling its products to retail stores and converting its 75 branch centers into retail outlets. The new arrangement meant that Avon's 50,000 sales representatives would lose their jobs.

Despite the obstacles, Avon and other companies are committed to opening the Chinese market. China accounted for only about 1.5 percent of Avon's sales in 1998, but the potential was huge. Most Chinese consumers have little money, no credit cards, no telephones, and no direct way to get merchandise. The most common means of distribution are the China Post Office, hand-delivered door drops, and on-street distribution. There are also few customer lists available that direct-marketing firms can use.

However, the Chinese population is developing into a discerning group that prefers quality products that meet their needs. Chinese customers believe that aggressive promotions cheapen a product. They like American-made products that companies promote tastefully. They particularly like cosmetics, jewelry, and entertainment products, especially if they are associated with celebrities.

Direct marketers are also learning that they should not view China as a single market. The stereotype of 1.3 billion, low-income people living in rural areas is simply not true. China has the largest urban population in the world. By 2000, savvy marketers realized that the true Chinese market is the 400 million consumers living in a set of urban centers along the Chinese coast.

Avon has shown its willingness to make changes and face challenges. Taking Barbie to China is just the latest challenge.

Questions

1. Which actors in Avon's microenvironment and forces in the macroenvironment have been important in shaping its marketing strategies?
2. What microenvironmental and macroenvironmental factors should Avon and Mattel consider as they enter international markets?
3. Assess Avon's marketing strategy in the United States What marketing recommendations would you make to help Avon improve its marketing strategy in the United States?
4. Assess Avon's marketing strategy in international markets. What marketing recommendations would you make to help Avon improve its marketing strategy in international markets, particularly China.

Sources: "Avon Gets a Green Light to Restart China Business," *WWD,* June 8, 1998, p. 27; William J. McDonald, "The Ban in China: How Direct Marketing Is Affected," *Direct Marketing,* June 1998, p. 16; Tara Parker-Pope, "Avon Is Calling with New Way to Make a Sale," *Wall Street Journal,* October 27, 1997, p. B1; Tara Parker-Pope and Lisa Bannon, "Avon's New Calling: Sell Barbie in China," *Wall Street Journal,* May 1, 1997, p. B1; Yumiko Ono, "Remember the Avon Lady? She's Back," *Wall Street Journal,* January 22, 1995; Suein L. Hwang, "Updating Avon Means Respecting History Without Repeating It," *Wall Street Journal,* April 4, 1994, p. A1.

Globalstar: Connecting Everyone, Everywhere

A SURPRISING ANNOUNCEMENT

On August 25, 1999, readers of the *Wall Street Journal* and other major newspapers were surprised to find an advertisement featuring a letter from John Richardson, Iridium's new CEO. Iridium was the wireless, satellite-based, global telephone system that the company had launched only nine months earlier. In the letter, Richardson wrote:

> Trailblazers, however, face unique challenges, and we have made some mistakes in launching our service. We recognize our missteps and are working diligently to correct them. Our single most important goal is to provide world-class service to our customers.
>
> To meet our goal, we must get our financial house in order. Iridium LLC recently filed for Chapter 11 reorganization in an effort to conclude a comprehensive financial restructuring under an orderly, court-supervised process. . . . I want to assure our customers, investors, and partners worldwide that Iridium will continue to provide its pioneering, high-quality global telecommunications service without interruption. We are still in business, and it is business as usual.

FALLING FROM ORBIT

Telecommunications developers had long envisioned a network of satellites in low-Earth orbit that would allow a person to make telephone calls from *any*place on Earth. Iridium and its backers, such as Motorola and Japanese components maker, Kyocera, had taken more than 12 years and invested over $5 billion to bring that dream to life. How could a company that blasted off with such fanfare crash so dramatically, so quickly?

Iridium's engineers designed a system that used 66 satellites to link a land-based cellular-phone network joining 200 service providers in 90 countries. The company organized its members around 15 regional gateways that were charged with promoting Iridium's service in their areas. Gateways were the ground-based switching systems that received and directed calls to and from the satellites.

Iridium's backers believed that there was a large potential market for its telephone service. In fact, a Merrill Lynch study predicted that by 2007, 32 million subscribers would be paying almost $32 billion a year for satellite phone service around the world. The study noted that 65 percent of the world's households did not have telephones. Cellular service has not penetrated many developing countries, and

even large areas of the United States and Europe have no cellular coverage.

Advertising agency Ammirati Puris Lintas (APL) worked with Iridium to design the marketing strategy. APL flew in eight managers from its offices in 77 countries to work with Iridium's managers. The APL team presented an analysis of 600 global travelers, VIPs who roamed the world conducting business. APL's research showed that these people worried about being out of touch when they traveled to faraway places. They were afraid of missing out on corporate developments back at the home office or being out of touch and, therefore, out of control. They were also worried about neglecting their families. They were people who had officer titles and were at least 35 years old, or people who had interesting occupations like oil exploration, shipping, or film production.

Iridium already had the product that would soothe these executives' fears and play to their desire for status. However, the one-pound phone the company developed resembled a brick with an antenna similar to a thick bread stick. Along with the phone, an executive had to carry a briefcase filled with a bewildering array of accessories and adapters. Further, to use the phone, the executive had to make sure the antenna pointed in the right direction, toward the satellite orbit, and that no buildings blocked the signal. Thus, a customer could not use the phone inside buildings or cars. Iridium did offer a roaming service, so that customers had access to cellular networks around the world and to a paging service. Customers had only one phone number for all these services worldwide and received only one bill.

Iridium was concerned about recovering its investment. Therefore, it followed a market-skimming pricing policy, charging up to $3,000 for the phone and up to $7 a minute for calls. The pricing also helped position the phone as a status symbol and attracted the early adopters who were willing to pay a premium to be the first people to get the new phones.

Under Iridium's organizational structure, the regional gateway organizations were responsible for developing distribution and marketing plans for their areas. However, as the initial September 1998 launch date approached, few had done so. Some of the partners lacked telecommunications experience.

Many managers thought it was essential to establish Iridium as a global brand as quickly as possible. Thus, to promote the project, Iridium allocated $125 million to fund a campaign in 50 countries. Double-page spreads in top magazines trumpeted the successful executive's need to be connected, in touch, and in control. The ads, television commercials, and direct mail pieces flattered and frightened the executives. One print ad noted, "If you are going to own the world, you'll need a phone that can follow you around it." APL varied the promotions by region (in as many as 20 languages), but the universal theme was the thrill and anxiety of global success.

The advertising started three months before the September launch in order to build excitement. Within a few weeks, more than a million customers inquired about Iridium. The company forwarded the inquiries to the regional partners but most of them were unable or unprepared to follow up. Further, when the company finally launched the service in November 1998, phones were in short supply. By August 1999, the company admitted it had only about 20,000 subscribers, well below the number it had predicted and the 500,000 customers it needed to cover its $1 billion annual operating costs and to pay the banks. The company dialed 911—filing for bankruptcy and seeking reorganization.

CAN GLOBALSTAR SUCCEED?

One reason for Iridium's haste was its knowledge that its competitors were right behind it. Globalstar, ICO Global Communications, Teledesic, and Ellipso were all preparing to build satellite telephone systems. ICO, however, followed Iridium into bankruptcy.

Globalstar, headquartered in San Jose, California, had a target launch date in 1999 and planned to invest $3.8 billion in its 48-satellite system. Loral Space and Communications and Qualcomm were the primary investors.

Globalstar's team is now trying to avoid Iridium's mistakes. Whereas Iridium targeted the traveling VIP executive wherever the executive might go, Globalstar is seeking to provide domestic service in developing countries, not international traffic. Bernard Schwartz, the CEO of Globalstar and Loral, argues that the primary customers are people who do not have phones, and who live in areas where there is no cellular service. These people are still integrated, through business or other relationships, with more populated business centers. Although VIPs may use the Globalstar's service, Schwartz wants to target people who live in the semimodern world, but who are missing instant communication. Schwartz believes that Mexico, Canada, Brazil, India, China, Indonesia, and Russia are key markets. Another Globalstar executive suggests that vertical markets such as natural-resource companies, offshore oil rigs, and construction companies will be important.

Globalstar has designed multimode phones that let users switch between cellular and satellite service, giving them the ability to get full coverage at the cheapest prices. The phone also has accessories that allow use in cars or on ships. In addition to vocal communication, Globalstar offers roaming,

positioning, facsimile, and data transmission services. The company has priced its phone at about $1,250, with service at about $1.25 per minute. Although these prices are still much higher than a $200 Nokia phone and $.10 per minute cellular service, Globalstar's target customers often don't have those choices.

To build its service infrastructure, Globalstar sells access to its system to regional and local telecom service companies worldwide. These companies partner with other local companies to provide the telecom services best suited to the local customers' needs. By complementing rather than competing with land-based telecom networks, Globalstar believes it will open up markets and bring telephone service to new areas.

The company figures it needs only about 200,000 subscribers to break even. However, getting those 200,000 customers is no sure thing. Schwartz and the other managers face numerous challenges. Getting 48 satellites in orbit is no small task. In September 1998, a Ukranian-made rocket took off from the Baikonur Cosmodrome launch complex in Kazakhstan with 12 of Globalstar's satellites. The rocket crashed and burned, destroying $100 million worth of satellites. The crash delayed Globalstar's liftoff because it needed 32 satellites in orbit to begin service. On October 11, 1999, the company announced the official introduction of its service, which it planned to roll out regionally in areas of the world served by its nine operational gateways.

Finally, on November 22, 1999, Globalstar announced that it had deployed four additional satellites, giving it a total of 48 in orbit. It will be able to start full commercial service in early 2000 after four additional backup satellites are in place.

Even with the satellites in place, Globalstar still has to deal with more than 100 government regulators, handle currency crises, and complete construction of its 36 gateways. Perhaps, however, the most difficult problem in the wake of Iridium's bankruptcy is to persuade investors to put up billions of dollars to support the venture.

Talk about a long-distance call! Iridium's failure has caused analysts to question whether there really is a market for satellite phone service. It's up to Globalstar to answer that question by proving that people everywhere want to be connected.

Questions

1. Chapter 1 develops the theme of "connectedness." What examples of connectedness do you see in the Globalstar case?
2. What customer needs and wants lead to the demand for satellite telephone service?
3. How have changes in the marketing environment affected demand for telephone services? Do you think there is a market for satellite telephone service?
4. What marketing mistakes did Iridium make? Why do you think it made these mistakes?

5. Outline Globalstar's marketing process, including its segmentation, targeting, positioning, and marketing mix decisions. Do you believe that it will be more successful than Iridium? Why or why not?

6. What marketing recommendations would you make to Globalstar?

Sources: Excerpts from Iridium advertisement, *Wall Street Journal,* August 25, 1999, p. B7. Other sources include James Surowiecki, "The Latest Satellite Startup Lifts Off. Will It Too Explode?" *Fortune,* October 25, 1999, pp. 236–38; "A New Satellite System Clambers onto the Launchpad," *Business Week,* September 6, 1999, p. 35; Quentin Hardy, "Surviving Iridium," *Forbes,* September 6, 1999, p. 216; Leslie Cauley, "Iridium's Downfall: The Marketing Took a Back Seat to Science," *Wall Street Journal,* August 18, 1999, p. A1, Sally Beatty, "Iridium Hopes Satellite Phone Will Hook Professionals," *Wall Street Journal,* June 22, 1998, p. B6; Quentin Hardy, "To Sell a World Phone, Play to Executive Fears of Being Out of Touch," *Wall Street Journal,* June 4, 1998, p. A1. Also see www.globalstar.com and www.iridium.com.

After reading this chapter, you should be able to
1. explain the importance of information to the company
2. define the marketing information system and discuss its parts
3. outline the steps in the marketing research process
4. compare the advantages and disadvantages of various methods of collecting information.
5. discuss the special issues some marketing researchers face, including public policy and ethics issues

CHAPTER 4

MARKETING RESEARCH AND INFORMATION SYSTEMS

In 1985, in what has now become an all-time classic marketing tale, the Coca-Cola Company made a major marketing blunder. After 99 successful years, it set aside its long-standing rule—"Don't mess with Mother Coke"—and dropped its original formula Coke! In its place came *New* Coke with a sweeter, smoother taste.

At first, amid the introductory flurry of advertising and publicity, New Coke sold well. But sales soon went flat, as a stunned public reacted. Coke began receiving sacks of mail and more than 1,500 phone calls each day from angry consumers. A group called "Old Cola Drinkers" staged protests, handed out T-shirts, and threatened a class-action suit unless Coca-Cola brought back the old formula. After only three months, the Coca-Cola Company brought old Coke back. Now called "Coke Classic," it sold side-by-side with New Coke on supermarket shelves. The company said that New Coke would remain its flagship brand, but consumers had a different idea. By the end of that year, Classic was outselling New Coke in supermarkets by two to one.

Quick reaction saved the company from potential disaster. It stepped up efforts for Coke Classic and slotted New Coke into a supporting role. Coke Classic again became the company's main brand, and the country's leading soft drink. New Coke became the company's "attack brand"—its Pepsi stopper—and ads boldly compared New Coke's taste with Pepsi's. Still, New Coke managed only a 2 percent market share. In the spring of 1990, the company repackaged New Coke and relaunched it as a brand extension with a new name, Coke II. Today, Coke Classic captures more than 20 percent of the U.S. soft drink market; Coke II holds a miniscule 0.1 percent.

Why was New Coke introduced in the first place? What went wrong? Many analysts blame the blunder on poor marketing research.

In the early 1980s, although Coke was still the leading soft drink, it was slowly losing market share to Pepsi. For years, Pepsi had successfully mounted the "Pepsi Challenge," a series of televised taste tests showing that consumers preferred the sweeter taste of Pepsi. By early 1985, although Coke led in the overall market, Pepsi led in share of supermarket sales by 2 percent. (That doesn't sound like much, but 2 percent of the huge U.S. soft drink market amounts to more than $1 billion in retail sales!) Coca-Cola had to do something to stop the loss of its market share, and the solution appeared to be a change in Coke's taste.

Coca-Cola began the largest new-product research project in the company's history. It spent more than two years and $4 million on research before settling on a new formula. It conducted some 200,000 taste tests—30,000 on the final formula alone. In blind tests, 60 percent of consumers chose the new Coke over the old, and 52 percent chose it over Pepsi. Research showed that New Coke would be a winner, and the company introduced it with confidence. So what happened?

Looking back, we can see that Coke defined its marketing research problem too narrowly. The research looked only at taste; it did not explore consumers' feelings about dropping the old Coke and replacing it with a new version. It took no account of the *intangibles*—Coke's name, history, packaging, cultural heritage, and image. However, to many people, Coke stands alongside baseball, hot dogs, and apple pie as an American institution; it represents the very fabric of America. Coke's symbolic meaning turned out to be more important to many consumers than its taste. Research addressing a broader set of issues would have detected these strong emotions.

Coke's managers may also have used poor judgment in interpreting the research and planning strategies around it. For example, they took the finding that 60 percent of consumers preferred New Coke's taste to mean that the new product would win in the marketplace, as when a political candidate wins with 60 percent of the vote. But it also meant that 40 percent still liked the original formula. By dropping the old Coke, the company trampled the taste buds of the large core of loyal Coke drinkers who didn't want a change. The company might have been wiser to leave the old Coke alone and introduce New Coke as a brand extension, as it later did successfully with Cherry Coke.

The Coca-Cola Company has one of the largest, best-managed, and most advanced marketing research operations in America. Good marketing research has kept the company atop the rough-and-tumble soft drink market for decades. But marketing research is far from an exact science. Consumers are full of surprises and figuring them out can be awfully tough. If Coca-Cola can make a large marketing research mistake, any company can.[1]

In order to produce superior value and satisfaction for customers, companies need information at almost every turn. As the New Coke story highlights, good products and marketing programs begin with a thorough understanding of consumer needs and wants. Companies also need an abundance of information on competitors, resellers, and other actors and forces in the marketplace.

Increasingly, marketers are viewing information not just as an input for making better decisions but also as an important strategic asset and marketing tool. In today's marketing, a company's information may prove to be its chief competitive advantage. Competitors can copy each other's equipment, products, and procedures, but they cannot duplicate the company's information and intellectual capital. Several companies have recently recognized this by appointing vice presidents of knowledge, learning, or intellectual capital.[2]

A century ago, most companies were small and knew their customers firsthand. Managers picked up marketing information by being around people, observing them, and asking questions. In more recent times, however, many factors have increased the need for more, better, and faster information. As companies become national or international in scope, they need more information on larger, more distant markets. As incomes increase and buyers become more selective, sellers need better information about how buyers respond to different products and appeals. As sellers use more complex marketing approaches and face more competition, they need information on the effectiveness of their marketing tools. Finally, in today's more rapidly changing environments, managers need more up-to-date information to make timely decisions.

Fortunately, increasing information requirements have been met by an explosion of information technologies. The past 30 years have witnessed the emergence of small but powerful computers, fax machines, CD-ROM drives, videoconferencing, the Internet, and a host of other advances that have revolutionized information handling. Using improved information systems, companies can now generate information in great quantities.

In fact, today's managers often receive too much information. For example, one study found that with all the companies offering data, and with all the information now available through supermarket scanners, a packaged-goods brand manager is bombarded with 1 million to 1 *billion* new numbers each week. Another study found that, on average, American office workers spend 60 percent of their time processing documents; a typical manager reads about a million words a week. The typical business Internet user receives 25 e-mails a day; 15 percent of users receive between 50 and 100 e-mails per day. Thus, the running out of information is not a problem but seeing through the "data smog" is.[3]

Despite this data glut, marketers frequently complain that they lack enough information of the *right* kind. For example, a recent survey of managers found that although half the respondents said they couldn't cope with the volume of information coming at them, two-thirds wanted even more. The researcher concluded that, "despite the volume, they're still not getting what they want."[4] Thus, most marketing managers don't need *more* information, they need *better* information. Companies have greater capacity to provide managers with good information, but often have not made good use of it. Many companies are now studying their managers' information needs and designing information systems to meet those needs.

THE MARKETING INFORMATION SYSTEM

Marketing information system (MIS)

People, equipment, and procedures to gather, sort, analyze, evaluate, and distribute needed, timely, and accurate information to marketing decision makers.

A **marketing information system (MIS)** consists of people, equipment, and procedures to gather, sort, analyze, evaluate, and distribute needed, timely, and accurate information to marketing decision makers. Figure 4.1 shows that the MIS begins and ends with marketing managers. First, it interacts with these managers to *assess information needs.* Next, it *develops needed information* from internal company data, marketing intelligence activities, marketing research, and information analysis. Finally, the MIS *distributes information* to managers in the right form at the right time to help them make better marketing decisions.

Assessing Information Needs

A good marketing information system balances the information managers would *like* to have against what they really *need* and what is *feasible* to offer. The company begins by interviewing managers to find out what information they would like. Some managers will ask for whatever information they can get without thinking carefully about what they really need. Too much information can be as harmful as too little. Other managers may omit things they ought to know or may not know to ask for some types of information they should have. For example, managers might need to know that a competitor plans to introduce a new product during the coming year. Because they do not know about the new product, they do not think to ask about it. The MIS must watch the marketing environment in order to provide decision makers with information they should have to make key marketing decisions.

FIGURE 4.1   The marketing information system

Sometimes the company cannot provide the needed information, either because it is not available or because of MIS limitations. For example, a brand manager might want to know how competitors will change their advertising budgets next year and how these changes will affect industry market shares. The information on planned budgets probably is not available. Even if it is, the company's MIS may not be advanced enough to forecast resulting changes in market shares.

Finally, the costs of obtaining, processing, storing, and delivering information can mount quickly. The company must decide whether the benefits of having additional information are worth the costs of providing it, and both value and cost are often hard to assess. By itself, information has no worth; its value comes from its *use*. In many cases, additional information will do little to change or improve a manager's decision, or the costs of the information may exceed the returns from the improved decision. Marketers should not assume that additional information will always be worth obtaining. Rather, they should weigh carefully the costs of additional information against the benefits resulting from it.

Developing Information

The information needed by marketing managers can be obtained from *internal data, marketing intelligence,* and *marketing research.* The information analysis system then processes this information to make it more useful for managers.

Internal Data

Internal databases
Computerized collections of information obtained from data sources within the company.

Many companies build extensive **internal databases,** computerized collections of information obtained from data sources within the company. Marketing managers can readily access and work with information in the database to identify marketing opportunities and problems, plan programs, and evaluate performance.

Information in the database can come from many sources. The accounting department prepares financial statements and keeps detailed records of sales, costs, and cash flows. Manufacturing reports on production schedules, shipments, and inventories. The sales force reports on reseller reactions and competitor activities. The marketing department furnishes information on customer demographics, psychographics, and buying behavior, and the customer service department keeps records of customer satisfaction or service problems. Research studies done for one department may provide useful information for several others.

Here is an example of how one company uses internal databases to make better marketing decisions:[5]

> ★ USAA, which provides financial services to U.S. military personnel and their families, maintains a customer database built from customer purchasing histories and from information collected directly from customers. To keep the database fresh, the organization regularly surveys its 3 million customers worldwide to learn such things as whether they have children (and if so, how old they are), if they have moved recently, and when they plan to retire. USAA uses the database to tailor marketing offers to the specific needs of individual customers. For example, if the family has college-age children, the USAA sends those children information on how to manage their credit cards. If the family has younger children, it sends booklets on things like financing a child's education. Or, for customers looking toward retirement, it sends information on estate planning. Through skillful use of its database, USAA serves each customer uniquely, resulting in high levels of customer loyalty—the roughly $7 billion company retains 97 percent of its customers. Says USAA's chief marketing executive, "We make it a point, in all of our materials, to let [customers] know that we're there for them as they make transactions."

Internal databases usually can be accessed more quickly and cheaply than other information sources, but they also present some problems. Because internal information was collected for other purposes, it may be incomplete or in the wrong form for making marketing decisions. For example, sales and cost data used by the accounting department for preparing financial statements must be adapted for use in evaluating product, sales force, or channel performance. Data ages quickly; keeping the database current requires a major effort. In addition, a large company produces mountains of information, and keeping track of it all is difficult. The database information must be well integrated and readily accessible through user-friendly interfaces so that managers can find it easily and use it effectively.

Every company contains more information than any manager can possibly know or analyze. The information is scattered in countless databases, plans, and records, and in heads of many longtime managers. The company must somehow bring order to its information gold mine so that its managers can more easily find answers to questions and make informed decisions. Increasingly, companies are creating *data warehouses* to house their customer data in a single, more accessible location. Then, using powerful *data mining* techniques, they search for meaningful patterns in the data and communicate them to managers (see Marketing Highlight 4.1).

Marketing Intelligence

Marketing intelligence is the systematic collection and analysis of publicly available information about competitors and developments in the marketing environment. A marketing intelligence system gathers, analyzes, and distributes information about the company's competitive, technological, customer, economic, social, and political and regulatory environments. Its goal is to improve strategic decision making, assess and track competitors' actions, and provide early warning of opportunities and threats. The

Marketing intelligence
Everyday information about developments in the marketing environment that helps managers prepare and adjust marketing plans.

DATA MINING: THERE'S GOLD IN THEM "THAR" DATABASES

Most companies are awash in information about their customers. The trouble is that this information is widely scattered across the organization. It's buried deep in the separate databases, plans, and records of many different company functions and departments. To remedy this problem, more and more companies are now developing *data warehouses* and using sophisticated *data mining* techniques to unearth data riches they didn't realize they had.

A data warehouse is a company-wide storehouse of customer information—a centralized database of finely detailed customer data that needs to be sifted through for gems. The purpose of a data warehouse is not to gather information—many companies have already amassed endless stores of information about their customers. Rather, the purpose is to allow managers to get at the information the company already has. Then, once the data warehouse brings the data together for analysis, the company uses high-powered data mining techniques to sift through the mounds of data and dig out interesting relationships and findings about customers.

Companies can gain many benefits from careful data warehousing and data mining. By understanding customers better, they can provide higher levels of customer service and develop deeper customer relationships. They can use the data to pinpoint high-value customers, target them more effectively, cross-sell the company's products, and create offers tailored to specific customer requirements.

For example, MCI Communications Corporation, the long-distance carrier, sifts through 1 trillion bytes of customer phoning data to craft new discount calling plans for different types of customers. Marriott's Vacation Club International has managed to reduce its volume of mail offers while at the same time increase its response rate by developing a model showing which customers in its database are most likely to respond to specific vacation

During the past few years, data warehousing and data mining have exploded onto the corporate research scene. Here, SPSS advertises data mining software, showing all of its potential uses.

offerings. Tesco, the British supermarket chain, notifies carefully selected groups, such as wine buyers or cheese buyers, when there will be a special sale of wine or cheese. Lands' End can tell which of its 2 million customers should receive special mailings of specific clothing items that would fit their wardrobe needs.

Here are some more detailed examples of companies that are benefiting from data warehousing and data mining.

- Companies such as the Limited, Federal Express, and U S West are now creating vast data warehouses that allow them to pinpoint which customers are profitable and which are not. For example, twice a year U S West sifts through its customer list looking for customers that have the potential to be more profitable. The company's database contains as many as 200 observations about each customer's calling patterns. By looking at demographic profiles, plus the mix of local versus long-distance calls or whether a consumer has voice mail, U S West can estimate potential spending. Next, the company determines how much of the customer's likely telecom budget is already coming its way. Armed with that knowledge, U S West sets a cutoff point for how much to spend marketing to this customer.

- Ping, the golf equipment manufacturer, has used data warehousing successfully for about two years. Its warehouse contains customer-specific data about every golf club it has manufactured and sold for the past 15 years. The database, which includes grip size and special assembly instructions, helps Ping design and build golf clubs specifically for each of its customers and allows for easy replacement. If a golfer needs a

new nine iron, for example, he or she can call in the serial number and Ping will ship an exact club to him or her within two days of receiving the order—a process that used to take two to three weeks. This faster processing of data has given Ping a competitive edge in a market saturated with new products. "We've been up; the golf market has been down," says Steve Bostwick, Ping's marketing manager. Bostwick estimates the golf market to be down about 15 percent, but he says Ping has experienced double-digit growth.

- A leading clothing catalog company with over 2 million customers invited IBM to mine its data and help it discover customer groupings. Instead of coming up with the usual 5 segments, or 50 niches, the IBM researchers identified 5,000 market cells. IBM found, for example, that 850 customers of the catalog company had purchased a blue shirt and a red tie! Now the reason this is interesting is that these buyers would probably be more interested in buying, say, a navy blue jacket than the average customer of the catalog company. It might pay for the cataloger to send a letter to just these 850 customers offering a very special price on a navy blue jacket. If the company is correct, the response rate in this market cell could be as high as 10 percent.

Most experts believe that a good data warehouse, by itself, can give a company a significant competitive advantage. No wonder that, at a secret location in Phoenix, security guards watch over American Express's 500 billion bytes of data on how its customers have used the company's 35 million green, gold, and platinum charge cards. Amex uses the database to include precisely

targeted offers in its monthly mailing of millions of customer bills.

Data warehousing and data mining benefits don't come without heavy cost, not only in collecting the original customer data but also in maintaining and mining it. But when it works, the benefits usually outweigh the costs. One recent study estimated that the average return on investment for a data warehouse over the course of three years is more than 400 percent. FedEx reports even more impressive returns, claiming that such techniques have helped it achieve an 8-to-1 return on its direct-marketing dollars.

During the past few years, data warehousing and data mining have exploded onto the corporate research scene. According to one recent study, over 90 percent of Fortune 2000 firms either have a data warehouse or are in the process of developing one. "No question that companies are getting tremendous value out of this," says David Bramblett, owner of Data Warehouse Solutions. "Companies [are] looking for ways to bring disparate sources of customer information together, then get it to all the customer touch points." Adds another data warehousing consultant, these powerful new techniques can unearth "a wealth of information to target that customer, to hit their hot button."

Sources: Quotes and excerpts from Sara Sellar, "Dust Off That Data," *Sales & Marketing Management,* May 1999, pp. 71–72; "What've You Done for Us Lately?" *Business Week,* September 14, 1998, pp. 142–48; and Philip Kotler, *Kotler on Marketing* (New York: Free Press, 1999), p. 29. Also see Stewart Deck, "Data Mining," *Computerworld,* March 29, 1999, p. 76; and Sunny Baker and Kim Baker, "The Best Little Warehouse in Business," *The Journal of Business Strategy,* March–April 1999, pp. 32–37.

marketing intelligence system determines what intelligence is needed, collects it by searching the environment, and delivers it to marketing managers.

Competitive intelligence gathering has grown dramatically as more and more companies are now busily snooping on their competitors. Techniques range from quizzing the company's own employees and benchmarking competitors' products to researching the Internet, lurking around industry trade shows, and rooting through rivals' trash bins.

Much intelligence can be collected from the company's own personnel—executives, engineers and scientists, purchasing agents, and the sales force. For example, a few years back, Xerox learned that listening to its own salespeople could pay off handsomely.

★ While talking with a Kodak copier salesperson, a Xerox technician learned that the salesperson was being trained to service Xerox products. The Xerox employee reported back to his boss, who in turn passed the news to Xerox's intelligence unit. Using such clues as a classified ad Kodak placed seeking new people with Xerox product experience, Xerox verified Kodak's plan—code-named Ulysses—to service Xerox copiers. To protect its profitable service business, Xerox designed a Total Satisfaction Guarantee, which allowed copier returns for any reason as long as *Xerox* did the servicing. By the time Kodak launched Ulysses, Xerox had been promoting its new program for three months.[6]

However, company people are often busy and fail to pass on important information. The company must sell its people on their importance as intelligence gatherers, train them to spot new developments, interact with them on an ongoing basis, and urge them to report intelligence back to the company.

The company can also get suppliers, resellers, and key customers to pass along important intelligence about competitors and their products. For example, prior to introducing its Good News disposable razor in the United States, Gillette told a large Canadian account about the planned U.S. introduction date. The Canadian distributor promptly called Bic and told it about the impending product launch. By putting on a crash program, Bic was able to start selling its razor shortly after Gillette did.

The company can obtain good information by observing competitors or analyzing physical evidence. It can buy and analyze competitors' products, monitor their sales, and check for new patents. For example, to design the first Taurus models, Ford compiled a list of more than 400 features its customers said they liked best about competing cars. Then it matched or topped the best of the competition. The result: Taurus soon became America's best-selling car.

Companies can also examine other types of physical evidence. For example, to gauge competitor shipping volumes, some companies have measured the rust on rails of railroad sidings to their competitors' plants or watched competitors' loading docks at the end of a quarter to see how much merchandise was being moved at the last minute. Other firms regularly check out competitors' parking lots—full lots might indicate plenty of work and prosperity; half-full lots might suggest hard times.[7]

Some companies even rifle their competitors' garbage, which is legally considered abandoned property once it leaves the premises. Although most companies now shred technical documents, they may overlook the almost-as-revealing refuse from the marketing or public relations departments. In one example of garbage snatching, Avon admitted that it had hired private detectives to paw through the dumpster of rival Mary Kay Cosmetics. An outraged Mary Kay sued to get its garbage back, but Avon claimed that it had done nothing illegal. The dumpster had been located in a public parking lot, and Avon had videotapes to prove it.[8]

Government agencies are another good intelligence source. For example, a company can't legally photograph a competitor's plant from the air. However, publicly available aerial photos are often on file with the U.S. Geological Survey or Environmental Protection Agency. In another instance, a company attempting to assess the capacity of a competitor's plant struck gold when it found that a publicly available Uniform Commercial Code filing the competitor had submitted to the state contained a detailed list of all the equipment in the competitor's plant.

Competitors themselves may reveal information through their annual reports, business publications, trade show exhibits, press releases, advertisements, and Web pages. The Internet is proving to be a vast new source of competitor-supplied information. Most companies now place volumes of information on their Web sites, providing details to attract customers, partners, suppliers, or franchisees, and that same information is available to competitors at the click of a mouse button. Press releases that never made it into the press are posted on Web sites, letting firms keep abreast of competitors' new products and organizational changes. Help wanted ads posted on the Web quickly reveal competitors' expansion priorities. For example, check Allied Signal's Web site and you'll find that it provides revenue goals and reveals the company's production-defect rate along with its plans to improve it. Mail Boxes Etc., a chain of mailing services, provides data on its average franchise, including square footage, number of employees, operating hours, and more—all valuable insights for a competitor.

It's not only company-sponsored Web sites that hold rich competitor intelligence booty. Researchers can also glean valuable nuggets of information from trade association Web sites. For example, when he was controller of Stone Container's specialty-packaging division, Gary Owen visited a trade association Web site and noticed that a rival had won an award for a new process using ultraviolet-resistant lacquers. The site revealed the machines' configuration and run rate, which Stone's engineers used to figure out how to replicate the process.[9]

Using Internet search engines such as Yahoo! or Infoseek, marketers can search specific competitor names, events, or trends and see what turns up. Intelligence seekers also pore through any of thousands of online databases. Some are free. For example, the U.S. Security and Exchange Commission's Edgar database (www.sec.gov) provides access to a huge stockpile of financial and other information on public companies. For a fee, companies can subscribe to any of more than 3,000 *online databases* and information search services such as Dialog, DataStar, LEXIS-NEXIS, Dow Jones News Retrieval, UMI ProQuest, and Dun & Bradstreet's Online Access. We discuss these and other online data services in more detail later in the chapter. Using such databases, companies can conduct complex information searches in a flash from the comfort of their keyboards.

One Internet site (www.fuld.com) provides a Competitive Intelligence Guide offering sleuthing tips. Another Web service—Company Sleuth (www.company sleuth.com)—provides users with a steady stream of intelligence data gleaned from the Internet. It searches the Web and gives users daily e-mail reports detailing the business activities, financial moves, and Internet dealings of competitors, prospects, and clients, often before the information is officially reported. "In today's information age, companies are leaving a paper trail of information online," says Joshua Kopelman, executive vice president of Infonautics, the company that offers the service. "Company Sleuth uncovers hard-to-find and seemingly hidden business news and information for users so they don't have to simply rely on old news or intuition when making investment and business decisions."[10]

Some companies set up an office to collect and circulate marketing intelligence. The staff scans major publications, searches the Internet, summarizes important news, and sends bulletins to marketing managers. It develops a file of intelligence information and helps managers evaluate new information. These services greatly improve the quality of information available to marketing managers.

The growing use of marketing intelligence raises a number of ethical issues. Although most of the preceding techniques are legal, and some are considered to be shrewdly competitive, many involve questionable ethics. Clearly, companies should take advantage of publicly available information. However, they should not stoop to snoop. With all the legitimate intelligence sources now available, a company does not have to break the law or accepted codes of ethics to get good intelligence.[11]

Marketing Research

In addition to information about competitors and environmental happenings, marketers often need formal studies of specific situations. For example, Toshiba wants to know how many and what kinds of people or companies will buy its new super-fast notebook computer. Or Barat College in Lake Forest, Illinois, needs to know what percentage of its target market has heard of Barat, how they heard, what they know, and how they feel about Barat. In such situations, the marketing intelligence system will not provide the detailed information needed. Managers will need marketing research.

Marketing research
The systematic design, collection, analysis, and reporting of data relevant to a specific marketing situation facing an organization.

We define **marketing research** as the systematic design, collection, analysis, and reporting of data relevant to a specific marketing situation facing an organization. Every marketer needs research. Marketing researchers engage in a wide variety of activities, ranging from market potential and market share studies, to assessments of customer satisfaction and purchase behavior, to studies of pricing, product, distribution, and promotion activities.

A company can conduct marketing research in its own research department or have some or all of it done outside, depending on its own research skills and resources. Although most large companies have their own marketing research departments, they often use outside firms to do special research tasks or special studies. A company with no research department has to buy the services of research firms.

Information Analysis

Information gathered by the company's marketing intelligence and marketing research systems often requires more analysis, and sometimes managers may need more help to apply the information to their marketing problems and decisions. This help may include advanced statistical analysis to learn more about both the relationships within a set of data and their statistical reliability. Such analysis allows managers to go beyond means and standard deviations in the data and to answer questions about markets, marketing activities, and outcomes.

Information analysis might also involve a collection of analytical models that will help marketers make better decisions. Each model represents some real system, process, or outcome. These models can help answer the questions of *what if* and *which is best*. During the past 20 years, marketing scientists have developed numerous models to help marketing managers make better marketing mix decisions, design sales territories and sales call plans, select sites for retail outlets, develop optimal advertising mixes, and forecast new-product sales.[12]

Company Sleuth intelligence service (www.companysleuth.com) provides users with a steady stream of intelligence data gleaned from the Internet.

Distributing Information

Marketing information has no value until managers use it to make better marketing decisions. The information gathered through marketing intelligence and marketing research must be distributed to the right marketing managers at the right time. Most companies have centralized marketing information systems that provide managers with regular performance reports, intelligence updates, and reports on the results of studies. Managers need these routine reports for making regular planning, implementation, and control decisions. But marketing managers may also need nonroutine information for special situations and on-the-spot decisions. For example, a sales manager having trouble with a large customer may want a summary of the account's sales and profitability over the past year. Or a retail store manager who has run out of a best-selling product may want to know the current inventory levels in the chain's other stores.

Developments in information technology have caused a revolution in information distribution. With recent advances in computers, software, and telecommunication, most companies have decentralized their marketing information systems. In most companies today, marketing managers have direct access to the information network, at any time and from virtually any location.

While working at a home office, in a hotel room, on an airplane—any place where they can turn on a laptop computer and phone in—today's managers can obtain information from company databases or outside information services, analyze the information using statistical packages and models, prepare reports using word processing and presentation software, and communicate with others in the network through electronic communications. Such systems offer exciting prospects. They allow managers to get the information they need directly and quickly and to tailor it to their own needs.

THE MARKETING RESEARCH PROCESS

The marketing research process (see Figure 4.2) has four steps: *defining the problem and research objectives, developing the research plan, implementing the research plan,* and *interpreting and reporting the findings.*

Defining the Problem and Research Objectives

The marketing manager and the researcher must work closely together to define the problem carefully, and they must agree on the research objectives. The manager best understands the decision for which information is needed; the researcher best understands marketing research and how to obtain the information.

Managers should know enough about marketing research to help in the planning and the interpretation of research results. If they know little about marketing research, they may obtain the wrong information, accept wrong conclusions, or ask for information that costs too much. Experienced marketing researchers who understand the manager's problem should also be involved at this stage. The researcher must be able to help the manager define the problem and suggest ways that research can help the manager make better decisions.

Defining the problem and research objectives is often the hardest step in the research process. The manager may know that something is wrong, without knowing the specific causes. For example, managers of a large discount retail store chain hastily decided that falling sales were caused by poor advertising, and they ordered research to test the company's advertising. When this research showed that current advertising was reaching the right people with the right message, the managers were puzzled. It turned out that the real problem was that the chain was not delivering the prices, products, and service promised in the advertising. Careful problem definition would have avoided the cost and delay of doing advertising research. In the classic New Coke case, Coca-Cola defined its research problem too narrowly, with disastrous results.

Exploratory research
Marketing research to gather preliminary information that will help define problems and suggest hypotheses.

Descriptive research
Marketing research to better describe marketing problems, situations, or markets, such as the market potential for a product or the demographics and attitudes of consumers.

Causal research
Marketing research to test hypotheses about cause-and-effect relationships.

After the problem has been defined carefully, the manager and researcher must set the research objectives. A marketing research project might have one of three types of objectives. The objective of **exploratory research** is to gather preliminary information that will help define the problem and suggest hypotheses. The objective of **descriptive research** is to describe things such as the market potential for a product or the demographics and attitudes of consumers who buy the product. The objective of **causal research** is to test hypotheses about cause-and-effect relationships. For example, would a 10 percent decrease in tuition at a private college result in an enrollment increase sufficient to offset the reduced tuition? Managers often start with exploratory research and later follow with descriptive or causal research.

The statement of the problem and research objectives guides the entire research process. The manager and researcher should put the statement in writing to be certain that they agree on the purpose and expected results of the research.

FIGURE 4.2   The marketing research process

Developing the Research Plan

The second step of the marketing research process calls for determining the information needed, developing a plan for gathering it efficiently, and presenting the plan to marketing management. The plan outlines sources of existing data and spells out the specific research approaches, contact methods, sampling plans, and instruments that researchers will use to gather new data.

Determining Specific Information Needs

Research objectives must be translated into specific information needs. For example, suppose Campbell decides to conduct research on how consumers would react to the company replacing its familiar red-and-white condensed soup can with a container more relevant to today's consumer lifestyles.[13] It's considering the introduction of new bowl-shaped plastic containers that it has used successfully for a number of its other products. The containers would cost more but would allow consumers to heat the soup in a microwave oven without adding water or milk and to eat it without using dishes. This research might call for the following specific information:

★ The demographic, economic, and lifestyle characteristics of current soup users. (Busy working couples might find the convenience of the new packaging worth the price; families with children might want to pay less and wash the pan and bowls.)

★ Consumer-usage patterns for soup: how much soup they eat, where, and when. (The new packaging might be ideal for adults eating lunch on the go, but less convenient for parents feeding lunch to several children.)

★ Retailer reactions to the new packaging. (Failure to get retailer support could hurt sales of the new package.)

★ Consumer attitudes toward the new packaging. (The red-and-white Campbell can has become an American institution—will consumers accept the new packaging?)

★ Forecasts of sales of both new and current packages. (Will the new packaging increase Campbell's profits?)

Campbell managers will need these and many other types of information to decide whether to introduce the new packaging.

Gathering Secondary Information

Secondary data
Information that already exists somewhere, having been collected for another purpose.

Primary data
Information collected for the specific purpose at hand.

To meet the manager's information needs, the researcher can gather secondary data, primary data, or both. **Secondary data** consist of information that already exists somewhere, having been collected for another purpose. **Primary data** consist of information collected for the specific purpose at hand.

Researchers usually start by gathering secondary data. The company's internal database provides a good starting point. However, the company can also tap a wide assortment of external information sources, ranging from company, public, and university libraries to government and business publications. Table 4.1 describes a number of other important sources of secondary data, including commercial data services, online database services, and Internet data sources.

Commercial Data Sources.   Companies can buy secondary data reports from outside suppliers. For example, Nielsen Marketing Research sells data on brand shares, retail prices, and percentages of stores stocking different brands. Information Resources, Inc. sells supermarket scanner purchase data from a panel of 60,000 households nationally, with measures of trial and repeat purchasing, brand loyalty,

TABLE 4.1   COMMERCIAL, ONLINE DATABASE, AND INTERNET DATA SOURCES

Commercial Data Services

Here are just a few of the dozens of commercial research houses selling data to subscribers:

AC Nielsen Corporation provides supermarket scanner data on sales, market share, and retail prices (ScanTrack), data on household purchasing (ScanTrack National Electronic Household Panel), data on television audiences (Nielsen National Television Index), and others.

Information Resources, Inc. provides supermarket scanner data for tracking grocery product movement (InfoScan) and single-source data collection (BehaviorScan).

The Arbitron Company provides local-market radio audience and advertising expenditure information, along with a wealth of other media and ad spending data.

PMSI/Source Infomatics provides reports on the movement of pharmaceuticals, hospital laboratory supplies, animal health products, and personal care products.

MMRI (Simmons Market Research Bureau) provides reports covering television markets, sporting goods, and proprietary drugs, giving lifestyle and geodemographic data by sex, income, age, and brand preferences (selective markets and media reaching them).

Dun & Bradstreet provides a database containing information on more than 50 million individual companies around the globe—who they are, where they are, and what they do.

Online Database Services

Here are only a few of the many online database services:

Dialog offers several services, including ABI/INFORM, which provides information on business management and administration from over 800 publications. The site also provides access to full-text reports and newsletters from 50 industries and a collection of U.S. public opinion surveys. In addition, subscribers can view Dun & Bradstreet data, such as census statistics and business directories, by searching through Donnelly Demographics and Dun's Electronic Business Directory.

LEXIS-NEXIS, in addition to providing access to articles from a wide range of business magazines and journals, features in-depth research reports from research firms, SEC filings, Standard & Poor's, and worldwide investment banks. Users can also access information from consumer goods and marketing trade publications. The service also includes PROMT/PLUS, which tracks competitors and industries, identifies trends, and evaluates advertising and promotion techniques.

CompuServe provides a variety of online database services. For example, its *Business Demographics* files summarize statistics on state employees by industry codes and categorize retail trade businesses by employee counts. By mining the *Neighborhood Report,* a user can access summaries of the demographics of any zip code in the United States. Other CompuServe databases offer full-text articles, news releases, and market and industry research report indices. The service also provides access to an additional 850 databases, ranging from newspapers and newsletters to government reports and patent records.

Dow Jones News Retrieval specializes in providing in-depth financial, historical, and operational information on public and private companies. The site offers Standard & Poor's profiles as well as Dun & Bradstreet profiles and company reports. In addition, the service compares stock price, volume, and data on companies and industries and summarizes same-day business and financial stories from both the United States and Japan.

Internet Data Sources

Most of the above online information services also provide Web-based versions. Literally thousands of other Web sites also offer data, often at little or no cost. The best way to locate such sources is by using Internet search engines to search specific topics. Here is just a tiny sampling of sites offering specialized information on a variety of business related topics.

The **U.S. Securities and Exchange Commission** Edgar database (www.sec.gov) provides financial information on public companies. The **Small Business Administration** (www.sbaonline.gov) site provides a rich variety of information for small business managers, along with links to dozens of other relevant sites. **Avenue Technologies** (www.com.avetech/avenue) presents summaries and full reports on over 25,000 public, private, and international companies. Similarly, **Dun & Bradstreet's Online Access** (www.dbisna.com/dbis/product/secure.html) offers short financial reports on 10 million U.S. companies. In addition to garnering financial information on companies and industries, Internet users can do real-time research. **Ecola's 24-Hour Newsstand** (www.ecola.com/news) links users to the Web sites of over 2,000 newspapers, journals, and computer publications. Researchers can view recent new articles online through *CNN Interactive* (www.cnn.com). Market researchers can visit the **American Demographics** site (www.demographics.com) and browse a directory of marketing experts.

Sources: See Christel Beard and Betsey Wiesendanger, "The Marketer's Guide to Online Databases," *Sales & Marketing Management,* January 1993, pp. 37–41; Susan Greco, "The Online Sleuth," *Inc.,* October 1996, pp. 88–89; Marydee Ojala, "The Daze of Future Business Research," *Online,* January–February 1998, pp. 78–80; Guy Kawasaki, "Get Your Facts Here," *Forbes,* March 23, 1998, p. 156; and Larry Kanaher, *Competitive Intelligence: How to Gather, Analyze, and Use Information to Move Your Business to the Top* (Touchstone Books, 1998).

and buyer demographics. The *Monitor* service by Yankelovich and Partners sells information on important social and lifestyle trends.[14] These and other firms supply high-quality data to suit a wide variety of marketing information needs.

Online databases

Computerized collections of information available from online commercial sources or via the Internet.

Online Databases and Internet Data Sources.   Using commercial **online databases,** marketing researchers can conduct their own searches of secondary data sources. A recent survey of marketing researchers found that 81 percent use such online services for conducting research.[15] A readily available online database exists to fill almost any marketing information need. General database services such as CompuServe, Dialog, and LEXIS-NEXIS put an incredible wealth of information at the keyboards of marketing decision makers. For example, a company doing business in Germany can check out CompuServe's German Company Library of financial and product information on over 48,000 German-owned firms. A U.S. auto parts manufacturer can punch up Dun & Bradstreet Financial Profiles and Company Reports to develop biographical sketches of key General Motors, Ford, and DaimlerChrysler executives. Just about any information a marketer might need—demographic data, today's Associated Press news wire reports, a list of active U.S. trademarks in the United States—is available from online databases.[16]

The Internet offers a mind-boggling array of databases and other secondary information sources, many free to the user. Beyond commercial Web sites offering information for a fee, almost every industry association, government agency, business publication, and news medium offers free information to those tenacious enough to find their Web sites. In fact, there are so many Web sites offering data that finding the right ones can become an almost overwhelming task.

Advantages and Disadvantages of Secondary Data.   Secondary data can usually be obtained more quickly and at a lower cost than primary data. For example, an Internet or online database search might provide all the information Campbell needs on soup usage, quickly and at almost no cost. A study to collect primary information might take weeks or months and cost thousands of dollars. Also, secondary sources sometimes can provide data an individual company cannot collect on its own—information that either is not directly available or would be too expensive to collect. For example, it would be too expensive for Campbell to conduct a continuing retail store audit to find out about the market shares, prices, and displays of

Online database services such as Compuserve, Dialog, and LEXIS-NEXIS put an incredible wealth of information at the keyboards of marketing decision makers.

competitors' brands. But it can buy the InfoScan service from Information Resources, Inc., which provides this information from thousands of scanner-equipped supermarkets in dozens of U.S. markets.

Secondary data can also present problems. The needed information may not exist—researchers can rarely obtain all the data they need from secondary sources. For example, Campbell will not find existing information about consumer reactions to new packaging that it has not yet placed on the market. Even when data can be found, they might not be very usable. The researcher must evaluate secondary information carefully to make certain it is *relevant* (fits research project needs), *accurate* (reliably collected and reported), *current* (up-to-date enough for current decisions), and *impartial* (objectively collected and reported).

Secondary data provide a good starting point for research and often help to define problems and research objectives. In most cases, however, the company must also collect primary data.

Planning Primary Data Collection

Good decisions require good data. Just as researchers must carefully evaluate the quality of secondary information, they also must take great care when collecting primary data to make sure that it will be relevant, accurate, current, and unbiased. Table 4.2 shows that designing a plan for primary data collection calls for a number of decisions on *research approaches, contact methods, sampling plan,* and *research instruments.*

Observational research
The gathering of primary data by observing relevant people, actions, and situations.

Research Approaches.   **Observational research** is the gathering of primary data by observing relevant people, actions, and situations. For example, a maker of personal care products might pretest its ads by showing them to people and measuring eye movements, pulse rates, and other physical reactions. Consumer packaged-goods marketers might visit supermarkets and observe shoppers as they browse the store, pick up products and examine packages, and make actual buying decisions. Or a bank might evaluate possible new branch locations by checking traffic patterns, neighborhood conditions, and the location of competing branches. Steelcase used observation to help design new office furniture for use by work teams.

> ★ To learn firsthand how teams actually operate, it set up video cameras at various companies and studied the tapes, looking for motions and behavior patterns that customers themselves might not even notice. It found that teams work best when they can do some work together and some privately. So Steelcase designed highly successful modular office units called Personal Harbor. These units are "rather like telephone booths in size and shape." They can be arranged around a common space where a team works, letting people work together but also alone when necessary. Says a Steelcase executive, "Market data wouldn't necessarily have pointed us that way. It was more important to know how people actually work."[17]

TABLE 4.2   PLANNING PRIMARY DATA COLLECTION

Research Approaches	Contact Methods	Sampling Plan	Research Instruments
Observation	Mail	Sampling unit	Questionnaire
Survey	Telephone	Sample size	Mechanical instruments
Experiment	Personal	Sampling procedure	
	Online		

Urban Outfitters, the fast-growing specialty clothing chain, prefers observation to other types of market research. "We're not after people's statements," notes the chain's president, "we're after their actions." The company develops customer profiles by videotaping and taking photographs of customers in its stores. This helps managers determine what people are actually wearing and allows them to make quick decisions on merchandise.[18]

Several companies sell information collected through *mechanical* observation. For example, Nielsen Media Research attaches *people meters* to television sets in selected homes to record who watches which programs. It then rates the size and demographic makeup of audiences for different television programs. The television networks use these ratings to judge program popularity and to set charges for advertising time. Advertisers use the ratings when selecting programs for their commercials. *Checkout scanners* in retail stores record consumer purchases in detail. Consumer products companies and retailers use scanner information to assess and improve product sales and store performance. Some marketing research firms now offer **single-source data systems** that electronically monitor both consumers' purchases and consumers' exposure to various marketing activities in an effort to better evaluate the link between the two (see Marketing Highlight 4.2).

Observational research can be used to obtain information that people are unwilling or unable to provide. In some cases, observation may be the only way to obtain the needed information. In contrast, some things simply cannot be observed, such as feelings, attitudes and motives, or private behavior. Long-term or infrequent behavior is also difficult to observe. Because of these limitations, researchers often use observation along with other data collection methods.

Survey research is the approach best suited for gathering *descriptive* information. A company that wants to know about people's knowledge, attitudes, preferences, or buying behavior can often find out by asking individuals directly.

Survey research is the most widely used method for primary data collection, and it is often the only method used in a research study. Researchers interview tens of millions of Americans each year in surveys. The major advantage of survey research is its flexibility. It can be used to obtain many different kinds of information in many different situations. Depending on the survey design, it also may

Single-source data systems
Electronic monitoring systems that link consumers' exposure to television advertising and promotion (measured using television meters) with what they buy in stores (measured using store checkout scanners).

Survey research
The gathering of primary data by asking people questions about their knowledge, attitudes, preferences, and buying behavior.

Observational research: Steelcase set up video cameras at various companies to study motions and behavior patterns that customers themselves might not even notice. The result was the highly successful Personal Harbor modular office units.

MARKETING HIGHLIGHT 4.2

SINGLE-SOURCE DATA SYSTEMS: A POWERFUL WAY TO MEASURE MARKETING IMPACT

Information Resources, Inc. knows all there is to know about the members of its panel households—what they eat for lunch; what they put in

Single-source data systems link marketing efforts directly with consumer buying behavior. Here a BehaviorScan panel member makes a purchase.

their coffee; and what they use to wash their hair, quench their thirsts, or make up their faces. The research company electronically monitors the television programs these people watch and tracks the brands they buy, the coupons they use, where they shop, and what newspapers and magazines they read. These households are a part of IRI's BehaviorScan service, a *single-source data system* that links consumers' exposure to television advertising, sales promotion, and other marketing efforts with their store purchases. BehaviorScan and other single-source data systems have revolutionized the way consumer products companies measure the impact of their marketing activities.

The basics of single-source research are straightforward, and the IRI BehaviorScan system provides a good example. IRI maintains a panel of 2,000 to 3,000 households in each of 7 markets. The company meters each home's television set to track who watches what and when,

provide information more quickly and at lower cost than observational or experimental research.

However, survey research also presents some problems. Sometimes people are unable to answer survey questions because they cannot remember or have never thought about what they do and why. Or people may be unwilling to respond to unknown interviewers or about things they consider private. Respondents may answer survey questions even when they do not know the answer in order to appear smarter or more informed. Or they may try to help the interviewer by giving pleasing answers. Finally, busy people may not take the time, or they might resent the intrusion into their privacy.

Whereas observation is best suited for exploratory research and surveys for descriptive research, **experimental research** is best suited for gathering *causal* information. Experiments involve selecting matched groups of subjects, giving them different treatments, controlling unrelated factors, and checking for differences in group responses. Thus, experimental research tries to explain cause-and-effect

Experimental research
The gathering of primary data by selecting matched groups of subjects, giving them different treatments, controlling related factors, and checking for differences in group responses.

and it quizzes family members to find out what they read. It carefully records important facts about each household, such as family income, age of children, lifestyle, and product and store buying history.

IRI also employs a panel of retail stores in each of its markets. For a fee, these stores agree to carry the new products that IRI wishes to test, and they allow IRI to control factors such as shelf placement, stocking, trade and consumer promotion, and pricing for these products.

Each BehaviorScan household receives an identification number. When household members shop for groceries in IRI panel stores, they give their identification number to the store checkout clerk. All the information about the family's purchases—brands bought, package sizes, prices paid—is recorded by the store's electronic scanner and immediately entered by computer into the family's purchase file. The system also records any other in-store factors that might affect purchase decisions, such as special competitor price promotions or shelf displays.

Thus, IRI builds a complete record of each household's demographic and psychographic makeup, purchasing behavior, media habits,

and the conditions surrounding purchase. But IRI takes the process a step farther. Through cable television, IRI controls the advertisements being sent to each household. It can beam different ads and promotions to different panel households and then use the purchasing information obtained from scanners to assess which ads had more or less impact and how various promotions affected different kinds of consumers. In short, from a single source, companies can obtain information that links their marketing efforts directly with consumer buying behavior.

BehaviorScan and other single-source systems have their drawbacks, and some researchers are skeptical. One hitch is that such systems produce truckloads of data, more than most companies can handle. Another problem is cost: Single-source data can cost marketers hundreds of thousands of dollars a year per brand. Also, because such systems are set up in only a few market areas, usually small cities, the marketer often finds it difficult to generalize from the measures and results. Finally, although single-source systems provide important information for assessing the impact of promotion and advertising, they shed lit-

tle light on the effects of other key marketing actions.

Despite these drawbacks, many companies rely on single-source data systems to test new products and new marketing strategies. Consumer researchers rely heavily on the data supplied by such systems in studies evaluating product performance and consumer buying behavior. When properly used, such systems can provide marketers with fast and detailed information about how their products are selling, who is buying them, and what factors affect purchase.

Sources: See Joanne Lipman, "Single-Source Ad Research Heralds Detailed Look at Household Habits," *Wall Street Journal,* February 16, 1988, p. 39; Magid H. Abraham and Leonard M. Lodish, "Getting the Most out of Advertising and Promotion," *Harvard Business Review,* May–June 1990, pp. 50–60; "Long-Term Effect of TV Advertising: Estimates from In-Market Experiments," *Stores,* January 1996, pp. RR1–RR3; Jack Honomichl, "The Honomichl 50," *Marketing News,* June 9, 1997, pp. H1–H6; and information obtained from the Information Resources Web site at www.infores.com, February 2000.

relationships. Observation and surveys may be used to collect information in experimental research.

Before adding a new sandwich to the menu, researchers at McDonald's might use experiments to answer questions such as the following:

★ How much will the new sandwich increase McDonald's sales?
★ How will the new sandwich affect the sales of other menu items?
★ Which advertising approach would have the greatest effect on sales of the sandwich?
★ How would different prices affect the sales of the product?
★ Should the new item be targeted toward adults, children, or both?

To test the effects of two different prices, McDonald's could set up a simple experiment: It could introduce the new sandwich at one price in its restaurants in one city and at another price in restaurants in another city. If the cities are similar, and if all other marketing efforts for the sandwich are the same, then differences in sales in the two cities could be related to the price charged. More complex experiments could be designed to include other variables and other locations.

Contact Methods.   Information can be collected by mail, telephone, personal interview, or online. Table 4.3 shows the strengths and weaknesses of each of these contact methods.

Mail questionnaires can be used to collect large amounts of information at a low cost per respondent. Respondents may give more honest answers to more personal questions on a mail questionnaire than to an unknown interviewer in person or over the phone. Also, no interviewer is involved to bias the respondent's answers. However, mail questionnaires are not very flexible—all respondents answer the same questions in a fixed order, and the researcher cannot adapt the questionnaire based on earlier answers. Mail surveys usually take longer to complete, and the response rate—the number of people returning completed questionnaires—is often very low. Finally, the researcher often has little control over the mail questionnaire sample. Even with a good mailing list, it is hard to control *who* at the mailing address fills out the questionnaire.

Telephone interviewing is one of the best methods for gathering information quickly, and it provides greater flexibility than mail questionnaires. Interviewers can explain difficult questions, and they can skip some questions or probe on others depending on the answers they receive. Response rates tend to be higher than with mail questionnaires, and telephone interviewing also allows greater sample control. Interviewers can ask to speak to respondents with the desired characteristics, or even by name.

However, with telephone interviewing, the cost per respondent is higher than with mail questionnaires. Also, people may not want to discuss personal questions with an interviewer. Using an interviewer also introduces interviewer bias—the way interviewers talk, how they ask questions, and other differences may affect respondents' answers. Finally, different interviewers may interpret and record responses differently, and under time pressures some interviewers might even cheat by recording answers without asking questions.

Personal interviewing takes two forms—individual and group interviewing. *Individual interviewing* involves talking with people in their homes or offices, on the street, or in shopping malls. Such interviewing is flexible. Trained interviewers can hold a respondent's attention for a long time and can explain difficult questions. They can

TABLE 4.3   STRENGTHS AND WEAKNESSES OF CONTACT METHODS

	Mail	Telephone	Personal	Online
Flexibility	Poor	Good	Excellent	Good
Quantity of data that can be collected	Good	Fair	Excellent	Good
Control of interviewer effects	Excellent	Fair	Poor	Fair
Control of Sample	Fair	Excellent	Fair	Poor
Speed of data collection	Poor	Excellent	Good	Excellent
Response rate	Fair	Good	Good	Good
Cost	Good	Fair	Poor	Excellent

Source: Adapted with permission from *Marketing Research: Measurement and Method,* 7th ed., by Donald S. Tull and Del I. Hawkins. Copyright 1993 by Macmillan Publishing Company.

guide interviews, explore issues, and probe as the situation requires. They can show subjects actual products, advertisements, or packages and observe reactions and behavior. In most cases, personal interviews can be conducted fairly quickly. However, individual personal interviews may cost three to four times as much as telephone interviews.

Group interviewing consists of inviting six to ten people to gather for a few hours with a trained moderator to talk about a product, service, or organization. The participants normally are paid a small sum for attending. The meeting is held in a pleasant place and refreshments are served to foster an informal setting. The moderator encourages free and easy discussion, hoping that group interactions will bring out actual feelings and thoughts. At the same time, the moderator "focuses" the discussion—hence the name **focus group interviewing.** The comments are recorded through written notes or on videotapes that are studied later.

Focus group interviewing has become one of the major marketing research tools for gaining insight into consumer thoughts and feelings. However, focus group studies usually employ small sample sizes to keep time and costs down, and it may be hard to generalize from the results. Because interviewers have more freedom in personal interviews, the problem of interviewer bias is greater.

Today, modern communications technology is changing the way that focus groups are conducted:

> In the old days, advertisers and agencies flew their staff to Atlanta or Little Rock to watch focus groups from behind one-way mirrors. The staff usually spent more time in hotels and taxis than they did doing research. Today, they are staying home. Videoconferencing links, television monitors, remote-control cameras, and digital transmission are boosting the amount of focus group research done over long-distance lines. [In a typical videoconferencing system], two cameras focused on the group are controlled by clients who hold a remote keypad. Executives in a far-off boardroom can zoom in on faces and pan the focus group at will. . . . A two-way sound system connects remote viewers to the backroom, focus group room, and directly to the monitor's earpiece. [Recently], while testing new product names in one focus group, the [client's] creative director . . . had an idea and contacted the moderator, who tested the new name on the spot.[19]

In addition, with the development of the Internet, many companies are now conducting online focus groups:

Focus group interviewing
Personal interviewing that involves inviting six to ten people to gather for a few hours with a trained interviewer to talk about a product, service, or organization.

Video-conference focus groups: Executives in a far-off boardroom can "sit in" on focus group sessions.

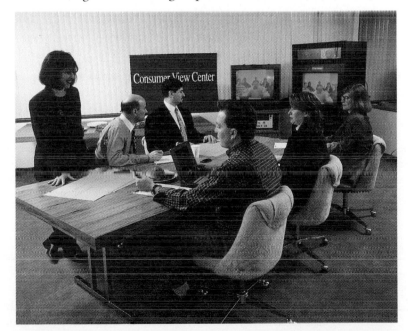

MARKETING HIGHLIGHT
4.3

MARKETING RESEARCH ON THE INTERNET

Like the Internet itself, performing marketing research on the Internet is still in its infancy. But as the use of the Internet and online services becomes more habit than hype for more and more U.S. consumers, online research is becoming a quick, easy, and inexpensive way to tap into their opinions. Web users are a desirable group, observes Paul Jacobson, an executive of Greenfield Online, an online research company. "There are a great number of companies which want to reach that group because they're early adopters and leading-edge consumers."

Online researchers don't pretend that Web users are representative of the U.S. population. Online users tend to be better educated, more affluent, and younger than the average consumer. However, these are highly important consumers to companies offering products and services online. They are also some of the hardest to reach when conducting research. Online surveys and chat sessions (or online focus groups) often prove effective in getting elusive teen, single, affluent, and well-educated audiences to participate.

"It's very solid for reaching hard-to-get segments," says Jacobson. "Doctors, lawyers, professionals—people you might have difficulty reaching because they are not interested in taking part in surveys. It's also a good medium for reaching working mothers and others who lead busy lives. They can do it in their own space and at their own convenience." Even researchers who prefer traditional methods agree that the Internet is a good medium for bringing together people from different parts of the country, especially those in higher income groups who can't spare the time to travel to a central site. For example, one virtual focus group convened by NFO Interactive to discuss the airline industry was made up of individuals with incomes of $150,000 per year. "You just can't get these kinds of people to come into your office," says NFO's president, "but we can get them online."

Online research isn't right for every company or product. For example, mass marketers who need to survey a representative cross-section of the population will find online research methodologies less useful. "If the target

for the product or service you're testing is inconsistent with the Internet user profile, then it's not the medium to use," Jacobson points out. "Is it the right medium to test Campbell's Chunky Soup? Probably not. But if you want to test how people feel about Campbell's Web site, yes."

When it is appropriate, online research offers marketers two distinct advantages over traditional surveys and focus groups: speed and cost-effectiveness. Online researchers routinely field quantitative studies and fill response quotas in only a matter of days. Online focus groups require some advance scheduling, but results are practically instantaneous. Notes an online researcher, "Online research is very fast, and time is what everybody wants now. Clients want the information yesterday."

Research on the Internet is also relatively inexpensive. Participants can dial in for a focus group from anywhere in the world, eliminating travel, lodging, and facility costs, making online chats cheaper than traditional focus groups. For surveys, the Internet eliminates most of the postage, phone, labor, and printing

Janice Gjersten, director of marketing for WP-Studio, an online entertainment company, wanted to conduct traditional focus groups to gauge reaction to a new Web site. However, she found that an online focus group netted more honest answers. Gjersten contacted Cyber Dialogue, which provided focus group respondents drawn from its 10,000-person database. The focus group was held in an online chat room, which Gjersten "looked in on" from her office computer. Gjersten could interrupt the moderator at any time with flash e-mails unseen by the respondents. Although the online focus group lacked voice and body cues, Gjersten says she will never conduct a traditional focus group again. Not only were respondents more honest, but the cost for the online group was one-third that of a traditional focus group and a full report came to her in one day, compared to four weeks.[20]

As this example suggests, the latest technology to hit marketing research is the fast-growing Internet. Increasingly, marketing researchers are collecting primary costs associated with other survey approaches. Moreover, sample size has little influence on costs. "There's not a huge difference between 10 and 10,000 on the Web," said Tod Johnson, head of NPD Group, a firm that conducts online research. "The cost [of research on the Web] can be anywhere from 10 percent to 80 percent less, especially when you talk about big samples."

However, using the Internet to conduct marketing research does have some drawbacks. One major problem is knowing who's in the sample. Tom Greenbaum, president of Groups Plus, recalls a cartoon in *The New Yorker* in which two dogs are seated at a computer: "On the Internet, nobody knows you are a dog," one says to the other. "If you can't see a person with whom you are communicating, how do know who they really are?" he says. Moreover, trying to draw conclusions from a "self-selected" sample of online users, those who clicked through to a questionnaire or accidentally landed in a chat room, can be troublesome. "Using a convenient sample is a way to do research quickly, but when you're done, you kind of scratch your head and ask what it means."

To overcome such sample and response problems, NPD and many other firms that offer online services construct panels of qualified Web regulars to respond to surveys and participate in online focus groups. NPD's panel consists of 15,000 consumers recruited online and verified by telephone; Greenfield Online picks users from its own database, then calls them periodically to verify that they are whom they say they are. Another online research firm, Research Connections, recruits in advance by telephone, taking time to help new users connect to the Internet, if necessary.

Even when using qualified respondents, focus group responses can lose something in the translation. "You're missing all of the key things that make a focus group a viable method," says Greenbaum. "You may get people online to talk to each other and play off each other, but it's very different to watch people get excited about a concept." Eye contact and body language are two direct, personal interactions of traditional focus group research that are lost in the online world. Although researchers can offer seasoned moderators, the Internet format—typed commentary and online "emoticons" (punctuation marks that express emotion, such as :-) to signify happiness)—greatly restrict respondent expressiveness. Similarly, technology limits researchers' capability to show visual cues to research subjects.

But just as it hinders the two-way assessment of visual cues, Web research can actually permit some participants the anonymity necessary to elicit an unguarded response. "There are reduced social effects online," Jacobson says. "People are much more honest in this medium." Another experienced online researcher agrees. When the subject is personal or sensitive, he suggests, online definitely has advantages. "People hiding behind a keyboard get pretty brave."

Some researchers are wildly optimistic about the prospects for marketing research on the Internet; others are more cautious. One expert predicts that in the next few years, 50 percent of all research will be done on the Internet. "Ten years from now, national telephone surveys will be the subject of research methodology folklore," he proclaims. "That's a little too soon," cautions another expert. "But in 20 years, yes."

Source: Portions adapted from Ian P. Murphy, "Interactive Research," *Marketing News,* January 20, 1997, pp. 1, 17. Selected quotes from "NFO Executive Sees Most Research Going to Internet," *Advertising Age,* May 19, 1997, p. 50; Kate Maddox, "Virtual Panels Add Real Insight for Marketers," *Advertising Age,* June 29, 1998, pp. 34, 40; and "Online or Off Target?" *American Demographics,* November 1998, pp. 20–21. Also see P. K. Kannan, "Marketing Information on the I-Way," *Communications of the ICM,* March 1998, pp. 35–40; Dick McCullough, "Web-Based Market Research Ushers in New Age," *Marketing News,* September 14, 1998, pp. 27–28; and Dana James," The Future of Online Research," *Marketing News,* January 3, 2000, pp. 1, 11.

Online (Internet) marketing research
Collecting primary data through Internet surveys and online focus groups.

data through **online (Internet) marketing research**—*Internet surveys* and *online focus groups.* Although online research offers much promise, and some analysts predict that the Internet will soon be the primary marketing research tool, others are more cautious. Marketing Highlight 4.3 summarizes the advantages, drawbacks, and prospects for conducting marketing research on the Internet.

Advances in computers and communications technology have also had a large impact on methods of obtaining information. For example, most research firms now do Computer Assisted Telephone Interviewing (CATI). Professional interviewers call respondents around the country, often using phone numbers drawn at random. When the respondent answers, the interviewer reads a set of questions from a video screen and types the respondent's answers directly into the computer.

Other firms use *computer interviewing* in which respondents sit down at a computer, read questions from a screen, and type their own answers into the computer.

The computers might be located at a research center, trade show, shopping mall, or retail location. For example, Boston Market uses touch-screen computers in its restaurants to obtain instant feedback from customers. Other researchers are conducting interactive focus groups using computers. Some researchers are even using Completely Automated Telephone Surveys (CATS), which employ voice response technology to conduct interviews. The recorded voice of an interviewer asks the questions, and respondents answer by pressing numbers on their push-button phones.[21]

Sampling Plan.   Marketing researchers usually draw conclusions about large groups of consumers by studying a small sample of the total consumer population. A **sample** is a segment of the population selected to represent the population as a whole. Ideally, the sample should be representative so that the researcher can make accurate estimates of the thoughts and behaviors of the larger population.

Sample
A segment of the population selected for marketing research to represent the population as a whole.

Designing the sample requires three decisions. First, *who* is to be surveyed (what *sampling unit*)? The answer to this question is not always obvious. For example, to study the decision-making process for a family automobile purchase, should the researcher interview the husband, wife, other family members, dealership salespeople, or all of these? The researcher must determine what information is needed and who is most likely to have it.

Second, *how many* people should be surveyed (what *sample size*)? Large samples give more reliable results than small samples. It is not necessary to sample the entire target market or even a large portion to get reliable results, however. If well chosen, samples of less than 1 percent of a population can often give good reliability.

Third, *how* should the people in the sample be *chosen* (what *sampling procedure*)? Table 4.4 describes different kinds of samples. Using *probability samples,* each population member has a known chance of being included in the sample, and researchers can calculate confidence limits for sampling error. But when probability sampling costs too much or takes too much time, marketing researchers often take *nonprobability samples,* even though their sampling error cannot be measured. These varied ways of drawing samples have different costs and time limitations as well as different accuracy and statistical properties. Which method is best depends on the needs of the research project.

Research Instruments.   In collecting primary data, marketing researchers have a choice of two main research instruments—the *questionnaire* and *mechanical devices.* The *questionnaire* is by far the most common instrument, whether administered in person, by phone, or online. Questionnaires are very flexible—there are many ways to ask questions. However, they must be developed carefully and tested before they can be used on a large scale. A carelessly prepared questionnaire usually contains several errors (see Table 4.5).

In preparing a questionnaire, the marketing researcher must first decide what questions to ask. Questionnaires frequently leave out questions that should be answered and include questions that cannot be answered, will not be answered, or need not be answered. Each question should be checked to see that it contributes to the research objectives.

The *form* of each question can influence the response. Marketing researchers distinguish between closed-end questions and open-end questions. *Closed-end questions* include all the possible answers, and subjects make choices among them. Examples include multiple-choice questions and scale questions. *Open-end questions* allow respondents to answer in their own words. In a survey of airline users, Delta might simply ask, "What is your opinion of Delta Airlines?" Or it might ask people to complete a sentence: "When I choose an airline, the most important considera-

TABLE 4.4   TYPES OF SAMPLES

Probability Sample	
Simple random sample	Every member of the population has a known and equal chance of selection.
Stratified random sample	The population is divided into mutually exclusive groups (such as age groups), and random samples are drawn from each group.
Cluster (area) sample	The population is divided into mutually exclusive groups (such as blocks), and the researcher draws a sample of the groups to interview.

Nonprobability Sample	
Convenience sample	The researcher selects the easiest population members from which to obtain information.
	The researcher uses his or her judgment to select population members who are good prospects for accurate information.
Judgment sample	The researcher finds and interviews a prescribed number of people in each of several categories.

tion is. . . ." These and other kinds of open-end questions often reveal more than closed-end questions because respondents are not limited in their answers. Open-end questions are especially useful in exploratory research, when the researcher is trying to find out *what* people think but not measuring *how many* people think in a certain way. Closed-end questions, on the other hand, provide answers that are easier to interpret and tabulate.

Researchers should also use care in the *wording* and *ordering* of questions. They should use simple, direct, unbiased wording. Questions should be arranged in a logical order. The first question should create interest if possible, and difficult or personal questions should be asked last so that respondents do not become defensive.

Although questionnaires are the most common research instrument, *mechanical instruments* also are used. We discussed two mechanical instruments, people meters and supermarket scanners, earlier in the chapter. Another group of mechanical devices measures subjects' physical responses. For example, a galvanometer measures the strength of interest or emotions aroused by a subject's exposure to different stimuli, such as an ad or picture. The galvanometer detects the minute degree of sweating that accompanies emotional arousal. The tachistoscope flashes an ad to a subject at an exposure range from less than one-hundredth of a second to several seconds. After each exposure, respondents describe everything they recall. Eye cameras are used to study respondents' eye movements to determine at what points their eyes focus first and how long they linger on a given item.

Presenting the Research Plan

At this stage, the marketing researcher should summarize the plan in a *written proposal*. A written proposal is especially important when the research project is large and complex or when an outside firm carries it out. The proposal should cover the management problems addressed and the research objectives, the information to be obtained, the sources of secondary information or methods for collecting primary

TABLE 4.5 TYPES OF QUESTIONS

A. Closed-End Questions

Name	Description	Example
Dichotomous	A question offering two answer choices.	"In arranging this trip, did you personally phone Delta?" Yes ☐ No ☐
Multiple choice	A question offering three or more answer choices.	"With whom are you traveling on this flight?" No one ☐ Children only ☐ Spouse ☐ Business associates/friends/relatives ☐ Spouse and children ☐ An organized tour group ☐
Likert scale	A statement with which the respondent shows the amount of agreement or disagreement.	"Small airlines generally give better service than large ones." Strongly disagree / Disagree / Neither agree nor disagree / Agree / Strongly agree 1 ☐ 2 ☐ 3 ☐ 4 ☐ 5 ☐
Semantic differential	A scale is inscribed between two bipolar words, and the respondent selects the point that represents the direction and intensity of his or her feelings.	*Delta Airlines* Large __X__ __ __ __ __ Small Experienced __ __ __ __X__ __ Inexperienced Modern __ __ __X__ __ __ Old-fashioned
Importance scale	A scale that rates the importance of some attribute from "not at all important" to "extremely important."	"Airline food service to me is" Extremely important / Very important / Somewhat important / Not very important / Not at all important 1 ___ 2 ___ 3 ___ 4 ___ 5 ___
Rating scale	A scale that rates some attribute from "poor" to "excellent."	"Delta's food service is" Excellent / Very good / Good / Fair / Poor 1 ___ 2 ___ 3 ___ 4 ___ 5 ___
Intention-to-buy scale	A scale that describes the respondent's intentions to buy.	"If in-flight, first-run movie service were available on a long flight, I would" Definitely buy / Probably buy / Not certain / Probably not buy / Definitely not buy 1 ___ 2 ___ 3 ___ 4 ___ 5 ___

B. Open-End Questions

Name	Description	Example
Completely unstructured	A question that respondents can answer in an almost unlimited number of ways.	"What is your opinion of Delta Airlines?"
Word association	Words are presented, one at a time, and respondents mention the first word that comes to mind.	"What is the first word that comes to mind when you hear the following?" Airline _____ Delta _____ Travel _____
Sentence completion	Incomplete sentences are presented, one at a time, and respondents complete the sentence.	"When I choose an airline, the most important consideration in my decision is _____"
Story completion	An incomplete story is presented, and respondents are asked to complete it.	"I flew Delta a few days ago. I noticed that the exterior and interior of the plane had very bright colors. This aroused in me the following thoughts and feelings." *Now complete the story.*
Picture completion	A picture of two characters is presented, with one making a statement. Respondents are asked to identify with the other and fill in the empty balloon.	Fill in the empty balloon.
Thematic Apperception Tests (TAT)	A picture is presented, and respondents are asked to make up a story about what they think is happening or may happen in the picture.	Make up a story about what you see.

Eye cameras determine where eyes land and how long they linger on a given item.

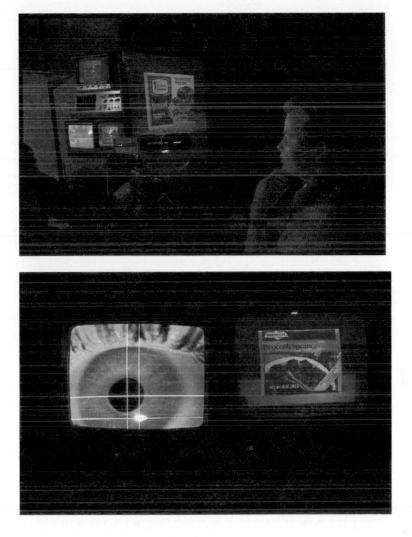

data, and the way the results will help management decision making. The proposal also should include research costs. A written research plan or proposal ensures that the marketing manager and researchers have considered all the important aspects of the research, and that they agree on why and how the research will be done.

Implementing the Research Plan

The researcher next puts the marketing research plan into action. This involves collecting, processing, and analyzing the information. Data collection can be carried out by the company's marketing research staff or by outside firms. The company keeps more control over the collection process and data quality by using its own staff. However, outside firms that specialize in data collection often can do the job more quickly and at a lower cost.

The data collection phase of the marketing research process is generally the most expensive and the most subject to error. The researcher should watch fieldwork closely to make sure that the plan is implemented correctly and to guard against problems with contacting respondents, with respondents who refuse to cooperate or who give biased or dishonest answers, and with interviewers who make mistakes or take shortcuts.

Researchers must process and analyze the collected data to isolate important information and findings. They need to check data from questionnaires for accuracy and completeness and code it for computer analysis. The researchers then tabulate the results and compute averages and other statistical measures.

Interpreting and Reporting the Findings

The researcher must now interpret the findings, draw conclusions, and report them to management. The researcher should not try to overwhelm managers with numbers and fancy statistical techniques. Rather, the researcher should present important findings that are useful in the major decisions faced by management.

However, interpretation should not be left only to the researchers. They are often experts in research design and statistics, but the marketing manager knows more about the problem and the decisions that must be made. In many cases, findings can be interpreted in different ways, and discussions between researchers and managers will help point to the best interpretations. The manager will also want to check that the research project was carried out properly and that all the necessary analysis was completed. Or, after seeing the findings, the manager may have additional questions that can be answered through further sifting of the data. Finally, the manager is the one who ultimately must decide what action the research suggests. The researchers may even make the data directly available to marketing managers so that they can perform new analyses and test new relationships on their own.

Interpretation is an important phase of the marketing process. The best research is meaningless if the manager blindly accepts faulty interpretations from the researcher. Similarly, managers may be biased—they might tend to accept research results that show what they expected and to reject those that they did not expect or hope for. Thus, managers and researchers must work together closely when interpreting research results, and both must share responsibility for the research process and resulting decisions.[22]

OTHER MARKETING RESEARCH CONSIDERATIONS

This section discusses marketing research in two special contexts: marketing research by small businesses and nonprofit organizations, and international marketing research. Finally, we look at public policy and ethics issues in marketing research.

Marketing Research in Small Businesses and Nonprofit Organizations

Managers of small businesses and nonprofit organizations often think that marketing research can be done only by experts in large companies with big research budgets. But many of the marketing research techniques discussed in this chapter also can be used by smaller organizations in a less formal manner and at little or no expense.

Managers of small businesses and nonprofit organizations can obtain good marketing information simply by *observing* things around them. For example, retailers can evaluate new locations by observing vehicle and pedestrian traffic. They can monitor competitor advertising by collecting ads from local media. They can evaluate their customer mix by recording how many and what kinds of customers shop in the store at different times. In addition, many small business managers routinely visit their rivals and socialize with competitors to gain insights. Tom Coohill, a chef who owns two Atlanta restaurants, gives managers a food allowance to dine out and bring back ideas. Atlanta jeweler Frank Maier Jr., who often visits out-of-town rivals, spotted and copied a dramatic way of lighting displays.[23]

Many associations, media, and government agencies provide special help to small organizations. Here the U.S. Small Business Administration offers a Web site that gives advice on topics ranging from starting, financing, and expanding a small business to ordering business cards.

Managers can conduct informal *surveys* using small convenience samples. The director of an art museum can learn what patrons think about new exhibits by conducting informal focus groups—inviting small groups to lunch and having discussions on topics of interest. Retail salespeople can talk with customers visiting the store; hospital officials can interview patients. Restaurant managers might make random phone calls during slack hours to interview consumers about where they eat out and what they think of various restaurants in the area.

Managers also can conduct their own simple *experiments.* For example, by changing the themes in regular fund-raising mailings and watching the results, a nonprofit manager can find out much about which marketing strategies work best. By varying newspaper advertisements, a store manager can learn the effects of things such as ad size and position, price coupons, and media used.

Small organizations can obtain most of the secondary data available to large businesses. In addition, many associations, local media, chambers of commerce, and government agencies provide special help to small organizations. The U.S. Small Business Administration offers dozens of free publications and a Web site (www.sbaonline.sba.gov) that give advice on topics ranging from starting, financing, and expanding a small business to ordering business cards. Local newspapers often provide information on local shoppers and their buying patterns. Finally, small businesses can collect a considerable amount of information at very little cost on the Internet. They can scour competitor and customer Web sites and use Internet search engines to research specific companies and issues.

In summary, secondary data collection, observation, surveys, and experiments can all be used effectively by small organizations with small budgets. Although these informal research methods are less complex and less costly, they still must be conducted carefully. Managers must think carefully about the objectives of the research, formulate questions in advance, recognize the biases introduced by smaller samples and less skilled researchers, and conduct the research systematically.[24]

International Marketing Research

International marketing researchers follow the same steps as domestic researchers, from defining the research problem and developing a research plan to interpreting and reporting the results. However, these researchers often face more and different problems. Whereas domestic researchers deal with fairly homogenous markets within a single country, international researchers deal with differing markets in many different countries. These markets often vary greatly in their levels of economic development, cultures and customs, and buying patterns.

In many foreign markets, the international researcher has a difficult time finding good *secondary data*. Whereas U.S. marketing researchers can obtain reliable secondary data from dozens of domestic research services, many countries have almost no research services at all. Some of the largest international research services operate in many countries. For example, AC Nielsen Corporation, the world's largest marketing research company, has offices in more than 80 countries, with over 72 percent of its revenues coming from outside the United States. Forty-seven percent of the revenues of the world's 25 largest marketing research firms comes from outside their own countries.[25] However, most research firms operate in only a relative handful of countries. Thus, even when secondary information is available, it usually must be obtained from many different sources on a country-by-country basis, making the information difficult to combine or compare.

Because of the scarcity of good secondary data, international researchers often must collect their own primary data. Here again, researchers face problems not found domestically. For example, they may find it difficult simply to develop good samples. U.S. researchers can use current telephone directories, census tract data, and any of several sources of socioeconomic data to construct samples. However, such information is largely lacking in many countries.

Once the sample is drawn, the U.S. researcher usually can reach most respondents easily by telephone, by mail, or in person. Reaching respondents is often not so easy in other parts of the world. Researchers in Mexico cannot rely on telephone and mail data collection—most data collection is door to door and concentrated in three or four of the largest cities. Most surveys in Mexico bypass the large segment of the population in which native tribes speak languages other than Spanish. In some countries, few people have phones; for example, there are only thirty-two phones per thousand people in Argentina. In other countries, the postal system is notoriously unreliable. In Brazil, for instance, an estimated 30 percent of the mail is never delivered. In many developing countries, poor roads and transportation systems make certain areas hard to reach, making personal interviews difficult and expensive.[26]

Cultural differences from country to country cause additional problems for international researchers. Language is the most obvious obstacle. For example, questionnaires must be prepared in one language and then translated into the languages of each country researched. Responses then must be translated back into the original language for analysis and interpretation. This adds to research costs and increases the risks of error.

Translating a questionnaire from one language to another is anything but easy. Many idioms, phrases, and statements mean different things in different cultures. For example, a Danish executive noted, "Check this out by having a different translator put back into English what you've translated from English. You'll get the shock of your life. I remember [an example in which] 'out of sight, out of mind' had become 'invisible things are insane.'"[27]

Buying roles and consumer decision processes vary greatly from country to country, further complicating international marketing research. Consumers in different countries also vary in their attitudes toward marketing research. People in one country may be very willing to respond; in other countries, nonresponse can be a major problem. For example, customs in some countries may prohibit people from talking with strangers. In certain cultures, research questions often are considered too personal. For example, in many Latin American countries, people may feel embarrassed to talk with researchers about their choices of shampoo, deodorant, or other personal care products. Even when respondents are

Some of the largest research services operate in many countries: Roper Starch Worldwide provides companies with information resources "from Brazil to Eastern Europe; from Cape Town to Beijing—if you are there, Roper Starch Worldwide is there."

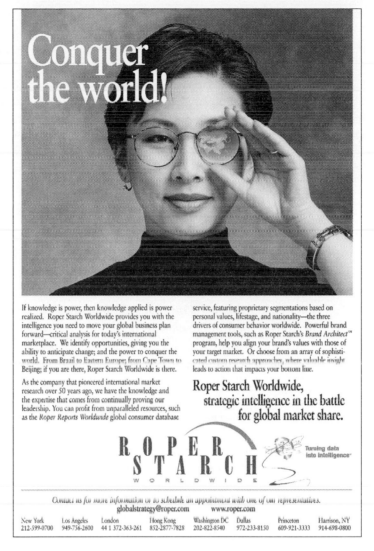

willing to respond, they may not be *able* to because of high functional illiteracy rates. Middle-class people in developing countries often make false claims in order to appear well off. For example, in a study of tea consumption in India, over 70 percent of middle-income respondents claimed that they used one of several national brands. However, the researchers had good reason to doubt these results—over 60 percent of the tea sold in India is unbranded generic tea.

Despite these problems, the recent growth of international marketing has resulted in a rapid increase in the use of international marketing research. Global companies have little choice but to conduct such research. Although the costs and problems associated with international research may be high, the costs of not doing it—in terms of missed opportunities and mistakes—might be even higher. Once recognized, many of the problems associated with international marketing research can be overcome or avoided.

Public Policy and Ethics in Marketing Research

Most marketing research benefits both the sponsoring company and its consumers. Through marketing research, companies learn more about consumers' needs, resulting in more satisfying products and services. However, the misuse of marketing research can also harm or annoy consumers. Two major public policy and ethics issues in marketing research are intrusions on consumer privacy and the misuse of research findings.

Intrusions on Consumer Privacy

Many consumers feel positively about marketing research and believe that it serves a useful purpose. Some actually enjoy being interviewed and giving their opinions. However, others strongly resent or even mistrust marketing research. A few consumers fear that researchers might use sophisticated techniques to probe our deepest feelings and then use this knowledge to manipulate our buying. Others may have been taken in by previous "research surveys" that actually turned out to be attempts to sell them something. Still other consumers confuse legitimate marketing research studies with telemarketing or database development efforts and say "no" before the interviewer can even begin. Most, however, simply resent the intrusion. They dislike mail or telephone surveys that are too long or too personal or that interrupt them at inconvenient times.

Increasing consumer resentment has become a major problem for the research industry. One recent poll found that 82 percent of Americans worry that they lack control over how businesses use their personal information, and 41 percent said that business had invaded their privacy. These concerns have led to lower survey response rates in recent years. One study found that 38 percent of Americans now refuse to be interviewed in an average survey, up dramatically from a decade ago. Another study found that 59 percent of consumers had refused to give information to a company because they thought it was not really needed or too personal, up from 42 percent just five years earlier.[28]

The research industry is considering several options for responding to this problem. One is to expand its "Your Opinion Counts" program to educate consumers about the benefits of marketing research and to distinguish it from telephone selling and database building. Another option is to provide a toll-free number that people can call to verify that a survey is legitimate. The industry also has considered adopting broad standards, perhaps based on Europe's International Code of Marketing and Social Research Practice. This code outlines researchers' responsibilities to respondents and to the general public. For example, it says that researchers should make their names and addresses available to participants, and it bans companies from representing activities such as database compilation or sales and promotional pitches as research.

Misuse of Research Findings

Research studies can be powerful persuasion tools; companies often use study results as claims in their advertising and promotion. Today, however, many research studies appear to be little more than vehicles for pitching the sponsor's products. In fact, in some cases, the research surveys appear to have been designed just to produce the intended effect. Few advertisers openly rig their research designs or blatantly misrepresent the findings; most abuses tend to be subtle "stretches." Consider the following examples:[29]

★ A study by Chrysler contends that Americans overwhelmingly prefer Chrysler to Toyota after test-driving both. However, the study included just 100 people in each of two tests. More importantly, none of the people surveyed owned a foreign car, so they appear to be favorably predisposed to U.S. cars.

★ A Black Flag survey asked: "A roach disk . . . poisons a roach slowly. The dying roach returns to the nest and after it dies is eaten by other roaches. In turn these roaches become poisoned and die. How effective do you think this type of product would be in killing roaches?" Not surprisingly, 79 percent said effective.

★ A poll sponsored by the disposable diaper industry asked: "It is estimated that disposable diapers account for less than 2 percent of the trash in today's landfills. In contrast, beverage containers, third-class mail, and yard waste are estimated to account for about 21 percent of the trash in landfills. Given this, in your opinion, would it be fair to ban disposable diapers?" Again, not surprisingly, 84 percent said no.

Thus, subtle manipulations of the study's sample, or the choice or wording of questions, can greatly affect the conclusions reached.

In others cases, so-called independent research studies actually are paid for by companies with an interest in the outcome. Small changes in study assumptions or in how results are interpreted can subtly affect the direction of the results. For example, at least four widely quoted studies compare the environmental effects of using disposable diapers to those of using cloth diapers. The two studies sponsored by the cloth diaper industry conclude that cloth diapers are more environmentally friendly. Not surprisingly, the other two studies, sponsored by the paper diaper industry, conclude just the opposite. Yet both appear to be correct *given* the underlying assumptions used.

Recognizing that surveys can be abused, several associations—including the American Marketing Association, the Council of American Survey Research Organizations, and the Marketing Research Association—have developed codes of research ethics and standards of conduct.[30] In the end, however, unethical or inappropriate actions cannot simply be regulated away. Each company must accept responsibility for policing the conduct and reporting of its own marketing research to protect consumers' best interests and its own.

REVIEW OF CONCEPT CONNECTIONS

In today's complex and rapidly changing environment, marketing managers need more and better information to make effective and timely decisions. This greater need for information has been matched by the explosion of information technologies for supplying information. Using today's new technologies, companies can now handle great quantities of information, sometimes even too much. Yet marketers often complain that they lack enough of the *right* kind of information or have an excess of the *wrong* kind. In response, many companies are now studying their managers' information needs and designing information systems to satisfy those needs.

1. Explain the importance of information to the company.

Good products and marketing programs start with a complete understanding of consumer needs and wants. Thus, the company needs sound information in order to produce superior value and satisfaction for customers. The company also requires information on competitors, resellers, and other actors and forces in the marketplace.

2. Define the marketing information system and discuss its parts.

The *marketing information system (MIS)* consists of people, equipment, and procedures to gather, sort, analyze, evaluate, and distribute needed, timely, and accurate information to marketing decision makers. A well-designed information system begins and ends with users. The MIS first *assesses information needs*, then *develops information* from internal databases, marketing intelligence activities, and marketing research. *Internal databases* provide information on the company's own sales, costs, inventories, cash flows, and accounts receivable and payable. Such data can be obtained quickly and cheaply but often need to be adapted for marketing decisions. *Marketing intelligence* activities supply everyday information about developments in the external marketing environment. *Marketing research* consists of collecting information relevant to a specific marketing problem faced by the company. Lastly, the MIS *distributes information* gathered from these sources to the right managers in the right form and at the right time to help them make better marketing decisions.

3. Outline the steps in the marketing research process.
The first step in the marketing research process involves *defining the problem and setting the research objectives,* which may be exploratory, descriptive, or causal. The second step consists of *developing a research plan* for collecting data from primary and secondary sources. The third step calls for *implementing the marketing research plan* by gathering, processing, and analyzing the information. The fourth step consists of *interpreting and reporting the findings.* Additional information analysis helps marketing managers apply the information and provides them with sophisticated statistical procedures and models from which to develop more rigorous findings.

4. Compare the advantages and disadvantages of various methods of collecting information.
Both *internal* and *external* secondary data sources often provide information more quickly and at a lower cost than primary data sources, and they can sometimes yield information that a company cannot collect by itself. However, needed information might not exist in secondary sources, and even if data can be found, they might be largely unusable. Researchers must also evaluate sec-ondary information to ensure that it is *relevant, accurate, current,* and *impartial.* Primary research must also be evaluated for these features. Each primary data collection method—*observational, survey,* and *experimental*—has its own advantages and disadvantages. Each of the various primary research contact methods—mail, telephone, personal interview, and online—also has its own advantages and drawbacks. Similarly, each contact method has its pluses and minuses.

5. Discuss the special issues some marketing researchers face, including public policy and ethics issues.
Some marketers face special marketing research situations, such as those conducting research in small business, nonprofit, or international situations. Marketing research can be conducted effectively by small businesses and nonprofit organizations with limited budgets. International marketing researchers follow the same steps as domestic researchers but often face more and different problems. All organizations need to respond responsibly to major public policy and ethical issues surrounding marketing research, including issues of intrusions on consumer privacy and misuse of research findings.

KEY TERMS

Causal research
Descriptive research
Experimental research
Exploratory research
Focus group interviewing
Internal databases

Marketing information system (MIS)
Marketing intelligence
Marketing research
Observational research
Online databases
Online (Internet) marketing research

Primary data
Sample
Secondary data
Single-source data systems
Survey research

ISSUES FOR DISCUSSION

1. Many companies build comprehensive internal databases that marketing managers can use to identify marketing opportunities and problems, plan strategies and programs, and evaluate performance. If you were the marketing manager for a large computer software producer, what types of information would you like to have available in your company's internal database? Explain.

2. Marketing intelligence has become increasingly important to marketing managers as an aid to formulating strategy. What other benefits are derived from the marketing intelligence function? Assume that you have been hired as a consultant to a company that is developing a new digital camera. What types of intelligence tips would you offer the firm?

3. Using commercial online databases, marketing researchers can conduct their own searches of secondary data sources. A recent survey of marketing researchers confirmed that at least three-quarters of them use online services for conducting research. Go online, find a marketing research database, describe the database, and evaluate the services offered. Was the database free or fee-based?

4. Name the type of research that would be appropriate in each of the following situations and explain why: (a) Kellogg wants to investigate the impact of young children on their parents' decisions to buy breakfast foods. (b) Your college bookstore wants to know how students would feel about adding a new "computer corner" in the bookstore staffed by Dell Computer personnel. (c) McDonald's is considering where to locate a new outlet in a fast-growing suburb. (d) Gillette wants to determine whether a new line of deodorant for teenagers will be profitable.

5. Research objectives must be translated into specific information needs. Assume that you are the marketing research director for Apple Computer. What specific

information might you need in order to pick two new colors for the popular iMac line of personal computers? List and briefly justify your choices.

6. Focus group interviewing is both widely used and widely criticized as a marketing research technique. List the advantages and disadvantages of focus groups. Suggest some kinds of questions that are suitable for exploration using focus groups.

7. Conducting marketing research on the Internet is still in its infancy. Assume that your company is interested in developing a Web site to reach teenagers for the purpose of selling teen fashion clothing. How could you obtain information about your target market via the Internet? How could you learn more about their specific reactions to your proposed Web site? Could you get the information for free, or would there be a cost?

8. Increasing consumer concern and resentment has become a major problem for the research industry. Design a "Consumer Bill of Rights" that would guide the research industry and specific marketing researchers.

MARKETING APPLICATIONS

1. The Internet provides a unique means for targeting minority market segments and gathering information about their preferences. All of the following sites are available to assist companies in their minority marketing and research efforts: www.minority.net—a large business-to-business e-commerce mall; www.twmall.com—a large Asian American mall that does business in several languages; www.collard-cards.com—this site sells greeting cards and cookbooks featuring upbeat black images; and www.demographics.com—a site that explores various demographic segments and trends that affect them.
   a. What seems to be the potential of marketing to minorities via the Internet?
   b. What unique features of the above sites might assist marketers wishing to reach minority markets?
   c. Using the *American Demographics* Web site (www.demographics.com), determine the potential size of the African American, Hispanic American, and Asian American Web-user markets. What other information about these important minorities can you find readily?
   d. Using information from your research, develop a brief marketing plan for FUBU Clothing (www.fubu.com), an African American clothing manufacturer, to expand beyond its current ethnic marketing approach.

2. American consumers are among the most researched subjects in the world. Companies spend millions of dollars each year to find out what they want, when they want it, and how much they will pay for it. Would you like to participate in the marketing research process yourself? Go to the following Web sites: www.pollingreport.com, www.gallup.com, and www.cnn.com.
   a. Which of these polls or questionnaires do you find most interesting? Why?
   b. Which was easiest to complete?
   c. Which of the polls could most easily be tied to marketing research? Why?
   d. Under what circumstances are you willing to provide information to an online researcher or Web site? Explain.
   e. You can test your advertising IQ by going to the Roper Starch Web site at www.roper.com. Once there, click to *Products and Services,* then click to *Starch Advertising and Media Research Service,* and finally click to *Tested Copy.* Take the online survey to test your skills in evaluating advertising that sells. The company will return your test results to you via e-mail.

 INTERNET CONNECTIONS

EVALUATING ONLINE RESEARCH

Shopping for stuff on the Web? Have you tried using BizRate? BizRate is a shopping portal that scientifically surveys Web shoppers to get their ratings of online merchants. BizRate surveys merchants' customers along ten dimensions in order to construct the BizRate ratings. The dimensions include ease of ordering, product selection, and price. The merchants voluntarily participate in this program and the aggregate results are published on BizRate's Web site. Deja.com also surveys online consumers (tag line: "Deja.com before you buy"). Visit BizRate at www.bizrate.com and Deja at www.deja.com and complete the following table.

	BizRate	Deja
Collect data about merchants? (yes/no)		
Collect data about products? (yes/no)		
Use random sample? (yes/no)		
Who gets surveyed?		
Survey administered at time of purchase? (yes/no)		
What is the privacy policy?		

FOR DISCUSSION

1. Locate a copy of BizRate's point-of-sale survey on its site. What is the purpose of this survey?
2. Locate the follow-up survey. Define a research problem that an online company might have to warrant this particular survey research.
3. What incentive do merchants have to participate in BizRate's program?
4. Are BizRate and Deja competitors or complementary services? Explain.
5. Which site has a better privacy policy? Explain.
6. Which survey results do you find more reliable? Why?
7. Which survey results do you find more helpful? Why?

SAVVY SITES

- The U.S. Securities and Exchange Commission (www.sec.gov) provides all financial statements for public companies in its EDGAR database, a good source for secondary data.
- Ever wondered which Internet search tool is best? The Search Engine Watch (www.searchenginewatch.com) provides ratings, features, and searching tips.
- American Consumer Opinion (www.acop.com) maintains a panel of Internet users who agree to complete online surveys. Sign up and see how it works!

NOTES

1. See "Coke 'Family' Sales Fly as New Coke Stumbles," *Advertising Age,* January 17, 1986, p. 1; Jack Honomichl, "Missing Ingredients in 'New' Coke's Research," *Advertising Age,* July 22, 1985, p. 1; Leah Rickard, "Remembering New Coke," *Advertising Age,* April 17, 1995, p. 6; Debra Goldman, "Power to the People," *Adweek,* October 6, 1997, p. 74; Kent Steinreide and Sarah Theodore, "1997 Soft Drink Wrap-Up," *Beverage Industry,* March 1998, pp. 36–42; and Rick Wise, "Why Things Go Better with Coke," *The Journal of Business Strategy,* January–February 1999, pp. 15–19.

2. See Philip Kotler, *Kotler on Marketing* (New York: Free Press, 1999), p. 73.

3. Joseph M. Winski, "Gentle Rain Turns into Torrent," *Advertising Age,* June 3, 1991, p. 34; David Shenk, *Data Smog: Surviving the Information Glut* (San Francisco: HarperSanFrancisco, 1997); Nancy Doucette, "Relieving Information Overload," *Rough Notes,* February 1998, pp. 26–27; and Diane Trommer, "Information Overload—Study Finds Intranet Users Overwhelmed with Data," *Electronic Buyers' News,* April 20, 1998, p. 98.

4. Alice LaPlante, "Still Drowning!" *Computer World,* March 10, 1997, pp. 69–70.

5. See Geoffrey Brewer, "The Customer Stops Here," *Sales & Marketing Management,* March 1998, pp. 31–36.

6. Stan Crock, "They Snoop to Conquer," *Business Week,* October 28, 1996, p. 172.

7. See Suzie Amer, "Masters of Intelligence," *Forbes,* April 5, 1999, p. 18.

8. Bruce Hager, "Dumpster Raids? That's Not Very Ladylike, Avon," *Business Week,* April 1, 1991, p. 32.

9. "Spy/Counterspy," *Context,* Summer 1998, pp. 20–21.

10. "Company Sleuth Uncovers Business Info for Free," *Link-Up,* January–February 1999, pp. 1, 8.

11. For more on marketing and competitive intelligence, see David B. Montgomery and Charles Weinberg, "Toward Strategic Intelligence Systems," *Marketing Management,* Winter 1998, pp. 44–52; Morris C. Attaway Sr., "A Review of Issues Related to Gathering and Assessing Competitive Intelligence," *American Business Review,* January 1998, pp. 25–35; and Larry Kanaher, *Competitive Intelligence: How to Gather, Analyze, and Use Information to Move Your Business to the Top* (Touchstone Books, 1998).

12. For a review of marketing models, see Gary Lilien, Philip Kotler, and Sridhar Moorthy, *Marketing Models* (Upper Saddle River, NJ: Prentice Hall, 1992); and Gary Lilien and Arvind Rangaswamy, *Marketing Engineering: Marketing Analysis and Planning in an Information Age* (Addison Wesley Longman, 1998).

13. See Judann Pollack, "Campbell Loses Its Appetite for Condensed Soup," *Advertising Age,* February 15, 1999, pp. 1, 42.

14. For more on research firms that supply marketing information, see Jack Honomichl, "Honomichl 50," special section, *Marketing News,* June 7, 1999, pp. H1–H39; and Honomichl, "Honomichl Global 25," special section, *Marketing News,* August 16, 1999, pp. H1–H23.

15. "Researching Researchers," *Marketing Tools,* September 1996, pp. 35–36.

16. See Marydee Ojala, "The Daze of Future Business Research," *Online,* January–February 1998, pp. 78–80; and Guy Kawasaki, "Get Your Facts Here," *Forbes,* March 23, 1998, p. 156.

17. Justin Martin, "Ignore Your Customer," *Fortune,* May 1, 1995, pp. 121–26; and "Even Executives Are Losing Their Offices," *HR Magazine,* March 1998, p. 77. Also see William B. Helmreich, "Louder Than Words: On-Site Observational Research," *Marketing News,* March 1, 1999, p. 16; Kenneth Labich, "Attention Shoppers: This Man Is Watching You," *Fortune,* July 19, 1999, pp. 131–34; and Kendra Parker, "How do You Like Your Beef?" *American Demographics,* January 2000, pp. 35–37.

18. Martin, "Ignore Your Customers," p. 126.

19. Rebecca Piirto Heather, "Future Focus Groups," *American Demographics,* January 1994, p. 6. For more on focus groups, see Thomas L. Greenbaum, "Focus Group by Video Next Trend of the '90s," *Marketing News,* July 29, 1996, p. 4; Howard Furmansky, "Debunking the Myths About Focus Groups," *Marketing News,* June 23, 1997, p. 2; and Judith Langer, "15 Myths of Qualitative Research: It's Conventional, but Is It Wisdom?" *Marketing News,* March 1, 1999, p. 13.

20. Sarah Schafer, "Communications: Getting a Line on Customers," *Inc. Technology,* 1996, p. 102. Also see "Online or Off Target?" *American Demographics,* November 1998, pp. 20–21; Langer, "15 Myths of Qualitative Research: It's Conventional, but Is It Wisdom?" pp. 13–14; and James Heckman, "Turning the Focus Online," *Marketing News,* February 28, 2000, p. 15.

21. Peter J. DePaulo and Rick Weitzer, "Interactive Phones Technology Delivers Survey Data Quickly," *Marketing News,* June 6, 1994, pp. 33–34; Peter Francese, "Managing Marketing Information," *American Demographics,* September 1995, pp. 56–62; Emil E. Becker, "Automated Interviewing Has Advantages," *Marketing News,* January 2, 1995, p. 9; and Thomas Kiely, "Wired Focus Groups," *Harvard Business Review,* January–February 1998, pp. 12–16.

22. For a discussion of the importance of the relationship between market researchers and research users, see Christine Moorman, Gerald Zaltman, and Rohit Deshpande, "Relationships Between Providers and Users of Market Research: The Dynamics of Trust Within and Between Organizations," *Journal of Marketing Research,* August 1992, pp. 314–28; Christine Moorman, Rohit Deshpande, and Gerald Zaltman, "Factors Affecting Trust in Market Research Relationships," *Journal of Marketing,* January 1993, pp. 81–101; Arlene Farber Sirkin, "Maximizing the Client–Researcher Partnership," *Marketing News,* September 13, 1994, p. 38; Pippa Considine, "Divided by a Common Cause," *Campaign,* September 19, 1997, p. 43; and Kevin P. Lonnie, "Researchers Must *Show* Their Findings to Clients," *Marketing News,* May 11, 1998, p. 4.

23. "Business Bulletin: Studying the Competition," *Wall Street Journal,* March 19, 1995, pp. A1, A5.

24. See Nancy Levenburg and Tom Dandridge, "Can't Afford Research? Try Miniresearch," *Marketing News,* March 31, 1997, p. 19; and Nancy Levenburg, "Research Resources Exist for Small Businesses," *Marketing News,* January 4, 1999, p. 19.

25. Honomichl, "Honomichl Global 25," pp. H1–H23; and the AC Nielsen Web page at www.acnielsen.com, February 2000.

26. Many of the examples in this section, along with others, are found in Subhash C. Jain, *International Marketing Management,* 3rd ed. (Boston: PWS-Kent Publishing Company, 1990), pp. 334–39. Also see Jack Honomichl, "Research Cultures Are Different in Mexico, Canada," *Marketing News,* May 5, 1993, pp. 12–13; Naghi Namakforoosh, "Data Collection Methods Hold Key to Research in Mexico," *Marketing News,* August 29, 1994, p. 28; Ken Gofton, "Going Global with Research," *Marketing,* April 15, 1999, p. 35; and Jack Edmonston, "U.S., Overseas Differences Abound," *Advertising Age's Business Marketing,* January 1998, p. 32.

27. Jain, *International Marketing Management,* p. 338.

28. See "MRA Study Shows Refusal Rates Are Highest at Start of Process," *Marketing News,* August 16, 1993, p. A15; "Private Eyes," *Marketing Tools,* January–February 1996, pp. 31–32; William O. Bearden, Charles S. Madden, and Kelly Uscategui, "The Pool Is Drying Up," *Marketing Research,* Spring 1998, pp. 26–33; and "Survey Results Show Consumers Want Privacy," *Direct Marketing,* March 1999, p. 10.

29. Cynthia Crossen, "Studies Galore Support Products and Positions, but Are They Reliable?" *Wall Street Journal,* November 14, 1991, pp. A1, A9. Also see Betsy Spethmann, "Cautious Consumers Have Surveyers Wary," *Advertising Age,* June 10, 1991, p. 34.

30. For example, see Betsy Peterson, "Ethics Revisited," *Marketing Research,* Winter 1996, pp. 47–48; and O. C. Ferrell, Michael D. Hartline, and Stephen W. McDaniel, "Codes of Ethics Among Corporate Research Departments, Marketing Research Firms, and Data Subcontractors: An Examination of a Three-Communities Metaphor," *Journal of Business Ethics,* April 1998, pp. 503–16. For discussion of a framework for ethical marketing research, see Naresh K. Malhotra and Gina L. Miller, "An Integrated Model of Ethical Decisions in Marketing Research," *Journal of Business Ethics,* February 1998, pp. 263–80.

COMPANY CASE

4

Enterprise Rent-A-Car: Measuring Service Quality

Kevin Kirkman wheeled his shiny, blue BMW coupe into his driveway, put the gear shift in the park position, set the parking brake, and got out to check his mailbox as he did every day when he got home. As he flipped through the deluge of catalogs and credit card offers, he noticed a letter from Enterprise Rent-A-Car.

THE WRECK

He wondered why Enterprise would be writing him. Then he remembered. Earlier that month, he'd been involved in a wreck. As he was driving to work one rainy morning, another car had been unable to stop on the slick pavement and had plowed into his car as he waited at a stoplight.

SERVICE QUALITY SURVEY

Please mark the box that best reflects your response to each question.

	Completely Satisfied	Somewhat Satisfied	Neither Satisfied Nor Dissatisfied	Somewhat Dissatisfied	Completely Dissatisfied
1. Overall, how satisfied were you with your recent car rental from Enterprise on January 1, 2000?	☐	☐	☐	☐	☐

2. What, if anything, could Enterprise have done better? (*Please be specific*) _____

_____

3a. Did you experience any problems during the rental process?	Yes ☐ No ☐	3b. If you mentioned any problems to Enterprise, did they resolve them to your satisfaction?	Yes ☐ No ☐ Did not mention ☐

	Excellent	Good	Fair	Poor	N/A
4. If you personally called Enterprise to reserve a vehicle, how would you rate the telephone reservation process?	☐	☐	☐	☐	☐

	Both at start and end of rental	Just at start of rental	Just at end of rental	Neither time	
5. Did you go to the Enterprise office	☐	☐	☐	☐	
6. Did an Enterprise employee give you a ride to help with your transportation needs	☐	☐	☐	☐	

7. After you arrived at the Enterprise office, how long did it take you to:	Less than 5 minutes	5–10 minutes	11–15 minutes	16–20 monutes	21–30 minutes	More than 30 minutes	N/A
◆ pick up your rental car?	☐	☐	☐	☐	☐	☐	☐
◆ return your rental car?	☐	☐	☐	☐	☐	☐	☐

8. How would you rate the ...	Excellent	Good	Fair	Poor	N/A
◆ timeliness with which you were either picked up at the start of the rental or dropped off afterwards?	☐	☐	☐	☐	☐
◆ timeliness with which the rental car was either brought to your location and left with you or picked up from your location afterwards?	☐	☐	☐	☐	☐
◆ Enterprise employee who handled your paperwork ...					
at the START of the rental?	☐	☐	☐	☐	☐
at the END of the rental?	☐	☐	☐	☐	☐
◆ mechanical condition of the car?	☐	☐	☐	☐	☐
◆ cleanliness of the car interior/exterior?	☐	☐	☐	☐	☐

	Yes	No	N/A		
9. If you asked for a specific type or size of vehicle, was Enterprise able to meet your needs?	☐	☐	☐		

10. For what reason did you rent this car?	Car repairs due to accident	All other car repairs/ maintenance	Car was stolen	Business	Leisure/ vacation	Some other reason
	☐	☐	☐	☐	☐	☐

11. The next time you need to pick up a rental car in the city or area in which you live, how likely are you to call Enterprise?	Definitely will call	Probably will call	Might or might not call	Probably will not call	Definitely will not call
	☐	☐	☐	☐	☐

12. Approximately how many times in total have you rented from Enterprise (including this rental)?	Once—this was first time	2 times	3–5 times	6–10 times	11 or more times
	☐	☐	☐	☐	☐

13. Considering all rental companies, approximately how many times within the past year have you rented a car in the city or area in which you live (including this rental)?	0 times	1 time	2 times	3–5 times	6–10 times	11 or more times
	☐	☐	☐	☐	☐	☐

Thankfully, neither Kevin nor the other driver had been hurt, but both cars had been considerably damaged. In fact, Kevin had not been able to drive his car.

Kevin had used his cellular phone to call the police; and while he waited for the officers to come, he had called his auto insurance agent. The agent assured Kevin that his policy included coverage to pay for a rental car while his car was being repaired. He told Kevin to have the car towed to a nearby auto repair shop and gave him the telephone number for the Enterprise Rent-A-Car office that served his area. The agent noted that his company recommended using Enterprise for replacement rentals and that Kevin's policy would cover up to $17.00 per day of the rental fee.

Once Kevin had checked his car in at the body shop and made the necessary arrangements, he telephoned the Enterprise office. Within 10 minutes, an Enterprise employee drove to the repair shop to pick him up. They returned to the Enterprise office where Kevin completed the paperwork to rent a Chevy Lumina. He drove the rental car for 12 days before the repair shop completed work on his car.

"Don't know why Enterprise would be writing me now," Kevin thought. "The insurance company paid the $17.00 per day, and I paid the extra because the Lumina cost a little more than that. Wonder what the problem could be?"

TRACKING CUSTOMER SATISFACTION

Kevin tossed the mail on the passenger's seat and drove up the driveway. Once inside his house, he opened the Enterprise letter to find that it was a survey to determine how satisfied he was with his rental experience. The survey came with a cover letter that thanked him for using Enterprise and asked him to complete the survey so that the company could continue to improve its service. The survey itself was just one page with 13 questions (see Exhibit 1).

Enterprise executives believe that the company has become the largest rental car company in the United States (in terms of revenue, number of cars in service, and number of rental locations) because of its laserlike focus on customer satisfaction and because of its concentration on serving the home-city replacement market. Enterprise aims to serve customers like Kevin, who are involved in wrecks and suddenly find themselves without a car. While the more well-known companies such as Hertz and Avis battled for business in the cutthroat airport market, Enterprise quietly built its business by cultivating insurance agents and body-shop managers as referral agents, so that when one of their clients or customers needed a replacement vehicle, the agents would recommend Enterprise. Although such replacement rentals account for about 80 percent of Enterprise's business, the company also serves the discretionary market (leisure/vacation rentals) and the business market (renting cars to businesses for their short-term needs).

Throughout its history, Enterprise has followed the advice of its founder, Jack Taylor. Taylor believed that if the company took care of its customers first and its employees second, profits would follow. So the company tracks customer satisfaction carefully.

About one in 20 customers will receive a letter as Kevin did. The letters are mailed to customers selected at random about 7 days following completion of a rental. On average, about 30 percent of the surveyed customers will return the completed survey in the enclosed postage-paid envelope. They mail the surveys to an outside service firm, which compiles the results and provides the company with monthly reports that employees in the branches can use to review their performance.

CONTINUOUS IMPROVEMENT

Enterprise has been using the survey form for several years. However, its managers wonder what they could do to improve the survey. Should the survey ask more questions? What could the company do to improve the response rate? Is the mail questionnaire the best way to collect customer satisfaction data? Are there any sampling issues or response biases in its system?

Kevin glanced through his living room window at his BMW sitting in the driveway. "That's amazing," he thought, "you could never tell it had been in a wreck. The repair shop did a great job, and I'm satisfied with Enterprise also. Guess I should complete this survey to let the company know."

Questions

1. Analyze Enterprise's Service Quality Survey. What information is it trying to gather? What are its research objectives?
2. What decisions has Enterprise made with regard to primary data collection—research approach, contact methods, sampling plan, and research instruments?
3. In addition to or instead of the mail survey, what other means could Enterprise use to gather customer satisfaction and other information about its customers and competitors?
4. What recommendations would you make to Enterprise with regard to its survey process and its data collection strategy?

Source: Officials at Enterprise Rent-A-Car contributed to and supported development of this case. See also the Part II Comprehensive Case for more details on Enterprise Rent-A-Car.

After studying this chapter, you should be able to
1. define the consumer market and construct a simple model of consumer buyer behavior
2. name the four major factors that influence consumer buyer behavior
3. list and understand the stages in the buyer decision process
4. describe the adoption and diffusion process for new products

CONSUMER MARKETS AND CONSUMER BUYER BEHAVIOR

Few brands engender such intense loyalty as that found in the hearts of Harley-Davidson owners. "The Harley audience is granitelike" in its devotion, laments the vice president of sales for competitor Yamaha. Observes the publisher of *American Iron,* an industry publication, "You don't see people tattooing Yamaha on their bodies." Each year, in early March, more than 400,000 Harley bikers rumble through the streets of Daytona Beach, Florida, to attend Harley-Davidson's Bike Week celebration. Bikers from across the nation lounge on their low-slung Harleys, swap biker tales, and sport T-shirts proclaiming "I'd rather push a Harley than drive a Honda."

Riding such intense emotions, Harley-Davidson has rumbled its way to the top of the fast-growing heavyweight motorcycle market. Harley's "Hogs" capture over one-fifth of all U.S. bike sales and more than half of the heavyweight segment. Both the segment and Harley's sales are growing rapidly. In fact, for several years running, sales have far outstripped supply, with customer waiting lists of up to three years for popular models and street prices running well above suggested list prices. "We've seen people buy a new Harley and then sell it in the parking lot for $4,000 to $5,000 more," says one dealer. Since its initial public stock offering in 1986, by the year 2000, Harley-Davidson shares had split 4 times and were up more than 7,100 percent.

Harley-Davidson's marketers spend a great deal of time thinking about customers and their buying behavior. They want to know who their customers are, what they think and how they feel, and why they buy a Harley rather than a Yamaha or a Suzuki or a big Honda American Classic. What is it that makes Harley buyers so fiercely loyal? These are difficult questions; even Harley owners themselves don't know exactly what motivates their buying. But Harley management puts top priority on understanding customers and what makes them tick.

Who rides a Harley? You might be surprised. It's no longer the Hell's Angels crowd—the burly, black-leather-jacketed rebels and biker chicks who once made up Harley's core clientele. Motorcycles are attracting a new breed of riders—older, more affluent, and better educated. Harley now appeals more to "rubbies"

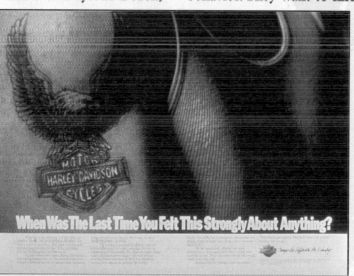

When Was The Last Time You Felt This Strongly About Anything?

(rich urban bikers) than to rebels. The average Harley customer is a 43-year-old husband with a median household income of $66,400. Harley's big, comfortable cruisers give these new consumers the easy ride, prestige, and twist-of-the-wrist power they want and can afford.

Harley-Davidson makes good bikes, and to keep up with its shifting market, the company has upgraded its showrooms and sales approaches. But Harley customers are buying a lot more than just a quality bike and a smooth sales pitch. To gain a better understanding of customers' deeper motivations, Harley-Davidson conducted focus groups in which it invited bikers to make cut-and-paste collages of pictures that expressed their feelings about Harley-Davidsons. (Can't you just see a bunch of hard-core bikers doing this?) It then mailed out 16,000 surveys containing a typical battery of psychological, sociological, and demographic questions as well as subjective questions such as "Is Harley more typified by a brown bear or a lion?" The research revealed seven core customer types: adventure-loving traditionalists, sensitive pragmatists, stylish status seekers, laid-back campers, classy capitalists, cool-headed loners, and cocky misfits. However, all owners appreciated their Harleys for the same basic reasons. "It didn't matter if you were the guy who swept the floors of the factory or if you were the CEO at that factory, the attraction to Harley was very similar," says a Harley executive. "Independence, freedom, and power were the universal Harley appeals."

These studies confirm that Harley customers are doing more than just buying motorcycles. They're making a lifestyle statement and displaying an attitude. As one analyst suggests, owning a Harley makes you "the toughest, baddest guy on the block. Never mind that [you're] a dentist or an accountant. You [feel] wicked astride all that power." Your Harley renews your spirits and announces your independence. As the Harley Web home page announces, "Thumbing the starter of a Harley-Davidson does a lot more than fire the engine. It fires the imagination." Adds a Harley dealer: "We sell a dream here. Our customers lead

hardworking professional or computer-oriented lives. Owning a Harley removes barriers to meeting people on a casual basis, and it gives you maximum self-expression in your own space.

The classic look, the throaty sound, the very idea of a Harley—all contribute to its mystique. Owning this "American legend" makes you a part of something bigger, a member of the Harley family. The fact that you have to wait to get a Harley makes it all that much more satisfying to have one. In fact, the company deliberately restricts its output. "Our goal is to eventually run production at a level that's always one motorcycle short of demand," says Harley-Davidson's chief executive.

Such strong emotions and motivations are captured in a recent Harley-Davidson advertisement. The ad shows a close-up of an arm, the bicep adorned with a Harley-Davidson tattoo. The headline asks, "When was the last time you felt this strongly about anything?" The ad copy outlines the problem and suggests a solution:

Wake up in the morning and life picks up where it left off. You do what has to be done. Use what it takes to get there. And what once seemed exciting has now become part of the numbing routine. It all begins to feel the same. Except when you've got a Harley-Davidson. Something strikes a nerve. The heartfelt thunder rises up, refusing to become part of the background. Suddenly things are different. Clearer. More real. As they should have been all along. The feeling is personal. For some, owning a Harley is a statement of individuality. For others, owning a Harley means being a part of a home-grown legacy that was born in a tiny Milwaukee shed in 1903. . . . To the uninitiated, a Harley-Davidson motorcycle is associated with a certain look, a certain sound. Anyone who owns one will tell you it's much more than that. Riding a Harley changes you from within. The effect is permanent. Maybe it's time you started feeling this strongly. Things are different on a Harley.[1]

The Harley-Davidson example shows that many different factors affect consumer buying behavior. Buying behavior is never simple, yet understanding it is the essential task of marketing management.

This chapter explores the dynamics of consumer behavior and the consumer market. **Consumer buying behavior** refers to the buying behavior of final consumers—individuals and households who buy goods and services for personal consumption. All of these final consumers combined make up the **consumer market.** The American consumer market consists of more than 273 million people who consume many trillions of dollars worth of goods and services each year, making it one of the most attractive consumer markets in the world. The world consumer market consists of more than *6 billion* people. At present growth rates, the world population will reach almost 8 billion people by 2025.[2]

Consumers around the world vary tremendously in age, income, education level, and tastes. They also buy an incredible variety of goods and services. How these diverse consumers connect with each other and with other elements of the world around them impacts their choices among various products, services, and companies. Here we examine the fascinating array of factors that affect consumer behavior.

Consumer buyer behavior
The buying behavior of final consumers—individuals and households who buy goods and services for personal consumption.

Consumer market
All the individuals and households who buy or acquire goods and services for personal consumption.

MODEL OF CONSUMER BEHAVIOR

Consumers make many buying decisions every day. Most large companies research consumer buying decisions in great detail to answer questions about what consumers buy, where they buy, how and how much they buy, when they buy, and why they buy. Marketers can study actual consumer purchases to find out what they buy, where, and how much. But learning about the *whys* of consumer buying behavior is not so easy—the answers are often locked deep within the consumer's head.

The central question for marketers is: How do consumers respond to various marketing efforts the company might use? The company that really understands how consumers will respond to different product features, prices, and advertising appeals has a great advantage over its competitors. The starting point is the stimulus–response model of buyer behavior shown in Figure 5.1. This figure shows that marketing and other stimuli enter the consumer's "black box" and produce certain responses. Marketers must figure out what is in the buyer's black box.[3]

Marketing stimuli consist of the four Ps: product, price, place, and promotion. Other stimuli include major forces and events in the buyer's environment: economic, technological, political, and cultural. All these inputs enter the buyer's black box, where they are turned into a set of observable buyer responses: product choice, brand choice, dealer choice, purchase timing, and purchase amount.

The marketer wants to understand how the stimuli are changed into responses inside the consumer's black box, which has two parts. First, the buyer's characteristics influence how he or she perceives and reacts to the stimuli. Second, the buyer's deci-

FIGURE 5.1 Model of buyer behavior

sion process itself affects the buyer's behavior. This chapter looks first at buyer characteristics as they affect buying behavior, and then discusses the buyer decision process.

CHARACTERISTICS AFFECTING CONSUMER BEHAVIOR

Consumer purchases are influenced strongly by cultural, social, personal, and psychological characteristics, as shown in Figure 5.2. For the most part, marketers cannot control such factors, but they must take them into account. We illustrate these characteristics for the case of a hypothetical consumer named Anna Flores. Anna is a married college graduate who works as a brand manager in a leading consumer packaged-goods company. She wants to find a new leisure-time activity that will provide some contrast to her working day. This need has led her to consider buying a camera and taking up photography. Many characteristics in her background will affect the way she evaluates cameras and chooses a brand.

Cultural Factors

Cultural factors exert the broadest and deepest influence on consumer behavior. The marketer needs to understand the role played by the buyer's *culture, subculture,* and *social class.*

Culture

Culture
The set of basic values, perceptions, wants, and behaviors learned by a member of society from family and other important institutions.

Culture is the most basic cause of a person's wants and behavior. Human behavior is largely learned. Growing up in a society, a child learns basic values, perceptions, wants, and behaviors from the family and other important institutions. A child in the United States normally learns or is exposed to the following values: achievement and success, activity and involvement, efficiency and practicality, progress, material comfort, individualism, freedom, humanitarianism, youthfulness, and fitness and health.

Every group or society has a culture, and cultural influences on buying behavior may vary greatly from country to country. Failure to adjust to these differences can result in ineffective marketing or embarrassing mistakes. For example, business representatives of a U.S. community trying to market itself in Taiwan found this out the hard way. Seeking more foreign trade, they arrived in Taiwan bearing gifts of green baseball caps. It turned out that the trip was scheduled a month before Taiwan

FIGURE 5.2   Factors influencing consumer behavior

elections, and that green was the color of the political opposition party. Worse yet, the visitors learned after the fact that according to Taiwan culture, a man wears green to signify that his wife has been unfaithful. The head of the community delegation later noted, "I don't know whatever happened to those green hats, but the trip gave us an understanding of the extreme differences in our cultures."[4] International marketers must understand the culture in each international market and adapt their marketing strategies accordingly.

Anna Flores's cultural background will affect her camera buying decision. Anna's desire to own a camera may result from her being raised in a modern society that has developed camera technology and a whole set of consumer learnings and values. Anna knows what cameras are. She knows how to read instructions, and her society has accepted the idea of women photographers.

Marketers are always trying to spot *cultural shifts* in order to discover new products that might be wanted. For example, the cultural shift toward greater concern about health and fitness has created a huge industry for exercise equipment and clothing, low-fat and more natural foods, and health and fitness services. The shift toward informality has resulted in more demand for casual clothing and simpler home furnishings. The increased desire for leisure time has resulted in more demand for convenience products and services, such as microwave ovens and fast food.

Subculture

Subculture

A group of people with shared value systems based on common life experiences and situations.

Each culture contains smaller **subcultures,** or groups of people with shared value systems based on common life experiences and situations. Subcultures include nationalities, religions, racial groups, and geographic regions. Many subcultures make up important market segments, and marketers often design products and marketing programs tailored to their needs. Here are examples of four such important subculture groups.

Hispanic Consumers. The U.S. Hispanic market—Americans of Cuban, Mexican, Central American, South American, and Puerto Rican descent—consists of 29 million consumers who buy more than $348 billion worth of goods and services each year. Expected to number almost 40 million by the year 2010, Hispanics are easy to reach through the growing selection of Spanish-language broadcast and print media that cater to them.[5]

Hispanics have long been a target for marketers of food, beverages, and household care products. But as the segment's buying power increases, Hispanics are now emerging as an attractive market for pricier products such as computers, financial services, photography equipment, large appliances, life insurance, and automobiles. Hispanic consumers tend to buy more branded, higher quality products—generics don't sell well to Hispanics. Perhaps more important, Hispanics are very brand loyal, and they favor companies who show special interest in them. Because of the segment's strong brand loyalty, companies that get the first foothold have an important head start in this fast-growing market.

Sears makes a special effort to market to Hispanic American consumers, especially for the 20 percent of its stores that are located in heavily Hispanic neighborhoods:

⭐ Sears was one of the first credit card providers to market cards to Hispanics, helping the retailer to build a formidable database of Hispanic consumers. Sears currently markets heavily to this attractive segment. Last year, it spent some $25 million on advertising to Hispanics—more than any other retailer—and it recently launched a Spanish-language Web site. In addition to advertising through local Spanish radio stations

Targeting important subcultures: Sears markets extensively to Hispanics—its Nuestra Gente *magazine is the nation's largest Spanish-language magazine.*

and newspapers, local Sears stores in Hispanic neighborhoods periodically hang Spanish-language ads on the doorknobs of area homes. These neighborhoods also receive regular visits from a Fiesta Mobile, a colorful Winnebago that plays music, gives out prizes, and promotes the Sears credit card. Sears also sponsors major Hispanic cultural festivals and concerts. However, one of its most successful marketing efforts is its magazine *Nuestra Gente*—which means Our People—the nation's largest Spanish-language magazine. The magazine features articles about Hispanic celebrities alongside glossy spreads of Sears fashions. Using a list culled from its database, Sears has built up a controlled circulation of about 700,000. The magazine is free, but subscriptions are available only by request. As a result of this careful cultivation of Hispanic consumers, although Sears has lost sales in recent years to discount retailers, the Hispanic segment has remained steadfastly loyal.[6]

Targeting Hispanics may also provide an additional benefit. With the passage of the North American Free Trade Agreement (NAFTA)—which reduced trade barriers between the United States, Mexico, and Canada—U.S. and Mexican companies have sought new opportunities to market "pan-American" brands. Companies on both sides of the border see the U.S. Hispanic population as a bridge for spanning U.S. and Latin American markets.

African American Consumers. If the U.S. population of African American consumers were a separate nation, its buying power of $500 billion annually would rank twelfth in the free world.[7] The black population in the United States is growing in affluence and sophistication. Although more price conscious than other segments, blacks are also strongly motivated by quality and selection. They place more importance on brand names, are more brand loyal, and do less "shopping around."

In recent years, many companies have developed special products and services, packaging, and appeals to meet the needs of African Americans. Hallmark launched its Afrocentric brand, Mahogany, with only 16 cards in 1987; it offers 800 cards today. Other companies are moving away from creating separate products for African Americans. Instead, they are offering more inclusive product lines within the same brand that goes out to the general market. For example, Sara Lee discontinued its separate Color-Me-Natural line of L'eggs pantyhose for black women and now offers shades and sheer styles popular among black women as half of the company's general-focus subbrands.[8]

A wide variety of magazines, television channels, and other media now target black consumers. Marketers are also reaching out to the African American virtual community. Per capita, black consumers spend twice as much as white consumers for online services. African Americans are increasingly turning to Web sites like The Black World Today (www.tbwt.com), a black *USA Today* on the Internet that address black culture in ways that network and cable TV rarely do. Other popular sites include Urban Sports Network, Net Noir, Afronet, and Black Voices.[9]

Asian American Consumers.   Asian Americans, the fastest-growing and most affluent U.S. demographic segment, now number more than 10 million with spending power of $110 billion annually. Chinese constitute the largest group, followed by Filipinos, Japanese, Asian Indians, and Koreans. Asian American family income exceeds the national average by 19 percent.[10] Long-distance telephone companies and financial services marketers have long targeted Asian American consumers, but until recently, packaged-goods firms, automobile companies, retailers, and fast-food chains have lagged in this segment. Language and cultural traditions appear to be the biggest barriers. For example, 66 percent of Asian Americans are foreign born, and 56 percent of those five years and older do not speak English fluently. Still, because of the segment's rapidly growing buying power, many firms are now looking seriously at this market.[11]

The 50-Plus Market.   As the U.S. population ages, mature consumers are becoming a very attractive market. Now 75 million strong, the 50-and-older population will swell to 115 million in the next 25 years. Mature consumers are better off financially than younger consumer groups. Because seniors have more time and money, they are an ideal market for exotic travel, restaurants, high-tech home entertainment products, leisure goods and services, designer furniture and fashions, financial services, and health care services.

Hallmark launched its Afrocentric brand, Mahogany, with only 16 cards in 1987. Today it offers 800 cards.

Their desire to look as young as they feel also makes more mature consumers good candidates for cosmetics and personal care products, health foods, fitness products, and other items that combat the effects of aging. The best strategy is to appeal to their active, multidimensional lives. For example, a recent Nike commercial features a senior weight lifter who proudly proclaims, "I'm not strong for my age. I'm strong!" Similarly, Kellogg aired a TV spot for All-Bran cereal in which individuals ranging in age from 53 to 81 are featured playing ice hockey, water skiing, running hurdles, and playing baseball, all to the tune of "Wild Thing." An Aetna commercial portrays a senior who, after retiring from a career as a lawyer, fulfills a life-long dream to become an archeologist.[12]

Anna Flores's buying behavior will be influenced by her subculture identification. These factors will affect her food preferences, clothing choices, recreation activities, and career goals. Subcultures attach different meanings to picture taking, and this could affect both Anna's interest in cameras and the brand she buys.

Social Class

Almost every society has some form of social class structure. **Social classes** are society's relatively permanent and ordered divisions whose members share similar values, interests, and behaviors. Social scientists have identified the seven American social classes (see Table 5.1).

> **Social classes**
> Relatively permanent and ordered divisions in a society whose members share similar values, interests, and behaviors.

Social class is not determined by a single factor, such as income, but is measured as a combination of occupation, income, education, wealth, and other variables. In some social systems, members of different classes are reared for certain roles and cannot change their social positions. In the United States, however, the lines between social classes are not fixed and rigid; people can move to a higher social class or drop into a lower one. Marketers are interested in social class because people within a given social class tend to exhibit similar buying behavior.[13]

Social classes show distinct product and brand preferences in areas such as clothing, home furnishings, leisure activity, and automobiles. Anna Flores's social class may affect her camera decision. If she comes from a high social class background, her family probably owned an expensive camera and she may have dabbled in photography.

Social Factors

A consumer's behavior also is influenced by social factors, such as the consumer's *small groups, family,* and *social roles* and *status.*

Groups

> **Group**
> Two or more people who interact to accomplish individual or mutual goals.

A person's behavior is influenced by many small **groups.** Groups that have a direct influence and to which a person belongs are called *membership groups.* In contrast, *reference groups* serve as direct (face-to-face) or indirect points of comparison or reference in forming a person's attitudes or behavior. People often are influenced by reference groups to which they do not belong. For example, an *aspirational group* is one to which the individual wishes to belong, as when a teenage basketball player hopes to play someday for the Utah Jazz. Marketers try to identify the reference groups of their target markets. Reference groups expose a person to new behaviors and lifestyles, influence the person's attitudes and self-concept, and create pressures to conform that may affect the person's product and brand choices.

> **Opinion leader**
> Person within a reference group who, because of special skills, knowledge, personality, or other characteristics, exerts influence on others.

The importance of group influence varies across products and brands. It tends to be strongest when the product is visible to others whom the buyer respects. Manufacturers of products and brands subjected to strong group influence must figure out how to reach **opinion leaders**—people within a reference group who,

TABLE 5.1 CHARACTERISTICS OF SEVEN MAJOR AMERICAN SOCIAL CLASSES

Upper Uppers (Less Than 1 Percent)

Upper uppers are the social elite who live on inherited wealth and have well-known family backgrounds. They give large sums to charity, run debutante balls, own more than one home, and send their children to the finest schools. They are a market for jewelry, antiques, homes, and vacations. They often buy and dress conservatively rather than showing off their wealth. Although small in number, upper uppers serve as a reference group for others.

Lower Uppers (About 2 Percent)

Lower uppers have earned high income or wealth through exceptional ability in the professions or business. They usually begin in the middle class. They tend to be active in social and civic affairs and buy for themselves and their children the symbols of status, such as expensive homes, schools, swimming pools, and automobiles. They include the new rich who consume conspicuously to impress those below them. They want to be accepted in the upper-upper stratum, a status more likely to be achieved by their children than by themselves.

Upper Middles (12 Percent)

Upper middles possess neither family status nor unusual wealth. They are primarily concerned with "career." They have attained positions as professionals, independent businesspersons, and corporate managers. They believe in education and want their children to develop professional or administrative skills. They are joiners and highly civic-minded. They are the quality market for good homes, clothes, furniture, and appliances.

Middle Class (32 Percent)

The middle class is made up of average-pay white- and blue-collar workers who live on "the better side of town" and try to "do the proper things." To keep up with the trends, they often buy products that are popular. Most are concerned with fashion, seeking the better brand names. Better living means owning a nice home in a nice neighborhood with good schools. They believe in spending more money on worthwhile experiences for their children and aiming them toward a college education.

Working Class (38 Percent)

The working class consists of those who lead a "working-class lifestyle" whatever their income, school background, or job. They depend heavily on relatives for economic and emotional support, for advice on purchases, and for assistance in times of trouble. The working class maintains sharper sex role division and stereotyping.

Upper Lower (9 Percent)

Upper lowers are working (are not on welfare), although their living standard is just above poverty. They perform unskilled work for very poor pay although they strive toward a higher class. Often, upper lowers lack education. Although they fall near the poverty line financially, they manage to "present a picture of self-discipline" and "maintain some effort at cleanliness."

Lower Lowers (7 Percent)

Lower lowers are on welfare, visibly poverty stricken, and usually out of work or have "the dirtiest jobs." Often they are not interested in finding a job and are permanently dependent on public aid or charity for income. Their homes, clothes, and possessions are "dirty," "raggedy," and "broken-down."

Sources: See Richard P. Coleman, "The Continuing Significance of Social Class to Marketing," *Journal of Consumer Research,* December 1983, pp. 265–80, © Journal of Consumer Research, Inc., 1983; and Leon G. Shiffman and Leslie Lazar Kanuk, *Consumer Behavior,* 6th ed. (Upper Saddle River, NJ: Prentice Hall, 1997), p. 388.

because of special skills, knowledge, personality, or other characteristics, exert influence on others.

Many marketers try to identify opinion leaders for their products and direct marketing efforts toward them. In other cases, advertisements can simulate opinion leadership, thereby reducing the need for consumers to seek advice from others. For example, the hottest trends in teenage music, language, and fashion start in America's inner cities, then quickly spread to more mainstream youth in the suburbs. Thus, clothing companies who hope to appeal to these fickle and fashion-conscious youth often make a concerted effort to monitor urban opinion leaders' style and behavior. Levi-Strauss is a good example:

> ★ In recent years, Levi-Strauss has been squeezed by the competition as teens and youth flock to designer labels and more "cool" brands. To revitalize sales for its Silver Tab line of clothing, the company's ad agency sent out employees to build a network of contacts familiar with the urban scene, including club-hoppers, stylists, photographers, and disk jockeys. The agency kept a scrapbook of people and looks and separated them into "tribes" defined by the music they like, including electronica, hip-hop and rap, and retro soul music. Its illustrated ads appealing to hip-hop and rap culture featured the statement "It's bangin', son," which means "cool," and teenagers clad in Silver Tab clothing—baggy pants, hip huggers, tiny tops—and wearing accessories such as nose rings, beepers, and chunky gold jewelry.[14]

The importance of group influence varies across products and brands. It tends to be strongest when the product is visible to others whom the buyer respects. Purchases of products that are bought and used privately are not much affected by group influences because neither the product nor the brand will be noticed by others. If Anna Flores buys a camera, both the product and the brand will be visible to others whom she respects, and her decision to buy the camera and her brand choice may be influenced strongly by some of her groups, such as friends who belong to a photography club.

Family

Family members can strongly influence buyer behavior. The family is the most important consumer buying organization in society, and it has been researched extensively. Marketers are interested in the roles and influence of the husband, wife, and children on the purchase of different products and services.

Husband–wife involvement varies widely by product category and by stage in the buying process. Buying roles change with evolving consumer lifestyles. In the United States, the wife traditionally has been the main purchasing agent for the family, especially in the areas of food, household products, and clothing. But with 70 percent of women holding jobs outside the home and the willingness of husbands to do more of the family's purchasing, all this is changing. For example, women now buy about 45 percent of all cars and men account for about 40 percent of food-shopping dollars.[15]

Such changes suggest that marketers who've typically sold their products to only women or only men are now courting the opposite sex. For example, with research revealing that women now account for nearly half of all hardware store purchases, home improvement retailers such as Home Depot and Builders Square have turned what once were intimidating warehouses into female-friendly retail outlets. The new Builders Square II outlets feature decorator design centers at the front of the store. To attract more women, Builders Square runs ads targeting women in *Home, House Beautiful, Woman's Day,* and *Better Homes and Gardens.* Home Depot even offers bridal registries.

Family buying influences: Children can exert a strong influence on family buying decisions. Chevrolet actively woos these "back-seat consumers" in its marketing for the Chevy Venture minivan.

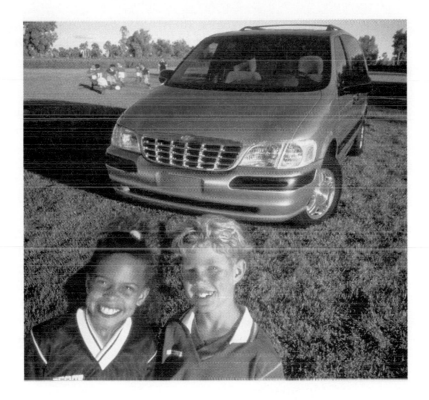

Similarly, after research indicated that women now make up 34 percent of the luxury car market, Cadillac has started paying more attention to this important segment. Male car designers at Cadillac are going about their work with paper clips on their fingers to simulate what it feels like to operate buttons, knobs, and other interior features with longer fingernails. The Cadillac Catera features an air-conditioned glove box to preserve such items as lipstick and film. Under the hood, yellow markings highlight where fluid fills go.[16]

Children may also have a strong influence on family buying decisions. Chevrolet recognizes these influences in marketing its Chevy Venture minivan. For example, it ran ads to woo these "back-seat consumers" in *Sports Illustrated for Kids,* which attracts mostly 8- to 14-year-old boys. "We're kidding ourselves when we think kids aren't aware of brands," says Venture's brand manager, adding that even she was surprised at how often parents told her that kids played a tie-breaking role in deciding which car to buy.[17]

In the case of expensive products and services, husbands and wives often make joint decisions. Anna Flores's husband may play an *influencer role* in her camera-buying decision. He may have an opinion about her buying a camera and about the kind of camera to buy. At the same time, she will be the primary decider, purchaser, and user.

Roles and Status

A person belongs to many groups—family, clubs, organizations. The person's position in each group can be defined in terms of both role and status. With her parents, Anna Flores plays the role of daughter; in her family, she plays the role of wife; in her company, she plays the role of brand manager. A *role* consists of the activities people are expected to perform according to the persons around them. Each of Anna's roles will influence some of her buying behavior.

Each role carries a *status* reflecting the general esteem given to it by society. People often choose products that show their status in society. For example, the role of brand manager has more status in our society than the role of daughter. As a brand manager, Anna will buy the kind of clothing that reflects her role and status.

Personal Factors

A buyer's decisions also are influenced by personal characteristics such as the buyer's *age* and *life-cycle stage, occupation, economic situation, lifestyle,* and *personality* and *self-concept.*

Age and Life-Cycle Stage

People change the goods and services they buy over their lifetimes. Tastes in food, clothes, furniture, and recreation are often age related. Buying is also shaped by the stage of the *family life cycle*—the stages through which families might pass as they mature over time. Table 5.2 lists the stages of the family life cycle. Marketers often define their target markets in terms of life-cycle stage and develop appropriate products and marketing plans for each stage. Traditional family life-cycle stages include young singles and married couples with children. Today, however, marketers are increasingly catering to a growing number of alternative, nontraditional stages such as unmarried couples, couples marrying later in life, childless couples, same-sex couples, single parents, extended parents (those with young adult children returning home), and others.

Occupation

A person's occupation affects the goods and services bought. Blue-collar workers tend to buy more rugged work clothes, whereas white-collar workers buy more business suits. Marketers try to identify the occupational groups that have an above-average interest in their products and services. A company can even specialize in making products needed by a given occupational group. Thus, computer software companies will design different products for brand managers, accountants, engineers, lawyers, and doctors.

Economic Situation

A person's economic situation will affect product choice. Anna Flores can consider buying an expensive Nikon if she has enough spendable income, savings, or borrowing power. Marketers of income-sensitive goods watch trends in personal income, savings, and interest rates. If economic indicators point to a recession, marketers can take steps to redesign, reposition, and reprice their products closely.

TABLE 5.2   FAMILY LIFE-CYCLE STAGES

Young	Middle-Aged	Older
Single	Single	Older married
Married without children	Married without children	Older unmarried
Married with children	Married with children	
Divorced with children	Married without dependent children	
	Divorced without children	
	Divorced with children	
	Divorced without dependent children	

Sources: Adapted from Patrick E. Murphy and William A. Staples, "A Modernized Family Life Cycle," *Journal of Consumer Research,* June 1979, p. 16; © Journal of Consumer Research, Inc., 1979. Also see Leon G. Shiffman and Leslie Lazar Kanuk, *Consumer Behavior,* 6th ed. (Upper Saddle River, NJ: Prentice Hall, 1997), pp. 360–69.

Lifestyle

Lifestyle
A person's pattern of living as expressed in his or her activities, interests, and opinions.

People coming from the same subculture, social class, and occupation may have quite different lifestyles. **Lifestyle** is a person's pattern of living as expressed in his or her psychographics. It involves measuring consumers' major *AIO dimensions—activities* (work, hobbies, shopping, sports, social events), *interests* (food, fashion, family, recreation), and *opinions* (about themselves, social issues, business, products). Lifestyle captures something more than the person's social class or personality. It profiles a person's whole pattern of acting and interacting in the world.

Several research firms have developed lifestyle classifications. The most widely used is the SRI Consulting's *Values and Lifestyles (VALS)*™ typology (see Figure 5.3). VALS classifies people according to how they spend their time and money. It divides consumers into eight groups based on two major dimensions: self-orientation and resources. *Self-orientation* groups include *principle-oriented* consumers who buy based on their views of the world; *status-oriented* buyers who base their purchases on the actions and opinions of others; and *action-oriented* buyers who are driven by their desire for activity, variety, and risk taking. Consumers within each orientation are further classified into those with *abundant resources* and those with *minimal resources,* depending on whether they have high or low levels of income, education, health, self-confidence, energy, and other factors. Consumers with either very high or very low levels of resources are classified without regard to

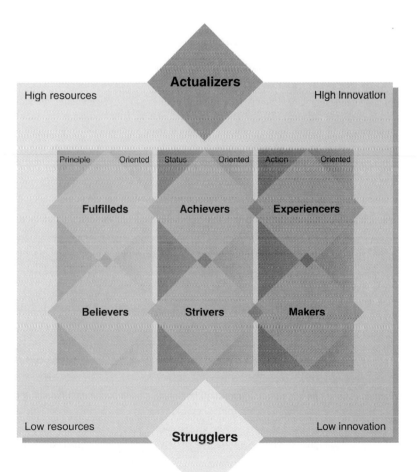

FIGURE 5.3   VALS lifestyle classifications

Source: Reprinted with permission of SRI International, Menlo Park, CA. VALS is a registered trademark of SRI International.

Lifestyles: Jeep targets people who want to "leave the civilized world behind."

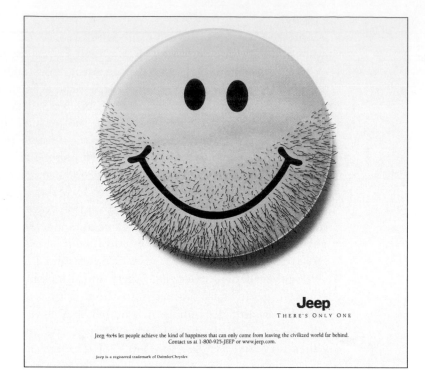

their self-orientations (actualizers, strugglers). Actualizers are people with so many resources that they can indulge in any or all self-orientations. In contrast, strugglers are people with too few resources to be included in any consumer orientation.

Iron City beer, a well-known brand in Pittsburgh, used VALS to update its image and improve sales. Iron City was losing sales—its aging core users were drinking less beer, and younger men weren't buying the brand. According to VALS research, experiencers drink the most beer, followed by strivers. To assess Iron City's image problems, the company interviewed men in these categories. It gave the men stacks of pictures of different kinds of people and asked them to identify first Iron City brand users and then people most like themselves. The men pictured Iron City drinkers as blue-collar steelworkers stopping off at the local bar. However, they saw themselves as more modern, hard working, and fun loving. They strongly rejected the outmoded, heavy-industry image of Pittsburgh. Based on this research, Iron City created ads linking its beer to the new self-image of target consumers. The ads mingled images of the old Pittsburgh with those of the new, dynamic city and scenes of young experiencers and strivers having fun and working hard. Within just one month of the start of the campaign, Iron City sales shot up by 26 percent.[18]

VALS can also be used to understand Internet behavior. SRI Consulting's 1999 Leading Edge survey showed that three-fourths of all Actualizers access the Internet but only one in six Believers do so. VALS also shows differences in how VALS groups use the Internet. For example, Actualizers and Fulfilleds are more likely to use the Internet to track investments whereas Experiencers and Strivers are more likely to visit chat sites. SRI's Web site (future.sri.com) allows visitors to complete the VALS questionnaire to determine their VALS type.[19] Others are developing tools for classifying consumers by "technology type" (see Marketing Highlight 5.1).

Lifestyle classifications are by no means universal—they can vary significantly from country to country. Advertising agency McCann-Erikson London, for example, found the following British lifestyles: Avant Guardians (interested in change); Pontificators (traditionalists, very British); Chameleons (follow the crowd); and Sleepwalkers (contented underachievers). The D'Arcy, Masius, Benton, & Bowles agency identified five categories of Russian consumers: Kuptsi (merchants),

Heavy coffee drinkers tend to be high on sociability, so to attract customers Starbucks and other coffeehouses create environments in which people can relax and socialize over a cup of steaming coffee.

Cossacks, Students, Business Executives, and Russian Souls. Cossacks are characterized as ambitious, independent, and status seeking; Russian Souls as passive, fearful of choices, and hopeful. Thus, a typical Cossack might drive a BMW, smoke Dunhill cigarettes, and drink Remy Martin liquor, whereas a Russian Soul would drive a Lada, smoke Marlboros, and drink Smirnoff vodka.[20]

When used carefully, the lifestyle concept can help the marketer understand changing consumer values and how they affect buying behavior. Anna Flores, for example, can choose to live the role of a capable homemaker, a career woman, or a free spirit—or all three. She plays several roles, and the way she blends them expresses her lifestyle. If she becomes a professional photographer, this would change her lifestyle, in turn changing what and how she buys.

Personality and Self-Concept

Personality

A person's distinguishing psychological characteristics that lead to relatively consistent and lasting responses to his or her own environment.

Each person's distinct personality influences his or her buying behavior. **Personality** refers to the unique psychological characteristics that lead to relatively consistent and lasting responses to one's own environment. Personality is usually described in terms of traits such as self-confidence, dominance, sociability, autonomy, defensiveness, adaptability, and aggressiveness. Personality can be useful in analyzing consumer behavior for certain product or brand choices. For example, coffee marketers have discovered that heavy coffee drinkers tend to be high on sociability. Thus, to attract customers, Starbucks and other coffeehouses create environments in which people can relax and socialize over a cup of steaming coffee.

Many marketers use a concept related to personality—a person's *self-concept* (also called *self-image*). The basic self-concept premise is that people's possessions contribute to and reflect their identities; that is, "we are what we have." Thus, in order to understand consumer behavior, the marketer must first understand the relationship between consumer self-concept and possessions. For example, the founder and chief executive of Barnes & Noble, the nation's leading bookseller, notes that people buy books to support their self-images:

> People have the mistaken notion that the thing you do with books is read them. Wrong.... People buy books for what the purchase says about them—their taste, their cultivation, their trendiness. Their aim ... is to connect themselves, or those to whom they give the books as gifts, with all the other refined owners of Edgar Allen Poe collections or sensitive owners of Virginia Woolf collections.... [The result is that] you can sell books as consumer

MARKETING
HIGHLIGHT
5.1

MOUSE POTATOES AND TECHNO-STRIVERS: WHAT MAKES TECHNOLOGY BUYERS *CLICK*?

Traditional market research may tell you who buys household computers. It may even tell you the kind of lifestyles they live. However, it won't tell you who in the household is using the computer and why. For example, it won't tell you that the wife is using the PC to take a distance-learning course, that the son is using it to download computer games from various Web sites, that the daughter is using it to log onto about a dozen chat groups, or that the husband, a confirmed technophobe, only logs on once in a blue moon to get

Technology buyer lifestyles: Forrester's "Technographics" approach segments consumers according to their motivation, desire, and ability to invest in technology

products, with seductive displays, flashy posters, an emphasis on the glamour of the book, and the fashionableness of the bestseller and the trendy author.[21]

Anna Flores may see herself as outgoing, creative, and active. Therefore, she will favor a camera that projects the same qualities. If the Nikon is promoted as a camera for outgoing, creative, and active people, then its brand image will match her self-image.

Psychological Factors

A person's buying choices are further influenced by four major psychological factors: *motivation, perception, learning,* and *beliefs* and *attitudes.*

stock quotes. A marketer who promotes the newest online gizmo to the husband will surely miss the mark.

Several new market research tools have emerged to help marketers of technology products get a better read on the buying habits of technology buyers and users. These new tools segment consumers based on technology types. Two of the most prominent approaches under development are Forrester Inc.'s "Technographics," which segments consumers according to motivation, desire, and ability to invest in technology, and SRI Consulting's iVALS, which focuses on attitudes, preferences, and behavior of online service and Internet users. Forrester Research developed its Technographics scheme by hiring NPD, a polling and research firm, to survey 131,000 consumers. The framework splits people into 10 categories, such as:

Fast Forwards are the biggest spenders on computer technology. Fast Forwards are early adopters of new technology for home, office, and personal use.

New Age Nurturers are also big spenders but focused on technology for home uses, such as a family PC.

Mouse Potatoes are consumers who are dedicated to interactive entertainment and willing to spend for the latest in "technotainment."

Techno-Strivers are consumers who use technology primarily to gain a career edge.

Handshakers are older consumers, typically managers, who don't touch computers at work and leave that to younger assistants.

SRI's iVALS also divides consumers into 10 segments, but the focus is on Internet use. Some of the iVALS segments are as follows:

Wizards are the most skilled and active Internet users for whom mastery of technology figures prominently in their identities.

Immigrants are recent arrivals to cyberspace who usually are familiar with only very specific parts of the Internet and are drawn online because they have to be for work or school.

Socialites are users who are strongly oriented toward social aspects of the Internet and who are prominent participants in online discussions. They are iVALS's youngest segment, mostly under 30 years of age.

Both Technographics and iVALS reinforce the idea of a dual-tier society, but one is based on knowledge, not income. For instance, people who are more computer savvy are perfect targets for an electronic banking product that allows them to pay bills, switch money between accounts, and check balances on the computer. Those who are not computer literate will still write checks by hand, send payments through "snail mail," and stand in line for a bank teller.

Yet the new market research tools reveal many shades in the spectrum between "the knows" and "the know nots." For instance, Delta Airlines wants to use Technographics to better target online ticket sales. It is creating marketing campaigns for time-strapped "Fast Forwards" and "New Age Nurturers," and it will eliminate those who are "technology pessimists" from its list of targets. "Traditional market research gives you a picture of the universe," says Paula Lai, manager of Delta's marketing research. But what good is that picture today, she adds, if it doesn't tell you who will book tickets online?

Sources: Andy Hines, "Do You Know Your Technology Type?" *The Futurist,* September–October 1997, pp. 10–11; Paul C. Judge, "Are Tech Buyers Different?" *Business Week,* January 26, 1998, pp. 64–65, 68; Josh Bernoff, Shelley Morrisette, and Kenneth Clemmer, "The Forrester Report," Forrester Research, Inc., 1998; the SRI Consulting Web site (future.sri.com), March 2000; and the Forrester Research Web site (www.forrester.com), February, 2000.

Motivation

We know that Anna Flores became interested in buying a camera. Why? What is she *really* seeking? What *needs* is she trying to satisfy?

A person has many needs at any given time. Some are *biological,* arising from states of tension such as hunger, thirst, or discomfort. Others are *psychological,* arising from the need for recognition, esteem, or belonging. Most of these needs will not be strong enough to motivate the person to act at a given point in time. A need becomes a *motive* when it is aroused to a sufficient level of intensity. A **motive** (or *drive*) is a need that is sufficiently pressing to direct the person to seek satisfaction. Psychologists have developed theories of human motivation. Two of the most popular—the theories of Sigmund Freud and Abraham Maslow—have quite different meanings for consumer analysis and marketing.

Motive (drive)
A need that is sufficiently pressing to direct the person to seek satisfaction of the need.

Freud's Theory of Motivation.   Freud assumed that people are largely unconscious about the real psychological forces shaping their behavior. He saw the person as growing up and repressing many urges. These urges are never eliminated or under perfect control; they emerge in dreams, in slips of the tongue, in neurotic and obsessive behavior, or ultimately in psychoses.

Thus, Freud suggests that a person does not fully understand his or her motivation. If Anna Flores wants to purchase an expensive camera, she may describe her motive as wanting a hobby or career. At a deeper level, she may be purchasing the camera to impress others with her creative talent. At a still deeper level, she may be buying the camera to feel young and independent again.

Motivation researchers collect in-depth information from small samples of consumers to uncover the deeper motives for their product choices. They use nondirective depth interviews and various "projective techniques" to throw the ego off guard—techniques such as word association, sentence completion, picture interpretation, and role playing. Motivation researchers have reached some interesting and sometimes odd conclusions about what may be in the buyer's mind regarding certain purchases. For example, one classic study concluded that consumers resist prunes because they are wrinkled looking and remind people of sickness and old age. Despite its sometimes unusual conclusions, motivation research remains a useful tool for marketers seeking a deeper understanding of consumer behavior (see Marketing Highlight 5.2).

Maslow's Theory of Motivation.   Abraham Maslow sought to explain why people are driven by particular needs at particular times. Why does one person spend much time and energy on personal safety and another on gaining the esteem of others? Maslow's answer is that human needs are arranged in a hierarchy, from the most pressing to the least pressing. Maslow's hierarchy of needs is shown in Figure 5.4. In order of importance, they are *physiological* needs, *safety* needs, *social* needs, *esteem* needs, and *self-actualization* needs. A person tries to satisfy the most important need first. When that need is satisfied, it will stop being a motivator and the person will then try to satisfy the next most important need. For example, starving people (physiological need) will not take an interest in the latest happenings in the art world (self-actualization needs), nor in how they are seen or esteemed by others (social or esteem needs), nor even in whether they are breathing clean air (safety needs). But as each important need is satisfied, the next most important need will come into play.

What light does Maslow's theory throw on Anna Flores's interest in buying a camera? We can guess that Anna has satisfied her physiological, safety, and social needs; they do not motivate her interest in cameras. Her camera interest might come from a strong need for more esteem. Or it might come from a need for self-actualization— she might want to be a creative person and express herself through photography.[22]

Perception

A motivated person is ready to act. How the person acts is influenced by his or her own perception of the situation. All of us learn by the flow of information through our five senses: sight, hearing, smell, touch, and taste. However, each of us receives, organizes, and interprets this sensory information in an individual way. **Perception** is the process by which people select, organize, and interpret information to form a meaningful picture of the world.

People can form different perceptions of the same stimulus because of three perceptual processes: selective attention, selective distortion, and selective retention. People are exposed to a great amount of stimuli every day. For example, the average person may be exposed to more than 1,500 ads in a single day. It is impossible

Perception
The process by which people select, organize, and interpret information to form a meaningful picture of the world.

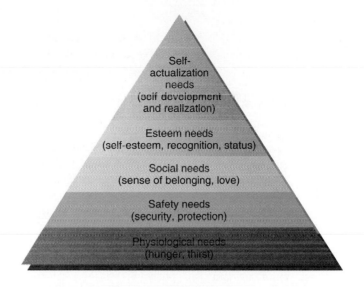

FIGURE 5.4   Maslow's hierarchy of needs

Source: From *Motivation and Personality* by Abraham H. Maslow. Copyright © 1970 by Abraham H. Maslow. Copyright 1954, 1987 by Harper & Row Publishers, Inc. Reprinted by permission of Addison-Wesley Educational Publishers Inc. Also see Barbara Marx Hubbard, "Seeking Our Future Potentials," *The Futurist,* May 1998, pp. 29–32.

for a person to pay attention to all these stimuli. *Selective attention*—the tendency for people to screen out most of the information to which they are exposed—means that marketers have to work especially hard to attract the consumer's attention.

Even noted stimuli do not always come across in the intended way. Each person fits incoming information into an existing mind-set. *Selective distortion* describes the tendency of people to interpret information in a way that will support what they already believe. Anna Flores may hear a salesperson mention some good and bad points about a competing camera brand. Because she already has a strong leaning toward Nikon, she is likely to distort those points in order to conclude that Nikon is the better camera. Selective distortion means that marketers must try to understand the mind-sets of consumers and how these will affect interpretations of advertising and sales information.

People also will forget much that they learn. They tend to retain information that supports their attitudes and beliefs. Because of *selective retention,* Anna is likely to remember good points made about the Nikon and to forget good points made about competing cameras. Because of selective exposure, distortion, and retention, marketers have to work hard to get their messages through. This fact explains why marketers use so much drama and repetition in sending messages to their market.

Interestingly, although most marketers worry about whether their offers will be perceived at all, some consumers worry that they will be affected by marketing messages without even knowing it—through *subliminal advertising.* In 1957, a researcher announced that he had flashed the phrases "Eat popcorn" and "Drink Coca-Cola" on a screen in a New Jersey movie theater every five seconds for 1/300th of a second. He reported that although viewers did not consciously recognize these messages, they absorbed them subconsciously and bought 58 percent more popcorn and 18 percent more Coke. Suddenly advertisers and consumer-protection groups became intensely interested in subliminal perception. People voiced fears of being brainwashed, and California and Canada declared the practice illegal. Although the researcher later admitted to making up the data, the issue has not died. Some consumers still fear that they are being manipulated by subliminal messages.

MARKETING HIGHLIGHT
5.2

"TOUCHY-FEELY" RESEARCH INTO CONSUMER MOTIVATIONS

The term *motivation research* refers to qualitative research designed to probe consumers' hidden, subconscious motivations. Consumers often don't know or can't describe just why they act as they do. Thus, motivation researchers use a variety of nondirective and projective techniques to uncover underlying emotions and attitudes toward brands and buying situations that will help them to form deeper, stronger connections with consumers. The techniques range from sentence completion, word association, and inkblot or cartoon interpretation tests, to having con-

Motivation research: When asked to sketch figures of typical cake mix users, subjects portrayed Pillsbury customers as grandmotherly types and Duncan Hines buyers as svelte and contemporary.

sumers describe typical brand users or form daydreams and fantasies about brands or buying situations. Some of these techniques verge on the bizarre. One writer offers the following tongue-in-cheek summary of a motivation research session:

Good morning, ladies and gentlemen. We've called you here today for a little consumer research. Now, lie down on the couch, toss your inhibitions out the window, and let's try a little free association. First, think about brands as if they were your *friends.* Imagine you could talk to your TV dinner. What would he say? And what would you say to him? . . . Now, think of your shampoo as an animal. Go on, don't be shy. Would it be a panda or a lion? A snake or a wooly worm? For our final exercise, let's all sit up and pull out our magic markers. Draw a picture of a typical cake-mix user. Would she wear an apron or a negligee? A business suit or a can-can dress?

Such projective techniques seem pretty goofy. But more and more, marketers are turning to these touchy-feely approaches to probe consumer psyches and develop better marketing strategies.

Many advertising agencies employ teams of psychologists, anthropologists, and other social scientists to carry out motivation research. One agency routinely conducts one-on-one, therapylike interviews to delve into the inner workings of consumers. Another agency asks consumers to describe their favorite brands as animals or cars (say, Cadillacs versus Chevrolets) in order to assess the prestige associated with various brands. Still another agency has consumers draw figures of typical brand users:

In one instance, the agency asked 50 interviewees to sketch likely buyers of two different brands of cake mixes. Consistently, the group portrayed Pillsbury customers as apron-clad, grandmotherly types, whereas they pictured Duncan Hines purchasers as svelte, contemporary women.

Some motivation research studies employ more basic techniques, such as simply mingling with or watching consumers to find out what makes them tick. For example, in the appliance industry, consumer brand loyalties have been built up over decades and passed on from generation to

---

Numerous studies by psychologists and consumer researchers have found no link between subliminal messages and consumer behavior. It appears that subliminal advertising simply doesn't have the power attributed to it by its critics. Most advertisers scoff at the notion of an industry conspiracy to manipulate consumers through "invisible" messages. As one advertising agency executive put it, "We have enough trouble persuading consumers using a series of up-front 30-second ads—how could we do it in 1/300th of a second?"

Learning
Changes in an individual's behavior arising from experience.

Learning

When people act, they learn. **Learning** describes changes in an individual's behavior arising from experience. Learning theorists say that most human behavior is learned. Learning occurs through the interplay of *drives, stimuli, cues, responses,* and *reinforcement.*

generation. To shake up entrenched market share and tap into consumers' often unexpressed needs, appliance giant Whirlpool Corporation went so far as to hire an anthropologist. A skilled observer, the anthropologist went to people's homes, observed how they used their appliances, and talked with all the household members. Whirlpool found that in busy families, women aren't the only ones doing the laundry. Armed with this knowledge, company engineers came up with color-coded washer and dryer controls to make it easier for kids and men to pitch in.

In an effort to understand the teenage consumer market better, ad agency BSB Worldwide videotaped teenagers' rooms in 25 countries. It found surprising similarities across countries and cultures:

From the steamy playgrounds of Los Angeles to the stately boulevards of Singapore, kids show amazing similarities in taste, language, and attitude.... From the gear and posters on display, it's hard to tell whether the rooms are in Los Angeles, Mexico City, or Tokyo. Basketballs sit alongside soccer balls. Closets overflow with staples from an international, unisex uniform: baggy Levi's or Deisel jeans, NBA jackets, and rugged shoes from Timberland or Doc Martens.

Bugle Boy found that traditional focus groups fail miserably in getting the scoop on teens and GenXers. These often-cynical young people are skeptical of sales pitches and just won't speak up in a conference room with two-way mirrors. Working with Chilton Research, Bugle Boy found an innovative solution. It plucked four young men out of obscurity, handed each of them an 8mm video camera, and told them to document their lives. The young amateurs were given only broad categories to work with: school, home, closet, and shopping. Bugle Boy then used the videos to prompt discussions of product and lifestyle issues in "free-form" focus groups held in unconventional locations, such as restaurants. Says one Bugle Boy ad manager, "I think this really helped us to get a handle on what these kids do. It let us see what their lives are all about, their awareness of the Bugle Boy brand, and how they perceive the brand."

Similarly, researchers at Sega of America's ad agency have learned a lot about video game buying behavior by hanging around with 150 kids in their bedrooms and by shopping with them in malls. Above all else, they learned, do everything fast. As a result, in Sega's most recent 15-second commercials, some images fly by so quickly that adults cannot recall seeing them, even after repeated showings. The kids, weaned on MTV, recollect them keenly.

Some marketers dismiss such motivation research as mumbo jumbo. These approaches do present some problems: They use small samples and researcher interpretations of results are often highly subjective, sometimes leading to rather exotic explanations of otherwise ordinary buying behavior. However, others believe strongly that these approaches can provide interesting nuggets of insight into the relationships between consumers and the brands they buy. To marketers who use them, motivation research techniques provide a flexible and varied means of gaining insights into deeply held and often mysterious motivations behind consumer buying behavior.

Sources: Excerpts from Annetta Miller and Dody Tsiantar, "Psyching Out Consumers," *Newsweek,* February 27, 1989, pp. 46–47; Shawn Tully, "Teens: The Most Global Market of All," *Fortune,* May 6, 1994, pp. 90–97; and Tobi Elkin, "Product Pampering," *Brandweek,* June 16, 1997, pp. 38–40. Also see "They Understand Your Kids," *Fortune,* special issue, Autumn–Winter 1993, pp. 29–30; Cyndee Miller, "Sometimes a Researcher Has No Alternative but to Hang Out in a Bar," *Marketing News,* January 3, 1994, pp. 16, 26; Ronald B. Lieber, "Storytelling: A New Way to Get Close to Your Customer," *Fortune,* February 3, 1997, pp. 102–8; Jerry W. Thomas, "Finding Unspoken Reasons for Consumers' Choices," *Marketing News,* June 8, 1998, pp. 10–11; Michele Marchetti, "Marketing's Weird Science," *Sales & Marketing Management,* May 1999, p. 87; and Kendra Parker, "How Do You Like Your Beef?" *American Demographics,* January 2000, pp. 35–37.

We saw that Anna Flores has a drive for self-actualization. A *drive* is a strong internal stimulus that calls for action. Her drive becomes a motive when it is directed toward a particular *stimulus object,* in this case a camera. Anna's response to the idea of buying a camera is conditioned by the surrounding cues. *Cues* are minor stimuli that determine when, where, and how the person responds. Seeing cameras in a shop window, hearing of a special sale price, and receiving her husband's support are all cues that can influence Anna's *response* to her interest in buying a camera.

Suppose Anna buys the Nikon. If the experience is rewarding, she will probably use the camera more and more. Her response to cameras will be *reinforced.* Then the next time she shops for a camera, binoculars, or some similar product, the probability is greater that she will buy a Nikon product.

The practical significance of learning theory for marketers is that they can build up demand for a product by associating it with strong drives, using motivating cues, and providing positive reinforcement.

Beliefs and Attitudes

Through doing and learning, people acquire beliefs and attitudes. These, in turn, influence their buying behavior. A **belief** is a descriptive thought that a person has about something. Anna Flores may believe that a Nikon camera takes great pictures, stands up well under hard use, and costs $450. These beliefs may be based on real knowledge, opinion, or faith, and may or may not carry an emotional charge. For example, Anna Flores's belief that a Nikon camera is heavy may or may not matter to her decision.

Marketers are interested in the beliefs that people formulate about specific products and services, because these beliefs make up product and brand images that affect buying behavior. If some of the beliefs are wrong and prevent purchase, the marketer will want to launch a campaign to correct them.

People have attitudes regarding religion, politics, clothes, music, food, and almost everything else. **Attitude** describes a person's relatively consistent evaluations, feelings, and tendencies toward an object or idea. Attitudes put people into a frame of mind of liking or disliking things, of moving toward or away from them. Thus, Anna Flores may hold attitudes such as "Buy the best," "The Japanese make the best products in the world," and "Creativity and self-expression are among the most important things in life." If so, the Nikon camera would fit well into Anna's existing attitudes.

Belief
A descriptive thought that a person holds about something.

Attitude
A person's consistently favorable or unfavorable evaluations, feelings, and tendencies toward an object or idea.

Attitudes are difficult to change, but the National Fluid Milk Processors' wildly popular milk mustache campaign succeeded in changing attitudes toward milk.

Milk isn't just for tadpoles.

Did you know 3 out of 4 adults don't get enough calcium? It takes at least 3 glasses of milk a day. I always keep some at my pad.

got milk?

Attitudes are difficult to change. A person's attitudes fit into a pattern, and to change one attitude may require difficult adjustments in many others. Thus, a company should usually try to fit its products into existing attitudes rather than attempt to change attitudes. Of course, there are exceptions in which the great cost of trying to change attitudes may pay off handsomely:

By 1994, milk consumption had been in decline for 25 years. The general perception was that milk was unhealthy, outdated, just for kids, or good only with cookies and cake. Beginning in 1994, the National Fluid Milk Processors Education Program (MilkPEP) began a $55 million print ad campaign featuring milk be-mustached celebrities like Cindy Crawford, Danny DeVito, Patrick Ewing, and Ivana Trump with the tag line "Milk: Where's your mustache?" The campaign has not only been wildly popular, it has been successful as well—not only did it stop the decline, milk consumption actually increased. By 1999, the campaign was still running and MilkPEP had upped spending on it to $110 million. Although initially the target market was women in their twenties, the campaign has been expanded to other target markets and has gained cult status with teens, much to their parents' delight. Teens collect the print ads featuring celebrities ranging from music stars Hanson and Leann Rimes, supermodel Tyra Banks, and Garfield to sports idols such as Mark McGuire, Jeff Gordon, Pete Sampras, Gabriela Sabatini, and Dennis Rodman. (Says Dennis, "Three glasses a day give the average man all the calcium he needs. Maybe I should drink six.") "Milking" the success of the print ads, milk producers set up Club Milk on a Web site (www.whymilk.com) where they limit membership only to those who pledge they will drink three glasses of the white fluid a day.[23]

We can now appreciate the many forces acting on consumer behavior. The consumer's choice results from the complex interplay of cultural, social, personal, and psychological factors.

TYPES OF BUYING DECISION BEHAVIOR

Buying behavior differs greatly for a tube of toothpaste, a tennis racket, an expensive camera, and a new car. More complex decisions usually involve more buying participants and more buyer deliberation. Figure 5.5 shows types of consumer buying behavior based on the degree of buyer involvement and the degree of differences among brands.[24]

Complex buying behavior
Consumer buying behavior in situations characterized by high consumer involvement in a purchase and significant perceived differences among brands.

Complex Buying Behavior

Consumers undertake **complex buying behavior** when they are highly involved in a purchase and perceive significant differences among brands. Consumers may be

FIGURE 5.5   Four types of buying behavior

Source: Adapted from Henry Assael, *Consumer Behavior and Marketing Action* (Boston: Kent Publishing Company, 1987), p. 87. Copyright © 1987 by Wadsworth, Inc. Printed by permission of Kent Publishing Company, a division of Wadsworth, Inc.

highly involved when the product is expensive, risky, purchased infrequently, and highly self-expressive. Typically, the consumer has much to learn about the product category. For example, a personal computer buyer may not know what attributes to consider. Many product features carry no real meaning: a "Pentium Pro chip," "super VGA resolution," or "megs of RAM."

This buyer will pass through a learning process, first developing beliefs about the product, then attitudes, and then making a thoughtful purchase choice. Marketers of high-involvement products must understand the information-gathering and evaluation behavior of high-involvement consumers. They need to help buyers learn about product-class attributes and their relative importance, and about what the company's brand offers on the important attributes. Marketers need to differentiate their brand's features, perhaps by describing the brand's benefits using print media with long copy. They must motivate store salespeople and the buyer's acquaintances to influence the final brand choice.

Dissonance-Reducing Buying Behavior

Dissonance-reducing buying behavior
Consumer buying behavior in situations characterized by high involvement but few perceived differences among brands.

Dissonance-reducing buying behavior occurs when consumers are highly involved with an expensive, infrequent, or risky purchase, but see little difference among brands. For example, consumers buying carpeting may face a high-involvement decision because carpeting is expensive and self-expressive. Yet buyers may consider most carpet brands in a given price range to be the same. In this case, because perceived brand differences are not large, buyers may shop around to learn what is available, but buy relatively quickly. They may respond primarily to a good price or to purchase convenience.

After the purchase, consumers might experience *postpurchase dissonance* (after-sale discomfort) when they notice certain disadvantages of the purchased carpet brand or hear favorable things about brands not purchased. To counter such dissonance, the marketer's after-sale communications should provide evidence and support to help consumers feel good about their brand choices.

Habitual Buying Behavior

Habitual buying behavior
Consumer buying behavior in situations characterized by low consumer involvement and few significant perceived brand differences.

Habitual buying behavior occurs under conditions of low consumer involvement and little significant brand difference. For example, take salt. Consumers have little involvement in this product category—they simply go to the store and reach for a brand. If they keep reaching for the same brand, it is out of habit rather than strong brand loyalty. Consumers appear to have low involvement with most low-cost, frequently purchased products.

In such cases, consumer behavior does not pass through the usual belief–attitude–behavior sequence. Consumers do not search extensively for information about the brands, evaluate brand characteristics, and make weighty decisions about which brands to buy. Instead, they passively receive information as they watch television or read magazines. Ad repetition creates *brand familiarity* rather than *brand conviction*. Consumers do not form strong attitudes toward a brand; they select the brand because it is familiar. Because they are not highly involved with the product, consumers may not evaluate the choice even after purchase. Thus, the buying process involves brand beliefs formed by passive learning, followed by purchase behavior, which may or may not be followed by evaluation.

Because buyers are not highly committed to any brands, marketers of low-involvement products with few brand differences often use price and sales promotions to stimulate product trial. In advertising for a low-involvement product, ad copy should stress only a few key points. Visual symbols and imagery are important because they can be remembered easily and associated with the brand. Ad campaigns should include high repetition of short-duration messages. Television is usually more effective than print media because it is a low-involvement medium suitable for passive learning. Advertising planning should be based on classical conditioning theory, in which buyers learn to identify a certain product by a symbol repeatedly attached to it.

Marketers can try to convert low-involvement products into higher-involvement ones by linking them to some involving issue. Procter & Gamble does this when it links Crest toothpaste to avoiding cavities. Or the product can be linked to some involving personal situation. Nestlé did this in its series of ads for Taster's Choice coffee, each consisting of a new soap-opera-like episode featuring the evolving romantic relationship between two neighbors. At best, these strategies can raise consumer involvement from a low to a moderate level. However, they are not likely to propel the consumer into highly involved buying behavior.

Variety-Seeking Buying Behavior

Variety-seeking buying behavior
Consumer buying behavior in situations characterized by low consumer involvement but significant perceived brand differences.

Consumers undertake **variety-seeking buying behavior** in situations characterized by low consumer involvement but significant perceived brand differences. In such cases, consumers often do a lot of brand switching. For example, when buying cookies, a consumer may hold some beliefs, choose a cookie brand without much evaluation, then evaluate that brand during consumption. But the next time, the consumer might pick another brand out of boredom or simply to try something different. Brand switching occurs for the sake of variety rather than because of dissatisfaction.

In such product categories, the marketing strategy may differ for the market leader and minor brands. The market leader will try to encourage habitual buying behavior by dominating shelf space, keeping shelves fully stocked, and running frequent reminder advertising. Challenger firms will encourage variety seeking by offering lower prices, special deals, coupons, free samples, and advertising that presents reasons for trying something new.

THE BUYER DECISION PROCESS

Now that we have looked at the influences that affect buyers, we are ready to look at how consumers make buying decisions. Figure 5.6 shows that the buyer decision process consists of five stages: *need recognition, information search, evaluation of alternatives, purchase decision,* and *postpurchase behavior.* Clearly, the buying process starts long before actual purchase and continues long after. Marketers need to focus on the entire buying process rather than on just the purchase decision.

The figure implies that consumers pass through all five stages with every purchase. But in more routine purchases, consumers often skip or reverse some of these stages. A woman buying her regular brand of toothpaste would recognize the need

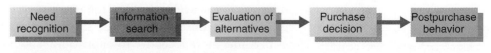

FIGURE 5.6   Buyer decision process

and go right to the purchase decision, skipping information search and evaluation. However, we use the model in Figure 5.6 because it shows all the considerations that arise when a consumer faces a new and complex purchase situation.

To illustrate this model, we will again follow Anna Flores and try to understand how she became interested in buying an expensive camera, and the stages she went through to make the final choice.

Need Recognition

Need recognition
The first stage of the buyer decision process in which the consumer recognizes a problem or need.

The buying process starts with **need recognition**—the buyer recognizes a problem or need. The buyer senses a difference between his or her *actual* state and some *desired* state. The need can be triggered by *internal stimuli* when one of the person's normal needs—hunger, thirst, sex—rises to a level high enough to become a drive. A need can also be triggered by *external stimuli*. Anna Flores might have felt the need for a new hobby when her busy season at work slowed down, and she thought of cameras after talking to a friend about photography or seeing a camera ad. At this stage, the marketer should research consumers to find out what kinds of needs or problems arise, what brought them about, and how they led the consumer to this particular product.

By gathering such information, the marketer can identify the factors that most often trigger interest in the product and can develop marketing programs that involve these factors.

Information Search

Information search
The stage of the buyer decision process in which the consumer is aroused to search for more information; the consumer may simply have heightened attention or may go into active information search.

An aroused consumer may or may not search for more information. If the consumer's drive is strong and a satisfying product is near at hand, the consumer is likely to buy it then. If not, the consumer may store the need in memory or undertake an **information search** related to the need.

At one level, the consumer may simply enter *heightened attention*. Here Anna Flores becomes more receptive to information about cameras. She pays attention to camera ads, cameras used by friends, and camera conversations. Or Anna may go into *active information search,* in which she looks for reading material, phones friends, and gathers information in other ways. The amount of searching she does will depend on the strength of her drive, the amount of information she starts with, the ease of obtaining more information, the value she places on additional information, and the satisfaction she gets from searching.

The consumer can obtain information from any of several sources. These include *personal sources* (family, friends, neighbors, acquaintances), *commercial sources* (advertising, salespeople, dealers, packaging, displays, Web sites), *public sources* (mass media, consumer-rating organizations), and *experiential sources* (handling, examining, using the product). The relative influence of these information sources varies with the product and the buyer. Generally, the consumer receives the most information about a product from commercial sources—those controlled by the marketer. The most effective sources, however, tend to be personal. Commercial sources normally *inform* the buyer, but personal sources *legitimize* or *evaluate* products for the buyer.

People often ask others—friends, relatives, acquaintances, professionals—for recommendations concerning a product or service. Thus, companies have a strong interest in building such *word-of-mouth sources.* These sources have two chief advantages. First, they are convincing: Word of mouth is the only promotion method that is *of* consumers, *by* consumers, and *for* consumers. Having loyal, satisfied customers that brag about doing business with you is the dream of every business owner. Not only are satisfied customers repeat buyers, but they are also walking, talking billboards for your business. Second, the costs are low. Keeping in touch with satisfied customers and turning them into word-of-mouth advocates costs the business relatively little.[25]

As more information is obtained, the consumer's awareness and knowledge of the available brands and features increases. In her information search, Anna Flores learned about the many camera brands available. The information also helped her drop certain brands from consideration. A company must design its marketing mix to make prospects aware of and knowledgeable about its brand. It should carefully identify consumers' sources of information and the importance of each source. Consumers should be asked how they first heard about the brand, what information they received, and what importance they placed on different information sources.

Evaluation of Alternatives

Alternative evaluation
The stage of the buyer decision process in which the consumer uses information to evaluate alternative brands in the choice set.

We have seen how the consumer uses information to arrive at a set of final brand choices. How does the consumer choose among the alternative brands? The marketer needs to know about **alternative evaluation**—that is, how the consumer processes information to arrive at brand choices. Unfortunately, consumers do not use a simple and single evaluation process in all buying situations. Instead, several evaluation processes are at work.

The consumer arrives at attitudes toward different brands through some evaluation procedure. How consumers go about evaluating purchase alternatives depends on the individual consumer and the specific buying situation. In some cases, consumers use careful calculations and logical thinking. At other times, the same consumers do little or no evaluating; instead they buy on impulse and rely on intuition. Sometimes consumers make buying decisions on their own; sometimes they turn to friends, consumer guides, or salespeople for buying advice.

Suppose Anna Flores has narrowed her choices to four cameras. Also suppose that she is primarily interested in four attributes—picture quality, ease of use, camera size, and price. Anna has formed beliefs about how each brand rates on each attribute. Clearly, if one camera rated best on all the attributes, we could predict that

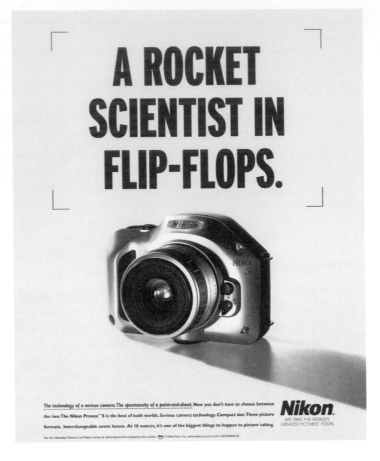

Evaluating alternatives: In some cases, consumers use careful calculations; in others they do little or no evaluating. In the small print, this Nikon ad emphasizes its serious camera technology, compact size, three picture-taking formats, and interchangeable zoom lenses—"The technology of a serious camera. The spontaneity of a point-and-shoot."

Anna would choose it. However, the brands vary in appeal. Anna might base her buying decision on only one attribute, and her choice would be easy to predict. If she wants picture quality above everything, she will buy the camera that she thinks has the best picture quality. But most buyers consider several attributes, each with different importance. If we knew the importance weights that Anna assigns to each of the four attributes, we could predict her camera choice more reliably.

Marketers should study buyers to find out how they actually evaluate brand alternatives. If they know what evaluative processes go on, marketers can take steps to influence the buyer's decision.

Purchase Decision

Purchase decision
The stage of the buyer decision process in which the consumer actually buys the product.

In the evaluation stage, the consumer ranks brands and forms purchase intentions. Generally, the consumer's **purchase decision** will be to buy the most preferred brand, but two factors can come between the purchase *intention* and the purchase *decision*. The first factor is the *attitudes of others*. If Anna Flores's husband feels strongly that Anna should buy the lowest priced camera, then the chances of Anna's buying a more expensive camera will be reduced.

The second factor is *unexpected situational factors*. The consumer may form a purchase intention based on factors such as expected income, expected price, and expected product benefits. However, unexpected events may change the purchase intention. Anna Flores may lose her job, some other purchase may become more urgent, or a friend may report being disappointed in her preferred camera. Or a close competitor may drop its price. Thus, preferences and even purchase intentions do not always result in actual purchase choice.

Postpurchase Behavior

Postpurchase behavior
The stage of the buyer decision process in which consumers take further action after purchase based their satisfaction or dissatisfaction.

The marketer's job does not end when the product is bought. After purchasing the product, the consumer will be satisfied or dissatisfied and will engage in **postpurchase behavior** of interest to the marketer. What determines whether the buyer is satisfied or dissatisfied with a purchase? The answer lies in the relationship between the *consumer's expectations* and the product's *perceived performance*. If the product falls short of expectations, the consumer is disappointed; if it meets expectations, the consumer is satisfied; if it exceeds expectations, the consumer is delighted.

The larger the gap between expectations and performance, the greater the consumer's dissatisfaction. This suggests that sellers should make product claims that faithfully represent the product's performance so that buyers are satisfied. Some sellers might even understate performance levels to boost consumer satisfaction with the product. For example, Boeing's salespeople tend to be conservative when they estimate the potential benefits of their aircraft. They almost always underestimate fuel efficiency—they promise a 5 percent savings that turns out to be 8 percent. Customers are delighted with better-than-expected performance; they buy again and tell other potential customers that Boeing lives up to its promises.

Cognitive dissonance
Buyer discomfort caused by postpurchase conflict.

Almost all major purchases result in **cognitive dissonance,** or discomfort caused by postpurchase conflict. After the purchase, consumers are satisfied with the benefits of the chosen brand and are glad to avoid the drawbacks of the brands not bought. However, every purchase involves compromise. Consumers feel uneasy about acquiring the drawbacks of the chosen brand and about losing the benefits of the brands not purchased. Thus, consumers feel at least some postpurchase dissonance for every purchase.[26]

Why is it so important to satisfy the customer? Such satisfaction is important because a company's sales come from two basic groups—*new customers* and *retained customers.* It usually costs more to attract new customers than to retain current ones, and the best way to retain current customers is to keep them satisfied. Customer satisfaction is a key to making lasting connections with consumers—to keeping and growing consumers and reaping their customer lifetime value. Satisfied customers buy a product again, talk favorably to others about the product, pay less attention to competing brands and advertising, and buy other products from the company. Many marketers go beyond merely *meeting* the expectations of customers—they aim to *delight* the customer. A delighted customer is even more likely to purchase again and to talk favorably about the product and company.

A dissatisfied consumer responds differently. Whereas, on average, a satisfied customer tells 3 people about a good product experience, a dissatisfied customer gripes to 11 people. In fact, one study showed that 13 percent of the people who had a problem with an organization complained about the company to more than 20 people.[27] Clearly, bad word of mouth travels farther and faster than good word of mouth and can quickly damage consumer attitudes about a company and its products.

Therefore, a company would be wise to measure customer satisfaction regularly. It cannot simply rely on dissatisfied customers to volunteer their complaints when they are dissatisfied. Some 96 percent of unhappy customers never tell the company about their problem. Companies should set up systems that *encourage* customers to complain (see Marketing Highlight 5.3). In this way, the company can learn how well it is doing and how it can improve. The 3M Company claims that over two-thirds of its new-product ideas come from listening to customer complaints. But listening is not enough—the company also must respond constructively to the complaints it receives.

MARKETING
HIGHLIGHT
5.3

GOT A PROBLEM? JUST PHONE, FAX, E-MAIL, OR "TELEWEB" US!

What should companies do with dissatisfied customers? Everything they can! Unhappy customers not only stop buying but also can quickly damage the company's image. Studies show that customers tell many more other people about bad experiences than about good ones. In contrast, dealing effectively with gripes can actually boost customer loyalty and the company's image. Thus, enlightened companies don't try to hide from dissatisfied customers. To the contrary, they go out of their way to *encourage* customers to complain, then bend over backward to make disgruntled buyers happy again.

The first opportunity to handle gripes often comes at the point of purchase. Many firms teach their customer-contact people how to resolve problems and diffuse customer anger. However, most companies have also set up call centers and Web sites to coax out and deal with consumer problems and questions.

Today, over two-thirds of all U.S. manufacturers offer toll-free numbers to handle complaints, inquiries, and orders. For example, now in its tenth year, the Gerber help line (1-800-GERBER) has received more than 4 million calls. Help-line staffers, most of them mothers or grandmothers themselves, handle customer concerns and provide baby care advice 24 hours a day, 365 days a year to more than 2,400 callers a day. The help line is staffed by English-, French-, and Spanish-speaking operators, and interpreters are available for most other languages. Callers include new parents, day care providers, and even health professionals. One in five of all calls to the help line comes from men.

Callers ask a wide variety of questions, from when to feed a baby specific foods to how to babyproof a home. "It used to be that mom or grandmom was right around the corner to answer your baby questions," notes the manager of the Gerber help line. "But more and more, that's not the case. For new or expectant parents, it's nice to know that they can pick up the phone any time of the day and talk to someone that understands and can help."

General Electric's Answer Center may be the most extensive 800-number system in the nation. It handles more than 3 million calls a year, only 5 percent of them complaints. At the heart of the system is a giant database that provides the center's service reps with instant access to more than 1 million answers concerning 8,500 models in 120 product lines. The center receives some unusual calls, as when a submarine off the Connecticut coast requested help fixing a motor. Still, according to GE, its people resolve 90 percent of complaints or inquiries on the first call, and complainers often become even more loyal customers. Although the company spends an average of $3.50 per call, it reaps two to three times that much in new sales and warranty savings. GE has also set up the GE Online Answer Center

Keeping customers happy: The Gerber help line has fielded more than 4 million calls providing baby care advice 24 hours a day, 365 days a year, to more than 2,400 callers a day.

(www.ge.com/oac) to help customers obtain information about its products and services, locate dealers, and get answers to frequently requested topics.

Companies like Famous Smoke Shop view their call centers as a tool not just for handling complaints but also for making the most out of each and every customer interaction. For example, whenever cigar enthusiast Cara Biden has called Famous Smoke Shops in search of highly coveted Short Stories cigars, they've been out of stock. Yet, this hasn't stopped Biden from staying loyal. Every time Biden phones Famous, a system known as an ACD (automatic call distributor) immediately kicks in to answer the call and route it to the appropriate contact person. Biden has been impressed with how fast the ACD funnels her to a customer service representative. She also enjoys chatting with the highly knowledgeable rep about alternatives to the tough-to-find cigars. The rep is knowledgeable not only about cigars but also about Biden—whenever she calls, her sales history and previous queries pop up on his computer screen.

Business-to-business marketers also go out of their way to give customers every opportunity for contact. For example, Indus International, a San Francisco–based maker of enterprise asset-management software, launched CareNet, a Web site designed to boost retention by simplifying customer contact. The site lets clients access product information, pose questions to service reps, and find solutions to specific problems. Customers are also encouraged to give feedback on the Web and post solutions to production problems. So far, Indus's clients are impressed. CareNet had 30 users

in its first month, but this number jumped to 600 just 10 months later.

Most call centers today are more than just a bank of phones that receive complaints. They are high-tech telemarketing operations that help companies to keep customers from defecting, lure customers from the competition, target the most profitable customers, and increase repeat customer purchases. In fact, they are "really more like contact centers," says one information-technology expert, "accommodating customers [making contact] via phone, fax, the Web, e-mail, even interactive video kiosk." The idea is to make customers' interactions with companies seamless and uniform, no matter which form of communication they choose.

Integrate the telephone—long a medium for developing customer relationships—with Web technology and you have a "teleweb" connection, an extremely powerful means of handling customer questions and concerns. This technology lets a customer browse a Web site on a PC at the same time that a customer service agent browses the site. The two can talk over a separate telephone line or an Internet connection to discuss problems or compare products. For example, Logistix, a California technology company, uses technology that allows it to synchronize Web screens viewed by the company's agents and customers as they talk. The technology even lets either party draw circles around words or pictures for both to see. This may not seem like a big deal, but when discussing a complex technological device, it really helps if customer and agent are viewing a common diagram. Logistix is pleased with the technology's ability to turn its call center into a central point of customer contact. "We're

growing like crazy," crows a Logistix executive, "and it's definitely because customers are coming to us through this technology."

Of course, the best way to keep customers happy is to provide good products and services in the first place. Short of that, however, a company must develop a good system for ferreting out problems and connecting with customers. Such a system is much more than just a necessary evil—customer happiness usually shows up on the company's bottom line. One recent study found that dollars invested in complaint handling and customer contact systems yield an average return of between 100 percent and 200 percent. Maryanne Rasmussen, vice president of worldwide quality at American Express, offers this formula: "Better complaint handling equals higher customer satisfaction equals higher brand loyalty equals higher performance."

Sources: Quote from "On Mother's Day, Advice Goes a Long Way," *PR Newswire,* Ziff Communications, May 2, 1995; Alessandra Bianchi, "Lines of Fire," *Inc. Technology,* 1988, pp. 36–48; and Matt Hamblen, "Call Centers and Web Sites Cozy Up," *Computerworld,* March 2, 1998, p. 1. Also see Roland T. Rust, Bala Subramanian, and Mark Wells, "Making Complaints a Management Tool," *Marketing Management,* Fall, 1992, pp. 41–45; Tibbett L. Speer, "They Complain Because They Care," *American Demographics,* May 1996, pp. 13–14; John F. Yarbrough, "Dialing for Dollars," *Sales & Marketing Management,* January 1997, pp. 60–67; Geoffrey Brewer, "The Customer Stops Here," *Sales & Marketing Management,* March 1998, pp. 31–36; and Marcia Stepanek, "You'll Wanna Hold Their Hands," *Business Week,* March 22, 1999, pp. EB30–EB31.

THE BUYER DECISION PROCESS FOR NEW PRODUCTS

New product
A good, service, or idea that is perceived by some potential customers as new.

Adoption process
The mental process through which an individual passes from first hearing about an innovation to final adoption.

We have looked at the stages buyers go through in trying to satisfy a need. Buyers may pass quickly or slowly through these stages, and some of the stages may even be reversed. Much depends on the nature of the buyer, the product, and the buying situation.

We now look at how buyers approach the purchase of new products. A **new product** is a good, service, or idea that is perceived by some potential customers as new. It may have been around for a while, but our interest is in how consumers learn about products for the first time and make decisions on whether to adopt them. We define the **adoption process** as "the mental process through which an individual passes from first learning about an innovation to final adoption,"[28] and *adoption* as the decision by an individual to become a regular user of the product.

Stages in the Adoption Process

Consumers go through five stages in the process of adopting a new product:

★ *Awareness:* The consumer becomes aware of the new product, but lacks information about it.
★ *Interest:* The consumer seeks information about the new product.
★ *Evaluation:* The consumer considers whether trying the new product makes sense.
★ *Trial:* The consumer tries the new product on a small scale to improve his or her estimate of its value.
★ *Adoption:* The consumer decides to make full and regular use of the new product.

This model suggests that the new-product marketer should think about how to help consumers move through these stages. A manufacturer of large-screen televisions may discover that many consumers in the interest stage do not move to the trial stage because of uncertainty and the large investment. If these same consumers were willing to use a large-screen television on a trial basis for a small fee, the manufacturer should consider offering a trial-use plan with an option to buy.

Individual Differences in Innovativeness

People differ greatly in their readiness to try new products. In each product area, there are "consumption pioneers" and early adopters. Other individuals adopt new products much later. People can be classified into the adopter categories shown in Figure 5.7. After a slow start, an increasing number of people adopt the new product. The number of adopters reaches a peak and then drops off as fewer nonadopters remain. Innovators are defined as the first 2.5 percent of the buyers to adopt a new idea (those beyond two standard deviations from mean adoption time); the early adopters are the next 13.5 percent (between one and two standard deviations); and so forth.

The five adopter groups have differing values. *Innovators* are venturesome—they try new ideas at some risk. *Early adopters* are guided by respect—they are opinion leaders in their communities and adopt new ideas early but carefully. The *early majority* are deliberate—although they rarely are leaders, they adopt new ideas before the

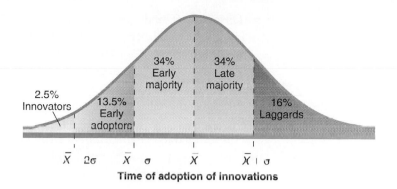

FIGURE 5.7   Adopter categorization on the basis of relative time of adoption of innovations

Source: Everett M. Rogers, *Diffusion of Innovations,* 4th ed. (New York: Free Press, 1995). Copyright© 1995 by Everett M. Rogers. Copyright© 1962, 1971, 1983 by The Free Press. Reprinted with the permission of The Free Press, a Division of Simon & Schuster.

average person. The *late majority* are skeptical—they adopt an innovation only after a majority of people have tried it. Finally, *laggards* are tradition bound—they are suspicious of changes and adopt the innovation only when it has become something of a tradition itself.

This adopter classification suggests that an innovating firm should research the characteristics of innovators and early adopters and should direct marketing efforts toward them. In general, innovators tend to be relatively younger, better educated, and higher in income than later adopters and nonadopters. They are more receptive to unfamiliar things, rely more on their own values and judgment, and are more willing to take risks. They are less brand loyal and more likely to take advantage of special promotions such as discounts, coupons, and samples.

Influence of Product Characteristics on Rate of Adoption

The characteristics of the new product affect its rate of adoption. Some products catch on almost overnight (Beanie Babies), whereas others take a long time to gain acceptance (high-density television, or HDTV). Five characteristics are especially important in influencing an innovation's rate of adoption. For example, consider the characteristics of HDTV in relation to the rate of adoption:

★ *Relative advantage:* The degree to which the innovation appears superior to existing products. The greater the perceived relative advantage of using HDTV—say, in picture quality and ease of viewing—the sooner such HDTVs will be adopted.

★ *Compatibility:* The degree to which the innovation fits the values and experiences of potential consumers. HDTV, for example, is highly compatible with the lifestyles found in upper-middle-class homes. However, it is not very compatible with the programming and broadcasting systems currently available to consumers.

★ *Complexity:* The degree to which the innovation is difficult to understand or use. HDTVs are not very complex and, therefore, once programming is available and prices come down, will take less time to penetrate U.S. homes than more complex innovations.

★ *Divisibility:* The degree to which the innovation may be tried on a limited basis. HDTVs are still very expensive. To the extent that people can lease them with an option to buy, their rate of adoption will increase.

★ *Communicability:* The degree to which the results of using the innovation can be observed or described to others. Because HDTV lends itself to demonstration and description, its use will spread faster among consumers.

Other characteristics influence the rate of adoption, such as initial and ongoing costs, risk and uncertainty, and social approval. The new-product marketer has to research all these factors when developing the new product and its marketing program.

CONSUMER BEHAVIOR ACROSS INTERNATIONAL BORDERS

Understanding consumer behavior is difficult enough for companies marketing within the borders of a single country. For companies operating in many countries, however, understanding and serving the needs of consumers can be daunting. Although consumers in different countries may have some things in common, their values, attitudes, and behaviors often vary greatly. International marketers must understand such differences and adjust their products and marketing programs accordingly.

Sometimes the differences are obvious. For example, in the United States, where most people eat cereal regularly for breakfast, Kellogg focuses its marketing on persuading consumers to select a Kellogg brand rather than a competitor's brand. In France, however, where most people prefer croissants and coffee or no breakfast at all, Kellogg advertising simply attempts to convince people that they should eat cereal for breakfast. Its packaging includes step-by-step instructions on how to prepare cereal. In India, where many consumers eat heavy, fried breakfasts and many consumers skip the meal altogether, Kellogg's advertising attempts to convince buyers to switch to a lighter, more nutritious breakfast diet.

Often, differences across international markets are more subtle. They may result from physical differences in consumers and their environments. For example, Remington makes smaller electric shavers to fit the smaller hands of Japanese consumers and battery-powered shavers for the British market, where few bathrooms have electrical outlets. Other differences result from varying customs. In Japan, for example, where humility and deference are considered great virtues, pushy, hard-hitting sales approaches are considered offensive. Failing to understand such differences in customs and behaviors from one country to another can spell disaster for a marketer's international products and programs.

Marketers must decide on the degree to which they will adapt their products and marketing programs to meet the unique cultures and needs of consumers in various markets. On the one hand, they want to standardize their offerings in order to simplify operations and take advantage of cost economies. On the other hand, adapting marketing efforts within each country results in products and programs that better satisfy the needs of local consumers. The question of whether to adapt or standardize the marketing mix across international markets has created a lively debate in recent years.

REVIEW OF CONCEPT CONNECTIONS

The American consumer market consists of more than 270 million people who consume many trillions of dollars worth of goods and services each year, making it one of the most attractive consumer markets in the world. The world consumer market consists of more than 5.9 *billion* people. Consumers around the world vary greatly in age, income, education level, and tastes. Understanding how these differences affect *consumer buying behavior* is one of the biggest challenges marketers face.

1. Define the consumer market and construct a simple model of consumer buyer behavior.

The *consumer market* consists of all the individuals and households who buy or acquire goods and services for personal consumption. The simplest model of consumer buyer behavior is the stimulus–response model. According to this model, marketing stimuli (the four Ps) and other major forces (economic, technological, political, cultural) enter the consumer's "black box" and produce certain responses. Once in the black box, these inputs produce observable buyer responses, such as product choice, brand choice, purchase timing, and purchase amount.

2. Name the four major factors that influence consumer buyer behavior.

Consumer buyer behavior is influenced by four key sets of buyer characteristics: cultural, social, personal, and psychological. Although many of these factors cannot be influenced by the marketer, they can be useful in identifying interested buyers and in shaping products and appeals to serve consumer needs better. *Culture* is the most basic determinant of a person's wants and behavior. It includes the basic values, perceptions, preferences, and behaviors that a person learns from family and other important institutions. *Subcultures* are "cultures within cultures" that have distinct values and lifestyles and can be based on anything from age to ethnicity. People with different cultural and subcultural characteristics have different product and brand preferences. As a result, marketers may want to focus their marketing programs on the special needs of certain groups.

Social factors also influence a buyer's behavior. A person's *reference groups*—family, friends, social organizations, professional associations—strongly affect product and brand choices. The buyer's age, life-cycle stage, occupation, economic circumstances, lifestyle, personality, and other *personal characteristics* influence his or her buying decisions. Consumer *lifestyles*—the whole pattern of acting and interacting in the world—are also an important influence on purchase decisions. Finally, consumer buying behavior is influenced by four major *psychological factors*—motivation, perception,

learning, and beliefs and attitudes. Each of these factors provides a different perspective for understanding the workings of the buyer's black box.

3. List and understand the stages in the buyer decision process.

When making a purchase, the buyer goes through a decision process consisting of *need recognition, information search, evaluation of alternatives, purchase decision,* and *postpurchase behavior.* The marketer's job is to understand the buyer's behavior at each stage and the influences that are operating. During *need recognition,* the consumer recognizes a problem or need that could be satisfied by a product or service in the market. Once the need is recognized, the consumer is aroused to seek more information and moves into the *information search* stage. With information in hand the consumer proceeds to *alternative evaluation,* during which the information is used to evaluate brands in the choice set. From there, the consumer makes a *purchase decision* and actually buys the product. In the final stage of the buyer decision process, *postpurchase behavior,* the consumer takes action based on satisfaction or dissatisfaction.

4. Describe the adoption and diffusion process for new products.

The product adoption process is comprised of five stages: awareness, interest, evaluation, trial, and adoption. Initially, the consumer must become aware of the new product. *Awareness* leads to *interest,* and the consumer seeks information about the new product. Once information has been gathered, the consumer enters the *evaluation* stage and considers buying the new product. Next, in the *trial* stage, the consumer tries the product on a small scale to improve his or her estimate of its value. If the consumer is satisfied with the product, he or she enters the *adoption* stage, deciding to use the new product fully and regularly.

With regard to diffusion of new products, consumers respond at different rates, depending on the consumer's characteristics and the product's characteristics. Consumers may be innovators, early adopters, early majority, late majority, or laggards. *Innovators* are willing to try risky new ideas; *early adopters*—often community opinion leaders—accept new ideas early but carefully; the *early majority*—rarely leaders—decide deliberately to try new ideas, doing so before the average person does; the *late majority* try an innovation only after a majority of people have adopted it; whereas *laggards* adopt an innovation only after it has become a tradition itself. Manufacturers try to bring their new products to the attention of potential early adopters, especially those who are opinion leaders.

KEY TERMS

Adoption process	Dissonance-reducing buying behavior	Opinion leader
Alternative evaluation	Group	Perception
Attitude	Habitual buying behavior	Personality
Belief	Information search	Postpurchase behavior
Cognitive dissonance	Learning	Purchase decision
Complex buying behavior	Lifestyle	Social classes
Consumer buying behavior	Motive (or drive)	Subculture
Consumer market	Need recognition	Variety-seeking buying behavior
Culture	New product	

ISSUES FOR DISCUSSION

1. List several factors that might be added to the model shown in Figure 5.1 to make it a more complete description of consumer behavior. Explain your reasoning.

2. Assume that you are the marketing manager for Kmart stores. Your objective is to compete more effectively against competitors Wal-Mart and Target by serving important subculture segments better. To assist your marketing team in preparing a marketing strategy to meet this objective, construct a profile of each of the following subcultures: (a) Hispanic consumers, (b) African American consumers, (c) Asian American consumers, and (d) the over-50 market.

3. In designing an advertising campaign for a soft drink, which would you find more useful: information about consumer demographics or information about consumer lifestyles? Give examples of how you would use each type of information.

4. The basic self-concept premise is that people's possessions contribute to and reflect their identities. How do advertisers on MTV use the idea of self-concept to market their products? Give specific illustrations (visit www.mtv.com for additional information). Assess MTV's approach to advertising.

5. Abraham Maslow sought to explain why people are driven by particular needs at particular times. Which level of Maslow's hierarchy applies best to the following situations: (a) purchasing the newest, fastest personal computer; (b) purchasing food at lunch time; (c) adjusting your clothing choices to reflect the latest trends; (d) serving on the United Way fund-raising board; and (e) purchasing a smoke detector for your home. Explain your choices.

6. Think about a very good or very bad experience you have had with a product. How did this experience shape your beliefs about the product, the purchasing process, or shopping in stores. How long will these beliefs last? What could make you change these beliefs?

7. Figure 5.5 shows types of consumer buying behavior based on the degree of buyer involvement and differences among brands. Which of the four types of consumer buying behavior is involved in each of the following situations: (a) You are about to purchase a new Lexus automobile. (b) You go into a candy store in the mall and purchase a new brand of candy bar. (c) You go to a tire retailer to purchase a set of tires. (d) During a break from class you purchase a soft drink from a vending machine. Explain your choices.

8. For many Americans, changing to a healthier lifestyle would constitute adopting an innovation. It might require changes in eating, exercise, smoking, and drinking habits. Discuss this innovation in terms of its relative advantage, compatibility, complexity, divisibility, and communicability. Is a healthy lifestyle likely to be adopted quickly by most Americans? Provide examples of the different adopter groups that might represent the various stages of healthy lifestyle acceptance (see Figure 5.7).

MARKETING APPLICATIONS

1. SRI has categorized Internet users according to iVALS segments, a VALS typology designed for Net users. Companies that market on the Web can use this information to develop their appeals, strategies, and promotions. The concept is that consumers purchases are shaped by the interplay of their psychological, physical, demographic, and material resources. Visit SRI at www.future.sri.com and follow the links to the iVALS questionnaire. Complete the survey to determine your iVals type. Answer the following questions:

   a. What is your iVALS type? Do you agree with the assessment? Why or why not?

   b. How do iVALS segments differ from the VALS segments discussed in this chapter?

   c. How can marketers use iVALS information to serve consumers better? Name five types of products or services for which iVALS information would be particularly useful. Explain.

   d. How could advertisers use iVALS or VALS information to communicate better with consumers. Find three advertising examples from Web sites or current magazines that might be designed around iVALS or VALS segments. Explain your reasoning.

   e. After having read Marketing Highlight 5.1, compare the iVALS approach to the Technographics scheme presented in the Highlight. Which do you prefer? Why?

2. What's holding up high-definition television (HDTV)? A year after its introduction, what was projected to be one of the greatest electronic viewing innovations since color, HDTV is struggling with low penetration, limited reception, scarce content, and heavy controversy. Why? Some blame poor marketing; others point to technical snafus. Whatever the reasons, digitalization of television pictures has been slow to develop and few consumers have been willing to plunk down $5,000 to watch the new and improved picture. (For more information on HDTV, see Sony at www.sony.com, Toshiba at www.toshiba.com, or Panosonic at www.panasonic.com.)

   a. Based on the information provided in the chapter, why is adoption of HDTV so slow to develop?

   b. Profile the characteristics of likely early adopters. As marketing manager for a large electronics superstore that carries HDTVs, devise a strategy to get early adopters into your store to see and preview this new form of television.

   c. When customers visit your store to see the new HDTVs, they are bound to have concerns that must be overcome before sales can occur. What might these concerns be? Considering the consumer behavior model presented in the chapter, design a strategy for overcoming these concerns.

   d. What do you think will be the future of HDTV? What other products and industries will HDTV impact?

 INTERNET CONNECTIONS

PSYCHOGRAPHIC CLASSIFICATION OF CONSUMERS

SRI Consulting, through the Business Intelligence Center online, features the Values and Lifestyles Program (VALS). Many marketers who wish to understand the psychographics of both existing and potential customers use this market segmentation program. Companies and advertisers on the Web can use this information to develop their sites. Visit SRI at sri.com and follow links to the VALS questionnaire. Take the survey to determine your type and then read all about your type. Use this information for the discussion questions below the table. Also of interest to marketers in the global economy are the psychographic differences among cultures. SRI recently created two new segmentation programs: Geo-VALS and Japan-VALS. Complete the following table about the nine Japan-VALS segments and characteristics as they are presented on the site.

Japan-VALS™ Type	% of Population	Characteristics

FOR DISCUSSION

1. What is your VALS type? Does it describe you well? Why or why not?

2. What four products have high indexes for your type? Do you buy these products?

3. How do the U.S.-based VALS segments differ from Japan-VALS segments? What does this say about consumer differences between the two cultures?

4. Why do you think SRI designed a separate typology for Japanese consumers?

5. Other than product design, how can marketers use information from Japan-VALS?

SAVVY SITES

- GeoCities (geocities.yahoo.com) offers free home pages to anyone who wants to be located in one of its "neighborhoods." These home page clusters are divided into 41 topics, from art to women. This is an interesting example of psychographic segmentation by self-selection.

- DoubleClick (www.doubleclick.com) serves ads from clients to users as they log onto various sites. Ads are targeted by psychographics and geographic location of user.

- Ad-Up (www.ad-up.com) provides psychographic and "affinity" targeting for advertisers wishing to find their markets among Web users.

NOTES

1. Quotes from Richard A. Melcher, "Tune-Up Time for Harley," *Business Week,* April 8, 1997, pp. 90–94; Ian P. Murphy, "Aided by Research, Harley Goes Whole Hog," *Marketing News,* December 2, 1996, pp. 16, 17; Dyan Machan, "Is the Hog Going Soft?" *Forbes,* March 10, 1997, pp. 114–19; and Linda Sandler, "Workspaces: Harley Shop," *Wall Street Journal,* April 21, 1999, p. B20; and the Harley-Davidson Web site (www.Harley-Davidson.com), September 1999. Also see Sarah Lorge, "Revving Up Customers," *Sales & Marketing Management,* June 1998, p. 15; and Leslie P. Norton, "Potholes Ahead?" *Barron's,* February 1, 1999, pp. 16–17.

2. For current population estimates, see the U.S. and world POP clocks at www.census.gov.

3. Several models of the consumer buying process have been developed by marketing scholars. For a summary, see Leon G. Schiffman and Leslie Lazar Kanuk, *Consumer Behavior,* 6th ed. (Upper Saddle River, NJ: Prentice Hall, 1997), pp. 560–64.

4. For this and other examples of the effects of culture in international marketing, see Philip R. Cateora, *International Marketing,* 8th ed. (Homewood, IL: Irwin, 1993), chap. 4; Sak Onkvisit and John J. Shaw, *International Marketing: Analysis and Strategy,* 3rd ed. (Upper Saddle River, NJ: Prentice Hall, 1997), chap. 6; and Greg Gimba, "Color in Marketing: Shades of Meaning," *Marketing News,* March 16, 1998, p. 6.

5. For examples, see Nancy Coltun Webster, "Multicultural," *Advertising Age,* November 17, 1997, pp. S1–S2; Rachel X. Weissman, "Los Ninos Go Shopping," *American Demographics,* May 1999, pp. 37–38; and Helene Stapinski, "Generación Latino," *American Demographics,* July 1999, pp. 63–68.

6. Calmetta Y. Coleman, "Attention Shoppers: Target Makes a Play for Minority Group Sears Has Cultivated," *Wall Street Journal,* April 12, 1999, p. A1.

7. Webster, "Multicultural," p. S1.

8. See "L'eggs Joins New Approach in Marketing to African-American Women," *Supermarket Business,* June 1998, p. 81; Beth Belton, "Black Buying Power Soaring," *USA Today,* July 30, 1998, p. 1B; and Dana Canedy, "The Courtship of Black Consumers," *New York Times,* August 11, 1998, pp. D1, D2.

9. See David Kiley, "Black Surfing," *Brandweek,* November 17, 1997, p. 36; Kim Cleland, "Narrow-Marketing Efforts Winning the Internet Savvy," *Advertising Age,* November 16, 1998, p. S26; and Chuck Ross, "BET Cries Foul, Hits Lack of Ad Commitment," *Advertising Age,* April 12, 1999, pp. S1, S16.

10. Webster, "Multicultural," p. S1; and Saul Gitlin, "A Yen for Brands," *Brandweek,* January 5, 1998, p. 17.

11. See Christy Fisher, "Marketers Straddle Asian-America Curtain," *Advertising Age,* November 7, 1994; John Steere, "How Asian-Americans Make Purchasing Decisions," *Marketing News,* March 13, 1995, p. 9; "Asian Demographics," *Media Week,* April 17, 1995, p. S1; and Brad Edmondson, "Asian Americans in 2001," *American Demographics,* February 1997, pp. 16–17.

12. See Rick Adler, "Stereotypes Won't Work with Seniors Anymore," *Advertising Age,* November 11, 1996, p. 32; Richard Lee, "The Youth Bias in Advertising," *American Demographics,* January 1997, pp. 47–50; D. Allen Kerr, "Where There's Gray, There's Green," *Marketing News,* May 25, 1998, p. 2; Jeff Brazil, "You Talkin' to Me?" *American Demographics,* December 1998, pp. 55–59; Heather Chaplin, "Centrum's Self-Inflicted Silver Bullet," *American Demographics,* March 1999, pp. 68–69; and Kendra Parker, "Reaping What They've Sown," *American Demographics,* December 1999, pp. 34–37.

13. For more on social class, see Leon G. Schiffman and Leslie L. Kanuk, *Consumer Behavior,* 6th ed. (Upper Saddle River, NJ: Prentice Hall, 1997), chap. 13; Michael R. Solomon, *Consumer Behavior,* 3rd ed. (Upper Saddle River, NJ: Prentice Hall, 1996), pp. 432–52; David Leonhardt, "Two-Tier Marketing," *Business Week,* March 17, 1997, p. 82; and Rebecca Piirto Heath, "The New Working Class," *American Demographics,* January 1998, pp. 51–55.

14. Courteny Kane, "Advertising: TBWA/Chiat Day Brings 'Street Culture' to a Campaign for Levi-Strauss Silver Tab Clothing," *New York Times,* August 14, 1998, p. D8.

15. Debra Goldman, "Spotlight Men," *Adweek,* August 13, 1990, pp. M1–M6; Nancy Ten Kate, "Who Buys the Pants in the Family?" *American Demographics,* January 1992, p. 12; and Laura Zinn, "Real Men Buy Paper Towels, Too," *Business Week,* November 9, 1992, pp. 75–76.

16. Jeffery Zbar, "Hardware Builds Awareness among Women," *Advertising Age,* July 11, 1994, p. 10, and Alan Alder, "Purchasing Power Women's Buying Muscle Shops Up in Car Design, Marketing," *Chicago Tribune,* September 29, 1996, p. A21.

17. David Leonhardt, "Hey Kids, Buy This," *Business Week,* June 30, 1997, pp. 62–67. Also see Kay M. Palan and Robert E. Wilkes, "Adolescent–Parent Interaction in Family Decisions," *Journal of Consumer Research,* September 1997, pp. 159–69; Chankon Kim and Hanjoon Lee, "Development of Family Triadic Measures for Children's Purchase Influence," *Journal of Marketing Research,* August 1997, pp. 307–21; and Judann Pollack, "Foods Targeting Children Aren't Just Child's Play," *Advertising Age,* March 1, 1999, p. 16.

18. This and other examples of companies using VALS can be found in Rebecca Piirto, "Measuring Minds in the 1990s," *American Demographics,* December 1990, pp. 35–39; and Rebecca Piirto, "VALS the Second Time," *American Demographics,* July 1991, p. 6. For good discussions of other lifestyle topics, see Basil G. Englis and Michael Solomon, "To Be or Not to Be: Lifestyle Imagery, Reference Groups, and the Clustering of America," *Journal of Advertising,* March 1995, p. 13; and Tom Miller, "Global Segments from 'Strivers' to 'Creatives,'" *Marketing News,* July 20, 1998, p. 11.

19. Piirto, "VALS the Second Time," p. 6; and Rebecca Piirto, "The Frontier of Psychographics," *American Demographics,* July 1996, pp. 38–43.

20. Stuart Elliot, "Sampling Tastes of a Changing Russia," *New York Times,* April 1, 1992, pp. D1, D19; and Miller, "Global Segments from 'Strivers' to 'Creatives,'" p. 11. For an excellent discussion of cross-cultural lifestyle systems, see Philip Kotler, Gary Armstrong, John Saunders, and Veronica Wong, *Principles of Marketing,* 2nd European ed. (London: Prentice Hall Europe, 1999), pp. 240–42.

21. Myron Magnet, "Let's Go for Growth," *Fortune,* March 7, 1994, p. 70. Also see Timothy R. Graeff, "Consumption Situations and the Effects of Brand Image on Consumers' Brand Evaluations," *Psychology and Marketing,* January 1997, pp. 49–70; Dun Gifford Jr., "Moving Beyond Loyalty," *Harvard Business Review,* March–April 1997, pp. 9–10; and Jennifer L. Aaker, "The Malleable Self: The Role of Self-Expression in Persuasion," *Journal of Marketing Research,* February 1999, pp. 45–57.

22. See Barbara Marx Hubbard, "Seeking Our Future Potentials," *The Futurist,* May 1998, pp. 29–32.

23. Jill Venter, "Milk Mustache Campaign Is a Hit with Teens," *St. Louis Post-Dispatch,* April 1, 1998, p. E1; Dave Fusaro, "The Milk Mustache," *Dairy Foods,* April 1997, p. 75; Judann Pollack, "Milk: Kurt Graetzer," *Advertising Age,* June 30, 1997, p. S1; and the Milk: Where's Your Mustache Web site (www.whymilk.com), February 2000.

24. See Henry Assael, *Consumer Behavior and Marketing Action* (Boston: Kent Publishing, 1987), chap. 4. An earlier classification of three types of consumer buying behavior—routine response behavior, limited problem solving, and extensive problem solving—can be found in John A. Howard and Jagdish Sheth, *The Theory of Consumer Behavior* (New York: John Wiley, 1969), pp. 27–28. Also see John A. Howard, *Consumer Behavior in Marketing Strategy* (Upper Saddle River, NJ: Prentice Hall, 1989).

25. For more on word-of-mouth sources, see Philip Kotler, *Marketing Management: Analysis, Planning, Implementation, and Control,* 10th ed. (Upper Saddle River, NJ: Prentice Hall, 2000), p. 560.

26. See Leon Festinger, *A Theory of Cognitive Dissonance* (Stanford, CA: Stanford University Press, 1957); Schiffman and Kanuk, *Consumer Behavior,* pp. 271–72; Jeff Stone, "A Radical New Look at Cognitive Dissonance," *The American Journal of Psychology,* Summer 1998, pp. 319–26; and Thomas R. Schultz, Elene Leveille, and Mark R. Lepper, "Free Choice and Cognitive Dissonance Revisited: Choosing 'Lesser Evils' Versus 'Greater Goods,'" *Personality and Social Psychology Bulletin,* January 1999, pp. 40–48.

27. See Frank Rose, "Now Quality Means Service Too," *Fortune,* April 22, 1991, pp. 97–108; Chip Walker, "Word of Mouth," *American Demographics,* July 1995, p. 40; Thomas O. Jones and W. Earl Sasser Jr., "Why Satisfied Customers Defect," *Harvard Business Review,* November–December 1995, pp. 88–99; and Roger Sant, "Did He Jump or Was He Pushed?" *Marketing News,* May 12, 1997, pp. 2, 21.

28. The following discussion draws heavily from Everett M. Rogers, *Diffusion of Innovations,* 3rd ed. (New York: Free Press, 1983). Also see Hubert Gatignon and Thomas S. Robertson, "A Propositional Inventory for New Diffusion Research," *Journal of Consumer Research,* March 1985, pp. 849–67; and Rogers, *Diffusion of Innovations,* 4th ed. (New York: Free Press, 1995).

Aibo: Looking for a Charged-up Spot?

FOR SALE: Puppy. Never needs to go outside, doesn't soil carpets, doesn't chew on furniture or slippers, doesn't eat. Can be turned off and put in the closet when you're on vacation. Contact—www.world.sony.com/robot/get/meet/html.

From the land of fascination with robots comes the latest twist on these machines—a puppy named Aibo, the entertainment robot. This is no simple animal or machine. Even the name has many possible meanings. Perhaps it stands for "artificial intelligence robot." Perhaps it refers to Aibo's camera eyes, which make it an "eye bot," or maybe it's just Japanese for companion or pal.

What can you do with Aibo? Well, you can play with it. Aibo has a favorite toy, a pink ball, which it will chase down, pick up in its mouth, and return to you just like any real dog would. If you praise Aibo, its tail wags, its eyes light up green, and it plays a happy melody. It's not exactly like a real dog, but close in the sense that Aibo responds visibly to your love and affection.

Because Aibo can respond to praise, it can learn. When you praise Aibo's behaviors, they become stronger and are more likely to be repeated. When scolded, Aibo is sometimes sad and plays a doleful melody. Other times, it responds to scolding by getting agitated and playing an angry melody while its eyes turn red. Although Aibo's responses may be different from a real dog's responses, they do represent the same emotions. Like a real dog, Aibo lets you know that it wants to play by jumping around. In addition to anger, sadness, and playfulness, Aibo can show joy (eyes turn green and it plays a happy melody), surprise (eyes light up and it plays a surprised melody and gives a start), discontent (its eyes turn angry red and it moves away), and fear (when it encounters a big hole or rolls onto its back and can't get up, it plays a scared melody).

Voice commands such as "stay," "sit," or "heel" won't work with Aibo because the puppy has no voice-response mechanism. Instead you give it commands through a sound controller. Aibo responds only to perfect tones, so the sound controller contains combinations of preset commands in perfect tones. If Aibo is in a bad mood, it will simply ignore you. When it is in a happy mood, it will perform tricks. Like most temperamental pets, Aibo will play or do tricks only if you're good to it.

When it's time to quit playing, you hit the pause button and Aibo lies down and goes to sleep. When not active, Aibo stays in its station, which serves as a battery charger. The robotic puppy comes with two lithium batteries so that one can be charged while the other is in use. A full charge lasts through about 1.5 hours of action.

Aibo comes in three colors (gray, metallic black, and silver gray); has stereo microphones for ears; can recognize colors and shapes; and emits a variety of bleeps and chirps. A sensor in its head can distinguish between an amiable pat and a reproachful slap. You can set Aibo to Performance Mode, in which it does tricks, or to Game Mode, in which you control its movements. By making Aibo run and kick, you can even play robot soccer.

Ready to buy an Aibo? You won't find one for sale in any store. It is available only on the Internet at www.world.sony.com/robot/get/meet/html. It's also a little pricey—250,000 Japanese yen or $2,500. Is anyone willing to pay such a stiff price? In June 1999 Sony offered 3,000 Aibos in Japan and 2,000 in the United States. All sold out in only 20 minutes. When Sony offered another 10,000 in November of 1999, it received more than 130,000 orders. Facing this greater than anticipated demand, Sony drew lots and selected winners in Japan, the United States, and Europe. There appear to be lots of robot-dog's best friends out there!

One of the appealing features of Aibo is its open architecture. Based on experiences with its PlayStation video-game business, Sony decided not to develop everything in-house. Instead, it has invited other developers to create new programs for Aibo. This has resulted in the rapid development of additional memory sticks (programs) that allow you to teach Aibo new tricks or movements.

What kinds of new behaviors could you teach Aibo? How about a hip-shaking dog that sings Elvis songs like— you guessed it—"You Ain't Nothing but a Hound Dog." Or how about a dog that really hates cats? Aibo could be programmed to recognize cats and react fiercely to them. In fact, two companies have created computerized cats, so we might soon have good old-fashioned dog and cat fights, but without the blood, gore, or veterinarian bills.

To test consumer reaction to their furless, high-tech critters before offering them for sale, Sony demonstrated Aibos at several trade shows. Uniform reaction to the pet was "That is *so* cute!" One enthusiastic consumer commented, "I love little robots. For me, it would be great. I'm single and I don't have time to keep a dog." Another said, "This is the coolest thing I've seen all day." Numerous journalists, privileged enough to play with Aibos, found them to be lots of fun—even if they can't do anything useful.

Although Aibo isn't likely to fetch your newspaper, bring you your shoes, or scare away burglars, this little puppy does have much promise from a marketing point of view. Sony hopes to create a whole new industry of entertainment robots, an industry that Sony management believes could be larger than the personal computer market.

These robots usher in the new era of digital creatures. Sure, there are robot fanatics who already gather for the annual Robocup—the World Cup for robots (www.robocup.org)—and robot sumo wrestling competitions in Japan. But those robots appeal only to consumers with specific and sometimes narrow interests. The new Aibo-like entertainment robots have broader appeal. More importantly, they may make people more comfortable with the idea of interacting with humanoid-like machines. Once that happens, robots could become nurses, maids, or bodyguards. They might even become partners who will play with and talk to us. There's more than a little bit of *Star Wars'* R2D2 in all this. Back in the eighties, however, R2D2 and his companions seemed a long way off. Now, Aibo and other animal-bots appear to be bringing us into that *Star Wars* world much sooner than we thought.

For those not able to afford an Aibo, Sharper Image has introduced the Wee Bot, which comes in families of adults and children. Wee Bots have big, bright, expressive eyes that move and an extraterrestrial language of beeps, burps, chirps, snores, coos, chortles, giggles, yips, snorts, purrs, and moans. What triggers these reactions? Your stroking, scratching, and tickling. They express happiness when petted, grouchiness when sleepy, and impatience when bored. They respond to commands from a silent wireless "translator" that converts your wishes into a language the robo-pet understands. The children, called PeeWee Bots, have their own routines and respond to beamed voice messages from the nearest grown-up Wee Bot. They like exercise and naps, and they eat by making slurping and gulping noises. When happy, they behave. When they are not happy, you need "special modes" to keep them in line.

Wee Bots don't look like any creature we're used to. They have round bodies, and the adults come in two models: Twirple, which has a purple body and green eyes, or Ziggle, which has an orange body and green eyes. Best of all, they don't cost too much. An adult Wee Bot is $39.95, a PeeWee Bot is $29.95, and a whole family (an adult and two children) is $99. Just call Sharper Image and you, too, can have a new age robo-pet companion.

Questions

1. How might personal factors affect the purchase of an Aibo? A Wee Bot?
2. What cultural and social-class factors might affect the decision to buy an Aibo or a Wee Bot?
3. How might reference groups affect a consumer's interest in robot pets or robots in general?
4. What motives or needs is an individual likely to be satisfying in purchasing a pet robot?
5. Why, do you think, did Sony chose to sell Aibos only over the Internet? How might this affect a consumer's buying decision process? Was this a wise decision?
6. How could Internet-only selling affect the rate of diffusion of Aibos? In creating its new industry, what could Sony do to speed the diffusion of entertainment robots?

Sources: Neil Gross and Irene Kunii, "Man's Best Friend—and No Scooper Needed," *Business Week,* July 20, 1998, p. 53+; Irene Kunii, "This Cute Little Pet Is a Robot," *Business Week,* May 24, 1999, pp. 56–57; Peter Landers, "At Last, a Dog That Barks, Wags Its Tail, and Never Has to Go Out," *Wall Street Journal,* May 12, 1999, p. B1; Ginny Parker, "In Japan, Robots Are Not Just for Factories Anymore," *Greensboro News and Record,* November 2, 1999, pp. B6 and B7; "Robots," *The Economist,* June 5, 1999, p. 78; Richard Shaffer, "Can't Anyone Make a Decent Robot?" *Fortune,* July 19, 1999, pp. 120–21; "Sony Launches Special Edition 'Aibo' Entertainment Robot," Sony press release, October 26, 1999; "Sony's Aibo Robot Dogs Draw 130,000 Orders in Japan Alone," *AsiaPulse News,* November 15, 1999, p. 100; and The Sharper Image, Holiday 1999 Catalog.

After studying this chapter, you should be able to
1. define the business market and explain how business markets differ from consumer markets
2. identify the major factors that influence business buyer behavior
3. list and define the steps in the business buying decision process
4. compare the institutional and government markets and explain how institutional and government buyers make their buying decisions

BUSINESS MARKETS AND BUSINESS BUYER BEHAVIOR

For more than 40 years, Gulfstream Aerospace Corporation has been the Rolls-Royce of corporate aviation. The original Gulfstream model—a twin-engine turboprop introduced in 1958—was the first jet designed expressly for corporate use. Gulfstream business jets come with price tags averaging $35 million. Identifying potential buyers isn't a problem—worldwide, only about 300 to 500 customers have the wherewithal to own and operate multimillion-dollar business aircraft. Customers include Disney, American Express, Coca-Cola, General Motors, IBM, and many others, including Bill Cosby and King Fahd of Saudi Arabia. Gulfstream's more difficult problems involve reaching key decision makers for jet purchases, understanding their complex motivations and decision processes, analyzing what factors will be important in their decisions, and designing marketing approaches.

Gulfstream recognizes the importance of *rational* motives and *objective* factors in buyers' decisions. Customers justify the expense of a corporate jet on utilitarian grounds, such as security, flexibility, responsiveness to customers, and efficient time use. A company buying a jet will evaluate Gulfstream aircraft on quality and performance, prices, operating costs, and service. At times, these "objective" factors may appear to be the only things that drive the buying decision. But having a superior product isn't enough to land the sale: Gulfstream also must consider the more subtle *human factors* that affect the choice of a jet.

The purchase process may be initiated by the chief executive officer (CEO), a board member wishing to increase efficiency or security, the company's chief pilot, or through Gulfstream efforts such as advertising or a sales visit. The CEO will be central in deciding whether to buy the jet, but he or she will be heavily influenced by the company's pilot, financial officer, and members of top management. The involvement of so many people in the purchase decision creates a group dynamic that Gulfstream must factor into its sales planning. Who makes up the buying group? How will the parties interact? Who will dominate and who submit? What priorities do the individuals have?

Each party in the buying process has subtle roles and needs. For example, the salespeople who try to impress both the CEO with depreciation schedules and the chief pilot with minimum runway statistics will almost certainly not sell a plane if they overlook the psychological and emotional components of the buying decision. The chief pilot, as an equipment expert, often has veto power over purchase decisions and may be able to stop the purchase of a certain brand of jet by simply expressing a negative opinion about, say, the plane's bad-weather capabilities. In this sense, the pilot not only influences the decision but also serves as an information "gatekeeper" by advising management on the equipment to select. The users of the jet—middle and upper management of the buying company, important customers, and others—may have at least an indirect role in choosing the equipment. Although the corporate legal staff will handle the purchase agreement and the purchasing department will acquire the jet, these parties may have little to say about whether or how the plane will be obtained and which type will be selected.

According to one salesperson, in dealing with the CEO, the biggest factor is not the plane's hefty price tag, but its image. You need all the numbers for support, but if you can't find the kid inside the CEO and excite him or her with the raw beauty of the new plane, you'll never sell the equipment. If you sell the excitement, you sell the jet.

Some buying influences may come as a big surprise. Gulfstream may never really know who is behind the purchase of a plane. Although many people inside the customer company can be influential, the most important influence may turn out to be the CEO's spouse. The typical buyer spends about $4 million to outfit the plane's interior. This covers top-of-the-line stereo sound and video systems, a lavish galley, and a bewildering array of custom-made furnishings. To help with such decisions, many CEOs hire designers and bring their spouses along to planning sessions. As one salesperson notes, "Wives are behind the CEO's decisions on a lot of things, not just airplanes. . . . A crucial moment in a deal comes when the CEO's wife takes off her shoes and starts decorating the plane."

In some ways, selling corporate jets to business buyers is like selling cars and kitchen appliances to families. Gulfstream asks the same questions as consumer marketers: Who are the buyers and what are their needs? How do buyers make their buying decisions and what factors influence these decisions? What marketing program will be most effective? But the answers to these questions are usually different for the business buyer. Thus, Gulfstream faces many of the same challenges as consumer marketers— and some additional ones. A solid understanding of the full dynamics of business buyer behavior has Gulfstream flying high these days. The company captures a lion's share of the top-of-the-line segment of the business-jet market and has amassed a $4.1 billion backlog of orders.[1]

Business market
All organizations that buy goods and services for use in the production of other products and services that are sold, rented, or supplied to others.

Business buying process
The decision-making process by which business buyers establish the need for purchased products and services and identify, evaluate, and choose among alternative brands and suppliers.

In one way or another, most large companies sell to other organizations. Many companies, such as DuPont, Xerox, Boeing, Motorola, and countless other firms, sell *most* of their products to other businesses. Even large consumer-products companies, which make products used by final consumers, must first sell their products to other businesses. For example, General Mills makes many familiar consumer products—Cheerios, Betty Crocker cake mixes, Gold Medal flour, and others. But to sell these products to consumers, General Mills must first sell them to the wholesalers and retailers that serve the consumer market. General Mills also sells products such as specialty chemicals directly to other businesses.

The **business market** comprises all the organizations that buy goods and services for use in the production of other products and services that are sold, rented, or supplied to others. It also includes retailing and wholesaling firms that acquire goods for the purpose of reselling or renting them to others at a profit. In the **business buying process,** business buyers determine which products and services their organizations need to purchase, and then find, evaluate, and choose among alternative suppliers and brands. Companies that sell to other business organizations must do their best to understand business markets and business buyer behavior.

BUSINESS MARKETS

The business market is *huge*. In fact, business markets involve far more dollars and items than do consumer markets. For example, think about the large number of business transactions involved in the production and sale of a single set of Goodyear tires. Various suppliers sell Goodyear the rubber, steel, equipment, and other goods that it needs to produce the tires. Goodyear then sells the finished tires to retailers, who in turn sell them to consumers. Thus, many sets of *business* purchases were made for only one set of *consumer* purchases. In addition, Goodyear sells tires as original equipment to manufacturers who install them on new vehicles, and as replacement tires to companies that maintain their own fleets of company cars, trucks, buses, or other vehicles.

Characteristics of Business Markets

In some ways, business markets are similar to consumer markets. Both involve people who assume buying roles and make purchase decisions to satisfy needs. However, business markets differ in many ways from consumer markets. The main differences, shown in Table 6.1 and discussed below, are in the *market structure and demand*, the *nature of the buying unit*, and the *types of decisions and the decision process* involved.

Market Structure and Demand
The business marketer normally deals with *far fewer but far larger buyers* than the consumer marketer does. For example, when Goodyear sells replacement tires to final consumers, its potential market includes the owners of the millions of cars currently

TABLE 6.1   CHARACTERISTICS OF BUSINESS MARKETS
Marketing Structure and Demand
Business markets contain *fewer but larger buyers*.   Business customers are *more geographically concentrated*.   Business buyer demand is *derived* from final consumer demand.   Demand in many business markets is *more inelastic*—not affected as much in the short run by price changes.   Demand in business markets *fluctuates more*, and more quickly.
Nature of the Buying Unit
Business purchases involve *more buyers*.   Business buying involves a *more professional purchasing effort*.
Types of Decisions and the Decision Process
Business buyers usually face *more complex buying decisions*.   The business buying process is *more formalized*.   In business buying, buyers and sellers work more closely together and build close long-run *relationships*.

in use in the United States. But Goodyear's fate in the business market depends on getting orders from one of only a few large automakers. Even in large business markets, a few buyers normally account for most of the purchasing.

Business markets are also *more geographically concentrated.* More than half the nation's business buyers are concentrated in eight states: California, New York, Ohio, Illinois, Michigan, Texas, Pennsylvania, and New Jersey. Further, business demand is **derived demand**—it ultimately derives from the demand for consumer goods. General Motors buys steel because consumers buy cars. If consumer demand for cars drops, so will the demand for steel and all the other products used to make cars. Therefore, business marketers sometimes promote their products directly to final consumers to increase business demand. For example, Intel's long-running "Intel Inside" advertising campaign sells personal computer buyers on the virtues of Intel microprocessors. The increased demand for Intel chips boosts demand for the PCs containing them, and both Intel and its business partners win.

Many business markets have *inelastic demand;* that is, total demand for many business products is not affected much by price changes, especially in the short run. A drop in the price of leather will not cause shoe manufacturers to buy much more leather unless it results in lower shoe prices that, in turn, will increase consumer demand for shoes.

Finally, business markets have more *fluctuating demand.* The demand for many business goods and services tends to change more—and more quickly—than the demand for consumer goods and services does. A small percentage increase in consumer demand can cause large increases in business demand. Sometimes a rise of only 10 percent in consumer demand can cause as much as a 200 percent rise in business demand during the next period.

Nature of the Buying Unit

Compared with consumer purchases, a business purchase usually involves *more decision participants* and a *more professional purchasing effort.* Often, business buying is done by trained purchasing agents who spend their working lives learning how to buy better. The more complex the purchase, the more likely that several people will participate in the decision-making process. Buying committees made up of technical experts and top management are common in the buying of major goods. As one observer notes, "It's a scary thought: Your customers may know more about your company and products than you do. . . . Companies are putting their best and

Derived demand
Business demand that ultimately comes from (derives from) the demand for consumer goods.

Derived demand: Intel's long-running "Intel Inside" logo advertising campaign boosts demand for Intel chips and for the PCs containing them. Now, HP and most other computer makers feature the logo in ads like this one.

brightest people on procurement patrol."[2] Therefore, business marketers must have well-trained salespeople to deal with well-trained buyers.

Types of Decisions and the Decision Process

Business buyers usually face *more complex* buying decisions than do consumer buyers. Purchases often involve large sums of money, complex technical and economic considerations, and interactions among many people at many levels of the buyer's organization. Because the purchases are more complex, business buyers may take longer to make their decisions. For example, the purchase of a large information technology system might take many months or more than a year to complete and could involve millions of dollars, thousands of technical details, and dozens of people ranging from top management to lower-level users.

The business buying process tends to be *more formalized* than the consumer buying process. Large business purchases usually call for detailed product specifications, written purchase orders, careful supplier searches, and formal approval. The buying firm might even prepare policy manuals that detail the purchase process.

Finally, in the business buying process, buyer and seller are often much *more dependent* on each other. Consumer marketers are often at a distance from their customers. In contrast, business marketers may roll up their sleeves and work closely with their customers during all stages of the buying process—from helping customers define problems, to finding solutions, to supporting after-sale operation. They often customize their offerings to individual customer needs. In the short run, sales go to suppliers who meet buyers' immediate product and service needs. However, business marketers also must build close *long-run* partnerships with customers. In recent years, relationships between customers and suppliers have been changing from downright adversarial to close and chummy:

★ Motoman, a leading supplier of industry robotic systems, and Stillwater Technologies, a contract tooling and machinery company and a key supplier to Motoman, are tightly integrated. Not only do they occupy office and manufacturing space in the same facility, they also link their telephone and computer systems and share a common lobby, conference room, and employee cafeteria. Philip Morrison, chairman and CEO of Motoman, says it's like "a joint venture without the paperwork." Short delivery distances are just one benefit of the unusual partnership. Also key is the fact that employees of both companies have ready access to each other and can share ideas on improving quality and reducing costs. This close relationship has also opened the

Business marketers often roll up their sleeves and work closely with their customers throughout the buying and consuming process. In this award-winning business-to-business ad, Fujitsu promises more than just high-tech products: "Our technology helps keep you moving upward. And our people won't let you down."

BUSINESS MARKETERS SELL CUSTOMER SUCCESS

In the late 1980s, the Dow Chemical Company realigned its dozen or so widely varied plastics businesses into a single business unit called Dow Plastics. One of the first things the Dow Chemical Company had to do was to decide how to position its new division competitively. Initial research with Dow's and competitors' customers showed that Dow Plastics rated a distant third in customer preference behind industry leaders DuPont and GE Plastics. The research also revealed, however, that customers were unhappy with the service, or lack thereof, that they received from all three suppliers. "Vendors peddled resins as a commodity," says the head of Dow Plastics' advertising agency. "They competed on price and delivered on time, but gave no service."

These findings led to a positioning strategy that went far beyond simply selling good products and delivering them on time. Dow Plastics set out to build deeper relationships with customers. The organization was selling not just products and services, but customer success. Says the agency executive, "Whether they're using Dow's plastics to make bags for Safeway or for complex aerospace applications, we have to help them succeed in their markets." This new thinking was summed up in the positioning statement, "We don't succeed unless you do."

The new positioning helped Dow Plastics to become a truly customer-oriented organization. It got Dow out of selling plastics and into selling customer success. The slogan and underlying philosophy created a unifying identity for the business— one based on building relationships with customers and helping them to succeed with their own businesses. Customer problems became more than just engineering challenges. Dow's customers sell to somebody else, so the company now faced new challenges of marketing to and helping satisfy customers' customers.

Because of its new customer relationship orientation, Dow Plastics has now become a leader in the plastics industry with over $9 billion in annual sales. The customer success philosophy permeates everything

door to new opportunities. Both companies had been doing work for Honda Motor Company, and Honda suggested that the two work together on systems projects. The symbiotic relationship makes the two bigger and better than they could be individually.[3]

In the long run, business marketers keep a customer's sales by meeting current needs *and* by working with customers to help them succeed with their own customers (see Marketing Highlight 6.1).

A Model of Business Buyer Behavior

At the most basic level, marketers want to know how business buyers will respond to various marketing stimuli. Figure 6.1 shows a model of business buyer behavior. In this model, marketing and other stimuli affect the buying organization and produce certain buyer responses. As with consumer buying, the marketing stimuli for business buying consist of the four Ps: product, price, place, and promotion. Other stimuli include major forces in the environment: economic, technological, political, cultural, and competitive. These stimuli enter the organization and are turned into buyer responses: product or service choice; supplier choice; order quantities; and delivery, service, and payment terms. In order to design good marketing mix strategies, the marketer must understand what happens within the organization to turn stimuli into purchase responses.

The slap-happy ski company from the island.

Dow Plastics tells customers, "We don't succeed unless you do." Building deeper relationships helped Dow become a leader in the plastics industry.

the business does. Whenever Dow Plastics people encounter a new product or market, the first question they always ask is, "How does this fit with 'We don't succeed unless you do'?" As Dow states simply on its Web page: "Dow Plastics is much more than just a supplier of plas-tics—we are dedicated to the success of our customers." Says a Dow manager, "This provides a competitive advantage not only for Dow, but most importantly, for our cus-tomers."

Source: Portions adapted from Nancy Arnott, "Getting the Picture: The Grand Design—We Don't Succeed Unless You Do," *Sales & Marketing Management,* June 1994, pp. 74–76. Also see the following Dow Plastics press releases accessed online at www.dow.com/plastics. "Dow Plastics Customer Succeed," June 16, 1997; "Dow Plastics Investing in Customer Success," December 12, 1997; and "Dow Plastics: Meeting the Changing Needs of Customers," January 26, 1999

Within the organization, buying activity consists of two major parts: the buying center, made up of all the people involved in the buying decision, and the buying decision process. The model shows that the buying center and the buying decision process are influenced by internal organizational, interpersonal, and individual factors as well as by external environmental factors.

FIGURE 6.1   Model of business buyer behavior

BUSINESS BUYER BEHAVIOR

The model in Figure 6.1 suggests four questions about business buyer behavior: What buying decisions do business buyers make? Who participates in the buying process? What are the major influences on buyers? How do business buyers make their buying decisions?

Major Types of Buying Situations

There are three major types of buying situations.[4] At one extreme is the *straight rebuy,* which is a fairly routine decision. At the other extreme is the *new task,* which may call for thorough research. In the middle is the *modified rebuy,* which requires some research.

Straight rebuy
A business buying situation in which the buyer routinely reorders something without any modifications.

In a **straight rebuy,** the buyer reorders something without any modifications. It is usually handled on a routine basis by the purchasing department. Based on past buying satisfaction, the buyer simply chooses from the various suppliers on its list. "In" suppliers try to maintain product and service quality. They often propose automatic reordering systems so that the purchasing agent will save reordering time. "Out" suppliers try to offer something new or exploit dissatisfaction so that the buyer will consider them. They try to get their foot in the door with a small order and then enlarge their purchase share over time.

Modified rebuy
A business buying situation in which the buyer wants to modify product specifications, prices, terms, or suppliers.

In a **modified rebuy,** the buyer wants to modify product specifications, prices, terms, or suppliers. The modified rebuy usually involves more decision participants than the straight rebuy. The in suppliers may become nervous and feel pressured to put their best foot forward to protect an account. Out suppliers may see the modified rebuy situation as an opportunity to make a better offer and gain new business.

New task
A business buying situation in which the buyer purchases a product or service for the first time.

A company buying a product or service for the first time faces a **new-task** situation. In such cases, the greater the cost or risk, the larger the number of decision participants and the greater their efforts to collect information will be. The new-task situation is the marketer's greatest opportunity and challenge. The marketer not only tries to reach as many key buying influences as possible but also provides help and information.

The buyer makes the fewest decisions in the straight rebuy and the most in the new-task decision. In the new-task situation, the buyer must decide on product specifications, suppliers, price limits, payment terms, order quantities, delivery times, and service terms. The order of these decisions varies with each situation, and different decision participants influence each choice.

Systems buying
Buying a packaged solution to a problem from a single seller.

Many business buyers prefer to buy a packaged solution to a problem from a single seller. Called **systems buying,** this practice began with government buying of major weapons and communication systems. Instead of buying and putting all the components together, the government asked for bids from suppliers who would supply the components *and* assemble the package or system.

Sellers increasingly have recognized that buyers like this method and have adopted systems selling as a marketing tool. Systems selling is a two-step process. First, the supplier sells a group of interlocking products. For example, the supplier sells not only glue, but also applicators and dryers. Second, the supplier sells a system of production, inventory control, distribution, and other services to meet the buyer's need for a smooth-running operation.

Systems selling is a key business marketing strategy for winning and holding accounts. The contract often goes to the firm that provides the most complete solution to customers' problems. For example, Enron, the $31 billion energy company, is best known for providing the natural gas and electricity that its customers use to power their buildings. However, Enron has discovered that companies actually spend far more on the other elements of their energy systems, including energy equipment inside their facilities and the employees who maintain it, than on paying for the energy itself. To help customers meet their complete power management needs, Enron started Enron Energy Services (EES), a division that offers entire energy management solutions. Now, customers can turn over all of their energy management needs to Enron. The systems package includes both the power and all the interior workings: the boilers, chillers, heating, ventilation, and air-conditioning equipment. The idea is, if it has to do with managing buildings, keeping them lit and warm in the winter and cool in the summer, it should be Enron's domain. Such systems selling has produced stunning results for Enron: In only the past three years, EES's sales have grown sevenfold to more than $8 billion.[5]

Participants in the Business Buying Process

Who does the buying of the trillions of dollars' worth of goods and services needed by business organizations? The decision-making unit of a buying organization is called its **buying center**: all the individuals and units that participate in the business decision-making process.

The buying center includes all members of the organization who play any of five roles in the purchase decision process.[6]

Buying center
All the individuals and units that participate in the business buying-decision process.

Users
Members of the organization who will use the product or service; users often initiate the buying proposal and help define product specifications.

Influencers
People in an organization's buying center who affect the buying decision; they often help define specifications and also provide information for evaluating alternatives.

Deciders
People in the organization's buying center who have formal or informal power to select or approve the final suppliers.

Gatekeepers
People in the organization's buying center who control the flow of information to others.

★ **Users** are members of the organization who will use the product or service. In many cases, users initiate the buying proposal and help define product specifications.
★ **Influencers** often help define specifications and also provide information for evaluating alternatives. Technical personnel are particularly important influencers.
★ **Buyers** have formal authority to select the supplier and arrange terms of purchase. Buyers may help shape product specifications, but their major role is in selecting vendors and negotiating. In more complex purchases, buyers might include high-level officers participating in the negotiations.
★ **Deciders** have formal or informal power to select or approve the final suppliers. In routine buying, the buyers are often the deciders, or at least the approvers.
★ **Gatekeepers** control the flow of information to others. For example, purchasing agents often have authority to prevent salespersons from seeing users or deciders. Other gatekeepers include technical personnel and even personal secretaries.

The buying center is not a fixed and formally identified unit within the buying organization. It is a set of buying roles assumed by different people for different purchases. Within the organization, the size and makeup of the buying center will vary for different products and for different buying situations. For some routine purchases, one person—say a purchasing agent—may assume all the buying center roles and serve as the only person involved in the buying decision. For more complex purchases, the buying center may include 20 or 30 people from different levels and departments in the organization. According to one survey, the average number of people involved in a buying decision ranges from about 3 (for services and items used in day-to-day operations) to almost 5 (for such high-ticket purchases as construction work and machinery). Another survey detected a trend toward team-based buying—87 percent of surveyed purchasing executives at Fortune 1000 companies expect teams of people from different functions to be making buying decisions in the year 2000.[7]

Business marketers working in global markets may face even greater levels of buying center influence. A study comparing the buying decision processes in the United States, Sweden, France, and Southeast Asia found that U.S. buyers may be lone eagles compared with their counterparts in some other countries. Sweden had the highest team buying effort, whereas the United States had the lowest, even though the Swedish and U.S. firms had very similar demographics. In making purchasing decisions, Swedish firms depended on technical staff, both their own and suppliers', much more than did the firms in other countries.[8]

The buying center concept presents a major marketing challenge. The business marketer must learn who participates in the decision, each participant's relative influence, and what evaluation criteria each decision participant uses. For example, Allegiance Healthcare Corporation, the large health care products and services company, sells disposable surgical gowns to hospitals. It identifies the hospital personnel involved in this buying decision as the vice president of purchasing, the operating room administrator, and the surgeons. Each participant plays a different role. The vice president of purchasing analyzes whether the hospital should buy disposable gowns or reusable gowns. If analysis favors disposable gowns, then the operating room administrator compares competing products and prices and makes a choice. This administrator considers the gown's absorbency, antiseptic quality, design, and cost, and normally buys the brand that meets requirements at the lowest cost. Finally, surgeons affect the decision later by reporting their satisfaction or dissatisfaction with the brand.

The buying center usually includes some obvious participants who are involved formally in the buying decision. For example, the decision to buy a corporate jet will probably involve the company's CEO, its chief pilot, a purchasing agent, some legal staff, a member of top management, and others formally charged with the buying decision. It may also involve less obvious, informal participants, some of

Buying center: Allegiance Healthcare Corporation deals with a wide range of buying influences, from purchasing executives and hospital administrators to the surgeons who actually use its products.

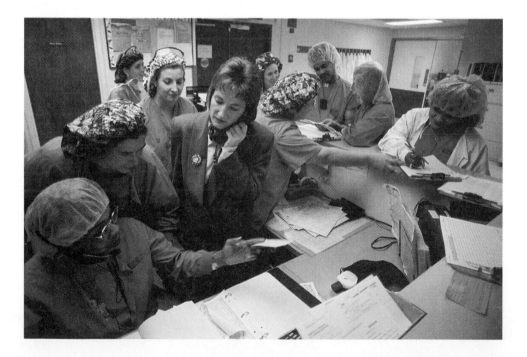

whom may actually make or strongly affect the buying decision. Sometimes, even the people in the buying center are not aware of all the buying participants. As the Gulfstream example showed, the decision about which corporate jet to buy may actually be made by a corporate board member who has an interest in flying and who knows a lot about airplanes. This board member may work behind the scenes to sway the decision. Many business buying decisions result from the complex interactions of ever-changing buying center participants.

Major Influences on Business Buyers

Business buyers are subject to many influences when they make their buying decisions. Some marketers assume that the major influences are economic. They think buyers will favor the supplier who offers the lowest price or the best product or the most service. They concentrate on offering strong economic benefits to buyers. However, business buyers actually respond to both economic and personal factors. Far from being cold, calculating, and impersonal, business buyers are human and social as well. They react to both reason and emotion.

Today, most business-to-business marketers recognize that emotion plays an important role in business buying decisions. For example, you might expect that an advertisement promoting large trucks to corporate truck fleet buyers would stress objective technical, performance, and economic factors. However, a recent ad for Volvo heavy-duty trucks shows two drivers arm wrestling and claims, "It solves all your fleet problems. Except who gets to drive." It turns out that, in the face an industrywide driver shortage, the type of truck a fleet provides can help it to attract qualified drivers. The Volvo ad stresses the raw beauty of the truck and its comfort and roominess, features that make it more appealing to drivers. The ad concludes that Volvo trucks are "built to make fleets more profitable and drivers a lot more possessive."

When suppliers' offers are very similar, business buyers have little basis for strictly rational choice. Because they can meet organizational goals with any supplier, buyers can allow personal factors to play a larger role in their decisions. However, when competing products differ greatly, business buyers are more accountable for their choice and tend to pay more attention to economic factors. Figure 6.2 lists various groups of influences on business buyers—environmental, organizational, interpersonal, and individual.[9]

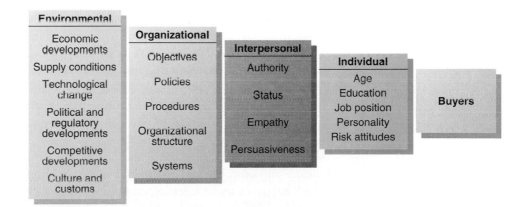

FIGURE 6.2   Major influences on business buyer behavior

MARKETING HIGHLIGHT 6.2

INTERNATIONAL MARKETING MANNERS: WHEN IN ROME, DO AS THE ROMANS DO

Scenario: Consolidated Amalgamation, Inc. thinks it's time that the rest of the world enjoyed the same fine products it has offered American consumers for two generations. It dispatches Vice President Harry E.

American companies must help their managers understand international needs, customers, and cultures. For example, Japanese people revere the business card as an extension of self—they do not hand it to people, they present it.

Slicksmile to Europe to explore the territory. Mr. Slicksmile stops first in London, where he makes short work of some bankers—he rings them up on the phone. He handles Parisians with similar ease: After securing a table at La Tour d'Argent, he greets his luncheon guest, the director of an industrial engineering firm, with the words, "Just call me Harry, Jacques."

In Germany, Mr. Slicksmile is a powerhouse. Whisking through a lavish, state-of-the-art marketing presentation, complete with the flip charts and audiovisuals, he shows them that this Georgia boy *knows* how to make a buck. Heading on to Milan, Harry strikes up a conversation with the Japanese businessman sitting next to him on the plane. He flips his card onto the guy's tray and, when the two say good-bye, shakes hands warmly and clasps the man's right arm. Later, for his appointment with the owner of an Italian packaging design firm, our hero wears his comfy corduroy sport coat, khaki

pants, and Topsiders. Everybody knows Italians are zany and laid back, right?

Wrong. Six months later, Consolidated Amalgamation has nothing to show for the trip but a pile of bills. In Europe, they weren't wild about Harry.

This hypothetical case has been exaggerated for emphasis. Americans are seldom such dolts. But experts say success in international business has a lot to do with knowing the territory and its people. By learning English and extending themselves in other ways, the world's business leaders have met Americans more than halfway. In contrast, Americans too often do little except assume that others will march to their music. "We want things to be 'American' when we travel. Fast. Convenient. Easy. So we become the 'ugly Americans' by demanding that others change," says one American world trade expert. "I think more business would be done if we tried harder."

Environmental Factors

Business buyers are influenced heavily by factors in the current and expected *economic environment,* such as the level of primary demand, the economic outlook, and the cost of money. As economic uncertainty rises, business buyers cut back on new investments and attempt to reduce their inventories.

An increasingly important environmental factor is shortages in key materials. Many companies now are more willing to buy and hold larger inventories of scarce materials to ensure adequate supply. Business buyers also are affected by technological, political, and competitive developments in the environment. Culture and customs can strongly influence business buyer reactions to the marketer's behavior and strategies, especially in the international marketing environment (see Marketing Highlight 6.2). The business marketer must watch these factors, determine how they will affect the buyer, and try to turn these challenges into opportunities.

Poor Harry tried, all right, but in all the wrong ways. The British do not, as a rule, make deals over the phone as much as Americans do. It's not so much a "cultural" difference as a difference in approach. A proper French businessperson neither likes instant familiarity—questions about family, church, or alma mater—nor refers to strangers by their first names. "That poor fellow, Jacques, probably wouldn't show anything, but he'd recoil. He'd *not* be pleased," explains an expert on French business practices. "It's considered poor taste," he continues. "Even after months of business dealings, I'd wait for him or her to make the invitation [to use first names]....You are always right, in Europe, to say 'Mister.' "

Harry's flashy presentation would likely have been a flop with the Germans, who dislike overstatement and ostentatiousness. According to one German expert, however, German businesspeople have become accustomed to dealing with Americans. Although differences in body language and customs remain, the past 20 years have softened them. "I hugged an American woman at a business meeting last night," he said. "That would be normal in France, but [older] Germans still have difficulty [with the cus-

tom]." He says that calling secretaries by their first names would still be considered rude: "They have a right to be called by the surname. You'd certainly ask—and get—permission first." In Germany, people address each other formally and correctly someone with two doctorates (which is fairly common) must be referred to as "Herr Doktor Doktor."

When Harry Slicksmile grabbed his new Japanese acquaintance by the arm, the executive probably considered him disrespectful and presumptuous. Japan, like many Asian countries, is a "no-contact culture" in which even shaking hands is a strange experience. Harry made matters worse by tossing his business card. Japanese people revere the business card as an extension of self and as an indicator of rank. They do not *hand* it to people, they *present* it—with both hands. In addition, the Japanese are sticklers about rank. Unlike Americans, they don't heap praise on subordinates in a room; they will praise only the highest-ranking official present.

Hapless Harry's last gaffe was assuming that Italians are like Hollywood's stereotypes of them. The flair for design and style that has characterized Italian culture for cen-

turies is embodied in the business-people of Milan and Rome. They dress beautifully and admire flair, but they blanch at garishness or impropriety in others' attire.

Thus, to compete successfully in global markets, or even to deal effectively with international firms in their home markets, companies must help their managers to understand the needs, customs, and cultures of international business buyers. The old advice is still good advice: When in Rome, do as the Romans do.

Sources: Adapted from Susan Harte, "When in Rome, You Should Learn to Do What the Romans Do," *Atlanta Journal-Constitution*, January 22, 1990, pp. D1, D6. Also see Terri Morrison, Wayne A. Conway, and George A. Borden, *Kiss, Bow, or Shake Hands: How to Do Business in 60 Countries* (Adams Media Corporation, 1994); Cynthia Kemper, "Global Sales Success Depends on Cultural Insight," *World Trade*, May 1998, pp. S2–S4; Ann Marie Sabath, *International Business Etiquette Europe: What You Need to Know to Conduct Business Abroad with Charm and Savvy* (Career Press, 1999); and Wayne A. Conway, Joseph J. Douress, and Terri Morrison, *Dun & Bradstreet's Guide to Doing Business Around the World*, rev. ed. (Upper Saddle River, NJ: Prentice Hall, 1999).

Organizational Factors

Each buying organization has its own objectives, policies, procedures, structure, and systems. The business marketer must know these *organizational factors* as thoroughly as possible. Questions such as these arise: How many people are involved in the buying decision? Who are they? What are their evaluative criteria? What are the company's policies and limits on its buyers?

Interpersonal Factors

The buying center usually includes many participants who influence each other. The business marketer often finds it difficult to determine what kinds of *interpersonal factors* and group dynamics enter into the buying process. As one writer notes, "Managers do not wear tags that say 'decision maker' or 'unimportant person.' The powerful are often invisible, at least to vendor representatives."[10] Nor does the buying center participant with the highest rank always have the most influence.

Participants may have influence in the buying decision because they control rewards and punishments, are well liked, have special expertise, or have a special relationship with other important participants. Interpersonal factors are often very subtle. Whenever possible, business marketers must try to understand these factors and design strategies that take them into account.

Individual Factors

Each participant in the business buying decision process brings in personal motives, perceptions, and preferences. These individual factors are affected by personal characteristics such as age, income, education, professional identification, personality, and attitudes toward risk. Also, buyers have different buying styles. Some may be technical types who make in-depth analyses of competitive proposals before choosing a supplier. Other buyers may be intuitive negotiators who are adept at pitting the sellers against one another for the best deal.

The Business Buying Process

Table 6.2 lists the eight stages of the business buying process.[11] Buyers who face a new-task buying situation usually go through all stages of the buying process. Buyers making modified or straight rebuys may skip some of the stages. We will examine these steps for the typical new-task buying situation.

Problem Recognition

Problem recognition
The first stage of the business buying process in which someone in the company recognizes a problem or need that can be met by acquiring a good or a service.

The buying process begins when someone in the company recognizes a problem or need that can be met by acquiring a specific product or service. **Problem recognition** can result from internal or external stimuli. Internally, the company may decide to launch a new product that requires new production equipment and materials. Or a machine may break down and need new parts. Perhaps a purchasing manager is unhappy with a current supplier's product quality, service, or prices. Externally, the buyer may get some new ideas at a trade show, see an ad, or receive a call from a salesperson who offers a better product or a lower price. In fact, in their advertising, business marketers often alert customers to potential problems and then show how their products provide solutions.

TABLE 6.2   MAJOR STAGES OF THE BUSINESS BUYING PROCESS IN RELATION TO MAJOR BUYING SITUATIONS

	Buying Situations		
Stages of the Buying Process	New Task	Modified Rebuy	Straight Rebuy
1. Problem recognition	Yes	Maybe	No
2. General need description	Yes	Maybe	No
3. Product specification	Yes	Yes	Yes
4. Supplier search	Yes	Maybe	No
5. Proposal solicitation	Yes	Maybe	No
6. Supplier selection	Yes	Maybe	No
7. Order-routine specification	Yes	Maybe	No
8. Performance review	Yes	Yes	Yes

Source: Adapted from Patrick J. Robinson, Charles W. Faris, and Yoram Wind, *Industrial Buying and Creative Marketing* (Boston: Allyn & Bacon, 1967), p. 14.

As this Andersen Consulting ad shows, business marketers often use advertising to alert customers to potential problems, then show how their products or services provide solutions.

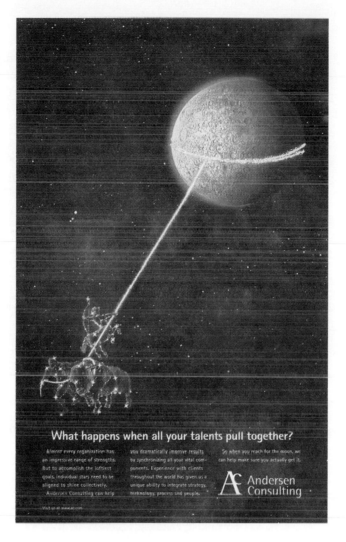

General Need Description

General need description
The stage in the business buying process in which the company describes the general characteristics and quantity of a needed item.

Having recognized a need, the buyer next prepares a **general need description** that describes the characteristics and quantity of the needed item. For standard items, this process presents few problems. For complex items, however, the buyer may have to work with others—engineers, users, consultants—to define the item. The team may want to rank the importance of reliability, durability, price, and other attributes desired in the item. In this phase, the alert business marketer can help the buyers define their needs and provide information about the value of different product characteristics.

Product Specification

Product specification
The stage of the business buying process in which the buying organization decides on and specifies the best technical product characteristics for a needed item.

The buying organization next develops the item's technical **product specifications,** often with the help of a value analysis engineering team. **Value analysis** is an approach to cost reduction in which components are studied carefully to determine if they can be redesigned, standardized, or made by less costly methods of production. The team decides on the best product characteristics and specifies them accordingly. Sellers, too, can use value analysis as a tool to help secure a new account. By showing buyers a better way to make an object, outside sellers can turn straight rebuy situations into new-task situations that give them a chance to obtain new business.

Value analysis
An approach to cost reduction in which components are studied carefully to determine if they can be redesigned, standardized, or made by less costly methods of production.

Supplier Search

Supplier search
The stage of the business buying process in which the buyer tries to find the best vendors.

The buyer now conducts a **supplier search** to find the best vendors. The buyer can compile a small list of qualified suppliers by reviewing trade directories, doing a computer search, or phoning other companies for recommendations. Today, more and more companies are turning to the Internet to find suppliers. For marketers, this has leveled the playing field—smaller suppliers have the same advantages as larger ones and can be listed in the same online catalogs for a nominal fee:

> ★ Worldwide Internet Solutions Network, better known as WIZnet (www.wiznet.net), has built an "interactive virtual library of business-to-business catalogs" that is global in coverage. At last report, its database included complete specifications for more than 10 million products and services from 45,000 manufacturers, distributors, and industrial service providers. For purchasing managers, who routinely receive a foot-high stack of mail each day, much of it catalogs, this kind of one-stop shopping will be an incredible time-saver (and price saver, because it allows easier comparison shopping). When told by a management consultant, "Do a search for 3.5-inch platinum ball valves available from a Michigan source," WIZnet found six Michigan sources for buying the exact product in about 15 seconds. More than just electric Yellow Pages, such as the Thomas Register or Industry.net, WIZnet includes all specifications for the products right in the system and offers secure e-mail to communicate directly with vendors to ask for requests for bids or to place an order. More than 10,000 product specs are added to WIZnet per week, and its database includes catalogs from Germany, Taiwan, the Czech Republic, and other countries.[12]

The newer the buying task, and the more complex and costly the item, the greater the amount of time the buyer will spend searching for suppliers. The supplier's task is to get listed in major directories and build a good reputation in the marketplace. Salespeople should watch for companies in the process of searching for suppliers and make certain that their firm is considered.

Many business buyers go to extremes in searching for and qualifying suppliers. Consider the hurdles that Xerox has set up in its qualifying suppliers:

> ★ Xerox qualifies only suppliers who meet ISO 9000 international quality standards (see chapter 18). But to win the company's top award—certification status—a supplier must first complete the Xerox Multinational Supplier Quality Survey. The survey

Using the Internet to find suppliers: WIZnet's eCommerce Portal provides quick access to more than 45,000 manufacturers, distributors, and industrial service providers.

requires the supplier to issue a quality assurance manual, adhere to continuous improvement principles, and demonstrate effective systems implementation. Once a supplier has been qualified, it must participate in Xerox's Continuous Supplier Involvement process, in which the two companies work together to create specifications for quality, cost, delivery times, and process capability. The final step toward certification requires a supplier to undergo additional quality training and an evaluation based on the same criteria as the Malcolm Baldrige National Quality Award. Not surprisingly, only 176 suppliers worldwide have achieved the 95 percent rating required for certification as a Xerox supplier.[13]

Proposal Solicitation

Proposal solicitation

The stage of the business buying process in which the buyer invites qualified suppliers to submit proposals.

In the **proposal solicitation** stage of the business buying process, the buyer invites qualified suppliers to submit proposals. In response, some suppliers will send only a catalog or a salesperson. However, when the item is complex or expensive, the buyer will usually require detailed written proposals or formal presentations from each potential supplier.

Business marketers must be skilled in researching, writing, and presenting proposals in response to buyer proposal solicitations. Proposals should be marketing documents, not just technical documents. Presentations should inspire confidence and should make the marketer's company stand out from the competition.

Supplier Selection

Supplier selection

The stage of the business buying process in which the buyer reviews proposals and selects a supplier or suppliers.

The members of the buying center now review the proposals and select a supplier or suppliers. During **supplier selection,** the buying center often will draw up a list of the desired supplier attributes and their relative importance. In one survey, purchasing executives listed the following attributes as most important in influencing the relationship between supplier and customer: quality products and services, on-time delivery, ethical corporate behavior, honest communication, and competitive prices. Other important factors include repair and servicing capabilities, technical aid and advice, geographic location, performance history, and reputation. The members of the buying center will rate suppliers against these attributes and identify the best suppliers.[14]

As part of the buyer selection process, buying centers must decide how many suppliers to use. In the past, many companies preferred a large supplier base to ensure adequate supplies and to obtain price concessions. These companies would insist on annual negotiations for contract renewal and would often shift the amount of business they gave to each supplier from year to year. Increasingly, however, companies are reducing the number of suppliers. Companies such as Ford, Motorola, and Allied Signal have cut the number of suppliers anywhere from 20 to 80 percent. These companies expect their preferred suppliers to work closely with them during product development and they value their suppliers' suggestions.

There is even a trend toward single sourcing, using one supplier. For example, whereas most newspapers rely on a variety of companies to supply the tons of newsprint they consume, the *Knoxville News-Sentinel* and the *New York Daily News* each rely on a single source for their newsprint.[15] With single sourcing there is only one supplier to handle and it is easier to control newsprint inventories. Using one source not only can translate into more consistent product performance, but it also allows press rooms to configure themselves for one particular kind of newsprint rather than changing presses for papers with different attributes.

Many companies, however, are still reluctant to use single sourcing. They fear that they may become too dependent on the single supplier or that the single-source supplier may become too comfortable in the relationship and lose its competitive edge.

Some marketers have developed programs that address these concerns. For example, GC Electronics of Rockford, Illinois, has a "one source lowest price guarantee program," which promotes the reduced transaction and purchasing costs of using it as a single source. However, if after being with the program for a while, distributors can show that they could have gotten a better deal elsewhere, GC offers them a 6 percent rebate.[16]

Order-Routine Specification

Order-routine specification
The stage of the business buying process in which the buyer writes the final order with the chosen supplier(s), listing the technical specifications, quantity needed, expected time of delivery, return policies, and warranties.

The buyer now prepares an **order-routine specification.** It includes the final order with the chosen supplier or suppliers and lists items such as technical specifications, quantity needed, expected time of delivery, return policies, and warranties. In the case of maintenance, repair, and operating items, buyers may use *blanket contracts* rather than periodic purchase orders. A blanket contract creates a long-term relationship in which the supplier promises to resupply the buyer as needed at agreed prices for a set time period. The seller holds the stock, and the buyer's computer automatically prints out an order to the seller when stock is needed. A blanket order eliminates the expensive process of renegotiating a purchase each time that stock is required. It also allows buyers to write more, but smaller, purchase orders, resulting in lower inventory levels and carrying costs.

Blanket contracting leads to more single-source buying and to buying more items from that source. This practice locks the supplier in tighter with the buyer and makes it difficult for other suppliers to break in unless the buyer becomes dissatisfied with prices or service.

Performance Review

Performance review
The stage of the business buying process in which the buyer rates its satisfaction with suppliers, deciding whether to continue, modify, or drop them.

In this stage, the buyer reviews supplier performance. The buyer may contact users and ask them to rate their satisfaction. The **performance review** may lead the buyer to continue, modify, or drop the arrangement. The seller's job is to monitor the same factors used by the buyer to make sure that the seller is giving the expected satisfaction.

We have described the stages that typically would occur in a new-task buying situation. The eight-stage model provides a simple view of the business buying decision process. The actual process is usually much more complex. In the modified rebuy or straight rebuy situation, some of these stages would be compressed or bypassed. Each organization buys in its own way, and each buying situation has unique requirements. Different buying center participants may be involved at different stages of the process. Although certain buying process steps usually do occur, buyers do not always follow them in the same order, and they may add other steps. Often, buyers will repeat certain stages of the process.

Business Buying on the Internet

During the past few years, incredible advances in information technology have changed the face of the business-to-business marketing process. Increasingly, business buyers are purchasing all kinds of products and services electronically, either through electronic data interchange (EDI) links or on the Internet. Such "cyberpurchasing" gives buyers access to new suppliers, lowers purchasing costs, and hastens order processing and delivery. In turn, business marketers are connecting with customers online to share marketing information, sell products and services, provide customer support services, and maintain ongoing customer relationships. In addition to their own Web pages on the Internet, they are establishing extranets that link a company's communications and data with its regular suppliers and distributors.

So far, most of the products bought by businesses through Internet and extranet connections are MRO materials—maintenance, repair, and operations. For instance, Los Angeles County purchases everything from chickens to lightbulbs over the Internet. National Semiconductor has automated almost all of the company's 3,500 monthly requisitions to buy materials ranging from the sterile booties worn in its fabrication plants to state-of-the-art software. The actual dollar amount spent on these types of MRO materials pales in comparison to the amount spent for items like airplane parts, computer systems, and steel tubing. Yet, MRO materials make up 80 percent of all business orders, and the transaction costs for order processing are high. Thus, companies have much to gain by streamlining the MRO buying process on the Web.

General Electric, one of the world's biggest purchasers, plans to be buying *all* of its general operating and industrial supplies online within the next two years. Five years ago, GE set up its Trading Process Network—a central Web site through which all GE business units could make their purchases. The site was so successful that GE has now opened it up to other companies, creating a vast electronic cyber-buying clearinghouse (see Marketing Highlight 6.3).

The rapid growth business-to-business cyberbuying promises many benefits. The cyberbuying juggernaut promises to[17]

★ *Shave transaction costs* for both buyers and suppliers. A Web-powered purchasing program eliminates the paperwork associated with traditional requisition and ordering procedures. At National Semiconductor, the $75 to $250 cost of processing each paper-based requisition has been cut to just $3 per electronic order.

★ *Reduce time between order and delivery:* Time savings are particularly dramatic for companies with many overseas suppliers. Adaptec, a leading supplier of computer storage, used an extranet to tie all of its Taiwanese chip suppliers together in a kind of virtual family. Now messages from Adaptec flow in seconds from its headquarters to its Asian partners, and Adaptec has reduced the time between the order and delivery of its chips from as long as 16 weeks to just 55 days—the same turnaround time for companies that build their own chips.

★ *Create more efficient purchasing systems:* One key motivation for GE's massive move to online purchasing has been a desire to get rid of overlapping purchasing systems across its many divisions. "We have too many purchasing systems to count," said Randy Rowe, manager of GE's corporate initiatives group. "We're looking to enable each division to manage its purchasing on extranets with financial data [concentrated in] a centralized platform."

★ *Forge more intimate relationships* between partners and buyers. Robert Mondavi Corporation puts satellite images of its vineyards out over its extranet so that its independent growers can pinpoint potential vineyard problems and improve the grapes Mondavi purchases from them.

★ *Level the playing field* between large and small suppliers. By using Internet technology to establish secure, standing information links between companies, extranets have helped firms do business with smaller suppliers. Currently most large manufacturers use EDI to order supplies, because it provides a secure means of coding and exchanging standardized business forms. However, EDI is an expensive system; it can cost as much as $50,000 to add a single trading partner to an EDI network, compared to $1,000 for a company to join GE's Trading Process Network. Moving business-to-business commerce onto the Web also levels the playing field between local and foreign suppliers, because purchasers can source materials from suppliers all over the globe for no additional transaction cost.

MARKETING HIGHLIGHT
6.3

GENERAL ELECTRIC'S BUSINESS-TO-BUSINESS CYBERBAZAAR

To most consumers, all the buzz about Internet buying has focused on Web sites selling computers, software, clothing, books, flowers, or other retail goods. However, consumer goods sales via the Web are dwarfed by the Internet sales of business goods. In fact, business-to-business cyberbuying now accounts for some 78 percent of the dollar value of all e-commerce transactions.

General Electric is among the pioneers in Internet purchasing. In early 1995, GE's Information Services division (GEIS) launched a Web site that allowed buyers in GE's many divisions to purchase industrial products electronically. This Web site let GE buyers snap out requests for bids to thousands of suppliers, who could then respond over the Internet. Such electronic purchasing has saved GE's many divisions money, time, and piles of paperwork. According to a *Forbes* account, here's how it works:

> Last month the machinery at a GE Lighting factory in Cleveland broke down. GE Lighting needed custom replacement parts, fast. In the past GE would have asked for bids from just four domestic suppliers. There was just too much hassle getting the paperwork and production-line blueprints together and sent out to [a long list of] suppliers. But this time it posted the specifications and "requests for quotes" on GE's Web site—and drew seven other bidders. The winner was a Hungarian [vendor] . . . that would not [even] have been contacted in the days of paper purchasing forms. The Hungarian firm's replacement parts arrived quicker, and GE Lighting paid just $320,000, a 20 percent savings.

Within little more than a year, GEIS's Internet purchasing system had logged more than $350 million worth of purchases by GE divisions, at a 10 percent to 15 percent savings in costs and a five-day reduction in average order time. In 1997, GE purchased $1 billion worth of materials via the Internet and by the end of 2000 expects to be buying $5 billion worth, a 20 percent savings over the old way.

Based on its own success, GE opened its online procurement services to other companies in the form of the Trading Process Network (TPN) (www.tpn.geis.com). TPN is an online purchasing service that lets member buyers prepare bids, select suppliers, and post orders to its Web site. Users can select items they wish to buy and use a purchasing card for payment. Once the order is placed, TPN sends a purchase order to a selected supplier or asks for bids from several qualified suppliers. Users of the

---

The rapidly expanding use of cybersourcing, however, also presents some problems. Here are a few of the negatives:

★ *Cut purchasing jobs* for millions of clerks and order processors. All these savings and efficiencies derived from cyberbuying don't come without a price. National Semiconductor reduced its purchasing staff by more than half when it took its purchasing activities online. On the other hand, for many purchasing professionals, going online means reducing drudgery and paperwork and spending more time managing inventory and working creatively with suppliers.

★ *Erode supplier–buyer loyalty:* At the same time that the Web makes it possible for suppliers and customers to share business data and even collaborate on product design, it can also erode decades-old customer–supplier relationships. Many firms are using the Web to search for better suppliers. Japan Airlines (JAL) has used the Internet to post orders for in-flight materials such as plastic cups. On its Web site it posts drawings and specifications that will attract proposals from any firm that comes across the site, rather than from just the usual Japanese suppliers.

★ *Create potential security disasters:* Over 80 percent of companies say security is the leading barrier to expanding electronic links with customers and partners.

TPN service have experienced up to a 50 percent reduction in order cycle times, 30 percent reduction in procurement costs, and 20 percent reduction in material costs.

Despite likely competition from such e-business giants as IBM and Microsoft, GEIS has developed a formidable head start in providing Internet purchasing services. According to Orville Bailey, who manages the TPN project, the toughest part of setting up such a system is just getting it started. Buyers don't want to sign on until plenty of suppliers are already on board, and vice versa. "It's the classic chicken-or-the-egg problem," says Bailey. Here, however, GE's tremendous size gives it a crucial advantage. GE's various divisions spend more than $30 billion a year buying goods and services from other companies. So when GE announced that it would be looking for bids over the Web, suppliers scurried to sign up. Now, with its own network of industrial goods suppliers already in place, GEIS has little difficulty reselling the Internet purchasing system to other compa-

nies that want to take advantage of what GE has built.

GEIS charges buyers an initial fee of $70,000 for access to its TPN site, plus an annual fee based on buying volume. Suppliers can sign on for free. The first outside buying firm to sign on with TPN was Textron Automotive, a subsidiary of the $9.3 billion Textron, Inc. According to Forbes, "Like GE, Textron Automotive buys a lot of raw materials and components: resin, ashtrays, metal clips, and other parts used in auto dashboards and paneling. By year end, Textron Automotive hopes to place all its orders—more than $500 million a year—over the GE Information Services Web site." Such big users, along with thousands of smaller ones, have put GEIS well on its way to creating a vast cyberbazaar.

Thus, the Internet promises to change greatly the face of business buying and hence the face of business-to-business marketing. As one expert suggests, "Internet presence is becoming as common as business cards and faxes." To stay in the game, business-to-business marketers will need a well-thought-out Internet

marketing strategy to support their other business marketing efforts. General Electric envisions a not-too-distant future in which hundreds of thousands of firms exchange trillions of dollars worth of industrial goods in cyberspace—with GEIS running the show, of course.

Sources: Extracts from Scott Woolley, "Double Click for Resin," *Forbes,* March 10, 1997, p. 132. Also see Dana Blankenhorn, "GE's E-commerce Network Opens Up to Other Marketers," *Advertising Age's Business Marketing,* May 1997, pp. M4, M11; "Consolidated Edison of New York Selects GE's Trading Process Network to Facilitate Internet Sourcing," press release, www.tpn.geis.com, February 10, 1998; Robert D. Hof, "The 'Click Here' Economy," *Business Week,* June 22, 1998, pp. 122–28; John Evan Frook, "Buying Behemoth—By Shifting $5B in Spending to Extranets, GE Could Ignite a Development Frenzy," *Internetweek,* August 17, 1998, p. 1; Richard Waugh and Scott Elliff, "Using the Internet to Achieve Purchasing Improvements at General Electric," *Hospital Materiel Management Quarterly,* November 1998, pp. 81–83; and James Carbone, "Internet Buying on the Rise," *Purchasing,* March 25, 1999, pp. 51–56.

Although e-mail and home banking transactions can be protected through basic encryption, the secure environment that businesses need to carry out confidential interactions is still lacking. However, security is of such high priority that companies are spending millions of research dollars on it. Companies are creating their own defensive strategies for keeping hackers at bay. Cisco Systems, for example, specifies the types of routers, firewalls, and security procedures that its partners must use to safeguard extranet connections. In fact, the company goes even further—it sends its own security engineers to examine a partner's defenses and holds the partner liable for any security breach that originates from its computer.

 INSTITUTIONAL AND GOVERNMENT MARKETS

So far, our discussion of organizational buying has focused largely on the buying behavior of business buyers. Much of this discussion also applies to the buying practices of institutional and government organizations. However, these two nonbusiness markets have additional characteristics and needs. In this final section, we address the special features of institutional and government markets.

Institutional Markets

Institutional market
Schools, hospitals, nursing homes, prisons, and other institutions that provide goods and services to people in their care.

The **institutional market** consists of schools, hospitals, nursing homes, prisons, and other institutions that provide goods and services to people in their care. Institutions differ from one another in their sponsors and in their objectives. For example, Humana hospitals are run for profit, whereas a nonprofit Sisters of Charity Hospital provides health care to the poor and a government-run hospital might provide special services to veterans.

Many institutional markets are characterized by low budgets and captive patrons. For example, hospital patients have little choice but to eat whatever food the hospital supplies. A hospital purchasing agent has to decide on the quality of food to buy for patients. Because the food is provided as a part of a total service package, the buying objective is not profit. Nor is strict cost minimization the goal—patients receiving poor-quality food will complain to others and damage the hospital's reputation. Thus, the hospital purchasing agent must search for institutional-food vendors whose quality meets or exceeds a certain minimum standard and whose prices are low.

Many marketers set up separate divisions to meet the special characteristics and needs of institutional buyers. For example, Heinz produces, packages, and prices its ketchup and other products differently to better serve the requirements of hospitals, colleges, and other institutional markets.

Government Markets

Government market
Governmental units—federal, state, and local—that purchase or rent goods and services for carrying out the main functions of government.

The **government market** offers large opportunities for many companies, both big and small. In most countries, government organizations are major buyers of goods and services. In the United States alone, federal, state, and local governments contain more than 82,000 buying units. Government buying and business buying are similar in many ways. But there are also differences that must be understood by companies that wish to sell products and services to governments. To succeed in the government market, sellers must locate key decision makers, identify the factors that affect buyer behavior, and understand the buying decision process.

Government organizations typically require suppliers to submit bids, and normally they award the contract to the lowest bidder. In some cases, the government unit will make allowance for the supplier's superior quality or reputation for completing contracts on time. Governments will also buy on a negotiated contract basis, primarily in the case of complex projects involving major R&D costs and risks, and in cases where there is little competition.

Government organizations tend to favor domestic suppliers over foreign suppliers. A major complaint of multinationals operating in Europe is that each country shows favoritism toward its nationals in spite of superior offers that are made by foreign firms. The European Economic Commission is gradually removing this bias.

Like consumer and business buyers, government buyers are affected by environmental, organizational, interpersonal, and individual factors. One unique thing about government buying is that it is carefully watched by outside publics, ranging from Congress to a variety of private groups interested in how the government spends taxpayers' money. Because their spending decisions are subject to public review, government organizations require considerable paperwork from suppliers, who often complain about excessive paperwork, bureaucracy, regulations, decision-making delays, and frequent shifts in procurement personnel. Given all the red tape, why would any firm want to do business with the U.S. government? Here's how a consultant who has helped clients obtain more than $30 billion in government contracts answers that question:

When I hear that question, I tell the story of the businessman who buys a hardware store after moving to a small town. He asks his new employees who the biggest hardware customer in town is. He is surprised to learn that the customer isn't doing business with his store. When the owner asks why not, his employees say the customer is difficult to do business with and requires that a lot of forms be filled out. I point out that the same customer is probably very wealthy, doesn't bounce his checks, and usually does repeat business when satisfied. That's the type of customer the federal government can be.

Most governments provide would-be suppliers with detailed guides describing how to sell to the government. For example, the U.S. Small Business Administration prints a booklet entitled *U.S. Government Purchasing, Specifications, and Sales Directory,* which lists thousands of items most frequently purchased by the government and the specific agencies most frequently buying them. The Government Printing Office issues the *Commerce Business Daily,* which lists major current and planned purchases and recent contract awards, both of which can provide leads to subcontracting markets. The U.S. Commerce Department publishes *Business America,* which provides interpretations of government policies and programs and gives concise information on potential worldwide trade opportunities. In several major cities, the General Services Administration operates *Business Service Centers* with staffs to provide a complete education on the way government agencies buy, the steps that suppliers should follow, and the procurement opportunities available. Various trade magazines and associations provide information on how to reach schools, hospitals, highway departments, and other government agencies. Almost all of these government organizations and associations maintain Internet sites offering up-to-date information and advice.

Still, suppliers have to master the system and find ways to cut through the red tape. For example, the U.S. government has always been ADI Technology Corporation's most important client—federal contracts account for about 90 percent of its nearly $6 million in annual revenues. Yet managers at this small professional services company often shake their heads at all the work that goes into winning the coveted government contracts. A comprehensive bid proposal will run from 500 to 700 pages because of federal paperwork requirements. The company's president estimates that the firm has spent as much as $20,000, mostly in worker hours, to prepare a single bid proposal. Fortunately, government buying reforms are being put in place that will simplify contracting procedures and make bidding more attractive, particularly to smaller vendors. These reforms include more emphasis on buying commercial off-the-shelf items instead of items built to the government's specs, online communication with vendors to eliminate the massive paperwork, and a "debriefing" from the appropriate government agency for vendors who lose a bid, enabling them to increase their chances of winning the next time around.[18]

Noneconomic criteria also play a growing role in government buying. Government buyers are asked to favor depressed business firms and areas; small business firms; minority-owned firms; and business firms that avoid race, sex, or age discrimination. Sellers need to keep these factors in mind when deciding to seek government business.

Many companies that sell to the government have not been marketing oriented for a number of reasons. Total government spending is determined by elected officials rather than by any marketing effort to develop this market. Government buying has emphasized price, making suppliers invest their effort in technology to bring costs down. When the product's characteristics are specified carefully, product differentiation is not a marketing factor. Nor do advertising or personal selling matter much in winning bids on an open-bid basis.

Dell Computer provides special Web pages for government buyers as well as individually customized sites for each city, state, or federal customer.

Several companies, however, have established separate government marketing departments. Rockwell, Kodak, and Goodyear are examples. These companies anticipate government needs and projects, participate in the product specification phase, gather competitive intelligence, prepare bids carefully, and produce stronger communications to describe and enhance their companies' reputations. Other companies have set up customized marketing programs for government buyers. For example, Dell Computer has specific business units tailored to meet the needs of federal as well as state and local government buyers. Dell offers its customers tailor-made Web pages that include special pricing, online purchasing, and service and support for each city, state, and federal government entity.[19]

During the past decade, some of the government's buying has gone online. For example, *Commerce Business Daily* is now online (cbd.cos.com) and the two federal agencies that act as purchasing agents for the rest of government have launched World Wide Web–based catalogs. The General Services Administration (www.gsa.gov) has set up an Advantage Web catalog, and the Defense Logistics Agency (www.dla.mil) offers one called Ascot. These Internet catalogs allow authorized defense and civilian agencies to buy everything from medical and office supplies to clothing through online purchasing. The GSA and DLA not only sell stocked merchandise through their Web sites but also create direct links between buyers and contract suppliers. For example, the branch of the DSA that sells 160,000 types of medical supplies to military forces transmits orders directly to vendors such as Bristol-Meyers. Such Internet systems promise to eliminate much of the hassle sometimes found in dealing with government purchasing.[20]

REVIEW OF CONCEPT CONNECTIONS

Business markets and consumer markets are alike in some key ways. For example, both include people in buying roles who make purchase decisions to satisfy needs. But business markets also differ in many ways from consumer markets. For one thing, the business market is *enormous,* far larger than the consumer market. Within the United States alone, the business market includes more than 13 million organizations that annually purchase trillions of dollars' worth of goods and services.

1. Define the business market and explain how business markets differ from consumer markets.

The *business market* comprises all organizations that buy goods and services for use in the production of other products and services or for the purpose of reselling or renting them to others at a profit. As compared to consumer markets, business markets usually have fewer, larger buyers who are more geographically concentrated. Business demand is *derived,* largely *inelastic,* and more *fluctuating.* More buyers are usually involved in the business buying decision, and business buyers are better trained and more professional than are consumer buyers. In general, business purchasing decisions are more complex, and the buying process is more formal than consumer buying.

2. Identify the major factors that influence business buyer behavior.

Business buyers make decisions that vary with the three types of buying situations: *straight rebuys, modified rebuys,* and *new tasks.* The buying center, which can consist of many different persons playing many different roles, is the decision-making unit of a buying organization. The business marketer needs to know the following: Who are the major participants? In what decisions do they exercise influence? What is their relative degree of influence? What evaluation criteria does each decision participant use? The business marketer also needs to understand the major environmental, organizational, interpersonal, and individual influences on the buying process.

3. List and define the steps in the business buying decision process.

The business buying decision process itself can be quite involved, with eight basic stages: (1) *problem recognition,* someone in the company recognizes a problem or need that can be met by acquiring a product or service; (2) *general need description,* the company determines the general characteristics and quantity of the needed item; (3) *product specification,* the buying organization decides on and specifies the best technical product characteristics for the needed item; (4) *supplier search,* the buyer seeks the best vendors; (5) *proposal solicitation,* the buyer invites qualified suppliers to submit proposals; (6) *supplier selection,* the buyer reviews proposals and selects a supplier or suppliers; (7) *order-routine specification,* the buyer writes the final order with the chosen supplier(s), listing the technical specifications, quantity needed, expected time of delivery, return policies, and warranties; and (8) *performance review,* the buyer rates its satisfaction with suppliers, deciding whether to continue, modify, or cancel them.

4. Compare the institutional and government markets and explain how institutional and government buyers make their buying decisions.

The *institutional market* comprises schools, hospitals, prisons, and other institutions that provide goods and services to people in their care. These markets are characterized by low budgets and captive patrons. The *government market,* which is vast, consists of government units—federal, state, and local—that purchase or rent goods and services for carrying out the main functions of government. Government buyers purchase products and services for defense, education, public welfare, and other public needs. Government buying practices are highly specialized and specified, with open bidding or negotiated contracts characterizing most of the buying. Government buyers operate under the watchful eye of Congress and many private watchdog groups. Hence, they tend to require more forms and signatures, and to respond more slowly and deliberately when placing orders.

KEY TERMS

Business buying process	Buying center	Gatekeepers
Business market	Deciders	General need description
Buyers	Derived demand	Government market

Influencers	Performance review	Supplier search
Institutional market	Problem recognition	Supplier selection
Modified rebuy	Product specification	Systems buying
New task	Proposal solicitation	Users
Order-routine specification	Straight rebuy	Value analysis

ISSUES FOR DISCUSSION

1. Although business markets are similar in many ways to consumers markets, there are also significant differences. What similarities and difference might Staples (www.staples.com) or Office Depot (www.officedepot.com) encounter in selling to the business market versus the consumer market for the following products: (a) a personal computer, (b) paper for a printer or photocopier, (c) a desk chair, and (d) paper clips?

2. Using the auto industry as an example, demonstrate the concept of derived demand. How might derived demand affect the industry in the following product categories: (a) steel, (b) CD players, (c) safety air bags, (d) On Star roadside assistance service, and (e) customized chrome wheels? What consumer trends would affect these products and their demand by the auto industry?

3. Compare Figure 5.1 (in the previous chapter) to Figure 6.1. What similarities and differences do you find in inputs and outputs of these two buying models? What additions would you recommend for either or both models? Explain.

4. Which of the major types of buying situations is represented by each of the following: (a) Chrysler's purchase of computers that go into cars and adjust engine performance to changing driving conditions, (b) Volkswagen's purchase of spark plugs for its line of minivans, and (c) Honda's purchase of lightbulbs for a new Acura model?

5. Using your university or college as an example, illustrate how the concept of systems buying might work if the university or college decided to purchase a new master computer system that would integrate all administrative, faculty, and student information requirements into a single system. The system could be accessed by users on or off campus. What would be the component parts of such a system. How would you go about selling such a system to the college or university?

6. Assume you are selling cars to a company for use as fleet cars by the company's sales force. The salespeople would like bigger, more comfortable cars, which would be more profitable for you. However, the company's fleet buyer prefers smaller, more economical cars. Who might be in the buying center for this purchase? How could you meet the varying needs of these participants?

7. More and more business buyers are now purchasing products and services electronically, either through electronic data interchange (EDI) links or on the Internet. What are the benefits of such "cyberpurchasing"? What are the negatives? What is the future of this growing field of commerce? Illustrate your view with an example.

MARKETING APPLICATIONS

1. Many companies now use outside suppliers to produce raw materials or parts instead of producing these components themselves. In the extreme, companies such as Dell Computer own no production facilities and have suppliers make everything to order. This type of company has been nicknamed a "virtual corporation."
   a. Do you think that buyers and suppliers are likely to be more cooperative or more adversarial in this type of corporate structure?
   b. List the advantages and disadvantages this sort of supplier relationship for both the buyer and the supplier.
   c. Explain how the supplier search process might work in the Dell "virtual corporation" example.

   d. Go to the Dell Web site at www.dell.com and review the information on the company. What can you determine about the "outside" parts that are contained in a Dell computer—for example, the processor, monitor, or CPU itself. Do buyers know which components are original Dell parts and which are not? Would this be of concern to potential buyers?
   e. In such a situation, what would be the most important considerations in supplier selections?

2. Performance review is one of the most critical stages in a business buying process. Perhaps nowhere is this more important than in the highly competitive aircraft manufacturing business. No matter what the size of the airplane,

once the purchase is made, the buyer is tied to the manufacturer for a long time because of service and parts requirements. "Air wars" are currently being fought between Europe's Airbus Industrie and America's Boeing. To a lesser extent the same competitive conflict exists in the smaller personal aircraft market between Cessna and Lear Jet. Who will eventually win these dramatic competitive struggles is still up in the air. (For additional information on these companies, see www.airbus.com, www.boeing.com, www.cessna.textron.com, and www.learjet.com.)

a. Apply Figure 6.1 to either of the preceding competitive situations and discuss the critical factors that might be found in such a business buying situation.

b. How would performance review be conducted in either of these situations? Who might be responsible for such a performance review?

c. Refer to Figure 6.2. Which specific components might be involved in a performance review of aircraft safety?

d. Find a recent example of "air war" competitiveness and bring the example to class for discussion. How does your example relate to business-to-business marketing and business buying?

 INTERNET CONNECTIONS

ONLINE DATABASES

Many business-to-business (B2B) marketers use the services of firms that provide information on other companies through their databases. Dun & Bradstreet is popular and has a fine reputation for both its paper and online company profiles. The Yellow Book, founded in 1930, also provides information for businesses seeking suppliers or other contacts. Finally, AskAlex Directory serves a niche market for businesses wanting a particular type of information. In this exercise you will visit all three online firms, check out their services, and evaluate their appropriateness for various business situations. Start by completing the table.

	Dun & Bradstreet www.dnb.com	Yellow Book www.yellowbook.com	AskAlex Directory askalex.co.uk
Database size			
Geographic coverage			
Cost for using the database			
Specific company profile information in database			
Three important services			
Useful for a supplier search?			
Useful for a supplier selection?			
Useful for finding prospective business customers?			
Database includes government market?			
Competitive edge			

DISCUSSION QUESTIONS

1. If your firm was looking for an office supply company in Manhattan to replace its current supplier, which of the three databases would you use? Explain.
2. If you wanted to quickly find the phone number of an office supply firm in Tampa, Florida, which database would you use? Why?
3. Which database offers the broadest range of services? Explain.
4. Under what circumstances would the AskAlex business database be useful to a company?
5. If you were a salesperson for IBM and prospecting for new business customers, which database would you use? Why?

6. Overall, which database company is the best in your opinion? Explain.
7. If you were going to start an online database firm to serve the B2B market, what would you do differently than these three firms?

SAVVY SITES

- EDS (www.eds.com), located in Dallas, Texas, "develops solutions for complex business issues" including management and solutions consulting, information solutions, and business process management.

- Ad-Up (www.ad-up.com) and Click-Through, Inc. (www.clickthrough.com) are online full-service advertising agencies that help business clients find appropriate sites for their banner advertisements. For a list of similar services, visit Advertising World at the University of Texas (advweb.cocomm.utexas.edu/world/).

- In addition to consumers, Intel (www.intel.com) provides lots of information on its Web site for business clients such as software and hardware developers, business computing, and channel members. It is especially helpful for e-business managers.

NOTES

1. Portions adapted from Thomas V. Bonoma, "Major Sales: Who Really Does the Buying," *Harvard Business Review,* May–June 1982. Copyright © 1982 by the President and Fellows of Harvard College; all rights reserved. Quotes from John Huey, "The Absolute Best Way to Fly," *Fortune,* May 30, 1994, pp. 121–28; and Anthony Bianco, "Gulfstream's Pilot," *Business Week,* April 14, 1997, pp. 64–76. Also see "My First Gulfstream," *Vanity Fair,* October 1998, pp. 236–58; and Steven Lipin and Andy Pasztor, "Defense Firm Set to Acquire Gulfstream," *Wall Street Journal,* May 17, 1999, p. A3.

2. Sarah Lorge, "Purchasing Power," *Sales & Marketing Management,* June 1998, pp. 43–46.

3. John H. Sheridan, "An Alliance Built on Trust," *Industry Week,* March 17, 1997, pp. 66–70.

4. Patrick J. Robinson, Charles W. Faris, and Yoram Wind, *Industrial Buying Behavior and Creative Marketing* (Boston: Allyn & Bacon, 1967). Also see Erin Anderson, Weyien Chu, and Barton Weitz, "Industrial Purchasing: An Empirical Exploration of the Buyclass Framework," *Journal of Marketing,* July 1987, pp. 71–86; Cynthia Webster, "Buying Involvement in Purchasing Success," *Industrial Marketing Management,* August 1993, p. 199; and Edward G. Brierty, Robert W. Eckles, and Robert R. Reeder, *Business Marketing,* 3rd ed. (Upper Saddle River, NJ: Prentice Hall, 1998), pp. 74–82.

5. Sarah Lorge, "Enron," *Sales & Marketing Management,* July 1999, pp. 48–52.

6. Frederick E. Webster Jr. and Yoram Wind, *Organizational Buying Behavior* (Upper Saddle River, NJ: Prentice Hall, 1972), pp. 78–80. Also see Michael D. Hutt and Thomas Speh, *Business Marketing Management,* 4th ed. (Fort Worth, TX: Dryden Press, 1992), pp. 104–12; and James C. Anderson and James A. Narus, *Business Market Management: Understanding, Creating and Delivering Value* (Upper Saddle River, NJ: Prentice Hall, 1998), chap. 3.

7. For results of both surveys, see "I Think You Have a Great Product, but It's Not My Decision," *American Salesman,* April 1994, pp. 11–13; and Tim Minahan, "OEM Buying Survey—Part 2: Buyers Get New Roles but Keep Old Tasks," *Purchasing,* July 16, 1998, pp. 208–9. For more on influence strategies within buying centers, see R. Venkatesh, Ajay K. Kohli, and Gerald Zaltman, "Influence Strategies in Buying Centers," *Journal of Marketing,* October 1995, pp. 71–82; John Monoky, "Who Does the Buying?" *Industrial Distribution,* October 1995, p. 48; and David I. Gilliland and Wesley J. Johnson, "Toward a Model of Business-to-Business Marketing Communications Effects," *Industrial Marketing Management,* January 1997, pp. 15–29; and Philip L. Dawes, Don Y. Lee, and Grahame R. Dowling, "Information Control and Influence in Emergent Buying Centers," *Journal of Marketing,* July 1998, pp. 55–68.

8. Melvin R. Matson and Esmail Salshi-Sangari, "Decision Making in Purchases of Equipment and Materials: A Four-Country Comparison," *International Journal of Physical Distribution & Logistics Management* 23, no. 8, 1993, pp. 16–30.

9. Webster and Wind, *Organizational Buying Behavior,* pp. 33–37. Also see Brierty, Eckles, and Reeder, *Business Marketing,* chap. 3.

10. Bonoma, "Major Sales," p. 114. Also see Ajay Kohli, "Determinants of Influence in Organizational Buying: A Contingency Approach," *Journal of Marketing,* July 1989, pp. 50–65.

11. Robinson, Faris, and Wind, *Industrial Buying Behavior and Creative Marketing,* p. 14.

12. John H. Sheridan, "Buying Globally Made Easier," *Industry Week,* February 2, 1998, pp. 63–64; and information accessed online at www.wiznet.net, September 1999.x

13. See "Xerox Multinational Supplier Quality Survey," *Purchasing,* January 1995, p. 112.

14. See "What Buyers Really Want," *Sales & Marketing Management,* October 1989, p. 30; "Purchasing Managers Sound Off," *Sales & Marketing Management,* February 1995, pp. 84–85; Thomas Y. Choi and Janet L. Hartley, "An Exploration of Supplier Selection Practices Across the Supply Chain," *Journal of Operations Management,* November 1996, pp. 333–43; Douglas M. Lambert, Ronald J. Adams, and Margaret A. Emmelhainz, "Supplier Selection Criteria in the Healthcare Industry: A Comparison of Importance and Performance," *International Journal of Purchasing and Materials Management,* Winter 1997, pp. 16–22; and Graig M. Gustin, Patricia J. Daugherty, and Alexander E. Ellinger, "Supplier Selection Decisions in Systems/Software," *International Journal of Purchasing and Materials Management,* Fall 1997, pp. 41–46.

15. Donna Del Moro, "Single-Source Newsprint Supply," *Editor & Publisher,* October 25, 1997, pp. 42–45.

16. See Kitty Vineyard, "Trends . . . in Single Sourcing," *Electrical Apparatus*, November 1996, p. 12; and Anne Millen Porter, "Supply Alliances Pose New Ethical Threats," *Purchasing*, May 20, 1999, pp. 20–23.

17. See Robert Yoegel, "The Evolution of B-to-B Selling on the 'Net," *Target Marketing*, August 1998, p. 34; Andy Reinhardt in San Mateo, "Extranets: Log On, Link Up, Save Big," *Business Week*, June 22, 1998, p. 134, "To Byte the Hand That Feeds," *The Economist*, January 17, 1998, pp. 61–62, John Evan Frook, "Buying Behemoth—By Shifting $5B in Spending to Extranets, GE Could Ignite a Development Frenzy," *Internetweek*, August 17, 1998, p. 1; John Jesitus, "Procuring an Edge," *Industry Week*, June 23, 1997, pp. 56–62; Ken Brack, "Source of the Future," *Industrial Distribution*, October 1998, pp. 76–80; and James Carbone, "Internet Buying on the Rise," *Purchasing*, March 25, 1999, pp. 51–56.

18. Laura M. Litvan, "Selling to Uncle Sam: New, Easier Rules," *Nation's Business*, March 1995, pp. 46–48; and Edward Robinson, "The Pentagon Finally Learns to Shop," *Fortune*, December 21, 1998, pp. 174–83.

19. For more on U.S. government buying, see Don Hill, "Who Says Uncle Sam's a Tough Sell?" *Sales & Marketing Management*, July 1988, pp. 56–60; Richard J. Wall and Carolyn M. Jones, "Navigating the Rugged Terrain of Government Contracts," *Internal Auditor*, April 1995, p. 32; and Wallace O. Keene, "New Bright Spot in Acquisition Reform," *Public Manager*, Spring 1999, pp. 45–46.

20. Ellen Messmer, "Feds Buy Online," *Network World*, April 15, 1996, p. 35; and "Government Surges Forward with Plans for Electronic Shopping Mall," *Supply Management*, March 18, 1999, p. 9. Also see Christina Couret, "Online Shopping Offers Governments 'Net' Gain," *The American City and County*, January 1999, pp. 20–23.

COMPANY CASE

6

Biofoam: Not Just Peanuts!

Like diamonds, polystyrene peanuts are forever and every year—the stash of them is growing at a rate of at least 50 million pounds (300 million cubic feet of peanuts) annually. Since their introduction in 1970, they have become one of the most popular forms of packaging material. They are lightweight, inexpensive, and resilient. They conform to any shape, protect superbly, resist shifting in transit, and leave no dusty residue on the goods they protect. Of course, too, they are indestructible. In fact, that's the problem. Nearly every one of those peanuts used since 1970 is still with us—blowing in the wind or taking up space in a landfill. Worse yet, they will be with us for another 500 years. They're wonderful, but they're just not environmentally sound.

A small firm in Phoenix, Arizona—Biofoam—thinks it has solved this problem. It sells a peanut made from grain sorghum that it calls, well, Biofoam. To make these sorghum peanuts, the company strips the grain of its nutritional value, presses it into pellets, and conveys it through a giant popper. The process creates a product that looks like tan cheese doodles, not so surprising given that the inventors started out to make a snack food. But no one wanted to eat these tan cheese doodles, so the inventors had to find other uses for them. According to Ed Alfke, Biofoam's CEO, the sorghum peanuts do just as good a job as the best foam peanuts and they don't cost any more. Moreover, they hold no electrostatic charge, so they won't cling to nylons or other synthetic fibers (such as your carpet or clothes). Better yet, they are "absolutely, frighteningly natural," says Tom Schmiegel, a veteran of the plastics industry.

To dispose of a Biofoam peanut, you can: (a) put it in your trash can, (b) throw it on your front lawn, (c) dump it into your compost bin, (d) put it in your dog's or cat's bowl, (e) set it out with salsa at your next party, or (f) simply wash it down your drain. The peanut dissolves in water and has some—although limited—nutritional value. Alfke bought into the company because of its environmentally positive stance. He is convinced that green companies will profit from a global regulatory climate that's increasingly hostile to polluters. "The writing is on the wall for companies that are not environmentally friendly," he says.

Biofoam initially targeted retailers who wanted to send an environmentally friendly message, helped along by the inclusion of a Biofoam pamphlet explaining the advantages of the Biofoam peanut. It targeted the heaviest users of Styrofoam peanuts, such as QVC and Home Shopping Network, which each consume 10 to 20 truckloads of loose fill a *day* at peak volume. To date, Biofoam has signed two major accounts—the Fuller Brush Company and computer reseller MicroAge.

Eventually, Biofoam will have to expand beyond environmentally sensitive firms into a broader market. To convince potential users to use Biofoam peanuts, Alfke has come up with a seemingly no-brainer option: to be environmentally responsible without having to pay more or sacrifice convenience. He is willing to install machines on the customer's premises to produce peanuts in-house—an arrangement that would give Biofoam rent-free production sites around the country. He'll even provide an employee to operate the machinery. Although this strategy might sound unusual, it has been used by other companies such as Haloid (now Xerox) to sell copies and Tetra Pak to sell juice boxes and milk cartons.

The in-house arrangement has benefits for the customer as well as for Biofoam. Users receive immediate, reliable, just-in-time delivery combined with on-site service and a five-year price guarantee with no intermediaries involved. With Biofoam on-site, users never run out of packaging, and they avoid the expense of stockpiling materials. Lower production costs make Biofoam's price competitive with that of polystyrene. For Biofoam, the arrangement provides a rent-free network of regional manufacturing facilities and an intimacy with each customer. Because the host company will only consume about one-third of the output, Biofoam plans to sell the excess to smaller firms in the host's area.

However, this in-house production arrangement is not without disadvantages. From the host's perspective, the machinery takes up 1,500 square feet of space that could be used to produce something else. Furthermore, some of the output of that 1,500 square feet goes to other firms, benefiting Biofoam but doing nothing for the host. Furthermore, the host has a nonemployee working in its plant. The peanut-making machinery is also intrusive. It consists of three machines—an extruder, a conditioning chamber, and a deduster—joined by ducts and conveyor belts. The machines make lots of noise (like a giant air conditioner), making conversation in the vicinity impossible. The process creates a smell rather like the inside of an old barn, and the machines produce heat, a potential problem. Thus, on closer inspection, the in-house arrangement is not entirely desirable. Without this arrangement, however, costs rise considerably. If it had to ship the peanuts to users, Biofoam would have to raise prices at least 10 percent, possibly 18 percent.

The polystyrene loose-fill industry is a dense, fragmented patchwork of diverse companies. It includes oil companies, chemical producers, fill manufacturers, and regional distributors—all of which would suffer from Biofoam's success. The industry is much more rough-and-tumble than CEO Alfke anticipated. So far, Biofoam has a microscopic market share. The company's 1995 sales totaled only $2.5 million—not much in an industry with potential sales of $150 to $500 million a year. But the $2.5 million represented a five-fold increase over the previous year, before Alfke hit the scene. Alfke now projects sales of $80 million in the year 2000, yielding 30 percent pretax profits. These projections include sales of products other than sorghum peanuts. Alfke plans to add injectible Biofoam and stiff Biofoam packaging materials. Other promising applications have been suggested, such as using Bifoam to absorb oil spills or in medicinal applications, but Alfke doesn't want to talk about those. For now, "It's important that we try to stay focused," he claims.

Can Alfke reach his ambitious goals? Many industry observers say no. Environmental claims, say these observers, don't have the impact that they used to have. "That was something we worried about three years ago," says a New Jersey purchasing agent. Even Biofoam's East Coast sales representatives are finding the market less environmentally concerned. Others, however, are more optimistic. For example, although she agrees that the novelty of environmentally responsible packaging has worn off, Nancy Pfund, general partner of Hambrecht and Quist's Environmental Technology Fund, thinks that many firms are still interested in environmentally friendly packaging. She notes that companies have "internalized a lot of environmental procedures without making a lot of noise about it. You also have younger people who grew up learning about the environment in school now entering the consumer market. That's a very strong trend." Such consumers will demand more responsible packaging.

Are companies that use Biofoam happy with it? Well, some yes, some no. On the positive side is MicroAge Computer. According to Mark Iaquinto, facilities manager, MicroAge had been searching for an acceptable alternative to polystyrene. Now that it's found Biofoam, he's convinced, it can stop searching. On the negative side, Norbert Schneider, president of Fuller Brush Company, has concerns about the way the product crumbles in boxes filled with sharp-pointed brushes. Alfke says that Biofoam is working on a solution, but if it doesn't find one soon, Fuller Brush may change packaging suppliers.

Other firms, such as Enviromold and American Excelsior have entered the market with biodegradable, water-soluble foams. Made from corn-starch-based thermoplastics, the products can be rinsed down the drain after use. They can be used in loose-fill packaging applications or be molded-in-place into shaped packaging. They compare favorably with traditional packaging materials in terms of cost and performance.

So, facing a stiffly competitive industry, new competitors, and a softening of environmental concerns, Biofoam will find the going hard. But none of this dents Alfke's enthusiasm. As the successful founder and developer of Rent-A-Wreck, Alfke was a multimillionaire before age 40. After selling his interest in Rent-A-Wreck, seeking another firm to buy into, he sank millions of his own money into Biofoam. "I've see a lot of deals," he claims, "and I've never, *ever* seen a deal as good as this one." As an experienced businessman, no doubt he *has* seen a lot of deals. He really believes in this one, but is he right?

Questions

1. Outline Biofoam's current marketing strategy. Which elements of the marketing mix are most important for Biofoam to focus on?

2. What is the nature of demand in the loose-fill packaging industry? What factors shape that demand?

3. If you were a buyer of packaging materials, would you agree to Biofoam's offer of machines inside your plant? If not, how could Biofoam overcome your objections?

4. What environmental and organizational factors are likely to affect the loose-fill packaging industry? How will these factors affect Biofoam?

5. Is Alfke right? Is this a good deal? Would you have bought into the firm? Why or why not?

Sources: "The Latest Trends in . . . Protective Packaging," *Modern Materials Handling,* October 1996, pp. P8–P12; "What the Experts Say," *Inc.,* October 1996, pp. 54–55; Robert D. Leaversuch, "Water-Soluble Foams Offer Cost-Effective Protection," *Modern Plastics,* April 1997, pp. 32–35; David Whitford, "The Snack Food That's Packing America," *Inc.,* October 1996, pp. 51–55.

After studying this chapter, you should be able to
1. define the three steps of target marketing: market segmentation, market targeting, and market positioning
2. list and discuss the major levels of market segmentation and bases for segmenting consumer and business markets
3. explain how companies identify attractive market segments and choose a market-coverage strategy
4. discuss how companies can position their products for maximum competitive advantage in the marketplace

MARKET SEGMENTATION, TARGETING, AND POSITIONING FOR COMPETITIVE ADVANTAGE

Procter & Gamble (P&G) sells eight brands of laundry detergent in the United States (Tide, Cheer, Bold, Gain, Era, Oxydol, Dreft, and Ivory Snow). It also sells six brands each of hand soap (Ivory, Safeguard, Camay, Oil of Olay, Zest, Coast) and shampoo (Pantene, Head & Shoulders, Ivory, Pert Plus, Vidal Sassoon, and Prell); four brands each of liquid dishwashing detergent (Dawn, Ivory, Joy, and Cascade), toothpaste (Crest, Gleam, Complete, and Denquel), and tissues and towels (Charmin, Bounty, Puffs, Royale); three brands each of floor cleaner (Spic & Span, Top Job, and Mr. Clean), deodorant (Secret, Sure, and Old Spice), and skin care potions (Oil of Olay, Noxema, and Clearasil); and two brands each of fabric softener (Downy and Bounce), disposable diapers (Pampers and Luvs), and cosmetics (Cover Girl and Max Factor). Moreover, P&G has many additional brands in each category for different international markets. For example, it sells 16 different laundry product brands in Latin America and 19 in Europe, the Middle East, and Africa. (See Procter & Gamble's Web site at www.pg.com for a full glimpse of the company's impressive lineup of familiar brands.)

These P&G brands compete with one another on the same supermarket shelves. But why would P&G introduce several brands in one category instead of concentrating its resources on a single leading brand? The answer lies in the fact that different people want different *mixes of benefits* from the products they buy. Take laundry detergents as an example. People use laundry detergents to get their clothes clean. But they also want other things from their detergents—such as economy, bleaching power, fabric softening, fresh smell, strength or mildness, and lots of suds or only a few. We all want *some* of every one of these benefits from our detergent, but we may have different *priorities* for each benefit. To some people, cleaning and bleaching power are most important; to others, fabric softening matters most; still others want a mild, fresh-scented detergent. Thus, there are groups—or segments—of laundry detergent buyers, and each segment seeks a special combination of benefits.

Procter & Gamble has identified at least eight important laundry detergent segments, along with numerous subsegments, and has developed a different brand designed to meet the special needs of each. The eight P&G brands are positioned for different segments as follows:

- *Tide* "helps keep clothes looking like new." It's the all-purpose family detergent that is "tough on greasy stains." *Tide with Bleach* is "so powerful, it whitens down to the fiber."
- *Cheer with Triple Color Guard* is the "color expert." It guards against fading, color transfer, and fuzzy buildup. *Cheer Free* is "dermatologist tested . . . contains no irritating perfume or dye."
- *Bold* is the detergent with built-in fabric softener. It's "for clean, soft, fresh-smelling clothes." *Bold* liquid adds "the fresh fabric softener scent."
- *Gain,* originally P&G's "enzyme" detergent, was repositioned as the detergent that gives you clean, fresh-smelling clothes. It "cleans and freshens like sunshine. It's not just plain clean, it's Gain clean."
- *Era* has "built-in stain removers." It's "the power tool for stains."
- *Oxydol* contains "stain-seeking bleach." It "combines the cleaning power of detergents with the whitening power of nonchlorine bleach, so your whites sparkle and your clothes look bright." So "don't reach for the bleach—grab a box of Ox!"
- *Dreft* also "helps remove tough baby stains . . . for a clean you can trust." It's "pediatrician recommended and the first choice of mothers." It "doesn't remove the flame resistance of children's sleepwear."
- *Ivory Snow* is "ninety-nine and forty-four one hundredths percent pure." It "gently cleans fine washables and baby clothes . . . leaving them feeling soft." It provides "safe and gentle care in the gentle cycle."

Within each segment, Procter & Gamble has identified even *narrower* niches. For example, you can buy regular Tide (in powder or liquid form) or any of several formulations:

- *Tide with Bleach* helps to "keep your whites white and your colors bright," "kills 99.9 percent of bacteria."
- *Tide Clean Rinse* "goes beyond stain removal to prevent dingy buildup on clothes."
- *Tide Mountain Spring* lets you "bring the fresh clean scent of the great outdoors inside—the scent of crisp mountain air and fresh wildflowers."
- *Tide High Efficiency* is "formulated for high efficiency top-loading machines"—it prevents oversudsing.
- *Tide Free* "provides all the stain removal benefits without any dyes or perfumes."

By segmenting the market and having several detergent brands, Procter & Gamble has an attractive offering for consumers in all important preference groups. As a result, P&G is really cleaning up in the $4.3 billion U.S. laundry detergent market. Tide, by itself, captures a whopping 38 percent market share. All P&G brands combined take a 57 percent share of the market—two and one-half times that of nearest rival Unilever and much more than any single brand could obtain by itself.[1]

Companies today recognize that they cannot appeal to all buyers in the marketplace, or at least not to all buyers in the same way. Buyers are too numerous, too widely scattered, and too varied in their needs and buying practices. Moreover, the companies themselves vary widely in their abilities to serve different segments of the market. Rather than trying to compete in an entire market, sometimes against superior competitors, each company must identify the parts of the market that it can serve best and most profitably.

Thus, most companies are being more choosy about the customers with whom they wish to connect. Most have moved away from mass marketing and toward *market segmentation and targeting*—identifying market segments, selecting one or more of them, and developing products and marketing programs tailored to each. Instead of scattering their marketing efforts (the "shotgun" approach), firms are focusing on the buyers who have greater interest in the values they create best (the "rifle" approach).

Figure 7.1 shows the three major steps in target marketing. The first is **market segmentation**—dividing a market into smaller groups of buyers with distinct

Market segmentation
Dividing a market into distinct groups of buyers on the basis of needs, characteristics, or behavior who might require separate products or marketing mixes.

FIGURE 7.1   Steps in market segmentation, targeting, and positioning

Market targeting
The process of evaluating each market segment's attractiveness and selecting one or more segments to enter.

Market positioning
Arranging for a product to occupy a clear, distinctive, and desirable place relative to competing products in the minds of target consumers.

needs, characteristics, or behaviors who might require separate products or marketing mixes. The company identifies different ways to segment the market and develops profiles of the resulting market segments. The second step is **market targeting**—evaluating each market segment's attractiveness and selecting one or more of the market segments to enter. The third step is **market positioning**—setting the competitive positioning for the product and creating a detailed marketing mix. We discuss each of these steps in turn.

 MARKET SEGMENTATION

Markets consist of buyers, and buyers differ in one or more ways. They may differ in their wants, resources, locations, buying attitudes, and buying practices. Through market segmentation, companies divide large, heterogeneous markets into smaller segments that can be reached more efficiently and effectively with products and services that match their unique needs. In this section, we discuss five important segmentation topics: levels of market segmentation, segmenting consumer markets, segmenting business markets, segmenting international markets, and requirements for effective segmentation.

Levels of Market Segmentation

Because buyers have unique needs and wants, each buyer is potentially a separate market. Ideally, then, a seller might design a separate marketing program for each buyer. However, although some companies attempt to serve buyers individually, many others face larger numbers of smaller buyers and do not find complete segmentation worthwhile. Instead, they look for broader classes of buyers who differ in their product needs or buying responses. Thus, market segmentation can be carried out at several different levels. Figure 7.2 shows that companies can practice no segmentation (mass marketing), complete segmentation (micromarketing), or something in between (segment marketing or niche marketing).

Mass Marketing

Companies have not always practiced target marketing. In fact, for most of the 1900s, major consumer products companies held fast to *mass marketing*—mass producing, mass distributing, and mass promoting about the same product in about the same way to all consumers. Henry Ford epitomized this marketing strategy when he offered the Model T Ford to all buyers; they could have the car "in any color as long as it is black." Similarly, Coca-Cola at one time produced only one drink for the whole market, hoping it would appeal to everyone.

The traditional argument for mass marketing is that it creates the largest potential market, which leads to the lowest costs, which in turn can translate into either

FIGURE 7.2   Levels of marketing segmentation

lower prices or higher margins. However, many factors now make mass marketing more difficult. For example, the world's mass markets have slowly splintered into a profusion of smaller segments—the baby boomers here, the GenXers there; here the Hispanic segment, there the African American segment; here working women, there single parents; here the Sun Belt, there the Rust Belt. Today, marketers find it very hard to create a single product or program that appeals to all of these diverse groups.

The proliferation of distribution channels and advertising media has also made it difficult to practice "one-size-fits-all" marketing. Today's consumers can shop at megamalls, superstores, or specialty shops; through mail catalogs or virtual stores on the Internet. They are bombarded with messages delivered via media ranging from old standards such as television, radio, magazines, newspapers, and telephone to newcomers like the Internet, fax, and e-mail. No wonder some have claimed that mass marketing is dying. Not surprisingly, many companies are retreating from mass marketing and turning to segmented marketing.

Segment Marketing

Segment marketing
Isolating broad segments that make up a market and adapting the marketing to match the needs of one or more segments.

A company that practices **segment marketing** isolates broad segments that make up a market and adapts its offers to more closely match the needs of one or more segments. Thus, Marriott markets to a variety of segments—business travelers, families, and others—with packages adapted to their varying needs. GM has designed specific models for different income and age groups. In fact, it sells models for segments with varied *combinations* of age and income. For instance, GM designed its Buick Park Avenue for older, higher-income consumers.

Segment marketing offers several benefits over mass marketing. The company can market more efficiently, targeting its products or services, channels, and communications programs toward only consumers that it can serve best and most profitably. The company can also market more effectively by fine-tuning its products, prices, and programs to the needs of carefully defined segments. The company may face fewer competitors if fewer competitors are focusing on this market segment.

Niche Marketing

Niche marketing
Focusing on subsegments or niches with distinctive traits that may seek a special combination of benefits.

Market segments are normally large, identifiable groups within a market—for example, luxury car buyers, performance car buyers, utility car buyers, and economy car buyers. **Niche marketing** focuses on subgroups within these segments. A *niche* is a more narrowly defined group, usually identified by dividing a segment into subsegments or by defining a group with a distinctive set of traits who may seek a special combination of benefits. For example, the utility vehicles segment might include light-duty pickup trucks and sport utility vehicles (SUVs). The sport utility vehicles subsegment might be further divided into standard SUV (as served by Ford and Chevrolet) and luxury SUV (as served by Lincoln and Lexus) niches.

Whereas segments are fairly large and normally attract several competitors, niches are smaller and normally attract only one or a few competitors.

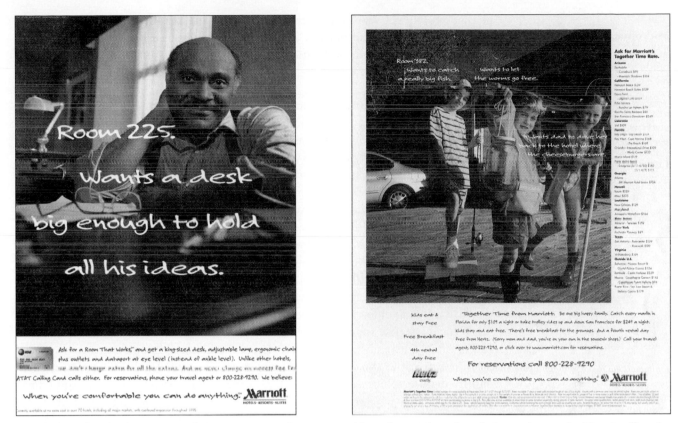

Segment marketing: Marriott markets to a variety of segments with packages adapted to their varying needs. Here it offers the business traveler a "king-sized desk, an ergonomic chair, and outlets and dataports at eye level." For the family traveler, it offers "Together time from Marriott: Kids eat and stay free."

Niche marketers presumably understand their niches' needs so well that their customers willingly pay a price premium. For example, the luxurious Bentley gets a high price for its cars because its loyal buyers feel that no other automobile comes close to offering the product–service–membership benefits that Bentley does.

Niching offers smaller companies an opportunity to compete by focusing their limited resources on serving niches that may be unimportant to or overlooked by larger competitors. However, large companies also serve niche markets. For example, American Express offers not only its traditional green cards but also gold cards, corporate cards, and even platinum cards aimed at a niche consisting of the top-spending 1 percent of its 28 million cardholders.[2] Nike makes athletic gear for basketball, running, and soccer but also for smaller niches such as biking and street hockey.

In many markets today, niches are the norm. As an advertising agency executive observed, "There will be no market for products that everybody likes a little, only for products that somebody likes a lot." Other experts assert that companies will have to "niche or be niched."[3]

Micromarketing

Segment and niche marketers tailor their offers and marketing programs to meet the needs of various market segments. At the same time, however, they do not customize their offers to each individual customer. Thus, segment marketing and niche

Micromarketing
The practice of tailoring products and marketing programs to suit the tastes of specific individuals and locations—includes *local marketing* and *individual marketing.*

Local marketing
Tailoring brands and promotions to the needs and wants of local customer groups—cities, neighborhoods, and even specific stores.

marketing fall between the extremes of mass marketing and micromarketing. **Micromarketing** is the practice of tailoring products and marketing programs to suit the tastes of specific individuals and locations. Micromarketing includes *local marketing* and *individual marketing.*

Local Marketing.   **Local marketing** involves tailoring brands and promotions to the needs and wants of local customer groups—cities, neighborhoods, and even specific stores. Thus, retailers such as Sears and Wal-Mart routinely customize each store's merchandise and promotions to match its specific clientele. Citibank provides different mixes of banking services in its branches depending on neighborhood demographics. Kraft helps supermarket chains identify the specific cheese assortments and shelf positioning that will optimize cheese sales in low-income, middle-income, and high-income stores and in different ethnic communities.

Local marketing has some drawbacks. It can drive up manufacturing and marketing costs by reducing economies of scale. It can also create logistics problems as companies try to meet the varied requirements of different regional and local markets. Further, a brand's overall image might be diluted if the product and message vary too much in different localities. Still, as companies face increasingly fragmented markets, and as new supporting technologies develop, the advantages of local marketing often outweigh the drawbacks. Local marketing helps a company to market more effectively in the face of pronounced regional and local differences in community demographics and lifestyles. It also meets the needs of the company's first-line customers—retailers—who prefer more fine-tuned product assortments for their neighborhoods.

Individual marketing
Tailoring products and marketing programs to the needs and preferences of individual customers—also labeled one-to-one marketing, customized marketing, and markets-of-one marketing.

Individual Marketing.   In the extreme, micromarketing becomes **individual marketing**—tailoring products and marketing programs to the needs and preferences of individual customers. Individual marketing has also been labeled *one-to-one marketing, customized marketing,* and *markets-of-one marketing.*[4]

The widespread use of mass marketing has obscured the fact that for centuries consumers were served as individuals: The tailor custom-made the suit, the cobbler designed shoes for the individual, the cabinetmaker made furniture to order. Today, however, new technologies are permitting many companies to return to customized marketing. More powerful computers, detailed databases, robotic production and flexible manufacturing, and immediate and interactive communication media such as e-mail, fax, and the Internet—all have combined to foster "mass customization." *Mass customization* is the process through which firms interact one-to-one with masses of customers to design products and services tailor-made to individual needs (see Marketing Highlight 7.1).

Thus, Dell Computer can deliver computers to individual customers loaded with customer-specified hardware and software. Peapod, the online grocery shopping and delivery service, lets customers create the virtual supermarket that best fits their individual needs. Ritz-Carlton Hotels creates custom-designed experiences for its delighted guests:

★ Check into any Ritz-Carlton hotel around the world, and you'll be amazed at how well the hotel's employees anticipate your slightest need. Without ever asking, they seem to know that you want a nonsmoking room with a king-size bed, a nonallergenic pillow, and breakfast with decaffeinated coffee in your room. How does Ritz-Carlton work this magic? The hotel employs a system that combines information technology and flexible operations to customize the hotel experience. At the heart of the system is a huge customer database, which contains information about guests gathered through the observations of hotel employees. Each day, hotel staffers—from those at the front desk to those in maintenance and housekeeping—discreetly record the unique habits, likes, and dislikes of each guest on small "guest preference pads." These observations are then transferred to a corporatewide "guest history database." Every morning, a "guest historian" at each hotel reviews the files of all new arrivals who have previously stayed at a Ritz-Carlton and prepares a list of suggested extra touches that might delight each guest. Guests have responded strongly to such markets-of-one service. Since inaugurating the guest-history system in 1992, Ritz-Carlton has boosted guest retention by 23 percent. An amazing 95 percent of departing guests report that their stay has been a truly memorable experience.

Business-to-business marketers are also finding new ways to customize their offerings. For example, Becton-Dickinson, a major medical supplier, offers to customize almost anything for its hospital customers. It offers custom-designed labeling, individual packaging, customized quality control, customized computer software, and customized billing. Motorola salespeople use a handheld computer to custom-design pagers following individual business customer wishes. The design data are transmitted to the Motorola factory and production starts within 17 minutes. The customized pagers are ready for shipment within two hours. John Deere manufactures seeding equipment that can be configured in more than 2 million versions to individual customer specifications. The seeders are produced one at a time, in any sequence, on a single production line.[5]

The move toward individual marketing mirrors the trend in consumer *self-marketing*. Increasingly, individual customers are taking more responsibility for determining which products and brands to buy. Consider two business buyers with two different purchasing styles. The first sees several salespeople, each trying to persuade him to buy his or her product. The second sees no salespeople but rather logs onto the Internet; searches for information on available products; interacts electronically with various suppliers, users, and product analysts; and then makes up her own mind about the best offer. The second purchasing agent has taken more responsibility for the buying process, and the marketer has had less influence over her buying decision.

As the trend toward more interactive dialogue and less advertising monologue continues, self-marketing will grow in importance. As more buyers look up consumer reports, join Internet product discussion forums, and place orders via phone or online, marketers will have to influence the buying process in new ways. They will need to involve customers more in all phases of the product development and buying processes, increasing opportunities for buyers to practice self-marketing. We will examine the trends toward one-to-one marketing and self-marketing further in chapter 17.

Segmenting Consumer Markets

There is no single way to segment a market. A marketer has to try different segmentation variables, alone and in combination, to find the best way to view the market structure. Table 7.1 outlines the major variables that might be used in segmenting consumer markets. Here we look at the major *geographic, demographic, psychographic,* and *behavioral variables.*

Geographic segmentation
Dividing a market into different geographical units such as nations, states, regions, counties, cities, or neighborhoods.

Geographic Segmentation
Geographic segmentation calls for dividing the market into different geographical units such as nations, regions, states, counties, cities, or neighborhoods. A company may decide to operate in one or a few geographical areas, or to operate in all areas but pay attention to geographical differences in needs and wants.

MARKETS OF ONE: "ANYTHING YOU CAN DIGITIZE, YOU CAN CUSTOMIZE"

Imagine walking into a booth that bathes your body in patterns of white light and, in a matter of seconds, captures your exact three-dimensional form. The resulting digitized data are imprinted on a credit card, which you then use to order customized clothing. No, this isn't a scene from the next *Star Wars* sequel; it's a peek ahead at how you will be able to buy clothing in the not-so-distant future. A consortium of over 100 apparel companies, including Levi-Strauss, has banded together to develop body scanning technology in the hope of making mass customization the norm.

Although body scanning technology and smart cards carrying customer measurements are still in development, many companies are now using existing technologies to tailor their products to individual customers. Here are just a few examples:

Levi-Strauss: Since 1994, Levi has made measure-to-fit women's jeans under its in-store Personal Pair program. The salesclerk takes a customer's measurements and enters them into a computer. Two days later, the customer receives jeans cut to her specific needs. She can order additional jeans at any time without visiting the store. Levi is now launching an expanded version of the system called Original Spin, which will offer even more style options and feature men's jeans as well. Whereas a fully stocked Levi's store carries 130 ready-to-wear pairs of jeans for a given waist and inseam, with Personal Pair the number jumps to 430. With Original Spin it will jump to 750.

Mattel: Since 1998, girls have been able to log onto www.barbie.com and design their own Special Friend of Barbie doll. They choose the doll's skin tone, eye color, hairdo and hair color, clothes, accessories, and name. They even fill out a questionnaire detailing their doll's likes and dislikes. When Barbie's Special Friend arrives in the mail, the girls find the doll's name on the packaging along with a computer-generated paragraph about her personality.

CDuctive: New York's hip, Tribeca-based CDuctive lets customers cut their own CDs online. If a customer likes acid jazz, he or she can click on the category, see 30 titles and sample a 45-second snatch of each. With a few keystrokes the customer can then order a $21 CD with all the tunes he or she has selected.

Paris Miki: At this Tokyo eyeglass store, special software allows technicians to design lenses and frames that conform to the shape of the customer's face. Using a monitor, various styles are superimposed on a scanned image of the person's face. The customer then chooses a style, the glasses are made up, and the person walks out with a pair of glasses designed and fitted for him or her alone.

Consumer goods marketers aren't the only ones going one-to-one. Business-to-business marketers are also providing customers with tailor-made goods, often more cheaply and quickly than it used to take to make standardized ones. Particularly for small companies, mass customization provides a way to stand out against larger competitors:

ChemStation: This small industrial-detergent company offers its industrial customers—ranging from car washes to the U.S. Air Force—individually concocted soap formulas. What cleans a car won't work to clean an airplane or equipment in a mine shaft. Information

Many companies today are localizing their products, advertising, promotion, and sales efforts to fit the needs of individual regions, cities, and even neighborhoods. For example, Campbell sells Cajun gumbo soup in Louisiana and Mississippi and makes its nacho cheese soup spicier in Texas and California. P&G sells Ariel laundry detergent primarily in Los Angeles, San Diego, San Francisco, Miami, and south Texas—areas with larger concentrations of Hispanic consumers. In the South, where customers tend to arrive later in the day and stay longer, Starbucks offers more desserts and larger, more comfortable coffee shops.[6]

collected by ChemStation sales-people about a specific customer's cleaning needs is fed into a customer database called the Tank Management System (TMS). Next, a company chemist develops a special "detergent recipe" for the customer, assigns it a number, and enters the formula into the TMS. Then, plant workers simply enter the customer's recipe number into a computer-controlled machine, which mixes up a batch of the special brew. ChemStation delivers the custom-made mixture to a tank installed at the customer's site. The company monitors usage and automatically refills the tank when supplies run low. At the same time that the customization system gives customers exactly what they need, it also reduces costs, resulting in higher margins. Since Chem Station began mass customizing in 1985, cost per customer has fallen nearly 25 percent while gross margins per customer have jumped to nearly 50 percent. Mass customization also helps ChemStation to lock out competitors. No one—not even the customer—knows what goes into each formula, making it hard for a customer to jump to competitors. "We tell [customers] it's a secret," says founder and CEO George Homan. "We're not as protective [about our formulas] as Coca-Cola, but we're close."

Two trends are behind the growth in one-to-one marketing. One is the ever-increasing emphasis on customer value and satisfaction. Today's consumers have very high expectations and, more and more, they are expecting products and services that meet their individual needs. Yet, it would be prohibitively expensive or downright impossible to meet these individual demands if it weren't for another trend: rapid advances in new technologies. Data warehouses allow companies to store trillions of bytes of customer information. Computer-controlled factory equipment and industrial robots can now quickly readjust assembly lines. Bar code scanners make it possible to track parts and products. Most important of all, the Internet ties it all together and makes it easy for a company to interact with customers, learn about their preferences, and respond.

Indeed, the Internet appears to be the ultimate one-to-one medium. The notion of personal service on the Internet might seem like an oxymoron, but it's rapidly becoming a reality. Consider the following example:

Soon after Jeri Capozzi logged onto the online nursery Garden Escape last winter, she was hooked. It wasn't just because the World Wide Web site offered unusual plants, such as hyacinth beans, firecracker, and dog's tooth violet. It's because Garden Escape created a personal store just for her. Greeted by name on her personal Web page when she visits, Capozzi can take notes on a private online notepad, tinker with garden plans using the site's interactive design program, and get answers from the Garden Doctor. So far, [she] has spent $600 at Garden Escape and has no plans to shop at any other nursery. With service that personal, she says, "I probably will never leave."

Thus, just as mass production was the marketing principle of the last century, mass customization is becoming the marketing principle for the twenty-first century. The world appears to be coming full circle—from the good old days when customers were treated as individuals, to mass marketing when nobody knew your name, and back again. As Joseph Pine, author of *Mass Customization*, concludes, "Anything you can digitize, you can customize."

Sources: See Erick Schonfeld, "The Customized, Digitized, Have-It-Your-Way Economy," *Fortune*, September 28, 1998, pp. 115–24; Luisa Kroll, "Digital Demin," *Forbes*, December 28, 1998, pp. 102–3; Jim Barlow, "Individualizing Mass Production," *Houston Chronicle*, April 13, 1997, p. E1; Marc Ballon, "Sale of Modern Music Keyed to Customization," *Inc.*, May 1998, pp. 23, 25; Robert D. Hof, "Now It's Your Web," *Business Week*, October 5, 1998, pp. 164–76; Don Peppers, Martha Rogers, and Bob Dorf, "Is Your Company Ready for One to One Marketing?" *Harvard Business Review*, January–February 1999, pp. 151–60; and Otis Port, "Customers Move into the Driver's Seat," *Business Week*, October 4, 1999, pp. 103–6.

Other companies are seeking to cultivate as-yet untapped territory. For example, many large companies are fleeing the fiercely competitive major cities and suburbs to set up shop in small-town America. Hampton Inns has opened a chain of smaller-format motels in towns too small for its standard-size units. For example, Townsend, Tennessee, with a population of only 329, is small even by small-town standards. But looks can be deceiving. Situated on a heavily traveled and picturesque route between Knoxville and the Smoky Mountains, the village serves both business and vacation travelers. Hampton Inns opened a unit in Townsend

TABLE 7.1 MAJOR SEGMENTATION VARIABLES FOR CONSUMER MARKETS

Geographic

World region or country	North America, Western Europe, Middle East, Pacific Rim, China, India, Canada, Mexico
Country region	Pacific, Mountain, West North Central, West South Central, East North Central, East South Central, South Atlantic, Middle Atlantic, New England
City or metro size	Under 5,000; 5,000–20,000; 20,000–50,000; 50,000–100,000; 100,000–250,000; 250,000–500,000; 500,000–1,000,000; 1,000,000–4,000,000; 4,000,000 or over
Density	Urban, suburban, rural
Climate	Northern, southern

Demographic

Age	Under 6, 6–11, 12–19, 20–34, 35–49, 50–64, 65+
Gender	Male, female
Family size	1–2, 3–4, 5+
Family life cycle	Young, single; young, married, no children; young, married with children; older, married with children; older, married, no children under 18; older, single; other
Income	Under $10,000; $10,000–$20,000; $20,000–$30,000; $30,000–$50,000; $50,000–$100,000; $100,000 and over
Occupation	Professional and technical; managers, officials, and proprietors; clerical, sales; craftspeople; supervisors; operatives; farmers; retired; students; homemakers; unemployed
Education	Grade school or less; some high school; high school graduate; some college; college graduate
Religion	Catholic, Protestant, Jewish, Muslim, Hindu, other
Race	Asian, Hispanic, Black, White
Generation	Baby boomer, Generation X, echo boomer
Nationality	North American, South American, British, French, German, Italian, Japanese

Psychographic

Social class	Lower lowers, upper lowers, working class, middle class, upper middles, lower uppers, upper uppers
Lifestyle	Achievers, strivers, strugglers
Personality	Compulsive, gregarious, authoritarian, ambitious

Behavioral

Occasions	Regular occasion, special occasion
Benefits	Quality, service, economy, convenience, speed
User status	Nonuser, ex-user, potential user, first-time user, regular user
Usage rate	Light user, medium user, heavy user
Loyalty status	None, medium, strong, absolute
Readiness stage	Unaware, aware, informed, interested, desirous, intending to buy
Attitude toward product	Enthusiastic, positive, indifferent, negative, hostile

and plans to open 100 more in small towns. It costs less to operate in these towns, and the company builds smaller units to match lower volume. The Townsend Hampton Inn, for example, has 54 rooms instead of the usual 135. Retailers from Home Depot to Saks Fifth Avenue are following suit. For example, Home Depot is testing four pint-size Villager's Hardware stores in New Jersey. Saks is implementing a new "Main Street" strategy, opening smaller stores in affluent suburbs and small towns that cannot support full-line Saks stores. Its new store in Greenwich, Connecticut, is less than one-third the size of regular stores found in malls and big cities.[7]

Geographic segmentation: Home Depot is opening pint-size Villager's Hardware shops in smaller towns.

Demographic Segmentation

Demographic segmentation
Dividing the market into groups based on demographic variables such as age, gender, family size, family life cycle, income, occupation, education, religion, race, and nationality.

Demographic segmentation divides the market into groups based on variables such as age, gender, family size, family life cycle, income, occupation, education, religion, race, and nationality. Demographic factors are the most popular bases for segmenting customer groups. One reason is that consumer needs, wants, and usage rates often vary closely with demographic variables. Another is that demographic variables are easier to measure than most other types of variables. Even when market segments are first defined using other bases, such as benefits sought or behavior, their demographic characteristics must be known in order to assess the size of the target market and to reach it efficiently.

Age and life-cycle segmentation
Dividing a market into different age and life-cycle groups.

Age and Life-Cycle Stage.   Consumer needs and wants change with age. Some companies use **age and life-cycle segmentation,** offering different products or using different marketing approaches for different age and life-cycle groups. For example, McDonald's targets children, teens, adults, and seniors with different ads and media. Its ads to teens feature dance-beat music, adventure, and fast-paced cutting from scene to scene; ads to seniors are softer and more sentimental. Procter & Gamble boldly targets its Oil of Olay ProVital Series subbrand at women over 50 years of age. It's "specially designed to meet the increased moisturization needs of more mature skin."[8]

Sega, the computer games giant, which has typically focused on the teen market, is now targeting older customers. According to a Sega licensing executive, Sega's core market of 10- to 18-year-olds "sit in their bedrooms playing games for hours." Then, however, "they turn 18 and discover girls . . . and the computer gets locked away." To retain these young customers as they move into new life-cycle stages, Sega is launching a range of products for adults under its Sega Sports brand, including clothing, shoes, watches, and sports equipment such as Sega Sports–branded footballs and basketballs.[9]

Marketers must be careful to guard against stereotypes when using age and life-cycle segmentation. For example, although some 70-year-olds require wheelchairs, others play tennis. Similarly, whereas some 40-year-old couples are sending their children off to college, others are just beginning new families. Thus, age is often a poor predictor of a person's life cycle, health, work or family status, needs, and buying power. Companies marketing to mature consumers usually employ positive images and appeals. For example, ads for Oil of Olay ProVital feature attractive older spokeswomen and uplifting messages. "Many women 50 and older have told us that as they age, they feel more confident, wiser, and freer than ever before," observes Olay's marketing director. "These women are redefining beauty."[10]

Gender segmentation
Dividing a market into different groups based on sex.

Gender.   **Gender segmentation** has long been used in clothing, cosmetics, toiletries, and magazines. For example, Procter & Gamble was among the first with

Secret, a brand specially formulated for a woman's chemistry, packaged and adver-tised to reinforce the female image. Recently, other marketers have noticed oppor-tunities for gender segmentation. For example, Merrill Lynch offers a *Financial Handbook for Women Investors* who want to "shape up their finances." Owens-Corning consciously aimed a major advertising campaign for home insulation at women after its study on women's role in home improvement showed that two-thirds were involved in materials installation, with 13 percent doing it themselves. Half the women surveyed compared themselves to Bob Vila, whereas less than half compared themselves to Martha Stewart.[11]

The automobile industry also uses gender segmentation extensively. Women buy half of all new cars sold in the United States and influence 80 per-cent of all new car purchasing decisions. "Selling to women should be no dif-ferent than selling to men," notes one analyst. "But there are subtleties that make a difference." Women have different frames, less upper-body strength, and greater safety concerns. To address these issues, automakers are designing cars with hoods and trunks that are easier to open, seat belts that fit women better, and an increased emphasis on safety features. Male car designers at Cadillac now go about their work with paper clips on their fingers to simulate what it feels like to operate buttons, knobs, and other interior features with longer fingernails. The Cadillac Catera features an air-conditioned glove box to preserve such items as lipstick and film. Under the hood, yellow markings highlight where fluid fills go.[12]

A growing number of Web sites also target women. For example, the Girls On Network (www.girlson.com) appeals to 18- to 34-year-old women with hip, twenty somethings-style film, television, and book reviews and features. After only two years, this site has 100,000 members and averages 5 million page views per month.

Gender segmentation: A growing number of Web sites are targeting women, such as Oxygen Media's fresh and hip Girls On Web site for twentysomethings and iVillage, the leading women's online community.

The leading women's online community, iVillage (www.iVillage.com), offers "real solutions for real women" and entreats visitors to "Join our community of smart, compassionate, real women." Various iVillage channels cover topics ranging from babies, food, fitness, pets, and relationships to careers, finance, and travel. The site now claims a membership of more than 1 million women across a broad demographic spectrum.[13]

Income segmentation
Dividing a market into different income groups.

Income. **Income segmentation** has long been used by the marketers of products and services such as automobiles, boats, clothing, cosmetics, financial services, and travel. Many companies target affluent consumers with luxury goods and convenience services. Stores such as Neiman Marcus pitch everything from expensive jewelry and fine fashions to glazed Australian apricots priced at $20 a pound. Prada's hot-selling black vinyl backpack sells for $450, and a front-row seat at a New York Knicks game at Madison Square Garden goes for $1,000.[14]

However, not all companies that use income segmentation target the affluent. Despite their lower spending power, the 25 percent of the nation's households that earn less that $25,000 per year offer an attractive market. For example, Greyhound Lines, with its inexpensive nationwide bus network, targets lower-income consumers. Almost half of its revenues come from people with annual incomes under $15,000. Many retailers also target this group, including chains such as Family Dollar, Dollar General, and Dollar Tree stores. When Family Dollar real estate experts scout locations for new stores, they look for lower-middle-class neighborhoods where people wear less expensive shoes and drive old cars that drip a lot of oil. The typical Family Dollar customer's household earns about $25,000 a year, and the average customer spends only about $8 per trip to the store. Yet the store's low-income strategy has made it one of the most profitable discount chains in the country.[15]

Psychographic Segmentation

Psychographic segmentation
Dividing a market into different groups based on social class, lifestyle, or personality characteristics.

Psychographic segmentation divides buyers into different groups based on social class, lifestyle, or personality characteristics. People in the same demographic group can have very different psychographic makeups.

In chapter 5, we discussed how the products people buy reflect their *lifestyles.* As a result, marketers often segment their markets by consumer lifestyles. For example, Duck Head apparel targets a casual student lifestyle claiming, "You can't get them old until you get them new." One forward-looking grocery store found that segmenting its self-service meat products by lifestyle had a big payoff:

★ Walk by the refrigerated self-service meat cases of most grocery stores and you'll usually find the offering grouped by type of meat. Pork is here, lamb is there, and chicken is over there. However, a Nashville, Tennessee, Kroger supermarket decided to experiment and offer groupings of different meats by lifestyle. For instance, the store had a section called "Meals in Minutes," one called "Cookin' Lite," another, filled with prepared products like hot dogs and ready-made hamburger patties, called "Kids Love This Stuff," and one called "I Like to Cook." By focusing on lifestyle needs and not on protein categories, Kroger's test store encouraged habitual beef and pork buyers to consider lamb and veal as well. As a result, the 16-foot service case has seen a substantial improvement in both sales and profits.[16]

Marketers also have used *personality* variables to segment markets. For example, the marketing campaign for Honda's Helix and Elite motor scooters *appears* to target hip and trendy 22-year-olds. But it is *actually* aimed at a much broader personality group. One ad, for example, shows a delighted child bouncing up and

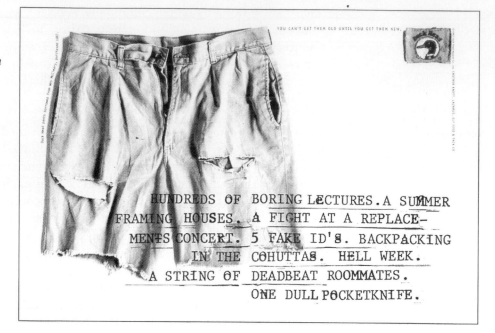

down on his bed while the announcer says, "You've been trying to get there all your life." The ad reminds viewers of the euphoric feelings they got when they broke away from authority and did things their parents told them not to do. It suggests that they can feel that way again by riding a Honda scooter. Thus, Honda is appealing to the rebellious, independent kid in all of us. As Honda notes on its Web page, "Fresh air, freedom, and flair—on a Honda scooter, every day is independence day!" In fact, more than half of Honda's scooter sales are to young professionals and older buyers—15 percent are purchased by the over-50 group.[17]

Behavioral Segmentation

Behavioral segmentation divides buyers into groups based on their knowledge, attitudes, uses, or responses to a product. Many marketers believe that behavior variables are the best starting point for building market segments.

Occasions.   Buyers can be grouped according to occasions when they get the idea to buy, actually make their purchase, or use the purchased item. **Occasion segmentation** can help firms build up product usage. For example, orange juice is most often consumed at breakfast, but orange growers have promoted drinking orange juice as a cool and refreshing drink at other times of the day. In contrast, Coca-Cola's "Coke in the Morning" advertising campaign attempts to increase Coke consumption by promoting the beverage as an early morning pick-me-up. Some holidays, such as Mother's Day and Father's Day, were originally promoted partly to increase the sale of candy, flowers, cards, and other gifts. Many food marketers prepare special offers and ads for holiday occasions. For example, Beatrice Foods runs special Thanksgiving and Christmas ads for Reddi-wip during November and December, months that account for 30 percent of all whipped cream sales.

Kodak, Konica, Fuji, and other camera makers use occasion segmentation in designing and marketing their single-use cameras. By mixing lenses, film speeds, and accessories, they have developed special disposable cameras for about any picture-taking occasion, from underwater photography to taking baby pictures.

Behavioral segmentation
Dividing a market into groups based on consumer knowledge, attitude, use, or response to a product.

Occasion segmentation
Dividing the market into groups according to occasions when buyers get the idea to buy, actually make their purchase, or use the purchased item.

Occasion segmentation: Beatrice Foods runs special Thanksgiving and Christmas ads for Reddi-wip during November and December, months that account for 30 percent of all whipped cream sales.

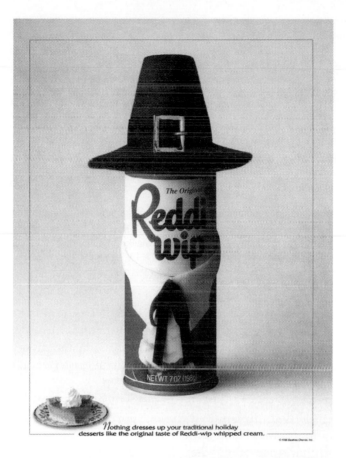

Nothing dresses up your traditional holiday desserts like the original taste of Reddi-wip whipped cream.

⭐ Standing on the edge of the Grand Canyon? Try Konica's Panoramic, which features a 17mm lens that takes in nearly 100 degrees horizontally. Going rafting, skiing, or snorkeling? You need Kodak's Max Sport, a rugged camera that can be used underwater to 14 feet. It has big knobs and buttons that let you use it with gloves. Want some pictures of the baby? Kodak offers a model equipped with a short focal-length lens and fast film requiring less light for parents who would like to take snapshots of their darlings without the disturbing flash. Need to check out your golf swing? Just point and shoot the QuickSnap Golf disposable camera, which snaps off eight frames per click showing how your body and club do during the swing. In one Japanese catalog aimed at young women, Kodak sells a package of five pastel-colored cameras, including a version with a fish-eye lens to create a rosy, romantic glow.[18]

Benefit segmentation
Dividing the market into groups according to the different benefits that consumers seek from the product.

Benefits Sought.   A powerful form of segmentation is to group buyers according to the different *benefits* that they seek from the product. **Benefit segmentation** requires finding the major benefits people look for in the product class, the kinds of people who look for each benefit, and the major brands that deliver each benefit. For example, one study of the benefits derived from travel uncovered three major market segments: those who travel to get away and be with family, those who travel for adventure or educational purposes, and people who enjoy the "gambling" and "fun" aspects of travel.[19]

One of the best examples of benefit segmentation was conducted in the toothpaste market (see Table 7.2). Research found four benefit segments: economic, medicinal, cosmetic, and taste. Each benefit group had special demographic, behavioral, and psychographic characteristics. For example, the people seeking to prevent decay

TABLE 7.2   BENEFIT SEGMENTATION OF THE TOOTHPASTE MARKET

Benefit Segments	Demographics	Behavior	Psychographics	Favored Brands
Economic (low price)	Men	Heavy users	High autonomy, value oriented	Brands on sale
Medicinal (decay prevention)	Large families	Heavy users	Hypochondriacal, conservative	Crest
Cosmetic (bright teeth)	Teens, young adults	Smokers	High sociability, active	Aqua-Fresh, Ultra Brite
Taste (good tasting)	Children	Spearmint lovers	High self-involvement hedonistic	Colgate, Aim

Source: Adapted from Russell J. Haley, "Benefit Segmentation: A Decision-Oriented Research Tool," *Journal of Marketing,* July 1968, pp. 30–35. Also see Haley, "Benefit Segmentation: Backwards and Forwards," *Journal of Advertising Research,* February–March 1984, pp. 19–25; and Haley, "Benefit Segmentation—20 Years Later," *Journal of Consumer Marketing* Vol. 1, 1984, pp. 5–14.

tended to have large families, were heavy toothpaste users, and were conservative. Each segment also favored certain brands. Most current brands appeal to one of these segments. For example, Crest toothpaste stresses protection and appeals to the family segment, whereas Aim looks and tastes good and appeals to children.

User Status.   Markets can be segmented into groups of nonusers, ex-users, potential users, first-time users, and regular users of a product. For example, one study found that blood donors are low in self-esteem, low risk takers, and more highly concerned about their health; nondonors tend to be the opposite on all three dimensions. This suggests that social agencies should use different marketing approaches for keeping current donors and attracting new ones. A company's market position also influences its focus. Market share leaders focus on attracting potential users, whereas smaller firms focus on attracting current users away from the market leader.

Usage Rate.   Markets can also be segmented into light, medium, and heavy product users. Heavy users are often a small percentage of the market but account for a high percentage of total consumption. Marketers usually prefer to attract one heavy user to their product or service rather than several light users. For example, a recent study of U.S.-branded ice cream buyers showed that heavy users make up only 18 percent of all buyers but consume 55 percent of all the ice cream sold. On average, these heavy users pack away 13 gallons of ice cream per year versus only 2.4 gallons for light users. Similarly, a travel industry study showed that frequent users of travel agents for vacation travel are more involved, more innovative, more knowledgeable, and more likely to be opinion leaders than less frequent users. Heavy users take more trips and gather more information about vacation travel from newspapers, magazines, books, and travel shows. Clearly, a travel agency would benefit by directing its marketing efforts toward heavy users, perhaps using telemarketing and special promotions.[20]

Loyalty Status.   A market can also be segmented by consumer loyalty. Consumers can be loyal to brands (Tide), stores (Wal-Mart), and companies (Ford). Buyers can be divided into groups according to their degree of loyalty. Some consumers are completely loyal—they buy one brand all the time. Others are somewhat loyal—they are loyal to two or three brands of a given product or favor one brand while sometimes buying others. Still other buyers show no loyalty to any brand. They either want something different each time they buy or they buy whatever's on sale.

A company can learn a lot by analyzing loyalty patterns in its market. It should start by studying its own loyal customers. Suppose Colgate finds that its loyal toothpaste buyers are more middle class, have larger families, and are more health conscious. These characteristics pinpoint the target market for Colgate. By studying its less loyal buyers, the company can detect which brands are most competitive with its own. If many Colgate buyers also buy Crest, Colgate can attempt to improve its positioning against Crest, possibly by using direct-comparison advertising. By looking at customers who are shifting away from its brand, the company can learn about its marketing weaknesses. As for nonloyals, the company may attract them by putting its brand on sale.

Using Multiple Segmentation Bases

Marketers rarely limit their segmentation analysis to only one or a few variables. Rather, they are increasingly using multiple segmentation bases in an effort to identify smaller, better-defined target groups. Thus, a bank may not only identify a group of wealthy retired adults but also, within that group, distinguish several segments depending on their current income, assets, savings and risk preferences, and lifestyles.

Companies often begin by segmenting their markets using a single base, then expand using other bases. Consider PageNet, the paging services provider, which found itself competing against communications giants such as Southwestern Bell and Pacific Telesis in the pager market:

> PageNet couldn't boast unique technology. Moreover, it was already competing on price, charging about 20 percent less than competitors. Instead, PageNet used smart segmentation to boost its competitive advantage. At first, it used geographic segmentation, targeting markets in Ohio and its home state of Texas where local competitors were vulnerable to PageNet's aggressive pricing. Once these markets were secure, the company targeted new geographical segments that promised the best growth potential. But PageNet's segmenting strategy didn't end with geography. The company next profiled major paging service user groups and targeted the most promising ones, such as salespeople, messengers, and service people. Flush with success, PageNet next used lifestyle segmentation to target additional consumer groups, such as parents who leave their babies with sitters, commuters who are out of reach while traveling to and from work, and elderly people living alone whose families want to keep an eye on them. The results of this multiple segmentation strategy: PageNet's subscriber base has expanded at a rate of 50 percent annually over the past 10 years. Now, with 10 million subscribers and sales approaching $1 billion, PageNet is the nation's largest wireless messaging and information services company.[21]

One of the most promising developments in multivariable segmentation is "geodemographic" segmentation. Several business information services have arisen to help marketing planners link U.S. Census data with lifestyle patterns to better segment their markets down to zip codes, neighborhoods, and even city blocks. One of the leading services is PRIZM by Claritas, Inc. (see Marketing Highlight 7.2).

Segmenting Business Markets

Consumer and business marketers use many of the same variables to segment their markets. Business buyers can be segmented geographically, demographically (industry, company size), or by benefits sought, user status, usage rate, and loyalty status.

MARKETING
HIGHLIGHT
7.2

BLUE BLOOD ESTATES TO SHOTGUNS & PICKUPS: SEGMENTING AMERICA'S NEIGHBORHOODS

Using a host of demographic and socioeconomic factors drawn from the U.S. Census data, the Claritas, Inc.'s PRIZM® system has classified every one of the over 260,000 U.S. neighborhood markets into one of 62 clusters.

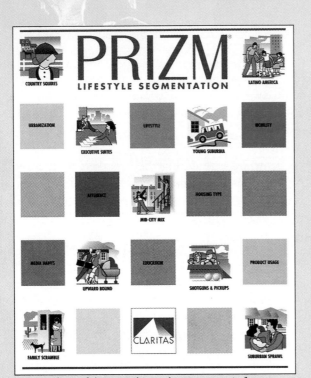

Using a host of demographic and socioeconomic factors drawn from U.S. Census data, Claritas, Inc.'s PRIZM system has classified every one of the more than 260,000 U.S. neighborhoods into one of 62 clusters.

You're 35 years old. The price tag on your suits shows that you're a success. You drive a Volvo. You know your way around the olive oil section of the store, buy fresh-ground coffee, and go on scuba-diving trips. You're living out your own, individual version of the good life in the suburbs. You're unique—not some demographic cliché. Wrong. You're a prime example of [PRIZM's] "Kids & Cul-de-Sacs.". . . If you consume, you can't hide from zip code seer Claritas.

The Kids & Cul-de-Sacs cluster points to a new migration to the suburbs. Other PRIZM clusters include "Blue Blood Estates," "Money & Brains," "Young Literati," "Shotguns & Pickups," "American Dreams," and "Gray Power." The clusters were formed by manipulating characteristics such as education, income, occupation, family life cycle, housing, ethnicity, and urbanization. For example, Blue Blood Estates neighborhoods are suburban areas populated mostly by active, college-educated, successful managers and professionals. They include some of America's wealthiest neighborhoods, areas characterized by low household density, highly homoge-

Yet, as Table 7.3 shows, business marketers also use some additional variables, such as customer *operating characteristics, purchasing approaches, situational factors,* and *personal characteristics.* The table lists major questions that business marketers should ask in determining which customers they want to serve.

By going after segments instead of the whole market, companies have a much better chance to deliver value to consumers and to receive maximum rewards for close attention to consumer needs. Thus, Hewlett-Packard's Computer Systems Division targets specific industries that promise the best growth prospects, such as telecommunications and financial services. Its "red team" sales force specializes in developing and serving major customers in these targeted industries.[22] Within the chosen industry, a company can further segment by *customer size* or *geographic loca-*

nous residents, a heavy family orientation, and mostly single-unit housing. In contrast, the Shotguns & Pickups cluster includes the blue-collar neighborhoods found in the Northeast, Southeast, Great Lakes, and Piedmont industrial regions of America. American Dreams reflects new waves of American immigrants; Young Literati taps Generation X. Each of the other clusters has a unique combination of characteristics.

Companies can combine these geodemographic PRIZM clusters with other data on product and service usage, media usage, and lifestyles to get a better picture of specific market areas. For example, the Shotguns & Pickups cluster is populated by lower-middle-class, blue-collar consumers who use chain saws and snuff and buy more canning jars, dried soups, and powdered soft drinks. The Hispanic Mix cluster prefers high-quality dresses, nonfilter cigarettes, and lip gloss. People in this cluster are highly brand conscious, quality conscious, and brand loyal. They have a strong family and home orientation.

Such geodemographic segmentation provides a powerful tool for segmenting markets, refining demand estimates, selecting target markets, and shaping promotion messages. For example, in marketing its Suave shampoo, Unilever's Helene Curtis division uses PRIZM to identify neighborhoods with high concentrations of working women. Such women respond best to advertising messages that Suave is inexpensive yet will make their hair "look like a million." Bookseller Barnes & Noble locates its stores where there are concentrations of Money & Brains consumers because they buy lots of books.

One large packaged-goods company used a similar system—Claritas, Inc.'s ClusterPLUS, in combination with Nielsen television ratings and data from Simmons Market Research Bureau—to more effectively market an ingredient used in baking cakes and cookies. The company first identified the clusters most likely to contain consumers who regularly bake from scratch. According to Simmons data, the top-ranking cluster is "Low-Mobility Rural Families"; of this group, 39 percent bake heavily from scratch, far greater than the 17 percent national average. Merging the 10 highest-ranking clusters, the company identified the best prospects as older, rural, and blue-collar consumers in the South and Midwest.

Next, using Nielsen ratings, the company examined the television viewing habits of the 10 best clusters. It turns out that the from-scratch bakers watch many highly rated programs, but some generally less popular programs are also popular with this group. The packaged-goods company improved its efficiency by running ads only on programs reaching large concentrations of from-scratch bakers, regardless of the size of the total audience. Thus, the ClusterPLUS–Simmons–Nielsen connection resulted in a basic shift in the company's television advertising, from a mass-media, "shotgun" approach to a more highly targeted one.

Sources: Quote from Christina Del Valle, "They Know Where You Live—And How You Buy," *Business Week,* February 7, 1994, p. 89. Also see Jonathon Marks, "Clusters Plus Nielsen Equals Efficient Marketing," *American Demographics,* September 1991, p. 16; Karen Dempsey, "Up Close and Personal," *Marketing,* direct marketing supplement, July 11, 1996, pp. III–IV, Leon G. Schiffman and Leslie Lazar Kanuk, *Consumer Behavior,* 6th ed. (Upper Saddle River NJ: Prentice Hall, 1997), pp. 66–67, and pp. 392–95; Philip Kotler, *Kotler on Marketing* (Upper Saddle River, NJ: Prentice Hall, 1999), pp. 78–79; Michael J. Weiss, *The Clustered World* (Boston: Little, Brown, 2000); and www.claritas.com, March 2000.

tion. For example, Hewlett-Packard's "blue team" telemarkets to smaller accounts and to those that don't fit neatly into the strategically targeted industries on which HP focuses.

A company might also set up separate systems for dealing with larger or multiple-location customers. For example, Steelcase, a major producer of office furniture, first segments customers into 10 industries, including banking, insurance, and electronics. Next, company salespeople work with independent Steelcase dealers to handle smaller, local, or regional Steelcase customers in each segment. But many national, multiple-location customers, such as Exxon or IBM, have special needs that may reach beyond the scope of individual dealers. So Steelcase uses national accounts managers to help its dealer networks handle its national accounts.

TABLE 7.3   MAJOR SEGMENTATION VARIABLES FOR BUSINESS MARKETS

Demographics

Industry: Which industries that buy this product should we focus on?
Company size: What size companies should we focus on?
Location: What geographical areas should we focus on?

Operating Variables

Technology: What customer technologies should we focus on?
User–nonuser status: Should we focus on heavy, medium, or light users or nonusers?
Customer capabilities: Should we focus on customers needing many services or few services?

Purchasing Approaches

Purchasing function organization: Should we focus on companies with highly centralized or decentralized purchasing?
Power structure: Should we focus on companies that are engineering dominated, financially dominated, or marketing dominated?
Nature of existing relationships: Should we focus on companies with which we already have strong relationships or simply go after the most desirable companies?
General purchase policies: Should we focus on companies that prefer leasing? Service contracts? Systems purchases? Sealed bidding?
Purchasing criteria: Should we focus on companies that are seeking quality? Service? Price?

Situational Factors

Urgency: Should we focus on companies that need quick delivery or service?
Specific application: Should we focus on certain applications of our product rather than all applications?
Size of order: Should we focus on large or small orders?

Personal Characteristics

Buyer–seller similarity: Should we focus on companies whose people and values are similar to ours?
Attitudes toward risk: Should we focus on risk-taking or risk-avoiding customers?
Loyalty: Should we focus on companies that show high loyalty to their suppliers?

Source: Adapted from Thomas V. Bonoma and Benson P. Shapiro, *Segmenting the Industrial Market* (Lexington, MA: Lexington Books, 1983). Also see John Berrigan and Carl Finkbeiner, *Segmentation Marketing: New Methods for Capturing Business* (New York: HarperBusiness, 1992).

Within a given target industry and customer size, the company can segment by purchase approaches and criteria. As in consumer segmentation, many marketers believe that *buying behavior* and *benefits* provide the best basis for segmenting business markets.[23]

Segmenting International Markets

Few companies have either the resources or the will to operate in all, or even most, of the countries that dot the globe. Although some large companies, such as Coca-Cola or Sony, sell products in as many as 200 countries, most international firms focus on a smaller set. Operating in many countries presents new challenges. Different countries, even those that are close together, can vary dramatically in their economic, cultural, and political makeup. Thus, just as they do within their domestic markets, international firms need to group their world markets into segments with distinct buying needs and behaviors.

Companies can segment international markets using one or a combination of several variables. They can segment by *geographic location,* grouping countries by regions such as Western Europe, the Pacific Rim, the Middle East, or Africa. Geographic segmentation assumes that nations close to one another will have many common traits and behaviors. Although this is often the case, there are many exceptions. For example, although the United States and Canada have much in common, both differ culturally and economically from neighboring Mexico. Even within a region, consumers can differ widely. For example, many U.S. marketers think that all Central and South American countries are the same, including their 400 million inhabitants. However, the Dominican Republic is no more like Brazil than Italy is like Sweden. Many Latin Americans don't speak Spanish, including 140 million Portuguese-speaking Brazilians and the millions in other countries who speak a variety of Indian dialects.

World markets can also be segmented on the basis of *economic factors.* For example, countries might be grouped by population income levels or by their overall level of economic development.[24] Some countries, such as the United States, Britain, France, Germany, Japan, Canada, Italy, and Russia, have established, highly industrialized economies. Other countries have newly industrialized or developing economies (Singapore, Taiwan, Korea, Brazil, Mexico). Still others are less developed (China, India). A company's economic structure shapes its population's product and service needs and, therefore, the marketing opportunities it offers.

Countries can be segmented by *political and legal factors* such as the type and stability of government, receptivity to foreign firms, monetary regulations, and the amount of bureaucracy. Such factors can play a crucial role in a company's choice of which countries to enter and how. *Cultural factors* can also be used, grouping markets according to common languages, religions, values and attitudes, customs, and behavioral patterns.

Segmenting international markets on the basis of geographic, economic, political, cultural, and other factors assumes that segments should consist of clusters of countries. However, many companies use a different approach called **intermarket segmentation.** Using this approach, they form segments of consumers who have similar needs and buying behavior even though they are located in different countries. For example, Mercedes-Benz targets the world's well-to-do, regardless of their country. MTV targets the world's teenagers. One study of more than 6,500 teenagers from 26 countries showed that teens around the world live surprisingly parallel lives. As one expert notes, "From Rio to Rochester, teens can be found enmeshed in much the same regimen: . . . drinking Coke, . . . dining on Big Macs, and surfin' the Net on their computers."[25] The world's teens have a lot *in common:* They study, shop, and sleep. They are exposed to many of the same major issues: love, crime, homelessness, ecology, and working parents. In many ways, they have more in common with each other than with their parents. MTV bridges the gap between cultures, appealing to what teens around the world have in common.[26]

Intermarket segmentation
Forming segments of consumers who have similar needs and buying behavior even though they are located in different countries.

Requirements for Effective Segmentation

Clearly, there are many ways to segment a market, but not all segmentations are effective. For example, buyers of table salt could be divided into blond and brunette customers. But hair color obviously does not affect the purchase of salt. Furthermore, if all salt buyers bought the same amount of salt each month, believed that all salt is the same, and wanted to pay the same price, the company would not benefit from segmenting this market.

To be useful, market segments must be:

★ *Measurable:* The size, purchasing power, and profiles of the segments can be measured. Certain segmentation variables are difficult to measure. For example, there are 32.5 million left-handed people in the United States—almost equaling the entire population of Canada. Yet few products are targeted toward this left-handed segment. The major problem may be that the segment is hard to identify and measure. There are no data on the demographics of lefties, and the U.S. Census Bureau does not keep track of left-handedness in its surveys. Private data companies keep reams of statistics on other demographic segments but not on left-handers.

★ *Accessible:* The market segments can be effectively reached and served. Suppose a fragrance company finds that heavy users of its brand are single men and women who stay out late and socialize a lot. Unless this group lives or shops at certain places and is exposed to certain media, its members will be difficult to reach.

★ *Substantial:* The market segments are large or profitable enough to serve. A segment should be the largest possible homogenous group worth pursuing with a tailored marketing program. It would not pay, for example, for an automobile manufacturer to develop cars for persons whose height is under four feet.

★ *Differentiable:* The segments are conceptually distinguishable and respond differently to different marketing mix elements and programs. If married and unmarried women respond similarly to a sale on perfume, they do not constitute separate segments.

★ *Actionable:* Effective programs can be designed for attracting and serving the segments. For example, although one small airline identified seven market segments, its staff was too small to develop separate marketing programs for each segment.

 # MARKET TARGETING

Market segmentation reveals the firm's market segment opportunities. The firm now has to evaluate the various segments and decide how many and which ones to target. We now look at how companies evaluate and select target segments.

Evaluating Market Segments

In evaluating different market segments, a firm must look at three factors: segment size and growth, segment structural attractiveness, and company objectives and resources. The company must first collect and analyze data on current segment sales, growth rates, and expected profitability for various segments. It will be interested in segments that have the right size and growth characteristics. (Appendix 1 discusses approaches for measuring and forecasting market demand.) But "right size and growth" is a relative matter. The largest, fastest-growing segments are not always the most attractive ones for every company. Smaller companies may lack the skills and resources needed to serve the larger segments or may find these segments too competitive. Such companies may select segments that are smaller and less attractive, in an absolute sense, but that are potentially more profitable for them.

The company also needs to examine major structural factors that affect long-run segment attractiveness.[27] For example, a segment is less attractive if it already contains many strong and aggressive *competitors.* The existence of many actual or potential *substitute products* may limit prices and the profits that can be earned in a segment. The relative *power of buyers* also affects segment attractiveness. Buyers with strong bargaining power relative to sellers will try to force prices down, demand more services, and set competitors against one another—all at the expense of seller profitability. Finally, a segment may be less attractive if it contains *powerful suppliers* who can control prices or reduce the quality or quantity of ordered goods and services.

Even if a segment has the right size and growth and is structurally attractive, the company must consider its own objectives and resources in relation to that segment. Some attractive segments could be dismissed quickly because they do not mesh with the company's long-run objectives. Even if a segment fits the company's objectives, the company must consider whether it possesses the skills and resources it needs to succeed in that segment. If the company lacks the strengths needed to compete successfully in a segment and cannot readily obtain them, it should not enter the segment. Even if the company possesses the *required* strengths, it needs to employ skills and resources *superior* to those of the competition in order to really win in a market segment. The company should enter only segments in which it can offer superior value and gain advantages over competitors.

Selecting Market Segments

Target market
A set of buyers sharing common needs or characteristics that the company decides to serve.

After evaluating different segments, the company must now decide which and how many segments to serve. This is the problem of *target market selection*. A **target market** consists of a set of buyers who share common needs or characteristics that the company decides to serve. Figure 7.3 shows that the firm can adopt one of three market-coverage strategies: *undifferentiated marketing, differentiated marketing,* and *concentrated marketing*.

A. Undifferentiated marketing

B. Differentiated marketing

C. Concentrated marketing

FIGURE 7.3 Three alternative market-coverage strategies

Undifferentiated Marketing

Undifferentiated marketing
A market-coverage strategy in which a firm decides to ignore market segment differences and go after the whole market with one offer.

Using an **undifferentiated marketing** (or mass-marketing) strategy, a firm might decide to ignore market segment differences and go after the whole market with one offer. This mass-marketing strategy focuses on what is *common* in the needs of consumers rather than on what is *different*. The company designs a product and a marketing program that will appeal to the largest number of buyers. It relies on mass distribution and mass advertising, and it aims to give the product a superior image in people's minds. As noted earlier in the chapter, most modern marketers have strong doubts about this strategy. Difficulties arise in developing a product or brand that will satisfy all consumers. Moreover, mass marketers often have trouble competing with more focused firms that do a better job of satisfying the need of specific segments and niches.

Differentiated Marketing

Differentiated marketing
A market-coverage strategy in which a firm decides to target several market segments and designs separate offers for each.

Using a **differentiated marketing** strategy, a firm decides to target several market segments or niches and designs separate offers for each. General Motors tries to produce a car for every "purse, purpose, and personality." Nike offers athletic shoes for a dozen or more different sports, from running, fencing, and aerobics to bicycling and baseball. Estée Lauder offers dozens of different products aimed at carefully defined niches:

★ The four best-selling prestige perfumes in the United States belong to Estée Lauder. So do seven of the top ten prestige makeup products and eight of the ten best-selling prestige skin care products. Estée Lauder is an expert in creating differentiated brands that serve the tastes of different market segments. There's the original Estée Lauder brand, which appeals to older, junior league types. Then there's Clinique, perfect for the middle-aged mom with a GMC Suburban and no time to waste. Then there's the hip M.A.C. line, which boasts as its spokesmodel RuPaul, a 6-foot, 7-inch drag queen. For the New Age type, there's upscale Aveda, with its aromatherapy line and earthy Origins, which the company expects will become a $1 billion brand. The company even offers downscale brands, such as Jane by Sassaby, for teens at Wal-Mart and Rite Aid.[28]

By offering product and marketing variations, these companies hope for higher sales and a stronger position within each market segment. Developing a stronger position within several segments creates more total sales than undifferentiated marketing across all segments. Procter & Gamble gets more total market share with eight brands of laundry detergent than it could with only one. But differentiated marketing also increases the costs of doing business. A firm usually finds it more expensive to develop and produce, say, 10 units of 10 different products than 100 units of one product. Developing separate marketing plans for the separate segments requires extra marketing research, forecasting, sales analysis, promotion planning, and channel management. Trying to reach different market segments with different advertising increases promotion costs. Thus, the company must weigh increased sales against increased costs when deciding on a differentiated marketing strategy.

Concentrated Marketing

Concentrated marketing
A market-coverage strategy in which a firm goes after a large share of one or a few submarkets.

A third market-coverage strategy, **concentrated marketing,** is especially appealing when company resources are limited. Instead of going after a small share of a large market, the firm goes after a large share of one or a few segments or niches. For example, Oshkosh Truck is the world's largest producer of airport rescue trucks and front-loading concrete mixers. Tetra sells 80 percent of the world's tropical fish

Concentrated marketing: Oshkosh Truck has found its niche as the world's largest producer of airport rescue trucks and front-loading concrete mixers.

food, and Steiner Optical captures 80 percent of the world's military binoculars market.

Today, the low cost of setting up shop on the Internet makes it even more profitable to serve seemingly minuscule niches. Small businesses, in particular, are realizing riches from serving small niches on the Web. Here are two "Webpreneurs" who achieved astonishing results:[29]

★ *Ostrichesonline.com.* Whereas Internet giants like music retailer CDnow and bookseller Amazon.com have yet to even realize a profit, Steve Warrington is earning a six-figure income online selling ostriches and every product derived from them (www.ostrichesonline.com). Launched for next to nothing on the Web, Warrington's business generated $4 million in sales last year. The site tells visitors everything they ever wanted to know about ostriches and much, much more—it supplies ostrich facts, ostrich pictures, an ostrich farm index, and a huge ostrich database and reference index. Visitors to the site can buy ostrich meat, feathers, leather jackets, videos, eggshells, and skin care products derived from ostrich body oil.

★ *Mesomorphosis.com.* At the age of 26, Millard Baker, a clinical psychology graduate student at the University of South Florida, launched a Web-based business selling body building supplements and oils (www.mesomorphosis.com). Although other Web sites peddled similar products, few offered articles and content, so Millard Baker added these elements to his site. Mesomorphosis.com has now grown into a full-fledged Internet publication as well as an online store. It provides subscribers with "scientifically-based articles about body building so that [they] can make informed decisions about training, nutrition, and supplementation." How successful is this Web nicher? Baker now pulls in more than $25,000 a month.

Concentrated marketing provides an excellent way for small new businesses to get a foothold against larger, more resourceful competitors. For example, Southwest Airlines began by concentrating on serving intrastate, no-frills commuters. PageNet got off to a successful start by concentrating on limited geographic areas. Wal-Mart got its start by bringing everyday low prices to small town and rural areas.

Through concentrated marketing, firms achieve strong market positions in the segments or niches they serve because of their greater knowledge of the segments' needs and the special reputations they acquire. They also enjoy many operating economies because of specialization in production, distribution, and promotion. If the segment is well chosen, firms can earn a high rate of return on their investments.

At the same time, concentrated marketing involves higher-than-normal risks. The particular market segment can turn sour. Or larger competitors may decide to enter the same segment. For example, California Cooler's success in the wine cooler segment attracted many large competitors, causing the original owners to sell to a larger company that had more marketing resources. For these reasons, many companies prefer to diversify in several market segments.

Choosing a Market-Coverage Strategy

Many factors need to be considered when choosing a market-coverage strategy. Which strategy is best depends on *company resources.* When the firm's resources are limited, concentrated marketing makes the most sense. The best strategy also depends on the degree of *product variability.* Undifferentiated marketing is more suited for uniform products such as grapefruit or steel. Products that can vary in design, such as cameras and automobiles, are more suited to differentiation or concentration. The *product's life-cycle stage* also must be considered.

When a firm introduces a new product, it is practical to launch only one version, and undifferentiated marketing or concentrated marketing makes the most sense. In the mature stage of the product life cycle, however, differentiated marketing begins to make more sense. Another factor is *market variability.* If most buyers have the same tastes, buy the same amounts, and react the same way to marketing efforts, undifferentiated marketing is appropriate. Finally, *competitors' marketing strategies* are important. When competitors use differentiated or concentrated marketing, undifferentiated marketing can be suicidal. Conversely, when competitors use undifferentiated marketing, a firm can gain an advantage by using differentiated or concentrated marketing.

Socially Responsible Target Marketing

Smart targeting helps companies to be more efficient and effective by focusing on the segments that they can satisfy best and most profitably. Targeting also benefits consumers—companies reach specific groups of consumers with offers carefully tailored to satisfy their needs. However, target marketing sometimes generates controversy and concern. Issues usually involve the targeting of vulnerable or disadvantaged consumers with controversial or potentially harmful products.

For example, over the years, the cereal industry has been heavily criticized for its marketing efforts directed toward children. Critics worry that premium offers and high-powered advertising appeals presented through the mouths of lovable animated characters will overwhelm children's defenses. The marketers of toys and other children's products have been similarly battered, often with good justification. Some critics have even called for a complete ban on advertising to children. To encourage responsible advertising to children, the Children's Advertising Review Unit, the advertising industry's self-regulatory agency, has published extensive children's advertising guidelines that recognize the special needs of child audiences.

Cigarette, beer, and fast-food marketers have also generated much controversy in recent years by their attempts to target inner-city minority consumers. For example, McDonald's and other chains have drawn criticism for pitching their high-fat, salt-laden fare to low-income, inner-city residents who are much more likely than suburbanites to be heavy consumers. R.J. Reynolds took heavy flak in the early 1990s when it announced plans to market Uptown, a menthol cigarette targeted toward low-income blacks. It quickly dropped the brand in the face of a loud public outcry and heavy pressure from black leaders. G. Heileman Brewing made a similar mistake with PowerMaster, a potent malt liquor. Because malt liquor had become the drink of choice among many in the inner city, Heileman focused its marketing efforts for PowerMaster on inner-city blacks. However, this group suffers disproportionately from liver diseases brought on by alcohol, and the inner city is already plagued by alcohol-related problems such as crime and violence. Thus, Heileman's targeting decision drew substantial criticism.[30]

The meteoric growth of the Internet and other carefully targeted direct media has raised fresh concerns about potential targeting abuses. The Internet allows increasing refinement of audiences and, in turn, more precise targeting. This might help makers of questionable products or deceptive advertisers to more readily victimize the most vulnerable audiences. As one expert observes, "In theory, an audience member could have tailor-made deceptive messages sent directly to his or her computer screen."[31]

Not all attempts to target children, minorities, or other special segments draw such criticism. In fact, most provide benefits to targeted consumers. For example, Colgate-Palmolive's Colgate Junior toothpaste has special features designed to get children to brush longer and more often—it's less foamy, has a milder taste, contains sparkles, and exits the tube in a star-shaped column.

Golden Ribbon Playthings has developed a highly acclaimed and very successful black character doll named "Huggy Bean" targeted toward minority consumers. Huggy comes with books and toys that connect her with her African heritage. Many cosmetics companies have responded to the special needs of minority segments by adding products specifically designed for African American, Hispanic, or Asian women. Black-owned ICE theaters noticed that although moviegoing by blacks has surged, there are few inner-city theaters. The chain has opened a theater in Chicago's South Side as well as two other Chicago theaters, and it plans to open in four more cities this year. ICE partners with the black communities in which it operates theaters, using local radio stations to promote films and featuring favorite food items at concession stands.[32]

Thus, in market targeting, the issue is not really *who* is targeted but rather *how* and for *what*. Controversies arise when marketers attempt to profit at the expense of targeted segments—when they unfairly target vulnerable segments or target them with questionable products or tactics. Socially responsible marketing calls for segmentation and targeting that serve not just the interests of the company but also the interests of those targeted.

POSITIONING FOR COMPETITIVE ADVANTAGE

Product position

The way the product is defined by consumers on important attributes—the place the product occupies in consumers' minds relative to competing products.

Once a company has decided which segments of the market it will enter, it must decide what positions it wants to occupy in those segments. A **product's position** is the way the product is *defined by consumers* on important attributes—the place the product occupies in consumers' minds relative to competing products. Positioning involves implanting the brand's unique benefits and differentiation in customers' minds. Thus, Tide is positioned as a powerful, all-purpose family detergent; Ivory Snow is positioned as the gentle detergent for fine washables and baby clothes. In the automobile market, Toyota Tercel and Subaru are positioned on economy, Mercedes and Cadillac on luxury, and Porsche and BMW on performance. Volvo positions powerfully on safety.

Consumers are overloaded with information about products and services. They cannot reevaluate products every time they make a buying decision. To simplify the buying process, consumers organize products into categories—they "position" products, services, and companies in their minds. A product's position is the complex set of perceptions, impressions, and feelings that consumers have for the product compared with competing products. Consumers position products with or without the help of marketers. But marketers do not want to leave their products' positions to chance. They must *plan* positions that will give their products the greatest advantage in selected target markets, and they must design marketing mixes to create these planned positions.

Choosing a Positioning Strategy

Some firms find it easy to choose their positioning strategy. For example, a firm well known for quality in certain segments will go for this position in a new segment if there are enough buyers seeking quality. But in many cases, two or more firms will go after the same position. Then, each will have to find other ways to set itself apart. Each firm must differentiate its offer by building a unique bundle of benefits that appeals to a substantial group within the segment.

The positioning task consists of three steps: identifying a set of possible competitive advantages upon which to build a position, choosing the right competitive advantages, and selecting an overall positioning strategy. The company must then effectively communicate and deliver the chosen position to the market.

Identifying Possible Competitive Advantages

Competitive advantage
An advantage over competitors gained by offering consumers greater value, either through lower prices or by providing more benefits that justify higher prices.

The key to winning and keeping customers is to understand their needs and buying processes better than competitors do and to deliver more value. To the extent that a company can position itself as providing superior value to selected target markets it gains **competitive advantage.** But solid positions cannot be built on empty promises. If a company positions its product as *offering* the best quality and service, it must then *deliver* the promised quality and service. Thus, positioning begins with actually *differentiating* the company's marketing offer so that it will give consumers more value than competitors' offers do.

To find points of differentiation, marketers must think through the customer's entire experience with the company's product or service. An alert company can find ways to differentiate itself at every point where it comes in contact with customers.[33] In what specific ways can a company differentiate its offer from those of competitors? A company or market offer can be differentiated along the lines of *product, services, channels, people,* or *image.*

Competitive advantages: Volvo positions powerfully on safety: All most people want from a car seat is "a nice, comfy place to put your gluteus maximus." However, when a Volvo is struck from behind, a sophisticated system "guides the front seats through an intricate choreography that supports the neck and spine, while helping to reduce dangerous collision impact forces."

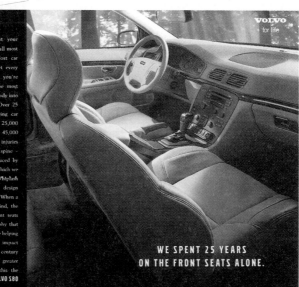

Product differentiation takes place along a continuum. At one extreme we find physical products that allow little variation: chicken, steel, aspirin. Yet even here some meaningful differentiation is possible. For example, Perdue claims that its branded chickens are better—fresher and more tender—and gets a 10 percent price premium based on this differentiation. At the other extreme are products that can be highly differentiated, such as automobiles, commercial machinery, and furniture. Such products can be differentiated on features, performance, or style and design. Thus, Volvo provides new and better safety features; Whirlpool designs its dishwasher to run more quietly; Bose speakers are positioned on striking design characteristics. Similarly, companies can differentiate their products on such attributes as *consistency, durability, reliability,* or *repairability.*

Beyond differentiating its physical product, a firm can also differentiate the services that accompany the product. Some companies gain *services differentiation* through speedy, convenient, or careful *delivery.* For example, BancOne has opened full-service branches in supermarkets to provide location convenience along with Saturday, Sunday, and weekday-evening hours. *Installation* can also differentiate one company from another, as can *repair* services. Many an automobile buyer will gladly pay a little more and travel a little farther to buy a car from a dealer that provides top-notch repair service. Some companies differentiate their offers by providing *customer training service* or *consulting services*—data, information systems, and advising services that buyers need. For example, McKesson Corporation, a major drug wholesaler, consults with its 12,000 independent pharmacists to help them set up accounting, inventory, and computerized ordering systems. By helping its customers compete better, McKesson gains greater customer loyalty and sales.

Firms that practice *channel differentiation* gain competitive advantage through the way they design their channel's coverage, expertise, and performance. Caterpillar's success in the construction-equipment industry is based on superior channels. Its dealers worldwide are renowned for their top-notch service. Dell Computer and Avon distinguish themselves by their high-quality direct channels. Iams pet food achieves success by going against tradition, distributing its products only through veterinarians and pet stores.

Companies can gain a strong competitive advantage through *people differentiation*—hiring and training better people than their competitors do. Thus, Disney people are known to be friendly and upbeat. Singapore Airlines enjoys an excellent reputation largely because of the grace of its flight attendants. IBM offers people who make sure that the solution customers want is the solution they get: "People Who Think. People Who Do. People Who Get It." People differentiation requires that a company select its customer-contact people carefully and train them well. For example, Disney trains its theme park people thoroughly to ensure that they are competent, courteous, and friendly. From the hotel check-in agents, to the monorail drivers, to the ride attendants, to the people who sweep Main Street USA, each employee understands the importance of understanding customers, communicating with them clearly and cheerfully, and responding quickly to their requests and problems. Each is carefully trained to "make a dream come true."

Even when competing offers look the same, buyers may perceive a difference based on company or brand *image differentiation.* A company or brand image should convey the product's distinctive benefits and positioning. Developing a strong and distinctive image calls for creativity and hard work. A company cannot plant an image in the public's mind overnight using only a few advertisements. If Ritz-Carlton means quality, this image must be supported by everything the company says and does. *Symbols*—such as McDonald's golden arches, the Prudential rock, or the Pillsbury doughboy—can provide strong company or brand recognition and image differentiation. The company might build a brand around a famous person, as Nike did with its Air Jordan basketball shoes. Some companies even become associated with colors, such as IBM (blue), Campbell (red and white), or Kodak (red and yellow). The chosen symbols, characters, and other image elements must be communicated through advertising that conveys the company's or brand's personality.

Choosing the Right Competitive Advantages

Suppose a company is fortunate enough to discover several potential competitive advantages. It now must choose the ones on which it will build its positioning strategy. It must decide *how many* differences to promote and *which ones*.

How Many Differences to Promote?   Many marketers think that companies should aggressively promote only one benefit to the target market. Ad man Rosser Reeves, for example, said a company should develop a *unique selling proposition (USP)* for each brand and stick to it. Each brand should pick an attribute and tout itself as "number one" on that attribute. Buyers tend to remember number one better, especially in an overcommunicated society. Thus, Crest toothpaste consistently promotes its anticavity protection and Volvo promotes safety. A company that hammers away at one of these positions and consistently delivers on it probably will become best known and remembered for it.

Other marketers think that companies should position themselves on more than one differentiating factor. This may be necessary if two or more firms are claiming to be the best on the same attribute. Today, in a time when the mass market is fragmenting into many small segments, companies are trying to broaden their positioning strategies to appeal to more segments. For example, Unilever introduced the first three-in-one bar soap—Lever 2000—offering cleansing, deodorizing, *and* moisturizing benefits. Clearly, many buyers want all three benefits, and the challenge was to convince them that one brand can deliver all three. Judging from Lever 2000's outstanding success,

Unilever positioned its best-selling Lever 2000 soap on three benefits in one: cleansing, deodorizing, and moisturizing benefits. It's good "for all your 2000 parts."

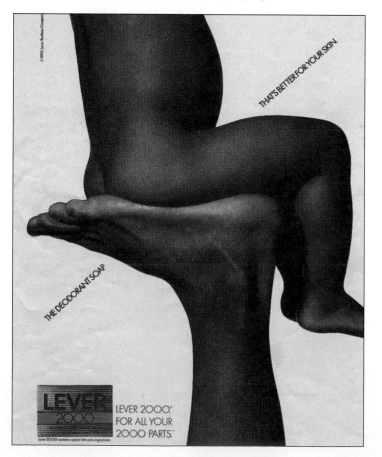

THE DEODORANT SOAP

THAT'S BETTER FOR YOUR SKIN.

LEVER 2000

LEVER 2000®
FOR ALL YOUR
2000 PARTS™

Unilever easily met the challenge. However, as companies increase the number of claims for their brands, they risk disbelief and a loss of clear positioning.

In general, a company needs to avoid three major positioning errors. The first is *underpositioning*—failing to ever really position the company at all. Some companies discover that buyers have only a vague idea of the company or that they do not really know anything special about it. The second error is *overpositioning*—giving buyers too narrow a picture of the company. Thus, a consumer might think that the Steuben glass company makes only fine art glass costing $1,000 and up, when in fact it makes affordable fine glass starting at around $50. Finally, companies must avoid *confused positioning*—leaving buyers with a confused image of a company. For example, over the past decade, Burger King has fielded six separate advertising campaigns, with themes ranging from "Herb the nerd doesn't eat here" to "Sometimes you've got to break the rules" and "BK Tee Vee." This barrage of positioning statements has left consumers confused and Burger King with poor sales and profits.

Which Differences to Promote?   Not all brand differences are meaningful or worthwhile; not every difference makes a good differentiator. Each difference has the potential to create company costs as well as customer benefits. Therefore, the company must carefully select the ways in which it will distinguish itself from competitors. A difference is worth establishing to the extent that it satisfies the following criteria:

★ *Important:* The difference delivers a highly valued benefit to target buyers.
★ *Distinctive:* Competitors do not offer the difference, or the company can offer it in a more distinctive way.
★ *Superior:* The difference is superior to other ways that customers might obtain the same benefit.
★ *Communicable:* The difference is communicable and visible to buyers.
★ *Preemptive:* Competitors cannot easily copy the difference.
★ *Affordable:* Buyers can afford to pay for the difference.
★ *Profitable:* The company can introduce the difference profitably.

Many companies have introduced differentiations that failed one or more of these tests. The Westin Stamford hotel in Singapore advertises that it is the world's tallest hotel, a distinction that is not important to many tourists—in fact, it turns many off. Polaroid's Polarvision, which produced instantly developed home movies, bombed too. Although Polarvision was distinctive and even preemptive, it was inferior to another way of capturing motion, namely, camcorders. When Pepsi introduced clear Crystal Pepsi some years ago, customers were unimpressed. Although the new drink was distinctive, consumers didn't see "clarity" as an important benefit in a soft drink. Thus, choosing competitive advantages upon which to position a product or service can be difficult, yet such choices may be crucial to success.

Selecting an Overall Positioning Strategy

Consumers typically choose products and services that give them the greatest value. Thus, marketers want to position their brands on the key benefits that they offer relative to competing brands. The full positioning of a brand is called the brand's **value proposition**—the full mix of benefits upon which the brand is positioned. It is the answer to the customer's question "Why should I buy your brand?" Volvo's value proposition hinges on safety but also includes reliability, roominess, and styling, all for a price that is higher than average but seems fair for this mix of benefits.

Figure 7.4 shows possible value propositions upon which a company might position its products. In the figure, the five green cells represent winning value propositions—positioning that gives the company competitive advantage. The

Value proposition
The full positioning of a brand—the full mix of benefits upon which it is positioned.

FIGURE 7.4   Possible value propositions

orange cells, however, represent losing value propositions, and the center cell represents at best a marginal proposition. In the following sections, we discuss the five winning value propositions companies can use to position their products: more for more, more for the same, the same for less, less for much less, and more for less.[34]

More for More.   "More for more" positioning involves providing the most upscale product or service and charging a higher price to cover the higher costs. Ritz-Carlton Hotels, Mont Blanc writing instruments, Mercedes-Benz automobiles—each claims superior quality, craftsmanship, durability, performance, or style and charges a price to match. Not only is the marketing offer high in quality, it also offers prestige to the buyer. It symbolizes status and a lofty lifestyle. Often, the price difference exceeds the actual increment in quality.

Sellers offering "only the best" can be found in every product and service category, from hotels, restaurants, food, and fashion to cars and kitchen appliances. Consumers are sometimes surprised, even delighted, when a new competitor enters a category with an unusually high-priced brand. Starbucks coffee entered as a very expensive brand in a largely commodity category; Häagen-Dazs came in as a premium ice cream brand at a price never before charged. In general, companies should be on the lookout for opportunities to introduce a "much more for much more" brand in any underdeveloped product or service category. For example, William-Sonoma's hottest-selling item this year is the $369 Dualit Toaster, a hand-assembled appliance that keeps toast warm for 10 minutes.[35]

Yet "more for more" brands can be vulnerable. They often invite imitators who claim the same quality but at a lower price. Luxury goods that sell well during good times may be at risk during economic downturns when buyers become more cautious in their spending.

More for the Same.   Companies can attack a competitor's more for more positioning by introducing a brand offering comparable quality but at a lower price. For example, Toyota introduced its Lexus line with a "more for the same" value proposition. Its headline read: "Perhaps the first time in history that trading a $72,000 car for a $36,000 car could be considered trading up." It communicated the high quality of its new Lexus through rave reviews in car magazines, through a widely distributed videotape showing side-by-side comparisons of Lexus and Mercedes-Benz automobiles, and through surveys showing that Lexus dealers were providing customers with better sales and service experiences than were Mercedes dealerships. Many Mercedes-Benz owners switched to Lexus, and the Lexus repurchase rate has been 60 percent, twice the industry average.

The Same for Less.   Offering "the same for less" can be a powerful value proposition—everyone likes a good deal. For example, Amazon.com sells the same book titles as its brick-and-mortar competitors but at lower prices, and Dell Computer offers equivalent quality at a better "price for performance." Discounts stores such as Wal-Mart and "category killers" such as Best Buy, Circuit City, and Sportmart also use this positioning. They don't claim to offer different or better products. Instead, they offer many of the same brands as department stores and specialty stores but at deep discounts based on superior purchasing power and lower-cost operations.

Other companies develop imitative but lower-priced brands in an effort to lure customers away from the market leader. For example, Advanced Micro Devices (AMD) and Cyrix make less expensive versions of Intel's market-leading microprocessor chips. Many personal computer companies make "IBM clones" and claim to offer the same performance at lower prices.

Less for Much Less.   A market almost always exists for products that offer less and therefore cost less. Few people need, want, or can afford "the very best" in everything they buy. In many cases, consumers will gladly settle for less than optimal performance or give up some of the bells and whistles in exchange for a lower price. For example, many travelers seeking lodgings prefer not to pay for what they consider unnecessary extras, such as a pool, cable television, attached restaurant, or mints on the pillow. Motel chains such as Motel 6 suspend some of these amenities and charge less accordingly.

"Less for much less" positioning involves meeting consumers' lower performance or quality requirements at a much lower price. For example, Family Dollar and Dollar General stores offer more affordable goods at very low prices. Sam's Club warehouse stores offer less merchandise selection and consistency, and much lower levels of service; as a result, they charge rock-bottom prices. Southwest Airlines, the nation's most profitable air carrier, also practices less for much less positioning. It charges incredibly low prices by not serving food, not assigning seats, and not using travel agents.

More for Less.   Of course, the winning value proposition would be to offer "more for less." Many companies claim to do this. For example, Dell Computer claims to have better products *and* lower prices for a given level of performance. Procter & Gamble claims that its laundry detergents provide the best cleaning *and* everyday low prices. In the short run, some companies can actually achieve such lofty positions. For example, when it first opened for business, Home Depot had arguably the best product selection and service *and* at the lowest prices compared to local hardware stores and other home improvement chains.

Yet in the long run, companies will find it very difficult to sustain such best-of-both positioning. Offering more usually costs more, making it difficult to deliver on the "for less" promise. Companies that try to deliver both may lose out to more focused competitors. For example, facing determined competition from Lowes stores, Home Depot must now decide whether it wants to compete primarily on superior service or on lower prices.

All said, each brand must adopt a positioning strategy designed to serve the needs and wants of its target markets. "More for more" will draw one target market, "less for much less" will draw another, and so on. Thus, in any market, there is usually room for many different companies, each successfully occupying different positions (see Marketing Highlight 7.3).

The important thing is that each company must develop its own winning positioning strategy, one that makes it special to its target consumers. Offering only "the same for the same" provides no competitive advantage, leaving the firm in the middle of the pack. Companies offering one of the three losing value propositions—"the

MARKETING HIGHLIGHT
7.3

AIRLINE POSITIONING: "MORE FOR MORE" OR "LESS FOR MUCH LESS"?

Southwest Airlines and Midwest Express Airlines couldn't be more different in their positioning. Southwest offers a classic "less for much less" value proposition. In contrast, Midwest Express offers "more for a tad more." What they have in common, however, is that both have consistently soared above their competitors. In an industry often plagued by huge losses, Southwest has experienced 26 straight years of profits; Midwest Express has turned a profit for 12 years in a row. Both owe their success to strong and clear positioning that serves a well-defined target segment. Here, we compare the alternative positions that have made these airlines so successful.

Southwest Airlines

Southwest Airlines knows its niche. From the start, it has positioned itself firmly as *the* short-haul, no-frills, low-price airline. Its average flight time is just one hour; its average

Southwest offers a classic "less for much less" value proposition. Southwest refuses to take itself seriously—here, happy-go-lucky CEO Herb Kelleher dons his Elvis suit.

one-way fare just $76. Southwest's passengers have learned to fly without the amenities. For example, the airline provides no meals—just peanuts. It also offers no first-class section, only three-across seating in all of its planes. There's no such thing as a reserved seat on a Southwest flight. Passengers receive numbered boarding passes—first come, first served—and are herded onto the plane in groups of 30. "Southwest will get you and your luggage where you're going," comments an industry analyst, "but we don't call their planes cattle cars for nothing. It's a mercy that Southwest is a short-haul airline, because you can get pretzelated on their planes p.d.q."

Why, then, do so many passengers love Southwest? Perhaps most importantly, Southwest excels at the basics of getting passengers where they want to go and on time. In 1992, Southwest received the U.S. Department of Transportation's first-ever Triple Crown Award for best on-time service, best baggage handling, *and* best customer service, a feat it repeated for the next five straight years. For more than a decade, Southwest has been an industry leader in on-time performance.

Beyond these basics, however, there are two key elements to Southwest's strong positioning. The analyst sums up Southwest's positioning this way: "It is not luxurious, . . . but it's cheap and it's fun." Southwest is a model of efficiency and low-cost operations. As a result, its prices are shockingly low. In fact, prices are so low that when Southwest enters a

new market, it actually increases total air traffic by attracting customers who might otherwise travel by car or bus. For example, when Southwest began its Louisville–Chicago flight at a one-way rate of $49 versus competitors' $250, total weekly air passenger traffic between the two cities increased from 8,000 to 26,000.

No frills and low prices, however, don't mean drudgery. To lighten things up, Southwest adds another key positioning ingredient—lots of good, clean fun. With its happy-go-lucky CEO, Herb Kelleher, leading the charge, Southwest refuses to take itself seriously. Cheerful employees go out of their way to amuse, surprise, or somehow entertain passengers. According to one account:

> Southwest employees are apt to dress as leprechauns on St. Patrick's Day, rabbits on Easter, and almost anything on Halloween. I have heard flight attendants sing the safety lecture as country music, blues, and rap; I have heard them compare the pilot to Rocky Raccoon and insist that passengers introduce themselves to one another, then hug, then kiss, then propose marriage.

Kelleher himself has been known to dress up as Elvis Presley to greet passengers.

During delays at the gate, ticket agents will award prizes to the passenger with the largest hole in his or her sock. Flight attendants have been known to hide in overhead luggage bins and then pop out when passengers start filing onboard. Veteran Southwest fliers have learned to listen up to announcements over the intercom. On a recent flight, the pilot suggested, "Flight attendants will please prepare their hair for departure." Later in the flight, he announced, "Good morning, ladies and gentlemen. Those of you who wish to smoke will please file out to our lounge on the wing, where you can enjoy our feature film, *Gone with the Wind*." Safety instructions from the flight attendant included the advice, "In the event of a water landing, please remember to paddle, kick, kick, paddle, kick, kick, all the way back."

As a result of its strong positioning, Southwest has grown to become the nation's fourth-largest domestic carrier. The company has successfully beaten off determined challenges from several major competitors who have tried to copy its winning formula, including Continental Lite, Delta Express, and Shuttle by United. Over the past 10 years, Southwest's revenues have grown 388 percent, its net earnings have soared 1,490 percent, and its stock has yielded an average annual return to investors of 29 percent.

Midwest Express Airlines

Midwest Express Airlines' positioning stands in stark contrast to Southwest's. Whereas Southwest offers no frills, low prices, and zany fun, Midwest Express provides all the creature comforts and calm, refined service at higher but still competitive prices. It targets older, more affluent business travelers—35 percent of Midwest Express fliers earn more than $100,000 per year and a majority are between the ages of 35 and 54. These fliers want more service and Midwest Express delivers it to them.

Flying Midwest Express is a special experience:

You slip into your leather seat. You don't tussle for the armrest with some sweaty stranger in the middle, because there is no middle; everyone sits two by two with loads of legroom. . . . On breakfast flights, the chilled champagne is free. At lunch and dinner, you can choose a quality merlot or Chardonnay poured from bottles with actual corks. Next comes the hot food on real china. Yes, food not pretzels or a deli bag, but lobster or salmon, served by certifiably cordial airline employees. You can cover your shirt with a linen napkin. And, in a burst of true genius, the glass you're drinking from is made of . . . glass! This isn't a frequent flier's fantasy; it's a real utopia on a shockingly civilized airline called Midwest Express.

Consistent with its motto, "The Best Care in the Air," Midwest Express provides high-quality, near first-class service to all passengers. All seats are leather and a full 21 inches wide, compared to the 17- to 18-inch-wide seats of competitors. There are no more than 4 seats per row, eliminating the dreaded middle seat. Congenial but reserved flight attendants serve hot and elegant meals with complimentary wine or champagne, followed by a helping of the airline's signature chocolate chip cookies, sinfully gooey from being baked right on board. Midwest Express spends about $10 per passenger meal—twice the industry average (Southwest boasts that its average food cost per passenger is about 20¢). In a recent survey rating airline comfort, Midwest Express rated 98 on a scale of 100 versus 67 to 74 for the major airlines.

Midwest Express is still a pretty small operation compared with Southwest and other major airlines. Unless you live in Milwaukee, Midwest's primary hub, you've probably never heard of it. Yet the classy lit-

tle airline has developed a devout following. Sales are growing steadily and the airline recently posted its twelfth consecutive year of profitability. Last year, Midwest's revenues were up 13 percent, income increased by 44 percent, and the airline flew a record 2 million passengers. Adding additional luster, three national travel magazines named it the best U.S. airline.

Midwest Express passengers pay more for its first-rate service. The airline's prices are a tad higher than those of competitors and the company sells very few economy seats. But to those who choose Midwest Express, the extras are well worth the additional costs. As for the future, Midwest Express is constantly on the lookout for new ways to please its already highly satisfied passengers. Says Tim Hoeksema, Midwest's president, "We're already looking for tomorrow's cookie—whatever makes somebody climb aboard . . . . and say, 'Wow.' "

Sources: Quotes from Molly Ivins, "From Texas, with Love and Peanuts," *New York Times,* March 14, 1999, p. 11; and Daniel Pedersen, "Cookies and Champagne," *Newsweek,* April 27, 1998, p. 60. Also see "One Midwest Carrier Proves That Smaller Can Be Better," *Money,* November 1997, p. 123; Ellen Jovin, "Buckling Up the Business Traveler," *American Demographics,* December 1998, pp. 48–51; Thomas A. Stewart, "America's Most Admired Companies," *Fortune,* March 2, 1998, pp. 70–73; Stephanie Gruner, "Have Fun, Make Money," *Inc.,* May 1998, p. 123; Chad Kaydo, "Riding High," *Sales & Marketing Management,* July 1998, pp. 64–69; "How Herb Keeps Southwest Hopping," *Money,* June 1999, pp. 61–62; *Southwest Airlines Fact Sheet—November 1999* at www.southwest.com; and "A Letter from the Chairman," accessed online from www.midwestexpress.com, February 2000.

same for more," "less for more," and "less for the same"—will inevitably fail. Here, customers soon realize that they've been underserved, tell others, and abandon the brand.

Communicating and Delivering the Chosen Position

Once it has chosen a position, the company must take strong steps to deliver and communicate the desired position to target consumers. All the company's marketing mix efforts must support the positioning strategy. Positioning the company calls for concrete action, not just talk. If the company decides to build a position on better quality and service, it must first *deliver* that position. Designing the marketing mix—product, price, place, and promotion—essentially involves working out the tactical details of the positioning strategy. Thus, a firm that seizes on a "for more" position knows that it must produce high-quality products, charge a high price, distribute through high-quality dealers, and advertise in high-quality media. It must hire and train more service people, find retailers who have a good reputation for service, and develop sales and advertising messages that broadcast its superior service. This is the only way to build a consistent and believable "more for more" position.

Companies often find it easier to come up with a good positioning strategy than to implement it. Establishing a position or changing one usually takes a long time. In contrast, positions that have taken years to build can quickly be lost. Once a company has built the desired position, it must take care to maintain the position through consistent performance and communication. It must closely monitor and adapt the position over time to match changes in consumer needs and competitors' strategies. However, the company should avoid abrupt changes that might confuse consumers. Instead, a product's position should evolve gradually as it adapts to the ever-changing marketing environment.

REVIEW OF CONCEPT CONNECTIONS

Marketers know that they cannot appeal to all buyers in their markets, or at least not to all buyers in the same way. Buyers are too numerous, too widely scattered, and too varied in their needs and buying practices. Therefore, most companies today are moving away from mass marketing. Instead, they practice *target marketing*—identifying market segments, selecting one or more of them, and developing products and marketing mixes tailored to each. In this way, sellers can develop the right product for each target market and adjust their prices, distribution channels, and advertising to reach the target market efficiently.

1. Define the three steps of target marketing: market segmentation, market targeting, and market positioning.
Market segmentation is the act of dividing a market into distinct groups of buyers with different needs, characteristics, or behavior who might require separate products or marketing mixes. Once the groups have been identified, *market targeting* evaluates each market segment's attractiveness and suggests one or more segments to enter. *Market positioning* consists of setting the competitive positioning for the product and creating a detailed marketing plan.

2. List and discuss the major levels of market segmentation and bases for segmenting consumer and business markets.
Market segmentation can be carried out at several different levels, including no segmentation (mass marketing), complete segmentation (micromarketing), or something in between (segment marketing or niche marketing). *Mass marketing* involves mass producing, mass distributing, and mass promoting about the same product in about the same way to all consumers. Using *segmented marketing,* the company tries to isolate broad segments that make up a market and adapts its offers to more closely match the needs of one or more segments. *Niche marketing* focuses on more narrowly defined subgroups within these segments, groups with distinctive sets of traits that may seek a special combination of benefits. *Micromarketing* is the practice of tailoring products and marketing programs to suit the tastes of specific individuals and locations. Micromarketing includes *local marketing* and *individual marketing.*

There is no single way to segment a market. Therefore, the marketer tries different variables to see which give the best segmentation opportunities. For consumer marketing, the major segmentation variables are geographic, demographic, psychographic, and behavioral. In *geographic segmentation,* the market is divided into different geographical units such as nations, states, regions, counties, cities, or neighborhoods. In *demographic segmentation,* the market is divided into groups based on demographic variables, including age, gender, family size, family life cycle, income, occupation, education, religion, race, and nationality. In *psychographic segmentation,* the market is divided into different groups based on social class, lifestyle, or personality characteristics. In *behavioral segmentation,* the market is divided into groups based on consumers' knowledge, attitudes, uses, or responses to a product.

Business marketers use many of the same variables to segment their markets. But business markets also can be segmented by business consumer *demographics* (industry, company size), *operating characteristics, purchasing approaches, situational factors,* and *personal characteristics.* The effectiveness of segmentation analysis depends on finding segments that are *measurable, accessible, substantial, differentiable,* and *actionable.*

3. Explain how companies identify attractive market segments and choose a market-coverage strategy.

To target the best market segments, the company first evaluates each segment's size and growth characteristics, structural attractiveness, and compatibility with company objectives and resources. It then chooses one of three market-coverage strategies. The seller can ignore segment differences (*undifferentiated marketing*), develop different market offers for several segments (*differentiated marketing*), or go after one or a few market segments (*concentrated marketing*). Much depends on company resources, product variability, product life-cycle stage, and competitive marketing strategies.

4. Discuss how companies can position their products for maximum competitive advantage in the marketplace.

Once a company has decided which segments to enter, it must decide on its *market positioning* strategy—on which positions to occupy in its chosen segments. The positioning task consists of three steps: identifying a set of possible competitive advantages upon which to build a position, choosing the right competitive advantages, and selecting an overall positioning strategy. The brand's full positioning is called its *value proposition*—the full mix of benefits upon which the brand is positioned. In general, companies can choose from one of five winning value propositions upon which to position their products: more for more, more for the same, the same for less, less for much less, or more for less. They must then effectively communicate and deliver the chosen position to the market.

KEY TERMS

Age and life-cycle segmentation
Behavioral segmentation
Benefit segmentation
Competitive advantage
Concentrated marketing
Demographic segmentation
Differentiated marketing
Gender segmentation
Geographic segmentation

Income segmentation
Individual marketing
Intermarket segmentation
Local marketing
Market positioning
Market segmentation
Market targeting
Micromarketing

Niche marketing
Occasion segmentation
Product position
Psychographic segmentation
Segment marketing
Target market
Undifferentiated marketing
Value proposition

ISSUES FOR DISCUSSION

1. Describe how the Ford Motor Company over the years has moved from mass marketing to segment marketing. Do you think the company will be able to move toward niche marketing or micromarketing? If so, how? How is the company using the Internet (see www.ford.com) to change its market segmentation approach.

2. Several years ago Samuel Adams Brewery led a charge of microbreweries in an attack on the brands of established brewers. How might such microbreweries use micromarketing? Evaluate the merits of such a strategy. (For more information, see www.samadams.com.)

3. How can a company devise a marketing strategy that will have a mass appeal yet recognize individual differences? One solution is to construct a strategy based on gender segmentation. Construct a brief gender-based strategy for a company attempting to market the following items: (a) a new blade razor, (b) a denim overshirt, (c) a Mazda Miata sports car, (d) life insurance, and (e) Oakley sunglasses.

4. Using Table 7.2 as a model, along with information found in the chapter-opening vignette, construct a benefit segmentation table for laundry detergent. Identify the major benefit segments, their characteristics, and their favored brands. Explain how you constructed your table and the potential benefits of your approach.

5. There are many ways to segment a market. However, not all segmentations are effective. Apply the five attributes listed in the text for effective segmentation to assess the usefulness of each of the following segments: (a) Internet users, (b) pager owners, (c) registered voters, and (d) adult students who return to college to get an undergraduate degree.

6. In 1994 Netscape appeared to be just another Silicon Valley start-up headed down the road to ruin. This was before the World Wide Web exploded to become the center of a generation's universe. As a result of this explosive Internet growth, Netscape's position in the marketplace has changed dramatically during the past several years. Choose one of the three market-coverage strategies described in the chapter and design a marketing strategy for Netscape for the next five years. Consider the market-coverage strategy of archrival Microsoft and other important competitors. Explain why your market-coverage strategy is best for the company. (See www.netscape.com for additional information.)

7. Social responsibility will be an important factor affecting the targeting marketing strategies of most firms in the new millennium. Provide an example of an organization that you believe takes a socially responsible approach to targeting markets. Explain your reasoning.

8. Apply the three steps for choosing and implementing a positioning strategy to assess in depth the positioning of one of the following products: (a) Dodge trucks, (b) Clausen pickles, (c) Amazon.com, and (d) American Express blue card. Explain your reasoning.

MARKETING APPLICATIONS

1. "Tweens"—youths aged 8 to 14—face pressures to grow up quickly. Research shows that the tweens are among the most targeted youth groups by today's marketers. They surround themselves with computers, electronic gadgets, music, clothing, magazines, and other gear that expresses their lifestyle. How do marketers reach this important group? Firms such as Nike, Gap, Sony, Pepsi, and Cover Girl have managed to strike the right notes. Primary influences on the tweens and their $12 billion in annual spending include friends, television and movies, and entertainment and sports idols. Such spending has commanded the attention of both traditional and Internet marketers. To learn more about marketing to tweens, visit the following Web sites: Gap—www.gap.com, Tommy Hilfiger—www.tommy.com, Delia's—www.delias.com, the Limited Too—www.limitedtoo.com, and Nintendo—www.nintendo.com.

   a. Using these and other data sources, profile the tweens market segment.
   b. How do companies appear to be marketing toward this segment?
   c. What strategies seem most popular with the Web sites mentioned above?
   d. Choose a company that currently markets to older youths and young adults. Explain how this company might go about attracting tweens to its products.

   e. What types of social responsibility issues might be encountered by a company targeting this group?

2. Is it time to trade in your highlighter for something more reliable? How many times during class or while studying do you underline a word, topic, or key phrase? Too many, right? Siemens (www.siemens.com) is betting that it has found a better way to process and store information. The Siemens Pocket Reader is a new portable digital highlighter. This small handheld scanner is easy to operate—you simply drag the battery-powered "pen" across the text you want to scan. The device stores up to 40,000 characters (about 20 pages) that you can then transfer to your PC for later processing and study. At $99.95 this new-age "highlighter" might well be worth the price.

   a. What market segments might be interested in this new product?
   b. What form of segmentation should Siemens employ?
   c. What market-coverage strategy makes the most sense?
   d. How should Siemens position the product?
   e. Outline the appeals that might be used in an advertising campaign for the product. What headline would be appropriate for an advertisement in your university or college newspaper?

INTERNET CONNECTIONS

ONLINE TARGET MARKETING

As the Internet becomes more mature, Web sites will focus to serve very specific target markets. College students are often surprised to learn that one of the most active groups online is older adults. ThirdAge is a Web site dedicated to this market segment. Visit www.thirdage.com and check out its media kit. Analyze how they characterize the demographic and psychographic profiles of their users. Now visit www.snowball.com (at the other end of the age spectrum) and complete the table for their users. You may also find useful information on these two market segments at American Demographics (www.demographics.com).

Statistic	Profile of a ThirdAge User	Profile of a Snowball User
Age		
Income		
Online purchase behavior		
Online investing		
Time spent online		
Online activities		
Psychographic characteristics		

FOR DISCUSSION

1. Who are some of the sponsors of the ThirdAge Web site? Of Snowball?
2. Browse around the sites. What types of products seem to appeal to ThirdAge users? To Snowball users?
3. Look at the list of the sites' sponsors. Do any of the brands that you find on the ThirdAge site also target the Snowball demographic? Give some examples.
4. In general, how do the articles differ in content for each market?
5. Based on questions 1–5, write a single-sentence positioning statement for each site.
6. What segmentation variable(s) is ThirdAge using for defining its target market?
7. How are the sites designed to appeal to their target audiences?

SAVVY SITES

- At TicketMaster's site (www.ticketmaster.com) one can locate *events* by *geographic location:* two important segmentation variables.
- The Yahoo search engine (www.yahoo.com) has a feature that allows users to receive a personalized Yahoo! page. This service, "My Yahoo," is a good example of micromarketing.
- Martha Stewart's site (www.marthastewart.com) targets a particular psycho-demographic: women who want to spend time beautifying their home or menus. Reading about her various media outlets is like reading a textbook study in market segmentation.

NOTES

1. See Kerri Walsh, "Soaps and Detergents," *Chemical Week,* January 28, 1998, pp. 27–29; Christine Bittar, "P&G Sets Anti-Fade Plan for Ailing Powder Detergents: New SKUs," *Brandweek,* March 22, 1999, p. 4; and information accessed online from www.pg.com and www.tide.com, February 2000.

2. Edward Baig, "Platinum Cards: Move Over AmEx," *Business Week,* August 19, 1996, p. 84; and "AmEx's No-Frills Snob Card," *Credit Card Management,* April 1997, pp. 12–14; and "AmEx Profit Up 25% in Quarter," *New York Times,* April 23, 1999, p. 4.

3. Laurel Cutler, quoted in "Stars of the 1980s Cast Their Light," *Fortune,* July 3, 1989, p. 76; and Robert E. Linneman and John L. Stanton Jr., *Making Niche Marketing Work: How to Grow Bigger by Acting Smaller* (New York: McGraw-Hill, 1991).

4. See Don Peppers and Martha Rogers, *The One-to-One Future: Building Relationships One Customer at a Time* (New York: Currency/Doubleday, 1993); B. Joseph Pine II, *Mass Customization* (Boston: Harvard Business School Press, 1993); B. Joseph Pine II, Don Peppers, and Martha Rogers, "Do You Want to Keep

Your Customers Forever?" *Harvard Business Review,* March–April 1995, pp. 103–14; James H. Gilmore and B. Joseph Pine II, "The Four Faces of Customization," *Harvard Business Review,* January–February 1997, pp. 91–101; and Don Peppers, Martha Rogers, and Bob Dorf, "Is Your Company Ready for One-to-One Marketing?" *Harvard Business Review,* January–February 1999, pp. 151–60.

5. See Philip Kotler, *Kotler on Marketing* (New York: Free Press, 1999), pp. 149–50.

6. Nelson D. Schwartz, "Still Perking After All These Years," *Fortune,* May 24, 1999, pp. 203–10.

7. See Bruce Hager, "Podunk Is Beckoning," *Business Week,* December 2, 1991, p. 76; David Greisling, "The Boonies Are Booming," *Business Week,* October 9, 1995, pp. 104–10; Leah Nathans Spiro, "Saks Tries on a Petite," *Business Week,* October 7, 1997, p. 8; and Stephanie Anderson Forest, "Look Who's Thinking Small," *Business Week,* May 17, 1999, pp. 68–70.

8. Accessed online at www.olay.com/facecare/fcbodytips.htm, November 1999.

9. "Sega to Target Adults with Brand Extensions," *Marketing Week,* March 12, 1998, p. 9.

10. Pat Sloan and Jack Neff, "With Aging Baby Boomers in Mind, P&G, Den-Mat Plan Launches," *Advertising Age,* April 13, 1998, pp. 3, 38.

11. Alice Z. Cuneo, "Advertisers Target Women, but Market Remains Elusive," *Advertising Age,* November 10, 1997, pp. 1, 24.

12. See "Automakers Learn Better Roads to Women's Market," *Marketing News,* October 12, 1992, p. 2; Alan Alder, "Purchasing Power Women's Buying Muscle Shops Up in Car Design, Marketing," *Chicago Tribune,* September 29, 1996, p. 21A; Jean Halliday, "GM Taps Harris to Help Lure Women," *Advertising Age,* February 17, 1997, pp. 1, 37; and Mary Louis Quinlin, "Women: We've Come a Long Way, Maybe," *Advertising Age,* February 13, 1999, p. 46.

13. "A Focus on Women at iVillage.com," *New York Times,* August 3, 1998, p. D6; Helene Stapinski, "Online Markets: You Go, Girls," *Sales & Marketing Management,* January 1999, pp. 47–48; and information accessed online at www.iVillage.com and www.girlson.com, February 2000.

14. See "The Wealthy," *Advertising Age,* April 3, 1995, p. S28; David Leonhardt, "Two-Tiered Marketing," *Business Week,* March 17, 1997, pp. 82–90; and Rebecca Piirto Heath, "Life on Easy Street," *American Demographics,* April 1997, pp. 33–37.

15. Brian Bremner, "Looking Downscale Without Looking Down," *Business Week,* October 8, 1990, pp. 62–67; Cyndee Miller, "The Have-Nots: Firms with the Right Products and Services Succeed Among Low-Income Consumers," *Marketing News,* August 1, 1994, pp. 1, 2; Wendy Zellner, "Leave the Driving to Lentzsch," *Business Week,* March 18, 1996, pp. 66–67; and Anne Faircloth, "Value Retailers Go Dollar for Dollar," *Fortune,* July 6, 1998, pp. 164–66.

16. "Lifestyle Marketing," *Progressive Grocer,* August 1997, pp. 107–10; and Philip Kotler, *Marketing Management: Analysis, Planning, Implementation, and Control,* 10th ed. (Upper Saddle River, NJ: Prentice Hall, 2000), pp. 266–67.

17. See Laurie Freeman and Cleveland Horton, "Spree: Honda's Scooters Ride the Cutting Edge," *Advertising Age,* September 5, 1985, pp. 3, 35; "Scooter Wars," *Cycle World,* February 1998, p. 26; and Honda's Web site at www.hondamotorcycle.com/scooter, November 1999.

18. See Mark Maremont, "The Hottest Thing Since the Flashbulb," *Business Week,* September 7, 1992; Bruce Nussbaum, "A Camera in a Wet Suit," *Business Week,* June 2, 1997, p. 109; Dan Richards, "The Smartest Disposable Cameras," *Travel Holiday,* December 1998, p. 20; and "Point and Click," *Golf Magazine,* February 1999, p. 102.

19. Stowe Shoemaker, "Segmenting the U.S. Travel Market According to Benefits Realized," *Journal of Travel Research,* Winter 1994, pp. 8–21.

20. See Ronald E. Goldsmith, Leisa Reinecke, and Mark Bonn, "An Empirical Study of Heavy Users of Travel Agencies," *Journal of Travel Research,* Summer 1994, pp. 38–43; and Warren Thayer, "Target Heavy Buyers!" *Frozen Food Age,* March 1998, pp. 22–24.

21. Norton Paley, "Cut Out for Success," *Sales & Marketing Management,* April 1994, pp. 43–44; Erick Schonfeld, "Paging Investors for a Smart Call," *Fortune,* January 15, 1996, p. 117; Michael J. Himowitz, "A Pager That Talks," *Fortune,* May 11, 1998, pp. 168–70; Joe Strupp, "Bloomberg Puts Stock in PageNet," *Editor & Publisher,* May 22, 1999, p. 16; and information from www.pagenet.com, November 1999.

22. Daniel S. Levine, "Justice Served," *Sales & Marketing Management,* May 1995, pp. 53–61.

23. For more on segmenting business markets, see John Berrigan and Carl Finkbeiner, *Segmentation Marketing: New Methods for Capturing Business* (New York: HarperBusiness, 1992); Rodney L. Griffith and Louis G. Pol, "Segmenting Industrial Markets," *Industrial Marketing Management* no. 23, 1994, pp. 39–46; Stavros P. Kalafatis and Vicki Cheston, "Normative Models and Practical Applications of Segmentation in Business Markets," *Industrial Marketing Management,* November 1997, pp. 519–30; and James C. Anderson and James A. Narus, *Business Market Management* (Upper Saddle River, NJ: Prentice Hall, 1999), pp. 44–47.

24. For example, see Philemon Oyewole, "Country Segmentation of the International Market Using ICP-Based Consumption Patterns," *Journal of Global Marketing,* 11, no. 4, 1998, pp. 75–94.

25. Cyndee Miller, "Teens Seen as the First Truly Global Consumers," *Advertising Age,* March 27, 1995, p. 9.

26. Shawn Tully, "Teens: The Most Global Market of All," *Fortune,* May 16, 1994, pp. 90–97. Also see Matthew Klein, "Teen Green," *American Demographics,* February 1998, p. 39.

27. See Michael Porter, *Competitive Advantage* (New York: Free Press, 1985), pp. 4–8, 234–36.

28. Nina Munk, "Why Women Find Lauder Mesmerizing," *Fortune,* May 25, 1998, pp. 97–106.

29. Paul Davidson, "Entrepreneurs Reap Riches from Net Niches," *USA Today,* April 20, 1998, p. B3; and information accessed online from www.ostrichesonline.com and www.mesomorphosis.com, February 2000.

30. See "PowerMaster," *Fortune,* January 13, 1992, p. 82; Herbert Rotfeld, "The FTC and Marketing Abuse," *Marketing News,* March 17, 1997, p. 4; and George G. Brenkert, "Marketing to Inner-City Blacks: PowerMaster and Moral Responsibility," *Business Ethics Quarterly,* January 1998, pp. 1–18.

31. Joseph Turow, "Breaking Up America: The Dark Side of Target Marketing," *American Demographics,* November 1997, pp. 51–54.

32. Roger O. Crockett, "They're Lining Up for Flicks in the 'Hood," *Business Week,* June 8, 1998, pp. 75–76.

33. For an interesting discussion of finding ways to differentiate marketing offers, see Ian C. MacMillan and Rita Gunther McGrath, "Discovering New Points of Differentiation," *Harvard Business Review,* July–August 1997, pp. 133–45.

34. See Philip Kotler, *Kotler on Marketing* (Upper Saddle River, NJ: Prentice Hall, 1999), pp. 59–63.

35. Mercedes M. Cardona and Jack Neff, "Everything's at a Premium," *Advertising Age,* August 2, 1999, pp. 12, 15.

COMPANY CASE

7

RJR's Eclipse: Rising from Premier's Ashes

PURSUING A BETTER CIGARETTE

In 1988, R. J. Reynolds Tobacco Company (RJR) capped a 10-year, $300 million investment program by introducing the Premier cigarette in several test markets. Reynolds and other tobacco companies had long dreamed of a better cigarette, one that would satisfy smokers without threatening their health or irritating others around them. RJR wanted to target Premier toward sophisticated, upscale, urban, educated, older (over-25) smokers. These smokers were hooked on smoking, but were looking for an alternative or trying to quit.

Premier was a very complex product to make and to use. It consisted of a small aluminum capsule that contained beads of glycerin impregnated with tobacco flavorings. The capsule was surrounded with tobacco. At the front end of the cigarette was a carbon tip that the smoker had to both light and heat properly during the lighting process. Air drawn through the cigarette was heated as it passed through the carbon. It then passed through the aluminum capsule where the heated air caused the glycerin beads to vaporize and carry the tobacco flavor through the cigarette's cooling filter to the smoker. Because only the carbon tip burned in the process, the cigarette did not burn down like a traditional cigarette. Also, because no tobacco was burning, the cigarette did not emit any "side-stream" smoke. Because of the cigarette's newness, packages carried instruction booklets that described the cigarette and explained how to light it properly.

Due to Premier's complexity and development cost, RJR priced it about 25 to 30 cents more per pack (about 25 percent) than other name-brand cigarettes. The company introduced the brand in Phoenix and Tucson, Arizona, and St. Louis, Missouri, in order to test its marketing strategy. It distributed the cigarettes through the normal cigarette distribution channels.

To promote Premier, RJR launched an expensive campaign. Contrary to most cigarette ads, Premier's ads contained lots of copy and "just the facts." They used the tag line, "The Cleaner Smoke," and encouraged smokers to try Premier for a week. To encourage trial, sales promotions offered two or more packs for the price of one.

However, despite all the time and money RJR put into developing and introducing Premier, smokers didn't buy it. They didn't like the taste or the difficulty they had in lighting and smoking the cigarettes. Rather than sticking with Premier for a week in order to get accustomed to Premier's taste, smokers decided quickly against the brand. After only five months, following consumer complaints that it smelled like burning lettuce and smoldering tennis shoes, RJR extinguished Premier.

IF AT FIRST YOU DON'T SUCCEED . . .

Despite Premier's costly failure, RJR continued to pursue its dream. During the next five years, it spent an estimated $200 million additional dollars on research and development to produce a better smokeless cigarette. During those five years, smokers increasingly felt like outcasts, as secondhand smoke became a bigger issue and more places banned smoking. In late 1994, the company announced its plan to introduce a new version in 1995 called Eclipse.

According to RJR, Eclipse targeted adult smokers over 35 with a slight skew toward women. The target smokers were "people who enjoy smoking but who'd rather not smell like a smoker" and people who did not want to expose friends and relatives to secondhand smoke. Reynolds did not, however, see Eclipse as a niche product. It claimed that the cigarette could eventually capture a 2 percent share of the nation's 46 million smokers. RJR's top brand, Camel, had just a 5 percent share, and Virginia Slims, a strong Philip Morris brand, had a 2.4 percent share.

Reynolds tested the new cigarette for more than a year, involving 12,000 smokers in 20 states in its research. It claimed that Eclipse scored well with smokers and their nonsmoking friends and family members, with more than 80 percent of both groups saying that the new product was a breakthrough. Although many smokers who tested the product did not believe it tasted as good as regular cigarettes, they indicated that it was a reasonable trade-off because there was less secondhand smoke—about 90 percent less than standard cigarettes.

Like Premier, the Eclipse has a charcoal tip wrapped in fiberglass insulation. When the consumer lights the charcoal, it heats to about 900 degrees Celsius, similar to a normal cigarette's burning temperature. However, the insulation contains the burning, so only hot air escapes as the smoker draws on the cigarette. The hot air passes through processed tobacco containing more than 50 percent glycerin that vaporizes at temperatures below those that burn tobacco. Unlike Premier, there is no aluminum capsule.

The heated glycerin makes a smokelike vapor that carries the tobacco flavor and nicotine. This is similar to water passing through coffee grounds in a coffee maker, picking up the coffee flavor but leaving the grounds behind. The vapor then passes through a standard filter into the smoker's mouth. Like Premier, the cigarette does not burn down. The tobacco taste simply goes away once the hot air has done its work. The smoker inhales and exhales smoke, but upon exhaling, the smoke quickly disappears, much as a person's smoky breath disappears on a cold morning. The company claimed that someone walking into a room where people were smoking Eclipses would notice only a faint aroma.

Like Premier, Eclipse does not burn tobacco; therefore it produces little side-stream smoke. Standard cigarette smoke is about 75 percent tars and related particles and about 25 percent water, glycerol, and nicotine. Eclipse's smoke is about 85 percent water, glycerol, and nicotine and about 15 percent tar. Observers pointed out, however, that other ultra-light cigarettes on the market had equally low tar and nicotine levels.

In mid-1996, RJR announced that Eclipse would enter the final testing phase in Chattanooga, Tennessee, a medium-size city where, it argued, the smokers were under societal pressure because of secondhand smoke. The company mailed smokers there a 15-minute video in which a female smoker complained that secondhand smoke was affecting her marriage to a nonsmoker, staining her walls and curtains, and permeating her clothes. The woman then told viewers about Eclipse's advantages.

Reynolds offered a free carton of Eclipse to smokers who agreed to participate in the test and to attend discovery groups of 50–100 people where RJR representatives explained and demonstrated the product. One spokesperson noted that getting consumers to try the product was very important. Because Eclipse was not a traditional product, it required a nontraditional approach.

Due to higher manufacturing costs, RJR priced Eclipse about 10 cents per pack above the price of premium brands. It spent about $110,000 on measured media in Chattanooga. Early ads showed a steaming teakettle with the copy, "Imagine a cigarette that smells like this." Later, the ad copy contained lines such as, "The smoke disappears. Your girlfriend doesn't."

In mid-1997, Reynolds added a second test market in Lincoln, Nebraska. One newspaper ad there showed a lone smoker at a table of friends with the taglines: "Smoke that disappears. Taste that doesn't." and "Less secondhand smoke. More firsthand pleasure." Billboards encouraged consumers to "Enjoy smoking without smelling like smoke," "Smoke on your couch, not on your porch," and "Smell like your cologne. Not your cigarettes."

Unlike the Chattanooga market, RJR limited distribution to about half of the tobacco sellers in Lincoln because it found that the product required explanation. In Chattanooga, it learned that unaided trial led to disappointed smokers. It also dropped the videos, realizing that smokers did not want to watch videos, and added more written instructions to the packs. RJR also priced Eclipse comparably to other premium brands.

DISAPPOINTING RESULTS

In late 1998, RJR announced it was rethinking Eclipse's marketing strategy, admitting that the cigarette was not meeting expectations and posed a vexing marketing challenge. Although some smokers liked Eclipse's flavor and the fact that it did not leave a tobacco smell in their homes and cars. Others panned the taste and complained about how difficult it was to light the cigarette. One tobacco dealer observed, "They were a novelty for a while. And a lot of people tried them. But now the new has worn off."

One RJR spokesperson noted, "It's a different cigarette. Smokers see its attributes but they compare it to their current cigarettes. They need to think of it as a different smoking experience. I think we've set wrong expectations." The spokesperson added, however, that the company was still committed to Eclipse. "We, by no means, have given up. We've put too much of an investment in it."

As of late 1999, Reynolds had not announced a decision as to Eclipse's future. However, it had test marketed the cigarette internationally. RJR tested the brand in Germany with the name Hi-Q. It licensed the technology in Japan and Sweden to other tobacco companies that were committed to marketing reduced-smoke cigarettes. In Japan, the cigarettes were called Airs. In Sweden they were called Inside.

It appears that Japan Tobacco (the Japanese licensee) has more confidence in the product than many people in the United States. In mid-1999, Japan Tobacco (JT) acquired RJR's international operations, including its German production facility and the Hi-Q brand. JT's Web site shows an illustration of the cigarette. Culturally, Japan stresses being polite and considerate of other people. One observer noted that perhaps the new Japanese cigarette is really a "considerette."

Questions

1. Analyze RJR's marketing strategy for Premier. What segmentation, targeting, and positioning problems do you see?
2. Analyze RJR's marketing strategy for Eclipse. What segmentation, targeting, and positioning problems do you see?
3. Compare the company's marketing strategies for the two cigarettes. How did it change the strategy for Eclipse?
4. Should RJR introduce Eclipse? What marketing recommendations would you make to the company if it decides to introduce the cigarette?
5. Do you believe Eclipse might be more successful in foreign markets? Why or why not?

Sources: Melanie Wells, "Low-Smoke Cigarette Lacks Sales Spark," *USA Today,* October 13, 1998, p. 5B; Melanie Wells, "RJR Takes Smokeless Test," *USA Today,* October 27, 1997, p. 1B; Judann Pollack, "RJR Expands Test of Low-Smoke Eclipse," *Advertising Age,* August 25, 1997, p. 1; Associated Press, "Smokeless Cigarettes Not Catching On with Consumers," *Marketing News TM,* August 4, 1997, p. 21; John Schwartz, "New Cigarette Clears the Smoke, but the Heat Is Still On," *Washington Post,* May 27, 1996, p. A03; Michelle Williams, "RJR Markets Smokeless Cigarette in Chattanooga," Associated Press, April 30, 1996; Richard Tomkins, "Tobacco's Holy Grail—A Look at the Lure of the Smokeless Cigarette, "*Financial Times* (London), December 2, 1994, p. 12; Stuart Elliott, "R.J. Reynolds Tobacco Renews Its Hope That Where There's Low Smoke, There's Marketing Fire," *New York Times,* November 29, 1994; Philip J. Hilts, "Little Smoke, Little Tar, but Full Dose of Nicotine," *New York Times,* November 27, 1994, p. 1; and Chris Burritt, "Don't Hold Your Breath . . . Low-Smoke Cigarette Still Doesn't Taste Right, Reynolds Says," *Atlanta Journal and Constitution,* November 28, 1994.

ENTERPRISE RENT-A-CAR: SELLING THE DREAM

IN THE FAST LANE

On a bright January 1998 morning, Dean Pittman, Enterprise Rent-A-Car's area rental manager for Durham/Chapel Hill, North Carolina, got out of his Dodge Intrepid at Enterprise's new office in Durham. He admired the line of clean cars and the new office with its green and white Enterprise sign. To Dean, it seemed that dreams really did come true.

A little over six years ago, Dean had graduated with a degree in industrial relations from the University of North Carolina at Chapel Hill. When he'd first scheduled a job interview with Enterprise, Dean had been skeptical. Although he didn't know much about the company, he wasn't certain that he'd like renting cars for a living or working a retail job that included washing cars. But he'd seen the potential to advance quickly, to develop strong management skills, and to learn about running a business.

Once hired, Dean had been promoted quickly to management assistant, then to branch manager at Enterprise's new office in Rocky Mount, North Carolina. A year ago, Enterprise had made him an area manager, giving him responsibility for the Durham/Chapel Hill area—supervising three branch offices with 22 employees, 495 cars, and annual revenues of more than $3 million. Dean felt as though he was running his own business. Enterprise gave its managers considerable autonomy and paid them based on a percentage of their branches' profits. Dean's starting salary had been in line with those of his classmates, but within three years his pay had doubled, and now it had tripled. There couldn't be many other companies, Dean thought, in which a person his age could have so much responsibility, so much fun, and such high earnings.

COMPANY BACKGROUND

Dean's good fortune mirrored that of Enterprise itself. The company's founder Jack Taylor started Enterprise in 1962 with a single location and 17 cars in St. Louis, Missouri. Since then, Enterprise had grown dramatically to become the nation's largest rental car company. In fact, Enterprise had grown at a compound annual rate of 25 percent for the past 11 years. By 1997, the company had more than 3,000 locations, 325,000 cars, $3.1 billion in sales, $5 billion in assets, and 30,000 employees.

A WINNING STRATEGY

Analysts attribute Enterprise's success to several factors. First, cars have become a more important part in people's lives. They just can't do without their cars, even for a day or two. And, as more and more families have both adults working or are single-parent families, there is often no one else in the family who can pick up people when they have car problems. Tied in to this, the courts ruled in the 1970s that insurance companies had to offer coverage so that insured motorists could rent a replacement car if they lost the use of their car. As a result, those insurance companies began to offer rental replacement coverage in their policies.

Beyond these environmental factors, the company's success resulted from its single-minded focus on one segment of the rental car market. Instead of following Hertz, Avis, and other rental car companies by setting up branches at airports to serve national travelers, Enterprise built an extensive network of neighborhood locations serving the "home-city" market—people who needed rental cars as replacements when their cars were wrecked, stolen, or in the shop being repaired. Because these customers were often stranded at a body shop or repair garage and had no easy way to get to a rental office, Enterprise offered to pick them up.

However, Enterprise's first customer in the replacement market is often the referral source—the insurance agent or auto body shop employee who recommends Enterprise to the stranded customer. Few of Enterprise's customers get up in the morning thinking they'll need to rent a car—but then they're involved in a wreck. So, employees visit the referral sources frequently, often taking them donuts or pizza as a way of thanking them for their business. They call on referral sources who may not be doing business with Enterprise, and they keep insurance agents apprised of a car's repair status.

Auto Rental News, an industry trade publication, estimates that the replacement market is growing at 10 to 15 percent per year (see Exhibit 1). The entire rental car market, including airport rentals and the travel segment, is about $14.6 billion.

Enterprise's rental rates in the replacement market tended to be lower than rates for comparable rentals at airport-based companies—some analysts estimated up to 30 percent lower. The company tended to locate its offices in city areas where

**EXHIBIT I   THE REPLACEMENT CAR RENTAL MARKET
COMPETITORS, REVENUE ESTIMATES, AND OTHER MARKET DATA[1]**

I.	Competitor	1996 U.S. Revenue	% Replacement[2]	Cars in Service (U.S.)
1.	Enterprise Rent-A-Car	$2.61 billion[3]	78%	315,000
2.	Ford and Chrysler Systems	$490 million	92	82,250
3.	Snappy Car Rental	$100 million	100	15,500
4.	U-Save Auto Rental	$115 million	60	13,500
5.	Rent-A-Wreck	$ 85 million	35	10,942
6.	Premier Car Rental	$ 66 million	100	9,500
7.	Advantage Rent-A-Car	$ 76 million	33	9,000
8.	Spirit Rent-A-Car	$ 50 million	100	7,500
9.	Super Star Rent-A-Car	$ 43 million	100	5,250
10.	Many independent companies	$750 million	53	
11.	Airport-based companies: Hertz, Avis, Budget, Dollar, National, Thrifty, Alamo[4]	$360 million	100	

II.   Industry Average Pricing

Estimated industry average price per day for replacement rentals, not including additional insurance coverages or other rentals, such as cellular phones: Industry average daily rental is $23. Industry average rental period for replacement rentals is 12 days. Additional insurance coverages produce about 5% of revenue, with other rental options producing about 2% of revenue. Per-day rental rates are often established through rational contracts with insurance companies or automobile manufacturers' or dealers' warranty reimbursement programs.

There are approximately 150 major U.S. airport rental markets. Airport-based rental rates vary widely depending on competition. Airport rental companies also negotiate corporate rates with individual companies.

III.   Overall Rent-A-Car Market

Overall 1996 U.S. market estimated at $14.62 billion broken down as follows:
Business rentals—40%, Leisure/Discretionary rentals—33%, Replacement rentals—27%

IV.   Advertising

Advertising Age estimated that U.S. car rental companies spent $384.4 million in measured advertising in 1994, about 2.8% of revenue. It estimated that Enterprise spent $22 million in 1994, up from $13 million in 1993. Enterprise's 1994 spending compared with $47 million spent by Hertz, $31 million by Alamo, and $24 million by Avis. (Sept. 27, 1995)

[1]Estimates provided by *Auto Rental News*. Data is for case discussion purposes only. Use in case does not imply certification of estimates by Enterprise.

[2]Replacement market includes insurance replacement rentals, mechanical repair rentals, dealer loaner rentals, and warranty rentals.

[3]*Auto Rental News* estimate of U.S. rental revenue excluding leasing. seven percent of revenue is from airport/traveler rentals, and 93% is from local market rentals. Local market includes replacement, business, and leisure rentals, with business and leisure about equal for Enterprise.

[4]Includes the portion of airport-based companies' revenue from local market operations that target the replacement market, including Hertz, $130,000; Budget, $126,000; National, $135,000; Dollar, $63,500; and Thrifty, $34,000.

Source: *Auto Rental News*

the rent was much lower than at the airport. It also kept its cars a little longer than the typical airport–rental company. These two factors, and a focus on efficient operations, helped it keep rates lower.

A second segment of the home–city market that Enterprise has begun to serve is the "discretionary" or "leisure/vacation" segment. Friends or relatives may visit and need a car, or the family may decide to take a vacation and feel that the family car is really not as dependable or comfortable as they would like. More and more people are renting for trips just to keep the extra miles off the family car.

Finally, Enterprise is also experiencing growth in the local corporate market. Many small businesses and some large ones have found that it's cheaper and easier for them to rent their fleets from Enterprise than to try to maintain their own fleets. Colleges and universities have realized that it's cheaper to rent a 15-passenger van when the soccer team travels than to keep a van full time for only occasional use.

Enterprise's success in the home-city market has attracted competition. Although Enterprise had the largest share of that market, a handful of major regional competitors, such as Spirit and Snappy, when combined, captured a large market share. The airport rental companies, such as Hertz, Avis, and Alamo, got only a small portion of the home-city business. Hertz is just starting a small operation that focuses on the home-city replacement market. Local "mom-and-pop" firms that often have just one office and a few cars serve the remainder of the market.

Enterprise grew very quietly, depending on its referral sources and word-of-mouth promotion. It wasn't until 1989 that the company did its first national advertising. At that time, marketing research demonstrated that if you showed people a list of company names and asked them to identify the rental car companies, only about 20 percent knew Enterprise. The company started advertising nationally but kept its ads low key. By 1997, it had more than quadrupled its annual advertising and promotion spending, using the theme "Pick Enterprise. We'll pick you up." However, although the company's research shows that Enterprise's overall awareness is up substantially, only about one-third of those surveyed are aware of the company's pick-up service, and only about one-third are aware that it has branches nearby.

THE IMPORTANCE OF CULTURE

Although the company's strategy worked well, that strategy was driven by Jack Taylor's philosophy. Taylor believed that the employees' and the company's first job was to serve the customer. From the beginning Taylor urged his employees to do whatever they had to do in order to make the customer happy. Sometimes it meant waiving charges. Other times, it meant stopping everything and running out to pick up a stranded customer. Employees knew that they needed to do whatever it took to make customers happy.

Further, Taylor believed that after customers came employees. He believed that to satisfy customers, a company had to have satisfied, challenged employees who worked as a team. All of Enterprise's branch employees, from assistant manager on up, earn a substantial portion of their pay based on branch profitability. In addition, the company has a profit-sharing plan for all employees. Enterprise hired primarily college graduates and promoted from within. Ninety-nine percent of its managers started as management trainees at the branch level, so they understand the customer-oriented culture. As important, they understand their local markets and the needs of customers in those markets.

Thus, Enterprise is really a collection of small, independent businesses, with the corporation providing capital and logistical support.

Finally, Taylor believed that if the company took care of its customers and employees, profits would follow. Sure enough, Enterprise has consistently been profitable in an industry where many firms have not been.

WHAT'S NEXT?

The question is, how can Enterprise continue to grow and prosper in the face of growing competition? The company believes it can double its revenues by the year 2001, but to do so it must wrestle with a number of growth related issues.

First, it must continue to attract and retain college graduates. The company needed to hire over 5,000 management trainees in 1997 alone, and that number will increase. Yet many college grads, like Dean Pittman, may know little or nothing about Enterprise and may have negative feelings about working for a rental car company. How can Enterprise do a better job of recruiting college graduates?

Second, Enterprise must examine its marketing strategy. Which markets should it target? How should it position itself in those markets? Are there new services it could offer that would make sense given its current strategy? How can it do a better job of increasing Enterprise's awareness among targeted customers? How should it respond as new competitors, including the airport-based firms such as Hertz, attack the home-city market?

Perhaps the most important question is how can Enterprise continue to grow without losing its focus and without losing the corporate culture that has been so important in helping it and its employees, like Dean Pittman, realize their dreams?

Questions

1. How are the buyer decision processes different for someone renting a replacement car because of a wreck, for someone renting a car for leisure/vacation purposes, for a business renting a car, and for a college graduate looking for a job?
2. What are the bases for segmenting the rental car market?
3. What marketing recommendations would you make to Enterprise to help it improve its recruiting?
4. What marketing recommendations would you make to Enterprise to improve its marketing strategy?
5. Will Enterprise's strategy work in international markets?

Source: Enterprise Rent-A-Car supported development of this case. *Auto Rental News* also provided information. This case is adapted from a longer case with the same title authored by Lew Brown, Gary Armstrong, and Philip Kotler, available from Enterprise.

After studying this chapter, you should be able to
1. define *product* and the major classifications of products and services
2. describe the roles of product and service branding, packaging, labeling, and product support services
3. explain the decisions companies make when developing product lines and mixes
4. identify the four characteristics that affect the marketing of a service
5. discuss the additional marketing considerations for services

PRODUCT AND SERVICES STRATEGY

Each year, cosmetics companies sell billions of dollars' worth of potions, lotions, and fragrances to consumers around the world. In one sense, these products are no more than careful mixtures of oils and chemicals that have nice scents and soothing properties. But the cosmetics companies know that they sell much more than just mixtures of ingredients—they sell the promise

a perfume's packaging is an important product attribute—the package and bottle are the most real symbols of the perfume and its image. The *name* is also important—fragrance names such as Obsession, Passion, Gossip, Wildheart, Opium, Joy, White Linen, Youth Dew, and Eternity suggest that the perfumes will do something more than just make you smell better.

5S own your mind and body*

of what these concoctions will do for the people who use them.

Of course, in the cosmetics business, like anywhere else, quality and performance contribute to success or failure. For example, perfume marketers agree, "No smell; no sell." However, $180-an-ounce perfume may cost no more than $10 to produce. Thus, to perfume consumers, many things beyond the scent and a few dollars' worth of ingredients add to a perfume's allure. For instance,

What *is* the promise of cosmetics? The following account by a *New York Times* reporter suggests the extent to which cosmetics take on meaning far beyond their physical makeup.

Last week I bathed in purple water (*I Trust* bubble bath, made by Philosophy) and powdered up with pink powder (*Rebirth,* by 5S, "to renew the spirit and recharge the soul"). My moisturizer was *Bliss* (Chakra VII by Aveda, for "the joyful enlightenment and soaring of the spirit"); my nail polish was *Spiritual* (by Tony and Tina, "to aid connection with the higher self"). My teeth were clean, my heart was open—however, my bathroom was so crowded with bottles and brochures, the latest tools and totems from the human potential movement, that I could hardly find my third eye.

If you are looking for enlightenment in all the wrong places, cosmetics companies are eager to help. Because today, feeling good is the new religion. And cosmetics companies are the newest of the new prophets, turning the old notion of hope in a jar on its head.

"Cosmetics are our satellite to the divine!" This is what you'll hear from Tony and Tina, for example. Tony and Tina (Anthony Gillis and Cristina Bornstein) are nice young artists. He's from London, she grew up in New York. Chakra nail polish, which they invented for an installation at the Gershwin Gallery in Manhattan two years ago, was intended as an ironic commentary on the beauty business. But then a friend suggested they get into the beauty business, and now Tony and Tina have a $2 million cosmetics company with a mission statement: "To aid in the evolution of human consciousness." Their products include nail polishes (Vibrational Remedies) in colors meant to do nice things to your chakras, as well as body glitter and hair mascara, lipstick and eyeshadow. You can buy them at Fred Segal, Nordstrom, and Bloomingdale's, where last month they outsold Hard Candy and Urban Decay. "We think color therapy is going to be the new medicine," said Tony.

Rainbows are proliferating as rapidly in the New Age as angels once did. Philosophy, a three-year-old Arizona company, makes a sort of head/heart kit—"a self-help program," the company insists—called the *Rainbow Connection.* You pay $45 for seven bottles of colored bubble bath in a metal box. "Choose your colored bath according to the area of your emotional life that needs attention, i.e., self-love, self-worth," the brochure reads. "My role as I see it," said Christina Carlino, Philosophy's founder, "is to help you stay on your destiny path. It's not about what you look like. Beauty is defined by your deeds."

5S, a new sprout of the Japanese cosmetics company Shiseido, offers a regimen that plays, the company says, on the "fundamental and mythical significance of 5" (Five Pillars of Islam, Five Classics of Confucianism, and so on) and which is organized into emotional rather than physical categories. At the 5S store in SoHo, you don't buy things for dry skin, you buy things that are "energizing" or "nurturing" or "adoring." The company also believes in color therapy. Hence, *Rebirth,* products tinted "nouveau pink" (the color of bubble gum). A customer can achieve rebirth with 5S pink soap, pink powder, and pink toner.

Here are products that are not intended to make you look better, but to make you act better, feel better, and be a better person. You don't need a month's visit to India to find your higher self; you need only buy this bubble bath, that lipstick, this night cream. The beauty business's old come-on (trap your man!) has been swept away in favor of a new pitch: I don't have wrinkles anymore. I've got a chakra blockage.

Of course, who knew about chakras before Aveda? In 1989, the plant-based, eco-friendly cosmetics company Aveda trademarked Chakras I through VII to use as titles for moisturizers and scents. Chakra products were perhaps a little ahead of their time back then. However, the purchase of Aveda nine months ago by the Estée Lauder Companies, the General Motors of the cosmetics world, suggests that the pendulum of history has finally caught up. "Aveda isn't a marketing idea," says Jeanette Wagner, the vice chairperson of Estée Lauder. "It is a passionately held belief." Estée Lauder plans to extend the Aveda concept through "lifestyle" stores built with sustainable woods and nontoxic elements, selling "beauty, health, lifestyle, you name it." "From my point of view," Wagner says, "the appeal is first the spirituality, and then the products."

All this might sound like only so much flim-flam, but the underlying point is legitimate. The success of such brands affirms that products really are more than just the physical entities. When a woman buys cosmetics, she really does buy much, much more than just oils, chemicals, and fragrances. The cosmetic's image, its promises and positioning, its ingredients, its name and package, the company that makes it, the stores that sell it—all become a part of the total cosmetic product. When Aveda, Philosophy, and 5S sell cosmetics, they sell more than just tangible goods. They sell lifestyle, self-expression, exclusivity, and spirituality; achievement, success, and status; romance, passion, and fantasy; memories, hopes, and dreams.[1]

Clearly, cosmetics are more than just cosmetics when Aveda sells them. This chapter begins with a deceptively simple question: *What is a product?* After answering this question, we look at ways to classify products in consumer and business markets. Then we discuss the important decisions that marketers make regarding individual products, product lines, and product mixes. Finally, we examine the characteristics and marketing requirements of a special form of product—services.

 # WHAT IS A PRODUCT?

Product
Anything that can be offered to a market for attention, acquisition, use, or consumption that might satisfy a want or need.

Service
Any activity or benefit that one party can offer to another that is essentially intangible and does not result in the ownership of anything.

A Sony CD player, a Ford Taurus, a Costa Rican vacation, a Caffé Mocha at Starbucks, Charles Schwab online investment services, and advice from your family doctor—all are products. We define a **product** as anything that can be offered to a market for attention, acquisition, use, or consumption and that might satisfy a want or need. Products include more than just tangible goods. Broadly defined, products include physical objects, services, events, persons, places, organizations, ideas, or mixes of these entities. Thus, throughout this text, we use the term *product* broadly to include any or all of these entities.

Because of their importance in the world economy, we give special attention to services. **Services** are a form of product that consist of activities, benefits, or satisfactions offered for sale that are essentially intangible and do not result in the ownership of anything. Examples are banking, hotel, tax preparation, and home repair services. We will look at services more closely in a section at the end of this chapter.

Products, Services, and Experiences

A company's offer to the marketplace often includes both tangible goods and services. Each component can be a minor or a major part of the total offer. At one extreme, the offer may consist of a *pure tangible good,* such as soap, toothpaste, or salt—no services accompany the product. At the other extreme are *pure services,* for which the offer consists primarily of a service. Examples include a doctor's exam or financial services. Between these two extremes, however, many goods and services combinations are possible.

For example, a company's offer may consist of a *tangible good with accompanying services.* Ford offers more than just automobiles. Its offer also includes repair and maintenance services, warranty fulfillment, showrooms and waiting areas, and a host of other support services. A *hybrid offer* consists of equal parts of goods and services. For instance, people patronize restaurants both for their food and their service. A *service with accompanying minor goods* consists of a major service along with supporting goods. For example, American Airlines passengers primarily buy transportation service, but the trip also includes some tangibles, such as food, drinks, and an airline magazine. The service also requires a capital intensive good—an airplane—for its delivery, but the primary offer is a service.

Today, as products and services become more and more commoditized, many companies are moving to a new level in creating value for their customers. To differentiate their offers, they are developing and delivering total customer *experiences.* Whereas products are tangible and services are intangible, experiences are memorable. Whereas products and services are external, experiences are personal and take place in the minds of individual consumers. Companies that market experiences realize that customers are really buying much more than just products and services. They are buying what those offers will *do* for them—the experiences they gain in purchasing and consuming these products and services (see Marketing Highlight 8.1).

BEYOND PRODUCTS AND SERVICES: WELCOME TO THE EXPERIENCE ECONOMY

In their book, *The Experience Economy,* Joseph Pine and James Gilmore argue that, as products and services become less and less differentiated, companies are moving to a new level in creating value for customers. As the next step in differentiating their offers, beyond simply making products and delivering services, companies are staging, marketing, and delivering memorable experiences. Consider the evolution of the birthday cake:

> [In an] *agrarian* economy, mothers made birthday cakes from scratch, mixing farm commodities (flour, sugar, butter, and eggs) that together cost mere dimes. As the *goods-based* industrial economy advanced, moms paid a dollar or two to Betty Crocker for premixed ingredients. Later, when the *service* economy took hold, busy parents ordered cakes from the bakery or grocery store, which, at $10 or $15, cost ten times as much as the packaged ingredients. Now, . . . time-

starved parents neither make the birthday cake nor even throw the party. Instead, they spend $100 or more to "outsource" the entire event to Chuck E. Cheese's, the Discovery Zone, the Mining Company, or some other business that stages a memorable event for the kids—and often throws in the cake for free. Welcome to the emerging *experience* economy. . . . From now on, leading-edge companies—whether they sell to consumers or businesses—will find that the next competitive battleground lies in staging experiences.

Experiences are sometimes confused with services, but experiences are as distinct from services as services are distinct from goods. Whereas products and services are external, experiences exist only in the mind of the individual. They are rich with emotional, physical, intellectual, or spiritual sensations created within the consumer. According to Pine and Gilmore:

An experience occurs when a company intentionally uses services as the stage, and goods as props, to engage individual customers in a way that creates a memorable event. . . . To appreciate the difference between services and experiences, recall the episode of the old television show *Taxi* in which Iggy, a usually atrocious (but fun-loving) cab driver, decided to become the best taxi driver in the world. He served sandwiches and drinks, conducted tours of the city, and even sang Frank Sinatra tunes. By engaging passengers in a way that turned an ordinary cab ride into a memorable event, Iggy created something else entirely—a distinct economic offering. The experience of riding in his cab was more valuable to his customers than the service of being transported by the cab—and in the TV show, at least, Iggy's customers happily responded by giving bigger tips. By asking to go around the block again, one patron even paid more for poorer service just to prolong his enjoyment. The service Iggy provided—taxi transportation—was simply the stage for the experience that he was really selling.

Experiences have always been important in the entertainment industry—Disney has long manufactured memories through its movies and theme parks. Today, however, all kinds of firms are recasting their traditional goods and services to create experiences. For example, restaurants create value well beyond the food they serve. Starbucks patrons are paying for more than just coffee. "Customers at Starbucks are paying for staged experiences," comments

Marketing experiences: Sony's METREON markets an "interactive entertainment experience: four floors and 350,000 square feet jam-packed with ways to entertain and escape into a whole new reality."

one analyst. "The company treats patrons to poetry on its wallpaper and tabletops, jaunty apron-clad performers behind the espresso machine, and an interior ambience that's both cozy and slick, marked by earth tones, brushed steel, and retro music (also for sale). Few people leave without feeling a little more affluent, sophisticated, or jazzed."

Many retailers also stage experiences. Niketown stores create "shoppertainment" by offering interactive displays, engaging activities, and promotional events in a stimulating shopping environment. At stores such as Sharper Image and Brookstone, "people play with the gadgets, listen to miniaturized stereo equipment, sit in massage chairs, and then leave without paying for what they valued, namely, the experience."

In San Francisco, Sony of America has developed Metreon, an "interactive entertainment experience," where visitors can shop, eat, drink, play, or simply soak up the experiences (check it out at www.metreon.com). The huge Metreon complex features 15 theaters, including a Sony-IMAX theatre, eight theme restaurants, and several interactive attractions, such as "Where the Wild Things Are" (an interactive playspace inspired by Maurice Sendak's popular children's book) and Moebius's Airtight Garage (an adventure zone featuring original interactive games inspired by French graphic novelist Jean Giraud). Visitors can also experience any of nine interactive stores, including the flagship Discovery Channel Store: "Destination San Francisco" (featuring interactive educational exhibits inspired by programming from the Discovery Channel, TLC,

and Animal Planet cable networks), Sony Style (a high-touch boutique of Sony products), and MicrosoftSF (where shoppers can play with the latest computer software and hardware). In all, Metreon offers a dazzling experience that far transcends the goods and services assortment it contains. Sony sums up the experience this way:

Use your eyes, ears, hands, and brain . . . sensory overload to a phenomenal degree. . . . Four floors and 350,000 square feet jam-packed with ways to entertain and escape into a whole new reality. Dazzle a date. Bring wonder to your kids. Shop in amazement. Have fun with your friends. Whenever you want real entertainment, head to Metreon.

The experience economy goes beyond the entertainment and retailing businesses. All companies stage experiences whenever they engage customers in a personal, memorable way:

In the travel business, former British Airways chairman Sir Colin Marshall has noted that the "commodity mind-set" is to "think that a business is merely performing a function in our case, transporting people from point A to point B on time and at the lowest possible price." What British Airways does, according to Sir Colin, is "to go beyond the function and compete on the basis of providing an experience." The company uses its base service (the travel itself) as the stage for a distinctive en route experience—one that attempts to transform air travel into a respite from the traveler's normally frenetic life.

Business-to-business marketers also stage experiences for their customers. For example, one Minneapolis computer installation and repair company has found a way to turn its otherwise

humdrum service into a memorable encounter. Calling itself the Geek Squad, it sends "special agents" dressed in white shirts with thin black ties and pocket protectors, carrying badges, and driving old cars. Similarly, Silicon Graphics creates an experience as elaborate as any Disney attraction:

[Its] Visionarium Reality Center at corporate headquarters in Mountain View, California, brings customers and engineers together in an environment where they can interact with real-time, three-dimensional product visualizations. Customers can view, hear, and touch—as well as drive, walk, or fly—through myriad product possibilities. [According to one Silicon Graphics executive,] "This is experiential computing at its ultimate, where our customers can know what their products will look like, sound like, and feel like before manufacturing."

Thus, as we move into the new millennium, marketers seeking new ways to bring value to customers must look beyond the goods and services they make and sell. They must find ways to turn their offers into total customer experiences. As the experience economy grows, Pine and Gilmore caution, it "threatens to render irrelevant those who relegate themselves to the diminishing world of goods and services."

Sources: Excerpts and quotes from "Welcome to the Experience Economy," *Harvard Business Review,* July–August 1998, pp. 97–105; Wade Roush, "Now Playing: Your Business," *Technology Review,* May–June 1999, p. 96; and Sony's METREON Web site, www.metreon.com, September 1999. Also see B. Joseph Pine and James H. Gilmore, *The Experience Economy* (New York: Free Press, 1999).

Levels of Product

Product planners need to think about products and services on three levels. The most basic level is the *core product,* which addresses the question *What is the buyer really buying?* As Figure 8.1 illustrates, the core product stands at the center of the total product. It consists of the core, problem-solving benefits that consumers seek when they buy a product or service. A woman buying lipstick buys more than lip color. Charles Revson of Revlon saw this early: "In the factory, we make cosmetics; in the store, we sell hope." Ritz-Carlton Hotels knows that it offers its guests more than simply rooms for rent—it provides "memorable travel experiences." Thus, when designing products, marketers must first define the core of *benefits* the product will provide to consumers. They must understand the total customer *experience* that surrounds the purchase and use of the product.

The product planner must next build an *actual product* around the core product. Actual products may have as many as five characteristics: a quality level, features, design, a brand name, and packaging. For example, a Sony camcorder is an actual product. Its name, parts, styling, features, packaging, and other attributes have all been combined carefully to deliver the core benefit—a convenient, high-quality way to capture important moments.

Finally, the product planner must build an *augmented product* around the core and actual products by offering additional consumer services and benefits. Sony must offer more than just a camcorder. It must provide consumers with a complete solution to their picture-taking problems. Thus, when consumers buy a Sony camcorder, Sony and its dealers also might give buyers a warranty on parts and workmanship, instructions on how to use the camcorder, quick repair services when needed, and a toll-free telephone number to call if they have problems or questions.

Therefore, a product is more than a simple set of tangible features. Consumers tend to see products as complex bundles of benefits that satisfy their needs. When developing products, marketers first must identify the *core* consumer needs the product will satisfy. They must then design the *actual* product and find ways to *augment* it in order to create the bundle of benefits that will best satisfy consumers.

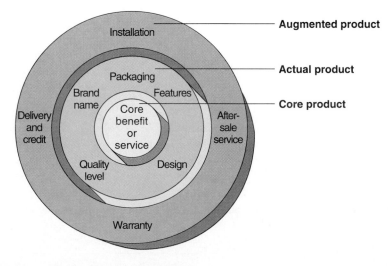

FIGURE 8.1   Three levels of product

PRODUCT CLASSIFICATIONS

Products and services fall into two broad classes based on the types of consumers that use them—*consumer products* and *industrial products.* Broadly defined, products also include other marketable entities such as experiences, organizations, persons, places, and ideas.

Consumer Products

Consumer products are those bought by final consumers for personal consumption. Marketers usually classify these goods further based on how consumers go about buying them. Consumer products include *convenience products, shopping products, specialty products,* and *unsought products.* These products differ in the ways consumers buy them and therefore in how they are marketed (see Table 8.1).

Convenience products are consumer products and services that the customer usually buys frequently, immediately, and with a minimum of comparison and buying effort. Examples include soap, candy, newspapers, and fast food. Convenience products are usually low priced, and marketers place them in many locations to make them readily available when customers need them.

Shopping products are less frequently purchased consumer products and services that customers compare carefully on suitability, quality, price, and style. When buying shopping products and services, consumers spend much time and effort in gathering information and making comparisons. Examples include furniture, clothing, used cars, major appliances, and hotel and motel services. Shopping products marketers usually distribute their products through fewer outlets but provide deeper sales support to help customers in their comparison efforts.

Consumer product
Product bought by final consumer for personal consumption.

Convenience product
Consumer product that the customer usually buys frequently, immediately, and with a minimum of comparison and buying effort.

Shopping product
Consumer good that the customer, in the process of selection and purchase, characteristically compares on such bases as suitability, quality, price, and style.

TABLE 8.1   MARKETING CONSIDERATIONS FOR CONSUMER PRODUCTS

Marketing Considerations	Type of Consumer Product			
	Convenience	**Shopping**	**Specialty**	**Unsought**
Customer buying behavior	Frequent purchase, little planning, little comparison or shopping effort, low customer involvement	Less frequent purchase, much planning and shopping effort, comparison of brands on price, quality, style	Strong brand preference and loyalty, special purchase effort, little comparison of brands, low price sensitivity	Little product awareness, knowledge (or, if aware, little or even negative interest)
Price	Low Price	Higher price	High price	Varies
Distribution	Widespread distribution, convenient locations	Selective distribution in fewer outlets	Exclusive distribution in only one or a few outlets per market area	Varies
Promotion	Mass promotion by the producer	Advertising and personal selling by both producer and resellers	More carefully targeted promotion by both producer and resellers	Aggressive advertising and personal selling by producer and resellers
Examples	Toothpaste, magazines, laundry detergent	Major appliances, televisions, furniture, clothing	Luxury goods, such as Rolex watches or fine crystal	Life insurance, Red Cross blood donations

Specialty product
Consumer product with unique characteristics or brand identification for which a significant group of buyers is willing to make a special purchase effort.

Specialty products are consumer products and services with unique characteristics or brand identification for which a significant group of buyers is willing to make a special purchase effort. Examples include specific brands and types of cars, high-priced photographic equipment, designer clothes, and the services of medical or legal specialists. A Lamborghini automobile, for example, is a specialty product because buyers are usually willing to travel great distances to buy one. Buyers normally do not compare specialty products. They invest only the time needed to reach dealers carrying the wanted products.

Unsought product
Consumer product that the consumer either does not know about or knows about but does not normally think of buying.

Unsought products are consumer products that the consumer either does not know about or knows about but does not normally think of buying. Most major new innovations are unsought until the consumer becomes aware of them through advertising. Classic examples of known but unsought products and services are life insurance and blood donations to the Red Cross. By their very nature, unsought products require a lot of advertising, personal selling, and other marketing efforts.

Industrial Products

Industrial product
Product bought by individuals and organizations for further processing or for use in conducting a business.

Industrial products are those purchased for further processing or for use in conducting a business. Thus, the distinction between a consumer product and an industrial product is based on the *purpose* for which the product is bought. If a consumer buys a lawn mower for use around home, the lawn mower is a consumer product. If the same consumer buys the same lawn mower for use in a landscaping business, the lawn mower is an industrial product.

Business services: ServiceMaster supplies business services for a wide range of organizations. This advertisement to schools and colleges offers services ranging from custodial, grounds, technology, and energy management services to maintenance and food services.

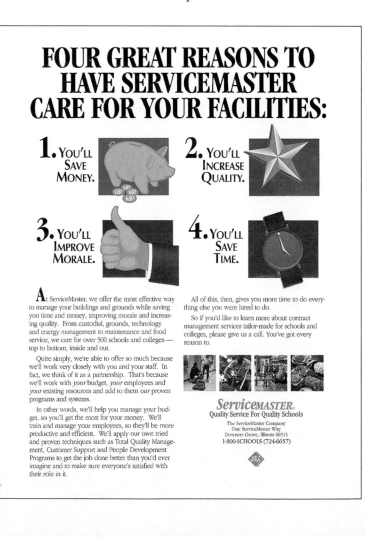

The three groups of industrial products and services include materials and parts, capital items, and supplies and services. *Materials and parts* include raw materials and manufactured materials and parts. Raw materials consist of farm products (wheat, cotton, livestock, fruits, vegetables) and natural products (fish, lumber, crude petroleum, iron ore). Manufactured materials and parts consist of component materials (iron, yarn, cement, wires) and component parts (small motors, tires, castings). Most manufactured materials and parts are sold directly to industrial users. Price and service are the major marketing factors; branding and advertising tend to be less important.

Capital items are industrial products that aid in the buyer's production or operations, including installations and accessory equipment. Installations consist of major purchases such as buildings (factories, offices) and fixed equipment (generators, drill presses, large computer systems, elevators). Accessory equipment includes portable factory equipment and tools (hand tools, lift trucks) and office equipment (fax machines, desks). They have a shorter life than installations and simply aid in the production process.

The final group of business products is *supplies and services.* Supplies include operating supplies (lubricants, coal, paper, pencils) and repair and maintenance items (paint, nails, brooms). Supplies are the convenience products of the industrial field because they are usually purchased with a minimum of effort or comparison. Business services include maintenance and repair services (window cleaning, computer repair) and business advisory services (legal, management consulting, advertising). Such services are usually supplied under contract.

Organizations, Persons, Places, and Ideas

In addition to tangible products and services, in recent years marketers have broadened the concept of a product to include other "marketable entities"—namely, organizations, persons, places, and ideas.

Organizations often carry out activities to "sell" the organization itself. *Organization marketing* consists of activities undertaken to create, maintain, or change the attitudes and behavior of target consumers toward an organization. Both profit and nonprofit organizations practice organization marketing. Business firms sponsor public relations or corporate advertising campaigns to polish their images. *Corporate image advertising* is a major tool companies use to market themselves to various publics. For example, Lucent puts out ads with the tag line, "We make the things that make communications work." IBM wants to establish itself as the company to turn to for "e-Business Solutions." Similarly, nonprofit organizations, such as churches, colleges, charities, museums, and performing arts groups, market their organizations in order to raise funds and attract members or patrons.

People can also be thought of as products. *Person marketing* consists of activities undertaken to create, maintain, or change attitudes or behavior toward particular people. All kinds of people and organizations practice person marketing. Presidents must be skillful in marketing themselves, their parties, and their platforms to get needed votes and program support. Entertainers and sports figures use marketing to promote their careers and improve their impact and incomes. Professionals such as doctors, lawyers, accountants, and architects market themselves in order to build their reputations and increase business. Business leaders use person marketing as a strategic tool to develop their companies' fortunes as well as their own. Businesses, charities, sports teams, fine arts groups, religious groups, and other organizations also use person marketing. Creating or associating with well-known personalities often helps these organizations achieve their goals better. Thus, brands such as Nike, Gatorade, McDonald's, Ball Park hot dogs, and Hanes have invested millions of dollars to link themselves with Michael Jordan.

Place marketing involves activities undertaken to create, maintain, or change attitudes or behavior toward particular places. Thus, cities, states, regions, and even entire nations compete to attract tourists, new residents, conventions, and company offices and factories. For example, today, almost every city, state, and country markets its tourist attractions. Texas has advertised "It's Like a Whole Other Country," Michigan has touted "YES M!CH!GAN—Great Lakes, Great Times," and New York State shouts "I Love New York!"[2] Stratford, Ontario, in Canada was a little-known town with one big marketing asset—its name and a river called Avon. This became the basis for an annual Shakespeare festival, which put Stratford on the tourist map. Most states and nations also operate industrial development offices that try to sell companies on the advantages of locating new plants in their states. For example, Ireland is an outstanding place marketer. The Irish Development Agency has attracted over 1,100 companies to locate their plants in Ireland. At the same time, the Irish Tourist Board has built a flourishing tourism business, and the Irish Export Board has created attractive markets for Irish exports.[3]

Ideas can also be marketed. In one sense, all marketing is the marketing of an idea, whether it be the general idea of brushing your teeth or the specific idea that Crest provides the most effective decay prevention. Here, however, we narrow our focus to the marketing of *social ideas,* such as public health campaigns to reduce smoking, alcoholism, drug abuse, and overeating; environmental campaigns

Place marketing: The Irish Tourist Board has built a flourishing tourism business— "Awaken to a different world, Ireland!"

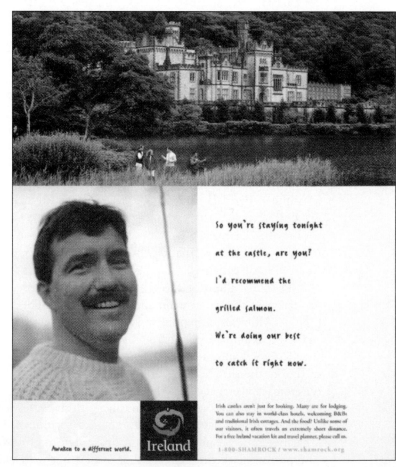

So you're staying tonight

at the castle, are you?

I'd recommend the

grilled salmon.

We're doing our best

to catch it right now.

Awaken to a different world.   Ireland

Irish castles aren't just for looking. Many are for lodging. You can also stay in world-class hotels, welcoming B&Bs and traditional Irish cottages. And the food? Unlike some of our visitors, it often travels an extremely short distance. For a free Ireland vacation kit and travel planner, please call us.

1-800-SHAMROCK / www.shamrock.org

Social marketing
The design, implementation, and control of programs seeking to increase the acceptability of a social idea, cause, or practice among a target group.

to promote wilderness protection, clean air, and conservation; and other campaigns such as family planning, human rights, and racial equality. This area has been called **social marketing,** which includes the creation and implementation of programs seeking to increase the acceptability of a social idea, cause, or practice within targeted groups.

The Ad Council of America has developed dozens of social advertising campaigns, including classics such as "Smokey Bear," "Keep America Beautiful," "Join the Peace Corps," "Don't Drive Drunk," and "Say No to Drugs." It now represents 35 causes, ranging from antidiscrimination, child abuse prevention, education reform, and youth fitness to recycling and organ donation (see www.adcouncil.org). But social marketing involves much more than just advertising. Many public marketing campaigns fail because they assign advertising the primary role and fail to develop and use all the marketing mix tools.[4]

INDIVIDUAL PRODUCT DECISIONS

Figure 8.2 shows the important decisions in the development and marketing of individual products and services. We will focus on decisions about *product attributes, branding, packaging, labeling,* and *product support services.*

Product Attributes

Developing a product or service involves defining the benefits that it will offer. These benefits are communicated and delivered by product attributes such as *quality, features,* and *style and design.*

Product Quality

Product quality
The ability of a product to perform its functions; it includes the product's overall durability, reliability, precision, ease of operation and repair, and other valued attributes.

Quality is one of the marketer's major positioning tools. **Product quality** has two dimensions—level and consistency. In developing a product, the marketer must first choose a *quality level* that will support the product's position in the target market. Here, product quality means *performance quality*—the ability of a product to perform its functions. For example, a Rolls-Royce provides higher performance quality than a Chevrolet: It has a smoother ride, handles better, and lasts longer. Companies rarely try to offer the highest possible performance quality level—few customers want or can afford the high levels of quality offered in products such as a Rolls-Royce automobile, a Sub Zero refrigerator, or a Rolex watch. Instead, companies choose a quality level that matches target market needs and the quality levels of competing products.

Beyond quality level, high quality also can mean high levels of quality *consistency.* Here, product quality means *conformance quality*—freedom from defects and *consistency* in delivering a targeted level of performance. All companies should strive for high levels of conformance quality. In this sense, a Chevrolet can have just as much quality as a Rolls-Royce. Although a Chevy doesn't perform as well as a Rolls, it can as consistently deliver the quality that customers pay for and expect.

FIGURE 8.2 Individual product decisions

During the past two decades, a renewed emphasis on quality has spawned a global quality movement. Most firms implemented "total quality management" (TQM) programs, efforts to improve product and process quality constantly in every phase of their operations. Recently, however, the total quality management movement has drawn criticism. Too many companies viewed TQM as a magic cure-all and created token total quality programs that applied quality principles only superficially. Today, companies are taking a "return on quality" approach, viewing quality as an investment and holding quality efforts accountable for bottom-line results.[5]

Beyond simply reducing product defects, the ultimate goal of total quality is to improve customer satisfaction and value. For example, when Motorola first began its total quality program in the early 1980s, its goal was to drastically reduce manufacturing defects. Later, however, Motorola's quality concept evolved into one of *customer-defined quality* and *total customer satisfaction*. "Quality," noted Motorola's vice president of quality, "has to do something for the customer. . . . Our definition of a defect is 'if the customer doesn't like it, it's a defect.'" Similarly, Siemans defines quality this way: "Quality is when our customers come back and our products don't."[6] As more and more companies have moved toward such customer-driven definitions of quality, their TQM programs are evolving into customer satisfaction and customer retention programs.

Thus, many companies today have turned customer-driven quality into a potent strategic weapon. They create customer satisfaction and value by consistently and profitably meeting customers' needs and preferences for quality. In fact, quality has now become a competitive necessity—in the twenty-first century, only companies with the best quality will thrive.

Product Features

A product can be offered with varying features. A stripped-down model, one without any extras, is the starting point. The company can create higher-level models by adding more features. Features are a competitive tool for differentiating the company's product from competitors' products. Being the first producer to introduce a needed and valued new feature is one of the most effective ways to compete.

How can a company identify new features and decide which ones to add to its product? The company should periodically survey buyers who have used the product and ask these questions: How do you like the product? Which specific features of the product do you like most? Which features could we add to improve the product? The answers provide the company with a rich list of feature ideas. The company can then assess each feature's *value* to customers versus its *cost* to the company. Features that customers value little in relation to costs should be dropped; those that customers value highly in relation to costs should be added.

Product Style and Design

Another way to add customer value is through distinctive *product style and design*. Some companies have reputations for outstanding style and design, such as Black & Decker in cordless appliances and tools, Steelcase in office furniture and systems, Bose in audio equipment, and Ciba Corning in medical equipment. Design can be one of the most powerful competitive weapons in a company's marketing arsenal.

Design is a larger concept than style. *Style* simply describes the appearance of a product. Styles can be eye catching or yawn producing. A sensational style may grab attention and produce pleasing aesthetics, but it does not necessarily make the product *perform* better. Unlike style, *design* is more than skin deep—it goes to the very heart of a product. Good design contributes to a product's usefulness as well as to its looks.

The dramatic iMac—with its sleek, egg-shaped, single-unit monitor and hard drive in a futuristic translucent casing— won raves for design and lured buyers in droves.

The thrill of surfing.
The agony of choosing a color.

Hop on an iMac and in just ten minutes you could be surfing the Internet and e-mailing everyone   and their brother. Now for the hard part: what color will it be? www.apple.com   Think different.

Good style and design can attract attention, improve product performance, cut production costs, and give the product a strong competitive advantage in the target market. For example, consider Apple's iMac personal computer:

> ★ Who said that computers have to be beige and boxy? Apple's iMac, is anything but. The iMac features a sleek, egg-shaped monitor and hard drive, all in one unit, in a futuristic translucent turquoise casing. There's no clunky tower or desktop hard drive to clutter up your office area. There's also no floppy drive—with more and more software being distributed via CDs or the Internet, Apple thinks the floppy is on the verge of extinction. Featuring one-button Internet access, this is a machine designed specifically for cruising the Internet (that's what the "i" in "iMac" stands for). The dramatic iMac won raves for design and lured buyers in droves. Only one month after the iMac hit the stores in the summer of 1998, it was the number-two best-selling computer. By mid-1999, it had sold more than a million units, marking Apple's reemergence as a legitimate contender in the personal computer industry.[7]

Branding

Perhaps the most distinctive skill of professional marketers is their ability to create, maintain, protect, and enhance brands of their products and services. A **brand** is a name, term, sign, symbol, or design, or a combination of these, that identifies the maker or seller of a product or service. Consumers view a brand as an important part of a product, and branding can add value to a product. For example, most consumers would perceive a bottle of White Linen perfume as a high-quality, expensive product. But the same perfume in an unmarked bottle would likely be viewed as lower in quality, even if the fragrance were identical.

Brand
A name, term, sign, symbol, or design, or a combination of these, that identifies the maker or seller of a product or service.

Brand

Branding has become so strong that today hardly anything goes unbranded. Salt is packaged in branded containers, common nuts and bolts are packaged with a distributor's label, and automobile parts—spark plugs, tires, filters—bear brand names that differ from those of the automakers. Even fruits, vegetables, and poultry are branded—Sunkist oranges, Dole pineapples, Chiquita bananas, Fresh Express salad greens, and Perdue chickens.

Branding helps buyers in many ways. Brand names help consumers identify products that might benefit them. Brands also tell the buyer something about product quality. Buyers who always buy the same brand know that they will get the same features, benefits, and quality each time they buy. Branding also gives the seller several advantages. The brand name becomes the basis on which a whole story can be built about a product's special qualities. The seller's brand name and trademark provide legal protection for unique product features that otherwise might be copied by competitors. Branding also helps the seller to segment markets. For example, General Mills can offer Cheerios, Wheaties, Total, Lucky Charms, and many other cereal brands, not just one general product for all consumers.

Brand Equity

Brand equity

The value of a brand, based on the extent to which it has high brand loyalty, name awareness, perceived quality, strong brand associations, and other assets such as patents, trademarks, and channel relationships.

Brands vary in the amount of power and value they have in the marketplace. A powerful brand has high **brand equity.** Brands have higher brand equity to the extent that they have higher brand loyalty, name awareness, perceived quality, strong brand associations, and other assets such as patents, trademarks, and channel relationships.

A brand with strong brand equity is a very valuable asset. Measuring the actual equity of a brand name is difficult. However, according to one estimate, the brand equity of Coca-Cola is $84 billion, Microsoft is $57 billion, and IBM is $44 billion. Other brands rating among the world's most valuable include McDonald's, Disney, Sony, Kodak, Intel, Gillette, and Budweiser.[8]

Although we normally think of brand equity as something accruing to products, service companies also prize it. As Wall Street competition intensifies, financial service companies are spending millions on their brand names in order to attract investors. Just as Coke wants you to reach for its soda when you're thirsty, Merrill Lynch and Charles Schwab want you to call them when you need financial know-how. Hence, brand-building advertising by financial services companies has soared in recent years.

High brand equity provides a company with many competitive advantages. A powerful brand enjoys a high level of consumer brand awareness and loyalty. Because consumers expect stores to carry the brand, the company has more leverage in bargaining with resellers. Because the brand name carries high credibility, the company can more easily launch line and brand extensions, as when Coca-Cola leveraged its well-known brand to introduce Diet Coke or when Procter & Gamble introduced Ivory dishwashing detergent. Above all, a powerful brand offers the company some defense against fierce price competition.

Some analysts see brands as *the* major enduring asset of a company, outlasting the company's specific products and facilities. Yet every powerful brand really represents a set of loyal customers. Therefore, the fundamental asset underlying brand equity is *customer equity.* This suggests that the proper focus of marketing planning is that of extending *loyal customer lifetime value,* with brand management serving as a major marketing tool.

Branding poses challenging decisions to the marketer. Figure 8.3 shows the key branding decisions.

Brand Name Selection

A good name can add greatly to a product's success. However, finding the best brand name is a difficult task. It begins with a careful review of the product and its benefits, the target market, and proposed marketing strategies.

Desirable qualities for a brand name include the following: (1) It should suggest something about the product's benefits and qualities. Examples: DieHard, Easy-Off, Craftsman, Sunkist, Spic and Span, Snuggles, Merrie Maids, and OFF! bug spray. (2) It should be easy to pronounce, recognize, and remember. Short names help.

FIGURE 8.3 Major branding decisions

Examples: Tide, Aim, Puffs. But longer ones are sometimes effective. Examples: "Love My Carpet" carpet cleaner, "I Can't Believe It's Not Butter" margarine, Better Business Bureau. (3) The brand name should be distinctive. Examples: Taurus, Kodak, Exxon. (4) The name should translate easily into foreign languages. Before spending $100 million to change its name to Exxon, Standard Oil of New Jersey tested several names in 54 languages in more than 150 foreign markets. It found that the name Enco referred to a stalled engine when pronounced in Japanese. (5) It should be capable of registration and legal protection. A brand name cannot be registered if it infringes on existing brand names.

Once chosen, the brand name must be protected. Many firms try to build a brand name that will eventually become identified with the product category. Brand names such as Kleenex, Levi's, Jell-O, Scotch Tape, Formica, and Fiberglas have succeeded in this way. However, their very success may threaten the company's rights to the name. Many originally protected brand names, such as cellophane, aspirin, nylon, kerosene, linoleum, yo-yo, trampoline, escalator, thermos, and shredded wheat, are now generic names that any seller can use.

Brand Sponsor

A manufacturer has four sponsorship options. The product may be launched as a *manufacturer's brand* (or national brand), as when Kellogg and IBM sell their output under their own manufacturer's brand names. Or the manufacturer may sell to resellers who give it a *private brand* (also called a *store brand* or *distributor brand*). Although most manufacturers create their own brand names, others market *licensed brands*. Finally, two companies can join forces and *co-brand* a product.

Manufacturer's Brands Versus Private Brands. Manufacturers' brands have long dominated the retail scene. In recent times, however, an increasing number of retailers and wholesalers have created their own **private brands** (or **store brands**). For example, Sears has created several names—DieHard batteries, Craftsman tools, Kenmore appliances, Weatherbeater paints. Wal-Mart offers its own Sam's American Choice and Great Value brands of beverages and food products to compete against major national brands. BASF Wyandotte, the world's second-largest antifreeze maker, sells its Alugard antifreeze through intermediaries that market the product under about 80 private brands, including Kmart, True Value, Pathmark, and Rite Aid. Private brands can be hard to establish and costly to stock and promote. However, they also yield higher profit margins for the reseller, and they give resellers exclusive products that cannot be bought from competitors, resulting in greater store traffic and loyalty.

In the so-called *battle of the brands* between manufacturers' and private brands, retailers have many advantages. They control what products they stock, where they go on the shelf, and which ones they will feature in local circulars. They charge manufacturers **slotting fees**—payments demanded by retailers before they will accept new products and find "slots" for them on the shelves. Retailers price their store brands lower than comparable manufacturers' brands, thereby appealing to

Private brand (or store brand)
A brand created and owned by a reseller of a product or service.

Slotting fees
Payments demanded by retailers before they will accept new products and find "slots" for them on the shelves.

Store brands: Loblaws's President's Choice brand has become so popular that the company now licenses it to retailers across the United States and in eight other countries where Loblaws has no stores of its own.

budget-conscious shoppers, especially in difficult economic times. Most shoppers believe that store brands are often made by one of the larger manufacturers anyway.

As store brands improve in quality and as consumers gain confidence in their store chains, store brands are posing a strong challenge to manufacturers' brands. Consider the case of Loblaws, the Canadian supermarket chain. Its President's Choice Decadent Chocolate Chip Cookies brand is now the leading cookie brand in Canada. Loblaws' private label President's Choice cola racks up 50 percent of Loblaws' canned cola sales. Based on this success, the private label powerhouse has expanded into a wide range of food categories. For example, it now offers more than 2,500 food items under the President's Choice label, ranging from cookies, paper, and frozen desserts to prepared foods and boxed meats. The brand has become so popular that Loblaw now licenses it to retailers across the United States and eight other countries where Loblaws has no stores of its own. For example, President's Choice Decadent Chocolate Chip Cookies are now sold by Jewel Food Stores in Chicago, where they are the number-one seller, beating out even Nabisco's Chips Ahoy brand.[9]

In U.S. supermarkets, taken as a single brand, private-label products are the number-one, -two, or -three brand in over 40 percent of all grocery product categories. In all, they capture over a 20 percent share of U.S. supermarket sales. Private labels are even more prominent in Europe, accounting for as much as 36 percent of supermarket sales in Britain and 24 percent in France. French retail giant Carrefour sells more than 3,000 in-house brands, ranging from cooking oil to car batteries. To fend off private brands, leading brand marketers will have to invest in R&D to bring out new brands, new features, and continuous quality improvements. They must design strong advertising programs to maintain high awareness and preference. They must find ways to "partner" with major distributors in a search for distribution economies and improved joint performance.[10]

Licensing. Most manufacturers take years and spend millions to create their own brand names. However, some companies license names or symbols previously created by other manufacturers, names of well-known celebrities, characters from popular movies and books—for a fee, any of these can provide an instant and proven brand name. Apparel and accessories sellers pay large royalties to adorn their products—from blouses to ties, and linens to luggage—with the names or initials of well-known fashion innovators such as Calvin Klein, Tommy Hilfiger, Gucci, or Armani. Sellers of children's products attach an almost endless list of character names to clothing, toys, school supplies, linens, dolls, lunch boxes, cereals, and other items. The character names range from classics such as Sesame Street, Disney, Peanuts, Winnie the Pooh, the Muppets, Scooby Doo, and Dr. Seuss characters to the more recent Teletubbies, Pokeman, Powderpuff Girls, Rugrats, and Blue's Clues characters. Almost half of all retail toy sales come from products based on television shows and movies such as *The Rugrats, Scooby Doo, Star Trek,* or *Star Wars.*

Name and character licensing has grown rapidly in recent years. Annual retail sales of licensed products in the United States and Canada has grown from only $4 billion in 1977 to $55 billion in 1987 and more than $71 billion today. The fastest-growing licensing category is corporate brand licensing, as more and more for-profit and nonprofit organizations are licensing their names to generate additional revenues and brand recognition (see Marketing Highlight 8.2). Even the Vatican engages in licensing: Heavenly images from its art collection, architecture, frescoes, and manuscripts are now imprinted on such earthy objects as T-shirts, ties, glassware, candles, and ornaments.[11]

Many companies have mastered the art of peddling their established brands and characters. For example, through savvy marketing, Warner Brothers has turned Bugs Bunny, Daffy Duck, Foghorn Leghorn, and its more than 100 other *Looney Tunes* characters into the world's favorite cartoon brand. The *Looney Tunes* license, arguably the most sought-after nonsports license in the industry, generates $4 billion in annual retail sales by more than 225 licensees. Warner Brothers has yet to tap the full potential of many of its secondary characters. The Tazmanian Devil, for example, initially appeared in only five cartoons. But through cross-licensing agreements with organizations such as Harley-Davidson and the NFL, Taz has become something of a pop icon. Warner Brothers sees similar potential for Michigan Frog or Speedy Gonzales for the Hispanic market.[12]

Co-branding
The practice of using the established brand names of two different companies on the same product.

Co-Branding.   Although companies have been **co-branding** products for many years, there has been a recent resurgence in co-branded products. Co-branding occurs when two established brand names of different companies are used on the same product. For example, Nabisco joined with Pillsbury to create Pillsbury Oreo Bars baking mix and with Kraft Foods' Post cereal division to create Oreo O's cereal. Kellogg joined forces with ConAgra to co-brand Healthy Choice from Kellogg's cereals. Ford and Eddie Bauer co-branded a sport utility vehicle—the Ford Explorer, Eddie Bauer edition. General Electric worked with Culligan to develop its Water by Culligan Profile Performance refrigerator with a built-in Culligan water filtration system. Mattel teamed with Coca-Cola to market Soda Fountain Sweetheart Barbie. In most co-branding situations, one company licenses another company's well-known brand to use in combination with its own.

Co-branding offers many advantages. Because each brand dominates in a different category, the combined brands create broader consumer appeal and greater brand equity. Co-branding also allows a company to expand its existing brand into a category it might otherwise have difficulty entering alone. For example, by licensing its Healthy Choice brand to Kellogg, ConAgra entered the breakfast segment with a solid product. In return, Kellogg could leverage the broad awareness of the Healthy Choice name in the cereal category.

Co-branding also has limitations. Such relationships usually involve complex legal contracts and licenses. Co-branding partners must carefully coordinate their

MARKETING
HIGHLIGHT
8 . 2

FROM HARLEY-DAVIDSON ARMCHAIRS TO COCA-COLA FISHING LURES: THE RISE OF CORPORATE BRANDING

When BMW bought the Rolls-Royce name—nothing else, just the *name*—for $60 million, it confirmed what savvy investors have always

Corporate brand licensing: Coca-Cola partners with some 320 licensees to produce more than 10,000 products in 57 countries. Products range from fashion apparel to holiday decorations and even a Coca-Cola Barbie doll.

known: A strong brand name is one of the most valuable assets a company has. Now companies are realizing that they shouldn't confine such assets only to their showrooms, stationery, business cards, or the company's core product. Instead, more and more companies, from the Fortune 500 to the not-for-profit sector, are licensing their names to generate additional brand recognition and revenues. That's why we're suddenly seeing products like Pillsbury doughboy potholders, Coca-Cola Picnic Barbie, Crayola house paints, Jeep bicycles, Royal Doulton perfume, and Harley-Davidson armchairs and baby clothes.

Last year, retail sales of all licensed products totaled $71 billion in the United States and Canada, more than $132 billion worldwide. Corporate brand licensing, the fastest-growing category, claimed 22 percent of that total, the same amount earned from entertainment property licensing. According to a licensing industry executive, at the recent L!CENSING 99 International licensing show, "The showroom floor [read] like a Fortune 500 directory, packed with such high-

profile corporate brands as Coca-Cola, Jeep, Chrysler, Anheuser-Busch, Pillsbury, Texaco, Popsicle, Harley-Davidson, Schwinn, McDonald's, Taco Bell, and many more."

When it comes to corporate brand licensing, few companies can equal Coca-Cola, whose extraordinary success has inspired hundreds of companies to follow suit. Yet few people know that Coca-Cola's entry into licensing was purely defensive. In the early 1980s, lawyers advised the company that if it didn't enter the Coca-Cola T-shirt market, others legally could. Coca-Cola responded by setting up a licensing program, which started modestly but now consists of a large department overseeing some 320 licensees in 57 countries producing more than 10,000 products, ranging from baby clothes and boxer shorts to earrings, a Coca-Cola Barbie doll, and even a fishing lure shaped like a tiny coke can. Last year alone, licensees sold 50 million licensed Coca-Cola products.

Although most companies have long sold promotional merchandise bearing their names and logos to dealers and distributors, full-scale

advertising, sales promotion, and other marketing efforts. Finally, when co-branding, each partner must trust the other will take good care of its brand. As one Nabisco manager puts it, "Giving away your brand is a lot like giving away your child—you want to make sure everything is perfect."[13]

Brand Strategy

A company has four choices when it comes to brand strategy (see Figure 8.4). It can introduce *line extensions* (existing brand names extended to new forms, sizes, and flavors of an existing product category), *brand extensions* (existing brand names extended to new product categories), *multibrands* (new brand names introduced in the same product category), or *new brands* (new brand names in new product categories).

retail merchandising is a real shift. Companies are making this shift both to capitalize on brand awareness in current markets and to extend their brands into new markets. For example, Caterpillar and John Deere, both companies with narrow markets, are now licensing a wide range of products aimed at generating additional sales among those already hooked on their brands. Caterpillar has set up licensing agreements with apparel and footwear companies to make Caterpillar work clothes and work boots. The "Cat" work boot is now Wolverine World Wide's (of Hush Puppies fame) hottest product. Visitors to the online John Deere Mall (mall.deere.com) will discover an array of licensed products that includes everything from logo hats, shirts, jackets, mugs, and watches to John Deere versions of Canon calculators, Victorinox penknives, Mini Mag-Lite flashlights, and hand-rubbed rosewood pens.

Sometimes companies get into licensing as a way to extend the brand to a new target market. Thus, although a Harley-Davidson armchair seems like an unlikely product, it's the motorcycle company's way of reaching out to women, who make up only 9 percent of the company's market. Harley also licenses toys, including a Barbie dressed in a "very feminine outfit" to appeal to future

generations of Harley purchasers. The ultimate goal is to sell more bikes to buyers who are not part of the core market. Similarly, Caterpillar is teaming up with Mattel to create a line of toys based on its construction equipment.

At the same time that corporate brand licensing lets companies reap some of the value they've built up in their brands, it also provides an additional tool for building even more brand value. For example, Unilever has invested heavily in advertising to create positioning and personality for its Snuggle fabric softener brand and for the cute little Snuggle Bear that appears on the label. Now, licensing the Snuggle Bear for use on other carefully selected products, says a Unilever brand manager, "will be another way to . . . help Snuggle leave lasting impressions long after our 30-second commercial is over."

What's in corporate licensing for the licensees, the manufacturers who pay large sums for the right to use corporate brand names or trademarks on their products? Compared to celebrity and entertainment names, corporate brands are much less risky. For example, what happens to a product brandishing a sports celebrity's name when that celebrity is busted for drugs? Or what can a manufacturer do with all its Godzilla backpacks after the

Godzilla movie flops (as it did)? Corporate brands are much safer bets. Many have been around for decades and have a proven, surprisingly strong appeal for customers. There are powerful forces behind the impulse to buy a Coke beach towel, a Good Humor die-cast truck, Harley Davidson boots, or Doulton perfume. Says Seth Siegel, co-chairman of the Beanstalk Group, which manages licensing for Coca-Cola and Harley-Davidson, "We live in a . . . society [where] people still love to surround themselves with icons that move them."

Sources: Quotes and other information from Constance L. Hays, "Licensing of Names Adds to Image and Profit," *New York Times,* June 12, 1998, p. D1; Carl Quintanilla, "Advertising: Caterpillar, Deere Break Ground in Consumer-Product Territory," *Wall Street Journal,* June 20, 1996, p. B2; Robert Oas, "Licensed Merchandise Sales Decrease, but Corporate Merchandise Is on the Rise," *Potentials,* April 1999, p. 8; Laura Petrecca, "'Corporate Brands' Put Licensing in the Spotlight," *Advertising Age,* June 14, 1999, p. 1; and "Licensing Industry Sets Trends for the Future at LICENSING 99 International," International Licensing Industry Merchandisers' Association press release, accessed online at www.licensing.org, June 8, 1999.

Line extension
Using a successful brand name to introduce additional items in a given product category under the same brand name, such as new flavors, forms, colors, added ingredients, or package sizes.

Line Extensions.   **Line extensions** occur when a company introduces additional items in a given product category under the same brand name, such as new flavors, forms, colors, ingredients, or package sizes. Thus, Dannon introduced several line extensions, including seven new yogurt flavors, a fat-free yogurt, and a large, economy-size yogurt. The vast majority of new-product activity consists of line extensions.

A company might introduce line extensions as a low-cost, low-risk way to introduce new products in order to meet consumer desires for variety, to utilize excess capacity, or simply to command more shelf space from resellers. However, line extensions involve some risks. An overextended brand name might lose its specific meaning or heavily extended brands can cause consumer confusion or frustration.

Product Category

		Existing	New
Brand Name	Existing	Line extension	Brand extension
	New	Multibrands	New brands

FIGURE 8.4   Four brand strategies

A consumer buying cereal at the local supermarket will be confronted by more than 150 brands, up to 30 different brands, flavors, and sizes of oatmeal alone. By itself, Quaker offers its original Quaker Oats, several flavors of Quaker instant oatmeal, and several dry cereals such as Oatmeal Squares, Toasted Oats, and Toasted Oats—Honey Nut. Another risk is that sales of an extension may come at the expense of other items in the line. A line extension works best when it takes sales away from competing brands, not when it "cannibalizes" the company's other items.

Brand extension
Using a successful brand name to launch a new or modified product in a new category.

Brand Extensions.   A **brand extension** involves the use of a successful brand name to launch new or modified products in a new category. Mattel has extended its incredibly popular and enduring Barbie Doll brand into new categories ranging from Barbie home furnishings, Barbie cosmetics, and Barbie electronics to Barbie books, Barbie sporting goods, and even a Barbie band—Beyond Pink. Honda uses its company name to cover different products such as its automobiles, motorcycles, snowblowers, lawn mowers, marine engines, and snowmobiles. This allows Honda to advertise that it can fit "six Hondas in a two-car garage." Swiss Army brand sunglasses, Disney Cruise Lines, Cosmopolitan low-fat dairy products, Century 21 home improvements, and Brinks home security systems—all are brand extensions.

A brand extension gives a new product instant recognition and faster acceptance. It also saves the high advertising costs usually required to build a new brand name. At the same time, a brand extension strategy involves some risk. Brand extensions such as Bic pantyhose, Heinz pet food, Life Savers gum, and Clorox laundry detergent met early deaths. The extension may confuse the image of the main brand. For example, when clothing retailer Gap saw competitors targeting its value-

Line extensions: Heavily extended brands can also cause consumer confusion or frustration. A consumer buying cereal at the local supermarket will be confronted by up to 30 different brands, flavors, and sizes of oatmeal alone.

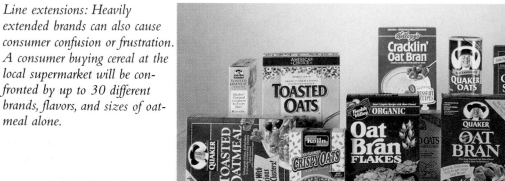

conscious customers with Gap-like fashions at lower prices, it began testing Gap Warehouse, which sold merchandise at a cut below Gap quality and price. However, the connection confused customers and eroded Gap image. As a result, the company renamed the stores Old Navy Clothing Company, a brand that has become enormously successful.[14]

If a brand extension fails, it may harm consumer attitudes toward the other products carrying the same brand name. Further, a brand name may not be appropriate to a particular new product, even if it is well made and satisfying—would you consider buying Texaco milk or Alpo chili? A brand name may lose its special positioning in the consumer's mind through overuse. Companies that are tempted to transfer a brand name must research how well the brand's associations fit the new product.[15]

Multibrands.   Companies often introduce additional brands in the same category. Thus, P&G markets many different brands in each of its product categories. *Multibranding* offers a way to establish different features and appeal to different buying motives. It also allows a company to lock up more reseller shelf space. Or the company may want to protect its major brand by setting up *flanker* or *fighter brands*. For example, Seiko uses different brand names for its higher-priced watches (Seiko Lasalle) and lower-priced watches (Pulsar) to protect the flanks of its mainstream Seiko brand. Finally, companies may develop separate brand names for different regions or countries, perhaps to suit different cultures or languages. For example, Procter & Gamble dominates the U.S. laundry detergent market with Tide, which in all its forms captures over a 40 percent market share. Outside North America, however, P&G leads the detergent category with its Ariel brand, now Europe's number-two packaged-goods brand behind Coca-Cola. In the United States, P&G targets Ariel to Hispanic markets.

A major drawback of multibranding is that each brand might obtain only a small market share, and none may be very profitable. The company may end up spreading its resources over many brands instead of building a few brands to a highly profitable level. These companies should reduce the number of brands they sell in a given category and set up tighter screening procedures for new brands.

New Brands.   A company may create a new brand name when it enters a new product category for which none of the company's current brand names are appropriate. For example, Japan's Matsushita uses separate names for its different families of products: Technics, Panasonic, National, and Quasar. Or, a company might believe that the power of its existing brand name is waning and a new brand name is needed. Finally, the company may obtain new brands in new categories through acquisitions. For example, S.C. Johnson & Son—marketer of Pledge furniture polish, Glade air freshener, Raid insect spray, Edge shaving gel, and many other well-known brands—added several new powerhouse brands through its acquisition of Drackett Company, including Windex, Drano, and Vanish toilet bowl cleaner.

As with multibranding, offering too many new brands can result in a company spreading its resources too thin. In some industries, such as consumer packaged goods, consumers and retailers have become concerned that there are already too many brands, with too few differences between them. Thus, Procter & Gamble, Frito-Lay, and other large consumer-product marketers are now pursuing *megabrand* strategies—weeding out weaker brands and focusing their marketing dollars only on brands that can achieve the number-one or -two market share positions in their categories.

Packaging

Packaging
The activities of designing and producing the container or wrapper for a product.

Packaging involves designing and producing the container or wrapper for a product. The package may include the product's primary container (the tube holding Colgate toothpaste); a secondary package that is thrown away when the product is about to be used (the cardboard box containing the tube of Colgate); and the shipping package necessary to store, identify, and ship the product (a corrugated box carrying six dozen tubes of Colgate toothpaste). Labeling, printed information appearing on or with the package, is also part of packaging.

Traditionally, the primary function of the package was to contain and protect the product. In recent times, however, numerous factors have made packaging an important marketing tool. Increased competition and clutter on retail store shelves means that packages must now perform many sales tasks—from attracting attention, to describing the product, to making the sale. Companies are realizing the power of good packaging to create instant consumer recognition of the company or brand. For example, in an average supermarket, which stocks 15,000 to 17,000 items, the typical shopper passes by some 300 items per minute, and 53 percent of all purchases are made on impulse. In this highly competitive environment, the package may be the seller's last chance to influence buyers. It becomes a "five-second commercial." The Campbell Soup Company estimates that the average shopper sees its familiar red and white can 76 times a year, creating the equivalent of $26 million worth of advertising. The package can also reinforce the product's positioning. Coca-Cola's familiar contour bottle speaks volumes about the product inside. "Even in a shadow, people know it's a Coke," observes a packaging expert. "It's a beautiful definition of how a package can influence the way a consumer perceives a product. People taste Coke differently from a contour bottle versus a generic package."[16]

Innovative packaging can give a company an advantage over competitors. Liquid Tide quickly attained a 10 percent share of the heavy-duty detergent market, partly because of the popularity of its container's innovative drip-proof spout and cap. In contrast, poorly designed packages can cause headaches for consumers and lost sales for the company (see Marketing Highlight 8.3). For example, Planters Lifesavers Company recently attempted to use innovative packaging to create an association between fresh-roasted peanuts and fresh-roasted coffee. It packaged its Fresh Roast Salted Peanuts in vacuum-packed "Brik-Pacs," similar to those used for ground coffee. Unfortunately, the coffeelike packaging worked too well: Consumers mistook the peanuts for a new brand of flavored coffee and ran them through supermarket coffee-grinding machines, creating a gooey mess, disappointed customers, and lots of irate store managers.[17]

Developing a good package for a new product requires making many decisions. First, the company must establish the *packaging concept,* which states what the package should *be* or *do* for the product. Should it mainly offer product protection, introduce a new dispensing method, suggest certain qualities about the product, or something else? Decisions then must be made on specific elements of the package, such as size, shape, materials, color, text, and brand mark. These elements must work together to support the product's position and marketing strategy. The package must be consistent with the product's advertising, pricing, and distribution.

In recent years, product safety has also become a major packaging concern. We have all learned to deal with hard-to-open "childproof" packages. After the rash of product tampering scares during the 1980s, most drug producers and food makers are now putting their products in tamper-resistant packages. In making packaging decisions, the company also must heed growing environmental concerns and make

Environmentally responsible packaging: Tetra Pak advertises the benefits of its packaging to consumers directly and initiates recycling programs to save the environment. As this ad to producers suggests, it's "more than just a package."

decisions that serve society's interests as well as immediate customer and company objectives. Shortages of paper, aluminum, and other materials suggest that marketers should try to reduce packaging. Many packages end up as broken bottles and crumpled cans littering the streets and countryside. All of this packaging creates a major problem in solid waste disposal, requiring huge amounts of labor and energy.

Fortunately, many companies have gone "green." For example, S.C. Johnson repackaged Agree Plus shampoo in a stand-up pouch using 80 percent less plastic. P&G eliminated outer cartons from its Secret and Sure deodorants, saving 3.4 million pounds of paperboard per year. Tetra Pak, a major Swedish multinational company, provides an example of the power of innovative packaging that takes environmental concerns into account.

⭐ Tetra Pak invented an "aseptic" package that enables milk, fruit juice, and other perishable liquid foods to be distributed without refrigeration or preservatives. Not only is this packaging more environmentally responsible, it also provides economic and distribution advantages. Aseptic packaging allows companies to distribute beverages over a wider area without investing in refrigerated trucks and warehouses. Supermarkets can carry Tetra Pak packaged products on ordinary shelves, allowing them to save expensive refrigerator space. Tetra's motto is "a package should save more than it cost." Tetra Pak promotes the benefits of its packaging to consumers directly and even initiates recycling programs to save the environment.

MARKETING HIGHLIGHT 8.3

THOSE FRUSTRATING, NOT-SO-EASY-TO-OPEN PACKAGES

Some things, it seems, will never change. This classic letter from an angry consumer to Robert D. Stuart, then chairman of Quaker Oats, beautifully expresses the utter frustration all of us have experienced in dealing with so-called easy-opening packages.

Dear Mr. Stuart:

I am an 86-year-old widow in fairly good health. (You may think of this as advanced age, but for me that description pertains to the years ahead. Nevertheless, if you decide to reply to this letter I wouldn't dawdle, actuarial tables being what they are.)

As I said, my health is fairly good. Feeble and elderly, as one understands these terms, I am not. My two Doberman Pinschers and I take a brisk 3-mile walk every day. They are two strong and energetic animals and it takes a bit of doing to keep "brisk" closer to a stroll than a mad dash. But I manage because as yet I don't lack the strength. You will shortly see why this fact is relevant.

I am writing to call your attention to the cruel, deceptive, and utterly [false] copy on your Aunt Jemima buttermilk complete pancake and waffle mix. The words on your package read, "to open—press here and pull back."

Mr. Stuart, though I push and press and groan and strive and writhe and curse and sweat and jab and push, poke and ram . . . whew!—I have never once been able to do what the package instructs—to "press here and pull back" the [blankety-blank]. It can't be done! Talk about failing strength! Have you ever tried and succeeded?

My late husband was a gun collector who among other lethal weapons kept a Thompson machine gun in a locked cabinet. It was a good thing that the cabinet was locked. Oh, the number of times I was tempted to give your package a few short bursts.

That lock and a sense of ladylike delicacy kept me from pursuing that vengeful fantasy. Instead, I keep a small cleaver in my pantry for those occasions when I need to open a package of your delicious Aunt Jemima pancakes.

For many years that whacking away with my cleaver served a dual purpose. Not only to open the [blankety-blank] package but also to vent my fury at your sadists who willfully and maliciously did design that torture apparatus that passes for a package.

Sometimes just for the [blank] of it I let myself get carried away. I don't stop after I've lopped off the top. I whack away until the package

is utterly destroyed in an outburst of rage, frustration, and vindictiveness. I wind up with a floorful of your delicious Aunt Jemima pancake mix. But that's a small price to pay for blessed release. (Anyway, the Pinschers lap up the mess.)

So many ingenious, considerate (even compassionate) innovations in package closures have been designed since Aunt Jemima first donned her red bandana. Wouldn't you consider the introduction of a more humane package to replace the example of marketing malevolence to which you resolutely cling? Don't you care, Mr. Stuart?

I'm really writing this to be helpful and in that spirit I am sending a copy to Mr. Tucker, president of Container Corp. I'm sure their clever young designers could be of immeasurable help to you in this matter. At least I feel it's worth a try.

Really, Mr. Stuart, I hope you will not regard me as just another cranky old biddy. I am The Public, the source of your fortunes.

Ms. Roberta Pavloff
Malvern, Pa.

Source: This letter was reprinted in "Some Designs Should Just Be Torn Asunder," *Advertising Age,* January 17, 1983, p. M54.

Labeling

Labels may range from simple tags attached to products to complex graphics that are part of the package. They perform several functions. At the very least, the label *identifies* the product or brand, such as the name Sunkist stamped on oranges. The label might also *describe* several things about the product—who made it, where it was made, when it was made, its contents, how it is to be used, and how to use it safely. Finally, the label might *promote* the product through attractive graphics.

There has been a long history of legal concerns about packaging and labels. The Federal Trade Commission Act of 1914 held that false, misleading, or deceptive labels or packages constitute unfair competition. Labels can mislead customers, fail to describe important ingredients, or fail to include needed safety warnings. As a result, several federal and state laws regulate labeling. The most prominent is the Fair Packaging and Labeling Act of 1966, which set mandatory labeling requirements, encouraged voluntary industry packaging standards, and allowed federal agencies to set packaging regulations in specific industries.

Labeling has been affected in recent times by *unit pricing* (stating the price per unit of standard measure), *open dating* (stating the expected shelf life of the product), and *nutritional labeling* (stating the nutritional values in the product). The Nutritional Labeling and Educational Act of 1990 requires sellers to provide detailed nutritional information on food products, and recent sweeping actions by the Food and Drug Administration regulate the use of health-related terms such as *low fat, light,* and *high-fiber.* Sellers must ensure that their labels contain all the required information.

Product Support Services

Customer service is another element of product strategy. A company's offer to the marketplace usually includes some services, which can be a minor or a major part of the total offer. Later in the chapter, we will discuss services as products in themselves. Here, we discuss *product support services*—services that augment actual products. More and more companies are using product support services as a major tool in gaining competitive advantage.

A company should design its product and support services to profitably meet the needs of target customers. The first step is to survey customers periodically to assess the value of current services and to obtain ideas for new ones. For example, Cadillac holds regular focus group interviews with owners and carefully watches complaints that come into its dealerships. From this careful monitoring, Cadillac has learned that buyers are very upset by repairs that are not done correctly the first time.

Once the company has assessed the value of various support services to customers, it must next assess the costs of providing these services. It can then develop a package of services that will both delight customers and yield profits to the company. For example, based on its consumer interviews, Cadillac has set up a system directly linking each dealership with a group of 10 engineers who can help walk mechanics through difficult repairs. Such actions helped Cadillac jump, in one year, from fourteenth to seventh in independent rankings of service.[18]

Many companies are now using the Internet to provide support services that were not possible before. For example, Kaiser-Permanente, the nation's largest health maintenance organization (HMO), has rolled out a Web site that lets members register online for office visits and send e-mail questions to nurses and pharmacists (and get responses within 24 hours). Kaiser also plans to give members access to lab results and pharmaceutical refills online. Similarly, American Airlines provides a support Web site for its frequent flier members. Members can streamline the booking process by creating profiles of their home airports, usual routes, and seating and meal preferences for themselves and their families. Beyond using the site to book tickets, members can check the status of their frequent flier accounts and take advantage of special member fares. Moreover, using these profiles, American can, say, offer discounts on flights to Disney World for parents whose children's school vacations start in a few weeks.[19]

Product Decisions and Social Responsibility

Product decisions have attracted much public attention. When making such decisions, marketers should consider carefully a number of public policy issues and regulations involving acquiring or dropping products, patent protection, product quality and safety, and product warranties.

Regarding the addition of new products, the government may prevent companies from adding products through acquisitions if the effect threatens to lessen competition. Companies dropping products must be aware that they have legal obligations, written or implied, to their suppliers, dealers, and customers who have a stake in the discontinued product. Companies must also must obey U.S. patent laws when developing new products. A company cannot make its product illegally similar to another company's established product.

Manufacturers must comply with specific laws regarding product quality and safety. The Federal Food, Drug, and Cosmetic Act protects consumers from unsafe and adulterated food, drugs, and cosmetics. Various acts provide for the inspection of sanitary conditions in the meat- and poultry-processing industries. Safety legislation has been passed to regulate fabrics, chemical substances, automobiles, toys, and drugs and poisons. The Consumer Product Safety Act of 1972 established a Consumer Product Safety Commission, which has the authority to ban or seize potentially harmful products and set severe penalties for violation of the law.

If consumers have been injured by a product that has been designed defectively, they can sue manufacturers or dealers. Product liability suits are now occurring in federal and state courts at the rate of almost 110,000 per year, with individual awards often running in the millions of dollars.[20] This phenomenon has resulted in huge increases in product liability insurance premiums, causing big problems in some industries. Some companies pass these higher rates along to consumers by raising prices. Others are forced to discontinue high-risk product lines.

Many manufacturers offer written product warranties to convince customers of their products' quality. To protect consumers, Congress passed the Magnuson-Moss Warranty Act in 1975. The act requires that full warranties meet certain minimum standards, including repair "within a reasonable time and without charge" or a replacement or full refund if the product does not work "after a reasonable number of attempts" at repair. Otherwise, the company must make it clear that it is offering only a limited warranty. The law has led several manufacturers to switch from full to limited warranties and others to drop warranties altogether as a marketing tool.

PRODUCT LINE DECISIONS

Product line
A group of products that are closely related because they function in a similar manner, are sold to the same customer groups, are marketed through the same types of outlets, or fall within given price ranges.

We have looked at product strategy decisions such as branding, packaging, labeling, and support services for individual products and services. But product strategy also calls for building a product line. A **product line** is a group of products that are closely related because they function in a similar manner, are sold to the same customer groups, are marketed through the same types of outlets, or fall within given price ranges. For example, Nike produces several lines of athletic shoes, Motorola produces several lines of telecommunications products, and AT&T offers several lines of long-distance telephone services. In developing product line strategies, marketers face a number of tough decisions.

The major product line decision involves *product line length*—the number of items in the product line. The line is too short if the manager can increase profits by adding items; the line is too long if the manager can increase profits by dropping items. Product line length is influenced by company objectives and resources.

Product lines tend to lengthen over time. The sales force and distributors may pressure the product manager for a more complete line to satisfy their customers. Or, the manager may want to add items to the product line to create growth in sales and profits. However, as the manager adds items, several costs rise: design and engineering costs, inventory costs, manufacturing changeover costs, transportation costs, and promotional costs to introduce new items. Eventually top management calls a halt to the mushrooming product line. Unnecessary or unprofitable items will be pruned from the line in a major effort to increase overall profitability. This pattern of uncontrolled product line growth followed by heavy pruning is typical and may repeat itself many times.

The company must manage its product lines carefully. It can systematically increase the length of its product line in two ways: by *stretching* its line and by *filling* its line. *Product line stretching* occurs when a company lengthens its product line beyond its current range. The company can stretch its line downward, upward, or both ways.

Many companies initially locate at the upper end of the market and later stretch their lines *downward*. A company may stretch downward to plug a market hole that otherwise would attract a new competitor or to respond to a competitor's attack on the upper end. Or it may add low-end products because it finds faster growth taking place in the low-end segments. Mercedes-Benz stretched downward for all these reasons. Facing a slow-growth luxury car market and attacks by Japanese automakers on its high-end positioning, Mercedes-Benz successfully introduced its C-Class cars at $30,000 without harming its ability to sell other Mercedes-Benz for $100,000 or more. In a joint venture with Switzerland's Swatch watchmaker, Mercedes-Benz launched the $10,000 Smart microcompact car, an environmentally correct second car. Just 7.5 feet long, and affectionately dubbed the "Swatchmobile," the Smart is "designed for two people and a crate of beer."[21]

Companies at the lower end of the market may want to stretch their product lines *upward*. Sometimes, companies stretch upward in order to add prestige to their current products. They may be attracted by a faster growth rate or higher margins at the higher end, or they may simply want to position themselves as full-line manufacturers. Thus, each of the leading Japanese auto companies introduced an upmarket automobile: Toyota launched Lexus; Nissan launched Infinity; and Honda launched Acura. They used entirely new names rather than their own names. Other companies have included their own names in moving upmarket. For example, Gallo introduced Ernest and Julio Gallo Varietals and priced these wines at more than twice the price of its regular wines. General Electric introduced GE Profile brand appliances targeted at the select few households earning more than $100,000 per year and living in houses valued at more than $400,000.[22]

Companies in the middle range of the market may decide to stretch their lines in *both directions*. Marriott did this with its hotel product line. Along with regular Marriott hotels, it added the Marriott Marquis line to serve the upper end of the market, and the Springhill Suites and Fairfield Inn lines to serve the moderate and lower ends. Each branded hotel line is aimed at a different target market. Marriott Marquis aims to attract and please top executives; Marriotts, middle managers; Courtyards, salespeople and other "road warriors"; and Fairfield Inns, vacationers and business travelers on a tight travel budget. Marriott's Residence Inn provides a home away from home for people who travel for a living, who are relocating, or who are on assignment and need inexpensive temporary lodging. The major risk with this strategy is that some travelers will trade down after finding that the lower-price hotels in the Marriott chain give them pretty much everything they want. However, Marriott would rather capture its customers who move downward than lose them to competitors.

Product line stretching: Mercedes introduced several smaller, lower-priced models, including the $10,000 Smart microcompact car in a joint venture with Swatch. Affectionately dubbed the "Swatchmobile," the Smart is "designed for two people and a crate of beer."

An alternative to product line stretching is *product line filling*—adding more items within the present range of the line. There are several reasons for product line filling: reaching for extra profits, satisfying dealers, using excess capacity, being the leading full-line company, and plugging holes to keep out competitors. Thus, Sony filled its Walkman line by adding solar-powered and waterproof Walkmans and an ultralight model that attaches to a sweatband for joggers, bicyclers, tennis players, and other exercisers. However, line filling is overdone if it results in cannibalization and customer confusion. The company should ensure that new items are noticeably different from existing ones.

PRODUCT MIX DECISIONS

Product mix (or product assortment)
The set of all product lines and items that a particular seller offers for sale.

An organization with several product lines has a product mix. A **product mix** (or **product assortment**) consists of all the product lines and items that a particular seller offers for sale. Avon's product mix consists of four major product lines: cosmetics, jewelry, fashions, and household items. Each product line consists of several sublines. For example, cosmetics breaks down into lipstick, eyeliner, powder, and so on. Each line and subline has many individual items. Altogether, Avon's product mix includes 1,300 items. In contrast, a typical Kmart stocks 15,000 items, 3M markets more than 60,000 products, and General Electric manufactures as many as 250,000 items.

A company's product mix has four important dimensions: width, length, depth, and consistency. Product mix *width* refers to the number of different product lines the company carries. For example, Procter & Gamble markets a fairly wide product mix consisting of many product lines, including paper, food, household cleaning, medicinal, cosmetics, and personal care products. Product mix *length* refers to the total number of items the company carries within its product lines. P&G typically carries many brands within each line. For example, it sells eight laundry detergents, six hand soaps, six shampoos, and four dishwashing detergents.

Product line *depth* refers to the number of versions offered of each product in the line. Thus, P&G's Crest toothpaste comes in three sizes and two formulations (paste and gel). Finally, the *consistency* of the product mix refers to how closely related the various product lines are in end use, production requirements, distribution channels, or some other way. P&G's product lines are consistent insofar as they are consumer products that go through the same distribution channels. The lines are less consistent insofar as they perform different functions for buyers.

These product mix dimensions provide the handles for defining the company's product strategy. The company can increase its business in four ways. It can add new product lines, thus widening its product mix. In this way, its new lines build on the company's reputation in its other lines. The company can lengthen its existing product lines to become a more full-line company. Or it can add more versions of each product and thus deepen its product mix. Finally, the company can pursue more product line consistency—or less—depending on whether it wants to have a strong reputation in a single field or in several fields.

SERVICES MARKETING

One of the major world trends in recent years has been the dramatic growth of services. As a result of rising affluence, more leisure time, and the growing complexity of products that require servicing, the United States has become the world's first service economy. Services now generate 74 percent of U.S. gross domestic product. Whereas service jobs accounted for 55 percent of all U.S. jobs in 1970, by 1993 they accounted for 79 percent of total employment. Services are growing even faster in the world economy, making up a quarter of the value of all international trade. In fact, a variety of service industries—from banking, insurance, and communications to transportation, travel, and entertainment—now accounts for well over 60 percent of the economy in developed countries around the world.[23]

Service industries vary greatly. *Governments* offer services through courts, employment services, hospitals, loan agencies, military services, police and fire departments, postal service, regulatory agencies, and schools. *Private nonprofit organizations* offer services through museums, charities, churches, colleges, foundations, and hospitals. A large number of *business organizations* offer services—airlines, banks, hotels, insurance companies, consulting firms, medical and law practices, entertainment companies, real estate firms, advertising and research agencies, and retailers. Some service businesses are very large, with total sales and assets in the billions of dollars. There are also tens of thousands of smaller service providers.

Nature and Characteristics of a Service

A company must consider four special service characteristics when designing marketing programs: *intangibility, inseparability, variability,* and *perishability.* These characteristics are summarized in Figure 8.5 and discussed in the following sections.

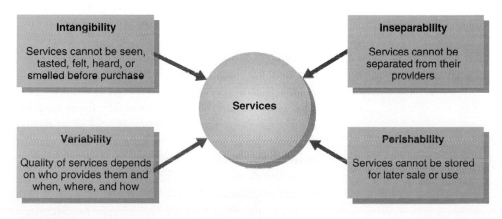

FIGURE 8.5   Four service characteristics

Service intangibility
A major characteristic of services—they cannot be seen, tasted, felt, heard, or smelled before they are bought.

Service intangibility means that services cannot be seen, tasted, felt, heard, or smelled before they are bought. For example, people undergoing cosmetic surgery cannot see the result before the purchase. Airline passengers have nothing but a ticket and the promise that they and their luggage will arrive safely at the intended destination, hopefully at the same time. To reduce uncertainty, buyers look for "signals" of service quality. They draw conclusions about quality from the place, people, price, equipment, and communications that they can see. Therefore, the service provider's task is to make the service tangible in one or more ways. Whereas product marketers try to add intangibles to their tangible offers, service marketers try to add tangibles to their intangible offers.

Physical goods are produced, then stored, later sold, and still later consumed. In contrast, services are first sold, then produced and consumed at the same time. **Service inseparability** means that services cannot be separated from their providers, whether the providers are people or machines. If a service employee provides the service, then the employee is a part of the service. Because the customer is also present as the service is produced, *provider–customer interaction* is a special feature of services marketing. Both the provider and the customer affect the service outcome.

Service inseparability
A major characteristic of services—they are produced and consumed at the same time and cannot be separated from their providers, whether the providers are people or machines.

Service variability
A major characteristic of services—their quality may vary greatly, depending on who provides them and when, where, and how.

Service variability means that the quality of services depends on who provides them as well as when, where, and how they are provided. For example, some hotels—say, Marriott—have reputations for providing better service than others. Still, within a given Marriott hotel, one registration-desk employee may be cheerful and efficient, whereas another standing just a few feet away may be unpleasant and slow. Even the quality of a single Marriott employee's service varies according to his or her energy and frame of mind at the time of each customer encounter.

Service perishability
A major characteristic of services—they cannot be stored for later sale or use.

Service perishability means that services cannot be stored for later sale or use. Some doctors charge patients for missed appointments because the service value existed only at that point and disappeared when the patient did not show up. The perishability of services is not a problem when demand is steady. However, when demand fluctuates, service firms often have difficult problems. For example, because of rush-hour demand, public transportation companies have to own much more equipment than they would if demand were even throughout the day. Thus, service firms often design strategies for producing a better match between demand and supply. For instance, hotels and resorts charge lower prices in the off-season to attract more guests. Restaurants hire part-time employees to serve during peak periods.

Marketing Strategies for Service Firms

Just like manufacturing businesses, good service firms use marketing to position themselves strongly in chosen target markets. Southwest Airlines positions itself as a no-frills, short-haul airline charging very low fares. Ritz-Carlton Hotels positions itself as offering a memorable experience that "enlivens the senses, instills well-being, and fulfills even the unexpressed wishes and needs of our guests." These and other service firms establish their positions through traditional marketing mix activities.

However, because services differ from tangible products, they often require additional marketing approaches. In a product business, products are fairly standardized and can sit on shelves waiting for customers. But in a service business, the customer and frontline service employee *interact* to create the service. Thus, service providers must interact effectively with customers to create superior value during service encounters. Effective interaction, in turn, depends on the skills of frontline service employees and on the service production and support processes backing these employees.

The Service-Profit Chain

Successful service companies focus their attention on *both* their customers and their employees. They understand the **service-profit chain,** which links service firm profits with employee and customer satisfaction. This chain consists of five links:[24]

Service-profit chain
The chain that links service firm profits with employee and customer satisfaction.

★ *Internal service quality:* superior employee selection and training, a quality work environment, and strong support for those dealing with customers, which results in . . .

★ *Satisfied and productive service employees:* more satisfied, loyal, and hard-working employees, which results in . . .

★ *Greater service value:* more effective and efficient customer value creation and service delivery, which results in . . .

★ *Satisfied and loyal customers:* satisfied customers who remain loyal, repeat purchase, and refer other customers, which results in . . .

★ *Healthy service profits and growth:* superior service firm performance.

Therefore, reaching service profits and growth goals begins with taking care of those who take care of customers (see Marketing Highlight 8.4).

All of this suggests that service marketing requires more than just traditional external marketing using the four Ps. Figure 8.6 shows that service marketing also requires *internal marketing* and *interactive marketing*. **Internal marketing** means that the service firm must effectively train and motivate its customer-contact employees and all the supporting service people to work as a *team* to provide customer satisfaction. For the firm to deliver consistently high service quality, marketers must get everyone in the organization to practice a customer orientation. In fact, internal marketing must *precede* external marketing. Thus, Ritz-Carlton orients its employees carefully, instills in them a sense of pride, and motivates them by recognizing and rewarding outstanding service deeds.

Internal marketing
Marketing by a service firm to train and effectively motivate its customer-contact employees and all the supporting service people to work as a team to provide customer satisfaction.

Interactive marketing means that service quality depends heavily on the quality of the buyer-seller interaction during the service encounter. In product marketing, product quality often depends little on how the product is obtained. But in services marketing, service quality depends on both the service deliverer and the quality of the delivery. Service marketers cannot assume that they will satisfy the customer simply by providing good technical service. They have to master interactive marketing skills as well. Thus, Ritz-Carlton selects only "people who care about people" and instructs them carefully in the fine art of interacting with customers to satisfy their every need.

Interactive marketing
Marketing by a service firm that recognizes that perceived service quality depends heavily on the quality of buyer-seller interaction.

Today, as competition and costs increase, and as productivity and quality decrease, more service marketing sophistication is needed. Service companies face

FIGURE 8.6   Three types of marketing in service industries

RITZ-CARLTON: TAKING CARE OF THOSE WHO TAKE CARE OF CUSTOMERS

Ritz-Carlton, a chain of luxury hotels renowned for outstanding service, caters to the top 5 percent of corporate and leisure travelers. The company's Credo sets lofty customer service goals: "The Ritz-Carlton Hotel is a place where the genuine care and comfort of our guests is our highest mission. We pledge to provide the finest personal service and facilities for our guests who will always enjoy a warm, relaxed yet refined ambience. The Ritz-Carlton experience enlivens the senses, instills well-being, and fulfills even the unexpressed wishes and needs of our guests." The company's Web page concludes: "Here a calm settles over you. The world, so recently at your door, is now at your feet."

The Credo is more than just words on paper—Ritz-Carlton delivers on its promises. In surveys of departing guests, some 95 percent report that they've had a truly memorable experience. In fact, at Ritz-Carlton, exceptional service encounters have become almost commonplace. Take the experiences of Nancy and Harvey Heffner of Manhattan, who stayed at the Ritz-Carlton Naples, in Naples, Florida (recently rated the best hotel in the United States, and fourth best in the world, by *Travel & Leisure* magazine). As reported in the *New York Times*:

"The hotel is elegant and beautiful," Mrs. Heffner said, "but more impor-

tant is the beauty expressed by the staff. They can't do enough to please you." When the couple's son became sick last year in Naples, the hotel staff brought him hot tea with honey at all hours of the night, she said. When Mr. Heffner had to fly home on business for a day and his return flight was delayed, a driver for the hotel waited in the lobby most of the night.

Such personal, high-quality service has also made the Ritz-Carlton a favorite among conventioneers. Comments one convention planner, "They not only treat us like kings when we hold our top-level meetings in their hotels, but we just never get any complaints."

In 1992, Ritz-Carlton became the first hotel company to win the Malcolm Baldrige National Quality Award. Since its incorporation in 1983, the company has received virtually every major award that the hospitality industry bestows. More importantly, service quality has resulted in high customer retention: Over 90 percent of Ritz-Carlton customers return. Despite its hefty room rates, the chain enjoys a 70 percent occupancy rate, almost nine points above the industry average.

Most of the responsibility for keeping guests satisfied falls to Ritz-

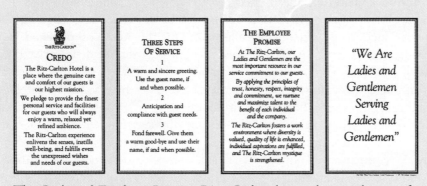

CREDO

The Ritz-Carlton Hotel is a place where the genuine care and comfort of our guests is our highest mission.

We pledge to provide the finest personal service and facilities for our guests who will always enjoy a warm, relaxed yet refined ambience.

The Ritz-Carlton experience enlivens the senses, instills well-being, and fulfills even the unexpressed wishes and needs of our guests.

THREE STEPS OF SERVICE

1
A warm and sincere greeting. Use the guest name, if and when possible.

2
Anticipation and compliance with guest needs.

3
Fond farewell. Give them a warm good-bye and use their name, if and when possible.

THE EMPLOYEE PROMISE

At The Ritz-Carlton, our Ladies and Gentlemen are the most important resource in our service commitment to our guests.

By applying the principles of trust, honesty, respect, integrity and commitment, we nurture and maximize talent to the benefit of each individual and the company.

The Ritz-Carlton fosters a work environment where diversity is valued, quality of life is enhanced, individual aspirations are fulfilled, and The Ritz-Carlton mystique is strengthened.

"We Are Ladies and Gentlemen Serving Ladies and Gentlemen"

The Credo and Employee Promise: Ritz-Carlton knows that to take care of customers, you must first take care of those who take care of customers.

three major marketing tasks: They want to increase their *competitive differentiation, service quality,* and *productivity.*

Managing Service Differentiation

In these days of intense price competition, service marketers often complain about the difficulty of differentiating their services from those of competitors. To the extent that customers view the services of different providers as similar, they care less about the provider than the price.

Carlton's customer-contact employees. Thus, the hotel chain takes great care in selecting its personnel. "We want only people who care about people," notes Patrick Mene, the company's vice president of quality. Once selected, employees are given intensive training in the art of coddling customers. New employees attend a two-day orientation, in which top management drums into them the "20 Ritz-Carlton Basics." Basic number one: "The Credo will be known, owned, and energized by all employees."

Employees are taught to do everything they can never to lose a guest. "There's no negotiating at Ritz-Carlton when it comes to solving customer problems," says Mene. Staff learn that *anyone* who receives a customer complaint *owns* that complaint until it's resolved (Ritz-Carlton Basic number eight). They are trained to drop whatever they're doing to help a customer—no matter what they're doing or what their department. Ritz-Carlton employees are empowered to handle problems on the spot, without consulting higher-ups. Each employee can spend up to $2,000 to redress a guest grievance, and each is allowed to break from his or her routine for as long as needed to make a guest happy. "We master customer satisfaction at the individual level," adds Mene. "This is our most sensitive listening post . . . our early warning system." Thus, while competitors are still reading guest comment cards to learn about customer problems, Ritz-Carlton has already resolved them.

Ritz-Carlton instills a sense of pride in its employees. "You serve," they are told, "but you are not servants." The company motto states, "We are ladies and gentlemen serving ladies and gentlemen." Employees understand their role in Ritz-Carlton's success. "We might not be able to afford a hotel like this," says employee Tammy Patton, "but we can make it so people who can afford it will want to keep coming here."

And so they do. When it comes to customer satisfaction, no detail is too small. Customer-contact people are taught to greet guests warmly and sincerely, using guest names when possible. They learn to use the proper language with guests—phrases such as *good morning, certainly, I'll be happy to, welcome back,* and *my pleasure,* never *Hi* or *How's it going?* The Ritz-Carlton Basics urge employees to escort guests to another area of the hotel rather than pointing out directions, to answer the phone within three rings and with a "smile," and to take pride and care in their personal appearance. As Jorge Gonzalez, general manager of the Ritz-Carlton Naples, puts it, "When you invite guests to your house, you want everything to be perfect."

Ritz-Carlton recognizes and rewards employees who perform feats of outstanding service. Under its 5-Star Awards program, outstanding performers are nominated by peers and managers, and winners receive plaques at dinners celebrating their achievements. For on-the-spot recognition, managers award

Gold Standard Coupons, redeemable for items in the gift shop and free weekend stays at the hotel. Ritz-Carlton further rewards and motivates its employees with events such as Super Sports Day, an employee talent show, luncheons celebrating employee anniversaries, a family picnic, and special themes in employee dining rooms. As a result, Ritz-Carlton's employees appear to be just as satisfied as its customers. Employee turnover is less than 30 percent a year, compared with 45 percent at other luxury hotels.

Ritz-Carlton's success is based on a simple philosophy: To take care of customers, you must first take care of those who take care of customers. Satisfied employees deliver high service value, which then creates satisfied customers. Satisfied customers, in turn, create sales and profits for the company.

Sources: Quotes from Edwin McDowell, "Ritz-Carlton's Keys to Good Service," *New York Times,* March 31, 1993, p. D1; Howard Schlossberg, "Measuring Customer Satisfaction Is Easy to Do—Until You Try," *Marketing News,* April 26, 1993, pp. 5, 8; Ginger Conlon, "True Romance," *Sales & Marketing Management,* May 1996, pp. 85–90; and the Ritz-Carlton Hotel Company, L.L.C. at www.ritzcarlton.com. Also see Don Peppers, "Digitizing Desire," *Forbes,* April 10, 1995, p. 76; and "Ritz-Carlton Hotels Reign in Three Categories of *Travel & Leisure's* 'World Best Awards' List," accessed online at www.ritz.carlton.com/corporate/worldbest.htm, February 2000.

The solution to price competition is to develop a differentiated offer, delivery, and image. The *offer* can include innovative features that set one company's offer apart from competitors' offers. For example, airlines have introduced innovations such as in-flight movies, advance seating, air-to-ground telephone service, and frequent flier award programs to differentiate their offers. British Airways even offers international travelers a sleeping compartment, hot showers, and cooked-to-order breakfasts.

Service companies can differentiate their service *delivery* by having more able and reliable customer-contact people, by developing a superior physical environment

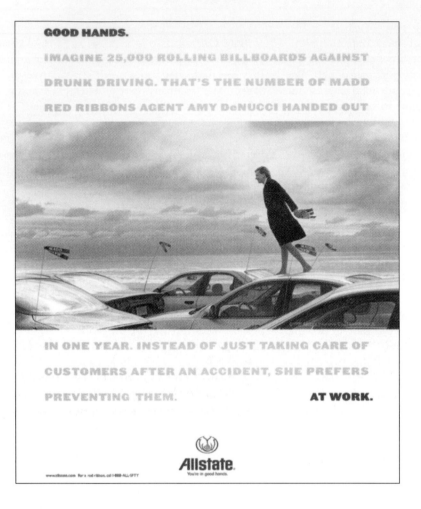

in which the service product is delivered, or by designing a superior delivery process. For example, many banks offer their customers electronic home banking as a better way to access banking services than having to drive, park, and wait in line.

Finally, service companies also can work on differentiating their *images* through symbols and branding. For example, the Harris Bank of Chicago adopted the lion as its symbol on its stationery, in its advertising, and even as stuffed animals offered to new depositors. The well-known Harris lion confers an image of strength on the bank. Other well-known service symbols include The Travelers' red umbrella, Merrill Lynch's bull, and Allstate's "good hands."

Managing Service Quality

One of the major ways a service firm can differentiate itself is by delivering consistently higher quality than its competitors do. Like manufacturers before them, most service industries have now joined the total quality movement. Like product marketers, service providers need to identify the expectations of target customers concerning service quality. Unfortunately, service quality is harder to define and judge than is product quality. For instance, it is harder to get agreement on the quality of a haircut than on the quality of a hair dryer. Customer retention is perhaps the best measure of quality—a service firm's ability to hang onto its customers depends on how consistently it delivers value to them.[25]

Service companies want to ensure that customers will receive consistently high-quality service in every service encounter. However, unlike product manufacturers who can adjust their machinery and inputs until everything is perfect, service quality will always vary, depending on the interactions between employees and customers. Problems will inevitably occur. As hard as they try, even the best companies will have an occasional late delivery, burned steak, or grumpy employee. However, although a company cannot always prevent service problems, it can learn to recover from them. Good *service recovery* can turn angry customers into loyal ones. In fact, good recovery can win more customer purchasing and loyalty than if things had gone well in the first place. Therefore, companies should take steps not only to provide good service every time but also to recover from service mistakes when they do occur.[26]

The first step is to *empower* frontline service employees—to give them the authority, responsibility, and incentives they need to recognize, care about, and tend to customer needs. At Marriott, for example, well-trained employees are given the authority to do whatever it takes, on the spot, to keep guests happy. They are also expected to help management ferret out the cause of guests' problems and to inform managers of ways to improve overall hotel service and guests' comfort.[27]

Studies of well-managed service companies show that they share a number of common virtues regarding service quality. Top service companies are *customer obsessed* and set *high service quality standards*. They do not settle merely for good service; they aim for 100 percent defect-free service. A 98 percent performance standard may sound good but, using this standard, 64,000 Federal Express packages would be lost each day, 10 words would be misspelled on each printed page, 400,000 prescriptions would be misfilled daily, and drinking water would be unsafe 8 days a year.[28]

Top service firms also *watch service performance closely*, both their own and that of competitors. They use methods such as comparison shopping, customer surveys, and suggestion and complaint forms. For example, General Electric sends out 700,000 response cards each year to households that rate their service people's performance. Citibank takes regular measures of "ART"—accuracy, responsiveness, and timeliness—and sends out employees who act as customers to check on service quality.

Good service companies also communicate their concerns about service quality to employees and provide performance feedback. At Federal Express, quality measurements are everywhere. When employees walk in the door in the morning, they see the previous week's on-time percentages. Then, the company's in-house television station gives them detailed breakdowns of what happened yesterday and any potential problems for the day ahead.

Managing Service Productivity

With their costs rising rapidly, service firms are under great pressure to increase service productivity. They can do so in several ways. The service providers can train current employees better or hire new ones who will work harder or more skillfully. Or the service providers can increase the quantity of their service by giving up some quality. Doctors working for health maintenance organizations (HMOs) have moved toward handling more patients and giving less time to each. The provider can "industrialize the service" by adding equipment and standardizing production, as in McDonald's assembly-line approach to fast-food retailing.

Finally, the service provider can harness the power of technology. Although we often think of technology's power to save time and costs in manufacturing companies, it also has great—and often untapped—potential to make service workers more productive. Consider this example:[29]

★ Using a help-desk computerized system called Apriori, Storage Dimensions (SD) can answer customer service questions on the spot. When a customer calls Storage Dimensions with a problem, the operator inputs keywords. If the customer's question has been asked and answered before by others, as so many have, a solution document "bubbles up" to the top of the PC screen and customer's problems get solved on the spot. Since installing Apriori, SD has reduced problem resolution time from an average of two hours to twenty minutes. As an added bonus, the company has also used information gleaned during the "help" conversations to generate sales leads and product development ideas.

Similarly, a well-designed Web site can allow customers to obtain buying information, narrow their purchase options, or even make a purchase directly, saving service provider time. For example, personal computer buyers can visit the Dell Web site (www.Dell.com), review the characteristics of various Dell models, check out prices, and organize their questions ahead of time. Even if they choose to call a Dell telesales representative rather than buying via the Web site, they are better informed and require less personal service.

However, companies must avoid pushing productivity so hard that doing so reduces quality. Attempts to industrialize a service or to cut costs can make a service company more efficient in the short run but reduce its longer run ability to innovate, maintain service quality, or respond to consumer needs and desires. In some cases, service providers accept reduced productivity in order to create more service differentiation or quality.

INTERNATIONAL PRODUCT AND SERVICES MARKETING

International product and service marketers face special challenges. First, they must figure out what products and services to introduce and in which countries. Then, they must decide how much to standardize or adapt their products and services for world markets. On the one hand, companies would like to standardize their offerings. Standardization helps a company to develop a consistent worldwide image. It also lowers manufacturing costs and eliminates duplication of research and development, advertising, and product design efforts. On the other hand, consumers around the world differ in their cultures, attitudes, and buying behaviors. Markets also vary in their economic conditions, competition, legal requirements, and physical environments. Companies must usually respond to these differences by adapting their product offerings. Something as simple as an electrical outlet can create big product problems:

> Those who have traveled across Europe know the frustration of electrical plugs, different voltages, and other annoyances of international travel. . . . Philips, the electrical appliance manufacturer, has to produce 12 kinds of irons to serve just its European market. The problem is that Europe does not have a universal [electrical] standard. The ends of irons bristle with different plugs for different countries. Some have three prongs, others two; prongs protrude straight or angled, round or rectangular, fat, thin, and sometimes sheathed. There are circular plug faces, squares, pentagons, and hexagons. Some are perforated and some are notched. One French plug has a niche like a keyhole; British plugs carry fuses.[30]

Packaging also presents new challenges for international marketers. Packaging issues can be subtle. For example, names, labels, and colors may not translate easily from one country to another. A firm using yellow flowers in its logo might fare well in the United States but meet with disaster in Mexico, where a yellow flower symbolizes death or disrespect. Similarly, although Nature's Gift might be an appealing name for gourmet mushrooms in America, it would be deadly in Germany, where *gift* means poison. Packaging may also have to be tailored to meet the physical characteristics of consumers in various parts of the world. For instance, soft drinks are sold in smaller cans in Japan to fit the smaller Japanese hand better. Thus, although product and package standardization can produce benefits, companies must usually adapt their offerings to the unique needs of specific international markets.

Service marketers also face special challenges when going global. Some service industries have a long history of international operations. For example, the commercial banking industry was one of the first to grow internationally. Banks had to provide global services in order to meet the foreign exchange and credit needs of their home country clients wanting to sell overseas. In recent years, many banks have become truly global operations. Germany's Deutsche Bank, for example, has branches in 41 countries. Thus, for its clients around the world who wish to take advantage of growth opportunities created by German reunification, Deutsche Bank can raise money not just in Frankfurt but also in Zurich, London, Paris, and Tokyo.

The travel industry also moved naturally into international operations. American hotel and airline companies grew quickly in Europe and Asia during the economic expansion that followed World War II. Credit card companies soon followed—the early worldwide presence of American Express has now been matched by Visa and MasterCard. Business travelers and vacationers like the convenience, and they have now come to expect that their credit cards will be honored wherever they go.

Professional and business services industries such as accounting, management consulting, and advertising have only recently globalized. The international growth of these firms followed the globalization of the manufacturing companies they serve. For example, as their client companies began to employ global marketing and advertising strategies, advertising agencies and other marketing services firms responded by globalizing their own operations.

Retailers are among the latest service businesses to go global. As their home markets become saturated with stores, American retailers such as Wal-Mart, Kmart,

Retailers are among the latest service businesses to go global. Here Asian shoppers buy American products in a Dutch-owned Makro store in Kuala Lumpur.

Toys "R" Us, Office Depot, Saks Fifth Avenue, and Disney are expanding into faster growing markets abroad. For example, every year since 1995, Wal-Mart has entered a new country; its international division's sales have now skyrocketed to more than $12 billion. Foreign retailers are making similar moves. The Japanese retailer Yaohan now operates the largest shopping center in Asia, the 21-story Nextage Shanghai Tower in China, and Carrefour of France is the leading retailer in Brazil and Argentina. Asian shoppers now buy American products in Dutch-owned Makro stores, now Southeast Asia's biggest store group with sales in the region of more than $2 billion.[31]

Service companies wanting to operate in other countries are not always welcomed with open arms. Whereas manufacturers usually face straightforward tariff, quota, or currency restrictions when attempting to sell their products in another country, service providers are likely to face more subtle barriers. In some cases, rules and regulations affecting international service firms reflect the host country's traditions. In others, they appear to protect the country's own fledgling service industries from large global competitors with greater resources. In still other cases, however, the restrictions seem to have little purpose other than to make entry difficult for foreign service firms.

A Turkish law, for example, forbids international accounting firms from bringing capital into the country to set up offices and requires them to use the names of local partners in their marketing rather than their own internationally known company names. To audit the books of a multinational company's branch in Buenos Aires, an accountant must have the equivalent of a high school education in Argentinean geography and history. In New Delhi, India, international insurance companies are not allowed to sell property and casualty policies to the country's fast-growing business community or life insurance to its huge middle class.[32]

Despite such difficulties, the trend toward growth of global service companies will continue, especially in banking, airlines, telecommunications, and professional services. Today service firms are no longer simply following their manufacturing customers. Instead, they are taking the lead in international expansion.

REVIEW OF CONCEPT CONNECTIONS

A product is more than a simple set of tangible features. In fact, many marketing offers consist of combinations of both tangible goods and services, ranging from *pure tangible goods* at one extreme to *pure services* at the other. Each product or service offered to customers can be viewed on three levels. The *core product* consists of the core problem-solving benefits that consumers seek when they buy a product. The *actual product* exists around the core and includes the quality level, features, design, brand name, and packaging. The *augmented product* is the actual product plus the various services and benefits offered with it, such as warranty, free delivery, installation, and maintenance.

1. Define *product* and the major classifications of products and services.

Broadly defined, a *product* is anything that can be offered to a market for attention, acquisition, use, or consumption that might satisfy a want or need. Products include physical objects, services, events, persons, places, organizations, ideas, or mixes of these entities. Services are products that consist of activities, benefits, or satisfactions offered for sale that are essentially intangible, such as banking, hotel, tax preparation, and home repair services.

Products and services fall into two broad classes based on the types of consumers that use them. *Consumer products*—those bought by final consumers—are usually classified according to consumer shopping habits (convenience products, shopping products, specialty products, and unsought products). *Industrial products*—purchased for further processing or use in conducting a business—are classified according to their cost and the way they enter the production process (materials and parts, capital items, and supplies and services). Other marketable entities—such as organizations, persons, places, and ideas—can also be thought of as products.

2. Describe the roles of product and service branding, packaging, labeling, and product support services.

Companies develop strategies for items in their product lines by making decisions about product attributes, branding, packaging, labeling, and product support services. *Product attribute decisions* involve the product quality, features, style, and design the company will offer. *Branding* decisions include selecting a brand name, garnering brand sponsorship, and developing a brand strategy. *Packaging* provides many key benefits, such as protection, economy, convenience, and promotion. Package decisions often include designing *labels,* which identify, describe, and possibly promote the product. Companies also develop *product support services* that enhance customer service and satisfaction and safeguard against competitors.

3. Explain the decisions companies make when developing product lines and mixes.

Most companies produce a product line rather than a single product. A *product line* is a group of products that are related in function, customer-purchase needs, or distribution channels. In developing a product line strategy, marketers face a number of tough decisions. *Line stretching* involves extending a line downward, upward, or in both directions to occupy a gap that might otherwise be filled by a competitor. In contrast, *line filling* involves adding items within the present range of the line. The set of product lines and items offered to customers by a particular seller make up the *product mix*. The mix can be described by four dimensions: width, length, depth, and consistency. These dimensions are the tools for developing the company's product strategy.

4. Identify the four characteristics that affect the marketing of a service.

As we move toward a *world service economy,* marketers need to know more about marketing services. *Services* are characterized by four key characteristics. First, services are *intangible*—they cannot be seen, tasted, felt, heard, or smelled. Services are also *inseparable* from their service providers. Services are *variable* because their quality depends on the service provider as well as the environment surrounding the service delivery. Finally, services are *perishable.* As a result, they cannot be inventoried, built up, or back ordered. Each characteristic poses problems and marketing requirements. Marketers work to find ways to make the service more tangible, to increase the productivity of providers who are inseparable from their products, to standardize the quality in the face of variability, and to improve demand movements and supply capacities in the face of service perishability.

5. Discuss the additional marketing considerations for services.

Good service companies focus attention on *both* customers and employees. They understand the *service-profit chain,* which links service firm profits with employee and customer satisfaction. Services marketing strategy calls not only for external marketing but also for *internal marketing* to motivate employees and *interactive marketing* to create service delivery skills among service providers. To succeed, service marketers must create *competitive differentiation,* offer high *service quality,* and find ways to increase *service productivity.*

KEY TERMS

Brand	Line extension	Service intangibility
Brand equity	Packaging	Service perishability
Brand extension	Private brand (or store brand)	Service-profit chain
Co-branding	Product	Service variability
Consumer product	Product line	Shopping product
Convenience product	Product mix (or product assortment)	Slotting fees
Industrial product	Product quality	Social marketing
Interactive marketing	Service	Specialty product
Internal marketing	Service inseparability	Unsought product

ISSUES FOR DISCUSSION

1. What are the primary differences between products and services? Give illustrations of marketing offers that highlight these differences. Provide an example of a "hybrid offer."

2. List and explain the "core, actual, and augmented products" of the educational experience that universities offer.

How are these different, if at all, from the "product" offered by junior colleges?

3. Because the various classes of consumer products differ in the ways that consumers buy them, they also differ in how they are marketed. (a) Select what might typically be considered an unsought product and suggest how a marketer

might convert this product into a specialty, shopping, or convenience product. (b) Explain how some personal computer manufacturers have been able to convert their specialty products into broader-based shopping products.

4. People can be thought of as "products." (a) Using the national election of 2000, indicate how the leading presidential candidates marketed themselves to the public. Think carefully about the tactics used, the advertising themes presented, and the images that were transmitted. (b) Construct a marketing profile of each of the major candidates. (c) From this analysis, what can you conclude about person marketing?

5. Brand name and symbol licensing has become a multi-billion-dollar worldwide business. Using information from the chapter and Marketing Highlight 8.2, devise a plan for licensing your school's logo, mascot, and other brand symbols. Your objective is to create toys, sportswear, gifts, and logo items that will have national appeal. Could co-branding also be an option? Explain.

6. For many years there was one type of Coca-Cola and one type of Tide. Now we find Coke Classic, Diet Coke, Cherry Coke, and several other versions of this popular soft drink. Tide detergent comes in Ultra, Liquid, Unscented, and several other formulations. It seems that almost every major brand has been greatly extended, some even past the breaking point. List some of the issues such brand extensions raise for manufacturers, retailers, and consumers.

7. Illustrate how a local theater can deal with the intangibility, inseparability, variability, and perishability characteristics of the service it provides. Give specific examples to illustrate your thoughts.

8. What are internal and interactive marketing? Give an example of how a specific firm or organization might use these concepts to increase the effectiveness of its services marketing. How might these concepts be linked to services differentiation?

MARKETING APPLICATIONS

1. The element of the "core product" in the automobile industry is transportation. The major problem-solving benefit is how to get from one place to another quickly and safely. However, most automobile manufacturers differentiate their products with additional service benefits. The various service approaches are almost as varied as are the automobile manufacturers themselves. Examine the Web sites for Ford (www.ford.com), General Motors (www.gm.com), Chrysler (www.chrysler.com), Honda (www.honda.com), Lexus (www.lexus.com), Mercedes-Benz (www.MBUSA.com), and Toyota (www.toyota.com). Look beyond the automobiles themselves and closely examine the manufacturers' services and service options.

   a. What primary services do the various automobile manufacturers offer? Prepare a grid that compares each company to the others.

   b. What services do the different companies appear to offer in common? What services do the various companies use to differentiate themselves from one another?

   c. Do any of the sites suggest that a company understands the service-profit chain? Explain.

   d. Do any of the auto companies employ interactive marketing with respect to the service component? Explain.

   e. Visit the Saturn Web site at www.saturn.com. Do you see anything that makes this company different from those you have already visited? What seems to

   be the company's focus and differential advantage? Suggest ways in which Saturn could use its service component to compete more effectively against the other competitors.

   f. What role does the Internet play in the product/service strategies of the companies in question 1?

2. In an attempt to expand beyond its core software business, Microsoft has created kiosks (boutiques) inside Tandy Corp.'s Radio Shack stores. Microsoft believes that if consumers receive information about the Web from sources other than just the Internet itself, they will more quickly accept the Internet as essential in their daily lives. It plans to construct 7,000 "stores within stores" to demonstrate Microsoft products and services. The kiosks will explain to consumers the various choices for connecting to the Web, including computers, hand held devices, MSN's WebTV, and other devices. See www.microsoft.com and www.radioshack.com for additional details.

   a. What benefits will this new retailing venture produce for Microsoft and Radio Shack? What difficulties?

   b. Describe the core, actual, or augmented products associated with this new partnership.

   c. Has a service-profit chain been created? Explain.

   d. Given recent court rulings against Microsoft, how might the Justice Department view this new partnership?

   e. How should Radio Shack's and Microsoft's competitors respond to this new retailing approach?

INTERNET CONNECTIONS

SERVICE STRATEGIES

The core service in the airline industry is transportation. The "problem-solving" benefit for the customer is travel from one place to another. To differentiate their services, airlines provide many additional benefits. If you wanted to visit Europe you might consider KLM Royal Dutch Airlines, British Airways, or Lufthansa. Review the Web sites of these airlines and complete the table to evaluate their services.

	KLM Royal Dutch Airlines www.klm.com	British Airways www.british-airways.com	Lufthansa www.lufthansa.com
Many destinations?			
Attractive frequent flyer program?			
Other service features			
Evidence of service quality			
Evidence of competitive positioning strategy			
Ways customers can give feedback to company at site			

FOR DISCUSSION

1. How would you classify airlines using consumer product categories: convenience, shopping, specialty, or unsought products?
2. Which airline brand name best conveys a quality image to you?
3. How does each airline differentiate itself from the others: KLM? British Airways? Lufthansa?
4. If Lufthansa decided to expand by developing a tourist hotel, would you recommend a brand extension or a new brand? Justify your choice.
5. Which airline would you choose for your European travel? Why?

SAVVY SITES

- Network solutions (www.networksolutions.com) manages many of the domain names on the Internet. In order for each of the airlines in this exercise to use its brand name as a domain name in its Web address, it had to register at this site.
- The Gap site (www.gap.com) contains lots of information about its product mix. It even allows you to dress a male or female figure in your favorite Gap clothes.
- E★Trade (www.etrade.com) is one of the first to offer investors online stock trading at a low price. Check out this site and see how it has grown to differentiate itself with a variety of services.

NOTES

1. Excerpt adapted from Penelope Green, "Spiritual Cosmetics. No Kidding," *New York Times,* January 10, 1999, p. 1.
2. Check out the tourism Web pages of these states at www.Travel Tex.com, www.michigan.org, and www.iloveny.state.ny.us.
3. See Philip Kotler, Irving J. Rein, and Donald Haider, *Marketing Places: Attracting Investment, Industry, and Tourism to Cities, States, and Nations* (New York: Free Press, 1993), pp. 202, 273.
4. See V. Rangan Kasturi, Sohel Karim, and Sheryl K. Sandberg, "Do Better at Doing Good," *Harvard Business Review,* May–June 1996, pp. 42 54; Alan R. Andreasen, *Marketing Social Change:*

Changing Behavior to Promote Health, Social Development, and the Environment (San Francisco: Jossey-Bass, 1995); Rance Crain, "Ruth Wooden Wheels and Deals to Lure Ad Council Sponsors," *Advertising Age,* March 9, 1998, p. 34; Alan R. Andreasen, Rob Gould, and Karen Gutierrez, "Social Marketing Has a New Champion," *Advertising Age,* February 7, 2000, p. 38 and information accessed online at www.adcouncil.org, February 2000.
5. See Roland T. Rust, Anthony J. Zahorik, and Timothy L. Keiningham, "Return on Quality (ROQ): Making Service Quality Financially Accountable," *Journal of Marketing,* April 1995,

pp. 58–70; Valerie A. Zeithaml, Leonard L. Berry, and A. Para-suraman, "The Behavioral Consequences of Service Quality," *Journal of Marketing,* April 1996, pp. 31–46; Otis Port, "The Baldrige's Other Reward," *Business Week,* March 10, 1997, p. 75; and George Thorne, "TQM Connects All Segments of Market-ing," *Advertising Age's Business Marketing,* March 1998, p. 34.

6. Philip Kotler, *Kotler on Marketing* (New York: Free Press, 1999), p. 17.

7. See "Hot R.I.P.: The Floppy Disk," *Rolling Stone,* August 20, 1998, p. 86; Owen Edwards, "Beauty and the Box," *Forbes,* October 5, 1998, p. 131; Bob Woods, "iMac Drives Apple's Q2 Results," *Computer Dealer News,* April 30, 1999, p. 39; and Eleft-heria Parpis, "Show Toppers," *Adweek,* May 10, 1999, pp. 31–32.

8. Kathleen Morris, "The Name's the Thing," *Business Week,* November 15, 1999, pp. 36–39. Also see David A. Aaker, *Manag-ing Brand Equity* (New York: Free Press, 1991); Terry Lefton and Weston Anson, "How Much Is Your Brand Worth?" *Brandweek,* January 26, 1996, pp. 43–44; Kevin Lane Keller, *Strategic Brand Management: Building, Measuring, and Managing Brand Equity* (Upper Saddle River, NJ: Prentice Hall, 1997); and David Kiley, "Q&A: Brand Value Rx," *Brandweek,* March 23, 1998, pp. 36–40.

9. Emily DeNitto, "They Aren't Private Labels Anymore—They're Brands," *Advertising Age,* September 13, 1993, p. 8; Warren Thayer, "Loblaws Exec Predicts: Private Labels to Surge," *Frozen Food Age,* May 1996, p. 1; "President's Choice Continues Brisk Pace," *Frozen Food Age,* March 1998, pp. 17–18; David Dunne and Chakravarthi Narasimhan, "The New Appeal of Private Labels," *Harvard Business Review,* May–June 1999, pp. 41–52; and Jack Neff, "Wal-Mart Stores Go Private Label," *Advertising Age,* November 29, 1999, pp. 1, 34.

10. See Patrick Oster, "The Eurosion of Brand Loyalty," *Business Week,* July 19, 1993, p. 22; Marcia Mogelonsky, "When Stores Become Brands," *American Demographics,* February 1995, pp. 32–38; John A. Quelch and David Harding, "Brands Versus Private Labels: Fighting to Win," *Harvard Business Review,* Janu-ary–February 1996, pp. 99–109; Stephanie Thompson, "Private Label Marketers Getting Savvier to Consumption Trends," *Brandweek,* November 24, 1997, p. 9; and David Dunne and Chakravarthi Narasimham, "The New Appeal of Private Labels," *Harvard Business Review,* May–June 1999, pp. 41–52.

11. See Silvia Sansoni, "Gucci, Armani, and . . . John Paul II?" *Busi-ness Week,* May 13, 1996, p. 61; Bart A. Lazar, "Licensing Gives Known Brands New Life," *Advertising Age,* February 16, 1998, p. 8; Robert Oas, "Licensed Merchandise Sales Decrease, but Corporate Merchandise Is on the Rise," *Potentials,* April 1999, p. 8; and Laura Petrecca, "'Corporate Brands' Put Licensing in the Spotlight," *Advertising Age,* June 14, 1999, p. 1.

12. Terry Lefton, "Warner Brothers' Not Very Looney Path to Licensing Gold," *Brandweek,* February 14, 1994, pp. 36–37; Robert Scally, "Warner Builds Brand Presence, Strengthens 'Tunes' Franchise," *Discount Store News,* April 6, 1998, p. 33; and Adrienne Mand, "Comet Cursors Bring WB Characters to Web," *Adweek,* April 19, 1999, p. 113.

13. Phil Carpenter, "Some Cobranding Caveats to Obey," *Marketing News,* November 7, 1994, p. 4; Karen Benezra, "Coke, Mattel Ink Pact for Collectable Barbie," *Brandweek,* October 14, 1996, p. 5; Tobi Elkin, "Brand Builders," *Brandweek,* February 2, 1998, pp. 16–18; Stephanie Thompson, "Brand Buddies," *Brandweek,* February 23, 1998, pp. 22–30; and Gabrielle Solomon, "Co-Branding Alliances: Arranged Marriages Made by Marketers," *Fortune,* October 12, 1998, p. 188.

14. See David Aaker, "Should You Take Your Brand to Where the Action Is?" *Harvard Business Review,* September–October 1997, pp. 135–45; Zeynep Gurhan-Canli and Durairaj Maheswaran, "The Effects of Extensions on Brand Name Dilution and Enhancement," *Journal of Marketing,* November 1998, pp. 464–73; and Lauren Goldstein, "Barbie's Secret Plan for World Domination," *Fortune,* November 23, 1998, pp. 38–39.

15. For more on the use of line and brand extensions and consumer attitudes toward them, see David A. Aaker and Kevin L. Keller, "Consumer Evaluations of Brand Extensions," *Journal of Market-ing,* January 1990, pp. 27–41; Susan M. Broniarczyk and Joseph W. Alba, "The Importance of Brand in Brand Extension," *Jour-nal of Marketing Research,* May 1994, pp. 214–28; Srinivas K. Reddy, Susan L. Holak, and Subodh Bhat, "To Extend or Not to Extend: Success Determinants of Line Extensions," *Journal of Marketing Research,* May 1994, pp. 243–62; Deborah Roedder John, Barbara Loken, and Christopher Joiner, *Journal of Market-ing,* January 1998, pp. 19–32; and Gurrhan-Canli and Mah-eswaran, "The Effects of Extensions on Brand Name Dilution and Enhancement," pp. 464–73.

16. See Joan Holleran, "Packaging Speaks Volumes," *Beverage Indus-try,* February 1998, p. 30.

17. Robert M. McMath, "Chock Full of (Pea)nuts," *American Demo-graphics,* April 1997, p. 60.

18. Bro Uttal, "Companies That Serve You Best," *Fortune,* Decem-ber 7, 1987, p. 116. For an excellent discussion of support ser-vices, see James C. Anderson and James A. Narus, "Capturing the Value of Supplementary Services," *Harvard Business Review,* January–February 1995, pp. 75–83.

19. Heather Green, "A Cyber Revolt in Health Care," *Business Week,* October 19, 1998, pp. 154–56; Robert D. Hof, "Now It's Your Web," *Business Week,* October 5, 1998, pp. 164–76; and George V. Hulme, Help! Companies Are Turning to Their Call Centers to Improve Customer Service on the Web," *Sales and Marketing Management,* February 2000, pp. 79–84.

20. See Paula Mergenbagen, "Product Liability: Who Sues?" *Ameri-can Demographics,* June 1995, p. 48; "Support Urged for Product Liability Reform," *Industrial Distribution,* April 1997, p. SA3; Owen Ullmann, "Product Liability Deadlock," *Business Week,* January 12, 1998, p. 51; and "A Primer on Product Liability Laws," *Purchasing,* May 6, 1999, pp. 32–34.

21. John Templeman, "A Mercedes in Every Driveway?" *Business Week,* August 26, 1996, pp. 38–40; and Sam Pickens and Dag-mar Mussey, "Swatch Taps Zurich Shop to Develop Euro Car Ads," *Advertising Age,* May 19, 1997, p. 32.

22. See Aaker, "Should You Take Your Brand to Where the Action Is?" pp. 135–43.

23. See Ronald Henkoff, "Service Is Everybody's Business," *Fortune,* June 27, 1994, pp. 48–60; Adrian Palmer and Catherine Cole, *Services Marketing: Principles and Practice* (Upper Saddle River, NJ: Prentice Hall, 1995), pp. 56–60; Valerie Zeithaml and Mary Jo Bitner, *Services Marketing* (New York: McGraw-Hill, 1996), pp. 8–9; and Michael van Biema and Bruce Greenwald, "Man-aging Our Way to Higher Service-Sector Productivity," *Harvard Business Review,* July–August 1997, pp. 87–95.

24. See James L. Heskett, Thomas O. Jones, Gary W. Loveman, W. Earl Sasser Jr., and Leonard A. Schlesinger, "Putting the Service-Profit Chain to Work," *Harvard Business Review,* March–April, 1994, pp. 164–74; and James L. Heskett, W. Earl Sasser Jr., and Leonard A. Schlesinger, *The Service Profit Chain: How Leading Companies Link Profit and Growth to Loyalty, Satisfaction, and Value* (New York:

Free Press, 1997). Also see Anthony J. Rucci, Steven P. Kirn, and Richard T. Quinn, "The Employee–Customer–Profit Chain at Sears," *Harvard Business Review,* January–February 1998, pp. 83–97.

25. For excellent discussions of service quality, see A. Parasuraman, Valerie A. Zeithaml, and Leonard L. Berry, "A Conceptual Model of Service Quality and Its Implications for Future Research," *Journal of Marketing,* Fall 1985, pp. 41–50; J. Joseph Cronin Jr. and Steven A. Taylor, "Measuring Service Quality: A Reexamination and Extension," *Journal of Marketing,* July 1992, pp. 55–68; Parasuraman, Zeithaml, and Berry, "Reassessment of Expectations as a Comparison Standard in Measuring Service Quality: Implications for Further Research," *Journal of Marketing,* January 1994, pp. 111–24; Zeithaml, Berry, and Parasuraman, "The Behavioral Consequences of Service Quality," pp. 31–46; and "Service Competitiveness: An Anglo-U.S. Study," *Business Strategy Review* 8, no. 1, 1997, pp. 7–22.

26. See Erika Rasmusson, "Winning Back Angry Customers," *Sales & Marketing Management,* October 1997, p. 131; and Stephen S. Tax, Stephen W. Brown, and Murali Chandrashekaran, "Customer Evaluations of Service Complaint Experiences: Implications for Relationship Marketing," *Journal of Marketing,* April 1998, pp. 60–76.

27. Ronald Henkoff, "Finding and Keeping the Best Service Workers," *Fortune,* October 3, 1994, pp. 110–22.

28. See James L. Heskett, W. Earl Sasser Jr., and Christopher W. L. Hart, *Service Breakthroughs* (New York: Free Press, 1990).

29. Nilly Landau, "Are You Being Served?" *International Business,* March 1995, pp. 38–40; and Omar A. El Sawy, "Redesigning the Customer Support Process for the Electronic Economy: Insights from Storage Dimensions," *MIS Quarterly,* December 1997, pp. 457–83. Also see Michael van Biema and Bruce Greenwald, "Managing Our Way to Higher Service-Sector Productivity," *Harvard Business Review,* July–August 1997, pp. 87–95.

30. Philip Cateora, *International Marketing,* 8th ed. (Homewood, IL: Irwin, 1993), p. 270.

31. See Carla Rapoport, "Retailers Go Global," *Fortune,* February 20, 1995, pp. 102–8; "Top 200 Global Retailers," *Stores,* January 1998, pp. S5–S12; Jeffery Adler, "The Americanization of Global Retailing," *Discount Merchandiser,* February 1998, p. 102; and Tony Lisanti, "Europe's Abuzz over Wal-Mart," *Discount Store News,* May 3, 1999, p. 11.

32. Lee Smith, "What's at Stake in the Trade Talks," *Fortune,* August 27, 1990, pp. 76–77.

COMPANY CASE

8

Swatchmobile: Is the Time Right for Small Cars?

If someone asked you what a Swatch watch and a Mercedes-Benz automobile have in common, you would probably answer, "not much." Perhaps you'd think the question was the lead in to a joke. After all, the Swatch is a disposable $35 to $50 fashion watch made on assembly lines from plastic parts. Mercedes, by contrast, prides itself on making the "best engineered cars in the world"—highly complex machines designed by engineers who cut no corners and make no compromises.

AN UNLIKELY MARRIAGE

Well, that's all true, but the Swiss Corporation for Microelectronics and Watchmaking Industries (SMH) and Mercedes do have one thing in common—the Swatchmobile. In 1994, the two companies announced that they would jointly develop an innovative, subcompact, economy car designed to reach speeds of up to 90 miles per hour while getting 80 miles per gallon and costing about $10,000. The idea behind the joint venture was to combine Mercedes' knowledge of how to design and build automobiles with SMH's knowledge of microtechnology design and automated production.

FROM THE DRAWING BOARD

The Swatchmobile concept results from the work of several dozen young jeans-and-sweatshirt-clad engineers who labored around the clock for three years in a secret garage in Biel, Switzerland. They conceived a two-seater car that would combine the safety features of a Mercedes with the funkiness of a Swatch watch. Besides reaching high speeds and getting great fuel economy, the Swatchmobile would be about 20 percent smaller than a typical subcompact—you could park it sideways in a typical parking space! To help accomplish all this, the engineers designed a 600cc, three-cylinder engine that would run on gasoline, electricity, or a combination of the two and weigh one-tenth the amount of a typical gas engine while achieving equal power.

The unlikely marriage is also the result of market realities. Swatch, following its success in watches, was searching for something else on which to put its name. It had tried telephones, pager watches, and sunglasses—all without much success. In the meantime, Mercedes watched its sales plummet 11 percent in the early 1990s because of stiff Japanese competition in the luxury car market. Mercedes felt it needed to attract buyers who could not afford its traditional cars. It had already announced plans to introduce a compact, four-seat model called the "Vision A" at a price of about $18,000 in 1997.

In addition, many car companies were beginning to work on concepts for smaller cars. The companies feared that large cities might ban conventional cars due to pollution concerns. Thus, the companies wanted to begin designing smaller cars that produced less pollution. Most were examining cars powered with electric engines.

MICROCOMPACT CARS

Swatch and Mercedes formed a joint venture known as Micro Compact Car AG (MCC) to develop the new car. Nicolas Hayek, the man who led Swatch to its success, initially owned 49 percent of the company with Mercedes owning 51 percent. Mercedes has since purchased the remaining interest in the company so that it now owns 100 percent. The company is headquartered in Biel, where it has 80 people on its staff. It also has a technical center in Renningen, Germany, where it employs 170 people.

MCC has invested about $507 million for research and development on the new car, and its suppliers have invested another $507 million for new plant and equipment. MCC will produce the car in Hambach, France. At full capacity, the plant will employ 2,000 people and produce 200,000 cars per year.

The companies changed the car's name to "Smart"—a combination of *Swatch, Mercedes,* and *art.* The Smart Car targets single people aged 18–36 and childless, dual-income couples living in urban areas who want a second car. The company wants to position the car as a fun but useful means of transportation in crowded cities. Although the car is small, it offers the crash protection of a Mercedes-Benz sedan.

Since the initial conception, the designers have abandoned the electric engine, because of the lack of adequate batteries, in favor of a small gasoline engine. Instead of using a conventional assembly line, assemblers will snap the cars together, much as you would a child's toy model car, using five subassembly modules that come from suppliers' factories located immediately around the assembly site in Hambach. Workers can assemble the car in just four and a half hours. Because the car snaps together, the company will offer customers the ability to change the cars' features. For example, if after a month or so the customer does not like the car's color, he or she can simply replace the panels with others of another color. The car's overall length is 98.4 inches. However, even though it is small on the outside, engineers say it is roomy on the inside. The Smart gets 47 to 49 miles per gallon with its 44–54 horsepower engines and has a top speed of 84 mph. Maintenance stops are guaranteed to take less than two hours.

The company expects to begin selling the car in March 1998 at a price between $9,405 and $11,402. At this price, the dealer margin is 16 percent. Dealers will offer a leasing package that includes the rental of a larger car for two weeks per year when the customer might want more seats and room for luggage. Financing, licensing, and insurance are available on site, so purchasing a Smart takes less than an hour.

MCC began signing up dealers in 1997, with a target of signing up 100 in Europe (not including the United Kingdom) in the first phase of developing distribution. Although it will give preference to Mercedes dealers, it has also advertised for interested entrepreneurs. Even Mercedes dealers, however, would have to set up separate dealerships to handle Smart. The second phase of distribution will cover the United Kingdom, Japan, and other right-hand-drive countries and the United States. The company has not indicated when this second phase will begin.

Dealers who want to distribute the Smart Car, as it is now called, will have to invest about $5 million to open a "Smart Centre." Of this amount, about $2 million is for land. MCC prefers that dealers build on land located near suburban shopping centers. The dealerships will be glass towers in which dealers can stack the brightly colored cars vertically, providing highly visible landmarks and convenient storage. The dealer will get an assigned geographic area capable of generating 1,000 unit sales per year with the expectation that sales will increase to 1,300 units per year by 2001. The dealer will need a staff of 15 people initially with the expectation that it will sell 1,000 units in the first year.

The franchise agreement is much like a fast-food franchise in that there are tight restrictions on showroom design and customer service. Dealers who violate provisions in the agreement can lose their franchise quickly. The agreement requires that the dealer pay a fee of $72 per new car and $36 per used car to MCC to support marketing campaigns. They will also have to pay about $42,000 to support marketing research.

Dealers will also have to establish two other locations where consumers can get information about the car. One location will have to be in an airport or railway station, and a second location will have to be in a shopping center.

To promote the car's eventual introduction in France, MCC began a $50 million "street awareness" campaign in October 1997 that featured promotion teams handing out postcards which merely read, "Reduce to the max," without mentioning the car's name. Early ads just depicted the car operating in urban environments.

MCC projects that after five years, the typical dealer will have sales of about $18.1 million, with a gross profit on sales of 15 percent, and a net return of 4 percent to 5 percent of sales, about $725,000.

WILL THE SMART CAR FLY?

Needless to say, there are plenty of skeptics who do not believe a tiny, two-seater car with almost no luggage space will make it in the highly competitive automobile market.

However, other manufacturers are also targeting the minicar market. Ford believes that tiny cars will eventually account for about one-third of the market. It has a factory in Valencia, Spain, that is already producing 200,000 Ka models per year, and it plans to increase capacity. Volkswagen, GM, BMW, and Rover all have minicar models under development. These companies are chasing Renault, which introduced its Twingo model minicar in 1993 and is selling 230,000 a year, about 2 percent of the West European car market.

It will be up to consumers to determine whether there is a market for these small cars or whether, like the Ford Edsel in the 1950s, the Smart Car will end up in museums as an example of one more time when car manufacturers missed the market.

Questions

1. What core product is MCC offering in the Smart Car? What are the actual and augmented parts of the product?

2. Into which consumer product classification does the Smart Car fall? What are the implications of this classification for MCC's marketing strategy?

3. What individual product decisions and product line decisions has MCC made for the Smart Car? Why did it make these decisions?

4. What marketing recommendations would you make to MCC?

5. What recommendations would you make to MCC when it decides to enter the U.S. market?

Sources: Thomas A. Sancton, "A Car, a Watch? Swatchmobile!" *Time,* March 28, 1994, p. 56; "Smaller Cars, Bigger Profits? European Cars," *The Economist,* November 9, 1996, p. 82; Luca Ciferri, "Smart to Get First Dealers This Spring," *Automotive News,* March 11, 1996, p. 20; Stefan Schlott, "Get Smart," *Automotive Industries,* August 1997, p. 75; Haig Simonian, "Mercedes-Benz May Play It Smart: Luxury Carmaker Hints at Developing Tiny Two-Seater into a 'Second Brand'," *Financial Times,* London Edition, October 6, 1997, p. 1; "Smart Car Builds Street Awareness," *Euromarketing Via E-mail,* October 17, 1997.

CONCEPT CONNECTIONS

After studying this chapter, you should be able to
1. explain how companies find and develop new-product ideas
2. list and define the steps in the new-product development process
3. describe the stages of the product life cycle
4. describe how marketing strategies change during the product's life cycle

CHAPTER 9

NEW-PRODUCT DEVELOPMENT AND PRODUCT LIFE-CYCLE STRATEGIES

"New products!" declares Gillette's chairman and CEO Alfred M. Zeien. "That's the name of the game." Since its founding in 1901, Gillette's heavy commitment to innovation has kept the company razor sharp. Gillette is best known for its absolute dominance of the razor-and-blades market. However, all of its divisions—Duracell batteries, Gillette toiletries and cosmetics (Right Guard, Soft & Dri), stationery products (Parker, Paper Mate, and Waterman pens), Oral-B toothbrushes, and Braun electrical appliances—share common traits: Each is profitable, fast growing, number one worldwide in its markets, and anchored by a steady flow of innovative new-product offerings. Zeien predicts that 50 percent of Gillette's new products will soon come from products that didn't exist five years ago—that's twice the level of innovation found at the average consumer-products company. "Gillette is a new-product machine," says one Wall Street analyst.

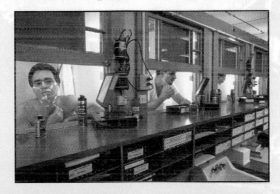

New products don't just happen at Gillette. New-product success starts with a company-wide culture that supports innovation. Whereas many companies try to protect their successful current products, Gillette encourages innovations that will cannibalize its established product hits. "They know that if they don't bring out a new zinger, someone else will," observes an industry consultant. Gillette also accepts blunders and dead ends as a normal part of creativity and innovation. It knows that it must generate dozens of new-product ideas to get just one success in the marketplace. The company scorns what CEO Zeien calls "putting blue dots in the soap powder"—attaching superficial frills to existing products and labeling them innovations. However, Gillette strongly encourages its people to take creative risks in applying cutting-edge technologies to find substantial improvements that make life easier for customers.

New-product development is complex and expensive, but Gillette's mastery of the process has put the company in a class of its own. For example, Gillette spent $275 million on designing and developing its Sensor family of razors, garnering 29 patents along the way. It spent an incredible $1 billion on the development of Sensor's successor, the triple-bladed Mach3, and applied for 35 more patents. Competing brands Bic and Wilkinson have managed to claim significant shares of the disposable-razor market, and Shick, Norelco, and Remington compete effectively in electric razors with Gillette's Braun unit. But Gillette, with its stunning technological superiority, operates with virtually no competition worldwide in the burgeoning cartridge-razor sector. Backed by Gillette's biggest new-product launch ever, the

Mach3 strengthened the company's stranglehold on this market. Within only a few months of its introduction, the new razor and blades were number-one sellers.

At Gillette, it seems that almost everyone gets involved in one way or another with new-product development. Even people who don't participate directly in the product design and development are likely to be pressed into service testing prototypes. Every working day at Gillette, 200 volunteers from various departments come to work unshaven, troop to the second floor of the company's gritty South Boston manufacturing and research plant, and enter small booths with a sink and mirror. There they take instructions from technicians on the other side of a small window as to which razor, shaving cream, or aftershave to use. The volunteers evaluate razors for sharpness of blade, smoothness of glide, and ease of handling. When finished, they enter their judgments into a computer. In a nearby shower room, women perform the same ritual on their legs, underarms, and what the company delicately refers to as the "bikini area." "We bleed so you'll get a good shave at home," says one Gillette employee.

Gillette also excels at bringing new products to market. The company understands that, once introduced, fledgling products need generous manufacturing and marketing support to thrive in the hotly competitive consumer products mar-
ketplace. To deliver the required support, Gillette has devised a formula that calls for R&D, capital investment, and advertising expenditures—which it refers to collectively as "growth drivers"—to rise in combination at least as fast as sales. Last year, spending on these growth drivers rose 16 percent as compared with a 12 percent rise in sales. The company spent a staggering $300 million on introductory advertising and marketing for the Mach3 alone.

Thus, over the decades, superior new products have been the cornerstone of Gillette's amazing success. The company commands the loyalty of more than 700 million shavers in 200 countries around the globe. These customers have purchased hundreds of millions of Gillette razors and billions of blades, giving Gillette more than 70 percent of the wet-shave market in the United States and 72 percent of the $7 billion worldwide market. Last year, Gillette was named by the American Marketing Association as its New Product Marketer of the Year.

Gillette's new-product prowess is so much a part of its image that it has even become the stuff of jokes. Quips down-home humorist Dave Barry, "One day soon the Gillette Company will announce the development of a razor that, thanks to a computer microchip, can actually travel ahead in time and shave beard hairs that don't even exist yet."[1]

A company has to be good at developing and managing new products. Every product seems to go through a life cycle—it is born, goes through several phases, and eventually dies as newer products come along that better serve consumer needs. This product life cycle presents two major challenges: First, because all products eventually decline, a firm must be good at developing new products to replace aging ones (the problem of *new-product development*). Second, the firm must be good at adapting its marketing strategies in the face of changing tastes, technologies, and competition as products pass through life-cycle stages (the problem of *product life-cycle strategies*). We first look at the problem of finding and developing new products and then at the problem of managing them successfully over their life cycles.

NEW-PRODUCT DEVELOPMENT STRATEGY

Given the rapid changes in consumer tastes, technology, and competition, companies must develop a steady stream of new products and services. A firm can obtain new products in two ways. One is through *acquisition*—by buying a whole company, a patent, or a license to produce someone else's product. The other is

New-product development
The development of original products, product improvements, product modifications, and new brands through the firm's own R&D efforts.

through **new-product development** in the company's own research and development department. By *new products* we mean original products, product improvements, product modifications, and new brands that the firm develops through its own research and development efforts. In this chapter, we concentrate on new-product development.

Innovation can be very risky. Ford lost $350 million on its Edsel automobile; RCA lost $580 million on its SelectaVision videodisc player; and Texas Instruments lost a staggering $660 million before withdrawing from the home computer business. Other costly product failures from sophisticated companies include New Coke (Coca-Cola Company), Eagle Snacks (Anheuser-Busch), Zap Mail electronic mail (Federal Express), Polarvision instant movies (Polaroid), Premier "smokeless" cigarettes (R.J. Reynolds), Clorox detergent (Clorox Company), and Arch Deluxe sandwiches (McDonald's).[2]

New products continue to fail at a disturbing rate. One source estimates that new consumer packaged goods (consisting mostly of line extensions) fail at a rate of 80 percent. Another study suggested that of the staggering 25,000 new consumer food, beverage, beauty, and health care products to hit the market each year, only 40 percent will be around five years later. Moreover, failure rates for new industrial products may be as high as 30 percent.[3] Why do so many new products fail? There are several reasons. Although an idea may be good, the market size may have been overestimated. Perhaps the actual product was not designed as well as it should have been. Or maybe it was incorrectly positioned in the market, priced too high, or advertised poorly. A high-level executive might push a favorite idea despite poor marketing research findings. Sometimes the costs of product development are higher than expected, and sometimes competitors fight back harder than expected.

Because so many new products fail, companies are anxious to learn how to improve their odds of new-product success. One way is to identify successful new products and find out what they have in common. Another is to study new-product failures to see what lessons can be learned (see Marketing Highlight 9.1). Various studies suggest that new-product success depends on developing a *unique superior product,* one with higher quality, new features, and higher value in use. Another key success factor is a *well-defined product concept* prior to development, in which the company carefully defines and assesses the target market, the product requirements, and the benefits before proceeding. Other success factors have also been suggested—senior management commitment, relentless innovation, and a smoothly functioning new-product development process.[4] In all, to create successful new products, a company must understand its consumers, markets, and competitors and develop products that deliver superior value to customers.

So companies face a problem—they must develop new products, but the odds weigh heavily against success. The solution lies in strong new-product planning and in setting up a systematic *new-product development process* for finding and growing new products. Figure 9.1 shows the eight major steps in this process.

Idea Generation

Idea generation
The systematic search for new-product ideas.

New-product development starts with **idea generation**—the systematic search for new-product ideas. A company typically has to generate many ideas in order to find a few good ones. At Gillette, of every 45 carefully developed new-product ideas, 3 make it into the development stage and only 1 eventually reaches the marketplace. DuPont has found that it can take as many as 3,000 raw ideas to produce just 2 winning commercial products, and pharmaceutical companies may require 6,000 to 8,000 starting ideas for every successful commercial new product.[5]

MR. FAILURE'S LESSONS FOR SWEET SUCCESS

Strolling the aisles at Robert McMath's New Product Showcase and Learning Center is like finding yourself in some nightmare version of a supermarket. There's Gerber food for adults (pureed sweet-and-sour pork and chicken Madeira), Hot Scoop microwaveable ice cream sundaes, Ben-Gay aspirin, Premier smokeless cigarettes, and Miller Clear Beer. How about Richard Simmons Dijon Vinaigrette Salad Spray, Look of Buttermilk shampoo, or garlic cake in a jar, parsnip chips, and aerosol mustard? Most of the 80,000 products on display were abject flops. Behind each of them are squandered dollars and hopes, but

McMath, the genial curator of this Smithsonian of consumerism, believes that even failure—or perhaps *especially* failure—offers valuable lessons.

The New Product Showcase and Learning Center is a place where product developers pay hundreds of dollars an hour to visit and learn from others' mistakes. McMath's unusual showcase represents $4 billion in product investment. From it he has distilled dozens of lessons for an industry that, by its own admission, has a very short memory. McMath "draws large audiences and commands a hefty speaking fee by decrying the convoluted thought

processes of marketers, package designers, and consumer-opinion pundits who brought these and thousands of other duds-in-the-making to market," comments one analyst. "He gets laughs when he asks, 'What were they thinking?'" For those who can't make the trip to the center or pay a steep consulting fee, McMath has now put his unique insights into a book by that same name, *What Were They Thinking?* Here are a few of the marketing lessons McMath espouses:

- *Offer real value:* Many classic flops failed to deliver what customers really wanted. New Coke flopped when Coca-Cola failed to see the real value of the Coke brand to customers—tradition as well as taste. Ford pitched its Edsel as revolutionary; consumers saw it as merely revolting. Consumers quickly snuffed out R.J. Reynolds's Premier smokeless cigarettes. It seemed like a good idea at the time—who could argue against a healthier, nonpolluting cigarette? But Premier didn't deliver what smokers really wanted—smoke. In the first place, in the words of RJR's CEO, the cigarettes "tasted like expletive!" Moreover, what is a cigarette without smoke? "It took them a while to figure out that

The New Product Showcase and Learning Center is like finding yourself in some nightmare version of a supermarket. Each product failure represents squandered dollars and hopes.

Major sources of new-product ideas include internal sources, customers, competitors, distributors and suppliers, and others. Using *internal sources,* the company can find new ideas through formal research and development. It can pick the brains of its executives, scientists, engineers, manufacturing, and salespeople. Some companies have developed successful "intrapreneurial" programs that encourage employees to think up and develop new-product ideas. For example, 3M's well-smokers actually like the smoke part of smoking," McMath notes. "The only people who loved the product were nonsmokers, and they somehow aren't the market RJR was trying to reach." In retrospect, what was RJR thinking?

- *Cherish thy brand!* The value of a brand is its good name, which it earns over time. People become loyal to it. They trust it to deliver a consistent set of attributes. Don't squander this trust by attaching your good name to something totally out of character. Louis Sherry No Sugar Added Gorgonzola Cheese Dressing was everything that Louis Sherry, known for its rich candies and ice cream, shouldn't be: sugarless, cheese, and salad dressing. Similarly, when you hear the name Ben-Gay, you immediately think of the way that Ben-Gay cream sears and stimulates your skin. Can you imagine swallowing Ben-Gay aspirin? Or how would you feel about quaffing a can of Exxon fruit punch or Kodak quencher? Cracker Jack cereal, Smucker's premium ketchup, and Fruit of the Loom laundry detergent were other misbegotten attempts to stretch a good name. What *were* they thinking?

- *Be different:* Me-too marketing is the number-one killer of new products. Most such attempts fail. The ones that succeed usually require resources and persistence beyond the capabilities of most marketers. Pepsi-Cola led a very precarious existence for decades

before establishing itself as the major competitor to Coca-Cola. More to the point, though, Pepsi is one of the few survivors among dozens of other brands that have challenged Coke for more than a century. Ever hear of Toca-Cola? Coco-Cola? Yum-Yum cola? French Wine of Cola? How about King-Cola, "the royal drink"? More recently, Afri Cola failed to attract African American soda drinkers and Cajun Cola pretty well flopped in the land of gumbo. All things equal, an established product has a distinct advantage over any new product that is not notably different.

- *But don't be too different:* Some products are notably different from the products, services, or experiences that consumers normally purchase. *Too* different. They fail because consumers don't relate to them. You can tell that some innovative products are doomed as soon as you hear their names: Toaster Eggs. Cucumber antiperspirant spray. Health-Sea sea sausage. Look of Buttermilk shampoo. Other innovative ideas have been victims of a brand's past success. For example, Nabisco's Oreo Little Fudgies, a confectionery product with a chocolate coating meant to compete with candy, sounds like a natural. But for many years Nabisco has encouraged people to pull apart Oreo cookies and lick out the filling. However, it's very messy to open an Oreo with a chocolate coating. What was *Nabisco* thinking?

- *Accentuate the positive:* Don't be fooled by the success of all the *Dummy's Guide to . . .* books. People usually don't buy products that remind them of their shortcomings. Gillette's For Oily Hair Only shampoo wavered because people did not want to confess that they had greasy hair. People will use products that discreetly say "for oily hair" or "for sensitive skin" in small print on containers that are otherwise identical to the regular product. But they don't want to be hit over the head with reminders that they are overweight, have bad breath, sweat too much, or are elderly. Nor do they wish to advertise their faults and foibles to other people by carrying such products in their grocery carts. Really, what were they thinking?

Sources: See Paul Lukas, "The Ghastliest Product Launches," *Fortune*, March 16, 1996, p. 44; Jan Alexander, "Failure Inc.," *Worldbusiness*, May June 1996, p. 46; Ted Anthony, "Where's Farrah Shampoo? Next to the Salsa Ketchup," *Marketing News*, May 6, 1996, p. 13. Quotes from Gary Slack, "Innovations and Idiocies," *Beverage World*, November 15, 1998; and Cliff Edwards, "Where Have All the Edsels Gone?" *Greensboro News Record*, May 24, 1999, p. B6. Bulleted points based on information found in Robert M. McMath and Thom Forbes, *What Were They Thinking? Money-Saving, Time-Saving, Face-Saving Marketing Lessons You Can Learn from Products That Flopped* (New York: Times Business, 1999), various pages.

known "15 percent rule" allows employees to spend 15 percent of their time "bootlegging"—working on projects of personal interest whether or not those projects directly benefit the company. The spectacularly successful Post-it notes evolved out of this program. Similarly, Texas Instruments's IDEA program provides funds for employees who pursue their own ideas. Among the successful new products to come out of the IDEA program was TI's Speak 'n' Spell, the first children's

FIGURE 9.1 Major stages in new-product development

toy to contain a microchip. Many other speaking toys followed, ultimately generating several hundred million dollars for TI.[6]

Good new-product ideas also come from watching and listening to *customers.* The company can analyze customer questions and complaints to find new products that better solve consumer problems. The company can conduct surveys or focus groups to learn about consumer needs and wants. Or company engineers or salespeople can meet with and work alongside customers to get suggestions and ideas. For example, United States Surgical Corporation (USSC) has developed most of its surgical instruments by working closely with surgeons. The company was quick to pick up on early experiments in laparoscopy—surgery performed by inserting a tiny TV camera into the body along with slim, long-handled instruments. USSC now captures about 58 percent of the single-use laparoscopy market.[7]

Finally, consumers often create new products and uses on their own, and companies can benefit by finding these products and putting them on the market. Customers can also be a good source of ideas for new product uses that can expand the market for and extend the life of current products. For example, Avon capitalized on new uses discovered by consumers for its Skin-So-Soft bath oil and moisturizer. For years, customers have been spreading the word that Skin-So-Soft bath oil is also a terrific bug repellent. Whereas some consumers were content simply to bathe in water scented with the fragrant oil, others carried it in their backpacks to mosquito-infested campsites or kept a bottle on the deck of their beach houses. Now, Avon offers a complete line of Skin-So-Soft Bug Guard products, including Bug Guard Plus, a combination moisturizer, insect repellent, and sunscreen.[8]

Competitors are another good source of new-product ideas. Companies watch competitors' ads and other communications to get clues about their new products. They buy competing new products, take them apart to see how they work, analyze their sales, and decide whether they should bring out a new product of their own. Finally, *distributors and suppliers* contribute many good new-product ideas. Resellers are close to the market and can pass along information about consumer problems and new-product possibilities. Suppliers can tell the company about new concepts, techniques, and materials that can be used to develop new products. Other idea sources include trade magazines, shows, and seminars; government agencies; new-product consultants; advertising agencies; marketing research firms; university and commercial laboratories; and inventors.

"Intrapreneurial" programs encourage employees to think up and develop new product ideas. 3M's spectacularly successful Post-it notes evolved out of such a program.

The search for new-product ideas should be systematic rather than haphazard. Otherwise, few new ideas will surface and many good ideas will sputter in and die. Top management can avoid these problems by installing an *idea management system* that directs the flow of new ideas to a central point where they can be collected, reviewed, and evaluated. In setting up such a system, the company can do any or all of the following:[9]

★ Appoint a respected senior person to be the company's idea manager.
★ Create a multidisciplinary idea management committee consisting of people from R&D, engineering, purchasing, operations, finance, and sales and marketing to meet regularly and evaluate proposed new-product and service ideas.
★ Set up a toll-free number for anyone who wants to send a new idea to the idea manager.
★ Encourage all company stakeholders—employees, suppliers, distributors, dealers—to send their ideas to the idea manager.
★ Set up formal recognition programs to reward those who contribute the best new ideas.

The idea manager approach yields two favorable outcomes. First, it helps create an innovation-oriented company culture. It shows that top management supports, encourages, and rewards innovation. Second, it will yield a larger number of ideas among which will be found some especially good ones. As the system matures, ideas will flow more freely. No longer will good ideas wither for the lack of a sounding board or a senior product advocate.

Idea Screening

Idea screening
Screening new-product ideas in order to spot good ideas and drop poor ones as soon as possible.

The purpose of idea generation is to create a large number of ideas. The purpose of the succeeding stages is to *reduce* that number. The first idea-reducing stage is **idea screening,** which helps spot good ideas and drop poor ones as soon as possible. Product development costs rise greatly in later stages, so the company wants to go ahead only with the product ideas that will turn into profitable products. As one marketing executive suggests, "Three executives sitting in a room can get 40 good ideas ricocheting off the wall in minutes. The challenge is getting a steady stream of good ideas out of the labs and creativity campfires, through marketing and manufacturing, and all the way to consumers."[10]

Many companies require their executives to write up new-product ideas on a standard form that can be reviewed by a new-product committee. The write-up describes the product, the target market, and the competition. It makes some rough estimates of market size, product price, development time and costs, manufacturing costs, and rate of return. The committee then evaluates the idea against a set of general criteria. For example, at Kao Company, the large Japanese consumer-products company, the committee asks questions such as these: Is the product truly useful to consumers and society? Is it good for our particular company? Does it mesh well with the company's objectives and strategies? Do we have the people, skills, and resources to make it succeed? Does it deliver more value to customers than do competing products? Is it easy to advertise and distribute? Many companies have well-designed systems for rating and screening new-product ideas.

Concept Development and Testing

Product concept
A detailed version of the new-product idea stated in meaningful consumer terms.

An attractive idea must be developed into a **product concept.** It is important to distinguish between a product idea, a product concept, and a product image. A *product idea* is an idea for a possible product that the company can see itself offering to the market. A *product concept* is a detailed version of the idea stated in meaningful consumer terms. A *product image* is the way consumers perceive an actual or potential product.

Concept Development
DaimlerChrysler is getting ready to commercialize its experimental fuel-cell-powered electric car. This car's low-polluting fuel-cell system runs directly off liquid hydrogen. It is highly fuel efficient (75 percent more efficient than gasoline engines) and gives the new car an environmental advantage over standard internal combustion engine cars. DaimlerChrysler is currently road testing its NECAR 4 (New Electric Car) subcompact prototype and plans to deliver the first fuel-cell cars to customers in 2004. Based on the tiny Mercedes A-Class, the car accelerates quickly, reaches speeds of 90 miles per hour, and has a 280-mile driving range, giving it a huge edge over battery-powered electric cars that travel only about 80 miles before needing 3 to 12 hours of recharging.[11]

DaimlerChrysler's task is to develop this new product into alternative product concepts, find out how attractive each concept is to customers, and choose the best one. It might create the following product concepts for the fuel-cell electric car:

Concept 1   A moderately priced subcompact designed as a second family car to be used around town. The car is ideal for running errands and visiting friends.

DaimlerChrysler's task is to develop its fuel-cell powered electric car into alternative product concepts, find out how attractive each is to customers, and choose the best one.

| Concept 2 | A medium-cost sporty compact appealing to young people. |
| Concept 3 | An inexpensive subcompact "green" car appealing to environmentally conscious people who want practical transportation and low pollution. |

Concept Testing

Concept testing calls for testing new-product concepts with groups of target consumers. The concepts may be presented to consumers symbolically or physically. Here, in words, is concept 3:

> An efficient, fun-to-drive, fuel-cell-powered electric subcompact car that seats four. This high-tech wonder runs on liquid hydrogen, providing practical and reliable transportation with almost no pollution. It goes up to 90 miles per hour and, unlike battery-powered electric cars, it never needs recharging. It's priced, fully equipped, at $20,000.

For some concept tests, a word or picture description might be sufficient. However, a more concrete and physical presentation of the concept will increase the reliability of the concept test. Today, some marketers are finding innovative ways to make product concepts more real to consumer subjects. For example, some are using virtual reality to test product concepts. Virtual reality programs use computers and sensory devices (such as gloves or goggles) to simulate reality. For example, a designer of kitchen cabinets can use a virtual reality program to help a customer "see" how his or her kitchen would look and work if remodeled with the company's products. Although virtual reality is still in its infancy, its applications are increasing daily.[12]

After being exposed to the concept, consumers then may be asked to react to it by answering questions such as those in Table 9.1. The answers will help the company decide which concept has the strongest appeal. For example, the last question asks about the consumer's intention to buy. Suppose 10 percent of the consumers said they "definitely" would buy and another 5 percent said "probably." The company could project these figures to the full population in this target group to estimate sales volume. Even then, the estimate is uncertain because people do not always carry out their stated intentions.

Many firms routinely test new-product concepts with consumers before attempting to turn them into actual new products. For example, each month Richard Saunders, Inc.'s Acu-Poll research system tests 35 new-product concepts in person on 100 nationally representative grocery store shoppers. In recent polls,

Concept testing
Testing new-product concepts with a group of target consumers to find out if the concepts have strong consumer appeal.

TABLE 9.1   QUESTIONS FOR FUEL-CELL ELECTRIC CAR CONCEPT TEST
1. Do you understand the concept of a fuel-cell-powered electric car?
2. Do you believe the claims about the car's performance?
3. What are the major benefits of the fuel-cell-powered electric car compared with a conventional car?
4. What are its advantages compared with a batter-powered electric car?
5. What improvements in the car's features would you suggest?
6. For what uses would you prefer a fuel-cell-powered electric car to a conventional car?
7. What would be a reasonable price to charge for the car?
8. Who would be involved in your decision to buy such a car? Who would drive it?
9. Would you buy such a car? (Definitely, probably, probably not, definitely not)

Nabisco's Oreo Chocolate Cones concept received a rare A+ rating, meaning that consumers think it is an outstanding concept that they would try and buy. Lender's Bake at Home Bagels were also a big hit. Other product concepts didn't fare so well. Nubrush Anti-Bacterial Toothbrush Spray disinfectant, from Applied Microdontics, received an F. Consumers found Nubrush to be overpriced, and most don't think they have a problem with "infected" toothbrushes. Another concept that fared poorly was Chef Williams 5 Minute Marinade, which comes with a syringe customers use to inject the marinade into meats. "I can't see that on grocery shelves," comments an Acu-Poll executive. Some consumers might find the thought of injecting something into meat a bit repulsive, and "it's just so politically incorrect to have this syringe on there."[13]

Marketing Strategy Development

Marketing strategy development
Designing an initial marketing strategy for a new product based on the product concept.

Suppose DaimlerChrysler finds that concept 3 for the fuel-cell-powered electric car tests best. The next step is **marketing strategy development,** designing an initial marketing strategy for introducing this car to the market.

The *marketing strategy statement* consists of three parts. The first part describes the target market; the planned product positioning; and the sales, market share, and profit goals for the first few years. Thus:

> The target market is younger, well-educated, moderate-to-high-income individuals, couples, or small families seeking practical, environmentally responsible transportation. The car will be positioned as more economical to operate, more fun to drive, and less polluting than today's internal combustion engine cars, and as less restricting than battery-powered electric cars, which must be recharged regularly. The company will aim to sell 100,000 cars in the first year, at a loss of not more than $15 million. In the second year, the company will aim for sales of 120,000 cars and a profit of $25 million.

The second part of the marketing strategy statement outlines the product's planned price, distribution, and marketing budget for the first year:

> The fuel-cell-powered electric car will be offered in three colors—red, white, and blue—and will have optional air-conditioning and power-drive features. It will sell at a retail price of $20,000—with 15 percent off the list price to dealers. Dealers who sell more than 10 cars per month will get an additional discount of 5 percent on each car sold that month. An advertising budget of $20 million will be split 50–50 between national and local advertising. Advertising will emphasize the car's fun and low emissions. During the first year, $100,000 will be spent on marketing research to find out who is buying the car and their satisfaction levels.

The third part of the marketing strategy statement describes the planned long-run sales, profit goals, and marketing mix strategy:

> DaimlerChrysler intends to capture a 3 percent long-run share of the total auto market and realize an after-tax return on investment of 15 percent. To achieve this, product quality will start high and be improved over time. Price will be raised in the second and third years if competition permits. The total advertising budget will be raised each year by about 10 percent. Marketing research will be reduced to $60,000 per year after the first year.

Business Analysis

Business analysis
A review of the sales, costs, and profit projections for a new product to find out whether these factors satisfy the company's objectives.

Once management has decided on its product concept and marketing strategy, it can evaluate the business attractiveness of the proposal. **Business analysis** involves a review of the sales, costs, and profit projections for a new product to find out whether they satisfy the company's objectives. If they do, the product can move to the product development stage.

To estimate sales, the company might look at the sales history of similar products and conduct surveys of market opinion. It can then estimate minimum and maximum sales to assess the range of risk. After preparing the sales forecast, management can estimate the expected costs and profits for the product, including marketing, R&D, operations, accounting, and finance costs. The company then uses the sales and costs figures to analyze the new product's financial attractiveness.

Product Development

Product development
A strategy for company growth by offering modified or new products to current market segments. Developing the product concept into a physical product in order to ensure that the product idea can be turned into a workable product.

So far, for many new-product concepts, the product may have existed only as a word description, a drawing, or perhaps a crude mock-up. If the product concept passes the business test, it moves into **product development.** Here, R&D or engineering develops the product concept into a physical product. The product development step, however, now calls for a large jump in investment. It will show whether the product idea can be turned into a workable product.

The R&D department will develop and test one or more physical versions of the product concept. R&D hopes to design a prototype that will satisfy and excite consumers and that can be produced quickly and at budgeted costs. Developing a successful prototype can take days, weeks, months, or even years. Often, products undergo rigorous functional tests to make sure that they perform safely and effectively. Here are some examples of such functional tests:[14]

★ A scuba-diving Barbie doll must swim and kick for 15 straight hours to satisfy Mattel that she will last at least one year. But because Barbie may find her feet in small owners' mouths rather than in the bathtub, Mattel has devised another, more torturous test: Barbie's feet are clamped by two steel jaws to make sure that her skin doesn't crack—and choke—potential owners.

★ At Shaw Industries, temps are paid $5 an hour to pace up and down 5 long rows of sample carpets for up to 8 hours a day, logging an average of 14 miles each. One regular reads 3 mysteries a week while pacing and shed 40 pounds in 2 years. Shaw Industries counts walkers' steps and figures that 20,000 steps equal several years of average carpet wear.

★ Acting on behalf of manufacturers, the Buyers Laboratory in Hackensack, New Jersey, an independent office products testing lab, tests the writing quality of ballpoint, felt-tip, and roller-ball pens. Its 50-pound "pen rig" measures a pen's life span.

Product testing: Shaw Industries pays temps to pace up and down 5 long rows of sample carpets for up to 8 hours a day, logging an average of 14 miles each.

The range fluctuates, but a medium-tip, made-in-the-U.S.A. ballpoint might last for 7,775 feet. In general, pens that blob, skip, and dot receive low ratings. Which pens fail the test altogether? "Some points are so fine they cut through the paper," says one supervisor, "and some felt-tips wear down long before the ink runs out."

The prototype must have the required functional features and also convey the intended psychological characteristics. The electric car, for example, should strike consumers as being well built, comfortable, and safe. Management must learn what makes consumers decide that a car is well built. To some consumers, this means that the car has "solid-sounding" doors. To others, it means that the car is able to withstand heavy impact in crash tests. Consumer tests are conducted in which consumers test-drive the car and rate its attributes.

Test Marketing

Test marketing
The stage of new-product development in which the product and marketing program are tested in more realistic market settings.

If the product passes functional and consumer tests, the next step is **test marketing,** the stage at which the product and marketing program are introduced into more realistic market settings. Test marketing gives the marketer experience with marketing the product before going to the great expense of full introduction. It lets the company test the product and its entire marketing program—positioning strategy, advertising, distribution, pricing, branding and packaging, and budget levels.

The amount of test marketing needed varies with each new product. Test marketing costs can be enormous, and it takes time that may allow competitors to gain advantages. When the costs of developing and introducing the product are low, or when management is already confident about the new product, the company may do little or no test marketing. Companies often do not test-market simple line extensions or copies of successful competitor products. For example, Procter & Gamble introduced its Folger's decaffeinated coffee crystals without test marketing, and Pillsbury rolled out Chewy granola bars and chocolate-covered Granola Dipps with no standard test market. However, when introducing a new product requires a big investment, or when management is not sure of the product or marketing program, a company may do a lot of test marketing. For instance, Lever USA spent two years testing its highly successful Lever 2000 bar soap in Atlanta before introducing it internationally. Frito-Lay did eighteen months of testing in three markets on at least five formulations before introducing its Baked Lays line of low-fat snacks.[15]

The costs of test marketing can be high, but they are often small when compared with the costs of making a major mistake. For example, Nabisco's launch of one new product without testing had disastrous—and soggy—results:[16]

> ★ Nabisco hit a marketing home run with its Teddy Grahams, teddy-bear-shaped graham crackers in several different flavors. So, the company decided to extend Teddy Grahams into a new area. In 1989, it introduced chocolate, cinnamon, and honey versions of Breakfast Bears Graham Cereal. When the product came out, however, consumers didn't like the taste enough, so the product developers went back to the kitchen and modified the formula. But they didn't test it. The result was a disaster. Although the cereal may have tasted better, it no longer stayed crunchy in milk, as the advertising on the box promised. Instead, it left a gooey mess of graham mush on the bottom of cereal bowls. Supermarket managers soon refused to restock the cereal, and Nabisco executives decided it was too late to reformulate the product again. So a promising new product was killed through haste to get it to market.

When using test marketing, consumer products companies usually choose one of three approaches—standard test markets, controlled test markets, or simulated test markets.

Standard Test Markets

Using standard test markets, the company finds a small number of representative test cities, conducts a full marketing campaign in these cities, and uses store audits, consumer and distributor surveys, and other measures to gauge product performance. The results are used to forecast national sales and profits, discover potential product problems, and fine-tune the marketing program.

Standard test markets have some drawbacks. They can be very costly and they may take a long time—some last as long as three years. Moreover, competitors can monitor test market results or even interfere with them by cutting their prices in test cities, increasing their promotion, or even buying up the product being tested. Finally, test markets give competitors a look at the company's new product well before it is introduced nationally. Thus, competitors may have time to develop defensive strategies, and may even beat the company's product to the market. For example, while Clorox was still test marketing its new detergent with bleach in selected markets, P&G launched Tide with Bleach nationally. Tide with Bleach quickly became the segment leader; Clorox later withdrew its detergent.

Despite these disadvantages, standard test markets are still the most widely used approach for major market testing. However, many companies today are shifting toward quicker and cheaper controlled and simulated test marketing methods.

Controlled Test Markets

Several research firms keep controlled panels of stores that have agreed to carry new products for a fee. Controlled test marketing systems like Nielsen's Scantrack and Information Resources, Inc.'s (IRI) BehaviorScan track individual behavior from the television set to the checkout counter. IRI keeps panels of 2,000 to 3,000 shoppers in 6 carefully selected markets.[17] It measures TV viewing in each panel household and can send special commercials to panel member television sets. Panel consumers buy from cooperating stores and show identification cards when making purchases.

Within test stores, IRI controls such factors as shelf placement, price, and in-store promotions. Detailed electronic scanner information on each consumer's

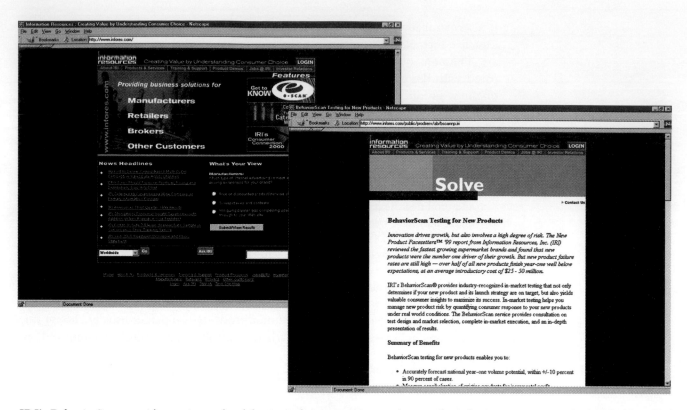

IRI's BehaviorScan provides an in-market laboratory for testing new products and marketing programs under highly controlled yet real-world conditions.

purchases is fed into a central computer, where it is combined with the consumer's demographic and TV viewing information and reported daily. Thus, BehaviorScan can provide store-by-store, week-by-week reports on the sales of new products being tested. Because the scanners record the specific purchases of individual consumers, the system also can provide information on repeat purchases and the ways that different types of consumers are reacting to the new product, its advertising, and various other elements of the marketing program.

Controlled test markets usually cost less than standard test markets and take less time (6 months to a year). A typical BehaviorScan test takes 16 to 24 months to complete. However, some companies are concerned that the limited number of small cities and panel consumers used by the research services may not be representative of their products' markets or target consumers. As in standard test markets, controlled test markets allow competitors to get a look at the company's new product.

Simulated Test Markets

Companies can also test new products in a simulated shopping environment. The company or research firm shows ads and promotions for a variety of products, including the new product being tested, to a sample of consumers. It gives consumers a small amount of money and invites them to a real or laboratory store where they may keep the money or use it to buy items. The researchers note how many consumers buy the new product and competing brands. This simulation provides a measure of trial and the commercial's effectiveness against competing commercials. The researchers then ask consumers the reasons for their purchase or nonpurchase. Some weeks later, they interview the consumers by phone to determine product attitudes, usage, satisfaction, and repurchase intentions. Using sophisticated computer models, the researchers then project national sales from results of the simulated test market. Recently, some marketers have begun to use interesting new high-tech approaches to simulated test market research, such as virtual reality and the Internet (see Marketing Highlight 9.2).

Simulated test markets overcome some of the disadvantages of standard and controlled test markets. They usually cost much less, can be run in eight weeks, and keep the new product out of competitors' view. Yet, because of their small samples and simulated shopping environments, many marketers do not think that simulated test markets are as accurate or reliable as larger, real-world tests. Still, simulated test markets are used widely, often as "pretest" markets. Because they are fast and inexpensive, they can be run to quickly assess a new product or its marketing program. If the pretest results are strongly positive, the product might be introduced without further testing. If the results are very poor, the product might be dropped or substantially redesigned and retested. If the results are promising but indefinite, the product and marketing program can be tested further in controlled or standard test markets.

Commercialization

Commercialization
Introducing a new product into the market.

Test marketing gives management the information needed to make a final decision about whether to launch the new product. If the company goes ahead with **commercialization**—introducing the new product into the market—it will face high costs. The company will have to build or rent a manufacturing facility. It may have to spend, in the case of a new consumer packaged good, between $10 million and $200 million for advertising, sales promotion, and other marketing efforts in the first year.

The company launching a new product must first decide on introduction *timing*. If DaimlerChrysler's new fuel-cell electric car will eat into the sales of the company's other cars, its introduction may be delayed. If the car can be improved further, or if the economy is down, the company may wait until the following year to launch it.

Next, the company must decide *where* to launch the new product—in a single location, a region, the national market, or the international market. Few companies have the confidence, capital, and capacity to launch new products into full national or international distribution. They will develop a planned *market rollout* over time. In particular, small companies may enter attractive cities or regions one at a time. Larger companies, however, may quickly introduce new models into several regions or into the full national market.

Companies with international distribution systems may introduce new products through global rollouts. Colgate-Palmolive uses a "lead-country" strategy. For example, it launched its Palmolive Optims shampoo and conditioner first in Australia, the Philippines, Hong Kong, and Mexico, then rapidly rolled it out into Europe, Asia,

Colgate-Palmolive introduces its new products internationally using a "lead country" strategy, launching the product first in a few important regions, followed by a swift global rollout.

MARKETING HIGHLIGHT
9 . 2

VIRTUAL REALITY TEST MARKETING: THE FUTURE IS NOW

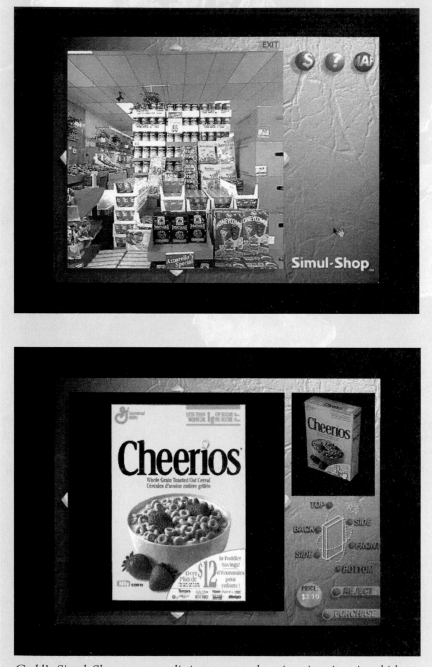

Gadd's Simul-Shop creates realistic on-screen shopping situations in which researchers can test consumers' reactions to factors such as product positioning, store layouts, and package designs. About the only thing consumers can't do is open the box and taste the cereal.

It's a steamy summer Saturday afternoon. Imagine that you're stopping off at the local supermarket to pick up some icy bottles of your favorite sports drink before heading to the tennis courts. You park the car, cross the parking lot, and walk through the store's automatic doors. You head for aisle 5, passing several displays along the way, and locate your usual sports drink brand. You pick it up, check the price, and take it to the checkout counter. Sounds like a pretty typical shopping experience, doesn't it? But in this case, the entire experience took place on your computer screen, not at the supermarket.

You've just experienced virtual reality—the wave of the future for test marketing and concept-testing research—courtesy of Gadd International Research. Gadd has developed a research tool called Simul-Shop, a CD-ROM virtual reality approach that recreates shopping situations in which researchers can test consumers' reactions to factors such as product positioning, store layouts, and package designs.

For example, suppose General Mills wants to test reactions to a new Cheerios package design and store shelf positioning. Using Simul-Shop on a standard desktop PC, test shoppers begin their shopping spree with a screen showing the outside of a grocery store. They click to enter the virtual store and are guided to the appropriate store section. Once there, they can scan the shelf, pick up various cereal packages, rotate them, study the labels—even look around to see what is on the shelf behind them. About the only thing they can't do is open the box and taste the cereal.

The virtual shopping trip includes full sound and video, along with a guide who directs users through the experience and answers their questions. Explains a Gadd's research director, "Once [users] move toward the item we want to test, [they] can look at different packaging, shelf layouts, and package colors. Depending on the activity, we can even ask users why they did what they did."

Virtual reality testing can take any of several forms. For example, Alternative Realities Corporation (ARC) has created a virtual reality amphitheater called the Vision Dome. The Dome offers 360 by 160 degrees of film projection, allowing as many as 40 people at one time to participate in a virtual reality experience. The Vision Dome is like an IMAX theater, but with one big difference—it's interactive. "When you use a computer to generate an image, . . . you have the advantage of making that image interactive," comments an ARC executive. When conducting research on a car, he suggests, "We can go into a Vision Dome, see that car in three dimensions, look at it from every angle, take it out for a test drive, and allow the customer to configure that car exactly the way he wants it." Caterpillar sees enormous potential for the Dome. "We can put one of our tractors in a VisionDome and actually have a customer sit in it and test it under whatever conditions they would use it for," says a Caterpillar design engineer. "The ability to immerse people in the product makes it a phenomenal [research and sales] tool."

Virtual reality as a research tool offers several advantages. For one, it's relatively inexpensive. For example, a firm can conduct a Simul-Shop study for only about $25,000,

including initial programming and the actual research on 75 to 100 people. This makes virtual reality research accessible to firms that can't afford full market-testing campaigns or the expense of creating actual mock-ups for each different product color, shape, or size. Another advantage is flexibility. A virtual reality store can display an almost infinite variety of products, sizes, styles, and flavors in response to consumers' desires and needs. Research can be conducted in almost any simulated surroundings, ranging from food store interiors and new car showrooms to farm fields or the open road. The technique also offers great interactivity, allowing marketers and consumers to work together via computer on designs of new products and marketing programs.

Finally, virtual reality has great potential for international research, which has often been difficult for marketers to conduct. With virtual reality, researchers can use a single standardized approach to evaluate products and programs worldwide. Consider the following example:

One multinational company has begun to conduct virtual-shopping studies in North and South America, Europe, Asia, and Australia. Researchers create virtual stores in each country and region using the appropriate local products, shelf layouts, and currencies. Once the stores are online, a product concept can be quickly tested across locations. When the studies are completed, the results are communicated to headquarters electronically. The analysis reveals which markets offer the greatest opportunity for a successful launch.

Virtual reality research also has its limitations. The biggest problem: Simulated shopping situations

never quite match the real thing. Observes one expert, "Just because it's technically [feasible], that doesn't mean that when you put [people] behind a computer you're going to get true responses. Any time you simulate an experience you're not getting the experience itself. It's still a simulation."

So what's ahead for virtual reality in marketing? Some pioneers are extremely enthusiastic about the technology—not just as a research tool, but as a place where even real buying and selling can occur. They predict that the virtual store may become a major channel for personal and direct interactions with consumers, interactions that encompass not only research but sales and service as well. They see great potential for conducting this type of research over the Internet, and virtual stores have become a reality on the Web. As one observer notes, "This is what I read about in science fiction books when I was growing up. It's the thing of the future." For many marketers, that future is already a virtual reality.

Sources: Quotes and extracts from Raymond R. Burke, "Virtual Shopping: Breakthrough in Marketing Research," *Harvard Business Review,* March–April, 1996, pp. 120–31; Tom Dellacave Jr., "Curing Market Research Headaches," *Sales & Marketing Management,* July 1996, pp. 84–85; Brian Silverman, "Get 'Em While They're Hot," *Sales & Marketing Management,* February 1997, pp. 47–48, 52; and Mike Hoffman, "Virtual Shopping," *Inc.,* July 1998, p. 88. Also see Tim Studt, "VR Speeds Up Car Designs," *Research & Development,* March 1998, p. 74; and Sara Sellar, "The Perfect Trade Show Rep," *Sales & Marketing Management,* April 1999, p. 11.

Latin America, and Africa. However, international companies are increasingly introducing their new products in swift global assaults. Procter & Gamble did this with its Pampers Phases line of disposable diapers, which it had on the shelf in 90 countries within just 12 months of introduction. Such rapid worldwide expansion solidified the brand's market position before foreign competitors could react. P&G has since mounted worldwide introductions of several other new products.[18]

Speeding Up New-Product Development

Sequential product development
A new-product development approach in which one company department works to complete its stage of the process before passing the new product along to the next department and stage.

Many companies organize their new-product development process into the orderly sequence of steps shown in Figure 9.1, starting with idea generation and ending with commercialization. Under this **sequential product development** approach, one company department works individually to complete its stage of the process before passing the new product along to the next department and stage. This orderly, step-by-step process can help bring control to complex and risky projects. But it also can be dangerously slow. In fast-changing, highly competitive markets, such slow-but-sure product development can result in product failures, lost sales and profits, and crumbling market positions. "Speed to market" and reducing new-product development cycle time have become pressing concerns to companies in all industries.

Simultaneous (or team-based) product development
An approach to developing new products in which various company departments work closely together, overlapping the steps in the product-development process to save time and increase effectiveness.

In order to get their new products to market more quickly, many companies are adopting a faster, team-oriented approach called **simultaneous (or team-based) product development.** Under this approach, company departments work closely together, overlapping the steps in the product development process to save time and increase effectiveness. Instead of passing the new product from department to department, the company assembles a team of people from various departments that stays with the new product from start to finish. Such teams usually include people from the marketing, finance, design, manufacturing, and legal departments, and even supplier and customer companies.

Top management gives the product development team general strategic direction but no clear-cut product idea or work plan. It challenges the team with stiff and seemingly contradictory goals—"turn out carefully planned and superior new products, but do it quickly"—and then gives the team whatever freedom and resources it needs to meet the challenge. In the sequential process, a bottleneck at one phase can seriously slow the entire project. In the simultaneous approach, if one functional area hits snags, it works to resolve them while the team moves on.

The Allen-Bradley Company, a maker of industrial controls, realized tremendous benefits by using simultaneous development. Under its old sequential approach, the company's marketing department handed off a new-product idea to designers, who worked in isolation to prepare concepts that they then passed along to product engineers. The engineers, also working by themselves, developed expensive prototypes and handed them off to manufacturing, which tried to find a way to build the new product. Finally, after many years and dozens of costly design compromises and delays, marketing was asked to sell the new product, which it often found to be too high priced or sadly out of date. Now, all of Allen-Bradley's departments work together to develop new products. The results have been astonishing. For example, the company recently developed a new electrical control in just two years; under the old system, it would have taken six years.

Black & Decker used the simultaneous approach—what it calls "concurrent engineering"—to develop its Quantum line of tools targeted toward serious do-it-yourselfers. B&D assigned a "fusion team," called Team Quantum and consist-

A Black & Decker "fusion team" developed the highly acclaimed Quantum tool line in only 12 months. The team included 85 marketers, engineers, finance people, and others from the United States, Britain, Germany, Italy, and Switzerland.

ing of 85 Black & Decker employees from around the world, to get the right product line to customers as quickly as possible. The team included engineers, finance people, marketers, designers, and others from the United States, Britain, Germany, Italy, and Switzerland. From idea to launch, including 3 months of consumer research, the team developed the highly acclaimed Quantum line in only 12 months.

The simultaneous approach does have some limitations. Superfast product development can be riskier and more costly than the slower, more orderly sequential approach. Moreover, it often creates increased organizational tension and confusion. The company also must take care that rushing a product to market doesn't adversely affect its quality—the objective is not just to create products faster, but to create them *better* and faster. Despite these drawbacks, in rapidly changing industries facing increasingly shorter product life cycles, the rewards of fast and flexible product development far exceed the risks. Companies that get new and improved products to the market faster than competitors often gain a dramatic competitive edge. They can respond more quickly to emerging consumer tastes and charge higher prices for more advanced designs. As one auto industry executive states, "What we want to do is get the new car approved, built, and in the consumer's hands in the shortest time possible. . . . Whoever gets there first gets all the marbles."[19]

PRODUCT LIFE-CYCLE STRATEGIES

Product life cycle (PLC)
The course of a product's sales and profits over its lifetime. It involves five distinct stages: product development, introduction, growth, maturity, and decline.

After launching the new product, management wants the product to enjoy a long and happy life. Although it does not expect the product to sell forever, the company wants to earn a decent profit to cover all the effort and risk that went into launching it. Management is aware that each product will have a life cycle, although the exact shape and length is not known in advance.

Figure 9.2 shows a typical **product life cycle (PLC),** the course that a product's sales and profits take over its lifetime. The product life cycle has five distinct stages:

FIGURE 9.2 **Sales and profits over the product's life from inception to demise**

1. *Product development* begins when the company finds and develops a new-product idea. During product development, sales are zero and the company's investment costs mount.
2. *Introduction* is a period of slow sales growth as the product is introduced in the market. Profits are nonexistent in this stage because of the heavy expenses of product introduction.
3. *Growth* is a period of rapid market acceptance and increasing profits.
4. *Maturity* is a period of slowdown in sales growth because the product has achieved acceptance by most potential buyers. Profits level off or decline because of increased marketing outlays to defend the product against competition.
5. *Decline* is the period when sales fall off and profits drop.

Not all products follow this product life cycle. Some products are introduced and die quickly; others stay in the mature stage for a long, long time. Some enter the decline stage and are then cycled back into the growth stage through strong promotion or repositioning.

The PLC concept can describe a *product class* (gasoline-powered automobiles), a *product form* (minivans), or a *brand* (the Ford Taurus). The PLC concept applies differently in each case. Product classes have the longest life cycles—the sales of many product classes stay in the mature stage for a long time. Product forms, in contrast, tend to have the standard PLC shape. Product forms such as "cream deodorants," the "dial telephone," and "phonograph records" passed through a regular history of introduction, rapid growth, maturity, and decline. A specific brand's life cycle can change quickly because of changing competitive attacks and responses. For example, although teeth-cleaning products (product class) and toothpastes (product form) have enjoyed fairly long life cycles, the life cycles of specific brands have tended to be much shorter.

The PLC concept also can be applied to what are known as styles, fashions, and fads. Their special life cycles are shown in Figure 9.3. A **style** is a basic and distinctive mode of expression. For example, styles appear in homes (colonial, ranch), clothing (formal, casual), and art (realist, surrealist, abstract). Once a style is invented, it may last for generations, passing in and out of vogue. A style has a cycle showing several periods of renewed interest. A **fashion** is a currently accepted or popular style in a given field. For example, the "preppie look" in the clothing of the 1980s gave way to the casual and layered look of the 1990s. Fashions tend to grow slowly, remain popular for a while, then decline slowly.

Style
A basic and distinctive mode of expression.

Fashion
A currently accepted or popular style in a given field.

Product life cycle: Companies want their products to enjoy long and happy life cycles. Hershey's chocolate bars have been "unchanged since 1899."

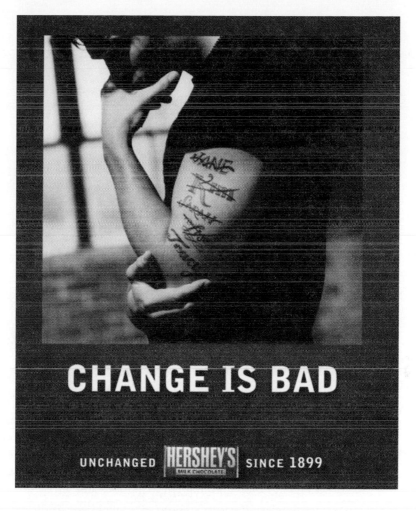

CHANGE IS BAD

UNCHANGED **HERSHEY'S** SINCE 1899

Fads

Fashions that enter quickly, are adopted with great zeal, peak early, and decline very fast.

Fads are fashions that enter quickly, are adopted with great zeal, peak early, and decline very quickly. They last only a short time and tend to attract only a limited following. "Pet rocks" have become the classic example of a fad. Upon hearing his friends complain about how expensive it was to care for their dogs, advertising copywriter Gary Dahl joked about his pet rock and was soon writing a spoof of a dog-training manual for it. Soon Dahl was selling some 1.5 million ordinary beach pebbles at $4 a pop. Yet the fad, which broke in October 1975, had sunk like a stone by the next February. Dahl's advice to those who want to succeed with a fad, "Enjoy it while it lasts." Other examples of fads include Rubik's Cubes and lava lamps. Most fads do not survive for long because they normally do not satisfy a strong need or satisfy it well.[20]

The PLC concept can be applied by marketers as a useful framework for describing how products and markets work. But using the PLC concept for forecasting product performance or for developing marketing strategies presents some practical problems.[21] For example, managers may have trouble identifying which stage of the PLC the product is in, pinpointing when the product moves into the next stage, and determining the factors that affect the product's movement through the stages. In practice, it is difficult to forecast the sales level at each PLC stage, the length of each stage, and the shape of the PLC curve.

Using the PLC concept to develop marketing strategy also can be difficult because strategy is both a cause and a result of the product's life cycle. The product's current PLC position suggests the best marketing strategies, and the resulting marketing strategies affect product performance in later life-cycle stages. Yet, when used

FIGURE 9.3   Styles, fashions, and fads

carefully, the PLC concept can help in developing good marketing strategies for different stages of the product life cycle.

We looked at the product development stage of the product life cycle in the first part of the chapter. We now look at strategies for each of the other life-cycle stages.

INTRODUCTION STAGE

Introduction stage
The product life-cycle stage in which the new product is first distributed and made available for purchase.

The **introduction stage** starts when the new product is first launched. Introduction takes time, and sales growth is apt to be slow. Well-known products such as instant coffee, frozen orange juice, and powdered coffee creamers lingered for many years before they entered a stage of rapid growth.

In this stage, as compared to other stages, profits are negative or low because of the low sales and high distribution and promotion expenses. Much money is needed to attract distributors and build their inventories. Promotion spending is relatively high to inform consumers of the new product and get them to try it. Because the market is not generally ready for product refinements at this stage, the company and its few competitors produce basic versions of the product. These firms focus their selling on those buyers who are the readiest to buy.

A company, especially the *market pioneer,* must choose a launch strategy that is consistent with the intended product positioning. It should realize that the initial strategy is just the first step in a grander marketing plan for the product's entire life cycle. If the pioneer chooses its launch strategy to make a "killing," it will be sacrificing long-run revenue for the sake of short-run gain. As the pioneer moves through later stages of the life cycle, it will have to continuously formulate new pricing, promotion, and other marketing strategies. It has the best chance of building and retaining market leadership if it plays its cards correctly from the start.[22]

Growth Stage

Growth stage
The product life-cycle stage in which a product's sales start climbing quickly.

If the new product satisfies the market, it will enter a **growth stage,** in which sales will start climbing quickly. The early adopters will continue to buy, and later buyers will start following their lead, especially if they hear favorable word of mouth. Attracted by the opportunities for profit, new competitors will enter the market. They will introduce new product features, and the market will expand. The increase in competitors leads to an increase in the number of distribution outlets, and sales jump just to build reseller inventories. Prices remain where they are or fall only slightly. Companies keep their promotion spending at the same or a slightly higher level. Educating the market remains a goal, but now the company must also meet the competition.

Profits increase during the growth stage, as promotion costs are spread over a large volume and as unit manufacturing costs fall. The firm uses several strategies to sustain rapid market growth as long as possible. It improves product quality and adds new product features and models. It enters new market segments and new distribution channels. It shifts some advertising from building product awareness to building product conviction and purchase, and it lowers prices at the right time to attract more buyers.

In the growth stage, the firm faces a trade-off between high market share and high current profit. By spending a lot of money on product improvement, promotion, and distribution, the company can capture a dominant position. In doing so, however, it gives up maximum current profit, which it hopes to make up in the next stage.

Maturity Stage

Maturity stage
The stage in the product life cycle in which sales growth slows or levels off.

At some point, a product's sales growth will slow down, and the product will enter a **maturity stage.** This maturity stage normally lasts longer than the previous stages, and it poses strong challenges to marketing management. Most products are in the maturity stage of the life cycle, and therefore most of marketing management deals with the mature product.

The slowdown in sales growth results in many producers with many products to sell. In turn, this overcapacity leads to greater competition. Competitors begin marking down prices, increasing their advertising and sales promotions, and upping their R&D budgets to find better versions of the product. These steps lead to a drop in profit. Some of the weaker competitors start dropping out, and the industry eventually contains only well-established competitors.

Although many products in the mature stage appear to remain unchanged for long periods, most successful ones are actually evolving to meet changing consumer needs (see Marketing Highlight 9.3). Product managers should do more than simply ride along with or defend their mature products—a good offense is the best defense. They should consider modifying the market, product, and marketing mix.

In *modifying the market,* the company tries to increase the consumption of the current product. It looks for new users and market segments, as when Johnson & Johnson targeted the adult market with its baby powder and shampoo. The manager also looks for ways to increase usage among present customers. Campbell does this by offering recipes and convincing consumers that "soup is good food." Or the company may want to reposition the brand to appeal to a larger or faster-growing segment, as Arrow did when it introduced its new line of casual shirts and announced, "We're loosening our collars."

The company might also try *modifying the product*—changing characteristics such as quality, features, or style to attract new users and to inspire more usage. It might improve the product's quality and performance—its durability, reliability, speed, or taste. Or it might add new features that expand the product's usefulness, safety, or convenience. For example, Sony keeps adding new styles and features to its Walkman and Discman lines, and Volvo adds new safety features to its cars. Finally, the company can improve the product's styling and attractiveness. Thus, car manufacturers restyle their cars to attract buyers who want a new look. The makers of consumer food and household products introduce new flavors, colors, ingredients, or packages to revitalize consumer buying.

Finally, the company can try *modifying the marketing mix*—improving sales by changing one or more marketing mix elements. It can cut prices to attract new users and competitors' customers. It can launch a better advertising campaign or use aggressive sales promotions—trade deals, cents-off, premiums, and contests. The company can also move into larger market channels, using mass merchandisers, if these channels are growing. Finally, the company can offer new or improved services to buyers.

AGE-DEFYING PRODUCTS OR JUST SKILLFUL PLC MANAGEMENT?

Some products are born and die quickly. Others, however, seem to defy the product life cycle, enduring for decades or even generations with little or no apparent change in their makeup or marketing. Look deeper, however, and you'll find that such products are far from unchanging. Rather, skillful product life-cycle management keeps them fresh, relevant, and appealing to customers. Here are examples of three products that might have been only fads but instead were turned into long-term market winners with plenty of staying power.

Beanie Babies

When Ty Inc. unleashed Beanie Babies on the market in 1993, most experts saw them as just a passing fad. Priced under $5, the tiny bean-filled creatures were designed by company founder Ty Warner as a back-to-basics toy that kids could buy with their own allowance money. Soon,

however, adults began compulsively collecting the floppy little animals, and the company couldn't get them onto store shelves fast enough.

Yet Ty quickly realized that scarcity would be the key to keeping the Beanie Babies craze going—and going and going. The company became adept at maintaining consumer demand by limiting distribution to small gift and specialty stores. Each store is limited to 36 toys of each style per month. Ty also adds to the hype by regularly retiring old characters and replacing them with many new ones. There are currently just over 200 styles of Beanie Babies, with about 150 of them retired. Retired models fetch as much as $1,000 from hard-core collectors. When new models or retirements are announced, visits to the company's Web site skyrocket. By mid-1999, the site had received almost 3 *billion* visits.

Thus, long after the experts would have predicted the demise of these cute little critters, avid collectors are still lining up to get their hands on new styles. In a typical scenario, Penny Madsen, who manages the gift shop at Adventureland Park in Des Moines, Iowa, says that she receives 15 or 20 calls a day asking whether the store has certain Beanies in stock. Even though Adventureland doesn't advertise its Beanie Babies, when new styles are expected, "People will be standing outside our gate at 6 in the morning, waiting until we open at 10," says Madsen. Even more impressive, they willingly pay the $20 gate admission just to get into the gift shop.

Barbie

Talk about age-defying products. Although Mattel's Barbie turned 40 in 1999, Mattel has kept Barbie both timeless and trendy. Since her creation in 1959, Barbie has mirrored girls' dreams of what they'd like to be when they grow up. Yet Barbie has changed as girls' dreams have changed. Her aspirations have evolved from jobs like stewardess, fashion model, and nurse to astronaut, rock singer, surgeon, and presidential candidate. These days, Barbie hardly notices her age—she's too busy being a WNBA basketball player, Olympic skater, and NASCAR race car driver.

Mattel introduces new Barbie dolls every year in order to keep up with the latest definitions of achievement, glamour, romance, adventure, and nurturing. Barbie also reflects

Some products seem to defy the product life cycle: Although Mattel's Barbie recently turned 40, she hardly notices her age—she's too busy being a WNBA basketball star, a NASCAR race car driver, a soccer player, and a pilot.

America's diverse and changing population. Mattel has produced African American Barbie dolls since 1968 and has since introduced Hispanic and Asian dolls as well. In recent years, Mattel has introduced Crystal Barbie (a gorgeous glamour doll), Puerto Rican Barbie (part of its "dolls of the world" collection), Great Shape Barbie (to tie into the fitness craze), Flight Time Barbie (a pilot), and Soccer Barbie (to tie in with the recent boom in girls' soccer). If none of these suit, girls can personalize their own Friend of Barbie dolls by clicking onto the Barbie Web site (www.barbie.com), where they can select the doll's hair color, eye color, and fashion—even give her a personality. Mattel will then custom-make the doll and send it out.

As a result of Mattel's adept product life-cycle handling, Barbie has kept her market allure as well as her youth. Available in 150 countries, Barbie now sells at a rate of two each second worldwide and racks up sales of more than $1.9 billion a year. If you placed head to foot every doll ever sold, Barbie and her friends would circle the globe 72 times.

Crayola Crayons

Over the past 100 years or so, Binney & Smith's Crayola crayons have become a household staple in more than 60 countries around the world. Few people can forget their first pack of "64s"—64 beauties neatly arranged in the familiar green and yellow flip-top box with a sharpener on the back. The aroma of a freshly opened Crayola box still drives kids into a frenzy and takes members of the older generation back to some of their fondest childhood memories.

In some ways, Crayola crayons haven't changed much since 1903, when they were sold in an eight-pack for a nickel. But a closer look reveals that Binney & Smith has made many adjustments to keep the brand out of decline. The company has added a steady stream of new colors, shapes, sizes, and packages. It has gradually increased the number of colors from the original eight in 1903 (red, yellow, blue, green, orange, black, brown, and white) to 96 in 1999. In 1962, as a result of the civil rights movement, it changed its crayon color "flesh" to "peach"; and in 1992, it added multicultural skin tones by which "children are able to build a positive sense of self and respect for cultural diversity." Binney & Smith has also extended the Crayola brand to new markets such as Crayola markers, watercolor paints, themed stamps and stickers, and stencils. The company has licensed the Crayola brand for use on everything from lunch boxes and children's apparel to house paints. Finally, the company has added several programs and services to help strengthen its relationships with Crayola customers. For example, its *Crayola Kids* magazine and Crayola Web site offer features for the children along with expert advice to parents on helping develop reading skills and creativity.

Not all of Binney & Smith's life-cycle adjustments have been greeted favorably by consumers. For example, in 1990, to make room for more modern colors, it retired eight colors from the time-honored box of 64—raw umber, lemon yellow, maize, blue grey, orange yellow, orange red, green blue, and violet blue—into the Crayola Hall of Fame. The move unleashed a groundswell of protest from loyal Crayola users, who formed such organizations as the RUMPS—the Raw Umber and Maize Preservation Society—and the National Committee to Save Lemon Yellow. Company executives were flabbergasted—"We were aware of the loyalty and nostalgia surrounding Crayola crayons," a spokesperson says, "but we didn't know we [would] hit such a nerve." The company reissued the old standards in a special collector's tin—it sold all of the 2.5 million tins made.

Thus, Crayola continues its long and colorful life cycle. Through smart product life cycle management, Binney & Smith, now a subsidiary of Hallmark, has dominated the crayon market for almost a century. Sixty-five percent of all American children between the ages of two and seven pick up a crayon at least once a day and color for an average of 28 minutes. Nearly 80 percent of the time, they pick up a Crayola crayon.

Sources: See Gary Samuels, "Mystique Marketing," *Forbes,* October 21, 1996, p. 276; Carole Schmidt and Lynn Kaladjian, "Ty Connects Hot-Property Dots," *Brandweek,* June 16, 1997, p. 26; Joyce Cohen, "Fans Still Lining Up to Haul in Beanie Babies," *Amusement Business,* January 18, 1999, p. 4; information accessed online at www.ty.com, February 2000; "Hue and Cry over Crayola May Revive Old Colors," *Wall Street Journal,* June 14, 1991, p. B1; Margaret O. Kirk, "Coloring Our Children's World Since '03," *Chicago Tribune,* October 29, 1986, sec. 5, p. 1; Becky Ebenkamp, "Crayola Heritage Tack Continues with $6–7M," *Brandweek,* February 1, 1999, p. 5; Crayola's Web site at www.crayola.com, February 2000; Gene Del Vecchio, "Keeping It Timeless, Trendy," *Advertising Age,* March 23, 1998, p. 24; Michele Neyer, "Barbie Hits 40," *Parenting,* March 1999, p. 31; the Barbie Web site at www.barbie.com, February 2000; and Alice Z. Cuneo and Laura Petrecca, "Barbie Has to Work Marder to Help Out Sagging Mattel," *Advertising Age,* March 6, 2000, pp. 4, 63.

Decline Stage

The sales of most product forms and brands eventually dip. The decline may be slow, as in the case of oatmeal cereal, or rapid, as in the case of phonograph records. Sales may plunge to zero, or they may drop to a low level where they continue for many years. This is the **decline stage.**

Sales decline for many reasons, including technological advances, shifts in consumer tastes, and increased competition. As sales and profits decline, some firms withdraw from the market. Those remaining may prune their product offerings. They may drop smaller market segments and marginal trade channels, or they may cut the promotion budget and reduce their prices further.

Carrying a weak product can be very costly to a firm, and not just in profit terms. There are many hidden costs. A weak product may take up too much of management's time. It often requires frequent price and inventory adjustments. It requires advertising and sales force attention that might be better used to make "healthy" products more profitable. A product's failing reputation can cause customer concerns about the company and its other products. The biggest cost may well lie in the future. Keeping weak products delays the search for replacements, creates a lopsided product mix, hurts current profits, and weakens the company's foothold on the future.

For these reasons, companies need to pay more attention to their aging products. The firm's first task is to identify those products in the decline stage by regularly reviewing sales, market shares, costs, and profit trends. Then, management must decide whether to maintain, harvest, or drop each of these declining products.

Management may decide to *maintain* its brand without change in the hope that competitors will leave the industry. For example, Procter & Gamble made good profits by remaining in the declining liquid soap business as others withdrew. Or management may decide to reposition or reformulate the brand in hopes of moving it back into the growth stage of the product life cycle. For instance, after watching sales of its Tostitos tortilla chips plunge 50 percent from their mid-1980s high, Frito-Lay reformulated the chips by doubling their size, changing their shape from round to triangular, and using white corn flour instead of yellow. The new Tostitos Restaurant Style Tortilla Chips have ridden the crest of the recent Tex-Mex food craze's record revenues. Similarly, facing a slumping market, Vlasic reinvented the sliced pickle:

★ Pickle consumption has been declining about 2 percent a year since the 1980s, but following successful new-product introductions, sales generally get a prolonged boost. Vlasic began its quest for a blockbuster pickle in the mid-1990s after focus groups revealed that people hate it when pickle slices slither out the sides of

Back to the growth stage: Facing a slumping market, Vlasic reinvented the sliced pickle.

Decline stage
The product life-cycle stage in which a product's sales decline.

hamburgers and sandwiches. At first the company decided to slice its average pickles horizontally into strips and marketed them as "Sandwich Stackers." The only problem was that the strips usually contained the soft seedy part of the cucumber, not the crunchy part. The company then embarked on "Project Frisbee," an effort to create a giant pickle chip. In 1998, after years of research and development, Vlasic created a cucumber ten times larger than the traditional pickle cucumber. The pickle slice, or "chip," is large enough to cover the entire surface of a hamburger and is stacked a dozen high in jars. The Sandwich Stackers line now accounts for about 20 percent of Vlasic's pickle sales.[23]

Management may decide to *harvest* the product, which means reducing various costs (plant and equipment, maintenance, R&D, advertising, sales force) and hoping that sales hold up. If successful, harvesting will increase the company's profits in the short run. Or management may decide to *drop* the product from the line. It can sell it to another firm or simply liquidate it at salvage value. If the company plans to find a buyer, it will not want to run down the product through harvesting.

Table 9.2 summarizes the key characteristics of each stage of the product life cycle. The table also lists the marketing objectives and strategies for each stage.[24]

TABLE 9.2 SUMMARY OF PRODUCT LIFE-CYCLE CHARACTERISTICS, OBJECTIVES, AND STRATEGIES

Characteristics	Introduction	Growth	Maturity	Decline
Sales	Low sales	Rapidly rising sales	Peak sales	Declining sales
Costs	High cost per customer	Average cost per customer	Low cost per customer	Low cost per customer
Profits	Negative	Rising profits	High profits	Declining profits
Customers	Innovators	Early adopters	Middle majority	Laggards
Competitors	Few	Growing number	Stable number beginning to decline	Declining number
Marketing Objectives				
	Create product awareness and trial	Maximize market share	Maximize profit while defending market share	Reduce expenditure and milk the brand
Strategies				
Product	Offer a basic product	Offer product extensions, service, warranty	Diversify brand and models	Phase out weak items
Price	Use cost-plus	Price to penetrate market	Price to match or beat competitors	Cut price
Distribution	Build selective distribution	Build intensive distribution	Build more intensive distribution	Go selective: phase out unprofitable outlets
Advertising	Build product awareness among early adopters and dealers	Build awareness and interest in the mass market	Stress brand differences and benefits	Reduce to level needed to retain hard-core loyals
Sales Promotion	Use heavy sales promotion to entice trial	Reduce to take advantage of heavy consumer demand	Increase to encourage brand switching	Reduce to minimal level

Source: Philip Kotler, *Marketing Management: Analysis, Planning, Implementation, and Control,* 10th ed. (Upper Saddle River, NJ: Prentice Hall, 2000), p. 316.

REVIEW OF CONCEPT CONNECTIONS

A company's current products face limited life spans and must be replaced by newer products. But new products can fail—the risks of innovation are as great as the rewards. The key to successful innovation lies in a total company effort, strong planning, and a systematic *new-product development* process.

1. Explain how companies find and develop new-product ideas.

Companies find and develop new-product ideas from a variety of sources. Many new-product ideas stem from *internal sources.* Companies conduct formal research and development, pick the brains of their employees, and brainstorm at executive meetings. By conducting surveys and focus groups and analyzing *customer* questions and complaints, companies can generate new-product ideas that will meet specific consumer needs. Companies track *competitors'* offerings and inspect new products, dismantling them, analyzing their performance, and deciding whether to introduce a similar or improved product. *Distributors and suppliers* are close to the market and can pass along information about consumer problems and new-product possibilities.

2. List and define the steps in the new-product development process.

The new-product development process consists of eight sequential stages. The process starts with *idea generation.* Next comes *idea screening,* which reduces the number of ideas based on the company's own criteria. Ideas that pass the screening stage continue through *product concept development,* in which a detailed version of the new-product idea is stated in meaningful consumer terms. In the next stage, *concept testing,* new-product concepts are tested with a group of target consumers to determine if the concepts have strong consumer appeal. Strong concepts proceed to *marketing strategy development,* in which an initial marketing strategy for the new product is developed from the product concept. In the *business analysis* stage, a review of the sales, costs, and profit projections for a new product is conducted to determine whether the new product is likely to satisfy the company's objectives. With positive results here, the ideas become more concrete through *product development* and *test marketing* and finally are launched during *commercialization.*

3. Describe the stages of the product life cycle.

Each product has a *life cycle* marked by a changing set of problems and opportunities. The sales of the typical product follow an S-shaped curve made up of five stages. The cycle begins with the *product development stage* when the company finds and develops a new-product idea. The *introduction stage* is marked by slow growth and low profits as the product is distributed to the market. If successful, the product enters a *growth stage,* which offers rapid sales growth and increasing profits. Next comes a *maturity stage* when sales growth slows down and profits stabilize. Finally, the product enters a *decline stage* in which sales and profits dwindle. The company's task during this stage is to recognize the decline and to decide whether it should maintain, harvest, or drop the product.

4. Describe how marketing strategies change during the product's life cycle.

In the *introduction stage,* the company must choose a launch strategy consistent with its intended product positioning. Much money is needed to attract distributors and build their inventories and to inform consumers of the new product and achieve trial. In the *growth stage,* companies continue to educate potential consumers and distributors. In addition, the company works to stay ahead of the competition and sustain rapid market growth by improving product quality, adding new product features and models, entering new market segments and distribution channels, shifting some advertising from building product awareness to building product conviction and purchase, and lowering prices at the right time to attract new buyers. In the *maturity stage,* companies continue to invest in maturing products and consider modifying the market, the product, and the marketing mix. When *modifying the market,* the company attempts to increase the consumption of the current product. When *modifying the product,* the company changes some of the product's characteristics—such as quality, features, or style—to attract new users or inspire more usage. When *modifying the marketing mix,* the company works to improve sales by changing one or more of the marketing mix elements. Once the company recognizes that a product has entered the *decline stage,* management must decide whether to *maintain* the brand without change, hoping that competitors will drop out of the market; *harvest* the product, reducing costs and trying to maintain sales; or *drop* the product, selling it to another firm or liquidating it at salvage value.

KEY TERMS

Business analysis	Decline stage	Growth stage
Commercialization	Fad	Idea generation
Concept testing	Fashion	Idea screening

Introduction stage	Product concept	Simultaneous (or team-based) product
Marketing strategy development	Product development	development
Maturity stage	Product life cycle (PLC)	Style
New-product development	Sequential product development	Test marketing

ISSUES FOR DISCUSSION

1. Select a familiar company and assume that you are an idea manager responsible for generating new-product ideas. How would you structure the new-product development process? What sources of new ideas would be most valuable?

2. Less than one-third of new-product ideas come from customers. Does this low percentage suggest that few companies employ the marketing concept philosophy of "find a need and fill it"? Why or why not?

3. Assume that you have been hired by General Motors to develop three alternative product concepts for a voice-activated, verbal Internet link it plans to make available in its luxury cars. This system would allow an automobile's occupants to access the Internet, e-mail, and e-shopping sites while driving or riding around. In developing the three concepts, think carefully about who would use such a system and when, where, and how. Which of your three concepts do you think has the greatest potential?

4. Discuss the advantages and disadvantages of the three approaches to test marketing. If you were the marketing research director for Frito-Lay, which of the three approaches would you use to test market a new brand of snack chips made from dried bananas? Explain.

5. Discuss the differences between a style, a fashion, and a fad. Then go to the Sharper Image Web site (www.sharperimage.com) and find examples of products that fit each category. Explain your choices.

6. Pick a soft drink, car, fashion, food product, or electronic appliance and trace the product's life cycle. Explain how you separated the stages of the product's evolution. Project where this life cycle will go from here.

7. What strategic options are open to the marketers of products in the mature stage of the product life cycle? Select a specific product (other than those mentioned in the chapter) that illustrates each of the strategic options that you have identified.

8. Which product life-cycle stage, if any, is the most important? Which stage is the riskiest? Which stage appears to hold the greatest profit potential? Which stage needs the greatest amount of "hands-on" management? Be certain to explain the thinking behind each of your answers.

MARKETING APPLICATIONS

1. In NASCAR driver Richard Petty's heyday, the Plymouth Road Runner was the "baddest boy" on the block. Recently, however, DaimlerChrysler announced that it would eliminate the Plymouth brand and transition Plymouth products into the Chrysler line. Many loyal customers are asking, "Why is this happening?" The short answer is that as Plymouth traded its muscle-car mystique for the more staid image that goes with affordable cars and minivans, it lost its positioning in the marketplace. Sales of Plymouth's major models—Breeze, Neon, and the Voyager minivan—have fallen off steadily in recent years.

   a. Go to the Plymouth Web site at www.plymouthcars.com and examine DaimlerChrysler's comments about the demise of the Plymouth brand. Summarize these comments.

   b. Examine the strategies presented in the chapter for a mature or declining product. Which of these did DaimlerChrysler try with Plymouth? What decline-phase strategies are now being used? What, if anything, might DaimlerChrysler have done differently with the Plymouth brand?

   c. If you were given the task of turning the Plymouth brand around, what actions would you take?

   d. If you were given the task of merging the Plymouth brand with the popular Chrysler brand, what actions would you take?

2. "Danger, Will Robinson! Danger!" might be one of the most memorable phrases ever uttered by a robot. However, today, the phrase would more likely be "Buy Me! Take Me Home!" Who will offer the first practical, affordable home robot? NASA? Intel? Sony? Lego? Did you say Lego? Yes, the same little company that developed those great plastic building blocks has now developed several models of home robots (such as the R2-D2 model from *Star Wars*) that sell for as little as $220. These Lego model kits contain Lego pieces, light and touch sensors, gears, and a minicomputer brick that forms the core of the system. The small, efficient robots already perform many hard-to-believe tasks (without complaining), and Lego is making daily upgrades. Copycat competitors have already begun a modification frenzy that will one day produce an awesome personal assistant. See www.lego.com, www.legomindstorms.com,

www.lugnet.com, and www.crynwr.com/lego-robotics for
more information.

a. Who might the first customers be for a Lego robot?
Explain.

b. Project the product life cycle for this new product.
Explain your thinking.

c. Outline a strategy for positioning this product away
from the toy category and into the "personal-device"
category.

d. What headline would you select for a first Lego robot
ad appearing in *USA Today?* In *Business Week?*

e. Design a quick test market study for the Lego robot
that would be administered at the annual computer
and software convention (COMDEX) in Las Vegas,
Nevada.

 INTERNET CONNECTIONS

NEW SERVICE OPPORTUNITY

One new service development on the Internet involves providing core business operations for other businesses. The
business receiving the service is said to be outsourcing a portion of its operations. Businesses may outsource anything
from order processing to shipping. In fact, it is possible to
outsource nearly all core operations. The outsourcing trend
is particularly prevalent among online storefronts.
Outsourcing makes a great deal of sense since most online
storefronts need virtually the same functionality. Why rein-
vent the wheel? Online storefronts need ways to find, support, bill, and collect payments from customers. Storefronts
also need to build inventories, keep them in warehouses, and
ship them when customers place orders. Finally, the technology to conduct electronic transactions and keep track of
the data is especially important for Internet selling. Two
companies rushing to provide these services include Digital
River and Pandesic. Visit these companies online and complete the following table to indicate which services they provide, using the marketing mix categories as a guideline. *Hint:*
Refer to other chapters in this book to see which services
might be appropriate in each of the four Ps.

Service	Pandesic www.pandesic.com	Digital River www. digitalriver.com
Product (e.g., sales analysis)		
Price (e.g., online pricing)		
Distribution place (e.g., warehousing)		
Promotion (e.g., attracting customers)		

FOR DISCUSSION

1. In which marketing mix strategies do these firms specialize?
2. What are the advantages of outsourcing key business
operations?
3. What are the disadvantages of outsourcing key business
operations?
4. Are outsourcing services better for start-up corporations
or for existing businesses?
5. Are outsourcing services better for large businesses or
small businesses?
6. If you were designing a new service firm to compete
with these companies, what services would you offer?
7. Which firm would you use if you wanted to start a new
company to sell products online?

SAVVY SITES

- The NPD Group (www.npd.com) provides custom
research for every product life cycle (PLC) stage. Of special interest is its Home Testing Institute (HTI) consumer
panel composed of 350,000 households.
- IBM (www.ibm.com) maintains an archive of U.S. Patent
& Trademark Office (USPTO) patent descriptions (and
some images) from 1971 to date. To access this patent
server, search for "patent" at the site.
- BUY.com (www.buy.com) is the "Internet Superstore,"
offering products at or near cost and selling advertising to
build revenue.

NOTES

1. Quotes from Lawrence Ingrassia, "Taming the Monster: How Big Companies Can Change," *Wall Street Journal,* December 10, 1992, pp. A1, A6; William H. Miller, "Gillette's Secret to Sharpness," *Industry Week,* January 3, 1994, pp. 24–30; Linda Grant, "Gillette Knows Shaving—and How to Turn Out Hot New Products," *Fortune,* October 14, 1996, pp. 207–10; and Dana Canedy, "Gillette's Strengths in Razors Undone by Troubles Abroad," *New York Times,* June 19, 1999, p. 3. Also see William C. Symonds, "Would You Spend $1.50 for a Razor Blade?" *Business Week,* April 27, 1998, p. 46; James Heckman, "Razor Sharp: Adding Value, Making Noise with Mach3 Intro," *Marketing News,* March 29, 1999, pp. E4, E13; and William C. Symonds, "The Big Trim at Gillette," *Business Week,* November 8, 1999, p. 42.

2. For these and other examples, see Cliff Edwards, "Where Have All the Edsels Gone?" *Greensboro News Record,* May 24, 1999, p. B6.

3. See Robert G. Cooper, "New Product Success in Industrial Firms," *Industrial Marketing Management,* 1992, pp. 215–23; William Bolding, Ruskin Morgan, and Richard Staelin, "Pulling the Plug to Stop the New Product Drain," *Journal of Marketing Research,* February 1997, pp. 164–76; Constance Gustke, "Built to Last," *Sales & Marketing Management,* August 1997, pp. 78–83; Philip Kotler, *Kotler on Marketing* (New York: Free Press, 1999), p. 51; and Martha Wirth Fellman, "Number of New Products Keeps Rising," *Marketing News,* March 29, 1999, p. 3.

4. See Robert G. Cooper and Elko J. Kleinschmidt, *New Product: The Key Factors in Success* (Chicago: American Marketing Association, 1990); X. Michael Song and Mark E. Perry, "A Cross-National Comparative Study of New Product Development Processes: Japan and the United States," *Journal of Marketing,* April 1997, pp. 1–18; Jerry Wind and Vijay Mahajan, "Issues and Opportunities in New Product Development," *Journal of Marketing Research,* February 1997, pp. 1–12; Jean-Marie Martino, "Not Only to Succeed but to Endure," *Across the Board,* January 1998, p. 55; and Don H. Lester, "Critical Success Factors for New Product Development," *Research Technology Management,* January–February 1998, pp. 36–43.

5. See Grant, "Gillette Knows Shaving—and How to Turn Out Hot New Products," pp. 207–10; Rosabeth Moss Kanter, "Don't Wait to Innovate," *Sales & Marketing Management,* February 1997, pp. 22–24; and Greg A. Stevens and James Burley, "3,000 Raw Ideas Equals 1 Commercial Success!" *Research-Technology Management,* May–June 1997, pp. 16–27.

6. See Tim Stevens, "Idea Dollars," *Industry Week,* February 16, 1998, pp. 47–49.

7. For this and other examples, see Jennifer Reese, "Getting Hot Ideas from Customers," *Fortune,* May 18, 1992, pp. 86–87; and Ken Miller, "Where You Really Need to Hear Customers," *Brandweek,* January 20, 1998, p. 17.

8. Pam Weisz, "Avon's Skin-So-Soft Bugs Out," *Brandweek,* June 6, 1994, p. 4; and information accessed online at www.avon.com, September 1999.

9. Kotler, *Kotler on Marketing,* pp. 43–44.

10. Brian O'Reilly, "New Ideas, New Products," *Fortune,* March 3, 1997, pp. 61–64.

11. See "DaimlerChrysler Plans '04 Launch of Fuel Cell Car," *Ward's Auto World,* April 1999, p. 25; and William J. Cook, "A Mercedes for the Future," *U.S. News & World Report,* March 29, 1999, p. 62.

12. See Raymond R. Burke, "Virtual Reality Shopping: Breakthrough in Marketing Research," *Harvard Business Review,* March–April 1996, pp. 120–31; Brian Silverman, "Get 'Em While They're Hot," *Sales & Marketing Management,* February 1997, pp. 47–52; and Mike Hoffman, "Virtual Shopping," *Inc.,* July 1998, p. 88.

13. Adrienne Ward Fawcett, "Oreo Cones Make Top Grade in Poll," *Advertising Age,* June 14, 1993, p. 30; "Fat-Free Cupcakes? OK; Frozen Incetea Bars? Nope." *Marketing News,* February 12, 1996, p. 14; and Becky Ebenkamp, "The New Gold Standards," *Brandweek,* April 19, 1999, p. 34.

14. See Faye Rice, "Secrets of Product Testing," *Fortune,* November 28, 1994, pp. 172–74.

15. Judann Pollack, "Baked Lays," *Advertising Age,* June 24, 1996, p. S2.

16. See Robert McMath, "To Test or Not to Test," *Advertising Age,* June 1998, p. 64.

17. Information on BehaviorScan accessed online at www.infores.com/public/prodserv/AB/bscan.htm, February 2000.

18. Jennifer Lawrence, "P&G Rushes on Global Diaper Rollout," *Advertising Age,* October 14, 1991, p. 6; Bill Saporito, "Behind the Tumult at P&G," *Fortune,* March 7, 1994, pp. 75–82; and George M. Chryssochoidis, "Rolling Out New Products Across Country Markets: An Empirical Study of Causes of Delays," *The Journal of Product Innovation Management,* January 1998, pp. 16–41.

19. For a good review of research on new-product development, see Shona L. Brown and Kathleen M. Eisenhardt, "Product Development: Past Research, Present Findings, and Future Directions," *Academy of Management Review,* April 1995, pp. 343–78; Jerry Wind and Vijay Mahajan, "Issues and Opportunities in New Product Development," *Journal of Marketing Research,* February 1997, pp. 1–12; Durward K. Sobek II, Jeffrey K. Liker, and Allen C. Ward, "Another Look at How Toyota Integrates Product Development," *Harvard Business Review,* July–August 1998, pp. 36–49; and Susanne Willsey, "Taking These 7 Steps Will Help You Launch a New Product," *Marketing News,* March 29, 1999, p. 17.

20. See Martin G. Letscher, "How to Tell Fads from Trends," *American Demographics,* December 1994, pp. 38–45; John Grossmann, "A Follow-up on Four Fabled Frenzies," *Inc.,* October 1994, pp. 66–67; and David Stipp, "The Theory of Fads," *Fortune,* October 14, 1996, pp. 49–52.

21. See George S. Day, "The Product Life Cycle: Analysis and Applications Issues," *Journal of Marketing,* Fall 1981, pp. 60–67; Chuck Ryan and Walter E. Riggs, "Redefining the Product Life Cycle: The Five-Element Product Wave," *Business Horizons,* September–October 1996, pp. 33–40; and Carole R. Hedden, "The Circle of (Product) Life," *American Demographics,* September 1996, pp. 26–30.

22. For an interesting discussion of how brand performance is affected by the product life-cycle stage at which the brand enters the market, see Venkatesh Shankar, Gregory S. Carpenter, and Lekshman Krishnamurthi, "The Advantages of Entry in the Growth Stage of the Product Life Cycle: An Empirical Analysis," *Journal of Marketing Research,* May 1999, pp. 269–76.

23. Vanessa O'Connell, "Food: After Years of Trial and Error, a Pickle Slice That Stays Put," *Wall Street Journal,* October 6,

1998, p. B1; "Vlasic's Hamburger-Size Pickles," *Wall Street Journal,* October 5, 1998, p. A26; and "Vlasic Foods International FY2000 New Products," accessed online at www.vlasic.com, July 1999.

24. For a more comprehensive discussion of marketing strategies over the course of the product life cycle, see Philip Kotler, *Marketing Management,* 10th ed. (Upper Saddle River, NJ: Prentice Hall, 2000), pp. 303–23.

COMPANY CASE

9

LifeSource Nutrition: Succeeding Where Campbell Soup Failed

MMM! SMART FOOD

How would you feel about eating a steady diet of frozen foods to improve your health? Well, that's what Campbell Soup wanted you to do when it cooked up a line of mostly frozen meals designed to reduce certain health risks such as heart disease and diabetes. Campbell introduced the product line, calling it Intelligent Quisine (IQ), in an Ohio test market in January 1997.

How IQ made it to the test market is an interesting story. In 1991, Campbell realized the soup market was mature and offered very little growth potential. As a result, the company began to beef up its research and development (R&D) efforts, devoting about 1 percent of sales to R&D. A senior vice president noted that the company's R&D efforts were guided by two objectives: "stay with the customer" and "focus on big opportunities."

While exploring diversification ideas related to its core business, CEO David W. Johnson stumbled onto the idea of "introducing the first and only meal program clinically proven to help people reduce cholesterol, blood pressure, and blood sugar." Johnson saw an explosive market potential for "functional food"—food that tasted good, was good for you, and was as effective therapeutically as a drug. Observers dubbed this type of food "nutraceuticals." Campbell thought it could offer a convenient meal program to a target market of 60 million people who suffered from a wide range of health problems like high cholesterol, high blood pressure, and hypertension. That number actually grew to 100 million when people who were at risk of getting these problems were factored in. In addition, research showed that 52 percent of the population believed food products could help reduce cancer and disease.

The company then spent two years gathering a medical advisory board that included specialists in heart disease, nutrition, and diabetes. The board also included representatives from organizations such as the American Heart Association. Campbell worked with the advisory board and conducted clinical research on 800 patients to help design the IQ products.

By 1997, Campbell had spent $55 million to develop the product line. It consisted of 41 meals, mostly frozen, that included breakfasts such as French toast or egg sandwiches, lunches such as chili or stew, and dinners such as pasta or chicken. It also included snacks such as pretzels and cookies.

During the 15-month Ohio test market, participants purchased 21 IQ meals each week for a price of about $80 per week. The participants had to agree to stick with the program for 4 to 10 weeks. With a discount, the recommended 10-week program actually cost about $700. Consumers had to commit to eating only IQ meals and to changing other habits. With each weekly order, Campbell included printed materials that offered advice on diet, exercise, and behavioral change. Participants could also use prepaid phone cards to talk to dietitians.

Campbell decided to distribute the meals directly to consumers using UPS to make weekly deliveries of the frozen meals. The company selected direct distribution because it believed that retailers would not be able to keep the complete line of 41 meals in stock.

Campbell used television, radio, and print ads to promote the program and an 800-number for consumers to call to place an order. The ads touted IQ's ability to reverse certain medical conditions such as high blood pressure and high blood sugar. "I ate cheesecake and my cholesterol went down 15 points," one ad proclaimed. In addition, the company had its sales representatives call on doctors and other health professionals, much as sales representatives for drug companies did.

At first glance, the test market seemed to be successful. In just 10 weeks, one consumer reported that she lost 10 pounds and saw her cholesterol drop from 240 to 200. Another consumer had her blood sugar drop from 300 to between 110 and 135. She was even able to stop taking a prescription medication.

Overall, however, Campbell considered the test market a failure. Although the company had a sales target of 40,000 orders, fewer than 2,500 people ordered just over six weeks of meals. Despite the homework that went into the project, it failed to meet Campbell's expectations. In early 1998, the company announced that it was pulling the plug on IQ. One analyst noted, "We are all waiting for the boom in nutraceuticals, but thus far there haven't been many opportunities to make money at it." Another analyst observed that it was never clear there would be a market for the product. "It never struck me as something that was very promising."

JUMPING INTO THE SOUP

Just as Campbell announced its decision, LifeSource Nutrition Solutions, an Emeryville, California-based company, announced it would tackle the problem of offering nutritionally balanced meals. LifeSource is a spin-off of Age Wave, a consulting company started in 1986 by Ken Dychtwald. Age Wave specialized in advising firms on how to market to people over 50. Once Age Wave reached $15 million in revenue, Dychtwald stopped consulting and started a business incubator to create businesses that would serve the mushrooming population of people over 50. Dychtwald commented that, "The food industry has typically catered to the needs and time pressures of young adults while often neglecting the taste and nutrient needs of mature women and men."

LifeSource, which is also funded by Monsanto, operates in San Francisco and Los Angeles. In its current markets, it runs two central production kitchens where culinarians and nutritionists prepare nutraceutical foods and beverages that meet or exceed the dietary requirements of the American Heart Association, National Institutes of Health, and American Diabetes Association. Each of its 24 nutrient-rich meals, which include soups and smoothie beverages, address common conditions such as congestive heart failure, coronary artery disease, and diabetes. The company also offers free nutritional counseling and nutrition materials.

Unlike Campbell Soup, however, LifeSource conducted no clinical research to help in developing its products. The company did, however, assemble a science advisory board to make sure it understood the link between diet and health.

LifeSource's meals target customers over 50 who have risk factors for diabetes and heart disease. These people either can't or don't want to cook for themselves, or they don't have the energy or the means to get to the grocery store. Of the $860 billion annual food market in the United States, only about $86 billion represents nutraceutical foods, and only about $14 billion of that amount is fortified foods (as opposed to natural fruits and vegetables). Moreover, there is a growing trend to "home meal replacements"—fully prepared foods that consumers purchase either to take home or for home delivery.

Once the company prepares the meals, it flash-freezes them in its own cold-storage facilities. Then, the company has its own fleet of vans and drivers deliver the meals. It decided on direct distribution to avoid problems with the freeze-thaw cycle. Controlling the food's temperature after production is critical to maintaining quality.

The company has not forgotten taste. Whereas a Meals-on-Wheels dinner of roast beef with red potatoes may not excite your taste buds, LifeSource's Creole cod, rice and red chile beans, and an orange mango smoothie makes for a flashier, tastier offering. Moreover, nothing on a Meals-on-Wheels menu is fortified.

However, the average cost of a Meals-on-Wheels dinner is $5.31, with the client paying only $1.25 (federal funds cover the balance of the cost). LifeSource, on the other hand, prices its dinners at $5.80 per entrée, its lunches from $3.20 to $4.20, its soups at $2.50, and its smoothies and desserts at $1.10 to $1.45. There is no delivery charge with a minimum

eight-item order. People over 50, the company notes, represent only 27 percent of the population but control 70 percent of the total net worth of U.S. households.

LifeSource promotes its products through direct mail, direct-response advertising, and public relations. It also has a Web site, www.lifesourcenutrition.com, where consumers can place orders and get other valuable information about health and nutrition.

Perhaps the most important difference between IQ and the LifeSource plan is that the company has positioned its plan as giving consumers free choice. Campbell's tied its meal program to a physician network. A LifeSource spokesperson noted, "There's a customization of diets to reach individuals' health goals, and if they want to substitute 15, 20, or 50 percent of their diet, it's up to them. It's not based on clinical research—it's voluntary compliance."

A SUCCESS OR ANOTHER FAILURE?

Will LifeSource succeed where Campbell failed? LifeSource reports that after experiencing a 50 percent reorder rate in its California markets, it is cautiously optimistic about its new products. In late 1999, it planned to expand to Seattle, Phoenix, and Salt Lake City; and, if all goes well, it plans a national rollout over the next four to seven years. Observers believe there is an opportunity for nutraceuticals and that Campbell's failure doesn't mean others will fail. However, a food industry analyst notes that, "It certainly is a niche that is extremely complex."

Questions

1. Outline Campbell Soup's marketing strategy for Intelligent Quisine and describe its new product development process. Why do you believe IQ failed?

2. Outline LifeSource Nutrition's marketing strategy for its products and describe its new product development process. How are its strategy and its new product development process alike or different from Campbell's?

3. Do you believe there is a market for nutraceuticals? Why or why not?

4. What marketing recommendations would you make to LifeSource Nutrition to help it be successful in this market?

Sources: "Takeout Meals for Specialized Diets," *Food Management,"* June 1999, p. 10; Rick Desloge, "Monsanto Puts $10 Million in Baby Boomers' Nutrition," *St. Louis Business Journal,* January 4, 1999, p. 6; Kitty Kevin, "A Golden Age for Meal Solutions," *Food Processing,* October 1998, p. 37; Jake Holden, "High-Tech Take-Out," *American Demographics,* October 1998; Claudia D. O'Donnell, "Campbell's R&D Cozies Up to the Consumer," *Prepared Foods,* September 1997, p. 26; Vanessa O'Connell, "Campbell Decides Its IQ Health Meals May Be Ahead of the Curve for Foods," *Wall Street Journal,* April 27, 1998, p. B8; Stephanie Thompson, "Eying an Aging America, Food Giants Broaden Inroads into Nutraceuticals," *Brandweek,* January 6, 1997, p. 8. See also, www.lifesourcenutrition.com.

After studying this chapter, you should be able to
1. identify and define the internal factors affecting a firm's pricing decisions
2. identify and define the external factors affecting pricing decisions, including the impact of consumer perceptions of price and value
3. contrast the three general approaches to setting prices

PRICING PRODUCTS: PRICING CONSIDERATIONS AND APPROACHES

F or decades preceding 1995, Kellogg was beloved on Wall Street—it was a virtual money machine. The cereal giant's 1995 sales of $7 billion represented its fifty-first straight year of rising revenues. Over the previous 30 years, Kellogg's sales had grown at one and a half times the industry growth rate and its share of the U.S. cereal market had consistently exceeded 40 percent. Over the preceding decade, annual returns to shareholders had averaged 19 percent, with gross margins running as high as 55 percent. In 1995, Kellogg held a 42 percent worldwide market share, with a 48 percent share in Asia and Europe and a mind-blowing 69 percent share in Latin America. Things, it seemed, could only get better for Kellogg.

Behind these dazzling numbers, however, Kellogg's cereal empire had begun to lose its luster. Much of its recent success, it now appears, had come at the expense of cereal customers. Kellogg's recent gains—and those of major competitors General Mills, Post, and Quaker—had come not from innovative new products, creative marketing programs, and operational improvements that added value for customers. Instead, these gains had come almost entirely from price increases that padded the sales and profits of the cereal makers.

Throughout most of the 1980s and early 1990s, Kellogg had boosted profit margins by steadily raising prices on its Rice Krispies, Special K, Raisin Bran, and Frosted Flakes—often twice a year. For example, by early 1996, a 14-ounce box of Raisin Bran that sold for $2.39 in 1985 was going for as much as $4.00 to $5.00, but with little or no change in the costs of the materials making up the cereal or its packaging.

Since World War II, no food category had had more price increases than cereal. The price increases were very profitable for Kellogg and the other cereal companies—on average, the cereal makers were reaping more than twice the operating margins of the food industry as a whole. However, the relentless price increases became increasingly difficult for customers to swallow.

So, not surprisingly, in 1994 the cereal industry's pricing policies began to backfire as frustrated consumers retaliated with a quiet fury. Cereal buyers began shifting away from branded cereals toward cheaper private-label brands; by 1995, private labels were devouring 10 percent of the American cereal market, up from a little more than 5 percent only five years earlier. Worse, many Americans switched to less expensive, more portable handheld breakfast foods, such as bagels, muffins, and breakfast bars. As a result, total American cereal sales began falling off by 3 to 4 percent a year. Kellogg's sales and profits sagged and its U.S. market share dropped to 36 percent. By early 1996, after what most industry analysts viewed as years of outrageous and self-serving pricing policies, Kellogg and the other cereal makers faced a full blown crisis.

Post Cereals was the first competitor to break away. Belated research showed that exorbitant pricing was indeed the cause of the industry's doldrums. "Every statistic, every survey we took only showed that our customers were becoming more and more dissatisfied," said Mark Leckie, then general manager of Post Cereals. "You can see them walking down cereal aisles, clutching fistfuls of coupons and looking all over the shelves, trying to match them with a specific brand." To boost its soggy sales, in April 1996 Post slashed the prices on its 22 cereal brands an average of 20 percent—a surprise move that rocked the industry.

At first, Kellogg, General Mills, and Quaker held stubbornly to their premium prices. However, cereal buyers began switching in droves to Post's lower-priced brands—Post quickly stole 4 points from Kellogg's market share alone. Kellogg and the others had little choice but to follow Post's lead. Kellogg announced price cuts averaging 19 percent on two-thirds of all brands sold in the United States, marking the start of what would become a long and costly industry price war. In recanting their previous pricing excesses, the cereal makers swung wildly in the opposite direction, caught up in layoffs, plant closings, and other cost-cutting measures and fresh rounds of price cutting. "It reminds me of one of those World War I battles where there's all this firing but when the smoke clears you can't tell who won," noted an industry analyst. In fact, it appears that nobody won, as the fortunes of all competitors suffered.

Kellogg was perhaps the hardest hit of the major competitors. Post Cereal's parent company, consumer-foods powerhouse Philip Morris, derived only about 2 percent of its sales and profits from cereals and could easily offset the losses elsewhere. However, Kellogg, which counted on domestic cereal sales for 42 percent of its revenues and 43 percent of its operating profits, suffered

enormously. Its operating margins were halved, and even after lowering its prices, Kellogg's revenues and profits continued to decline.

Now, several years after the initial price rollbacks, Kellogg and the cereal industry are still feeling the aftershocks. Entering the new millennium, the total American cereal market is growing at a meager 1 percent a year, private brands now capture an impressive 18 percent market share, and alternative breakfast foods continue their strong growth. Kellogg's market share has slumped to 32 percent, down from 42 percent in 1988, and its sales and profits are flat. During the past several years, Kellogg has watched its stock price languish while the stock market as a whole has more than tripled.

Recently, Kellogg and the other cereal titans have quietly begun pushing ahead with modest price increases. The increases are needed, they argue, to fund the product innovation and marketing support necessary to stimulate growth in the stagnant cereal category. But there's an obvious risk. Consumers have long memories, and if the new products and programs aren't exciting enough, the higher prices may well push consumers further toward less expensive private-label cereals and alternative breakfast foods. "It's almost a no-win situation," says another analyst.

Despite its problems, Kellogg remains the industry leader. The Kellogg brand name is still one of the world's best known and most respected. Kellogg's recent initiatives to cut costs, get reacquainted with its customers, and develop innovative new products and marketing programs—all of which promise to add value for customers rather than simply cutting prices—has Wall Street cautiously optimistic about Kellogg's future. But events of the past five years teach an important lesson. When setting prices, as when making any other marketing decisions, a company can't afford to focus on its own costs and profits. Instead, it must focus on customers' needs and the value they receive from the company's total marketing offer. If a company doesn't give customers full value for the price they're paying, they'll go elsewhere. In this case, Kellogg stole profits by steadily raising prices without also increasing customer value. Customers paid the price in the short run—but Kellogg is paying the price in the long run.[1]

All profit organizations and many nonprofit organizations must set prices on their products or services. *Price* goes by many names:

> Price is all around us. You pay *rent* for your apartment, *tuition* for your education, and a *fee* to your physician or dentist. The airline, railway, taxi, and bus companies charge you a *fare;* the local utilities call their price a *rate;* and the local bank charges you *interest* for the money you borrow. The price for driving your car on Florida's Sunshine Parkway is a *toll,* and the company that insures your car charges you a *premium.* The guest lecturer charges an *honorarium* to tell you about a government official who took a *bribe* to help a shady character steal *dues* collected by a trade association. Clubs or societies to which you belong may make a special *assessment* to pay unusual expenses. Your regular lawyer may ask for a *retainer* to cover her services. The "price" of an executive is a *salary,* the price of a salesperson may be a *commission,* and the price of a worker is a *wage.* Finally, although economists would disagree, many of us feel that *income taxes* are the price we pay for the privilege of making money.[2]

Price

The amount of money charged for a product or service, or the sum of the values that consumers exchange for the benefits of having or using the product or service.

In the narrowest sense, **price** is the amount of money charged for a product or service. More broadly, price is the sum of all the values that consumers exchange for the benefits of having or using the product or service. Historically, price has been the major factor affecting buyer choice. This is still true in poorer nations, among poorer groups, and with commodity products. However, nonprice factors have become more important in buyer-choice behavior in recent decades.

Throughout most of history, prices were set by negotiation between buyers and sellers. *Fixed price* policies—setting one price for all buyers—is a relatively modern idea that arose with the development of large-scale retailing at the end of the nineteenth century. Now, some one hundred years later, the Internet promises to reverse the fixed pricing trend and take us back to an era of *dynamic pricing*—charging different prices depending on individual customers and situations (see Marketing Highlight 10.1). The Internet, corporate networks, and wireless setups are connecting sellers and buyers as never before. Web sites like Compare.Net and PriceScan.com allow buyers to quickly and easily compare products and prices. Online auction sites like eBay.com and Amazon.com make it easy for buyers and sellers to negotiate prices on thousands of items—from refurbished computers to antique tin trains. At the same time, new technologies allow sellers to collect detailed data about customers' buying habits, preferences—even spending limits—so they can tailor their products and prices.[3]

Price is the only element in the marketing mix that produces revenue; all other elements represent costs. Price is also one of the most flexible elements of the marketing mix. Unlike product features and channel commitments, price can be changed quickly. At the same time, pricing and price competition is the number-one problem facing many marketing executives. Yet, as the chapter-opening Kellogg example illustrates, many companies do not handle pricing well. The most common mistakes are pricing that is too cost oriented rather than customer-value oriented; prices that are not revised often enough to reflect market changes; pricing that does not take the rest of the marketing mix into account; and prices that are not varied enough for different products, market segments, and purchase occasions.

In this chapter and the next, we focus on the problem of setting prices. This chapter looks at the factors marketers must consider when setting prices and at general pricing approaches. In the next chapter, we examine pricing strategies for new-product pricing, product mix pricing, price adjustments for buyer and situational factors, and price changes.

MARKETING HIGHLIGHT 10.1

BACK TO THE FUTURE: DYNAMIC PRICING ON THE WEB

The Internet is more than simply a new "marketspace"—it's actually changing the rules of commerce. Take pricing, for example. From the mostly fixed pricing policies of the nineteenth century, the Web seems now to be taking us back—into a new age of fluid pricing. "Potentially, [the Internet] could push aside sticker prices and usher in an era of dynamic pricing," says *Business Week* writer Robert Hof, "in which a wide range of goods would be priced according to what the market will bear—instantly, constantly." Here's how the Internet is changing the rules of pricing for both sellers and buyers.

Sellers Can . . .

- **charge lower prices, reap higher margins.** Web buying and selling can result in drastically lower costs, allowing online merchants to charge lower prices and still make higher margins. "The vastly lower cost of selling online provides plenty of riches to go around," observes Hof. "Thanks to their Internet connections, buyers and sellers around the world can connect at almost no cost—making instant bargaining [economically feasible]." Reduced inventory and distribution costs add to the savings. For example, by selling online and making its computers to order, Dell Computer greatly reduces inventory costs and eliminates retail markups. It shares the savings with buyers in the form of the "lowest price per performance."

- **monitor customer behavior and tailor offers to individuals.** With the help of new technologies, Web merchants can now target special prices to specific customers. For example, Personify Inc. has software that allows Internet sellers such as Amazon.com or Virtual Vineyards to assess each visitor's "clickstream," the way the person navigates the Web site, then instantaneously tailor products and prices to that shopper's specific behavior. If a visitor behaves like a price-sensitive shopper, he or she may be offered a lower price. The Internet also lets sellers give certain customers special access to special prices. For example, CDnow, the online music vendor, e-mails a special Web site address with lower prices to certain buyers—say, new buyers that it wants to encourage or heavy users that it wants to reward. If you don't know the secret address, you pay full price.

- **change prices on the fly according to changes in demand or costs.** Just ask online catalog retailers such as Lands' End, Spiegel, or Fingerhut. With printed catalogs, a price is a price, at least until the next catalog is printed. Online sellers, however, can change prices for specific items on a day-by-day or even hour-by-hour basis. Such flexible pricing lets sellers adjust quickly to changing costs, drop prices and offer promotions to boost sales for slow-moving items, and nudge prices upward to improve margins on hot-selling goods. Many business marketers use their extranets—the private networks that link them with suppliers and customers—to get a precise handle on inventory, costs, and demand at any given moment and adjust prices instantly.

The Internet is ushering in a new era of fluid pricing. MySimon is an independent site that provides product comparisons and guides and searches all merchant sites for the best prices.

Both Sellers and Buyers Can . . .

- **negotiate prices in online auctions and exchanges.** Want to sell that antique pickle jar that's been collecting dust for generations? Post it on www.eBay.com, the world's biggest online flea market. Want to purchase vintage baseball cards at a bargain price? Go to Boekhout's Collectibles Mall at www.azww.com. Want to dump that excess inventory? Try adding an auction feature to your own Web site—Sharper Image claims it's getting 40 percent of retail for excess goods sold via its online auction site, compared with only 20 percent from liquidators.

Suddenly the centuries-old art of haggling is back in vogue. Experts predict that in the year 2002, more than $129 billion worth of goods and services will be sold through Internet auctions, up from only $3.8 billion in 1998. Of the thousands of Internet auction sites, Onsale, eBay, and Amazon.com Auctions are the largest. More than 12 million bids have been placed on Onsale since it opened for business in 1995. At eBay, which began when its owner used the Web to find a market for his girlfriend's vintage Pez dispenser collection, about a million registered users bid on 700,000 items in more than 1,000 categories.

Buyers like auctions because, quite simply, they like the bargains they find. Sellers like auctions because, over the Internet, the cost per transaction drops dramatically. Thus, it becomes practical—even profitable—to auction an item for mere dollars rather than thousands of dollars. For example, the seller can program its computers to accept the 3,000 best bids higher than $2.10 for 3,000 pieces of costume jewelry. Business marketers, whose transactions account for 68 percent of online auction sales, also use auctions to offer time-sensitive deals

and gauge interest on possible price points for new products.

Buyers Can . . .

- **get instant price comparisons from thousands of vendors.** The Internet gives consumers access to reams of data about products and prices. According to Hof, "In the physical world, buyers face all kinds of obstacles to getting the best deal—far-flung suppliers, limited time to do research, middlemen who keep a tight lid on information. . . . On the Web, shopping's a snap. Buyers can quickly compare information about products and vendors almost anywhere." New online comparison guides—such as CompareNet and PriceScan—spring up daily, giving product and price comparisons at the click of a mouse. CompareNet, for instance, lets consumers compare prices on more than 100,000 consumer products. Other sites offer intelligent shopping agents—such as MySimon, Junglee, and Jango—that seek out products, prices, and reviews. MySimon (www.mySimon. com), for instance, takes a buyer's criteria for a PC, camcorder, or collectible Barbie, then roots through top sellers' sites to find the best match at the best price.

- **find and negotiate lower prices.** With market information and access come buyer power. In addition to simply finding the vendor with the best price, customers armed with price information can often negotiate lower prices. Here are examples of both consumers and industrial buyers exercising this newfound power:

In search of the best possible deal on a Palm Pilot organizer, Stephen Manes first checked PriceSCAN.com, an online price comparison site, where he learned that buysoware.com had the high-tech gadget for only $358. Buysoware, however, was "out of stock," as was the second lowest priced vendor, mcglen.com. Undaunted, Stephen skipped to the other end of the list

where he found that PC Zone was offering the device for $449, and it was in stock. "Time to haggle," said Stephen. "I picked up the phone. In seconds, an eager salesperson quoted me the official price. 'I saw it at buy.com for $358,' I said, omitting mention of the word[s 'out of stock'].'I don't know if I can match buy.com,' came the response. 'But we can do it for $375.'" Stephen snapped up the offer, saving himself a bundle off the store price.

Business buying on the Internet dwarfs consumer buying, so it's no wonder that business buyers have also learned the price advantages of shopping the Web. For example, hoping to save some money, United Technologies Corporation tried something new last year. Instead of the usual haggling with dozens of individual vendors to secure printed circuit boards for various subsidiaries worldwide, UTC put the contract out on FreeMarkets, an online marketplace for industrial goods. To the company's delight, bids poured in from 39 suppliers, saving UTC a cool $10 million off its initial $24 million estimate. Says a UTC executive, "The technology drives the lowest price in a hurry."

Will dynamic pricing sweep the marketing world? "Not entirely," says Hof. "It takes a lot of work to haggle—which is why fixed prices happened in the first place." However, he continues, "Pandora's e-box is now open, and pricing will never be the same. For many . . . products, millions of buyers figure a little haggling is a small price to pay for a sweet deal."

Sources: Quotes and extracts from Robert D. Hof, "Going, Going, Gone," *Business Week,* April 12, 1999, pp. 30–32; Robert D. Hof, "The Buyer Always Wins," *Business Week,* March 22, 1999, pp. EB26–EB28; and Stephen Manes, "Off-Web Dickering," *Forbes,* April 5, 1999, p. 134. Also see Amy E. Cortese, "Good-Bye to Fixed Pricing?" *Business Week,* May 4, 1998, pp. 71–84; Scott Woolley, "I Got It Cheaper Than You," *Forbes,* November 2, 1998, pp. 82–84; Scott Woolley, "Price War!" *Forbes,* December 14, 1998, pp. 182–84; and Michael Krauss, "Web Offers Biggest Prize in Product Pricing Game," *Marketing News,* July 6, 1998, p. 8.

FACTORS TO CONSIDER WHEN SETTING PRICES

A company's pricing decisions are affected by both internal company factors and external environmental factors (see Figure 10.1).[4]

Internal Factors Affecting Pricing Decision

Internal factors affecting pricing include the company's marketing objectives, marketing mix strategy, costs, and organizational considerations.

Marketing Objectives

Before setting price, the company must decide on its strategy for the product. If the company has selected its target market and positioning carefully, then its marketing mix strategy, including price, will be fairly straightforward. For example, if General Motors decides to produce a new sports car to compete with European sports cars in the high-income segment, this suggests charging a high price. Motel 6, Econo Lodge, and Red Roof Inn have positioned themselves as motels that provide economical rooms for budget-minded travelers; this position requires charging a low price. Thus, pricing strategy is largely determined by decisions on market positioning.

At the same time, the company may seek additional objectives. The clearer a firm is about its objectives, the easier it is to set price. Examples of common objectives are *survival, current profit maximization, market share leadership,* and *product quality leadership.*

Companies set *survival* as their major objective if they are troubled by too much capacity, heavy competition, or changing consumer wants. To keep a plant going, a company may set a low price, hoping to increase demand. In this case, profits are less important than survival. As long as their prices cover variable costs and some fixed costs, they can stay in business. However, survival is only a short-term objective. In the long run, the firm must learn how to add value that consumers will pay for or face extinction.

Many companies use *current profit maximization* as their pricing goal. They estimate what demand and costs will be at different prices and choose the price that will produce the maximum current profit, cash flow, or return on investment. In all cases, the company wants current financial results rather than long-run performance. Other companies want to obtain *market share leadership.* They believe that the company with the largest market share will enjoy the lowest costs and highest long-run profit. To become the market share leader, these firms set prices as low as possible.

A company might decide that it wants to achieve *product quality leadership.* This normally calls for charging a high price to cover higher performance quality and the high cost of R&D. For example, Hewlett-Packard focuses on the high-quality,

FIGURE 10.1   Factors affecting price decisions

Product-quality leadership: Maytag targets the higher quality end of the appliance market. Its ads use the long-running slogan "Built to last longer" and feature Ol' Lonely, the Maytag repairman.

high-price end of the hand-held calculator market. Gillette's product superiority lets it price its Mach3 razor cartridges at a 50 percent premium over its own SensorExcel and competitors' cartridges. Maytag has long built high-quality washing machines and priced them higher. Its ads use the long-running Maytag slogan "Built to last longer" and feature the lonely Maytag repairman (who's lonely because no one ever calls him for service). The ads point out that washers are custodians of what is often a $300 to $400 load of clothes, making them worth the higher price tag. For instance, at $1,099, Maytag's new Neptune, a front-loading washer without an agitator, sells for double what most other washers cost because the company's marketers claim that it uses less water and electricity and prolongs the life of clothing by being less abrasive.[5]

A company might also use price to attain other, more specific objectives. It can set prices low to prevent competition from entering the market or set prices at competitors' levels to stabilize the market. Prices can be set to keep the loyalty and support of resellers or to avoid government intervention. Prices can be reduced temporarily to create excitement for a product or to draw more customers into a retail store. One product may be priced to help the sales of other products in the company's line. Thus, pricing may play an important role in helping to accomplish the company's objectives at many levels.

Nonprofit and public organizations may adopt a number of other pricing objectives. A university aims for *partial cost recovery,* knowing that it must rely on private gifts and public grants to cover the remaining costs. A nonprofit hospital may aim for *full cost recovery* in its pricing. A nonprofit theater company may price its productions to fill the maximum number of theater seats. A social service agency may set a *social price* geared to the varying income situations of different clients.

Marketing Mix Strategy

Price is only one of the marketing mix tools that a company uses to achieve its marketing objectives. Price decisions must be coordinated with product design, distribution, and promotion decisions to form a consistent and effective marketing program. Decisions made for other marketing mix variables may affect pricing decisions. For example, producers using many resellers who are expected to support and promote their products may have to build larger reseller margins into their prices. The decision to position the product on high-performance quality will mean that the seller must charge a higher price to cover higher costs.

Target costing
Pricing that starts with an ideal selling price, then targets costs that will ensure that the price is met.

Companies often position their products on price and then base other marketing mix decisions on the prices they want to charge. Here, price is a crucial product-positioning factor that defines the product's market, competition, and design. Many firms support such price-positioning strategies with a technique called **target costing,** a potent strategic weapon. Target costing reverses the usual process of first designing a new product, determining its cost, and then asking, "Can we sell it for that?" Instead, it starts with an ideal selling price based on customer considerations, then targets costs that will ensure that the price is met.

The original Swatch watch provides a good example of target costing. Rather than starting with its own costs, Swatch surveyed the market and identified an unserved segment of watch buyers who wanted "a low-cost fashion accessory that also keeps time." Armed with this information about market needs, Swatch set out to give consumers the watch they wanted at a price they were willing to pay, and it managed the new product's costs accordingly. Like most watch buyers, targeted consumers were concerned about precision, reliability, and durability. However, they were also concerned about fashion and affordability. To keep costs down, Swatch designed fashionable simpler watches that contained fewer parts and that were constructed from high-tech but less expensive materials. It then developed a revolutionary automated process for mass producing the new watches and exercised strict cost controls throughout the manufacturing process. By managing costs carefully, Swatch was able to create a watch that offered just the right blend of fashion and function at a price consumers were willing to pay. As a result of its initial major success, consumers have placed increasing value on Swatch products, allowing the company to introduce successively higher-priced designs.[6]

Other companies deemphasize price and use other marketing mix tools to create *nonprice* positions. Often, the best strategy is not to charge the lowest price, but rather to differentiate the marketing offer to make it worth a higher price. For example, for years Johnson Controls, a producer of climate-control systems for office buildings, used initial price as its primary competitive tool. However, research showed that customers were more concerned about the total cost of installing and maintaining a system than about its initial price. Repairing broken systems was expensive, time-consuming, and risky. Customers had to shut down the heat or air conditioning in the whole building, disconnect a lot of wires, and face the dangers of electrocution. Johnson decided to change its strategy. It designed an entirely new system called "Metasys." To repair the new system, customers need only pull out an old plastic module and slip in a new one—no tools required. Metasys costs more to make than the old system, and customers pay a higher initial price, but it costs less to install and maintain. Despite its higher asking price, the new Metasys system brought in $500 million in revenues in its first year.[7]

Thus, the marketer must consider the total marketing mix when setting prices. If the product is positioned on nonprice factors, then decisions about quality, promotion, and distribution will strongly affect price. If price is a crucial positioning factor, then price will strongly affect decisions made about the other marketing mix elements. However, even when featuring price, marketers need to remember that customers rarely buy on price alone. Instead, they seek products that give them the best value in terms of benefits received for the price paid. Thus, in most cases, the company will consider price along with all the other marketing-mix elements when developing the marketing program.

Costs

Costs set the floor for the price that the company can charge for its product. The company wants to charge a price that both covers all its costs for producing, distributing, and selling the product and delivers a fair rate of return for its effort and risk. A company's costs may be an important element in its pricing strategy. Many companies, such as Southwest Airlines, Wal-Mart, and Union Carbide, work to become the "low-cost producers" in their industries. Companies with lower costs can set lower prices that result in greater sales and profits.

Fixed costs
Costs that do not vary with production or sales level.

Variable costs
Costs that vary directly with the level of production.

Total costs
The sum of the fixed and variable costs for any given level of production.

Types of Costs.   A company's costs take two forms, fixed and variable. **Fixed costs** (also known as overhead) are costs that do not vary with production or sales level. For example, a company must pay each month's bills for rent, heat, interest, and executive salaries, whatever the company's output. **Variable costs** vary directly with the level of production. Each personal computer produced by Compaq involves a cost of computer chips, wires, plastic, packaging, and other inputs. These costs tend to be the same for each unit produced. They are called variable because their total varies with the number of units produced. **Total costs** are the sum of the fixed and variable costs for any given level of production. Management wants to charge a price that will at least cover the total production costs at a given level of production. The company must watch its costs carefully. If it costs the company more than competitors to produce and sell its product, the company will have to charge a higher price or make less profit, putting it at a competitive disadvantage.

Costs at Different Levels of Production.   To price wisely, management needs to know how its costs vary with different levels of production. For example, suppose Texas Instruments (TI) has built a plant to produce 1,000 calculators per day. Figure 10.2a shows the typical short-run average cost curve (SRAC). It shows that the cost per calculator is high if TI's factory produces only a few per day. But as production moves up to 1,000 calculators per day, average cost falls. This is because fixed costs are spread over more units, with each one bearing a smaller share of the fixed cost. TI can try to produce more than 1,000 calculators per day, but average costs will increase because the plant becomes inefficient. Workers have to wait for machines, the machines break down more often, and workers get in each other's way.

If TI believed it could sell 2,000 calculators a day, it should consider building a larger plant. The plant would use more efficient machinery and work arrangements. Also, the unit cost of producing 2,000 calculators per day would be lower than the unit cost of producing 1,000 units per day, as shown in the long-run average cost (LRAC) curve (Figure 10.2b). In fact, a 3,000-unit capacity plant would even be more efficient, according to Figure 10.2b. But a 4,000-unit daily production plant would be less efficient because of increasing diseconomies of scale—too many workers to manage, paperwork slows things down, and so on. Figure 10.2b shows that a 3,000-unit daily production plant is the best size to build if demand is strong enough to support this level of production.

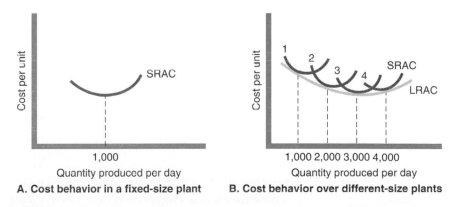

A. Cost behavior in a fixed-size plant   **B. Cost behavior over different-size plants**

FIGURE 10.2   **Cost per unit at different levels of production per period**

Costs as a Function of Production Experience.   Suppose TI runs a plant that produces 3,000 calculators per day. As TI gains experience in producing calculators, it learns how to do it better. Workers learn shortcuts and become more familiar with their equipment. With practice, the work becomes better organized, and TI finds better equipment and production processes. With higher volume, TI becomes more efficient and gains economies of scale. As a result, average cost tends to fall with accumulated production experience. This is shown in Figure 10.3.[8] Thus, the average cost of producing the first 100,000 calculators is $10 per calculator. When the company has produced the first 200,000 calculators, the average cost has fallen to $9. After its accumulated production experience doubles again to 400,000, the average cost is $7. This drop in the average cost with accumulated production experience is called the **experience curve** (or the **learning curve**).

If a downward-sloping experience curve exists, this is highly significant for the company. Not only will the company's unit production cost fall, but it will fall faster if the company makes and sells more during a given time period. But the market has to stand ready to buy the higher output. To take advantage of the experience curve, TI must get a large market share early in the product's life cycle. This suggests the following pricing strategy. TI should price its calculators low; its sales will then increase, and its costs will decrease through gaining more experience, and then it can lower its prices further.

Some companies have built successful strategies around the experience curve. For example, Bausch & Lomb solidified its position in the soft contact lens market by using computerized lens design and steadily expanding its one Soflens plant. As a result, its market share climbed steadily to 65 percent. However, a single-minded focus on reducing costs and exploiting the experience curve will not always work. Experience curve pricing carries some major risks. The aggressive pricing might give the product a cheap image. The strategy also assumes that competitors are weak and not willing to fight it out by meeting the company's price cuts. Finally, while the company is building volume under one technology, a competitor may find a lower-cost technology that lets it start at prices lower than the market leader's, who still operates on the old experience curve.

Organizational Considerations

Management must decide who within the organization should set prices. Companies handle pricing in a variety of ways. In small companies, prices are often set by top management rather than by the marketing or sales departments. In large companies, pricing is typically handled by divisional or product line managers. In industrial markets, salespeople may be allowed to negotiate with customers within

Experience curve (learning curve)

The drop in the average per-unit production cost that comes with accumulated production experience.

FIGURE 10.3   Cost per unit as a function of accumulated production: The experience curve

certain price ranges. Even so, top management sets the pricing objectives and policies, and it often approves the prices proposed by lower-level management or salespeople. In industries in which pricing is a key factor (aerospace, railroads, oil companies), companies often have a pricing department to set the best prices or help others in setting them. This department reports to the marketing department or top management. Others who have an influence on pricing include sales managers, production managers, finance managers, and accountants.

External Factors Affecting Pricing Decisions

External factors that affect pricing decisions include the nature of the market and demand, competition, and other environmental elements.

The Market and Demand

Whereas costs set the lower limit of prices, the market and demand set the upper limit. Both consumer and industrial buyers balance the price of a product or service against the benefits of owning it. Thus, before setting prices, the marketer must understand the relationship between price and demand for its product. In this section, we explain how the price–demand relationship varies for different types of markets and how buyer perceptions of price affect the pricing decision. We then discuss methods for measuring the price–demand relationship.

Pricing in Different Types of Markets.   The seller's pricing freedom varies with different types of markets. Economists recognize four types of markets, each presenting a different pricing challenge.

Under *pure competition,* the market consists of many buyers and sellers trading in a uniform commodity such as wheat, copper, or financial securities. No single buyer or seller has much effect on the going market price. A seller cannot charge more than the going price because buyers can obtain as much as they need at the going price. Nor would sellers charge less than the market price because they can sell all they want at this price. If price and profits rise, new sellers can easily enter the market. In a purely competitive market, marketing research, product development, pricing, advertising, and sales promotion play little or no role. Thus, sellers in these markets do not spend much time on marketing strategy.

Under *monopolistic competition,* the market consists of many buyers and sellers who trade over a range of prices rather than a single market price. A range of prices occurs because sellers can differentiate their offers to buyers. Either the physical product can be varied in quality, features, or style, or the accompanying services can be varied. Buyers see differences in sellers' products and will pay different prices for them. Sellers try to develop differentiated offers for different customer segments and, in addition to price, freely use branding, advertising, and personal selling to set their offers apart. For example, H.J. Heinz, Vlasic, and several other national brands of pickles compete with dozens of regional and local brands, all differentiated by price and nonprice factors. In services, Kinko's differentiates its offer through strong branding and advertising, reducing the impact of pricing. Because there are many competitors in such markets, each firm is less affected by competitors' marketing strategies than in oligopolistic markets.

Under *oligopolistic competition,* the market consists of a few sellers who are highly sensitive to each other's pricing and marketing strategies. The product can be uniform (steel, aluminum) or nonuniform (cars, computers). There are few sellers because it is difficult for new sellers to enter the market. Each seller is alert to competitors' strategies and moves. If a steel company slashes its price by 10 percent, buy-

Monopolistic competition: Kinko's differentiates its offer through strong branding and advertising, reducing the impact of pricing.

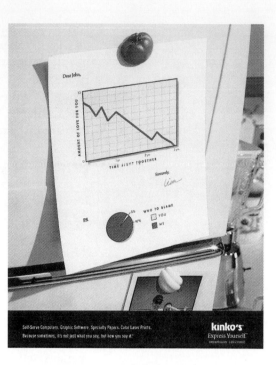

ers will quickly switch to this supplier. The other steelmakers must respond by lowering their prices or increasing their services. An oligopolist is never sure that it will gain anything permanent through a price cut. In contrast, if an oligopolist raises its price, its competitors might not follow this lead. The oligopolist then would have to retract its price increase or risk losing customers to competitors.

In a *pure monopoly,* the market consists of one seller. The seller may be a government monopoly (the U.S. Postal Service), a private regulated monopoly (a power company), or a private nonregulated monopoly (DuPont when it introduced nylon). Pricing is handled differently in each case. A government monopoly can pursue a variety of pricing objectives. It might set a price below cost because the product is important to buyers who cannot afford to pay full cost. Or the price might be set either to cover costs or to produce good revenue. It can even be set quite high to slow down consumption. In a regulated monopoly, the government permits the company to set rates that will yield a "fair return," one that will let the company maintain and expand its operations as needed. Nonregulated monopolies are free to price at what the market will bear. However, they do not always charge the full price for a number of reasons: a desire to not attract competition, a desire to penetrate the market faster with a low price, or a fear of government regulation.[9]

Consumer Perceptions of Price and Value.   In the end, the consumer will decide whether a product's price is right. Pricing decisions, like other marketing mix decisions, must be buyer oriented. When consumers buy a product, they exchange something of value (the price) to get something of value (the benefits of having or using the product). Effective, buyer-oriented pricing involves understanding how much value consumers place on the benefits they receive from the product and setting a price that fits this value.

A company often finds it hard to measure the values customers will attach to its product. For example, calculating the cost of ingredients in a meal at a fancy restaurant is relatively easy. But assigning a value to other satisfactions such as taste, environment, relaxation, conversation, and status is very hard. These values will vary both for different consumers and different situations. Still, consumers will use these

A. Inelastic demand

B. Elastic demand

FIGURE 10.4 Demand curves

values to evaluate a product's price. If customers perceive that the price is greater than the product's value, they will not buy the product. If consumers perceive that the price is below the product's value, they will buy it, but the seller loses profit opportunities.

Analyzing the Price–Demand Relationship. Each price the company might charge will lead to a different level of demand. The relationship between the price charged and the resulting demand level is shown in the **demand curve** in Figure 10.4. The demand curve shows the number of units the market will buy in a given time period at different prices that might be charged. In the normal case, demand and price are inversely related; that is, the higher the price, the lower the demand. Thus, the company would sell less if it raised its price from P_1 to P_2. In short, consumers with limited budgets probably will buy less of something if its price is too high.

Demand curve

A curve that shows the number of units the market will buy in a given time period at different prices that might be charged.

In the case of prestige goods, the demand curve sometimes slopes upward. Consumers think that higher prices mean more quality. For example, Gibson Guitar Corporation recently toyed with the idea of lowering its prices to compete more effectively with Japanese rivals like Yamaha and Ibanez. To its surprise, Gibson found that its instruments didn't sell as well at lower prices. "We had an inverse [price–demand relationship]," noted Gibson's chief executive officer. "The more we charged, the more product we sold." Gibson's slogan promises: "The world's finest musical instruments." It turns out that low prices simply aren't consistent with "Gibson's century old tradition of creating investment-quality instruments that represent the highest standards of imaginative design and masterful craftsmanship."[10] Still, if the company charges too high a price, the level of demand will be lower.

Most companies try to measure their demand curves by estimating demand at different prices. The type of market makes a difference. In a monopoly, the demand curve shows the total market demand resulting from different prices. If the company faces competition, its demand at different prices will depend on whether competitors' prices stay constant or change with the company's own prices.

In measuring the price–demand relationship, the market researcher must not allow other factors affecting demand to vary. For example, if Sony increased its advertising at the same time that it lowered its television prices, we would not know how much of the increased demand was due to the lower prices and how much was due to the increased advertising. The same problem arises if a holiday weekend occurs when the lower price is set—more gift giving over the holidays causes people to buy more televisions. Economists show the impact of nonprice factors on demand through shifts in the demand curve rather than movements along it.

The demand curve sometimes slopes upward. Gibson was surprised to learn that its high-quality instruments didn't sell as well at lower prices.

Price elasticity

A measure of the sensitivity of demand to changes in price.

Price Elasticity of Demand.   Marketers also need to know **price elasticity**—how responsive demand will be to a change in price. Consider the two demand curves in Figure 10.4. In Figure 10.4a, a price increase from P_1 to P_2 leads to a relatively small drop in demand from Q_1 to Q_2. In Figure 10.4b, however, the same price increase leads to a large drop in demand from Q'_1 to Q'_2. If demand hardly changes with a small change in price, we say the demand is *inelastic*. If demand changes greatly, we say the demand is *elastic*. The price elasticity of demand is given by the following formula:

$$\text{Price Elasticity of Demand} = \frac{\%\ \text{Change in Quantity Demanded}}{\%\ \text{Change in Price}}$$

Suppose demand falls by 10 percent when a seller raises its price by 2 percent. Price elasticity of demand is therefore –5 (the minus sign confirms the inverse relation between price and demand) and demand is elastic. If demand falls by 2 percent with a 2 percent increase in price, then elasticity is –1. In this case, the seller's total revenue stays the same: The seller sells fewer items but at a higher price that preserves the same total revenue. If demand falls by 1 percent when price is increased by 2 percent, then elasticity is –½ and demand is inelastic. The less elastic the demand, the more it pays for the seller to raise the price.

What determines the price elasticity of demand? Buyers are less price sensitive when the product they are buying is unique or when it is high in quality, prestige, or exclusiveness. They are also less price sensitive when substitute products are hard to find or when they cannot easily compare the quality of substitutes. Finally, buyers are less price sensitive when the total expenditure for a product is low relative to their income or when the cost is shared by another party.[11]

If demand is elastic rather than inelastic, sellers will consider lowering their price. A lower price will produce more total revenue. This practice makes sense as long as the extra costs of producing and selling more do not exceed the extra revenue. At the same time, most firms want to avoid pricing that turns their products into commodities. In recent years, forces such as deregulation and the instant price comparisons afforded by the Internet and other technologies have increased consumer price sensitivity, turning products ranging from telephones and computers to new automobiles into commodities in consumers' eyes. Marketers need to work harder than ever to differentiate their offerings when a dozen competitors are selling virtually the same product at a comparable or lower price. More than ever, companies need to understand the price sensitivity of their customers and prospects and the trade-offs people are willing to make between price and product characteristics. In the words of marketing consultant Kevin Clancy, those who target only the price sensitive are "leaving money on the table."

Even in the energy marketplace, where you would think that a kilowatt is a kilowatt is a kilowatt, some utility companies are beginning to wake up to this fact. They are differentiating their power, branding it, marketing it, and providing unique services to customers, even if it means higher prices. For example, Green Mountain Power (GMP), a small Vermont utility, is approaching the deregulated consumer energy marketplace with the firm belief that even kilowatt hours can be differentiated. GMP conducted extensive marketing research and uncovered a large segment of prospects who were not only concerned with the environment but were willing to support their attitudes with dollars. Because GMP is a "green" power provider— a large percentage of its power is hydroelectric—customers had an opportunity to ease the environmental burden by purchasing GMP power. GMP has already participated in two residential power-selling pilot projects in Massachusetts and New Hampshire, successfully competing against "cheaper" brands that focused on more price-sensitive consumers.[12]

Competitors' Costs, Prices, and Offers

Another external factor affecting the company's pricing decisions is competitors' costs and prices and possible competitor reactions to the company's own pricing moves. A consumer who is considering the purchase of a Canon camera will evaluate Canon's price and value against the prices and values of comparable products made by Nikon, Minolta, Pentax, and others. In addition, the company's pricing strategy may affect the nature of the competition it faces. If Canon follows a high-price, high-margin strategy, it may attract competition. A low-price, low-margin strategy, however, may stop competitors or drive them out of the market.

Canon needs to benchmark its costs against its competitors' costs to learn whether it is operating at a cost advantage or disadvantage. It also needs to learn the price and quality of each competitor's offer. Once Canon is aware of competitors' prices and offers, it can use them as a starting point for its own pricing. If Canon's cameras are similar to Nikon's, it will have to price close to Nikon or lose sales. If Canon's cameras are not as good as Nikon's, the firm will not be able to charge as much. If Canon's products are better than Nikon's, it can charge more. Basically, Canon will use price to position its offer relative to the competition.

Other External Factors

When setting prices, the company also must consider other factors in its external environment. *Economic conditions* can have a strong impact on the firm's pricing strategies. Economic factors such as boom or recession, inflation, and interest rates affect pricing decisions because they affect both the costs of producing a product and consumer perceptions of the product's price and value. The company must also consider what impact its prices will have on other parties in its environment. How will *resellers* react to various prices? The company should set prices that give resellers a fair profit, encourage their support, and help them to sell the product effectively.

The *government* is another important external influence on pricing decisions. Finally, *social concerns* may have to be taken into account. In setting prices, a company's short-term sales, market share, and profit goals may have to be tempered by broader societal considerations.

GENERAL PRICING APPROACHES

The price the company charges will be somewhere between one that is too low to produce a profit and one that is too high to produce any demand. Figure 10.5 summarizes the major considerations in setting price. Product costs set a floor to the price; consumer perceptions of the product's value set the ceiling. The company must consider competitors' prices and other external and internal factors to find the best price between these two extremes.

Companies set prices by selecting a general pricing approach that includes one or more of three sets of factors. We examine these approaches: the *cost-based approach* (cost-plus pricing, break-even analysis, and target profit pricing); the *buyer-based approach* (value-based pricing); and the *competition-based approach* (going-rate and sealed-bid pricing).

Cost-Based Pricing

Cost-Plus Pricing

Cost-plus pricing
Adding a standard markup to the cost of the product.

The simplest pricing method is **cost-plus pricing**—adding a standard markup to the cost of the product. Construction companies, for example, submit job bids by estimating the total project cost and adding a standard markup for profit. Lawyers, accountants, and other professionals typically price by adding a standard markup to their costs. Some sellers tell their customers they will charge cost plus a specified markup; for example, aerospace companies price this way to the government.

To illustrate markup pricing, suppose a toaster manufacturer had the following costs and expected sales:

Variable cost	$10
Fixed costs	$300,000
Expected unit sales	50,000

Then the manufacturer's cost per toaster is given by:

$$\text{Unit Cost} = \text{Variable Cost} + \frac{\text{Fixed Costs}}{\text{Unit Sales}} = \$10 + \frac{\$300,000}{50,000} = \$16$$

Product costs	Competitors' prices and other internal and external factors	Consumer perceptions of value
Price floor No profits below this price		**Price ceiling** No demand above this price

FIGURE 10.5   Major considerations in setting price

Now suppose the manufacturer wants to earn a 20 percent markup on sales. The manufacturer's markup price is given by:[13]

$$\text{Markup Price} = \frac{\text{Unit Cost}}{(1 - \text{Desired Return on Sales})} = \frac{\$16}{1 - 0.2} = \$20$$

The manufacturer would charge dealers \$20 a toaster and make a profit of \$4 per unit. The dealers, in turn, will mark up the toaster. If dealers want to earn 50 percent on sales price, they will mark up the toaster to \$40 (\$20 + 50% of \$40). This number is equivalent to a *markup on cost* of 100 percent (\$20/\$20).

Does using standard markups to set prices make sense? Generally, no. Any pricing method that ignores demand and competitor prices is not likely to lead to the best price. Suppose the toaster manufacturer charged \$20 but sold only 30,000 toasters instead of 50,000. Then the unit cost would have been higher because the fixed costs are spread over fewer units, and the realized percentage markup on sales would have been lower. Markup pricing works only if that price actually brings in the expected level of sales.

Still, markup pricing remains popular for many reasons. First, sellers are more certain about costs than about demand. By tying the price to cost, sellers simplify pricing—they do not have to make frequent adjustments as demand changes. Second, when all firms in the industry use this pricing method, prices tend to be similar and price competition is thus minimized. Third, many people feel that cost-plus pricing is fairer to both buyers and sellers. Sellers earn a fair return on their investment but do not take advantage of buyers when buyers' demand becomes great.

Break-even Analysis and Target Profit Pricing

Break-even pricing (target profit pricing)
Setting price to break even on the costs of making and marketing a product; or setting price to make a target profit.

Another cost-oriented pricing approach is **break-even pricing** (or a variation called **target profit pricing**.) The firm tries to determine the price at which it will break even or make the target profit it is seeking. Such pricing is used by General Motors, which prices its automobiles to achieve a 15 to 20 percent profit on its investment. This pricing method is also used by public utilities, which are constrained to make a fair return on their investment.

Target pricing uses the concept of a *break-even chart,* which shows the total cost and total revenue expected at different sales volume levels. Figure 10.6 shows a break-even chart for the toaster manufacturer discussed here. Fixed costs are \$300,000 regardless of sales volume. Variable costs are added to fixed costs to form total costs, which rise with volume. The total revenue curve starts at zero and rises with each unit sold. The slope of the total revenue curve reflects the price of \$20 per unit.

The total revenue and total cost curves cross at 30,000 units. This is the *break-even volume.* At \$20, the company must sell at least 30,000 units to break even; that is, for total revenue to cover total cost. Break-even volume can be calculated using the following formula:

$$\text{Break-even Volume} = \frac{\text{Fixed Cost}}{\text{Price} - \text{Variable Cost}} = \frac{\$300,000}{\$20 - \$10} = 30,000$$

If the company wants to make a target profit, it must sell more than 30,000 units at \$20 each. Suppose the toaster manufacturer has invested \$1,000,000 in the business and wants to set price to earn a 20 percent return, or \$200,000. In that case, it must sell at least 50,000 units at \$20 each. If the company charges a higher price,

FIGURE 10.6   Break-even chart for determining target price

it will not need to sell as many toasters to achieve its target return. But the market may not buy even this lower volume at the higher price. Much depends on the price elasticity and competitors' prices.

The manufacturer should consider different prices and estimate break-even volumes, probable demand, and profits for each. This is done in Table 10.1. The table shows that as price increases, break-even volume drops (column 2). But as price increases, demand for the toasters also falls off (column 3). At the $14 price, because the manufacturer clears only $4 per toaster ($14 less $10 in variable costs), it must sell a very high volume to break even. Even though the low price attracts many buyers, demand still falls below the high break-even point, and the manufacturer loses money. At the other extreme, with a $22 price the manufacturer clears $12 per toaster and must sell only 25,000 units to break even. But at this high price, consumers buy too few toasters, and profits are negative. The table shows that a price of $18 yields the highest profits. Note that none of the prices produce the manufacturer's target profit of $200,000. To achieve this target return, the manufacturer will have to search for ways to lower fixed or variable costs, thus lowering the break-even volume.

Value-Based Pricing

Value-based pricing

Setting price based on buyers' perceptions of value rather than on the seller's cost.

An increasing number of companies are basing their prices on the product's perceived value. **Value-based pricing** uses buyers' perceptions of value, not the seller's cost, as the key to pricing. Value-based pricing means that the marketer cannot design a product and marketing program and then set the price. Price is considered along with the other marketing mix variables *before* the marketing program is set.

Figure 10.7 compares cost-based pricing with value-based pricing. Cost-based pricing is product driven. The company designs what it considers to be a good product, totals the costs of making the product, and sets a price that covers costs plus a target profit. Marketing must then convince buyers that the product's value at that price justifies its purchase. If the price turns out to be too high, the company must settle for lower markups or lower sales, both resulting in disappointing profits.

Value-based pricing reverses this process. The company sets its target price based on customer perceptions of the product value. The targeted value and price then drive decisions about product design and what costs can be incurred. As a result, pricing begins with analyzing consumer needs and value perceptions, and price is set to match consumers' perceived value.

TABLE 10.1   BREAK-EVEN VOLUME AND PROFITS AT DIFFERENT PRICES

(1) Price	(2) Unit Demand Needed to Break Even	(3) Expected Unit Demand at Given Price	(4) Total Revenues (1) × (3)	(5) Total costs*	(6) Profit (4) − (5)
$14	75,000	71,000	$ 994,000	$1,010,000	−$ 16,000
16	50,000	67,000	1,072,000	970,000	102,000
18	37,500	60,000	1,080,000	900,000	180,000
20	30,000	42,000	840,000	720,000	120,000
22	25,000	23,000	506,000	530,000	−24,000

A company using value-based pricing must find out what value buyers assign to different competitive offers. However, measuring perceived value can be difficult. Sometimes, consumers are asked how much they would pay for a basic product and for each benefit added to the offer. Or a company might conduct experiments to test the perceived value of different product offers. If the seller charges more than the buyers' perceived value, the company's sales will suffer. Many companies overprice their products, and their products sell poorly. Other companies underprice. Underpriced products sell very well, but they produce less revenue than they would have if price were raised to the perceived-value level.

During the past decade, marketers have noted a fundamental shift in consumer attitudes toward price and quality. Many companies have changed their pricing approaches to bring them into line with changing economic conditions and consumer price perceptions. According to Jack Welch, CEO of General Electric, "The value decade is upon us. If you can't sell a top-quality product at the world's best price, you're going to be out of the game. . . .The best way to hold your customers is to constantly figure out how to give them more for less."[14]

Value pricing
Offering just the right combination of quality and good service at a fair price.

Thus, more and more, marketers have adopted **value pricing** strategies—offering just the right combination of quality and good service at a fair price. In many cases, this has involved the introduction of less expensive versions of established, brand-name products. Campbell introduced its Great Starts Budget frozen-food line, Holiday Inn opened several Holiday Express budget hotels, Revlon's Charles of the Ritz offered the Express Bar collection of affordable cosmetics, and fast-food restaurants such as Taco Bell and

FIGURE 10.7   Cost-based versus value-based pricing
Source: Thomas T. Nagle and Reed K. Holden, *The Strategy and Tactics of Pricing*, 2nd ed. (Upper Saddle River, NJ: Prentice Hall, 1995), p. 5.

MARKETING HIGHLIGHT
10.2

PRICING POWER: THE VALUE OF VALUE ADDED

When a company finds its major competitors offering a similar product at a lower price, the natural tendency is to try to match or beat that price. Although the idea of undercutting competitor's prices and watching customers flock to you is tempting, there are dangers. Successive rounds of price cutting can lead to price wars that erode the profit margins of all competitors in an industry. Or worse, discounting a product can cheapen it in the minds of customers, greatly reducing the seller's power to

maintain profitable prices in the long term. "It ends up being a losing battle," notes one marketing executive. "You focus away from quality, service, prestige—the things brands are all about."

So, how can a company keep its pricing power when a competitor undercuts its price? Often, the best strategy is not to price below the competitor, but rather to price above and convince customers that the product is worth it. The company should ask, "What is the value of the product to the customer?" then

stand up for what the product is worth. In this way, the company shifts the focus from price to value.

But what if the company is operating in a "commodity" business, in which the products of all competitors seem pretty much alike? In such cases, the company must find ways to "decommoditize" its products—to create superior value for customers. It can do this by developing value-added features and services that differentiate its offer and justify higher prices and margins. Here are some examples of how suppliers are using value-added features and services to give them a competitive edge:

- *Caterpillar:* Caterpillar is a master at charging premium prices for its heavy construction and mining equipment and convincing customers that its products and service justify every additional cent—or, rather, the extra tens of thousands of dollars. Caterpillar typically reaps a 20 to 30 percent price premium over competitors—that can amount to an extra $200,000 dollars or more on one of those huge yellow million-dollar dump trucks. When a large potential customer says, "I can get it for less from a competitor," rather than discounting the price, the Caterpillar dealer explains that, even at the higher price, Cat

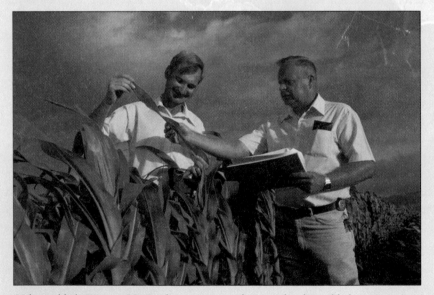

Value-added: Pioneer Hi-Bred's superior products and value-added services give it plenty of pricing power. Beyond selling seeds, the company's reps provide advice and information that help farmers do a better job of farm management.

McDonald's offered "value menus." In other cases, value pricing has involved redesigning existing brands in order to offer more quality for a given price or the same quality for less.

In many business-to-business marketing situations, the pricing challenge is to find ways to maintain the company's *pricing power*—its power to maintain or even raise prices without losing market share. To retain pricing power—to escape price competition and to justify higher prices and margins—a firm must retain or build the value of its marketing offer. This is especially true for suppliers of commodity products, which are characterized by little differentiation and intense price competition.

offers the best value. Caterpillar equipment is designed with modular componentry that can be removed and repaired quickly, minimizing machine downtime. Caterpillar dealers carry an extensive parts inventory and guarantee delivery within 48 hours anywhere in the world, again minimizing downtime. Cat's products are designed to be rebuilt, providing a "second life" that competitors cannot match. As a result, Caterpillar used-equipment prices are often 20 to 30 percent higher. In all, the dealer explains, even at the higher initial price, Caterpillar equipment delivers the lowest total cost per cubic yard of earth moved, ton of coal uncovered, or mile of road graded over the life of the product—guaranteed! Most customers seem to agree with Caterpillar's value proposition—the company dominates its markets with a more than 40 percent worldwide market share.

- *Pioneer Hi-Bred International:* A major supplier of corn seed and other agricultural commodities, Pioneer Hi-Bred hardly acts like a commodity supplier. Its patented hybrid seeds yield 10 percent more corn than competitors' seeds. Beyond producing a superior product, Pioneer Hi-Bred provides a bundle of value-added services. For example, it equips its sales representatives with notebook computers that allow them to provide farmers with customized information and advice. The rep can plug in the type of

hybrid that a farmer is using, along with information about pricing, acreage, and yield characteristics, then advise the farmer on how to do a better job of farm management. The reps can also supply farmers with everything from agricultural research reports to assistance in comparison shopping. Its superior products and value-added services give Pioneer Hi-Bred plenty of pricing power. Despite charging a significant price premium—or perhaps because of it—the company's share of the North American corn market has grown from 35 percent during the mid-1980s to its current level of 44 percent.

- *Jefferson Smurfit Corporation:* When General Electric expanded a no-frost refrigerator line in 1990, it needed more shipping boxes, and fast. Jefferson Smurfit Corporation, a $4.5 billion packaging supplier, assigned a coordinator to juggle production from three of its plants—and sometimes even divert product intended for other customers—to keep GE's Decatur plant humming. This kind of value-added hustling helped Jefferson Smurfit win the GE appliance unit's "Distinguished Supplier Award." It also has sheltered Smurfit from the bruising struggle of competing only on price. "Today, it's not just getting the best price but getting the best value—and there are a lot of pieces to value," says a vice president for procurement at Emerson Electric Company, a major Smurfit customer that has cut its supplier count by 65 percent.

- *Microsystems Engineering Company:* "The way we sell on value is by differentiating ourselves," says Mark Beckman, director of sales for Microsystems, a software company. "My product is twice as much as my nearest competitor's, but we sell as much—if not more than—our competition." Rather than getting into price wars, Microsystems adds value to its products by adding new components and services. "[Customers] get more for their money," says Beckman. "We get the price because we understand what people want." When customers see the extra value, price becomes secondary. Ultimately, Beckman asserts, "Let the customer decide whether the price you're charging is worth all the things they're getting." What if the answer is no? Beckman would suggest that dropping price is the last thing you want to do. Instead, look to the value of value added.

Sources: Jim Morgan, "Value Added: From Cliché to the Real Thing," *Purchasing,* April 3, 1997, pp. 59–61; James E. Ellis, "There's Even a Science to Selling Boxes," *Business Week,* August 3, 1992, pp. 51–52; John Jesitus, "Close Connections," *Industry Week,* October 6, 1997, pp. 28–34; Darren McDermott, "Cost-Consciousness Beats 'Pricing Power,'" *Wall Street Journal,* May 3, 1999, p. A1; James C. Anderson and James A. Narus, "Business Marketing: Understand What Customers Value," *Harvard Business Review,* November–December 1998, pp. 53–65; and Tom Nagle, "How to Pull It Off," *Across the Board,* March 1999, pp. 53–56.

In such cases, many companies adopt *value-added* strategies. Rather than cutting prices to match competitors, they attach value-added services to differentiate their offers and thus support higher margins (see Marketing Highlight 10.2).[15]

An important type of value pricing at the retail level is *everyday low pricing (EDLP)*. EDLP involves charging a constant, everyday low price with few or no temporary price discounts. In contrast, *high–low pricing* involves charging higher prices on an everyday basis but running frequent promotions to temporarily lower prices on selected items below the EDLP level.[16] In recent years, high–low pricing has given way to EDLP in retail settings ranging from Saturn car dealerships to upscale department stores such as Nordstrom. Retailers adopt EDLP for many reasons, the most important of which is that constant sales and promotions are costly and have eroded consumer confidence in the credibility of everyday shelf prices. Consumers also have less time and patience for such time-honored traditions as watching for supermarket specials and clipping coupons.

The king of EDLP is Wal-Mart, which practically defined the concept. Except for a few sale items every month, Wal-Mart promises everyday low prices on everything it sells. In contrast, Sears's attempts at EDLP in 1989 failed. To offer everyday low prices, a company must first have everyday low costs. Wal-Mart's EDLP strategy works well because its expenses are only 15 percent of sales. Sears, however, was spending 29 percent of sales to cover administrative and other overhead costs. As a result, Sears now offers everyday *fair* pricing, under which it tries to offer customers differentiated products at a consistent, fair price with fewer markdowns.

Competition-Based Pricing

Competition-based pricing
Setting prices based on the prices that competitors charge for similar products

Consumers will base their judgments of a product's value on the prices that competitors charge for similar products. One form of **competition-based pricing** is *going-rate pricing,* in which a firm bases its price largely on competitors' prices, with less attention paid to its own costs or to demand. The firm might charge the same, more, or less than its major competitors. In oligopolistic industries that sell a commodity such as steel, paper, or fertilizer, firms normally charge the same price. The smaller firms follow the leader: They change their prices when the market leader's prices change, rather than when their own demand or costs change. Some firms may charge a bit more or less, but they hold the amount of difference constant. Thus, minor gasoline retailers usually charge a few cents less than the major oil companies, without letting the difference increase or decrease.

Going-rate pricing is quite popular. When demand elasticity is hard to measure, firms feel that the going price represents the collective wisdom of the industry concerning the price that will yield a fair return. They also feel that holding to the going price will prevent harmful price wars.

Competition-based pricing is also used when firms *bid* for jobs. Using *sealed-bid pricing,* a firm bases its price on how it thinks competitors will price rather than on its own costs or on the demand. The firm wants to win a contract, and winning the contract requires pricing less than other firms. Yet the firm cannot set its price below a certain level. It cannot price below cost without harming its position. In contrast, the higher the company sets its price above its costs, the lower its chance of getting the contract.

REVIEW OF CONCEPT CONNECTIONS

Price can be defined narrowly as the amount of money charged for a product or service, or more broadly, as the sum of the values that consumers exchange for the benefits of having and using the product or service. Despite the increased role of nonprice factors in the modern marketing process, price remains an important element in the marketing mix. It is the only element in the marketing mix that produces revenue; all other elements represent costs. Price is also one of the most flexible elements of the mar-keting mix. Unlike product features and channel commitments, price can be raised or lowered quickly. Even so, many companies are not good at handling pricing—pricing decisions and price competition are major problems for many marketing executives. Pricing problems often arise because prices are too cost oriented, not revised frequently enough to reflect market changes, not consistent with the rest of the marketing mix, or not varied enough for differing products, market segments, and purchase occasions.

1. Identify and define the internal factors affecting a firm's pricing decisions.

Many internal factors influence the company's pricing decisions, including the firm's *marketing objectives, marketing mix strategy, costs,* and *organization for pricing.* The pricing strategy is largely determined by the company's *target market* and *positioning objectives.* Pricing decisions affect and are affected by product design, distribution, and promotion decisions. Therefore, pricing strategies must be carefully coordinated with the other marketing mix variables when designing the marketing program.

Costs set the floor for the company's price—the price must cover all the costs of making and selling the product, plus a fair rate of return. Common pricing objectives include survival, current profit maximization, market share leadership, and product quality leadership.

In order to coordinate pricing goals and decisions, management must decide who within the organization is responsible for setting price. In large companies, some pricing authority may be delegated to lower-level managers and salespeople, but top management usually sets pricing policies and approves proposed prices. Production, finance, and accounting managers also influence pricing decisions.

2. Identify and define external factors affecting pricing decisions, including the impact of consumer perceptions of price and value.

External factors that influence pricing decisions include the nature of the *market and demand; competitors' prices and offers;* and factors such as the *economy, reseller needs,* and *government actions.* The seller's pricing freedom varies with different types of markets. Pricing is especially challenging in markets characterized by monopolistic competition or oligopoly.

Ultimately, the consumer decides whether the company has set the right price. The consumer weighs the price against the perceived values of using the product—if the price exceeds the sum of the values, consumers will not buy the product. The more *inelastic* the demand, the higher the company can set its price. Therefore, *demand* and *consumer value perceptions* set the ceiling for prices. Consumers differ in the values they assign to different product features, and marketers often vary their pricing strategies for different price segments. When assessing the market and demand, the company estimates the demand curve, which shows the probable quantity purchased per period at alternative price levels. Consumers also compare a product's price to the prices of *competitors'* products. As a result, a company must learn the price and quality of competitors' offers and use them as a starting point for its own pricing.

3. Contrast the three general approaches to setting prices.

A company can select one or a combination of three general pricing approaches: the *cost-based approach* (cost-plus pricing, break-even analysis, and target profit pricing); the *value-based approach;* and the *competition-based approach.* Cost-based pricing sets prices based on the seller's cost structure, whereas value-based pricing relies on consumer perceptions of value to drive pricing decisions. Competition-based pricing has two major variations: In *going-rate pricing,* the firm sets prices based on what competitors are charging. *Sealed-bid pricing* forces the company to set prices based on what they think the competition will charge.

KEY TERMS

Break-even pricing (target profit pricing)
Competition-based pricing
Cost-plus pricing
Demand curve

Experience curve (learning curve)
Fixed costs
Price
Price elasticity
Target costing

Total costs
Value pricing
Value-based pricing
Variable costs

ISSUES FOR DISCUSSION

1. Assume the role of the vice president for financial affairs at a major college or university. For the past three years, enrollments and revenue have declined steadily at a rate of about 10 percent per year. You are under great pressure to raise tuition to compensate for the falling revenues. However, you suspect that raising tuition might only make matters worse. What internal and external pricing factors should you consider before you make your decision? Explain.

2. Discuss the typical pricing objectives outlined in the chapter. Which of these objectives do you believe: (a) is the most commonly used; (b) is the most difficult to achieve; and (c) has the greatest potential for long-term growth of the organization? Explain.

3. Detergent A is priced at $2.19 for 32 ounces, whereas detergent B is priced at $1.99 for 26 ounces. Which brand appears most attractive? Assuming equal quality,

which is the better value? Is there a psychological reason to price this way?

4. Explain the concept of an experience curve (or learning curve) as it applies to pricing. Apply this concept to: (a) a Texas Instrument's calculator (see www.ti.com); (b) a Toyota Camry automobile (www.toyota.com); and (c) Peapod's Internet grocery shopping and delivery service (www.peapod.com).

5. A seller's pricing freedom varies with type of market. Economists generally recognize four types of markets, each presenting a different pricing challenge. Identify each of these market forms and discuss the pricing challenges facing each one.

6. Genentech, a high-technology pharmaceutical company, has developed a clot-dissolving drug called TPA. This drug can halt a heart attack in progress. It has been proven that TPA saves lives, minimizes hospital stays, and reduces damage to the heart itself. It was initially priced at $2,200 per dose. What pricing approach does Genentech appear to be using? Is this approach justified? Is demand for this drug likely to be price elastic?

7. Discuss the three general pricing approaches and select an example to illustrate the primary characteristics unique to each general approach.

8. The federal government has accused Microsoft of monopolistic practices in tying (or bundling) the sales of its popular Windows 95, 98, and 2000 operating systems software to its Web browser product. In a controversial ruling, a federal judge has agreed that Microsoft is acting like a monopolist. What pricing strategy does Microsoft seem to be using? Take a side in the monopoly debate and state how you would resolve this ongoing problem.

MARKETING APPLICATIONS

1. Conduct a pricing survey of several gasoline stations in your town. Check prices at stations near exit ramps on a major highway, at stations on your local commercial strip, at a convenience store, smaller stations that are not located near other stations, and at a truck stop. Record the brand of gasoline, prices of regular and premium grades, type of location, distance to the nearest competitor, and the competitors' prices.

    a. What patterns do you detect for the pricing of gasoline at the various outlets?

    b. Do these stations appear to be using cost-based, buyer-based, or going-rate pricing?

    c. Talk to several station operators. What factors do they think usually trigger a price war? How much control do the station operators have over pricing?

    d. Report your results in class.

2. As Marketing Highlight 10.1 indicates, the Internet is having an impact on pricing. Consider the effect of the Internet and its associated technology on pricing in the music business. Music is sold in retail stores such as Wherehouse Music (www.wherehouse.com) or Tower Records (www.towerrecords.com), in discount and electronics outlets such as Best Buy (www.bestbuy.com) or Circuit City (www.circuitcity.com), and via the Internet on such sites as Columbia House (www.columbiahouse.com)

or CDNow (www.cdnow.com). All of these sellers price music differently. However, recently developed MP3 technology (www.mp3.com) has drastically altered the music retailing business. Using this technology, any music enthusiast with a computer and CD rewritable capability can download music directly via the Internet directly from the source and copy it to a CD, cutting out retailers and other intermediaries. Projections are that this same technology will eventually impact the videotape and movie businesses in much the same way. The recording and entertainment industry may never be the same.

    a. Visit the Web sites mentioned previously. What can you tell about their pricing policies? What strategies seem to be in place?

    b. How will MP3 technology affect pricing strategies of traditional distributors?

    c. The music industry is concerned that MP3 technology, while having substantial promise for legitimate distribution, might result in a dramatic increase in music piracy and bootlegging. What ethics issues are associated with this technology and its use on the Internet?

    d. Considering the demand for music, design a pricing strategy that could be used by a music retailer to compete with and music producer using MP3 technology to sell directly to consumers.

 INTERNET CONNECTIONS

ELASTICITY OF DEMAND

Airline tickets are a price-driven market for most customers. Many will trade off nonstop flights, preferred travel times, and choice of airline to get the lowest possible price.

Therefore, airlines offer advance purchase discounts to make sure they fill as many seats as possible. Demand tends to be very elastic, as evidenced by the heavy reservation activity that takes place during fare wars. Notable exceptions include first-class travelers and business travelers. First class travelers are easily segmented—they get a better seat; but business travelers often sit in coach. Ever wonder why you get a cheaper fare when you have a Saturday night stay? It's because the business traveler is willing to pay a premium to fly out and return home in the same workweek. Vacation travelers by contrast are willing to spend Saturday night. In this exercise we are going to plan a flight online in order to observe the price elasticity in this industry.

Expedia is a comprehensive travel site developed by Microsoft and then spun off as a separate company. The site allows consumers to book flights, reserve hotel rooms and rent cars online. Sign onto the Expedia Web site at www.expedia.com. Register a new account; it's free. Then price a round-trip flight from New York (any airport) to Paris (any airport) traveling coach class, departing tomorrow, and returning one day after you arrive. Record Expedia's response in the table below. Then press the Search Again button and vary the criteria to complete the rest of the table.

Class	Departing	Returning After	Airline and Departure Flight	Price
Coach	Tomorrow	I day		
Coach	Tomorrow	I week		
Coach	Next month	I day		
Coach	Next month	I week		
First	Tomorrow	I day		
First	Tomorrow	I week		
First	Next month	I day		
First	Next month	I week		

FOR DISCUSSION

1. What can you conclude from this example about the elasticity of demand for coach fares? For first-class fares?

2. Do you think the higher price for a first-class seat is justified by higher costs to the airline?

3. How do the prices differ for one day versus one week trips? How can you explain this?

4. For first class, do the prices differ for trips departing tomorrow versus next month? Why or why not?

5. What pricing approach(es) mentioned in the chapter might the airlines be using based on your research?

SAVVY SITES

- American Airlines has a competitive site called Travelocity (www.travelocity.com)

- Want to find the cheapest place online to purchase your textbooks? Try the shopping agent MySimon (www.mysimon.com).

- Another good online shopping agent is PriceScan (www.pricescan.com).

NOTES

1. See John Greenwald, "Cereal Showdown," *Time,* April 29, 1996, p. 60; "Cereal Thriller," *The Economist,* June 15, 1996, p. 59; Gretchen Morgenson, "Denial in Battle Creek," *Forbes,* October 7, 1996, p. 44; Judann Pollack, "Post's Price Play Rocked Category, but Did It Work?" *Advertising Age,* December 1, 1997, p. 24; Carleen Hawn, "General Mills Tests Limits," *Forbes,* April 6, 1998, p. 48; Judann Pollack, "Price Cuts Unsettling to Cereal Business," *Advertising Age,* September 28, 1998, p. S10; Rekha Balu, "Kellogg Increases Prices on Majority of Cereal Brands," *Wall Street Journal,* December 15, 1998, p. B23; Susan Pulliam, "Kellogg, Long Treated as Stale by Wall Street, Shows Signs of Putting Some Snap in Its Walk," *Wall Street Journal,* February 16, 1999, pp. C2, C3; Terril Yue Jones, "Outside the Box," *Forbes,* June 14, 1999, pp. 52–53; and Amy Kover, "Why the Cereal Business Is Soggy," *Fortune,* March 6, 2000.

2. See David J. Schwartz, *Marketing Today: A Basic Approach,* 3rd ed. (New York: Harcourt Brace Jovanovich, 1981), pp. 270–73.

3. See Amy E. Cortese, "Good-Bye to Fixed Pricing?" *Business Week,* May 4, 1998, pp. 71–84; Robert D. Hof, "The Buyer Always Wins," *Business Week,* March 22, 1999, pp. EB26–EB28; and Robert D. Hof, "Going, Going, Gone," *Business Week,* April 12, 1999, pp. 30–32.

4. For an excellent discussion of factors affecting pricing decisions, see Thomas T. Nagle and Reed K. Holden, *The Strategy and Tactics of Pricing,* 2nd ed. (Upper Saddle River, NJ: Prentice Hall, Inc., 1995), chap. 1.

5. See Steve Gelsi, "Spin-Cycle Doctor," *Brandweek,* March 10, 1997, pp. 38–40. Tim Stevens, "From Reliable to 'Wow,'" *Industry Week,* June 22, 1998, pp. 22–26; and William C. Symonds, "'Build a Better Mousetrap' Is No Claptrap," *Business Week,* February 1, 1999, p. 47.

6. See Timothy M. Laseter, "Supply Chain Management The Ins and Outs of Target Costing," *Purchasing,* March 12, 1998, pp. 22–25. Also check out the Swatch Web page at www.swatch.com.

7. Brian Dumaine, "Closing the Innovation Gap," *Fortune,* December 2, 1991, pp. 56–62.

8. Here accumulated production is drawn on a semilog scale so that equal distances represent the same percentage increase in output.

9. See Luis M. B. Cabral, David J. Salant, and Glenn A. Woroch, "Monopoly Pricing with Network Externalities," *International Journal of Industrial Organization,* February 1999, pp. 199–214.

10. Joshua Rosenbaum, "Guitar Maker Looks for a New Key," *Wall Street Journal,* February 11, 1998, p. B1; and information obtained online from www.gibson.com, February 2000.

11. See Nagle and Holden, *The Strategy and Tactics of Pricing,* chap. 4.

12. Kevin J. Clancy, "At What Profit Price?" *Brandweek,* June 23, 1997, pp. 24–28; and information obtained from www.gmpvt.com, February 2000.

13. The arithmetic of markups and margins is discussed in Appendix 2, "Marketing Arithmetic."

14. See Philip Kotler, *Kotler on Marketing* (New York: Free Press, 1999), p. 54.

15. See Darren McDermott, "Cost-Consciousness Beats 'Pricing Power,'" *Wall Street Journal,* May 3, 1999, p. A1.

16. See Stephen J. Hoch, Xavier Drèze, and Mary E. Purk, "EDLP, Hi-Lo, and Margin Arithmetic," *Journal of Marketing,* October 1994, pp. 16–27.

COMPANY CASE

10

PeoplePC: Is There a Free Lunch?

WHAT'S GOING ON?

Economists tell us that there is no such thing as a free lunch. Well, perhaps, but it certainly seems that many personal computer and Internet companies are trying to come up with one. The December 22, 1999, issue of the *Wall Street Journal* carried a full-page ad with the words "100% Off" in bold letters centered on the page. The ad from Juno Online Services, Inc., went on to advise, "Starting now, Juno is offering full Internet access for free. From free Web access to premium dial-up and broadband services, everybody's getting it."

But perhaps not everyone is getting it. How can a company give away a service for which millions of people have been paying about $20 per month? What's going on? How can Juno and other companies make these offers? And what about Egreetings Network, Inc.? In 1998, when this Internet company began offering email birthday cards for $.50 to $2.50 each, only 300,000 people signed up for the service. Then, the company decided to ditch its pricing strategy and give its cards away for free. By mid-1999, it had 7,000,000 registered users. Egreeting's CEO Gordon Tucker admits, "Charging for cards was a small idea. Giving them away is a really big idea."

GIVING THINGS AWAY

Is this some form of cyber-suicide? You might argue that a company giving away an electronic greeting card is not really giving away very much. But how do you explain the offer by Free-PC? The price of personal computers was already plummeting. In fact, computers priced below $1,000 were accounting for the majority of sales—some were as cheap as $500. Then, along came Free-PC. In February 1999, the company announced that it would give away 10,000 personal computers. All that interested consumers had to do was to register at its Web site, www.freepc.com and provide detailed demographic information about themselves and their families including name, address, sex, age, e-mail address, marital status, makes and models of family cars, and lifestyle information from a list of 26 categories.

The company indicated it would review the applications it received and implied that it would select them to create a pool of users who would be attractive to advertisers. The company also announced that it planned to charge 200 advertisers $10,000 each for a 90-day period, a time during which Free-PC would direct their ads to the lucky 10,000. Free-PC guaranteed the advertisers one million impressions during the period. It argued that it provided real targeting using the 60 pieces of demographic data it tracked, along with response data on each variable. Moreover, advertisers could deliver media-rich ads and test different ad messages to see which got the best responses.

When Free-PC opened its Web site, over 1.2 million people logged-on and applied for the 10,000 free PCs. Applicants the company selected received a full-featured Compaq Presario Internet PC with preinstalled software and unlimited access to the Internet, which included e-mail service and technical support.

Consumers had to agree to log on to the Internet at least 10 hours per month. If customers did not live up to this commitment, FreePC would ask them to return their PCs. Whenever they surfed the Internet, consumers' monitor screens contained a bar down the right side and across the bottom, occupying about 40 percent of the screen in total, that displayed ads and other marketing messages. The company called the Free-PC network the first permission-based, one-to-one targeted marketing network. Free-PCs Web site explained, by having so much information "you will help us to make sure that the ads and services that appear in the small frame around the screen are relevant to you. And, just like you don't want to waste your time with meaningless ads, advertisers don't want to waste money displaying ads to people who aren't interested in their products."

JUMPING ON THE BANDWAGON

More than a dozen companies quickly jumped on the free-PC bandwagon, with some adding new twists. Enchilada (www.enchilada.com) threw in Internet access along with the computer to offer "the whole enchilada" for $399. The offer includes the computer and three years of Internet access. However, you have to pay extra for a monitor, warranty, and extended technical support.

InterSquid (www.intersquid.com) offers a PC and Internet access for $29.95 per month with a 30-month commitment. You must commit to a costly credit check, or you can pay the total amount, about $900, up front. MyFreePC.com (www.myfreepc.com) provides a low-end computer and Internet access for $26.79 per month. However, you must commit to 19 months of service and, to avoid an interest-bearing loan, pay up front.

PEOPLEPC

In late 1999, Nicholas Grouf, a 31-year-old Harvard MBA, launched PeoplePC and added the latest twist. PeoplePC offers a brand-name PC, such as Compaq or Toshiba, including a monitor and free Internet service through MCI Worldcom's UUNet. In addition to the computer and Internet access, PeoplePC subscribers get around-the-clock technical support and even in-home computer repair service if required. It is the only company offering in-home repair service. The cost is $24.95 per month for three years. After the three-year period, PeoplePC will give you a new computer if you want to sign up again. The company planned to sign up 400,000 people in its first wave.

PeoplePC's plan differs in several ways from FreePC's plan. PeoplePC's program requires only a minimum amount of personal information as a part of the registration process. Second, PeoplePC will not use an ad-supported business model. That is, it will not require that buyers devote some of their screen space to ads, or pledge to be online for a certain number of hours per month. Rather, PeoplePC sees itself as a membership-based model in which it will use its members' buying power to get them good deals on products and services. In a sense, the company serves as an Internet shopping club. It will earn money by getting a fee from the product or service provider whenever a PeoplePC member buys something. For example, at the PeoplePC home page, a member can click on a button marked, "Special Offers for PeoplePC Members." Offers include 5 percent off at wine.com, 10 percent off at chipshot.com, 15 percent off at Ashford.com, and a $100 sign-up bonus from E★Trade.

With E★Trade, for example, PeoplePC will earn between $50 and $100 for each member who signs up with E★Trade. That's much less than the average $400 most online brokers must spend to acquire a new customer. Moreover, the company lets each e-tailer decide how much to pay PeoplePC. Although this might seem to encourage e-tailers to take advantage of the company, Nicholas Grouf argues that the more a company pays, the harder PeoplePC will work for it. "Every company knows just how much it pays in customer acquisition costs. If it costs $1,000 to get a customer, and we get just 10 percent of that for doing the same work, it's still a lucrative business." PeoplePC will also have three-year commitments from customers, allowing it to sell that receivable to a bank and get its money quickly.

To attract members, PeoplePC kicked off a $40 million multimedia promotion campaign in late 1999, starting with spots during game three of the World Series. Additional television, newspaper, and online ads that followed those spots used the tag line: "It's for people." In November 1999, the company reported that phone calls were coming in at four times the predicted rate, and it had increased the number of representatives answering phones from 100 to 500.

A FREE-FOR-ALL

One observer noted, "Time and again, do-it-for-free companies are coming in and spoiling an industry for everyone else. But it's a fact on the Internet: People expect a lot of things for free. And if you don't give it away, some other start-up will." Internet companies rush to sign up large numbers of people and earn money either by selling advertising or earning fees from online vendors. One wonders what consumers expect for free. Moreover, are there enough advertising revenues or indirect fees to support all these Web sites? With MP3.com giving away music, e Fax.com giving away fax service, and Juno.com giving away Internet access, we may soon find out how much a free lunch really costs.

Questions:

1. What internal and external factors affect e-commerce pricing decisions?

2. What marketing objectives and pricing approaches are PeoplePC and FreePC pursuing?

3. What is the nature of costs for a company like PeoplePC? Which costs are fixed and which are variable? What are the implications of this cost structure?

4. How can companies like PeoplePC make offers that appear to be free or almost free? What are the true costs to the consumer?

5. What marketing recommendations would you make to PeoplePC?

Sources: "PeoplePC Energizes Personal Computer Shopping This Holiday Season," *PR Newswire,* December 14, 1999, p. 1460; Nikhil Hutheesing, "Matchmaker," *Forbes,* November 15, 1999, p. 222; "PeoplePC to Unveil Investors' Backing Totaling $65 Million," *Wall Street Journal,* November 1, 1999, p. B13; Tobi Elkin, "Newcomer PeoplePC Rolls $40 Mil Campaign: Online Discounts and Ecard Offer Form Backbone of Trouble-Free PC-Buying Pitch," *Advertising Age,* October 11, 1999, p. 85; Cade Metz, "Nearly Free PCs," *PC Magazine,* September 1, 1999, p. 177; George Anders, "Eager to Boost Traffic, More Internet Firms Give Away Services," *Wall Street Journal,* July 28, 1999, p. A1; Makoto Ushida, "Cyberslice: Free-PC Wave Hits Japanese Shore," *Asahi Shimbun/Asahi Evening News,* July 26, 1999, p. ASAH6396762. Also see www.FreePC.com, www.peoplepc.com, and home.peoplepc.com.

After studying this chapter, you should be able to
1. describe the major strategies for pricing imitative and new products
2. explain how companies find a set of prices that maximizes the profits from the total product mix
3. discuss how companies adjust their prices to take into account different types of customers and situations
4. discuss the key issues related to initiating and responding to price changes

PRICING PRODUCTS: PRICING STRATEGIES

Procter & Gamble, the huge consumer packaged-goods producer, is part of a complex food industry distribution channel consisting of producers, wholesale food distributors, and grocery retailers. In early 1992, P&G's relations with many of its resellers took a decided turn for the worse. "We think that [P&G] will end up where most dictators end up—in trouble," fumed the chairman of Stop & Shop, a chain of 119 groceries in the Northeast. Hundreds of miles away, the assistant manager of Paulbeck's SuperValu in International Falls, Minnesota, shared these harsh feelings: "We should drop their top dogs—like half the sizes of Tide—and say 'Now see who put you on the shelf and who'll take you off of it.' "

The cause of the uproar was P&G's new everyday fair-pricing policy, tabbed "value pricing" by the company. Under this sweeping new plan, the company began phasing out most of the large promotional discounts that it had offered resellers in the past. At the same time, it lowered its everyday wholesale list prices for these products by 10 percent to 25 percent. P&G insists that price fluctuations and promotions had gotten out of hand. During the previous decade, average trade discounts had more than tripled. Some 44 percent of all marketing dollars spent by manufacturers went to trade promotions, up from 24 percent only a decade earlier.

Manufacturers had come to rely on price-oriented trade promotions to differentiate their brands and boost short-term sales. In turn, wholesalers and retail chains were conditioned to wait for manufacturers' "deals." Many perfected "forward buying"—stocking up during manufacturers' price promotions on far more merchandise than they could sell, then reselling it to consumers at higher prices once the promotion was over. Such forward buying created costly production and distribution inefficiencies. P&G's factories had to gear up to meet the resulting huge demand swings. Meanwhile, supermarkets needed more buyers to find the best prices and extra warehouses to store and handle merchandise bought "on deal." The industry's "promotion sickness" also infected consumers. Wildly fluctuating retail prices eroded brand loyalty by teaching consumers to shop for what's on sale, rather than to assess the merits of each brand.

Through value pricing, P&G sought to restore the price integrity of its brands and to begin weaning the industry and consumers from discount pricing. But the strategy came into conflict with the pricing strategies of P&G's distribution channels. Discounts are the bread and butter of many retailers and wholesalers, who had used products purchased from P&G at special low prices for weekly sales to lure value-minded consumers into supermarkets or stores. In other cases, retailers and wholesalers relied on the discounts to pad their profits through forward buying. Although the average costs of products to resellers remained unchanged, resellers lost promotional dollars that they—not P&G—controlled. Thus, the new system gave P&G greater control over how its products were marketed but reduced retailer and wholesaler pricing flexibility.

P&G's new strategy was risky. It alienated some of the very businesses that sell its wares to the public, and it gave competitors an opportunity to take advantage of the ban on promotions by highlighting their own specials. P&G counted on its enormous market clout—retailers could ill afford, the company hoped, to eliminate heavily advertised and immensely popular brands such as Tide detergent, Crest toothpaste, Folgers coffee, Pantene shampoo, and Ivory soap. But even P&G's size and power were sorely tested. Some large chains such as A&P, Safeway, and Rite Aid drugstores began pruning out selected P&G sizes or dropping marginal brands such as Prell and Gleem. Certified Grocers, a Midwestern wholesaler, dropped about 50 of the 300 P&G varieties it stocked. Numerous other chains considered moving P&G brands from prime, eye-level space to less visible shelves, stocking more profitable private-label brands and competitors' products in P&G's place. SuperValu, the nation's largest wholesaler, which also runs retail stores, added surcharges to some P&G products and pared back orders to make up for profits it says it lost.

Despite these strong reactions, P&G stayed the course with its bold new pricing approach, and the strategy appears to be paying off. After an initial drop in sales and market shares, P&G's products in most categories are again growing steadily and producing healthier profits. The company claims that under the new pricing scheme it cut list prices an average of 6 percent across its product portfolio, saving consumers $6 billion. Given this success at home, P&G later introduced value pricing to its European markets. It received the same blistering response from European retailers that it had received from U.S. retailers five years earlier. For example, Germany's largest retailer, Rewe, and its major supermarket chain, Spar, immediately "delisted" several P&G brands, including Ariel, Vizir, and Lenor laundry products, Bess toilet paper, and Tempo tissues. As happened in the United States, initial European sales and market shares dipped as angry retailers responded.

P&G's struggle to reshape the industry's distorted pricing system demonstrates the dynamic forces shaping today's pricing decisions. Ideally, P&G should set its prices at the level that will reflect and enhance the value consumers perceive in its brands. But such value is difficult to assess. Which offers more value: higher regular prices with frequent sales or lower everyday prices? What impact will each pricing strategy have on consumer perceptions of brand quality? P&G's pricing decisions would be difficult enough if the company had only to set its own prices and gauge customer reactions. However, P&G's pricing decisions affect not just its own sales and profits but those of its marketing partners as well. Thus, P&G must work with resellers to find the pricing strategy that is best for all. In the end, customers will judge whether prices accurately reflect the value they receive. Which is the best pricing strategy? Customers will vote with their food-budget dollars.[1]

As the Procter & Gamble example illustrates, pricing decisions are subject to an incredibly complex array of environmental and competitive forces. A company sets not a single price, but rather a *pricing structure* that covers different items in its line. This pricing structure changes over time as products move through their life cycles. The company adjusts product prices to reflect changes in costs and demand and to account for variations in buyers and situations. As the competitive environment changes, the company considers when to initiate price changes and when to respond to them.

This chapter examines the major dynamic pricing strategies available to management. In turn, we look at *new-product pricing strategies* for products in the introductory stage of the product life cycle, *product mix pricing strategies* for related products in the product mix, *price-adjustment strategies* that account for customer differences and changing situations, and strategies for initiating and responding to *price changes.*[2]

NEW-PRODUCT PRICING STRATEGIES

Pricing strategies usually change as the product passes through its life cycle. The introductory stage is especially challenging. Companies bringing out a new product face the challenge of setting prices for the first time. They can choose between two broad strategies: *market-skimming pricing* and *market-penetration pricing*.

Market-Skimming Pricing

Market-skimming pricing
Setting a high price for a new product to skim maximum revenues layer by layer from the segments willing to pay the high price; the company makes fewer but more profitable sales.

Many companies that invent new products initially set high prices to "skim" revenues layer by layer from the market. Intel is a prime user of this strategy, called **market-skimming pricing.** One analyst describes Intel's pricing strategy this way: "The chip giant introduces a new, higher-margin microprocessor every 12 months and sends older models down the food chain to feed demand at lower price points."[3] When Intel first introduces a new computer chip, it charges as much as $1,000 for each chip, a price that makes it *just* worthwhile for some segments of the market to adopt computers containing the chip. The new chips power top-of-the-line PCs and servers purchased by customers who just can't wait. As initial sales slow down, and as competitors threaten to introduce similar chips, Intel lowers the price to draw in the next price-sensitive layer of customers. Prices eventually bottom out at less than $200 per chip, making the chip a hot mass-market processor. In this way, Intel skims a maximum amount of revenue from the various segments of the market.[4]

Market skimming makes sense only under certain conditions. First, the product's quality and image must support its higher price, and enough buyers must want the product at that price. Second, the costs of producing a smaller volume cannot be so high that they cancel the advantage of charging more. Finally, competitors should not be able to enter the market easily and undercut the high price.

Market-Penetration Pricing

Market-penetration pricing
Setting a low price for a new product in order to attract a large number of buyers and a large market share.

Rather than setting a high initial price to *skim* off small but profitable market segments, some companies use **market-penetration pricing.** They set a low initial price in order to *penetrate* the market quickly and deeply—to attract a large number of buyers quickly and win a large market share. The high sales volume results in falling costs, allowing the company to cut its price even further. For example, Dell used penetration pricing to enter the personal computer market, selling high-quality computer products through lower-cost direct channels. Its sales soared when IBM, Compaq, Apple, and other competitors selling through retail stores could not match its prices. Wal-Mart and other discount retailers also use penetration pricing.

Several conditions must be met for this low-price strategy to work. First, the market must be highly price sensitive so that a low price produces more market growth. Second, production and distribution costs must fall as sales volume increases. Finally, the low price must help keep out the competition, and the penetration pricer must maintain its low-price position—otherwise, the price advantage may be only temporary. For example, Dell faced difficult times when IBM and Compaq established their own direct distribution channels. However, through its dedication to low production and distribution costs, Dell has retained its price advantage and established itself as the industry's fastest-growing computer maker and number two in personal computers behind Compaq.

PRODUCT MIX PRICING STRATEGIES

The strategy for setting a product's price often has to be changed when the product is part of a product mix. In this case, the firm looks for a set of prices that maximizes the profits on the total product mix. Pricing is difficult because the various products have related demand and costs and face different degrees of competition. We now take a closer look at the five product mix pricing situations summarized in Table 11.1.

Product Line Pricing

Companies usually develop product lines rather than single products. For example, Snapper makes many different lawn mowers, ranging from simple walk-behind versions priced at $259.95, $299.95, and $399.95, to elaborate riding mowers priced at $1,000 or more. Each successive lawn mower in the line offers more features. Kodak offers not just one type of film, but an assortment, including regular Kodak film, higher-priced Kodak Royal Gold film for special occasions, and still higher-priced Advantix APS film for Advanced Photo System cameras. It offers each of these brands in a variety of sizes and film speeds. In **product line pricing,** management must decide on the price steps to set between the various products in a line.

The price steps should take into account cost differences between the products in the line, customer evaluations of their different features, and competitors' prices. In many industries, sellers use well-established *price points* for the products in their

Product line pricing
Setting the price steps between various products in a product line based on cost differences between the products, customer evaluations of different features, and competitors' prices.

Product line pricing: Kodak makes many different types of film priced at different levels.

TABLE 11.1 PRODUCT MIX PRICING STRATEGIES	
Strategy	**Description**
Product line pricing	Setting price steps between product line items
Optional-product pricing	Pricing optional or accessory products sold with the main product
Captive-product pricing	Pricing products that must be used with the main product
By-product pricing	Pricing low-value by-products to get rid of them
Product bundle pricing	Pricing bundles of products sold together

line. Thus, men's clothing stores might carry men's suits at three price levels: $185, $325, and $495. The customer will probably associate low-, average-, and high-quality suits with the three price points. Even if the three prices are raised a little, men normally will buy suits at their own preferred price points. The seller's task is to establish perceived quality differences that support the price differences.

Optional-Product Pricing

Optional-product pricing
The pricing of optional or accessory products along with a main product.

Many companies use **optional-product pricing**—offering to sell optional or accessory products along with their main product. For example, a car buyer may choose to order power windows, cruise control, and a CD changer. Pricing these options is a sticky problem. Automobile companies have to decide which items to include in the base price and which to offer as options. Until recent years, General Motors' normal pricing strategy was to advertise a stripped-down model at a base price to pull people into showrooms and then devote most of the showroom space to showing option-loaded cars at higher prices. The economy model was stripped of so many comforts and conveniences that most buyers rejected it. More recently, however, GM and other U.S. carmakers have followed the example of the Japanese and German automakers and included in the sticker price many useful items previously sold only as options. The advertised price now often represents a well-equipped car.

Captive-Product Pricing

Captive-product pricing
Setting a price for products that must be used along with a main product, such as blades for a razor and film for a camera.

Companies that make products that must be used along with a main product are using **captive-product pricing.** Examples of captive products are razor blades, camera film, video games, and computer software. Producers of the main products (razors, cameras, video game consoles, and computers) often price them low and set high markups on the supplies. Thus, Polaroid prices its cameras low because it makes its money on the film it sells. Gillette sells low-priced razors but makes money on the replacement cartridges. U-Haul rents out trucks at low rates but commands high margins on accessories such as boxes, pads, insurance, and storage space rental. Nintendo sells its game consoles at low prices and makes money on video game titles. In fact, whereas Nintendo's margins on its consoles run a mere 1 percent to 5 percent, margins on its game cartridges run close to 45 percent. Video game sales contribute more than half the company's profits.[5]

In the case of services, this strategy is called *two-part pricing*. The price of the service is broken into a *fixed fee* plus a *variable usage rate*. Thus, a telephone company charges a monthly rate—the fixed fee—plus charges for calls beyond some minimum number—the variable usage rate. Amusement parks charge admission plus fees for food, midway attractions, and rides over a minimum. Theaters charge admission, then generate additional revenues from concessions. The service firm must decide how much to charge for the basic service and how much for the variable usage. The fixed amount should be low enough to induce usage of the service; profit can be made on the variable fees.

By-Product Pricing

By-product pricing
Setting a price for by-products in order to make the main product's price more competitive.

In producing processed meats, petroleum products, chemicals, and other products, there are often by-products. If the by-products have no value and if getting rid of them is costly, this will affect the pricing of the main product. Using **by-product pricing,** the manufacturer will seek a market for these by-products and should accept any price that covers more than the cost of storing and delivering them. This practice allows the seller to reduce the main product's price to make it more competitive. By-products can even turn out to be profitable. For example, many lumber mills have begun to sell bark chips and sawdust profitably as decorative mulch for home and commercial landscaping.

Sometimes, companies don't realize how valuable their by-products are. For example, most zoos don't realize that one of their by-products—their occupants' manure—can be an excellent source of additional revenue. But the Zoo-Doo Compost Company has helped many zoos understand the costs and opportunities involved with these by-products. Zoo-Doo licenses its name to zoos and receives royalties on manure sales. "Many zoos don't even know how much manure they are producing or the cost of disposing of it," explains president and founder Pierce Ledbetter. Zoos are often so pleased with any savings they can find on disposal that they don't think to move into active by-product sales. However, sales of the fragrant by-product can be substantial. So far, novelty sales have been the largest, with tiny containers of Zoo Doo (and even "Love, Love Me Doo" valentines) available in 160 zoo stores and 700 additional retail outlets. You can also buy Zoo Doo products online ("the easiest way to buy our crap," says Zoo Doo). For the long-term market, Zoo-Doo looks to organic gardeners who buy 15 to 70 pounds of manure at a time. Zoo-Doo is already planning a "Dung of the Month" club to reach this lucrative by-products market.[6]

By-product pricing: Zoo Doo sells tiny containers of zoo "by-products"—even "Love Me Doo" valentines—through 160 zoo stores and 700 additional retail outlets.

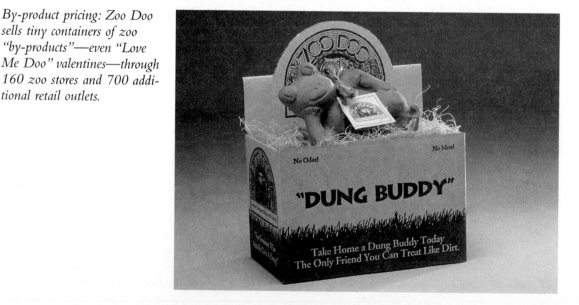

Product Bundle Pricing

Product bundle pricing
Combining several products and offering the bundle at a reduced price.

Using **product bundle pricing,** sellers often combine several of their products and offer the bundle at a reduced price. Thus, theaters and sports teams sell season tickets at less than the cost of single tickets; hotels sell specially priced packages that include room, meals, and entertainment; computer makers include attractive software packages with their personal computers. Price bundling can promote the sales of products consumers might not otherwise buy, but the combined price must be low enough to get them to buy the bundle.[7]

PRICE-ADJUSTMENT STRATEGIES

Companies usually adjust their basic prices to account for various customer differences and changing situations. Table 11.2 summarizes six price-adjustment strategies: *discount and allowance pricing, segmented pricing, psychological pricing, promotional pricing, geographical pricing,* and *international pricing.*

Discount and Allowance Pricing

Most companies adjust their basic price to reward customers for certain responses, such as early payment of bills, volume purchases, and off-season buying. These price adjustments—called *discounts* and *allowances*—can take many forms.

Cash discount
A price reduction to buyers who pay their bills promptly.

A **cash discount** is a price reduction to buyers who pay their bills promptly. A typical example is "2/10, net 30," which means that although payment is due within 30 days, the buyer can deduct 2 percent if the bill is paid within 10 days. The discount must be granted to all buyers meeting these terms. Such discounts are customary in many industries and help to improve the sellers' cash situation and reduce bad debts and credit-collection costs.

Quantity discount
A price reduction to buyers who buy large volumes.

A **quantity discount** is a price reduction to buyers who buy large volumes. A typical example might be "$10 per unit for less than 100 units, $9 per unit for 100 or more units." By law, quantity discounts must be offered equally to all customers and must not exceed the seller's cost savings associated with selling large quantities. These savings include lower selling, inventory, and transportation expenses. Discounts provide an incentive to the customer to buy more from one given seller, rather than from many different sources.

TABLE 11.2 PRICE-ADJUSTMENT STRATEGIES	
Strategy	**Description**
Discount and allowance pricing	Reducing prices to reward customer responses such as paying early or promoting the product
Segmented pricing	Adjusting prices to allow for differences in customers, products, or locations
Psychological pricing	Adjusting prices for psychological effect
Promotional pricing	Temporarily reducing prices to increase short-run sales
Geographical pricing	Adjusting prices to account for the geographic location of customers
International pricing	Adjusting prices for international markets

Functional discount
A price reduction offered by the seller to trade channel members who perform certain functions such as selling, storing, and record keeping.

Seasonal discount
A price reduction to buyers who purchase merchandise or services out of season.

Allowance
Promotional money paid by manufacturers to retailers in return for an agreement to feature the manufacturer's products in some way.

Segmented pricing
Selling a product or service at two or more prices, where the difference in prices is not based on differences in costs.

A **functional discount** (also called a *trade discount*) is offered by the seller to trade channel members who perform certain functions, such as selling, storing, and record keeping. Manufacturers may offer different functional discounts to different trade channels because of the varying services they perform, but manufacturers must offer the same functional discounts within each trade channel.

A **seasonal discount** is a price reduction to buyers who buy merchandise or services out of season. For example, lawn and garden equipment manufacturers offer seasonal discounts to retailers during the fall and winter months to encourage early ordering in anticipation of the heavy spring and summer selling seasons. Hotels, motels, and airlines will offer seasonal discounts in their slower selling periods. Seasonal discounts allow the seller to keep production steady during an entire year.

Allowances are another type of reduction from the list price. For example, *trade-in allowances* are price reductions given for turning in an old item when buying a new one. Trade-in allowances are most common in the automobile industry but are also given for other durable goods. *Promotional allowances* are payments or price reductions to reward dealers for participating in advertising and sales support programs.

Segmented Pricing

Companies will often adjust their basic prices to allow for differences in customers, products, and locations. In **segmented pricing,** the company sells a product or service at two or more prices, even though the difference in prices is not based on differences in costs (see Marketing Highlight 11.1).

Segmented pricing takes several forms. Under *customer-segment* pricing, different customers pay different prices for the same product or service. Museums, for example, will charge a lower admission for students and senior citizens. Under *product-form pricing,* different versions of the product are priced differently but not according to differences in their costs. For instance, Black & Decker prices its most expensive iron at $54.98, which is $12 more than the price of its next most expensive iron. The top model has a self-cleaning feature, yet this extra feature costs only a few more dollars to make. Using *location pricing,* a company charges different prices for different locations, even though the cost of offering at each location is the same. For instance, theaters vary their seat prices because of audience preferences for certain locations, and state universities charge higher tuition for out-of-state students. Finally, using *time pricing,* a firm varies its price by the season, the month, the day, and even the hour. Public utilities vary their prices to commercial users by time of day and weekend versus weekday. The telephone company offers lower off-peak charges, and resorts give seasonal discounts.

For segmented pricing to be an effective strategy, certain conditions must exist. The market must be segmentable, and the segments must show different degrees of demand. Members of the segment paying the lower price should not be able to turn around and resell the product to the segment paying the higher price. Competitors should not be able to undersell the firm in the segment being charged the higher price. Nor should the costs of segmenting and watching the market exceed the extra revenue obtained from the price difference. Of course, the segmented pricing must also be legal. Most importantly, segmented prices should reflect real differences in customers' perceived value. Otherwise, in the long run, the practice will lead to customer resentment and ill will.

Psychological Pricing

Price says something about the product. For example, many consumers use price to judge quality. A $100 bottle of perfume may contain only $3 worth of scent, but some people are willing to pay the $100 because this price indicates something special.

Psychological pricing
A pricing approach that considers the psychology of prices and not simply the economics; the price is used to say something about the product.

In using **psychological pricing,** sellers consider the psychology of prices and not simply the economics. For example, one study of the relationship between price and quality perceptions of cars found that consumers perceive higher-priced cars as having higher quality.[8] By the same token, higher-quality cars are perceived to be even higher priced than they actually are. When consumers can judge the quality of a product by examining it or by calling on past experience with it, they use price less to judge quality. When consumers cannot judge quality because they lack the information or skill, price becomes an important quality signal:

⭐ Heublein produces Smirnoff, America's leading vodka brand. Some years ago, Smirnoff was attacked by another brand. Wolfschmidt, priced at one dollar less per bottle, claimed to have the same quality as Smirnoff. To hold on to market share, Heublein considered either lowering Smirnoff's price by one dollar or holding Smirnoff's price but increasing advertising and promotion expenditures. Either strategy would lead to lower profits and it seemed that Heublein faced a no-win situation. At this point, however, Heublein's marketers thought of a third strategy. They *raised* the price of Smirnoff by one dollar! Heublein then introduced a new brand, Relska, to compete with Wolfschmidt. Moreover, it introduced yet another brand, Popov, priced even *lower* than Wolfschmidt. This clever strategy positioned Smirnoff as the elite brand and Wolfschmidt as an ordinary brand, producing a large increase in Heublein's overall profits. The irony is that Heublein's three brands are pretty much the same in taste and manufacturing costs. Heublein knew that a product's price signals its quality. Using price as a signal, Heublein sells roughly the same product at three different quality positions.

Reference prices
Prices that buyers carry in their minds and refer to when they look at a given product.

Another aspect of psychological pricing is **reference prices**—prices that buyers carry in their minds and refer to when looking at a given product. The reference price might be formed by noting current prices, remembering past prices, or assessing the buying situation. Sellers can influence or use these consumers' reference prices when setting price. For example, a company could display its product

Psychological pricing: What do the prices marked on this tag suggest about the product and buying situation?

SEGMENTED PRICING: THE RIGHT PRODUCT TO THE RIGHT CUSTOMER AT THE RIGHT TIME FOR THE RIGHT PRICE

Many companies would love to raise prices across the board—but fear losing business. When the Washington Opera Company, located in the nation's capital, was considering increasing ticket prices after a difficult season, Ticket Services Manager Jimmy Legarreta decided there had to be a better way. He found one after carefully reviewing opera economics. Legarreta knew—and his computer system confirmed—that the company routinely turned away people for Friday and Saturday night performances, particularly for prime seats. Meanwhile, midweek tickets went begging.

Legarreta also knew that not all seats were equal, even in the sought-after orchestra section. So the ticket manager and his staff sat in every one of the opera house's 2,200 seats and gave each a value according to the view and the acoustics. With his revenue goal in mind, Legarreta played with ticket prices until he arrived at nine levels, up from five. In the end, the opera raised prices for its most coveted seats by as much as 50 percent but also dropped the prices of some 600 seats. The gamble paid off in a 9 percent revenue increase during the next season.

Legarreta didn't have a name for it, but he was practicing "segmented pricing," an approach that also has many other labels. Airlines, hotels, and restaurants call it "yield management" and practice it religiously. Robert Cross, a longtime consultant to the airlines, calls it "revenue management." In a book by that name, Cross argues that all companies should apply revenue-management concepts, which emphasize an aggressive micromarket approach to maximizing sales. "Revenue management," Cross writes, "assures that companies will sell the right product to the right consumer at the right time for the right price."

Segmented pricing and yield management aren't really new ideas. For instance, Marriott Corporation used seat-of-the-pants yield-management

Segmented pricing: Not all seats in an opera house are equal. After sitting in every one of the Washington Opera House's 2,200 seats, management arrived at nine pricing levels. The result was a 9 percent revenue increase.

next to more expensive ones in order to imply that it belongs in the same class. Department stores often sell women's clothing in separate departments differentiated by price: Clothing found in the more expensive department is assumed to be of better quality. Companies can also influence consumers' reference prices by stating high manufacturer's suggested prices, by indicating that the product was originally priced much higher, or by pointing to a competitor's higher price.

Even small differences in price can suggest product differences. Consider a stereo priced at $300 compared to one priced at $299.95. The actual price differ-approaches long before it installed its current sophisticated system. Back when J. W. "Bill" Marriott was a young man working at the family's first hotel, the Twin Bridges in Washington, DC, he sold rooms from a drive-up window. As Bill tells it, the hotel charged a flat rate for a single occupant, with an extra charge for each additional person staying in the room. When room availability got tight on some nights, Bill would lean out the drive-up window and assess the cars waiting in line. If some of the cars were filled with passengers, Bill would turn away vehicles with just a single passenger to sell his last rooms to those farther back in line who would be paying for multiple occupants. He might have accomplished the same result by charging a higher rate at peak times, regardless of the number of room occupants.

Cross's underlying premise: No two customers value a product or service exactly the same way. Furthermore, the perceived value of a product results from many variables that change over time. Some of Cross's clients use sophisticated yield-management simulation models and high-powered computer systems to predict sales at different price levels, but the technique doesn't have to be rocket science. If you understand your customers' motivation for buying and you keep careful sales records, it's possible to adjust prices to remedy supply-and-demand imbalances. Legarreta, for example, ended his midweek slump by making

opera affordable for more people, yet he accurately predicted that the Washington in-crowd would pay higher prices for the best weekend seats.

Probably the simplest form of segmented pricing is off-peak pricing, common in the entertainment and travel industries. Marc Epstein, owner of the Milk Street Cafe in Boston, discovered that technique more than 10 years ago, when he noticed he had lines out the door at noon but a near-empty restaurant around his 3 P.M. closing time. After some experimentation, Epstein settled on a 20 percent discount for the hours just before noon and after 2 P.M.—and he's pleased with the results. "If we didn't offer this, our overall revenue would be less," he argues. Epstein did not feel he could simultaneously raise prices during the lunch rush; instead, he has expanded the corporate catering side of his business, where he can charge more per sandwich because "the perceived value of a catered lunch is higher."

Many other companies could conceivably segment their prices to increase revenues and profits. Cross cites examples ranging from a one-chair barbershop, to an accounting firm, to a health center. But there are risks. When you establish a range of prices, customers who pay the higher ones may feel cheated. "It can't be a secret that you're charging different prices for the same service," Cross advises. "Customers must

know, so they can choose when to use a service."

Even so, promotions designed to shift customer traffic to off-peak times can backfire. Rick Johnson, owner of Madison Car Wash in Montgomery, Alabama, describes his experience with a "Wonderful Wednesday" special: "The incentive was too good. It took away from the rest of the week and made Wednesday a monster day; it was a horrible strain on my facility and my people. I played around with the discount, but it was still a problem. So I finally dropped it."

The moral of the story? You can never know too much about your customers and the different values they assign to your product or service. With that customer knowledge comes power—to make the best pricing decisions.

Source: Portions adapted with permission from Susan Greco, "Are Your Prices Right?" *Inc.,* January 1997, pp. 88–89. Copyright 1997 by Goldhirsh Group, Inc., 38 Commercial Wharf, Boston, MA 02110. Other information from Robert G. Cross, *Revenue Management: Hard-Core Tactics for Market Domination* (New York: Broadway Books, 1998); and William J. Quain, Michael Sansbury, and Dennis Quinn, "Revenue Enhancement, Part 3: Picking Low-Hanging Fruit—A Simple Approach to Yield Management," *Cornell Hotel and Restaurant Administration Quarterly,* April 1999, pp. 76–83. Also see Ramarao Desiraju and Steven M. Shugan, "Strategic Service Pricing and Yield Management," *Journal of Marketing,* January 1999, pp. 44–56.

ence is only 5 cents, but the psychological difference can be much greater. For example, some consumers will see the $299.95 as a price in the $200 range rather than the $300 range. The $299.95 will more likely be seen as a bargain price, whereas the $300 price suggests more quality. Some psychologists argue that each digit has symbolic and visual qualities that should be considered in pricing. Thus, 8 is round and even and creates a soothing effect, whereas 7 is angular and creates a jarring effect.[9]

Promotional Pricing

Promotional pricing
Temporarily pricing products below the list price, and sometimes even below cost, to increase short-run sales.

With **promotional pricing,** companies will temporarily price their products below list price and sometimes even below cost. Promotional pricing takes several forms. Supermarkets and department stores will price a few products as *loss leaders* to attract customers to the store in the hope that they will buy other items at normal markups. Sellers will also use *special-event pricing* in certain seasons to draw more customers. Thus, linens are promotionally priced every January to attract weary Christmas shoppers back into stores.

Manufacturers will sometimes offer *cash rebates* to consumers who buy the product from dealers within a specified time; the manufacturer sends the rebate directly to the customer. Rebates have been popular with automakers and producers of durable goods and small appliances, but they are also used with consumer packaged goods. Some manufacturers offer *low-interest financing, longer warranties,* or *free maintenance* to reduce the consumer's "price." This practice has recently become a favorite of the auto industry. Or, the seller may simply offer *discounts* from normal prices to increase sales and reduce inventories.

Promotional pricing, however, can have adverse effects. Used too frequently and copied by competitors, price promotions can create "deal-prone" customers who wait until brands go on sale before buying them. Or, constantly reduced prices can erode a brand's value in the eyes of customers. Marketers sometimes use price promotions as a quick fix instead of sweating through the difficult process of developing effective longer-term strategies for building their brands. In fact, one observer notes that price promotions can be downright addicting to both the company and the customer: "Price promotions are the brand equivalent of heroin: easy to get into but hard to get out of. Once the brand and its customers are addicted to the short-term high of a price cut it is hard to wean them away to real brand building. . . . But continue and the brand dies by 1,000 cuts."[10]

Jack Trout, a well-known marketing author and consultant, cautions that some categories tend to self-destruct by always being on sale. Discount pricing has become routine for a surprising number of companies. Furniture, automobile tires, and many other categories of goods are rarely sold at anything near list price, and when automakers get rebate happy, the market just sits back and waits for a deal. Even Coca-Cola and Pepsi, two of the world's most popular brands, engage in regular price wars that ultimately tarnish their brand equity. Trout offers several "Commandments of Discounting," such as "Thou shalt not offer discounts because everyone else does," "Thou shalt be creative with your discounting," "Thou shalt put time limits on the deal," and "Thou shalt stop discounting as soon as you can."[11] The point is that promotional pricing can be an effective means of generating sales in certain circumstances but can be damaging if taken as a steady diet.

Geographical Pricing

A company also must decide how to price its products for customers located in different parts of the country or world. Should the company risk losing the business of more distant customers by charging them higher prices to cover the higher shipping costs? Or should the company charge all customers the same prices regardless of location? We will look at five geographical pricing strategies for the following hypothetical situation:

★   The Peerless Paper Company is located in Atlanta, Georgia, and sells paper products to customers all over the United States. The cost of freight is high and affects the companies from whom customers buy their paper. Peerless wants to establish a geographical pricing policy. It is trying to determine how to price a $100 order to three specific customers: Customer A (Atlanta); Customer B (Bloomington, Indiana), and Customer C (Compton, California).

One option is for Peerless to ask each customer to pay the shipping cost from the Atlanta factory to the customer's location. All three customers would pay the same factory price of $100, with Customer A paying, say, $10 for shipping; Customer B, $15; and Customer C, $25. Called **FOB-origin pricing,** this practice means that the goods are placed *free on board* (hence, *FOB*) a carrier. At that point the title and responsibility pass to the customer, who pays the freight from the factory to the destination. Because each customer picks up its own cost, supporters of FOB pricing feel that this is the fairest way to assess freight charges. The disadvantage, however, is that Peerless will be a high-cost firm to distant customers.

Uniform-delivered pricing is the opposite of FOB pricing. Here, the company charges the same price plus freight to all customers, regardless of their location. The freight charge is set at the average freight cost. Suppose this is $15. Uniform-delivered pricing therefore results in a higher charge to the Atlanta customer (who pays $15 freight instead of $10) and a lower charge to the Compton customer (who pays $15 instead of $25). Although the Atlanta customer would prefer to buy paper from another local paper company that uses FOB-origin pricing, Peerless has a better chance of winning over the California customer. Other advantages of uniform-delivered pricing are that it is fairly easy to administer and it lets the firm advertise its price nationally.

Zone pricing falls between FOB-origin pricing and uniform-delivered pricing. The company sets up two or more zones. All customers within a given zone pay a single total price; the more distant the zone, the higher the price. For example, Peerless might set up an East Zone and charge $10 freight to all customers in this zone, a Midwest Zone in which it charges $15, and a West Zone in which it charges $25. In this way, the customers within a given price zone receive no price advantage from the company. For example, customers in Atlanta and Boston pay the same total price to Peerless. The complaint, however, is that the Atlanta customer is paying part of the Boston customer's freight cost.

Using **basing-point pricing,** the seller selects a given city as a "basing point" and charges all customers the freight cost from that city to the customer location, regardless of the city from which the goods are actually shipped. For example, Peerless might set Chicago as the basing point and charge all customers $100 plus the freight from Chicago to their locations. This means that an Atlanta customer pays the freight cost from Chicago to Atlanta, even though the goods may be shipped from Atlanta. If all sellers used the same basing-point city, delivered prices would be the same for all customers and price competition would be eliminated. Industries such as sugar, cement, steel, and automobiles used basing-point pricing for years, but this method has become less popular today. Some companies set up multiple basing points to create more flexibility: They quote freight charges from the basing-point city nearest to the customer.

Finally, the seller who is anxious to do business with a certain customer or geographical area might use **freight-absorption pricing.** Using this strategy, the seller absorbs all or part of the actual freight charges in order to get the desired business. The seller might reason that if it can get more business, its average costs will

FOB-origin pricing
A geographical pricing strategy in which goods are placed free on board a carrier; the customer pays the freight from the factory to the destination.

Uniform-delivered pricing
A geographical pricing strategy in which the company charges the same price plus freight to all customers, regardless of their location.

Zone pricing
A geographical pricing strategy in which the company sets up two or more zones. All customers within a zone pay the same total price; the more distant the zone, the higher the price.

Basing-point pricing
A geographical pricing strategy in which the seller designates some city as a basing point and charges all customers the freight cost from that city to the customer location, regardless of the city from which the goods are actually shipped.

Freight-absorption pricing
A geographical pricing strategy in which the seller absorbs all or part of the actual freight charges in order to get the desired business.

fall and more than compensate for its extra freight cost. Freight-absorption pricing is used for market penetration and to hold on to increasingly competitive markets.

International Pricing

Companies that market their products internationally must decide what prices to charge in the different countries in which they operate. In some cases, a company can set a uniform worldwide price. For example, Boeing sells its jetliners at about the same price everywhere, whether in the United States, Europe, or a third-world country. However, most companies adjust their prices to reflect local market conditions and cost considerations.

The price that a company should charge in a specific country depends on many factors, including economic conditions, competitive situations, laws and regulations, and development of the wholesaling and retailing system. Consumer perceptions and preferences also may vary from country to country, calling for different prices. Or the company may have different marketing objectives in various world markets, which require changes in pricing strategy. For example, Sony might introduce a new product into mature markets in highly developed countries with the goal of quickly gaining mass-market share—this would call for a penetration-pricing strategy. In contrast, it might enter a less developed market by targeting smaller, less price-sensitive segments; in this case, market-skimming pricing makes sense.

Costs play an important role in setting international prices. Travelers abroad are often surprised to find that goods that are relatively inexpensive at home may carry outrageously higher price tags in other countries. A pair of Levi's selling for $30 in the United States goes for about $63 in Tokyo and $88 in Paris. A McDonald's Big Mac selling for a modest $2.25 here costs $5.75 in Moscow, and an Oral-B toothbrush selling for $2.49 at home costs $10.00 in China. Conversely, a Gucci handbag going for only $60 in Milan, Italy, fetches $240 in the United States. In some cases, such *price escalation* may result from differences in selling strategies or market conditions. In most instances, however, it is simply a result of the higher costs of selling in foreign markets—the additional costs of modifying the product, higher shipping and insurance costs, import tariffs and taxes, costs associated with exchange-rate fluctuations, and higher channel and physical distribution costs.

For example, Campbell found that its distribution costs in the United Kingdom were 30 percent higher than in the United States. U.S. retailers typically purchase

Companies that market products internationally must decide what prices to charge in the different countries.

soup in large quantities—48-can cases of a single soup by the dozens, hundreds, or carloads. In contrast, English grocers purchase soup in small quantities—typically in 24-can cases of *assorted* soups. Each case must be handpacked for shipment. To handle these small orders, Campbell had to add a costly extra wholesale level to its European channel. The smaller orders also mean that English retailers order two or three times as often as their U.S. counterparts, bumping up billing and order costs. These and other factors caused Campbell to charge much higher prices for its soups in the United Kingdom.[12]

Thus, international pricing presents some special problems and complexities. We discuss international pricing issues in more detail in chapter 19.

PRICE CHANGES

After developing their pricing structures and strategies, companies often face situations in which they must initiate price changes or respond to price changes by competitors.

Initiating Price Changes

In some cases, the company may find it desirable to initiate either a price cut or a price increase. In both cases, it must anticipate possible buyer and competitor reactions.

Initiating Price Cuts

Several situations may lead a firm to consider cutting its price. One such circumstance is excess capacity. In this case, the firm needs more business and cannot get it through increased sales effort, product improvement, or other measures. It may drop its "follow-the-leader pricing"—charging about the same price as its leading competitor—and aggressively cut prices to boost sales. But as the airline, construction equipment, fast-food, and other industries have learned in recent years, cutting prices in an industry loaded with excess capacity may lead to price wars as competitors try to hold on to market share.

Another situation leading to price changes is falling market share in the face of strong price competition. Several American industries—automobiles, consumer electronics, cameras, watches, and steel, for example—lost market share to Japanese competitors whose high-quality products carried lower prices than did their American counterparts. In response, American companies resorted to more aggressive pricing action. A company may also cut prices in a drive to dominate the market through lower costs. Either the company starts with lower costs than its competitors or it cuts prices in the hope of gaining market share that will further cut costs through larger volume. Bausch & Lomb used an aggressive low-cost, low-price strategy to become an early leader in the competitive soft contact lens market.

Initiating Price Increases

A successful price increase can greatly increase profits. For example, if the company's profit margin is 3 percent of sales, a 1 percent price increase will increase profits by 33 percent if sales volume is unaffected. A major factor in price increases is cost inflation. Rising costs squeeze profit margins and lead companies to pass cost increases along to customers. Another factor leading to price increases is overdemand: When a company cannot supply all its customers' needs, it can raise its prices, ration products to customers, or both.

Companies can increase their prices in a number of ways to keep up with rising costs. Prices can be raised almost invisibly by dropping discounts and adding higher-priced units to the line. Or prices can be pushed up openly. In passing price increases on to customers, the company must avoid being perceived as a price gouger. Companies also need to think of who will bear the brunt of increased prices. As the Kellogg example in the previous chapter suggests, customer memories are long, and they will eventually turn away from companies or even whole industries that they perceive as charging excessive prices.

There are some techniques for avoiding this problem. One is to maintain a sense of fairness surrounding any price increase. Price increases should be supported with a company communication program telling customers why prices are being increased and customers should be given advance notice so they can do forward buying or shop around. Making low-visibility price moves first is also a good technique: Eliminating discounts, increasing minimum order sizes, curtailing production of low-margin products are some examples. Contracts or bids for long-term projects should contain escalator clauses based on such factors as increases in recognized national price indexes. The company sales force should help business customers find ways to economize.[13]

Wherever possible, the company should consider ways to meet higher costs or demand without raising prices. For example, it can consider more cost-effective ways to produce or distribute its products. It can shrink the product instead of raising the price, as candy bar manufacturers often do. It can substitute less expensive ingredients or remove certain product features, packaging, or services. Or it can "unbundle" its products and services, removing and separately pricing elements that were formerly part of the offer. IBM, for example, now offers training and consulting as separately priced services.

Buyer Reactions to Price Changes

Whether the price is raised or lowered, the action will affect buyers, competitors, distributors, and suppliers and may interest government as well. Customers do not always interpret prices in a straightforward way. They may view a price *cut* in several ways. For example, what would you think if Sony were suddenly to cut its VCR

Buyer reactions to price changes: What would you think if the price of Joy was suddenly cut in half?

prices in half? You might think that these VCRs are about to be replaced by newer models or that they have some fault and are not selling well. You might think that Sony is abandoning the VCR business and may not stay in this business long enough to supply future parts. You might believe that quality has been reduced. Or you might think that the price will come down even further and that it will pay to wait and see.

Similarly, a price *increase,* which would normally lower sales, may have some positive meanings for buyers. What would you think if Sony *raised* the price of its latest VCR model? On the one hand, you might think that the item is very "hot" and may be unobtainable unless you buy it soon. Or you might think that the VCR is an unusually good value. On the other hand, you might think that Sony is greedy and charging what the traffic will bear.[14]

Competitor Reactions to Price Changes

A firm considering a price change has to worry about the reactions of its competitors as well as its customers. Competitors are most likely to react when the number of firms involved is small, when the product is uniform, and when the buyers are well informed.

How can the firm anticipate the likely reactions of its competitors? If the firm faces one large competitor, and if the competitor tends to react in a set way to price changes, that reaction can be easily anticipated. But if the competitor treats each price change as a fresh challenge and reacts according to its self-interest, the company will have to figure out just what makes up the competitor's self-interest at the time.

The problem is complex because, like the customer, the competitor can interpret a company price cut in many ways. It might think the company is trying to grab a larger market share, that the company is doing poorly and trying to boost its sales, or that the company wants the whole industry to cut prices to increase total demand.

When there are several competitors, the company must guess each competitor's likely reaction. If all competitors behave alike, this amounts to analyzing only a typical competitor. In contrast, if the competitors do not behave alike—perhaps because of differences in size, market shares, or policies—then separate analyses are necessary. However, if some competitors will match the price change, there is good reason to expect that the rest will also match it.

Responding to Price Changes

Here we reverse the question and ask how a firm should respond to a price change by a competitor. The firm needs to consider several issues: Why did the competitor change the price? Was it to take more market share, to use excess capacity, to meet changing cost conditions, or to lead an industrywide price change? Is the price change temporary or permanent? What will happen to the company's market share and profits if it does not respond? Are other companies going to respond? What are the competitor's and other firms' responses to each possible reaction likely to be?

Besides these issues, the company must make a broader analysis. It has to consider its own product's stage in the life cycle, the product's importance in the company's product mix, the intentions and resources of the competitor, and the possible consumer reactions to price changes. The company cannot always make an extended analysis of its alternatives at the time of a price change, however. The competitor may have spent much time preparing this decision, but the company may have to react within hours or days. About the only way to cut down reaction

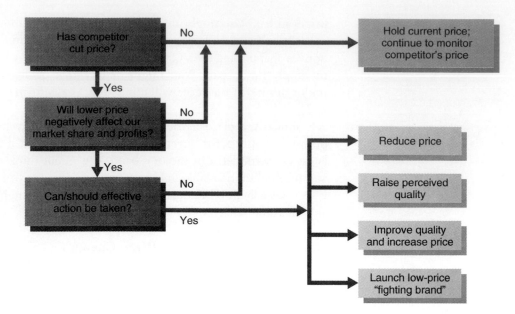

FIGURE 11.1   Assessing and responding to competitor's price changes

time is to plan ahead for both possible competitor's price changes and possible responses.

Figure 11.1 shows the ways a company might assess and respond to a competitor's price cut. Once the company has determined that the competitor has cut its price and that this price reduction is likely to harm company sales and profits, it might simply decide to hold its current price and profit margin. The company might believe that it will not lose too much market share, or that it would lose too much profit if it reduced its own price. It might decide that it should wait and respond when it has more information on the effects of the competitor's price change. For now, it might be willing to hold on to good customers, while giving up the poorer ones to the competitor. The argument against this holding strategy, however, is that the competitor may get stronger and more confident as its sales increase and that the company might wait too long to act.

If the company decides that effective action can and should be taken, it might make any of four responses. First, it could *reduce its price* to match the competitor's price. It may decide that the market is price sensitive and that it would lose too much market share to the lower-priced competitor. Or it might worry that recapturing lost market share later would be too hard. Cutting the price will reduce the company's profits in the short run. Some companies might also reduce their product quality, services, and marketing communications to retain profit margins, but this will ultimately hurt long-run market share. The company should try to maintain its quality as it cuts prices.

Alternatively, the company might maintain its price but *raise the perceived quality* of its offer. It could improve its communications, stressing the relative quality of its product over that of the lower-price competitor. The firm may find it cheaper to maintain price and spend money to improve its perceived value than to cut price and operate at a lower margin.

Or, the company might *improve quality and increase price,* moving its brand into a higher-price position. The higher quality justifies the higher price, which in turn preserves the company's higher margins. Or the company can hold price on the current product and introduce a new brand at a higher-price position.

Fighting brands: When challenged on price by store brands and other low-priced entrants, Procter & Gamble turned a number of its brands into fighting brands, including Luvs disposable diapers.

Finally, the company might launch a low-price "fighting brand." Often, one of the best responses is to add lower-price items to the line or to create a separate lower-price brand. This is necessary if the particular market segment being lost is price sensitive and will not respond to arguments of higher quality. Thus, when challenged on price by store brands and other low-price entrants, Procter & Gamble turned a number of its brands into fighting brands, including Luvs disposable diapers, Joy dishwashing detergent, and Camay beauty soap. In response to price pressures, Miller cut the price of its High Life brand by 20 percent in most markets, and sales jumped 9 percent in less than a year.[15]

PUBLIC POLICY AND PRICING

Price competition is a core element of our free-market economy. In setting prices, companies are not usually free to charge whatever prices they wish. Many federal, state, and even local laws govern the rules of fair play in pricing. In addition, companies must consider broader societal pricing concerns (see Marketing Highlight 11.2). The most important pieces of legislation affecting pricing are the Sherman, Clayton, and Robinson-Patman acts, initially adopted to curb the formation of monopolies and to regulate business practices that might unfairly restrain trade. Because these federal statutes can be applied only to interstate commerce, some states have adopted similar provisions for companies that operate locally.

MARKETING
HIGHLIGHT
11.2

PRICING PHARMACEUTICAL PRODUCTS:
MORE THAN SALES AND PROFITS

The U.S. pharmaceutical industry has historically been one of the nation's most profitable industries. However, critics claim that this success has come at the expense of consumers. The U.S. population spent more than $100 billion on prescription medications last year, and prescription prices have risen steadily over the years at higher-than-inflation rates. The critics claim that competitive forces do not operate well in the pharmaceutical market, allowing companies to charge excessive prices.

Consumers don't usually shop for the best deal on medicines—they simply take what the doctor orders. Because physicians who write the prescriptions don't pay for the med-icines they recommend, they have little incentive to be price conscious. Moreover, third-party payers—insurance companies, health plans, and government programs—often pay all or part of the bill. In the pharmaceutical industry, the huge investment and time needed to develop, test, and market a new drug discourages competitors from challenging the market leader and forcing lower prices. Finally, expensive advertising and promotional efforts dictate higher prices at the same time that they build demand for expensive therapies, knock out the competition, and permit companies to charge the higher prices. These market factors leave pharmaceutical companies free to practice monop-oly pricing, the critics claim, result-ing in seemingly outlandish cases of price gouging.

One classic case involved the drug levamisole. Forty years ago, Johnson & Johnson introduced levamisole as a drug used to deworm sheep. When farmers using the drug noticed that dewormed sheep also suffered fewer cases of shipping fever, researchers began investigating the drug for human use. Under the sponsorship of the National Cancer Institute, and with free pills provided by Johnson & Johnson, Dr. Charles Moertel of the Mayo Comprehensive Cancer Center tested levamisole in combination with another drug as a treatment for cancer. The combination proved effective for patients with advanced colon cancer. It reduced recurrence of the disease by 40 percent and cut deaths by a third.

The FDA quickly approved lev-amisole for human use. In 1990, the Janssen division of Johnson & Johnson introduced the drug under the brand name Ergamisol. All went well until an Illinois farm woman noticed that her cancer pills con-tained the same active ingredient as the medicine she used to deworm her sheep. It wasn't the fact that both humans and sheep were using the drug that disturbed her. What really rankled her was that the sheep med-icine sold for pennies a pill, whereas the human medicine sold for $5 to $6 per tablet. In a year's time, humans had to spend $1,250 to $3,000 for Ergamisol; the cost for treating sheep was only about $14.95.

The price discrepancy caused quite a stir. At the annual meetings

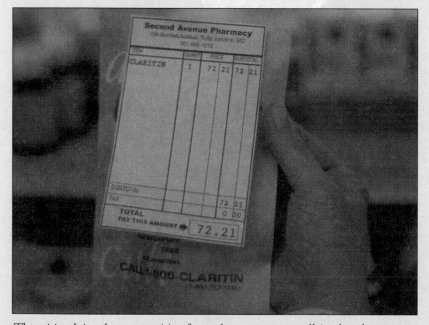

The critics claim that competitive forces do not operate well in the pharmaceu-tical market, allowing companies to charge excessive prices.

of the American Society for Clinical Oncology in May 1992, Dr. Moertel blasted Johnson & Johnson for its unconscionable pricing of the drug. In August 1992, Chicago consumer Frank Glickman filed suit against Janssen. He claimed that he was forced to pay "an outrageous, unconscionable, and extortionate price for a lifesaving drug" that is sold at a fraction of the cost for treating sheep.

Janssen replied that the cost of Ergamisol was reasonable when compared to other lifesaving drugs such as AZT, which at the time cost $6,000 to $8,000 a year. The company also claimed that the price reflected decades of costly research and testing conducted to determine if levamisole could be used to treat humans. The company said it had conducted over 1,400 studies with 40,000 subjects. Dr. Moertel disagreed. He claimed that the Cancer Institute, funded by the American taxpayer, sponsored the levamisole studies. Further, he asserted, FDA approval was obtained on the basis of his research, which cost Janssen only pennies. He also pointed out that Janssen had 25 years to recoup its investment before it ever sold the drug to humans.

The levamisole case may be extreme, but at one time or another we've all gulped at the prices we've had to pay for prescription drugs. Even when doctors or pharmacists recommend less expensive generic drugs, consumers may pay substantial markups. One recent study found that drugstores and pharmacies are marking up the price of some generics by over 1,000 percent. For example, stores charge an average of $18.08 for a prescription of the generic version of the antipsychotic drug Haldol, 2,800 percent more than the $.62 cost the generic man-

ufacturer charges. A prescription for the generic version of Zovirax, an antiviral drug, sells at pharmacies for an average of $61.64, more than eight times the manufacturer's price of $7.22. Not only do pharmacies pocket a handsome profit, but they look like good guys when they encourage customers to use a generic drug to save money. Indeed, the generic drug is still cheaper than the brand-name counterpart. For their part, pharmacies argue that the high gross margins for generics doesn't tell the whole story. Just as a patient who visits a doctor and gets handed a Band-Aid is not billed for just the Band-Aid, a pharmacy customer has to pay for the pharmacist's time and other expenses of maintaining a pharmacy department.

These examples highlight many important drug-pricing issues. Most consumers appreciate the steady stream of beneficial drugs produced by the U.S. pharmaceutical industry. There is no question that developing new drugs is a risky endeavor, involving legions of scientists, expensive technology, and often years of effort with no certainty of success. However, there is much concern that the industry may be taking advantage of its monopoly-pricing power. Unlike purchases of other consumer products, drug purchases cannot be postponed. Nor can consumers shop around to save money. Because of patents and FDA approvals, few competing brands exist, and they don't go on sale. Perhaps the most serious concern is that high drug prices may have life-and-death consequences. Without levamisole, many of the 22,000 patients diagnosed with advanced colon cancer each year would die. Thus, some critics claim that drug company profits may come at the expense of human life.

As a result, the industry is facing ever-greater pressure from the federal government, insurance companies, managed care providers, and consumer advocates to exercise restraint in setting prices. Legislation has been passed to curb drug pricing and more is pending. Rather than waiting for tougher legislation on prices, some forward-thinking drug companies have taken action on their own by agreeing to keep their average price hikes at or below inflation. Others have voluntarily provided discounts to agencies such as the U.S. Public Health Service and to federally funded drug- and alcohol-treatment centers. Still other companies make free drugs available to people who cannot afford them. These companies recognize that in setting prices, their short-term sales, market share, and profit goals must be tempered by broader societal considerations. They know that in the long run, socially responsible pricing will benefit both the consumer and the company.

Sources: Marilyn Chase, "Doctor Assails J&J Price Tag on Cancer Drug," *Wall Street Journal,* May 20, 1992, p. B1; "Cancer Patient Sues Johnson & Johnson over Drug Pricing," *Wall Street Journal,* August 13, 1992, p. B6; Mike King, "Colon Cancer Drug: 5 Cents for an Animal, $5 for Humans," *Atlanta Constitution,* March 11, 1991, p. E1; Elyse Tanouye, "Drugs: Steep Markups on Generics Top Branded Drugs," *Wall Street Journal,* December 31, 1998, p. B1; Jill Wechsler, "Policy Issues for 1999," *Pharmaceutical Executive,* January 1999, pp. 20–26; "Bill Mulled for Uniform Prescription Drug Pricing," *Chemical Market Reporter,* May 24, 1999, p. 17; and Elyse Tanouye and Philip Connors, "Drugs: New Price Data on Prescriptions Show Big Hike for Many Drugs of Inflation," *Wall Street Journal,* June 19, 1999, p. B1.

FIGURE 11.2   Public policy issues in pricing

Source: Adapted from Dhruv Grewel and Larry D. Compeau, "Pricing and Public Policy: A Research Agenda and Overview of Special Issue," *Journal of Marketing and Public Policy,* Spring 1999, pp. 3–10.

Figure 11.2 shows the major public policy issues in pricing. These include potentially damaging pricing practices within a given level of the channel (price-fixing and predatory pricing) and across levels of the channel (retail price maintenance, discriminatory pricing, and deceptive pricing).[16]

Pricing Within Channel Levels

Federal legislation on *price-fixing* states that sellers must set prices without talking to competitors. Otherwise, price collusion is suspected. Price-fixing is illegal per se—that is, the government does not accept any excuses for price-fixing. Companies found guilty of such practices can receive heavy fines. For example, when the U.S. Justice Department recently found that Archer Daniels Midland Company and three of its competitors had met regularly in the early 1990s to illegally fix prices, the four companies paid more than $100 million to settle the charges.[17]

Even a simple conversation between competitors can have serious consequences. For example, during the early 1980s, American Airlines and Braniff were immersed in a price war in the Texas market. In the heat of the battle, American's CEO, Robert Crandall, called the president of Braniff and said, "Raise your . . . fares 20 percent. I'll raise mine the next morning. You'll make more money and I will, too." Fortunately for Crandall, the Braniff president warned him off, saying, "We can't talk about pricing!" As it turns out, the phone conversation had been recorded, and the U.S. Justice Department began action against Crandall and American for price-fixing. The charges were eventually dropped—the courts ruled that because Braniff had rejected Crandall's proposal, no actual collusion had occurred and that a proposal to fix prices was not an actual violation of the law. Still, as part of the settlement, for two years Crandall was required to keep a detailed log of his conversations with fellow airline chiefs.[18] Such cases have made most executives very reluctant to discuss prices in any way with competitors.

Sellers are also prohibited from using *predatory pricing*—selling below cost with the intention of punishing a competitor or gaining higher long-run profits by putting competitors out of business. This protects small sellers from larger ones who might sell items below cost temporarily or in a specific locale to drive them out of business. The biggest problem is determining just what constitutes predatory pricing behavior. Selling below cost to sell off excess inventory is not considered predatory; selling below cost to drive out competitors is. Thus, the same action may or may not be predatory depending on intent, and intent can be very difficult to determine or prove.

In recent years, several large and powerful companies have been accused of this practice. For example, Wal-Mart has been sued by dozens of small competitors charging that it lowered prices in their specific areas to drive them out of business. In another case, the Justice Department sued American Airlines in 1999 for allegedly using predatory pricing to muscle three small competitors—Vanguard Airlines, Sun Jet, and Western Pacific—out of its huge Dallas–Fort Worth hub. American contended that it was just being a tough competitor.[19] Giant Microsoft has also been a Justice Department target:

> When Microsoft targets a market for domination, it frequently wins over customers with an irresistible offer: free products. In 1996, Microsoft started giving away Internet Explorer, its Web browser—and in some cases arguably even "paid" people to use it by offering free software and marketing assistance. The strategy was crucial in wresting market dominance from Netscape Communications Corporation. Netscape constantly revised its pricing structure but "better than free" is not the most appealing sales pitch. Most of Microsoft's giveaways were offered as part of its effort to gain share in the interactive corporate computing market. For instance, the company offered free Web server software to customers who purchase the Windows NT network operating system. Netscape was selling a higher-powered version of the same software for $4,100. Although such pricing and promotion strategies might be viewed as shrewd marketing by some, competitors saw them as purely predatory. They noted that in the past, once Microsoft had use these tactics to gain a lion's share of the market, it had tended to raise prices *above* market levels. For example, the wholesale price it charged PC makers for its Windows operating system (in which is bundled the Internet Explorer) has doubled during the past seven years.[20]

Pricing Across Channel Levels

The Robinson-Patman Act seeks to prevent unfair *price discrimination* by ensuring that sellers offer the same price terms to customers at a given level of trade. For example, every retailer is entitled to the same price terms from a given manufacturer, whether the retailer is Sears or the local bicycle shop. However, price discrimination is allowed if the seller can prove that its costs are different when selling to different retailers—for example, that it costs less per unit to sell a large volume of bicycles to Sears than to sell a few bicycles to a local dealer. Or the seller can discriminate in its pricing if the seller manufactures different qualities of the same product for different retailers. The seller has to prove that these differences are proportional. Price differentials may also be used to "match competition" in "good faith," provided the price discrimination is temporary, localized, and defensive rather than offensive.

Resale price maintenance is also prohibited—a manufacturer cannot require dealers to charge a specified retail price for its product. Although the seller can propose a manufacturer's *suggested* retail price to dealers, it cannot refuse to sell to a dealer who takes independent pricing action, nor can it punish the dealer by shipping late or denying advertising allowances. For example, in 1996 the Federal Trade Commission (FTC) charged that New Balance had engaged in fixing resale prices for its athletic shoes. Its agreements with retailers required that the retailers raise the price of New Balance products, maintain prices at levels set by New Balance, and not discount the products.

Deceptive pricing occurs when a seller states prices or price savings that mislead consumers or are not actually available to consumers. This might involve bogus reference or comparison prices, as when a retailer sets artificially high "regular" prices then announces "sale" prices close to its previous everyday prices. Such comparison pricing is widespread:

Open any Sunday newspaper and find hundreds of such promotions being offered by a variety of retailers, such as supermarkets, office supply stores, furniture stores, computer stores, appliance stores, pharmacies and drug stores, car dealers, department stores, and others. Surf the Internet and see similar price promotions. Watch the shopping channels on television and find more of the same. It seems that, today, selling prices rarely stand alone. Instead retailers are using an advertised reference price (e.g., regular price, original price, manufacturer's suggested price) to suggest that buyers will save money if they take advantage of the "deal" being offered.[21]

Such claims are legal if they are truthful. However, the FTC's *Guides Against Deceptive Pricing* warns sellers not to advertise a price reduction unless it is a saving from the usual retail price, not to advertise "factory" or "wholesale" prices unless such prices are what they are claimed to be, and not to advertise comparable value prices on imperfect goods.

Other deceptive pricing issues include *scanner fraud* and price confusion. The widespread use of scanner-based computer checkouts has lead to increasing complaints of retailers overcharging their customers. Most of these overcharges result from poor management—from a failure to enter current or sale prices into the system. Other cases, however, involve intentional overcharges. *Price confusion* results when firms employ pricing methods that make it difficult for consumers to understand just what price they are really paying. For example, consumers are sometimes mislead regarding the real price of a home mortgage or car leasing agreement. In other cases, important pricing details may be buried in the "fine print."

Many federal and state statutes regulate against deceptive pricing practices. For example, the Automobile Information Disclosure Act requires automakers to attach a statement to new car windows stating the manufacturer's suggested retail price, the prices of optional equipment, and the dealer's transportation charges. However, reputable sellers go beyond what is required by law. Treating customers fairly and making certain that they fully understand prices and pricing terms is an important part of building strong and lasting customer relationships.[22]

REVIEW OF CONCEPT CONNECTIONS

Pricing decisions are subject to an incredibly complex array of environmental and competitive forces. A company sets not a single price, but rather a *pricing structure* that covers different items in its line. This pricing structure changes over time as products move through their life cycles. The company adjusts product prices to reflect changes in costs and demand and to account for variations in buyers and situations. As the competitive environment changes, the company considers when to initiate price changes and when to respond to them.

1. Describe the major strategies for pricing imitative and new products.
Pricing is a dynamic process. Companies design a *pricing structure* that covers all their products. They change this structure over time and adjust it to account for different cus-

tomers and situations. Pricing strategies usually change as a product passes through its life cycle. The company can decide on one of several price–quality strategies for introducing an imitative product, including premium pricing, economy pricing, good value, or overcharging. In pricing innovative new products, it can follow a *skimming policy* by initially setting high prices to "skim" the maximum amount of revenue from various segments of the market. Or it can use *penetration pricing* by setting a low initial price to penetrate the market deeply and win a large market share.

2. Explain how companies find a set of prices that maximizes the profits from the total product mix.
When the product is part of a product mix, the firm searches for a set of prices that will maximize the profits from the

total mix. In *product line pricing*, the company decides on price steps for the entire set of products it offers. In addition, the company must set prices for *optional products* (optional or accessory products included with the main product), *captive products* (products that are required for use of the main product), *by products* (waste or residual products produced when making the main product), and *product bundles* (combinations of products at a reduced price).

3. Discuss how companies adjust their prices to take into account different types of customers and situations.
Companies apply a variety of *price-adjustment strategies* to account for differences in consumer segments and situations. One is *discount and allowance pricing*, whereby the company establishes cash, quantity, functional, or seasonal discounts, or varied types of allowances. A second strategy is *segmented pricing*, where the company sells a product at two or more prices to accommodate different customers, product forms, locations, or times. Sometimes companies consider more than economics in their pricing decisions, using *psychological pricing* to better communicate a product's intended position. In *promotional pricing*, a company offers discounts or temporarily sells a product below list price as a special event, sometimes even selling below cost as a loss leader. Another approach is *geographical pricing*, whereby the company decides

how to price to distant customers, choosing from such alternatives as FOB pricing, uniform-delivered pricing, zone pricing, basing-point pricing, and freight-absorption pricing. Finally, *international pricing* means that the company adjusts its price to meet different conditions and expectations in different world markets.

4. Discuss the key issues related to initiating and responding to price changes.
When a firm considers initiating a *price change*, it must consider customers' and competitors' reactions. There are different implications for *initiating price cuts* and *initiating price increases*. Buyer reactions to price changes are influenced by the meaning customers see in the price change. Competitors' reactions flow from a set reaction policy or a fresh analysis of each situation.

There are also many factors to consider in responding to a competitor's price changes. The company that faces a price change initiated by a competitor must try to understand the competitor's intent as well as the likely duration and impact of the change. If a swift reaction is desirable, the firm should pre-plan its reactions to different possible price actions by competitors. When facing a competitor's price change, the company might sit tight, reduce its own price, raise perceived quality, improve quality and raise price, or launch a fighting brand.

KEY TERMS

Allowance	Functional discount	Psychological pricing
Basing-point pricing	Market-penetration pricing	Quantity discount
By product pricing	Market-skimming pricing	Reference prices
Captive-product pricing	Optional-product pricing	Seasonal discount
Cash discount	Product bundle pricing	Segmented pricing
FOB-origin pricing	Product line pricing	Uniform-delivered pricing
Freight-absorption pricing	Promotional pricing	Zone pricing

ISSUES FOR DISCUSSION

1. Which pricing strategy—market skimming or market penetration—does each of the following companies use? (a) McDonald's, (b) Curtis Mathes (television and other home electronics), (c) Bic Corporation (disposable pens, lighters, razors, and related products), and (d) IBM (personal computers). Are these the right strategies for each company? Explain.

2. A clothing store sells men's suits at three price levels: $180, $250, and $340. If shoppers use these price points as reference prices when comparing different suits, what would be the effect of adding a new line of suits priced to sell at $280. Would you expect sales of the $250 suits to increase, decrease, or stay the same? Why? What would be the effect of adding a line of suits priced at $450?

3. Which of the five product mix pricing situations found in Table 11.1 apply to the following examples? (a) Ben & Jerry's sells the residue or sludge produced in the ice cream manufacturing process to farmers for use as animal feed. (b) Sony offers to sell its latest 32-inch color television set with a set of additional six speakers to enhance DVD sound. (c) Sega's video game system will only play Sega games. (d) At many of its popular resorts, Marriott offers weekend packages that include a two-night stay, a complementary breakfast, valet parking, and two tickets to a local theme park.

4. Consider the following scenario: Each week of the year, the owner of a small gift store orders a case of 24 candles from its supplier. The supplier offers a cash discount of 2/10 net 30 to encourage prompt payment. Each case of candles costs $24.00 before the discount. The 2 percent discounts seems so small that the owner rarely takes it, instead waiting to pay the bill on the 30th day. Should the owner take the discount or not? Why?

5. Companies will often adjust their basic prices to allow for differences in customers, products, and locations. List and briefly describe the different forms of segmented pricing. Provide an example (other than those provided in the text) of each of these forms. Which forms might be used in pricing products on the Internet? Explain.

6. Houston's Gallery Furniture not only sells from its showroom and warehouse facility but also promotes its products nationwide via an elaborate Web site (www.gallery-furniture.com). When visiting the Web site, consumers can see showroom furniture in real time via robotic cameras. Locally, Gallery Furniture boasts, "Buy it today, receive it by tonight!" Recently, it declared that one of its new goals was to expand statewide and nationwide with aggressive pricing policies. Which of the geographical pricing methods described in the chapter should Gallery Furniture use in this expansion?

7. Formulate rules that might govern (a) initiating a price cut, (b) initiating a price increase, (c) a negative reaction on the part of buyers to a price change by your company, (d) a competitor's response to your price change, and (e) your response to a competitor's price change. State the assumptions underlying your proposed rules.

8. Some analysts see predatory pricing by a strong, competitive marketer extremely damaging to competition and well-functioning economy. Others view it simply as good, healthy competition. Take a stand on this issue and discuss your view. Consider questions of ethics, long-term survival, the competitive environment, consumer benefits and welfare, and stockholder profit.

INTERACTIVE MARKETING APPLICATIONS

1. If you want the best airfare deals, look to the Internet—many others are. Experts say that the key to getting the best fares is to avoid locking yourself into a single approach, whether it's using a reservation call center, a flesh-and-blood travel agent, an online agent, or an airline's Web site. Smart consumers do their homework, paying attention to full-fare prices, markdown rates, restrictions, and competitive booking options. Currently, the top airline sites for domestic travel are Continental Airlines (www.continental.com), American Airlines (www.AA.com), United Airlines (www.ual.com), Delta Airlines (www.delta-air.com), and fast-growing Southwest Airlines (www.iflyswa.com). Non-airline sites include AOL Travel (www.aol.com), Travelocity (www.travelocity.com), Expedia (www.expedia.com), Lowestfare (www.lowestfare.com), and Cheaptickets (www.cheaptickets.com).

a. Investigate a sampling of these Web sites. What can you determine about the ticket-pricing policies of airlines? Do they apply any of the pricing strategies discussed in the chapter?

b. Design a hypothetical trip and use several of the sites to book tickets (cancel when it comes time to pay). Critique your experience. How much does pricing have to do with your choice of a booking procedure and airline? What other factors are important?

c. Which of the sites for obtaining airline tickets seems the best?

d. How should travel agencies deal with the increasing use of online ticket purchasing?

e. What is the future of online booking and the travel agency industry. What impact will this have on airline pricing?

2. The computer printer industry is intensively competitive with respect to pricing. Only a few years ago, consumers were often shocked to find that a good printer could account for up to 50 percent of the cost of an entire home computer setup. No more! Recently, companies such as Epson, Hewlett-Packard, Canon, Tektronix, and Xerox have all introduced expanded lines of technologically advanced but less expensive models. Despite dramatic improvements in speed, quality, and optional features, today's printers sell at much lower prices than their predecessors. The industry is even producing high-quality, portable, color models at reasonable prices.

   a. What role does pricing play in a consumer's selection of a home printer? An office printer? A portable printer to be taken on business trips?

   b. What pricing strategies are Epson, Hewlett-Packard, Canon, Xerox and other companies using to sell color printers, personal computers, home offices, and mobile offices? (Visit each Web site to get additional information.) Which companies appear to have the most effective pricing strategies? Explain.

   c. Assume that you are the marketing manager of a company that is introducing a new line of color printers and is seeking quick entry into the small color-printer market. Assume that your products are comparable to those of primary competitors and that your have the funds necessary to compete with the industry leaders. Design a pricing strategy for capturing business in the home computer, home office, and mobile office markets. What factors would be critical to your product's success? How could you combat competitive reaction to your entry?

 INTERNET CONNECTIONS

PRODUCT MIX PRICING STRATEGIES

In the automotive industry, slightly altered versions of the same vehicle are sometimes marketed under different brand names. For example, the Ford Explorer and the Mercury Mountaineer are essentially the same vehicle. The Mountaineer is shipped with a greater number of standard features and a higher price tag. It was designed to appeal to women and contains many safety features important to this target group. Visit Edmund's car buying service at www.edmunds.com. Look under new trucks for the Ford Explorer and the Mercury Mountaineer. Find the least expensive base model for each vehicle and complete the chart below. For each feature on which you compare the vehicles, list that feature by name. Then indicate which of the models is equipped with the feature.

Item	Ford Explorer	Mercury Mountaineer
Price (MSRP)		
Feature (specify)		
Feature (specify)		
Feature (specify)		
Feature (specify)		

FOR DISCUSSION

1. What new product pricing strategy do you think Mercury used when it introduced the Mountaineer?
2. Do you think the extra features listed above cost the manufacturer the difference in price charged?
3. Is the manufacturer using psychological pricing as well? How?
4. Why do you think Ford introduced its "Explorer look-alike" under the Mercury brand rather than extending the Explorer line and using product-form pricing?

SAVVY SITES

- The Robinson-Patman Act (RPA) concerns price discrimination. The LawMall (www.lawmall.com/rpa) maintains a special RPA section that targets businesses.
- Online auctions are huge business and demonstrate the Internet's ability to allow different prices for different surfers. See eBay (www.ebay.com) to compare prices on various auctions for one product.
- At Priceline (www.priceline.com) customers can name their own prices for airline tickets, hotel rooms, cars, and more.

NOTES

1. Portions adapted from Valerie Reitman, "Retail Resistance: Eliminated Discounts on P&G Goods Annoy Many Who Sell Them," *Wall Street Journal,* August 11, 1992, pp. A1, A3. Also see Zachary Schiller, "Not Everyone Loves a Supermarket Special," *Business Week,* February 17, 1992, pp. 64–68; Karen Benezra, "Beyond Value," *Brandweek,* October 7, 1996, pp. 14–16; Dagmar Mussey, "Heat's on Value Pricing," *Advertising Age International,* January 1997, pp. i21–i22; and Cathy Bond, "P&G's Gamble: Price or Promotion?" *Marketing,* February 13, 1997, pp. 30–33. For additional interesting insights, see Kusum L. Aliwadi, Donald R. Lehmann, and Scott A. Neslin, "Understanding Market Response to a Long-Term Change in Marketing Mix: An Analysis of P&G's Value Pricing Strategy," working paper, Dartmouth University, August 5, 1999.

2. For a comprehensive discussion of pricing strategies, see Thomas T. Nagle and Reed K. Holden, *The Strategy and Tactics of Pricing,* 2nd ed. (Upper Saddle River, NJ: Prentice Hall, 1995). Also see Joshua D. Libresco, "The Pricing Game, Have I Got a Deal for You," *Marketing News,* December 8, 1997, p. 10.

3. Andy Reinhardt, "Pentium: The Next Generation," *Business Week,* May 12, 1997, pp. 42–43.

4. See Marcia Savage, "Intel Set to Slash Pentium II Prices," *Computer Reseller News,* February 8, 1999, pp. 1, 10.

5. Seanna Browder, "Nintendo: At the Top of Its Game," *Business Week,* June 9, 1997, pp. 72–73; and Orit Gadiesh and James L. Gilbert, "Profit Pools: A Fresh Look at Strategy," *Harvard Business Review,* May–June 1999, p. 140.

6. Susan Krafft, "Love, Love Me Doo," *American Demographics,* June 1994, pp. 15–16; Damon Darlin, "Zoo Doo," *Forbes,* May 22, 1995, p. 92; and the Zoo Doo Web site (www.zoodoo.com), March 2000.

7. See Nagle and Holden, *The Strategy and Tactics of Pricing,* pp. 225–28; and Manjit S. Yadav and Kent B. Monroe, "How Buyers Perceive Savings in a Bundle Price: An Examination of a Bundle's Transaction Value," *Journal of Marketing Research,* August 1993, pp. 350–58.

8. See Gary M. Erickson and Johnny K. Johansson, "The Role of Price in Multi-Attribute Product Evaluations," *Journal of Consumer Research,* September 1985, pp. 195–99.

9. For more reading on reference prices and psychological pricing, see K. N. Rajendran and Gerard J. Tellis, "Contextual and Temporal Components of Reference Price," *Journal of Marketing,* January 1994, pp. 22–34; Richard A. Briesch, Lakshman Krishnamurthi, Tridib Mazumdar, and S. P. Raj, "A Comparative Analysis of Reference Price Models," *Journal of Consumer Research,* September 1997, pp. 202–14; John Huston and Nipoli Kamdar, "$9.99: Can 'Just-Below' Pricing Be Reconciled with Rationality?" *Eastern Economic Journal,* Spring 1996, pp. 137–45; Robert M. Schindler and Patrick N. Kirby, "Patterns of Right-Most Digits Used in Advertised Prices: Implications for Nine-Ending Effects," *Journal of Consumer Research,* September 1997, pp. 192–201; Michel Wedel and Peter S. H. Leeflang, "A Model for the Effects of Psychological Pricing in Gabor-Granger Price Studies," *Journal of Economic Psychology,* April 1998, pp. 237–60; and Dhruv Grewal, Kent B. Monroe, Chris Janiszewski, and Donald R. Lichtenstein, "A Range Theory of Price Perception," *Journal of Consumer Research,* March 1999, pp. 353–68.

10. Tim Ambler, "Kicking Price Promotion Habit Is Like Getting Off Heroin—Hard," *Marketing,* May 27, 1999, p. 24.

11. Jack Trout, "Prices: Simple Guidelines to Get Them Right," *The Journal of Business Strategy,* November–December 1998, pp. 13–16.

12. Philip R. Cateora, *International Marketing,* 7th ed. (Homewood, IL: Richard D. Irwin, 1990), p. 540. Also see S. Tamer Cavusgil, "Pricing for Global Markets," *Columbia Journal of World Business,* Winter 1996, pp. 66–78; and Sak Onkvisit and John R. Shaw, *International Marketing: Analysis and Strategy* (Upper Saddle River, NJ: Prentice Hall, 1997), chap. 16.

13. Eric Mitchell, "How Not to Raise Prices," *Small Business Reports,* November 1990, pp. 64–67.

14. For an interesting discussion of buyer perceptions of price increases, see Margaret C. Campbell, "Perceptions of Price Unfairness: Antecedents and Consequences," *Journal of Marketing Research,* May 1999, pp. 187–99.

15. Jonathon Berry and Zachary Schiller, "Attack of the Fighting Brands," *Business Week,* May 2, 1994, p. 125; and Jeff Ansell, "Luvs," *Advertising Age,* June 30, 1997, p. S16.

16. For an excellent discussion of these issues, see Dhruv Grewel and Larry D. Compeau, "Pricing and Public Policy: A Research Agenda and Overview of Special Issue," *Journal of Marketing and Public Policy,* Spring 1999, pp. 3–10.

17. David Barboza, "Archer Daniels Executive Said to Tell of Price-Fixing Talks with Cargill Counterpart," *New York Times,* June 17, 1999, p. 6.

18. Holman W. Jenkins Jr., "Business World: Flying the 'Angry' Skies," *Wall Street Journal,* April 29, 1998, p. A23.

19. John Greenwald, "Bird of Prey," *Time,* May 24, 1999, p. 66.

20. Mike France, "Does Predatory Pricing Make Microsoft a Predator?" *Business Week,* November 23, 1998, pp. 130–32.

21. Grewel and Compeau, "Pricing and Public Policy: A Research Agenda and Overview of Special Issue," p. 8.

22. For more on public policy and pricing, see Louis W. Stern and Thomas L. Eovaldi, *Legal Aspects of Marketing Strategy* (Upper Saddle River, NJ: Prentice Hall, 1984), chap. 5; Robert J. Posch, *The Complete Guide to Marketing and the Law* (Upper Saddle River, NJ: Prentice Hall, 1988), chap. 28; Nagle and Holden, *The Strategy and Tactics of Pricing,* chap. 14; Joseph P. Guiltinan and Gregory Gunlach, "Aggressive and Predatory Pricing: A Framework for Analysis," *Journal of Marketing,* July 1996, pp. 87–102; Bruce Upbin, "Vindication," *Forbes,* November 17, 1997, pp. 52–56; and Grewel and Compeau, "Pricing and Public Policy: A Research Agenda and Overview of Special Issue," pp. 3–10.

Circuit City: Selling Used Cars Like Stereos

A HASSLE!

Buying a used car. Just mention the subject, and anyone with experience will probably frown and immediately launch into a sad story about his or her last purchase. The used-car salesperson, in fact, is often what people have in mind when they think about marketing's excesses.

So why would Circuit City, a company that has succeeded in selling stereos, televisions, car radios, and other electronic items through its 300 superstores, suddenly try selling used cars? Why, when management consultants advise companies to "stick to their knitting," would an electronics retailer try its hand at used cars?

THE USED CAR MARKET

The answer is simple: new car prices. During the past ten years, the average new car price has risen 70 percent to about $19,500. Government mandated pollution controls and safety features have driven the price increases. Over that same period, however, median family income and the consumer price index have risen only about 40 percent. For some consumers, today's new cars cost as much as their houses! Consumers also understand that new-car quality has improved and that the average used car on dealers' lots today is only 3.5 years old. Thus, they reason, they can get a low-mileage used car that will be very reliable and save $5,000 to $10,000 in the process. Moreover, surveys show that the value consumers place on new cars as a status symbol has steadily declined and that used cars have increased in status.

Besides growing demand for used cars, supply has also increased. To encourage consumers to buy new cars, many manufacturers and dealers have turned to leasing programs that allow consumers to drive new cars and turn them in after two to three years. The dealers then resell the used cars. Further, the growth of the rental car business has resulted in a growing supply of used rental cars as the companies turn over their fleets.

Moreover, although it used to be difficult to finance used cars, banks and finance companies are offering financing for used cars at interest rates only slightly above those they charge for new car loans. Whereas lenders once saw used car buyers as higher credit risks, today's new car buyers actually have higher loan default rates.

Finally, dealers may earn more net profit by selling a used car. A recent survey indicated that a used-car sale produced an average net profit of $265, versus a $130 profit for a new car.

PLUGGING INTO A NEW WAY

Despite these changes in demand and supply, however, the process of selling and buying used cars has not changed much. Because most consumers buy cars infrequently, they often are at a disadvantage dealing with used-car salespeople. Consumers have to negotiate the price of the used car as well as the price the dealer will pay for any trade-in that is involved. Consumers worry about whether they are paying too much or getting too little. They worry about the car's quality. The process produces hassled, worried, and dissatisfied customers.

Circuit City believes it can change all this by applying the principles of electronics retailing to selling used cars. In 1993, the company started CarMax, the Auto Superstore, to carry out its vision. It opened its first CarMax store in Richmond, Virginia, and a second in Raleigh, North Carolina, in 1994.

A SIMPLE STRATEGY

CarMax's strategy is straightforward. It located its Raleigh store, for example, on the city's outskirts where the company could buy a large piece of land on a major highway. On the nine-acre tract, CarMax displays up to 500 used cars, a selection far larger than the typical used-car lot. The typical store serves a market area with a 25- to 40-mile radius.

Customers enter an attractive display room, similar to one in a new-car dealership. If they bring their children along, there is an attended child-care area complete with toys and video games. A sales associate clad in a blue polo shirt and khakis greets customers and escorts them to a computer kiosk. The associate finds out what type of car the consumer is seeking. Using a computer touch screen, the associate can call up a full listing of all the cars or trucks in stock that meet the customer's criteria. For example, if the customer is interested in late-model sport-utility vehicles priced between $12,000 and $17,000, the computer will quickly display each such model in inventory by brand and model. The display shows a color picture of the vehicle; lists its features, such as four-wheel drive; and details its specifications, such as engine type and EPA gas-mileage estimates.

The screen also presents CarMax's price for the vehicle, a price based on the average retail price in the NADA "Blue Book" that car dealers use. The company says its prices are $500 to $1,000 lower than the average retail book value. The customer can print a copy of the information, including the picture and the vehicle's location on CarMax's lot. The customer is then free to look at the vehicle, which is located in a specified parking place on the lot. In addition, all similar vehicles, such as other sport-utility vehicles, are located in the same area rather than being spread haphazardly across the lot. CarMax pays its salespeople commissions based on the number of cars they sell, not based on the profit from each sale. Thus, the salesperson has no incentive to push the customer to look at more expensive vehicles.

Before putting cars it buys on its lot, CarMax's mechanics carry out a 110-point inspection and thorough cleaning, even cleaning the engine. The employees add new tires or make other repairs as needed. No car on the lot is more than five years old. CarMax offers a five-day money-back guarantee and a 30-day comprehensive warranty. For an additional cost, it also offers extended warranties that stretch up to three years.

If the customer decides to buy the vehicle, there is no haggling over price. The price CarMax sets is its sales price. There is no negotiation. There are no hidden or extra fees, just state sales tax, title, and tag charges. Circuit City has its own financing company, and the CarMax associate can arrange financing for the purchase in 20 minutes. The company has also started offering leases for used cars. If the customer wants to sell his or her current car, CarMax will make an offer based on that car's Blue Book value. Each store has 8 to 15 full-time vehicle buyers and appraisers. The offer is not dependent on the customer purchasing a car. CarMax will purchase the car even if the customer does not want to buy another car from CarMax. The company also offers on-site car insurance service. Customers find that the entire sales process can take less than an hour.

THE BOTTOM LINE

Circuit City started CarMax as an experiment. Many traditional new and used car dealers argued that the majority of buyers want to negotiate and that, in fact, "no-haggle" prices would not produce lower prices for consumers. Others argued that there simply were not enough good locations with the 15-acre parcels needed for used-car superstores available in large urban areas.

But so far the results look good. Customers report that they like the no-pressure sales approach, and cars are flying off CarMax lots. The company opened its fifth store in March 1996 and reported sales at its first four stores totaled $304.5 million for the year ending February 29, 1996. This

represented the first time Circuit City had provided detailed information about CarMax's operations. Many observers were surprised by the higher-than-expected sales numbers and by CarMax's lower-than-expected loss of $7 million. Analysts attributed the loss to the significant start-up expenses associated with establishing dealerships. Analysts estimated that it cost up to $10 million to open a superstore. By late 1999, CarMax had expanded to 38 stores and had plans to have 80 to 90 stores by 2002. In addition, CarMax had entered the new-car sales arena by buying new-car franchises. CarMax President W. Austin Ligon reported that all the stores that had been open more than a year were profitable, but that the costs of expansion and implementing standardized systems had been greater than projected. For the nine months ending in November 1999, CarMax reported sales of $1.51 billion versus $1.09 billion for the nine months ending November 1998. The company reported earning $2.8 million for the nine-month period ending in November 1999 versus a loss of $13.5 million for the nine months ending in November 1998. CarMax's sales were 80 percent used cars and 20 percent new cars for the period ending November 1999. Ligon also indicated that a typical CarMax store needs to sell 400 to 600 cars a month when it is fully established, a process that takes about three to four years. By comparison, a typical new car dealer would sell about 700 used cars in a year.

Circuit City's experiment has attracted competition. Wayne Huizenga, the founder of Blockbuster video, jumped into the used-car business by starting AutoNation in late 1995 and announced plans to have 80 to 90 superstores by 2000, up from seven in early 1997. In late December 1999, however, AutoNation shocked the industry by announcing that it would close 23 of its used-car superstores and convert the remaining six into new-car franchises. Company officials indicated the superstores had been losing money.

Several new-car dealers who became concerned about the new trend teamed up to form Driver's Mart in early 1996. Rather than opening company-owned superstores like CarMax and AutoNation, Driver's Mart has established a strict franchise agreement and is looking for new car dealers with high customer satisfaction ratings who want to sign up for exclusive territories. Driver's Mart intends to locate in the top 100 U.S. markets by 2000. The typical dealer will have to invest about $4 million in land and buildings and $6 million in a 350-to-600 car inventory. That dealer will need to sell about 4,000 cars per year at average prices of $13,000 to $15,000.

Industry observers are divided over whether or not CarMax and its competitors can make money with their used-car superstores. They are also divided over whether there are enough customers who want a no-haggle car-buying experience to support the companies' aggressive expansion plans. Moreover, the analysts wonder if the superstores can really be profitable with only one profit center—used cars. Perhaps that is why CarMax has moved to sell new cars also. Some analysts noted that many car manufacturers were holding the line on new-car prices and offering so many incentives that monthly costs for a new car could be less than for a used car. Will the bottom line be satisfied customers and profitable superstores, or will the industry return to its traditional operating model—lots of small dealers with limited selections negotiating with buyers in a high-pressure environment?

Questions

1. What product-mix pricing strategies do automobile dealers and manufacturers typically follow?
2. What price adjustment strategies do car dealers use?
3. How is CarMax changing the used-car industry's pricing strategies? How have buyers and competitors reacted to these changes?
4. What marketing recommendations would you make to CarMax?

Sources: Douglas Lavin, "Cars Are Sold Like Stereos by Circuit City," *Wall Street Journal,* June 8, 1994, p. B1; Douglas Lavin, "Stiff Showroom Prices Drive More Americans to Purchase Used Cars," *Wall Street Journal,* November 1, 1994, p. A1; J. Ward Best, "Maxed Out? Circuit City Bets Used Car Market Is Far from It," *Raleigh News and Observer,* November 6, 1994, p. F1; Gabriella Stern, " 'Nearly New' Autos for Sale: Dealers Buff Up Their Marketing of Used Cars," *Wall Street Journal,* February 17, 1995, p. B1; Bradford Wernle, "Dealers Launch Used-Car Chain," *Automotive News,* February 12, 1996, p. 1; Gregory J. Gilligan, "Circuit City's CarMax Superstores Pass $300 Million in Yearly Sales," *Knight-Ridder/Tribune Business News,* April 5, 1996, p. 4050139; Michael Rose, "Trio of Used-Car Superstores Peels Across U.S.," *Business Journal-Portland,* April 4, 1997, p. 19; David Welsh, "CarMax Roars into the Tarrant County, Texas, Auto Sales Arena," *Knight-Ridder/Tribune Business News,* December 9, 1997, p. 1029B1132; Terry Box, "Used-Car Megastores Take on Look of New-Car Dealerships," *Knight-Ridder/Tribune Business News,* June 14, 1999, p. OKRB9916503C; "Circuit City Stores, Inc. Reports Third Quarter Results for the Group and the CarMax Group," *PR Newswire,* December 17, 1999, p. 4714.

After studying this chapter, you should be able to
1. explain why companies use distribution channels and discuss the functions these channels perform
2. discuss how channel members interact and how they organize to perform the work of the channel
3. identify the major channel alternatives open to a company
4. discuss the nature and importance of physical distribution
5. analyze integrated logistics, including how it may be achieved and its benefits to the company

DISTRIBUTION CHANNELS AND LOGISTICS MANAGEMENT

For more than half a century, Caterpillar has dominated the world's markets for heavy construction and mining equipment. Its familiar yellow tractors, crawlers, loaders, and trucks are a common sight at any construction area. With sales of $21 billion, Caterpillar is half again as large as its nearest competitor. It now captures over a 40 percent share of the world's heavy-construction equipment market, selling more than 300 products in nearly 200 countries. Caterpillar has posted 6 straight record years of record sales.

Many factors contribute to Caterpillar's enduring success— high-quality products, flexible and efficient manufacturing, a steady stream of innovative new products, and a lean organization that is responsive to

customer needs. Although Caterpillar charges premium prices for its equipment, its high-quality and trouble-free operation provide greater long-term value. Yet these are not the most important reasons for Caterpillar's dominance. Instead, Caterpillar Chairman and CEO Glen Barton credits the company's focus on customers and its worldwide distribution system, which does a superb job of taking care of every

customer need. Former CEO Donald Fites agrees: "The biggest reason for Caterpillar's success has been our system of distribution and product support and the close customer relationships its fosters. . . . The backbone of that system is our 195 dealers around the world who sell and service our [equipment]."

Caterpillar's dealers provide a wide range of important services to customers. Fites summarizes:

After the product leaves our door, the dealers take over. They are the ones on the frontline. They're the ones who live with the product for its lifetime. They're the ones customers see. Although we offer financing and insurance, they arrange those deals for customers. They're out there making sure that when a machine is delivered, it's in the condition it's supposed to be in. They're out there training a customer's operators. They service a product frequently throughout its life, carefully monitoring a machine's health and scheduling repairs to prevent costly downtime. The customer . . . knows that there is a $20-billion-plus company called Caterpillar. But the dealers create the image of a company that doesn't just stand behind its products but with its products, anywhere in the world. Our dealers are the reason that our motto—Buy the Iron, Get the Company—is not an empty slogan.

Caterpillar's dealers build strong customer relationships in their communities. "Our independent dealer in Novi, Michigan, or in Bangkok, Thailand, knows so much more about the requirements of customers in those locations than a huge corporation like Caterpillar could," says Fites. Competitors often bypass their dealers and sell directly to big customers to cut costs or make more profits for themselves. However, Caterpillar wouldn't think of going around its dealers. "The knowledge of the local market and the close relations with customers that our dealers provide are worth every penny," he asserts with passion. "We'd rather cut off our right arm than sell directly to customers and bypass our dealers."

Caterpillar and its dealers work in close harmony to find better ways to bring value to customers. Says Fites, "We genuinely treat our system and theirs as one." The entire system is linked by a single worldwide computer network. For example, working at their desktop computers, Caterpillar managers can check to see how many Cat machines in the world are waiting for parts. Closely linked dealers play a vital role in almost every aspect of Caterpillar's operations, from product design and delivery, to product service and support, to market intelligence and customer feedback.

In the heavy-equipment industry, in which equipment downtime can mean big losses, Caterpillar's exceptional service gives it a huge advantage in winning and keeping customers. For example, consider Freeport-McMoRan, a Cat customer that operates one of the world's largest copper and gold mines, 24 hours a day, 365 days a year. High in the mountains of Indonesia, the mine is accessible only by aerial cableway or helicopter. Freeport-McMoRan relies on more than 500 pieces of Caterpillar mining and construction equipment—worth several hundred million dollars—including loaders, tractors, and mammoth 240-ton, 2,000-plus-horsepower trucks. Many of these machines cost well over $1 million apiece. When equipment breaks down, Freeport-McMoRan loses money fast. Thus, Freeport-McMoRan gladly pays a premium price for machines and service on which it can count. It knows that it can count on Caterpillar and its outstanding distribution network for superb support.

The close working relationship between Caterpillar and its dealers comes down to more than just formal contracts and business agreements. According to Fites, the powerful partnership rests on a handful of basic principles and practices:

- *Dealer profitability:* Caterpillar's rule: "Share the gain as well as the pain." When times are good, Caterpillar shares the bounty with its dealers rather than trying to grab all the riches for itself. When times are bad, Caterpillar protects its dealers. For example, in the mid-1980s, facing a depressed global construction-equipment market and cutthroat competition, Caterpillar sheltered its dealers by absorbing much of the economic damage. It lost almost $1 billion in just three years but didn't lose a single dealer. In contrast, competitors' dealers struggled and many failed. As a result, Caterpillar emerged with its distribution system intact and its competitive position stronger than ever.

- *Extraordinary dealer support:* Nowhere is this support more apparent than in the company's parts delivery system, the fastest and most reliable in the industry. Caterpillar maintains 22 parts facilities around the world, which stock 320,000 different parts and ship 84,000 items per day, about one per second every day of the year. In turn, dealers have made huge investments in inventory, warehouses, fleets of trucks, service bays, diagnostic and service equipment, and information technology. Together, Caterpillar and its dealers guarantee parts delivery within 48 hours anywhere in the world. The company ships 80 percent of parts orders immediately and 99 percent on the same day the order is received. In contrast, it's not unusual for competitors' customers to wait four or five days for a part.

- *Communications:* Caterpillar communicates with its dealers—fully, frequently, and honestly. According to Fites, "There are no secrets between us and our dealers. We have the financial statements and key operating data of every dealer in the world. . . . In addition, virtually all Caterpillar and dealer employees have real-time access to continually updated databases of service information, sales trends and forecasts, customer satisfaction surveys, and other critical data. . . . [Moreover,] virtually everyone from the youngest design engineer to the CEO now has direct contact with somebody in our dealer organizations."

- *Dealer performance:* Caterpillar does all it can to ensure that its dealerships are run well. It closely monitors each dealership's sales, market position, service capability, financial situation, and other performance measures. It genuinely wants each dealer to succeed, and when it sees a problem, it jumps in to help. As a result, Caterpillar dealerships, many of which are family businesses, tend to be stable and profitable. The average Caterpillar dealership has remained in the hands of the same family for more than 50 years. Some actually predate the 1925 merger that created Caterpillar.

- *Personal relationships:* In addition to more formal business ties, Cat forms close personal ties with its dealers in a kind of family relationship. Fites relates the following example: "When I see Chappy Chapman, a retired executive vice-president . . ., out on the golf course, he always asks about particular dealers or about their children, who may be running the business now. And every time I see those dealers, they inquire, 'How's Chappy?' That's the sort of relationship we have. . . . I consider the majority of dealers personal friends."

Thus, Caterpillar's superb distribution system serves as a major source of competitive advantage. The system is built on a firm base of mutual trust and shared dreams. Caterpillar and its dealers feel a deep pride in what they are accomplishing together. As Fites puts it, "There's a camaraderie among our dealers around the world that really makes it more than just a financial arrangement. They feel that what they're doing is good for the world because they are part of an organization that makes, sells, and tends to the machines that make the world work."[1]

Marketing channel decisions are among the most important decisions that management faces. A company's channel decisions are linked with every other marketing decision. The company's pricing depends on whether it uses mass merchandisers or high-quality specialty stores. The firm's sales force and advertising decisions depend on how much persuasion, training, motivation, and support the dealers need. Whether a company develops or acquires certain new products may depend on how well those products fit the capabilities of its channel members.

Companies often pay too little attention to their distribution channels, however, sometimes with damaging results. In contrast, many companies have used imaginative distribution systems to *gain* a competitive advantage. Federal Express's creative and imposing distribution system made it the leader in the small-package delivery industry. General Electric gained a strong advantage in selling its major appliances by supporting its dealers with a sophisticated computerized order-processing and delivery system. Dell Computer revolutionized its industry by selling personal computers directly to consumers rather than through retail stores. Charles Schwab & Company pioneered the delivery of financial services via the Internet.

Distribution channel decisions often involve long-term commitments to other firms. For example, companies such as Ford, IBM, or McDonald's can easily change their advertising, pricing, or promotion programs. They can scrap old products and introduce new ones as market tastes demand. But when they set up distribution channels through contracts with franchisees, independent dealers, or large retailers, they cannot readily replace these channels with company-owned stores if conditions change. Therefore, management must design its channels carefully, with an eye on tomorrow's likely selling environment as well as today's.

This chapter examines four major questions concerning distribution channels: What is the nature of distribution channels? How do channel firms interact and organize to do the work of the channel? What problems do companies face in designing and managing their channels? What role does physical distribution play in attracting and satisfying customers? In chapter 13, we will look at distribution channel issues from the viewpoint of retailers and wholesalers.

THE NATURE OF DISTRIBUTION CHANNELS

Distribution channel
A set of interdependent organizations involved in the process of making a product or service available for use or consumption by the consumer or business user.

Most producers use intermediaries to bring their products to market. They try to forge a **distribution channel**—a set of interdependent organizations involved in the process of making a product or service available for use or consumption by the consumer or business user.[2]

Why Are Marketing Intermediaries Used?

Why do producers give some of the selling job to intermediaries? After all, doing so means giving up some control over how and to whom the products are sold. The use of intermediaries results from their greater efficiency in making goods available to target markets. Through their contacts, experience, specialization, and scale of operation, intermediaries usually offer the firm more than it can achieve on its own.

Figure 12.1 shows how using intermediaries can provide economies. Figure 12.1a shows three manufacturers, each using direct marketing to reach three customers. This system requires nine different contacts. Figure 12.1b shows the three manufacturers working through one distributor, who contacts the three customers. This system requires only six contacts. In this way, intermediaries reduce the amount of work that must be done by both producers and consumers.

From the economic system's point of view, the role of marketing intermediaries is to transform the assortments of products made by producers into the assortments wanted by consumers. Producers make narrow assortments of products in large quan-

A. Number of contacts without a distributor
$M \times C = 3 \times 3 = 9$

B. Number of contacts with a distributor
$M + C = 3 + 3 = 6$

= Manufacturer   = Customer   = Distributor

FIGURE 12.1   How a marketing intermediary reduces the number of channel transactions

tities, but consumers want broad assortments of products in small quantities. In the distribution channels, intermediaries buy large quantities from many producers and break them down into the smaller quantities and broader assortments wanted by consumers. Thus, intermediaries play an important role in matching supply and demand.

The concept of distribution channels is not limited to the distribution of tangible products. Producers of services and ideas also face the problem of making their output available to target populations. In the private sector, retail stores, hotels, banks, and other service providers take great care to make their services conveniently available to target customers. In the public sector, service organizations and agencies develop "educational distribution systems" and "health care delivery systems" for reaching sometimes widely dispersed populations. Hospitals must be located to serve various patient populations, and schools must be located close to the children who need to be taught. Communities must locate their fire stations to provide rapid response to fires and polling stations must be placed where people can vote conveniently.

Distribution Channel Functions

The distribution channel moves goods and services from producers to consumers. It overcomes the major time, place, and possession gaps that separate goods and services from those who would use them. Members of the marketing channel perform many key functions. Some help to complete transactions.

* *Information:* gathering and distributing marketing research and intelligence information about actors and forces in the marketing environment needed for planning and aiding exchange.
* *Promotion:* developing and spreading persuasive communications about an offer.
* *Contact:* finding and communicating with prospective buyers.
* *Matching:* shaping and fitting the offer to the buyer's needs, including activities such as manufacturing, grading, assembling, and packaging.
* *Negotiation:* reaching an agreement on price and other terms of the offer so that ownership or possession can be transferred.

Others help to fulfill the completed transactions:

* *Physical distribution:* transporting and storing goods.
* *Financing:* acquiring and using funds to cover the costs of the channel work.
* *Risk taking:* assuming the risks of carrying out the channel work.

The question is not *whether* these functions need to be performed—they must be—but rather *who* will perform them. To the extent that the manufacturer performs these functions, its costs go up and its prices have to be higher. At the same time, when some of these functions are shifted to intermediaries, the producer's costs and prices may be lower, but the intermediaries must charge more to cover the costs of their work. In dividing the work of the channel, the various functions should be assigned to the channel members who can perform them most efficiently and effectively to provide satisfactory assortments of goods to target consumers.

Channel level
A layer of intermediaries that performs some work in bringing the product and its ownership closer to the final buyer.

Number of Channel Levels

Distribution channels can be described by the number of channel levels involved. Each layer of marketing intermediaries that performs some work in bringing the product and its ownership closer to the final buyer is a **channel level.** Because the

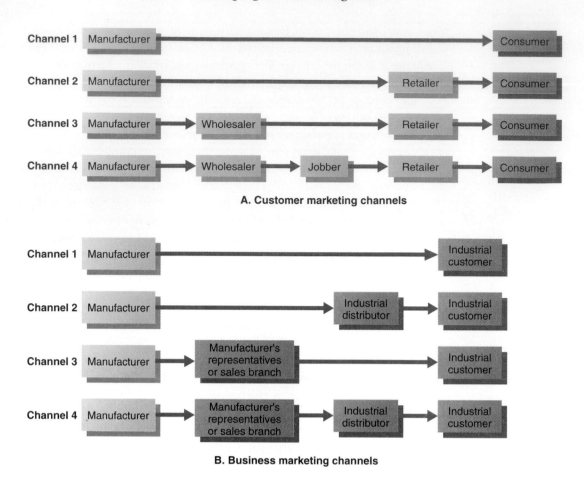

A. Customer marketing channels

B. Business marketing channels

FIGURE 12.2   Consumer and business marketing channels

Direct marketing channel
A marketing channel that has no intermediary levels.

Indirect marketing channel
Channel containing one or more intermediary levels.

producer and the final consumer both perform some work, they are part of every channel. We use the *number of intermediary levels* to indicate the *length* of a channel. Figure 12.2a shows several consumer distribution channels of different lengths.

Channel 1, called a **direct marketing channel,** has no intermediary levels. It consists of a company selling directly to consumers. For example, Avon, Amway, and Tupperware sell their products door to door or through home and office sales parties; Lands' End and Fingerhut sell products direct through mail order, telephone, or at their Web sites; and Singer sells its sewing machines through its own stores. The remaining channels in Figure 12.2a are **indirect marketing channels.** Channel 2 contains one intermediary level. In consumer markets, this level is typically a retailer. For example, the makers of televisions, cameras, tires, furniture, major appliances, and many other products sell their goods directly to large retailers such as Wal-Mart and Sears, which then sell the goods to final consumers. Channel 3 contains two intermediary levels, a wholesaler and a retailer. This channel is often used by small manufacturers of food, drugs, hardware, and other products. Channel 4 contains three intermediary levels. In the meatpacking industry, for example, jobbers buy from wholesalers and sell to smaller retailers who generally are not served by larger wholesalers. Distribution channels with even more levels are sometimes found, but less often. From the producer's point of view, a greater number of levels means less control and greater channel complexity.

Figure 12.2b shows some common business distribution channels. The business marketer can use its own sales force to sell directly to business customers. It can also sell to industrial distributors, who in turn sell to business customers. It can sell through manufacturer's representatives or its own sales branches to business customers, or it can use these representatives and branches to sell through industrial distributors. Thus, business markets commonly include multilevel distribution channels.

All of the institutions in the channel are connected by several types of *flows*. These include the *physical flow* of products, the *flow of ownership*, the *payment flow*, the *information flow*, and the *promotion flow*. These flows can make even channels with only one or a few levels very complex.

CHANNEL BEHAVIOR AND ORGANIZATION

Distribution channels are more than simple collections of firms tied together by various flows. They are complex behavioral systems in which people and companies interact to accomplish individual, company, and channel goals. Some channel systems consist only of informal interactions among loosely organized firms; others consist of formal interactions guided by strong organizational structures. Moreover, channel systems do not stand still—new types of intermediaries emerge and whole new channel systems evolve. Here we look at channel behavior and at how members organize to do the work of the channel.

Channel Behavior

A distribution channel consists of firms that have banded together for their common good. Each channel member is dependent on the others. For example, a Ford dealer depends on the Ford Motor Company to design cars that meet consumer needs. In turn, Ford depends on the dealer to attract consumers, persuade them to buy Ford cars, and service cars after the sale. The Ford dealer also depends on other dealers to provide good sales and service that will uphold the reputation of Ford and its dealer body. In fact, the success of individual Ford dealers depends on how well the entire Ford distribution channel competes with the channels of other auto manufacturers.

Each channel member plays a role in the channel and specializes in performing one or more functions. For example, Compaq's role is to produce personal computers that consumers will like and to create demand through national advertising. Best Buy's role is to display these Compaq computers in convenient locations, to answer buyers' questions, and to close sales. The channel will be most effective when each member is assigned the tasks it can do best.

Ideally, because the success of individual channel members depends on overall channel success, all channel firms should work together smoothly. They should understand and accept their roles, coordinate their goals and activities, and cooperate to attain overall channel goals. By cooperating, they can more effectively sense, serve, and satisfy the target market.

However, individual channel members rarely take such a broad view. They are usually more concerned with their own short-run goals and their dealings with those firms closest to them in the channel. Cooperating to achieve overall channel goals sometimes means giving up individual company goals. Although channel members are dependent on one another, they often act alone in their own short-run best interests. They often disagree on the roles each should play—on who should do what and for what rewards. Such disagreements over goals and roles generate **channel conflict.**

Channel conflict
Disagreement among marketing channel members on goals and roles—who should do what and for what rewards.

Horizontal conflict occurs among firms at the same level of the channel. For instance, some Ford dealers in Chicago might complain about other dealers in the city who steal sales from them by being too aggressive in their pricing and advertising or by selling outside their assigned territories. Or Holiday Inn franchisees might complain about other Holiday Inn franchisees overcharging guests or giving poor service, hurting the overall Holiday Inn image.

Vertical conflict, conflicts between different levels of the same channel, is even more common. For example, McDonald's came into conflict with some of its California dealers when its aggressive expansion plans called for placing new stores in areas that took business from existing locations. Similarly, office furniture maker Herman Miller created conflict with its dealers when it opened an online store—www.hmstore.com—and began selling its products directly to customers. Although Herman Miller believed that the Web site was reaching only smaller customers who weren't being served by current channels, dealers complained loudly. To help resolve the conflict, Herman Miller embarked on a communication campaign to educate dealers on how the online efforts would help them rather than hurt them.[3]

Some conflict in the channel takes the form of healthy competition. Such competition can be good for the channel—without it, the channel could become passive and noninnovative. But sometimes conflict can damage the channel, as it did in the case of Motorola's StarTAC phone. For the channel as a whole to perform well, each channel member's role must be specified and channel conflict must be managed. Cooperation, role assignment, and conflict management in the channel are attained through strong channel leadership. The channel will perform better if it includes a firm, agency, or mechanism that has the power to assign roles and manage conflict.

Vertical Marketing Systems

Historically, distribution channels have been loose collections of independent companies, each showing little concern for overall channel performance. These *conventional distribution channels* have lacked strong leadership and have been troubled by damaging conflict and poor performance. One of the biggest recent channel developments has been the *vertical marketing systems* that have emerged to challenge conventional marketing channels. Figure 12.3 contrasts the two types of channel arrangements.

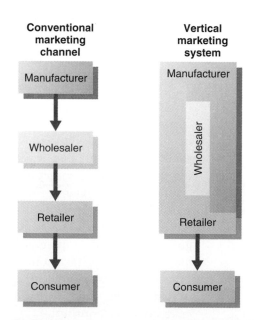

FIGURE 12.3 A conventional marketing channel versus a vertical marketing system

Conventional distribution channel

A channel consisting of one or more independent producers, wholesalers, and retailers, each a separate business seeking to maximize its own profits even at the expense of profits for the system as a whole.

Vertical marketing system (VMS)

A distribution channel structure in which producers, wholesales, and retailers act as a unified system. One channel member owns the others, has contracts with them, or has so much power that they all cooperate

Corporate VMS

A vertical marketing system that combines successive stages of production and distribution under single ownership channel leadership is established through common ownership.

Contractual VMS

A vertical marketing system in which independent firms at different levels of production and distribution join together through contracts to obtain more economies or sales impact than they could achieve alone.

A **conventional distribution channel** consists of one or more independent producers, wholesalers, and retailers. Each is a separate business seeking to maximize its own profits, even at the expense of profits for the system as a whole. No channel member has much control over the other members, and no formal means exists for assigning roles and resolving channel conflict. In contrast, a **vertical marketing system (VMS)** consists of producers, wholesalers, and retailers acting as a unified system. One channel member owns the others, has contracts with them, or wields so much power that they must all cooperate. The VMS can be dominated by the producer, wholesaler, or retailer. Vertical marketing systems came into being to control channel behavior and manage channel conflict.

We look now at three major types of VMSs: *corporate, contractual,* and *administered.* Each uses a different means for setting up leadership and power in the channel. We now take a closer look at each type of VMS.

Corporate VMS

A **corporate VMS** combines successive stages of production and distribution under single ownership. Coordination and conflict management are attained through regular organizational channels. For example, Sears obtains over 50 percent of its goods from companies that it partly or wholly owns. Giant Food Stores operates an ice-making facility, a soft drink bottling operation, an ice cream plant, and a bakery that supplies Giant stores with everything from bagels to birthday cakes.

E. J. Gallo, the world's largest wine maker, grows its own grapes to produce wine, which it pours into Gallo-made bottles topped with caps produced in Gallo's wholly owned Midcal Aluminum Company plant. Gallo's Fairbanks Trucking Company hauls wine out of Gallo wineries and raw materials back in. The raw materials include lime from Gallo's quarry near Sacramento. Thus, Gallo participates in every aspect of producing and selling "short of whispering in the ear of each imbiber."

Contractual VMS

A **contractual VMS** consists of independent firms at different levels of production and distribution who join together through contracts to obtain more economies or sales impact than each could achieve alone. Coordination and conflict management are attained through contractual agreements among channel members. There are

Contractual VMS: Hardware wholesaler Do it Best Corp. has organized a voluntary chain of 4,400 independently owned hardware stores, helping them to compete with large chain organizations.

three types of contractual VMSs: wholesaler-sponsored voluntary chains, retailer cooperatives, and franchise organizations.

In *wholesaler-sponsored voluntary chains,* wholesalers organize voluntary chains of independent retailers to help them compete with large chain organizations. The wholesaler develops a program in which independent retailers standardize their selling practices and achieve buying economies that let the group compete effectively with chain organizations. Examples include the Independent Grocers Alliance (IGA), Western Auto, and Do it Best hardwares.

In *retailer cooperatives,* retailers organize a new, jointly owned business to carry on wholesaling and possibly production. Members buy most of their goods through the retailer co-op and plan their advertising jointly. Profits are passed back to members in proportion to their purchases. Examples include Certified Grocers, Associated Grocers, and Ace Hardware.

In **franchise organizations,** a channel member called a *franchiser* links several stages in the production-distribution process. The more than 500,000 franchise operations in the United States now account for nearly $760 billion in sales, about 40 percent of all U.S. retail sales.[4] Almost every kind of business has been franchised—from motels and fast-food restaurants to dental centers and dating services, from wedding consultants and maid services to funeral homes and fitness centers.

There are three forms of franchises. The first form is the *manufacturer-sponsored retailer franchise system,* as found in the automobile industry. Ford, for example, licenses dealers to sell its cars; the dealers are independent businesspeople who agree to meet various conditions of sales and service. The second type of franchise is the *manufacturer-sponsored wholesaler franchise system,* as found in the soft drink industry. Coca-Cola, for example, licenses bottlers (wholesalers) in various markets who buy Coca-Cola syrup concentrate and then carbonate, bottle, and sell the finished product to retailers in local markets. The third franchise form is the *service-firm-sponsored retailer franchise system,* in which a service firm licenses a system of retailers to bring its service to consumers. Examples are found in the auto-rental business (Hertz, Avis); the fast-food service business (McDonald's, Burger King); and the motel business (Holiday Inn, Ramada Inn).

The fact that most consumers cannot tell the difference between contractual and corporate VMSs shows how successfully the contractual organizations compete with corporate chains. Chapter 13 presents a fuller discussion of the various contractual VMSs.

Administered VMS

An **administered VMS** coordinates successive stages of production and distribution, not through common ownership or contractual ties but through the size and power of one of the parties. In an *administered VMS,* leadership is assumed by one or a few dominant channel members. Manufacturers of a top brand can obtain strong trade cooperation and support from resellers. For example, General Electric, Procter & Gamble, and Kraft can command unusual cooperation from resellers regarding displays, shelf space, promotions, and price policies. Large retailers like Wal-Mart and Barnes & Noble can exert strong influence on the manufacturers that supply the products they sell.

Horizontal Marketing Systems

Another channel development is the **horizontal marketing system,** in which two or more companies at one level join together to follow a new marketing opportunity. By working together, companies can combine their capital, production

---

Franchise organization
A contractual vertical marketing system in which a channel member, called a franchiser, links several stages in the production-distribution process.

Administered VMS
A vertical marketing system that coordinates successive stages of production and distribution, not through common ownership or contractual ties but through the size and power of one of the parties.

Horizontal marketing system
A channel arrangement in which two or more companies at one level join together to follow a new marketing opportunity.

Horizontal marketing systems: Nestlé jointly sells General Mills cereal brands in markets outside North America.

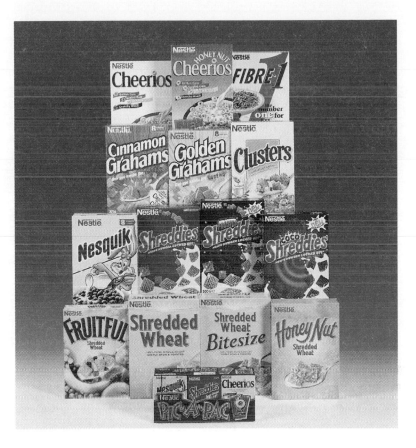

capabilities, or marketing resources to accomplish more than any one company could alone. Companies might join forces with competitors or noncompetitors. They might work with each other on a temporary or permanent basis, or they may create a separate company. For example, the Lamar Savings Bank of Texas arranged to locate its savings offices and automated teller machines in Safeway stores. Lamar gained quicker market entry at a low cost, and Safeway was able to offer in-store banking convenience to its customers.

Such channel arrangements also work well globally. For example, because of its excellent coverage of international markets, Nestlé jointly sells General Mills cereal brands in markets outside North America. Coca-Cola and Nestlé formed a joint venture to market ready-to-drink coffee and tea worldwide. Coke provides worldwide experience in marketing and distributing beverages, and Nestlé contributes two established brand names—Nescafé and Nestea. Similarly, Coca-Cola and Procter & Gamble have created distribution systems linking Coca-Cola soft drinks and Pringles potato crisps in global markets. Seiko Watch's distribution partner in Japan, K. Hattori, markets Schick's razors there, giving Schick the leading market share in Japan, despite Gillette's overall strength in many other markets.[5]

Hybrid Marketing Systems

Hybrid marketing channel
Multichannel distribution system in which a single firm sets up two or more marketing channels to reach one or more customer segments.

In the past, many companies used a single channel to sell to a single market or market segment. Today, with the proliferation of customer segments and channel possibilities, more and more companies have adopted *multichannel distribution systems*—often called **hybrid marketing channels.** Such multichannel marketing occurs when a single firm sets up two or more marketing channels to reach one or more customer segments. The use of hybrid channel systems has increased greatly in recent years.

FIGURE 12.4   **Hybrid marketing channel**

Figure 12.4 shows a hybrid channel. In the figure, the producer sells directly to consumer segment 1 using direct-mail catalogs and telemarketing and reaches consumer segment 2 through retailers. It sells indirectly to business segment 1 through distributors and dealers and to business segment 2 through its own sales force.

IBM uses such a hybrid channel effectively. For years, IBM sold computers only through its own sales force, which sold its large systems to business customers. However, the market for computers and information technology has now exploded into a profusion of products and services for dozens of segments and niches, ranging from large corporate buyers to small businesses to home and home office buyers. As a result, IBM has had to dramatically rethink the way it goes to market. To serve the diverse needs of these many segments, IBM added 18 new channels in less than 10 years. For example, in addition to selling through the vaunted IBM sales force, IBM also sells through a comprehensive network of distributors and value-added resellers, which sell IBM computers, systems, and services to a variety of special business segments. Final customers can buy IBM personal computers from spe-

Hybrid channels: In addition to its sales force, IBM sells through distributors and value-added resellers, specialty computer stores and large retailers, telemarketing, and its ShopIBM Web site.

cialty computer stores or any of several large retailers, including Wal-Mart, Circuit City, and Office Depot. IBM uses telemarketing to service the needs of small and medium-size business. Both business and final consumers can buy online from the company's ShopIBM Web site (www.direct.ibm.com).[6]

Hybrid channels offer many advantages to companies facing large and complex markets. With each new channel, the company expands its sales and market coverage and gains opportunities to tailor its products and services to the specific needs of diverse customer segments. But such hybrid channel systems are harder to control, and they generate conflict as more channels compete for customers and sales. For example, when IBM began selling directly to customers through catalogs, telemarketing, and its own Web site, many of its retail dealers cried "unfair competition" and threatened to drop the IBM line or to give it less emphasis. Many outside salespeople felt that they were being undercut by the new "inside channels."

Changing Channel Organization

Disintermediation

The elimination of a layer of intermediaries from a marketing channel or the displacement of traditional resellers by radically new types of intermediaries.

Changes in technology and the explosive growth of direct and online marketing are having a profound impact on the nature and design of marketing channels. One major trend is toward **disintermediation**—a big term with a clear message and important consequences. Disintermediation means that more and more, product and service producers are bypassing intermediaries and going directly to final buyers, or that radically new types of channel intermediaries are emerging to displace traditional ones.

Thus, in many industries, traditional intermediaries are dropping by the way side. For example, companies like Dell Computer are selling directly to final buyers, eliminating retailers from their marketing channels. E-commerce merchants are growing rapidly in number and size, displacing traditional brick-and-mortar retailers. Consumers can buy flowers from 1-800-Flowers.com; books, videos, CDs, toys, and other goods from Amazon.com; household products from Wal-Mart; groceries from Peapod.com or webvan.com; clothes from Gap or Eddie Bauer; and consumer electronics from buy.com, all without ever visiting a store.

Disintermediation presents problems and opportunities for both producers and intermediaries (see Marketing Highlight 12.1). To avoid being swept aside, traditional intermediaries must find new ways to add value in the supply chain. To remain competitive, product and service producers must develop new channel opportunities, such as Internet and other direct channels. However, developing these new channels often brings them into direct competition with their established channels, resulting in conflict. To ease this problem, companies often look for ways to make going direct a plus for both the company and its channel partners:

★ Going direct is rarely an all-or-nothing proposition. For example, to trim costs and add business, Hewlett-Packard opened three direct-sales Web sites—Shopping Village (for consumers), HP Commerce Center (for businesses buying from authorized resellers), and Electronic Solutions Now (for existing contract customers). However, to avoid conflicts with its established reseller channels, HP forwards all its Web orders to resellers, who complete the orders, ship the products, and get the commissions. In this way, HP gains the advantages of direct selling but also boosts business for resellers.

However, although this compromise system reduces conflicts, it also creates inefficiencies. "That all sounds great and everyone's happy," says a distribution con-

MARKETING HIGHLIGHT 12.1

DISINTERMEDIATION: A FANCY WORD BUT A CLEAR MESSAGE

Belair/Empress Travel in Bowie, Maryland, typifies the kind of business most threatened by the advent of new marketing channels, particularly the surge in Internet selling. Like other traditional travel agencies, Belair/Empress faces some scary new competitors: giant online travel supersites such as Expedia or Travelocity, that let consumers surf the Web for rock-bottom ticket prices. To make matters worse, the airlines' themselves are opening Web sites to sell seats, not only their own seats but competitors' seats as well. For example, visitors to the United Airlines' Web site can purchase tickets on more than 500 other airlines. These new channels give consumers more choices, but they threaten the very existence of Belair/Empress Travel and other traditional travel agents.

Resellers in dozens of industries face similar situations as new channel forms threaten to make them obsolete. There's even a fancy 17-letter word to describe this phenomenon: *disintermediation*. Strictly speaking, disintermediation means the elimination of a layer of intermediaries from a marketing channel. For example, for years personal computer makers assumed that customers needed hands-on buying experience, with lots of point-of-sale inventory and hand-holding sales assistance from retailers. Then, along came Dell Computer with a

new distribution formula: Bypass retailers and sell made-to-order computers directly to consumers. By eliminating retailers, Dell eliminated many costs and inefficiencies from the traditional computer supply chain.

More broadly, disintermediation includes not just the elimination of channel levels through direct marketing but also the displacement of traditional resellers by radically new types of intermediaries. For example, the publishing industry had for decades assumed that book buyers wanted to purchase their books from small, intimate neighborhood bookshops. Then, along came the book superstores—Barnes & Noble and Borders—with their huge inventories and low prices. Disintermediation occurred as the new intermediaries rapidly displaced traditional independent booksellers. Then, most recently, online bookseller Amazon.com emerged to threaten the category killers. Amazon.com doesn't eliminate the retail channel—it's actually a new type of retailer that increases consumers' channel choices rather than reducing them. Still, disintermediation has occurred as Amazon.com and superstores' own Web sites are displacing traditional brick-and-mortar retailers.

Disintermediation is often associated with the surge in e-commerce and online selling. In fact, the Internet is a major disinterme-

diating force. By facilitating direct contact between buyers and sellers, the Internet is displacing channels in industries ranging from books, apparel, toys, drugs, and consumers electronics to travel, stock brokerage, and real estate services. However, disintermediation can involve almost any new form of channel competition. For example, Dell bypassed retailers through telephone and mail-order selling long before it took to the Internet.

Disintermediation works only when a new channel form succeeds in bringing greater value to consumers. Thus, if Amazon.com weren't giving buyers greater convenience, selection, and value, it wouldn't be able to lure customers away from traditional retailers. If Dell's direct channel weren't more efficient and effective in serving the needs of computer buyers, traditional retail channels would have little to fear. However, the huge success of these new channels suggests that they *are* bringing greater value to significant segments of consumers.

From a producer's viewpoint, although eliminating unneeded intermediaries makes sense, disintermediation can be very difficult. One analyst summarizes this way:

You thought electronic commerce would bring nothing but good news.

sultant, "but kicking the customer over to the reseller . . . is a lot more expensive than letting customers order directly from the manufacturer. HP is spending a fair chunk of change to set this up, plus the business partner still wants eight percent margins for getting the product to the customer."[7] To be truly efficient in the long run, HP eventually will have to find ways for its resellers to add value or drop them from the direct channel.

Here at last, you reasoned, is a way to add customers, boost market share, and cut sales costs. All manufacturers have to do is set up an electronic conduit between themselves and their customers and voila, instant sales channel. There's just one little hitch. Those same thoughts terrify the retailers, distributors, and resellers that account for up to 90 percent of manufacturers' revenues. They fear that their role between company and customer will be rendered obsolete by the virtual marketplace. And that puts manufacturers in a bind. Either they surrender to the seductions of e-commerce and risk a mutiny from those valuable partners, or they do nothing and risk the wrath of [successful e-commerce competitors].

Thus, Dell had the advantage of starting from scratch in designing its direct channel—it didn't have to jump from one channel model to another. However, for Compaq, IBM, and other computer producers that are already locked into traditional retail channels, disintermediation presents real problems. To compete more effectively with Dell, both Compaq and IBM have now developed their own direct sales operations. For instance, Compaq has shifted its ratio of traditional channel sales to direct sales from 98 to 2 only a year ago to about 80 to 20 today. However, although the direct channel helps Compaq to compete better with Dell, it worries and displeases the established retail partners that Compaq counts on for the bulk of its sales.

Still, most producers know that when more effective channels come along, they have no choice but to change. There is a Dell at work or in

waiting in every industry, and traditional producers can't afford to wait very long to get inefficiencies out of their distribution channels. Despite the risks, most companies are more afraid of being late to the party than of angering their channel partners. Hugh McColl—chairman and CEO of Bank of America—has said that he would rather put himself out of business with electronic banking than have someone else do it to him. The major question often is not whether to move to a new, high-growth channel but how quickly and what to do with the established channel.

What about traditional resellers? How can they avoid being "Amazoned"? The answer lies in continually looking for new ways to create real customer value. Many companies threatened by Internet competitors have themselves learned to leverage the Web to serve customers better. For example, Belair/Express Travel plans to de-emphasize airline ticket sales and become a market nicher specializing in specialty cruises. The owner plans to do what computers can't—get to know his customers so well that he can provide personal advice on the cruises he books. Still, he'll use a Web site to launch his newly reformulated travel business.

Discount brokerage Charles Schwab & Company also proves the value point. Facing a horde of price-cutting e-commerce competitors who got there first—including E★Trade and Ameritrade—Schwab jumped into the Internet with both feet. However, instead of becoming just

another no-frills Internet trading operation, Schwab has done competitors one better. It has plied customers with a wealth of financial and company information, helping them to research and manage their accounts and assuming the role of investment adviser. Schwab is even teaching courses on Web trading at some of its 300 branches. Thus, rather than dragging its feet or fighting the change, Schwab embraced the new channel as a competitive opportunity. The gamble paid off handsomely. Schwab remains the nation's largest discount stockbroker and ranks number one online with a 28 percent share of the online market, twice the share of nearest competitor E★Trade.

Thus, disintermediation is a big word but the meaning is clear. Those who continually seek new ways to add real value for customers have little to fear. However, those who fall behind in adding value risk being swept aside by their customers and channel partners.

Sources: Quotes from Rochelle Garner, "Mad as Hell," *Sales & Marketing Management,* June 1999, pp. 55–61; and Maricris G. Briones, "What Technology Wrought: Distribution Channel in Flux," *Marketing News,* February 1, 1999, pp. 3, 15. Also see Evan I. Schwartz, "How Middlemen Can Come Out on Top," *Business Week,* February 9, 1998, pp. ENT4–ENT7; James Champy, "How to Fire Your Dealers," *Forbes,* June 14, 1999, p. 141; Stewart Alsop, "Is There an Amazon.com for Every Industry?" *Fortune,* January 11, 1999, pp. 159–60; and Daniel Roth, "E★Trade's Plan for World Domination," *Fortune,* August 2, 1999, pp. 95–98.

CHANNEL DESIGN DECISIONS

We now look at several channel decisions manufacturers face. In designing marketing channels, manufacturers struggle between what is ideal and what is practical. A new firm with limited capital usually starts by selling in a limited market area.

Deciding on the *best* channels might not be a problem: The problem might simply be how to convince one or a few good intermediaries to handle the line.

If successful, the new firm might branch out to new markets through the existing intermediaries. In smaller markets, the firm might sell directly to retailers; in larger markets, it might sell through distributors. In one part of the country, it might grant exclusive franchises; in another, it might sell through all available outlets. In this way, channel systems often evolve to meet market opportunities and conditions. However, for maximum effectiveness, channel analysis and decision making should be more purposeful. Designing a channel system calls for analyzing consumer service needs, setting channel objectives and constraints, identifying major channel alternatives, and evaluating them.

Analyzing Consumer Service Needs

As noted previously, marketing channels can be thought of as *customer value delivery systems* in which each channel member adds value for the customer. Thus, designing the distribution channel starts with finding out what targeted consumers want from the channel. Do consumers want to buy from nearby locations or are they willing to travel to more distant centralized locations? Would they rather buy in person, over the phone, through the mail, or via the Internet? Do they value breadth of assortment or do they prefer specialization? Do consumers want many add-on services (delivery, credit, repairs, installation) or will they obtain these elsewhere? The faster the delivery, the greater the assortment provided, and the more add-on services supplied, the greater the channel's service level.

But providing the fastest delivery, greatest assortment, and most services may not be possible or practical. The company and its channel members may not have the resources or skills needed to provide all the desired services. Also, providing higher levels of service results in higher costs for the channel and higher prices for consumers. The company must balance consumer service needs not only against the feasibility and costs of meeting these needs but also against customer price preferences. The success of off-price and discount retailing shows that consumers are often willing to accept lower service levels if this means lower prices.

Setting Channel Objectives and Constraints

Channel objectives should be stated in terms of the desired service level of target consumers. Usually, a company can identify several segments wanting different levels of channel service. The company should decide which segments to serve and the best channels to use in each case. In each segment, the company wants to minimize the total channel cost of meeting customer service requirements.

The company's channel objectives are also influenced by the nature of the company, its products, marketing intermediaries, competitors, and the environment. For example, the company's size and financial situation determine which marketing functions it can handle itself and which it must give to intermediaries. Companies selling perishable products may require more direct marketing to avoid delays and too much handling. In some cases, a company may want to compete in or near the same outlets that carry competitors' products. In other cases, producers may avoid the channels used by competitors. Avon, for example, set up a profitable door-to-door selling operation rather than going head to head with other cosmetics makers for scarce positions in retail stores. Finally, environmental factors such as economic conditions and legal constraints may affect channel objectives and design. For exam-

Product characteristics affect channel decisions: Fresh flowers must be delivered quickly with a minimum of handling.

ple, in a depressed economy, producers want to distribute their goods in the most economical way, using shorter channels and dropping unneeded services that add to the final price of the goods.

Identifying Major Alternatives

When the company has defined its channel objectives, it should next identify its major channel alternatives in terms of *types* of intermediaries, the *number* of intermediaries, and the *responsibilities* of each channel member.

Types of Intermediaries

A firm should identify the types of channel members available to carry out its channel work. For example, suppose a manufacturer of test equipment has developed an audio device that detects poor mechanical connections in machines with moving parts. Company executives think this product would have a market in all industries in which electric, combustion, or steam engines are made or used. The company's current sales force is small, and the problem is how best to reach these different industries. The following channel alternatives might emerge from management discussion:

> *Company sales force:* Expand the company's direct sales force. Assign outside salespeople to territories and have them contact all prospects in the area or develop separate company sales forces for different industries. Or, add an inside telesales operation in which telephone salespeople handle small or midsize companies.
>
> *Manufacturer's agency:* Hire manufacturer's agents—independent firms whose sales forces handle related products from many companies—in different regions or industries to sell the new test equipment.
>
> *Industrial distributors:* Find distributors in the different regions or industries who will buy and carry the new line. Give them exclusive distribution, good margins, product training, and promotional support.

Number of Marketing Intermediaries

Companies must also determine the number of channel members to use at each level. Three strategies are available: intensive distribution, exclusive distribution, and selective distribution.

Producers of convenience products and common raw materials typically seek **intensive distribution**—a strategy in which they stock their products in as many outlets as possible. These goods must be available where and when consumers want them. For example, toothpaste, candy, and other similar items are sold in millions of outlets to provide maximum brand exposure and consumer convenience. Procter & Gamble, Coca-Cola, and other consumer goods companies distribute their products in this way.

By contrast, some producers purposely limit the number of intermediaries handling their products. The extreme form of this practice is **exclusive distribution,** in which the producer gives only a limited number of dealers the exclusive right to distribute its products in their territories. Exclusive distribution is often found in the distribution of new automobiles and prestige women's clothing. For example, Bentley dealers are few and far between—even large cities may have only one or two dealers. By granting exclusive distribution, Bentley gains stronger distributor selling support and more control over dealer prices, promotion, credit, and services. Exclusive distribution also enhances the car's image and allows for higher markups.

Between intensive and exclusive distribution lies **selective distribution**—the use of more than one, but fewer than all, of the intermediaries who are willing to carry a company's products. Most television, furniture, and small-appliance brands are distributed in this manner. For example, Maytag, Whirlpool, and General

Intensive distribution
Stocking the product in as many outlets as possible.

Exclusive distribution
Giving a limited number of dealers the exclusive right to distribute the company's products in their territories.

Selective distribution
The use of more than one, but fewer than all, of the intermediaries who are willing to carry the company's products.

Exclusive distribution: Luxury car makers sell exclusively through a limited number of dealerships. Such limited distribution enhances the car's image and generates stronger dealer support.

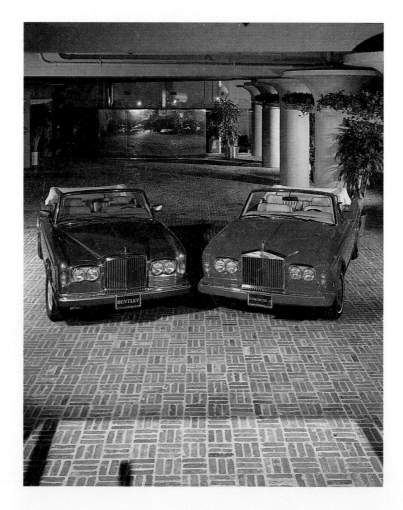

Electric sell their major appliances through dealer networks and selected large retailers. By using selective distribution, they do not have to spread their efforts over many outlets, including many marginal ones. They can develop good working relationships with selected channel members and expect a better-than-average selling effort. Selective distribution gives producers good market coverage with more control and less cost than does intensive distribution.

Responsibilities of Channel Members

The producer and intermediaries need to agree on the terms and responsibilities of each channel member. They should agree on price policies, conditions of sale, territorial rights, and specific services to be performed by each party. The producer should establish a list price and a fair set of discounts for intermediaries. It must define each channel member's territory, and it should be careful about where it places new resellers. Mutual services and duties need to be spelled out carefully, especially in franchise and exclusive distribution channels. For example, McDonald's provides franchisees with promotional support, a record-keeping system, training, and general management assistance. In turn, franchisees must meet company standards for physical facilities, cooperate with new promotion programs, provide requested information, and buy specified food products.

Evaluating the Major Alternatives

Suppose a company has identified several channel alternatives and wants to select the one that will best satisfy its long-run objectives. Each alternative should be evaluated against economic, control, and adaptive criteria.

Using *economic criteria,* a company compares the likely profitability of different channel alternatives. It estimates the sales that each channel would produce and the costs of selling different volumes through each channel. The company must also consider *control issues.* Using intermediaries usually means giving them some control over the marketing of the product, and some intermediaries take more control than others. Other things being equal, the company prefers to keep as much control as possible. Finally, the company must apply *adaptive criteria.* Channels often involve long-term commitments to other firms, making it hard to adapt the channel to the changing marketing environment. The company wants to keep the channel as flexible as possible. Thus, to be considered, a channel involving long-term commitment should be greatly superior on economic and control grounds.

Designing International Distribution Channels

International marketers face many additional complexities in designing their channels. Each country has its own unique distribution system that has evolved over time and changes very slowly. These channel systems can vary widely from country to country. Thus, global marketers must usually adapt their channel strategies to the existing structures within each country. In some markets, the distribution system is complex and hard to penetrate, consisting of many layers and large numbers of intermediaries. Consider Japan:

> The Japanese distribution system stems from the early seventeenth century when cottage industries and a [quickly growing] urban population spawned a merchant class.... Despite Japan's economic achievements, the distribution system has remained remarkably faithful to its antique pattern.... [It] encompasses a wide range of wholesalers and other agents, brokers, and retailers, differing more in number than in function from

The Japanese distribution system has remained remarkably traditional. A profusion of tiny retail shops are supplied by an even greater number of small wholesalers.

their American counterparts. There are myriad tiny retail shops. An even greater number of wholesalers supplies goods to them, layered tier upon tier, many more than most U.S. executives would think necessary. For example, soap may move through three wholesalers plus a sales company after it leaves the manufacturer before it ever reaches the retail outlet. A steak goes from rancher to consumers in a process that often involves a dozen middle agents. . . . The distribution network . . . reflects the traditionally close ties among many Japanese companies . . . [and places] much greater emphasis on personal relationships with users. . . . Although [these channels appear] inefficient and cumbersome, they seem to serve the Japanese customer well. . . . Lacking much storage space in their small homes, most Japanese homemakers shop several times a week and prefer convenient [and more personal] neighborhood shops.[8]

Many Western firms have had great difficulty breaking into the closely knit, tradition-bound Japanese distribution network.

At the other extreme, distribution systems in developing countries may be scattered and inefficient, or altogether lacking. For example, China and India would appear to be huge markets, each with populations in the hundreds of millions. In reality, however, these markets are much smaller than the population numbers suggest. Because of inadequate distribution systems in both countries, most companies can profitably access only a small portion of the population located in each country's most affluent cities.[9]

Thus, international marketers face a wide range of channel alternatives. Designing efficient and effective channel systems between and within various country markets poses a difficult challenge. We discuss international distribution decisions further in chapter 19.

CHANNEL MANAGEMENT DECISIONS

Once the company has reviewed its channel alternatives and decided on the best channel design, it must implement and manage the chosen channel. Channel management calls for selecting and motivating individual channel members and evaluating their performance over time.

Selecting Channel Members

Producers vary in their ability to attract qualified marketing intermediaries. Some producers have no trouble signing up channel members. For example, when Toyota first introduced its Lexus line in the United States, it had no trouble attracting new dealers. In fact, it had to turn down many would-be resellers. In some cases, the promise of exclusive or selective distribution for a desirable product will draw plenty of applicants.

At the other extreme are producers who have to work hard to line up enough qualified intermediaries. When Polaroid started, for example, it could not get photography stores to carry its new cameras, and it had to go to mass-merchandising outlets. Similarly, when the U.S. Time Company first tried to sell its inexpensive Timex watches through regular jewelry stores, most jewelry stores refused to carry them. The company then managed to get its watches into mass-merchandise outlets. This turned out to be a wise decision because of the rapid growth of mass merchandising.

When selecting intermediaries, the company should determine what characteristics distinguish the better ones. It will want to evaluate each channel member's years in business, other lines carried, growth and profit record, cooperativeness, and reputation. If the intermediaries are sales agents, the company will want to evaluate the number and character of other lines carried and the size and quality of the sales force. If the intermediary is a retail store that wants exclusive or selective distribution, the company will want to evaluate the store's customers, location, and future growth potential.

Motivating Channel Members

Once selected, channel members must be motivated continuously to do their best. The company must sell not only *through* the intermediaries but *to* them. Most companies see their intermediaries as first-line customers. Some use the carrot-and-stick approach: At times they offer *positive* motivators such as higher margins, special deals, premiums, cooperative advertising allowances, display allowances, and sales contests. At other times they use *negative* motivators, such as threatening to reduce margins, to slow down delivery, or to end the relationship altogether. A producer using this approach usually has not done a good job of studying the needs, problems, strengths, and weaknesses of its distributors.

More advanced companies try to forge long-term partnerships with their distributors to create a marketing system that meets the needs of both the manufacturer *and* the distributors. Thus, Procter & Gamble and Wal-Mart work together to create superior value for final consumers. They jointly plan merchandising goals and strategies, inventory levels, and advertising and promotion plans. Similarly, GE Appliances works closely with its independent dealers to help them be successful in selling the company's products (see Marketing Highlight 12.2). In managing its channels, a company must convince distributors that they can make their money by being part of an advanced marketing system.[10]

Evaluating Channel Members

The producer must regularly check the channel member's performance against standards such as sales quotas, average inventory levels, customer delivery time, treatment of damaged and lost goods, cooperation in company promotion and training programs, and services to the customer. The company should recognize and reward

GE APPLIANCES FORGES STRONG PARTNERSHIPS WITH DEALERS

Before the late 1980s, General Electric's appliance division worked at selling *through* its dealers rather than *to* them or *with* them. GE Appliances operated a traditional system of trying to load up the channel with its appliances on the premise that "loaded dealers are loyal dealers." Loaded dealers would have less space to feature other brands and would recommend GE appliances to reduce their high inventories. To load its dealers, GE Appliances would offer the lowest price when the dealer ordered a full truckload of products.

GE eventually realized that this approach created many problems, especially for smaller, independent appliance dealers who could ill afford to carry a large stock. These dealers were hard pressed to meet price competition from larger, multibrand dealers. Rethinking its strategy from the point of view of creating dealer satisfaction and profitability, GE created an alternative distribution system to serve its dealers—a system now called GE CustomerNet.

GE CustomerNet gives dealers instant online access to GE Appliances' distribution and order-processing system, 24 hours a day, 7 days a week. By logging onto the

Creating dealer satisfaction and profitability: Using GE's CustomerNet system, dealers can access GE's order-processing system 24 hours a day, check on model availability, and place orders for next-day delivery. They can also get GE's best price, financing from GE Credit, and no interest charges for the first 90 days.

intermediaries who are performing well. Those who are performing poorly should be assisted or, as a last resort, replaced. A company may periodically "requalify" its intermediaries and prune the weaker ones.

Finally, manufacturers need to be sensitive to their dealers. Those who treat their dealers lightly risk not only losing their support but also causing some legal problems. The next section describes various rights and duties pertaining to manufacturers and their channel members.

PUBLIC POLICY AND DISTRIBUTION DECISIONS

For the most part, companies are legally free to develop whatever channel arrangements suit them. In fact, the laws affecting channels seek to prevent the exclusionary tactics of some companies that might keep another company from using a desired channel. Most channel law deals with the mutual rights and duties of the channel members once they have formed a relationship.

GE CustomerNet Web site, dealers can obtain product specifications, photos, feature lists, and side-by-side model comparisons for hundreds of GE appliance models. They can check on product availability and prices, place orders, review order status, and even download "advertising slicks"—professionally prepared GE appliance ads ready for insertion in local media. Says Brian Kelly, sales vice president for GE Appliances, "With this system, we're putting all our backroom capabilities right in the store with our [dealers]. We want [them] to get closer to us and have better access to our data."

GE CustomerNet yields substantial benefits to dealers. Instead of loading them up with big inventories, the system gives them a large "virtual inventory" from which to satisfy their customers' needs. GE promises next-day delivery on most appliance models, so dealers need carry only display models in their stores and can rely on the virtual inventory to fill orders. This greatly reduces inventory costs, making even small dealers more price competitive. GE CustomerNet also helps dealers to sell GE appliances more easily and effectively. A dealer can put a computer terminal on the showroom floor, where salespeople

and customers together can use the system to dig through detailed product specifications and check availability for GE's entire line of appliances. As one dealer states, "You can quickly tell customers whether or not a product is available, and you can print them a great looking picture with the click of a button."

GE Appliances also benefits from the new system. GE CustomerNet dramatically decreases the volume of costly and time-consuming phone inquiries and orders, and the electronic order-entry system saves the company substantial clerical costs. GE Appliances now knows the actual sales of its goods at the retail level, which helps it to schedule production more accurately. It now can produce in response to demand rather than to meet inventory replenishment rules. GE has been able to simplify its warehouse locations, so it can deliver appliances to 90 percent of the United States within 24 hours.

Perhaps the biggest benefit to GE Appliances, however, is that the system builds strong bonds between the company and its dealers and motivates dealers to put more push behind the company's products. Beyond its sales support features, GE CustomerNet contains an online

feedback system that lets dealers communicate promptly and regularly with GE Appliances about anything related to products, service, or the Web site. Notes Kelly, "We want to make it simple and easy for [dealers] who have questions, complaints, and suggestions. This helps us constantly enhance relationships with our customers."

The GE CustomerNet system now handles upward of 50,000 transactions per week. As a result of the system, dealer profit margins have skyrocketed. Thus, over the past decade, GE Appliances has replaced the old "us-against-them" mentality with a passion for partnerships that benefits both the company and its dealers.

Sources: Michael Treacy and Fred Wiersema, "Customer Intimacy and Other Discipline Values," *Harvard Business Review,* January–February 1993, pp. 84–93; Robert D. Buzzell and Gwen Ortmeyer, "Channel Partnerships Streamline Distribution," *Sloan Management Review,* Spring 1995, pp. 85–96; Cathy Ciccolella, "GE to Offer Online Dealer Support with CustomerNet," *Twice,* April 21, 1997, p. 88; Cathy Ciccolella, "GE Online Support Wins Dealers Over," *Twice,* February 9, 1998, p. 38; and information supplied by GE Appliances, July 1999.

Many producers and wholesalers like to develop exclusive channels for their products. When the seller allows only certain outlets to carry its products, this strategy is called *exclusive distribution.* When the seller requires that these dealers not handle competitors' products, its strategy is called *exclusive dealing.* Both parties can benefit from exclusive arrangements: The seller obtains more loyal and dependable outlets, and the dealers obtain a steady source of supply and stronger seller support. But exclusive arrangements also exclude other producers from selling to these dealers. This situation brings exclusive dealing contracts under the scope of the Clayton Act of 1914. They are legal as long as they do not substantially lessen competition or tend to create a monopoly and as long as both parties enter into the agreement voluntarily.

Exclusive dealing often includes *exclusive territorial agreements.* The producer may agree not to sell to other dealers in a given area or the buyer may agree to sell only in its own territory. The first practice is normal under franchise systems as a way to increase dealer enthusiasm and commitment. It is also perfectly legal—a seller has no legal obligation to sell through more outlets than it wishes. The second practice, whereby the producer tries to keep a dealer from selling outside its territory, has become a major legal issue.

Producers of a strong brand sometimes sell it to dealers only if the dealers will take some or all of the rest of the line. This is called full-line forcing. Such *tying agreements* are not necessarily illegal, but they do violate the Clayton Act if they tend to lessen competition substantially. The practice may prevent consumers from freely choosing among competing suppliers of these other brands.

Finally, producers are free to select their dealers, but their right to terminate dealers is somewhat restricted. In general, sellers can drop dealers "for cause." However, they cannot drop dealers if, for example, the dealers refuse to cooperate in a doubtful legal arrangement, such as exclusive dealing or tying agreements.[11]

PHYSICAL DISTRIBUTION AND LOGISTICS MANAGEMENT

In today's global marketplace, selling a product is sometimes easier than getting it to customers. Companies must decide on the best way to store, handle, and move their products and services so that they are available to customers in the right assortments, at the right time, and in the right place. Logistics effectiveness has a major impact on both customer satisfaction and company costs. Here we consider the *nature and importance of marketing logistics, goals of the logistics system, major logistics functions,* and the need for *integrated logistics management.*

Nature and Importance of Physical Distribution and Marketing Logistics

Physical distribution (or marketing logistics)
The tasks involved in planning, implementing, and controlling the physical flow of materials, final goods, and related information from points of origin to points of consumption to meet customer requirements at a profit.

To some managers, physical distribution means only trucks and warehouses. But modern logistics is much more than this. **Physical distribution**—or **marketing logistics**—involves planning, implementing, and controlling the physical flow of materials, final goods, and related information from points of origin to points of consumption to meet customer requirements at a profit. In short, it involves getting the right product to the right customer in the right place at the right time.

Traditional physical distribution typically started with products at the plant and then tried to find low-cost solutions to get them to customers. However, today's marketers prefer *market logistics* thinking, which starts with the marketplace and works backward to the factory. Logistics addresses not only the problem of outbound distribution (moving products from the factory to customers) but also the problem of inbound distribution (moving products and materials from suppliers to the factory). It involves the management of entire *supply chains,* value-added flows from suppliers to final users, as shown in Figure 12.5. Thus, the logistics manager's task is to coordinate activities of suppliers, purchasing agents, marketers, channel members, and customers. These activities include forecasting, information systems, purchasing, production planning, order processing, inventory, warehousing, and transportation planning.

Companies today are placing greater emphasis on logistics for several reasons. First, customer service and satisfaction have become the cornerstones of marketing strategy, and distribution is an important customer service element. More and more, companies are finding that they can attract and keep customers by giving better service or lower prices through better physical distribution.

Second, logistics is a major cost element for most companies. According to one study, in a recent year American companies "spent $670 billion—a gaping 10.5 percent

Value-added flows of materials,
final goods, and related information
through coordination of forecasting,
information systems, purchasing,
production planning, order processing,
inventory, warehousing, and transportation

FIGURE 12.5   Marketing logistics: Managing supply chains

of gross domestic product—to wrap, bundle, load, unload, sort, reload, and transport goods."[12] About 15 percent of an average product's price is accounted for by shipping and transport alone. Poor physical distribution decisions result in high costs. Improvements in physical distribution efficiency can yield tremendous cost savings for both the company and its customers.

Third, the explosion in product variety has created a need for improved logistics management. For example, in 1911 the typical A&P grocery store carried only 270 items. The store manager could keep track of this inventory on about 10 pages of notebook paper stuffed in a shirt pocket. Today, the average A&P carries a bewildering stock of more than 16,700 items.[13] Ordering, shipping, stocking, and controlling such a variety of products presents a sizable logistics challenge.

Finally, improvements in information technology have created opportunities for major gains in distribution efficiency. The increased use of computers, point-of-sale scanners, uniform product codes, satellite tracking, electronic data interchange (EDI), and electronic funds transfer (EFT) has allowed companies to create advanced systems for order processing, inventory control and handling, and transportation routing and scheduling.

Goals of the Logistics System

Some companies state their logistics objective as providing maximum customer service at the least cost. Unfortunately, no logistics system can *both* maximize customer service *and* minimize distribution costs. Maximum customer service implies rapid delivery, large inventories, flexible assortments, liberal returns policies, and other services—all of which raise distribution costs. In contrast, minimum distribution costs imply slower delivery, smaller inventories, and larger shipping lots—which represent a lower level of overall customer service.

The goal of the marketing logistics system should be to provide a targeted level of customer service at the least cost. A company must first research the importance of various distribution services to its customers and then set desired service levels for each segment. The company normally will want to offer at least the same level of service as its competitors do. But the objective is to maximize *profits*, not sales. Therefore, the company must weigh the benefits of providing higher levels of service against the costs. Some companies offer less service than their competitors and charge a lower price. Other companies offer more service and charge higher prices to cover higher costs.

Major Logistics Functions

Given a set of logistics objectives, the company is ready to design a logistics system that will minimize the cost of attaining these objectives. The major logistics functions include *order processing, warehousing, inventory management,* and *transportation*.

Order Processing
Orders can be submitted in many ways—by mail or telephone, through salespeople, or via computer and EDI. In some cases, the suppliers might actually generate orders for their customers:

> One Kmart quick response program calls for selected suppliers to manage the retailer's inventory replenishment for their products. Kmart transmits daily records of product sales to the vendor, who analyzes the sales information, comes up with an order, and sends it back to Kmart through EDI. Once in Kmart's system, the order is treated as though Kmart itself created it. Says a Kmart executive, "We don't modify the order, and we don't question it. . . . Our relationship with those vendors is such that we trust them to create the type of order that will best meet our inventory needs."[14]

Once received, orders must be processed quickly and accurately. Both the company and its customers benefit when order processing is carried out efficiently. Most companies now use computerized order-processing systems that speed up the order–shipping–billing cycle. For example, General Electric operates a computer-based system that, on receipt of a customer's order, checks the customer's credit standing as well as whether and where the items are in stock. The computer then issues an order to ship, bills the customer, updates the inventory records, sends a production order for new stock, and relays the message back to the salesperson that the customer's order is on its way—all in less than 15 seconds.

Warehousing
Every company must store its goods while they wait to be sold. A storage function is needed because production and consumption cycles rarely match. For example, Snapper, Toro, and other lawn mower manufacturers must produce all year long and store up their product for the heavy spring and summer buying seasons. The storage function overcomes differences in needed quantities and timing.

Distribution center
A large, highly automated warehouse designed to receive goods from various plants and suppliers, take orders, fill them efficiently, and deliver goods to customers as quickly as possible.

A company must decide on *how many* and *what types* of warehouses it needs and *where* they will be located. The company might use either *storage warehouses* or *distribution centers*. Storage warehouses store goods for moderate to long periods. **Distribution centers** are designed to move goods rather than just store them. They are large and highly automated warehouses designed to receive goods from various plants and suppliers, take orders, fill them efficiently, and deliver goods to customers as quickly as possible. For example, Wal-Mart operates huge distribution centers. One center, which serves the daily needs of 165 Wal-Mart stores, contains some 28 acres of space under a single roof. Laser scanners route as many as 190,000 cases of goods per day along 11 miles of conveyer belts, and the center's 1,000 workers load or unload 310 trucks daily.[15]

Warehousing facilities and equipment technology have improved greatly in recent years. Older, multistoried warehouses with outdated materials-handling methods are facing competition from newer, single-storied *automated warehouses* with advanced materials-handling systems under the control of a central computer. In these warehouses, only a few employees are necessary. Computers read orders and direct lift trucks, electric hoists, or robots to gather goods, move them to loading docks, and issue invoices. These warehouses have reduced worker injuries, labor costs, theft, and breakage and have improved inventory control.

Inventory

Inventory levels also affect customer satisfaction. The major problem is to maintain the delicate balance between carrying too much inventory and carrying too little. Carrying too much inventory results in higher-than-necessary inventory-carrying costs and stock obsolesence. Carrying too little may result in stock outs, costly emergency shipments or production, and customer dissatisfaction. In making inventory decisions, management must balance the costs of carrying larger inventories against resulting sales and profits.

During the past decade, many companies have greatly reduced their inventories and related costs through *just-in-time* logistics systems. Through such systems, producers and retailers carry only small inventories of parts or merchandise, often only enough for a few days of operations. New stock arrives exactly when needed, rather than being stored in inventory until being used. Just-in-time systems require accurate forecasting along with fast, frequent, and flexible delivery so that new supplies will be available when needed. However, these systems result in substantial savings in inventory-carrying and handling costs.

Transportation

Marketers need to take an interest in their company's *transportation* decisions. The choice of transportation carriers affects the pricing of products, delivery performance, and condition of the goods when they arrive—all of which will affect customer satisfaction. In shipping goods to its warehouses, dealers, and customers, the company can choose among five transportation modes: rail, truck, water, pipeline, and air.

Railroads are the nation's largest carrier, accounting for 26 percent of total cargo ton-miles moved.[16] They are one of the most cost-effective modes for shipping large amounts of bulk products—coal, sand, minerals, farm and forest products—over long distances. In recent years, railroads have increased their customer services by designing new equipment to handle special categories of goods, providing flatcars for carrying truck trailers by rail (piggyback), and providing in-transit services such as the diversion of shipped goods to other destinations en route and the processing of goods en route. Thus, after decades of losing out to truckers, railroads appear ready for a comeback.[17]

Roadway and other trucking firms have added many services in recent years, such as satellite tracking of shipments and sleeper tractors that keep freight moving around the clock.

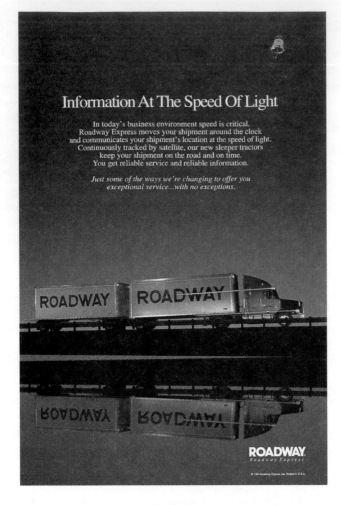

Trucks have increased their share of transportation steadily and now account for 24 percent of total cargo ton-miles (over 52 percent of actual tonnage). They account for the largest portion of transportation *within* cities as opposed to *between* cities. Each year in the United States, trucks travel more than 600 billion miles—equal to nearly 1.3 million round trips to the moon—carrying 2.5 billion tons of freight.[18] Trucks are highly flexible in their routing and time schedules, and they can usually offer faster service than railroads. They are efficient for short hauls of high-value merchandise. Trucking firms have added many services in recent years. For example, Roadway Express now offers satellite tracking of shipments and sleeper tractors that move freight around the clock.

Water carriers transport large amounts of goods by ships and barges on U.S. coastal and inland waterways. Mississippi River barges alone account for 15 percent of the freight shipped in the United States. Although the cost of water transportation is very low for shipping bulky, low-value, nonperishable products such as sand, coal, grain, oil, and metallic ores, water transportation is the slowest mode and may be affected by the weather.

Pipelines are a specialized means of shipping petroleum, natural gas, and chemicals from sources to markets. Most pipelines are used by their owners to ship their own products.

Although *air* carriers transport less than 1 percent of the nation's goods, they are becoming more important as a transportation mode. Air freight rates are much higher than rail or truck rates, but air freight is ideal when speed is needed or distant markets have to be reached. Among the most frequently air-freighted products are perishables (fresh fish, cut flowers) and high-value, low-bulk items (technical instruments, jewelry). Companies find that air freight also reduces inventory levels, packaging costs, and the number of warehouses needed.

Intermodal transportation
Combining two or more modes of transportation.

Shippers increasingly are using **intermodal transportation**—combining two or more modes of transportation. *Piggyback* describes the use of rail and trucks; *fishyback,* water and trucks; *trainship,* water and rail; and *airtruck,* air and trucks. Combining modes provides advantages that no single mode can deliver. Each combination offers advantages to the shipper. For example, not only is piggyback cheaper than trucking alone but it also provides flexibility and convenience.

In choosing a transportation mode for a product, shippers must balance many considerations: speed, dependability, availability, cost, and others. Thus, if a shipper needs speed, air and truck are the prime choices. If the goal is low cost, then water or pipeline might be best.

Integrated Logistics Management

Integrated logistics management
The logistics concept that emphasizes teamwork, both inside the company and among all the marketing channel organizations, to maximize the performance of the entire distribution system.

Today, more and more companies are adopting the concept of **integrated logistics management.** This concept recognizes that providing better customer service and trimming distribution costs requires *teamwork,* both inside the company and among all the marketing channel organizations. Inside, the company's various functional departments must work closely together to maximize the company's own logistics performance. Outside, the company must integrate its logistics system with those of its suppliers and customers to maximize the performance of the entire distribution system.

Cross-Functional Teamwork Inside the Company

In most companies, responsibility for various logistics activities is assigned to many different functional units—marketing, sales, finance, manufacturing, purchasing. Too often, each function tries to optimize its own logistics performance without regard for the activities of the other functions. However, transportation, inventory, warehousing, and order-processing activities interact, often in an inverse way. For example, lower inventory levels reduce inventory-carrying costs. But they may also reduce customer service and increase costs from stock outs, back orders, special production runs, and costly fast-freight shipments. Because distribution activities involve strong trade-offs, decisions by different functions must be coordinated to achieve superior overall logistics performance.

The goal of integrated logistics management is to harmonize all of the company's distribution decisions. Close working relationships among functions can be achieved in several ways. Some companies have created permanent logistics committees made up of managers responsible for different physical distribution activities. Companies can also create management positions that link the logistics activities of functional areas. For example, Procter & Gamble has created supply managers, who manage all of the supply chain activities for each of its product categories. Many companies have a vice president of logistics with cross-functional authority. The important thing is that the company coordinate its logistics and marketing activities to create high market satisfaction at a reasonable cost.

Building Channel Partnerships

The members of a distribution channel are linked closely in delivering customer satisfaction and value. One company's distribution system is another company's supply system. The success of each channel member depends on the performance of the entire supply chain. For example, Wal-Mart can charge the lowest prices at retail only if its entire supply chain—consisting of thousands of merchandise suppliers, transport companies, warehouses, and service providers—operates at maximum efficiency.

Companies must do more than improve their own logistics. They must also work with other channel members to improve whole-channel distribution. Today, smart companies are coordinating their logistics strategies and building strong partnerships with suppliers and customers to improve customer service and reduce channel costs.

These channel partnerships can take many forms. Many companies have created *cross-functional, cross-company teams.* For example, Procter & Gamble has a team of almost 100 people living in Bentonville, Arkansas, home of Wal-Mart. The P&Gers work with their counterparts at Wal-Mart to jointly find ways to squeeze costs out of their distribution system. Working together benefits not only P&G and Wal-Mart but also their final consumers. Haggar Apparel Company has a similar system called "multiple points of contact," in which a Haggar team works with JCPenney people at corporate, divisional, and store levels. As a result of this partnership, JCPenney now receives Haggar merchandise within 18 days of placing an order—10 days fewer than its next-best supplier. Haggar ships the merchandise "floor ready"—hangered and pretagged—reducing the time it takes JCPenney to move the stock from receiving docks to the sales floor from four days to just one.[19]

Other companies partner through *shared projects.* For example, many larger retailers are working closely with suppliers on in-store programs. Home Depot

Western Publishing Group partners with Toys "R" Us to create mini-bookstore sections-called Books "R" Us—within each store. Toys "R" Us provides the space and customers; Western serves as distributor and servicer for the Books "R" Us sections.

allows key suppliers to use its stores as a testing ground for new merchandising programs. The suppliers spend time at Home Depot stores watching how their product sells and how customers relate to it. They then create programs specially tailored to Home Depot and its customers. Western Publishing Group, publisher of "Little Golden Books" for children, formed a similar partnership with Toys "R" Us. Western and the giant toy retailer coordinated their marketing strategies to create minibookstore sections—called Books "R" Us—within each Toys "R" Us store. Toys "R" Us provides the locations, space, and customers; Western serves as distributor, consolidator, and servicer for the Books "R" Us program.[20] Clearly, both the supplier and customer benefit from such partnerships.

Channel partnerships may also take the form of *information sharing* and *continuous inventory replenishment* systems. Companies manage their supply chains through information. Suppliers link up with customers to share information and coordinate their logistics decisions. Here are just two examples:

★ The Branded Apparel division of giant Sara Lee Corporation says that retailer Dayton Hudson's willingness to share information with suppliers separates this company from its competitors. Dayton's Global Merchandising System (GMS), its supply chain management system, consists of more than 60 applications, including forecasting, ordering, and trend analysis. A Dayton company, such as Target stores, can use GMS to order a certain number of sweatshirts from Sara Lee Branded Apparel without specifying more than style. As the delivery date draws near, Target analyzes trends for colors and sizes. Based on those forecasts, Sara Lee makes trial lots and Target starts to sell them. If customers buy more navy sweatshirts than initially predicted, Target adjusts its order. The result: Both Sara Lee and Target have fewer goods in inventory while at the same time doing a better job of meeting customer preferences, which in turn results in fewer markdowns.[21]

★ Bailey Controls, a manufacturer of control systems for big factories, from steel and paper mills to chemical and pharmaceutical plants, . . . treats some of its suppliers almost like departments of its own plants. Bailey has plugged two of its main electronics suppliers into itself. Future Electronics is hooked in through an electronic data interchange system. Every week, Bailey electronically sends Future its latest forecasts of what materials it will need for the next six months so that Future can stock up in time. Bailey itself stocks only enough inventory for a few days of operation, as opposed to the three or four months' worth it used to carry. Whenever a bin of parts falls below a designated level, a Bailey employee passes a laser scanner over the bin's bar code, instantly alerting Future to send the parts at once. Arrow Electronics . . . is plugged in even more closely: It has a warehouse in Bailey's factory, stocked according to Bailey's twice-a-month forecasts. Bailey provides the space, Arrow the warehouseman and the $500,000 of inventory.[22]

Today, as a result of such partnerships, many companies have switched from *anticipatory-based distribution systems* to *response-based distribution systems*.[23] In anticipatory distribution, the company produces the amount of goods called for by a sales forecast. It builds and holds stock at various supply points, such as the plant, distribution centers, and retail outlets. A response-based distribution system, in contrast, is *customer triggered*. The producer continuously builds and replaces stock as orders arrive. It produces what is currently selling. For example, Japanese carmakers take orders for cars, then produce and ship them within four days. Benetton, the Italian fashion house, uses a *quick-response system,* dyeing its sweaters in the colors that are currently selling instead of trying to guess far in advance which colors people will want. Producing for order rather than for forecast substantially cuts down inventory costs and risks.

GO RYDER, AND LEAVE THE DELIVERING TO US

Most big companies love to make and sell their products. But many loathe the associated logistics "grunt work"—the bundling, loading, unloading, sorting, storing, reloading, transporting, and tracking required to supply their factories and to get products out to customers. They hate it so much that 60 percent of the Fortune 500 now outsource some or all of these functions. Increasingly, companies are handing over their logistics to suppliers that specialize in helping them tighten up sluggish, overstuffed supply chains, slash inventories, and get products to customers more quickly and reliably. Following are some examples:

Saturn: Saturn's just-in-time production system allows for almost no parts inventory at the plant. Instead, it relies on a world-class logistics system to keep parts flowing into the factory at precisely the times they're needed. Saturn is so adroit in managing its supply chain that in four years it has had to halt production just once—for only 18 minutes—because the right part failed to arrive at the right time. Most of the credit, however, goes to Ryder Integrated Logistics, the nation's largest logistics management firm. Ryder, best known for renting trucks, manages Saturn's far-ranging supply chain, moving the automaker's materials, parts, and products efficiently and reliably from supplier to factory to dealer showroom.

To keep Saturn's assembly lines humming, Ryder transports thousands of preinspected and presorted parts—more than 2,200 receiving dock transactions every day—hitting delivery windows as narrow as five minutes. Ryder keeps its parts, people, and trucks in a nearly constant blur of high-tech motion. For example, according to one account, when delivering service parts to Saturn dealerships, Ryder's long-haul drivers "plug a plastic key, loaded with electronic data, into an onboard computer. The screen tells them exactly where to go, which route to take, and how much time to spend getting there." Ryder's effective supply chain management results in lower costs, improved operations, more productive dealers, and—in the end—more satisfied customers.

Cisco Systems: This vendor of computer networking equipment and network management software ships tons of routers to Europe daily. It needs to know where each box is at any given time and may have to reroute orders on short notice to fill urgent customer requests. Moreover, Cisco's customers need to know exactly when orders will arrive. When Cisco handled its own logistics, deliveries took up to three weeks. Now, the company contracts its complex distribution process to UPS Worldwide Logistics. Leveraging its knowledge of international plane, train, and trucking schedules, UPS Worldwide can speed routers to European customers in fewer than four days. If its own planes or trucks can't make the fastest delivery, UPS

Third-Party Logistics

Third-party logistics provider
An independent logistics provider that performs any or all of the functions required to get their clients' product to market.

Over 90 percent of U.S. businesses perform their own logistics functions. However, a growing number of firms now outsource some or all their logistics to **third-party logistics providers** such as Ryder Systems, UPS Worldwide Logistics, FedEx Logistics, Roadway Logistics Services, or Emory Global Logistics (see Marketing Highlight 12.3). Such integrated logistics companies perform any or all of the functions required to get their clients' product to market. For example, Emory's Global Logistics unit provides clients with coordinated, single-source logistics services including supply chain management, customized information technology, inventory control, warehousing, transportation management, customer service and fulfillment, and freight auditing and control. Last year, U.S. manufacturers and distributors spent more than $39 billion on third-party logistics (also called *outsourced logistics* or *contract logistics*) services, and the market is expected to grow by at least 20 percent per year through the year 2004.[24]

subcontracts the job to Lufthansa, KLM, or Danzas, a European trucking firm. Such superfast delivery saves Cisco Systems a bundle on inventories. Soon, UPS Worldwide will begin installing custom software into Cisco's routers at its warehouse in the Netherlands, letting Cisco cut its inventories even more.

Cisco's reaps some additional advantages from the logistics partnership. For example, UPS Worldwide has extensive knowledge of local customs laws and import duties. It recently arranged with Dutch customs to aggregate Cisco's import duties into a monthly bill, paid once customers receive shipments instead of each time the routers land at the airport. The result: even more savings in time and paperwork.

National Semiconductor: In the early 1990s, National Semiconductor—whose chips end up inside everything from cars and computers to telecommunications gear—faced a logistics nightmare. National produced and assembled chips at 13 plants located in the United States, Britain, Israel, and Southeast Asia. Finished products were then shipped to an array of large customers—IBM, Toshiba, Compaq, Ford, Siemens—each with factories scattered around the globe. On their way to customers, chips traveled any of 20,000 direct routes, mostly in the cargo holds of planes flown by 12 airlines, stopping along the way at 10 different warehouses. National's logistics performance left much to be desired: Ninety-five percent of its products were delivered within 45 days of the order. The other 5 percent took as long as 90 days. Because customers never knew which 5 percent would be late, they demanded 90 days' worth of inventory in everything. "We had buffer stocks all along the line," comments a National executive. "The whole system was awash in inventory."

National's management set out to overhaul its global logistics network. It decided that all finished products would be transported to a central distribution center in Asia, where they would be sorted and air-freighted to customers. Although strategically sound, the plan created some big practical problems: National knew a lot about making chips but very little about air freight. "To do that," says the executive, "we would have had to make our company into FedEx." Instead, National *hired* FedEx to handle its global distribution. FedEx Logistics now runs National's distribution center in Singapore, conducting all storage, sorting, and shipping activities. The results have been startling. Within two years, National's distribution costs fell 27 percent. At the same time, sales jumped by $584 million and delivery performance improved dramatically. National can now move products from the factory to customers in an average of 4 days or less, and it's well on its way toward its goal of a 72-hour turnaround. Thus, by outsourcing its distribution to a firm that specializes in efficient logistics, National Semiconductor has both cut its costs and improved its service to customers.

Sources: Quotes and other information from Ronald Henkoff, "Delivering the Goods," *Fortune,* November 28, 1994, pp. 64–77; Lisa H. Harrington, "Special Report on Contract Logistics," *Transportation & Distribution,* September 1996, pp. A–N; Scott Woolley, "Replacing Inventory with Information," *Forbes,* March 24, 1997, pp. 54–58; Allen Allnoch, "Third-Party Logistics Industry Poised for Growth in U.S. and Abroad," *IIE Solutions,* January 1998, p. 10; and Martha Celestino, "Choosing a Third-Party Logistics Provider," *World Trade,* July 1999, pp. 54–56. Also see Sandor Boyson, Thomas Corsi, Martin Dresner, and Elliott Rabinovich, "Managing Effective Third Party Logistics Relationships: What Does It Take?" *Journal of Business Logistics,* 20, no. 1, 1999, pp. 73–101.

Companies may use third-party logistics providers for several reasons. First, because getting the product to market is their main focus, these providers can often do it more efficiently and at lower cost than clients whose strengths lie elsewhere. According to one study, outsourcing warehousing alone typically results in 10 percent to 15 percent cost savings. Another expert estimates that companies can save 15 percent to 25 percent in their total logistics costs by outsourcing.[25] Second, outsourcing logistics frees a company to focus more intensely on its core business. Finally, integrated logistics companies understand increasingly complex logistics environments. This can be especially helpful to companies attempting to expand their global market coverage. For example, companies distributing their products across Europe face a bewildering array of environmental restrictions that affect logistics, including packaging standards, truck size and weight limits, and noise and emissions pollution controls. By outsourcing its logistics, a company can gain a complete pan-European distribution system without incurring the costs, delays, and risks associated with setting up its own system.[26]

Third-party logistics: Many companies are now outsourcing logistics tasks to companies like Ryder Integrated Logistics. Here, Ryder describes a system it designed to keep Friendly's refrigerated trucks on the road. "Thanks to Ryder, Friendly's doesn't have to worry about break-downs. Or meltdowns."

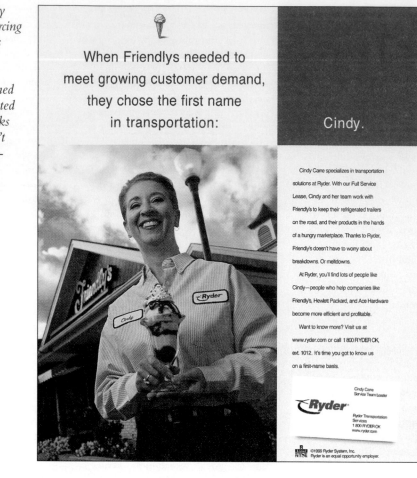

When Friendlys needed to meet growing customer demand, they chose the first name in transportation: Cindy.

Cindy Carre specializes in transportation solutions at Ryder. With our Full Service Lease, Cindy and her team work with Friendly's to keep their refrigerated trailers on the road, and their products in the hands of a hungry marketplace. Thanks to Ryder, Friendly's doesn't have to worry about breakdowns. Or meltdowns.

At Ryder, you'll find lots of people like Cindy—people who help companies like Friendly's, Hewlett Packard, and Ace Hardware become more efficient and profitable.

Want to know more? Visit us at www.ryder.com or call 1 800 RYDER OK, ext. 1012. It's time you got to know us on a first-name basis.

Ryder

Cindy Carre
Service Team Leader

Ryder Transportation
Services
1 800 RYDER OK
www.ryder.com

©1999 Ryder System, Inc.
Ryder is an equal opportunity employer.

REVIEW OF CONCEPT CONNECTIONS

Marketing channel decisions are among the most important decisions that management faces. A company's channel decisions directly affect every other marketing decision. Each channel system creates a different level of revenues and costs and reaches a different segment of target consumers. Management must make channel decisions carefully, incorporating today's needs with tomorrow's likely selling environment. Some companies pay too little attention to their distribution channels, but others have used imaginative distribution systems to gain competitive advantage.

1. Explain why companies use distribution channels and discuss the functions that these channels perform.

Most producers use intermediaries to bring their products to market. They try to forge a *distribution channel*—a set of interdependent organizations involved in the process of making a product or service available for use or consumption by the consumer or business user. Through their contacts, experience, specialization, and scale of operation, intermediaries

usually offer the firm more than it can achieve on its own. Distribution channels perform many key functions. Some help *complete* transactions by gathering and distributing *information* needed for planning and aiding exchange; by developing and spreading persuasive *communications* about an offer; by performing *contact* work—finding and communicating with prospective buyers; by *matching*—shaping and fitting the offer to the buyer's needs; and by entering into *negotiation* to reach an agreement on price and other terms of the offer so that ownership can be transferred. Other functions help to *fulfill* the completed transactions by offering *physical distribution*—transporting and storing goods; *financing*—acquiring and using funds to cover the costs of the channel work; and *risk taking*—assuming the risks of carrying out the channel work.

2. Discuss how channel members interact and how they organize to perform the work of the channel.

The channel will be most effective when each member is assigned the tasks it can do best. Ideally, because the success of individual channel members depends on overall channel success, all channel firms should work together smoothly. They should understand and accept their roles, coordinate their goals and activities, and cooperate to attain overall channel goals. By cooperating, they can more effectively sense, serve, and satisfy the target market. In a large company, the formal organization structure assigns roles and provides needed leadership. But in a distribution channel made up of independent firms, leadership and power are not formally set. Traditionally, distribution channels have lacked the leadership needed to assign roles and manage conflict. In recent years, however, new types of channel organizations have appeared that provide stronger leadership and improved performance.

3. Identify the major channel alternatives open to a company.

Each firm identifies alternative ways to reach its market. Available means vary from direct selling to using one, two, three, or more intermediary *channel levels*. Marketing channels face continuous and sometimes dramatic change. Three of the most important trends are the growth of *vertical, horizontal,* and *hybrid marketing systems*. These trends affect channel cooperation, conflict, and competition. *Channel design* begins with assessing customer channel-service needs and company channel objectives and constraints. The company then identifies the major channel alternatives in terms of the *types* of intermediaries, the *number* of intermediaries, and the *channel responsibilities* of each. Each channel alternative must be evaluated according to economic, control, and adaptive criteria. Channel management calls for selecting qualified intermediaries and motivating them. Individual channel members must be evaluated regularly.

4. Discuss the nature and importance of physical distribution.

Just as firms are giving the marketing concept increased recognition, more business firms are paying attention to the *physical distribution,* or *marketing logistics*. Logistics is an area of potentially high cost savings and improved customer satisfaction. Marketing logistics involves coordinating the activities of the entire *supply chain* to deliver maximum value to customers. No logistics system can both maximize customer service and minimize distribution costs. Instead, the goal of logistics management is to provide a *targeted* level of service at the least cost. The major logistics functions include *order processing, warehousing, inventory management,* and *transportation*.

5. Analyze integrated logistics, including how it may be achieved and its benefits to the company.

The *integrated logistics concept* recognizes that improved logistics requires teamwork in the form of close working relationships across functional areas inside the company and across various organizations in the supply chain. Companies can achieve logistics harmony among functions by creating cross-functional logistics teams, integrative supply manager positions, and senior-level logistics executives with cross-functional authority. Channel partnerships can take the form of cross-company teams, shared projects, and information-sharing systems. Through such partnerships, many companies have switched from *anticipatory-based distribution systems* to customer-triggered *response-based distribution systems*. Today, some companies are outsourcing their logistics functions to third-party logistics providers to save costs, increase efficiency, and gain faster and more effective access to global markets.

KEY TERMS

Administered VMS	Distribution center	Intensive distribution
Channel conflict	Distribution channel	Intermodal transportation
Channel level	Exclusive distribution	Physical distribution (or marketing
Contractual VMS	Franchise organization	logistics)
Conventional distribution channel	Horizontal marketing system	Selective distribution
Corporate VMS	Hybrid marketing channel	Third-party logistics provider
Direct marketing channel	Indirect marketing channel	Vertical marketing system (VMS)
Disintermediation	Integrated logistics management	

ISSUES FOR DISCUSSION

1. The Book of the Month Club (BOMC) has successfully marketed books by mail for more than 50 years. Suggest reasons why BOMC has survived competition from chains such as B. Dalton, Waldenbooks, Borders, Barnes & Noble, and other large booksellers in recent years. How do you think BOMC will fare against online booksellers such as Amazon.com? What changes, if any, should BOMC make to meet this new competitive threat?

2. List and briefly discuss the marketing channel functions that involved creating and completing transactions. Discuss the channel functions that involve fulfilling completed transactions. Which set of functions applies most

in each of the following situations? (a) A retailer puts in a rush reorder for a needed Christmas item that is in short supply. (b) An Internet marketer seeks ways to identify and contact its market. (c) A small retailer wants to expand its order size but does not currently have funds needed to pay for the expanded order. (d) A business buyer attends a large trade show wanting to buy higher quality products on a limited budget.

3. Describe the kinds of horizontal and vertical channel conflict that might occur in one of the following: (a) the personal computer industry, (b) the automobile industry, (c) the music industry, or (d) the clothing industry. How would you remedy the problems you have just described?

4. Give your own example of each of the three major forms of vertical marketing system described in the chapter. What advantages do such systems have over traditional channel organizations?

5. What is disintermediation? Give an example other than those discussed in the chapter. What opportunities and

problems does disintermediation present for traditional retailers? Explain.

6. Which distribution strategy—intensive, selective, or exclusive—is used for each of the following products and why? (a) Piaget watches, (b) Acura automobiles, and (c) Snickers candy bars.

7. The chapter discusses four basic logistics functions. Which of these functions is most important for: (a) Quicken's Turbo Tax income tax preparation software; (b) Faith Hill's newest country music release; (c) a Toyota Camry; and (d) an issue of *Wired* magazine (see www.wired.com).

8. Regarding outsourcing: (a) Why would a company choose to outsource its distribution function? (b) What major factors contribute to a successful outsourcing relationship? What are the potential dangers of such a relationship? (c) Give an example of a company that could benefit from outsourcing its logistics, and suggest some practical outsourcing alternatives for the company. (For more information on outsourcing, see the Outsourcing Institute's Web site at www.outsourcing.com.)

MARKETING APPLICATIONS

1. Internet giant Amazon.com has thrown open its doors not only to its customers but also to its competitors. Recent expansions by this "Wal-Mart of the Web" include zShops where any other retailers can set up shop on Amazon.com's site; an All Product Search feature that helps shoppers to find any product for sale on the Web no matter where it is sold; the addition of toy, consumer electronics, and home improvement items to the Amazon site; the addition of a live auction to the site; and investment in and links to numerous "dotcom" retailers, including a sports site Gear.com (www.gear.com), Pets.com (www.pets.com), HomeGrocer.com (www.homegrocer.com), and Drugstore.com (www.drugstore.com). Amazon is betting that these moves will make it more like a mall on the Internet. It's ambitious goal is to sell everything to everyone on the Internet. Despite many potential hurdles, Amazon.com has become a force with which even Wal-Mart must reckon.

   a. Review Amazon.com's expansion strategy. What are the benefits and challenges of each expansion move?

   b. How is Amazon.com using distribution to it's advantage?

   c. Review the Amazon.com Web site at www.amazon.com. What other changes or expansion would you recommend? Why?

   d. How is Amazon.com affecting traditional retail distribution channels? How should Wal-Mart react to Amazon.com?

2. You know about the Internet, but have you ever heard of an extranet? An extranet occurs when a company opens part of its own internal network (or intranet) to trusted suppliers, distributors, and other selected external business partners. Via such extranets, a company can communicate quickly and efficiently with its partners, complete transactions, and share data. A supplier might analyze the customer's inventory needs. (Boeing booked $100 million in parts orders from airline customers in one year.) Partners might swap customer lists for interrelated products and services or share purchasing systems to gain savings through more efficient purchasing. (General Electric claims that $500 million of purchasing costs can be saved using an extranet.) Imagine the strategic advantages created when virtual partners communicate in nanoseconds about shifting supply and demand situations, customer requests and opportunities, and just-in-time inventory needs. Purchase processing times can be reduced from weeks to minutes at enormous cost savings, which can then be passed along to consumers.

   a. What role will extranets play in distribution decisions for retailers, wholesalers, and manufacturers?

   b. Discuss the potential dangers and benefits of an extranet system.

c. How might Home Depot employ an extranet in its dealings with suppliers? What types of activities and information might be shared on this extranet? How might this save time and costs?

d. How does the extranet concept fit with outsourcing (if at all)?

 INTERNET CONNECTIONS

HYBRID MARKETING CHANNELS

Many companies have adopted multichannel distribution systems or hybrid marketing channels. This allows companies to reach different customer segments simultaneously. One segment that publishers would like to reach is college students. Traditionally, students have been reached through the campus bookstore, which is probably where you bought this book. But what if the bookstore was out of stock and you needed the text right away? You have alternatives. For example, you can purchase the book directly from Prentice Hall by phone, or you can order it online from a Web bookstore. Visit Prentice Hall at www.prenhall.com to explore these options. Get price quotes from at least three of the online retailers listed.

Retailer	Price	Shipping Charge	Shipping Time
Campus bookstore			
Prentice Hall by phone			
Amazon www.amazon.com			
Barnes & Noble (online) www.barnesandnoble.com			
Borders (online) www.borders.com			
Bookstore at another college (if online, specify)			

FOR DISCUSSION

1. Which distribution channel offers the lowest prices (don't forget to include shipping charges)?
2. Is the shipping time for the off-campus channels substantial enough to present a hardship for the college student segment?
3. Are there advantages to the campus bookstore that the off-campus channels cannot provide?
4. What are the advantages to the publisher for maintaining a multichannel distribution system? Disadvantages?
5. Why doesn't Prentice Hall display the text on its site and simply charge users for using and printing it?

SAVVY SITES

- Bertelsmann (www.bertelsmann.de) is one of the largest multimedia giants, owning sites such as www.bugjuice.com for alternative music in the United States, and other hot Web properties all over the globe.
- The *New York Times* (www.nyt.com) and the *Wall Street Journal* (www.wsj.com) both deliver their news products online. Interestingly, the pricing differs between their online and traditional channels. Also, users must buy an annual subscription to the WSJ prior to using the site.
- Want to get global news before online media get it? Search Reuters, (www.reuters.com), a premier news service. Their archives are helpful for research projects.

 NOTES

1. Quotes from Donald V. Fites, "Make Your Dealers Your Partners," *Harvard Business Review,* March–April 1996, pp. 84–95; and De Ann Weimer, "A New Cat on the Hot Seat," *Business Week,* March 1998, pp. 56–62. Also see Peter Elstrom, "This Cat Keeps on Purring," *Business Week,* January 20, 1997, pp. 82–84; "Caterpillar CEO Optimistic About Company's Future," press release accessed online at www.cat.com, April 14, 1999; and "Best Sales Forces: Caterpillar," *Sales & Marketing Management,* July 1999, p. 64.

2. See Louis Stern, Adel I. El-Ansary, and Anne Coughlin, *Marketing Channels*, 5th ed. (Upper Saddle River, NJ: Prentice Hall, 1996), p. 3.

3. Greg Burns, "Fast-Food Fight," *Business Week*, June 2, 1997, pp. 34–36; Patricia Sellers, "McDonald's Starts Over," *Fortune*, June 22, 1998, pp. 34–35; and Rochelle Garner, "Mad as Hell," *Sales & Marketing Management*, June 1999, pp. 55–59.

4. See Stern, El-Ansary, and Coughlin, *Marketing Channels*, p. 251.

5. See Allan J. Magrath, "Collaborative Marketing Comes of Age—Again," *Sales & Marketing Management*, September 1991, pp. 61–64; Andrew E. Serwer, "What Price Loyalty?" *Fortune*, January 10, 1995, pp. 103–4; and Judann Pollack and Louise Kramer, "Coca-Cola and Pringles Eye Global Brand Linkup," *Advertising Age*, June 15, 1998, pp. 1, 73.

6. See Rowland T. Moriarity and Ursula Moran, "Managing Hybrid Marketing Systems," *Harvard Business Review*, November–December 1990, pp. 146–55; Frank V. Cespedes and E. Raymond Corey, "Managing Multiple Channels," *Business Horizons*, July–August 1990, pp. 67–77; Geoffrey Brewer, "Lou Gerstner Has His Hands Full," *Sales & Marketing Management*, May 1998, pp. 36–41; and the ShopIBM Web site at www.direct.ibm.com.

7. See Garner, "Mad as Hell," pp. 55–61.

8. Subhash C. Jain, *International Marketing Management*, 3rd ed. (Boston, MA: PWS-Kent Publishing, 1990), pp. 489–91. Also see Emily Thornton, "Revolution in Japanese Retailing," *Fortune*, February 7, 1994, pp. 143–47; and "Ever-Shorter Channels—Wholesale Industry Restructures," *Focus Japan*, July–August 1997, pp. 3–4.

9. For examples, see Philip Cateora, *International Marketing*, 7th ed. (Homewood, IL: Richard D. Irwin, 1990), pp. 570–71; and Dexter Roberts, "Blazing Away at Foreign Brands," *Business Week*, May 12, 1997, p. 58.

10. See James A. Narus and James C. Anderson, "Turn Your Industrial Distributors into Partners," *Harvard Business Review*, March–April 1986, pp. 66–71; Jan B. Heide, "Interorganizational Governance in Marketing Channels," *Journal of Marketing*, January 1994, pp. 71–85; Nirmalya Kumar, "The Power of Trust in Manufacturer–Retailer Relationships," *Harvard Business Review*, November–December 1996, pp. 92–106; James A. Narus and James C. Anderson, "Rethinking Distribution," *Harvard Business Review*, July–August 1996, pp. 112–20; and James C. Anderson and James A. Narus, *Business Market Management* (Upper Saddle River, NJ: Prentice Hall, 1999), pp. 276–88.

11. For a full discussion of laws affecting marketing channels, see Stern, El-Ansary, and Coughlin, *Marketing Channels*, chap. 8.

12. Ronald Henkoff, "Delivering the Goods," *Fortune*, November 18, 1994, pp. 64–78. Also see Shlomo Maital, "The Last Frontier of Cost Reduction," *Across the Board*, February 1994, pp. 51–52.

13. Maital, "The Last Frontier of Cost Reduction," p. 52.

14. See "Linking with Vendors for Just-in-Time Service," *Chain Store Age Executive*, June 1993, pp. 22A–24A; Ken Cottrill, "Reforging the Supply Chain," *The Journal of Business Strategy*, November–December 1997, pp. 35–39; and "Kmart to Outsource Most EDI Tasks," *Chain Store Age*, April 1998, pp. 74–76.

15. John Huey, "Wal-Mart: Will It Take Over the World?" *Fortune*, January 30, 1989, pp. 52–64. Also see "Distribution Centers," *Chain Store Age*, October 1996, pp. 4–10.

16. For statistics on freight shipments, see *Transportation Statistics Annual Report: 1998*, U.S. Department of Transportation, Bureau of Transportation Statistics, (Washington, DC: 1998). A copy can be obtained from www.fedstats.gov.

17. Shawn Tully, "Comeback Ahead for Railroads," *Fortune*, June 17, 1991, pp. 107–13; and Joseph Weber, "Highballing Toward Two Big Railroads," *Business Week*, March 17, 1997, pp. 32–33.

18. See "Trucking Deregulation: A Ten-Year Anniversary," *Fortune*, August 13, 1990, pp. 25–35; and Brian O'Reilly and Alicia Hills Moore, "On the Road Again," *Fortune*, April 27, 1998, pp. 182–95.

19. See Sandra J. Skrovan, "Partnering with Vendors: The Ties That Bind," *Chain Store Age Executive*, January 1994, pp. 6MH–9MH; Robert D. Buzzell and Gwen Ortmeyer, "Channel Partnerships Streamline Distribution," *Sloan Management Review*, March 22, 1995, p. 85; and Ken Cottrill, "Reforging the Supply Chain," *The Journal of Business Strategy*, November–December 1997, pp. 35–39.

20. Skrovan, "Partnering with Vendors," p. 6MH; and Susan Caminiti, "After You Win, the Fun Begins," *Fortune*, May 2, 1994, p. 76.

21. Tom Stein and Jeff Sweat, "Killer Supply Chains—Six Companies Are Using Supply Chains to Transform the Way They Do Business," *Information Week*, November 11, 1998, p. 36.

22. Myron Magnet, "The New Golden Rule of Business," *Fortune*, February 21, 1994, pp. 60–64. For a related example, see Justin Martin, "Are You as Good as You Think You Are?" *Fortune*, September 1996, pp. 145–46.

23. Based on an address by Professor Donald J. Bowersox at Michigan State University on August 5, 1992. For a general discussion of improving supply chain performance, see Marshall L. Fisher, "What Is the Right Supply Chain for Your Product?" *Harvard Business Review*, March–April 1997, pp. 105–16.

24. Brian Milligan, "New Study Says 3PL Services Keep Growing," *Purchasing*, June 3, 1999, pp. 89–90.

25. See Martha Celestino, "Choosing a Third-Party Logistics Provider," *World Trade*, July 1999, pp. 54–56.

26. See Stern, El-Ansary, and Coughlin, *Marketing Channels*, p. 160; and Sandor Boyson, Thomas Corsi, Martin Dresner, and Elliott Rabinovich, "Managing Effective Third Party Logistics Relationships: What Does It Take?" *Journal of Business Logistics*, 20, no. 1, 1999, pp. 73–101.

COMPANY CASE

12

Icon Acoustics: Bypassing Tradition

THE DREAM

Like most entrepreneurs, Dave Fokos dreams a lot. He imagines customers eagerly phoning Icon Acoustics in Billerica, Massachusetts, to order his latest, custom-made stereo speakers. He sees sales climbing, cash flowing, and hundreds of happy workers striving to produce top-quality products that delight Icon's customers.

Like most entrepreneurs, Dave has taken a long time to develop his dream. While majoring in electrical engineering at Cornell, Dave discovered that he had a strong interest in audio engineering. Following graduation, Dave landed a job as a speaker designer with Conrad-Johnson, a high-end audio-equipment manufacturer. Within four years, Dave had designed 13 speaker models and decided to start his own company.

Dave identified a market niche that he felt other speaker firms had overlooked. The niche consisted of "audio-addicts"—people who love to listen to music and appreciate first-rate stereo equipment. These affluent, well-educated customers are genuinely obsessed with their stereo equipment. "They'd rather buy a new set of speakers than eat," Dave observes.

Dave faced one major problem—how to distribute Icon's products. He had learned from experience at Conrad-Johnson that most manufacturers distribute their equipment primarily through stereo dealers. Dave did not hold a high opinion of most such dealers; he felt that they too often played hardball with manufacturers, forcing them to accept thin margins. Furthermore, the dealers concentrated on only a handful of well-known producers who provided mass-produced models. This kept those firms that offered more customized products from gaining access to the market. Perhaps most disturbing, Dave felt that the established dealers often sold not what was best for customers, but whatever they had in inventory that month.

Dave dreamed of offering high-end stereo loudspeakers directly to the audio-obsessed, bypassing the established dealer network. By going directly to the customers, Dave could avoid the dealer markups and offer top-quality products and service at reasonable prices.

THE PLAN

At the age of 28, Dave set out to turn his dreams into reality. Some customers who had gotten to know Dave's work became enthusiastic supporters of his dream and invested $189,000 in Icon. With their money and $10,000 of his own, Dave started Icon in a rented facility in an industrial park.

The Market. Approximately 335 stereo-speaker makers compete for a $3 billion annual U.S. market for audio components. About 100 of these manufacturers sell to the low- and midrange segments of the market, which account for 90 percent of the market's unit volume and about 50 percent of its value. In addition to competing with each other, U.S. manufacturers also compete with Japanese firms that offer products at affordable prices. The remaining 235 or so manufacturers compete for the remaining 10 percent of the market's unit volume and 50 percent of the value—the high end—where Dave hopes to find his customers.

Icon's Marketing Strategy. To serve the audio-addicts segment, Dave offers only the highest-quality speakers. He has developed two models: The Lumen and the Parsec. The Lumen stands 18 inches high, weighs 26 pounds, and is designed for stand mounting. The floor-standing Parsec is 47 inches high and weighs 96 pounds. Both models feature custom-made cabinets that come in natural or black oak and American walnut. Dave can build and ship two pairs of the Lumen speakers or one pair of the Parsec speakers per day by himself. In order to have an adequate parts inventory, he had to spend $50,000 of his capital on the expensive components.

Dave set the price of the Lumen and Parsec at $795 and $1,795 per pair, respectively. He selected these prices to provide a 50 percent gross margin. He believes that traditional dealers would sell equivalent speakers at retail at twice those prices. Customers can call Icon on a toll-free 800 number to order speakers or to get advice directly from Dave. Icon pays for shipping and any return freight via Federal Express—round-trip freight for a pair of Parsecs costs $486.

Dave offers to pay for the return freight because a key part of his promotional strategy is a 30-day, in-home, no-

EXHIBIT 12.1 ICON ACOUSTIC'S PRO FORMA FINANCIALS ($ IN THOUSANDS)					
Year	**1**	**2**	**3**	**4**	**5**
Pairs of Speakers Sold	224	435	802	1,256	1,830
Total Sales Revenue	$303	$654	$1,299	$2,153	$3,338
Cost of Sales					
Materials and Packaging	$130	$281	$561	$931	$1,445
Shipping	$43	$83	$157	$226	$322
Total Cost of Sales	$173	$364	$718	$1,157	$1,767
Gross Profit	$130	$290	$581	$996	$1,571
Gross Margin	43%	44%	45%	46%	47%
Expenses					
New Property and Equipment	$3	$6	$12	$15	$18
Marketing	$13	$66	$70	$109	$135
General and Administrative	$51	$110	$197	$308	$378
Loan Repayment	$31	$31	$0	$0	$0
Outstanding Payables	$30	$0	$0	$0	$0
Total Expenses	$128	$213	$279	$432	$531
Pretax Profit	$2	$77	$302	$564	$1,040
Pretax Margin	1%	12%	23%	26%	31%

obligation trial. In his ads, Dave calls this "The 43,200 Minute, No Pressure Audition." The trial period allows customers to listen to the speakers in their actual listening environment. In a dealer's showroom, the customer must listen in an artificial environment and often feels pressure to make a quick decision.

Dave believes that typical high-end customers may buy speakers for "nonrational" reasons: They want a quality product and good sound, but they also want an image. Thus, Dave has tried to create a unique image through the appearance of his speakers and to reflect that image in all of the company's marketing. He spent over $40,000 on distinctive stationery, business cards, a brochure, and a single display ad. He also designed a laminated label he places just above the gold-plated input jack on each speaker. The label reads: "This loudspeaker was handcrafted by [the technician's name who assembled the speaker goes here in his/her own handwriting]. Made in the United States of America by Icon Acoustics, Inc., Billerica, Mass."

To get the word out, Dave concentrates on product reviews in trade magazines and on trade shows, such as the High End Hi-Fi show in New York. Attendees at the show cast ballots to select "The Best Sound at the Show." In the balloting, among 200 brands, Icon's Parsec speakers finished fifteenth. Among the top 10 brands, the least expensive was a pair priced at $2,400, and six of the systems were priced from $8,000 to $18,000. A reviewer in an issue of *Stereophile* magazine evaluated Icon's speakers and noted: "The overall sound was robust and dynamic, with a particularly potent low end. Parts and construction quality appeared to be first rate. Definitely a company to watch."

Dave made plans to invest in a slick, four-color display ad in *Stereo Review,* the consumer magazine with the highest circulation (600,000). He also expected another favorable review in *Stereophile* magazine.

THE REALITY

Dressed in jeans and a hooded sweatshirt, Dave pauses in the middle of assembling a cardboard shipping carton, pulls up a chair, and leans against the concrete-block wall of his manufacturing area. Reflecting on his experiences during his first year in business, Dave realizes he's learned a lot in jumping all the hurdles the typical entrepreneur faces. Dave experienced quality problems with the first cabinet supplier. Then, he ran short of a key component after a mixup with a second supplier. Despite his desire to avoid debt, he had to borrow $50,000 from a bank. Prices for his cabinets and some components had risen, and product returns had been higher than expected (19 percent for the past six months). These price and cost increases put pressure on his margins, forcing Dave to raise his prices (to those quoted earlier). Despite the price increases, his margins remained below his 50 percent target.

Still, Dave feels good about his progress. The price increase does not seem to have affected demand. The few ads and word-of-mouth advertising appear to be working. Dave receives about five phone calls per day, with one in seven calls leading to a sale. Dave also feels the stress of the long hours and the low pay, however. He is not able to pay himself a high salary—just $9,500 this year.

Dave reaches over and picks up his most recent financial projections from a workbench (see Exhibit 1). He believes that this will be a breakeven year—then he'll have it made. As Dave sets the projections back on the workbench, his mind drifts to his plans to introduce two exciting new speakers—The Micron ($2,495 per pair) and the Millennium ($7,995 per pair). He also wonders if there is a foreign market for his speakers. Should he use his same direct-marketing strategy for foreign markets, or should he consider distributors? The dream continues.

Questions

1. What functions do traditional stereo dealers perform?
2. Why has Dave Fokos decided to establish a direct channel? What objectives and constraints have shaped his decision?
3. What consumer service needs do Dave's customers have?
4. What problems will Dave face as a result of his channel decisions? What changes would you recommend in Dave's distribution strategy, if any? Will his strategy work in foreign markets?
5. What other changes would you recommend in Dave's marketing strategy?

Source: Adapted from "Sound Strategy," *Inc.,* May 1991, pp. 46–56. © 1991 by Goldhirsh Group, Inc. Used with permission. Dave Fokos also provided information.

RETAILING AND WHOLESALING

Home Depot, the giant do-it-yourself home improvement retail chain, is one of the world's hottest retailers. It's one of a breed of retailers called *category killers*—giant retailers that offer a huge selection of merchandise in a single product category at such low prices that they destroy the competition. At first glance, a cavernous Home Depot store doesn't look like much. With its cement floors and drafty, warehouselike interior, the store offers all the atmosphere of an airplane hangar. But the chances are good that you'll find exactly what you're looking for, priced to make it a real value. Home Depot carries a huge assortment of more than 35,000 items— anything and everything related to home improvement. Its prices run 20 to 30 percent below those of local hardware stores.

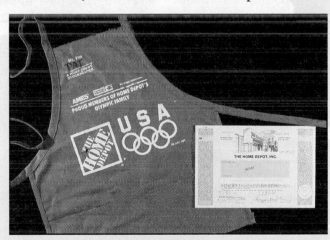

Home Depot provides more than the right products at the right prices, however. Perhaps the best part of shopping at Home Depot is the high quality of its customer service. Home Depot is more than just customer driven—it's customer *obsessed*. In the words of cofounder and chief executive Bernie Marcus, "All of our people understand what the Holy Grail is. It's not the bottom line. It's an almost blind, passionate commitment to taking care of customers." Arthur Blank, Home Depot's other cofounder and president, gives all new store managers the following six pieces of advice: "Serve the customer, serve the customer, serve the customer, serve the customer, serve the customer. And number 6, kick [butt]."

Bernie Marcus and Arthur Blank founded Home Depot with the simple mission of helping customers solve their home improvement problems. Their goal: "To take ham-handed homeowners who lack the confidence to do more than screw in a lightbulb and transform them into Mr. and Ms. Fixits." Accomplishing this mission takes more than simply peddling the store's products and taking the customers' money. It means building lasting customer relationships.

Bernie and Arthur understand the importance of customer satisfaction. They calculate that a satisfied customer is worth more than $25,000 in customer lifetime value ($38 per store visit, times 30 visits per year, times about 22 years of patronage). Customer satisfaction, in turn, results from interactions with well-trained, highly motivated employees who consistently provide good value and high-quality service. "The most important part of our formula," says Arthur, "is the quality of caring that takes place in our stores between the employee and the customer." Thus, at Home Depot, taking care of customers begins with taking care of employees.

Home Depot attracts the best salespeople by paying above-average salaries; then it trains them thoroughly. All employees take regular "product knowledge" classes to gain hands-on experience with problems customers will face. When it comes to creating customer value and satisfaction, Home Depot treats its employees as partners. All full-time employees receive at least 7 percent of their annual salary in company stock. As a result, Home Depot employees take ownership in the business of serving customers. Each employee wears a bright orange apron that says, "Hello, I'm _____ , a Home Depot stockholder. Let me help you."

Bernie and Arthur have become energetic crusaders in the cause of customer service. For example, four Sundays a year at 6:30 A.M., the two don their own orange aprons and air *Breakfast with Bernie and Art*—a good old-fashioned revival broadcast live over closed-circuit TV to the company's more than 100,000 employees nationwide. According to one account, "Bernie regularly rouses his disciples with the following: 'Where do you go if you want a job?' They yell back: 'Sears . . . Lowe's . . . Builders Square.' 'Where do you go if you want a *career?*' 'HOME DEPOT!' they roar. At times, when the excitement becomes feverish, Marcus has been known to grab a resisting Blank, plant a noisy kiss on his cheek, and exclaim, 'Arthur, I love you!'"

Home Depot avoids the high-pressure sales techniques used by some retailers. Instead, it encourages salespeople to build long-term relationships with customers—to spend whatever time it takes, visit after visit, to solve customer problems. Home Depot pays employees a straight salary so that they can spend as much time as necessary with customers without worrying about making the sale. Bernie Marcus declares, "The day I'm dead with an apple in my mouth is the day we'll pay commissions." In fact, rather than pushing customers to *overspend,* employees are trained to help customers spend *less* than they expected. "I love it when shoppers tell me they were prepared to spend $150 and our people showed them how to do the job for four or five bucks," says Bernie.

Home Depot has also extended its high-grade relationship-building efforts to the Internet. In addition to selling goods online, the company's Web site also offers plenty of how-to tips for household projects: how to fix it, build it, grow it, decorate it, or install it. It provides useful tools, such as calculators for figuring out how much paint or wallpaper is needed to cover a given amount of space. Home Depot also sends e-mail to regular site users alerting them to how-to workshops or other events at nearby stores.

Taking care of customers has made Home Depot one of today's most successful retailers. Founded in 1978, in little more than 20 years it has grown explosively to become the nation's largest do-it-yourself chain, with more than 820 stores reaping more than $30 billion in sales. Home Depot sales have grown 36 percent annually over the past decade, with 10-year average annual returns to shareholders of almost 45 percent. The company's stock price has rocketed up 28,000 percent—yes, 28,000 percent—since the company went public in 1981! In fact, a current problem in some stores is too many customers—some outlets are generating an astounding $600 of sales per square foot (compared with Wal-Mart at $250 and Kmart at $150). This has created problems with clogged aisles, stock outs, too few salespeople, and long checkout lines. Although many retailers would welcome this kind of problem, it bothers Bernie and Arthur greatly, and they've quickly taken corrective action. Continued success, they know, depends on the passionate pursuit of customer satisfaction. Bernie will tell you, "Every customer has to be treated like your mother, your father, your sister, or your brother." You certainly wouldn't want to keep your mother waiting in line.[1]

The Home Depot story provides many insights into the workings of one of today's most successful retailers. This chapter looks at *retailing* and *wholesaling.* In the first section, we look at the nature and importance of retailing, major types of store and nonstore retailers, the decisions retailers make, and the future of retailing. In the second section, we discuss these same topics as they relate to wholesalers.

RETAILING

Retailing
All activities involved in selling goods or services directly to final consumers for their personal, nonbusiness use.

Retailer
Business whose sales come *primarily* from retailing.

What is retailing? We all know that Wal-Mart, Sears, and Kmart are retailers, but so are Avon representatives, Amazon.com, the local Holiday Inn, and a doctor seeing patients. **Retailing** includes all the activities involved in selling goods or services directly to final consumers for their personal, nonbusiness use. Many institutions—manufacturers, wholesalers, and retailers—do retailing. But most retailing is done by **retailers:** businesses whose sales come *primarily* from retailing.

Although most retailing is done in retail stores, in recent years *nonstore retailing* has been growing much faster than has store retailing. Nonstore retailing includes selling to final consumers through direct mail, catalogs, telephone, home TV shopping shows, home and office parties, door-to-door contact, vending machines, online services and the Internet, and other direct retailing approaches. We discuss such direct-marketing approaches in detail in chapter 17. In this chapter, we focus on store retailing.

TYPES OF RETAILERS

Retail stores come in all shapes and sizes, and new retail types keep emerging. The most important types of retail stores are described in Table 13.1 and discussed in the following sections. They can be classified in terms of several characteristics, including the *amount of service* they offer, the breadth and depth of their *product lines,* the *relative prices* they charge, and how they are organized.

Amount of Service

Different products require different amounts of service, and customer service preferences vary. Retailers may offer one of three levels of service—self-service, limited service, and full service.

Self-service retailers serve customers who are willing to perform their own "locate-compare-select" process to save money. Self-service is the basis of all discount operations and is typically used by sellers of convenience goods (such as supermarkets) and nationally branded, fast-moving shopping goods (such as Best Buy or Service Merchandise).

Limited-service retailers, such as Sears or JCPenney, provide more sales assistance because they carry more shopping goods about which customers need information. Their increased operating costs result in higher prices. In *full-service retailers,* such as specialty stores and first-class department stores, salespeople assist customers in every phase of the shopping process. Full-service stores usually carry more specialty goods for which customers like to be "waited on." They provide more services resulting in much higher operating costs, which are passed along to customers as higher prices.

TABLE 13.1 MAJOR TYPES OF RETAILERS

Type	Description	Examples
Specialty stores	Carry a narrow product line with a deep assortment within that line: apparel stores, sporting-goods stores, furniture stores, florists, and bookstores. Specialty stores can be subclassified by the degree of narrowness in their product line. A clothing store would be a *single-line store*; a men's clothing store would be a *limited-line store*; and a men's custom-shirt store would be a *superspecialty store*.	Athlete's Foot (sport shoes only), Tall Men (tall men's clothing), The Limited (women's clothing), The Body Shop (cosmetics and bath supplies)
Department stores	Carry several product lines—typically clothing, home furnishings, and household goods—with each line operated as a separate department managed by specialist buyers or merchandisers.	Sears, Saks Fifth Avenue, Marshall Fields, May's, JCPenney, Nordstrom, Macy's
Supermarkets	Relatively large, low-cost, low-margin, high-volume, self-service operations designed to serve the consumers total needs for food, laundry, and household maintenance products.	Safeway, Kroger, A&P, Winn-Dixie, Publix, Food Lion, Vons, Jewel
Convenience stores	Relatively small stores that are located near residential areas, open long hours seven days a week, and carry a limited line of high-turnover convenience products. Their long hours and their use by consumers mainly for "fill-in" purchases make them relatively high-price operations.	7-Eleven, Circle K, Stop-N-Go, White Hen Pantry
Superstores	Larger stores that aim at meeting consumers' total needs for routinely purchased food and nonfood items. They include *supercenters*, combined supermarket and discount stores, which feature cross-merchandising. They also include so-called *category killers* that carry a very deep assortment of a particular line. Another superstore variation is *hypermarkets*, huge stores that combine supermarket, discount, and warehouse retailing to sell routinely purchased goods as well as furniture, large and small appliances, clothing, and many other items.	*Supercenters:* Wal-Mart Supercenters, and Super Kmart Centers; *Category killers:* Toys "R" Us (toys), Petsmart (pet supplies), Staples (office supplies), Home Depot (home improvements), Best Buy (consumer electronics); *Hypermarkets:* Carrefour (France), Pyrca (Spain), Meijer's (Netherlands)
Discount stores	Sell standard merchandise at lower prices by accepting lower margins and selling higher volumes. A true discount store *regularly* sells its merchandise at lower prices, offering mostly national brands, not inferior goods. Discount retailers include both general merchandise and specialty merchandise stores.	*General discount stores:* Wal-Mart, Kmart, Target; *Specialty discount stores:* Circuit City (electronics), Crown Book (books)
Off-price retailers	Sell a changing and unstable collection of higher-quality merchandise, often leftover goods, overruns, and irregulars obtained at reduced prices from manufacturers or other retailers. They buy at less-than-regular wholesale prices and charge consumers less than retail. They include three main types:	
Independent off-price retailers	Owned and run either by entrepreneurs or by divisions of larger retail corporations.	T.J. Maxx, Filene's Basement, Loehmann's, Hit or Miss
Factory outlets	Owned and operated by manufacturers and normally carry the manufacturer's surplus, discontinued, or irregular goods. Such outlets increasingly group together in *factory outlet malls*, where dozens of outlet stores offer prices as much as 50 percent below retail on a broad range of items.	Mikasa (dinnerware), Dexter (shoes), Ralph Lauren and Liz Claiborne (upscale apparel)
Warehouse clubs (or wholesale clubs)	Sell a limited selection of brand-name grocery items, appliances, clothing, and a hodgepodge of other goods at deep discounts to members who pay $25 to $50 annual membership fees. They serve small businesses and other club members out of huge, low-overhead, warehouselike facilities and offer few frills or services.	Wal-Mart-owned Sam's Club, Costco, BJ's Wholesale Club

Product Line

Retailers also can be classified by the length and breadth of their product assortments. Some retailers, such as **specialty stores,** carry narrow product lines with deep assortments within those lines. Today, specialty stores are flourishing. The increasing use of market segmentation, market targeting, and product specialization has resulted in a greater need for stores that focus on specific products and segments.

Specialty store
A retail store that carries a narrow product line with a deep assortment within that line.

In contrast, **department stores** carry a wide variety of product lines. In recent years, department stores have been squeezed between more focused and flexible specialty stores on the one hand, and more efficient, lower-priced discounters on the other. In response, many have added "bargain basements" and promotional events to meet the discount threat. Others have set up store brand programs, "boutiques" and "designer shops" (such as Tommy Hilfiger or Polo shops within department stores), and other store formats that compete with specialty stores. Still others are trying mail-order, telephone, and Web site selling. Service remains the key differentiating factor. Department stores such as Nordstrom, Saks, Neiman Marcus, and other high-end department stores are doing well by emphasizing high-quality service.

Department store
A retail organization that carries a wide variety of product lines—typically clothing, home furnishings, and household goods; each line is operated as a separate department managed by specialist buyers or merchandisers.

Supermarkets are the most frequently shopped type of retail store. Today, however, they are facing slow sales growth because of slower population growth and an increase in competition from convenience stores, discount food stores, and superstores. Supermarkets also have been hit hard by the rapid growth of out-of-home eating. Thus, most supermarkets are making improvements to attract more customers. In the battle for "share of stomachs," most large supermarkets have moved upscale, providing from-scratch bakeries, gourmet deli counters, and fresh seafood departments. Others are cutting costs, establishing more efficient operations, and lowering prices in order to compete more effectively with food discounters.

Supermarket
Large, low-cost, low-margin, high-volume, self-service store that carries a wide variety of food, laundry, and household products.

Convenience stores are small stores that carry a limited line of high-turnover convenience goods. In the 1990s, the convenience store industry suffered from overcapacity as its primary market of young, blue-collar men shrunk. As a result, many chains have redesigned their stores with female customers in mind. They are dropping the image of a "truck stop" where men go to buy beer, cigarettes, and magazines, and instead offer fresh, prepared foods and cleaner, safer environments. Many convenience chains also are experimenting with micromarketing—tailoring each store's merchandise to the specific needs of its surrounding neighborhood. For example, a Stop-N-Go in an affluent neighborhood carries fresh produce, gourmet pasta sauces, chilled Evian water, and expensive wines. Stop-N-Go stores in Hispanic neighborhoods carry Spanish-language magazines and other goods catering to the specific needs of Hispanic consumers.[2]

Convenience store
A small store, located near a residential area, that is open long hours seven days a week and carries a limited line of high-turnover convenience goods.

Superstores are much larger than regular supermarkets and offer a large assortment of routinely purchased food products, nonfood items, and services. Examples include Safeway's Pak 'N Pay and Pathmark Super Centers. Wal-Mart, Kmart, and other discount retailers are now opening *supercenters,* combination food and discount stores that emphasize cross-merchandising. For example, at a Super Kmart Center, toasters are above the fresh-baked bread, kitchen gadgets are across from produce, and infant centers carry everything from baby food to clothing. Supercenters are growing in the United States at an annual rate of 25 percent, compared with a supermarket industry growth rate of only 1 percent. Wal-Mart, which opened its first supercenter in 1988, had opened more than 700 such stores by 2000, capturing almost two-thirds of all supercenter volume. By 2005, the retailing giant will likely be operating 1,200 to 1,500 supercenters.[3]

Superstore
A store almost twice the size of a regular supermarket that carries a large assortment of routinely purchased food and nonfood items and offers services such as dry cleaning, post offices, photo finishing, check cashing, bill paying, lunch counters, car care, and pet care.

Category killers, such as Best Buy, feature stores the size of airplane hangars that carry a very deep assortment of a particular line.

Category killer
Giant specialty store that carries a very deep assortment of a particular line and is staffed by knowledgeable employees.

Recent years have also seen the explosive growth of superstores that are actually giant specialty stores, the so-called **category killers.** They feature stores the size of airplane hangers that carry a very deep assortment of a particular line with a knowledgeable staff. Category killers are prevalent in a wide range of categories, including books, baby gear, toys, electronics, home improvement products, linens and towels, party goods, sporting goods, even pet supplies. Another superstore variation, *hypermarkets,* are huge superstores, perhaps as large as *six* football fields. Although hypermarkets have been very successful in Europe and other world markets, they have met with little success in the United States.

Finally, for some retailers, the product line is actually a service. Service retailers include hotels and motels, banks, airlines, colleges, hospitals, movie theaters, tennis clubs, bowling alleys, restaurants, repair services, hair care shops, and dry cleaners. Service retailers in the United States are growing faster than product retailers.

Relative Prices

Retailers can also be classified according to the prices they charge. Most retailers charge regular prices and offer normal-quality goods and customer service. Others offer higher-quality goods and service at higher prices. The retailers that feature low prices are discount stores, "off-price" retailers, and catalog showrooms (see Table 13.1).

Discount Stores

Discount store
A retail institution that sells standard merchandise at lower prices by accepting lower margins and selling at higher volume.

A **discount store** sells standard merchandise at lower prices by accepting lower margins and selling higher volume. The early discount stores cut expenses by offering few services and operating in warehouselike facilities in low-rent, heavily traveled districts. In recent years, facing intense competition from other discounters and department stores, many discount retailers have "traded up." They have improved decor, added new lines and services, and opened suburban branches, which have led to higher costs and prices.

Off-Price Retailers

Off-price retailer
Retailer that buys at less-than-regular wholesale prices and sells at less than retail.

When the major discount stores traded up, a new wave of **off-price retailers** moved in to fill the low-price, high-volume gap. Ordinary discounters buy at regular wholesale prices and accept lower margins to keep prices down. In contrast,

Factory outlet malls and value-added centers have blossomed in recent years, making them one of retailing's hottest growth areas.

off-price retailers buy at less-than-regular wholesale prices and charge consumers less than retail. Off-price retailers can be found in all areas, from food, clothing, and electronics to no-frills banking and discount brokerages.

The three main types of off-price retailers are *independents, factory outlets,* and *warehouse clubs.* **Independent off-price retailers** are either owned and run by entrepreneurs or are divisions of larger retail corporations. Although many off-price operations are run by smaller independents, most large off-price retailer operations are owned by bigger retail chains. Examples include Loehmann's (owned by Associated Dry Goods, owner of Lord & Taylor), Filene's Basement (Federated Department Stores), and T.J. Maxx (TJX Cos).

Factory outlets—such as the Burlington Coat Factory Warehouse, Manhattan's Brand Name Fashion Outlet, and the factory outlets of Levi-Strauss, Carters, and Ship 'n' Shore—sometimes group together in *factory outlet malls* and *value-retail centers,* where dozens of outlet stores offer prices as low as 50 percent below retail on a wide range of items. Whereas outlet malls consist primarily of manufacturers' outlets, value-retail centers combine manufacturers' outlets with off-price retail stores and department store clearance outlets. Factory outlet malls have become one of the hottest growth areas in retailing.

The malls now are moving upscale, narrowing the gap between factory outlets and more traditional forms of retailers. As the gap narrows, the discounts offered by outlets are getting smaller. However, a growing number of factory outlets now feature brands such as Coach, Esprit, Liz Claiborne, Calvin Klein, and Nike, causing department stores to protest to the manufacturers of these brands. Given their higher costs, the department stores have to charge more than the off-price outlets. Manufacturers counter that they send last year's merchandise and seconds to the factory outlet malls, not the new merchandise that they supply to the department stores. The malls are also located far from urban areas, making travel to them more difficult. Still, the department stores are concerned about the growing number of shoppers willing to make weekend trips to stock up on branded merchandise at substantial savings.[4]

Warehouse clubs (or *wholesale clubs,* or *membership warehouses*), such as Sam's Club and Costco, operate in huge, drafty, warehouselike facilities and offer few frills.

Independent off-price retailer

Off-price retailer that is either owned and run by entrepreneurs or is division of larger retail corporation.

Factory outlet

Off-price retailing operation that is owned and operated by a manufacturer and that normally carries the manufacturer's surplus, discontinued, or irregular goods.

Warehouse club

Off-price retailer that sells a limited selection of brand name grocery items, appliances, clothing, and a hodgepodge of other goods at deep discounts to members who pay annual membership fees.

Customers themselves must wrestle furniture, heavy appliances, and other large items to the checkout line. Such clubs make no home deliveries and accept no credit cards, but they do offer rock-bottom prices. Warehouse clubs took the country by storm in the 1980s, but growth slowed considerably in the 1990s as a result of growing competition among warehouse store chains and effective reactions by supermarkets and discount stores.[5]

Retail Organizations

Although many retail stores are independently owned, an increasing number are banding together under some form of corporate or contractual organization. The major types of retail organizations—*corporate chains, voluntary chains* and *retailer cooperatives, franchise organizations,* and *merchandising conglomerates*—are described in Table 13.2.

Chain stores
Two or more outlets that are owned and controlled in common, have central buying and merchandising, and sell similar lines of merchandise.

Chain stores are two or more outlets that are commonly owned and controlled. They have many advantages over independents. Their size allows them to buy in large quantities at lower prices. They can afford to hire corporate-level specialists to deal with areas such as pricing, promotion, merchandising, inventory control, and sales forecasting. Corporate chains gain promotional economies because their advertising costs are spread over many stores and over a large sales volume.

The great success of corporate chains caused many independents to band together in one of two forms of contractual associations. One is the *voluntary chain*—a wholesaler-sponsored group of independent retailers that engages in group buying and common merchandising. The other form of contractual association is the *retailer cooperative*—a group of independent retailers that bands together to set up a jointly owned, central wholesale operation and conducts joint merchandising and

TABLE 13.2 MAJOR TYPES OF RETAIL ORGANIZATIONS

Type	Description	Examples
Corporate chain stores	Two or more outlets that are commonly owned and controlled, employ central buying and merchandising, and sell similar lines of merchandise. Corporate chains appear in all types of retailing, but they are strongest in department stores, variety stores, food stores, drugstores, shoe stores, and women's clothing stores.	Tower Records, CVS Pharmacy, Pottery Barn (dinnerware and home furnishings)
Voluntary chains	Wholesaler-sponsored groups of independent retailers engaged in bulk buying and common merchandising.	Independent Grocers Alliance (IGA), Sentry Hardwares, Western Auto, Tru Value
Retailer cooperatives	Groups of independent retailers who set up a central buying organization and conduct joint promotion efforts.	Associated Grocers (groceries), ACE (hardware)
Franchise organizations	Contractual association between a *franchiser* (a manufacturer, wholesaler, or service organization) and *franchisees* (independent businesspeople who buy the right to own and operate one or more units in the franchise system). Franchise organizations are normally based on some unique product, service, or method of doing business, or on a trade name or patent, or on goodwill that the franchiser has developed.	McDonald's, Subway, Pizza Hut, Jiffy Lube, Meineke Mufflers, 7-Eleven
Merchandising conglomerates	A free-form corporation that combines several diversified retailing lines and forms under central ownership, along with some integration of their distribution and management functions.	Dayton-Hudson, the Venator Group

promotion efforts. These organizations give independents the buying and promotion economies they need to meet the prices of corporate chains.

Franchise
A contractual association between a manufacturer, wholesaler, or service organization (a franchiser) and independent businesspeople (franchisees) who buy the right to own and operate one or more units in the franchise system.

Another form of contractual retail organization is a **franchise.** The main difference between franchise organizations and other contractual systems (voluntary chains and retail cooperatives) is that franchise systems are normally based on some unique product or service; on a method of doing business; or on the trade name, goodwill, or patent that the franchiser has developed. Franchising has been prominent in fast foods, video stores, health or fitness centers, haircutting, auto rentals, motels, travel agencies, real estate, and dozens of other product and service areas. Franchising is described in detail in Marketing Highlight 13.1.

Finally, *merchandising conglomerates* are corporations that combine several different retailing forms under central ownership. Examples include Dayton-Hudson, JCPenney, and the Venator Group. For example, Dayton-Hudson operates Target (upscale discount stores), Mervyn's (middle-market apparel and soft goods), and three department stores—Dayton's, Hudson's, and Marshall Fields. The Venator Group owns numerous specialty chains, including Foot Locker, Northern Reflections, Champs Sports, Afterthoughts (targeting American teenage girls), Eastbay (catalog and online sales), and a dozen others. Diversified retailing, which provides superior management systems and economies that benefit all the separate retail operations, is likely to increase in the new millennium.

RETAILER MARKETING DECISIONS

Retailers are searching for new marketing strategies to attract and hold customers. In the past, retailers attracted customers with unique products, more or better services than their competitors offered, or credit cards. Today, national-brand manufacturers, in their drive for volume, have placed their branded goods everywhere. Thus, stores offer more similar assortments—national brands are found not only in department stores but also in mass-merchandise and off-price discount stores. As a result, stores are looking more and more alike.

Service differentiation among retailers has also eroded. Many department stores have trimmed their services, whereas discounters have increased theirs. Customers have become smarter and more price sensitive. They see no reason to pay more for identical brands, especially when service differences are shrinking. For all these reasons, many retailers today are rethinking their marketing strategies.

As shown in Figure 13.1, retailers face major marketing decisions about their *target markets* and *positioning, product assortment and services, price, promotion,* and *place.*

FIGURE 13.1 Retailer marketing decisions

FRANCHISE FEVER

Once considered upstarts among independent businesses, franchises now command 35 percent of all retail sales in the United States. These days, it's nearly impossible to stroll down a city block or drive on a suburban street without seeing a McDonald's, Subway, Jiffy Lube, or Holiday Inn. One of the best-known and most successful franchisers, McDonald's, now has 24,500 stores in 116 countries and racks up more than $36 billion in systemwide sales. Over 80 percent of McDonald's restaurants worldwide are owned and operated by franchisees. Gaining fast is Subway Sandwiches and Salads, one of the fastest-growing franchises, with nearly 14,000 shops in 71 countries. Franchising is even moving into new areas such as education. For example, LearnRight Corporation, in State College, Pennsylvania, franchises its methods for teaching students thinking skills.

How does a franchising system work? The individual franchises are a tightly knit group of enterprises whose systematic operations are planned, directed, and controlled by the operation's innovator, called a *franchiser.* Generally, franchises are distinguished by three characteristics:

1. *The franchiser owns a trade or service mark and licenses it to franchisees in return for royalty payments.*
2. *The franchisee is required to pay for the right to be part of the system.* Yet this initial fee is only a small part of the total amount that franchisees invest when they sign a franchising contract. Start-up costs include rental and lease of equipment and fixtures and sometimes a regular license fee. McDonald's franchisees may invest as much as $600,000 in initial start-up costs. The franchisee then pays McDonald's a service fee and a rental charge that equal 11.5 percent of the franchisee's sales volume. Subway's success is partly due to its low start-up cost average, just $100,000, which is lower than 70 percent of other franchise system start-up costs. However, Subway franchisees pay an 8 percent royalty on gross sales, the highest in the food franchise industry, plus a 3.5 percent advertising fee.
3. *The franchiser provides its franchisees with a marketing and operations system for doing business.* McDonald's requires franchisees to attend its "Hamburger University" in Oak Brook, Illinois, for three weeks to learn how to manage the business. Franchisees must also adhere to certain procedures in buying materials.

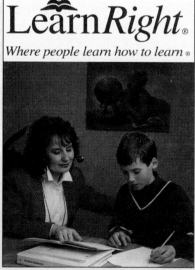

Franchising fever: Most of us encounter dozens of franchised businesses each day, from familiar fast-food restaurants to franchised educational systems such as LearnRight.

In the best cases, franchising is mutually beneficial to both franchiser and franchisee. Franchisers can cover a new territory in little more than the time it takes the franchisee to sign a contract. They can achieve enormous purchasing power (consider the purchase order that Holiday Inn is likely to make for bed linens, for instance). Franchisers also benefit from the franchisees' familiarity with local communities and conditions and from the motivation and hard work of employees who are entrepreneurs rather than "hired hands." Similarly, franchisees benefit from buying into a proven business with a well-known and accepted brand name. And they receive ongoing support in areas ranging from marketing and advertising to site selection, staffing, and financing.

As a result of the franchise explosion in recent years, many types of franchisers (such as fast-food franchisers) are facing worrisome market saturation. One indication is the number of franchisee complaints filed with the Federal Trade Commission against parent companies, which has been growing by more than 50 percent annually since 1990. The most common complaint: Franchisers "encroach" on existing franchisees' territory by bringing in another store. For example, McDonald's franchisees in California and other states recently complained when the company decided to open new company-owned stores in their areas.

Or franchisees may object to parent company marketing programs that may adversely affect their local operations. For instance, franchisees strongly resisted McDonald's "Campaign 55" promotion, in

which the company reduced prices on Big Macs and Egg McMuffins to 55 cents in an effort to revive stagnant sales. Many franchisees believed that the promotion might cheapen McDonald's image and unnecessarily reduce their profit margins.

Another complaint is higher-than-advertised failure rates. Subway, in particular, has been criticized for misleading its franchisees by telling them that it has only a 2 percent failure rate when the reality is much different. In addition, some franchisees feel that they've been misled by exaggerated claims of support, only to feel abandoned after the contract is signed and $100,000 is invested.

There will *always* be a conflict between the franchisers, who seek systemwide growth, and the franchisees, who want to earn a good living from their individual franchises. Some new directions that may deliver both franchiser growth and franchisee earnings include:

- *Strategic alliances with major outside corporations:* An example is the alliance between film company Fuji USA and Moto Photo, a one-hour photo developer. Fuji gained instant market penetration through Moto Photo's 400 locations and Moto Photo franchisees enjoyed Fuji's brand-name recognition and advertising reach.
- *Expansion abroad:* Fast-food franchises have become very popular throughout the world. For example, Domino's has entered Japan with master franchisee Ernest Higa, who owns 106 stores in Japan with combined sales of

$140 million. Part of Higa's success can be attributed to adapting Domino's product to the Japanese market, where food presentation is everything. Higa carefully charted the placement of pizza toppings and made cutmark perforations in the boxes for perfectly uniform slices.

- *Nontraditional site locations:* Franchises are opening in airports, convenience stores, truck stops, college campuses, sporting facilities, hospitals, military bases, gambling casinos, theme parks, convention halls, and even on riverboats.

Thus, it appears, franchise fever will not cool down soon. Experts expect that by the early 2000s, franchises will capture almost 50 percent of all U.S. retail sales.

Sources: Norman D. Axelrad and Robert E. Weigand, "Franchising—A Marriage of System Members," in Sidney Levy, George Frerichs, and Howard Gordon, eds., *Marketing Managers Handbook,* 3rd ed. (Chicago: Dartnell, 1994), pp. 919–34; Andrew E. Serwer, "McDonald's Conquers the World," *Fortune,* October 17, 1994, pp. 103–16; Roberta Maynard, "The Decision to Franchise," *Nation's Business,* January 1997, pp. 49–53; Cliff Edwards, "'Campaign 55' Flop Shows Growing Power of Franchisees," *Marketing News,* July 7, 1997, p. 9; Patrick J. Kaufmann and Sevgin Eroglu, "Standardization and Adaptation in Business Format Franchising," *Journal of Business Venturing,* January 1999, pp. 69–85; information accessed online at www.subway.com, December 1999; and "McDonald's Commitment to Franchising," accessed online at www.mcdonalds.com, December 1999.

Target Market and Positioning Decision

Retailers first must define their target markets and then decide how they will position themselves in these markets. Should the store focus on upscale, midscale, or downscale shoppers? Do target shoppers want variety, depth of assortment, convenience, or low prices? Until they define and profile their markets, retailers cannot make consistent decisions about product assortment, services, pricing, advertising, store decor, or any of the other decisions that must support their positions.

Too many retailers fail to define their target markets and positions clearly. They try to have "something for everyone" and end up satisfying no market well. In contrast, successful retailers define their target markets well and position themselves strongly. For example, in 1963, Leslie H. Wexner borrowed $5,000 from his aunt to create *The Limited,* which started as a single store targeted to young, fashion-conscious women. All aspects of the store—clothing assortment, fixtures, music, colors, personnel—were orchestrated to match the target consumer. He continued to open more stores, but a decade later his original customers were no longer in the "young" group. To catch the new "youngs," he started the Limited Express. Over the years, he has started or acquired other highly targeted store chains, including Lane Bryant, Victoria's Secret, Lerner, Express, Structure, Bath & Body Works, and others to reach new segments. Today The Limited, Inc. operates more than 5,300 stores in several different segments of the market, with sales of almost $10 billion.[6]

Even large stores such as Wal-Mart, Sears, Kmart, and Target must define their major target markets in order to design effective marketing strategies. In fact, in recent years, thanks to strong targeting and positioning, Wal-Mart has zoomed past Sears and Kmart to become the world's largest retailer (see Marketing Highlight 13.2). How can any discounter hope to compete with the likes of huge and dominating Wal-Mart? Again, the answer is good targeting and positioning. For example, rather than facing Wal-Mart head-on, Target aims for a seemingly oxymoronic niche—the "upscale discount" segment.

★ Target—or Tar-*zhay* as many fans call it—has developed its own distinct interpretation of the discount retailing. "Going to Target is a cool experience, and everybody now considers it cool to save money," says one retailing consultant. "On the other hand, is it cool to save at Kmart, at Wal-Mart? I don't think so." Wal-Mart and other rival "marts" achieve growth with expanded stores, inventory prowess, and rock-bottom prices. But Target isn't Wal-Mart, the giant that wooed suburbia with its acres of guns and gummy bears. And it definitely isn't Kmart, which still seems downscale despite its Martha Stewart tea-towel sets. Target's aim is more subtle: Stick to low prices, of course, but rise above the discount fray with upmarket style and design and higher-grade service. In other words, price like a discounter, but don't think like one. Target's ability to position itself as an upscale alternative really separates it from its mass-merchant peers. The payoff is that Target's "expect more, pay less" creed is appealing to more affluent consumers than those frequenting other discounters. The chain's average customer is typically female, 40, and college educated, with a household income approaching $50,000. On average, Target customers spend $40 a visit, almost twice that of other mass merchants. With nearly 1,000 stores nationwide, Target accounted for an impressive 75 percent of parent company Dayton-Hudson's sales and earnings. "People used to say, 'Ooh, a Nordstrom's coming to town,'" says another consultant. "Those same people now say, 'Ooh, we're getting a Target!' "[7]

Target—or Tar-zhay as many fans call it—has developed its own distinct positioning as an "upscale discounter." Its trendy ads appeal to more affluent consumers who spend more than twice as much per visit as those frequenting other discounters. Its familiar bulls-eye design is a registered trademark.

Product Assortment and Services Decision

Retailers must decide on three major product variables: *product assortment, services mix,* and *store atmosphere.*

The retailer's *product assortment* should match target shoppers' expectations. In its quest to differentiate itself from competitors, a retailer can use any of several product-differentiation strategies. For one, it can offer merchandise that no other competitor carries—its own private brands or national brands on which it holds exclusives. For example, The Limited designs most of the clothes carried by its store and Saks gets exclusive rights to carry a well-known designer's labels. Second, the retailer can feature blockbuster merchandising events—Bloomingdale's is known for running spectacular shows featuring goods from a certain country, such as India or China. Or the retailer can offer surprise merchandise, as when Loehmann's offers surprise assortments of seconds, overstocks, and closeouts. Finally, the retailer can differentiate itself by offering a highly targeted product assortment—Lane Bryant carries goods in larger sizes; Brookstone offers an unusual assortment of gadgets in what amounts to an adult toy store.

Retailers also must decide on a *services mix* to offer customers. The old mom-and-pop grocery stores offered home delivery, credit, and conversation—services that today's supermarkets ignore. The services mix is one of the key tools of non-price competition for setting one store apart from another.

The *store's atmosphere* is another element in its product arsenal. Every store has a physical layout that makes moving around in it either hard or easy. Each store has

MARKETING
HIGHLIGHT
13.2

WAL-MART: THE WORLD'S LARGEST RETAILER

In 1962, Sam Walton and his brother opened the first Wal-Mart discount store in small-town Rogers, Arkansas. It was a big, flat, warehouselike store that sold everything from apparel to automotive supplies to small appliances at very low prices. Experts gave the fledgling retailer little chance—conventional wisdom suggested that discount stores could succeed only in large cities. Yet, from these modest beginnings, the chain expanded rapidly, opening new stores in one small southern town after another.

By the mid-1980s, Wal-Mart had exploded onto the national retailing

scene. Incredibly, Wal-Mart's annual sales now exceed $140 billion—more than those of Sears, Kmart, JCPenney, and Target combined—making it the world's fourth largest company. Each year in the United States, Wal-Mart sells one out of every four quarts of motor oil, one out of every five deodorants, and one out of every four replacement toilet seats. It sells a Timex watch every 7.4 seconds and a Barbie Doll every 2 seconds.

Wal-Mart's phenomenal growth shows few signs of slowing. In recent years, the company has taken its winning formula into new growth areas.

For example, the company is now well established in larger cities and is expanding rapidly into international markets. Within only a few years of entering the grocery business with its supercenters—and more recently with its smaller Neighborhood Market stores—Wal-Mart is now the nation's number-two grocery retailer. Wal-Mart is beginning to flex its cybermuscles. The retailing giant already sells a selection of merchandise on its Web site (www.wal-mart.com), and it recently formed an alliance with Fingerhut, known for its expertise in distributing individual orders straight to customers' homes. Many industry experts believe that Wal-Mart will soon dominate Internet marketspaces in the same way that it now dominants the physical marketplace. "At the end of the next four years," predicts one retailing industry consultant, "Wal-Mart will be number one on land and online."

Such sparkling performance has rewarded investors handsomely. An investment of $1,650 in Wal-Mart stock in 1970 would be worth more than $5 million today! What are the secrets behind this spectacular success? Wal-Mart listens to and takes care of its customers, treats employees as partners, and keeps a tight rein on costs.

Listening to and Taking Care of Customers

Wal-Mart positioned itself strongly in a well-chosen target market. Initially, Sam Walton focused on value-conscious consumers in small-town America. The chain built a strong everyday low-price position long before it became fashionable in retailing. It grew rapidly by bringing the lowest possible prices to towns ignored by national discounters—

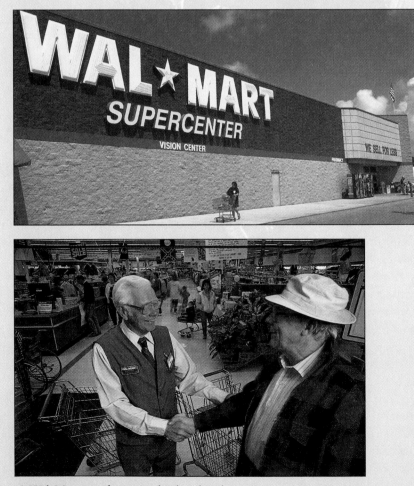

A Wal-Mart people greeter lends a hand.

towns such as Van Buren, Arkansas, and Idabel, Oklahoma.

Wal-Mart knows its customers and takes good care of them. As one analyst puts it, "The company gospel . . . is relatively simple: Be an agent for customers, find out what they want, and sell it to them for the lowest possible price." Thus, the company listens carefully—for example, each top Wal-Mart executive spends at least two days a week visiting stores, talking directly with customers, and getting a firsthand look at operations. Then, Wal-Mart delivers what customers want: a broad selection of carefully selected goods at unbeatable prices. Concludes Wal-Mart's current president and chief executive, "We're obsessed with delivering value to customers."

But the right merchandise at the right price isn't the only key to Wal-Mart's success. Wal-Mart also provides the kind of service that keeps customers satisfied. A sign reading "Satisfaction Guaranteed" hangs prominently at each store's entrance. Another sign inside the store reads "At Wal-Mart, our goal is: You're always next in line!" Customers are often welcomed by "people greeters" eager to lend a helping hand or just to be friendly. Sure enough, the store opens extra checkout counters to keep waiting lines short.

Treating Employees as Partners

Wal-Mart believes that, in the final accounting, the company's people are what really make it better. Thus, it works hard to show employees that it cares about them. Wal-Mart was first to call employees "associates," a practice now widely copied by competitors. The associates work as partners, become deeply involved in operations, and share rewards for good performance.

Everyone at Wal-Mart [is] an associate—from [the CEO] . . . to a cashier named Janet at the Wal-Mart on Highway 50 in Ocoee, Florida. "We," "us," and "our" are the operative words. Wal-Mart department heads,

hourly associates who look after one or more of 30-some departments ranging from sporting goods to electronics, see figures that many companies never show general managers: costs, freight charges, profit margins. The company sets a profit margin for each store, and if the store exceeds it, then the hourly associates share part of the additional profit.

The partnership concept is deeply rooted in the Wal-Mart corporate culture. Wal-Mart's concern for its employees translates into high employee satisfaction, which in turn translates into greater customer satisfaction.

Keeping a Tight Rein on Costs

Wal-Mart has the lowest cost structure in the industry. Thus, Wal-Mart can charge lower prices but still reap higher profits, allowing it to offer better service. Wal-Mart's lower prices and better service attract more shoppers, producing more sales, making the company more efficient, and enabling it to lower prices even more.

Wal-Mart's low costs result in part from superior management and more sophisticated technology. Its Bentonville, Arkansas, headquarters contains a computer communications system that the Defense Department would envy, giving managers around the country instant access to sales and operating information. Its huge, fully automated distribution centers employ the latest technology to supply stores efficiently. Wal-Mart also spends less than competitors on advertising—only 0.5 percent of sales, compared to 2.5 percent at Kmart and 3.8 percent at Sears. Because Wal-Mart has what customers want at the prices they'll pay, its reputation has spread rapidly by word of mouth. It has not needed more advertising.

Finally, Wal-Mart keeps costs down through good old "tough buying." Whereas the company is known for the warm way it treats customers, it is equally well known for the cold, calculated way it wrings low prices from suppliers. The fol-

lowing passage describes a visit to Wal-Mart's buying offices:

Don't expect a greeter and don't expect friendly. . . . Once you are ushered into one of the spartan little buyers' rooms, expect a steely eye across the table and be prepared to cut your price. "They are very, very focused people, and they use their buying power more forcefully than anyone else in America," says the marketing vice president of a major vendor. "All the normal mating rituals are [forbidden]. Their highest priority is making sure everyone at all times in all cases knows who's in charge, and it's Wal-Mart. They talk softly, but they have piranha hearts, and if you aren't totally prepared when you go in there, you'll have your [head] handed to you."

Some observers wonder whether Wal-Mart can be so big and still retain its focus and positioning. They wonder if an ever-larger Wal-Mart can stay close to its customers and employees. The company's managers are betting on it. No matter where it operates, Wal-Mart's announced policy is to take care of customers "one store at a time." Says one top executive: "We'll be fine as long as we never lose our responsiveness to the consumer."

Sources: Quoted material from Bill Saporito, "Is Wal-Mart Unstoppable?" *Fortune,* May 6, 1991, pp. 50–59; John Huey, "Wal-Mart: Will It Take Over the World?" *Fortune,* January 30, 1998, pp. 52–61; Jay L. Johnson, "A Borderless Wal-Mart," *Discount Merchandiser,* April 1998, p. 43; and Alice Z. Cuneo, "Wal-Mart's Goal: To Reign Over the Web," *Advertising Age,* July 5, 1999, pp. 1, 27. Also see Joan Bergmann, "Food for Thought: Going into the Grocery Business," *Discount Merchandiser,* May 1999, pp. 36–40; Joe Ronning, "Understanding Wal-Mart," *Discount Merchandiser,* April 1999, pp. 48–50; Karen Lowry Miller, "When Wal-Mart Flexes Its Cybermuscles. . . ," *Business Week,* July 26, 1999, pp. 82–87; and Kerry Capell and Heidi Dawley, "Wal-Mart's Not-So-Secret British Weapon," *Business Week,* January 24, 2000, p. 132.

a "feel"; one store is cluttered, another charming, a third plush, a fourth somber. The store must have a planned atmosphere that suits the target market and moves customers to buy.

Increasingly, retailers are turning their stores into theaters that transport customers into unusual, exciting shopping environments. For example, Barnes & Noble uses atmospherics to turn shopping for books into entertainment. It has found that "to consumers, shopping is a social activity. They do it to mingle with others in a prosperous-feeling crowd, to see what's new, to enjoy the theatrical dazzle of the display, to treat themselves to something interesting or unexpected." Thus, Barnes & Noble stores are designed with "enough woody, traditional, soft-colored library touches to please book lovers; enough sophisticated modern architecture and graphics, sweeping vistas, and stylish displays to satisfy fans of the theater of consumption. And for everyone, plenty of space, where they can meet other people and feel at home. . . . [Customers] settle in at heavy chairs and tables to browse through piles of books; they fill the cafes [designed] to increase the festivities. . . ." As one Barnes & Noble executive notes: "The feel-good part of the store, the quality of life contribution, is a big part of the success."[8]

Perhaps the most dramatic conversion of stores into theater is the Mall of America near Minneapolis. Containing more than 500 specialty stores, the mall is a veritable playground. Under a single roof, it shelters a seven-acre Knott's Berry Farm amusement park featuring 23 rides and attractions, an ice-skating rink, an Underwater World featuring hundreds of marine specimens and a dolphin show, and a two-story miniature golf course. One of the stores, Oshman Supersports USA, features a basketball court, a boxing gym, a baseball batting cage, a 50-foot archery range, and a simulated ski slope.[9]

All of this confirms that retail stores are much more than simply assortments of goods. They are environments to be experienced by the people who shop in them. Store atmospheres offer a powerful tool by which retailers can differentiate their stores from those of competitors.

Price Decision

A retailer's price policy is a crucial positioning factor and must be decided in relation to its target market, its product and service assortment, and its competition. All retailers would like to charge high markups and achieve high volume, but the two seldom go together. Most retailers seek *either* high markups on lower volume (most specialty stores) *or* low markups on higher volume (mass merchandisers and discount stores). Thus, Bijan's on Rodeo Drive in Beverly Hills prices men's suits starting at $1,000 and shoes at $400—it sells a low volume but makes a hefty profit on each sale. At the other extreme, T.J. Maxx sells brand-name clothing at discount prices, settling for a lower margin on each sale but selling at a much higher volume.

Promotion Decision

Retailers use the normal promotion tools—advertising, personal selling, sales promotion, public relations, and direct marketing—to reach consumers. They advertise in newspapers, magazines, radio, and television. Advertising may be supported by newspaper inserts and direct-mail pieces. Personal selling requires careful training of salespeople in how to greet customers, meet their needs, and handle their complaints. Sales promotions may include in-store demonstrations, displays, contests, and visiting celebrities. Public relations activities, such as press conferences and speeches, store openings, special events, newsletters, magazines, and public service activities, are always available to retailers. Many retailers have also set up Web sites, offering customers information and other features and sometimes selling merchandise directly.

Place Decision

Retailers often cite three critical factors in retailing success: *location, location,* and *location!* A retailer's location is key to its ability to attract customers. The costs of building or leasing facilities have a major impact on the retailer's profits. Thus, site-location decisions are among the most important the retailer makes. Small retailers may have to settle for whatever locations they can find or afford. Large retailers usually employ specialists who select locations using advanced methods. Two of the savviest location experts in recent years have been the off-price retailer T.J. Maxx and toy-store giant Toys "R" Us. Both put the majority of their new locations in rapidly growing areas where the population closely matches their customer base. The undisputed winner in the "place race" has been Wal Mart, whose strategy of being the first mass merchandiser to locate in small and rural markets was one of the key factors in its phenomenal early success.

Most stores today cluster together to increase their customer pulling power and to give consumers the convenience of one-stop shopping. *Central business districts* were the main form of retail cluster until the 1950s. Every large city and town had a central business district with department stores, specialty stores, banks, and movie theaters. When people began to move to the suburbs, however, these central business districts, with their traffic, parking, and crime problems, began to lose business. Downtown merchants opened branches in suburban shopping centers, and the decline of the central business districts continued. In recent years, many cities have joined with merchants to try to revive downtown shopping areas by building malls and providing underground parking.

A **shopping center** is a group of retail businesses planned, developed, owned, and managed as a unit. A *regional shopping center,* the largest and most dramatic shopping center, contains from 40 to over 200 stores. It is like a covered minidowntown and attracts customers from a wide area. A *community shopping center* contains between 15 and 40 retail stores. It normally contains a branch of a department store

Shopping center
A group of retail businesses planned, developed, owned, and managed as a unit.

Shopping centers: The spectacular Mall of America contains more than 500 stores, 45 restaurants, 7 theaters, and a 7-acre indoor theme park. It attracts more than 35 million visitors a year.

or variety store, a supermarket, specialty stores, professional offices, and sometimes a bank. Most shopping centers are *neighborhood shopping centers* or *strip malls* that generally contain between 5 and 15 stores. They are close and convenient for consumers. They usually contain a supermarket, perhaps a discount store, and several service stores—dry cleaner, self-service laundry, drugstore, video-rental outlet, barber or beauty shop, hardware store, or other stores.

Combined, all shopping centers now account for about one-third of all retail sales, but they may have reached their saturation point. Through the past decade, on average, consumers have been going to traditional malls less often, staying a shorter period of time, and visiting fewer stores. Why are people using shopping malls less? First, with more dual-income households, people have less time to shop. "You have two workers in every family and no one has time to go to the mall for four hours anymore," observes one industry analyst. "People who used to go to the mall 20 times a year now go two or three times."[10]

Second, shoppers appear to be tiring of traditional malls, which are too big, too crowded, and too much alike. Today's large malls offer great selection but are less comfortable and convenient. Finally, today's consumers have many alternatives to traditional malls, ranging from online shopping to so-called *power centers*. These huge unenclosed shopping centers consist of a long strip of retail stores, including large, free-standing anchors such as Wal-Mart, Home Depot, Best Buy, Michaels, OfficeMax, and CompUSA. Each store has its own entrance with parking directly in front for shoppers who wish to visit only one store. Power centers have increased rapidly during the past few years to challenge traditional indoor malls. "Malls have been hit hard by competition from street shopping and from recent retail innovations—especially power centers," concludes the analyst. "And . . . malls in the same city may no longer be differentiated by their anchors; they seem to have the same stores. Add to all this the emergence of Internet shopping, and the concept of the shopping mall is beginning to look dated."[11] Thus, despite the recent development of many new "megamalls," such as the spectacular Mall of America, the current trend is toward value-oriented outlet malls, power centers, and smaller malls located in medium-size and smaller cities in fast-growing areas such as the Southwest.

THE FUTURE OF RETAILING

Retailers operate in a harsh and fast-changing environment, which offers threats as well as opportunities. For example, the industry suffers from chronic overcapacity, resulting in fierce competition for customer dollars. Consumer demographics, lifestyles, and shopping patterns are changing rapidly, as are retailing technologies. To be successful, then, retailers will have to choose target segments carefully and position themselves strongly. They will have to take the following retailing developments into account as they plan and execute their competitive strategies.

New Retail Forms and Shortening Retail Life Cycles

New retail forms continue to emerge to meet new situations and consumer needs, but the life cycle of new retail forms is getting shorter. Department stores took about 100 years to reach the mature stage of the life cycle; more recent forms, such as warehouse stores, reached maturity in about 10 years. In such an environment, seemingly solid retail positions can crumble quickly. Of the top 10 discount retailers in 1962 (the year that Wal-Mart and Kmart began), not one still exists today.

Consider the Price Club, the original warehouse store chain. When Sol Price opened his first warehouse store outside San Diego in 1976, he launched a retailing revolution. Selling everything from tires and office supplies to five-pound tubs of peanut butter at superlow prices, his store chain was generating $2.6 billion a year in sales within 10 years. But Price refused to expand beyond its California base. As the industry quickly matured, Price ran headlong into wholesale clubs run by such retail giants as Wal-Mart and Kmart. Only 17 years later, in a stunning reversal of fortune, a faltering Price sold out to competitor Costco. Price's rapid rise and fall "serves as a stark reminder to mass-market retailers that past success means little in a fiercely competitive and rapidly changing industry."[12] Thus, retailers can no longer sit back with a successful formula. To remain successful, they must keep adapting.

Wheel of retailing concept
A concept of retailing that states that new types of retailers usually begin as low-margin, low-price, low-status operations but later evolve into higher-priced, higher-service operations, eventually becoming like the conventional retailers they replaced.

Many retailing innovations are partially explained by the **wheel of retailing concept.**[13] According to this concept, many new types of retailing forms begin as low-margin, low-price, low-status operations. They challenge established retailers that have become "fat" by letting their costs and margins increase. The new retailers' success leads them to upgrade their facilities and offer more services. In turn, their costs increase, forcing them to increase their prices. Eventually, the new retailers become like the conventional retailers they replaced. The cycle begins again when still newer types of retailers evolve with lower costs and prices. The wheel of retailing concept seems to explain the initial success and later troubles of department stores, supermarkets, and discount stores, and the recent success of off-price retailers.

Growth of Nonstore Retailing

Although most retailing still takes place the old-fashioned way across countertops in stores, consumers now have an array of alternatives, including mail order, television, phone, and online shopping (see Marketing Highlight 13.3). "Some Americans never face a single crowd at holiday time; they do all of their gift shopping via phone or computer. A few may never even talk to a human being; they can punch in their order and credit card numbers on a Web site and have gifts delivered to recipients. This might remove some of the personal touch from the process, but it sure saves time."[14] Although such advances may threaten some traditional retailers, they offer exciting opportunities for others. Most store retailers are now actively exploring direct retailing channels.

Increasing Intertype Competition

Today's retailers increasingly face competition from many different forms of retailers. For example, a consumer can buy CDs at specialty music stores, discount music stores, electronics superstores, general merchandise discount stores, video-rental outlets, and through dozens of Web sites. They can buy books at stores ranging from independent local bookstores to discount stores such as Wal-Mart, superstores such as Barnes & Noble or Borders, or Web sites such as Amazon.com. When it comes to brand-name appliances, department stores, discount stores, off-price retailers, or electronics superstores all compete for the same customers. Suggests one industry expert, "What we're seeing is cross-shopping—consumers buying one item at Neiman Marcus and another at Wal-Mart or General Dollar."[15]

The competition between chain superstores and smaller, independently owned stores has become particularly heated. Because of their bulk buying power and high sales volume, chains can buy at lower costs and thrive on smaller margins. The arrival of a superstore can quickly force nearby independents out of business. For

MARKETING HIGHLIGHT
13.3

SHOPPING IN CYBERSPACE

Most of us still make the majority of our purchases the old-fashioned way: We go to the store, find what we want, wait patiently in line to plunk down our cash or credit card, and bring home the goods. However, a growing number of online retailers are providing an attractive alternative—one that lets us browse, select, order, and pay with little more effort than it takes to apply an index finger to a mouse button. They sell a rich variety of goods ranging from books, CDs, flowers, and food to stereo equipment, kitchen appliances, airplane tickets, auto parts, and bags of cement. Here are just a few examples.

Books: Amazon.com, (www.amazon.com) offers 4 million titles online—more than 18 times the number carried by the largest superstore—and discounts best-sellers up to 50 percent. Amazon attracts almost 10 million visitors a month, has annual sales of more than $1 billion, and is growing fast. Customers usually receive books two to three days after ordering. Although Amazon.com can't offer couches and coffee, it has authors post comments on their books, encourages customers to share opinions on books, and recommends titles to individual customers based on each customer's profile. The company even tracks down hard-to-find books. "Businesses can do things on the Web that simply cannot be done any other way," says founder and CEO Jeff Bezos.

"We are changing the way people buy." Although Amazom.com started by selling only books, in an effort to leverage its large 11-million-person customer base, the fast-growing online marketer now also sells CDs, videos, gifts, toys and games, consumers electronics, and home improvement products, as well as hosting an online auction site.

Music: CDNow's cyberstore (www.cdnow.com) offers Web shoppers more than 500,000 CD titles, including every jazz album in the United States and 20,000 imports. Customers place their orders online, CDNow contacts the distributor, and customers receive their music within 24 hours. Jason Olim, the company's 29-year-old founder, started CDNow five years ago with $12,000 in savings, an $8,000

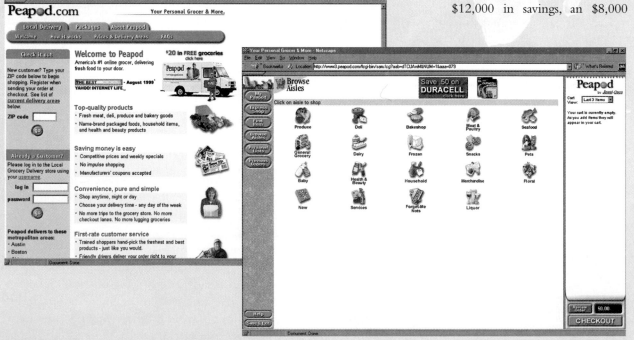

Online retailers provide an attractive alternative to shopping the old-fashioned way. Peapod, the nation's first and largest online grocery and delivery service, operates in several major cities and has attracted more than 90,000 members.

loan from his parents, and maxed-out credit cards. The online music merchant now averages more than 120,000 visitors daily to its Web site and had sales of more than $100 million last year. CDNow's biggest challenge comes from fellow cybermerchant Amazon.com, which sold $50 million worth of CDs within its first 6 months of entering the music business.

Flowers: One-fourth of all flowers sold in the United States are now ordered on the Internet. *1-800 FLOWERS* (www.1-800-flowers.com) president and owner Jim McCann, who created a $300 million company from one that was $7 million in debt in 1987, started selling flowers online in 1992. Now customers can find 1-800 FLOWERS on interactive services such as America Online, eWorld, and the Plaza on the Microsoft Network. They can choose from some 150 different gift arrangements, from roses and daisies to balloons and fruit baskets, with same-day delivery in most locations. In Arthur Andersen's latest *International Trends in Retailing,* McCann discusses taking the shopping experience on line. "For many businesses—for flowers, certainly—" he writes, "moving that [shopping] experience to an electronic medium is a bear. It just doesn't translate that directly. . . . We learned that to achieve the result we want, we would have to think about marketing in a new way. . . . Where we [used to have] actual conversations, we now would have to provide a constant, changing stream of relevant information and entertainment. What has to happen, in other words, is that retailers must learn how to recreate the physical retail experience online."

Apparel: Many basic apparel items already move like wildfire via cat-alogs. Most catalog retailers—L.L. Bean, Lands' End, and others—have already put their catalogs online. However, other noncatalog specialty retailers are also setting up to sell online. For example, Gap now uses its Web site (www.gap.com) to sell a wide range of products, from jeans and khakis, T-shirts, socks, and sweaters to accessories and fragrances. Since launching its Web site, Gap has mapped visitor usage patterns and found that, on average, people stayed 50 percent longer at Gap's site than at other sites. This statistic bodes well for the chain's chances at online retailing. Gap's entry into online retail is a natural, asserts one industry analyst. "It's about time," says the analyst. "The Gap is a marquee brand and an excellent demographic fit" with Web users. The challenge will be to develop ways to spark impulse buys, which often add significantly to sales.

Food: Consumers could buy most of their groceries without touching them. Half of European food retailers surveyed recently by the *Financial Times* believe that home delivery will represent 20 percent of volume by 2005. Several online food retailers—Peapod, NetGrocer, Webvan, Food Express—have already sprung up in the United States. *Peapod* (www.peapod.com), which has teamed with supermarkets in several major cities, has more than 90,000 members. The supermarkets receive orders by fax or over Peapod's software. They pack the orders and Peapod makes the delivery. Webvan in California plans to cut grocery stores out of the process by setting up its own distribution centers, where it will pack orders and deliver them to customers. Its Oakland distribution center includes 4½ miles of conveyor belts and temperature-sensitive rooms to store items such as wine, cigars, and ice cream. The center covers a market area of 40 square miles and serves as many customers as 20 supermarkets. Webvan provides free delivery for orders over $50 and will eventually offer about 50,000 items—including everything from the basics to 300 varieties of fresh fruit, 750 kinds of cheese, 500 types of cereals, and 700 cuts of fresh meat and fish, including live lobsters.

Still, succeeding online is anything but a given. "The online success stories in retail are few and far between," cautions another analyst. Those who fare well tend to be catalog companies with internal structures and staff to deal with orders. However, he admits, with each passing day, technological advances make it a bit easier for retailers to make their bottom lines online.

Source: Portions based on Joy A. Scansaroli and Vicky Eng, "Interactive Retailing: Marketing Products," *Chain Store Age,* January 1997, pp. 9A–10A. Gap example and quotes from Alice Z. Cuneo, "The Gap Readies Electronic Commerce Plan for Web Site," *Advertising Age,* June 23, 1997, p. 18; and Louise Lee, "Clicks and Mortar at Gap.com," *Business Week,* October 18, 1999, pp. 150–52. Other information from "My Flower Shop Blooms at Modified 1-800-Flowers," *Advertising Age,* November 9, 1998, p. 70; Andrea Peterson, "Two Web Sellers of CDs, Tapes Plan a Duet," *Wall Street Journal,* March 17, 1999, p. B1; Bill Spindle, "E-Commerce (A Special Report)," *Wall Street Journal,* July 12, 1999, p. R22; Greg Lindsay, "Will the Net Really Bring Home the Bacon?" *Fortune,* November 22, 1999, p. 354; Wendy Zellner and Stephanie Anderson Forest, "The Big Guys Go Online," *Business Week,* September 6, 1999, pp. 30–32; and Robert D. Hof, "Suddenly Amazon's Books Look Better," *Business Week,* February 21, 2000, pp. 78–84.

example, the decision by Best Buy, the electronics superstore, to sell CDs as loss leaders at rock-bottom prices pushed a number of specialty record store chains into bankruptcy.[16] Yet the news is not all bad for smaller companies. Many small, independent retailers are thriving. Independents are finding that sheer size and marketing muscle are often no match for the personal touch small stores can provide or the specialty niches that small stores fill for a devoted customer base.

The Rise of Megaretailers

The rise of huge mass merchandisers and specialty superstores, the formation of vertical marketing systems and buying alliances, and a rash of retail mergers and acquisitions have created a core of superpower megaretailers. Through their superior information systems and buying power, these giant retailers are able to offer better merchandise selections, good service, and strong price savings to consumers. As a result, they grow even larger by squeezing out their smaller, weaker competitors. The megaretailers also are shifting the balance of power between retailers and producers. A relative handful of retailers now controls access to enormous numbers of consumers, giving them the upper hand in their dealings with manufacturers. For example, in the United States, Wal-Mart's revenues are more than three times those of Procter & Gamble. Wal-Mart can, and often does, use this power to wring concessions from P&G and other suppliers.[17]

Growing Importance of Retail Technology

Retail technologies are becoming critically important as competitive tools. Progressive retailers are using computers to produce better forecasts, control inventory costs, order electronically from suppliers, send e-mail between stores, and even sell to customers within stores. They are adopting checkout scanning systems, online transaction processing, electronic funds transfer, electronic data interchange, in-store television, and improved merchandise-handling systems.

One innovative scanning system now in use is the shopper scanner, a radar-like system that counts store traffic. When a New Jersey Saks Fifth Avenue used one such system, ShopperTrak, it learned that there was a shopper surge between the hours of 11 A.M. and 3 P.M. To better handle the shopper flow, the store varied lunch hours for its counter clerks. Pier One Imports uses the same system to test, among other things, the impact of newspaper ads on store traffic. By combining traffic and sales data, retailers say they can find out how well the store converts browsers into buyers.[18]

Perhaps the most startling advances in retailing technology concern the ways in which today's retailers are connecting with customers:

> In the past, life was simple. Retailers connected with their customers through stores, through their salespeople, through the brands and packages they sold, and through direct mail and advertising in the mass media. But today, life is more complex. There are dozens of new ways to attract and engage consumers. . . . Indeed, even if one omits the obvious—the Web—retailers are still surrounded by technical innovations that promise to redefine the way they and manufacturers interact with customers. Consider, as just a sampling, touch screen kiosks, electronic shelf labels and signs, handheld shopping assistants, smart cards, self-scanning systems, virtual reality displays, and intelligent agents. So, if we ask the question, Will technology change the way [retailers] interface with customers in the future? The answer has got to be yes.[19]

Retail technology: Video-based shopper scanner systems such as ShopperTrak help manage store traffic, measure the impact of advertising, and convert browsers into buyers.

Global Expansion of Major Retailers

Retailers with unique formats and strong brand positioning are increasingly moving into other countries. Many are expanding internationally to escape mature and saturated home markets. Over the years, several giant U.S. retailers—McDonald's, Gap, Toys "R" Us—have become globally prominent as a result of their great marketing prowess. Others, such as Wal-Mart and Kmart, are rapidly establishing a global presence. Wal-Mart, which now operates more than 700 stores in 8 countries abroad, sees exciting global potential. Its international division racked up 1999 sales of more than $12 billion, an increase of 63 percent over the previous year. Here's what happened when it recently opened two new stores in Shenzhen, China:[20]

> [Customers came] by the hundreds of thousands—up to 175,000 on Saturdays alone—to China's first Wal-Mart Supercenter and Sam's Club. They broke the display glass to snatch out chickens at one store and carted off all the big-screen TVs before the other store had been open an hour. The two outlets . . . were packed on Day One and have been bustling ever since.

However, U.S retailers are still significantly behind Europe and Asia when it comes to global expansion. Only 18 percent of the top U.S. retailers operate globally, compared to 40 percent of European retailers and 31 percent of Asian retailers. Among foreign retailers that have gone global are Britain's Marks and Spencer, Italy's Benetton, France's Carrefour hypermarkets, Sweden's IKEA home furnishings stores, and Japan's Yaohan supermarkets.[21] Marks and Spencer, which started out as a penny bazaar in 1884, grew into a chain of variety stores over the decades and now has a thriving string of 150 franchised stores around the world, which sell mainly its private-label clothes. It also runs a major food business. IKEA's well-constructed but fairly inexpensive furniture has proven very popular in the United States, where shoppers often spend an entire day in an IKEA store.

Retail Stores as "Communities" or "Hangouts"

With the rise in the number of people living alone, working at home, or living in isolated and sprawling suburbs, there has been a resurgence of establishments that, regardless of the product or service they offer, also provide a place for people to get together. These places include cafes, tea shops, juice bars, bookshops, superstores, children's play spaces, brew pubs, and urban greenmarkets. Brew pubs such as New York's Zip City Brewing and Seattle's Trolleyman Pub (run by Red Hook Brewery) offer tastings and a place to pass the time. The Discovery Zone, a chain of children's play spaces, offers indoor spaces where kids can go wild without breaking anything and stressed-out parents can exchange stories. Today's bookstores have become part bookstore, part library, and part living room.

> Welcome to today's bookstore. The one featuring not only shelves and cash registers but also cushy chairs and coffee bars. It's where backpack-toting high school students come to do homework, where retirees thumb through the gardening books and parents read aloud to their toddlers. If no one actually buys books, that's just fine, say bookstore owners and managers. They're offering something grander than ink and paper, anyway. They're selling comfort, relaxation, community.[22]

Denver's two Tattered Cover Bookstores host more than 250 events annually, from folk dancing to women's meetings.

Stores as communities: Today's bookstores offer something grander than just ink and paper—they're selling comfort, relaxation, and community.

WHOLESALING

Wholesaling
All activities involved in selling goods and services to those buying for resale or business use.

Wholesaler
A firm engaged *primarily* in wholesaling activity.

Wholesaling includes all activities involved in selling goods and services to those buying for resale or business use. We call **wholesalers** those firms engaged *primarily* in wholesaling activity.

Wholesalers buy mostly from producers and sell mostly to retailers, industrial consumers, and other wholesalers. But why are wholesalers used at all? For example, why would a producer use wholesalers rather than selling directly to retailers or consumers? Quite simply, wholesalers are often better at performing one or more of the following channel functions:

★ *Selling and promoting:* Wholesalers' sales forces help manufacturers reach many small customers at a low cost. The wholesaler has more contacts and is often more trusted by the buyer than the distant manufacturer.
★ *Buying and assortment building:* Wholesalers can select items and build assortments needed by their customers, thereby saving the consumers much work.
★ *Bulk-breaking:* Wholesalers save their customers money by buying in carload lots and breaking bulk (breaking large lots into small quantities).
★ *Warehousing:* Wholesalers hold inventories, thereby reducing the inventory costs and risks of suppliers and customers.
★ *Transportation:* Wholesalers can provide quicker delivery to buyers because they are closer than the producers.
★ *Financing:* Wholesalers finance their customers by giving credit, and they finance their suppliers by ordering early and paying bills on time.
★ *Risk bearing:* Wholesalers absorb risk by taking title and bearing the cost of theft, damage, spoilage, and obsolescence.
★ *Market information:* Wholesalers give information to suppliers and customers about competitors, new products, and price developments.
★ *Management services and advice:* Wholesalers often help retailers train their salesclerks, improve store layouts and displays, and set up accounting and inventory control systems.

Merchant wholesaler
Independently owned business that takes title to the merchandise it handles.

Broker
A wholesaler who does not take title to goods and whose function is to bring buyers and sellers together and assist in negotiation

TYPES OF WHOLESALERS

Agent
A wholesaler who represents buyers or sellers on a relatively permanent basis, performs only a few functions, and does not take title to goods.

Manufacturer's sales branches and offices
Wholesaling by sellers or buyers themselves rather than through independent wholesalers.

Wholesalers fall into three major groups (see Table 13.3): *merchant wholesalers, brokers and agents,* and *manufacturers' sales branches and offices.* **Merchant wholesalers** are the largest single group of wholesalers, accounting for roughly 50 percent of all wholesaling. Merchant wholesalers include two broad types: full-service wholesalers and limited-service wholesalers. *Full-service wholesalers* provide a full set of services, whereas the various *limited-service wholesalers* offer fewer services to their suppliers and customers. The several different types of limited-service wholesalers perform varied specialized functions in the distribution channel.

Brokers and *agents* differ from merchant wholesalers in two ways: They do not take title to goods, and they perform only a few functions. Like merchant wholesalers, they generally specialize by product line or customer type. A **broker** brings buyers and sellers together and assists in negotiation. **Agents** represent buyers or sellers on a more permanent basis. *Manufacturers' agents* (also called manufacturers' representatives) are the most common type of agent wholesaler. The third major type of wholesaling is that done in **manufacturers' sales branches and offices** by sellers or buyers themselves rather than through independent wholesalers.

TABLE 13.3   MAJOR TYPES OF WHOLESALERS

Type	Description
Merchant wholesalers	Independently owned businesses that take title to the merchandise they handle. In different trades they are called *jobbers, distributors,* or *mill supply houses.* Include full-service wholesalers and limited-service wholesalers:
Full-service wholesalers	Provide a full line of services: carrying stock, maintaining a sales force, offering credit, making deliveries, and providing management assistance. There are two types:
Wholesale merchants	Sell primarily to retailers and provide a full range of services. *General-merchandise wholesalers* carry several merchandise lines, whereas *general-line wholesalers* carry one or two lines in greater depth. *Specialty wholesalers* specialize in carrying only part of a line. (Examples: health food wholesalers, seafood wholesalers.)
Industrial distributors	Sell to manufacturers rather than to retailers. Provide several services, such as carrying stock, offering credit, and providing delivery. May carry a broad range of merchandise, a general line, or a specialty line.
Limited-service wholesalers	Offer fewer services than full-service wholesalers. Limited-service wholesalers are of several types:
Cash-and-carry wholesalers	Carry a limited line of fast-moving goods and sell to small retailers for cash. Normally do not deliver. Example: A small fish store retailer may drive to a cash-and-carry fish wholesaler, buy fish for cash, and bring the merchandise back to the store.
Truck wholesalers (or truck jobbers)	Perform primarily a selling and delivery function. Carry a limited line of semiperishable merchandise (such as milk, bread, snack foods), which they sell for cash as they make their rounds to supermarkets, small groceries, hospitals, restaurants, factory cafeterias, and hotels.
Drop shippers	Do not carry inventory or handle the product. On receiving an order, they select a manufacturer, who ships the merchandise directly to the customer. The drop shipper assumes title and risk from the time the order is accepted to its delivery to the customer. They operate in bulk industries, such as coal, lumber, and heavy equipment.
Rack jobbers	Serve grocery and drug retailers, mostly in nonfood items. They send delivery trucks to stores, where the delivery people set up toys, paperbacks, hardware items, health and beauty aids, or other items. They price the goods, keep them fresh, set up point-of-purchase displays, and keep inventory records. Rack jobbers retain title to the goods and bill the retailers only for the goods sold to consumers.
Producers' cooperatives	Owned by farmer members and assemble farm produce to sell in local markets. The co-op's profits are distributed to members at the end of the year. They often attempt to improve product quality and promote a co-op brand name, such as Sun Maid raisins, Sunkist oranges, or Diamond walnuts.
Mail-order wholesalers	Send catalogs to retail, industrial, and institutional customers featuring jewelry, cosmetics, specialty foods, and other small items. Maintain no outside sales force. Main customers are businesses in small outlying areas. Orders are filled and sent by mail, truck, or other transportation.
Brokers and agents	Do not take title to goods. Main function is to facilitate buying and selling, for which they earn a commission on the selling price. Generally, specialize by product line or customer types.
Brokers	Chief function is bringing buyers and sellers together and assisting in negotiation. They are paid by the party who hired them, and do not carry inventory, get involved in financing, or assume risk. Examples: food brokers, real estate brokers, insurance brokers, and security brokers.
Agents	Represent either buyers or sellers on a more permanent basis than brokers do. There are several types:
Manufacturers' agents	Represent two or more manufacturers of complementary lines. A formal written agreement with each manufacturer covers pricing, territories, order handling, delivery service and warranties, and commission rates. Often used in such lines as apparel, furniture, and electrical goods. Most manufacturers' agents are small businesses, with only a few skilled salespeople as employees. They are hired by small manufacturers who cannot afford their own field sales forces, and by large manufacturers who use agents to open new territories or to cover territories that cannot support full-time salespeople.

TABLE 13.3 *(continued)* **MAJOR TYPES OF WHOLESALERS**	
Type	**Description**
Selling agents	Have contractual authority to sell a manufacturer's entire output. The manufacturer either is not interested in the selling function or feels unqualified. The selling agent serves as a sales department and has significant influence over prices, terms, and conditions of sale. Found in product areas such as textiles, industrial machinery and equipment, coal and coke, chemicals, and metals.
Purchasing agents	Generally have a long-term relationship with buyers and make purchases for them, often receiving, inspecting, warehousing, and shipping the merchandise to the buyers. They provide helpful market information to clients and help them obtain the best goods and prices available.
Commission merchants	Take physical possession of products and negotiate sales. Normally, they are not employed on a long-term basis. Used most often in agricultural marketing by farmers who do not want to sell their own output and do not belong to producers' cooperatives. The commission merchant takes a truckload of commodities to a central market, sells it for the best price, deducts a commission and expenses, and remits the balance to the producer.
Manufacturers' and retailers' branches and offices	Wholesaling operations conducted by sellers or buyers themselves rather than through independent wholesalers. Separate branches and offices can be dedicated to either sales or purchasing.
Sales branches and offices	Set up by manufacturers to improve inventory control, selling, and promotion. Sales branches carry inventory and are found in industries such as lumber and automotive equipment and parts. Sales offices do not carry inventory and are most prominent in dry-goods and notions industries.
Purchasing offices	Perform a role similar to that of brokers or agents but are part of the buyer's organization. Many retailers set up purchasing offices in major market centers such as New York and Chicago.

WHOLESALER MARKETING DECISIONS

Wholesalers have experienced mounting competitive pressures in recent years. They have faced new sources of competition, more demanding customers, new technologies, and more direct-buying programs on the part of large industrial, institutional, and retail buyers. As a result, they have had to improve their strategic decisions on target markets and positioning, and on the marketing mix—product assortments and services, price, promotion, and place (see Figure 13.2).

Target Market and Positioning Decision

Like retailers, wholesalers must define their target markets and position themselves effectively—they cannot serve everyone. They can choose a target group by size of customer (only large retailers), type of customer (convenience food stores only), need for service (customers who need credit), or other factors. Within the target group, they can identify the more profitable customers, design stronger offers, and build better relationships with them. They can propose automatic reordering systems, set up management-training and advising systems, or even sponsor a voluntary chain. They can discourage less profitable customers by requiring larger orders or adding service charges to smaller ones.

FIGURE 13.2   Wholesaler marketing decisions

Marketing Mix Decisions

Like retailers, wholesalers must decide on product assortment and services, prices, promotion, and place. The wholesaler's "product" is the assortment of *products and services* that it offers. Wholesalers are under great pressure to carry a full line and to stock enough for immediate delivery. But this practice can damage profits. Wholesalers today are cutting down on the number of lines they carry, choosing to carry only the more profitable ones. Wholesalers are also rethinking which services count most in building strong customer relationships and which should be dropped or charged for. The key is to find the mix of services most valued by their target customers.

Price is also an important wholesaler decision. Wholesalers usually mark up the cost of goods by a standard percentage—say, 20 percent. Expenses may run 17 percent of the gross margin, leaving a profit margin of 3 percent. In grocery wholesaling, the average profit margin is often less than 2 percent. Wholesalers are trying new pricing approaches. They may cut their margin on some lines in order to win important new customers. They may ask suppliers for special price breaks when they can turn them into an increase in the supplier's sales.

Although *promotion* can be critical to wholesaler success, most wholesalers are not promotion minded. Their use of trade advertising, sales promotion, personal selling, and public relations is largely scattered and unplanned. Many are behind the times in personal selling—they still see selling as a single salesperson talking to a single customer instead of as a team effort to sell, build, and service major accounts. Wholesalers also need to adopt some of the nonpersonal promotion techniques used by retailers. They need to develop an overall promotion strategy and to make greater use of supplier promotion materials and programs.

Finally, *place* is important—wholesalers must choose their locations and facilities carefully. Wholesalers typically locate in low-rent, low-tax areas and tend to invest little money in their buildings, equipment, and systems. As a result, their materials-handling and order-processing systems are often outdated. In recent years, however, large and progressive wholesalers are reacting to rising costs by investing in automated warehouses and online ordering systems. Orders are fed from the retailer's system directly into the wholesaler's computer, and the items are picked up by mechanical devices and automatically taken to a shipping platform where they are assembled. Most large wholesalers use computers to carry out accounting, billing, inventory control, and forecasting. Modern wholesalers are adapting their services to the needs of target customers and finding cost-reducing methods of doing business.

Merchant wholesalers: A typical Fleming Companies, Inc., wholesale food distribution center. The average Fleming warehouse contains 500,000 square feet of floor space (with 30-foot-high ceilings), carries 16,000 different food items, and serves 150 to 200 retailers within a 500-mile radius.

TRENDS IN WHOLESALING

As the thriving wholesaling industry moves into the twenty-first century, it faces considerable challenges. The industry remains vulnerable to one of the most enduring trends of the 1990s—fierce resistance to price increases and the winnowing out of suppliers based on cost and quality. Progressive wholesalers constantly watch for better ways to meet the changing needs of their suppliers and target customers. They recognize that, in the long run, their only reason for existence comes from adding value by increasing the efficiency and effectiveness of the entire marketing channel. To achieve this goal, they must constantly improve their services and reduce their costs.

McKesson HBOC, the nation's leading wholesaler of pharmaceuticals, health and beauty care, and home health care products, provides an example of progressive wholesaling. To survive, McKesson HBOC had to remain more cost-effective than manufacturers' sales branches. Thus, the company automated its 36 warehouses, established direct computer links with 225 drug manufacturers, designed a computerized accounts-receivable program for pharmacists, and provided drugstores with computer terminals for ordering inventories. Retailers can even use the McKesson HBOC computer system to maintain medical profiles on their customers. Thus, McKesson HBOC has delivered better value to both manufacturers and retail customers.

One study predicts several developments in the wholesaling industry.[23] Geographic expansion will require that distributors learn how to compete effectively over wider and more diverse areas. Consolidation will significantly reduce the number of wholesaling firms. Surviving wholesalers will grow larger, primarily through acquisition, merger, and geographic expansion. The trend toward vertical integration, in which manufacturers try to control their market share by owning the intermediaries that bring their goods to market, remains strong. In health care, for

To improve both efficiency and service, drug wholesaler McKesson set up direct computer links with drugstores. Retailers can order merchandise directly and even use the McKesson computer system to maintain medical profiles on their customers.

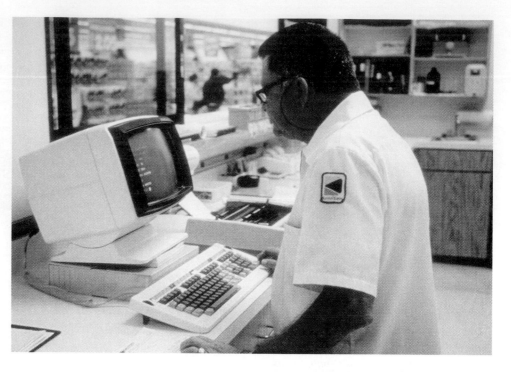

instance, drug makers have purchased drug-distribution and pharmacy-management companies. This trend began in 1993 when drug-industry giant Merck acquired Medco Containment Services, a drug-benefits manager and mail-order distributor. The surviving wholesaler-distributors in this sector and in others will be bigger and will provide more services for their customers.[24]

The distinction between large retailers and large wholesalers continues to blur. Many retailers now operate formats such as wholesale clubs and hypermarkets that perform many wholesale functions. In return, many large wholesalers are setting up their own retailing operations. SuperValu and Flemming, both leading food wholesalers, now operate their own retail outlets. In fact, SuperValu, the nation's largest food wholesaling company, is also the country's eleventh largest food retailer. Almost 30 percent of the company's $17.4 billion in sales comes from its Bigg's, Cub Foods, Shop 'n Save, Farm Fresh, Hornbacher's, Save-A-Lot, Laneco, and Scott's supermarket operations.[25]

Wholesalers will continue to increase the services they provide to retailers—retail pricing, cooperative advertising, marketing and management information reports, accounting services, online transactions, and others. Rising costs on the one hand, and the demand for increased services on the other, will put the squeeze on wholesaler profits. Wholesalers who do not find efficient ways to deliver value to their customers will soon drop by the wayside. However, the increased use of computerized, automated, and Internet systems will help wholesalers to contain the costs of ordering, shipping, and inventory holding, boosting their productivity.

Finally, facing slow growth in their domestic markets and such developments as the North American Free Trade Agreement, many large wholesalers are now going global. For example, in 1991, McKesson HBOC bought out its Canadian partner, Provigo. The company now receives about 3 percent of its total revenues from Canada.

REVIEW OF CONCEPT CONNECTIONS

Although many retail stores are independently owned, an increasing number are now banding together under some form of corporate or contractual organization. Wholesalers, too, have experienced recent environmental changes, most notably mounting competitive pressures. They have faced new sources of competition, more demanding customers, new technologies, and more direct-buying programs on the part of large industrial, institutional, and retail buyers.

1. Explain the roles of retailers and wholesalers in the distribution channel.

Retailing and wholesaling consist of many organizations bringing goods and services from the point of production to the point of use. *Retailing* includes all activities involved in selling goods or services directly to final consumers for their personal, nonbusiness use. *Wholesaling* includes all the activities involved in selling goods or services to those who are buying for the purpose of resale or for business use. Wholesalers perform many functions, including selling and promoting, buying and assortment building, bulk breaking, warehousing, transporting, financing, risk bearing, supplying market information, and providing management services and advice.

2. Describe the major types of retailers and give examples of each.

Retailers can be classified as *store retailers* and *nonstore retailers*. Although most goods and services are sold through stores, nonstore retailing has been growing much faster than has store retailing. Store retailers can be further classified by the *amount of service* they provide (self-service, limited service, or full service); *product line sold* (specialty stores, depart-ment stores, supermarkets, convenience stores, superstores, and service businesses); and *relative prices* (discount stores, off-price retailers, and catalog showrooms). Today, many retailers are banding together in corporate and contractual *retail organizations* (corporate chains, voluntary chains and retailer cooperatives, franchise organizations, and merchandising conglomerates).

3. Identify the major types of wholesalers and give examples of each.

Wholesalers fall into three groups. First, *merchant wholesalers* take possession of the goods. They include *full-service wholesalers* (wholesale merchants, industrial distributors) and *limited-service wholesalers* (cash-and-carry wholesalers, truck wholesalers, drop shippers, rack jobbers, producers' cooperatives, and mail-order wholesalers). Second, *brokers* and *agents* do not take possession of the goods but are paid a commission for aiding buying and selling. Finally, *manufacturers' sales branches and offices* are wholesaling operations conducted by nonwholesalers to bypass the wholesalers.

4. Explain the marketing decisions facing retailers and wholesalers.

Each retailer must make decisions about its target markets, product assortment and services, price, promotion, and place. Retailers need to choose target markets carefully and position themselves strongly. Today, wholesaling is holding its own in the economy. Progressive wholesalers are adapting their services to the needs of target customers and are seeking cost-reducing methods of doing business. Faced with slow growth in their domestic markets and developments such as the North American Free Trade Association, many large wholesalers are also now going global.

KEY TERMS

Agent
Broker
Category killer
Chain stores
Convenience store
Department store
Discount store
Factory outlet

Franchise
Independent off-price retailer
Manufacturers' sales branches and offices
Merchant wholesaler
Off-price retailer
Retailer
Retailing

Shopping center
Specialty store
Supermarket
Superstore
Warehouse club
Wheel of retailing concept
Wholesaler
Wholesaling

ISSUES FOR DISCUSSION

1. Warehouse clubs such as Costco and Sam's are restricted to members only and are growing rapidly. They offer a very broad but shallow line of products, often in institutional packaging, at very low prices. Some members buy for resale, others buy to supply a business, and still others buy for personal use. Are such store chains wholesalers or retailers? Explain.

2. Answer the following questions about category killers: (a) How is a category killer different from other types of retailers? (b) Why has this form of retailing grown so rapidly? (c) What types of retailers are most threatened by category killers and why? (d) How will online retailing affect category killers? Give an example of a category killer that has been affected by online marketing.

3. How has the growth of other types of large retailers affected the willingness of manufacturers to sell to off-price retailers at or below regular wholesale rates? What policy should Sony set for selling the following products to off-price retailers: (a) HDTV televisions, (b) big screen televisions, (c) regular televisions, (d) Walkman cassette players. Explain.

4. Compare the basic marketing decisions made by retailers and wholesalers to those made by manufacturers. Give examples that show the similarities and differences in decisions made by these groups.

5. Use the "wheel of retailing" concept to assess the emergence and evolution of outlet malls. What do you predict will be the future of outlet malls? Explain.

6. In only the past few years, online retailing has boomed. (a) How will retailers going online change the competitive balance between retailers, direct and catalog marketers, wholesalers, and manufacturers? (b) What are the major advantages of online retailing? The pitfalls? (c) What do you think is the future of online retailing?

7. Many U.S. retailers are significantly behind European and Asian retailers when it comes to global expansion. (a) Why is this so? (b) Which U.S. retailers are positioned for global expansion? Explain. (c) How will online retailing affect global retail expansion? (d) Study Sweden's IKEA home furnishings stores (www.ikea.com). Why has IKEA been so successful in expanding into the U.S. market?

8. List and describe each of the channel functions that have been traditionally assigned to wholesalers. How will wholesalers have to change in order to meet the threat of increasing competition from larger retailers? From direct marketers?

MARKETING APPLICATIONS

1. As American consumers demand more and more service and customization, virtual retailing seems to have an ever-brighter future. Through virtual retailing, a seller can come directly into your home, at your convenience, and allow you to participate in designing your own personalized product and shopping experience. This sounds great—no more ill-fitting bathing suits or greeting cards that seem like they were written for someone else, no high-pressure salespeople, no congested parking lots. At virtual retail sites, you can spend as much or as little time as you need to make up your mind. Virtual retailing has made mass customization a reality. All you have to do is point and click. Take a look at the following Web sites for more information on customizing clothing products: Gap (www.gap.com), Interactive Custom Clothes (www.ic3d.com), Lands' End (www.landsend.com),

QVC's Fashion Advisor (www.QVC.com), and Macy's (www.macys.com). Then answer the following questions.

a. How does virtual retailing compare with more traditional shopping formats? What are its primary advantages and disadvantages for consumers?

b. What target markets would be most interested in virtual retailing? Do the Web sites you just visited appear to be appealing to those segments? Explain.

c. Compare the marketing strategies of the various Web retailers you just visited.

d. Pick one of the Web sites and design your own article of clothing. Discuss the pros and cons of your experience. How was this experience different from buying in a retail store? Would you be willing to purchase the item you designed?

2. When Wal-Mart flexes its cybermuscles, everyone pays attention. After three years of careful study, Wal-Mart is finally jumping into cyberspace. Its new beefed-up Web site will now sell everything from toothpaste to apparel to consumer electronics. Long-range plans call for Wal-Mart's Web site to rival its brick-and-mortar stores. Wal-Mart has signed deals with order-processing expert Fingerhut Business Services to get the kinks out of its logistics, and with partners such as Books-A-Million to add depth to its cyberline. These moves have already brought the giant retailer into competition with Web-only merchants such as Amazon.com. However, Wal-Mart believes that customers have spoken, and they're saying, "Move to the Web." When the customer speaks, Wal-Mart listens.

a. Compare Wal-Mart's Web site (www.walmart.com) to those of competitors Kmart (www.kmart.com) and Target (www.targetstores.com).

b. What are the similarities and differences between the Amazon.com (www.amazon.com) and Wal-Mart Web sites?

c. Are the markets for Wal-Mart's brick-and-mortar stores different from those of its cyberstore? How?

d. What opportunities do you see for Wal-Mart on the Web? What difficulties?

 ## INTERNET CONNECTIONS

ONLINE STORE

In this exercise you are going to build your own online store. Yahoo! Store is a comprehensive solution for small businesses seeking to establish an online storefront. Visit Yahoo! Store at store.yahoo.com. Go ahead and create a free online store (it expires in 10 days). You can sell anything you want at your store—but don't worry, no one can place a real order. Looking for ideas? How about some stuff you have lying around your room? Once you have created the store make a printout of the home page and give it to your professor along with the URL. The URL will read like this: store.yahoo.com/yourusername. Now complete the following chart listing the retail functions provided by Yahoo! Store.

Function	Provided by Yahoo! Store? (y/n)
Web store design	
Web store hosting	
Order processing	
Electronic shopping cart	
Secure order form	
Credit authorization	
Warehouse notification	
Order fulfillment	
Merchandising	
Relationship marketing	
Data warehousing and data mining	
Customer Service	

DISCUSSION QUESTIONS

1. What type of retail operation defines your store (e.g., department store)? Explain in terms of amount of service and product line.

2. Who is your target market and what position will you occupy for this store?

3. What is the cost of running a store on Yahoo! Store?

4. Who are some of Yahoo! Store's more prominent clients?

5. What steps would you take to advertise your store?

6. Yahoo! Store domain names are store.yahoo.com/ mystore. For an additional charge you can register a domain name such as www.mystore.com. Which approach would be better for your business? Why?

SAVVY SITES

Try these sites for some cool trends in online retailing.
- Lands' End (www.landsend.com), the catalog retailer allows Internet female shoppers to build a model according to their own body shape and coloring, and then dress the model with recommended outfits.
- The award winning Virtual Reality Mall (www.vr-mall.com) gives Internet shoppers something they miss from brick-and-mortar malls: ambiance. Note you'll need a VRML plug-in for your Web browser to get the best effects.
- The Sharper Image (www.sharperimage.com) offers three-dimensional views and animations for selected products.

NOTES

1. Quotes in this Home Depot tale are from Patricia Sellers, "Companies That Serve You Best," *Fortune,* May 31, 1993, pp. 74–88; and Patricia Sellers, "Can Home Depot Fix Its Sagging Stock?" *Fortune,* March 4, 1996, pp. 139–46. Also see Graham Button, "The Man Who Almost Walked Out on Ross Perot," *Forbes,* November 22, 1993, pp. 68–76; Roy S. Johnson, "Home Depot Renovates," *Fortune,* November 23, 1998, pp. 200–12; Thomas H. Nodine, "Home Depot's Leading Indicators of Value," *Harvard Business Review,* March–April 1999, p. 100; "Home Depot to Sell Wares on Site Beginning in the Fall," *Wall Street Journal,* June 30, 1999, p. A4; and Bernie Marcus, Arthur Blank, and Bob Andelman, *Built from Scratch: How a Couple of Regular Guys Grew the Home Depot from Nothing to $30 Billion* (New York: Random House, 1999).
2. See "Stop-N-Go Micromarkets New Upscale Mix," *Chain Store Age Executive,* January 1990, p. 145; Matt Nannery, "Convenience Stores Get Fresh," *Chain Store Age,* August 1996, pp. 18A–19A; Wendy Zellner, "How Classy Can 7-Eleven Get?" *Business Week,* September 1, 1997, pp. 74–75; and "Convenience Stores," *Chain Store Age,* January 1998, pp. 8A–9A.
3. "Traditional Discount Stores Take a Back Seat to Supercenters," *Discount Store News,* March 3, 1997, p. 43; and Laura Liebeck, "After a Long Warm-Up, Large Units Ready to Race," *Discount Store News,* June 7, 1999, pp. 89, 128.
4. See Duke Ratliff, "Evolution of Off-Price Retailers," *Discount Merchandising,* March 1996, pp. 22–30; Roberta Maynard, "A Growing Outlet for Small Firms," *Nation's Business,* August 1996, pp. 45–48; Charles V. Bagli, "Discount Mania," *New York Times,* April 5, 1998, p. 12; and Howard Banks, "The Malling of Europe," *Forbes,* February 22, 1999, p. 66.
5. "Warehouse Clubs Experience Renewed Sales Growth," *Discount Store News,* March 9, 1998, pp. 7, 10; Robert Scally, "Costco Ready to Grow Clubs and Expand Private Label," *Discount Store News,* February 8, 1999, pp. 1, 72; and Laura Liebeck, "New Leader Hopes to Take Member Club Out of Middle Ground," *Discount Store News,* June 7, 1999, pp. 92, 139.
6. Rebecca Quick, "Limited to Spin Off Chain as It Disposes of Its Noncore Businesses," *Wall Street Journal,* May 4, 1999, p. B10; and information accessed online from www.limited.com, February 2000.
7. Based on Shelly Branch, "How Target Got Hot," *Fortune,* May 24, 1999, pp. 169–74.
8. Myron Magnet, "Let's Go for Growth," *Fortune,* March 7, 1994, pp. 60–72. Also see Dierdre Donahue, "Bookstores: A Haven for the Intellect," *USA Today,* July 10, 1997, pp. D1, D2; and Christina Nifong, "Beyond Browsing," *Raleigh News & Observer,* May 25, 1999, p. E1.
9. "It's Not Just a Mall. It's Mallville, U.S.A.," *New York Times Magazine,* February 8, 1998, p. 19; Kristen Ostendorf, "Not Wed to Tradition," Gannett News Service, January 5, 1998; and "The History of Mall of America," www.mallofamerica.com, February 2000.
10. Steven Bergsman, "Slow Times at Sherman Oaks: What's Ailing the Big Malls of America?" *Barron's,* May 17, 1999, p. 39.
11. Ibid., p. 39.
12. Amy Barrett, "A Retailing Pacesetter Pulls Up Lame," *Business Week,* July 12, 1993, pp. 122–23.
13. See Malcolm P. McNair and Eleanor G. May, "The Next Revolution of the Retailing Wheel," *Harvard Business Review,* September–October 1978, pp. 81–91; Stephen Brown, "The Wheel of Retailing: Past and Future," *Journal of Retailing,* Summer 1990, pp. 143–47; Stephen Brown, "Variations on a Marketing Enigma: The Wheel of Retailing Theory," *The Journal of Marketing Management* 7, no. 2, 1991, pp. 131–55; Stanley C. Hollander, "The Wheel of Retailing," reprinted in *Marketing Management,* Summer 1996, pp. 63–66; and Jennifer Negley, "Retrenching, Reinventing and Remaining Relevant," *Discount Store News,* April 5, 1999, p. 11.
14. Diane Crispell, "Retailing's Next Decade," *American Demographics,* May 1997, p. 9. Also see Barbara Martinez, "REIT Interest: Will the Internet Kill All the Shopping Centers?" *Wall Street Journal,* February 17, 1999, p. B12.
15. Stephanie Anderson Forest and Keith Naughton, "I'll Take That and That and That and . . . ," *Business Week,* June 22, 1998, p. 38.
16. Tim Carvell, "The Crazy Record Business: These Prices Really Are Insane," *Fortune,* August 4, 1997, pp. 109–16.
17. See Nirmalya Kumar, "The Power of Trust in Manufacturer–Retailer Relationships," *Harvard Business Review,* November–December 1996, pp. 92–106; and "The Fortune 500," *Fortune,* April 26, 1999, p. F1.
18. "Business Bulletin: Shopper Scanner," *Wall Street Journal,* February 18, 1995, pp. A1, A5; and Kenneth Labich, "Attention Shoppers: This Man Is Watching You," *Fortune,* July 19, 1999, pp. 131–34.
19. Regina Fazio Maruca, "Retailing: Confronting the Challenges that Face Bricks-and-Mortar Stores," *Harvard Business Review,* July–August 1999, pp. 159–68.
20. James Cox, "Red-Letter Day as East Meets West in the Aisles," *USA Today,* September 11, 1996, p. B1; "Everybody's Hometown Store," Wal-Mart 1999 Annual Report, accessed online at www.walmart.com/corporate/annual_1999; and Jeremy Kahn,

"Wal-Mart Goes Shopping in Europe," *Fortune,* June 7, 1999, pp. 105–12.

21. Shelby D. Coolidge, "Facing Saturated Home Markets, Retailers Look to Rest of World," *Christian Science Monitor,* February 14, 1994, p. 7; Carla Rapoport, "Retailers Go Global," *Fortune,* February 20, 1995, pp. 102–8; and Joseph H. Ellis, "Global Retailing's Winners and Losers," *Chain Store Age,* December 1997, pp. 27–29.

22. Christina Nifong, "Beyond Browsing," *Raleigh News & Observer,* May 25, 1999, p. E1.

23. See Arthur Andersen & Co., *Facing the Forces of Change: Beyond Future Trends in Wholesale Distribution* (Washington, DC: Distribution Research and Education Foundation, 1987), p. 7. Also see Joseph Weber, "Its 'Like Somebody Had Shot the Postman,' " *Business Week,* January 13, 1992, p. 82; and Michael Mandel, "Don't Cut Out the Middleman," *Business Week,* September 16, 1996, p. 30.

24. Richard A. Melcher, "The Middlemen Stay on the March," *Business Week,* January 9, 1995, p. 87.

25. Facts accessed online from www.supervalu.com, February 2000.

COMPANY CASE

13

Delia's: Hitting the Sweet Spot with Teens

Hitting the right target market makes all the difference in marketing. Consider the case of Christopher Edgar and Steve Kahn, two college roommates who started a catalog business selling to college girls—specifically, sorority sisters. Sales were at best ho-hum until they realized that it was actually the little sisters of the college girls who were buying the merchandise. Sensing an opportunity, they shifted targets and aimed their catalog, named Delia's, at the 12 to 24-year-old market. Since that decision in 1994, Delia's has become *the* shopping place for teens. According to one teen shopper, Addie, "If it's in Delia's, it's all right to wear, but if it's not in Delia's, you take a chance in wearing it."

How does Delia's hit the teens' sweet spot? Primarily through its edgy image. It uses fresh-faced, wide-eyed models with whipped up hair that is sometimes green and sometimes blue. No glam dolls here! Styles include wide-legged pants, clunky shoes, baby-doll dresses, ankle-length skirts, striped T-shirts, and the like—all very hip and high-spirited, but not overly sexy. Even the order form at Delia's is something special. There you can find tips on how to order pants so that they droop well below the hips with hems dragging. The under-16 crowd, especially 12-year-olds, find the catalog most appealing, but their older sisters look at it too—just to see what's there. You never know what you might find.

When their catalogs arrive, girls haul them to school to giggle and coo over new styles and decide what they really need. In their own minds they identify strongly with the models, so Delia's can become very special to them. The company encourages this attitude by hiring high school and college girls to answer the telephones, chat, answer questions, and provide shoppers with fashion tips. In turn, Delia's customers are fanatically loyal. They send the catalogers photos of themselves, letters, critiques of the clothes, suggestions for new merchandise, and tons of e-mail. Specially designated Delia's employees answer each letter and e-mail, a major investment in relationship building with what is often a very fickle market. Staying in touch with the market becomes extremely important when the target is so young and fast changing.

Delia's hits the sweet spot in other ways, including its brand portfolio and ever-widening merchandise assortment, plus multiple paths to market. Only about 30 percent of the merchandise sold through the catalog carries the Delia's label. Eager readers find a host of other desirable brands such as Roxy by Quiksilver, Free People, Dollhouse, 26 Redsugar, Sugartooth, and Greed Girl. With each brand, Delia's spreads its risk. If one brand doesn't appeal, others might, so the catalog does not depend solely on Delia's buyers and designers guessing right on the market's fashion wants.

Initially, Delia's catalog was passed around from hand to hand, but by 1996, it had developed a stable database. That database is one of the catalog retailer's key strengths. Over the years, the company has compiled the database from telephone requests (sometimes 5,000 a day). By mid-1999, Delia's had a database of 11 million individuals, including more than 1 million actual buyers. To maintain the loyalty of its customers, Delia's does not sell or share the database. Communications and transactions with Delia's are kept private and confidential.

To expand their market, Steve and Chris have pursued two additional strategies. First, they have moved into brick-and-mortar retailing by acquiring TSI Soccer Corp.—a soccer apparel and equipment retailer. Purchasing TSI Soccer achieved placement in malls, exposure to the male half of the teen market, and a broadened merchandise assortment that includes items associated with teens' primary sport—soccer. Later, Delia's purchased Screeem!, a retail chain that contained 11 stores under that name and 15 under the name Jeans Country. Whereas TSI Soccer was primarily a southeastern chain, Screeem! stores were found in a corridor from Massachusetts to Pennsylvania. By adding Screeem!, Delia's expanded its geographic locations to include most of the East Coast and gained access to the slightly older crowd that shops at Screeem! stores.

Finally, Delia's opened its first Delia's store in the Westchester Mall in White Plains, New York, in February 1999. The merchandise assortment included not only clothing but also cosmetics, bath products, posters, candy, novelty home accessories, and underwear. The stores look like three-dimensional versions of the catalog. The Delia's logo is featured throughout the brightly lit stores. Ceilings are festooned with pink parachute fabric and inflatable pink and yellow armchairs hang from the walls. From the start, products flew off Delia's store shelves. At the time, store manager Danielle Gorman commented, "Virtually everything is selling well. What didn't sell in the first week, sold in the second. We are going to be needing constant deliveries because of the kind of traffic we are seeing." Satisfied that sales revenues had exceeded targets, the company opened eight more Delia's stores before the end of 1999 and began to convert its Screeem! stores to the Delia's format.

For its second major new strategy, Delia's began adding Internet services to its arsenal of direct-marketing weapons. All Internet activities are grouped under a subsidiary called ITurf. First, Delia's purchased gURL.com—a Web site for teenage girls that features news, chat rooms, and a link to the new Delia's Web site. The Delia's.com site mostly entertains, but it also sells some merchandise. The print catalog remains the main selling vehicle. By 1999, only 3 to 4 percent of sales were made online.

Delia's has also introduced contentsonline.com, a home furnishings Web site, and droog.com, a boys' Web site. These were paired with Contents, a print furnishings catalog aimed primarily at girls, and Droog, a catalog for young males. According to Delia's founders, young girls like to furnish their own rooms, so a furnishings catalog that includes inflatable and bean bag chairs and throw rugs should appeal to loyal Delia's customers. The latest Internet launch is dotdotdash.com, which is aimed at 7- to 11-year-olds. As if all this Internet activity were not enough, Delia's is also available in the teen shopping category on Yahoo!.

Steve and Chris are onto a good thing with this market. The 10- to 24-year-old GenY market is 55 million large, and half are women. Moreover, teens spent about $141 billion a year—$94 billion of their own money and $47 billion of their parents' money. It's a large and affluent market and it could be a long-run market as well if Delia's can hang onto these youths throughout their lifetimes.

Delia's rapid expansion comes at a high price. Stores are much more capital intensive than direct sales channels. They require major up-front investments in leases, furnishings, inventory, and sales personnel. A catalog with slow-selling merchandise can be quickly replaced, but a store with slow-selling merchandise suffers from the sales and markdowns needed to move inventory. Although the Delia's stores appear to be a roaring success, the conversion of the Screeem! stores necessitated many markdowns and additional promotions to move merchandise, leading to a $13.7 million after-tax charge in the first quarter of 1999.

The Internet operations are another drain on resources. The ITurf subsidiary required the building of an expensive infrastructure. Although investors seem willing to let Internet companies spend millions to build customer bases and infrastructure, the lack of sales (remember the 3 to 4 percent?) is an important issue. So is the fact that Internet sites frequently compete for the same customers as the catalogs.

Combined with the losses resulting from store conversions and Internet sites, Delia's core catalog business softened in late 1998 for a major operating loss. With that year's holiday catalog, however, the company seemed to recover somewhat. Even with the losses in late 1998 and 1999, Delia's continued to be a darling of the stock market, where it's offerings were highly regarded and it stayed on investment analysts' buy lists.

Still, there are serious problems in dealing with this fickle market which can turn on a retailer instantly. Even young Addie, who was so sold on Delia's, is becoming disillusioned. She says "having all my friends dress out of the same catalog ended up meaning that everybody has the same stuff. Out of the winter [catalog], I bought this sweater and six people in my school had it, and they all wore it on the same day, and I'd rather be original with my clothes."

Interviews with teens reveal that they frequently pore over catalogs and then tell their mothers what to order for them. Some say it's too much trouble to order over the Internet. In addition, this is a market that is highly sociable—teens likes to hang out in groups and visit stores. The Internet may not offer the social interaction that going to the mall or sharing catalogs does. Thus, Delia's could be betting heavily on a marketing channel that will not provide sufficient return on equity. Perhaps it should spend more money on stores and catalogs rather than on the Internet.

Questions

1. Check out the many Delia's Web sites. How are they similar? How do they differ?

2. Does expanding to the male market using catalogs or the Internet make sense? Do boys want to shop in those medias?

3. From a consumer's viewpoint, what advantages does the Internet offer? What disadvantages?

4. What are the advantages of retail stores? The disadvantages?

5. Is a firm likely to be successful in selling to multiple targets, such as 7- to 11-year olds and then 12- to 24-year olds? Will customers grow out of the Delia's catalog when they turn 12?

6. What marketing strategy and mix recommendations would you make for Delia's?

Sources: "ITurf IPO Lifts Delia's Profits," *WWD*, June 10, 1999, p. 9; "Delia's 2nd Quarter Loss Deepens," *WWD*, September 2, 1999, p. 5; "We Are Going to Own this Genereation," *Business Week*, Feburary 15, 1999, p. 88; "Delia's Screeem! and Jeans Country Acquisition a Done Deal," *Daily News Record*, August 3, 1998, p. 8; "Gullemin Promoted to President of Delia's," *WWD*, March 22, 1999, p. 44; "Internet, Retail Costs Dampen Delia's 3rd Quarter Earnings," *WWD*, December 10, 1998, p. 15; Catherine Curan, "Delia's Buys TSI Soccer, WWW site," *WWD*, December 31, 1997, p. 3; Thomas Cunningham, "Internet May Spur More Fashion IPO's," *WWD*, July 19, 1999, p. 24; Yolanda Gault, "Market Drops as Delia's Shops, but Analysts Stand By Cataloger: Marketer to Teens Makes Move to Stores," *Crain's New York Business,* June 8, 1998, p. 23; Lawrence Gould, "How 2 Grown Men Mastered Girl Talk: Apparel Catalog for Generation Y Producing Totally Awesome Results," *Crain's New York Business,* October 27, 1997, p. 4; Denise Lavoie, "Agency Aims to Get Inside Minds of Teens During Shopping Spree," *Greensboro News and Record,* September 7, 1999, pp. B6, B7; Patricia McLaughlin, "12-Year-Olds Dig Delia's Look," *St. Louis Post-Dispatch,* September 18, 1997, p. 2; Karen Parr, "New Catalogs Target Gen Y," *WWD*, July 24, 1997, p. 12; Cynthia Redecker, "Delia's Opens First Retail Unit," *WWD*, February 25, 1999, p. 11; and Cynthia Redecker, "Delia's Widens Web Effort," *WWD*, December 3, 1998, p. 13.

After studying this chapter, you should be able to
1. name and define the tools of the marketing communications mix
2. discuss the process and advantages of integrated marketing communications
3. outline the steps in developing effective marketing communication
4. explain the methods for setting the promotion budget and factors that affect the design of the promotion mix

INTEGRATED MARKETING COMMUNICATIONS STRATEGY

Jim Lesinski, director of Marketing Communications and Research for Volvo Trucks North America, first proposed putting an ad for Volvo's heavy-duty trucks on the Super Bowl in 1994. His bosses at Swedish parent AB Volvo, who were not familiar with the hype and frenzy that surrounds American football, must have thought he'd gone a little ditzy. "How much will it cost?" they asked. "About $1.3 million in media costs," replied Lesinski, "plus another $500,000 or so to produce the ad." "And how long and how often will the ad run?" they asked. "Just once," said Lesinski, "for 30 seconds." With eyebrows raised and mouths agape, Volvo's top management respectfully rejected Lesinski's proposal.

In fact, early on, Lesinski himself had some doubts. *Did* it make sense to spend almost a third of his annual marketing budget on a single ad? Given the narrow target market for Volvo's huge, $120,000 trucks, *was* it wise to advertise in the granddaddy of mass-media spectacles, amidst the glitzy showcase ads run by big-spending consumer-product companies selling to the masses? Volvo Trucks' target market constituted a mere 1 percent of the total

Super Bowl audience. Moreover, no other heavy-duty truck manufacturer was advertising on television, let alone on the Super Bowl.

But the more he thought about it, the more convinced Lesinski became. Volvo had been selling heavy trucks in the United States since 1981 under a variety of nameplates, including Volvo, Autocar, and White/GMC. Its early trucks lacked quality, sold at relatively low prices, and had gained a reputation as low-status "fleet trucks." In recent years, however, Volvo Trucks had consolidated its various nameplates under the Volvo brand and had developed a new line of premium trucks—the VN Series. These new Volvo trucks were superior to competing premium brands in overall quality, design, safety, and driving comfort. Now, all that remained was to raise Volvo Trucks' old low-status image to match the new high-quality reality. That task, Lesinski knew, would take something dramatic—something like the Super Bowl. He persisted and finally won approval to place a single ad in the 1998 Super Bowl.

The target market for heavy-duty trucks consists of truck fleet buyers and independent owner-operators. However, truck drivers themselves are perhaps the most important buying influence. The industry faces a severe driver shortage, and firms perceived as having better-performing, more comfortable, higher-status trucks have a big edge in attracting and holding good drivers. As a result, truck buyers are swayed by driver perceptions. Thus, Lesinski's communications goal was to improve the image of Volvo's VN Series trucks, not just among truck buyers but also among drivers. No other event reaches this audience more completely than the Super Bowl. In fact, nearly 70 percent of all truck drivers watch some or all of an average Super Bowl game.

Still, Jim Lesinski knew that a single Super Bowl ad, by itself, wasn't likely to have much lasting impact on buyer and driver perceptions. Instead—and this is the real story—he designed a comprehensive, carefully targeted, four-month integrated promotional campaign, with Super Bowl advertising as its centerpiece (see figure below). Called *The Best Drive in the Game Sweepstakes,* the promotion offered truck drivers a chance to win a new Volvo VN770 truck worth $120,000. Lesinski began promoting the Best Drive sweepstakes in September 1997, using a wide range of carefully coordi-

nated media, including trucker magazines and radio stations. Drivers could enter the sweepstakes by responding to print or radio ads, by visiting a Volvo Truck dealer or participating truck stop, or by clicking onto the Volvo Trucks Web site (a large proportion of truckers use the Internet regularly to schedule loads). To create additional interest, Volvo Trucks sponsored a national truck tour, consisting of two caravans of three VN770s each, that visited major truck stops around the country, encouraging truck drivers to enter the Best Drive sweepstakes and giving them a chance to experience a new Volvo VN770 firsthand.

The campaign attracted more than 48,700 entrants. Each entrant received a wallet-size entry card with one of 40 "Volvo Truths" printed on it—each emphasizing a key VN770 positioning point. If the phrase on a driver's card matched the winning phrase revealed in the Super Bowl commercial, the driver became a finalist eligible for the grand prize. To further encourage drivers to watch the commercial, Volvo Trucks sponsored Super Bowl parties at 40 Flying J truck stops around the country. It also had Volvo VN770s at each truck stop so that dri-

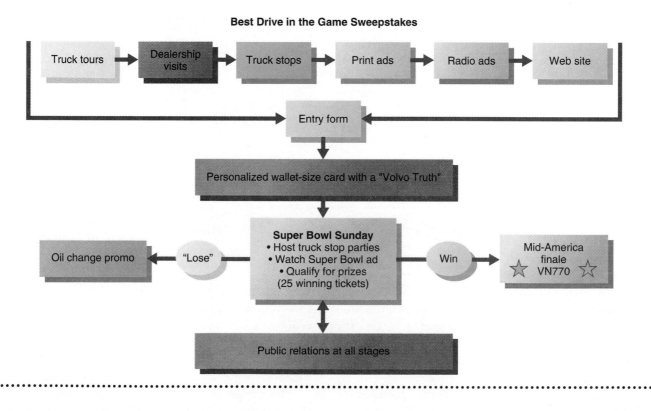

Best Drive in the Game Sweepstakes

vers could see the truck that was causing all the commotion.

On Super Bowl Sunday 1998, Jim Lesinski found himself at a Greensboro, North Carolina, truck stop, anxiously awaiting the fourth-quarter airing of his ad. He sat shoulder to shoulder with a standing-room-only crowd of truckers, clustered around a lounge television with their Best Drive wallet cards in hand. To Lesinski's dismay, a clever ad for Tabasco Sauce preceded the Volvo ad (remember the exploding mosquito?) and the crowd was still laughing as the Volvo commercial began. Lesinski still remembers counting off the missed seconds (at a cost of some $60,000 apiece!) waiting for the group to settle their attention on his ad.

The Volvo Trucks ad itself used soft humor to make the quality point. It featured an experienced and approachable professional driver named Gus, driving a new Volvo VN770 down a desert highway. Gus talked sagely about "what 30 years on the road have taught me," and advised "always run the best truck you can." During the 30-second spot, the scenes shifted to show both the sleek, handsome exterior of the truck and its luxurious interior. "But success hasn't spoiled me," Gus concluded. "I still put my pants on one leg at a time." As Gus delivered this last line, a uniformed butler approached from the sleeper area of the truck, presenting a small silver box on a pillow. "Your toothpick, sir," he intoned. The winning phrase, "Volvo—Drive Safely," appeared on the screen as the commercial ended.

To Jim's enormous relief, the drivers at the truck stop seemed to really like the commercial. They were pleased that it portrayed professional truck drivers and their huge, sometimes scary trucks in positive light. More importantly, the ad got the drivers buzzing about the VN770 truck and the winning phrase. In the month following the Super Bowl, the 10 finalists holding winning phrases received all-expense-paid trips to the trucking industry's premier trade show, the Mid-America Truck Show in Louisville, Kentucky. Volvo stole the show, sponsoring a Brooks and Dunn concert at which company officials held an on-stage drawing in front of 20,000 truckers to select the grand prize winner.

In all, the Best Drive in the Game Sweepstakes cost Volvo Trucks North America $2.4 million—$1.8 million for the ad alone. Was it worth the cost? Lesinski and his bosses at AB Volvo certainly think so. Later research showed that the campaign had a sizable, positive impact on both trucker and public perceptions. More than 30 million U.S. adults recalled seeing the Super Bowl ad. Just that one ad created a 98 percent increase in the general public's awareness of Volvo trucks and significantly improved public perceptions of Volvo drivers as intelligent, safe, successful, and friendly.

Perhaps more importantly, the ad was viewed by 1.4 million truck drivers, almost half the target market. Twenty-three percent of these drivers talked about the ad with someone else, generating more than 325,000 conversations about the commercial. After the Best Drive campaign, substantially higher proportions of drivers and buyers perceive the Volvo VN770 as being like a "Hilton" rather than a "Motel 6," and as a "sleek, aerodynamic, friendly vehicle" versus a "work truck." The campaign created 30 percent driver preference for Volvo trucks, higher than preferences for competitors Freightliner (25 percent), Peterbilt (23 percent), and Kenworth (16 percent). By the end of 1998, sales of Volvo trucks were up 44.5 percent compared with the previous year; market share rose 2.5 points to 12 percent. Based on these results, Volvo Trucks North America sponsored a repeat promotion, *The Best Drive in the Game II,* the following year, including a brand new ad in the 1999 Super Bowl.

Why did the Best Drive promotion work so well? Success resulted from much, much more than just a single Super Bowl ad. "The ad was definitely the main attraction," says Jim Lesinski, "but it was really just the lure that pulled drivers into the full Best Drive promotion and got them into our trucks." By blending Super Bowl advertising with a full slate of other carefully targeted ads, promotions, and events, Lesinski created a complete integrated marketing communications campaign that had a larger and more lasting impact than any single ad could ever have achieved.[1]

Modern marketing calls for more than just developing a good product, pricing it attractively, and making it available to target customers. Companies must also *communicate* with current and prospective customers, and what they communicate should not be left to chance. For most companies, the question is not *whether* to communicate, but *how much to spend* and *in what ways*. All of their communications efforts must be blended into a consistent and coordinated communications program.

THE MARKETING COMMUNICATIONS MIX

Marketing communications mix (promotion mix)
The specific mix of advertising, personal selling, sales promotion, public relations, and direct-marketing tools a company uses to pursue its advertising and marketing objectives.

Advertising
Any paid form of nonpersonal presentation and promotion of ideas, goods, or services by an identified sponsor.

Personal selling
Personal presentation by the firm's sales force for the purpose of making sales and building customer relationships.

Sales promotion
Short-term incentives to encourage the purchase or sale of a product or service.

Public relations
Building good relations with the company's various publics by obtaining favorable publicity, building up a good corporate image, and handling or heading off unfavorable rumors, stories, and events.

Direct marketing
Direct communications with carefully targeted individual consumers to obtain an immediate response, and cultivate lasting customer relationships.

A company's total **marketing communications mix**—also called its **promotion mix**—consists of the specific blend of advertising, personal selling, sales promotion, public relations, and direct-marketing tools that the company uses to pursue its advertising and marketing objectives. Definitions of the five major promotion tools follow:[2]

> **Advertising:** Any paid form of nonpersonal presentation and promotion of ideas, goods, or services by an identified sponsor.
> **Personal selling:** Personal presentation by the firm's sales force for the purpose of making sales and building customer relationships.
> **Sales promotion:** Short-term incentives to encourage the purchase or sale of a product or service.
> **Public relations:** Building good relations with the company's various publics by obtaining favorable publicity, building up a good corporate image, and handling or heading off unfavorable rumors, stories, and events.
> **Direct marketing:** Direct connections with carefully targeted individual consumers to both obtain an immediate response and cultivate lasting customer relationships—the use of telephone, mail, fax, e-mail, the Internet, and other tools to communicate directly with specific consumers.

Each category involves specific tools. For example, advertising includes print, broadcast, outdoor, and other forms. Personal selling includes sales presentations, trade shows, and incentive programs. Sales promotion includes point-of-purchase displays, premiums, discounts, coupons, specialty advertising, and demonstrations. Direct marketing includes catalogs, telemarketing, fax, kiosks, the Internet, and more. Thanks to technological breakthroughs, people can now communicate through traditional media (newspapers, radio, telephone, television), as well as through newer media forms (fax machines, cellular phones, pagers, and computers). The new technologies have encouraged more companies to move from mass communication to more targeted communication and one-to-one dialogue.

At the same time, communication goes beyond these specific promotion tools. The product's design, its price, the shape and color of its package, and the stores that sell it—*all* communicate something to buyers. Thus, although the promotion mix is the company's primary communication activity, the entire marketing mix—promotion *and* product, price, and place—must be coordinated for the greatest communication impact.

In this chapter, we begin by examining the rapidly changing marketing communications environment, the concept of integrated marketing communications, and the marketing communication process. Next, we discuss the factors that marketing communicators must consider in shaping an overall communication mix. Finally, we summarize the legal, ethical, and social responsibility issues in marketing communications. In chapter 15, we look at *mass-communication tools*—advertising, sales promotion, and public relations. Chapter 16 examines the *sales force* as a communication and promotion tool.

INTEGRATED MARKETING COMMUNICATIONS

During the past several decades, companies around the world have perfected the art of mass marketing—selling highly standardized products to masses of customers. In the process, they have developed effective mass-media advertising techniques to support their mass-marketing strategies. These companies routinely invest millions of dollars in the mass media, reaching tens of millions of customers with a single ad. However, as we move into the twenty-first century, marketing managers face some new marketing communications realities.

The Changing Communications Environment

Two major factors are changing the face of today's marketing communications. First, as mass markets have fragmented, marketers are shifting away from mass marketing. More and more, they are developing focused marketing programs designed

The relatively few mass magazines of past decades have been replaced today by thousands of magazines targeting special-interest audiences. IIMP alone publishes these and more than 20 other magazines reaching 17 different markets and more than 47 million readers, not to mention a wide range of online, broadcast, outdoor, and other media.

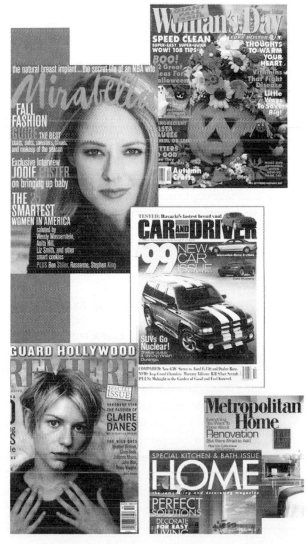

to build closer relationships with customers in more narrowly defined micromarkets. Second, vast improvements in information technology are speeding the movement toward segmented marketing. Today's information technology helps marketers to keep closer track of customer needs—more information about consumers at the individual and household levels is available than ever before. New technologies also provide new communications avenues for reaching smaller customer segments with more tailored messages.

The shift from mass marketing to segmented marketing has had a dramatic impact on marketing communications. Just as mass marketing gave rise to a new generation of mass-media communications, the shift toward one-to-one marketing is spawning a new generation of more specialized and highly targeted communications efforts.[3]

Given this new communications environment, marketers must rethink the roles of various media and promotion mix tools. Mass-media advertising has long dominated the promotion mixes of consumer product companies. However, although television, magazines, and other mass media remain very important, their dominance is now declining. *Market* fragmentation has resulted in *media* fragmentation—in an explosion of more focused media that better match today's targeting strategies. For example, in 1975 what used to be the three major TV networks (ABC, CBS, and NBC) attracted 82 percent of the 24-hour viewing audience. By 1995 that number had dropped to only 35 percent, as cable television and satellite broadcasting systems offered advertisers dozens or even hundreds of alternative channels that reach smaller, specialized audiences. It's expected to drop even further, down to 25 percent by the year 2005. Similarly, the relatively few mass magazines of the 1940s and 1950s—*Look, Life, Saturday Evening Post*—have been replaced by more than 18,600 special-interest magazines reaching more focused audiences. Beyond these channels, advertisers are making increased use of new, highly targeted media, ranging from video screens on supermarket shopping carts to CD-ROM catalogs and Web sites on the Internet.[4]

More generally, advertising appears to be giving way to other elements of the promotion mix. In the glory days of mass marketing, consumer product companies spent the lion's share of their promotion budgets on mass-media advertising. Today, media advertising captures only about 26 percent of total promotion spending.[5] The rest goes to various sales promotion activities, which can be focused more effectively on individual consumer and trade segments. They are using a richer variety of focused communication tools in an effort to reach their diverse target markets. In all, companies are doing less *broadcasting* and more *narrowcasting.*

The Need for Integrated Marketing Communications

The shift from mass marketing to targeted marketing, and the corresponding use of a richer mixture of communication channels and promotion tools, poses a problem for marketers. Consumers are being exposed to a greater variety of marketing communications from and about the company from a broader array of sources. However, customers don't distinguish between message sources the way marketers do. In the consumer's mind, advertising messages from different media such as television, magazines, or online sources blur into one. Messages delivered via different promotional approaches—such as advertising, personal selling, sales promotion, public relations, or direct marketing—all become part of a single message about the company. Conflicting messages from these different sources can result in confused company images and brand positions.

All too often, companies fail to integrate their various communications channels. The result is a hodgepodge of communications to consumers. Mass advertisements say one thing, a price promotion sends a different signal, a product label creates still another message, company sales literature says something altogether different, and the company's Web site seems out of sync with everything else.

The problem is that these communications often come from different company sources. Advertising messages are planned and implemented by the advertising department or advertising agency. Personal selling communications are developed by sales management. Other functional specialists are responsible for public relations, sales promotion, direct marketing, online sites, and other forms of marketing communications. Recently, such functional separation has been a major problem for many companies and their Internet communications activities, which are often split off into separate organizational units. "These new, forward-looking, high-tech functional groups, whether they exist as part of an established organization or as a separate new business operation, commonly are located in separate space, apart from the traditional operation," observes one IMC expert. "They generally are populated by young, enthusiastic, technologically proficient people with a burning desire to 'change the world,' " he adds, but "the separation and the lack of cooperation and cohesion" can be a *dis*integrating force in marketing communications (see Marketing Highlight 14.1).

Integrated marketing communications (IMC)

The concept under which a company carefully integrates and coordinates its many communications channels to deliver a clear, consistent, and compelling message about the organization and its products.

In the past, no one person was responsible for thinking through the communication roles of the various promotion tools and coordinating the promotion mix. Today, however, more companies are adopting the concept of **integrated marketing communications (IMC).** Under this concept, as illustrated in Figure 14.1, the company carefully integrates and coordinates its many communications channels to deliver a clear, consistent, and compelling message about the organization and its products.[6] As one marketing executive puts it, "IMC builds a strong brand identity in the marketplace by tying together and reinforcing all your images and

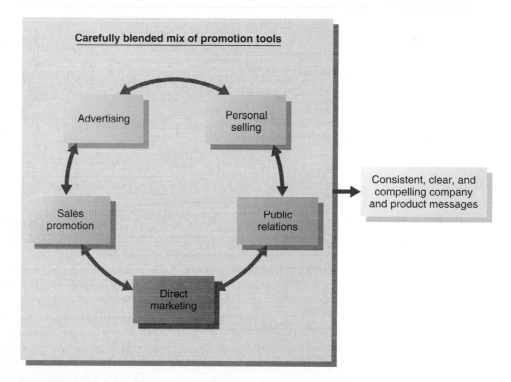

FIGURE 14.1 Integrated marketing communications

THE INTERNET, INTERACTIVITY, AND ALL THOSE NETS AND "DOT-COMS": *DIS*INTEGRATED MARKETING COMMUNICATIONS?

Ever had a day when you couldn't get a TV commercial out of your head? Or do ad jingles from yesteryear sometimes stick in your cranium, like "I'd like to buy the world a Coke," or "Plop, plop, fizz, fizz. Oh what a relief it is"? Or do long lost words like "Two all beef patties, special sauce, lettuce, cheese, pickles, onions, on a sesame seed bun" suddenly and inexplicably burst from your mouth? If you're like most people, you sop up more than a fair share of TV advertising.

Now, try to remember the last ad you saw while surfing the Internet. Drawing a blank? That's not surprising. The Web's ineffectiveness as a major brand-building tool is one of

The Internet can rarely stand alone as a brand-building tool. Even companies that rely primarily on e-commerce for sales are conducting most of their branding efforts offline.

today's hottest marketing issues. Still, some firms are treating the Internet as if it were the "one and only" communication medium of the future. The problem? According to integrated marketing communication guru Don Schultz, all the special attention this new medium is getting may be resulting in *dis*integrated marketing communications. Says Schultz:

My mailbox has filled with brochures, invitations, meetings, get-togethers, and debates all promising to explain interactivity, new media, e-commerce and electronic media. Each . . . promises to give me the full picture of how to do the Internet, the Web, extranets, intranets, and all the other "nets" that are popping up everywhere. Not one has even suggested how all this new stuff might fit with, coordinate alongside, relate to, or be integrated with the existing media systems. Nothing on how to combine or bring together existing programs and existing customers with the brave new world of the 21st century.

Most troubling is that many firms are organizing their new e-communications operations into separate groups or divisions, isolating them from mainstream marketing activities. "It is . . . the apartness that concerns me," Schultz observes. "We seem to be creating the same problems with new media, new marketing, and new commerce that

we created years ago when we developed separate sales promotion groups, separate direct-marketing activities, separate public relations departments, separate events organizations, and so on. . . . In my view, we are well on the way to disintegrating our marketing and communication programs and processes all over again." However, whereas companies appear to be compartmentalizing the new communications tools, customers won't. According to Schultz:

New media, the Internet, interactivity and all the Nets and "dot-coms" are critical to marketing and communication practice, but they are not the be-all-and-end-all of marketing and marketing communication. They . . . are not going to instantaneously replace all our current techniques, approaches or media systems. . . . The real issue for most [marketers] and consumers is transition, from what they do now to what they likely will do in the future. And, the truth is, most [consumers] won't compartmentalize their use of the new systems. They won't say, "Hey, I'm going off to do a bit of Net surfing. Burn my TV, throw out all my radios, cancel all my magazine subscriptions and, by the way, take out my telephone and don't deliver any mail anymore." It's not that kind of world for consumers, and it shouldn't be the kind of world for marketers either.

To be sure, the new Internet promises exciting marketing com-

messages. IMC means that all your corporate messages, positioning and images, and identity are coordinated across all [marketing communications] venues. It means that your PR materials say the same thing as your direct mail campaign, and your advertising has the same 'look and feel' as your Web site."[7]

The IMC solution calls for recognizing all contact points where the customer may encounter the company, its products, and its brands. Each *brand contact* will munications potential. However, marketers trying to use the Web to build brands face many challenges. One limitation is that the Internet doesn't build mass brand awareness. Instead, it's like having millions of private conversations. The Web simply can't match the impact of the Super Bowl, where tens of millions of people see the same 30-second Coca-Cola or Hallmark ad at the same time. Thus, using the Internet, it's hard to establish the universal meanings—like "Always Coca-Cola" or "When you care enough to send the very best"—that are at the heart of brand recognition and brand value. That's why tactics that have worked on TV have failed on the Web. For example, Bell Atlantic developed an online soap opera that revolved around yuppie newlyweds Troy and Linda. Although the site won raves from critics and had lots of fans, Bell Atlantic's research showed it did little to boost the brand.

Another Internet limitation is format and quality constraints. Web ads are still low in quality and impact. Procter & Gamble and other large advertisers have been pushing to get Internet publishers to allow larger, more complex types of ads with high-quality sound and full-motion video. So far, however, ads on the Internet are all too ignorable. Even if advertisers could put larger, richer ads on the Web, they would likely face a consumer backlash. In the digital world, consumers control ad exposure. Many consumers who've grown up with the Internet are skeptical of ads in general and resentful of Web ads in particular.

Internet advertisers face an uphill battle in getting such consumers to click onto their ads. In fact, a recent survey found that 21 percent of Internet users polled said they never clicked on Internet ads and another 51 percent said they clicked only rarely.

Facing such realities, most marketers opt for fuller promotion campaigns to build their brands. Even companies that rely primarily on e-commerce for sales are conducting most of their branding efforts offline. Business-to-business e-commerce star Cisco Systems spends ad money for full page ads in the *Wall Street Journal* rather than on Web banners. Dell Computer is one of the largest ad spenders in tech trade magazines and runs a $100 million-plus branding campaign almost entirely on TV. Dell hopes to conduct 50 percent of all transactions online and contends that it can't generate that kind of volume with Web advertising.

Similarly, most traditional marketers are adding the Web as an enhancement to their more traditional communication media. They wed the emotional pitch and impact of traditional brand marketing with real service offered online. For example, television ads for Saturn still offer the same old-fashioned humorous appeal. But now they point viewers to the company's Web site, which offers lots of help and very little hype. The site helps serious car buyers select a model, calculate payments, and find a dealer online. Even marketers that can't really sell their goods via the Web are using the Internet as an effective

customer communication and relationship enhancer. For example, Procter & Gamble has turned Pampers.com into the Pampers Parenting Institute, addressing various issues of concern to new or expectant parents.

Thus, although the Internet offers electrifying prospects for marketing communication, it can rarely stand alone as a brand-building tool. Instead, it must be carefully integrated into the broader marketing communications mix. Schultz makes this plea: "My cry is to integrate, not isolate. Yes, we need to explore and develop the new media and new approaches, but we need to . . . integrate [them] with the old, melding e-commerce and across-the-counter commerce. There never has been a greater need for integration than there is today. Let's recognize and develop the new electronic forms on the basis of what they are—alternatives and perhaps enhancements for the existing approaches presently in place—and nothing more. Then again, they are nothing less, either."

Sources: Quotes and excerpts from Don E. Schultz, "New Media, Old Problem: Keep Marcom Integrated," *Marketing News,* March 29, 1999, p. 11. Also see Jeffrey O'Brien, "Web Advertising and the Branding Mission," *Upside,* September 1998, pp. 90–94; Saul Hansell, "Selling Soap Without the Soap Operas, Mass Marketers Seek Ways to Build Brands on the Web," *New York Times,* August 24, 1998, pp. D1–D2; Ellen Neuborne, "Branding on the Net," *Business Week,* November 9, 1998, pp. 76–86; and Bradley Johnson, "Boom or Bust?" *Advertising Age,* November 1, 1999, pp. 1, 52.

deliver a message, whether good, bad, or indifferent. The company must strive to deliver a consistent and positive message at all contact points.

To help implement integrated marketing communications, some companies appoint a marketing communications director—or *marcom manager*—who has overall responsibility for the company's communications efforts. Integrated marketing communications produces better communications consistency and greater sales impact. It places the responsibility in someone's hands—where none existed before—to unify the company's image as it is shaped by thousands of company activities. It leads to a total marketing communication strategy aimed at showing how the company and its products can help customers solve their problems.

A VIEW OF THE COMMUNICATION PROCESS

Integrated marketing communications involves identifying the target audience and shaping a well-coordinated promotional program to elicit the desired audience response. Too often, marketing communications focus on overcoming immediate awareness, image, or preference problems in the target market. But this approach to communication has limitations: It is too short term and too costly, and most messages of this type fall on deaf ears. Today, marketers are moving toward viewing communications as *managing the customer relationship over time,* during the preselling, selling, consuming, and postconsumption stages. Because customers differ, communications programs need to be developed for specific segments, niches, and even individuals. Given the new interactive communications technologies, companies must ask not only "How can we reach our customers?" but also "How can we find ways to let our customers reach us?"

Thus, the communications process should start with an audit of all the potential contacts target customers may have with the company and its brands. For example, someone purchasing a new computer may talk to others, see television ads, read articles and ads in newspapers and magazines, visit various Web sites, and try out computers in one or more stores. The marketer needs to assess the influence that each of these communications experiences will have at different stages of the buying process. This understanding will help marketers allocate their communication dollars more efficiently and effectively.

To communicate effectively, marketers need to understand how communication works. Communication involves the nine elements shown in Figure 14.2. Two of these elements are the major parties in a communication—the *sender* and the *receiver.* Another two are the major communication tools—the *message* and the

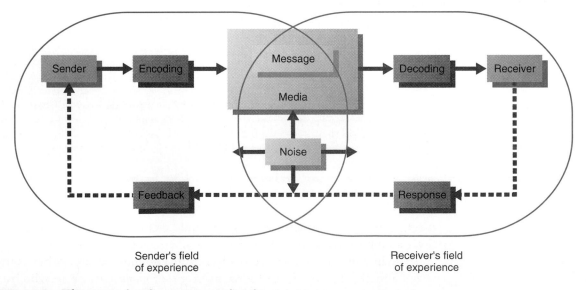

FIGURE 14.2 Elements in the communication process

media. Four more are major communication functions—*encoding, decoding, response,* and *feedback*. The last element is *noise* in the system. Definitions of these elements follow and are applied to an ad for Hewlett-Packard (HP) color copiers.

★ *Sender:* The *party sending the message* to another party—here, HP.
★ *Encoding:* The process of *putting thought into symbolic form*—HP's advertising agency assembles words and illustrations into an advertisement that will convey the intended message.
★ *Message:* The *set of symbols* that the sender transmits—the actual HP copier ad.
★ *Media:* The *communication channels* through which the message moves from sender to receiver—in this case, the specific magazines that HP selects.
★ *Decoding:* The process by which the receiver *assigns meaning to the symbols* encoded by the sender—a consumer reads the HP copier ad and interprets the words and illustrations it contains.
★ *Receiver:* The *party receiving the message* sent by another party—the home office or business customer who reads the HP copier ad.
★ *Response:* The *reactions of the receiver* after being exposed to the message—any of hundreds of possible responses, such as the consumer is more aware of the attributes of HP copiers, actually buys an HP copier, or does nothing.
★ *Feedback:* The part of the *receiver's response communicated back to the sender*—HP research shows that consumers are struck by and remember the ad, or consumers write or call HP praising or criticizing the ad or HP's products.
★ *Noise:* The *unplanned static or distortion* during the communication process, which results in the receiver's getting a different message than the one the sender sent—the consumer it distracted while reading the magazine and misses the HP ad or its key points.

For a message to be effective, the sender's encoding process must mesh with the receiver's decoding process. Thus, the best messages consist of words and other symbols that are familiar to the receiver. The more the sender's field of experience overlaps with that of the receiver, the more effective the message is likely to be. Marketing communicators may not always *share* their consumer's field of experience. For example, an advertising copywriter from one social stratum might create ads for consumers from another stratum—say, blue-collar workers or wealthy business owners. However, to communicate effectively, the marketing communicator must *understand* the consumer's field of experience.

This model points out several key factors in good communication. Senders need to know what audiences they wish to reach and what responses they want. They must be good at encoding messages that take into account how the target audience decodes them. They must send messages through media that reach target audiences, and they must develop feedback channels so that they can assess the audience's response to the message.

STEPS IN DEVELOPING EFFECTIVE COMMUNICATION

We now examine the steps in developing an effective integrated communications and promotion program. The marketing communicator must do the following: Identify the target audience; determine the communication objectives; design a message; choose the media through which to send the message; select the message source; and collect feedback.

Identifying the Target Audience

A marketing communicator starts with a clear target audience in mind. The audience may be potential buyers or current users, those who make the buying decision or those who influence it. The audience may be individuals, groups, special publics, or the general public. The target audience will heavily affect the communicator's decisions on *what* will be said, *how* it will be said, *when* it will be said, *where* it will be said, and *who* will say it.

Determining the Communication Objectives

Once the target audience has been defined, the marketing communicator must decide what response is sought. Of course, in many cases, the final response is *purchase.* But purchase is the result of a long process of consumer decision making. The marketing communicator needs to know where the target audience now stands and to what stage it needs to be moved. The target audience may be in any of six **buyer-readiness stages,** the stages consumers normally pass through on their way to making a purchase. These stages include *awareness, knowledge, liking, preference, conviction,* and *purchase* (see Figure 14.3).

> **Buyer-readiness stages**
> The stages consumers normally pass through on their way to purchase, including awareness, knowledge, liking, preference, conviction, and purchase.

The marketing communicator's target market may be totally unaware of the product, know only its name, or know one or a few things about it. The communicator must first build *awareness* and *knowledge.* For example, when Nissan introduced its Infiniti automobile line, it began with an extensive "teaser" advertising campaign to create name familiarity. Initial ads for the Infiniti created curiosity and awareness by showing the car's name but not the car. Later ads created knowledge by informing potential buyers of the car's high quality and many innovative features.

Assuming target consumers *know* the product, how do they *feel* about it? Once potential buyers knew about the Infiniti, Nissan's marketers wanted to move them through successively stronger stages of feelings toward the car. These stages included *liking* (feeling favorable about the Infiniti), *preference* (preferring Infiniti to other car brands), and *conviction* (believing that Infiniti is the best car for them). Infiniti marketers used a combination of the promotion mix tools to create positive feelings and conviction. Advertising extolled the Infiniti's advantages over competing brands. Press releases and other public relations activities stressed the car's innovative features and performance. Dealer salespeople told buyers about options, value for the price, and after-sale service.

Finally, some members of the target market might be convinced about the product, but not quite get around to making the *purchase.* Potential Infiniti buyers might have decided to wait for more information or for the economy to improve. The communicator must lead these consumers to take the final step. Actions might include offering special promotional prices, rebates, or premiums. Salespeople might call or write to selected customers, inviting them to visit the dealership for a spe-

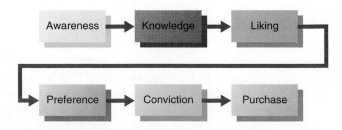

FIGURE 14.3   Buyer-readiness stages

Moving consumers toward purchase: Nissan created awareness for Infiniti using teaser ads that didn't show the car. Later ads created liking, preference, and conviction by comparing the Infiniti's features to those of competitors.

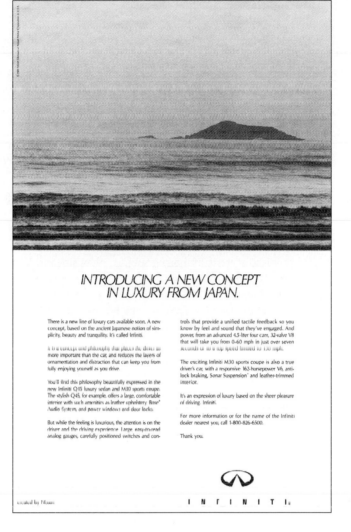

cial showing. The Infiniti Web site (www.infiniti.com) tells potential buyers, "Own one and you'll understand," explains various financing options, and invites them to visit the local dealer's showroom.

Of course, marketing communications alone cannot create positive feelings and purchases for Infiniti. The car itself must provide superior value for the customer. In fact, outstanding marketing communications can actually speed the demise of a poor product. The more quickly potential buyers learn about the poor product, the more quickly they become aware of its faults. Thus, good marketing communication calls for "good deeds followed by good words."

Designing a Message

Having defined the desired audience response, the communicator turns to developing an effective message. Ideally, the message should get *Attention,* hold *Interest,* arouse *Desire,* and obtain *Action* (a framework known as the *AIDA model*). In practice, few messages take the consumer all the way from awareness to purchase, but the AIDA framework suggests the desirable qualities of a good message. In putting the message together, the marketing communicator must decide what to say (*message content*) and how to say it (*message structure* and *format*).

Message Content

The communicator has to figure out an appeal or theme that will produce the desired response. There are three types of appeals: rational, emotional, and moral. *Rational appeals* relate to the audience's self-interest. They show that the product will produce the desired benefits. Examples are messages showing a product's quality, economy, value, or performance. Thus, in its ads, Mercedes offers automobiles that are "engineered like no other car in the world," stressing engineering design, performance, and safety.

Emotional appeals attempt to stir up either negative or positive emotions that can motivate purchase. Communicators may use positive emotional appeals such as love, pride, joy, and humor. For example, advocates for humorous messages claim that they attract more attention and create more liking and belief in the sponsor. Consider the recent series of ads from Hartford Financial Services Group:

> The insurer's new . . . ads use humor to talk about what for most people is either a deadly serious or eternally boring subject. New slogan: "Whatever life brings. Bring it on." In [one] spot, a kangaroo escapes from the zoo and starts bouncing through a crowd. "Possibility one: He flattens your car. Your Hartford auto policy covers the damage. Possibility two: He flattens your hot dog stand. Your Hartford small-business insurance helps you rebuild. Possibility three: He flattens your Great Aunt Edna. Might we suggest investing your inheritance in one of our top-selling annuities?" Funny, no? Hartford's chairman and chief executive . . . thinks so. "Insurance ads often portray fires—mishaps if you will," he says. Now, "there is nothing humorous about a fire or a hurricane," he quickly adds. But "because everybody's ads are so serious" in the insurance business "we thought it would be neat if we portrayed a more energetic, confident, invigorating attitude to life. We wanted people to remember us, and we thought humor would bring that out." Insurance "is such a low-interest category, bordering on no interest," adds [an executive at Hartford's ad agency]. . . . "Creatively, you better make people cry or make them laugh, or it's not going to be memorable," she says. Hartford says consumer tests found the company's message—that it's in the financial-services industry and not just in insurance—came through clearly. What's more, she says, the ads "seemed to warm up the company's personality, and we want people to identify with us."[8]

Cliff Freeman, the adman responsible for a decade's worth of humorous Little Caesars' "Pizza, Pizza" ads, as well as more recent side splitters for companies like Staples and Outpost.com, contend that "Humor is a great way to bound out of the starting gate. When you make people laugh, and they feel good after seeing the commercial, they like the association with the product." But others maintain that humor can detract from comprehension, wear out its welcome fast, and overshadow the product.[9]

Communicators can also use negative emotional appeals, such as fear, guilt, and shame that get people to do things they should (brush their teeth, buy new tires) or to stop doing things they shouldn't (smoke, drink too much, eat fatty foods). For example, a Crest ad invokes mild fear when it claims, "There are some things you just can't afford to gamble with" (cavities). Etonic ads ask, "What would you do if you couldn't run?" They go on to note that Etonic athletic shoes are designed to avoid injuries—they're "built so you can last." The American Academy of Dermatology advertises, "One in every five Americans will develop skin cancer. Don't be the one."

Moral appeals are directed to the audience's sense of what is "right" and "proper." They are often used to urge people to support social causes such as a cleaner environment, better race relations, equal rights for women, and aid to the disadvantaged. An example of a moral appeal is the March of Dimes appeal, "God made you whole. Give to help those He didn't."

Message Structure

The communicator must also decide how to handle three message structure issues. The first is whether to draw a conclusion or leave it to the audience. Early research showed that drawing a conclusion was usually more effective. More recent research, however, suggests that in many cases the advertiser is better off asking questions and letting buyers come to their own conclusions. The second message structure issue is whether to present a one-sided argument (mentioning only the product's strengths) or a two-sided argument (touting the product's strengths while also admitting its shortcomings). Usually, a one-sided argument is more effective in sales presentations—except when audiences are highly educated or likely to hear opposing claims, or when the communicator has a negative association to overcome. In this spirit, Heinz ran the message "Heinz Ketchup is slow good" and Listerine ran the message "Listerine tastes bad twice a day."[10] In such cases, two-sided messages can enhance the advertiser's credibility and make buyers more resistant to competitor attacks. The third message structure issue is whether to present the strongest arguments first or last. Presenting them first gets strong attention but may lead to an anticlimactic ending.

Message Format

The marketing communicator also needs a strong *format* for the message. In a print ad, the communicator has to decide on the headline, copy, illustration, and color. To attract attention, advertisers can use novelty and contrast; eye-catching pictures and headlines; distinctive formats; message size and position; and color, shape, and movement. If the message is to be carried over the radio, the communicator has to choose words, sounds, and voices. The "sound" of an announcer promoting banking services should be different from one promoting quality furniture.

Message format: To attract attention, advertisers can use distinctive formats, novelty, and eye-catching pictures, as in this award-winning Volkswagen ad.

If the message is to be carried on television or in person, then all these elements plus body language have to be planned. Presenters plan their facial expressions, gestures, dress, posture, and hairstyle. If the message is carried on the product or its package, the communicator has to watch texture, scent, color, size, and shape. For example, color plays a major communication role in food preferences. When consumers sampled four cups of coffee that had been placed next to brown, blue, red, and yellow containers (the coffee samples were identical, but the consumers did not know this), 75 percent felt that the coffee next to the brown container tasted too strong; nearly 85 percent judged the coffee next to the red container to be the richest; nearly everyone felt that the coffee next to the blue container was mild; and the coffee next to the yellow container was judged as weak. Thus, if a coffee company wants to communicate that its coffee is rich, it should probably use a red container along with label copy boasting the coffee's rich taste.[11]

Choosing Media

The communicator now must select *channels of communication*. There are two broad types of communication channels—*personal* and *nonpersonal*.

Personal Communication Channels

Personal communication channels
Channels through which two or more people communicate directly with one another, whether face to face, by telephone, by mail, or via the Internet.

In **personal communication channels,** two or more people communicate directly with each other. They might communicate face to face, over the telephone, through the mail, or even through an Internet "chat." Personal communication channels are effective because they allow for personal addressing and feedback.

Some personal communication channels are controlled directly by the company. For example, company salespeople contact buyers in the target market. But other personal communications about the product may reach buyers through channels not directly controlled by the company. These might include independent experts—consumer advocates, consumer buying guides, and others—making statements to target buyers. Or they might be neighbors, friends, family members, and associates talking to target buyers. This last channel, known as **word-of-mouth influence,** has considerable effect in many product areas.

Word-of-mouth influence
Personal communication about a product between target buyers and neighbors, friends, family members, and associates.

Personal influence carries great weight for products that are expensive, risky, or highly visible. For example, buyers of automobiles and major appliances often go beyond mass-media sources to seek the opinions of knowledgeable people.

Companies can take steps to put personal communication channels to work for them. For example, they can create *opinion leaders*—people whose opinions are sought by others—by supplying certain people with the product on attractive terms. For instance, they can work through community members such as local radio personalities, class presidents, and heads of local organizations. They can use influential people in their advertisements or develop advertising that has high "conversation value."

Nonpersonal Communication Channels

Nonpersonal communication channels
Media that carry messages without personal contact or feedback, including major media, atmospheres, and events.

Nonpersonal communication channels are media that carry messages without personal contact or feedback. They include major media, atmospheres, and events. Major *media* include print media (newspapers, magazines, direct mail), broadcast media (radio, television), display media (billboards, signs, posters), and online media (online services, Web sites). *Atmospheres* are designed environments that create or reinforce the buyer's leanings toward buying a product. Thus, lawyers' offices and banks are designed to communicate confidence and other qualities that might be valued by their clients. *Events* are staged occurrences that communicate messages to target audiences. For example, public relations departments arrange press conferences, grand openings, shows and exhibits, public tours, and other events.

Nonpersonal communication affects buyers directly. In addition, using mass media often affects buyers indirectly by causing more personal communication. Communications first flow from television, magazines, and other mass media to opinion leaders and then from these opinion leaders to others. Thus, opinion leaders step between the mass media and their audiences and carry messages to people who are less exposed to media. This suggests that mass communicators should aim their messages directly at opinion leaders, letting them carry the message to others.

Selecting the Message Source

In either personal or nonpersonal communication, the message's impact on the target audience is also affected by how the audience views the communicator. Messages delivered by highly credible sources are more persuasive. Thus, marketers hire celebrity endorsers—well-known athletes, actors, and even cartoon characters—to deliver their messages (see Marketing Highlight 14.2). Many food companies promote to doctors, dentists, and other health care providers to motivate these professionals to recommend their products to patients.

Campbell Soup Company did this to promote its Intelligent Quisine (IQ) meal plan program of prepackaged, healthy frozen entrées and snacks delivered weekly via UPS to customers' homes. The 40 or so meals are tailored to nutritional guidelines limiting fat, cholesterol, and salt. To win over physicians, Campbell consulted with the American Heart Association and the American Diabetes Association and sponsored research on the program's effectiveness. Campbell salespeople visit health care professionals regularly, urging them to recommend the Intelligent Quisine program to their patients.[12]

Collecting Feedback

After sending the message, the communicator must research its effect on the target audience. This involves asking the target audience members whether they remember the message, how many times they saw it, what points they recall, how they felt about the message, and their past and present attitudes toward the product and company. The communicator would also like to measure behavior resulting from the message—how many people bought a product, talked to others about it, or visited the store.

Feedback on marketing communications may suggest changes in the promotion program or in the product offer itself. For example, US Airways uses television and newspaper advertising to inform area consumers about the airline, its routes, and its fares. Suppose feedback research shows that 80 percent of all fliers in an area recall seeing the airline's ads and are aware of its flights and prices. Sixty percent of these aware fliers have flown US Airways, but only 20 percent of those who tried it were satisfied. These results suggest that although promotion is creating *awareness,* the airline isn't giving consumers the *satisfaction* they expect. Therefore, US Airways needs to improve its service while staying with the successful communication program. In contrast, suppose the research shows that only 40 percent of area consumers are aware of the airline, only 30 percent of those aware have tried it, but 80 percent of those who have tried it return. In this case, US Airways needs to strengthen its promotion program to take advantage of its power to create customer satisfaction.

MARKETING HIGHLIGHT 14.2

ATHLETES AS ENDORSERS: NICE GUYS FINISH FIRST

Companies today are paying big bucks to have their products associated with big-name athletes. With so much money riding on athletes as pitchpersons, companies are taking great care to put their money on endorsers with the right stuff. Consider the following example from *Forbes*:

"Kid, you've got the talent, but you've got a problem," barks Bill Laimbeer, one of basketball's all-time dirtiest players, at young superstar Grant Hill during a commercial for Fila. "You're too nice." A series of drills follows in which Laimbeer tries to teach Hill elbowing, tripping, referee abuse, cameraman pushing, nose piercing—all the skills needed for today's modern athletes to make big money off the court and playing field. But the joke is on Laimbeer. A follow-up spot shows Hill calling his mom, asking her to rescue him. The next commercial in the series depicts Hill finally break-

ing free of Laimbeer's hold, despite 52 days of brainwashing at "Camp Tough Guy." "I've got to play with decency, honesty," he says as a ray of light dawns upon him. "I've got to play clean." Clean is now cool. Clean is also lucrative. For endorsing Fila's sneakers, Hill will get about $25 million over 5 years.

Thus, despite what a rogues' gallery of other thuggish professional athletes might have you believe, it's the nice guys who are finishing first. In fact, a majority of today's endorsement dollars are going to athletes with sterling reputations. Picking the wrong spokesperson can result in embarrassment and a tarnished image. Hertz found this out when it entrusted its good name to the care of O. J. Simpson. Pepsi and Kodak faced similar embarrassment when their spokesperson, boxer Mike Tyson, was accused of beating his wife and was later jailed for rape. When Dallas

Cowboys star Michael Irvin was caught some years ago in a motel with go-go dancers and drugs, 13 Toyota dealerships that had paid Irvin $120,000 to do a series of commercials had little choice but to pull the ads—swallowing $400,000 in production costs. The dealers' next spokesperson? A cartoon monkey—no unpleasant surprises that way.

Manufacturers and advertisers seek an endorser's "halo effect"—the positive association that surrounds a product after a popular sports celebrity has pitched it. *Forbes* notes:

The trend toward nice is very good news for good guys like baseball's iron man, Cal Ripken, Jr. ... Ripken is a known quantity, a safe bet. ... Throughout his 18-year career, Ripkin has taken only endorsement deals that would create and reinforce the image he desired. In his rookie year Ripken turned down a chance to make big money endorsing Jockey underwear with his then-

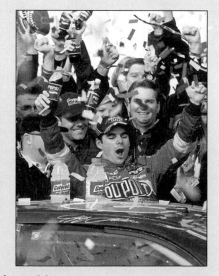

Celebrity endorsers Tiger Woods, Mia Hamm, and Jeff Gordon. Nice is now cool—and lucrative.

teammate Jim Palmer. "I couldn't see myself (promoting) underwear," says Ripken. "I chose a milk radio spot instead because that's the kind of person I am." Now the image is paying off. Ripken's endorsement fees have taken off, jetting from $1 million to $6 million in 3 years.

Few embody the new breed of superstar nice guy better than Grant Hill. His father played football at Yale, then with the Dallas Cowboys. Growing up, Grant practiced basketball, then the piano. Hill's idols back then included nice guys Michael Jordan, Julius Erving, and Arthur Ashe. That was the profile Fila was looking for in 1994, when it hired Hill on. Says Howe Burch, Fila's vice president for advertising, "We don't care if they're the best athlete in the world if he or she is a solid citizen." Hill's impact? With Hill as spokesperson, Fila has become the third-largest sneaker maker domestically. Hill's namesake shoe trails only Nike's Air Jordans in sales. . . . "He's played a big role in our success," says Burch.

Another sports nice guy cashing in on the trend is Pete Sampras, one of the world's top tennis players, who pulled down $8 million in endorsements this year, twice his haul of four years ago. "You don't have to be a jerk," Sampras advises. Then there's super nice-guy phenom Tiger Woods. To go with his tremendous talent, Woods has "brains, cover-boy style, a smile to die for, and charm for days," notes one sports journalist. After winning the 1997 Masters, the charismatic Woods landed sponsorship contracts with Nike, Titleist, American Express, and other companies totaling close to $100 million over five years.

Perhaps the latest beneficiary of niceness is NASCAR's Jeff Gordon. According to Forbes:

NASCAR driver Jeff Gordon is one of the most sought-after endorsers in professional sports—behind only Michael Jordan, Tiger Woods, and Arnold Palmer. Deals including Pepsi, Ray-Ban, and Unilever will bring Gordon endorsement and licensing income of $8.3 million this year. . . . Handsome and self effacing, Gordon is a refreshing change from almost a decade of arrogant, spoiled-brat athletes. [His] squeaky clean, nice guy personality is a positive for him. It shows: More than most celebrity endorsers, Gordon really moves the merchandise. Just ask Jenny German, a dental hygienist from Jasper, Alabama. . . . A Gordon fan since he started on the Winston Cup circuit in 1993, she actively seeks any product he endorses. She drinks Pepsi instead of Coke, eats Edy's ice cream for dessert, and owns a pair of Ray-Ban sunglasses. "If they sold underwear with the number 24 on it, I'd have it on," German says. Unilever's Close-Up, which signed Gordon last year to appear on toothpaste boxes, had to increase production by 40 percent when orders started flooding in from retailers all over the country. In targeted accounts, the toothpaste, which has a market share nationwide of about 2.2 percent, saw it jump to 15 percent; at some retailers the number hit 50 percent.

Another newcomer on the nice-guy front is U.S. women's soccer star Mia Hamm. According to one recent account, "She's a hero, a role model, and a superstar soccer player with everything from a Barbie doll with shin guards to a humongous new building on the Nike campus named after her. But [more], Mia Hamm, the Olympic gold medalist and spokewoman for Nike, Gatorade, and several other brands is an exceedingly modest and team-focused woman." Hamm's commercial appeal soared following the U.S. team's inspiring victory in the 1999 Women's World Cup. Significantly, much of her commercial appeal stems from the fact that she seems so wholesomely noncommercial. Despite her legions of fans and status as number-one scorer (male or female) in international soccer history, Hamm shuns the spotlight. "I'm no better than a lot of people on this U.S. team," she demures. In fact, the entire U.S. women's soccer team seems to represent only the very best in sports. "They didn't argue, they didn't bad mouth anybody, they were always going out of their way to be gracious. The whole idea of the teamwork aspect captured the fancy of the public," says an advertising executive. As a result, the team—individually and collectively—has been courted by advertisers ranging from Nike and Gatorade to Disney and General Mills's Wheaties.

Perhaps the ultimate advantage of having a likable personality is that it extends beyond the athlete's career. Arnold Palmer hasn't played golf seriously in 20 years, but sponsors still pay $15 million a year for his good-guy aura. Even after retirement from his long and venerable career, Michael Jordan, the granddaddy of celebrity endorsers, still pulls down more than $42 million a year from endorsements for such blue-chip sponsors as Nike, McDonald's, Quaker Oats, Sara Lee, and Wilson Sporting Goods. Jordan's enduring wholesomeness and universal appeal have made him a "superbrand" in his own right. His appeal will extend well into his retirement—most of his endorsement contracts extend 5 to 10 years into the future. Says one analyst, "He's another Arnold Palmer and Jack Nicklaus. He'll be around forever."

Sources: Extracts and quotes from Lane Randall, "Nice Guys Finish First," *Forbes,* December 16, 1996, pp. 236–42; Peter Spiegel, "Heir Gordon," *Forbes,* December 14, 1998, pp. 188 97; Barbara Lippart, "Team Mia," *Adweek,* June 21, 1999, pp. 42–46; and "Soccer Team Becomes Hot Property with Advertisers," *Raleigh News and Observer,* July 14, 1999, p. C8.

SETTING THE TOTAL PROMOTION BUDGET AND MIX

We have looked at the steps in planning and sending communications to a target audience. But how does the company decide on the total *promotion budget* and its division among the major promotional tools to create the *promotion mix?* By what process does it blend the tools to create integrated marketing communications? We now look at these questions.

Setting the Total Promotion Budget

One of the hardest marketing decisions facing a company is how much to spend on promotion. John Wanamaker, the department store magnate, once said, "I know that half of my advertising is wasted, but I don't know which half. I spent $2 million for advertising, and I don't know if that is half enough or twice too much." Thus, it is not surprising that industries and companies vary widely in how much they spend on promotion. Promotion spending may be 20 to 30 percent of sales in the cosmetics industry and only 2 or 3 percent in the industrial machinery industry. Within a given industry, both low and high spenders can be found.[13]

How does a company decide on its promotion budget? We look at four common methods used to set the total budget for advertising: the *affordable method,* the *percentage-of-sales method,* the *competitive-parity method,* and the *objective-and-task method.*[14]

Affordable Method

Affordable method
Setting the promotion budget at the level management thinks the company can afford.

Some companies use the **affordable method:** They set the promotion budget at the level they think the company can afford. Small businesses often use this method, reasoning that the company cannot spend more on advertising than it has. They start with total revenues, deduct operating expenses and capital outlays, and then devote some portion of the remaining funds to advertising.

Unfortunately, this method of setting budgets completely ignores the effects of promotion on sales. It tends to place advertising last among spending priorities, even in situations in which advertising is critical to the firm's success. It leads to an uncertain annual promotion budget, which makes long-range market planning difficult. Although the affordable method can result in overspending on advertising, it more often results in underspending.

Percentage-of-Sales Method

Percentage-of-sales method
Setting the promotion budget at a certain percentage of current or forecasted sales or as a percentage of the unit sales price.

Other companies use the **percentage-of-sales method,** setting their promotion budget at a certain percentage of current or forecasted sales. Or they budget a percentage of the unit sales price. The percentage-of-sales method has advantages. It is simple to use and helps management think about the relationships between promotion spending, selling price, and profit per unit.

Despite these claimed advantages, however, the percentage-of-sales method has little to justify it. It wrongly views sales as the *cause* of promotion rather than as the *result.* "A study in this area found good correlation between investments in advertising and the strength of the brands concerned—but it turned out to be effect and cause, not cause and effect. . . . The strongest brands had the highest sales and could afford the biggest investments in advertising!"[15] Thus, the percentage-of-sales budget is based on availability of funds rather than on opportunities. It may prevent the increased spending sometimes needed to turn around falling sales. Because the budget varies with year-to-year sales, long-range planning is difficult. Finally, the method does not provide any basis for choosing a *specific* percentage, except what has been done in the past or what competitors are doing.

Competitive-Parity Method

Competitive-parity method
Setting the promotion budget to match competitors' outlays.

Still other companies use the **competitive-parity method,** setting their promotion budgets to match competitors' outlays. They monitor competitors' advertising or get industry promotion spending estimates from publications or trade associations, and then set their budgets based on the industry average.

Two arguments support this method. First, competitors' budgets represent the collective wisdom of the industry. Second, spending what competitors spend helps prevent promotion wars. Unfortunately, neither argument is valid. There are no grounds for believing that the competition has a better idea of what a company should be spending on promotion than does the company itself. Companies differ greatly, and each has its own special promotion needs. Finally, there is no evidence that budgets based on competitive parity prevent promotion wars.

Objective-and-Task Method

Objective-and-task method
Developing the promotion budget by (1) defining specific objectives, (2) determining the tasks that must be performed to achieve these objectives, and (3) estimating the costs of performing these tasks. The sum of these costs is the proposed promotion budget.

The most logical budget-setting method is the **objective-and-task method,** whereby the company sets its promotion budget based on what it wants to accomplish with promotion. This budgeting method entails (1) defining specific promotion objectives, (2) determining the tasks needed to achieve these objectives, and (3) estimating the costs of performing these tasks. The sum of these costs is the proposed promotion budget.

The objective-and-task method forces management to spell out its assumptions about the relationship between dollars spent and promotion results. But it is also the most difficult method to use. Often, it is hard to figure out which specific tasks will achieve specific objectives. For example, suppose Sony wants 95 percent awareness for its latest camcorder model during the six-month introductory period. What specific advertising messages and media schedules should Sony use to attain this objective? How much would these messages and media schedules cost? Sony management must consider such questions, even though they are hard to answer.

Setting the Overall Promotion Mix

The company now must divide the total promotion budget among the major promotion tools—advertising, personal selling, sales promotion, public relations, and direct marketing. The concept of integrated marketing communications suggests that it must blend the promotion tools carefully into a coordinated *promotion mix*. But how does the company determine what mix of promotion tools it will use? Companies within the same industry differ greatly in the design of their promotion mixes. For example, Avon spends most of its promotion funds on personal selling and direct marketing, whereas Revlon spends heavily on consumer advertising. Compaq Computer relies on advertising and promotion to retailers, whereas Dell Computer uses only direct marketing. We now look at factors that influence the marketer's choice of promotion tools.

The Nature of Each Promotion Tool

Each promotion tool has unique characteristics and costs. Marketers must understand these characteristics in selecting their tools.

Advertising.   Advertising can reach masses of geographically dispersed buyers at a low cost per exposure, and it enables the seller to repeat a message many times. For example, television advertising can reach huge audiences. More than 127 million Americans tuned into the most recent Super Bowl and about 78 million people watched at least part of the past Academy Awards broadcast. "If you want to get to the mass audience," says a media services executive, "broadcast TV is where you have to be." He adds, "For anybody introducing anything who has to lasso an audience in a hurry—a new product, a new campaign, a new movie—the networks are still the biggest show in town."[16]

Beyond its reach, large-scale advertising says something positive about the seller's size, popularity, and success. Because of advertising's public nature, consumers tend to view advertised products as more legitimate. Advertising is also very expressive—it allows the company to dramatize its products through the artful use of visuals, print, sound, and color. On the one hand, advertising can be used to build up a long-term image for a product (such as Coca-Cola ads). On the other hand, advertising can trigger quick sales (as when Sears advertises a weekend sale).

Advertising also has some shortcomings. Although it reaches many people quickly, advertising is impersonal and cannot be as directly persuasive as company salespeople. For the most part, advertising can carry on only a one-way communication with the audience, and the audience does not feel that it has to pay attention or respond. In addition, advertising can be very costly. Although some advertising forms, such as newspaper and radio advertising, can be done on smaller budgets, other forms, such as network TV advertising, require very large budgets.

Personal Selling.   Personal selling is the most effective tool at certain stages of the buying process, particularly in building up buyers' preferences, convictions, and actions. It involves personal interaction between two or more people, so each person can observe the other's needs and characteristics and make quick adjustments. Personal selling also allows all kinds of relationships to spring up, ranging from a matter-of-fact selling relationship to personal friendship. The effective salesperson keeps the customer's interests at heart in order to build a long-term relationship.

With personal selling, the customer feels a greater need to listen and respond, even if the response is a polite "no thank you."

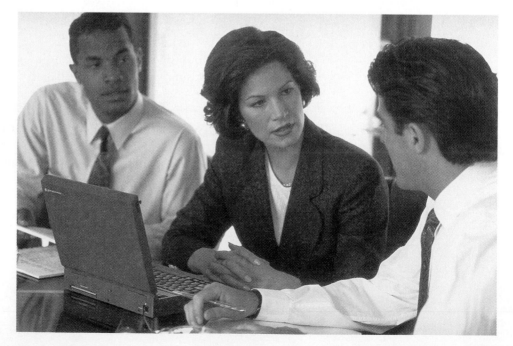

Finally, with personal selling the buyer usually feels a greater need to listen and respond, even if the response is a polite "no thank you."

These unique qualities come at a cost, however. A sales force requires a longer-term commitment than does advertising—advertising can be turned on and off, but sales force size is harder to change. Personal selling is also the company's most expensive promotion tool, costing companies $165 on average per sales call.[17] U.S. firms spend up to three times as much on personal selling as they do on advertising.

Sales Promotion.   Sales promotion includes a wide assortment of tools—coupons, contests, cents-off deals, premiums, and others—all of which have many unique qualities. They attract consumer attention, offer strong incentives to purchase, and can be used to dramatize product offers and to boost sagging sales. Sales promotions invite and reward quick response—whereas advertising says, "Buy our product," sales promotion says, "Buy it now." Sales promotion effects are often short lived, however, and often are not as effective as advertising or personal selling in building long-run brand preference.

Public Relations.   Public relations is very believable—news stories, features, and events seem more real and believable to readers than ads do. Public relations can also reach many prospects who avoid salespeople and advertisements—the message gets to the buyers as "news" rather than as a sales-directed communication. As with advertising, public relations can dramatize a company or product. Marketers tend to underuse public relations or to use it as an afterthought. Yet a well-thought-out public relations campaign used with other promotion mix elements can be very effective and economical.

Direct Marketing.   Although there are many forms of direct marketing—telemarketing, direct mail, electronic marketing, online marketing, and others—they all share four distinctive characteristics. Direct marketing is *nonpublic:* The message is normally addressed to a specific person. Direct marketing also is *immediate* and *customized:* Messages can be prepared very quickly, and they can be tailored to appeal to specific consumers. Finally, direct marketing is *interactive:* It allows a dialogue between the marketing and the consumer, and messages can be altered depending on the consumer's response. Thus, direct marketing is well suited to highly targeted marketing efforts and to building one-to-one customer relationships.

Promotion Mix Strategies

Push strategy
A promotion strategy that calls for using the sales force and trade promotion to push the product through channels.

Pull strategy
A promotion strategy that calls for spending a lot on advertising and consumer promotion to build up consumer demand, which pulls the product through the channels.

Marketers can choose from two basic promotion mix strategies—*push* promotion or *pull* promotion. Figure 14.4 contrasts the two strategies. The relative emphasis on the specific promotion tools differs for push and pull strategies. A **push strategy** involves "pushing" the product through distribution channels to final consumers. The producer directs its marketing activities (primarily personal selling and trade promotion) toward channel members to induce them to carry the product and to promote it to final consumers. Using a **pull strategy,** the producer directs its marketing activities (primarily advertising and consumer promotion) toward final consumers to induce them to buy the product. If the pull strategy is effective, consumers will then demand the product from channel members, who will in turn demand it from producers. Thus, under a pull strategy, consumer demand "pulls" the product through the channels.

Some small industrial goods companies use only push strategies; some direct-marketing companies use only pull. However, most large companies use some combination of both. For example, Frito-Lay uses mass-media advertising to pull its

FIGURE 14.4 Push versus pull promotion strategy

products and a large sales force and trade promotions to push its products through the channels. In recent years, consumer goods companies have been decreasing the pull portions of their promotion mixes in favor of more push.

Companies consider many factors when developing their promotion mix strategies, including *type of product–market* and the *product life-cycle stage.* For example, the importance of different promotion tools varies between consumer and business markets. Consumer goods companies usually "pull" more, putting more of their funds into advertising, followed by sales promotion, personal selling, and then public relations. In contrast, business-to-business marketers tend to "push" more, putting more of their funds into personal selling, followed by sales promotion, advertising, and public relations. In general, personal selling is used more heavily with expensive and risky goods and in markets with fewer and larger sellers.

The effects of different promotion tools also vary with stages of the product life cycle. In the introduction stage, advertising and public relations are good for producing high awareness, and sales promotion is useful in promoting early trial. Personal selling must be used to get the trade to carry the product. In the growth stage, advertising and public relations continue to be powerful influences, whereas sales promotion can be reduced because fewer incentives are needed. In the mature stage, sales promotion again becomes important relative to advertising. Buyers know the brands, and advertising is needed only to remind them of the product. In the decline stage, advertising is kept at a reminder level, public relations is dropped, and salespeople give the product only a little attention. Sales promotion, however, might continue strong.

Integrating the Promotion Mix

Having set the promotion budget and mix, the company must now take steps to see that all of the promotion mix elements are smoothly integrated. Here is a checklist for integrating the firm's marketing communications.[18]

★ *Analyze trends—internal and external—that can affect your company's ability to do business:* Look for areas where communications can help the most. Determine the strengths and weaknesses of each communications function. Develop a combination of promotional tactics based on these strengths and weaknesses.

★ *Audit the pockets of communications spending throughout the organization:* Itemize the communications budgets and tasks and consolidate these into a single budgeting process. Reassess all communications expenditures by product, promotional tool, stage of the life cycle, and observed effect.

★ *Identify all contact points for the company and its brands:* Work to ensure that communications at each point are consistent with your overall communications strategy and that your communications efforts are occurring when, where, and how your customers want them.

★ *Team up in communications planning:* Engage all communications functions in joint planning. Include customers, suppliers, and other stakeholders at every stage of communications planning.

★ *Create compatible themes, tones, and quality across all communications media:* Make sure each element carries your unique primary messages and selling points. This consistency achieves greater impact and prevents the unnecessary duplication of work across functions.

★ *Create performance measures that are shared by all communications elements:* Develop systems to evaluate the combined impact of all communications activities.

★ *Appoint a director responsible for the company's persuasive communications efforts:* This move encourages efficiency by centralizing planning and creating shared performance measures.

 # SOCIALLY RESPONSIBLE MARKETING COMMUNICATION

In shaping its promotion mix, a company must be aware of the large body of legal and ethical issues surrounding marketing communications. Most marketers work hard to communicate openly and honestly with consumers and resellers. Still, abuses may occur, and public policy makers have developed a substantial body of laws and regulations to govern advertising, sales promotion, personal selling, and direct-marketing activities. In this section, we discuss issues regarding advertising, sales promotion, and personal selling. Issues regarding direct marketing are addressed in chapter 17.

Advertising and Sales Promotion

By law, companies must avoid false or deceptive advertising. Advertisers must not make false claims, such as suggesting that a product cures something when it does not. They must avoid ads that have the capacity to deceive, even though no one actually may be deceived. An automobile cannot be advertised as getting 32 miles per gallon unless it does so under typical conditions, and a diet bread cannot be advertised as having fewer calories simply because its slices are thinner.

Sellers must avoid bait-and-switch advertising that attracts buyers under false pretenses. For example, a large retailer advertised a sewing machine at $179. However, when consumers tried to buy the advertised machine, the seller downplayed its features, placed faulty machines on showroom floors, understated the machine's performance, and took other actions in an attempt to switch buyers to a more expensive machine. Such actions are both unethical and illegal.

A company's trade promotion activities also are closely regulated. For example, under the Robinson-Patman Act, sellers cannot favor certain customers through their use of trade promotions. They must make promotional allowances and services available to all resellers on proportionately equal terms.

Beyond simply avoiding legal pitfalls, such as deceptive or bait-and-switch advertising, companies can use advertising to encourage and promote socially responsible programs and actions. For example, State Farm joined with the National Council for Social Studies, National Science Teachers Association, and other national teachers' organizations to create a Good Neighbor Award to recognize primary and secondary teachers for innovation, leadership, and involvement in their profession. State Farm promotes the award through a series of print advertisements. Similarly, Caterpillar is one of several companies and environmental groups forming the Tropical Forest Foundation, which is working to save the great Amazon rain forest. It uses advertising to promote the cause and its involvement.

Personal Selling

A company's salespeople must follow the rules of "fair competition." Most states have enacted deceptive sales acts that spell out what is not allowed. For example, salespeople may not lie to consumers or mislead them about the advantages of buying a product. To avoid bait-and-switch practices, salespeople's statements must match advertising claims.

Different rules apply to consumers who are called on at home versus those who go to a store in search of a product. Because people called on at home may be taken by surprise and may be especially vulnerable to high-pressure selling techniques, the Federal Trade Commission (FTC) has adopted a *three-day cooling-off rule* to give special protection to customers who are not seeking products. Under this rule, customers who agree in their own homes to buy something costing more than $25 have 72 hours in which to cancel a contract or return merchandise and get their money back, no questions asked.

Much personal selling involves business-to-business trade. In selling to businesses, salespeople may not offer bribes to purchasing agents or to others who can influence a sale. They may not obtain or use technical or trade secrets of competitors through bribery or industrial espionage. Finally, salespeople must not disparage competitors or competing products by suggesting things that are not true.[19]

REVIEW OF CONCEPT CONNECTIONS

Modern marketing calls for more than just developing a good product, pricing it attractively, and making it available to target customers. Companies also must *communicate* with current and prospective customers, and what they communicate should not be left to chance. For most companies, the question is not *whether* to communicate, but *how much to spend* and *in what ways*.

1. Name and define the tools of the marketing communications mix.

A company's total *marketing communications mix*—also called its *promotion mix*—consists of the specific blend of *advertising, personal selling, sales promotion, public relations,* and *direct-marketing* tools that the company uses to pursue its advertising and marketing objectives. Advertising includes any paid form of nonpersonal presentation and promotion of ideas, goods, or services by an identified sponsor. Personal selling is any form of personal presentation by the firm's sales force for the purpose of making sales and building customer relationships. Firms use sales promotion to provide short-term incentives to encourage the purchase or sale of a product or service. Public relations focuses on building good relations with the company's various publics by obtaining favorable unpaid publicity. Finally, firms seeking immediate response from targeted individual customers use nonpersonal direct-marketing tools to communicate with customers.

2. Discuss the process and advantages of integrated marketing communications.

Recent shifts in marketing strategy from mass marketing to targeted or one-on-one marketing, coupled with advances in information technology, have had a dramatic impact on marketing communications. Although still important, the mass media are giving way to a profusion of smaller, more focused media. Companies are doing less *broadcasting* and more *narrowcasting.* As marketing communicators adopt richer but more fragmented media and promotion mixes to reach their diverse markets, they risk creating a communications hodgepodge for consumers. To prevent this, more companies are adopting the concept of *integrated marketing communications,* which calls for carefully integrating all sources of company communication to deliver a clear and consistent message to target markets.

To integrate its external communications effectively, the company must first integrate its internal communications activities. The company then works out the roles that the various promotional tools will play and the extent to which each will be used. It carefully coordinates the promotional activities and the timing of when major campaigns take place. Finally, to help implement its integrated marketing strategy, the company appoints a marketing communications director who has overall responsibility for the company's communications efforts.

3. Outline the steps in developing effective marketing communications.

In preparing marketing communications, the communicator's first task is to *identify the target audience* and its characteristics. Next, the communicator has to determine the *communication objectives* and define the response sought, whether it be *awareness, knowledge, liking, preference, conviction,* or *purchase.* Then a *message* should be constructed with an effective content and structure. *Media* must be selected, both for personal and nonpersonal communication. The communicator must find highly credible sources to deliver the message. Finally, the communicator must collect *feedback* by watching how much of the market becomes aware, tries the product, and is satisfied in the process.

4. Explain the methods for setting the promotion budget and factors that affect the design of the promotion mix.

The company has to decide how much to spend for promotion. The most popular approaches are to spend what the company can afford, to use a percentage of sales, to base promotion on competitors' spending, or to base it on an analysis and costing of the communication objectives and tasks.

The company has to divide the *promotion budget* among the major tools to create the *promotion mix.* Companies can pursue a *push* or a *pull* promotional strategy, or a combination of the two. The best specific blend of promotion tools depends on the type of product–market, the buyer's readiness stage, and the product life-cycle stage.

People at all levels of the organization must be aware of the many legal and ethical issues surrounding marketing communications. Companies must work hard and proactively at communicating openly, honestly, and agreeably with their customers and resellers.

KEY TERMS

Advertising	Marketing communications mix	Public relations
Affordable method	(promotion mix)	Pull strategy
Buyer-readiness stages	Nonpersonal communication channel	Push strategy
Competitive-parity method	Objective-and-task method	Sales promotion
Direct marketing	Percentage-of-sales method	Word-of-mouth influence
Integrated marketing communications	Personal communication channel	
(IMC)	Personal selling	

ISSUES FOR DISCUSSION

1. The shift from mass marketing to targeted marketing, and the corresponding use of a richer mixture of promotion tools and communication channels, poses problems for many marketers. Using all of the promotion-mix elements suggested in the chapter, propose a plan for integrating marketing communications at one of the following: (a) your university or college, (b) McDonald's (see www.mcdonalds.com), (c) Burton Snow Boards (see www.burton.com), or (d) a local zoo, museum, theater, or civic event. Discuss your plan in class.

2. Which form of marketing communications does each of the following represent? (a) a Limp Bizkit T-shirt sold at a concert, (b) a *Rolling Stone* interview with Eric Clapton arranged by his manager, (c) a scalper auctioning tickets via eBay (ebay.com) for a Korn concert, (d) a music store selling Boyz II Men albums for $2 off during the week their latest music video debuts on MTV, and (e) Shania Twain's development of a Web page to keep fans aware of her concert tours, latest recordings, and line of signature clothing products.

3. Using Figure 14.2, describe the communications process for (a) a local newspaper ad for new cars, (b) a phone call from a representative of MCI requesting service sign up, (c) a salesperson in Sears attempting to sell you a television set, and (d) Microsoft's Web page (www.microsoft.com), allows you to ask questions about products.

4. List and briefly describe each of the six buyer-readiness stages through which consumers pass on their way to making a purchase. Provide your own example that illustrates how a consumer passes through these stages.

5. The marketing communicator can use one or more types of appeals or themes to produce a desired response. (a) What are these types of appeals? (b) When should each be used? (c) Provide an example of each type of appeal using three different magazine ads.

6. Michael Jordan, Tiger Woods, Jeff Gordon, and numerous Olympic athletes have had a huge impact on advertising and endorsements. Explain the positive and negative consequences of using celebrity sports figures to promote a company's products. What impact does the use of sports celebrity endorsers have on the average person? Is this different from the impact of other types of celebrity endorsers?

7. Decide which of the promotional budget models described in the text would be most appropriate for (a) a small retail gift store, (b) an office supply company that has had a consistent sales and promotion pattern during each of the past five years, (c) a grocery store that has faced intense competition from three competitors in its immediate market area, and (d) an electronics manufacturer that is seeking to expand its market base and national appeal. Explain.

8. Each promotional tool has unique characteristics and costs. Marketers must understand these characteristics in selecting their tools. Using Coca-Cola as an example, demonstrate how each of the promotional tools might be used to create an integrated marketing communications approach for the upcoming year.

MARKETING APPLICATIONS

1. The markets for personal and handheld computers are exploding. It seems that there will soon be a PC for every desk or pocket. However, tomorrow's computers will probably be as different from today's as today's laptops are from yesterday's old "punch card" machines. But how do you tell consumers in plain terms what they need to know about new generations of products without boring them? Computer manufacturers have learned that most consumers do not respond well to the detailed descriptions that are often needed to explain complex technological features and differences. The answer may be as close as the computer company's Web site. Experts predict that more and more consumers will be surfing the Web for product information and that fewer will use traditional information sources. Examine the following Web sites: Sharp (www.sharp-usa.com), IBM (www.ibm.com), NEC Computer Systems (www.nec.com), Casio (www.casio.com), Apple (www.apple.com), and Sony (www.sony.com).

   a. How are the marketing communications at these Web sites different from those found in traditional advertising media? Develop a grid that compares and critiques the two forms of marketing communication. Assess the advantages and disadvantages of each form.

   b. Which of these Web sites is the most effective? Explain.

   c. After reviewing each site, pick a product that you might like to own (such as a laptop or handheld computer). Based solely on the Web sites above, which company and product most grabs your attention and purchasing interest? Critique your information-gathering experience: What information was most useful? How could the communication be improved? Would you be willing to purchase the product via the Internet? Why or why not?

2. In five short years Charles Brewer has turned MindSpring Enterprises (www.mindspring.com) from a one-room operation into one of the nation's largest Internet service providers (ISP). When Mindspring recently merged with EarthLink Network, it jumped past industry giants such as Microsoft, AT&T, and Prodigy to become the nation's number-two ISP behind mammoth AOL (www.aol.com). However, with 3 million customers as compared to AOL's 20 million, catching up will take careful strategic planning—and a bit of luck. MindSpring/EarthLink plans to spend $300 million (half of its annual revenues) on promotion to encourage AOL customers (approximately 1 million defect from AOL each month) to join the ISP "with better service." EarthLink also plans to attack AOL's small business market by offering customized e-mail addresses, home pages, and applications that AOL doesn't currently provide. Will these moves move MindSpring/EarthLink closer to the top or will the AOL juggernaut continue to roll unchecked? Only time will tell.

   a. What successful communications strategies does MindSpring/EarthLink appear to be using now? How could MindSpring/EarthLink use integrated marketing communications (IMC) to challenge AOL?

   b. What other areas of AOL vulnerability might MindSpring/EarthLink attack?

   c. If you were AOL's CEO, what would you do to meet the threat?

   d. If you were to give one piece of advice to an ISP that wanted to get your business, what would the advice be? What would be the best way for MindSpring/EarthLink to communicate in response to your advice?

INTERNET CONNECTIONS

INTEGRATED MARKETING COMMUNICATIONS

McDonald's is one of the most powerful brands in the world. In addition to its product mix, wide distribution of restaurants, and value pricing, McDonald's has extremely effective communications with important audiences. The concept of integrated marketing communications recognizes that customers are only one group to whom a firm wants to disseminate persuasive information. In addition to targeting kids and their parents, McDonald's is concerned with stockholders, potential franchisees, potential employees, and the communities in which the restaurants reside. Visit McDonald's online (www.mcdonalds.com) and see how it communicates to various audiences. View each page in the table and then formulate a sentence to describe your opinion about the overall communication content and desired response.

Audience	One-sentence message to this audience	Desired response from this audience
Customer: Kids		
Customer: Adults		
Investors		
Potential franchisees (corporate)		
Potential employees		
Community		
Other (specify)		
Other (specify)		

FOR DISCUSSION

1. Why do you think McDonald's wants to communicate with each of the noncustomer groups?
2. Although the specific messages may differ, is the overall appeal of its messages consistent to all audiences (rational/emotional tone, visuals, color, brand name, and image)? What is the overall feeling you get from viewing its site?
3. Is McDonald's online message to consumers consistent with what you've seen on TV and elsewhere?
4. Have you seen any of McDonald's promotions or packages that direct consumers to the Web site? Specify where you've seen it.

SAVVY SITES

- Want to see some Web sites that don't do a good job at attracting and keeping visitors? Visit Web Pages That Suck (www.webpagesthatsuck.com) for an interesting and humorous look at the Web's worst.
- Check out Advertising Age (www.adage.com) and AdWeek (www.adweek.com) online editions to learn more about what is happening in integrated marketing communications worldwide.

NOTES

1. Based on information supplied by Jim Lesinski at Volvo Trucks North America.
2. The first four of these definitions are adapted from Peter D. Bennett, *Dictionary of Marketing Terms* (Chicago: American Marketing Association, 1995).
3. For more discussion, see Don E. Schultz, Stanley I. Tannenbaum, and Robert F. Lauterborn, *Integrated Marketing Communication* (Chicago, IL: NTC, 1992), pp. 11, 17; Larry Percy, *Strategies for Implementing Integrated Marketing Communication* (Chicago, IL: NTC, 1997); and James R. Ogdan, *Developing a Creative and Innovative Integrated Marketing Communications Plan* (Upper Saddle River, NJ: Prentice Hall, 1998).
4. Michael Kubin, "Simple Days of Retailing on TV Are Long Gone," *Marketing News,* February 17, 1997, pp. 2, 13; Elizabeth Lesly Stevens and Ronald Glover, "The Entertainment Glut," *Business Week,* February 16, 1998, pp. 88–95; Ronald Glover, "If These Shows Are Hits, Why Do They Hurt So Much?" *Business Week,* April 13, 1998, p. 36; Stuart Elliott, "Fewer Viewers, More Commercials," *New York Times,* June 8, 1999, p. 1; Joe Mandese, "Networks Facing a Most Uncertain Fate," *Advertising Age,* February 14, 2000, pp. 54, 516; and information accessed online at www.magazine.org, March 2000.
5. "Promotion Practices Condensed," *Potentials,* November 1998, p. 6.

6. See Schultz, Tannenbaum, and Lauterborn, *Integrated Marketing Communication*, chaps. 3 and 4.

7. P. Griffith Lindell, "You Need Integrated Attitude to Develop IMC," *Marketing News*, May 26, 1997, p. 6.

8. Sally Beatty, "'Serious' Super Bowl Advertisers to Try Humor in Making Pitches," *Wall Street Journal*, January 28, 1999, p. B16.

9. Kevin Goldman, "Advertising: Knock, Knock. Who's There? The Same Old Funny Ad Again," *Wall Street Journal*, November 2, 1993, p. B10; Melanie Wells, "Little Caesars Ads Aim for Pizza Lust," *USA Today*, November 16, 1998, p. 8B; and "Comedy Dominates the Best," *Advertising Age*, May 31, 1999, p. S2.

10. See Ayn E. Crowley and Wayne D. Hoyer, "An Integrative Framework for Understanding Two-Sided Persuasion," *Journal of Consumer Research*, March 1994, pp. 561–74.

11. Philip Kotler, *Marketing Management: Analysis, Planning, Implementation, and Control*, 10th ed. (Upper Saddle River, NJ: Prentice Hall, 2000), p. 559.

12. Joseph Weber, "Now, Campbell's Makes House Calls," *Business Week*, June 16, 1997, pp. 144–46; and Chad Kaydo, "Selling a Lifestyle Change," *Sales & Marketing Management*, December 1997, p. 95.

13. "1999 Advertising-to-Sales Ratios for the 200 Largest Ad Spending Industries," *Advertising Age*, June 28, 1999, p. 58.

14. For more on setting promotion budgets, see George S. Low and Jakki J. Mohr, "Brand Managers' Perceptions of the Marketing Communications Budget Allocation Process," Marketing Science Institute, Report No. 98-105, March 1998; and J. Thomas Russell and W. Ronald Lane, *Kleppner's Advertising Procedure*, 14th ed. (Upper Saddle River, NJ: Prentice Hall, 1999), chap. 6.

15. David Allen, "Excessive Use of the Mirror," *Management Accounting*, June 1966, p. 12. Also see Laura Petrecca, "4A's Will Study Financial Return on Ad Spending," *Advertising Age*, April 7, 1997, pp. 3, 52; and Dana W. Hayman and Don E. Schultz, "How Much Should You Spend on Advertising," *Advertising Age*, April 26, 1999, p. 32.

16. Stuart Elliott, "Fewer Viewers, More Commercials," *New York Times*, June 8, 1999, p. 1.

17. Michele Marchetti, "The Costs of Doing Business," *Sales & Marketing Management*, September 1999, p. 56.

18. Based on Matthew P. Gonring, "Putting Integrated Marketing Communications to Work Today," *Public Relations Quarterly*, Fall 1994, pp. 45–48.

19. For more on the legal aspects of promotion, see Louis W. Stern and Thomas I. Eovaldi, *Legal Aspects of Marketing Policy* (Upper Saddle River, NJ: Prentice Hall, 1984), chaps. 7 and 8; Robert J. Posch, *The Complete Guide to Marketing and the Law* (Upper Saddle River, NJ: Prentice Hall, 1988), chaps. 15 to 17; and William Wells, John Burnett, and Sandra Moriarty, *Advertising Principles and Practice*, 4th ed. (Upper Saddle River, NJ: Prentice Hall, 1998), chap. 2.

COMPANY CASE

14

Mailboxes, Etc.: Making Communications More Effective

For Jeremy Kraus, it was the dream of a lifetime. He would appear in a television commercial before millions of people, sandwiched between Budweiser's Louie the Lizard and the Oscar Meyer Wienermobile on Super Bowl XXXIII to pitch his Jeremy's MicroBatch Ice Creams. Incredibly, it wouldn't cost him a cent. In fact, he would *receive* $5,000 to hawk his product. How can the owner of a small business, which employs only four full-time and five part-time employees, afford an advertising opportunity like this? The simple answer is that he can't. However, Mailboxes, Etc. (MBE) can, and it chose to feature Jeremy's business in a 15-second segment contained within it's own 30-second Super Bowl ad.

Why does MBE give away advertising space that costs more than $1 million a minute? It is attempting to raise credibility for its own slogan, "Making business easier worldwide." MBE is showing that the slogan is more than just words; it's backing the words with actions. By giving one entrepreneur each year an opportunity to score big with a Super Bowl appearance, MBE really does make business easier for that small company. At the same time, it is grabbing the attention of millions of potential MBE customers with what some observers call the best idea in Super Bowl advertising.

With more than 3,700 centers in 59 countries, MBE is the world's largest nonfood franchise operation. Besides mailboxes, it offers all forms of shipping (FedEx, UPS, U.S. Postal Service), packaging, communication (voice mail, fax, Internet, Western Union, secretarial and answering services), and other office services such as color copying, office supplies, and design and printing of cards and stationery.

To supplement it's free-standing franchise locations, MBE recently introduced MBE Business Express—a superkiosk that dispenses business services. It features 24-hour, credit card–activated access to a PC, laser printer, fax, photocopier, laptop hookup, and high-speed Internet connection. Currently located in hotels, MBE Business Express enables hospitality providers who can't afford a full-service business center of their own to provide business services to travelers. It also answers the prayers of business travelers when they need services outside a hotel's regular hours. In the future, you'll find these superkiosks everywhere—in convenience stores, convention centers, and supermarkets—making MBE services available to individual consumers as well as business customers. Through contracts with the U.S. Postal Service, eBay.com, and Hewlett-Packard to become recycling centers for toner cartridges, MBE has broadened its market to include more services for final consumers as well as to small businesses.

With its "See your small business on the Super Bowl search," MBE invites all of its franchisees' customers to enter the contest. The winner gets $5,000 and appears on the Super Bowl; the two runners up get $2,000 each. Potential entrants must have fewer than 20 employees and be regular customers of an MBE franchise. To enter, they simply answer two questions: First, they must tell how their business demonstrates the entrepreneurial spirit of small business in America. Second, they must explain in 25 words or less what they would say about their business to the 130 million Super Bowl viewers.

For three years running, MBE has purchased Super Bowl ad time. The first year, prior to the contests, its ad featured a testimonial from Wilderness Air in Alaska. That ad didn't stand out from the Super Bowl clutter as well as the more recent contest winner ads. Also, according to Pete Devaris, owner of the Wilderness Air, the ad didn't do anything for the airline's business. The next year, MBE came up with the Super Bowl search contest. The winner was Pump Products, which makes a handheld basketball-inflating pocket pump. In contrast to the MBE's first Super Bowl ad, the Pump Products ad struck gold, resulting in tens of thousands of dollars in sales. "We're still catching our breath," say Robert Lange and Chuck Davey, owners of Pump Products.

More than four months before the Super Bowl, MBE uses its regular advertising campaign to kick off the contest. These ads air on television, news, sports, prime time network TV programming, print, and national cable. Entry forms are disseminated using a combination of radio and point-of-purchase advertising in stores. Press releases on the MBE Web site (www.mbe.com) back up the campaign.

The first two contests have attracted considerable industry notice and have been the subject of articles in *Advertising Age*, *Nation's Business*, *Adweek*, and *Marketing News*, all of which helped publicize the contests and provide promotion for MBE. MBE has also promoted the contests by sending mailings to franchisees and their regular customers. As a result, the contests gain continued media attention after MBE announces its 10 finalists and picks a winner.

Promotional efforts do not end with the Super Bowl ads. Through the contests, MBE has built a database of franchise customers to whom it can send future mailings and offerings. The first year of the campaign alone, for a promotion that cost only $3 million, including production of the Super Bowl commercial, MBE received more than 3,500 entries.

Through its Web site, MBE is able to coordinate promotions and the contest. Entrants can submit their essays on the Internet and check there for contest updates. In addition, the site disseminates information about MBE, attracts new employees, and facilitates communication with customers, potential franchisees, and current franchise owners. To facilitate internal communications, MBE established a chat room on its Internet site, where franchisees can discuss problems, share information, and help each other. In addition, MBE uses its extranet to direct communications from headquarters in San Diego to franchisees and issue the monthly "Notes and News" containing relevant business articles. It also has the capability to tailor an individual store's home page to the special services that it offers in addition to the regular MBE services.

For business travelers outside the United States, MBE moved from Main Street to High Street (United Kingdom) as early as 1996. Beginning with locations in Europe—particularly southern Europe—it now has offices on nearly every continent. In late 1998, MBE signed contracts with Svenska Tjanstebutiker AB to expand into Scandinavia and with SK Global Co. to enter the Korean market. All of this demonstrates a commitment to the company's goal of making business easier worldwide for both local businesses and for U.S. business people abroad.

How can MBE tie these non-U.S. operations into its promotion mix? Its much-lauded contest and Super Bowl ads really seem to be aimed at the U.S. market—all the contestants have been in the United States. Because the Super Bowl is shown around the world, franchisees worldwide could be encouraged to enter, but American football doesn't command the same high involvement and strong following outside the United States. Perhaps MBE could sponsor multiple regional contests (one for Europe, one for Asia, and so on). Or perhaps there's some other worldwide event on which MBE could advertise that would attract contestants globally.

Another issue for MBE is wearout. How long will the contest continue to attract attention and motivate entrants? After several years, it might lose its attractiveness in the United States. Notably, a lot of the 1998 final contestants were the same as those of 1997. If that's true, maybe it's time for MBE to design a new U.S. campaign by either dropping the contest idea or continuing it only outside the United States.

Questions

1. What are the target audiences for an MBE Super Bowl ad? For the contests?
2. What is the message of these Super Bowl ads? Of the contests? Of the other associated promotions, such as the direct mail pieces?
3. What forms of promotion is MBE using in its integrated marketing communications campaign? How does each form contribute?
4. What response does MBE want from the contests? From the Super Bowl ads?
5. Why did the initial MBE testimonial ad for Wilderness Air not result in additional sales? In contrast, why was the ad for Pump Products so successful?
6. Has the contest idea worn out in the United States? Should MBE extend the contest idea to its non-U.S. markets? Explain.

Sources: "A Super Contest," *Nation's Business,* October 1997, p. 13; Alison Ashton, "Office Services to Go," *Home Office Computing,* May 1998, p. 24; Alice Cuneo, "Promotion Prize: Super Bowl Ad," *Advertising Age,* September 1, 1997, p. 29; Emily Fromm, "Super Sunday," *Adweek,* January 25, 1999, pp. 30–31; Bob Garfield, "Bud Lizards Electrify Super Bowl Ads," *Advertising Age,* January 26, 1998, pp. 1, 53; Ryan Peal, "Mail Boxes, Etc. Announces Master License Agreement for Sweden with Founder of McDonald's Sweden and Two Former CEOs of Volvo," *MBE Press Release;* Ryan Peal, "Republic of Korea Master License Agreement Announced by Mail Boxes, Etc." *MBE Press Release;* Skip Wollenberg, "Volvo Trucks, Mail Boxes, Etc. Make Big Bets on Lone Commercials During Super Bowl," *Marketing News,* January 5, 1998, p. 25.

After studying this chapter, you should be able to
1. define the roles of advertising, sales promotion, and public relations in the promotion mix
2. describe the major decisions involved in developing an advertising program
3. explain how sales-promotion campaigns are developed and implemented
4. explain how companies use public relations to communicate with their publics

ADVERTISING, SALES PROMOTION, AND PUBLIC RELATIONS

The senior marketing manager for M&M/Mars knew she was on to something when she got a call from her daughter at school. It seems that the kids in her daughter's class were picking up the phrase, "Not going anywhere for a while? Grab a Snickers." This was music to the woman behind the now highly successful Snickers advertising campaign.

In its "Not going anywhere for a while?" theme—later simplified to "Hungry? Why Wait?"— Snickers had found the elusive "big idea"—a creative approach that turns a solid advertising strategy into a great ad campaign. During the past three years, the idea has become the basis for a series of wonderfully engaging, award-winning commercials that spill over with brand personality. Such commercials are crucial in today's cluttered and chaotic TV advertising environ-

ment, in which the average U.S. adult is exposed to as many as 247 ads a day. Before an ad can even start to communicate a selling proposition, it must first break through the din of commercials and other distractions to capture viewer attention. Humor is often the best clutter buster, and the Snickers ads are delightfully funny.

The campaign has consisted of several humorous variations on a central premise: Through circumstances beyond their control, characters in the ads find themselves stuck in one place for a long time, without access to a meal. The first spot in the campaign featured Buffalo Bills coach Marv Levy—who had taken teams to the Super Bowl four times without a win—lecturing his players that nobody would leave until they figured out how to win the big game. The ad was funny. It was also very expensive— football stars don't come cheap. So the creative team at BBDO Worldwide, the Snickers ad agency, set out to reduce production expenses. "We have a great idea," said the ad agency's creative director to his team. "Let's simplify it." The team responded with five new spots that not only cost less to produce but also allowed more effective use of 15-second media slots versus 30-second ones, thus saving on media costs as well. The lower budget created a kind of modesty and simplicity in the Snickers campaign that made the new ads even more appealing than the original.

One of these ads, set in a football locker room, took a good-natured poke at political correctness. In the ad, a gruff, crew-cut head coach announces, "Listen up. This year we gotta be a little more 'politically correct' with the team prayer." He turns to a priest standing behind him and says, "Hit it, Padre." The priest begins his prayer, but before he can go on, the coach butts in to introduce a second clergyman. "All right, Rabbi. Let's go." The rabbi too is cut off, this time in favor of a Native American spiritualist, who in turn gives way to a Buddhist monk. "That was very touching," growls the coach. As the camera pans the room to reveal a long line of spiritual leaders waiting to bless the team, the voice-over says, "Not going anywhere for a while? Grab a Snickers."

Some may take the Snickers campaign as comedy for comedy's sake, but beneath the funny lines is a very serious selling proposition. The stakes are high and so is the investment—M&M/Mars spends tens of millions of dollars each year on advertising for Snickers. The campaign's objective is to advance Snickers' long-time hunger-satisfaction positioning—it's what to eat to satisfy your between-meal hunger. Previous advertising portrayed idealized role models such as firefighters and investigative reporters scarfing down Snickers bars before committing nougat-fortified acts of heroism. Those ads were neither entertaining nor relevant to the brand's primary target market of males 18 to 22 years old. The new ads are both. They give Snickers a less serious tone and position the brand more credibly and believably as a hunger-relieving stop-gap measure. "We moved [our positioning] from [damping] a preoccupying hunger to satisfying hunger in an enjoyable way," says the senior marketing manager.

Perhaps the most memorable ad was "Chefs." The ad opens with Clarence, the "Chiefs'" elderly end zone painter, painstakingly reproducing the team logo beneath the goal posts. As he steps back finally to admire

his work, a player walks up behind him. "Hey, that's great," says the beefy player, "but who are the Chefs?" Yes, he left out the "i," which is amusing, but his reaction is hilarious. "Great googily moogily," he grumbles. (It's a line one member of the ad team remembered hearing an old uncle exclaim.) Disgusted that he's not going anywhere for a while, he gnaws on a Snickers.

A more recent ad taps the old gag of an umpire needing eyeglasses. A long-suffering but patient optometrist deals with a ref in a striped shirt who keeps seeing cows on the letter chart. "No, there are no cows," says the doctor gently. Meanwhile, his bored assistant looks outside the examination room to see a dozen officials in the waiting room. As the announcer asks "Hungry? Why Wait?" the assistant takes a big chomp out of a super-size Snickers bar.

Lots of people *are* chomping a Snickers, it would appear. The aggressive ad campaign has helped make Snickers one of the best-performing candy and snack brands in the country. The campaign seems to have captured the minds and imaginations of American consumers. "Enjoyability, memorability, and awareness of the thing have gone through the roof," says the director of marketing for the brand.

Thus, the Snickers advertising campaign amounts to much more than just funny ads. Bob Garfield, ad reviewer for *Advertising Age,* concludes, "The annals of advertising record very few . . . enduring 'big ideas,' but soon you may add to the list [Hungry? Why Wait?]. . . . As the campaign inexorably develops—and it will, over many years—this [big] idea will be revealed to have more than charm. It will have depth, scope, and the endless power of surprise. So grab a Snickers and enjoy. This advertising isn't going away for a long, long time." In 1999, for the third year in a row, a Snickers "Hungry? Why Wait?" ad was selected as the Ad Age Best TV Spot in the packaged-goods category.[1]

Companies must do more than make good products—they must inform consumers about product benefits and carefully position products in consumers' minds. To do this, they must skillfully use the mass-promotion tools of *advertising, sales promotion,* and *public relations.* In this chapter, we take a closer look at each of these tools.

ADVERTISING

Advertising
Any paid form of nonpersonal presentation and promotion of ideas, goods, or services by an identified sponsor.

Advertising can be traced back to the very beginnings of recorded history. Archaeologists working in the countries around the Mediterranean Sea have dug up signs announcing various events and offers. The Romans painted walls to announce gladiator fights, and the Phoenicians painted pictures promoting their wares on large rocks along parade routes. A Pompeii wall painting praised a politician and asked for votes. During the Golden Age in Greece, town criers announced the sale of cattle, crafted items, and even cosmetics. An early "singing commercial" went as follows: "For eyes that are shining, for cheeks like the dawn/For beauty that lasts after girlhood is gone/For prices in reason, the woman who knows/Will buy her cosmetics from Aesclyptos."

Modern advertising, however, is a far cry from these early efforts. U.S. advertisers now run up an estimated annual advertising bill of more than $212 billion; worldwide ad spending exceeds $414 billion.[2] Although advertising is used mostly by business firms, it also is used by a wide range of nonprofit organizations, professionals, and social agencies that advertise their causes to various target publics. In fact, the twenty-fifth largest advertising spender is a nonprofit organization—the U.S. government. Advertising is a good way to inform and persuade, whether the purpose is to sell Coca-Cola worldwide or to get consumers in a developing nation to drink milk or use birth control.

Large national advertisers spend huge amounts to position their brands and influence buyers. General Motors, the nation's top advertiser, spends $2.9 billion annually in the United States alone. Number-two Procter & Gamble spends $2.7 billion in the United States and more than twice that amount worldwide.[3] Other major spenders are found in the retailing, auto, food, and entertainment industries. Advertising as a percentage of sales varies greatly by industry. For example, percentage spending is low in the auto industry but high in food, drugs, toiletries, and cosmetics.

Marketing management must make four important decisions when developing an advertising program (see Figure 15.1): *setting advertising objectives, setting advertising budgets, developing advertising strategy* (*message decisions* and *media decisions*), and *evaluating advertising campaigns.*

FIGURE 15.1   Major advertising decisions

Setting Advertising Objectives

The first step is to set *advertising objectives.* These objectives should be based on past decisions about the target market, positioning, and marketing mix, which define the job that advertising must do in the total marketing program.

Advertising objective
A specific communication *task* to be accomplished with a specific *target* audience during a specific period of *time*.

An **advertising objective** is a specific communication *task* to be accomplished with a specific *target* audience during a specific period of *time*. Advertising objectives can be classified by primary purpose—whether the aim is to *inform, persuade, or remind.* Table 15.1 lists examples of each of these objectives.

Informative advertising is used heavily when introducing a new product category. In this case, the objective is to build primary demand. Thus, producers of CD players first informed consumers of the sound and convenience benefits of CDs. *Persuasive advertising* becomes more important as competition increases. Here, the company's objective is to build selective demand. For example, once CD players were established, Sony began trying to persuade consumers that *its* brand offered the best quality for their money.

Some persuasive advertising has become *comparative advertising,* in which a company directly or indirectly compares its brand with one or more other brands. Comparative advertising has been used for products ranging from soft drinks and computers to batteries, pain relievers, long-distance telephone services, car rentals, and credit cards. For example, in its classic comparative campaign, Avis positioned itself against market-leading Hertz by claiming, "We're number two, so we try harder." More recently, Buick ran a "Century Challenge" campaign in which it compared the Buick Century directly against the Ford Taurus and other midsize cars. The aggressive ads take jabs at Taurus's smaller truck and at aspects of the Toyota Camry and Honda Accord that Buick contends compare unfavorably with its Century. In its long-running comparative campaign, Visa has advertised, "American Express is offering you a new credit card, but you don't have to accept it. Heck, 7 million merchants don't." American Express has responded with ads bashing Visa,

TABLE 15.1 POSSIBLE ADVERTISING OBJECTIVES	
To Inform	
Telling the market about a new product	Describing available services
Suggesting new uses for a product	Correcting false impressions
Informing the market of a price change	Reducing buyers' fears
Explaining how the product works	Building a company image
To Persuade	
Building brand preference	Persuading customers to purchase now
Encouraging switching to your brand	Persuading customers to receive a sales call
Changing customer perceptions of product attributes	
To Remind	
Reminding customers that the product may be needed in the near future	Keeping the product in customers' minds during off-seasons
Reminding customers where to buy the product	Maintaining top-of-mind product awareness

Comparative advertising: This ad compares Tylenol—very favorably—to Excedrin.

recommended most:

\,rek·a·men'd·ed mõst\ adj : a course of action doctors subscribe to or advocate above all others for a particular ailment or condition.

TYLENOL®	**EXCEDRIN®**
BRAND RECOMMENDED MOST FOR:	BRAND RECOMMENDED MOST FOR:
1. Headache	1. None
2. Osteoarthritis pain	
3. Back pain	
4. Post-surgery pain	
5. Fever	
6. Flu	
7. Gastrointestinal patients with mild to moderate pain	
8. Sore throat pain	
9. Musculoskeletal pain	
10. Traumatic injury pain	
11. Common cold discomfort	
12. Carpal tunnel syndrome pain	
13. General pain (mild to moderate)	
14. Burn pain	
15. Contusion pain	
16. Otitis media pain	
17. Fracture pain	

Doctors recommend Tylenol more than any other pain reliever for a wide range of ailments and conditions. Tylenol is simply the most trusted combination of safety and strength in pain relief today.

TYLENOL®
Take Comfort in Our Strength.

noting that AmEx's cards offer benefits not available with Visa's regular card, such as rapid replacement of lost cards and higher credit limits. As often happens with comparative advertising, both sides complain that the other's ads are misleading.[4]

Reminder advertising is important for mature products—it keeps consumers thinking about the product. Expensive Coca-Cola ads on television are designed primarily to remind people about Coca-Cola, not to inform or persuade them.

Setting the Advertising Budget

After determining its advertising objectives, the company next sets its *advertising budget* for each product. Four commonly used methods for setting promotion budgets are discussed in chapter 14. Here we discuss some specific factors that should be considered when setting the advertising budget.

A brand's advertising budget often depends on its *stage in the product life cycle.* For example, new products typically need large advertising budgets to build awareness and to gain consumer trial. In contrast, mature brands usually require lower budgets as a ratio to sales. *Market share* also impacts the amount advertising needed: Because building the market or taking share from competitors requires larger advertising spending than does simply maintaining current share, high-share brands usually need more advertising spending as a percentage of sales. Also, brands in a market with many competitors and high advertising clutter must be advertised more heavily to be noticed above the noise in the market. Undifferentiated brands—those that closely resemble other brands in their product class (beer, soft drinks, laundry detergents)—may require heavy advertising to set them apart. When the product differs greatly from competitors, advertising can be used to point out the differences to consumers.

No matter what method is used, setting the advertising budget is no easy task. How does a company know if it is spending the right amount? Some critics charge that large consumer packaged-goods firms tend to spend too much on advertising and business-to-business marketers generally underspend on advertising. They claim that, on the one hand, the large consumer companies use lots of image advertising without really knowing its effects. They overspend as a form of "insurance" against not spending enough. On the other hand, business advertisers tend to rely too heavily on their sales forces to bring in orders. They underestimate the power of company and product image in preselling to industrial customers. Thus, they do not spend enough on advertising to build customer awareness and knowledge.

Companies such as Coca-Cola and Kraft have built sophisticated statistical models to determine the relationship between promotional spending and brand sales, and to help determine the "optimal investment" across various media. Still, because so many factors affect advertising effectiveness, some controllable and others not, measuring the results of advertising spending remains an inexact science. In most cases, managers must rely on large doses of judgment along with more quantitative analysis when setting advertising budgets.[5]

Developing Advertising Strategy

Advertising strategy consists of two major elements: creating advertising *messages* and selecting advertising *media*. In the past, companies often viewed media planning as secondary to the message-creation process. The creative department first created good advertisements, then the media department selected the best media for carrying these advertisements to desired target audiences. This often caused friction between creatives and media planners.

Today, however, media fragmentation, soaring media costs, and more focused target marketing strategies have promoted the importance of the media-planning function. In some cases, an advertising campaign might start with a great message idea, followed by the choice of appropriate media. In other cases, however, a campaign might begin with a good media opportunity, followed by advertisements designed to take advantage of that opportunity. Increasingly, companies are realizing the benefits of planning these two important elements *jointly*.

Thus, more and more advertisers are orchestrating a closer harmony between their messages and the media that deliver them. Media planning is no longer an after-the-fact complement to a new ad campaign. Media planners are now working more closely than ever with creatives to allow media selection to help shape the creative process, often before a single ad is written. In some cases, media people are even initiating ideas for new campaigns.

Among the more noteworthy ad campaigns based on tight media–creative partnerships is the pioneering campaign for Absolut vodka, marketed by Seagram.

★ The Absolut team and its ad agency meet once each year with a slew of magazines to set Absolut's media schedule. The schedule consists of up to 100 magazines, ranging from consumer and business magazines to theater playbills. The agency's creative department is charged with creating media-specific ads. The result is a wonderful assortment of very creative ads for Absolut, tightly targeted to audiences of the media in which they appear. For example, an "Absolut Bravo" ad in playbills has roses adorning a clear bottle, whereas business magazines contain an "Absolut Merger" foldout. In New York–area magazines, "Absolut Manhattan" ads feature a satellite photo of Manhattan, with Central Park assuming the distinctive outline of an Absolut bottle. In Chicago, the windy city, ads show an Absolut bottle with the letters on the label blown

Media planners for Absolut vodka work with creatives to design ads targeted to specific media audiences. "Absolut Bravo"
appears in theater playbills. "Absolut Chicago" targets the Windy City.

askew. An "Absolute Primary" ad run during the political season featured the well-known bottle spattered with mud. In some cases, the creatives even developed ads for magazines not yet on the schedule, such as a clever "Absolut Centerfold" ad for *Playboy* magazine. The ad portrayed a clear, unadorned playmate bottle ("11-inch bust, 11-inch waist, 11-inch hips"). In all, Absolut has developed more than 500 ads for the almost two-decade-old campaign. At a time of soaring media costs and cluttered communication channels, a closer cooperation between creative and media people has paid off handsomely for Absolut. Largely as a result of its breakthrough advertising, Absolut now captures a 63 percent share of the imported vodka market.[6]

Creating the Advertising Message

No matter how big the budget, advertising can succeed only if commercials gain attention and communicate well. Good advertising messages are especially important in today's costly and cluttered advertising environment. The average number of television channels beamed into U.S. homes has skyrocketed from 3 in 1950 to 47 today, and consumers have 18,600 magazines from which to choose.[7] Add the countless radio stations and a continuous barrage of catalogs, direct mail and online ads, and out-of-home media, and consumers are being bombarded with ads at home, at work, and at all points in between.

If all this advertising clutter bothers some consumers, it also causes big problems for advertisers. Take the situation facing network television advertisers. They regularly pay $200,000 or more for 30 seconds of advertising time during a popular prime-time program, even more if it's an especially popular program such as *ER* ($545,000 per 30-second spot), *Friends* ($510,000), *Frasier* ($466,000 per spot), *The*

Drew Carey Show ($370,000), or a mega-event such as the Super Bowl (more than $1.6 million).[8] Then, their ads are sandwiched in with a clutter of some 60 other commercials, announcements, and network promotions per hour.

Until recently, television viewers were pretty much a captive audience for advertisers. Viewers had only a few channels from which to choose. But with the growth in cable and satellite TV, VCRs, and remote-control units, today's viewers have many more options. They can avoid ads by watching commercial-free cable channels. They can "zap" commercials by pushing the fast-forward button during taped programs. With remote control, they can instantly turn off the sound during a commercial or "zip" around the channels to see what else is on. In fact, a recent study found that half of all television viewers now switch channels when the commercial break starts.[9]

Thus, just to gain and hold attention, today's advertising messages must be better planned, more imaginative, more entertaining, and more rewarding to consumers. "Today we have to entertain and not just sell, because if you try to sell directly and come off as boring or obnoxious, people are going to press the remote on you," points out one advertising executive. "When most TV viewers are armed with remote channel switchers, a commercial has to cut through the clutter and seize the viewers in one to three seconds, or they're gone," comments another.[10] Some advertisers even create intentionally controversial ads to break through the clutter and gain attention for their products (see Marketing Highlight 15.1).

Message Strategy. The first step in creating effective advertising messages is to decide what general message will be communicated to consumers—to plan a *message strategy*. The purpose of advertising is to get consumers to think about or react to the product or company in a certain way. People will react only if they believe that they will benefit from doing so. Thus, developing an effective message strategy begins with identifying customer *benefits* that can be used as advertising appeals. Ideally, advertising message strategy will follow directly from the company's broader positioning strategy.

Message strategy statements tend to be plain, straightforward outlines of benefits and positioning points that the advertiser wants to stress. The advertiser must next develop a compelling *creative concept*—or *"big idea"*—that will bring the message strategy to life in a distinctive and memorable way. At this stage, simple message ideas become great ad campaigns. Usually, a copywriter and art director will team up to generate many creative concepts, hoping that one of these concepts will turn out to be the big idea. The creative concept may emerge as a visualization, a phrase, or a combination of the two.

The creative concept will guide the choice of specific appeals to be used in an advertising campaign. *Advertising appeals* should have three characteristics: First, they should be *meaningful,* pointing out benefits that make the product more desirable or interesting to consumers. Second, appeals must be *believable*—consumers must believe that the product or service will deliver the promised benefits. However, the most meaningful and believable benefits may not be the best ones to feature. Appeals should also be *distinctive*—they should tell how the product is better than the competing brands. For example, the most meaningful benefit of owning a wristwatch is that it keeps accurate time, yet few watch ads feature this benefit. Instead, based on the distinctive benefits they offer, watch advertisers might select any of a number of advertising themes. For years, Timex has been the affordable watch that "Takes a lickin' and keeps on tickin'." In contrast, Swatch has featured style and fashion, and Rolex stresses luxury and status.

Message Execution.   The advertiser now has to turn the big idea into an actual ad execution that will capture the target market's attention and interest. The creative people must find the best style, tone, words, and format for executing the message. Any message can be presented in different *execution styles,* such as the following:

★ *Slice of life:* This style shows one or more "typical" people using the product in a normal setting. For example, two mothers at a picnic discuss the nutritional benefits of Jif peanut butter.

★ *Lifestyle:* This style shows how a product fits in with a particular lifestyle. For example, an ad for Mongoose mountain bikes shows a serious biker traversing remote and rugged but beautiful terrain and states, "There are places that are so awesome and so killer that you'd like to tell the whole world about them. But please, *don't.*"

★ *Fantasy:* This style creates a fantasy around the product or its use. For instance, many ads are built around dream themes. Gap even introduced a perfume named Dream. Ads show a woman sleeping blissfully and suggests that the scent is "the stuff that clouds are made of."

★ *Mood or image:* This style builds a mood or image around the product, such as beauty, love, or serenity. No claim is made about the product except through suggestion. Bermuda tourism ads create such moods.

★ *Musical:* This style shows one or more people or cartoon characters singing about the product. For example, one of the most famous ads in history was a Coca-Cola ad built around the song "I'd Like to Teach the World to Sing."

★ *Personality symbol:* This style creates a character that represents the product. The character might be *animated* (the Jolly Green Giant, Cap'n Crunch, Garfield the Cat) or *real* (the Marlboro man, Ol' Lonely the Maytag repairman, Betty Crocker, Morris the 9-Lives Cat, Taco Bell's Chihuahua).

★ *Technical expertise:* This style shows the company's expertise in making the product. Thus, Maxwell House shows one of its buyers carefully selecting coffee beans, and Gallo tells about its many years of wine-making experience.

★ *Scientific evidence:* This style presents survey or scientific evidence that the brand is better or better liked than one or more other brands. For years, Crest toothpaste has used scientific evidence to convince buyers that Crest is better than other brands at fighting cavities.

Execution styles: Harley-Davidson uses humor to get its "the legend rolls on" message across.

MARKETING HIGHLIGHT
15.1

ADVERTISING ON THE EDGE: YOU EITHER HATE 'EM OR LOVE 'EM

You may remember the ad. It opens with a calm, deep-voiced announcer sitting comfortably in a leather chair in a library setting. The spot cuts to a concrete wall with "Outpost.com" emblazoned on it. "Hello," he intones, "we want you to remember our name—Outpost.com." To the shock of some viewers and to the surprised delight of others, he continues, "That's why we've decided to fire gerbils out of this cannon through the 'o' in Outpost." He gives a nod, and his assistant fires a nearby cannon. "Boom!" The cannon hurls a gerbil toward the hole. "Splat!" A near miss—the gerbil hits the wall, then falls to the ground and scurries away. "Cute little guy," says the

announcer, smiling warmly. "Again," he instructs. "Boom!" This time, a gerbil sails high over the wall. "Boom!" "Splat!" "Boom!" "Splat!" "So close," affirms the announcer. Finally, the cannon blasts a gerbil cleanly through the "O," setting off a fanfare of sirens, buzzers, and flashing lights. The ad closes with an invitation to viewers to "Send complaints to Outpost.com—the cool place to buy computer stuff online."

It was all pretend, of course, but complain people did. These ads by Outpost.com—the Internet company that sells computer technology products and consumer electronics online—set off a flurry of controversy on Madison Avenue and among animal-protection groups.

"They do a slick job of depicting violence to animals . . . it's heinous," says an ASPCA spokesperson, who led a letter-writing effort against the campaign. PETA (People for Ethical Treatment of Animals) called it "one of the most reckless ad campaigns in years." Despite the criticism, however, the ads did draw attention—Outpost.com rocketed from near obscurity into the national spotlight in a matter of weeks.

Outpost.com's commercials are just the latest examples of a new genre of irreverent, cutting-edge advertising: commercials that intentionally create controversy, even if it means turning off some potential customers. In today's cluttered advertising environment, these ads go to extremes to get attention—you either love 'em or hate 'em. "It's the age-old question of breaking through the clutter," says the creative director of the ad agency that developed the Outpost.com ads. You turn to "anything you can to get noticed," he says. The ads follow a series of movie and television hits that feature crudeness, lewdness, black humor, or violence—*There's Something About Mary, American Pie, South Park.* "With such entertainment fare pushing the limits of bad taste, increasingly rude, nasty, or just plain boorish behavior is showing up in advertising campaigns as well," notes one analyst.

Indeed, the Outpost.com campaign is just one of many controversial ad efforts. Other examples abound. While flipping through your favorite magazine you might encounter a Toyota ad targeting echo boomers with the headline "Attention nose

Ads on the edge: These ads go to extremes to bust through the clutter—either you love 'em or you hate 'em.

pickers. . . ." On the next page is a boundary-pushing ad from Candies, featuring company spokesmodel Jenny McCarthy sitting on a toilet with her pants around her calves, wearing little more than her bright orange Candies shoes. A Fox Sports television ad shows an able-bodied young guy, engrossed in his Fox Sports Web site, casually ignoring an old man just a few feet away struggling to get a jar down from a shelf. An Orange Slice "twisted taste" commercial opens with the camera panning across a row of squeamish students in a science class, frog legs dangling from their dissection trays. As the teacher drones on about ruptured spleens and green discharges, one kid lunches on his lab project.

For pure gross-out value, few ads top the "Blind Date" spot from SmartBeep, the retail paging-services provider. The spot, which generated enormous response, is part of a wacky five-part campaign that contrasts smart versus not-so-smart behavior to promote SmartBeep's free pagers and low rates on paging services. In it, a woman climbs into the front seat of her blind date's car. While he's crossing around to the other side, thinking she is alone, she leans to one side and lets rip a frat house blast of gas. When her date hops in the car, she hesitates then turns red with embarrassment as he introduces her to another couple in the back seat. "You guys meet? Gregg, Janice?" he asks, to which Janice in the back seat responds, "We sure did." The announcer concludes, "That was stupid. . . . This is smart. A beeper service for just $1.99 a month." The ad closes: "We've got chemistry here. You feel it?" says the blind-date guy. "I felt it!" says Janice from the back seat.

Outpost.com's ads—three in all—themselves rated pretty high on the irreverence meter. The gerbils ad wasn't the only one to set fur flying.

In a second ad, a tattoo artist attempted to make the Outpost.com name more memorable by inscribing it on the foreheads of six-year-old kids at a daycare center, reducing them to tears. In a third, a high school marching band spelling out the company's name on a football field is attacked by "a pack of ravenous wolves," who jump on band members, tearing at their limbs. "Ha, ha, ha," says the announcer, "That's good stuff."

Outpost.com's marketers knew that the ads would be controversial—that was the point. "Our intent was to create memorable ads that would force people to remember our name," says an Outpost.com spokesperson. The agency creative director adds, "We told the people at Outpost that we didn't know if these ads were good or bad. What we told them was that they were memorable—they'll get people to your Web site."

Mission accomplished. Outpost.com received 13,000 e-mails during the 10-week campaign; a surprising 60 percent of them were positive. More important, by the end of the campaign, business was booming. Outpost.com signed 15,000 new customers in the two weeks after the commercials first aired, and 30,000 new customers by the end of the campaign. At the end of the fiscal year, the company had nearly quadrupled its sales over the previous year. Moreover, as a testament to its cutting-edge creativity, the campaign amassed more than a dozen of the ad industry's highest awards and spawned many competitors.

Some industry critics did question the campaign's long-term effectiveness. It appealed to only a narrow segment of viewers, they claimed, and did little to position Outpost.com or to tell people what it had to sell. In fact, Outpost.com

has now shifted to a more informational campaign which positions the company more firmly on its products and free overnight delivery policy.

Still, Outpost.com's initial irreverent advertising appears to have done its job. "Clearly we accomplished our strategic goal," says Outpost.com's founder. "[The creative team] accomplished the goal of making the Outpost.com's name unforgettable, using humor and irreverence. The highly memorable and provocative commercials helped the company to raise brand awareness, increase traffic to the site, and quickly stir significant controversy."

What about viewers who find such "gross-out" ads unsettling? "Some people need to loosen up," shrugs one marketing executive who is under fire for a recent commercial run by his company. "[People] aren't stupid. They can work out what's going on." Says another executive after receiving a pile of complaints about a "gross-out" commercial, "We did nothing, except air the commercial even more, because we knew people were watching it."

Sources: Melanie Wells, "Wanted: Television Ad Complaints," *USA Today,* January 11, 1999, p. 4B; Dottie Enrico, "Creature Feature," *TV Guide,* January 23, 1999, p. 13; Hank Kim, "Creature Feature," *Adweek,* November 23, 1998, p. 20; Anthony Vagnoni, " 'Something About' This Advertising," *Advertising Age,* February 8, 1999, p. 30; Sara Sellar, "Pop Goes the Gerbil," *Sales & Marketing Management,* May 1999, p. 15; Tom Kurtz, "Unsettling TV Commercials: And Now, a Gross-Out from Our Sponsor," *New York Times,* July 25, 1999, p. 7; Stephanie Eads, "Eighty-Six the Flying Gerbils," *Business Week,* December 6, 1999, p. 52; and Debra Ako Williamson, "Outpost.com Drops Gerbils and Wolves, Touts Free Shipping," *Advertising Age,* January 31, 2000, p. 70.

★ *Testimonial evidence or endorsement:* This style features a highly believable or likable source endorsing the product. It could be ordinary people saying how much they like a given product ("My doctor said Mylanta") or a celebrity presenting the product. Many companies use actors or sports celebrities as product endorsers.

The advertiser also must choose a *tone* for the ad. Procter & Gamble always uses a positive tone: Its ads say something very positive about its products. P&G usually avoids humor that might take attention away from the message. In contrast, Taco Bell ads use humor, in the form of an odd but cute little Chihuahua that has put the phrase "Yo quiero Taco Bell," along with millions of tacos, on the tongues of U.S. consumers.

The advertiser must use memorable and attention-getting *words* in the ad. For example, rather than claiming simply that "a BMW is a well-engineered automobile," BMW uses more creative and higher-impact phrasing: "The ultimate driving machine." Instead of stating plainly that Hanes socks last longer than less expensive ones, Hanes suggests, "Buy cheap socks and you'll pay through the toes." It's not that Häagen-Dazs is "a good-tasting luxury ice cream," it's "Our passport to indulgence: passion in a touch, perfection in a cup, summer in a spoon, one perfect moment."

Finally, *format* elements make a difference on an ad's impact as well as on its cost. A small change in ad design can make a big difference in its effect. The *illustration* is the first thing the reader notices—it must be strong enough to draw attention. Next, the *headline* must effectively entice the right people to read the copy. Finally, the *copy*—the main block of text in the ad—must be simple but strong and convincing. Moreover, these three elements must effectively work *together*.

Selecting Advertising Media

The major steps in media selection are (1) deciding on *reach, frequency,* and *impact;* (2) choosing among major *media types;* (3) selecting specific *media vehicles;* and (4) deciding on *media timing.*

Deciding on Reach, Frequency, and Impact.   To select media, the advertiser must decide what reach and frequency are needed to achieve advertising objectives. *Reach* is a measure of the *percentage* of people in the target market who are exposed to the ad campaign during a given period of time. For example, the advertiser might try to reach 70 percent of the target market during the first three months of the campaign. *Frequency* is a measure of how many *times* the average person in the target market is exposed to the message. For example, the advertiser might want an average exposure frequency of three. The advertiser also must decide on the desired *media impact*—the *qualitative value* of a message exposure through a given medium. For example, for products that need to be demonstrated, messages on television may have more impact than messages on radio because television uses sight *and* sound. The same message in one magazine (say, *Newsweek*) may be more believable than in another (say, *The National Enquirer*). In general, the more reach, frequency, and impact the advertiser seeks, the higher the advertising budget will have to be.

Choosing Among Major Media Types.   The media planner has to know the reach, frequency, and impact of each of the major media types. As summarized in Table 15.2, the major media types are newspapers, television, direct mail, radio, magazines, outdoor, and the Internet. Each medium has advantages and limitations.

TABLE 15.2 PROFILES OF MAJOR MEDIA TYPES

Medium	Advantages	Limitations
Newspapers	Flexibility; timeliness; good local market coverage; broad acceptability; high believability	Short-life; poor reproduction quality; small pass-along audience
Television	Good mass-market coverage; low cost per exposure; combines sight, sound, and motion; appealing to the senses	High absolute costs; high clutter; fleeting exposure; less audience selectivity
Direct mail	High audience selectivity; flexibility; no ad competition within the same medium; allows personalization	Relatively high cost per exposure; "junk mail" image
Radio	Good local acceptance; high geographic and demographic selectivity; low cost	Audio only, fleeting exposure; low attention ("the half-heard" medium); fragmented audiences
Magazines	High geographic and demographic selectivity; credibility and prestige; high-quality reproduction; long life and good pass-along readership	Long ad purchase lead time; high cost; no guarantee of position
Outdoor	Flexibility; high repeat exposure; low cost; low message competition; good positional selectivity	Little audience selectivity; creative limitations
Internet	High selectivity; low cost; immediacy; interactive capabilities	Small, demographically skewed audience; relatively low impact; audience controls exposure

Media planners consider many factors when making their media choices. The *media habits of target consumers* will affect media choice—advertisers look for media that reach target consumers effectively. So will the *nature of the product*—for example, fashions are best advertised in color magazines, and automobile performance is best demonstrated on television. Different *types of messages* may require different media. A message announcing a major sale tomorrow will require radio or newspapers; a message with a lot of technical data might require magazines, direct mailings, or an online ad and Web site. *Cost* is another major factor in media choice. For example, network television is very expensive, whereas newspaper or radio advertising costs much less but also reaches fewer consumers. The media planner looks both at the total cost of using a medium and at the cost per thousand exposures— the cost of reaching 1,000 people using the medium.

Media impact and cost must be reexamined regularly. For a long time, television and magazines have dominated in the media mixes of national advertisers, with other media often neglected. Recently, however, the costs and clutter of these media have gone up, audiences have declined, and marketers are adopting strategies beamed at narrower segments. As a result, advertisers are increasingly turning to alternative media—ranging from cable TV and outdoor advertising to parking meters and shopping carts—that cost less and target more effectively (see Marketing Highlight 15.2).

Selecting Specific Media Vehicles. The media planner now must choose the best *media vehicles*—specific media within each general media type. For example, television vehicles include *ER* and *ABC World News Tonight*. Magazine vehicles include *Newsweek, People, In Style,* and *Sports Illustrated.*

Media planners must compute the cost per thousand persons reached by a vehicle. For example, if a full-page, four-color advertisement in *Time* costs $162,000 and *Time's* readership is 4 million people, the cost of reaching each group of 1,000 persons is $40. The same advertisement in *Business Week* may cost only $81,000 but

MARKETING HIGHLIGHT 15.2

ADVERTISERS SEEK ALTERNATIVE MEDIA

As network television costs soar and audiences shrink, many advertisers are looking for new ways to reach consumers. The move toward micromarketing strategies, focused more narrowly on specific consumer groups, has also fueled the search for alternative media to replace or supplement network television. Advertisers are shifting larger portions of their budgets to media that cost less and target more effectively.

Three media benefiting greatly from the shift are outdoor advertising, cable television, and digital satellite television systems. Billboards have undergone a resurgence in recent years. Gone are the ugly eyesores of the past; in their place we now see cleverly designed, colorful attention grabbers. Outdoor advertising provides an excellent way to reach important local consumer segments at a fraction of the cost per exposure of other major media. Cable television and digital satellite systems are also booming. Such systems allow narrow programming formats such as all sports, all news, nutrition, arts, gardening, cooking, travel, history, and others that target select groups. Advertisers can take

Marketers have discovered a dazzling array of "alternative media."

reach only 875,000 persons—at a cost per thousand of about $93. The media planner ranks each magazine by cost per thousand and favor those magazines with the lower cost per thousand for reaching target consumers.[11]

The media planner must also consider the costs of producing ads for different media. Whereas newspaper ads may cost very little to produce, flashy television ads may cost millions. On average, U.S. advertisers pay $308,000 to produce a single 30-second television commercial. A few years ago, Nike paid a cool $2 million to make a single ad called "The Wall."[12]

In selecting media vehicles, the media planner must balance media cost measures against several media impact factors. First, the planner should balance costs against the media vehicle's *audience quality.* For a baby lotion advertisement, for example, *New Parents* magazine would have a high-exposure value; *Gentlemen's Quarterly* would have a low-exposure value. Second, the media planner should consider *audience attention.* Readers of *Vogue,* for example, typically pay more attention to ads than do *Newsweek* readers. Third, the planner should assess the vehicle's *editorial quality*—*Time* and the *Wall Street Journal* are more believable and prestigious than *The National Enquirer.*

advantage of such "narrowcasting" to "rifle in" on special market segments rather than use the "shotgun" approach offered by network broadcasting.

Outdoor, cable, and satellite media seem to make good sense. But, increasingly, ads are popping up in far less likely places. In their efforts to find less costly and more highly targeted ways to reach consumers, advertisers have discovered a dazzling collection of "alternative media." As consumers, we're used to ads on television, in magazines and newspapers, on the radio, and along the roadways. But these days, no matter where you go or what you do, you probably will run into some new form of advertising.

Tiny billboards attached to shopping carts, ads on shopping bags, and even advertising tiles on supermarket floors urge you to buy Jell-O Pudding Pops or Pampers. Signs atop parking meters hawk everything from Jeeps to Minolta cameras to Recipe dog food. A city bus rolls by, fully painted as a traveling ad for the Cezanne exhibit at your local art museum. You escape to the ballpark, only to find billboard-size video screens running Budweiser ads while

a blimp with an electronic message board circles lazily overhead. How about a quiet trip in the country? Sorry—you find an enterprising farmer using his milk cows as four-legged billboards mounted with ads for Ben & Jerry's ice cream.

You pay to see a movie at your local theater, but first you view a two-minute science-fiction fantasy that turns out to be an ad for General Electric portable stereo boxes. Then the movie itself is full of not-so-subtle promotional plugs for Pepsi, Domino's Pizza, MasterCard, Fritos, BMWs, Ray Ban sunglasses, or any of a dozen other products. At the airport you're treated to the CNN Airport Network; at the local rail station, it's the Commuter Channel. Boats cruise along public beaches flashing advertising messages for Sundown Sunscreen or Snapple as sunbathers spread their towels over ads for Skippy peanut butter pressed into the sand. Even church bulletins carry ads for Campbell soup.

These days, you're likely to find ads—well, anywhere. Ad space is being sold on video cases, parking lot tickets, golf scorecards, delivery trucks, gas pumps, and municipal garbage cans. Some of these alterna-

tive media seem a bit farfetched, and they sometimes irritate consumers. But for many marketers, these media can save money and provide a way to hit selected consumers where they live, shop, work, and play. Of course, this may leave you wondering if there are any commercial-free havens remaining for ad weary consumers. The back seat of a taxi, perhaps, or public elevators, or stalls in a public restroom? Forget it! Each has already been invaded by innovative marketers.

Sources: See John P. Cortez, "Ads Head for the Bathroom," *Advertising Age,* May 18, 1992, p. 24; Cristina Merrill, "Alternative Reality," *Adweek,* February 3, 1997, pp. 23–30; Ellen Neuborne, "Saturday Night at the Ads," *Business Week,* September 15, 1997, pp. 63–64; Andy Fry, "Choose Your Weapon," *Marketing,* April 16, 1998, pp. 31–34; Marc Gunther, "The Great Outdoors," *Fortune,* March 1, 1999, pp. 150–50, and Skip Wollenberg, "Cost, Clutter Push Ads into—Well, Anywhere," *Charlotte Observer,* May 28, 1999, p. 1D, 3D.

Deciding on Media Timing.   The advertiser must also decide how to schedule the advertising over the course of a year. Suppose sales of a product peak in December and drop in March. The firm can vary its advertising to follow the seasonal pattern, to oppose the seasonal pattern, or to be the same all year. Most firms do some seasonal advertising. Some do *only* seasonal advertising: For example, Hallmark advertises its greeting cards only before major holidays.

Finally, the advertiser has to choose the pattern of the ads. *Continuity* means scheduling ads evenly within a given period. *Pulsing* means scheduling ads unevenly over a given time period. Thus, 52 ads could either be scheduled at one per week during the year or pulsed in several bursts. The idea is to advertise heavily for a short period to build awareness that carries over to the next advertising period. Those who favor pulsing feel that it can be used to achieve the same impact as a steady schedule but at a much lower cost. However, some media planners believe that although pulsing achieves minimal awareness, it sacrifices depth of advertising communications.

Recent advances in technology have had a substantial impact on the media planning and buying functions. Today, for example, new computer software applications called *optimizers* allow media planners to evaluate vast combinations of television programs and prices. Such programs help advertisers to make better decisions about which mix of networks, programs, and day parts will yield the highest reach per ad dollar.[13]

Evaluating Advertising

The advertising program should evaluate both the communication effects and the sales effects of advertising regularly. Measuring the *communication effects* of an ad—*copy testing*—tells whether the ad is communicating well. Copy testing can be done before or after an ad is printed or broadcast. Before the ad is placed, the advertiser can show it to consumers, ask how they like it, and measure recall or attitude changes resulting from it. After the ad is run, the advertiser can measure how the ad affected consumer recall or product awareness, knowledge, and preference.

But what *sales* are caused by an ad that increases brand awareness by 20 percent and brand preference by 10 percent? The *sales effects* of advertising are often harder to measure than the communication effects. Sales are affected by many factors besides advertising—such as product features, price, and availability.

One way to measure the sales effect of advertising is to compare past sales with past advertising expenditures. Another way is through experiments. For example, to test the effects of different advertising spending levels, Coca-Cola could vary the amount it spends on advertising in different market areas and measure the differences in the resulting sales levels. It could spend the normal amount in one market area, half the normal amount in another area, and twice the normal amount in a third area. If the three market areas are similar, and if all other marketing efforts in the area are the same, then differences in sales in the three areas could be related to advertising level. More complex experiments could be designed to include other variables, such as difference in the ads or media used.

Other Advertising Considerations

In developing advertising strategies and programs, the company must address two additional questions. First, how the company will organize its advertising function—who will perform which advertising tasks? Second, how will the company adapt its advertising strategies and programs to the complexities of international markets?

Organizing for Advertising

Different companies organize in different ways to handle advertising. In small companies, advertising might be handled by someone in the sales department. Large companies set up advertising departments whose job it is to set the advertising budget, work with the ad agency, and handle other advertising not done by the agency. Most large companies use outside advertising agencies because they offer several advantages.

Advertising agency
A marketing services firm that assists companies in planning, preparing, implementing, and evaluating all or portions of their advertising programs.

How does an **advertising agency** work? Advertising agencies were started in the mid-to-late 1800s by salespeople and brokers who worked for the media and received a commission for selling advertising space to companies. As time passed, the salespeople began to help customers prepare their ads. Eventually, they formed agencies and grew closer to the advertisers than to the media. Today's agencies employ specialists who can often perform advertising tasks better than the company's own staff. Agencies also bring an outside point of view to solving the company's problems, along with lots of experience from working with different clients and situations. Thus, today, even companies with strong advertising departments of their own use advertising agencies.

Some ad agencies are huge—the largest U.S. agency, Grey Advertising, has an annual income of $422 million on billings (the dollar amount of advertising placed for clients) of more than $2.8 billion. In recent years, many agencies have grown by gobbling up other agencies, thus creating huge agency holding companies. The largest of these agency "megagroups," Omnicom Group, includes several large advertising, public relations, and promotion agencies—DDB Needham, BBDO, TBWA, and several others—with combined worldwide gross income of $4.8 billion on billings exceeding $37 billion.[14]

Most large advertising agencies have the staff and resources to handle all phases of an advertising campaign for their clients, from creating a marketing plan to developing ad campaigns and preparing, placing, and evaluating ads. Agencies usually have four departments: *creative,* which develops and produces ads; *media,* which selects media and places ads; *research,* which studies audience characteristics and wants, and *business,* which handles the agency's business activities. Each account is supervised by an account executive, and people in each department are usually assigned to work on one or more accounts.

Ad agencies traditionally have been paid through commissions and fees. In the past, the agency typically received 15 percent of the media cost as a rebate. For example, suppose the agency bought $60,000 of magazine space for a client. The magazine would bill the advertising agency for $51,000 ($60,000 less 15 percent), and the agency would then bill the client for $60,000, keeping the $9,000 commission. If the client bought space directly from the magazine, it would have paid $60,000 because commissions are paid only to recognized advertising agencies.

However, both advertisers and agencies have become more and more unhappy with the commission system. Larger advertisers complain that they pay more for the same services received by smaller ones simply because they place more advertising. Advertisers also believe that the commission system drives agencies away from low-cost media and short advertising campaigns. Another factor is vast changes in how ad agencies reach consumers that go way beyond network TV or magazine advertising. "The commission formula tends to encourage costly media buys and has been criticized for overlooking important emerging mediums such as the Internet," say one advertising analyst. Therefore, she continues, "The 15 percent commission on media spending that . . . was once standard in the advertising business . . . is about as dead as the three-martini lunch." New agency payment methods may include anything from fixed retainers or straight hourly fees for labor to incentives keyed to performance of the agencies' ad campaigns, or some combination of these.[15]

Another trend is affecting the advertising agency business: Many agencies have sought growth by diversifying into related marketing services. These new diversified agencies offer a complete list of integrated marketing and promotion services under one roof, including advertising, sales promotion, marketing research, public relations, and direct and online marketing. Some have even added marketing consulting, television production, and sales training units in an effort to become full "marketing partners" to their clients.

However, agencies are finding that most advertisers don't want much more from them than traditional media advertising services plus direct marketing, sales promotion, and sometimes public relations. Thus, many agencies have recently limited their diversification efforts in order to focus more on traditional services. Some have even started their own "creative boutiques," smaller and more independent agencies that can develop creative campaigns for clients free of large-agency bureaucracy.

International Advertising Decisions

International advertisers face many complexities not encountered by domestic advertisers. The most basic issue concerns the degree to which global advertising should be adapted to the unique characteristics of various country's markets. Some large advertisers have attempted to support their global brands with highly standardized worldwide advertising, with campaigns that work as well in Bangkok as they do in Baltimore. For example, Jeep has created a worldwide brand image of ruggedness and reliability; Coca-Cola's Sprite brand uses standardized appeals to target the world's youth. Gillette's ads for its Sensor Excel for Women are almost identical worldwide, with only minor adjustments to suit the local culture. Ericsson, the Swedish telecommunications giant, spent $100 million on a standardized global television campaign with the tag line "make yourself heard," which features Agent 007, James Bond.

Standardization produces many benefits—lower advertising costs, greater global advertising coordination, and a more consistent worldwide image. But it also has drawbacks. Most importantly, it ignores the fact that country markets differ greatly in their cultures, demographics, and economic conditions. Thus, most international advertisers "think globally but act locally." They develop global advertising *strategies* that make their worldwide advertising efforts more efficient and consistent. Then they adapt their advertising *programs* to make them more responsive to consumer needs and expectations within local markets.

For example, Coca-Cola has a pool of different commercials that can be used in or adapted to several different international markets. Some can be used with only minor changes—such as language—in several different countries. Local and regional managers decide which commercials work best for which markets.

Gillette Sensor Excel for Women ads are almost identical worldwide, with only minor adjustments to suit the local culture.

Recently, in a reverse of the usual order, a series of Coca-Cola commercials developed for the Russian market, using a talking bear and a man who transforms into a wolf, was shown in the United States. "This approach fits perfectly with the global nature of Coca-Cola," says the president of Coca-Cola's Nordic division. "[It] offers people a special look into a culture that is different from their own."[16]

Global advertisers face several special problems. For instance, advertising media costs and availability differ vastly from country to country. Countries also differ in the extent to which they regulate advertising practices. Many countries have extensive systems of laws restricting how much a company can spend on advertising, the media used, the nature of advertising claims, and other aspects of the advertising program. Such restrictions often require advertisers to adapt their campaigns from country to country.

For example, alcoholic products cannot be advertised or sold in Muslim countries. Tobacco products are subjected to strict regulation in many countries—the United Kingdom now wants not only to ban tobacco advertising but also to outlaw sports sponsorship by tobacco companies. In many countries, Norway and Sweden, for example, no TV ads may be directed at children under 12. Moreover, Sweden is lobbying to extend that ban to all EU member countries. To play it safe, McDonald's advertises itself as a family restaurant in Sweden.

Comparative ads, while acceptable and even common in the United States and Canada, are less commonly used in the United Kingdom, unacceptable in Japan, and illegal in India and Brazil. PepsiCo found that its comparative taste test ad in Japan was refused by many television stations and actually led to a lawsuit. China has restrictive censorship rules for TV and radio advertising; for example, the words *the best* are banned, as are ads that "violate social customs" or present women in "improper ways." Coca-Cola's Indian subsidiary was forced to end a promotion that offered prizes, such as a trip to Hollywood, because it violated India's established trade practices by encouraging customers to buy in order to "gamble."[17]

Thus, although advertisers may develop global strategies to guide their overall advertising efforts, specific advertising programs must usually be adapted to meet local cultures and customs, media characteristics, and advertising regulations.

SALES PROMOTION

Sales promotion
Short-term incentives to encourage the purchase or sale of a product or service.

Advertising and personal selling often work closely with another promotion tool, sales promotion. **Sales promotion** consists of short-term incentives to encourage the purchase or sale of a product or service. Whereas advertising and personal selling offer reasons to buy a product or service, sales promotion offers reasons to buy *now*.

Examples of sales promotions are found everywhere. A freestanding insert in the Sunday newspaper contains a coupon offering 50 cents off Folgers coffee. An e-mail from CDNow offers $5.00 off your next CD purchase over $9.99. The end-of-the-aisle display in the local supermarket tempts impulse buyers with a wall of Coke cartons. An executive who buys a new Compaq laptop computer gets a free carrying case, or a family buys a new Taurus and receives a rebate check for $500. A hardware store chain receives a 10 percent discount on selected Black & Decker portable power tools if it agrees to advertise them in local newspapers. Sales promotion includes a wide variety of promotion tools designed to stimulate earlier or stronger market response.

Rapid Growth of Sales Promotion

Sales promotion tools are used by most organizations, including manufacturers, distributors, retailers, trade associations, and nonprofit institutions. They are targeted toward final buyers (*consumer promotions*), business customers (*business promotions*), retailers and wholesalers (*trade promotions*), and members of the sales force *(sales force promotions)*. Today, in the average consumer packaged-goods company, sales promotion accounts for 74 percent of all marketing expenditures.[18]

Several factors have contributed to the rapid growth of sales promotion, particularly in consumer markets. First, inside the company, product managers face greater pressures to increase their current sales, and promotion is viewed as an effective short-run sales tool. Second, externally, the company faces more competition and competing brands are less differentiated. Increasingly, competitors are using sales promotion to help differentiate their offers. Third, advertising efficiency has declined because of rising costs, media clutter, and legal restraints. Finally, consumers have become more deal oriented and ever-larger retailers are demanding more deals from manufacturers.

The growing use of sales promotion has resulted in *promotion clutter,* similar to advertising clutter. Consumers are increasingly tuning out promotions, weakening their ability to trigger immediate purchase. Manufacturers are now searching for ways to rise above the clutter, such as offering larger coupon values or creating more dramatic point-of-purchase displays.

In developing a sales promotion program, a company must first set sales promotion objectives and then select the best tools for accomplishing these objectives.

Sales Promotion Objectives

Sales promotion objectives vary widely. Sellers may use consumer promotions to increase short-term sales or to help build long-term market share. Objectives for trade promotions include getting retailers to carry new items and more inventory, getting them to advertise the product and give it more shelf space, and getting them to buy ahead. For the sales force, objectives include getting more sales force support for current or new products or getting salespeople to sign up new accounts. Sales promotions are usually used together with advertising or personal selling. Consumer promotions must usually be advertised and can add excitement and pulling power to ads. Trade and sales force promotions support the firm's personal selling process.

In general, sales promotions should be *consumer relationship building.* Rather than creating only short-term sales or temporary brand switching, they should help to reinforce the product's position and build long-term relationships with consumers. Increasingly, marketers are avoiding "quick fix," price-only promotions in favor of promotions designed to build brand equity. Even price promotions can be designed to help build customer relationships. Examples include all of the "frequency marketing programs" and clubs that have mushroomed in recent years. For example, Waldenbooks sponsors a Preferred Reader Program, which has attracted more than 4 million members, each paying $5 to receive mailings about new books, a 10 percent discount on book purchases, toll-free ordering, and many other services. American Express's Custom Extras program automatically awards customers deals and discounts based on frequency of purchases at participating retailers. Norwegian Cruise Lines sponsors a loyalty program called Latitudes, a co-branding effort with Visa. The program includes a two-for-one cruise offer and a Latitudes Visa card that rewards users with points redeemable for discounts on NCL cruises.

If properly designed, every sales promotion tool has the potential to build consumer relationships. Here's another example of a loyalty-building promotion:[19]

★ The Valley View Center Mall in Dallas sponsors the Smart Shoppers Club, a program that rewards customers who tap onto its computerized interactive touchscreen kiosks. To obtain a membership and personal identification number, mallgoers fill out a short application that asks simple demographic and psychographic questions. Then, each time members visit the mall, they input their ID number into one of the mall's three touch-screen kiosks and receive daily discount retail coupons, prizes awarded randomly each week, and a calendar of events. While customers reap discounts and prizes, Valley View retailers get valuable marketing information about their customers. The shopping center is one of only about 10 of the nation's 35,000 malls to use this high-tech consumer loyalty program.

Major Sales Promotion Tools

Many tools can be used to accomplish sales promotion objectives. Descriptions of the main consumer, trade, and business promotion tools follow.

Consumer Promotion Tools

The main consumer promotion tools include samples, coupons, cash refunds, price packs, premiums, advertising specialties, patronage rewards, point-of-purchase displays and demonstrations, and contests, sweepstakes, and games.

Sample
A small amount of a product offered to consumers for trial.

Samples are offers of a trial amount of a product. Sampling is the most effective—but most expensive—way to introduce a new product. Some samples are free; for others, the company charges a small amount to offset its cost. The sample might be delivered door-to-door, sent by mail, handed out in a store, attached to another product, or featured in an ad. Sometimes, samples are combined into sample packs, which can then be used to promote other products and services. Procter & Gamble has even distributed samples via the Internet:[20]

★ When Procter & Gamble decided to relaunch Pert Plus shampoo, it extended its $20 million ad campaign by constructing a new Web site (www.pertplus.com). P&G had three objectives for the Web site: to create awareness for reformulated Pert Plus, get consumers to try the product, and gather data about Web users. The site's first page invites visitors to place their heads against the computer screen in a mock attempt to measure the cleanliness of their hair. After "tabulating the results," the site tells visitors that they "need immediate help." The solution: "How about a free sample of new Pert Plus?" Visitors obtain the sample by filling out a short demographic form. The site offers other interesting features as well. For example, clicking "get a friend in a lather" produces a template that will send an e-mail to a friend with an invitation to visit the site and receive a free sample. How did the sampling promotion work out? Even P&G was shocked by the turnout. Within just two months of launching the site, 170,000 people visited and 83,000 requested samples. More surprising, given that the site is only 10 pages deep, the average person visited the site 1.9 times and spent a total of 7.5 minutes each visit.

Coupon
Certificate that gives buyers a saving when they purchase a specified product.

Coupons are certificates that give buyers a saving when they purchase specified products. Most consumers love coupons: They clipped 4.8 billion of them last year with an average face value of 70 cents, for a total savings of $3.4 billion.[21] Coupons can stimulate sales of a mature brand or promote early trial of a new brand. However, as a result of coupon clutter, redemption rates have been declining in recent years. Thus, most major consumer goods companies are issuing fewer coupons and targeting them more carefully.

Internet sampling: Within just two months, this Pert Plus site generated 170,000 visits and 83,000 sample requests.

In the past, marketers have relied almost solely on mass-distributed coupons delivered through the mail or on freestanding inserts or ads in newspapers and magazines. Today, however, although Sunday newspapers still account for 80 percent of all coupons, marketers are cultivating new outlets. They are increasingly distributing coupons through shelf dispensers at the point of sale, by electronic point-of-sale coupon printers, or through "paperless coupon systems." An example is Catalina Marketing Network's Checkout Direct system, which dispenses personalized discounts to targeted buyers at the checkout counter in stores. Some companies are now offering coupons on their Web sites or through online coupon services such as coolsavings.com, valupage.com, hotcoupons.com, and directcoupons.com. For example, participants in CoolSavings include JCPenney, Toys "R" Us, Boston Market, Domino's Pizza, and H&R Block.[22]

Cash refund offer (rebate)
Offer to refund part of the purchase price of a product to consumers who send a "proof of purchase" to the manufacturer.

Cash refund offers (or **rebates**) are like coupons except that the price reduction occurs after the purchase rather than at the retail outlet. The consumer sends a "proof of purchase" to the manufacturer, who then refunds part of the purchase price by mail. For example, Toro ran a clever preseason promotion on some of its snowblower models, offering a rebate if the snowfall in the buyer's market area turned out to be below average. Competitors were not able to match this offer on such short notice, and the promotion was very successful.

Price pack (cents-off deal)
Reduced price that is marked by the producer directly on the label or package.

Price packs (also called **cents-off deals**) offer consumers savings off the regular price of a product. The reduced prices are marked by the producer directly on the label or package. Price packs can be single packages sold at a reduced price (such as two for the price of one), or two related products banded together (such as a toothbrush and toothpaste). Price packs are very effective—even more so than coupons—in stimulating short-term sales.

Premium
Good offered either free or at low cost as an incentive to buy a product.

Premiums are goods offered either free or at low cost as an incentive to buy a product, ranging from toys included with kids' products to phone cards, compact disks, and computer CD-ROMs. A premium may come inside the package (in-pack), outside the package (on-pack), or through the mail. In its "Treasure Hunt" promotion, for example, Quaker Oats inserted $5 million worth of gold and silver coins in Ken-L Ration dog food packages. In another premium promotion, Cutty Sark offered a brass tray with the purchase of one bottle of its scotch and a desk lamp with the purchase of two. Last year, United Airlines rewarded Chicago-area 75,000 Mileage Plus frequent flier club members with a custom compact disk. The 10-song, Chicago-themed compilation disk, entitled "Chicago—Our Kind of Town," was widely played on local radio stations. It became so popular that United ended up selling it at record stores. The airline plans similar custom-designed premiums for four other major cities it serves.[23]

Advertising specialties are useful articles imprinted with an advertiser's name given as gifts to consumers. Typical items include pens, calendars, key rings, matches, shopping bags, T-shirts, caps, nail files, and coffee mugs. Such items can be very effective. In a recent study, 63 percent of all consumers surveyed were either carrying or wearing an ad specialty item. More than three-quarters of those who had an item could recall the advertiser's name or message before showing the item to the interviewer.[24]

Patronage rewards are cash or other awards offered for the regular use of a certain company's products or services. For example, airlines offer frequent flier plans, awarding points for miles traveled that can be turned in for free airline trips. Marriott Hotels has adopted an honored-guest plan that awards points to users of their hotels. Baskin-Robbins offers frequent-purchase awards—for every 10 purchases, customers receive a free quart of ice cream.

Point-of-purchase (POP) promotions include displays and demonstrations that take place at the point of purchase or sale. An example is a five-foot-high cardboard display of Cap'n Crunch next to Cap'n Crunch cereal boxes. Unfortunately, many retailers do not like to handle the hundreds of displays, signs, and posters they receive from manufacturers each year. Manufacturers have responded by offering better POP materials, tying them in with television or print messages, and offering to set them up.

Contests, sweepstakes, and **games** give consumers the chance to win something, such as cash, trips, or goods, by luck or through extra effort. A *contest* calls for consumers to submit an entry—a jingle, guess, suggestion—to be judged by a panel that will select the best entries. A *sweepstakes* calls for consumers to submit their names for a drawing. A *game* presents consumers with something—bingo numbers, missing letters—every time they buy, which may or may not help them win a prize. A sales contest urges dealers or the sales force to increase their efforts, with prizes going to the top performers.

Trade Promotion Tools

More sales promotion dollars are directed to retailers and wholesalers (68 percent) than to consumers (32 percent). Trade promotion can persuade resellers to carry a brand, give it shelf space, promote it in advertising, and push it to consumers. Shelf space is so scarce these days that manufacturers often have to offer price offs, allowances, buy-back guarantees, or free goods to retailers and wholesalers to get products on the shelf and, once there, to stay on it.

Manufacturers use several trade promotion tools. Many of the tools used for consumer promotions—contests, premiums, displays—can also be used as trade promotions. Or the manufacturer may offer a straight **discount** off the list price on each case purchased during a stated period of time (also called a *price-off, off-invoice,* or *off-list*). The offer encourages dealers to buy in quantity or to carry a new item. Dealers can use the discount for immediate profit, for advertising, or for price reductions to their customers.

Advertising specialty
Useful article imprinted with an advertiser's name, given as a gift to consumers.

Patronage reward
Cash or other award for the regular use of a certain company's products or services.

Point-of-purchase (POP) promotion
Display and demonstration that takes place at the point of purchase or sale.

Contests, sweepstakes, games
Promotional events that give consumers the chance to win something—such as cash, trips, or goods—by luck or through extra effort.

Discount
A straight reduction in price on purchases during a stated period of time.

Allowance
Promotional money paid by
manufacturers to retailers in
return for an agreement to
feature the manufacturer's
products in some way.

Manufacturers also may offer an **allowance** (usually so much off per case) in return for the retailer's agreement to feature the manufacturer's products in some way. An *advertising allowance* compensates retailers for advertising the product. A *display allowance* compensates them for using special displays.

Manufacturers may offer *free goods,* which are extra cases of merchandise, to resellers who buy a certain quantity or who feature a certain flavor or size. They may offer *push money*—cash or gifts to dealers or their sales forces to "push" the manufacturer's goods. Manufacturers may give retailers free *specialty advertising items* that carry the company's name, such as pens, pencils, calendars, paperweights, matchbooks, memo pads, and yardsticks.

Business Promotion Tools

Companies spend billions of dollars each year on promotion to industrial customers. These business promotions are used to generate business leads, stimulate purchases, reward customers, and motivate salespeople. Business promotion includes many of the same tools used for consumer or trade promotions. Here, we focus on two additional major business promotion tools—conventions and trade shows, and sales contests.

Many companies and trade associations organize *conventions and trade shows* to promote their products. Firms selling to the industry show their products at the trade show. More than 4,300 trade shows take place every year, drawing as many as 85 million people. Vendors receive many benefits, such as opportunities to find new sales leads, contact customers, introduce new products, meet new customers, sell more to present customers, and educate customers with publications and audio-visual materials. Trade shows also help companies reach many prospects not reached through their sales forces. About 90 percent of a trade show's visitors see a company's salespeople for the first time at the show. Business marketers may spend as much as 35 percent of their annual promotion budgets on trade shows.[25]

A *sales contest* is a contest for salespeople or dealers to motivate them to increase their sales performance over a given period. Sales contests motivate and recognize good company performers, who may receive trips, cash prizes, or other gifts. Some companies award points for performance, which the receiver can turn in for any of

More than 4,300 trade shows take place every year, drawing as many as 85 million people, giving sellers chances to introduce new products and meet new customers. At this consumer electronics trade show, 2,000 exhibitors attracted more than 91,000 professional visitors.

a variety of prizes. Sales contests work best when they are tied to measurable and achievable sales objectives (such as finding new accounts, reviving old accounts, or increasing account profitability).

Developing the Sales Promotion Program

The marketer must make several other decisions in order to define the full sales promotion program. First, the marketer must decide on the *size of the incentive*. A certain minimum incentive is necessary if the promotion is to succeed; a larger incentive will produce more sales response. The marketer also must set *conditions for participation*. Incentives might be offered to everyone or only to select groups.

The marketer must decide how to *promote and distribute the promotion* program itself. A 50-cents-off coupon could be given out in a package, at the store, by mail, or in an advertisement. Each distribution method involves a different level of reach and cost. Increasingly, marketers are blending several media into a total campaign concept. The *length of the promotion* is also important. If the sales promotion period is too short, many prospects (who may not be buying during that time) will miss it. If the promotion runs too long, the deal will lose some of its "act now" force.

Evaluation is also very important. Yet many companies fail to evaluate their sales promotion programs, and others evaluate them only superficially. Manufacturers can use one of many evaluation methods. The most common method is to compare sales before, during, and after a promotion. Suppose a company has a 6 percent market share before the promotion, which jumps to 10 percent during the promotion, falls to 5 percent right after, and rises to 7 percent later on. The promotion seems to have attracted new triers and more buying from current customers. After the promotion, sales fell as consumers used up their inventories. The long-run rise to 7 percent means that the company gained some new users. If the brand's share had returned to the old level, then the promotion would have changed only the *timing* of demand rather than the *total* demand.

Consumer research would also show the kinds of people who responded to the promotion and what they did after it ended. *Surveys* can provide information on how many consumers recall the promotion, what they thought of it, how many took advantage of it, and how it affected their buying. Sales promotions also can be evaluated through *experiments* that vary factors such as incentive value, length, and distribution method.

Clearly, sales promotion plays an important role in the total promotion mix. To use it well, the marketer must define the sales promotion objectives, select the best tools, design the sales promotion program, implement the program, and evaluate the results. Moreover, sales promotion must be coordinated carefully with other promotion mix elements within the integrated marketing communications program.

PUBLIC RELATIONS

Another major mass-promotion tool is *public relations*—building good relations with the company's various publics by obtaining favorable publicity, building up a good corporate image, and handling or heading off unfavorable rumors, stories, and events. Public relations departments may perform any or all of the following functions:[26]

★ *Press relations or press agentry:* Creating and placing newsworthy information in the news media to attract attention to a person, product, or service.
★ *Product publicity:* Publicizing specific products.

Public relations involves many functions beyond product publicity, including public affairs, lobbying, and investor relations. For example, most company Web sites feature special sections for current and potential investors—like this one for IBM.

★ *Public affairs:* Building and maintaining national or local community relations.
★ *Lobbying:* Building and maintaining relations with legislators and government officials to influence legislation and regulation.
★ *Investor relations:* Maintaining relationships with shareholders and others in the financial community.
★ *Development:* Public relations with donors or members of nonprofit organizations to gain financial or volunteer support.

Public relations is used to promote products, people, places, ideas, activities, organizations, and even nations. Trade associations have used public relations to rebuild interest in declining commodities such as eggs, apples, milk, and potatoes. New York City turned its image around when its "I Love New York!" campaign took root, bringing millions more tourists to the city. Johnson & Johnson's masterly use of public relations played a major role in saving Tylenol from extinction after its product-tampering scare. Nations have used public relations to attract more tourists, foreign investment, and international support.

Public relations can have a strong impact on public awareness at a much lower cost than advertising (see Marketing Highlight 15.3). The company does not pay for the space or time in the media. Rather, it pays for a staff to develop and circulate information and to manage events. If the company develops an interesting story, it could be picked up by several different media, having the same effect as advertising that would cost millions of dollars. It would have more credibility than advertising. Public relations results can sometimes be spectacular.

Despite its potential strengths, public relations is often described as a marketing stepchild because of its limited and scattered use. The public relations department is usually located at corporate headquarters. Its staff is so busy dealing with various publics—stockholders, employees, legislators, city officials—that public relations programs to support product marketing objectives may be ignored. Marketing managers and public relations practitioners do not always talk the same language. Many public relations practitioners see their job as simply communicating. In contrast, marketing managers tend to be much more interested in how advertising and public relations affect sales and profits.

This situation is changing, however. Many companies now want their public relations departments to manage all of their activities with a view toward marketing the company and improving the bottom line. They know that good public relations can be a powerful brand-building tool. Two well-known marketing consultants provide the following advice, which points to the potential power of public relations as a first step in building brands:

> Just because a heavy dose of advertising is associated with most major brands doesn't necessarily mean that advertising built the brands in the first place. The birth of a brand is usually accomplished with [public relations], not advertising. Our general rule is [PR] first, advertising second. [Public relations] is the nail, advertising the hammer. [PR] creates the credentials that provide the credibility for advertising. . . . Anita Roddick built the Body Shop into a major brand with no advertising at all. Instead, she traveled the world on a relentless quest for publicity. . . . Until recently Starbucks Coffee Co. didn't spend a hill of beans on advertising, either. In 10 years, the company spent less than $10 million on advertising, a trivial amount for a brand that delivers annual sales of $1.3 billion. Wal-Mart Stores became the world's largest retailer . . . with very little advertising. . . . In the toy field, Furby, Beanie Babies, and Tickle Me Elmo became highly successful . . . and on the Internet, Yahoo!, Amazon.com, and Excite became powerhouse brands, [all] with virtually no advertising.[27]

Thus, some companies are setting up special units called *marketing public relations* to support corporate and product promotion and image making directly. Many companies hire marketing public relations firms to handle their PR programs or to assist the company public relations team.

Major Public Relations Tools

Public relations professionals use several tools. One of the major tools is *news*. PR professionals find or create favorable news about the company and its products or people. Sometimes news stories occur naturally, and sometimes the PR person can suggest events or activities that would create news. *Speeches* can also create product and company publicity. Increasingly, company executives must field questions from

The birth of a brand is often accomplished with public relations, not advertising. For example, Beanie Babies have been highly successful with virtually no advertising.

MARKETING HIGHLIGHT 15.3

PUBLIC RELATIONS: STRETCHING THE MARKETING BUDGET

The Italian sports car maker, Lamborghini, sells fewer than 100 of its cars each year in the United States. Marketing Lamborghinis is no simple matter. The car is pure poetry in motion—but at a steep price. The Diablo VT's 530-horsepower engine delivers a top speed of 202 mph and goes from 0 to 62 miles per hour in just 3.9 seconds. The price: $295,000. Just to lease a Diablo VT runs $3,700 a month with a $64,000 down payment. Moreover, because so few Lamborghinis are sold, most people rarely see one. Thus, to gain exposure and persuade would-be buyers, the company must invest its modest $600,000 U.S. marketing budget carefully.

Lamborghini's eventual goal is to sell 1,500 to 2,000 units a year in the United States. To reach this ambitious sales goal, however, the car maker will need to increase its exposure and awareness. It currently advertises in several selective business, travel, and lifestyle magazines, emphasizing the car's speed and sensual beauty. In addition, the company recently fielded a direct-mail campaign to 50,000 prospective buyers with median household incomes of $1.5 million.

When it comes to advertising, however, $600,000 doesn't go far.

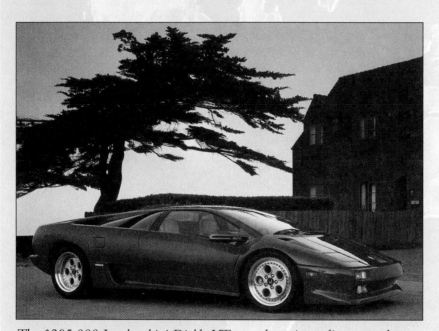

The $295,000 Lamborghini Diablo VT moved one journalist to say that "on the beauty meter . . . it rates rates right up there with a roomful of Matisse originals. . . . Neighbors I have never met come rushing out of their homes to get a closer look."

the media or give talks at trade associations or sales meetings, and these events can either build or hurt the company's image.

Another common PR tool is *special events,* ranging from news conferences, press tours, grand openings, and fireworks displays to laser shows, hot air balloon releases, multimedia presentations and star-studded spectaculars, or educational programs designed to reach and interest target publics. Here's an example of an interesting public relations program launched by Levi-Strauss & Company:

★ In the increasingly more casual business world, as companies relax their dress codes, they are often dismayed to find employees showing up at the office in anything from sweatsuits to torn jeans. Where can they turn for a little fashion advice? Levi-Strauss & Company to the rescue! The world's largest apparel maker has put together an elaborate and stealthy program to help companies advise their people on

So Lamborghini stretches its limited marketing budget with an assortment of less expensive public relations efforts. The company actively courts the press. For example, it makes the car available to auto journalists for test drives. This resulted in a *New York Times* review describing the car as "kinetic sculpture, proof of affluence, and amusement park ride wrapped into one." A *Fortune* journalist wrote, "On the beauty meter, the screaming lemon-yellow Diablo rates right up there with a roomful of Matisse originals. . . . Neighbors I have never met come rushing out of their homes to get a closer look." After riding with Lamborghini's chief U.S. test driver, another journalist reported, "He fired up the engine and shot out of Lamborghini's vast and immaculate garage. He slammed the car sideways through the parking lot [and] a split second later straightened the Diablo out with a snap and hammered ahead. No swaying, no rolling, no hesitation, just unadulterated energy. It was an all-sensory extravaganza." After a test drive on the twisty byways of the Italian island of Sardinia as a guest of Lamborghini, a *Car and Driver* reporter filed this ecstatic account:

My right foot stomps the accelerator hard against the narrow floorboard three times in rapid succession as I clang the long-throw shifter up through its heavy-toothed gate. Behind us, 5.7 liters' worth of V-12 roars like the angry hooves and snorts of a hundred bulls bouncing off the walls of Pamplona. As we pass through 160 mph, an approaching blind curve prompts us to switch pedals. At that moment, a tiny dip in the pavement jounces the front tires into contact with the fender liners, and a whiff of rubber wafts into the cabin. Four of the five senses confirm that we're not dreaming.

Lamborghini also sponsors tasteful public relations events. For example, it recently held a cocktail party for 200 people at a Georgio Armani store in Boston, with an invitation list put together by the store and *The Robb Report,* a publication devoted to the lifestyles of the wealthy.

Lamborghini is constantly seeking new ways to expose the car to its affluent audience. As a result of good public relations efforts, the Lamborghini Diablo VT was designated as a pace car for the 1995 PPG Indy Car World Series. This gave Lamborghini exposure at 15 race sites and allowed local dealers to give prospective buyers a ride around the track in the days before a race. Says a Lamborghini executive, "We sold three cars by doing that last year at the Detroit Grand Prix." Also, for the first time, Lamborghini is making a demonstrator available to its 19 U.S. dealers so that prospects can test-drive the car without the dealer worrying about mileage and insurance costs.

Lamborghini's total annual U.S. *sales* of $22 million amount to only a tiny fraction of the *advertising budgets* of the major car makers. However, through the innovative use of public relations, the company successfully stretches its modest marketing budget to gain exposure among affluent buyers.

Sources: Quotes from Raymond Serafin, "Even Lamborghini Must Think Marketing," *Advertising Age,* May 1, 1995, p. 4; Faye Rice, "Lamborghini's Sales Drive," *Fortune,* June 12, 1995, p. 13; Sue Zesiger, "Driving with the Devil," *Fortune,* February 17, 1997, pp. 170–71; and Frank Markus, "Lamborghini Diablo," *Car and Driver,* March 1999, pp. 75–77. Also see Jean Halliday, "Ultraluxury Cars Avoid Traditional Marketing Path," *Advertising Age,* April 27, 1998, p. 27; and "Prestige Brands Such as Ferrari, Rolls, Lambo Spend Little on Ads," *Automotive News,* May 11, 1998, p. 8B.

how to dress casually without being sloppy. To promote the program initially, Levi mailed a newsletter to 65,000 human resource managers and sent videos to some 7,000 companies. Since 1992, the company has provided information and advice to more than 30,000 companies, including Charles Schwab & Company, IBM, Nynex, and Aetna Life & Casualty. Through the program, Levi offers snazzy brochures and videos showing how to dress casually. Other activities range from putting on fashion shows and manning a toll-free number for employees who have questions about casual wear to holding seminars for human resource directors. Levi also created a Web page from which human resources managers can obtain advice and Levi's Casual Businesswear Kit, a detailed guide for starting and maintaining company dress policies. Levi's avoids outright product pitches. Instead, the company explains, it's simply "trying to create a dress code for dress-down wear." Of course, it wouldn't hurt if that wear had the Levi label attached.[28]

A company's Web site can be a good public relations vehicle. Butterball's site, which features cooking and carving tips, received more than 500,000 visits in one day during Thanksgiving week last year.

Public relations people also prepare *written materials* to reach and influence their target markets. These materials include annual reports, brochures, articles, and company newsletters and magazines. *Audiovisual materials,* such as films, slide-and-sound programs, and video- and audiocassettes, are being used increasingly as communication tools. *Corporate identity materials* can also help create a corporate identity that the public immediately recognizes. Logos, stationery, brochures, signs, business forms, business cards, buildings, uniforms, and company cars and trucks—all become marketing tools when they are attractive, distinctive, and memorable. Finally, companies can improve public goodwill by contributing money and time to *public service activities.*

A company's Web site can be a good public relations vehicle. Consumers and members of other publics can visit the site for information and entertainment. Such sites can be extremely popular. For example, Butterball's site (www.butterball.com), which features cooking and carving tips, received 550,000 visitors in one day during Thanksgiving week last year. Web sites can also be ideal for handling crisis situations. For example, when several bottles of Odwalla apple juice sold on the West Coast were found to contain *E. coli* bacteria, Odwalla initiated a massive product recall. Within only three hours, it set up a Web site laden with information about the crisis and Odwalla's response. Company staffers also combed the Internet looking for newsgroups discussing Odwalla and posted links to the site. In another example, American Home Products quickly set up a Web site to distribute accurate information and advice after a model died reportedly after inhaling its Primatene Mist. The Primatene site, up less than 12 hours after the crisis broke, remains in place today (www.primatene.com). In all, notes one analyst, "Today, public relations is reshaping the Internet and the Internet, in turn, is redefining the practice of public relations." Says another, "People look to the Net for information, not salesmanship, and that's the real opportunity for public relations."[29]

As with the other promotion tools, in considering when and how to use product public relations, management should set PR objectives, choose the PR messages and vehicles, implement the PR plan, and evaluate the results. The firm's publics relations should be blended smoothly with other promotion activities within the company's overall integrated marketing communications effort.

REVIEW OF CONCEPT CONNECTIONS

Companies must do more than make good products—they have to inform consumers about product benefits and carefully position products in consumers' minds. To do this, they must skillfully employ three mass-promotion tools in addition to personal selling, which targets specific buyers: *advertising, sales promotion,* and *public relations.*

1. Define the roles of advertising, sales promotion, and public relations in the promotion mix.

Advertising—the use of paid media by a seller to inform, persuade, and remind about its products or organization—is a strong promotion tool. American marketers spend more than $212 billion each year on advertising, and it takes many forms and has many uses. *Sales promotion* covers a wide variety of short-term incentive tools—coupons, premiums, contests, allowances—designed to stimulate final and business consumers, the trade, and the company's own sales force. Sales promotion spending has been growing faster than advertising spending in recent years. *Public relations*—gaining favorable publicity and creating a favorable company image—is the least used of the major promotion tools, although it has great potential for building consumer awareness and preference.

2. Describe the major decisions involved in developing an advertising program.

Advertising decision making involves decisions about the objectives, the budget, the message, the media, and, finally, the evaluation of results. Advertisers should set clear *objectives* as to whether the advertising is supposed to inform, persuade, or remind buyers. The advertising *budget* can be based on what is affordable, on sales, on competitors' spending, or on the objectives and tasks. The *message decision* calls for plan-

ning a message strategy and executing it effectively. The *media decision* involves defining reach, frequency, and impact goals; choosing major media types; selecting media vehicles; and deciding on media timing. Message and media decisions must be closely coordinated for maximum campaign effectiveness. Finally, *evaluation* calls for evaluating the communication and sales effects of advertising before, during, and after the advertising is placed.

3. Explain how sales promotion campaigns are developed and implemented.

Sales promotion campaigns call for setting sales promotions objectives (in general, sales promotions should be *consumer relationship building);* selecting tools; developing and implementing the sales promotion program by using trade promotion tools (*discounts, allowances, free goods, push money*) and business promotion tools (*conventions, trade shows, sales contests*) as well as deciding on such things as the size of the incentive, the conditions for participation, how to promote and distribute the promotion package, and the length of the promotion. After this process is completed, the company evaluates the results.

4. Explain how companies use public relations to communicate with their publics.

Companies use public relations to communicate with their publics by setting PR objectives, choosing PR messages and vehicles, implementing the PR plan, and evaluating PR results. To accomplish these goals, public relations professionals use several tools such as *news, speeches,* and *special events.* They also prepare *written, audiovisual,* and *corporate identity materials* and contribute money and time to *public service activities.*

KEY TERMS

Advertising	Cash refund offer (rebate)	Point-of-purchase (POP) promotion
Advertising agency	Contests, sweepstakes, games	Premium
Advertising objective	Coupon	Price pack (cents-off deal)
Advertising specialty	Discount	Sales promotion
Allowance	Patronage reward	Sample

ISSUES FOR DISCUSSION

1. Advertising objectives can be classified by primary purpose: to inform, persuade, or remind. Using your local newspaper, find examples of ads pursuing each of the above objectives. Apply Table 15.1 to explain your answers.

2. What are the benefits and drawbacks of comparison advertising? Find a comparison ad in your favorite magazine. (a) Which has more to gain from using comparison advertising—the leading brand in a market or a lesser brand? Why? (b) In the ad you found, what is the relative market position of the ad's sponsor? (c) Is it an appropriate use of comparison advertising? Explain.

3. Surveys show that many Americans are skeptical of advertising claims. (a) Do you trust advertising? Explain. (b) What types of advertising do you trust the most? The least? (c) Suggest some things the advertising industry could do to increase advertising credibility.

4. Advertisers must develop compelling creative concepts—or "big ideas"—that will bring their message strategies to life in a distinctive way. Sony has just developed a robot pet dog. Priced at $2,500, the robopet can bark for attention, sit up, lie down, scratch its face, wag its tail, play ball, express emotion through changing eye colors, and learn as it grows. Sony is betting that robopets will soon be as hot as video games. Name Sony's new robopet and develop a compelling message strategy and creative concept that will aid Sony (www.sony.com) in developing a nationwide advertising campaign for the upcoming Christmas season.

5. Pick one of the execution styles suggested in the chapter that best fits the following situations and explain your choice: (a) Schwinn bicycles wishes to demonstrate the pleasure and freedom found in trail riding; (b) Lexus wants to demonstrate the benefits of leasing versus purchasing one of its cars; (c) Caterpillar wishes to demonstrate the quality and maintenance-free benefits of its huge earth-moving machines; and (d) Bank of America wants to demonstrate the security and ease of using its online banking services.

6. Which factors call for more frequency in an advertising media schedule and which factors call for more reach? Can you increase one without sacrificing the other or increasing the advertising budget?

7. Which of the sales promotion tools described in the chapter would be best for stimulating sales of the following products and services? (a) A dry cleaner that wishes to emphasize low prices on washed and pressed dress shirts, (b) Gummi Bears's new Black Cherry flavor, (c) Procter & Gamble's efforts to bundle laundry detergents and fabric softeners together in a combined marketing effort, and (d) online merchant eToys's efforts to engage customers in helping it to develop a new advertising jingle.

8. The Internet is the latest public relations frontier. Web users now routinely share their experiences and problems with a company's products, service, prices, and warranties on electronic bulletin boards and chat rooms and at various Web sites. What kinds of special public relations problems and opportunities does the Internet present to today's marketers? How can companies use their own Web sites to deal with these problems and opportunities? Find a good example of a company that uses its Web site as a public relations tool.

MARKETING APPLICATIONS

1. Total toothpaste's market-leading position has lots of people at Colgate-Palmolive smiling these days. However, achieving this position was not easy. To move to number one in the huge $1.6 billion toothpaste market, Total had to unseat Procter & Gamble's long-time market-leading Crest brand. Colgate spent $120 million launching Total. Perhaps more importantly, beyond obtaining the usual American Dental Association's Seal of Approval, Total was the first toothpaste to earn the U.S. Food and Drug Administration's permission to claim that it could prevent gingivitis (the early stages of gum disease). When first introducing the brand, Colgate skipped its warehouses and shipped 46 million tubes of Total to 13,000 stores in just three days. It shipped the product directly to 130,000 promotional displays (about five times the usual amount) strategically placed in retail outlets. At the same time, it blitzed the market with billboards, transit posters, television commercials, print ads, and coupons, announcing that Total was "so advanced it even works when you're not brushing." Colgate plans to use the Total name on line extensions in the future. Colgate toothpaste brands now capture 30 percent of

the market, and Colgate is betting that consumers will keep smiling over Total for many years to come.

a. Evaluate Total's integrated marketing communication strategy. What has been the secret to Colgate's success with Total?

b. Visit the Colgate Web site (www.colgate.com) and evaluate the company's efforts to extend its communications efforts to the Internet.

c. As a competitor, how would you respond to Colgate's success with Total? (See Procter & Gamble's Web site at www.pg.com and its Crest site at www.crestsmiles.com for additional information.) What media would you use? Explain.

2. Philip Morris Company is the world's largest tobacco company. It's also one of the most controversial. Philip Morris is full of apparent contradictions. For example, it recently spent $100 million to persuade children not to smoke; it contributes $60 million in cash and $15 million in food each year to fight hunger, combat domestic violence, and support the arts; and it has paid $8.5 billion to reimburse states for the costs of treating smoking-related illnesses. Even its employees have given $5 million to charities. Such numbers are impressive by any standard. So why is Philip Morris on every social crusader's hit list? The answer: the tobacco culture that engulfs the organization. For years Philip Morris operated under a siege mentality, closing itself off from the questions and criticism coming from the outside world. Recently, however, this culture has slowly begun to change. The $74.3 billion company is now renewing its efforts to change its image. However, being a responsible corporate citizen and changing the company's culture, products, and image will not be easy.

a. What public relations issues does Philip Morris face?

b. On its Web site (www.philipmorris.com), Philip Morris's admits that "cigarette smoking is addictive." What kind of public relations advantages does this admission create? What problems?

c. Outline a public relations program for gaining public trust and shareholder interest.

d. Visit the Web sites of other Philip Morris companies. What public relations synergies do you see? What problems might these synergies create?

 INTERNET CONNECTIONS

ONLINE ADVERTISING

Diverse content and advertising on the Web make it similar to television, magazines, and other traditional media. Web advertising comes in many forms such as banners and sponsorships. The online advertising market has grown quickly but still represents a small proportion of all media advertising expenditures. Content providers sell online advertising to businesses that wish to target a particular audience. DoubleClick, one of the largest online advertising firms, specializes in targeted advertising. It even holds patented techniques for targeting ads online. Visit the Web site at www.doubleclick.com and complete the following table to indicate seven of the possible ways DoubleClick targets ads using audience psychographics and behavior. *Hint:* Look for this information in the section for advertisers.

Targeting method (Market description)	Definition/options

FOR DISCUSSION

1. If you were buying ad space for your university in order to increase enrollment, which DoubleClick market/method would you use? Justify.

2. For your university ad, would you rather buy a banner or a sponsorship? Explain.

3. For the university ad, would you rather buy an online ad or place a magazine or radio ad? Explain.

4. What type of targeting are you able to do with DoubleClick's Boomerang service?

5. How does DoubleClick monitor the performance of your ad? What type of information can they provide?

6. DoubleClick claims to be able to target to an audience of one person. Explain how they do this.

SAVVY SITES

- The Web is becoming a great place for sales promotions. Check out Playhere's giveaway page (www.playhere.com) for lots of coupons, contests and sweepstakes.

- NetRatings (www.netratings.com), in association with A.C. Nielsen, provides statistics on the top banner ads online.

- For a killer media property, visit ZDNet (www.zdnet.com): This media firm has over 7 million unique visitors a month and sells lots of advertising.

NOTES

1. Portions adapted from "The Marketing 100: Snickers' Santa Cruz Hughes," *Advertising Age,* June 30, 1997, p. S32; Bob Garfield, "Snickers Ads Grab the Elusive 'Big Idea,'" *Advertising Age,* September 2, 1996, p. 37; Bob Garfield, "Best TV: Snickers," *Advertising Age,* May 26, 1997, p. S1; and "A Sure Thing? Hunger Pangs Have One Answer: Snickers Satisfies," *Advertising Age,* May 31, 1999, pp. S2, S12.

2. Robert J. Coen, "Spending Spree," *Advertising Age Special Issue: The Advertising Century,* 1999, p. 126.

3. Statistical information in this section on advertising's size and composition draws from information accessed online from http://adage.com/dataplace, December 1999.

4. See Dhruv Grewel, Sukumar Kavanoor, Edward F. Fern, Carolyn Costley, and James Barnes, "Comparative Versus Noncomparative Advertising: A Meta-Analysis," *Journal of Marketing,* October 1997, pp. 1–15; "Attribute Upgrading Through Across-Class, Within-Category Comparison Advertising," *Journal of Advertising Research,* March–April 1998, pp. 6–16; Stuart Van Auken and Arthur J. Adams, "Across- Versus Within-Class Comparative Advertising: Insights into Prestige Class Anchoring," *Psychology & Marketing,* August 1999, p. 429–50; and Jeff Green, "Buick Aims 'Challenge' at Rivals," *Brandweek,* June 21, 1999, p. 10.

5. See Andrew Ehrenberg, Neil Barnard, and John Scriven, "Justifying Our Advertising Budgets," *Marketing & Research Today,* February 1997, pp. 38–44; and Dana W. Hayman and Don E. Schultz, "How Much Should You Spend on Advertising?" *Advertising Age,* April 26, 1999, p. 32.

6. Information from Gary Levin, "'Meddling' in Creative More Welcome," *Advertising Age,* April 9, 1990, pp. S4, S8; Lynne Roberts, "New Media Choice: Absolut Vodka," *Marketing,* April 9, 1998, p. 12; Eleftheria Parpis, "TBWA: Absolut," *Adweek,* November 9, 1998, p. 172; and the Q&A section at www.absolutvodka.com, March 2000.

7. "Swimming the Channels," *American Demographics,* June 1998, p. 37; and information obtained online at www.magazine.org, February 2000.

8. "1999–2000 Network TV Price Estimates," *Advertising Age,* September 20, 1999, p. 12.

9. Richard Cook, "Tackling the Problem of Increased TV Zapping," *Campaign,* September 25, 1998, p. 16.

10. Edward A. Robinson, "Frogs, Bears, and Orgasms: Think Zany If You Want to Reach Today's Consumers," *Fortune,* June 9, 1997, pp. 153–56. Also see Marc Gunther, "What's Wrong with This Picture?" *Fortune,* January 12, 1998, pp. 107–14; John Consoli, "A Crescendo of Clutter," *Mediaweek,* March 16, 1998, pp. 4–5 and Chuck Ross, "TV Commercial Clutter Has Ad Buyers Worried," *Advertising Age,* December 6, 1999, p. 77.

11. For current magazines rates and circulations, see each magazine's media kit, accessed through www.magazinedata.com.

12. See *Television Production Cost Survey* (New York: American Association of Advertising Agencies, 1998); and the 4A's Web site at www.aaaa.org/resources.

13. See Gary Schroeder, "Behavioral Optimization," *American Demographics,* August 1998, pp. 34–36; and Erwin Ephron, "Ad World Was Ripe for Its Conversion to Optimizers," *Advertising Age,* February 22, 1999, p. S16.

14. Information on advertising agency income and billings obtained online at http://adage/dataplace, December 1999.

15. Patricia Winters Lauro, "New Method of Agency Payments Drive a Stake Through the Heart of the Old 15% Commission," *New York Times,* April 2, 1999, p. 2.

16. Patti Bond, "Today's Topic: From Russia with Fizz, Coke Imports Ads," *Atlanta Journal and Constitution,* April 4, 1998, pp. E2. Also see Jack Neff, "P&G Hammers Last Nail into Commission Coffin," *Advertising Age,* September 20, 1999, p. 4.

17. See "U.K. Tobacco Ad Ban Will Include Sports Sponsorship," *AdAgeInternational.com,* May 1997; "Coca-Cola Rapped for

Running Competition in India," *AdAgeInternational.com,* February 1997; Naveen Donthu, "A Cross Country Investigation of Recall of and Attitude Toward Comparative Advertising," *Journal of Advertising,* 27, June 22, 1998, pp. 111; John Shannon, "Comparative Ads Call for Prudence," *Marketing Week,* May 6, 1999, p. 32 and "A Trojan Horse for Advertisers," *Business Week,* April 3, 2000, p. 10.

18. "Promotion Practices Condensed," *Potentials,* November 1998, p. 6.

19. For these and other examples, see Cyndee Miller, "Rewards for the Best Customers," *Marketing News,* July 5, 1993, pp. 1, 6; Louise O'Brien and Charles Jones, "Do Rewards Really Create Loyalty?" *Harvard Business Review,* May–June 1995, pp. 75–82; Grahame R. Dowling and Mark Uncles, "Do Customer Loyalty Programs Really Work?" *Sloan Management Review,* Summer 1997, pp. 71–82; and "Building Brand Loyalty," *Advertising Age's Business Marketing,* May 1998, pp. S1–S3; and Richard G. Barlow, "Future Looks Bright for Frequency Marketing," *Marketing News,* July 5, 1999, p. 14.

20. Debra Aho Williamson, "P&G's Reformulated Pert Plus Builds Consumer Relationships," *Advertising Age,* June 28, 1999, p. 52.

21. "DSN Charts: Coupons," *Discount Store News,* May 3, 1999, p. 4.

22. See "Loyal Shoppers Can Score by Using In-Store Kiosks," *Advertising Age,* May 1998, p. S4; "1998 Gallery of Excellence: Catalina Marketing Corp.," *Supermarket Business,* November 1998, p. 19; Gregg Cebrzyski, "Domino's to Join Other Chains in Testing Internet Coupons," *Nation's Restaurant News,* May 25, 1998, p. 12; and "Electronic Coupon Clipping," *USA Today,* May 11, 1999, p. 1B.

23. See Kate Bertrand, "Premiums Prime the Market," *Advertising Age's Business Marketing,* May 1998, p. S6; and Paul Nolan, "Promotions Come Alive with the Sound of Music," *Potentials,* April 1999, p. 10.

24. See "Power to the Key Ring and T-Shirt," *Sales & Marketing Management,* December 1989, p. 14; and Chad Kaydo, "Your Logo Here," *Sales & Marketing Management,* April 1998, pp. 65–70.

25. See Richard Szathmary, "Trade Shows," *Sales & Marketing Management,* May 1992, pp. 83–84; Srinath Gopalakrishna, Gary L. Lilien, Jerome D. Williams, and Ian Sequeira, "Do Trade Shows Pay Off?" *Journal of Marketing,* July 1995, pp. 75–83; Barbara Axelson, "Trade Shows Gain Larger Share of Marketing Budgets: Computers Help Make Manufacturing Top Category," *Advertising Age's Business Marketing,* May 1999, p. S14; and Peter Jenkins, "Making the Most of Trade Shows," *Nation's Business,* June 1999, p. 8.

26. Adapted from Scott Cutlip, Allen Center, and Glen Broom, *Effective Public Relations,* 8th ed. (Upper Saddle River, NJ: Prentice Hall, 1999), chap. 1.

27. Al Ries and Laura Ries, "First Do Some Publicity," *Advertising Age,* February 8, 1999, p. 42.

28. Linda Himelstein, "Levi's vs. the Dress Code," *Business Week,* April 1, 1996, pp. 57–58; "Dressing for Success," *LAB Online Advertising Guide,* Spring 1998, p. 29A, and www.levistrauss.com/casual/casual.html, December 1999.

29. Mark Gleason, "Edelman Sees Niche in Web Public Relations," *Advertising Age,* January 20, 1997, p. 30; and Michael Krauss, "Good PR Critical to Growth on the Net," *Marketing News,* January 18, 1999, p. 8.

COMPANY CASE

15

Procter & Gamble: Rushing to Prevent Rash

THE DIAPER WARS

Ever since Procter & Gamble (P&G) introduced the first commercially successful disposable diaper over 35 years ago, P&G and Kimberly-Clark (K-C) have been slugging it out for the lion's share of the approximately $4 billion market. With brand names like Pampers, Luvs, and Huggies, P&G and K-C have pursued value-added strategies arguing that their brands fit better, are more absorbent, or control leakage better than the other brands. Although P&G developed innovative diapers like Extra Absorbent Daytime, Improved Newborn, or Quilted Pampers, in the early 1990s, it found itself trailing K-C in the super-premium segment. K-C's Huggies Supremes dominated that segment. As a result, K-C had the dominant overall market share. A host of smaller competitors, led by Drypers, pursued value-pricing strategies to target more price-sensitive consumers.

By 1997, however, even the companies using the value-price strategy offered fit, absorbency, and leakage-control features similar to P&G's and K-C's products. Moreover, the disposable diaper market flattened due to price competition and population growth of only 1 percent per year. Consumer concern over the environmental impact of disposable diapers and other products had also slowed market growth. However, some studies that used a technique called "life cycle assessment" concluded that although disposable diapers generated four times as much solid waste as reusables, they utilized only about half the energy and one-fourth as much water and caused half the air pollution. Given these factors, the competition for market share intensified.

A NEW FRONT

Then, Drypers opened a new front in the diaper wars. It introduced several varieties of diapers that used aloe vera to soothe the baby's skin and baking soda to control odor. Drypers' innovation introduced skin care as the next big thing in disposable diapers. P&G confirmed that Drypers was onto something when, just three months later, it introduced Pampers Gentle Touch diapers.

P&G trumpeted Gentle Touch with television and magazine ads that informed consumers that the diapers had liners that contained a patented combination of three skin-soothing ingredients to transfer a nongreasy lotion evenly to the baby's skin. The lotion would protect babies against wetness and keep their bottoms "soft, smooth, and clearer-looking."

LEADING THE FOLLOWERS

Although Drypers had beaten P&G to the skin care punch, P&G was already working on the concept. In fact, it had introduced "breathable" diapers in 1996 that let air into the diaper, allowing the skin to dry. Then, it had introduced Gentle Touch in response to Drypers' move. In addition, the company had been working for several years on a new product concept. By early 1999, it had conducted six clinical trials, worked with over 800 babies, and spent four years developing a new product it called Pampers Rash Guard diapers. To make medical claims for the diapers, P&G had to comply with Food and Drug Administration guidelines.

The company's research found that approximately two-thirds of all babies experienced some form of diaper rash monthly. This meant that babies experienced diaper rash more frequently than colds. One-third of parents believed that their babies suffered diaper rash frequently. Moreover, P&G's researchers discovered that diaper rash was more than a medical condition. Even though many factors that could cause diaper rash were out of a parent's control, such as, teething, changes in diet, or the use of antibiotics, the parents still felt guilty when their babies got the rash. Parents often felt depressed and blamed themselves. Thus, diaper rash

was a miserable experience for the parents as well as for the babies. Prior to these revelations, P&G had believed that parents were primarily concerned about leakage prevention.

Diaper rash is caused partly by irritants that penetrate the skin. The pH level in a wet, soiled diaper increases, activating enzymes that attack the skin. The process can cause minor irritation or painful sores that require medical attention. Using its research, P&G patented a process to transfer a hypoallergenic skin protectant, petrolatum, and a skin conditioner, stearate, from the diaper's top sheet and cuff areas to the baby's skin with each diaper change. Stripes inside the diaper's lining and cuffs hold the ingredients while funneling the baby's waste into the diaper. The baby's body heat and movements cause the continuous transfer, which keeps the skin healthy and protected from moisture and irritants that can cause diaper rash. Even if the baby already has diaper rash, the diaper's skin protectant can help heal the irritated skin. The company claims that its diapers are better than skin creams and lotions, which can clog a diaper and affect its leak protection. Moreover, most parents don't use the creams and lotions until the baby already has diaper rash.

All this protection isn't cheap, however. A jumbo package of Rash Guards with 36 diapers costs $13.25, about $.37 per diaper. This compares with a price of about $.24 per diaper for P&G's basic diapers—a hefty 54 percent premium. Pamper's Premium diapers sell for about $.30 a diaper.

P&G plans to introduce Rash Guards in all food and drug stores and mass merchandisers. Interestingly, in the early days of disposable diapers, retailers were not sure exactly where to place them in the store. Consumers often found them in the convenience section, the food aisle, the paper product section, or even in the drug section.

THE BOTTOM LINE

Even though this advanced diaper's promised benefits sound good, some mothers are skeptical. Some suggest the secret to preventing diaper rash is simply to change the diaper frequently. Another mother suggests she would try cornstarch or other ointments before she would spend money for an expensive diaper. "I'm very cynical about this kind of stuff," she says. "It's a poo-poo diaper. It's not their education."

Educating the consumer about Rash Guard and countering skepticism and price resistance will be challenges for P&G. How should it communicate with consumers on the delicate and emotional subject of diaper rash?

Questions

1. Who are P&G's target audiences for its Pampers Rash Guard diapers? What should its communication objectives be?

2. What elements of the promotion mix should P&G use in designing its marketing mix strategy? What issues should it consider in designing its promotional messages?

3. How can P&G integrate its marketing communications for Rash Guard?

4. What promotion recommendations would you make to P&G? Design an overall promotion strategy for Rash Guard.

Sources: Tara Parker-Pope, "A New Front in Diaper Wars: Preventing Rash," *Wall Street Journal,* February 26, 1999, p. B1; Laurie Freeman, "Flanking Maneuver," *Marketing News,* October 27, 1997, p. 1; David Wellman, "Baby Needs," *Supermarket Business,* September 1997, p. 53; and Mark Duda, "From Cradle to Grave: Measuring Products' Environmental Impact," *USA Today,* May 17, 1997, p. 54. See also www.pampers.com.

After studying this chapter, you should be able to
1. discuss the role of a company's salespeople in creating value for customers and building customer relationships
2. explain how companies design sales force strategy and structure
3. explain how companies recruit, select, and train salespeople
4. describe how companies compensate and supervise salespeople, and how they evaluate sales force effectiveness
5. discuss the personal selling process, distinguishing between transaction-oriented marketing and relationship marketing

PERSONAL SELLING AND SALES MANAGEMENT

When someone says "salesperson," what image comes to mind? Perhaps it's the stereotypical "traveling salesman"—the fast-talking, ever-smiling peddler who travels his territory foisting his wares on reluctant customers. Such stereotypes, however, are sadly out of date. Today, most professional salespeople are well-educated, well-trained men and women who work to build long-term, value-producing relationships with their customers. They succeed not by taking customers in but by helping them out—by assessing customer needs and solving customer problems.

Consider Lear Corporation, one of the largest, fastest-growing, and most successful automotive suppliers in the world. Each year, Lear produces more than $12 billion worth of automotive interiors—seat systems, instrument panels, door panels, floor and acoustic systems, overhead systems, and electronic and electrical distribution systems. Its customers include most of the world's leading automotive companies, from Ford, General Motors, Fiat, and Volvo to Mercedes-Benz, Ferrari, Rolls-Royce, Toyota, and more than a dozen others. Lear now operates more than 300 facilities in 33 countries around the globe. During the past few years, Lear has achieved record-breaking sales and earnings growth. Lear's sales during the past five years have more than tripled, and its "average content per car" in North America has increased more than fourfold

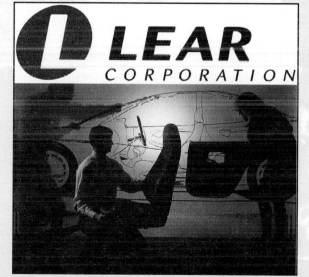

since 1990. It currently owns about a 30 percent share of the North American interior components market.

Lear Corporation owes its success to many factors, including a strong customer orientation and a commitment to continuous improvement, teamwork, and customer value. But perhaps more than any other part of the organization, it's Lear's outstanding sales force that makes the company's credo, "Consumer driven. Customer focused," ring true. In fact, Lear's sales force was recently rated by *Sales & Marketing Management* magazine as one of "America's Best Sales Forces." What makes this an outstanding sales force? Lear knows that good selling these days takes much more than just a sales rep covering a territory and convincing customers to buy the product. It takes teamwork, relationship building, and doing what's best for the customer. Lear's sales force excels at these tasks.

Lear's sales depend completely on the success of its customers. If the automakers don't sell cars, Lear doesn't sell interiors. So the Lear sales force strives to create not just sales, but customer success. In fact, Lear salespeople aren't "sales reps," they're "account managers" who function more as consultants than as order getters. "Our salespeople don't really close deals," notes a senior marketing executive. "They consult and work with customers to learn exactly what's needed and when."

To more fully match up with customers' needs, Lear has diversified its product line to become a kind of "one-stop shopping" source.

Until a few years ago, Lear supplied only seats; now it sells almost everything for a car's interior. Providing complete interior solutions for customers also benefits Lear. "It used to be that we'd build a partnership and then get only a limited amount of revenue from it," the executive says. "Now we can get as much as possible out of our customer relationships."

Lear is heavily customer focused, so much so that it's broken up into separate divisions dedicated to specific customers. For example, there's a Ford division and a General Motors division, and each operates as its own profit center. Within each division, high-level "platform teams"—made up of salespeople, engineers, and program managers—work closely with their customer counterparts. These platform teams are closely supported by divisional manufacturing, finance, quality, and advanced technology groups. Lear's limited customer base, consisting of only a few dozen customers in all, allows Lear's sales teams to get very close to their customers. "Our teams don't call on purchasers; they're linked to customer operations at all levels," the marketer notes. "We try to put a system in place that creates continuous contact with customers." In fact, Lear often locates its sales offices in customers' plants. For example, the team that handles GM's light truck division works at GM's truck operation campus. "We can't just be there to give quotes and ask for orders," the marketing executive says. "We need to be involved with customers every step of the way—from vehicle concept through launch."

Lear's largest customers are worth billions of dollars in annual sales to the company. Maintaining profitable relationships with such large customers takes much more than a nice smile and a firm handshake. Certainly there's no place for the "smoke and mirrors" or "flimflam" sometimes mistakenly associated with personal selling. Success in such a selling environment requires careful teamwork among well-trained, dedicated sales professionals who are bent on profitably taking care of their customers.[1]

Robert Louis Stevenson once noted that "everyone lives by selling something." We are all familiar with the sales forces used by business organizations to sell products and services to customers around the world. But sales forces are also found in many other kinds of organizations. For example, colleges use recruiters to attract new students, and churches use membership committees to attract new members. Hospitals and museums use fund-raisers to contact donors and raise money. Even governments use sales forces. The U.S. Postal Service, for instance, uses a sales force to sell Express Mail and other services to corporate customers, and the Agricultural Extension Service sends agricultural specialists to sell farmers on new farming methods. In this chapter, we examine the role of personal selling in the organization, sales force management decisions, and basic principles of personal selling.

THE ROLE OF PERSONAL SELLING

There are many types of personal selling jobs, and the role of personal selling can vary greatly from one company to another. Here, we look at the nature of personal selling positions and at the role the sales force plays in modern marketing organizations.

The Nature of Personal Selling

Selling is one of the oldest professions in the world. The people who do the selling go by many names: *salespeople, sales representatives, account executives, sales consultants, sales engineers, agents, district managers, marketing representatives,* and *account development reps,* to name just a few.

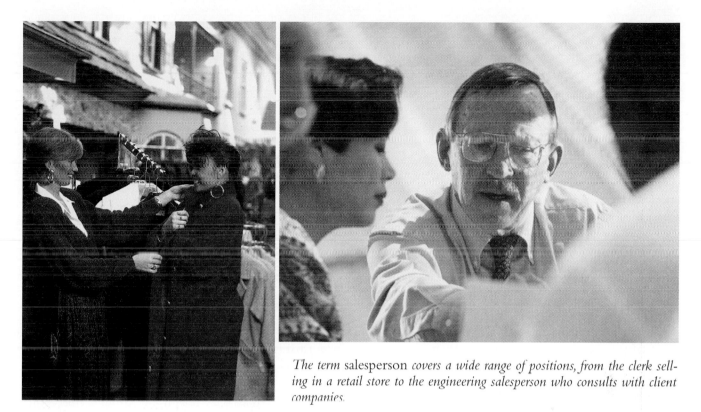

The term salesperson *covers a wide range of positions, from the clerk selling in a retail store to the engineering salesperson who consults with client companies.*

People hold many stereotypes of salespeople—including some unfavorable ones. "Salesman" may bring to mind the image of Arthur Miller's pitiable Willy Loman in *Death of a Salesman*. Or you might think of Meredith Willson's cigar-smoking, back-slapping, joke-telling Harold Hill in *The Music Man*. Both examples depict salespeople as loners, traveling their territories, trying to foist their wares on unsuspecting or unwilling buyers.

However, modern salespeople are a far cry from these unfortunate stereotypes. Today, most salespeople are well-educated, well-trained professionals who work to build and maintain long-term customer relationships by listening to their customers, assessing customer needs, and organizing the company's efforts to solve customer problems. Consider Boeing, the aerospace giant that dominates the world-wide commercial aircraft market with a 55 percent market share. It takes more than a friendly smile and a firm handshake to sell expensive airplanes:

> ★ Selling high-tech aircraft at $70 million or more a copy is complex and challenging. A single big sale can easily run into billions of dollars. Boeing salespeople head up an extensive team of company specialists—sales and service technicians, financial analysts, planners, engineers—all dedicated to finding ways to satisfy airline customer needs. The salespeople begin by becoming experts on the airlines, much like Wall Street analysts would. They find out where each airline wants to grow, when it wants to replace planes, and details of its financial situation. The team runs Boeing and competing planes through computer systems, simulating the airline's routes, cost per seat, and other factors to show that their planes are most efficient. Then the high-level negotiations begin. The selling process is nerve-rackingly slow—it can take two or three years from the first sales presentation to the day the sale is announced. Sometimes top executives from both the airline and Boeing are brought in to close the deal. After getting the order, salespeople then must stay in almost constant touch to keep track of the account's equipment needs and to make certain the customer

stays satisfied. Success depends on building solid, long-term relationships with customers, based on performance and trust. According to one analyst, Boeing's salespeople "are the vehicle by which information is collected and contacts are made so all other things can take place."[2]

Salesperson
An individual acting for a company by performing one or more of the following activities: prospecting, communicating, servicing, and information gathering.

The term **salesperson** covers a wide range of positions. At one extreme, a salesperson might be largely an *order taker,* such as the department store salesperson standing behind the counter. At the other extreme are *order getters,* whose positions demand the *creative selling* of products and services ranging from appliances, industrial equipment, or airplanes to insurance, advertising, or consulting services. Other salespeople engage in *missionary selling:* These salespeople are not expected or permitted to take an order but only build goodwill or educate buyers. An example is a salesperson for a pharmaceutical company who calls on doctors to educate them about the company's drug products and to urge them to prescribe these products to their patients. Here, we focus on the more creative types of selling and on the process of building and managing an effective sales force.

The Role of the Sales Force

Personal selling is the interpersonal arm of the promotion mix. Advertising consists of one-way, nonpersonal communication with target consumer groups. In contrast, personal selling involves two-way, personal communication between salespeople and individual customers—whether face-to-face, by telephone, through video conferences, or by other means. Personal selling can be more effective than advertising in more complex selling situations. Salespeople can probe customers to learn more about their problems. They can adjust the marketing offer to fit the special needs of each customer and can negotiate terms of sale. They can build long-term personal relationships with key decision makers.

The role of personal selling varies from company to company. Some firms have no salespeople at all—for example, companies that sell only through mail-order catalogs or companies that sell through manufacturer's reps, sales agents, or brokers. In most firms, however, the sales force plays a major role. In companies that sell business products, such as Xerox or DuPont, the company's salespeople work directly with customers. In fact, to many customers, salespeople may be the only contact. To these customers, the sales force *is* the company. In consumer product companies such as Procter & Gamble or Nike that sell through intermediaries, final consumers rarely meet salespeople or even know about them. Still, the sales force plays an important behind-the-scenes role. It works with wholesalers and retailers to gain their support and to help them be more effective in selling the company's products.

The sales force serves as a critical link between a company and its customers. In many cases, salespeople serve both masters—the seller and the buyer. First, they *represent the company to customers.* They find and develop new customers and communicate information about the company's products and services. They sell products by approaching customers, presenting their products, answering objections, negotiating prices and terms, and closing sales. In addition, salespeople provide services to customers, carry out market research and intelligence work, and fill out sales call reports.

At the same time, salespeople *represent customers to the company,* acting inside the firm as "champions" of customers' interests. Salespeople relay customer concerns about company products and actions back to those who can handle them. They learn about customer needs and work with others in the company to develop greater customer value. The salesperson often acts as an "account manager" who manages the relationship between the seller and buyer. Thus, salespeople must work closely with other marketing and nonmarketing people within the firm.

As companies move toward a stronger market orientation, their sales forces are becoming more market focused and customer oriented. The old view was that salespeople should worry about sales and the company should worry about profit. However, the current view holds that salespeople should be concerned with more than just producing *sales*—they also must know how to produce *customer satisfaction* and *company profit*. Beyond winning new customers and making sales, they must be able to help the company to create long-term, profitable relationships with customers.

MANAGING THE SALES FORCE

Sales force management
The analysis, planning, implementation, and control of sales force activities.

We define **sales force management** as the analysis, planning, implementation, and control of sales force activities. It includes designing sales force strategy and structure and recruiting, selecting, training, compensating, supervising, and evaluating the firm's salespeople. These major sales force management decisions are shown in Figure 16.1 and are discussed in the following sections.

Designing Sales Force Strategy and Structure

Marketing managers face several sales force strategy and design questions. How should salespeople and their tasks be structured? How big should the sales force be? Should salespeople sell alone or work in teams with other people in the company? Should they sell in the field or by telephone? We address these issues below.

Sales Force Structure

A company can divide up sales responsibilities along any of several lines. The decision is simple if the company sells only one product line to one industry with customers in many locations. In that case the company would use a *territorial sales force structure*. However, if the company sells many products to many types of customers, it might need either a *product sales force structure*, a *customer sales force structure*, or a combination of the two.

Territorial sales force structure
A sales force organization that assigns each salesperson to an exclusive geographic territory in which that salesperson sells the company's full line.

Territorial Sales Force Structure. In the **territorial sales force structure,** each salesperson is assigned to an exclusive geographic area and sells the company's full line of products or services to all customers in that territory. This organization has many advantages. It clearly defines the salesperson's job, and because only one salesperson works the territory, he or she gets all the credit or blame for territory sales. The territorial structure also increases the salesperson's desire to build local business relationships that, in turn, improve selling effectiveness. Finally, because each salesperson travels within a limited geographic area, travel expenses are relatively small.

A territorial sales organization is often supported by many levels of sales management positions. For example, Campbell Soup uses a territorial structure in which each salesperson is responsible for selling all Campbell Soup products. Starting at the bottom of the organization, *sales merchandisers* report to *sales representatives,* who report to *retail supervisors,* who report to *directors of retail sales operations,* who report to 1 of 22 *regional sales managers*. Regional sales managers, in turn, report to 1 of 4 *general sales managers* (West, Central, South, and East), who report to a *vice president* and *general sales manager.*

FIGURE 16.1 **Major steps in sales force management**

Product sales force structure
A sales force organization under which salespeople specialize in selling only a portion of the company's products or lines.

Product Sales Force Structure.   Salespeople must know their products—especially when the products are numerous and complex. This need, together with the growth of product management, has led many companies to adopt a **product sales force structure,** in which the sales force sells along product lines. For example, Kodak uses different sales forces for its film products than for its industrial products. The film products sales force deals with simple products that are distributed intensively, whereas the industrial products sales force deals with complex products that require technical understanding.

The product structure can lead to problems, however, if a single large customer buys many different company products. For example, Baxter International, a hospital supply company, has several product divisions, each with a separate sales force. Several Baxter salespeople might end up calling on the same hospital on the same day. This means that they travel over the same routes and wait to see the same customer's purchasing agents. These extra costs must be compared with the benefits of better product knowledge and attention to individual products.

Customer sales force structure
A sales force organization under which salespeople specialize in selling only to certain customers or industries.

Customer Sales Force Structure.   More and more companies are now using a **customer sales force structure,** in which they organize the sales force along customer or industry lines. Separate sales forces may be set up for different industries, for serving current customers versus finding new ones, and for major accounts versus regular accounts.

Organizing the sales force around customers can help a company to become more customer focused and build closer relationships with important customers. For example, giant ABB, the $30-billion-a-year Swiss-based industrial equipment maker, changed from a product-based to a customer-based sales force. The new structure resulted in a stronger customer orientation and improved service to clients:

> ★ Until four months ago, David Donaldson sold boilers for ABB. . . . After 30 years, Donaldson sure knew boilers, but he didn't know much about the broad range of other products offered by ABB's U.S. Power Plant division. Customers were frustrated because as many as a dozen ABB salespeople called on them at different times to peddle their products. ABB's bosses decided that this was a poor way to run a sales force. So [recently], David Donaldson and 27 other power plant salespeople began new jobs. [Donaldson] now also sells turbines, generators, and three other product lines. He handles six major accounts . . . instead of a [mixed batch] of 35. His charge: Know the customer intimately and sell him the products that help him operate productively. Says Donaldson: "My job is to make it easy for my customers to do business with us. . . . I show them where to go in ABB whenever they have a problem." The president of ABB's power plant businesses [adds]: "If you want to be a customer-driven company, you have to design the sales organization around individual buyers rather than around your products."[3]

IBM made a similar shift from a product-based structure to a customer-based one. Before the shift, droves of salespeople representing different IBM software, hardware, and services divisions might call on a single large client, creating confusion and frustration. Such large customers wanted a "single face," one point of contact for all of IBM's vast array of products and services. Following the restructuring, a single IBM "client executive" works with each large customer and manages a team of IBMers—product reps, systems engineers, consultants, and others—who work with the customer. The client executive becomes an expert in the customer's industry. Greg Buseman, a client executive in the distribution industry who spends most of his time working with a major consumer packaged-goods customer, describes his role this way: "I am the owner of the business relationship with the client. If the client has a problem, I'm the one who pulls together software or hardware specialists or consultants. At the customer I work most closely with, we usually have 15 to

This Procter & Gamble "customer business development team" serves a major southeastern grocery retailer. It consists of a customer business development manager and five account executives (shown here), along with specialists from other functional areas.

20 projects going at once, and I have to manage them."[4] Such an intense focus on customers is widely credited for IBM's dramatic turnaround in recent years.

Procter & Gamble has also moved to a customer sales force structure in recent years. P&G sales reps are now organized into "customer business development teams." Each CBD team is assigned to a major P&G customer. Each team consists of a customer business development manager, several account executives (each responsible for a specific category of P&G products), and specialists in marketing strategy, operations, information systems, logistics, and finance. This organization places the focus on serving the complete needs of each important customer.

Complex Sales Force Structures. When a company sells a wide variety of products to many types of customers over a broad geographic area, it often combines several types of sales force structures. Salespeople can be specialized by customer and territory, by product and territory, by product and customer, or by territory, product, and customer. No single structure is best for all companies and situations. Each company should select a sales force structure that best serves the needs of its customers and fits its overall marketing strategy.

Sales Force Size

Once the company has set its structure, it is ready to consider *sales force size.* Salespeople constitute one of the company's most productive—and most expensive—assets. Therefore, increasing their number will increase both sales and costs.

In recent years, sales forces have been shrinking in size. One study revealed that, in just the two years from 1996 to 1998, the average company's sales force decreased by a whopping 26 percent.[5] One cause is advances in selling technology, such as selling on the Internet or the use of account management software, which make salespeople more efficient in handling customers or replace the salespeople altogether. Another cause is recent merger mania, on both the seller and customer sides. When two sellers merge, they rarely need a doubled sales force. "When you merge two sales forces, you'll have about one and a half sales forces when you're done," says a sales consultant.[6] Similarly, the merging of two customer firms means fewer customers, and fewer customers means that fewer salespeople are needed to call on them.

Workload approach
An approach to setting sales force size in which the company groups accounts into different size classes and then determines how many salespeople are needed to call on each class of accounts the desired number of times.

Many companies use some form of **workload approach** to set sales force size. Using this approach, a company first groups accounts into different classes according to size, account status, or other factors related to the amount of effort required to maintain them. It then determines the number of salespeople needed to call on each class of accounts the desired number of times. The company might think as follows: Suppose we have 1,000 Type-A accounts and 2,000 Type-B accounts. Type-A accounts require 36 calls a year and Type-B accounts require 12 calls a year. In this case, the sales force's *workload*—the number of calls it must make per year—is

60,000 calls [(1,000 $\times$ 36) + (2,000 $\times$ 12) = 36,000 + 24,000 = 60,000]. Suppose our average salesperson can make 1,000 calls a year. Thus, the company needs 60 salespeople (60,000 ÷ 1,000).

Other Sales Force Strategy and Structure Issues

Sales management must also decide who will be involved in the selling effort and how various sales and sales support people will work together.

Outside sales force

Outside salespeople who travel to call on customers. Also known as *field sales force*.

Inside sales force

Inside salespeople who conduct business from their offices via telephone or visits from prospective buyers.

Telemarketing

Using the telephone to sell directly to customers.

Outside and Inside Sales Forces.   The company may have an **outside sales force** (or *field sales force*), an **inside sales force,** or both. Outside salespeople travel to call on customers. Inside salespeople conduct business from their offices via telephone or visits from prospective buyers.

To reduce time demands on their outside sales forces, many companies have increased the size of their inside sales forces. Inside salespeople include technical support people, sales assistants, and telemarketers. *Technical support people* provide technical information and answers to customers' questions. *Sales assistants* provide clerical backup for outside salespeople. They call ahead and confirm appointments, conduct credit checks, follow up on deliveries, and answer customers' questions when outside salespeople cannot be reached. *Telemarketers* use the phone to find new leads and qualify prospects for the field sales force, or to sell and service accounts directly.

The inside sales force frees outside salespeople to spend more time selling to major accounts and finding major new prospects. Depending on the complexity of the product and customer, a telemarketer can make from 20 to 33 decision-maker contacts a day, compared to the average of 4 that an outside salesperson can make. For many types of products and selling situations, **telemarketing** can be as effective as a personal call but much less expensive. Whereas the average personal sale costs about $165, a routine industrial telemarketing call costs only about $5 and a complex call about $20.[7] Notes a DuPont telemarketer: "I'm more effective on the phone. [When you're in the field], if some guy's not in his office, you lose an hour. On the phone, you lose 15 seconds. . . . Through my phone calls, I'm in the field as much as the rep is." There are other advantages. "Customers can't throw things at you," quips the rep, "and you don't have to outrun dogs."[8]

Telemarketing can be used successfully by both large and small companies:

★ IBM's traditional image has long been symbolized by the salesman in the blue suit, crisp white shirt, and red tie—an imposing fellow far more comfortable in Corporate America's plush executive suites than in the cramped quarters of some fledgling entrepreneur. Small businesses were often ignored. Typical is the Fess Parker Winery & Vineyard, a $4.5 million company in Los Olivos, California, that employs 25 people. "I never would've thought of IBM as someone to call for a business our size" says general manager Charlie Kears. To sell its electronic-business solutions to such small businesses, IBM is now boosting emphasis on its telemarketing effort. Stroll through the IBM call center in suburban Atlanta, with its sea of cubicles, and a new image of the IBM salesperson emerges: Men and women, many recent college grads, sporting golf shirts and khakis or—gasp!—blue jeans. They wear headsets and talk on the phone with customers they'll likely never meet in person. Phone selling, once deemed a poor stepchild at IBM, is now in vogue. IBM's roughly 1,200 phone reps now generate 30 percent of IBM's revenues from small and midsize businesses. The reps focus on specific industries and each calls on as many as 300 accounts. They nurture client relationships, pitch IBM solutions, and, when needed, refer customers to product and service specialists within the call center or to resellers in their region. How do customers like dealing with telesales reps? According to Kears, it's been "terrific"—he's never on hold for long, and the reps are very helpful, he says. "Plus, I get a lot of e-mails from my rep in Atlanta, and I usually hear from someone there every other week."[9]

Experienced telemarketers sell complex chemical products by phone at DuPont's Customer Telecontact Center. Quips one, "I'm more effective on the phone . . . and you don't have to outrun dogs."

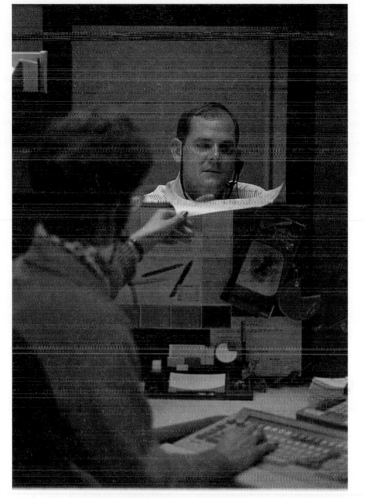

★ Climax Portable Machine Tools has proven that a small company can use telemarketing to save money and still lavish attention on buyers. Under the old system, Climax sales engineers spent one-third of their time on the road, training distributor salespeople and accompanying them on calls. They could make about 4 contacts a day. Now, each of 5 sales engineers on Climax's telemarketing team calls about 30 prospects a day, following up on leads generated by ads and direct mail. Because it takes about 5 calls to close a sale, the sales engineers update a prospect's computer file after each contact, noting the degree of commitment, requirements, next call date, and personal comments. "If anyone mentions he's going on a fishing trip, our sales engineer enters that in the computer and uses it to personalize the next phone call," says Climax's president, noting that's just one way to build good relations. Another is that the first mailing to a prospect includes the sales engineer's business card with his picture on it. Of course, it takes more than friendliness to sell $15,000 machine tools over the phone (special orders may run $200,000), but the telemarketing approach is working well. When Climax customers were asked, "Do you see the sales engineer often enough?" the response was overwhelmingly positive. Obviously, many people didn't realize that the only contact they'd had with Climax had been on the phone.[10]

Just as telemarketing is changing the way that many companies go to market, the Internet offers explosive potential for restructuring sales forces and conducting sales operations. More and more companies are now using the Internet to support their personal selling efforts—not just for selling, but for everything from training salespeople to conducting sales meetings and servicing accounts (see Marketing Highlight 16.1).

**MARKETING
HIGHLIGHT**

16.1

POINT, CLICK, AND SELL: WELCOME TO THE WEB-BASED SALES FORCE

There are few rules at Fisher Scientific International's sales training sessions. The chemical company's salespeople are allowed to show up for new workshops in their pajamas. No one flinches if they stroll in at midnight for their first class, take a dozen breaks to call clients, or invite the family cat to sleep in their laps while they take an exam. Sound unorthodox? It would be if Fisher's salespeople were trained in a regular classroom. But for the past year and a half, the company has been using the Internet to teach the majority of its salespeople in the privacy of their homes, cars, hotel rooms, or wherever else they bring their laptops.

To get updates on Fisher's pricing or refresh themselves on one of the company's highly technical products, all salespeople have to do is log onto the Web site and select from the lengthy index. Any time of the day or night, they can get information on a new product, take an exam, or post messages for product experts—all without ever entering a corporate classroom. Welcome to the new world of the Web-based sales force.

In the past few years sales organizations around the world have begun saving money and time by using a host of new Web approaches to train reps, hold sales meetings, and even conduct live sales presentations.

"Web-based technologies are becoming really hot in sales because they save salespeople's time," says technology consultant Tim Sloane. Web-based technologies help companies save time and travel costs while keeping reps up to speed on their company's new products and sales strategies. Fisher Scientific's reps can dial up the Web site at their leisure, and whereas newer reps might spend hours online going through each session in order, more seasoned sellers might just log on for a quick refresher on a specific product before a sales call. "It allows them to manage their time better, because they're only getting training when they need it, in the doses they need it in," says John Pavlik, director of the company's training department. If salespeople are spending less time on training, Pavlik says, they're able to spend more time on what they do best: selling.

Training is only one of the ways sales organizations are using the Internet. Many companies are using the Web to make sales presentations and service accounts. For example, Digital Equipment Corporation's salespeople used to spend a great deal of time traveling to the offices of clients and prospects. But since 1997 the company (now a division of Compaq) has been delivering sales pitches by combining teleconferences with Web presentations. For example, when Digital's account team in Connecticut needed to see what marketing manager Joe Batista and his team in Massachusetts had

Internet selling support: Sales organizations around the world are now using a host of new Web approaches to train reps, hold sales meetings, and even conduct live sales presentations.

prepared for a client, Batista input his ideas into a PowerPoint presentation and uploaded it using Internet Conference Center, Web-based software provided by Contigo Software. The account team joined Batista via teleconference and used their own computers to log onto the Web site Batista specified.

Once everyone was logged on, Batista was able to take control of the browsers and lead the reps through the presentation in real time, highlighting and pointing out specific items as he went. The account reps added their comments, based on their more detailed knowledge of the client, and the revised presentation was then shown online to the client. The beauty of the whole process? It's so fast. "The use of [the Web] clearly helps shorten our sales cycle," Batista says. Presentations are created and delivered in less time   sometimes weeks less than the process would take face-to-face—and salespeople are able to close deals more quickly.

Other companies are using Web-based sales presentations to find new prospects. Oracle Corporation, the $8 billion software and information technology services company, conducts online, live product seminars for prospective clients. Prospects can scan the high-tech company's Web site to see which seminars they might want to attend, then dial in via modem and telephone at the appropriate time (Oracle pays for the cost of the phone call). The seminars, which usually consist of a live lecture describing the product's applications followed by a question-and-answer session, average about 125 prospective clients apiece. Once a seminar is completed, prospects are directed to another part of Oracle's

Web site, from which they can order products. "It costs our clients nothing but time," says Oracle's manager of Internet marketing programs, "and we're reaching a much wider audience than we would if we were doing in-person seminars."

The Internet can also be a handy way to hold sales strategy meetings. Consider Cisco Systems, which provides networking solutions for the Internet. Sales meetings used to take an enormous bite out of Cisco's travel budget. Now the company saves about $1 million per month by conducting many of those sessions on the Web using PlaceWare virtual conference center software. Whenever Cisco introduces a new product, it holds a Web meeting to update salespeople, in groups of 100 or more, on the product's marketing and sales strategy.

Usually led by the product manager or a vice president of sales, the meetings typically begin with a 10-minute slide presentation that spells out the planned strategy. Then, salespeople spend the next 50 or so minutes asking questions via teleconference. The meeting's leader can direct attendees' browsers to competitors' Web sites or ask them to vote on certain issues by using the software's instant polling feature. "Our salespeople are actually meeting more online then they ever were face-to-face," says Mike Mitchell, Cisco's distance learning manager, adding that some salespeople who used to meet with other reps and managers only a few times a quarter are meeting online nearly every day. "That's very empowering for the sales force, because they're able to make suggestions at every step of the way about where we're going with our sales and marketing strategies."

Thus, Web-based technologies can produce big organizational benefits for sales forces. They help conserve salespeople's valuable time, save travel dollars, and give salespeople a new vehicle for selling and servicing accounts. But the technologies also have some drawbacks. For starters, they're not cheap. Setting up a Web based system can cost up to several hundred thousand dollars. Such systems also can intimidate low-tech salespeople or clients. "You must have a culture that is comfortable using computers," says one marketing communications manager. "As simple as it is, if your salespeople or clients aren't comfortable using the Web, you're wasting your money." Also, Web tools are susceptible to server crashes and other network difficulties, not a happy event when you're in the midst of an important sales meeting or presentation.

For these reasons, some high-tech experts recommend that sales executives use Web technologies for training, sales meetings, and preliminary client sales presentations, but resort to old-fashioned, face-to-face meetings when the time draws near to close the deal. "When push comes to shove, if you've got an account worth closing, you're still going to get on that plane and see the client in person," says sales consultant Sloane. "Your client is going to want to look you in the eye before buying anything from you, and that's still one thing you just can't do online."

Source: Adapted from Melinda Ligos, "Point, Click, and Sell," *Sales & Marketing Management,* May 1999 pp. 51–55. Also see Chad Kaydo, "You've Got Sales," *Sales & Marketing Management,* October 1999, pp. 29–39 and Ginger Conlon, "How to Move Customers Online," *Sales & Marketing Management, March 2000, pp. 27–28.*

Team Selling.   For years, the customer has been solely in the hands of the salesperson. The salesperson identified the prospect, arranged the call, explored the customer's needs, created and proposed a solution, closed the deal, and turned cheerleader as others delivered what he or she promised. For selling relatively simple products, this approach can work well. But if the products are more complex and the service requirements greater, the salesperson simply can't go it alone. Instead, most companies now are using **team selling** to service large, complex accounts.

Team selling
Using teams of people from sales, marketing, engineering, finance, technical support, and even upper management to service large, complex accounts.

More and more, companies are finding that sales teams can unearth problems, solutions, and sales opportunities that no individual salesperson could. Such teams might include experts from any area or level of the selling firm—sales, marketing, technical and support services, R&D, engineering, operations, finance, and others. In team selling situations, the salesperson shifts from "soloist" to "orchestrator."[11]

In many cases, the move to team selling mirrors similar changes in customers' buying organizations. According to the director of sales education at Dow Chemical, over 80 percent of purchasing decisions are now being made by multifunctional buying teams, including purchasing, engineering, and financial management staff. To sell effectively to such selling teams, he states, "Our sellers . . . have to captain selling teams. There are no more lone wolves."[12]

Some companies, like IBM, Xerox, and Procter & Gamble have used teams for a long time. Others have only recently reorganized to adopt the team concept. For example, Cutler-Hammer, which supplies circuit breakers, motor starters, and other electrical equipment to heavy industrial manufacturers such as Ford Motor, recently developed "pods" of salespeople that focus on a specific geographical region, industry, or market. Each pod member contributes unique expertise and knowledge about a product or service that salespeople can leverage when selling to increasingly sophisticated buying teams.[13]

Team selling does have some pitfalls. For example, selling teams can confuse or overwhelm customers who are used to working with only one salesperson. Salespeople who are used to having customers all to themselves may have trouble learning to work with and trust others on a team. Finally, difficulties in evaluating individual contributions to the team selling effort can create some sticky compensation issues.

Still, team selling can produce dramatic results. For example, Dun & Bradstreet, the world's largest marketer of business information and related services, recently established sales teams made up of representatives from its credit, collection, and marketing business units, which up to then had worked separately. Their mission was to work as a team to call on higher-ups in customer organizations, learn about customer needs, and offer solutions. The teams concentrated on D&B's top 50 customers.

When one of the D&B sales teams asked to meet with the chief financial officer of a major telecommunications company, the executive responded, "I'm delighted you asked, but why talk?" He found out after a one-hour meeting. The D&B team listened as he discussed problems facing his organization, and by the end of the information-seeking session, the team had come up with several solutions for the executive and had identified $1.5 million in D&B sales opportunities from what had been a $700,000 customer. More teams met with more clients, creating more opportunities. About a year after the program started, D&B's marketing department had targeted $200 million in sales opportunities, about half of which would not have been found under the old system. Now these teams are getting together with D&B's top 200 customers.[14]

Recruiting and Selecting Salespeople

At the heart of any successful sales force operation is the recruitment and selection of good salespeople. The performance difference between an average salesperson and a top salesperson can be substantial. In a typical sales force, the top 30 percent of the salespeople might bring in 60 percent of the sales. Thus, careful salesperson selection can greatly increase overall sales force performance. Beyond the differences in sales performance, poor selection results in costly turnover. When a salesperson quits, the costs of finding and training a new salesperson—plus the costs of lost sales—can run as high as $50,000 to $75,000. Also, a sales force with many new people is less productive.[15]

What Makes a Good Salesperson?

Selecting salespeople would not be a problem if the company knew what traits to look for. If it knew that good salespeople were outgoing, aggressive, and energetic, for example, it could simply check applicants for these characteristics. But many successful salespeople are bashful, soft-spoken, and laid back.

Still, the search continues for the magic list of traits that spells sure-fire sales success. One survey suggests that good salespeople have a lot of enthusiasm, persistence, initiative, self-confidence, and job commitment. They are committed to sales as a way of life and have a strong customer orientation. Another study suggests that good salespeople are independent and self-motivated and are excellent listeners. Still another study advises that salespeople should be a friend to the customer as well as persistent, enthusiastic, attentive, and—above all—honest. They must be internally motivated, disciplined, hardworking, and able to build strong relationships with customers. Finally, studies show that good salespeople are team players rather than loners.[16]

How can a company find out what traits salespeople in its industry should have? Job *duties* suggest some of the traits a company should look for. Does the job require a lot of planning and paperwork? Does it call for much travel? Will the salesperson face a lot of rejections? Will the salesperson be working with high-level buyers? The successful salesperson should be suited to these duties. The company also should look at the characteristics of its most successful salespeople for clues to needed traits.

Recruiting Procedures

After management has decided on needed traits, it must *recruit* salespeople. The human resources department looks for applicants by getting names from current salespeople, using employment agencies, placing classified ads, and contacting college students. Another source is to attract top salespeople from other companies. Proven salespeople need less training and can be immediately productive.

Until recently, companies sometimes found it hard to sell college students on selling. Many thought that selling was a job and not a profession, that salespeople had to be deceitful to be effective, and that selling involved too much insecurity and travel. In addition, some women believed that selling was a man's career. To counter such objections, recruiters now offer high starting salaries and income growth and note that more than one-fourth of the presidents of large U.S. corporations started out in marketing and sales. They point out that over 23 percent of all professional salespeople in the United States are women. Women account for a much higher percentage of the sales force in some industries, such as lodging (63 percent), banking and financial services (53 percent), and health services (52 percent).[17]

Selecting Salespeople

Recruiting will attract many applicants from whom the company must select the best. The selection procedure can vary from a single informal interview to lengthy testing and interviewing. Many companies give formal tests to sales applicants. Tests typically measure sales aptitude, analytical and organizational skills, personality traits, and other characteristics. Test results count heavily in companies such as IBM, Prudential, Procter & Gamble, and Gillette. Gillette claims that tests have reduced turnover by 42 percent and that test scores have correlated well with the later performance of new salespeople. But test scores provide only one piece of information in a set that includes personal characteristics, references, past employment history, and interviewer reactions.[18]

Training Salespeople

Many companies used to send their new salespeople into the field almost immediately after hiring them. They would be given samples, order books, and general instructions ("sell west of the Mississippi"). To many companies, a training program translated into high expense for instructors, materials, space, and salary for a person who was not yet selling, and a loss of sales opportunities because the person was not in the field.

Today's new salespeople, however, may spend anywhere from a few weeks or months to a year or more in training. The average training period is four months. In all, U.S. companies spend more than $7 billion annually on training salespeople and devote more than 33 hours per year to the average salesperson.[19] Although

Sales training: U.S. companies spend more than $7 billion annually on training salespeople and devote more than 33 hours per year to the average salesperson.

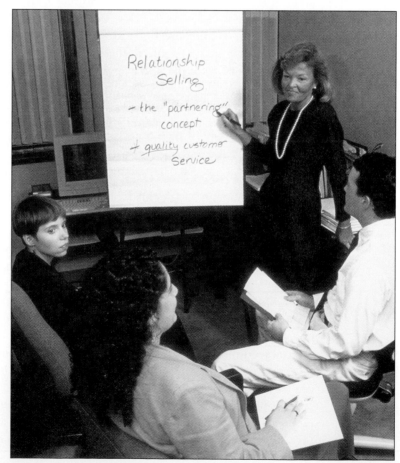

training can be expensive, it can also yield dramatic returns on the training investment. For example, Nabisco did an extensive analysis of the return on investment of its two-day Professional Selling Program, which teaches sales reps how to plan for and make professional presentations to their retail customers. Although it cost about $1,000 to put each sales rep through the program, the training resulted in additional sales of more than $122,000 per rep and yielded almost $21,000 of additional profit per rep.[20]

Training programs have several goals. Salespeople need to know and identify with the company, so most training programs begin by describing the company's history and objectives, its organization, its financial structure and facilities, and its chief products and markets. Salespeople also need to know the company's products, so sales trainees are shown how products are produced and how they work. They also need to know customers' and competitors' characteristics, so the training program teaches them about competitors' strategies and about different types of customers and their needs, buying motives, and buying habits. Because salespeople must know how to make effective presentations, they are trained in the principles of selling. Finally, salespeople need to understand field procedures and responsibilities. They learn how to divide time between active and potential accounts and how to use an expense account, prepare reports, and route communications effectively.

Compensating Salespeople

To attract salespeople, a company must have an appealing compensation plan. These plans vary greatly both by industry and by companies within the same industry. The level of compensation must be close to the "going rate" for the type of sales job and needed skills. To pay less than the going rate would attract too few quality salespeople; to pay more would be unnecessary.

Compensation is made up of several elements—a fixed amount, a variable amount, expenses, and fringe benefits. The fixed amount, usually a salary, gives the salesperson some stable income. The variable amount, which might be commissions or bonuses based on sales performance, rewards the salesperson for greater effort. Expense allowances, which repay salespeople for job-related expenses, let salespeople undertake needed and desirable selling efforts. Fringe benefits, such as paid vacations, sickness or accident benefits, pensions, and life insurance, provide job security and satisfaction.

Management must decide what *mix* of these compensation elements makes the most sense for each sales job. Different combinations of fixed and variable compensation give rise to four basic types of compensation plans—straight salary, straight commission, salary plus bonus, and salary plus commission. A study of sales force compensation plans showed that 70 percent of all companies surveyed use a combination of base salary and incentives. The average plan consisted of about 60 percent salary and 40 percent incentive pay.[21]

The sales force compensation plan can both motivate salespeople and direct their activities. For example, if sales management wants salespeople to emphasize new account development, it might pay a bonus for opening new accounts. Thus, the compensation plan should direct the sales force toward activities that are consistent with overall marketing objectives.

Table 16.1 illustrates how a company's compensation plan should reflect its overall marketing strategy. For example, if the overall strategy is to grow rapidly and gain market share, the compensation plan should reward high sales performance and encourage salespeople to capture new accounts. This might suggest a larger commission component coupled with new-account bonuses. In contrast, if the marketing goal is to maximize profitability of current accounts, the compensation plan

TABLE 16.1   THE RELATIONSHIP BETWEEN OVERALL MARKETING STRATEGY AND SALES FORCE COMPENSATION

	STRATEGIC GOAL		
	To Gain Market Share Rapidly	**To Solidify Market Leadership**	**To Maximize Profitability**
Ideal salesperson	◆ An independent self-starter	◆ A competitive problem solver	◆ A team player ◆ A relationship manager
Sales focus	◆ Deal making ◆ Sustained high effort	◆ Consultative selling	◆ Account penetration
Compensation role	◆ To capture accounts ◆ To reward high performance	◆ To reward new and existing account sales	◆ To manage the product mix ◆ To encourage team selling ◆ To reward account management

Source: Adapted from Sam T. Johnson, "Sales Compensation: In Search of a Better Solution," *Compensation & Benefits Review,* November–December 1993, pp. 53–60. Copyright © 1998 American Management Association, NY, http://www.amanet.org. All Rights reserved, used with permission.

might contain a larger base-salary component, with additional incentives based on current account sales or customer satisfaction. In fact, more and more companies are moving away from high commission plans that may drive salespeople to make short-term grabs for business. Notes one sales force expert, "The last thing you want is to have someone ruin a customer relationship because they're pushing too hard to close a deal." Instead, companies are designing compensation plans that reward salespeople for building customer relationships and growing the long-run value of each customer.[22] (See Marketing Highlight 16.2.)

Supervising Salespeople

New salespeople need more than a territory, compensation, and training—they need *supervision*. Through supervision, the company *directs* and *motivates* the sales force to do a better job.

Directing Salespeople

How much should sales management be involved in helping salespeople manage their territories? It depends on everything from the company's size to the experience of its sales force. Thus, companies vary widely in how closely they supervise their salespeople.

Many companies help their salespeople in identifying customer targets and setting call norms. In addition, companies may specify how much time their sales forces should spend prospecting for new accounts. Companies may also direct salespeople in how to use their time efficiently. One tool is the *annual call plan* that shows which customers and prospects to call on in which months and which activities to carry out. Activities include taking part in trade shows, attending sales meetings, and carrying out marketing research. Another tool is *time-and-duty analysis*. In addition to time spent selling, the salesperson spends time traveling, waiting, eating, taking breaks, and doing administrative chores.

Figure 16.2 shows how salespeople spend their time. On average, actual face-to-face selling time accounts for less than 30 percent of total working time! If selling time could be raised from 30 percent to 40 percent, this would be a 33

MARKETING HIGHLIGHT

16.2

PAYING FOR CUSTOMER VALUE

For years, companies have paid their salespeople based on sales volume and dollar sales. Both are worthy goals, as long as the primary objective is selling the product. However, as the emphasis shifts to adding customer value, retaining customers and building strong relationships, and building "share of customer" (percentage of the customer's total business captured), companies are adding a new set of measures to their sales compensation equations. More and more, salespeople are being evaluated and compensated based on the following kinds of measures:

Long-term customer satisfaction: This requires a salesperson not to over-sell customers in the short run in order to satisfy a sales quota but to look out for customers' best interests and focus on helping them to achieve their goals.

Full customer service: This requires that the salesperson provide whatever customers need by working within the firm as well as building alliances with other companies that offer complementary products and services needed by customers. The goal: Never send a customer out the door to become someone else's customer.

Retention rates: The salesperson's goal becomes making sure that once a customer buys from the company, the customer doesn't buy from anyone else.

Growth of customer value: This involves increasing each customer's value to the company by increasing the customer's overall volume of business and capturing a greater share of that business. To make this happen, the salesperson must build strong relationships based on real value and customer success.

To see how including such measures in the compensation formula might affect a salesperson's performance, imagine rewarding a car salesperson differently. Most car dealerships reward salespeople for selling cars—each car sale results in a commission. Once the commission is paid, the salesperson turns to finding a new customer for the next sale. But what if, in addition to a token commission, the dealership rewarded the sales associate for long-term customer satisfaction, such as high 18-month satisfaction scores? Such rewards would motivate the salesperson to follow up with the customer, to make sure the service department was handling the customer well, and to identify and resolve a host of other problems that might upset the customer.

Suppose the dealership further rewarded the sales associate for share of customer. The associate would then find out what else is in the customer's garage and concentrate on ways to use the dealership's products to build "share of garage." If rewarded for such smart selling, the associate would find service, repair, and accessories for a customer and get them all under the dealership's roof. The dealership would know what the customer wanted next, and when. In addition, the sales associate would feed customer information into the dealership's database so that the customer would be served well even when the associate was on a well-earned vacation. Then, the dealership and the associate could work together to track customer needs electronically.

Most importantly, suppose that the dealership rewarded this salesperson for increasing long-term customer value to the dealership—perhaps by paying a tiny percentage of every dollar ever spent at the dealership by the customer on cars, financing, insurance, service, and repair. The salesperson would thus be motivated not just to make the sale but to make sure that each customer came back to this dealership for everything, forever.

To be sure, reaching this level of sophistication in sales force compensation will not be easy. Such measures are difficult to track and apply. However, salespeople usually do what they are rewarded for doing. Sales compensation plans can help motivate salespeople to build real relationships between customers and the company, increasing the value of each customer to the company.

Source: Adapted from Don Peppers and Martha Rogers, "The Money Trap," *Sales & Marketing Management,* May 1997, pp. 58–60. Also see James Champy, "Taking Sales to New Heights," *Sales & Marketing Management,* July 1998, p. 26; and Don Peppers and Martha Rogers, "The Price of Customer Service," *Sales & Marketing Management,* April 1999, pp. 20–21.

FIGURE 16.2   How salespeople spend their time
Source: Dartnell Corporation, 30th Sales Force Compensation Survey. © 1998 Dartnell Corporation.

percent increase in the time spent selling. Companies always are looking for ways to save time—using phones instead of traveling, simplifying record-keeping forms, finding better call and routing plans, and supplying more and better customer information.

Many firms have adopted *sales force automation systems,* computerized sales force operations for more efficient order-entry transactions, improved customer service, and better salesperson decision-making support. Salespeople use computers to profile customers and prospects, analyze and forecast sales, manage account relationships, schedule sales calls, make presentations, enter orders, check inventories and order status, prepare sales and expense reports, process correspondence, and carry out many other activities. Sales force automation not only lowers sales force costs and improves productivity, it also improves the quality of sales management decisions. Here is an example of successful sales force automation:[23]

> ★ Owens-Corning recently put its sales force online with FAST—its newly developed Field Automation Sales Team system. FAST gives Owens-Corning salespeople a constant supply of information about their company and the people they're dealing with. Using laptop computers, each salesperson can access three types of programs. First, FAST gives them a set of *generic tools,* everything from word processing to fax and e-mail transmission to creating presentations online. Second, it provides *product information*—tech bulletins, customer specifications, pricing information, and other data that can help close a sale. Finally, it offers up a wealth of *customer information*—buying history, types of products ordered, and preferred payment terms. Reps previously stored such information in loose-leaf books, calendars, and account cards. FAST makes working directly with customers easier than ever. Salespeople can prime themselves on backgrounds of clients; call up prewritten sales letters; transmit orders and resolve customer-service issues on the spot during customer calls; and have samples, pamphlets, brochures, and other materials sent to clients with a few keystrokes.

Perhaps the fastest-growing sales force technology tool is the Internet. In a survey by Dartnell Corporation of 1,000 salespeople, 61 percent reported using the Internet regularly in their daily selling activities. The most common uses include gathering competitive information, monitoring customer Web sites, and researching industries and specific customers. As more and more companies pro-

Sales force automation: Owens-Corning's FAST sales force automation system makes working directly with customers easier than ever.

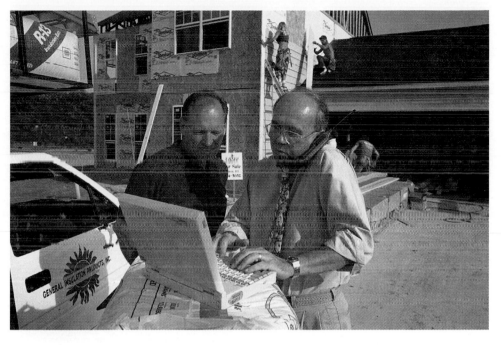

vide their salespeople with Web access, experts expect continued growth in sales force Internet usage.[24]

Motivating Salespeople

Some salespeople will do their best without any special urging from management. To them, selling may be the most fascinating job in the world. But selling can also be frustrating. Salespeople often work alone, and they must sometimes travel away from home. They may face aggressive competing salespeople and difficult customers. They sometimes lack the authority to do what is needed to win a sale and may thus lose large orders they have worked hard to obtain. Therefore, salespeople often need special encouragement to do their best.

Management can boost sales force morale and performance through its organizational climate, sales quotas, and positive incentives. *Organizational climate* describes the feeling that salespeople have about their opportunities, value, and rewards for a good performance within the company. Some companies treat salespeople as if they are not very important. Other companies treat their salespeople as their prime movers and allow virtually unlimited opportunity for income and promotion. Not surprisingly, in companies that hold their salespeople in low esteem, there is high turnover and poor performance. Where salespeople are held in high esteem, there is less turnover and higher performance.

Sales quotas

Standards set for salespeople, stating the amount they should sell and how sales should be divided among the company's products.

Many companies motivate their salespeople by setting **sales quotas**—standards stating the amount they should sell and how sales should be divided among the company's products. Compensation is often related to how well salespeople meet their quotas. Companies also use various *positive incentives* to increase sales force effort. *Sales meetings* provide social occasions, breaks from routine, chances to meet and talk with "company brass," and opportunities to air feelings and to identify with a larger group. Companies also sponsor *sales contests* to spur the sales force to make a selling effort above what would normally be expected. Other incentives include honors, merchandise and cash awards, trips, and profit-sharing plans.[25]

Sales force incentives: Many companies offer cash, trips, or merchandise as incentives. American Express suggests that companies reward out-standing sales performers with high-tech Persona Select cards—electronically prepaid reward cards that allow recipients to purchase whatever they want most.

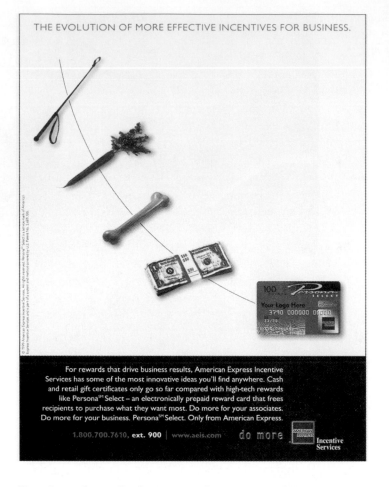

Evaluating Salespeople

We have thus far described how management communicates what salespeople should be doing and how it motivates them to do it. This process requires good feedback. Good feedback means getting regular information about salespeople to evaluate their performance. Management gets information about its salespeople in several ways. The most important source is *sales reports,* including weekly or monthly work plans and longer-term territory marketing plans. Salespeople also write up their completed activities on *call reports* and turn in *expense reports* for which they are partly or wholly repaid. Additional information comes from personal observation, customer surveys, and talks with other salespeople.

The sales manager might begin with a *qualitative evaluation,* looking at a salesperson's knowledge of the company, products, customers, competitors, territory, and tasks. Personal traits—manner, appearance, speech, and temperament—can be rated. The sales manager can also review any problems in motivation or compliance. Each company must decide what would be most useful to know. It should communicate these criteria to salespeople so that they understand how their performance is evaluated and can make an effort to improve it.

Using sales force reports and other information, sales management can also conduct a more *formal evaluation* of members of the sales force. Formal evaluation produces several benefits. It forces management to develop and communicate clear standards for judging performance and to gather well-balanced information about each salesperson. Formal evaluation gives salespeople constructive feedback that helps them to improve future performance. Finally, salespeople are motivated to perform well because they know they will have to sit down with the sales manager and explain their performance.

One type of formal evaluation compares and ranks the sales performance of one salesperson against others. Such comparisons can be misleading, however. Salespeople may perform differently because of differences in territory potential, workload, level of competition, company promotion effort, and other factors. Furthermore, sales are not usually the best indicator of achievement. Management should be more interested in how much each salesperson contributes to net profits, a concern that requires looking at each salesperson's sales mix and expenses.

A second type of formal evaluation compares a salesperson's current performance with past performance. Such a comparison should directly indicate the person's progress. Table 16.2 provides an example. The sales manager can learn many things about Chris Bennett from this table. Bennett's total sales increased every year (line 3). This does not necessarily mean that Bennett is doing a better job. The product breakdown shows that Bennett has been able to push the sales of product B further than those of product A (lines 1 and 2). According to the quotas for the two products (lines 4 and 5), the success in increasing product B sales may be at the expense of product A sales. According to gross profits (lines 6 and 7), the company earns twice as much gross profit (as a ratio to sales) on A as it does on B. Bennett may be pushing the higher-volume, lower-margin product at the expense of the more profitable product. Although Bennett increased total sales by $1,100 between 1998 and 1999 (line 3), the gross profits on these total sales actually decreased by $580 (line 8).

Sales expense (line 9) shows a steady increase, although total expense as a percentage of total sales seems to be under control (line 10). The upward trend in Bennett's total dollar expenses does not seem to be explained by any increase in the number of calls (line 11), although it may be related to his success in acquiring new customers (line 14). However, there is a possibility that in prospecting for new customers, Bennett is neglecting present customers, as indicated by an upward trend in the annual number of lost customers (line 15).

The last two lines in the table show the level and trend in Bennett's sales and gross profits per customer. These figures become more meaningful when they are compared with overall company averages. If Chris Bennett's average gross profit per

TABLE 16.2   EVALUATING SALESPEOPLE'S PERFORMANCE

Territory: Midland	Salesperson: Chris Bennett 1996	1997	1998	1999
1. Net sales product A	$251,300	$253,200	$270,000	$263,100
2. Net sales product B	$423,200	$439,200	553,900	561,900
3. Net sales total	$674,500	$692,400	$823,900	$825,000
4. Percent of quota product A	95.6	92.0	88.0	84.7
5. Percent of quota product B	120.4	122.3	134.9	130.8
6. Gross profits product A	$ 50,260	$ 50,640	$ 54,000	$ 52,620
7. Gross profits product B	$ 42,320	$ 43,920	$ 53,390	$ 56,190
8. Gross profits total	$ 92,580	$ 94,560	$109,390	$108,810
9. Sales expense	$ 10,200	$ 11,100	$ 11,600	$ 13,200
10. Sales expense to total sales (%)	1.5	1.6	1.4	1.6
11. Number of calls	1,675	1,700	1,680	1,660
12. Cost per call	$ 6.09	$ 6.53	$ 6.90	$ 7.95
13. Average number of customers	320	324	328	334
14. Number of new customers	13	14	15	20
15. Number of lost customers	8	10	11	14
16. Average sales per customer	$ 2,108	$ 2,137	$ 2,512	$ 2,470
17. Average gross profit per customer	$ 289	$ 292	$ 334	$ 326

customer is lower than the company's average, Chris may be concentrating on the wrong customers or may not be spending enough time with each customer. Looking back at the annual number of calls (line 11), Bennett may be making fewer calls than the average salesperson. If distances in the territory are not much different, this may mean Chris is not putting in a full workday, is poor at planning routing or minimizing waiting time, or spends too much time with certain accounts.

PRINCIPLES OF PERSONAL SELLING

We now turn from designing and managing a sales force to the actual personal selling process. Personal selling is an ancient art that has spawned a large body of literature and many principles. Effective salespeople operate on more than just instinct—they are highly trained in methods of territory analysis and customer management.

The Personal Selling Process

Most companies take a *customer-oriented approach* to personal selling. They train salespeople to identify customer needs and to find solutions. This approach assumes that customer needs provide sales opportunities, that customers appreciate good suggestions, and that customers will be loyal to salespeople who have their long-term interests at heart. The problem-solver salesperson fits better with the marketing concept than does a hard-sell salesperson or the glad-handing extrovert. Buyers today want solutions, not smiles; results, not razzle-dazzle. They want salespeople who listen to their concerns, understand their needs, and respond with the right products and services.

Selling process
The steps that the salesperson follows when selling, which include prospecting and qualifying, preapproach, approach, presentation and demonstration, handling objections, closing, and follow-up.

Steps in the Selling Process

Most training programs view the **selling process** as consisting of several steps that the salesperson must master (see Figure 16.3). These steps focus on the goal of getting new customers and obtaining orders from them. However, most salespeople spend much of their time maintaining existing accounts and building long-term customer *relationships*. We discuss the relationship aspect of the personal selling process in a later section.

Prospecting
The step in the selling process in which the salesperson identifies qualified potential customers.

Prospecting and Qualifying
The first step in the selling process is **prospecting**—identifying qualified potential customers. Approaching the right potential customers is crucial to selling success. As one expert puts it: "If the sales force starts chasing anyone who is breathing and

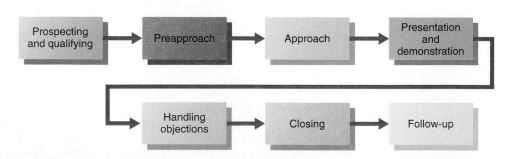

FIGURE 16.3 Major steps in effective selling

seems to have a budget, you risk accumulating a roster of expensive-to-serve, hard-to-satisfy customers who never respond to whatever value proposition you have." He continues, "The solution to this isn't rocket science. [You must] train salespeople to actively scout the right prospects. If necessary, create an incentive program to reward proper scouting."[26]

The salesperson must often approach many prospects to get just a few sales. Although the company supplies some leads, salespeople need skill in finding their own. They can ask current customers for referrals. They can build referral sources, such as suppliers, dealers, noncompeting salespeople, and bankers. They can join organizations to which prospects belong or can engage in speaking and writing activities that will draw attention. They can search for names in newspapers or directories and use the telephone and mail to track down leads. Or they can drop in unannounced on various offices (a practice known as "cold calling").

Salespeople also need to know how to *qualify* leads—that is, how to identify the good ones and screen out the poor ones. Prospects can be qualified by looking at their financial ability, volume of business, special needs, location, and possibilities for growth.

Preapproach

Preapproach
The step in the selling process in which the salesperson learns as much as possible about a prospective customer before making a sales call.

Before calling on a prospect, the salesperson should learn as much as possible about the organization (what it needs, who is involved in the buying) and its buyers (their characteristics and buying styles). This step is known as the **preapproach.** The salesperson can consult standard industry and online sources, acquaintances, and others to learn about the company. The salesperson should set *call objectives,* which may be to qualify the prospect, to gather information, or to make an immediate sale. Another task is to decide on the best approach, which might be a personal visit, a phone call, or a letter. The best timing should be considered carefully because many prospects are busiest at certain times. Finally, the salesperson should give thought to an overall sales strategy for the account.

Approach

Approach
The step in the selling process in which the salesperson meets and greets the buyer to get the relationship off to a good start.

During the **approach** step, the salesperson should know how to meet and greet the buyer and get the relationship off to a good start. This step involves the salesperson's appearance, opening lines, and the follow-up remarks. The opening lines should be positive, such as "Mr. Johnson, I am Chris Bennett from the Alltech Company. My company and I appreciate your willingness to see me. I will do my best to make this visit profitable and worthwhile for you and your company." This opening might be followed by some key questions to learn more about the customer's needs or by showing a display or sample to attract the buyer's attention and curiosity.

Presentation and Demonstration

Presentation
The step in the selling process in which the salesperson tells the product "story" to the buyer, showing how the product will make or save money for the buyer.

During the **presentation** step of the selling process, the salesperson tells the product "story" to the buyer, showing how the product will make or save money. The salesperson describes the product features but concentrates on presenting customer benefits. Using a *need-satisfaction approach,* the salesperson starts with a search for the customer's needs by getting the customer to do most of the talking.

This approach calls for good listening and problem-solving skills. "I think of myself more as a . . . well, psychologist," notes one experienced salesperson. "I listen to customers. I listen to their wishes and needs and problems, and I try to figure out a solution. If you're not a good listener, you're not going to get the order." Another salesperson suggests, "It's no longer enough to have a good relationship with a client. You have to understand their problems. You have to feel their pain."[27]

In the sales presentation, the salesperson tells the product story to the buyers.

The qualities that purchasing agents *dislike most* in salespeople include being pushy, late, and unprepared or disorganized. The qualities they *value most* include empathy, honesty, dependability, thoroughness, and follow-through.[28] Sales presentations can be improved with demonstration aids, such as booklets, flip charts, slides, videotapes or videodiscs, and product samples. If buyers can see or handle the product, they will better remember its features and benefits.

Sales presentations can be improved with product samples or demonstrations. Visual aids can show how a product performs and provide other information about it. Booklets and brochures remain useful as "leave behinds" for customer reference. Today, advanced presentation technologies allow for full multimedia presentations to only one or a few people. Audio and videocassettes, laptop computers with presentation software, and online presentation technologies have replaced the flip chart. Advanced Sterilization Products, a Johnson & Johnson company, even provides its sales force with a virtual reality presentation, called the STERRAD Experience. Originally designed for use at conferences, the presentation equipment has been redesigned for sales calls and consists of a small video player with five headsets, all easily transported in an ordinary-size briefcase. Prospects don a helmet for a virtual reality tour of the inner workings of the STERRAD Sterilization System for medical devices and surgical instruments. The presentation provides more information in a more engaging way than could be done by displaying the actual machinery.[29]

Handling Objections

Handling objections
The step in the selling process in which the salesperson seeks out, clarifies, and overcomes customer objections to buying.

Customers almost always have objections during the presentation or when asked to place an order. The problem can be either logical or psychological, and objections are often unspoken. In **handling objections,** the salesperson should use a positive approach, seek out hidden objections, ask the buyer to clarify any objections, take objections as opportunities to provide more information, and turn the objections into reasons for buying. Every salesperson needs training in the skills of handling objections.

Closing

Closing
The step in the selling process in which the salesperson asks the customer for an order.

After handling the prospect's objections, the salesperson now tries to close the sale. Some salespeople do not get around to **closing** or do not handle it well. They may lack confidence, feel guilty about asking for the order, or fail to recognize the right moment to close the sale. Salespeople should know how to recognize closing signals from the buyer, including physical actions, comments, and questions. For exam-

New sales presentation technologies: Advanced Sterilization Products, a Johnson & Johnson Company, provides its sales force with a presentation in which prospects don a helmet for a virtual reality tour of the inner workings of the STERRAD Sterilization System for medical devices and surgical instruments.

ple, the customer might sit forward and nod approvingly or ask about prices and credit terms. Salespeople can use one of several closing techniques. They can ask for the order, review points of agreement, offer to help write up the order, ask whether the buyer wants this model or that one, or note that the buyer will lose out if the order is not placed now. The salesperson may offer the buyer special reasons to close, such as a lower price or an extra quantity at no charge.

Follow-up

The last step in the selling process—**follow-up**—is necessary if the salesperson wants to ensure customer satisfaction and repeat business. Right after closing, the salesperson should complete any details on delivery time, purchase terms, and other matters. The salesperson then should schedule a follow-up call when the initial order is received to make sure there is proper installation, instruction, and servicing. This visit would reveal any problems, assure the buyer of the salesperson's interest, and reduce any buyer concerns that might have arisen since the sale.

Relationship Marketing

The principles of personal selling as just described are *transaction oriented*—their aim is to help salespeople close a specific sale with a customer. But in many cases, the company is not seeking simply a sale: It has targeted a major customer that it would like to win and keep. The company would like to show that it has the capabilities to serve the customer over the long haul in a mutually profitable *relationship*.

Most companies today are moving away from transaction marketing, with its emphasis on making a sale. Instead, they are practicing **relationship marketing,** which emphasizes maintaining profitable long-term relationships with customers by creating superior customer value and satisfaction. They are realizing that when operating in maturing markets and facing stiffer competition, it costs a lot more to wrest new customers from competitors than to keep current customers.

Today's customers are large and often global. They prefer suppliers who can sell and deliver a coordinated set of products and services to many locations. They favor suppliers who can quickly solve problems that arise in their different parts of the nation or world, and who can work closely with customer teams to improve products and processes. For these customers, the sale is only the beginning of the relationship.

Follow-up

The last step in the selling process in which the salesperson follows up after the sale to ensure customer satisfaction and repeat business.

Relationship marketing

The process of creating, maintaining, and enhancing strong, value-laden relationships with customers and other stakeholders.

MARKETING HIGHLIGHT 16.3

GREAT SALESPEOPLE—DRIVE, DISCIPLINE, AND RELATIONSHIP-BUILDING SKILLS

What sets great salespeople apart from all the rest? What separates the masterful from the merely mediocre? In an effort to profile top sales performers, Gallup Management Consulting, a division of the well-known Gallup polling organization, has interviewed as many as half a million salespeople. Its research suggests that the best salespeople possess four key talents: intrinsic motivation, disciplined work style, the ability to close a sale, and, perhaps most important, the ability to build relationships with customers.

Intrinsic Motivation

"Different things drive different people—pride, happiness, money, you name it," says one expert. "But all great salespeople have one thing in common: an unrelenting drive to excel." This strong, internal drive can be shaped and molded, but it can't be taught. The source of the motivation varies—some are driven by money, some by hunger for recognition, some by a yearning to build relationships.

The Gallup research revealed four general personality types, all high performers, but all with different sources of motivation. *Competitors* are people who not only want to win but crave the satisfaction of beating specific rivals—other companies *and* their fellow salespeople. They'll come right out and say to a colleague, "With all due respect, I know you're salesperson of the year, but I'm going after your title." The *ego driven* are salespeople who just want to experience the glory of winning. They want to be recognized as being the best, regardless of the competition. *Achievers* are a rare breed who are almost completely self-motivated. They like accomplishment and routinely set goals that are higher than what is expected of them. They often make the best sales managers because they don't mind seeing other people

succeed, as long as the organization's goals are met. Finally, *service-oriented* salespeople are those whose strength lies in their ability to build and cultivate relationships. They are generous, caring, and empathetic. "These people are golden," says the national training manager of Minolta Corporation's business equipment division. "We need salespeople who will take the time to follow up on the 10 questions a customer might have, salespeople who love to stay in touch."

No one is purely a competitor, an achiever, ego driven, or service driven. There's at least some of each in most top performers. "A *competitor* with a strong sense of *service* will probably bring in a lot of business while doing a great job of taking care of customers," observes the managing director of the Gallup Management Consulting Group. "Who could ask for anything more?"

Unfortunately, some companies are not set up for these developments. They often sell their products through separate sales forces, each working independently to close sales. Their technical people may not be willing to lend time to educate a customer. Their engineering, design, and manufacturing people may have the attitude that "it's our job to make good products and the salesperson's to sell them to customers." However, other companies are recognizing that winning and keeping accounts requires more than making good products and directing the sales force to close lots of sales. It requires a carefully coordinated whole-company effort to create value-laden, satisfying relationships with important customers.

Disciplined Work Style

Whatever their motivation, if salespeople aren't organized and focused, and if they don't work hard, they can't meet the ever-increasing demands customers are making these days. Great salespeople are tenacious about laying out detailed, organized plans, then following through in a timely, disciplined way. There's no magic here, just solid organization and hard work. "Our best sales reps never let loose ends dangle," says the president of a small business equipment firm. "If they say they're going to make a follow-up call on a customer in six months, you can be sure that they'll be on the doorstep in six months." Top sellers rely on hard work, not luck or gimmicks. "Some people say it's all technique or luck," notes one sales trainer. "But luck happens to the best salespeople when they get up early, work late, stay up till two in the morning working on a proposal, or keep making calls when everyone is leaving at the end of the day."

The Ability to Close the Sale

Other skills mean little if a seller can't ask for the sale. No close, no sale. Period. So what makes for a great closer? For one thing, an unyielding persistence, say managers and sales consultants. Claims one, "Great closers are like great athletes. They're not afraid to fail, and they don't give up until they close." Part of what makes the failure rate tolerable for top performers is their deep-seated belief in themselves and what they are selling. Great closers have a high level of self-confidence and believe that they are doing the right thing. They also have got a burning need to make the sale happen—to do whatever it takes within legal and ethical standards to get the business.

The Ability to Build Relationships

Perhaps most important in today's relationship-marketing environment, top salespeople are customer problem solvers and relationship builders. They have an instinctive understanding of their customers' needs. Talk to sales executives and they'll describe top performers in these terms: Empathetic. Patient. Caring. Responsive. Good listeners. Even *honest*. Top sellers can put themselves on the buyer's side of the desk and see the world through their customers' eyes. Today, customers are looking for business partners, not golf partners. "At the root of it all," says a Dallas sales consultant, "is an integrity of intent. High performers don't just want to be liked, they want to add value." High-performing salespeople, he adds, are "always thinking about the big picture, where the customer's organization is going, and how they can help them get there."

Sources: Adapted from Geoffrey Brewer, "Mind Reading: What Drives Top Salespeople to Greatness?" *Sales & Marketing Management,* May 1994, pp. 82–88. Also see Barry J. Farber, "Success Stories for Salespeople," *Sales & Marketing Management,* May 1995, pp. 30–31; Roberta Maynard, "Finding the Essence of Good Salespeople," *Nation's Business,* February 1998, p. 10; Jeanie Casison, "Closest Thing to Cloning," *Incentive,* June 1999, p. 7; and Erika Rasmusson, "The 10 Traits of Top Salespeople," *Sales & Marketing Management,* August 1999, pp. 34–37.

Relationship marketing is based on the premise that important accounts need focused and ongoing attention. Studies have shown that the best salespeople are those who are highly motivated and good closers, but more than this, they are customer problem solvers and relationship builders (see Marketing Highlight 16.3). Good salespeople working with key customers do more than call when they think a customer might be ready to place an order. They also study the account and understand its problems. They call or visit frequently, work with the customer to help solve the customer's problems and improve its business, and take an interest in customers as people.

REVIEW OF CONCEPT CONNECTIONS

Selling is one of the world's oldest professions. People who do the selling are called by a variety of names, including *salespeople, sales representatives, account executives, sales consultants, sales engineers, agents, district managers,* and *marketing representatives.* Regardless of their titles, members of the sales force play a key role in modern marketing organizations.

The term *salesperson* covers a wide spectrum of positions. Salespeople may be *order takers,* such as the department store salesperson who stands behind the counter. Or they may be *order getters,* salespeople engaged in the *creative selling* of products and services such as appliances, industrial equipment, advertising, or consulting services, and so forth. Other salespeople do *missionary selling,* in which they are not involved in taking an order but in building goodwill or educating buyers. To be successful in these more creative forms of selling, a company must first build and then manage an effective sales force.

1. Discuss the role of a company's salespeople in creating value for customers and building customer relationships.

Most companies use salespeople, and many companies assign them an important role in the marketing mix. For companies selling business products, the firm's salespeople work directly with customers. Often, the sales force is the customer's only direct contact with the company and, therefore, may be viewed by customers as representing the company itself. In contrast, for consumer product companies that sell through intermediaries, consumers usually do not meet salespeople or even know about them. But the sales force works behind the scenes, dealing with wholesalers and retailers to obtain their support and helping them become effective in selling the firm's products.

As an element of the marketing mix, the sales force is very effective in achieving certain marketing objectives and carrying out such activities as prospecting, communicating, selling and servicing, and information gathering. But with companies becoming more market oriented, a market-focused sales force also works to produce *customer satisfaction* and *company profit.* To accomplish these goals, the sales force needs skills in marketing analysis and planning in addition to the traditional selling skills.

The high cost of the sales force calls for an effective *sales management process* consisting of six steps: *designing sales force strategy and structure, recruiting and selecting, training, compensating, supervising,* and *evaluating* salespeople.

2. Explain how companies design sales force strategy and structure.

In designing a sales force, sales management must address issues such as what type of sales force structure will work best (territorial, product, customer, or complex structured);

how large the sales force should be; who will be involved in the selling effort and how its various sales and sales support people will work together (inside or outside sales forces and team selling).

3. Explain how companies recruit, select, and train salespeople.

To hold down the high costs of hiring the wrong people, salespeople must be *recruited* and *selected* carefully. In recruiting salespeople, a company may look to job duties and the characteristics of its most successful salespeople to suggest the traits it wants in its salespeople and then look for applicants through recommendations of current salespeople, employment agencies, classified ads, and by contacting college students. In the selection process, the procedure can vary from a single informal interview to lengthy testing and interviewing. After the selection process is complete, *training* programs familiarize new salespeople not only with the art of selling but also with the company's history, its products and policies, and the characteristics of its market and competitors.

4. Describe how companies compensate and supervise salespeople, and how they evaluate sales force effectiveness.

The sales force *compensation* system helps to reward, motivate, and direct salespeople. In compensating salespeople, companies try to have an appealing plan, usually close to the going rate for the type of sales job and needed skills. In addition to compensation, all salespeople need *supervision,* and many need continuous encouragement because they must make many decisions and face many frustrations. Periodically, the company must *evaluate* their performance to help them do a better job. In evaluating salespeople the company relies on getting regular information gathered through sales reports, personal observations, customers' letters and complaints, customer surveys, and conversations with other salespeople.

5. Discuss the personal selling process, distinguishing between transaction-oriented marketing and relationship marketing.

The art of selling involves a seven-step *selling process: prospecting and qualifying, preapproach, approach, presentation and demonstration, handling objections, closing,* and *follow-up.* These steps help marketers close a specific sale and as such are *transaction oriented.* However, a seller's dealings with customers should be guided by the larger concept of *relationship marketing.* The company's sales force should help to orchestrate a whole-company effort to develop profitable long-term relationships with key customers based on superior customer value and satisfaction.

KEY TERMS

Approach	Preapproach	Sales quotas
Closing	Presentation	Selling process
Customer sales force structure	Product sales force structure	Team selling
Follow-up	Prospecting	Telemarketing
Handling objections	Relationship marketing	Territorial sales force structure
Inside sales force	Sales force management	Workload approach
Outside sales force	Salesperson	

ISSUES FOR DISCUSSION

1. What did Robert Louis Stevenson mean when he said "everyone lives by selling something"? Describe all the various roles the modern salesperson might be required to fill or play.

2. The term *salesperson* covers a wide range of positions. List and briefly describe the positions that are normally filled by a salesperson. Provide an example of each of these positions. State what your career ambition is and briefly state how you might be involved in selling.

3. One of the most pressing issues that sales managers face is how to structure salespeople and their tasks. Evaluate the methods described in the text. For each method, provide (a) a brief description of its chief characteristics, (b) an example of how it's used, and (c) a critique of its effectiveness.

4. Telemarketing and Web-based selling (see Marketing Highlight 16.1) provide marketers with opportunities to reach customers at work and in their homes. Critique each of these approaches, discussing the advantages and disadvantages of each. Provide an example of product or service marketing that uses each approach and discuss how the selling process works in these examples.

5. What is team selling and what are its advantages and disadvantages? How would recruiting and training for a sales team differ from recruiting and training for individual selling?

6. Many people think that they do not have the attributes and abilities required for successful selling. What role does training play in helping a person develop selling skills and ability?

7. List and briefly describe the steps involved in the personal selling process. Which step do you think is most difficult for the average salesperson? Which step is the most critical to successful selling? Which step do you think is usually done most correctly? Explain each of your choices.

8. Explain the meaning of relationship marketing. Describe how relationship marketing might be used in (a) selling a personal computer to a final consumer, (b) selling a new car, (c) providing a student with a college education, and (d) selling season tickets to a local drama theater.

MARKETING APPLICATIONS

1. Being a stock broker can be an exciting and challenging occupation. In years past, young broker trainees received extensive training on the technical workings of the stock market and the characteristics of potential clients. One of the most difficult tasks for new brokers was finding and developing clients. This involved long and often discouraging hours on the telephone "prospecting" and "cold-calling" potential clients. Today, however, things are changing. The rapid expansion of investment and information alternatives have made the broker's job more challenging. Most major investment services brokerages are now online and brokers can now help information-hungry investors in ways that would have been unimaginable only a few years ago. Visit the following

Web sites: E★Trade (www.etrade.com), Fidelity Investments (www.fidelity.com), DLJ Direct (www.dljdirect.com), Charles Schwab (www.schwab.com), Suretrade (www.suretrade.com), Datek (www.datek.com), and Waterhouse (www.waterhouse.com).

a. How have such sites changed the brokerage business? How is the selling function in the brokerage business changing?

b. How can online brokerage services help the average broker to be a more effective salesperson? What sales strategies appear to be most appropriate for the broker who wishes to use personal contact and online connections to do business?

c. Which Web site did you find to be the most "user friendly?" Why? Which of the sites would make it easiest for you to get in touch with a broker in your local area? How could the local broker find out that you had been using his or her company's online service?

d. Prepare an analysis grid that compares the above sites on sales stimulation, information services, cost, graphic design, responsiveness, security, and relationship marketing. Which site is best? Why?

2. Jonathan Ellermann was excited about his new job as a personal communication consultant for Nokia (www.nokia.com), the giant phone producer that captures a quarter of the global market and half the profits. Rivals such as Ericsson (www.ericsson.se), Vodafone (www.vodaphone.com), Panasonic (www.panasonic.com), and Motorola (www.motorola.com) have vowed to make things tougher for Nokia in the coming year. They've developed new designs, communications applications, and strategic alliances between hardware and software makers in an effort to lure fickle consumers away from Nokia.

a. Ellermann is attempting to sell Nokia's latest model personal communication device to Shell Oil's Houston branch (approximately 5,000 phones). What sales strategy and plan should Ellermann recommend? In your answer, consider the advantages and disadvantages of Nokia's product.

b. Would you recommend that Nokia employ individual selling or team selling? Explain.

c. Which step of the sales process do you think will be most critical to Ellermann's success?

d. What could Ellermann do to establish a strong relationship with local Shell representatives?

 INTERNET CONNECTION

PROSPECTING ONLINE

One interesting way to build a prospect list online is to find out which Web sites are linked to your site. By placing a link to your site, the business has demonstrated an interest in your product and, therefore, is a potential customer. The AltaVista search engine (www.altavista.com) provides a feature that automatically constructs this list. Herman Miller, Inc. sells office furniture and systems to businesses, and it might use this feature to develop leads for the salespeople. In the AltaVista search box type "link:www.hermanmiller.com" to find out which sites are linked to Herman Miller's home page. From that list, select four sites that might be good prospects and explain why you chose them.

Company	Web address	Reason for inclusion

FOR DISCUSSION

1. How could Herman Miller use the same search feature to find out which prospective customers have an interest in competitive office furniture stores? Would these constitute good prospects for Herman Miller? Why or why not?

2. What is the next step after building the prospect list?

3. How could Herman Miller identify prospects directly on its own Web site?

4. How could Herman Miller use e-mail to move prospects closer to purchase?

SAVVY SITES

- *Sales & Marketing Management* (www.salesandmarketing. com) is a "magazine for executives who want to build sales, stay ahead of the competition, keep up with technology, and market their companies to today's tough customers."

- Looking for a job in sales? Some of the best sites for finding jobs in any field are www.monster.com, www.careerpath. com, and www.careermosaic.com.

- Dale Carnegie (www.dalecarnegie.com) is the master of sales training. At this site you can get tips as well as take some interesting tests such as "Are you a workaholic?"

NOTES

1. Quotes from Andy Cohen, "Top of the Charts: Lear Corporation," *Sales & Marketing Management,* July 1998, p. 40. Also see Sarah Lorge, "Better Off Branded," *Sales & Marketing Management,* March 1998, pp. 39–42; Terril Yue Jones, "The Forbes Platinum: Consumer Durables: Low-Cost Supplier," *Forbes,* January 11, 1999, pp. 156–58; "Lear Corporation," *Sales & Marketing Management,* July 1999, p. 62; and "This Is Lear," accessed online at www.lear.com/d.htm, March 2000.

2. See Bill Kelley, "How to Sell Airplanes, Boeing-Style," *Sales & Marketing Management,* December 9, 1985, pp. 32–34; Andy Cohen, "Boeing," *Sales & Marketing Management,* October 1997, p. 68; and Laurence Zukerman, "On Center Runway, Boeing's Little 717," *New York Times,* June 15, 1999, p. 6.

3. Patricia Sellers, "How to Remake Your Sales Force," *Fortune,* May 4, 1992, p. 96. Also see Charles Fleming and Leslie Lopez, "The Corporate Challenge—No Boundaries. ABB's Dramatic Plan Is to Recast Its Business Structure Along Global Lines," *Wall Street Journal,* September 28, 1998, p. R16; and "Employing 200,000 People in over 100 Countries," accessed online at www.abb.com, September 1999.

4. Geoffrey Brewer, "Love the Ones You're With," *Sales & Marketing Management,* February 1997, pp. 38–45.

5. Melinda Ligos, "The Incredible Shrinking Sales Force," *Sales & Marketing Management,* December 1998, p. 15.

6. Ibid., p. 15.

7. See Michele Marchetti, "The Costs of Doing Business," *Sales & Marketing Management,* September 1999, p. 56.

8. See Martin Everett, "Selling by Telephone," *Sales & Marketing Management,* December 1993, pp. 75–79.

9. Geoffrey Brewer, "Lou Gerstner Has His Hands Full," *Sales & Marketing Management,* May 8, 1998, pp. 36–41.

10. See "A Phone Is Better Than a Face," *Sales & Marketing Management,* October 1987, p. 29. Also see Brett A. Boyle, "The Importance of the Industrial Inside Sales Force: A Case Study," *Industrial Marketing Management,* September 1996, pp. 339–48; Victoria Fraza, "Upgrading Inside Sales," *Industrial Distribution,* December

1997, pp. 44–49; and Michele Marchetti, "Look Who's Calling," *Sales & Marketing Management,* May 1998, pp. 43–46.

11. Richard C. Whiteley, "Orchestrating Service," *Sales & Marketing Management,* April 1994, pp. 29–30.

12. Rick Mullin, "From Lone Wolves to Team Players," *Chemical Week,* January 14, 1998, pp. 33–34.

13. Robert Hiebeler, Thomas B. Kelly, and Charles Ketteman, *Best Practices: Building Your Business with Customer-focused Solutions* (New York: Arthur Andersen/Simon & Schuster, 1998), pp. 122–24. Also see Richard C. Whiteley, "Orchestrating Service," *Sales & Marketing Management,* April 1994, pp. 29–30; Mark A. Moon and Susan Forquer Gupta, "Examining the Formation of Selling Centers: A Conceptual Framework," *Journal of Personal Selling and Sales Management,* Spring 1997, pp. 31–41; and Donald W. Jackson Jr., Scott M. Widmier, Ralph Giacobbe, and Janet E. Keith, "Examining the Use of Team Selling by Manufacturers' Representatives: A Situational Approach," *Industrial Marketing Management,* March 1999, pp. 155–64.

14. See Christopher Meyer, "How the Right Measures Help Teams Excel," *Harvard Business Review,* May–June 1994, pp. 95–103; Michele Marchetti, "Why Teams Fail," *Sales & Marketing Management,* June 1997, p. 91; Melinda Ligos, "On with the Show," *Sales & Marketing Management,* November 1998, pp. 70–76; and Jackson, Widmier, Giacobbe, and Keith, "Examining the Use of Team Selling by Manufacturers' Representatives: A Situational Approach," pp. 155–64.

15. See George H. Lucas Jr., A. Parasuraman, Robert A. Davis, and Ben M. Enis, "An Empirical Study of Sales Force Turnover," *Journal of Marketing,* July 1987, pp. 34–59; Lynn G. Coleman, "Sales Force Turnover Has Managers Wondering Why," *Marketing News,* December 4, 1989, p. 6; Thomas R. Wotruba and Pradeep K. Tyagi, "Met Expectations and Turnover in Direct Selling," *Journal of Marketing,* July 1991, pp. 24–35; and Chad Kaydo, "Overturning Turnover," *Sales & Marketing Management,* November 1997, pp. 50–60.

16. See Geoffrey Brewer, "Mind Reading: What Drives Top Salespeople to Greatness?" *Sales & Marketing Management,* May 1994, pp. 82–88; Barry J. Farber, "Success Stories for Salespeople," *Sales & Marketing Management,* May 1995, pp. 30–31; Roberta Maynard, "Finding the Essence of Good Salespeople," *Nation's Business,* February 1998, p. 10; and Jeanie Casison, "Closest Thing to Cloning," *Incentive,* June 1999, p. 7.

17. "23 Percent of U.S. Salespeople Are Women," *American Salesman,* April 1995, p. 8. Also see Nancy Arnott, "It's a Woman's World," *Sales & Marketing Management,* March 1995, pp. 55–59; "Selling Sales to Students," *Sales & Marketing Management,* January 1998, p. 15; and Ray Holley, "Corporate Pirates Wage Battles for Top Salespeople," *Computer Reseller News,* June 21, 1999, p. 107.

18. See "To Test or Not to Test," *Sales & Marketing Management,* May 1994, p. 86.

19. Sarah Lorge, "Getting into Their Heads," *Sales & Marketing Management,* February 1998, pp. 58–67.

20. Robert Klein, "Nabisco Sales Soar After Sales Training," *Marketing News,* January 6, 1997, p. 23.

21. Christen P. Heide, "All Levels of Sales Reps Post Impressive Earnings," press release, www.dartnell.com, May 5, 1997; and *Dartnell's 30th Sales Force Compensation Survey,* Dartnell Corporation, August 1998.

22. Geoffrey Brewer, "Brain Power," *Sales & Marketing Management,* May 1997, pp. 39–48; Don Peppers and Martha Rogers, "The Money Trap," *Sales & Marketing Management,* May 1997, pp. 58–60; Michele Marchetti, "No Commissions? Are You Crazy?" *Sales & Marketing Management,* May 1998, p. 83; and Don Peppers and Martha Rogers, "The Price of Customer Service," *Sales & Marketing Management,* April 1999, pp. 20–21.

23. Tony Seideman, "Who Needs Managers?" *Sales & Marketing Management,* part 2, June 1994, pp. 15–17. Also see Tim McCollum, "High-Tech Marketing Hits the Target," *Nation's Business,* June 1997, pp. 39–42; Ginger Conlon, "Plug and Play," *Sales & Marketing Management,* December 1998, pp. 64–67; and Erika Rasmusson, "The 5 Steps to Successful Sales Force Automation," *Sales & Marketing Management,* March 1999, pp. 34–40.

24. Christen Heide, "Rep Use of the Internet Up 226 Percent in 2 Years," *Sales & Marketing Management Executive Report,* August 19, 1998, pp. 8–9; and Melinda Ligos, "Point, Click, and Sell," *Sales & Marketing Management,* May 1999, pp. 51–56.

25. For more on sales incentives, see Vincent Alonzo, "Money Isn't Everything," *Sales & Marketing Management,* January 1999, pp. 28–29; and James Champy, "Are Your Sellers Devoted to the Cause?" *Sales & Marketing Management,* May 1999, p. 22.

26. Bob Donath, "Delivering Value Starts with Proper Prospecting," *Marketing News,* November 10, 1997, p. 5. Also see Sarah Lorge, "The Best Way to Prospect," *Sales & Marketing Management,* January 1998, p. 80.

27. David Stamps, "Training for a New Sales Game," *Training,* July 1997, pp. 46–52.

28. Brewer, "Brain Power," p. 42; and Rosemay P. Ramsey and Ravipreet S. Sohi, "Listening to Your Customers: The Impact of Perceived Salesperson Listening Behavior on Relationship Outcomes," *Journal of the Academy of Marketing Science,* Spring 1997, pp. 127–37.

29. "Briefcase Full of Views: Johnson & Johnson Uses Virtual Reality to Give Prospects an Inside Look at Its Products," *American Demographics,* April 1997.

COMPANY CASE

16

CDW: Restructuring the Sales Force

THE THIRD INTERVIEW

Brady Hilshire stared at the pages before him and sighed. His interview process had gone very well so far. In fact, he was beginning the third step in the interview process with CDW Computer Centers, Inc. The company had just moved up to number 11 from number 36 on *Fortune* magazine's list of the "100 Best Companies to Work for in America," and he wanted a job offer. This interview, he believed, would be the clincher.

To begin this third step, the CDW recruiter had given Brady a brief case study on the company. His instructions were to read the case carefully, identify a crucial problem facing CDW, develop several solutions to the problem, pick the best solution, and write up his recommendation to the company. Brady took a deep breath and began to read.

A SHOOTING STAR

Things had gone very well for CDW since its humble beginnings on CEO Michael Krasny's kitchen table in 1982. Krasny sold his first computer, a used IBM PC, through a classified ad in the *Chicago Tribune,* discovering that he could add value and make money by reselling computers. Over the years, CDW gradually transformed into a direct marketer of brand-name computers, accessories, peripherals, and software from companies such as Compaq, IBM, Hewlett-Packard, Microsoft, and Toshiba. By 1988, the company's growth dictated a move to a new 28,000-square-foot facility in Northbrook, Illinois; and by 1991 it had 143 employees. In May 1993 CDW successfully went public, ending the year with $270 million in sales and 247 employees. That was only the beginning.

Each year following its initial public offering, CDW set new performance records. In 1995, CDW was among the first US companies to launch an e-business Web site. In 1996, the company won *Computer Shopper's* Best Buy award for Best Vendor Web Site. In 1997, CDW reached $1 billion in sales; *Fortune* recognized it as one of "America's 100 Fastest-Growing Companies," and *Computer Retail Week* selected it as the Retailer of the Year. In 1998, CDW joined the *Fortune* 1000 at number 868, and *PC Magazine* recognized it as one of America's "100 Most Influential Companies." Analysts estimated that CDW, a company that started with a single man and a single computer, finished 1999 with an estimated $2.5 billion in sales, more than 2,000 employees, some 600,000 customers, thousands of products, and a sales growth rate more than twice that of the industry!

A SUCCESSFUL CORPORATE STRATEGY

Glancing over his case study, Brady noted that from the beginning CDW had held fast to its CEO's original business model—what the company called a win–win philosophy among CDW's co-workers, customers, vendors, and shareholders. The company expressed this philosophy in its mission statement: "To be one of the nation's highest-volume computer resellers selling brand-name products; to provide a fun and challenging work environment and above-average earnings; and to maintain a high net profit by running a lean, highly automated, systems-oriented company." Brady reflected that the mission statement was supported by a dozen or so "philosophies of success" that he had seen posted throughout the colorful work areas in the 318,000-square foot facility in Vernon Hills, Illinois—sayings such as "It's only good if it's win–win!" and "Smile! People can hear your smile through the phone."

The company's true basis for its success, however, rested on CDW's Circle of Service, meaning that everything CDW did revolved around providing the best customer service possible. That meant the right support and excellent execution—as defined by the customer. To this end, CDW had invested in warehouse automation, in-depth training of its sales force, sales force automation, and other innovations to provide unparalleled expertise and unmatched response time focused on relevant customer concerns. The company's goal was to "treat every customer as if they were your *only* customer." CDW refined that treatment on an ongoing basis by following the philosophy that "success means never being satisfied."

THE SALES FORCE STRUCTURE

Analysts attributed much of CDW's success to a highly trained, highly competent inside sales force that reached customers through inbound/outbound calling and direct-mail catalogs. CDW targeted its selling efforts toward business clients, maintaining a core strength in small and medium-size businesses and continued growth and concentration in large business customers. The sales force worked out of the Chicago area in either Buffalo Grove or Vernon Hills with all operations and shipping handled out of their headquarters in Vernon Hills. The company trained its sales force of approximately 850 account managers as generalists to assist virtually any customer, drawing where necessary on technical support from dedicated vendor hotlines, vendor representatives, electronic information available on the Web, and dedicated presales network technicians. The company trained each of its account managers to take a proactive, entrepreneurial selling approach—but maintained its goal of cooperation and a fun work environment by assigning account managers to teams with street, city, and state names. For example, one team was Fisherman's Wharf, a part of the San Francisco group, which was part of California state. There were typically eight or fewer salespeople in a "street," three to four streets in a "city," and three to four cities in a "state." "Street contests" pitted street against street in a variety of lively competitions, such as company- or vendor-sponsored sales contests to promote new products or to increase attention on company focus areas.

CDW's customers interfaced with the sales force in a variety of ways. The company assigned call-in customers to the account manager who answered the customer's original call. Additionally, account managers proactively developed accounts by profiling business needs and providing business assistance through a broad range of technical products and value added services. Account managers picked up Internet customers via random assignment. That is, once a new customer (a new company) made its first purchase on the Web site, the CDW information system automatically posted the company and contact person's name and randomly assigned the company to a salesperson who was Web certified (i.e., had passed the tests on basic CDW Web page use). Typically, developing a profitable account base took an account manager between 6 and 18 months, depending on account complexity and account manager tenure. Account managers maintained account ownership as long as the customer was satisfied and actively purchasing. No matter the initial type of contact, however, account managers worked to identify short- and long-term opportunities, building strong relationships with their customers and seeking to provide full solutions.

CDW recruited both experienced salespeople and recent college graduates. To hire experienced salespeople, the recruiting staff generated a resume stream through an

Internet presence, local job fairs, and newspapers. The staff recruited on college campuses fall and midwinter seeking to build long-term relationships with a select group of schools. New hires, after three to six months of intensive training, began as account managers. The company assigned them randomly, or based on need, to one of the street teams. After two years of selling experience, account managers could earn the right to be "street leaders."

CDW paid their account managers on a monthly commission basis. The company guaranteed each account manager a minimum predetermined commission level and a substantial draw. An account manager earned commission based on his or her gross profit shipped. Within guidelines, each account manager could control profit margins based on customer volume and needs. However, although CDW wanted to offer competitive prices, it did not want to compete based on price alone. The commission rate could increase significantly based on sales goals achieved, certification, and the ability to act as a value-added business consultant for the client. Successful salespeople could move out of direct selling and into sales management. Sales managers assumed responsibility for all streets within a given city. Senior sales managers assumed responsibility for all cities within a given state, and the general sales manager coordinated the entire sales force, reporting to the vice president of sales.

Brady noted that the company emphasized technical training for the sales force, establishing its own CDW University in 1990. Furthermore, it focused on personal development of its salespeople through a variety of certifications, ongoing training, and development of management skills. Brady also noted that in 1998, CDW had modified its selling structure by creating CDW-G, a subsidiary focused exclusively on meeting the needs of government and education customers. Analysts predicted that CDW would increase the total number of account managers by more than 40 percent by the end of 2000.

A WEB PRESENCE

In 1995, CDW developed its Web site, www.cdw.com, to support the sales force's efforts to provide excellent customer service. The company maintained a focus on e-business, which it defined as providing added value for its business partners through a variety of Web support services—moving beyond the traditional e-commerce models that often amounted to discrete, unassisted retail sales on the Web. Although any individual or company could go to the site and make a purchase, CDW believed that if a customer did any significant business with the company, it would have to have the technical assistance that its salespeople and technical specialists could offer. CDW wanted to build relationships with its customers.

The company's early entry into e-business started with Web site access to consumer product information and specifications. Later in 1995, CDW added other site capabilities to allow consumers to track the status of orders placed through account managers, and in 1996 the company expanded its Web site's capabilities to include direct sales. At that time, the company added online account creation and ordering capabilities to the existing advertising and marketing information.

Late in 1996, without restructuring its sales force, the company made a strategic push toward focusing on business customers. To complement the focus, CDW enhanced its Web site to focus on business-to-business relationships. The company improved the Web site's functionality by introducing new tools for business customers. For example, the site notified buyers of pertinent price cuts, provided support for direct returns to vendors, and listed full product catalogs. At the end of 1998, CDW introduced extranets—direct, secured links between the customer and CDW that facilitated the customer's procurement process. The extranets provided customers with better access to critical business information, including more detailed order status information, serial-number tracking, and purchase acquisition summaries. A staff of 25 IT support people worked continuously on enhancing and perfecting Web site support for CDW's business customers. In 1999, direct Web sales averaged about 6 percent of total sales, and *PC Week* ranked CDW's Web site as the number-one e-commerce site for IT buyers.

THE CHALLENGE

Brady sat back and looked at the case study, considering the dilemma of finding a problem with a company that seemed to have done just about everything right. Nonetheless, he thought, the challenges for all companies involved with computers were very real. Industry issues for CDW would have to include problems such as margin erosion in high-technology goods, limited product availability as a result of vendor production capabilities, volatile overseas markets, new entrants into the computer reselling business, and a growing interest in direct Internet sales, among others. Direct challenges within the company itself would likely include recruiting, training, and developing hundreds of account managers, meeting continued needs for increased capacity, maintaining superior customer service, and keeping a sales force structure supportive of CDW's goals.

After reviewing the case information one last time, Brady decided to focus on the issue of sales force structure for his interview question. As he began to think about CDW's customers and to envision himself as a member of one of

CDW's street teams, he wondered what sales force strategy CDW should use to sustain its phenomenal growth and earnings while still maintaining outstanding customer service and a highly motivated sales force.

Questions

1. What problems do you see with CDW's current sales force strategy and structure?
2. What blend of inside selling and Web site support would generate the most customer satisfaction for CDW's business customers? Would you recommend encouraging e-commerce rather than e-business as the case defines the two terms?
3. What impact would the upcoming rapid increase in the size of CDW's sales force have on your recommendations for a sales force strategy and structure?
4. Given your recommendations, what actions would you take to ensure a highly motivated sales force?

Sources: Dr. Barbara Dyer, Assistant Professor, Ohio University, developed this case in cooperation with CDW.

After studying this chapter, you should be able to
1. discuss the benefits of direct marketing to customers and companies and the trends fueling its rapid growth
2. define a customer database and list the four ways companies use databases in direct marketing
3. identify the major forms of direct marketing
4. compare the two types of online marketing channels and explain the effect of the Internet on electronic commerce
5. identify the benefits of online marketing to consumers and marketers and the four ways marketers can conduct online marketing
6. discuss the public policy and ethical issues facing direct marketers

DIRECT AND ONLINE MARKETING: THE NEW MARKETING MODEL

When 19-year-old Michael Dell began selling personal computers out of his college dorm room in 1984, few would have bet on his chances for success. In those days, most computer makers sold their PCs through an extensive network of all-powerful distributors and resellers. Even as the fledgling Dell Computer Corporation began to grow, competitors and industry insiders scoffed at the concept of mail-order computer marketing. PC buyers, they contended, needed the kind of advice and hand-holding that only full-service channels could provide.

Yet young Michael Dell has proved the skeptics wrong—way wrong. In little more than a decade and a half, he has turned his dorm-room mail-order business into a burgeoning, $22 billion computer empire. Dell Computer is now the world's largest direct marketer of computer systems, the number-two PC maker, and the world's fastest-growing computer manufacturer. Over the past three years, Dell's sales have increased at an average of 53 percent per year, twice as fast as any competitor and five times the industry average. Profits have skyrocketed 89 percent per year. Since 1990, Dell's stock has risen an incredible 29,600 percent! Direct buyers now account for nearly a third of all PC sales, and Dell's

once-skeptical competitors are now scrambling to build their own direct-marketing systems.

What's the secret to Dell's stunning success? Anyone at Dell can tell you without hesitation: It's the company's radically different business model—the *direct model*. "We have a tremendously clear business model," says Michael Dell, the 34-year-old founder. "There's no confusion about what the value proposition is, what the company offers, and why it's great for customers. That's a very simple thing, but it has tremendous power and appeal." It also garners tremendous success for the company.

Dell's direct-marketing approach delivers greater customer value through an unbeatable combination of product customization, low prices, fast delivery, and award-winning customer service. A customer can talk by phone with a Dell representative on Monday morning; order a fully customized, state-of-the-art PC to suit his or her special needs; and have the machine delivered to his or her doorstep by Wednesday—all at a price that's 10 to 15 percent below competitors' prices for a comparably performing PC. Dell backs its products with high-quality service and support. As a result, Dell consistently ranks among the industry leaders in product reliability and service, and its customers are routinely among the industry's most satisfied.

Dell customers get exactly the machines they need. Michael Dell's initial idea was to serve individual buyers by letting them customize machines with the special features they wanted at low prices. However, this one-to-one approach also appeals strongly to corporate buyers, because Dell can so easily preconfigure each computer to precise requirements. Dell routinely preloads machines with a company's own software and even undertakes tedious tasks such as pasting inventory tags onto each machine so that computers can be delivered directly to a given employee's desk. As a result, nearly two-thirds of Dell's sales now come from large corporate, government, and educational buyers.

Direct selling results in more efficient selling and lower costs, which translate into lower prices for customers. Because Dell builds machines to order, it carries barely any inventory. Dealing one-to-one with customers helps the company react immediately to shifts in demand, so Dell doesn't get stuck with PCs no one wants. Finally, by selling directly, Dell has no dealers to pay. As a result, on average, Dell's costs are 12 percent lower than those of Compaq, its leading PC competitor.

Dell knows that time is money, and the company is obsessed with "speed." For example, Dell has long been a model of just-in-time manufacturing and efficient supply chain management. It has also mastered the intricacies of today's lightning-fast electronic commerce. The combination makes Dell a lean and very fast operator. According to one account, "Dell calls it 'velocity'—squeezing time out of every step in the process—from the moment an order is taken to collecting the cash. [By selling direct, manufacturing to order, and] tapping credit cards and electronic payment, Dell converts the average sale to cash in less than 24 hours. By contrast, Compaq Computer Corp., which sells primarily through dealers, takes 35 days, and even mail-order rival Gateway 2000 takes 16.4 days." Such blazing speed results in more satisfied customers and still lower costs. For example, customers are often delighted to find their new computers arriving within as few as 36 hours of placing an order. And because Dell doesn't order parts until an order is booked, it can take advantage of ever-falling component costs. On average, its parts are 60 days newer than those in competing machines, and, hence, 60 days farther down the price curve. This gives Dell a 6 percent profit advantage from parts costs alone.

Flush with success, Dell has taken its direct-marketing formula a step further. It's selling PCs on the Internet—lots of PCs. Now, by simply clicking the "Buy a Dell" icon at Dell's Web site (www.dell.com), customers can design and price customized computer systems electronically. Then, with a click on the "purchase" button, they can submit an order, choosing from online payment options that include a credit card, company purchase order, or corporate lease. Dell dashes out a digital confirmation to customers within five minutes of receiving the order. After receiving confirmation, customers can check the status of the order online at any time.

The Internet is a perfect extension of Dell's direct-marketing model. Customers who are already comfortable buying direct from Dell now have an even more powerful way to do so. "The Internet," says Michael Dell, "is the ultimate direct model. . . . [Customers] like the immediacy, convenience, savings, and personal touches that the [Internet] experience provides. Not only are some sales done completely online, but people who call on the phone after having visited Dell.com are twice as likely to buy."

The direct-marketing pioneer now sells more than $30 million worth of computers daily from its Web site, accounting for over 40 percent of revenues. In just a single quarter last year, Dell.com received some 25 million visits at more than 50 country-specific sites. Buyers range from individuals purchasing home computers to large business users buying high-end $30,000 servers. Michael Dell sees online marketing as the next great conquest in the company's direct-marketing crusade. "The Internet is like a booster rocket on our sales and growth," he proclaims. "Our vision is to have *all* customers conduct *all* transactions on the Internet, globally."

As you might imagine, competitors are no longer scoffing at Michael Dell's vision of the future. It's hard to argue with success, and Michael Dell has been very successful. By following his hunches, at the tender age of 34 he has built one of the world's hottest computer companies. In the process, he's amassed a personal fortune exceeding $16.5 billion.[1]

Many of the marketing tools that we've examined in previous chapters were developed in the context of *mass marketing:* targeting broad markets with standardized messages and offers distributed through intermediaries. Today, however, with the trend toward more narrowly targeted or one-to-one marketing, more and more companies are adopting *direct marketing,* either as a primary marketing approach or as a supplement to other approaches. Increasingly, companies are turning to direct marketing in an effort to reach carefully targeted customers more efficiently and to build stronger, more personal, one-to-one relationships with them.

In this chapter, we explore the exploding world of direct marketing. We look at the nature, role, and growing applications of direct marketing and its newest form, Internet marketing and e-commerce. We address the following questions: What is direct marketing? What are its benefits to companies and their customers? How do customer databases support direct marketing? What channels do direct marketers use to reach individual prospects and customers? What marketing opportunities do online and Internet channels provide? How can companies use integrated direct marketing for competitive advantage? What public and ethical issues are raised by direct and online marketing?

WHAT IS DIRECT MARKETING?

Mass marketers have typically sought to reach masses of buyers with a single product and a standard message delivered through the mass media. Thus, Procter & Gamble originally launched Crest toothpaste in one version with a single message ("Crest fights cavities"), hoping that hundreds of millions of Americans would get the message and buy the brand from their local retailer. P&G did not need to know its customers' names or anything else about them, only that they wanted to take good care of their teeth. Under this mass-marketing model, most marketing involved one-way connections aimed *at* consumers, not two-way interactions *with* them.

Direct marketing

Direct communications with carefully targeted individual consumers to obtain an immediate response and cultivate lasting customer relationships.

In contrast, **direct marketing** consists of direct connections with carefully targeted individual consumers to both obtain an immediate response and cultivate lasting customer relationships. Direct marketers communicate directly with customers, often on a one-to-one, interactive basis. Using detailed databases, they tailor their marketing offers and communications to the needs of narrowly defined segments or even individual buyers. Beyond brand and image building, they usually seek a direct, immediate, and measurable consumer response. For example, Dell Computer interacts directly with customers, by telephone or through its Web site, to design built-to-order systems that meet customers' individual needs. Buyers order directly from Dell, and Dell quickly and efficiently delivers the new computers to their homes or offices.

The New Direct-Marketing Model

Early direct marketers—catalog companies, direct mailers, and telemarketers—gathered customer names and sold goods mainly through the mail and by telephone. Today, however, fired by rapid advances in database technologies and new marketing media—especially the Internet and other electronic channels—direct marketing has undergone a dramatic transformation.

In previous chapters, we've discussed direct marketing as direct distribution, as marketing channels that contain no intermediaries. We've also included direct

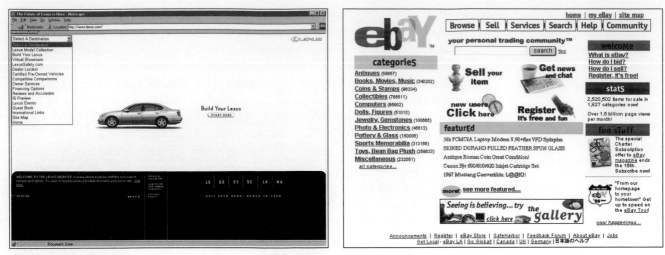

For companies like Lexus, direct marketing and the Web supplement other marketing efforts. But for the so-called e-corporations, such as online auctioneer eBay, they constitute a new and complete model for doing business.

marketing as one element of the marketing communications mix—as an approach for communicating directly with consumers. In fact, direct marketing is both these things. Most companies still use direct marketing as a supplementary channel or medium for marketing their goods. Thus, Lexus markets mostly through mass-media advertising and its high-quality dealer network but also supplements these channels with direct marketing. Its direct marketing includes promotional videos and other materials mailed directly to prospective buyers and a Web page (www.lexus.com) that provides consumers with information about various models, competitive comparisons, financing, and dealer locations. Similarly, Barnes & Noble conducts most of its business through brick-and-mortar bookstores but also markets directly through its Web site. Compaq Computer advertises heavily and makes most of its sales through retailers but also sells directly to consumers via telemarketing and the Internet. Most department stores sell the majority of their merchandise off their store shelves but also mail out catalogs.

However, for many companies today, direct marketing is much more than just a supplementary channel or medium. For these companies, direct marketing—especially in its newest transformation, Internet marketing and e-commerce—constitutes a new and complete model for doing business. "The Internet is not just another marketing channel; it's not just another advertising medium; it's not just a way to speed up transactions," says one strategist. "The Internet is the foundation for a new industrial order. [It] will change the relationship between consumers and producers in ways more profound than you can yet imagine."[2] This new *direct model*, suggests another analyst, is "revolutionizing the way we think about . . . how to construct relationships with suppliers and customers, how to create value for them, and how to make money in the process; in other words, [it's] revolutionizing marketing."[3]

Whereas most companies use direct marketing and the Internet as supplemental approaches, firms employing the direct model use it as the *only* approach. Some of these companies, such as Dell Computer, Amazon.com, and the so-called e-corporations (eBay, eToys, eTrade, and others), began as only direct marketers. Other companies—such as Cisco Systems, Charles Schwab, IBM, and many others—are rapidly transforming themselves into direct-marketing superstars.

As our chapter-opening story suggests, perhaps the company that best exemplifies this new direct marketing model is Dell Computer. On its Web page, Dell explains its direct model this way:

★ Dell's award-winning customer service, industry-leading growth, and financial performance continue to differentiate the company from competitors. At the heart of that performance is Dell's unique *direct-to-customer business model*. "Direct" refers to the company's relationships with its customers, from home-PC users to the world's largest corporations. There are no retailers or other resellers adding unnecessary time and cost, or diminishing Dell's understanding of customer expectations. Why are computer-systems customers and investors increasingly turning to Dell and its unique direct model? There are several reasons: (1) *Price for Performance:* By eliminating resellers, retailers, and other costly intermediary steps, together with the industry's most efficient procurement, manufacturing, and distribution process, Dell offers its customers more powerful, more richly configured systems for the money than competitors. (2) *Customization:* Every Dell system is built to order—customers get exactly, and only, what they want. (3) *Service and Support:* Dell uses knowledge gained from direct contact before and after the sale to provide award-winning, tailored customer service. (4) *Latest Technology:* Dell's efficient model means the latest relevant technology is introduced in its product lines much more quickly than through slow-moving indirect distribution channels. Inventory is turned over every 10 or fewer days, on average, keeping related costs low. (5) *Superior Shareholder Value:* During the past fiscal year, the value of Dell common stock more than doubled. In [the previous two years], Dell was the top-performing stock among the Standard & Poor's 500 and Nasdaq 100, and represented the top-performing U.S. stock on the Dow Jones World Stock Index.

Thus, Dell has built its entire approach to the marketplace around direct marketing. This direct model has proven highly successful, not just for Dell, but for the fast-growing number of other companies that employ it.

Many strategists have hailed direct marketing as the marketing model of the new millennium. They envision a day when all buying and selling will involve direct connections between companies and their customers. According to one account, the new model "will fundamentally change customers' expectations about convenience, speed, comparability, price, and service. Those new expectations will reverberate throughout the economy, affecting every business." Comparing the adoption of the Internet and other new direct-marketing technologies to the early days of the airplane, Amazon.com CEO Jeff Bezos says, "It's the Kitty Hawk era of electronic commerce." Even those offering more cautious predictions agree that the Internet and e-commerce will have a tremendous impact on future business strategies.

BENEFITS AND GROWTH OF DIRECT MARKETING

Whether employed as a complete business model or as a supplement to a broader integrated marketing mix, direct marketing brings many benefits to both buyers and sellers. As a result, direct marketing is growing very rapidly.

Benefits to Buyers

Direct marketing benefits buyers in many ways. It is *convenient:* Customers don't have to battle traffic, find parking spaces, and trek through stores and aisles to find and examine products. They can do comparative shopping by browsing through mail catalogs or surfing Web sites. Direct marketers never close their doors. Buying is *easy* and *private:* Customers encounter fewer buying hassles and don't have to face salespeople or open themselves up to persuasion and emotional pitches. Business buyers can learn about available products and services without waiting for and tying up time with salespeople.

Direct marketing often provides shoppers with greater *product access and selection*. For example, the world's the limit for the Web. Unrestrained by physical boundaries, cyberstores can offer an almost unlimited selection. Try comparing the incredible selections offered by Web merchants such as Amazon.com, CDNow, or Virtual Vineyards to the more meager assortments of their counterparts in the brick-and-mortar world.

Beyond a broader selection of sellers and products, online and Internet channels also give consumers access to a wealth of comparative *information,* information about companies, products, and competitors. Good sites often provide more information in more useful forms than even the most solicitous salesclerk can. eToys, for example, offers parents toy recommendations from consumer and educational groups. CDNow offers best-seller lists and record reviews.

Finally, online buying is *interactive* and *immediate.* Consumers often can interact with the seller's site to create exactly the configuration of information, products, or services they desire, then order or download them on the spot. Moreover, the Internet and other forms of direct marketing give consumers a greater measure of control. "The Internet will empower consumers like nothing else ever has," notes one analyst. "Think about this: Already 16 percent of car buyers shop online before showing up at a dealership, and they aren't comparing paint jobs—they're arming themselves with information on dealer costs. . . . The new reality is consumer control."[4]

Benefits to Sellers

Direct marketing also yields many benefits to sellers. First, direct marketing is a powerful tool for *customer relationship building*. Direct marketers build or buy databases containing detailed information about potentially profitable customers. Using these databases, they build strong, ongoing customer relationships. With today's technology, a direct marketer can select small groups or even individual consumers, personalize offers to their special needs and wants, and promote these offers through individualized communications.

For example, Mead Johnson's "Enfamil Family Beginnings" direct-mail program builds relationships with expectant and new mothers. It begins with a note of congratulations to expectant mothers, followed by a series of mailings rich with information about infant nutrition and health. Samples of Enfamil are timed to the mother's expected due date. "Now we're number one [in sales]," says Mead Johnson's director of consumer relationship marketing. "This program has had a huge impact on that."[5] Similarly, P&G's Pampers Parenting Institute Web site (www.pampers.com) builds relationships by offering parents of young children more than just product information. It gives ongoing advice on baby development, health, and safety; a newsletter; a resource library; and an "ask our experts" feature where they can get answers to personal parenting questions.

Direct marketing can also be timed to reach prospects at just the right moment. Because they reach more interested consumers at the best times, direct-marketing materials receive higher readership and response. Direct marketing also permits easy testing of alternative media and messages.

Because of its one-to-one, interactive nature, the Internet is an especially potent direct-marketing tool. Companies can interact online with customers to learn more about specific needs and wants. In turn, online customers can ask questions and volunteer feedback. Based on this ongoing interaction, companies can increase customer value and satisfaction through product and service refinements.

Direct marketing via the Internet and other electronic channels yields additional advantages, such as *reducing costs* and *increasing speed and efficiency*. Online mar-

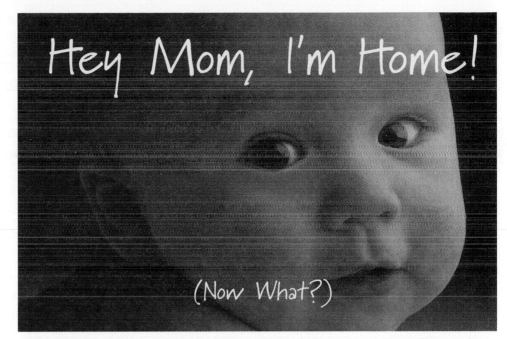

Building direct relationships: Mead Johnson's "Enfamil Family Beginnings" direct mail program builds relationships with expectant and new mothers.

keters avoid the expense of maintaining a store and the accompanying costs of rent, insurance, and utilities. Online retailers such as Amazon.com reap the advantage of a negative operating cycle: Amazon receives cash from credit card companies just a day after customers place an order. Then it can hold on to the money for 46 days until it pays suppliers, the book distributors and publishers.

By using the Internet to link directly to suppliers, factories, distributors, and customers, businesses like Dell Computer and General Electric are wringing waste out of the system and passing on savings to customers. Because customers deal directly with sellers, online marketing often results in lower costs and improved efficiencies for channel and logistics functions such as order processing, inventory handling, delivery, and trade promotion. Finally, communicating electronically often costs less than communicating on paper through the mail. For instance, a company can produce digital catalogs for much less than the cost of printing and mailing paper ones.

Online marketing also offers greater *flexibility*, allowing the marketer to make ongoing adjustments to its offers and programs. For example, once a paper catalog is mailed, the products, prices, and other catalog features are fixed until the next catalog is sent. However, an online catalog can be adjusted daily or even hourly, adapting product assortments, prices, and promotions to match changing market conditions.

Finally, the Internet is a truly *global* medium that allows buyers and sellers to click from one country to another in seconds. A Web surfer from Paris or Istanbul can access a Lands' End catalog as easily as someone living on 1 Lands' End Lane in Dodgeville, Wisconsin, the direct retailer's hometown. Thus, even small online marketers find that they have ready access to global markets.

The Growth of Direct Marketing

Sales through traditional direct-marketing channels (telephone marketing, direct mail, catalogs, direct-response television, and others) have been growing rapidly.

Whereas U.S. retail sales over the past five years have grown at about 6 percent annually, direct-marketing sales grew at about 8 percent annually. These sales include sales to the consumer market (55 percent) and business-to-business sales (45 percent).[6]

While direct marketing through traditional channels is growing rapidly, online marketing is growing explosively. The number of U.S. households with access to the Internet has grown from only about 6 million in 1994 to more than 40 million today, to a projected 60 million by 2003. Sales via the Internet are expected to grow at an incredible 60 percent per year over the next five years.[7] We will examine online and Internet marketing more closely later in this chapter.

In the consumer market, the extraordinary growth of direct marketing is a response to rapid advances in technology and to the new marketing realities discussed in previous chapters. Market "demassification" has resulted in an ever-increasing number of market niches with distinct preferences. Direct marketing allows sellers to focus efficiently on these minimarkets with offers that better match specific consumer needs.

Other trends have also fueled the rapid growth of direct marketing in the consumer market. Higher costs of driving, traffic congestion, parking headaches, lack of time, a shortage of retail sales help, and lines at checkout counters all encourage at-home shopping. Consumers are responding favorably to direct marketers' toll-free phone numbers, their willingness to accept telephone orders 24 hours a day, 7 days a week, and their growing commitment to customer service. The growth of 24-hour and 48-hour delivery via Federal Express, Airborne, UPS, DHL, and other express carriers has made direct shopping fast as well as easy. Finally, the growth of affordable computer power and customer databases has enabled direct marketers to single out the best prospects for any product they wish to sell.

Direct marketing has also grown rapidly in business-to-business marketing, partly in response to the ever-increasing costs of reaching business markets through the sales force. When personal sales calls cost $165 per contact, they should be made only when necessary and to high-potential customers and prospects. Lower cost-per-contact media—such as telemarketing, direct mail, and the newer electronic media—often prove more cost effective in reaching and selling to more prospects and customers.

CUSTOMER DATABASES AND DIRECT MARKETING

Table 17.1 lists the main differences between mass marketing and so-called *one-to-one marketing*.[8] Companies that know about individual customer needs and characteristics can customize their offers, messages, delivery modes, and payment methods to maximize customer value and satisfaction. Today's companies also have a very powerful tool for accessing pertinent information about individual customers and prospects: the customer database.

Customer database
An organized collection of comprehensive data about individual customers or prospects, including geographic, demographic, psychographic, and behavioral data.

A **customer database** is an organized collection of comprehensive data about individual customers or prospects, including geographic, demographic, psychographic, and behavioral data. The database can be used to locate good potential customers, tailor products and services to the special needs of targeted consumers, and maintain long-term customer relationships. *Database marketing* is the process of building, maintaining, and using customer databases and other databases (products, suppliers, resellers) for the purpose of contacting and transacting with customers.

Many companies confuse a customer mailing list with a customer database. A customer mailing list is simply a set of names, addresses, and telephone numbers. A customer

TABLE 17.1 MASS MARKETING VERSUS ONE-TO-ONE MARKETING	
Mass Marketing	**One-to-One Marketing**
Average customer	Individual customer
Customer anonymity	Customer profile
Standard product	Customized market offering
Mass production	Customized production
Mass distribution	Individualized distribution
Mass advertising	Individualized message
Mass promotion	Individualized incentives
One-way message	Two-way messages
Economies of scale	Economies of scope
Share of market	Share of customer
All customers	Profitable customers
Customer attraction	Customer retention

Source: Adapted from Don Peppers and Martha Rogers, *The One-to-One Future* (New York: Doubleday/Currency, 1993).

database contains much more information. In business-to-business marketing, the salesperson's customer profile might contain the products and services the customer has bought; past volumes and prices; key contacts (and their ages, birthdays, hobbies, and favorite foods); competitive suppliers; status of current contracts; estimated customer spending for the next few years; and assessments of competitive strengths and weaknesses in selling and servicing the account. In consumer marketing, the customer database might contain a customer's demographics (age, income, family members, birthdays), psychographics (activities, interests, and opinions), buying behavior (past purchases, buying preferences), and other relevant information. For example, the catalog company Fingerhut maintains a database containing some 1,300 pieces of information about each of 30 million households (see Marketing Highlight 17.1). Ritz-Carlton's database holds more than 500,000 individual customer preferences. And Pizza Hut's database lets it track the purchases of more than 50 million customers.[9]

Database marketing is most frequently used by business-to-business marketers and service retailers (hotels, banks, and airlines). Increasingly, however, other kinds of companies are also employing database marketing. Armed with the information in their databases, these companies can identify small groups of customers to receive fine-tuned marketing offers and communications. Kraft Foods has amassed a list of more than 30 million users of its products who have responded to coupons or other Kraft promotions. Based on their interests, the company sends these customers tips on issues such as nutrition and exercise, as well as recipes and coupons for specific Kraft brands. Blockbuster, the massive entertainment company, uses its database of 36 million households and 2 million daily transactions to help its video-rental customers select movies and to steer them to other Blockbuster subsidiaries. American Express uses its database to tailor offers to cardholders. In Belgium, it is testing a system that links cardholder spending patterns with postal-zone data. If a new restaurant opens, for example, the company might offer a special discount to cardholders who live within walking distance and who eat out a lot. And FedEx uses its sophisticated database to create 100 highly targeted, customized direct-mail and telemarketing campaigns each year to its nearly 5 million customers shipping to 212 countries. By analyzing customers carefully and reaching the right customers at the right

MARKETING HIGHLIGHT 17.1

DATABASE MARKETING: FINGERHUT BUILDS STRONG CUSTOMER RELATIONSHIPS

As Betty Holmes of Detroit, Michigan, sifts through the day's stack of mail, one item in particular catches her eye. It's only a catalog

Fingerhut's database stores millions of facts on tens of millions of consumers.

but it's speaking directly to her. A laser-printed personal message on the catalog's cover states: "Thank you, Mrs. Holmes, for your recent purchase of women's apparel. To show our thanks, we are offering you up to 5 free gifts, plus deferred payment until July 31st." The note goes on with amazing accuracy, to refer Betty to specific items in the catalog that will likely interest her.

The catalog is from Fingerhut, the giant direct-mail retailer and master database marketer. A typical Fingerhut catalog offers products ranging from $20 toy phones to $2,000 big-screen TVs. Fingerhut operates on a *huge* scale: It sends out some 558 million mailings each year, more than 1.5 million per day. When new customers first respond to a direct-mail offer, Fingerhut asks them to fill out a questionnaire about the kinds of products that interest them. Using information from this questionnaire and from other sources, along with information about later purchases, Fingerhut has built an impressive marketing database. The database contains up to 3,000 variables on more than 65 million active and potential customers. It's filled to the brim with the usual demographic details such as address,

age, marital status, number of children, and previous transactions but also tracks hobbies, interests, birthdays, and other seemingly obscure facts.

The database allows Fingerhut to target the most likely buyers with products that interest them most. Instead of sending out the same catalogs and letters to all of its customers, Fingerhut tailors its offers based on what each customer is likely to buy. Moreover, promotions such as the Birthday Club provide opportunities to create special offers that sell more products. A month before a child's birthday, Birthday Club customers receive a free birthday gift for their child if they agree to try any one of the products Fingerhut offers in an accompanying mailing. A customer who responds to these and other offers might become one of millions of "promotable" customers who receive Fingerhut mailings. As a result of such skillful use of its database, Fingerhut achieves direct-mail response rates that are three times the industry average. Says one retailing consultant, "Fingerhut is one of those pioneering companies that is making intense knowledge of their customer a core competency."

time with the right promotions, FedEx achieves response rates of 20 to 25 percent and earns an 8-to-1 return on its direct-marketing dollars.[10]

Smaller companies can also make good use of database marketing. Here are two examples:[11]

★ Over the last few years, nearly 9,000 grocery chains have introduced frequent-shopper programs. Now they're rifling through household shopping histories as fast as they can to tell cardholders what's running low in the pantry. Dick's Supermarkets, an eight-store chain in Wisconsin, uses transaction data from its loyalty-card program to personalize shopping lists that it mails every two weeks to nearly 30,000 members. The shopping lists . . . contain timed offers based on past purchases. A consumer who bought Tide several weeks ago, for example, may be offered a $1.50

Fingerhut uses its database to build long-term customer relationships that go well beyond its merchandise. It stays in continuous touch with preferred customers through regular special promotions an annual sweepstakes, free gifts, a deferred-billing promotion, and others. These special offers are all designed with one goal in mind: to create a reason for Fingerhut to be in the customer's mailbox. Once in the mailbox, the personalized messages and targeted offers get attention.

Credit is an important cornerstone of Fingerhut's relationship with customers. The average Fingerhut customer has a household income of just $25,000. Whereas many retailers and credit companies are reluctant to extend credit to this moderate-income group, Fingerhut encourages credit. Catalogs list monthly payments in bold type and actual prices in fine print. Customers can spread a $40 sneaker purchase over 13 months with payments of just $4.79 per month. Thus, Fingerhut regularly extends credit to people who would otherwise have to pay cash. "When I started out, Fingerhut was the only place that would give me credit," says Marilyn Gnat from Eagle River, Wisconsin, a loyal Fingerhut customer who raised nine children on a modest income.

Despite selling to consumers of modest means, Fingerhut turns credit into a competitive advantage by using its huge database to effectively control credit risks. Some 40 percent of Fingerhut customers have had so little credit that they don't even have credit reports. Thus, the company's extensive database helps it to do a better job than its competitors can of predicting customers' creditworthiness. Fingerhut further controls credit risks by what it offers to whom. When a new customer makes a first order, the amount of credit allowed may be limited to $50. If the customer pays promptly, the next mailing offers higher-ticket items. Good customers, who pay their bills regularly, get cards and rewards to reinforce this behavior. For example, an award envelope cheers "Congratulations! You've been selected to receive our 'exceptional customer award'!" and contains a certificate suitable for framing.

Recently, Fingerhut has begun applying its database touch to the Internet. Customers can now log on to the Fingerhut Online Web site (www.fingerhut.com) and order products from the catalog using an online order form. The company's popular Andy's Garage Sale site (www.andysgarage.com) even customizes its interactions with Web customers. "If you are repeatedly buying golf equipment and I'm buying boat supplies, it'll show you golf bags, and it'll show me life jackets," explains Fingerhut's vice president of marketing.

The skillful use of database marketing and relationship building have made Fingerhut one of the nation's largest direct-mail marketers. Founded in 1948 by brothers Manny and William Fingerhut, and currently a division of Federated Department Stores, Inc., it now sells more than $2 billion worth of mail-order and Web merchandise each year, making it the nation's second-largest consumer catalog company behind JCPenney. In fact, one in every six U.S. households has *bought* something from the company. Fingerhut's success is no accident. "Most of our competitors use a full catalog; they could care less about what the individuals want," notes a Fingerhut executive. "Fingerhut finds out what each customer wants and builds an event around each promotion."

Sources: Quotes from Eileen Norris, "Fingerhut Gives Customers Credit," *Advertising Age,* March 6, 1986, p. 19; Susan Chandler, "Data Is Power. Just Ask Fingerhut," *Business Week,* June 3, 1996, p. 69; Mitch Wagner, "Repeat Traffic Is Goal of Customerized Web Sites," *Computerworld,* November 25, 1996, p. 48; and Jennifer Lach, "Data Mining Digs In," *American Demographics,* July 1999, pp. 38–45. Also see Gene G. Marcial, "Fingerhut Gets a Grip on the Net," *Business Week,* December 14, 1998, p. 128; and "Retailer Buys Fingerhut Marketing Company," *Marketing News,* March 15, 1999, p. 15.

---

coupon to restock. If that customer buys laundry detergent every week, he or she may be offered twice as much to purchase a larger size of Tide, or two packages of the size normally purchased.

★ Some grocers are going a step further, tweaking promotions based on past responses as well as purchase data. Nature's NorthWest health food chain [uses its database] to distribute custom-printed newsletters at its checkouts. When the cashier scans a frequent shopper card, the card's transaction history triggers a newsletter reflecting that consumer's purchase history and areas of interest (individuals can check off interests on their application for the card). Bought herbal supplements and organic meat on your last visit? Interested in exercise? Your newsletter might have a schedule of local exercise classes, a recipe for meat, and a coupon for more herbs. The newsletter prints at the checkout counter in seven seconds, faster than a cashier can make change and bag the groceries. Nature's NorthWest tracks which bar coded coupons are redeemed from the newsletter, and then adjusts the newsletter each time to better suit that shopper.

Companies use their databases in four ways:[12]

1. *Identifying prospects:* Many companies generate sales leads by advertising their products or offers. Ads generally have some sort of response feature, such as a business reply card or toll-free phone number. The database is built from these responses. The company sorts through the database to identify the best prospects, then reaches them by mail, phone, or personal calls in an attempt to convert them into customers.

2. *Deciding which customers should receive a particular offer:* Companies identify the profile of an ideal customer for an offer. Then they search their databases for individuals most closely resembling the ideal type. By tracking individual responses, the company can improve its targeting precision over time. Following a sale, it can set up an automatic sequence of activities: One week later, send a thank-you note; five weeks later, send a new offer; ten weeks later (if the customer has not responded), phone the customer and offer a special discount.

3. *Deepening customer loyalty:* Companies can build customers' interest and enthusiasm by remembering their preferences and by sending appropriate information, gifts, or other materials. For example, Mars, a market leader in pet food as well as candy, maintains an exhaustive pet database. In Germany, the company has compiled the names of virtually every German family that owns a cat. It has obtained these names by contacting veterinarians, via its Katzen-Online.de Web site, and by offering the public a free booklet titled "How to Take Care of Your Cat." People who request the booklet fill out a questionnaire, providing their cat's name, age, birthday, and other information. Mars then sends a birthday card to each cat in Germany each year, along with a new cat food sample and money-saving coupons for Mars brands. The result is a lasting relationship with the cat's owner.

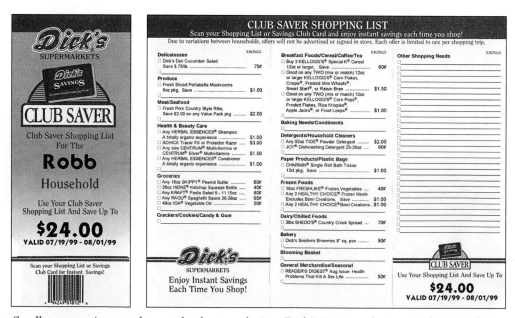

Smaller companies can also use database marketing: Dick's Supermarkets, an eight-store chain in Wisconsin, uses transaction data to create personalized shopping lists for each of its nearly 30,000 members.

4. *Reactivating customer purchases:* The database can help a company make attractive offers of product replacements, upgrades, or complementary products just when customers might be ready to act. For example, a General Electric customer database contains each customer's demographic and psychographic characteristics along with an appliance purchasing history. Using this database, GE marketers assess how long specific customers have owned their current appliances and which past customers might be ready to purchase again. They can determine which customers need a new GE videorecorder, compact disc player, stereo receiver, or something else to go with other recently purchased electronics products. Or they can identify the best past GE purchasers and send them gift certificates or other promotions to apply against their next GE purchases. A rich customer database allows GE to build profitable new business by locating good prospects, anticipating customer needs, cross-selling products and services, and rewarding loyal customers.

Like many other marketing tools, database marketing requires a special investment. Companies must invest in computer hardware, database software, analytical programs, communication links, and skilled personnel. The database system must be user friendly and available to various marketing groups, including those in product and brand management, new-product development, advertising and promotion, direct mail, telemarketing, field sales, order fulfillment, and customer service. A well-managed database should lead to sales gains that will more than cover its costs.

FORMS OF DIRECT MARKETING

The major forms of direct marketing—as shown in Figure 17.1—include *face-to-face selling, telemarketing, direct-mail marketing, catalog marketing, direct-response television marketing, kiosk marketing,* and *online marketing.*

FIGURE 17.1   Forms of direct marketing

Face-to-Face Selling

The original and oldest form of direct marketing is the sales call, which we examined in the previous chapter. Today most business-to-business marketers rely heavily on a professional sales force to locate prospects, develop them into customers, build lasting relationships, and grow the business. Or they hire manufacturers' representatives and agents to carry out the direct-selling task. In addition, many consumer companies use a direct-selling force to reach final consumers: insurance agents, stockbrokers, and salespeople working part- or full-time for direct-sales organizations such as Avon, Amway, Mary Kay, and Tupperware.

Telemarketing

Telemarketing
Using the telephone to sell directly to customers.

Telemarketing—using the telephone to sell directly to consumers—has become the major direct-marketing communication tool. Telephone marketing now accounts for over 38 percent of all direct-marketing media expenditures.[13] We're all familiar with telemarketing directed toward consumers, but business-to-business marketers also use telemarketing extensively.

Marketers use *outbound* telephone marketing to sell directly to consumers and businesses. *Inbound* toll-free 800 numbers are used to receive orders from television and radio ads, direct mail, or catalogs. The use of 800 numbers has taken off in recent years as more and more companies have begun using them, and as current users have added new features such as toll-free fax numbers. Residential use has also grown. To accommodate this rapid growth, new toll-free area codes (888, 877, 866) have been added. After the 800 area code was established in 1967, it took almost 30 years before its 8 million numbers were used up. In contrast, 888 area code numbers, established in 1996, were used up in only 2 years.[14]

Other marketers use 900 numbers to sell consumers information, entertainment, or the opportunity to voice an opinion on a pay-per-call basis. For example, for a charge, consumers can obtain weather forecasts from American Express (900-WEATHER—$.75 a minute), pet care information from Quaker Oats (900-990-PETS—$.95 a minute), advice on snoring and other sleep disorders from Somnus (900-USA-SLEEP—$2.00 for the first minute, then $1.00 a minute), golf lessons from *Golf Digest* (900-454-3288—$.95 a minute), or individual answers to nutrition questions from a registered dietician sponsored by the American Dietetic Association (900-CALL-AN-RD—$1.95 for the first minute, then $.95 a minute). In addition to its 800 number and Internet site, Nintendo offers a 900 number, for $1.50 per minute, for game players wanting assistance with the company's video games. Ronald McDonald House Charities uses a 900 number to raise funds. Each call to 900-CALL-RMHC results in a $15.00 contribution, which is simply charged to the caller's local phone bill. Overall, the use of 900 numbers has grown by more than 10 percent a year over the past five years.[15]

Many consumers appreciate many of the offers they receive by telephone. Properly designed and targeted telemarketing provides many benefits, including purchasing convenience and increased product and service information. However, the recent explosion in unsolicited telephone marketing has annoyed many consumers who object to the almost daily "junk phone calls" that pull them away from the dinner table or fill their answering machines. Lawmakers around the country are responding with legislation ranging from banning unsolicited telemarketing calls during certain hours to letting households sign up for "Do not call" lists. Most telemarketers support some action against random and poorly targeted telemarketing. As a Direct Marketing Association executive notes, "We want to target people who want to be targeted."[16]

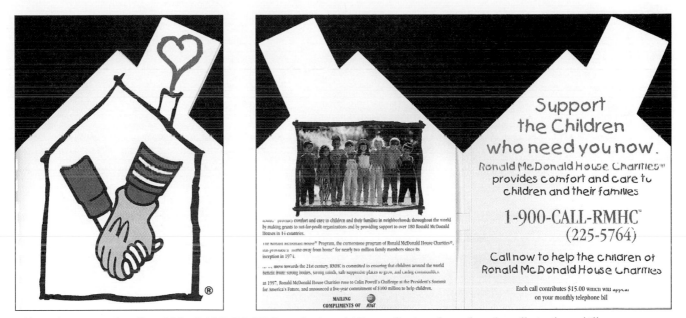

Telemarketing: Each call to 900-CALL-RMHC results in a $15 contribution charged to the caller's phone bill.

Direct-Mail Marketing

Direct-mail marketing
Direct marketing through single mailings that include letters, ads, samples, foldouts, and other "salespeople with wings" sent to prospects on mailing lists.

Direct-mail marketing involves sending an offer, announcement, reminder, or other item to a person at a particular address. Using highly selective mailing lists, direct marketers send out millions of mail pieces each year—letters, ads, samples, foldouts, and other "salespeople with wings." Direct mail accounts for over 24 percent of all direct-marketing media expenditures. Together, telemarketing and direct-mail marketing account for over 60 percent of direct-marketing expenditures and 66 percent of direct-marketing sales.[17]

Direct mail is well suited to direct, one-to-one communication. It permits high target-market selectivity, can be personalized, is flexible, and allows easy measurement of results. Whereas the cost per thousand people reached is higher than with mass media such as television or magazines, the people who are reached are much better prospects. Direct mail has proved successful in promoting all kinds of products, from books, magazine subscriptions, and insurance to gift items, clothing, gourmet foods, and industrial products. Direct mail is also used heavily by charities to raise billions of dollars each year. The following example shows the power of direct mail in obtaining contributions, in this case for an ailing public TV–radio station:

★ When planning its capital improvement campaign, public TV–radio station WFYI set what it thought was an ambitious five-year, $5 million fund-raising goal. The results, however, far outstripped projections. Instead of sending out the usual glossy, full-color brochures, WFYI used a brutally frank approach centering on its dire financial straits. It used cardboard, rubber stamps, and duct tape to create an introductory mailer. A silvery, die-cut TV set illustrated the message, "In 1969, Indianapolis was the largest city in the nation without a public television station." Turning the page, the copy continued "It could be again," with the TV now held together with duct tape. An inexpensively printed follow-up brochure showed a time line of the station's 18-year history. Above the line in black were milestones and accomplishments. Below, in red, equipment failures. When the time line hit 1996, expenses had become an angry, unreadable blotch of red ink. The direct approach worked: Despite sending out only 500 mailers, the campaign raised some $3.5 million in only the first nine months. That's an astounding return of $7,000 per piece.[18]

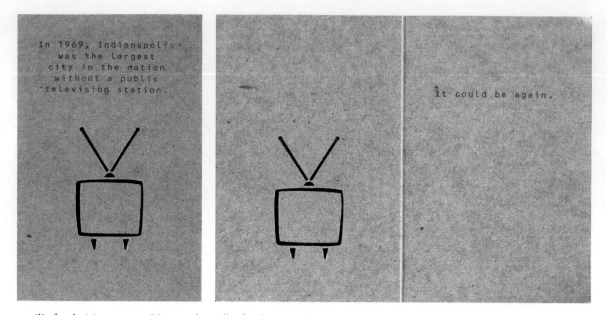

Direct mail's fundraising power: Using a brutally frank approach centering on its dire financial straits, public TV–radio station WFYI far outstripped what it thought was an ambitious five-year fundraising goal.

The direct-mail industry constantly seeks new methods and approaches. For example, videocassettes and CDs are now among the fastest-growing direct-mail media. With VCRs now in most American homes, marketers mailed out tens of millions of cassettes each year. For instance, to introduce its Donkey Kong Country video game, Nintendo of America created a 13-minute MTV-style video and sent 2 million copies to avid video game players. This direct-mail video helped Nintendo sell 6.1 million units of the game in only 45 days, making it the fastest-selling game in industry history.[19] Some direct marketers even mail out computer diskettes. For example, Ford sends a computer diskette called "Disk Drive Test Drive" to consumers responding to its ads in computer publications. The diskette's menu provides technical specifications and attractive graphics about Ford cars and answers frequently asked questions.

Until recently, all mail was paper based and handled by the U.S. Post Office, telegraphic services, or for-profit mail carriers such as Federal Express, DHL, or Airborne Express. Recently, however, three new forms of mail delivery have become popular:

★ *Fax mail:* Fax machines allow delivery of paper-based messages over telephone lines. Fax mail has one major advantage over regular mail: The message can be sent and received almost instantaneously. Marketers now routinely send fax mail announcing offers, sales, and other events to prospects and customers with fax machines. Fax numbers of companies and individuals are now available through published directories. However, some prospects and customers resent receiving unsolicited fax mail, which ties up their machines and consumes their paper.

★ *E-mail:* E-mail (short for *electronic mail*) allows users to send messages or files directly from one computer to another. Messages arrive almost instantly and are stored until the receiving person retrieves them. Many marketers now send sales announcements, offers, product information, and other messages to e-mail addresses—sometimes to a few individuals, sometimes to large groups. As people begin to receive more e-mail messages, including unimportant ones, they may look for an "agent" software program to sort out the more important messages from those that can be ignored or discarded.

★ *Voice mail:* Voice mail is a system for receiving and storing oral messages at a telephone address. Telephone companies sell this service as a substitute for answering machines. The person with a voice mail account can check messages by dialing into the voice mail system and entering a personal code. Some marketers have set up automated programs that exclusively target voice mail boxes and answering machines with prerecorded messages. These systems target homes between 10 A.M. and 4 P.M. and businesses between 7 P.M. and 9 P.M. when people are least likely to answer. If the automated dialer hears a live voice, it disconnects. Such systems thwart hang-ups by annoyed potential customers. However, they can also create substantial ill will.[20]

These new forms deliver direct mail at incredible speeds compared to the post office's "snail mail" pace. Yet, much like mail delivered through traditional channels, they may be resented as "junk mail" if sent to people who have no interest in them. For this reason, marketers must carefully identify appropriate targets so as not to waste their money and recipients' time (see Marketing Highlight 17.2).

Catalog Marketing

Catalog marketing
Direct marketing through print, video, or electronic catalogs that are mailed to select customers, made available in stores, or presented online.

Rapid advances in technology, along with the move toward personalized, one-to-one marketing, have resulted in dramatic changes in **catalog marketing.** *Catalog Age* magazine used to define a *catalog* as "a printed, bound piece of at least eight pages, selling multiple products, and offering a direct ordering mechanism." Today, only a few years later, this definition is sadly out of date. With the stampede to the Internet, although printed catalogs remain the primary medium, more and more catalogs are going electronic. Many traditional print catalogers have added Web-based catalogs to their marketing mixes and a variety of new Web-only catalogers have emerged.

Catalog marketing has grown explosively during the past 25 years. Annual catalog sales (both print and electronic) are expected to grow from a current $80 billion to more than $107 billion by 2002.[21] Some huge general-merchandise retailers—such as JCPenney and Spiegel—sell a full line of merchandise through catalogs. More recently, the giants have been challenged by thousands of specialty catalogs that serve highly specialized market niches. Consumers can buy just about anything from a catalog. Sharper Image sells $2,400 jet-propelled surfboards. The Banana Republic Travel and Safari Clothing Company features everything you would need to go hiking in the Sahara or the rain forest. And each year Lillian Vernon sends out 33 editions of its catalogs with total circulation of 178 million copies to its 20-million person database, selling everything from shoes to decorative lawn birds and monogrammed oven mitts.[22]

Specialty department stores, such as Neiman Marcus, Bloomingdale's, and Saks Fifth Avenue, use catalogs to cultivate upper-middle-class markets for high-priced, often exotic, merchandise. Several major corporations have also developed or acquired catalog divisions. For example, Avon now issues 10 women's fashion catalogs along with catalogs for children's and men's clothes. Walt Disney Company mails out over 6 million catalogs each year featuring videos, stuffed animals, and other Disney items.

*MIS*DIRECTED MARKETING: MY DEAD DOG MAY ALREADY BE A WINNER!

Poor database management and wrongly targeted direct marketing not only aggravates consumers, it costs companies millions of dollars each year and sometimes makes them look downright foolish. Take the following account, written by Lee Coppola, the bemused recipient of some of this misdirected mania:

Every wonder what happens when a pet takes on a persona? Ashley could have told you, if he could have talked. Ashley was the family mutt, an SPCA special, part beagle and part spaniel. For years, most of them after he died, he also served as the family's representative in the local telephone book. He was picked for the role quite haphazardly one day when I tried to keep my number out of the book to avoid getting business calls at home. When I balked at the $60-a-year-fee, the cheery telephone company representative suggested I list the number in one of my children's names.

I was munching on a sandwich at the time and Ashley followed me around the kitchen waiting for a crumb to fall. "Can I put the phone in any name?" I asked the rep as I sidestepped Ashley. "Certainly," she answered, and therein gave birth to 10 years of telephone calls and mail to a dog.

"A remarkable new book about the Coppolas since the Civil War is about to make history—and you, Ashley Coppola, are in it," touted one letter asking Ashley to send $10 right away for "this one-time offer." Ashley received hundreds of pieces of mail, the bulk soliciting his money.

The most ironic pitches for cash were from the SPCA and the Buffalo Zoo, a kind of animal-helping-animal scenario. And we wondered how the chief executive of a local cemetery might react if he knew he was asking a canine to buy a plot to give his family "peace of mind." Or a local lawn service's thoughts about asking a dog who daily messed the grass, "Is your lawn as attractive as it could be?" Then there was the letter offering Ashley "reliable electronic security to protect your home." One of the kids asked if that wasn't Ashley's job.

The kids soon got into the swing of having their dog receive mail and telephone calls. "He's sleeping under the dining room table," one would tell telemarketers. "He's out in the backyard taking a whiz," was the favorite reply of another. My wife would have nothing of that frivolity, preferring to simply reply, "He's deceased."

But that tack backfired on her one day when our youngest child took an almost pleading call from a survey-company employee looking for Ashley. "I'm Ashley," the 17-year-old politely replied, taking pity on the caller. He dutifully gave his age and answered a few questions before he realized he was late for an appointment and hurriedly cut short the conversation. "Can I call you again?" the surveyor asked. "OK," our son said as he hung up.

Sure enough, the surveyor called again the next day and asked for Ashley. But this time Mom answered and gave her standard reply. "Oh, my God," exclaimed the caller. "I'm so, so sorry." The surveyor's horrified grief puzzled my wife until our son explained how he had been a healthy teenage Ashley the day before.

Sometimes we worried about our dog's fate. You see, he broke several chain letters urging him to copy and send 20 others or risk some calamity. After all, Ashley was warned, didn't one person die nine days after throwing out the letter?

Did I mention credit cards? Ashley paid his bills on time, judging from the $5,000 lines-of-credit for which he "automatically" qualified. Made us wonder about the scrutiny of the nation's credit-card industry.

Of course, Ashley was no ordinary dog. He was an Italian dog. How else to explain the solicitation to Mr. Coppola Ashley that came all the way from Altamura, Italy, and sought donations to an orphanage? Then there was the offer to obtain his family's cherished crest, "fashioned hundreds of years ago in Italy," and purchase the Coppola family registry that listed him along with all the other Coppolas in America.

Is there some message to all this? Think of the saplings that were sacrificed to try to squeeze money from a canine. Or the time, energy, and money that were wasted each time a postage or bulk-mail stamp was affixed to an envelope being sent to a mutt. We did feel sheepish about the deception when the mail came from the self-employed trying to make a buck. We wondered if a local dentist really would have given Ashley a "complete initial consultation, exam, and bitewing X-rays for ONLY THREE DOLLARS." And what might have been the expression on the saleswoman's face if Ashley had shown up for his complimentary Mary Kay facial?

Ashley did appreciate, however, the coupon for dog food.

Source: Lee Coppola, "My Dead Dog May Already Be a Winner!" *Newsweek,* July 5, 1999, p. 11.

The Internet has had a tremendous impact on catalog selling. In the face of increasing competition from Internet retailing, one expert even predicts "catalogs are doomed . . . mail-order catalogs as we know them today won't even survive."[23] Thus, even traditional catalogers are adding Wed-based catalogs. In fact, more than three-quarters of all catalog companies now present merchandise and take orders over the Internet. For example, the Lands' End Web site, which debuted in 1995, now gets 180,000 e-mail queries a year, surpassing its print mail response.[24] Here's another example that illustrates this dramatic shift in catalog marketing:

When novelty gifts marketer Archie McPhee launched its Web site in September 1995, response was "underwhelming," says Mark Pahlow, president of the catalog company. "But when we added the shopping basket ordering feature in summer 1997, it came alive." You might say it roared to life. According to Pahlow, the site now has 35,000 unique visitors each month, generating 55 percent of the cataloger's total sales. In fact, the Web numbers are so positive that Archie McPhee has slashed circulation of its print catalog from 1 million to less than 300,000, and reduced the frequency from five issues a year to three. Archie McPhee's Web-based catalog makes good sense for many reasons. "We did the math," Pahlow says. The Web site has saved the company more than 50 percent in the costs of producing, printing, and mailing its color catalog, which had been as high as $700,000 annually. Using the Web site, Archie McPhee can also offer interactive features, such as "The Nerd Test" and a fortune-telling ball, as well as much more merchandise. "A 48-page catalog would show fewer than 200 items, whereas the Web site offers more than 500," Pahlow notes. Another benefit of the site is its real-time inventory feature. "The day a new product arrives, it is shown on the site. The moment we run out of an item, we pull it off. We are also able to show items we have small quantities of as Web-only specials."[25]

Along with the benefits, however, Web-based catalogs also present challenges. Whereas a print catalog is intrusive and creates its own attention, Web catalogs are passive and must be marketed. "Attracting new customers is much more difficult to do with a Web catalog," says an industry consultant. "You have to use advertising,

Web-based catalogs: Most catalog companies now present merchandise and take orders over the Internet. Novelty gifts marketer Archie McPhee's site attracts 35,000 unique visitors each month and generates 55 percent of the cataloger's total sales.

linkage, and other means to drive traffic to it." Thus, even catalogers who are sold on the Web are not likely to abandon their print catalogs completely. For example, Archie McPhee relies on its print catalogs to promote its site. "I think we will always produce at least one catalog a year," Pahlow says.

Direct-Response Television Marketing

Direct-response television marketing

Direct marketing via television, including *direct-response television advertising* or *infomercials* and *home shopping channels.*

Direct-response television marketing takes one of two major forms. The first is *direct-response advertising.* Direct marketers air television spots, often 60 or 120 seconds long, that persuasively describe a product and give customers a toll-free number for ordering. Television viewers often encounter 30-minute advertising programs, or *infomercials,* for a single product.

Some successful direct-response ads run for years and become classics. For example, Dial Media's ads for Ginsu knives ran for seven years and sold almost 3 million sets of knives worth more than $40 million in sales; its Armourcote cookware ads generated more than twice that much. The current infomercial champ?

> ★ It's three o'clock in the morning. Plagued with insomnia, you grab the remote and flip around until a grinning blonde in an apron catches your attention: "I'm going to show you something you won't believe! Juicy meals in minutes! Something else you won't believe . . . George Foreman!" The studio roars, and boxing's elder statesman, in a red apron, shows off his Lean Mean Fat-Reducing Grilling Machine and highlights the grease caught in the pan below. "Eew!" the audience screams. It can be yours for three easy payments of $19.95 (plus shipping and handling). Don't laugh. [This infomercial has] notched $200 million in sales of Foreman grills in less than four years.[26]

For years, infomercials have been associated with somewhat questionable pitches for juicers and other kitchen gadgets, get-rich-quick schemes, and nifty ways to stay in shape without working very hard at it. Recently, however, a num-

Some successful direct-response television ads run for years and become classics. Infomercials for George Foreman's Lean Mean Fat-Reducing Grilling Machine have notched $200 million in sales in less than four years.

ber of large companies—GTE, Johnson & Johnson, MCA Universal, Sears, Procter & Gamble, Revlon, Apple Computer, Cadillac, Volvo, Anheuser-Busch, even the U.S. Navy—have begun using infomercials to sell their wares over the phone, refer customers to retailers, or send out coupons and product information.[27]

Home shopping channels, another form of direct-response television marketing, are television programs or entire channels dedicated to selling goods and services. Some home shopping channels, such as the Quality Value Channel (QVC) and the Home Shopping Network (HSN), broadcast 24 hours a day. On HSN, the program's hosts offer bargain prices on products ranging from jewelry, lamps, collectible dolls, and clothing to power tools and consumer electronics—usually obtained by the home shopping channel at closeout prices. The show is upbeat, with the hosts honking horns, blowing whistles, and praising viewers for their good taste. Viewers call a toll-free number to order goods. At the other end of the operation, 400 operators handle more than 1,200 incoming lines, entering orders directly into computer terminals. Orders are shipped within 48 hours. QVC sells more than $1.6 billion worth of merchandise each year and averages 113,000 orders per day. Sears, Kmart, JCPenney, Spiegel, and other major retailers are now looking into the home shopping industry.[28]

Beyond infomercials, home shopping channels, and other direct-response television marketing approaches, many experts think that advances in two-way, interactive television and linkages with Internet technology will one day make television shopping one of the major forms of direct marketing.[29]

Kiosk Marketing

Some companies place information and ordering machines—called *kiosks* (in contrast to vending machines, which dispense actual products)—in stores, airports, and other locations. Hallmark and American Greetings use kiosks to help customers create and purchase personalized greeting cards. Tower Records has listening kiosks that let customers listen to the music before purchase. Kiosks in the do-it-yourself ceramics stores of California-based Color Me Mine Inc. contain clip-art images that customers can use to decorate the ceramics pieces they purchase in the store. At Car Max, the used car superstore, customers use a kiosk with a touch-screen computer to get information about its vast inventory of as many as 1,000 cars and trucks. Customers can choose a handful and print out photos, prices, features, and locations on the store's lot. The use of such kiosks is expected to increase fivefold during the next three years.[30]

Business marketers also use kiosks. For example, Dow Plastics places kiosks at trade shows to collect sales leads and to provide information on its 700 products. The kiosk system reads customer data from encoded registration badges and produces technical data sheets that can be printed at the kiosk or faxed or mailed to the customer. The system has resulted in a 400 percent increase in qualified sales leads.[31]

Like about everything else these days, kiosks are also going online, as many companies merge the powers of the real and virtual worlds. For example, in some Levi-Strauss stores, you can plug your measurements into a Web kiosk and have custom-made jeans delivered to your home within two weeks. Gap has installed interactive kiosks, called Web lounges, in some of its stores that provide gift ideas or let customers match up outfits without trying them on in dressing rooms. Outdoor equipment retailer REI recently outfitted its stores with kiosks that provide customers with product information and let them place orders online.[32]

ONLINE MARKETING AND ELECTRONIC COMMERCE

Online marketing
Marketing conducted through interactive online computer systems, which link consumers with sellers electronically.

Commercial online services
Services that offer online information and marketing services to subscribers who pay a monthly fee, such as America Online, CompuServe, and Prodigy.

Internet
The vast and burgeoning global web of computer networks with no central management or ownership.

World Wide Web (the Web)
The user-friendly Internet access standard.

Online marketing is conducted through interactive online computer systems, which link consumers with sellers electronically. There are two types of online marketing channels: commercial online services and the Internet.

Commercial online services offer online information and marketing services to subscribers who pay a monthly fee. The best known online service provider is giant America Online, which has more than 21 million subscribers. Microsoft Network (MSN) and Prodigy trail far behind AOL with 2.45 million and 1 million subscribers, respectively.[33] These online services provide subscribers with information (news, libraries, education, travel, sports, reference), entertainment (fun and games), shopping services, dialogue opportunities (bulletin boards, forums, chat boxes), and e-mail.

After growing rapidly through the mid-1990s, the commercial online services have now been overtaken by the **Internet** as the primary online marketing channel. In fact, all of the online service firms now offer Internet access as a primary service. The Internet is a vast and burgeoning global web of computer networks. It evolved from a network created by the Defense Department during the 1960s, initially to link government labs, contractors, and military installations. Today, this huge, public computer network links computer users of all types all around the world. Anyone with a PC, a modem, and the right software can browse the Internet to obtain or share information on almost any subject and to interact with other users.[34]

Internet usage surged with the development of the user-friendly **World Wide Web** (the **Web**) and Web browser software such as Netscape Navigator and Microsoft Internet Explorer. Today, even novices can surf the Internet and experience fully integrated text, graphics, images, and sound. Users can send e-mail, exchange views, shop for products, and access news, food recipes, art, and business information. The Internet itself is free, although individual users usually must pay a commercial access provider to be hooked up to it.

Commercial online services: Leader America Online has more than 19 million subscribers who pay a monthly fee for its information and marketing services.

Rapid Growth of Online Marketing

Although still in their infancy, Internet usage and online marketing are growing explosively. Today, some 40 million U.S. households are dialing into the Internet, up from just 6 million in 1994. The U.S. Internet population is expected to swell to some 60 million households by the year 2002. Total U.S. purchasing on the Web is expected to skyrocket from zero in 1994 and about $130 billion in 1999 to $1.4 trillion by 2003.[35]

Electronic commerce (e-commerce)
The general term for a buying and selling process that is supported by electronic means.

This explosion of Internet usage heralds the dawning of a new world of *electronic commerce*. **Electronic commerce** is the general term for a buying and selling process that is supported by electronic means. *Electronic markets* are "market*spaces*," rather than physical "market*places*," in which sellers offer their products and services electronically, and buyers search for information, identify what they want, and place orders using a credit card or other means of electronic payment.

The electronic commerce explosion is all around us. Here are just a few examples:

★ A reporter wants to buy a 35mm camera. She turns on her computer, logs onto the Shopper's Advantage Web site, clicks on cameras, then clicks on 35mm cameras. A list of all the major brands appears, along with information about each brand. She can retrieve a photo of each camera and reviews by experts. Finding the camera she wants, she places an order by typing in her credit card number, address, and preferred shipping mode.

★ An affluent investor decides to do his own banking and investing. He signs onto discount brokerage Charles Schwab Company's SchwabNOW Web site (www.schwab. com), checks the current status of his investment account, and obtains reports on several stocks he is considering buying. After completing his research, he reviews current stock prices and places his buy and sell orders.

★ An executive is planning a trip to London and wants to locate a hotel that meets her needs. She signs onto the Travelocity Web site (www.travelocity.com) and inputs her criteria (rate, location, amenities, safety). The computer produces a list of appropriate hotels, and she can book a room once she has made her choice. Eventually, videos giving a "guided tour" of each hotel will be included in the program.

E-commerce is exploding: The Charles Schwab Web site allows clients to check the status of their accounts, research stocks, receive investment advice, place buy and sell orders, and create their own customized home pages.

According to one study, nearly 60 percent of all Internet users have used the Web to shop, a 15 percent increase over just a year ago.[36] Whereas business-to-consumer e-commerce is growing rapidly, business-to-business Internet commerce is exploding. Business buyers are far and away the largest Web users, accounting for more than 90 percent of all e-commerce.[37]

The Online Consumer

When people envision the typical Internet user, some mistakenly envision a pasty-faced computer nerd or "cyberhead." Others envision a young, techy, upscale male professional. Such stereotypes are sadly outdated.

The Internet population does differ demographically from the general population. As a whole, the Internet population is still younger, more affluent, better educated, and more male than the general population. However, as more and more people find their way onto the Internet, the cyberspace population is becoming more mainstream and diverse. For example, one recent study of Internet "newbies"—those who started using the Internet in the past year—found that 71 percent had no college degree, 65 percent earn less than $50,000 a year, and only 25 percent were younger than 30.[38] An industry analyst summarizes:

> The Internet isn't just a geek's playground anymore. These days, everybody's logging on. . . . Doral Main, a 51-year-old mother of two and office manager of a low-income property company in Oakland, CA, saves precious time by shopping the Internet for greeting cards and getaways. Her Net-newbie father, Charles, 73, goes online to buy supplies for his wood-carving hobby. Even niece Katrina, 11, finds excitement on the Web, picking gifts she wants from the Disney.com site. "It's addictive," Main says of the Net. [Indeed,] the Web isn't mostly a hangout for techno-nerds anymore.[39]

Thus, increasingly, the Internet provides online marketers with access to a broad range of demographic segments. For example, 46 percent of Internet users are women, up from only 37 percent three years ago. And although more than half of all users are professionals or managers, this percentage is decreasing.[40]

Internet users come from all age groups. For example, the populations of almost 9 million "Net kids" and more than 8 million teens (predicted to reach almost 22 million and 17 million, respectively, by the year 2002) have attracted a host of online marketers. America Online offers a Kids Only area featuring homework help and online magazines along with the usual games, software, and chat rooms. The Microsoft Network site carries Disney's Daily Blast, which offers kids games, stories, comic strips with old and new Disney characters, and current events tailored to preteens. Nickelodeon (www.nick.com) offers Natalie's Backseat Traveling Web Show, which includes games based on a Nickelodeon character named Natalie. "Similar to the offline market," observes one expert, "kids and teens have a profound impact on online purchasing decisions. . . . Instead of grabbing parents' coat sleeves, today's kids ask parents for credit card numbers in place of an allowance and buy products online."[41]

Although Internet users are younger on average than the population as a whole, seniors age 55 to 64 make up some 22 percent of today's online households and that number will grow to 40 percent by 2003. Whereas younger groups are more likely to use the Internet for entertainment and socializing, older Internet surfers go online for more serious matters. For example, 24 percent of people in this age group use the Internet for investment purposes, compared with only 3 percent of those 25 to 29. Thus, older Netizens make an attractive market for Web businesses, ranging from florists and automotive retailers to financial services providers.[42]

Internet users also differ psychographically from the general consumer population. As discussed in chapter 5 (see Marketing Highlight 5.1), Forrester Research and SRI Consulting have developed approaches for measuring attitudes, preferences, and behavior of online service and Internet users. SRI Consulting's Web site (www.future.sri.com/VALS/survey/html) allows visitors to take the VALS 2 questionnaire and get immediate feedback on their VALS 2 type. The firm has identified 10 different psychographic segments ranging from Wizards, skilled users who identify strongly with the Internet, to Socialites, who are strongly oriented toward social aspects of the Internet.[43]

Finally, Internet consumers differ in their approaches to buying and in their responses to marketing. They are empowered consumers who have greater control over the marketing process. People who use the Internet place greater value on information and tend to respond negatively to messages aimed only at selling. Whereas traditional marketing targets a somewhat passive audience, online marketing targets people who actively select which Web sites they will visit and which ad banners they will click on. They decide what marketing information they will receive about which products and services and under what conditions. Thus, in online marketing, the consumer controls more of the interaction.

Internet search engines such as Yahoo! Go Network, and Excite give consumers access to varied information sources, making them better informed and more discerning shoppers. In fact, online buyers are increasingly creators of product information, not just consumers of it. As greater numbers of consumers join Internet interest groups that share product-related information, "word of Web" is joining "word of mouth" as an important buying influence. Thus, the new world of e-commerce will require new marketing approaches.

Conducting Online Marketing

Marketers can conduct online marketing in four ways: by creating an electronic presence online; placing ads online; participating in Internet forums, newsgroups, or "Web communities"; or using online e-mail or Webcasting.

Creating an Electronic Online Presence

A company can establish an electronic online presence in two ways: It can buy space on a commercial online service or it can open its own Web site. Buying a location on a commercial online service involves either renting storage space on the online service's computer or establishing a link from the company's own computer to the online service's shopping mall. JCPenney, for example, has links to America Online, Microsoft Network, and Prodigy, gaining access to the millions of consumers who subscribe to these services. The online services typically design the storefront for the company and introduce it to their subscribers. For these services, the company pays the online service an annual fee plus a small percentage of the company's online sales.

In addition to buying a location on an online service, or as an alternative, most companies have now created their own Web sites. These sites vary greatly in purpose and content. The most basic type is a **corporate Web site.** These sites are designed to build customer goodwill and to supplement other sales channels rather than to sell the company's products directly. For example, you can't buy ice cream at www.benjerrys.com, but you can learn all about Ben & Jerry's company philosophy, products, and locations; send a free E-card to a friend or subscribe to the Chunk Mail newsletter; and while away time in the Fun Stuff area, playing "Ask Habeeni" or "The Phish Game." Similarly, Nabisco's LifeSavers Candystand Web site

Corporate Web site
Web site that seeks to build customer goodwill and to supplement other sales channels rather than to sell the company's products directly.

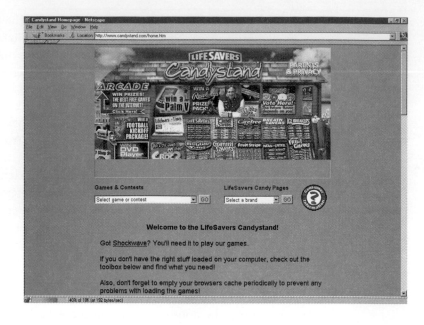

Corporate Web site: The highly entertaining Candystand Web site doesn't sell LifeSavers products. However, it does offer a rich variety of features that create an entertaining online experience for children and teenagers. It also gathers useful customer feedback.

doesn't sell candy but does generate consumer excitement and goodwill, as well as valuable feedback to LifeSavers brand managers:

> ★ Nabisco's highly entertaining LifeSavers Candystand Web site (www.candystand.com) features a rich variety of more than 27 interactive games, along with a variety of informational features and promotions, primarily designed to interest children and teenagers. Candystand contains 11 themed sections, each dedicated to a particular LifeSavers brand. "Our philosophy is to create an exciting online experience that reflects the fun and quality associated with the LifeSavers brands," says Silvio Bonvini, senior manager of new media at LifeSavers Company. "For the production cost of about two television spots we have a marketing vehicle that lives 24 hours a day, 7 days a week, 365 days a year." Candystand attracts more than 300,000 unique visitors a month. The site also offers LifeSavers an efficient channel for gathering customer feedback. Its "What Do You Think?" feature has generated 180,000 responses since the site launched in March 1997. "It's instant communication that we pass along directly to our brand people," Bonvini says. "It's not filtered by an agency or edited in any way." Comments collected from the Web site have resulted in improved packaging of one LifeSavers product and the resurrection of the abandoned Wintergreen flavor in the Carefree sugarless gum line.[44]

Corporate Web sites typically offer a rich variety of information and other features in an effort to answer customer questions, build closer customer relationships, and generate excitement about the company. They generally provide information about the company's history, its mission and philosophy, and the products and services that it offers. They might also tell about current events, company personnel, financial performance, and employment opportunities. Most corporate Web sites also provide entertainment features to attract and hold visitors. Finally, the site might also provide opportunities for customers to ask questions or make comments through e-mail before leaving the site.

Marketing Web site
Web site designed to engage consumers in an interaction that will move them closer to a purchase or other marketing outcome.

Other companies create a **marketing Web site.** These sites are designed to engage consumers in an interaction that will move them closer to a purchase or other marketing outcome. Such a site might include a catalog, shopping tips, and promotional features such as coupons, sales events, or contests. Companies aggressively promote their marketing Web sites in print and broadcast advertising and through "banner-to-site" ads that pop up on other Web sites. Consumers can find a Web site for buying almost anything—clothing from Lands' End or JCPenney, books from Barnes & Noble, or flowers from Grant's Flowers to be sent anywhere in the world.

Toyota operates a marketing Web site at www.toyota.com. Once a potential customer clicks in, the car maker wastes no time trying to turn the inquiry into a sale. The site offers plenty of entertainment and useful information, from cross-country trip guides and tips for driving with kids to events such as a Golf Skills Challenge and a Bike Express. But the site is also loaded with more serious selling features, such as detailed descriptions of current Toyota models and information on dealer locations and services, complete with maps and dealer Web links. Visitors who want to go further can use the Shop@Toyota feature to choose a Toyota, select equipment, and price it, then contact a dealer and even apply for credit. Or they fill out an online order form (supplying name, address, phone number, and e-mail address) for brochures and a free, interactive CD-ROM that shows off the features of Toyota models. The chances are good that before the CD-ROM arrives, a local dealer will call to invite the prospect in for a test drive. Toyota's Web site has now replaced its 800 number as the number-one source of customer leads.

Business-to-business marketers also make good use of marketing Web sites. For example, corporate buyers can visit Sun Microsystems' Web site (www.sun.com), select detailed descriptions of Sun's products and solutions, request sales and service information, and interact with staff members. Customers visiting GE Plastics' Web site (www.ge.com/plastics) can draw on more than 1,500 pages of information to get answers about the company's products anytime and from anywhere in the world. FedEx's Web site (www.fedex.com) allows customers to schedule their own shipments, request a courier, and track their packages in transit.[45]

Creating a Web site is one thing; getting people to *visit* the site is another. The key is to create enough value and excitement to get consumers to come to the site, stick around, and come back again. This means that companies must constantly update their sites to keep them fresh and exciting. Doing so involves time and expense, but the expense is necessary if the online marketer wishes to cut through the increasing online clutter. In addition, many online marketers spend heavily on good old-fashioned advertising and other offline marketing avenues to attract visitors to their sites. Says one analyst, "The reality today is you can't build a brand simply on the Internet. You have to go offline."[46]

For some types of products, attracting visitors is easy. Consumers buying new cars, computers, or financial services will be open to information and marketing initiatives from sellers. Marketers of lower-involvement products, however, may face a difficult challenge in attracting Web site visitors. As one veteran notes, "If you're shopping for a computer and you see a banner that says, 'We've ranked the top 12 computers to purchase,' you're going to click on the banner. [But] what kind of banner could encourage any consumer to visit dentalfloss.com?"[47] For such low-interest products, the company should create a corporate Web site to answer customer questions and build goodwill, using it only to supplement selling efforts through other channels.

Online ads

Ads that appear while subscribers are surfing online services or Web sites, including banners, pop-up windows, "tickers," and "roadblocks."

Placing Advertisements Online

Companies can use online advertising to build their Internet brands or to attract visitors to their Web sites. **Online ads** pop up while Internet users are surfing online services or Web sites. Such ads include banner ads, pop-up windows, "tickers" (banners that move across the screen), and "roadblocks" (full-screen ads that

Banner ads: While booking airline tickets on Travelocity.com, site visitors are exposed to ads from VISA, Disney Vacation Club, Palm VII, and others. However, such ads are easily overlooked.

users must pass through to get to other screens they wish to view). For example, a Web user or America Online subscriber who is looking up airline schedules or fares might find a flashing banner on the screen exclaiming, "Rent a car from Alamo and get up to 2 days free!" To attract visitors to its own Web site, Toyota sponsors Web banner ads on other sites, ranging from ESPN SportZone (www.espn.com) to Parent Soup (www.parentsoup.com), a kind of online coffee klatch through which moms and dads exchange views. Another form of Web advertising is *content sponsorships.* For example, Advil sponsors ESPN SportZone's Injury Report and Oldsmobile sponsors AOL's Celebrity Circle.

Companies spent almost $2 billion on Web advertising in 1998, and spending is expected to increase to almost $8.9 billion by 2002.[48] Still, this represents only a tiny fraction of overall advertising media expenditures when compared with the more than $40 billion each spent for advertising in newspapers and on broadcast television. Many marketers still question the value of Internet advertising as an effective tool. Costs are reasonable compared with those of other advertising media. For example, Web advertising on ESPNet SportZone, which attracts more than 500,000 Web surfers and 20 million "hits"—the number of times the site is accessed—per week, costs about $300,000 per year. However, Web surfers can easily ignore these banner ads and often do. Moreover, the industry has yet to come up with good measures of Web advertising impact—of who clicks on Web ads and how the ads affect them. Thus, although many firms are experimenting with Web advertising, it still plays only a minor role in their promotion mixes.

Participating in Forums, Newsgroups, and Web Communities

Companies may decide to participate in or sponsor Internet forums, newsgroups, and bulletin boards that appeal to specific special-interest groups. Such activities may be organized for commercial or noncommercial purposes. *Forums* are discussion groups located on commercial online services. A forum may operate a library, a "chat room" for real-time message exchanges, and even a classified ad directory.

For example, America Online boasts some 14,000 chat rooms, which account for a third of its members' online time. It also provides "buddy lists," which alert members when friends are online, allowing them to exchange instant messages. Most forums are sponsored by special-interest groups. Thus, as a major musical instruments manufacturer, Yamaha might start a forum on classical music.

Newsgroups are the Internet version of forums. However, such groups are limited to people posting and reading messages on a specified topic, rather than managing libraries or conferencing. Internet users can participate in newsgroups without subscribing. There are thousands of newsgroups dealing with every imaginable topic, from healthful eating and caring for your Bonsai tree to collecting antique cars or exchanging views on the latest soap opera happenings.

Bulletin board systems (BBSs) are specialized online services that center on a specific topic or group. There are over 60,000 BBSs originating in the United States, dealing with topics such as vacations, health, computer games, and real estate. Marketers might want to identify and participate in newsgroups and BBSs that attract subscribers who fit their target markets. However, newsgroups and BBS users often resent commercial intrusions on their Net space, so the marketer must tread carefully, participating in subtle ways that provide real value to participants.

The popularity of forums and newsgroups has resulted in a rash of commercially sponsored Web sites called *Web communities*. Such sites allow members to congregate online and exchange views on issues of common interest. They are the cyberspace equivalent to a Starbucks coffeehouse, a place where everybody knows your e-mail address. For example, iVillage is a Web community in which "smart, compassionate, real women" can obtain information and exchange views on families, fitness, relationships, travel, finances, or just about any other topic. The site reaches 7.3 million unique visitors per month, greater than the combined monthly average paid circulation of *Cosmopolitan, Glamour, Vogue,* and *Marie Claire* magazines. Tripod is an online hangout for twentysomethings, offering chat rooms and free home pages for posting job resumés. Parent Soup is an online community of more than 200,000 parents who spend time online gathering parenting information, chatting with other parents about kid-related issues, and linking with other related sites.

Visitors to these Internet neighborhoods develop a strong sense of community. Such communities are attractive to advertisers because they draw consumers with common interests and well-defined demographics. For example, Parent Soup provides an ideal environment for the Web ads of Johnson & Johnson, Gerber's, Wal-Mart, and other companies targeting family audiences. Moreover, cyberhood consumers visit frequently and stay online longer, increasing the chance of meaningful exposure to the advertiser's message.

Web communities can be either social or work related. One successful work-related community is Agriculture Online (or @griculture Online). This site offers commodity prices, recent farm news, and chat rooms of all types. Rural surfers can visit the Electronic Coffee Shop and pick up the latest down-on-the-farm joke or join a hot discussion on controlling soybean cyst nematodes. @griculture Online has been highly successful, attracting as many as 5 million hits per month.[49]

Using E-mail and Webcasting

A company can encourage prospects and customers to send questions, suggestions, and even complaints to the company via e-mail. Customer service representatives can quickly respond to such messages. The company may also develop Internet-based electronic mailing lists of customers or prospects. Such lists provide an excellent opportunity to introduce the company and its offerings to new customers and to build ongoing relationships with current ones. Using the lists, online marketers can send out customer newsletters, special product or promotion offers based on customer purchasing histories, reminders of service requirements or warranty renewals, or announcements of special events.

3Com Corporation, a manufacturer of high-tech computer hardware, made good use of e-mail to generate and qualify customer leads for its Network Interface Cards. The company used targeted e-mail and banner ads on 18 different computer-related Web sites to attract potential buyers to its own Web site featuring a "3Com Classic" sweepstakes, where by filling out the entry form, visitors could register to win a 1959 Corvette. The campaign generated 22,000 leads, which were further qualified using e-mail and telemarketing. "Hot" leads were passed along to 3Com's inside sales force. "[Sales reps] were very skeptical," says a 3Com marketing manager, "but they were blown away by how well the contest did." Of the 482 leads given to reps, 71 turned into actual sales that totaled $2.5 million. What's more, states the manager, "Now I've got 22,000 names in my e-mail database that I can go back and market to."[50]

Webcasting

The automatic downloading of customized information of interest to recipients' PCs, affording an attractive channel for delivering Internet advertising or other information content.

Companies can also sign on with any of a number of **"Webcasting"** services, such as PointCast and Ifusion, which automatically download customized information to recipients' PCs. For a monthly fee, subscribers to these services can specify the channels they want—news, company information, entertainment, and others—and the topics they're interested in. Then, rather than spending hours scouring the Internet, they can sit back while the Webcaster automatically delivers information of interest to their desktops.[51]

Webcasting, also known as "push" programming, affords an attractive channel through which online marketers can deliver their Internet advertising or other information content. The major commercial online services are also beginning to offer Webcasting to their members. For example, America Online offers a feature called Driveway that will fetch information, Web pages, and e-mail based on members' preferences and automatically deliver it to their PCs.

As with other types of online marketing, companies must be careful that they don't cause resentment among Internet users who are already overloaded with "junk e-mail." Warns one analyst, "There's a fine line between adding value and the consumer feeling that you're being intrusive."[52] Companies must beware of irritating consumers by sending unwanted e-mail to promote their products. Netiquette, the unwritten rules that guide Internet etiquette, suggests that marketers should ask customers for permission to e-mail marketing pitches—and tell recipients how to stop the flow of e-mail promotions at any time. This approach, known as permission-based marketing, is emerging as a new model for e-mail marketing (see Marketing Highlight 17.3).

The Promise and Challenges of Online Marketing

Online marketing offers great promise for the future. Its most ardent apostles envision a time when the Internet and e-commerce will replace magazines, newspapers, and even stores as sources of information and buying. Yet despite all the hype and promise, online marketing may be years away from realizing its full potential. Even then, it is unlikely to fulfill such sweeping predictions. To be sure, online marketing will become a full and complete business model for some companies; Internet firms such as Amazon.com, eBay, Yahoo!, and Netscape; and direct-marketing companies such as Dell Computer. Michael Dell's goal is one day "to have *all* customers conduct *all* transactions on the Internet, globally." But for most companies, online marketing will remain just one important approach to the marketplace that works alongside other approaches in a fully integrated marketing mix.

For many marketers, including fast-growing Internet superstars such as Amazon.com, the Web is still not a money-making proposition. According to one report, less than half of today's Web sites are profitable.[53] Here are just some of the challenges that online marketers face:

★ *Limited consumer exposure and buying:* Although expanding rapidly, online marketing still reaches only a limited marketspace. Moreover, many Web users do more window browsing than actual buying. One source estimates that although 65 percent of current Internet users have used the Web to check out products and compare prices prior to a purchase decision, only 14 percent of Internet users have actually purchased anything online. Still fewer have used their credit card.[54]

★ *Skewed user demographics and psychographics:* Although the Web audience is becoming more mainstream, online users still tend to be more upscale and technically oriented than the general population. This makes online marketing ideal for marketing computer hardware and software, consumer electronics, financial services, and certain other classes of products. However, it makes online marketing less effective for selling mainstream products.

★ *Chaos and clutter:* The Internet offers millions of Web sites and a staggering volume of information. Thus, navigating the Internet can be frustrating, confusing, and time consuming for consumers. In this chaotic and cluttered environment, many Web ads and sites go unnoticed or unopened. Even when noticed, marketers will find it difficult to hold consumer attention. One study found that a site must capture Web surfers' attention within eight seconds or lose them to another site. That leaves very little time for marketers to promote and sell their goods.

★ *Security:* Consumers still worry that unscrupulous snoopers will eavesdrop on their online transactions or intercept their credit card numbers and make unauthorized purchases. In turn, companies doing business online fear that others will use the Internet to invade their computer systems for the purposes of commercial espionage or even sabotage. Online marketers are developing solutions to such security problems. However, there appears to be an ongoing competition between the technology of Internet security systems and the sophistication of those seeking to break them.

★ *Ethical concerns:* Privacy is a primary concern. Marketers can easily track Web site visitors, and many consumers who participate in Web site activities provide extensive personal information. This may leave consumers open to information abuse if companies make unauthorized use of the information in marketing their products or exchanging electronic lists with other companies. There are also concerns about segmentation and discrimination. The Internet currently serves upscale consumers well. However, poorer consumers have less access to the Internet, leaving them increasingly less informed about products, services, and prices.[55]

Despite these challenges, companies large and small are quickly integrating online marketing into their marketing mixes. As it continues to grow, online marketing will prove to be a powerful tool for building customer relationships, improving sales, communicating company and product information, and delivering products and services more efficiently and effectively.

PERMISSION-BASED MARKETING: CLICK HERE FOR OUR PITCH

Companies that send marketing pitches via e-mail walk a fine and dangerous line. One false move—such as sending e-mail to a customer who didn't request it—can quickly damage a company's reputation. Yet, more and more companies are now walking that fine line, and for good reason. Done right, an e-mail campaign can build profitable customer relationships at a fraction of the cost of a "d-mail" (direct-mail) campaign.

E-mail marketing offers several real benefits. The Internet gives marketers immediate access to millions of customers and prospects. Studies show that 80 percent of Internet users respond to e-mail within 36 hours, compared with a 2 percent response rate for the average direct-mail campaign. Also, compared to other forms of online promotion, e-mail is usually a hands-down winner. Consider the "click-through" rate. A click-through occurs whenever a user follows links—whether they are provided through a site's ad banners or e-mail—to a company's home page or sales site. The average click-through

rate for ad banners has dropped to less than 1 percent whereas click-through rates for e-mail are running around 80 percent. Then there's cost. Paper, printing, and postage are expensive and getting more so every year. In contrast, e-mail costs almost nothing to produce and send. For example, Microsoft used to spend approximately $70 million a year on paper-driven campaigns. Now, the software giant sends out 20 million pieces of e-mail every month at a significant savings over the costs of paper-based campaigns.

There is a catch, though. In order to achieve stellar click-throughs and to get recipients to respond quickly—or even at all—marketers must follow the cardinal rule of e-mail marketing: Get the consumer's permission. In fact, Seth Godin, a pioneer of direct marketing on the Web and CEO of Yoyodyne Entertainment Inc. (recently acquired by Yahoo!), has even come up with a term—"permission-based marketing"—to define the new e-mail marketing model. According to

Godin, whose company specializes in developing Web-based marketing relationships for its clients, consumers are weary of unwanted marketing pitches. Permission-based marketing provides the perfect remedy by using the interactivity of the Internet to let consumers have a say in what is sent to them. Godin compares permission-based marketing to dating; if a company conducts itself well in its first contact with consumers, it will build up trust that encourages them to open up to subsequent offers.

One company that has been successful in using permission-based e-mail marketing campaigns is Iomega Corporation, which markets computer storage devices such as the popular Zip drive. Iomega always starts its e-mail campaigns with its base of registered customers. From this select list, it mails only to those who have given Iomega permission to send them e-mail. By targeting customers who actively agree to receive e-mail, companies can increase their chances of getting a

INTEGRATED DIRECT MARKETING

Too often, a company's individual direct-marketing efforts are not well integrated with one another or with other elements of its marketing and promotion mixes. For example, a firm's media advertising may be handled by the advertising department working with a traditional advertising agency. Meanwhile, its direct-mail and catalog business efforts may be handled by direct-marketing specialists while its Web site is developed and operated by an outside Internet firm.

Integrated direct marketing
Direct-marketing campaigns that use multiple vehicles and multiple stages to improve response rates and profits.

Within a given direct-marketing campaign, too many companies use only a "one-shot" effort to reach and sell a prospect or a single vehicle in multiple stages to trigger purchases. For example, a magazine publisher might send a series of four direct-mail notices to a household to get a subscriber to renew before giving up. A more powerful approach is **integrated direct marketing,** which involves using carefully coordinated multiple-media, multiple-stage campaigns. Such campaigns positive response or sale and avoid being blackballed on the Internet.

Whereas most consumers who are peeved at getting junk mail simply toss it in the trash, really angry consumers can strike back online in new, alarmingly effective ways. With just a quick e-mail to friends, all those on their list serve, or to other Web sites—or by setting up an anti-company Web site—an irate consumer can give offending companies a bad reputation almost instantaneously. For this reason, effective e-mail marketers not only restrict their mailings to those who "opt in" but also offer recipients the chance to "opt out" at every turn. At Iomega, for instance, every single e-mail, even those sent to people on record as consenting to additional mailings, provides customers with an easy opt-out option.

Yet, it takes much more than simply asking permission and providing an opt-out escape to craft a successful e-mail marketing campaign. Most important: As in any direct marketing offer, you must offer something of value. Here are some other important guidelines followed by pioneering e-mail marketers.

Give the customer a reason to respond: Yoyodyne offers surfers powerful incentives for reading e-mail pitches and online ads. The innovative direct-marketing firm uses e-mail trivia games, scavenger hunts, and instant-win sweepstakes to lure customers. So far, more than a million Internet surfers have agreed to wade through product information from companies such as Sprint, Readers Digest, and Major League Baseball to become eligible for prizes such as a trip to the Caribbean or a bag of gold.

Personalize the content of your e-mails: The Web allows companies to personalize e-mails based on past interactions, and customers are more receptive to personalized pitches. Cyberstore Amazon.com has gained a loyal following by sending willing customers personalized recommendations based on past purchases. IBM's "Focusing on You News Digest" is distributed directly through customers' office e-mail, delivering to them only "the news they choose." Customers who agree to receive the newsletter select from topics listed on an interest profile.

Offer something the customer couldn't get via direct mail: Direct-mail campaigns take a lot of time to plan, carry out, and mail. Because e-mail campaigns can be carried out more quickly, they can offer time-sensitive information. Travelocity, a travel site on the Web, sends frequent e-mails called Fare Watchers, which pitch last-minute cheap airfares. Club Med uses e-mail to pitch unsold, discounted vacation packages to the 34,000 people in its database.

Playing by such rules, many direct marketers have turned e-mail into a hot new marketing media. Rather than resenting it, many customers and prospects actively seek to be put on the e-mail lists of their favorite companies.

Sources: Nicole Harris, "Spam That You Might Not Delete," *Business Week,* June 15, 1998, pp. 115–18; Matt Barthel, "Marketer: Banks Miss Web's Real Strength—Relationships," *American Banker,* October 21, 1998, p. 19; Jay Winchester, "Point, Click, Sell," *Sales & Marketing Management,* November 1998, pp. 100–101; Michelle L. Smith, "One to One: Put the Customer in the Information Driver Seat and Build Better Relationships," *Direct Marketing,* January 1998, pp. 37–39; Roberta Fusaro, "More Sites Use E-Mail for Marketing," *Computerworld,* October 19, 1998, pp. 51–54; and Mary Kuntz, "Point, Click—And Here's the Pitch," *Business Week,* February 9, 1998, pp. ENT8–ENT10.

can greatly improve response. Whereas a direct-mail piece alone might generate a 2 percent response, adding a Web site and toll-free phone number might raise the response rate by 50 percent. Then, a well-designed outbound telemarketing effort might lift response by an additional 500 percent. Suddenly, a 2 percent response has grown to 15 percent or more by adding interactive marketing channels to a regular mailing.

More elaborate integrated direct-marketing campaigns can be used. Consider the multimedia, multistage campaign shown in Figure 17.2. Here, the paid ad

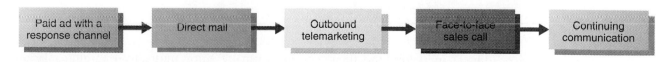

FIGURE 17.2   An integrated direct-marketing campaign

MARKETING HIGHLIGHT

AMERICAN STANDARD'S INTEGRATED DIRECT MARKETING: ANYTHING BUT STANDARD

You probably haven't thought much about your bathroom—it's not something that most of us get all that inspired about. But as it turns out, you probably have a relationship with your bathroom unlike that with any other room in your house. It's where you start and end your day, primp and preen and admire yourself, escape from the rigors of everyday life, and do some of your best thinking. The marketers at American Standard, the plumbing fixtures giant, understand this often-overlooked but special little room. A few years back they set out upon a mission to help people design bathrooms worthy of their finest moments.

Working with its ad agency, Carmichael Lynch, American Standard created a wonderfully warm and highly effective but not-so-standard integrated marketing campaign. The campaign, called "We want you to love your bathroom," targeted men and women age 25 to 54 from households planning to remodel bathrooms or replace fixtures. The campaign employed a carefully integrated mix of brand-image and direct-response media ads, direct mailings, and per-

sonal contacts to create a customer database, generate sales leads, gently coax customers into its retail showrooms, and build sales and market share.

The campaign began with a series of humorous, soft-sell, brand-image ads in home and shelter magazines such as *Home, House Beautiful,* and *Country Living,* which reach a high percentage of readers undertaking remodeling projects. Featuring simple but artistic shots of ordinary bathroom fixtures and scenes, the ads positioned American Standard as a company that understands the special relationships we have with our bathrooms. For example, one ad showed a white toilet and a partially unwound roll of toilet paper, artfully arranged in a corner against plain blue-gray walls. "We're not in this business for the glory," proclaimed the headline. "Designing a toilet or sink may not be as glamorous as, say, designing a Maserati. But to us, it's every bit as important. After all, more people will be sitting on our seats than theirs."

Another ad showed the feet of a man standing on a white tile bathroom floor wearing his goofy-looking,

floppy-eared dog slippers. "The rest of the world thinks you're a genius," noted the ad. But "after a long day of being brilliant, witty, and charming, it's nice just to be comfortable. The right bathroom understands. And accepts you unconditionally." Each simple but engaging ad included a toll-free phone number and urged readers to call for a free guidebook "overflowing with products, ideas, and inspiration."

Whereas the brand-image ads positioned American Standard and its products, when it came to generating inquiries, the real workhorses were the one-third-page, couponlike direct-response ads that ran in the same magazines. One such ad noted, "You will spend seven years of your life in the bathroom. You will need a good book." Readers could obtain the free guidebook by mailing in the coupon or calling the toll-free number listed in the ad.

Consumers who responded found that they'd taken the first step in a carefully orchestrated relationship-building venture. First, they received the entertaining, highly informative, picture-filled 30-page guidebook *We Want You to Love Your Bathroom* along

creates product awareness and stimulates inquiries. The company immediately sends direct mail to those who inquire. Within a few days, the company follows up with a phone call seeking an order. Some prospects will order by phone; others might request a face-to-face sales call. In such a campaign, the marketer seeks to improve response rates and profits by adding media and stages that contribute more to additional sales than to additional costs (see Marketing Highlight 17.4).

PUBLIC POLICY AND ETHICAL ISSUES IN DIRECT MARKETING

Direct marketers and their customers usually enjoy mutually rewarding relationships. Occasionally, however, a darker side emerges. The aggressive and sometimes with a folksy letter thanking them for their interest and noting the locations of nearby American Standard dealers. The guidebook's purpose was straightforward—"Walk into your bathroom, turn the knob and suddenly, for a moment or an hour, the world stops turning. You should love the place. If you don't, well, American Standard wants to further your relationship. Thumb through this book. In the bathroom, perhaps. . . ."

The guidebook was chock full of helpful tips on bathroom design, starting with answers to some simple questions: What kind of lavatory—what color? The bathtub—how big; big enough for two? The toilet—sleek one-piece or familiar two-piece? The faucet? "You'll fumble for it every morning, so be particular about how it operates." To spice things up, the guidebook also contained loads of entertaining facts and trivia. An example: Did you know that "you will spend seven years in your bathroom . . . here's hoping your spouse doesn't sneak in first!" Another example: "During the Middle Ages, Christianity preached that to uncover your skin, even to bathe it, was an invitation to sin. Thank heavens for perfume. These days, we average about 4 baths or 7.5 showers a week." Of course, the guidebook contained plenty of information on American Standard products, along with a tear-out card that

prospective customers could return to obtain more detailed guides and product catalogs.

In addition to the guidebook, customers received a carefully coordinated stream of communications from American Standard, starting with a series of "Bathroom Reading" bulletins, each containing information on specific bathroom design issues. For example, one issue contained information and tips on how to make a bathroom safer; another offered "10 neat ways to save water."

Meanwhile, information about prospective customers and their remodeling projects collected by the 1-800 operator or from the coupon went into American Standard's customer database. The database generated leads for salespeople at American Standard's showrooms around the country. The company marketed the program to key distributors and kitchen and bath dealers, motivating them to follow up on leads and training them how to do it effectively. The key was to get customers who'd made inquiries to come into the showroom. Not long after making their inquiries, prospective customers typically received a handwritten postcard—or perhaps even a phone call—from a local dealer's showroom consultant, who extended a personal invitation to

visit, see American Standard products firsthand, and discuss bathroom designs. Thus, the integrated direct-marketing program built relationships not just with buyers but with dealers as well.

American Standard's integrated direct-marketing campaign did wonders for the company's positioning and performance. After the campaign began, American Standard's plumbing division experienced steady increases in sales and earnings. The campaign generated tens of thousands of qualified leads for local showrooms—more than a half million qualified leads in the first two years.

Research has confirmed significant shifts in consumer perceptions of American Standard and its products—from "boring and institutional" to well designed and loaded with "personal spirit." According to Bob Srenaski, group vice president of marketing at American Standard, the campaign "has totally repositioned our company and established a momentum and winning spirit that is extraordinary." Joe Summary, an account manager at Carmichael Lynch, says, "The campaign has been incredible. It's given American Standard and its products a more personal face, one that's helped us to build closer relationships with customers and dealers. From the first ad to the last contact with our dealers, the campaign was designed to help customers create bathrooms they'd love."

shady tactics of a few direct marketers can bother or harm consumers, giving the entire industry a black eye. Abuses range from simple excesses that irritate consumers to instances of unfair practices or even outright deception and fraud. During the past few years, the direct-marketing industry has also faced growing concerns about invasion of privacy issues.[56]

Irritation, Unfairness, Deception, and Fraud

Direct-marketing excesses sometimes annoy or offend consumers. Most of us dislike direct-response TV commercials that are too loud, too long, and too insistent. Especially bothersome are dinnertime or late-night phone calls. Beyond irritating consumers, some direct marketers have been accused of taking unfair advantage of impulsive or less sophisticated buyers. TV shopping shows and program-long "infomercials" seem to be the worst culprits. They feature smooth-talking hosts, elaborately staged demonstrations, claims of drastic price reductions, "while they last" time limitations, and unequaled ease of purchase to inflame buyers who have low sales resistance.

Worse yet, so-called heat merchants design mailers and write copy intended to mislead buyers. Political fund-raisers, among the worst offenders, sometimes use gimmicks such as "look-alike" envelopes that resemble official documents, simulated newspaper clippings, and fake honors and awards. Other direct marketers pretend to be conducting research surveys when they are actually asking leading questions to screen or persuade consumers. Fraudulent schemes, such as investment scams or phony collections for charity, have also multiplied in recent years. Crooked direct marketers can be hard to catch: Direct-marketing customers often respond quickly, do not interact personally with the seller, and usually expect to wait for delivery. By the time buyers realize that they have been bilked, the thieves are usually somewhere else plotting new schemes.

Invasion of Privacy

Invasion of privacy is perhaps the toughest public policy issue now confronting the direct-marketing industry. These days, it seems that almost every time consumers enter a sweepstakes, apply for a credit card, take out a magazine subscription, or order products by mail, telephone, or the Internet, their names are entered into some company's already bulging database. Using sophisticated computer technologies, direct marketers can use these databases to "microtarget" their selling efforts.

Consumers often benefit from such database marketing—they receive more offers that are closely matched to their interests. However, many critics worry that marketers may know *too* much about consumers' lives and that they may use this knowledge to take unfair advantage of consumers. At some point, they claim, the extensive use of databases intrudes on consumer privacy.

For example, they ask, should AT&T be allowed to sell marketers the names of customers who frequently call the 800 numbers of catalog companies? Should a company like American Express be allowed to make data on its 175 million American cardholders available to merchants who accept AmEx cards? Is it right for credit bureaus to compile and sell lists of people who have recently applied for credit cards—people who are considered prime direct-marketing targets because of their spending behavior? Or is it right for states to sell the names and addresses of driver's license holders, along with height, weight, and gender information, allowing apparel retailers to target tall or overweight people with special clothing offers?

In their drives to build databases, companies sometimes get carried away. For example, when first introduced, Intel's new Pentium III chip contained an imbedded serial number that allowed the company to trace users' equipment. When privacy advocates screamed, Intel disabled the feature. Similarly, Microsoft caused substantial privacy concerns when it introduced its Windows 95 software. It used a "Registration Wizard," which allowed users to register their new software online. However, when users went online to register, without their knowledge, Microsoft took the opportunity to "read" the configurations of their PCs. Thus, the company gained instant knowledge of the major software products running on each customer's system. When users learned of this invasion, they protested loudly and Microsoft abandoned the practice. Such actions have spawned a quiet but determined "privacy revolt" among consumers and public policy makers.[57]

In one survey of consumers, 79 percent of respondents said that they were concerned about threats to their personal privacy. In a survey of Internet users, 71 percent of respondents said there should be laws to protect Web privacy and a full 84 percent objected to firms selling information about users to other companies. In yet another survey, *Advertising Age* asked advertising industry executives how they felt about database marketing and the privacy issue. The responses of two executives show that even industry insiders have mixed feelings:[58]

> There are profound ethical issues relating to the marketing of specific household data—financial information, for instance. . . . For every household in the United States, the computer can guess with amazing accuracy things like credit use, net worth, and investments, the kind of information most people would never want disclosed, let alone sold to any marketer.
>
> It doesn't bother me that people know I live in a suburb of Columbus, Ohio, and have X number of kids. It [does] bother me that these people know the names of my wife and kids and where my kids go to school. They . . . act like they know me when the bottom line is they're attempting to sell me something. I do feel that database marketing has allowed companies to cross the fine line of privacy. . . . [And] in a lot of cases, I think they know they have crossed it.

The direct-marketing industry is addressing issues of ethics and public policy. For example, the Direct Marketing Association (DMA)—the largest association for businesses interested in interactive and database marketing with more than 4,600 member companies—recently developed its "Privacy Promise to American Consumers." This initiative, an effort to build consumer confidence in shopping direct, requires that all DMA members adhere to a carefully developed set of consumer privacy rules. The Privacy Promise requires that members notify customers when any personal information is rented, sold, or exchanged with others. Members must also honor consumer requests not to receive mail, telephone, or other solicitations again.

Direct marketers know that, left untended, such problems will lead to increasingly negative consumer attitudes, lower response rates, and calls for more restrictive state and federal legislation. More importantly, most direct marketers want the same things that consumers want: honest and well-designed marketing offers targeted only toward consumers who will appreciate and respond to them. Direct marketing is just too expensive to waste on consumers who don't want it.

The DMA recently developed its "Privacy Promise to American Consumers," which attempts to build consumer confidence by requiring that all DMA members adhere to certain carefully developed consumer privacy rules.

REVIEW OF CONCEPT CONNECTIONS

Mass marketers have typically tried to reach millions of buyers with a single product and a standard message communicated via the mass media. Consequently, most mass-marketing communications were one-way communications directed *at* consumers rather than two-way communications *with* consumers. Today, many companies are turning to direct marketing in an effort to reach carefully targeted customers more efficiently and to build stronger, more personal, one-to-one relationships with them.

1. Discuss the benefits of direct marketing to customers and companies and the trends fueling its rapid growth.

Customers benefit from direct marketing in many ways. For consumers, home shopping is fun, convenient, hassle-free; saves time; and gives them a bigger selection of merchandise. It allows them to comparison shop using mail catalogs and online shopping services, then order products and services without dealing with salespeople. Sellers also benefit. Direct marketers can target almost any group, customize offers to special wants and needs, and then use individualized communications to promote these offers. Direct marketers can also build an ongoing relationship with each customer; time offers to reach prospects at the right moment, thereby receiving higher readership and response; and easily test alternative media and messages. Finally, direct marketers gain privacy because their offer and strategy are less visible to competitors.

Various trends have led to the rapid growth of direct marketing. Market "demassification" has produced a constantly increasing number of market niches with specific preferences. Direct marketing enables sellers to focus efficiently on these minimarkets with offers that better match particular consumer wants and needs. Other trends encouraging at-home shopping include higher costs of driving, traffic and parking congestion, lack of time, a shortage of retail sales help, and long lines at checkout counters. Consumers like the convenience of direct marketers' toll-free phone numbers, their acceptance of orders round the clock, and their commitment to customer service. The growth of quick delivery via express carriers has also made direct shopping fast and easy. The increased affordability of computers and customer databases has allowed direct marketers to single out the best prospects for each of their products. Finally, in business-to-business marketing, lower cost-per-contact media has proven more cost effective in reaching and selling to more prospects and customers than using a sales force.

2. Define a customer database and list the four ways companies use databases in direct marketing.

A *customer database* is an organized collection of comprehensive data about individual customers or prospects, including geographic, demographic, psychographic, and behavioral data. Companies use databases to identify prospects, decide which customers should receive a particular offer, deepen customer loyalty, and reactivate customer purchases.

3. Identify the major forms of direct marketing.

The main forms of direct marketing include *face-to-face selling, telemarketing, direct-mail marketing, catalog marketing, direct-response television marketing, kiosk marketing,* and *online marketing.* Most companies today continue to rely heavily on *face-to-face selling* through a professional sales force, or they hire manufacturers' representatives and agents. *Telemarketing* consists of using the telephone to sell directly to consumers. *Direct-mail marketing* consists of the company sending an offer, announcement, reminder, or other item to a person at a specific address. Recently, three new forms of mail delivery have become popular—*fax mail, e-mail,* and *voice mail.* Some marketers rely on *catalog marketing,* or selling through catalogs mailed to a select list of customers or made available in stores. *Direct-response television marketing* has two forms: *direct-response advertising* or *infomercials* and *home shopping channels. Kiosks* are information and ordering machines that direct marketers place in stores, airports, and other locations. *Online marketing* involves online channels and electronic commerce and is usually conducted through interactive online computer systems, which electronically link consumers with sellers.

4. Compare the two types of online marketing channels and explain the effect of the Internet on electronic commerce.

The two types of online marketing channels are *commercial online services* and the *Internet. Commercial online services* provide online information and marketing services to subscribers for a monthly fee. The *Internet* is a vast global and public web of computer networks. In contrast to commercial online services, use of the Internet is free—anyone with a PC, a modem, and the right software can browse the Internet to obtain or share information on almost any subject and to interact with other users. The explosion of Internet usage has created a new world of *electronic commerce,* a term that refers to the buying and selling process that is supported by electronic means. In this process, *electronic markets* become "marketspaces" in which sellers offer products and services electronically, whereas buyers search for information, identify their wants and needs, and then place orders using a credit card or other form of electronic payment.

5. Identify the benefits of online marketing to consumers and marketers and the four ways marketers can conduct online marketing.

For consumers, online marketing is beneficial for many reasons. It is *interactive, immediate,* and provides access to an abundance of comparative *information* about products, companies, and competitors. Marketers also benefit from online marketing. For them, it helps *consumer relationship building, reduces costs, increases efficiency,* provides more *flexibility,* and is, in the form of the Internet, a *global* medium that enables buyers and sellers in different countries to interact with each other in seconds. Marketers can conduct online marketing by creating an electronic storefront; placing ads online; participating in Internet forums, newsgroups, or "Web communities"; or using online e-mail or Webcasting.

6. Discuss the public policy and ethical issues facing direct marketers.

Direct marketers and their customers have typically forged mutually rewarding relationships. However, there remains a potential for customer abuse, ranging from irritation and unfair practices to deception and fraud. In addition, there have been growing concerns about invasion of privacy, perhaps the most difficult public policy issue currently facing the direct-market industry.

KEY TERMS

Catalog marketing
Commercial online services
Corporate Web site
Customer database
Direct-mail marketing
Direct marketing

Direct-response television marketing
Electronic commerce (e-commerce)
Integrated direct marketing
Internet
Marketing Web site

Online ads
Online marketing
Telemarketing
Webcasting
World Wide Web (the Web)

ISSUES FOR DISCUSSION

1. The chapter suggests that a new direct marketing model has been created. Answer the following questions: (a) What is direct marketing? (b) How is it different from other forms of marketing delivery? (c) How will the new direct marketing model impact our emerging electronic marketplace?

2. As part of an integrated marketing mix, direct marketing brings many benefits to both buyers and sellers. Describe these benefits. Provide three examples of direct marketing firms that demonstrate strong marketing benefits for their customers. Describe and explain the benefits fully.

3. Companies that know about individual customer needs and characteristics can customize their offers, messages, delivery modes, and payment methods to maximize customer value and satisfaction. Pick two of these organizations and answer the following questions about them: (a) State Farm Insurance, (b) IBM, (c) the New York Metropolitan Opera, (d) the American Cancer Society, and (e) Lexus. What information should these companies keep in their customer databases? Where would they get this information? How might they use the databases? How much would it cost to build such databases?

4. List and briefly describe each of the major forms of direct marketing. Pick one of the following companies and demonstrate how it could use each form of direct marketing to sell its products and services: (a) Microsoft, (b) General Motors, or (c) Gap.

5. Direct-mail marketing used to mean sending an offer, announcement, reminder, or item to a person through the mail. Today, however, we are fast becoming a paperless society and new forms of direct communication are emerging. Critique (a) fax mail, (b) e-mail, and (c) voice mail as forms of direct mail. Discuss the advantages, disadvantages, customer profiles, costs, and future of each form.

6. Contact one of the personal computer direct marketers (such as Dell Computer at www.dell.com or Gateway at www.gateway.com). (a) How does the company make it easy to order its products? (b) What differentiates this company from traditional retailers or manufacturers? (c) What are the company's chief advantages and disadvantages? (d) How does it provide security (or not)? (e) Based on this experience, what is your opinion of online marketers?

7. In the past year there has been a dramatic increase in the number of Web communities (commercially sponsored Web sites). If you were (a) Nike, (b) Citicorp, (c) British Airways, or (d) Fuji, what type of Web communities would you be interested in sponsoring? What would be the possible advantages and disadvantages of doing this? Find a Web community and evaluate its site. Discuss your conclusions in class.

8. Online marketing offers great promise for the future. Assume that you are the sales manager for a local travel agency. Make a case that would persuade your superiors that going online would be a good investment. Cite the potential positive and negative outcomes.

MARKETING APPLICATIONS

1. In the past many consumers have dreaded anniversaries, birthdays, Mother's Day, Valentine's Day, and seemingly countless other gift-giving occasions because of the hassles associated with trying to find the perfect gift. E-commerce is beginning to change all that. Today, when you need to send flowers or small gifts at the last minute, the Internet is definitely the way to go. For example, a fast-growing number of florist Web sites provide the e-shopper with a convenient way to search by price, occasion, or types of flowers. Last-minute gift givers no longer have to rely on the florist's judgment or even to visit the florist to pick out arrangements. The florist Web sites let buyers make their own selections without leaving home or the office. Most of these Web retailers offer event reminder services (via e-mail) so that buyers will never forget important dates and occasions. Visit the following Web sites for more information: 1-800-Flowers (www.1800flowers.com), PC Flowers & Gifts (www.pcflowers.com), 2G Roses (www.freshroses.com), and GiftTree (www.gifttree.com).

   a. How does purchasing floral arrangements via the Internet compare with buying them by telephone or in person? Compare these channels in terms of cost, speed of delivery, selection of merchandise, freshness, dependability, ease of ordering, and ability to personalize requests?

   b. What are the difficulties in using the Internet for this type of purchasing? How could these difficulties be overcome?

   c. Which of the above Web sites seem to be the most user friendly? Why? Which site would you be most willing to use? Why?

   d. What future do you see for marketing flowers and gifts via the Internet? If you were a local florist, would you invest in a Web page? Why or why not? If you did invest in a Web page, how would you get old and new customers to use it?

2. Do you hate bulky PCs and laptops? Do you want something more mobile? Japanese camera maker Olympus (www.olympus.com) and computer maker IBM (www.ibm.com) have developed a computer you can wear. The screen is a monocle that fits over one eye and the computer itself is a pocketbook-size box with two buttons. This wearable PC weighs only 13 ounces, has an Intel Pentium processor, 64 megabytes of memory, and runs the Microsoft Windows operating system. To use the system, the wearer flips out the tiny eye screen from a headset and manipulates a banana-shaped handle with a touchpad and two buttons to select icons on the "Eye Trek" virtual screen. Keyboards are under development, although not currently available. Users can open and look at files and play audio and video. The wearable PC seems to be a step in the right direction for accomplishing Olympus's objective of getting in on the ground floor of the "virtual world" that is overtaking our society.

   a. What is the target market for the wearable PC? What uses do you foresee for the device? What would you name it?

   b. How might such a device advance society's use of the Internet? The use of online purchasing?

   c. Propose an integrated direct marketing campaign for introducing the wearable PC to the target market.

   d. What opportunities should an e-marketer see in such a device?

   e. Would you buy one of these PCs? Explain.

INTERNET CONNECTIONS

ONLINE MARKETING

Online marketing can bring benefits to customers that other channels cannot. A good example is online music stores, where customers can listen to clips of selected tracks before buying a CD. Other online benefits are ease of communication with customers and adaptability to marketplace changes. Visit CDNow (www.cdnow.com) and look up three CDs of your choosing. For each CD, record below the total number of tracks on that CD and the number of tracks that CDNow will let you sample.

CD title	Total tracks	Tracks available to sample

FOR DISCUSSION

1. Does CDNow offer other benefits that you might not find at a traditional retail music store? If so, what are they?
2. If you were to purchase a CD, how could CDNow use the information from your visit to develop a one-to-one relationship with you?
3. Are CDNow's prices competitive?
4. How could traditional music stores offer some of the same benefits as CDNow? Would it be cost-effective for them to do so?
5. Do you think CDNow should open a traditional store in addition to its online store? Why or why not?
6. Visit www.bizrate.com and see how CDNow rates against the competition. How do they place?

SAVVY SITES

- Did-it (www.did-it.com) gives Webmasters lots of ways to publicize their new Web sites. Among them are 50 different e-mail lists that target either consumers or businesses—the cyberspace version of direct mail.
- Direct Marketing World (www.dmworld.com) is an information center for the direct marketing industry.
- IBM has a great site for people thinking of starting an e-business (advisor.internet.ibm.com/inet.nsf). Visit the site and evaluate several options for your Internet business plan.

NOTES

1. Quotes and Dell performance statistics from Gary McWilliams, "Whirlwind on the Web," *Business Week,* April 7, 1997, pp. 132–36; Bill Robbins and Cathie Hargett, "Dell Internet Sales Top $1 Million a Day," press release, Dell Computer Corporation, March 4, 1997; "The InternetWeek Interview—Michael Dell," *InternetWeek,* April 13, 1999, p. 8; and information accessed online at www.dell.com/corporate/access/factpak/index.htm, January 2000. Also see "Nerdy Like a Fox," *Business Week,* January 1999, p. 74; James Cox, "Technology, Stock Market Click for World's Richest," *USA Today,* June 21, 1999, p. 2A; Melanie Warner, "The Young and the Loaded," *Fortune,* September 27, 1999, p. S12 and David Rynecki, "Has Dell Become Just Another Growth Stock?" *Fortune,* February 21, 2000, pp. 317–318.

2. Gary Hamel and Jeff Sampler, "The E-Corporation: More Than Just Web-Based, It's Building a New Industrial Order," *Fortune,* December 7, 1998, pp. 80–92.

3. Alan Mitchell, "Internet Zoo Spawns New Business Models," *Marketing Week,* January 21, 1999, pp. 24–25.

4. Hamel and Sampler, "The E-Corporation: More Than Just Web-Based, It's Building a New Industrial Order," p. 82.

5. Carol Krol, "Mead Johnson Finds Winning Formula for Reaching Moms," *Advertising Age,* April 26, 1999, p. 25.

6. See *Economic Impact: U.S. Direct Marketing Today,* Direct Marketing Association, 1999, accessed online at www.the-dma.org/services/libres-ecoimpact1b1a.shtml.

7. Facts on Internet usage and sales found in *Economic Impact: U.S. Direct Marketing Today,* 1999; and furnished by Forrester Research, August 1999.

8. See Don Peppers and Martha Rogers, *The One-to-One Future* (New York: Doubleday/Currency, 1993).

9. Carol Krol, "Pizza Hut's Database Makes Its Couponing More Efficient," *Advertising Age,* November 30, 1998, p. 27.

10. For these and other examples, see Jonathan Berry, "A Potent New Tool for Selling: Database Marketing," *Business Week,* September 4, 1994, pp. 56–62; Weld F. Royal, "Do Databases Really Work?" *Sales & Marketing Management,* October 1995, pp. 66–74; Daniel Hill, "Love My Brand," *Brandweek,* January

19, 1998, pp. 26–29; and "FedEx Taps into Data Warehousing," *Advertising Age's Business Marketing,* January 1999, p. 25.

11. Betsy Spethmann, "Can We Talk?" *American Demographics,* March 1999, pp. 42–44. Also see Tricia Campbell, "Database Marketing for the Little Guys," *Sales & Marketing Management,* June 1999, p. 69.

12. See Joe Schwartz, "Databases Deliver the Goods," *American Demographics,* September 1989, pp. 23–25; Gary Levin, "Database Draws Fevered Interest," *Advertising Age,* June 8, 1992, p. 31; Jonathan Berry, "A Potent New Tool for Selling: Database Marketing," *Business Week,* September 5, 1994, pp. 56–62; Richard Cross and Janet Smith, "Customer Bonding and the Information Core," *Direct Marketing Magazine,* February, 1995, p. 28; Frederick Newell, *The New Rules of Marketing* (New York: McGraw-Hill, 1997); R. M. Gordon, "Consumer Guidance," *Marketing Management,* Spring 1998, pp. 59–60; and Sara Sellar, "Dust Off That Data," *Sales & Marketing Management,* May 1999, p. 69.

13. *Economic Impact: U.S. Direct Marketing Today.*

14. Matthew L. Wald, "Third Area Code Is Added in the Land of the Toll-Free," *New York Times,* April 4, 1998, p. 10.

15. Kevin R. Hopkins, "Dialing in to the Future," *Business Week,* July 28, 1997, p. 90; and Holly McCord, "1-900-CALL-AN-RD," *Prevention,* August 1997, p. 54.

16. See James Heckman, "How Telemarketers Are Coping with the Rising Tide of State Regs," *Marketing News,* April 12, 1999, p. 4; and Catherine Siskos, "Pulling the Plug on Telemarketers," *Kiplinger's Personal Finance Magazine,* July 1999, pp. 18–20.

17. *Economic Impact: U.S. Direct Marketing Today.*

18. Debra Ray, " 'Poor Mouth' Direct Mail Brochure Nets $3.5 Million in Contributions," *Direct Marketing,* February 1998, pp. 38–39.

19. Junu Bryan Kim, "Marketing with Video: The Cassette Is in the Mail," *Advertising Age,* May 22, 1995, p. S1. Also see Albert Fried-Cassorla, "The Bright Future of Direct Mail: (Yes, Even in the Online Era!)," *Direct Marketing,* March 1998, pp. 40–42.

20. Kruti Trivedi, "Telemarketers Don't Want You, Just Your Answering Machine," *Wall Street Journal,* August 6, 1999, p. B1.

21. *Economic Impact: U.S. Direct Marketing Today.*

22. "Lillian Vernon Announces New Catalog Title," *Direct Marketing,* April 1998, pp. 15–16.

23. Irwin Helford, "Your Catalogs Are Doomed!" *Catalog Age,* August 1999, pp. 101, 106.

24. Bruce Horovitz, "Catalog Craze Delivers Holiday Deals," *USA Today,* December 1, 1998, p. 3B.

25. Example adapted in part from Moira Pascale, "Archie's Online Boom Cuts Circulation," accessed online at www.catalogagemag.com, August 1999.

26. Erika Brown, "Ooh! Aah!" *Forbes,* March 8, 1999, p. 56.

27. See Timothy R. Hawthorne, "Opening Doors to Retail Sales," *Direct Marketing,* January 1998, pp. 48–51; Jacqueline M. Graves, "The Fortune 500 Opt for Infomercials," *Fortune,* March 6, 1995, p. 20; "Infomercials," *Advertising Age,* September 8, 1997, pp. A1–A2; Carol Krol, "Navy Infomercial Aims at Prospective Recruits," *Advertising Age,* May 31, 1999, p. 12; Dave Guilford, "Cadillac Takes New Route for Sevill STS: Infomercial," *Advertising Age,* August 23, 1999, p. 8; and Jean Halliday, "Volvo Ready to Act on Leads After Infomercial Success," *Advertising Age,* January 25, 1999, p. 61.

28. See Dale D. Buss, "Capturing Customers with TV Retailing," *Nation's Business,* February 1997, pp. 29–32; "Shopping from the Sofa," *American Demographics,* April 1997, pp. 31–32; Doreen Carvajal, "Publishers Find New Market Through Television Shopping Network," *New York Times,* February 14, 1998, p. D1; and John Lippman, "Home Shopping's Held Steps Down as CEO, Chairman," *Wall Street Journal,* March 8, 1999.

29. See Frank Rose, "The End of TV as We Know It," *Fortune,* December 23, 1996, pp. 58–68; Elizabeth Lesly and Robert D. Hof, "Is Digital Convergence for Real?" *Business Week,* June 23, 1997, pp. 42–43; Amy Cortese, "Not @Home Alone: Bill Comes Knocking," *Business Week,* July 14, 1997, p. 24; B. G. Yovovich, "Webbed Feet: Marketing Opportunities Emerge from Interactive Television Applications and Services," *Marketing News,* January 19, 1998, pp. 1, 18; and Horst Stipp, "Should TV Marry PC?" *American Demographics,* July 1998, pp. 16–18.

30. DeAnn Weimer, "Can You Keep 'Em Down on the Mall?" *Business Week,* December 15, 1997, pp. 66–70; "Lining Up for Interactive Kiosks," *Nation's Business,* February 1998, p. 46; Warren S. Hersch, "Kiosks Poised to Be a Huge Growth Market," *Computer Reseller News,* May 18, 1998, p. 163; and Catherine Yang, "No Web Site Is an Island, *Business Week,* March 22, 1999, p. EB38.

31. "Interactive: Ad Age Names Finalists," *Advertising Age,* February 27, 1995, pp. 12–14.

32. Yang, "No Web Site Is an Island," p. EB38.

33. See Matt Richtel, "Small Internet Providers Survive Among Giants," *New York Times,* August 16, 1999, p. 1; Dean Foust and David Ricks, "In a Squeeze at Mindspring," *Business Week,* September 20, 1999, pp. 139–42; and Timothy J. Mullaney, "AOL Rules!" *Business Week,* April 3, 2000, pp. EB134–EB136.

34. For more on the basics of using the Internet, see Raymond D. Frost and Judy Strauss, *The Internet: A New Marketing Tool—2000* (Upper Saddle River, NJ: Prentice Hall, 2000).

35. Internet usage statistics provided by Forrester Research, August 1999.

36. "Females Lead Online Growth Spurt," CommerceNet and Nielsen Media Research, June 17, 1999, accessed online at www.cyberatlas.com.

37. Information provided by Forrester Research, August 1999. Also see Laura Cohn, "B2B: The Hottest Net Bet Yet?" *Business Week,* January 17, 2000, pp. 36–37.

38. Sharon Machlis, "Web Retailers Retool for Mainstream Users," *Computerworld,* March 22, 1999, p. 40.

39. Roger O. Crockett, "A Web That Looks Like the World," *Business Week,* March 22, 1999, pp. EB46–EB47.

40. See "Females Lead Online Growth Spurt," CommerceNet and Nielsen Media Research, June 17, 1999, accessed online at www.cyberatlas.com.

41. "Kids and Teens to Spend More Online," June 7, 1999, accessed online at www.cyberatlas.com. Also see Roger O. Crockett, "Forget the Mall. Kids Shop the Net," *Business Week,* July 26, 1999, p. EB14; Eryn Brown, "The Future of Net Shopping? Your Teens," *Fortune,* April 12, 1999, p. 152: and "Just Surfin' Through" *American Demographic,* January 2000, p.12.

42. See Crockett, "A Web That Looks Like the World," p. EB47; and Joanne Cleaver, "Surfing for Seniors," *Marketing News,* July 19, 1999, pp. 1, 7.

43. See Rebecca Piirto Heath, "The Frontiers of Psychographics," *American Demographics,* July 1996, pp. 38–43; Paul C. Judge, "Are Tech Buyers Different?" *Business Week,* January 26, 1998, pp. 64–65, 68; and the SRI Consulting Web site (future.sri.com), June 1999.

44. Don Peppers and Martha Rogers, "Opening the Door to Consumers," *Sales & Marketing Management,* October 1998, pp. 22–29.

45. Melanie Berger, "It's Your Move," *Sales & Marketing Management,* March 1998, pp. 45–53.

46. Laurie Freeman, "Why Internet Brands Take Offline Avenues," *Marketing News,* July 1999, p. 4; and Paul C. Judge, "The Name's the Thing," *Business Week,* November 15, 1999, pp. 35–39.

47. John Deighton, "The Future of Interactive Marketing," *Harvard Business Review,* November–December 1996, p. 154.

48. Online advertising expenditure figures were obtained online at www.emarketer.com/stats, September 1999.

49. See Ian P. Murphy, "Web 'Communities' a Target Marketer's Dream," *Advertising Age,* July 7, 1997, p. 2; Patricia Riedman, "Web Communities Offer Shopping Options for Users," *Advertising Age,* October 26, 1998, p. S10; Neil Cross, "Building Global Communities," *Business Week,* March 22, 1999, pp. EB42–EB43; and Richard Siklos, "Weaving Yet Another Web for Women," *Business Week,* January 17, 2000, p. 101.

50. Erika Rasmusson, "Tracking Down Sales," *Sales & Marketing Management,* June 1998, p. 19.

51. See Mary J. Cronin, "Using the Web to Push Key Data to Decision Makers," *Fortune,* September 19, 1997, p. 254; and Tim McCollum, "All the News That's Fit to Print," *Nation's Business,* June 1998, pp. 59–61.

52. Amy Cortese, "It's Called Webcasting, and It Promises to Deliver the Info You Want, Straight to Your PC," *Business Week,* February 24, 1997, pp. 95–104. Also see Kenneth Leung, "Marketing with Electronic Mail Without Spam," *Marketing News,* January 19, 1998, p. 11; Philip M. Perry, "E-mail Hell: The Dark Side of the Internet Age," *Folio: The Magazine for Magazine Management,* June 1998, pp. 74–75; and Chad Kaydo, "As Good As It Gets," *Sales & Marketing Management,* March 2000, pp. 55–60.

53. Heather Green, "Cyberspace Winners: How They Did It," *Business Week,* June 22, 1998, pp. 154–60; and "Believe It or Not, Web Stores Can Make Money," *Computerworld,* December 7, 1998, p. 4. Also see Michael D. Donahue, "Adapting the Internet to the Needs of Business," *Advertising Age,* February 2, 1998, p. 26; Shikhar Ghosh, "Making Business Sense of the Internet," *Harvard Business Review,* March–April 1998, pp. 126–35; and Lisa Bransten, "E-Commerce (A Special Report)—A New Model—The Bottom Line: If They Built It, Will Profits Come?" *Wall Street Journal,* July 12, 1999, p. R8.

54. "eCommerce: Consumers and Shopping Online," accessed online at www.emarketer.com/estats/ec_shop.html, September 1999.

55. See "Digital Divide Persists in the U.S.," obtained online at www.cyberatlas.com, July 8, 1999; "Privacy: On-Line Groups Are Offering Up Privacy Plans," *Wall Street Journal,* June 22, 1998, p. B1; Edward C. Baig, Marcia Stepanek, and Neil Gross, "Privacy: The Internet Wants Your Personal Information. What's in It for You?" *Business Week,* April 5, 1999, pp. 84–90; and Marcia Stepanek, "A Small Town Reveals America's Digital Divide," *Business Week,* October 4, 1999, pp. 188–98.

56. Portions of this section are based on Terrence H. Witkowski, "Self-Regulation Will Suppress Direct Marketing's Downside," *Marketing News,* April 24, 1989, p. 4. Also see Katie Muldoon, "The Industry Must Rebuild Its Image," *Direct,* April 1995, p. 106; Jim Castelli, "How to Handle Personal Information," *American Demographics,* March 1996, pp. 50–57; and Elyssa Yoon-Jung Lee, "How Do You Say 'Leave Me Alone?' " *Money,* June 1998, p. 140.

57. John Hagel III and Jeffrey F. Rayport, "The Coming Battle for Customer Information," *Harvard Business Review,* January–February 1997, pp. 53–65; Bruce Horovitz, "AmEx Kills Database Deal After Privacy Outrage," *USA Today,* July 15, 1998, p. B1; Carol Krol, "Consumers Reach the Boiling Point," *Advertising Age,* March 29, 1999, p. 22; and Heather Green, Mike France, and Marcia Stepanek, "It's Time for Rules in Wonderland," *Business Week,* March 20, 2000, pp. 83–96.

58. Melanie Rigney, "Too Close for Comfort, Execs Warn," *Advertising Age,* January 13, 1992, p. 31. Also see "Summary of '1992 Harris-Equifax Consumer Privacy Survey'," *Marketing News,* August 16, 1993, p. A18; and Jennifer Lach, "The New Gatekeepers," *American Demographics,* June 1999, pp. 41–42.

COMPANY CASE

17

Cars Direct.com: Shaking Up the Competition

Not that long ago, buying a car was an onerous task. When consumers visited a dealership, they were at a disadvantage. Not only did they have little information, they also had few negotiation skills. Because consumers buy cars infrequently, few develop strong negotiation skills and most forget what they learned the last time around.

Even consumers who took the time and effort to gather information and who were skillful negotiators found themselves embroiled in a long, tedious purchase process. They made visits to the car lot, haggled with the salesperson, and then haggled some more with the business manager over financing. The process could take hours, even days. At the end, many consumers were exhausted and believed that they had been taken advantage of by the dealer, who had all the power.

ALONG COMES THE INTERNET

The Internet let consumer-oriented organizations distribute information easily. *Consumer Reports* (www.consumerreports.com), *Consumer's Digest* (www.consumersdigest.com), AutoSite (www.autosite.com), *Car and Driver* (www.caranddriver.com), *Kelley Blue Book* (www.kbb.com), and *Edmund's* (www.edmunds.com) quickly set up Web sites offering consumers performance, pricing, and dealer information. Carforums.com (www.carforums.com) even offered model-specific chat rooms so that consumers could talk with one another about their cars and car problems.

Although helping consumers get more information was fine, savvy e-commerce entrepreneurs saw that the Internet offered a way to begin to change the car-buying process itself. Autobytel (www.autobytel.com) was one of the first companies to offer car-buying assistance. Other companies, such as CarPoint (carpoint.msn.com), AutoConnect (www.autoconnect.com), AutoWeb (www.autoweb.com), and AutoVantage (www.autovantage.com) quickly followed. In fact, analysts estimated that there were soon more than 100 automotive Web sites offering some type of car-shopping help. Autobytel and similar services signed up dealers who agreed to participate and pay fees for referrals. The sites helped consumers identify dealers in their areas who had the cars they were seeking. The services would either notify the dealer about an interested consumer or simply let the consumer know where to find the dealer. Some sites allowed consumers to submit electronic, "no-haggle" bids to dealers. Using these services, however, the consumer still had to visit the dealer to conclude the negotiations and take possession of the car.

CARS DELIVERED FRESH DAILY

It was only a matter of time until some bold entrepreneur took the next logical step. As a result of having gone through the traditional car-buying process himself, Internet entrepreneur Bill Gross realized there had to be a better way. Mr. Gross had previously founded the Pasadena, California-based

Internet incubator Idealab!, which had already spawned companies such as eToys, GoTo.com, and Free-PC. Gross and other investors, including Michael Dell of Dell Computer, established CarsDirect.com (www.carsdirect.com).

Rather than just serving as an electronic middleman, CarsDirect actually closes the sale and delivers the car to the consumer. A consumer visiting the CarsDirect Web site finds a simple, three-step process to follow. First, the site guides the consumer through the process of selecting the vehicle. Using information and guidance that the site provides, consumers can choose from a complete selection of production vehicles available in the United States. Consumers who want a specialty vehicle, such as a Ferrari, or who don't find the vehicle they are seeking, can e-mail the company directly. A service advisor will contact them within 24 hours.

Once a consumer selects a car, CarsDirect negotiates with the 1,700 dealers in its network to find the car. CarsDirect tries to set a price to the consumer that is in the bottom 10 percent of the market price range for the particular vehicle. Its substantial buying power allows CarsDirect to get the vehicle from the dealer at an even lower price, then make a profit on the difference between what it pays the dealer and what it charges the consumer. One dealer reported selling 53 cars to CarsDirect over a three-month period. Selling to CarsDirect lowers the dealer's costs because the dealer doesn't have to pay the sales commission it would normally pay to salespeople.

Having found a car and set a price, CarsDirect offers the car to the consumer. Consumers can lock in the price by making a fully refundable $50 deposit. They can pay cash, use their own financing, such as through a local bank, or select a lease or loan package that CarsDirect.com offers. Consumers who want to use a CarsDirect financing package can fill out an application online.

Finally, the consumer must decide how to take delivery. The company offers consumers the option of going to a local CarsDirect Priority Dealer to pick up the vehicle. Or, depending on where they live and the vehicle purchased, CarsDirect will deliver the vehicle to a consumer's home or office. (In Los Angeles, CarsDirect delivery trucks display the slogan, "Cars Delivered Fresh Daily.") No matter which option consumers select, they will be able to inspect their vehicles, find out about service options, and ask questions.

Thus, CarsDirect was the first company to offer the consumer the opportunity to purchase a vehicle, finance the purchase, and take delivery without ever leaving home.

WILL THIS WORK?

Although CarsDirect sold its first car in December 1998, its official launch was in May 1999. By August 1999, total sales revenue had topped $100 million and the company was reaping daily revenues of more than $1.5 million. The company projected total revenues would top $400 million in its first year.

Although these numbers are impressive, especially for an Internet-based company, the average daily rate of $1.5 million represents only about 52 vehicles per day, given the average vehicle price of about $29,000. CarsDirect gets only about 2 percent of this amount to cover its expenses and generate a profit.

CarsDirect raised $30 million in its first two rounds of start-up funding and expects to raise another $150 million. Like other e-commerce ventures, it remains in the red and the founders don't anticipate profits until 2001.

Profits or not, however, CarsDirect is already shaking up the car-buying industry. CarPoint.com (a Microsoft site) responded by joining forces with Ford Motor Company. Together, they are looking into developing a site that would allow consumers to order cars online directly from the factory. Trilogy Software of Austin, Texas, is funding CarOrder.com, a company that intends to spend up to $600 million to buy underperforming dealerships in smaller markets. CarOrder.com will then use these dealerships to create regional distribution centers, transforming these dealers into online retailers to serve large territories. Like CarsDirect, CarOrder would take online orders. However, it would ship the cars to its own dealerships and deliver them to customers from those dealerships.

Yet another competitor, AutoNation, of Fort Lauderdale, Florida, is putting the inventory in its 270 dealerships online and encouraging other independent dealers to sell on its Web site. Autobytel reported that it is also testing a direct-sales method. Even Ford and GM have launched new units that will buy dealerships and operate them as factory-owned stores, allowing them to test Internet selling.

Moreover, several companies are experimenting with e-commerce car-buying strategies in foreign markets. GM is testing strategies in Taiwan, where it already sells 10 percent of its vehicles via the Internet. It plans to begin building cars to order in 2000. Ford has set up a seamless e-commerce system in the Philippines that links consumers, dealers, Ford, and its suppliers. Meanwhile, Autobytel has moved into Europe. There, European Union laws enable manufacturers to restrict new car sales to captive dealers. Such laws have led to inflated prices in many markets, as much as 25 percent higher on average than in the United States. When this exemption expires in 2002, Autobytel hopes to be able to offer direct sales over the Internet.

WHERE TO FROM HERE?

Where will all this lead? No one's sure. An analyst for one company argues that, "All [CarsDirect has] is motivated salespeople in a call center" who try to get dealers to sell cars for less than CarsDirect's customer is paying. Other analysts note that although the number of new-vehicle buyers using the Internet to shop has risen from 25 percent in 1998 to 40 percent in 1999, the number of people using the Internet to actually buy a vehicle is still relatively small. Further, CarsDirect and other online vehicle retailers face restrictive state franchise laws, some of which ban Internet sales. They also face political and legal actions by some of the 20,000 established dealers and complicated ordering systems by which automakers require dealers to take unwanted cars in order to get hot-selling models.

Finally, CarsDirect has proven that some consumers will make a five-figure purchase over the Internet without having seen the car. However, some analysts still wonder: Are there enough such consumers out there for CarsDirect to become profitable?

Questions

1. How do customers and CarsDirect each benefit from online marketing?
2. Outline CarsDirect's marketing strategy. What problems do you see with its strategy?
3. What marketing recommendations would you make to CarsDirect? Specifically, how can CarsDirect get more people to visit its site and purchase cars using its service?

4. What advantages or disadvantages will CarsDirect and its competitors face in foreign markets?
5. What ethical issues does CarsDirect face? How should it deal with those issues?

Sources: CarsDirect.com home page, www.carsdirect.com; Edward Harris, "Web Car-Shopping Puts Buyers in Driver's Seat," *Wall Street Journal,* April 15, 1999, p. B10; Daniel Taub, "Firm Proves People Are Ready to Buy Cars on the Web," *Los Angeles Business Journal,* August 23, 1999, p. 5; John Couretas, "CarsDirect Tops Online Buying List from Gomez," *Automotive News,* September 20, 1999, p. 10; Fara Warner, "Internet Auto Retailer CarOrder.com Receives Funds to Acquire Dealerships," *Wall Street Journal,* September 29, 1999, p. B2; Tim Burt, "Autobytel to Push Online Car Sales in Europe," *Financial Times,* October 8, 1999, p. 30; Fara Warner, "New Tactics Shake Up Online Auto Retailing," *Wall Street Journal,* October 18, 1999, p. B1; and Fara Warner, "GM Tests E-Commerce Plans in Emerging Markets," *Wall Street Journal,* October 25, 1999, p. B6.

SMITH'S HOME FOODS: BRINGING HOME THE BACON

Ronald Smith, president of Smith's Country Hams[1] in Ashton, North Carolina, walked into his daughter's office and plopped down in one of the chairs across from her desk. "Christy," he said, "I've just been looking at last month's numbers, and they are pretty discouraging. We've got to find a way to get the home foods business moving. I'm not sure what's wrong, but I think we've somehow got the cart before the horse. I'm convinced that if we could just find the right button, and push it, everything would work well."

Christy Smith looked across the desk at her casually dressed father. "Dad, I am just as frustrated as you are," she replied. "Nothing we try seems to work right. Even when we do attract new customers, they are the wrong kind."

Christy was a very busy person. In addition to her duties at Smith's, she commuted daily to a major university located in a neighboring city, where she was a senior business major. Although she had worked in the family business for as long as she could remember, she had been pleased and surprised when her father had asked her to take over the newly formed Smith's Home Foods operation. Glancing at the calendar on her desk, she noted the date—April 4, 1997. She could hardly believe that five months had passed since taking on the assignment. Although pleased with her father's confidence in her, she knew that he felt frustrated about the slow development of the Smith's Home Foods business.

As Christy and her father talked, Sonny Jones, one of the Home Foods' two full-time salespeople, entered the office and joined the conversation. He seemed upset. "We just got two more turn-downs from the finance company," he grumbled. "They rejected both of the families I sold plans to last night. We just can't seem to get onto the right side of the street."

"What do you mean?" Ronald asked.

"It's the same old story," Sonny replied. "Both families I called on last night live in Dogwood Acres—they're nice people and all, but they don't have very high incomes. We have to find a way to attract the higher-income folks who live across the road in Ashton Estates."

Ronald Smith rose to leave. "Whatever the problem is, I'm depending on the two of you to figure it out and tell me what we need to do. And you need to get moving quickly."

BACKGROUND

Smith's Country Hams, a 25-year-old family business that focuses on wholesale meat products such as ham, bacon, and

[1]Company name and location are disguised.

other pork products, sells to restaurants and fast-food operations in eastern North Carolina. In July 1996, seeking growth opportunities, Ronald Smith started a new division—Smith's Home Foods. He got the idea from an employee who had previously worked for another home-delivered foods company. Ronald, who is always looking for new ways to make money, believed the idea had potential. He knew that people these days are seeking more convenience. Therefore, a service that provides home-delivered meats, vegetables, and fruits should be in considerable demand. He also realized that he could use his own meat products in the business, thereby providing new sales for Smith's Country Hams.

Ronald reconditioned an old production facility that had been idle and set up offices there for Smith's Home Foods. He put the employee who had the idea in charge of the business. However, by October 1996, the employee had failed to meet Ronald's expectations and had resigned. Ronald then asked Christy to take over. He knew this would be a challenging assignment for her. She was still a full-time university student. As a result, she could devote only afternoons and whatever time she could squeeze from her evenings to manage Smith's Home Foods.

THE HOME FOODS BUSINESS

The home-delivered foods business centers on providing families with prearranged assortments of foods that are delivered to their homes. Smith's Home Foods offers 11 standard packages, containing various combinations of frozen meats, vegetables, and fruits. The packages differ in size and cost, but each provide a four-month food supply. Exhibit III-1 shows the items in a typical package. Exhibit III-2 summarizes the characteristics of each of the 11 packages.

When Christy first assumed management of the operation, she wondered why everything was sold in four-month packages. According to Sonny Jones, who had once worked with a competing food service, most competitors offer similar four-month packages. As a result, the quantity of food delivered with each package requires that customers own a freezer or purchase one. Therefore, Smith's Home Foods, like other home-foods companies, also sells a 21-cubic-foot freezer on an installment payment plan. In general, the requirement of having a freezer does not appear to be a barrier to food-package sales.

Christy believes that customers gain many benefits from the home delivery of food. First, it's convenient—customers can make fewer trips to the store because Smith's Home Foods packages make a large variety of foods readily avail-

EXHIBIT III.1 CONTENTS OF A TYPICAL SMITH'S HOME FOODS PACKAGE

107	Pounds Net Weight Beef
6	Chuck Roasts (2 lb avg.)
4	Shoulder Roasts (2 lb avg.)
1	Sirloin Tip Roast (3 lb avg.)
1	Eye of Round Roast (3 lb avg.)
1	Bottom Round Roast (3 lb avg.)
20	Ribeye Steaks (8 oz)
12	T-Bone Steaks (12 oz)
	Cube Steak (8 lb)
	BLS Stew Beef (10 lb)
18	Chopped Beef Steaks (8 oz; 9 lb case)
	Ground Beef (32 lb; 1 lb rolls or 4 oz patties)
	Pork Chops (6 lb)
	BLS Pork Chops (6 lb)
	Dinner Ham (5 lb)
30	Misc. Meats
20	Fryers
1	Seafood
60	Vegetables (16 oz)
12	Fruits
32	Juices (12 oz)
	Cheese (6 lb)
	Margarine (6 lb)

Bank	$1,094.38
Tax	54.71
	1,149.09
Deposit	35.00
Amount Financed	1,114.09
Finance Charge	56.23
Deferred Payment	1,170.32
Total Price	1,205.32

Four Payments at $292.58
$68.04 per Week

EXHIBIT III.2 CHARACTERISTICS OF SMITH'S HOME FOODS PACKAGES

Food Package Number	Pounds of Meat per Week	Minimum Freezer Size	Family Size	Package Price*
1	14	21 cu ft	3–4	$1,205
2	12	18	3–4	1,088
3	12	18	3	1,070
4	10	15	2–3	940
5	17	21	4–5	1,532
6	6.5	12	2	655
7	8	15	2–3	1,093
8	9.5	12	2–3	825
9	11	15	2–3	809
10	11	15	2–3	834
11	13	21	4–5	958

*Price for four-month package, including tax and finance charges able in the home. Therefore, the person who does the cooking has fewer worries about whether enough food is available. Second, Christy believes that Smith's offers superior quality products, especially meats, compared with those consumers typically find at grocery stores. She and her father carefully select the meat offered in the packages. Of course, they supply their own high-quality Smith's Country Ham products. All other meats are purchased from other quality wholesalers, either in individually wrapped portions, such as eight-ounce T-bone steaks, or in "family portions," such as five-pound rib roasts. The wholesalers vacuum pack the meats with plastic shrink wrap to protect their freshness and flavor. Meats packed this way and frozen will maintain their freshness indefinitely. Smith's Home Foods packages feature brand-name meats, such as Morrell, Armour, Jimmy Dean, and Fishery products. The packages also include brandname fruits and vegetables, such as Dulany and McKenzie, which are purchased from wholesalers. Smith's guarantees the quality of its food, stating that it will replace any food that fails to completely satisfy the customer.

Finally, Christy argues, purchasing food through a home food service saves consumers money. Because customers buy in large quantities, they receive lower prices. And they escape any price increases that occur during the four-month period covered by their food packages. Making fewer trips to the store also helps customers avoid expensive impulse purchases.

SMITH'S HOME FOODS' MARKETING PROGRAM

Smith's priced its food packages at $655 to $1,532, including tax and finance charges, with an average price of $1,000. Smith's cost of goods sold averages 48 percent for the 11 packages, not including a variable cost of $30 per package for delivery. Customers can pay cash, or they can charge or finance their purchases. Although Smith's accepts Visa and MasterCard, customers seldom use these cards to purchase the food packages. Another option allows customers to pay one half in cash on signing the contract and the final half within 30 days without an interest charge.

Smith's provides credit to qualified customers through the Fair Finance Company of Akron, Ohio, one of the few finance companies that finances food purchases. Customers who opt for financing make a $35 down payment and fill out a credit application. If Fair approves the application, the customer makes the first payment—one-fourth of the amount financed—30 days after the delivery of the food. Thus, on a $1,200 food package financed by Fair, the customer makes four $300 payments. Because the first payment is not due until a month after delivery, the financing plan allows the customer to save $75 a week for food in each of the four weeks leading up to the first payment, and so forth for the remaining three payments. Although the finance company absorbs the risks of the purchase, Smith's assumes the risk until the first payment is made. That is, if a customer receives the food but does not make the first payment,

Smith's accepts responsibility for the entire amount financed and must take whatever action it can to obtain payment or reclaim the food.

When a salesperson submits an order for a food package, if the customer wants to finance it, Smith's faxes a copy of the order to Fair Finance Company. Typically, the finance company approves or rejects the application within one business day. If credit is approved, a clerk completes a "pull sheet," which tells warehouse employees which package the customer purchased and what items are included. Typically, the warehouse manager holds orders until five or six are ready to be pulled and then sets a delivery date with the customer.

For customers who want to purchase freezers, Smith's sells a 21-cubic-foot freezer for approximately $800, with a cost of goods sold at $435. This freezer can also be financed through a separate finance company—consumers pay $12.95 down and make 24 monthly payments of about $33. When a customer orders a freezer and credit is approved, Smith's calls a local appliance store that delivers the freezer to the customer and installs it. Once installed, the freezer must run for about three days before it reaches the appropriate temperature to receive the food. Therefore, Smith's must coordinate food delivery with delivery of the freezer.

Smith's stores its inventory in the Smith's Country Hams warehousing and cold-storage facilities. It has a one-ton pickup truck equipped with a freezer box to make the delivery to customers. Two Smith's Country Hams employees make the deliveries, personally placing the food in the customer's freezer.

Smith's Home Foods uses both personal and mass-selling techniques to promote its services. Its two full-time salespeople, Sonny Jones and Barbara Johnson, both earn salaries plus commission on their own sales. Sonny and Barbara have also recruited four other part-time, commission-only salespeople. Smith's pays its salespeople a $100 commission on each package sold. It also pays an additional $25 commission to both Sonny and Barbara for each sale made by the part-time salespeople. The same commissions are paid on each freezer sold.

When the salespeople make a call, they must often meet with the customers in the evening, spending as long as two hours discussing the service and completing the applications. Each salesperson carries a three-ring binder that contains all the information needed for a sales presentation. The binder includes 12 pages of beef and pork product pictures, 6 pages of poultry and fish product pictures, 3 pages of vegetable and fruit product pictures, and 1 page of dessert pictures. Additional pages describe the costs and terms for each of the 11 packages. The binder also contains pictures of freezers and lists substitutions allowed in the packages.

To generate leads for the sales force, Smith's uses several mass-selling techniques. First, it has advertised three times recently in the local Ashton paper, which also serves the small adjoining community of Wolfsburg and the surrounding county with a total population of about 100,000. Each insert costs about $.04. The inserts stress the money-saving features of the service and include a detachable postcard that consumers can mail, postage paid, to the company.

More recently, the company has contracted with the local Welcome Wagon to distribute a $10-off coupon for Smith's products along with the other promotions that it gives to newlyweds, families who have just had babies, and new arrivals to the community. Finally, Christy also prepared a flyer that outlines the service. Salespeople place these flyers in various locations around the community, such as beauty parlors.

Christy does not feel that Smith's Home Foods faces any direct competition in the Ashton area. Another large, well-established company, Southern Foods of Greensboro, North Carolina, operates a home foods service very similar to Smith's. However, although Southern Foods also operates in some other states and has customers throughout North Carolina, it does not directly target the Ashton area. In fact, Christy feels that Southern Foods has probably helped her business—it has developed the market generally and acquainted potential customers with the kinds of services that Smith's offers.

When Christy took over, she made a number of immediate changes in an effort to improve performance. She redesigned the food packages to make them more attractive and developed the newspaper insert, flyer, and sales book. Despite these efforts, however, the business has developed very slowly.

Although only about eight families had contracted for the service when Christy took over, Smith's now has 60 customers. However, many of the families who signed up since she arrived would soon be finishing their first package. Christy was concerned about how many of these customers would reorder. She was also worried about how long her father's patience would last. He had told her that he would invest as much as $250,000 to get this business going. He had already invested $25,000 in inventory. Furthermore, she estimated that Smith's Home Foods annual fixed costs amounted to $57,000, including salaries, rent and utilities, and other overhead. Christy wondered about the business's profitability and about how many customers she needed to reach to break even.

Questions

1. Outline Smith's Home Foods' marketing strategy. What is Smith's Home Foods really selling?
2. What problems, if any, do you see with each element of the strategy?
3. Using information given in the case, calculate the average contribution per food package and the number of customers Smith's Home Foods needs to break even.
4. Based on your analysis, what steps would you recommend that Christy take to improve her marketing strategy and Smith's performance?

After studying this chapter, you should be able to

1. discuss customer value and satisfaction and how companies attract, retain, and grow profitable customers

2. explain the roles of the company value chain, value-delivery network, and total quality in delivery of customer value and satisfaction

3. discuss the need to understand competitors as well as customers through competitor analysis

4. explain the fundamentals of competitive marketing strategies based on creating value for customers

5. illustrate the need for balancing customer and competitor orientations in becoming a truly market-centered organization

COMPETITIVE STRATEGIES: ATTRACTING, RETAINING, AND GROWING CUSTOMERS

Entering the new millennium, PC maker Gateway, Inc. faces some daunting challenges—plummeting PC prices that put the squeeze on profit margins; the exploding and often baffling Internet; and deep-pockets competitors like IBM, Compaq, and Dell, all vying for shares of the consumer's computer budget. To survive and thrive, Gateway will need a strong, customer-focused marketing strategy—and it appears to have found one. Call it an "own the customer" strategy, one that focuses not just on gaining share of the market but also on growing "share of customer" and capturing customer lifetime value.

"At the core of [Gateway's] strategy is a simple idea," writes *Business Week* analyst Steven Brull. "Grab customers early on and keep them generating incremental revenue through a variety of services. The relationship starts with the purchase of a PC. . . . Then Gateway [locks] in those customers through financing, Internet access, and a personalized portal that will steer them to Gateway's e-commerce sites."

Thus, Gateway has devised a three-phase strategy for attracting, retaining, and growing customers. Phase one centers on PC sales. Gateway attracts new buyers through media advertising, telemarketing, online selling, and its national network of almost 200 Gateway Country retail stores. It targets primarily first-time buyers and small businesses, customers who have not yet formed strong brand loyalties. Gateway's low prices, financing, and training classes make it easy for these new buyers to get started on a Gateway machine. Gateway was the first computer company to introduce consumer-PC leases—it lets buyers pay for their computers in monthly installments as low as $28 over a two-year period. When the two years are up, buyers can keep the machine or receive trade-in value toward a new model. To help novice buyers figure out how to use their new computers, Gateway offers training courses that start at $75 for three hours. This extended financing and training relationship serves buyers well. It also benefits Gateway: Higher margins on credit and training revenues help offset the razor-thin margins Gateway gets on its low-priced PCs.

The PC purchase is just the first stop on what Gateway hopes will be a lifelong journey with the customer. In phase two, the connection lengthens. To entice buyers online, and to develop a more permanent relationship, Gateway offers a free one-year subscription to Gateway.net, the company's Internet access service. About 400,000 customers already subscribe to Gateway.net and the company is mounting a direct-marketing campaign to woo its 5 million customers who are not yet subscribers. It is also courting non-Gateway customers with sales pitches at its Gateway Country stores. After the free year ends, customers pay $17.95 a month to continue, creating additional sales and a longer-term customer connection for Gateway. The company expects to have as many as 3 million subscribers by the end of 2000, making it the number-two Internet service provider behind America Online.

In phase three, the relationship deepens. Beyond selling computers and linking customers to the Internet through Gateway.net, Gateway goes all out to earn a big share of customers' e-commerce business. "The big dollars can be earned after the PC is plugged into the Net," says analyst Brull. "To keep customers coming back, Gateway offers each customer a customized home page created in partnership with portal Yahoo!" When completing a PC sale, Gateway reps collect information for tailoring home pages to individual preferences. "When we deliver a PC," adds Jeffrey Weitzen, Gateway's president and chief operating officer, "we want you to be registered on the Net, with software loaded and a personalized portal for news, weather, and stocks."

Of course, the personalized Web page also puts customers within a mouse click of the company's SpotShop.com site. Once there, they can buy any of more than 30,000 items, including computer hardware, software, and accessories but also office and personal technology products, ranging from digital cameras and pro-

jectors to personal digital assistants. Moreover, it looks as though Gateway might have plans for garnering an even greater share of customers' online dollars in other categories. For example, the company has registered such Web addresses as spotgames.com, travelinfospot.com, and spotedu.com.

Thus, Gateway isn't just a PC company anymore—its interests in the customer go far beyond the initial sale. In fact, Gateway anticipates that within the next two years or so services such as training, consulting, and Internet access will account for more than a third of its sales and half its profits. "Smart marketers build lifetime customer relationships, rather than trying to drive a [specific] purchase event," says another analyst. "In the past (or for those still living there), the goal . . . was to make the phone ring, or cause the prospect to buy a product in the shortest possible time. The reality today is that as growth slows, the requirement changes from finding sales to growing customers . . . from 'selling' to 'managing lifetime value.' [More than any other PC company,] Gateway has been focused on the ongoing relationship."

Says Gateway's president, "Gateway works harder than anyone to build lifelong relationships with consumers based on trust and complete personalization. Our clients have responded to that relationship with repeat purchases and by recommending us to friends, family members, and business associates. We're going to continue working harder than ever to remain worthy of our client's loyalty." Gateway's "own the customer" strategy appears to be working well. The company's sales have grown by more than 20 percent in each of the last two years, and over the past five years its stock price has jumped eightfold. Perhaps more importantly, the relationship between Gateway and its customers appears to go both ways. In a recent study by AC Nielsen's Tech★Watch, Gateway ranked number one in customer loyalty among major PC makers.[1]

Today's companies face their toughest competition ever. In previous chapters, we argued that to succeed in today's fiercely competitive marketplace, companies will have to move from a *product and selling philosophy* to a *customer and marketing philosophy.* This chapter spells out in more detail how companies can go about outperforming competitors in order to win and keep customers. To win in today's marketplace, companies must become adept not just in *building products,* but in *building customers.* The answer lies in doing a better job than competitors do of delivering customer value and satisfaction.

We first address several important questions relating *customer relationship marketing.* What are the key building blocks for attracting, retaining, and growing profitable customers? What are customer value and satisfaction? How is customer satisfaction related to customer loyalty and retention? How can a company grow its "share of customer"? Who in the organization is responsible for building and maintaining customer relationships? What is the role of total quality marketing? Next, we examine *competitive marketing strategies*—how companies analyze their competitors and develop successful, value-based strategies for attracting, retaining, and growing customers.

CUSTOMER RELATIONSHIP MARKETING

Relationship marketing
The process of creating, maintaining, and enhancing strong, value-laden relationships with customers and other stakeholders.

Traditional marketing theory and practice have focused on attracting new customers rather than retaining existing ones. Today, however, although attracting new customers remains an important marketing task, the emphasis has shifted toward **relationship marketing**—creating, maintaining, and enhancing strong relationships with customers and other stakeholders. Beyond designing strategies to *attract* new customers and create *transactions* with them, companies are going all out to *retain* current customers and build profitable, long-term *relationships* with them. The new view is that marketing is the science and art of finding, retaining, *and* growing profitable customers.

Why the new emphasis on retaining and growing customers? In the past, many companies took their customers for granted. Facing an expanding economy and rapidly growing markets, companies could practice a "leaky bucket" approach to marketing. Growing markets meant a plentiful supply of new customers. Companies could keep filling the marketing bucket with new customers without worrying about losing old customers through holes in the bottom of the bucket.

However, companies today are facing some new marketing realities. Changing demographics, more sophisticated competitors, and overcapacity in many industries—all of these factors mean that there are fewer customers to go around. Many companies are now fighting for shares of flat or fading markets. Thus, the costs of attracting new consumers are rising. In fact, it costs five times as much to attract a new customer as it does to keep a current customer satisfied.[2]

Companies are also realizing that losing a customer means losing more than a single sale: It means losing the entire stream of purchases that the customer would make over a lifetime of patronage. For example, here is a dramatic illustration of **customer lifetime value:**

Customer lifetime value
The amount by which revenues from a given customer over time will exceed the company's costs of attracting, selling, and servicing that customer.

⭐ Stew Leonard, who operates a highly profitable single-store supermarket, says that he sees $50,000 flying out of his store every time he sees a sulking customer. Why? Because his average customer spends about $100 a week, shops 50 weeks a year, and remains in the area for about 10 years. If this customer has an unhappy experience and switches to another supermarket, Stew Leonard has lost $50,000 in revenue. The loss

Customer lifetime value: Stew Leonard's does all it can to keep customers satisfied.

can be much greater if the disappointed customer shares the bad experience with other customers and causes them to defect.

Similarly, the customer lifetime value of a Taco Bell customer exceeds $12,000. Lexus estimates that a single satisfied and loyal customer is worth $600,000 in lifetime sales.[3] Thus, working to retain and grow customers makes good economic sense. A company can lose money on a specific transaction but still benefit greatly from a long-term relationship.

Attracting, Retaining, and Growing Customers

The key to building lasting relationships is the creation of superior customer value and satisfaction. Satisfied customers are more likely to be loyal customers, and loyal customers are more likely to give the company a larger share of their business. We now look more closely at the concepts of customer value and satisfaction, loyalty and retention, and share of customer.

Relationship Building Blocks: Customer Value and Satisfaction

Attracting and retaining customers can be a difficult task. Today's customers face a vast array of product and brand choices, prices, and suppliers. The company must answer a key question: How do customers make their choices? The answer is that customers choose the marketing offer that they believe will give them the most value. They are satisfied with and continue to buy offers that consistently meet or exceed their value expectations. Let's look more closely at customer value and satisfaction.

Customer Value.   Consumers buy from the firm that they believe offers the highest **customer delivered value**—the difference between total customer value and total customer cost (see Figure 18.1).[4] For example, suppose that a large construction firm wants to buy a bulldozer. It will buy the bulldozer from either Caterpillar or Komatsu. The salespeople for the two companies carefully describe their respective offers to the buyer. The construction firm evaluates the two competing bull-

Customer delivered value
The difference between total customer value and total customer cost of a marketing offer—"profit" to the customer.

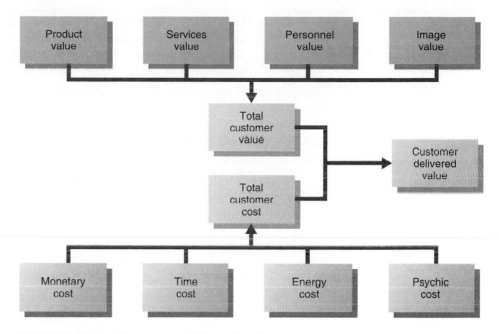

FIGURE 18.1   Customer delivered value

dozer offers to assess which one delivers the greatest value. It adds all the values from four sources—product, services, personnel, and image. First, it judges that Caterpillar's bulldozer provides higher reliability, durability, and performance. It also decides that Caterpillar has better accompanying services—delivery, training, and maintenance. The customer views Caterpillar personnel as more knowledgeable and responsive. Finally, it places higher value on Caterpillar's reputation. Thus, the customer decides that Caterpillar offers more *total customer value* than does Komatsu.

Does the construction firm buy the Caterpillar bulldozer? Not necessarily. The firm also will examine the **total customer cost** of buying Caterpillar's bulldozer versus Komatsu's. The total customer cost consists of more than just monetary costs. As Adam Smith observed more than two centuries ago, "The real price of anything is the toil and trouble of acquiring it." Total customer cost also includes the buyer's anticipated time, energy, and psychic costs. The construction firm evaluates these costs along with monetary costs to form a complete estimate of its costs.

The buying firm now compares total customer value to total customer cost and determines the total delivered value associated with Caterpillar's bulldozer. In the same way, it assesses the total delivered value for the Komatsu bulldozer. The firm then buys from the company that offers the highest delivered value.

Some marketers might rightly argue that this concept of how buyers choose among product alternatives is too rational. They might cite examples in which buyers did not choose the offer with the highest delivered value. For example, suppose that the Caterpillar salesperson convinces the construction firm that Caterpillar's bulldozer offers a higher delivered value. Nonetheless, the customer decides to buy the Komatsu bulldozer. Why would the buyer make such a decision? There are many possible explanations. Perhaps the construction firm's buyers enjoy a long-term friendship with the Komatsu salesperson. Or the firm's buyers might be under strict orders to buy at the lowest price. Or perhaps the construction firm rewards its buyers for short-term performance, causing them to choose the less expensive Komatsu bulldozer, even though the Caterpillar machine will perform better and be less expensive to operate in the long run.

Total customer cost
The total of all the monetary, time, energy, and psychic costs associated with a marketing offer.

Clearly, buyers operate under various constraints and sometimes make choices that give more weight to their personal benefit than to company benefit. However, the customer delivered value framework applies to many situations and yields rich insights. It suggests that sellers must first assess the total customer delivered value associated with their own and competing marketing offers to determine how their own offers stack up. If competitors deliver greater value, the firm must act.

How might Caterpillar use this concept of buyer decision making to help it succeed in selling its bulldozer to this buyer? It can improve its offer in either of two ways. First, it can increase total customer value by strengthening or augmenting the product, services, personnel, or image benefits of its offer. Second, it can reduce total customer cost by lowering its price or by lessening the buyer's time, energy, and psychic costs. In fact, although Caterpillar products cost more than competing brands, the company claims that its higher quality, superior service, and strong reputation make its products a better value in the long run. Its goal is to provide customers with the lowest total cost per cubic yard of earth moved, ton of coal uncovered, or mile of road graded over the life of the product.[5]

Customer satisfaction
The extent to which a product's perceived performance matches a buyer's expectations.

Customer Satisfaction.   Thus, consumers form expectations about the value of marketing offers and make buying decisions based on these expectations. **Customer satisfaction** with a purchase depends on the product's actual performance relative to a buyer's expectations. A customer might experience various degrees of satisfaction. If the product's performance falls short of expectations, the customer is dissatisfied. If performance matches expectations, the customer is satisfied. If performance exceeds expectations, the customer is highly satisfied or delighted.[6]

But how do buyers form their expectations? Expectations are based on the customer's past buying experiences, the opinions of friends and associates, and marketer and competitor information and promises. Marketers must be careful to set the right level of expectations. If they set expectations too low, they may satisfy those who buy but fail to attract enough buyers. In contrast, if they raise expectations too high, buyers are likely to be disappointed. For example, Holiday Inn ran a campaign a few years ago called "No Surprises," which promised consistently trouble-free accommodations and service. However, Holiday Inn guests still encountered a host of problems, and the expectations created by the campaign only made customers more dissatisfied. Holiday Inn had to withdraw the campaign.

The American Customer Satisfaction Index, which tracks customer satisfaction in more than two dozen U.S. manufacturing and service industries, shows that overall customer satisfaction has been declining slightly in recent years.[7] It is unclear whether this has resulted from a decrease in product and service quality or from an increase in customer expectations. In either case, it presents an opportunity for companies that can consistently deliver superior customer value and satisfaction.

Today's most successful companies are raising expectations—and delivering performance to match. These companies embrace *total customer satisfaction*. For example, Honda claims "One reason our customers are so satisfied is that we aren't." Cigna vows "100% Satisfaction. 100% of the Time." Such companies track their customers' expectations, perceived company performance, and customer satisfaction. However, although the customer-centered firm seeks to deliver high customer satisfaction relative to competitors, it does not attempt to *maximize* customer satisfaction. A company can always increase customer satisfaction by lowering its price or increasing its services, but this may result in lower profits. Thus, the purpose of marketing is to generate customer value profitably. This requires a very delicate balance:

The marketer must continue to generate more customer value and satisfaction but not "give away the house."

Customer Loyalty and Retention

Highly satisfied customers produce several benefits for the company. Satisfied customers are less price sensitive, talk favorably to others about the company and its products, and remain loyal for a longer period. However, the relationship between customer satisfaction and loyalty varies greatly across industries and competitive situations. Figure 18.2 shows the relationship between customer satisfaction and loyalty in five different markets.[8] In all cases, as satisfaction increases, so does loyalty. In highly competitive markets, such as those for automobiles and personal computers, there is surprisingly little difference between the loyalty of less satisfied customers and those who are merely satisfied. However, there is a tremendous difference between the loyalty of *satisfied* customers and *completely satisfied* customers.

Even a slight drop from complete satisfaction can create an enormous drop in loyalty. For example, one study showed that completely satisfied customers are nearly 42 percent more likely to be loyal than merely satisfied customers. Another study by AT&T showed that 70 percent of customers who say they are satisfied with a product or service are still willing to switch to a competitor; customers who are *highly* satisfied are much more loyal. Xerox found that its totally satisfied customers are six times more likely to repurchase Xerox products over the next 18 months than its satisfied customers.[9] This means that companies must aim high if they want to hold on to their customers. Customer *delight* creates an emotional affinity for a product or service, not just a rational preference, and this creates high customer loyalty.

FIGURE 18.2 **The relationship between customer satisfaction and customer loyalty**

Source: Thomas O. Jones and W. Earl Sasser Jr., "Why Satisfied Customers Defect," *Harvard Business Review,* November–December 1995, p. 91. Copyright © 1997 by the President and Fellows of Harvard College; all rights reserved. Reprinted by permission of *Harvard Business Review.*

Figure 18.2 also shows that in noncompetitive markets, such as those served by regulated monopolies or those dominated by powerful or patent-protected brands, customers tend to remain loyal no matter how dissatisfied they are. This might seem like an ideal situation for the protected or dominant firm. However, such firms may pay a high price for customer dissatisfaction in the long run.

For example, during the 1960s and 1970s, Xerox flourished under the protection of patents on its revolutionary photocopy process. Customers had no choice but to remain loyal to Xerox, and sales and profits soared despite customer dissatisfaction over machine malfunctions and rising prices. In fact, customer dissatisfaction led to even *greater* short-run profits for Xerox: Disgruntled customers were forced to pay for service when machines broke down, and some even leased extra machines as backups. But as the 1980s dawned, Xerox paid dearly for its failure to keep its customers satisfied. Japanese competitors skirted patents and entered the market with higher quality copiers sold at lower prices. Dissatisfied customers gleefully defected to the new competitors. Xerox's share of the world copier market plunged from over 80 percent to less than 35 percent in just five years.[10] Thus, even highly successful companies must pay close attention to customer satisfaction and its relationship to customer loyalty. Xerox has now developed industry-leading, customer-driven quality, customer satisfaction, and customer retention programs. As a result, although it has lost its dominance, it is once again a profitable industry leader.

At the same time, a high customer satisfaction rating doesn't guarantee customer loyalty. A major insurance firm learned this when comparing its performance to competitor State Farm:

★ A study comparing the competitor to State Farm showed only a 6.5 point spread between the percentage of respondents who were totally satisfied with the competitor and the percent totally satisfied with State Farm. So, how can we explain State Farm's consistently higher profitability over the years? The answer lies in customer loyalty. By using discounts and guarantees for long-term loyal customers and an agent compensation plan that encourages customer retention, State Farm has created strong customer loyalty. Although the study showed fairly minor differences in those totally satisfied, loyalty measures widened the gap between the companies. When customers were asked how strongly they preferred their life insurance company over others, there was an 11 percent spread between the competitor and State Farm. The gulf widened to a 15 percentage point State Farm lead on the statement, "I am very loyal to my company, it would take a lot to get me to switch." Twice as many respondents strongly agreed with the statement, "I would go out of my way to stay with my life insurance company," for State Farm than for the competitor.[11]

Thus, customer satisfaction remains an extremely important component in customer loyalty—a company will find it difficult to earn customer loyalty without first earning high levels of customer satisfaction. However, companies should also carefully examine customer loyalty itself, which often is a better indicator of customer attitudes and behavior.

Growing "Share of Customer"

Beyond simple attracting and retaining good customers, marketers want to constantly increase their *share of customer*. They want to capture a greater share of the customer's purchasing in their product categories, either by becoming the sole supplier of products the customer is currently buying or by persuading the customer to purchase additional company products. Thus, banks want a greater "share of wallet," supermarkets want to increase their "share of stomach," car companies want a greater "share of garage," and airlines want a greater "share of travel."

Growing "share of customer": American Airline's Airpass program benefits both the company and its customers. The customer gets better rates and more services; American gets most of the customer's business.

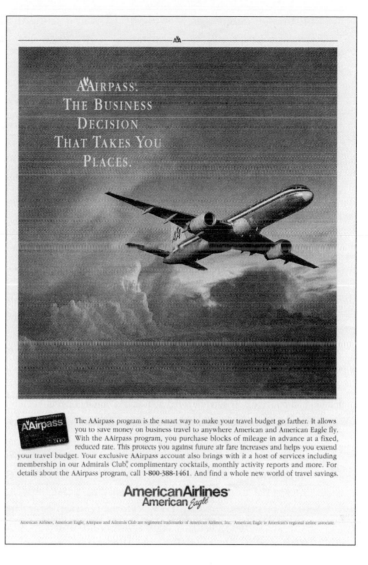

★ Today, the goal isn't to win some business from a lot of customers—it's to win all the business of current customers. Feverishly chasing market share is out; trying to maximize share of customers is in. For example, seeking maximum share of Perot System's travel dollars, American Airlines sold the company a program called Airpass. Now, unless a travel schedule demands otherwise, all Perot employees fly American. It works like this: When Perot employees book flights, they don't have to bother waiting for tickets; they simply present a card at the ticket counter or gate. Miles are automatically credited to their American frequent flier accounts. Upgrades are readily available and, to complete the package, American allows all Perot employees to use its Ambassadors Clubs for business and leisure travel. For all of this, Perot gets charged at a discounted travel rate against a corporate commitment for a specified number of travel miles. In return, American gets most of Perot's business. It's a winning proposition for everyone—except American's competitors. They just got excluded from a lot of Perot's travel business.[12]

One of the best ways to increase share of customer is through cross-selling. Cross-selling means getting more business from current customers of one product or service by selling them additional offerings. For example, the recent merger between Citibank and Travelers is helping both units of the Citibank Group to cross-sell the company's services.[13] A new Travelers Financial Edge program allows independent Travelers agents to introduce a number of Citibank products to their insurance clients, such as credit cards and student loans, as well as an equipment leasing program for commercial customers. Similarly, under a new Citibank Partners program, Citibank representatives can offer a fuller slate of financial services to their customers, such as insurance from Travelers and mutual funds from Salomon Smith Barney (another Citibank Group unit). To support the effort to cross-sell a broader range of services for customers, Citibank's personal bankers will be dubbed "client financial analysts" and its branches will be called "Citibank Financial Centers." As a result, Citibank Group will obtain a larger share of each customer's financial services dollars.

Building Lasting Customer Relationships

We can now see the importance of not just finding customers, but of keeping and growing them as well. Relationship marketing is oriented toward the long term. Today's smart companies not only want to create customers, they want to "own" them for life.

In this section, we discuss several questions about how companies actually build lasting customer relationships. What levels of relationships can companies build with their customers and what relationship-building tools do they use? Who is responsible for delivering customer value and satisfaction? What is the role of total marketing quality?

Customer Relationship Levels and Tools

Companies can build customer relationships at many levels—economic, social, technical, and legal—depending on the nature of the target market. At one extreme, a company with many low-margin customers may seek to develop *basic relationships* with them. For example, Procter & Gamble does not phone all of its Tide customers to get to know them personally and express its appreciation for their business. Instead, P&G creates relationships through brand-building advertising, sales promotions, a 1-800 customer response number, and its Tide ClothesLine Web site (www.tide.com). At the other extreme, in markets with few customers and high margins, sellers want to create *full partnerships* with key customers. For example, P&G customer teams work closely with Wal-Mart, Safeway, and other

Basic relationships: Procter & Gamble doesn't get to know Tide customers personally, but it does create close relationships through brand-building advertising, sales promotions, a 1-800 customer response number, and its Tide ClothesLine Web site.

large retailers. Boeing works closely with American Airlines, Delta, and other airlines in designing its airplanes and ensuring that Boeing airplanes fully satisfy their requirements. In between these two extreme situations, other levels of relationship marketing are appropriate.

Today, more and more companies are developing customer loyalty and retention programs. Beyond offering consistently high value and satisfaction, marketers can use a number of specific marketing tools to develop stronger bonds with consumers.[14] First, a company might build value and satisfaction by adding *financial benefits* to the customer relationship. For example, many companies now offer *frequency marketing programs* that reward customers who buy frequently or in large amounts. Airlines offer frequent flier programs, hotels give room upgrades to their frequent guests, and supermarkets give patronage refunds.

Other companies sponsor *club marketing programs* that offer members special discounts and other benefits. For example:[15]

★ Swiss watchmaker, Swatch, uses its club to cater to collectors, who on average buy nine of the company's quirky watches every year. Club members can buy exclusives, such as the "Garden Turf" watch, a clear watch with an Astroturf band. They also receive the *World Journal,* a magazine filled with Swatch-centric news from the four corners of the globe. Swatch counts on enthusiastic word of mouth from club members as a boost to business. "Our members are like walking billboards," says the manager of Swatch's club, Trish O'Callaghan. "They love, live, and breathe our product. They are ambassadors for Swatch."

★ Upon submitting a $25 fee to the Volkswagen Club, members receive the first issue of a club magazine, *Volkswagen World,* a T-shirt, a road atlas and decal, a phone card, and discount offers on travel and recreation. Members can also take advantage of discounts on parts and service from local dealers, and, as a particularly nifty touch, members can apply for a club Visa card with a picture of their own VW on the front.

★ Thanks in part to its magic club aimed at children, Spain's Telepizza now claims a 65 percent share of the Spanish pizza market compared to less than 20 percent for Pizza Hut. As the largest membership club in Spain, with 3 million children enrolled, the magic club offers children small prizes, usually simple magic tricks, with every order.

★ Harley-Davidson sponsors the Harley Owners Group (HOG), which now numbers 330,000 members, about a third of all Harley owners. The first-time buyer of a Harley-Davidson motorcycle gets a free one-year membership with annual renewal costing $40. HOG benefits include a magazine (*Hog Tales*), a copy of the *H.O.G. Touring Handbook,* a complete *H.O.G. World Atlas,* an emergency pickup service, a specially designed insurance program, theft reward service, discount hotel rates, and a *Fly & Ride* program enabling members to rent Harleys while on vacation.

A second approach is to add *social benefits* as well as financial benefits. Here the company increases its social bonds with customers by learning individual customers' needs and wants and then personalizing its products and services. For example, to build better relationships with its customers, in the summer of 1994 and again in 1999 Saturn invited all of its owners to a "Saturn Homecoming" at its manufacturing facility in Spring Hill, Tennessee. The two-day affair included family events, plant tours, entertainment, and physical challenge activities designed to build trust and a team spirit. Says Saturn's manager of corporate communications, "The Homecoming party is another way of building . . . relationships, and it shows that we treat our customers differently than any other car company." More than 60,000 people attended the most recent homecoming, traveling from as far as Alaska and Taiwan, with another 150,000 celebrating the occasion at the dealerships where they bought their cars.[16]

A third approach to building customer relationships is to add *structural ties* as well as financial and social benefits. For example, a business marketer might supply customers with special equipment or computer linkages that help them manage their orders, payroll, or inventory. McKesson Corporation, a leading pharmaceutical wholesaler, has invested millions of dollars in its electronic data interchange (EDI) system to help small pharmacies manage their inventory, their order entry, and their shelf space. FedEx offers Web links to its customers to keep them from defecting to competitors such as UPS. Customers can use the Web site to link with FedEx's computers, arrange shipments, and check the status of their FedEx packages.

Relationship marketing means that marketers must focus on managing their customers as well as their products. At the same time, they don't want relationships with every customer. In fact, there are undesirable customers for every company. Ultimately, marketing involves attracting, keeping, and growing *profitable* customers. Thus, in addition to assessing the value that it delivers *to* customers, a firm should actively measure the value *of* individual customers to the firm (see Marketing Highlight 18.1). Once it has identified profitable customers, it can create attractive offers and special handling to bind these customers to the company for a lifetime. But what should the company do with unprofitable customers? If it can't turn them into profitable ones, it may even want to "fire" customers that are too unreasonable or that cost more to serve than they are worth.

Figure 18.3 shows a useful type of analysis for assessing the value of a customer to a firm.[17] Customers make up the columns of the figure and products or services make up the rows. Each cell contains a symbol for the profitability of selling a given product or service to a given customer. Customer C_1 is very profitable—he or she buys three profit-making products, products $P_1, P_2,$ and P_3. Customer C_2 yields mixed profitability, buying one profitable product and one unprofitable product. Customer C_3 generates losses by purchasing one profitable product and two unprofitable ones ("loss leaders"). What can the company do about consumers like C_3? First, the company should consider raising the prices of its less profitable products or eliminating them. Second, the company also can try to cross-sell its profit-making products to its unprofitable customers. If these actions cause customers like C_3 to defect, it may be for the good. In fact, the company might benefit by *encouraging* its unprofitable customers to switch to competitors.[18]

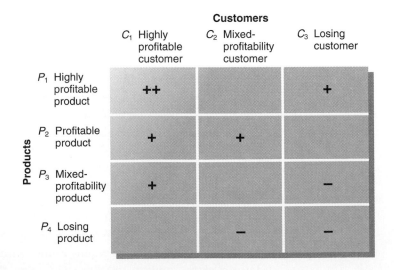

FIGURE 18.3   Customer–product profitability analysis

Delivering Customer Value and Satisfaction

Marketers alone cannot deliver superior customer value and satisfaction. Although it plays a leading role, marketing can be only a partner in attracting, keeping, and growing customers. Relationship marketing requires that marketers must work closely with other company departments to form an effective *value chain* that serves the customer. Moreover, the company can be effective only to the extent that it works effectively with its marketing system partners to form a competitively superior *value-delivery network*. We now take a closer look at the concepts of a company value chain and value-delivery network.

Value chain

A major tool for identifying ways to create more customer value.

Company Value Chain.   Each company department can be thought of as a link in the company's **value chain**.[19] That is, each department carries out value-creating activities to design, produce, market, deliver, and support the firm's products. The firm's success depends not only on how well each department performs its work, but also on how well the activities of various departments are coordinated.

For example, we learned previously that the goal of Ritz-Carlton Hotels is to deliver "a truly memorable experience." Marketers make up an important link in the Ritz-Carlton value chain that creates this experience. They conduct research to learn about customer needs, design services to meet these needs, advertise to inform guests about services and locations, and perform other value-creating activities.

However, other departments must also perform well in order to make the Ritz-Carlton experience a reality. For example, the Ritz-Carlton housekeeping and maintenance staffs make certain that everything at the Ritz-Carlton looks and works just right, meeting customers' exacting standards for room cleanliness and functioning. The human resources department hires people-oriented employees, trains them carefully, and motivates them to ferret out and attend to even the slightest customer want. Ritz-Carlton employees treat customers as individuals, not as nameless, faceless members of a mass market. Whenever possible, they refer to guests by name and give each guest a warm welcome every day. Finally, the information systems department maintains an extensive customer database, which holds more than 500,000 individual customer preferences, accessible by all hotels in the worldwide Ritz chain. A frequent guest who requests a specific type of room at the Ritz in San Francisco will be delighted to find a similar room assigned when he or she checks into the Atlanta Ritz months later, arranged just the way that he or she likes it.[20]

A company's value chain is only as strong as its weakest link. Success depends on how well each department performs its work of adding value for customers and on how well the activities of different departments are coordinated. At Ritz-Carlton, if customer-contact people are poorly selected or trained, or if rooms are anything less than spotless, marketers cannot fulfill their promise of a truly memorable experience.

Customer Value-Delivery Network.   In its search for competitive advantage, the firm needs to look beyond its own value chain and into the value chains of its suppliers, distributors, and ultimately customers. Consider McDonald's. People do not swarm to the world's 24,500 McDonald's restaurants only because they love the chain's hamburgers. In fact, according to one national survey, consumers rank McDonald's behind Burger King and Wendy's in taste preference.[21] Still, McDonald's commands over a 16 percent share of the nation's fast-food business and over 40 percent of the burger segment. Consumers flock to the McDonald's *system,* not just to its food products. Throughout the world, McDonald's finely

WANTED: PROFITABLE CUSTOMERS ONLY

All customers are created equal—right? Wrong! Whereas traditional marketing strategies have involved casting a wide net to lure as many customers as possible, today's smart companies now focus on keeping and growing only the most profitable customers they already have. "They are aggressively mining their vast databases to weed out losers, or at least to charge them more, and to target the best customers for pampering," says Rick Brooks of the *Wall Street Journal*. "Of course, some industries have a long tradition of favoring 'good' customers over less profitable ones," he adds. "Airlines, credit-card issuers, and

mail-order companies have thrown loads of tailored services to so-called platinum and premier customers. . . . But only recently has technology developed to the point where companies can compare profit-and-loss statements on every customer and weed out the money-losers."

Here are some examples of how companies are using customer profitability analysis to weed out losing customers and target the winning ones for pampering.

- Two years ago, shipping giant FedEx began analyzing the returns on its business for about

30 large customers that generate about 10 percent of its total volume. It found that certain customers, including some requiring lots of residential deliveries, weren't bringing in as much revenue as they had promised when they first negotiated discounted rates. So FedEx went on the offensive, demanding that some customers pay higher rates and imposing double-digit increases in a handful of instances. A couple of big customers who refused to budge were told they could take their shipping business elsewhere. "We were willing to risk a point or two of market share to correct the problem," says a spokesperson for FedEx. "You have to be willing to suck it up and walk away."

- At Thomas Cook Travel, differentiating between best and worst customers required a huge change in the company's culture. Agents had always been coached to deliver top-level service to everyone. Realizing that such an attitude just isn't profitable anymore, the agency divided its customers into As (those who bring in $750 or more in annual revenues), Bs (those bringing in $250–$749), and Cs (those who bring in less than $250). It found that 80 percent of its customers were Cs. "It's not that you don't want them, it's just that you differentiate," says Wendy White, marketing manager for Thomas Cook Travel Canada. You still deliver professional service, she observes, but not every client requires—or deserves—two hours' worth of service to purchase an airline ticket. The travel agents at Thomas Cook now know which customers deserve

Selective relationship management: BancOne uses targeted marketing to strengthen relationships with its most profitable customers. It lets Premier One customers know that they are "special, exclusive, privileged, valued"— "Expect a little more . . . you deserve it."

the full treatment and which ones don't. When C clients demand time-consuming services, for example, asking an agent to research a trip they're not positive they want to take, they are now asked for a $25 deposit. Clients who are serious pay up; the fee simply goes toward their booking cost. If they're not serious and don't pay, it frees up agents to deal with more profitable A and B clients. Agents also receive a quarterly printout from a database that lists the company's top 500 clients and the revenue each generates. It helps agents look for missed sales opportunities and "get a handle on the target and their needs," White adds. The change in focus has been lucrative for Thomas Cook Travel, resulting in 20 percent growth in the company's A and B level clients. "When you look at the bottom line, that's a very tangible result," say White.

- Imagex, a distributor of presentation graphics and document management equipment, tracks total dollars spent, profit dollars made, and the profit margin for each of its customers. Those who bring in the highest margins are the brightest stars in Imagex's constellation of customers. The analysis has helped Imagex pinpoint customer segments that are no longer worth the time and effort of its reps. For example, the firm estimates that 80 to 90 percent of its business historically has come from large companies with their own procurement departments. But those companies focus heavily on price and require time-consuming product demos before bids are even put out. Imagex no longer pursues new business from these less profitable large companies. Instead, it focuses on the more profitable business it gets from small and medium-size companies at which

the end user, not a purchasing department, makes purchase decisions. That allows for a higher-margin, value-added sale where service, and not just price, plays into the purchasing equation.

- Banks are by far the biggest industry yet to use profit data to make customer service decisions. For banks, a typical "bad" customer makes frequent branch visits, keeps less than $1,000 in the bank, and calls often to check on account balances. The most profitable customers keep several thousand dollars in their accounts, use a teller less than once a month, and hardly ever use the call center. The top 20 percent of typical bank customers produce as much as 150 percent of overall profit, whereas the bottom 20 percent of customers drain about 50 percent from the bank's bottom line. Thus, many banks now actively separate preferred customers from the nonpreferred. For example, BancOne has redesigned its 218 branches in Louisiana so that "Premier One" customers, after presenting a special gold card to the "concierge" near the front door, can be whisked away to a special teller window with no line or to the desk of a specially trained bank officer. At Westamerica Bancorp. in San Rafael, California, about 5,000 "VIP" customers get a secret toll-free number allowing them to jump ahead of unprofitable callers. BankAmerica routes calls from preferred and unprofitable customers to different operators; a personal-identification number entered by each caller allows the bank to determine, among other things, the customer's profitability ranking.

This sorting out process, of course, has many risks. For one,

future profits are hard to predict. A high school student on his or her way to a Harvard MBA and a plum job on Wall Street might be unprofitable now but worth courting for the future. So might an unprofitable customer who suddenly inherits a lot of money and wants to plunk it in CDs or other products. "That shabby-looking guy might actually be or become an eccentric billionaire. But as a result of using this technology, do you give him the bum's rush?" asks one analyst. Still, most banks believe that the benefits outweigh the risks. For example, after First Chicago imposed a $3 teller fee in 1995 on some of its money-losing customers, 30,000 of them—or close to 3 percent of the bank's total customers—closed their accounts. Many marginal customers became profitable by boosting their account balances high enough to avoid the fee or by visiting ATMs instead of tellers. On balance, imposing the fee improved the profitability of the bank's customer base.

Thus, today's marketers are looking closely at the profitability of their customers. Analyst Erika Rasmusson summarizes: "All men may be created equal, but increasingly, all customers are not. . . . Learning where your customers rank in terms of profitability is the future of business, and companies that are doing it now have a distinct advantage over their competitors. Call it *selective* relationship management—companies need to pick wisely which customers they're going to have relationships with— and what kind of relationships."

Sources: Examples adapted from Rick Brooks, "Unequal Treatment: Alienating Customers Isn't Always a Bad Idea, Many Firms Discover," *Wall Street Journal*, January 7, 1999, p. A1; and Erika Rasmusson, "Wanted: Profitable Customers," *Sales & Marketing Management*, May 1999, pp. 28–34.

tuned system delivers a high standard of what the company calls QSCV—quality, service, cleanliness, and value. McDonald's is effective only to the extent that it successfully partners with its franchisees, suppliers, and others to jointly deliver exceptionally high customer value.

Value-delivery network
The network made up of the company, suppliers, distributors, and ultimately customers who "partner" with each other to improve the performance of the entire system.

More companies today are "partnering" with the other members of the supply chain to improve the performance of the customer **value-delivery network.** For example, Honda has designed a program for working closely with its suppliers to help them reduce their costs and improve quality. When Honda chose Donnelly Corporation to supply all of the mirrors for its U.S.-made cars, it sent engineers swarming over Donnelly's plants, looking for ways to improve its products and operations. This helped Donnelly reduce its costs by 2 percent in the first year. As a result of its improved performance, Donnelly's sales to Honda have grown from $5 million annually to more than $60 million in less than 10 years. In turn, Honda has gained an efficient, low-cost supplier of quality components. As a result of Honda's partnerships with Donnelly and other suppliers, Honda customers receive greater value in the form of lower-cost, higher-quality cars.[22]

Increasingly in today's marketplace, competition no longer takes place between individual competitors. Rather, it takes place between the entire value-delivery networks created by these competitors. Thus, Honda's performance against another automaker —say Toyota—depends on the quality of Honda's overall value-delivery network versus Toyota's. Companies no longer compete—their entire marketing networks do.

Total Quality Marketing

Customer relationships and company profitability are linked closely to product and service quality. Higher levels of quality result in greater customer satisfaction, while at the same time supporting higher prices and often lower costs. Therefore, *quality improvement programs* normally increase profitability. Today's executives view the task of improving product and service quality as a top priority.

Japan was the first country to award a national quality prize, the Deming prize, named after the American statistician who taught the importance of quality to postwar Japan. The quest for quality paid off handsomely. Consumers around the world flocked to buy high-quality Japanese products, leaving many American and European firms playing catch-up. In recent years, however, Western firms have closed the quality gap. Many have started their own quality programs in an effort to compete both globally and at home with the Japanese.

In the mid-1980s, the United States established the Malcolm Baldrige National Quality Award, which encourages U.S. firms to implement quality practices. Not wanting to be left out of the quality race, Europe developed the European Quality Award in 1993. It also initiated an exacting set of quality standards called ISO 9000. Whereas the Baldrige and other quality awards measure less tangible aspects of quality, such as customer satisfaction and continuous improvement, ISO 9000 is a set of specific international standards on quality management and quality assurance. More than 74 countries have officially recognized ISO 9000 as an international standard for quality systems. Many companies in these countries are now demanding ISO certification as a prerequisite for doing business with a seller. To earn ISO 9000 certification, sellers must undergo a quality audit every six months by a registered ISO (International Standards Organization) assessor. Thus, total quality has become a truly global concern.[23]

Most customers will no longer accept or tolerate average quality. If companies want to stay in the race, let alone be profitable, they have no choice but to adopt

Quality
The totality of features and characteristics of a product or service that bear on its ability to satisfy stated or implied needs.

quality concepts. But what exactly is quality? Various experts have defined *quality* as "fitness for use," "conformance to requirements," and "freedom from variation." The American Society for Quality defines **quality** as the totality of features and characteristics of a product or service that bear on its ability to satisfy stated or implied needs.[24] This is clearly a customer-centered definition of quality. It suggests that a company has delivered quality whenever its product and service meet or exceed customers' needs, requirements, and expectations.

It is important to distinguish between performance quality and conformance quality. *Performance quality* refers to the *level* at which a product performs its functions. For example, a Mercedes provides higher performance quality than a Honda Civic: It has a smoother ride, handles better, and lasts longer. It is more expensive and sells to a market with higher means and requirements. *Conformance quality* refers to freedom from defects and the *consistency* with which a product delivers a specified level of performance. Thus, a Mercedes and a Honda Civic can be said to offer equivalent conformance quality to their respective markets to the extent that each consistently delivers what its market expects. A $50,000 car that meets all of its requirements is a quality car; so is an $18,000 car that meets all of its requirements. But if the Mercedes handles badly, or if the Honda gives poor fuel efficiency, then both cars have failed to deliver quality, and customer satisfaction suffers accordingly.

Total quality management (TQM) swept the corporate boardrooms of the 1980s. Many companies adopted the language of TQM but not the substance. Others viewed TQM as a cure-all for all the company's problems. Still others became obsessed with narrowly defined TQM principles and lost sight of broader concerns for customer value and satisfaction. As a result, many TQM programs begun in the 1980s failed, causing a backlash against TQM. Still, when applied in the context of creating customer satisfaction, total quality principles remain a requirement for success. Although many firms don't use the TQM label anymore, for most top companies customer-driven quality has become a way of doing business. They apply the notion of *return on quality (ROQ)*, and they make certain that the quality they offer is the quality that customers want. This quality, in turn, results in improved sales and profits.[25]

Total quality is the key to creating customer value, satisfaction, and retention. Just as marketing is everyone's job, total quality is everyone's job:

> Marketers who don't learn the language of quality improvement, manufacturing, and operations will become as obsolete as buggy whips. The days of functional marketing are gone. We can no longer afford to think of ourselves as market researchers, advertising people, direct marketers, marketing strategists—we have to think of ourselves as customer satisfiers—customer advocates focused on whole processes.[26]

Marketers play a major role in helping their companies define and deliver high-quality products and services to target customers. First, marketers bear the major responsibility for correctly identifying the customers' needs and requirements and for communicating customer expectations correctly to product designers. They must take part in designing strategies and programs that help the company win through total quality excellence. Marketers must be the customer's watchdog or guardian, complaining loudly for the customer when the product or the service is not right. Second, marketing must deliver marketing quality as well as production quality. It must perform each marketing activity—marketing research, sales training, advertising, customer service, and others—to high-quality standards.

COMPETITIVE MARKETING STRATEGIES

Competitor analysis
The process of identifying key competitors; assessing their objectives, strategies, strengths and weaknesses, and reaction patterns; and selecting which competitors to attack or avoid.

Competitive marketing strategies
Strategies that strongly position the company against competitors and that give the company the strongest possible strategic advantage.

Today, understanding customers is crucial, but it's not enough. Under the marketing concept, companies gain competitive advantage by satisfying target consumer needs *better than competitors do.* Thus, marketing strategies must consider not only the needs of target consumers but also the strategies of competitors. The first step is **competitor analysis,** the process of identifying, assessing, and selecting key competitors. The second step is developing **competitive marketing strategies** that strongly position the company against competitors and give it the greatest possible competitive advantage.

Competitor Analysis

To plan effective competitive marketing strategies, the company needs to find out all it can about its competitors. It must constantly compare its products, prices, channels, and promotion with those of close competitors. In this way the company can find areas of potential competitive advantage and disadvantage. As shown in Figure 18.4, competitor analysis involves first identifying and assessing competitors and then selecting which competitors to attack or avoid.

Identifying Competitors

Normally, it would seem a simple task for a company to identify its competitors. At the narrowest level, a company can define its competitors as other companies offering similar products and services to the same customers at similar prices. Thus, Coca-Cola might view Pepsi as a major competitor, but not Budweiser or Kool-Aid. Buick might see Ford as a major competitor, but not Mercedes or Hyundai.

But companies actually face a much wider range of competitors. The company might define competitors as all firms making the same product or class of products. Thus, Buick would see itself as competing against all other automobile makers. Even more broadly, competitors might include all companies making products that supply the same service. Here Buick would see itself competing not only against other automobile makers but also against companies that make trucks, motorcycles, or even bicycles. Finally, and still more broadly, competitors might include all companies that compete for the same consumer dollars. Here Buick would see itself competing with companies that sell major consumer durables, new homes, or vacations abroad.

Companies must avoid "competitor myopia." A company is more likely to be "buried" by its latent competitors than its current ones. For example, in its detergent business, Unilever has worried most about growing competition from Procter & Gamble and other detergent manufacturers. But Unilever may face a much greater threat from research being done on an ultrasonic washing machine. If perfected, this machine would wash clothes in water with little or no detergent. What greater threat is there to the detergent business than detergentless washing?

FIGURE 18.4 Steps in analyzing competitors

Competitor myopia: Encyclopedia Britannica's sales plunged when it failed to recognize that its real competitor was computer and CD-ROM applications such as Microsoft Encarta.

Similarly, Encyclopedia Britannica viewed itself as competing with other publishers of printed encyclopedia sets selling for as much as $2,200 per set. However, it learned a hard lesson when Microsoft Encarta, an encyclopedia on CD-ROM, was introduced and sold for only $50. It seems that parents bought the *Britannica* less for its intellectual content than out of a desire to do what's right for their children. Although less comprehensive than the *Britannica,* Encarta and other CD-ROM encyclopedias served this "do what's right" purpose well. By the time *Britannica* introduced its own CD-ROM and online versions, its sales plunged by more than 50 percent. Thus, Encyclopedia Britannica's real competitor was the computer.[27]

Assessing Competitors

Having identified the main competitors, marketing management now asks: What does each competitor seek in the marketplace? What is each competitor's strategy? What are various competitor's strengths and weaknesses, and how will each react to actions the company might take?

Each competitor has a mix of objectives. The company wants to know the relative importance that a competitor places on current profitability, market share growth, cash flow, technological leadership, service leadership, and other goals. Knowing a competitor's mix of objectives reveals whether the competitor is satisfied with its current situation and how it might react to different competitive actions. A company also must monitor its competitors' objectives for various segments. If the company finds that a competitor has discovered a new segment, this might be an opportunity. If it finds that competitors plan new moves into segments now served by the company, it will be forewarned and, hopefully, forearmed.

The more that one firm's strategy resembles another firm's strategy, the more the two firms compete. In most industries, the competitors can be sorted into groups that pursue different strategies. For example, in the major appliance industry, General Electric, Whirlpool, and Maytag all belong to the same strategic group. Each produces a full line of medium-price appliances supported by good service. Sub Zero and KitchenAid, on the other hand, belong to a different strategic group. They produce a narrower line of higher-quality appliances, offer a higher level of service, and charge a premium price.

Some important insights emerge from identifying strategic groups. For example, if a company enters one of the groups, the members of that group become its key competitors. Thus, the company needs to look at all of the dimensions that identify strategic groups within the industry. It needs to know each competitor's product quality, features, and mix; customer services; pricing policy; distribution coverage; sales force strategy; and advertising and sales promotion programs. It also must study the details of each competitor's R&D, manufacturing, purchasing, financial, and other strategies.

Marketers need to assess each competitor's strengths and weaknesses carefully in order to answer the critical question: What *can* our competitors do? Companies normally learn about their competitors' strengths and weaknesses through secondary data, personal experience, and hearsay. They also can conduct primary marketing research with customers, suppliers, and dealers. Or they can **benchmark** themselves against other firms, comparing the company's products and processes to those of competitors or leading firms in other industries to find ways to improve quality and performance. Benchmarking has become a powerful tool for increasing a company's competitiveness.

Finally, the company wants to know: What *will* our competitors do? A competitor's objectives, strategies, and strengths and weaknesses go a long way toward explaining its likely actions, as well as its likely reactions to company moves such as price cuts, promotion increases, or new-product introductions. In addition, each competitor has a certain philosophy of doing business, a certain internal culture and guiding beliefs. Marketing managers need a deep understanding of a given competitor's mentality if they want to anticipate how the competitor will act or react.

Each competitor reacts differently. Some do not react quickly or strongly to a competitor's move. They may feel their customers are loyal; they may be slow in noticing the move; they may lack the funds to react. Some competitors react only to certain types of moves and not to others. Other competitors react swiftly and strongly to any action. Thus, Procter & Gamble does not let a new detergent come easily into the market. Many firms avoid direct competition with P&G and look for easier prey, knowing that P&G will react fiercely if challenged.

In some industries, competitors live in relative harmony; in others, they fight constantly. Knowing how major competitors react gives the company clues on how best to attack competitors or how best to defend the company's current positions.

Selecting Competitors to Attack and Avoid

A company has already largely selected its major competitors through prior decisions on customer targets, distribution channels, and marketing mix strategy. These decisions define the strategic group to which the company belongs. Management now must decide which competitors to compete against most vigorously.

The company can focus on one of several classes of competitors. Most companies prefer to aim their shots at their *weak competitors*. This requires fewer resources and less time. But in the process, the firm may gain little. The argument could be made that the firm also should compete with *strong competitors* in order to sharpen its abilities. Furthermore, even strong competitors have some weaknesses, and succeeding against them often provides greater returns.

Most companies will compete with *close competitors*—those that resemble them most—rather than *distant competitors*. Thus, Chevrolet competes more against Ford than against Lexus. At the same time, the company may want to avoid trying to "destroy" a close competitor. For example, in the late 1970s, Bausch & Lomb moved aggressively against other soft lens manufacturers with great success. However, this forced weak competitors to sell out to larger firms such as Schering-Plough and Johnson & Johnson. As a result, Bausch & Lomb faced much larger competitors—and it suffered the consequences. Johnson & Johnson acquired Vistakon, a small nicher

Benchmarking
The process of comparing the company's products and processes to those of competitors or leading firms in other industries to find ways to improve quality and performance.

with only $20 million in annual sales. Backed by Johnson & Johnson's deep pockets, however, the small but nimble Vistakon developed and introduced its innovative Acuvue disposable lenses. According to one analyst, "The speed of the [Acuvue] roll-out and the novelty of [Johnson & Johnson's] big-budget ads left giant Bausch & Lomb . . . seeing stars." By 1992, Vistakon was number one in the fast-growing disposable segment and had captured about 25 percent of the entire U.S. contact lens market.[28] In this case, success in hurting a close rival brought in tougher competitors.

A company really needs and benefits from competitors. The existence of competitors results in several strategic benefits. Competitors may help increase total demand. They may share the costs of market and product development and help to legitimize new technologies. They may serve less attractive segments or lead to more product differentiation. Finally, they lower the antitrust risk and improve bargaining power versus labor or regulators. For example, Intel's recent aggressive pricing on low-end computer chips has sent smaller rivals like MD and 3Com reeling. However, Intel may want to be careful not to knock these competitors completely out. "If for no other reason than to keep the feds at bay," notes one analyst, "Intel needs AMD, 3Com, and other rivals to stick around." Says another: "Intel may have put the squeeze on a little too hard. If AMD collapsed, the FTC would surely react."[29]

However, a company may not view all of its competitors as beneficial. An industry often contains *"well-behaved" competitors* and *"disruptive" competitors.*[30] Well-behaved competitors play by the rules of the industry. Disruptive competitors, in contrast, break the rules. They try to buy share rather than earn it, take large risks, and in general shake up the industry. For example, American Airlines finds Delta and United to be well-behaved competitors because they play by the rules and attempt to set their fares sensibly. But American finds Continental and America West disruptive competitors because they destabilize the airline industry through continual heavy price discounting and wild promotional schemes. The implication is that "well-behaved" companies would like to shape an industry that consists of only well-behaved competitors. A company might be smart to support well-behaved competitors, aiming its attacks at disruptive competitors. Thus, some analysts claim that American used huge fare discounts from time to time intentionally designed to teach disruptive airlines a lesson or to drive them out of business altogether.

Competitive Strategies

Having identified and evaluated its major competitors, the company now must design broad competitive marketing strategies by which it can gain competitive advantage by offering superior customer value. But what broad marketing strategies might the company use? Which ones are best for a particular company, or for the company's different divisions and products?

No one strategy is best for all companies. Each company must determine what makes the most sense given its position in the industry and its objectives, opportunities, and resources. Even within a company, different strategies may be required for different businesses or products. Johnson & Johnson uses one marketing strategy for its leading brands in stable consumer markets and a different marketing strategy for its new high-tech health care businesses and products. We now look at broad competitive marketing strategies companies can use.

Basic Competitive Strategies

More than a decade ago, Michael Porter suggested four basic competitive positioning strategies that companies can follow—three winning strategies and one losing one.[31] The three winning strategies include:

Overall cost leadership: Here the company works hard to achieve the lowest costs of production and distribution so that it can price lower than its competitors and win a large market share. Texas Instruments, Dell Computer, and Wal-Mart are leading practitioners of this strategy.

Differentiation: Here the company concentrates on creating a highly differentiated product line and marketing program so that it comes across as the class leader in the industry. Most customers would prefer to own this brand if its price is not too high. IBM and Caterpillar follow this strategy in information technology products and services and heavy construction equipment, respectively.

Focus: Here the company focuses its effort on serving a few market segments well rather than going after the whole market. For example, Ritz-Carlton focuses on the top 5 percent of corporate and leisure travelers. Glassmaker AFG Industries focuses on users of tempered and colored glass—it makes 70 percent of the glass for microwave oven doors and 75 percent of the glass for shower doors and patio tabletops.

Companies that pursue a clear strategy—one of the above—are likely to perform well. The firm that carries out that strategy best will make the most profits. But firms that do not pursue a clear strategy—*middle-of-the-roaders*—do the worst. Sears, Holiday Inn, and International Harvester encountered difficult times because they did not stand out as the lowest in cost, highest in perceived value, or best in serving some market segment. Middle-of-the-roaders try to be good on all strategic counts, but end up being not very good at anything.

More recently, two marketing consultants, Michael Treacy and Fred Wiersema, offered a new classification of competitive marketing strategies.[32] They suggest that companies gain leadership positions by delivering superior value to their customers. Companies can pursue any of three strategies—called *value disciplines*—for delivering superior customer value. These are:

Operational excellence: The company provides superior value by leading its industry in price and convenience. It works to reduce costs and to create a lean and efficient value-delivery system. It serves customers who want reliable, good-quality products or services, but who want them cheaply and easily. Examples include Wal-Mart and Dell Computer.

Customer intimacy: The company provides superior value by precisely segmenting its markets and then tailoring its products or services to match exactly the needs of targeted customers. It specializes in satisfying unique customer needs through a close relationship with and intimate knowledge of the customer. It builds detailed customer databases for segmenting and targeting, and empowers its marketing people to respond quickly to customer needs. It serves customers who are willing to pay a premium to get precisely what they want, and it will do almost anything to build long-term customer loyalty and to capture customer lifetime value. Examples include Nordstrom department stores, Lands' End outfitters, and Kraft General Foods (see Marketing Highlight 18.2).

Product leadership: The company provides superior value by offering a continuous stream of leading-edge products or services that make their own and competing products obsolete. It is open to new ideas, relentlessly pursues new solutions, and works to reduce cycle times so that it can get new products to market quickly. It serves customers who want state-of-the-art products and services, regardless of the costs in terms of price or inconvenience. Examples include Intel, Motorola, and Nike.

*Customer intimacy:
Nordstrom delivers superior
value through a close relationship with and intimate
knowledge of its customers.*

Some companies successfully pursue more than one value discipline at the same time. For example, Federal Express excels at both operational excellence and customer intimacy. However, such companies are rare—few firms can be the best at more than one of these disciplines. By trying to be *good at all* of the value disciplines, a company usually ends up being *best at none.*

Treacy and Wiersema have found that leading companies focus on and excel at a single value discipline, while meeting industry standards on the other two. Such companies design their entire value-delivery network to single-mindedly support the chosen discipline. For example, Wal-Mart knows that customer intimacy and product leadership are important. Compared with other discounters, it offers very good customer service and an excellent product assortment. Still, it offers less customer service and less depth in its product assortment than do Lands' End or Nordstrom, which pursue customer intimacy. Instead, Wal-Mart focuses obsessively on operational excellence—on reducing costs and streamlining its order-to-delivery process in order to make it convenient for customers to buy just the right products at the lowest prices.

Classifying competitive strategies as value disciplines is appealing. It defines marketing strategy in terms of the single-minded pursuit of delivering superior value to customers. It recognizes that management must align every aspect of the company with the chosen value discipline—from its culture, to its organizational structure, to its operating and management systems and processes.

Competitive Positions

Firms competing in a given target market, at any point in time, differ in their objectives and resources. Some firms are large, others small. Some have many resources, others are strapped for funds. Some are old and established, others new and fresh. Some strive for rapid market share growth, others for long term profits. The firms occupy different competitive positions in the target market.

We now examine competitive strategies based on the roles firms play in the target market—that of leading, challenging, following, or niching. Every industry contains a **market leader,** the firm with the largest market share. Most also contain

Market leader

The firm in an industry with the largest market share; it usually leads other firms in price changes, new product introductions, distribution coverage, and promotion spending.

MARKETING
HIGHLIGHT
1 8 . 2

KRAFT GENERAL FOODS: IN PURSUIT OF CUSTOMER INTIMACY

An investigation of your pantry or refrigerator will likely unearth a dozen or more Kraft products. Well-known Kraft brands such as Miracle Whip, Kool-Aid, Jell-O, Maxwell House, Velveeta, Cracker Barrel, Philadelphia, Good Seasons, Country Time, and Oscar Mayer have become household words to most of us. Not surprisingly, Kraft pursues a strategy of customer intimacy. It gets to know its customers well, segments and targets its markets precisely, and tailors its products and merchandising programs closely to match the needs of targeted customers.

At the heart of Kraft's customer-intimacy strategy is an extensive, centralized customer information system, which keeps track of the whos, whats, and hows of customer buying. The information system consists of three databases. The first database contains customer purchase information collected from individual stores, broken out by store, category, and product. It also shows how purchases are affected by displays, price promotions, and other merchandising factors. A second database, supplied by an outside research firm, contains geodemographic data by zip code. The final and most extensive database contains demographic and purchasing information on more than 30 million Kraft customers who have supplied their names when sending in coupons or responding to some other Kraft promotion.

Kraft's marketers use this information to create carefully tailored and targeted marketing offers. They development direct-marketing programs—clubs, newsletters, premium offers, and coupon mailings—to increase customer purchasing and loyalty. For example, based on the interests they express in surveys, Kraft customers receive regular tips on topics such as exercise and nutrition, along with recipes and coupons for specific brands. Kraft also uses its information system to shape individual retail store assortments and merchandising programs.

Like most other customer-intimate companies, Kraft has decentralized its marketing organization, empowering its marketers and salespeople with the information, authority, and merchandising tools required to meet customer needs in specific segments.

[Kraft] has created the capacity to tailor its advertising, merchandising, and operations in a single store, or in several stores within a supermarket chain, to the needs of those stores' particular customers. Kraft has the information systems, analytical capability, and educated sales force to allow it to develop as many different so-called micro-merchandising programs for a chain . . . as the chain has stores. The program can be different for every neighborhood outlet. . . . Instead of pushing one-size-fits-all sales-promotion programs, Kraft salespeople now work with individual store managers and regional managers to create customized promotional programs from an extensive computerized menu of program models.

At . . . headquarters, [Kraft's] trade marketing team sorts and integrates the information from [its] databases and uses the results to supply sales teams with [an assortment] of usable programs, products, value-added ideas, and selling tools. For instance, the . . . team sorted all shoppers into six distinct groups, with names such as full-margin shoppers, planners and dine-outs, and commodity shoppers. Kraft then determined for its major accounts which shopper groups frequented each of their stores. A Kraft sales team even persuaded one chain to create a drive-through window in stores where planners and dine-outs—people who plan their shopping trips and dine out often—were a large segment, making it more convenient for them to pick up staples between big shopping trips.

Kraft is also able to develop promotion packages for store clusters for special events like the Superbowl. It can design a product mix more likely to succeed in one cluster than another. Pinpointing which store gets which products reduces inventory and delivers the right product to the right place at the right time.

Thus, in pursuit of customer intimacy, Kraft delivers superior customer value by first acquiring a detailed understanding of customer needs in precisely defined segments and then developing a flexible and responsive organization that closely meets those needs.

Sources: Excerpts from Michael Treacy and Fred Wiersema, "Customer Intimacy and Other Value Disciplines," *Harvard Business Review,* January–February 1993, pp. 84–93. Copyright © 1993 by the President and Fellows of Harvard College; all rights reserved. Also see Irene B. Rosenfeld, "Brand Management in a Marketplace War Zone," *Journal of Advertising Research,* September–October 1997, pp. 85–89; Judann Pollack, "The Food Chain," *Advertising Age,* May 6, 1996, pp. 28–30; and the Kraft Foods Web page at www.kraftfoods.com.

Market challenger
A runner-up firm in an industry that is fighting hard to increase its market share.

Market follower
A runner-up firm in an industry that wants to hold its share without rocking the boat.

Market nicher
A firm in an industry that serves small segments that other firms overlook or ignore.

one or more **market challengers,** runner-up firms that are fighting hard to increase their market share. **Market followers** are runner-up firms that want to hold their share without rocking the boat. Finally, **market nichers** serve small segments not being pursued by other firms.

We now look at specific marketing strategies that are available to market leaders, challengers, followers, and nichers (see Table 18.1).[33] Remember, however, that these classifications often do not apply to a whole company, but only to its position in a specific industry. Large and diversified companies such as IBM, Microsoft, Procter & Gamble, or Disney might be leaders in some markets and nichers in others. For example, Procter & Gamble leads in many segments, such as dishwashing and laundry detergents, disposable diapers, and shampoo, but it challenges Lever in the hand soaps and Kimberly-Clark in facial tissues. Such companies often use different strategies for different business units or products, depending on the competitive situations of each.

Market Leader Strategies

Most industries contain an acknowledged market leader. The leader has the largest market share and usually leads the other firms in price changes, new-product introductions, distribution coverage, and promotion spending. The leader may or may not be admired or respected, but other firms concede its dominance. Competitors focus on the leader as a company to challenge, imitate, or avoid. Some of the best-known market leaders are General Motors (autos), Kodak (photography), IBM (computers and information technology services), Caterpillar (earth-moving equipment), Coca-Cola (soft drinks), Wal-Mart (retailing), McDonald's (fast food), and Gillette (razors and blades).

A leader's life is not easy. It must maintain a constant watch. Other firms keep challenging its strengths or trying to take advantage of its weaknesses. The market leader can easily miss a turn in the market and plunge into second or third place. A product innovation may come along and hurt the leader (as when Nokia's and Ericcon's digital phones took the lead from Motorola's analog models). The leader might grow arrogant or complacent and misjudge the competition (as when Sears lost its lead to Wal-Mart and other emerging retailers). Or the leader might look old-fashioned against new and peppier rivals (as when Levi's lost serious ground to more current or stylish brands like Gap, Lees, Tommy Hilfiger, DKNY, or Guess).

To remain number one, leading firms can take any of three actions. First, they can find ways to expand total demand. Second, they can protect their current market share through good defensive and offensive actions. Third, they can try to expand their market share further, even if market size remains constant.

Expanding the Total Market.   The leading firm normally gains the most when the total market expands. If Americans take more pictures, Kodak stands to gain the most because it sells over 80 percent of this country's film. If Kodak can convince

TABLE 18.1   STRATEGIES FOR MARKET LEADERS, CHALLENGERS, FOLLOWERS, AND NICHERS

Market Leader Strategies	Market Challenger Strategies	Market Follower Strategies	Market Nicher Strategies
Expand total market	Full frontal attack	Follow closely	By customer, market,
Protect market share	Indirect attack	Follow at a distance	quality–price, service
Expand market share			Multiple niching

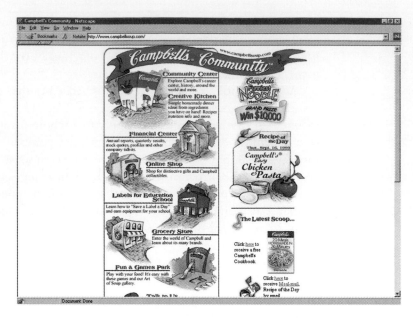

more Americans to take pictures, or to take pictures on more occasions, or to take more pictures on each occasion, it will benefit greatly.

Market leaders can expand the market by developing new users, new uses, and more usage of its products. They usually can find *new users* in many places. For example, Revlon might find new perfume users in its current markets by convincing women who do not use perfume to try it. It might find users in new demographic segments, such as by producing cologne for men. Or it might expand into new geographic segments, perhaps by selling its perfume in other countries.

Marketers can expand markets by discovering and promoting *new uses* for the product. For example, Intel invests heavily to develop new PC applications, which in turn increases the demand for microprocessors. It knows that it will get a 90 percent share of the new computer chip business. Another example of new-use expansion is Arm & Hammer baking soda. Its sales had flattened after 125 years; then the company discovered that consumers were using baking soda as a refrigerator deodorizer. It launched a heavy advertising and publicity campaign focusing on this use and persuaded consumers in half of America's homes to place an open box of baking soda in their refrigerators and to replace it every few months. Today, its Web site (www.armandhammer.com) regularly features new uses, from removing residue left behind by hairstyling products and sweetening garbage disposals, laundry hampers, refrigerators, and trash cans to creating a home spa in your bathroom.

Finally, marketer leaders can encourage *more usage* by convincing people to use the product more often or to use more per occasion. For example, Campbell urges people to eat soup more often by running ads containing new recipes and by offering a toll-free hot line (1-888-MMM-GOOD), staffed by live "recipe representatives" who offer recipes to last-minute cooks at a loss for meal ideas. Gillette's new Mach3 shaving system encourages more usage by actually "telling" consumers when a cartridge is worn out. Each Mach3 Cartridge features a blue stripe that slowly fades with repeated use. After about a dozen shaves, it fades away completely, signaling the user to move on to the next cartridge in order to continue getting "the optimal Mach3 shaving experience." The more users change the cartridge, the more cartridges Gillette sells.

Protecting Market Share.   While trying to expand total market size, the leading firm also must constantly protect its current business against competitors' attacks.

Coca-Cola must also constantly guard against PepsiCo; Gillette against Bic; Kodak against Fuji; McDonald's against Burger King; General Motors against Ford.

What can the market leader do to protect its position? First, it must prevent or fix weaknesses that provide opportunities for competitors. It needs to keep its costs down and its prices in line with the value the customers see in the brand. The leader should "plug holes" so that competitors do not jump in. But the best defense is a good offense, and the best response is *continuous innovation*. The leader refuses to be content with the way things are and leads the industry in new products, customer services, distribution effectiveness, and cost cutting. It keeps increasing its competitive effectiveness and value to customers.

For example, International Gaming Technology (IGT) is a company that manufactures slot machines and video poker machines for casinos around the world. It has achieved the daunting 75 percent market share in its mature market. Unlike the people who use its products, IGT doesn't rely on luck. Instead, it has formed partnerships with both casino operators and competitive gaming manufacturers to develop innovative new equipment to replace the old. IGT spends aggressively on R&D, allocating $31 million annually to create new games. "We know months, years, in advance what our customers want," says Robert Shay, a sales director for IGT. In this way, IGT takes the offensive, sets the pace, and exploits competitors' weaknesses.[34]

Expanding Market Share. Market leaders also can grow by increasing their market shares further. In many markets, small market share increases mean very large sales increases. For example, in the coffee market, a 1 percent increase in market share is worth $48 million; in soft drinks, $500 million!

Studies have shown that, on average, profitability rises with increasing market share. Because of these findings, many companies have sought expanded market shares to improve profitability. General Electric, for example, declared that it wants to be at least number one or two in each of its markets or else get out. GE shed its computer, air-conditioning, small appliances, and television businesses because it could not achieve top-dog position in these industries.

Companies must not think, however, that gaining increased market share will improve profitability automatically. Much depends on their strategy for gaining increased share. There are many high share companies with low profitability and many low-share companies with high profitability. The cost of buying higher market share may far exceed the returns. Higher shares tend to produce higher profits only when unit costs fall with increased market share, or when the company offers a superior-quality product and charges a premium price that more than covers the cost of offering higher quality.

Market Challenger Strategies

Firms that are second, third, or lower in an industry are sometimes quite large, such as Colgate, Ford, Kmart, Avis, Dell, and PepsiCo. These runner-up firms can adopt one of two competitive strategies: They can challenge the leader and other competitors in an aggressive bid for more market share (market challengers). Or they can play along with competitors and not rock the boat (market followers). We now look at competitive strategies for market challengers.

A market challenger must first define which competitors to challenge and its strategic objective. The challenger can attack the market leader, a high-risk but potentially high-gain strategy that makes good sense if the leader is not serving the market well. To succeed with such an attack, a company must have some sustainable competitive advantage over the leader—a cost advantage leading to lower prices or the ability to provide better value at a premium price. If the company goes after the market leader, its objective may be to wrest a certain market share. Bic knows that it can't topple Gillette in the razor market—it simply wants a larger share. Or the challenger's goal might be to take over market leadership. Wal-Mart began as a nicher in small towns in the Southwest, grew rapidly to challenge market leader Sears, and finally assumed market leadership, all within a span of less than 25 years.

Alternatively, the challenger can avoid the leader and instead challenge firms its own size, or smaller local and regional firms. These smaller firms may be underfinanced and not serving their customers well. Several of the major beer companies grew to their present size not by challenging large competitors, but by gobbling up small local or regional competitors. If the company goes after a small local company, its objective may be to put that company out of business. The important point remains: The challenger must choose its opponents carefully and have a clearly defined and attainable objective.

How can the market challenger best attack the chosen competitor and achieve its strategic objectives? It may launch a full *frontal attack,* matching the competitor's product, advertising, price, and distribution efforts. It attacks the competitor's strengths rather than its weaknesses. The outcome depends on who has the greater strength and endurance. If the market challenger has fewer resources than the competitor, a frontal attack makes little sense. For example, the runner-up razor-blade manufacturer in Brazil attacked Gillette, the market leader. The attacker was asked if it offered the consumer a better razor blade. "No," was the reply. "A lower price?" "No." "A better package?" "No." "A clever advertising campaign?" "No." "Better allowances to the trade?" "No." "Then how do you expect to take share away from Gillette?" "Sheer determination" was the reply. Needless to say, the offensive failed. Even great size and strength may not be enough to challenge a firmly entrenched, resourceful competitor successfully.

Rather than challenging head on, the challenger can make an *indirect attack* on the competitor's weaknesses or on gaps in the competitor's market coverage. For example, PepsiCo often finds it difficult to go head-to-head against market leader Coca-Cola. So in 1998 it tried the indirect approach by acquiring juice giant Tropicana. As the world's largest juice company, Tropicana arms PepsiCo with a powerful new weapon in the war against Coca-Cola. In the $3 billion market for orange juice, Tropicana's 42 percent share blows away Coke-owned Minute-Maid, which has only 24 percent share. The purchase gave PepsiCo at least one way to beat Coca-Cola.[35]

Similarly, rather than copying the competitor's product and mounting a costly frontal attack, the challenger might diversify into unrelated products or leapfrog into new technologies to replace existing products. Thus, Minolta toppled Canon from the lead in the 35mm SLR camera market when it introduced its technologically advanced autofocusing Maxxum camera. Canon's market share dropped toward 20 percent while Minolta's zoomed past 30 percent. It took Canon three years to introduce a matching technology. Such indirect challenges make good sense when the company has fewer resources than the competitor.

Market Follower Strategies

Not all runner-up companies want to challenge the market leader. Challenges are never taken lightly by the leader. If the challenger's lure is lower prices, improved service, or additional product features, the leader can quickly match these to diffuse the attack. The leader probably has more staying power in an all-out battle for customers. A hard fight might leave both firms worse off. Thus, many firms prefer to follow rather than challenge the leader.

A follower can gain many advantages. The market leader often bears the huge expenses of developing new products and markets, expanding distribution, and educating the market. The market follower, on the other hand, can learn from the leader's experience and copy or improve on the leader's products and programs, usually with much less investment. Although the follower will probably not overtake the leader, it often can be as profitable. A good example of a follower is Dial Corporation, maker of such well-known brands as Dial, Tone, and Pure & Natural hand soaps, Armour Star canned meats, Purex laundry products, and Renuzit air freshener:

> ★ Flashy it isn't. "We want to be the dullest story in America," declares Dial's CEO. Dial doesn't try to come up with innovative new products. . . . It doesn't spend zillions to make its offerings household names across the nation. Instead, Dial prefers to coast in the slipstream of giant rivals, such as Procter & Gamble. [Its] lineup consists largely of me-too products and second-tier regional brands. . . . Instead of spending big on research and development or marketing, Dial leaves it to others. . . . And Dial lets other companies educate consumers about new products. P&G, for instance, introduced concentrated powder detergents in 1990. Dial followed over a year later with its own concentrated version, Purex—priced as much as one-third lower than P&G's Tide. Despite this low profile, the company does well in its markets. For example, Dial soap is America's number-one antibacterial soap and Purex has staked out a leadership position in the value segment of the laundry detergent market. Renuzit is the nation's number-two air freshener brand and Amour Star is number two in canned meats.[36]

Following is not the same as being passive or a carbon copy of the leader. The follower has to define a growth path, but one that does not create competitive retaliation. A market follower must know how to hold current customers and win a fair share of new ones. It must find the right balance between following closely enough to win customers from the market leader but following at enough of a distance to avoid retaliation. Each follower tries to bring distinctive advantages to its target market—location, services, financing. The follower is often a major target of attack by challengers. Therefore, the market follower must keep its manufacturing costs low and its product quality and services high. It must also enter new markets as they open up.

Market Nicher Strategies

Almost every industry includes firms that specialize in serving market niches. Instead of pursuing the whole market, or even large segments, these firms target subsegments. Nichers are often smaller firms with limited resources. But smaller divisions of larger firms also may pursue niching strategies. Firms with low shares of the total market can be highly profitable through smart niching (see Marketing Highlight 18.3).

Why is niching profitable? The main reason is that the market nicher ends up knowing the target customer group so well that it meets their needs better than other firms that casually sell to this niche. As a result, the nicher can charge a substantial markup over costs because of the added value. Whereas the mass marketer achieves *high volume,* the nicher achieves *high margins.*

Nichers try to find one or more market niches that are safe and profitable. An ideal market niche is big enough to be profitable and has growth potential. It is one that the firm can serve effectively. Perhaps most importantly, the niche is of little interest to major competitors. The firm can build the skills and customer goodwill to defend itself against a major competitor as the niche grows and becomes more attractive. Here are just a few examples of profitable nichers:[37]

MARKETING HIGHLIGHT
1 8 . 3

JOLLIBEE: SMALL CAN BE BEAUTIFUL

When someone says "fast-food restaurant," what's the first name that comes to mind? Chances are good that it's McDonald's, the world's largest food service organization. McDonald's holds a more than 40 percent share of the U.S. fast-food burger market, many times the share of its nearest competitor, Burger King, and is rapidly expanding its worldwide presence. Ask the same question in the Philippines, however, and the first name uttered likely will be Jollibee. That's right, Jollibee. In the grand scheme of global commerce, Jollibee Foods Corporation isn't exactly a household name. But in its niche, the Philippines, it's king of the burger market.«

At first glance, the rivalry between Jollibee and McDonald's looks like no contest. McDonald's has more than 24,500 outlets in 116 countries, 2,735 of them in Asia alone, and nearly $36 billion in annual systemwide sales. By comparison, Jollibee has fewer than 250 restaurants contributing about $350 million in annual revenues. Its sales equal only a fraction of the $1 billion or more that McDonald's spends annually just on U.S. advertising. Despite these lopsided numbers, in the Philippines, small Jollibee is giving giant McDonald's more than it can handle. Jollibee captures a 75 percent share of the Philippines' hamburger chain market and 53 percent of the fast-food market as a whole. Its sales are growing rapidly and profitably. "Jollibee is one of only two or three examples in the world of a fast-food company that is able to compete with McDonald's," comments an industry analyst.

What's Jollibee's secret? Smart niching. Whereas McDonald's exports largely standardized fare to consumers around the world, Jollibee is relentlessly local—it concentrates on serving the unique tastes of Filipino consumers. In

Market nicher Jollibee is king of the burger market in the Philippines. The Jollibee burger is similar to "what a Filipino mother would cook at home."

★ Logitech has become a $450 million global success story by focusing on human interface devices—computer mice, game controllers, keyboards, and others. It makes every variation of computer mouse imaginable. Logitech turns out mice for left- and right-handed people, cordless mice that use radio waves, mice shaped like real mice for children, and 3-D mice that let the user appear to move behind screen objects. This year, the company's 200 millionth mouse will roll off the production line. Breeding computer mice has been so successful that Logitech dominates the world market, with Microsoft as its runner-up.

★ By focusing on hospital face masks, Tecnol Medical Products competes against two giants: Johnson & Johnson and 3M. Tecnol has transformed an ordinary face mask into a lucrative line of specialty masks that shield health care workers from infection. Now the little-known company has surpassed Johnson & Johnson and 3M to become the top mask supplier to U.S. hospitals.

★ In his book *Hidden Champions,* Herman Simon documents the surprising number of German companies that are barely known but have strong profits and global mar-many ways, Jollibee's operations mirror those of McDonald's: Both offer cleanliness, fast service, and convenient locations. Jollibee's Champ burger competes with the Big Mac and its peach-mango pie replicates McDonald's apple version. However, in contrast to the fairly bland fare that McDonald's serves so successfully worldwide, Jollibee's menu and flavors are specially suited to Filipino tastes. The local chain cooks up sweet, spicy burgers and serves seasoned chicken and spaghetti with sweet sauce, the way Filipinos like it. It serves these meals with rice or noodles, not french fries. "We've designed these products, which are really all-American delights, to suit the Filipino palate," says Jollibee's marketing vice president. Some items, however, are uniquely Filipino. For example, Jollibee's Palabok Fiesta meal, featuring noodles with fish and shrimp, is very popular in the Philippines. Most Americans wouldn't like it because it smells of fish.

Beyond its special understanding of the Filipino palate, Jollibee has also mastered the country's culture and lifestyle. "What happens in the normal Filipino family is that weekends are especially for children," notes a Philippines business analyst, "and parents try to ask their children where they want to eat." Jollibee

lures kids with in-store play activities and a cast of captivating characters. Its hamburger-headed Champ, complete with boxing gloves, goes head-to-head with McDonald's Hamburglar. Its massive orange-jacketed bee and a blond spaghetti-haired girl named Hetti are better known and loved in the Philippines than Ronald McDonald.

Jollibee has some additional advantages in this seemingly unfair rivalry. Although much smaller in global terms than McDonald's, Jollibee concentrates most of its limited resources within the Philippines, where its restaurants outnumber McDonald's two to one. It also receives a measure of protection through government regulations that limit McDonald's and other foreign competitors. But its primary advantage comes from simply doing a better job of giving Filipino consumers what they want. Small can be beautiful, and Jollibee has shown that through smart niching small players can compete effectively against industry giants.

In an effort to conquer Jollibee's niche, McDonald's is launching a comeback. It's rapidly adding new locations and introducing its own Filipino-style dishes—spicy fried chicken with rice, sweet-tasting spaghetti, and a heavily seasoned burger called the McDo. However,

Jollibee managers don't seem overly worried about their rival's new moves. McDonald's may have greater universal appeal, but Jollibee knows its niche. "Maybe they'll gain market share," says Jollibee's chief executive, "but I don't think anybody can beat us out because, in the final analysis, the customer is the one deciding." For most Filipinos, the choice is clear. Notes the business analyst, "The Jollibee burger is similar to what a Filipino mother would cook at home."

Sources: Quotes from Hugh Filman, "Happy Meals for McDonald's Rival," *Business Week,* July 29, 1996, p. 77; Cris Prystay and Sanjay Kumar, "Asia Bites Back," *Asian Business,* January 1997, pp. 58–60; and Dominic Jones and Nicholas Bradbury, "Blue Chips of the Future," *Euromoney,* December 1998, pp. 99–102. Also see Andrew Tanzer, "Bee Bites Clown," *Forbes,* October 20, 1997, pp. 182–183; David Leonhardt, "McDonald's: Can It Regain Its Golden Touch?" *Business Week,* March 9, 1998, pp. 70–77; Rogoberto Tiglao, "Hamburger Heaven," *Far Eastern Economic Review,* December 31, 1999, pp. 76–78; and James Leung and Tony Jordan, "AMAC: Asia's Most Admired Companies," *Asian Business,* May 1999, pp. 24–32.

ket shares exceeding 50 percent in their respective niches. Tetra has 80 percent of the world tropical fish market; Hohner owns a stunning 85 percent of the harmonica market; Bechner makes 50 percent of the world's umbrellas; and Steiner Optical make 80 percent of the world's military field glasses.

The key idea in niching is specialization. A market nicher can specialize along any of several market, customer, product, or marketing mix lines. For example, it can specialize in serving one type of *end user,* as when a law firm specializes in the criminal, civil, or business law markets. The nicher can specialize in serving a given *customer-size* group—many nichers specialize in serving small customers who are neglected by the majors. Some nichers focus on one or a few *specific customers,* selling their entire output to a single company, such as Wal-Mart or General Motors. Still other nichers specialize by *geographic market,* selling only in a certain locality, region, or area of the world. *Quality–price* nichers operate at the low or high end of the market. For example, Hewlett-Packard specializes in the high-quality, high-price end of the hand-calculator market. Finally, *service nichers* offer services not available from other firms. An example is a bank that takes loan requests over the phone and hand delivers the money to the customer.

Niching carries some major risks. For example, the market niche may dry up, or it might grow to the point that it attracts larger competitors. That is why many companies practice *multiple niching*. By developing two or more niches, a company increases its chances for survival. Even some large firms prefer a multiple niche strategy to serving the total market. For example, Alberto Culver is a midsize company that has used a multiple niching strategy to grow profitably without incurring the wrath of the market leader. CEO Howard Bernick explains the Alberto Culver philosophy this way: "We know who we are and, perhaps more importantly, we know who we are not. We know that if we try to out-Procter Procter, we will fall flat on our face." Instead, the company known mainly for its Alberto VO5 hair products has focused its marketing muscle on acquiring a stable of small niche brands. Its other items include flavor enhancers Molly McButter and Mrs. Dash, static-cling fighter Static Guard, and Consort men's hairspray. Each of these brands is number one in its niche.[38]

Profitable nichers: Small but profitable Hohner owns a stunning 85 percent of the harmonica market.

BALANCING CUSTOMER AND COMPETITOR ORIENTATIONS

Competitor-centered company

A company whose moves are mainly based on competitors' actions and reactions.

Customer-centered company

A company that focuses on customer developments in designing its marketing strategies and on delivering superior value to its target customers.

Market-centered company

A company that pays balanced attention to both customers and competitors in designing its marketing strategies.

Whether a company is a market leader, challenger, follower, or nicher, it must watch its competitors closely and find the competitive marketing strategy that positions it most effectively. It must continually adapt its strategies to the fast-changing competitive environment. This question now arises: Can the company spend too much time and energy tracking competitors, damaging its customer orientation? The answer is yes! A company can become so competitor centered that it loses its even more important customer focus.

A **competitor-centered company** is one that spends most of its time tracking competitors' moves and market shares and trying to find strategies to counter them. This approach has some pluses and minuses. On the positive side, the company develops a fighter orientation. It trains its marketers to be on a constant alert, watching for weaknesses in their own position, and searching out competitors' weaknesses. On the negative side, the company becomes too reactive. Rather than carrying out its own customer-oriented strategy, it bases its own moves on competitors' moves. As a result, because so much depends on what the competitors do, the company does not move in a planned direction toward a goal. It may end up simply matching or extending industry practices rather than seeking innovative new ways to bring more value to customers.

A **customer-centered company,** by contrast, focuses more on customer developments in designing its strategies. Clearly, the customer-centered company is in a better position to identify new opportunities and set long run strategies that make sense. By watching customer needs evolve, it can decide what customer groups and what emerging needs are the most important to serve, then concentrate its resources on delivering superior value to target customers. In practice, today's companies must be **market-centered companies,** watching both their customers and their competitors. They must not let competitor watching blind them to customer focusing.

Figure 18.5 shows that companies have moved through four orientations over the years. In the first stage, they were product oriented, paying little attention to either customers or competitors. In the second stage, they became customer oriented and started to pay attention to customers. In the third stage, when they started to pay attention to competitors, they became competitor oriented. Today, companies need to be market oriented, paying balanced attention to both customer and competitors. Rather than simply watching competitors and trying to beat them on current ways of doing business, they need to watch customers and find innovative ways to deliver more value than competitors do.[39]

FIGURE 18.5   Evolving company orientations

REVIEW OF CONCEPT CONNECTIONS

Today's companies face their toughest competition ever. To survive, a company has to win customers and outperform competitors, often by moving from a product and selling philosophy to a customer and marketing philosophy. Winning companies in today's marketplace have become adept at developing and implementing strategies for *building customers*, not merely *building products*. Today, the focus is shifting toward customer *relationship marketing*. The new view is that marketing is the science and art of finding, retaining, *and* growing customers.

1. Discuss customer value and satisfaction and how companies attract, retain, and grow profitable customers.

The key to building lasting relationships is the creation of superior *customer value* and *satisfaction,* and companies need to understand the determinants of these important elements. Faced with a growing range of choices of products and services, consumers base their buying decisions on their perceptions of *value. Customer delivered value* is the difference between *total customer value* and *total customer cost*. Customers will usually choose the offer that maximizes their delivered value.

Customer satisfaction results when a company's performance has fulfilled a buyer's expectations. Customers are dissatisfied if performance is below expectations, satisfied if performance equals expectations, and delighted if performance exceeds expectations.

Satisfied customers buy more, are less price sensitive, talk favorably about the company, and remain loyal longer. Companies not only strive to gain customers but, perhaps more importantly, to retain and grow "share of customer." Companies must decide the level at which they want to build relationships with different market segments and individual customers, ranging from basic relationships to full partnerships. Which is best depends on a customer's lifetime value relative to the costs required to attract and keep that customer. Today's marketers use a number of specific marketing tools to develop stronger bonds with customers by adding *financial* and *social benefits* or *structural ties.*

2. Explain the roles of the company value chain, value-delivery network, and total quality in delivery of customer value and satisfaction.

To create customer value and satisfaction, and to retain customers, companies must manage their value chains and value-delivery networks in a customer-orientated way. Each company department can be seen as a link in the firm's *value chain*. That is, each department carries out value-creating activities to design, produce, market, deliver, and support the firm's products. The firm's success depends on how well each department performs its work and on how well the activities of various departments are coordinated.

In seeking a competitive advantage, a company must also look beyond its own value chain and into the *customer value-delivery network,* the system made up of the value chains of its suppliers, distributors, and, ultimately, customers. Today most companies are "partnering" with the other members of the supply chain to improve the performance of the customer value-delivery network.

Total quality management is a major approach to providing customer satisfaction and company profitability. Companies need to understand and meet consumer quality expectations. To be successful companies must therefore do a better job of meeting consumer quality expectations than competitors do. Besides measurement and reward systems, delivering quality requires total management and employee commitment. Marketers perform a critical role in their company's effort to achieve higher quality by helping design strategies and programs that help the company win through total quality excellence and by delivering market quality as well as production quality.

3. Discuss the need to understand competitors as well as customers through competitor analysis.

In order to prepare an effective marketing strategy, a company must consider its competitors as well as its customers. It must continuously analyze competitors and develop *competitive marketing strategies* that position it effectively against competitors and give it the strongest possible *competitive advantage.*

Competitive analysis first involves identifying the company's major competitors. The company then assesses competitors' objectives, strategies, strengths and weaknesses, and reaction patterns. Using this information, it can select competitors to attack or avoid. Next, having identified and assessed its main competitor, the company must decide how it wants to deliver value to target customers and fashion a broad competitive strategy by which it can gain competitive advantage.

4. Explain the fundamentals of competitive marketing strategies based on creating value for customers.

Which *competitive marketing strategy* makes the most sense depends on the company's industry, and on whether it is a market leader, challenger, follower, or nicher. A *market leader* has to mount strategies to expand the total market, protect market share, and expand market share. A *market challenger* is a firm that tries aggressively to expand its market share by attacking the leader, other runner-up companies, or smaller firms in the industry. The challenger can select from a variety of direct or indirect attack strategies. A *market follower* is a runner-up firm that chooses not to rock the boat, usually from fear that it stands to lose more than it might gain. But the follower is not without a strategy and seeks to use its particular skills to gain market growth. Some followers enjoy a higher rate of return than the leaders in their industry. A *market nicher* is a smaller firm that is unlikely to attract the attention of larger firms. Market nichers often become specialists in some end use, customer size, specific customer, geographic area, or service.

5. Illustrate the need for balancing customer and competitor orientations in becoming a truly market-centered organization.

A competitive orientation is important in today's markets, but companies should not overdo their focus on competitors. Companies are more likely to be hurt by emerging consumer needs and new competitors than by existing competitors. *Market-centered companies* that balance consumer and competitor considerations are practicing a true market orientation.

KEY TERMS

Benchmarking	Customer lifetime value	Market nicher
Competitive marketing strategy	Customer satisfaction	Quality
Competitor analysis	Market-centered company	Relationship marketing
Competitor-centered company	Market challenger	Total customer cost
Customer-centered company	Market follower	Value chain
Customer delivered value	Market leader	Value-delivery network

ISSUES FOR DISCUSSION

1. More than three decades ago, Peter Drucker observed that a company's first task is "to create customers." How do the following companies create customers: (a) Intel, (b) Delta Airlines, (c) a university or college, and (d) America Online? Explain.

2. Most universities and colleges seek strong relationships with their alumni. Considering the relationship-marketing approaches suggested in your text, formulate a plan that would keep you as a loyal alumnus of your university or college.

3. Explain the difference between customer value and customer satisfaction. How does an organization provide total customer satisfaction? Give an example of an organization that accomplishes this feat. Explain your choice.

4. Customer loyalty is an extremely important asset for any company. How does a company grow customer loyalty? How can a company increase its "share of customer?"

5. Select a company and describe the "value chain" that links the company to its customers. Explain the significance of each link in the chain.

6. Explain the concept of competitor myopia. Provide an original example of (a) an organization that appears to be competitively myopic and (b) an organization that is not. How do your examples relate to Michael Porter's four basic competitive strategies?

7. The chapter describes competitive strategies for firms playing the role of market leader, challenger, follower, or nicher. Answer the following questions for either the personal computer, cellular phone, automobile, or beer industry. (a) Which firms in the industry assume each of the roles listed above? (b) What competitive strategy does each major competitors use? (c) What are the strengths and weaknesses of each competitor?

8. The company's goal under the marketing concept is to satisfy customer wants and needs. What is the goal of a firm adopting a competitor orientation? Do the marketing concept and a competitor orientation conflict? Explain.

MARKETING APPLICATIONS

1. Have you ever found yourself lost on some unknown and lonely road with no idea of how to get where you're trying to go? If so, you're just one of many consumers looking for a more certain and safer way to travel. Now, there's a solution. Auto navigation systems will not only plot your course, they'll help get you there on time and even book a room for you. Sound too good to be true? OnStar's on-board concierge system helps drivers answer all the irritating questions that plague most travelers. OnStar combines cutting-edge technology with attentive personal service to provide the travelers with safety, security, and convenience. Using global positioning satellites, OnStar can not only tell where you are, it can help you get where you're going through personal directions delivered via an on-board telephone system. OnStar also provides remote diagnostics, remote door unlock, stolen vehicle tracking, roadside assistance, accident assistance, and many other services. In the future, the best friend a motorist may have is that friendly

voice from OnStar that says "May I be of assistance?" (Visit www.onstar.com for more information.)

a. What customer value does OnStar deliver? How does it create customer satisfaction? How does it build relationships with customers?

b. What is OnStar's overall competitive strategy? What consumers should it target? What's the best way to reach this target market: through ads, via the Internet, via automobile dealers, or something else? Explain.

c. How does the value chain concept apply to OnStar's operation?

d. How does OnStar use the marketing concept to enhance its business?

2. In the rapidly expanding world of the Internet and personal information and communications devices, America Online's plan is to get inside every information appliance. According to AOL's CEO, "We want to be as pervasive as the telephone or TV, but even more valuable in people's lives." To this end, AOL is partnering with a broad range of companies. For example, in addition to its already established relationships with Netscape and Sun Systems, AOL will invest $800 million in Gateway over two years to help develop and co-market Internet appli-

ances. It will partner with 3Com to put its online services on Palm handheld devices. AOL's instant message service will now be part of all new Motorola smart wireless devices, and AOL has joined with DirecTV, Hughes Network Systems, and Philips Electronics to preload set-top boxes with AOL features and access. However, all will not be easy for America Online. AOL is going up against Microsoft with its deep pockets, and its recent moves have gotten the attention of Yahoo! All three competitors plan to spread their services to all manner of information devices early in the twenty-first century. For more information, visit www.aol.com.

a. What do you see as the major strengths and weaknesses of America Online? How do those strengths and weaknesses match those of Microsoft and Yahoo!?

b. What competitive position does America Online hold in its industry? Does this position change as it partners across industry lines?

c. Which of the competitive strategies outlined in the chapter is AOL using? How will competitors respond?

d. Propose one additional partnership that you think would make sense for AOL. Explain.

 INTERNET CONNECTIONS

CUSTOMER SATISFACTION

In the highly competitive world of Internet content providers, customer satisfaction is key. Therefore, content providers must continuously innovate to meet or exceed customer expectations. Portals such as Yahoo! have added numerous services to their portfolios–many of them free in an effort to build lasting customer relationships. Visit Yahoo! and record five of its services that you would consider using. For each service you choose, find a competitor providing the same service and compare strengths and weaknesses. Finally, suggest Yahoo!'s competitive strategy for each service (e.g., market leader).

Service that interests you	Competitor providing the same service	Compare strengths/weaknesses	Yahoo! competitive strategy

FOR DISCUSSION

1. In general, how would Yahoo! define and thus identify its competitors?

2. There is no charge for many Yahoo! services. What benefits does Yahoo! realize from providing these services?

3. Yahoo! has acquired some of its services through purchasing smaller Web companies. Is this a strategy you would recommend that it continue? Why or why not?

4. Is it important for Yahoo! to be the market leader in each service area? Why or why not?

5. One way that Yahoo! builds customer satisfaction is its consistently high ratings for speed of page downloads over the Internet. What are other ways Yahoo! builds relationships with customers?

SAVVY SITES

- One way to evaluate the competition is to review financial analysts' comments at investment firms. Some firms that offer industry and individual firm analyses are Charles Schwab (www.schwab.com), Merrill Lynch (www.merrill lynch.com), and E★Trade (www.etrade.com).

- Arthur Andersen Consulting (www.arthurandersen.com) helps businesses understand their competitors and develop appropriate strategies.

NOTES

1. Quotes and other information from "Gateway Ranks #1 in Both Client Loyalty and U.S. Consumer Desktop Shipments," press release accessed online at www.gateway.com, June 15, 1999; Steven V. Brull, "A Net Gain for Gateway," *Business Week,* July 19, 1999, pp. 77–78; Aaron Goldberg, "Going Long," *MC Technology Marketing Intelligence,* May 1999, p. 14; and Gary McWilliams, "Gateway Managers to Smooth Out Earnings and Bull Ahead in Internet-Service Business," *Wall Street Journal,* July 12, 1999, p. C2.

2. See Kevin J. Clancy and Robert S. Shulman, "Breaking the Mold," *Sales & Marketing Management,* January 1994, pp. 82–84; Thomas O. Jones and W. Earl Sasser Jr., "Why Satisfied Customers Defect," *Harvard Business Review,* November–December 1995, pp. 88–99; Susan Fournier, Susan Dobscha, and David Glen Mick, "Preventing the Premature Death of Relationship Marketing," *Harvard Business Review,* January–February 1998, pp. 42–50; and Erika Rasmusson, "Complaints Can Build Relationships," *Sales & Marketing Management,* September 1999, p. 89.

3. Libby Estell, "This Call Center Accelerates Sales," *Sales & Marketing Management,* February 1999, p. 72.

4. For a thorough discussion on defining value, see Howard E. Butz Jr. and Leonard D. Goodstein, "Measuring Customer Value: Gaining Strategic Advantage," *Organizational Dynamics,* Winter 1996, pp. 63–77; and Robert B. Woodruff, "Customer Value: The Next Source of Competitive Advantage," *Journal of the Academy of Marketing Science,* Spring 1997, pp. 139–53.

5. See Donald V. Fites, "Make Your Dealers Your Partners," *Harvard Business Review,* March–April 1996, pp. 84–95; De Ann Weimer, "A New Cat on the Hot Seat," *Business Week,* March 1998, pp. 56–62; Woodruff, "Customer Value: The Next Source of Competitive Advantage," pp. 139–53; and James C. Anderson and James A. Narus, "Business Marketing: Understand What Customers Value," *Harvard Business Review,* November–December 1998, pp. 53–61.

6. For an excellent discussion of the determinants of customer satisfaction, see Richard A. Spreng, Scott B. MacKenzie, and Richard W. Olshavsky, "A Reexamination of the Determinants of Customer Satisfaction," *Journal of Marketing,* July 1996, pp. 15–32; and Ruth N. Bolton and Katherine N. Lemon, "A Dynamic Model of Customers' Usage of Services: Usage as an Antecedent and Consequence of Satisfaction," *Journal of Marketing,* May 1999, pp. 171–86.

7. See Claes Fornell, Michael D. Johnson, Eugene W. Anderson, Jaesung Cha, and Barbara Everitt Bryant, "The American Customer Satisfaction Index: Nature, Purpose, and Findings," *Journal of Marketing,* October 1996, pp. 7–18; Kevin Heubusch, ". . . But Quality Is Down," *American Demographics,* May 1998, p. 42; and Mike Campbell, "Happy Bank Customers? Think Again," *Bank Marketing,* April 1999, p. 10.

8. Jones and Sasser, Jr. "Why Satisfied Customers Defect," pp. 88–99. Also see Thomas A. Stewart, "A Satisfied Customer Isn't Enough," *Fortune,* July 21, 1997, pp. 112–13.

9. Jones and Sasser, "Why Satisfied Customers Defect," p. 91. For other examples, see Roger Sant, "Did He Jump or Was He Pushed?" *Marketing News,* May 12, 1997, pp. 2, 21.

10. See Joseph Juran, "Made in the U.S.A.: A Renaissance in Quality," *Harvard Business Review,* July–August 1993, pp. 42–50.

11. Harry Seymour and Laura Rifkin, "Study Shows Satisfaction Not the Same as Loyalty," *Marketing News,* October 26, 1998, pp. 40, 42.

12. Example based on James Champy, "Taking Sales to New Heights," *Sales & Marketing Management,* July 1998, p. 26.

13. See Philip Kotler, *Kotler on Marketing* (New York: Free Press, 1999), pp. 129–39; Don Peppers and Martha Rogers, "Growing Revenues with Cross-Selling," *Sales & Marketing Management,* February 1999, p. 24; Phil Zinkewicz, "Travelers Agents Begin Getting Access to Citicorp Products," *Rough Notes,* February 1999, pp. 22, 26; and Tara Siegel, "Citigroup Is Ready to Realize Benefits of Cross Selling," *Wall Street Journal,* March 15, 1999, p. B11.

14. Leonard L. Berry and A. Parasuraman, *Marketing Services: Competing Through Quality* (New York: Free Press, 1991), pp. 136–42.

15. See Louise O'Brien and Charles Jones, "Do Rewards Really Create Loyalty?" *Harvard Business Review,* May–June 1995, pp. 75–82; "Harley Owners Journey to Meet Their Maker . . . Again and Again," *Colloquy,* 5, no. 4, 1997, pp. 13–14; Constance L. Hays, "What Companies Need to Know Is in the Pizza Dough," *New York Times,* July 26, 1998, p. 3, and Richard G. Barlow, "Future Looks Bright for Frequency Marketing," *Marketing News,* July 5, 1999, p. 14.

16. Andy Cohen, "It's Party Time for Saturn," *Sales & Marketing Management,* June 1994, p. 19; T. L. Stanley, Betsy Spethman, Terry Lefton, and Karen Benezra, "Brand Builders," *Brandweek,* March 20, 1995, p. 20; Michelle Krebs, "Another Hoedown at Saturn Ranch," *New York Times,* March 14, 1999; and information accessed online at www.saturn.com/homecoming, January 2000.

17. See Thomas M. Petro, "Profitability: The Fifth 'P' of Marketing," *Bank Marketing,* September 1990, pp. 48–52.

18. See Rick Brooks, "Unequal Treatment: Alienating Customers Isn't Always a Bad Idea, Many Firms Discover," *Wall Street Journal,* January 7, 1999, p. A1; and Erika Rasmusson, "Wanted: Profitable Customers," *Sales & Marketing Management,* May 1999, pp. 28–34.

19. Michael E. Porter, *Competitive Advantage: Creating and Sustaining Superior Performance* (New York: Free Press, 1985); and Michael E. Porter, "What Is Strategy?" *Harvard Business Review,* November–December 1996, pp. 61–78.

20. Edwin McDowell, "Ritz-Carlton's Keys to Good Service," *New York Times,* March 31, 1993, p. 1; Don Peppers, "Digitizing Desire," *Forbes,* April 10, 1995, p. 76; Ginger Conlon, "True Romance," *Sales & Marketing Management,* May 1996, pp. 85–89; and "Ritz-Carlton Hotels Reign in Three Categories of *Travel & Leisure*'s 'World Best

Awards' List," accessed online at www.ritz.carlton.com/corporate/worldbest.htm, September 1999.

21. Jennifer Waters, "High-Tech Test Restaurant Offers Customer Orders, More Efficiency," *Advertising Age,* April 14, 1997, p. 49.

22. Myron Magnet, "The New Golden Rule of Business," *Fortune,* February 21, 1994, pp. 60–63. For more on supply chain management and strategic alliances, see also Rosabeth Moss Kanter, "Why Collaborate?" *Executive Excellence,* April 1999, p. 8; and Gabor Gari, "Leveraging the Rewards of Strategic Alliances," *The Journal of Business Strategy,* April 1999, pp. 40–43.

23. See Otis Port, "Baldrige's Other Reward," *Business Week,* March 10, 1997, p. 75; "ISO 9000 and Quality: A World Class Advantage," special section, *Industrial Distribution,* January 1998, p. 61; Zhiwei Zhu and Larry Scheuermann, "A Comparison of Quality Programmes: Total Quality Management and ISO 9000," *Total Quality Management,* March 1999, pp. 291–97; and "Standards and Certification: ISO 9000," American Society for Quality, accessed online at www.asq.com, January 2000.

24. Accessed online at the American Society for Quality's Web site at www.asq.org, January 2000. See this excellent site for information on a wide range of quality topics.

25. See Melissa Larson, "Whatever Happened to TQM?" *Quality,* June 1999, pp. 32–35; "TQM Is Alive," *Quality,* February 1999, p. 12; Roland T. Rust, Anthony J. Zahorik, and Timothy L. Keiningham, "Return on Quality (ROQ): Making Service Quality Financially Accountable," *Journal of Marketing,* April 1995, pp. 58–70; and Roland T. Rust, Timothy Keiningham, Stephen Clemens, and Anthony Zahorik, "Return on Quality at Chase Manhattan Bank," *Interfaces,* March–April 1999, pp. 62–72.

26. J. Daniel Beckham, "Expect the Unexpected in Health Care Marketing Future," *The Academy Bulletin,* July 1992, p. 3.

27. Philip B. Evans and Thomas S. Wurster, "Strategy and the New Economics of Information," *Harvard Business Review,* September–October 1997, pp. 70–83; Michael Krantz, "Click Till You Drop," *Time,* July 20, 1998, pp. 34–39; Ed Tallent, "Encyclopedia Britannica Online," *Library Journal,* May 15, 1999, pp. 138–39; and "Withering Britannica Bets It All on the Web," *Fortune,* November 22, 1999, p. 344. For more on identifying competitors, see "Bruce H. Clark and David Montgomery, "Managerial Identification of Competitors," *Journal of Marketing,* July 1999, pp. 67–83.

28. See Porter, *Competitive Advantage,* pp. 226–27; and Joseph Weber, "How J&J's Foresight Made Contact Lenses Pay," *Business Week,* May 4, 1992, p. 132.

29. Andy Reinhardt, "Intel Is Taking No Prisoners," *Business Week,* July 12, 1999, p. 38.

30. See Porter, *Competitive Advantage,* chap. 6.

31. Michael E. Porter, *Competitive Strategy: Techniques for Analyzing Industries and Competitors* (New York: Free Press, 1980), chap. 2; and Porter, "What Is Strategy?" Also see James Surowiecki, "The Return of Michael Porter," *Fortune,* February 1, 1999, pp. 135–38.

32. Michael Treacy and Fred Wiersema, "Customer Intimacy and Other Value Disciplines," *Harvard Business Review,* January–February 1993, pp. 84–93; Michael Treacy and Fred Wiersema, "How Market Leaders Keep Their Edge," *Fortune,* February 6, 1995, pp. 88–98; Michael Treacy and Fred Wiersema, *The Discipline of Market Leaders: Choose Your Customers, Narrow Your Focus, Dominate Your Market* (Perseus Press, 1997); and Fred Wiersema, *Customer Intimacy: Pick Your Partners, Shape Your Culture, Win Together* (Knowledge Exchange, 1998).

33. For more discussion on defense and attack strategies, see Philip Kotler, *Marketing Management: Analysis, Planning, Implementation, and Control,* 10th ed. (Upper Saddle River, NJ: Prentice Hall, 2000), chap. 8.

34. Erika Rasmusson, "The Jackpot," *Sales & Marketing Management,* June 1998, pp. 35–41.

35. Holman W. Jenkins Jr., "Business World: On a Happier Note, Orange Juice," *Wall Street Journal,* September 23, 1998, p. A23.

36. Amy Barrett, "Dial Succeeds by Stepping in Bigger Footsteps," *Business Week,* June 13, 1994, pp. 82–83; Seth Lubove, "Cleaning Up," *Forbes,* December 28, 1998, p. 110; and "The Dial Corporation: Company Profile," accessed online at www.dialcorp.com, January 2000.

37. Stephanie Anderson, "Who's Afraid of J&J and 3M?" *Business Week,* December 5, 1994, pp. 66–68; Hermann Simon, *Hidden Champions* (Boston: Harvard Business School Press, 1996); and information accessed online from "Financial Highlights" and "Company Fact Sheet" on the Logitech Web site at www.logitech.com, January 2000.

38. Jim Kirk, "Company Finds Itself, Finds Success: Alberto-Culver Adopts Strategy of Knowing Its Strengths and Promoting Small Brands, Rather Than Tackling Giants," *Chicago Tribune,* January 22, 1998, Business Section, p. 1; and information obtained from the Alberto Culver Web site at www.alberto-culver.com, January 2000.

39. For interesting discussions, see W. Cahn Kim and Renée Mauborgne, "Value Innovation: The Strategic Logic of High Growth," *Harvard Business Review,* January–February 1997, pp. 103–12; and W. Chan Kim and Renee Mauborgne, "Creating New Market Space," *Harvard Business Review,* January–February 1999, pp. 83–93.

COMPANY CASE

18

Lowe's Companies: Battling Home Depot

GOING SHOPPING

Joanne Miles had been telling her husband Bud for months that they needed to improve their Greensboro, North Carolina, home by turning their screened porch into a sunroom. Joanne had scoured home decor magazines and clipped articles on how to design and build sunrooms. Finally, Bud had consented to take on the project.

Bud fancied himself as a very good handyman. He was skilled at the typical do-it-yourself projects such as plumbing, painting, wallpapering, and even fixing sheetrock. Bud realized that Joanne's porch project would take all his skill. But he figured that with some good advice and a home equity loan, he would be able to complete the project himself.

Bud made a list of materials and prepared to go to a home improvement store to get advice and prices. He invited Joanne to go with him and to pick out the color of the terra cotta floor tile. As they prepared to leave, Joanne asked, "By the way, which store are we going to? Both Lowe's and Home Depot are located right together there on Wendover Road."

"I hadn't really thought about it. Do you have any preference?" Bud answered.

"Not really. From what I've seen, both stores seem to have pretty good selections and prices. Both offer lots of advice. Let's just get in the car and see how the spirit moves us."

THE HOME IMPROVEMENT BATTLEFIELD

Bud and Joanne are just one more target in the increasingly competitive battle for the do-it-yourself (DIY) home improvement market. Lowe's, Home Depot, Builder's Square, and other building supply/home improvement chains; independent retailers affiliated with wholesaler groups such as Ace Hardware and Tru Value; and individual hardware stores—all are trying to attract DIY baby boomers like Bud and Joanne.

The Home Improvement Research Institute, a trade association, and Management Horizons, a consulting firm, estimate that the DIY homeowner and building contractor repair and remodel (R&R) markets would grow from $126 billion in 1994 to an estimated $163 billion by 1999, a compound annual growth rate of 4.9 percent. The DIY portion of the market alone will grow from $70 billion to $113 billion during that period, a 5.5 percent growth rate. Analysts speculate that this market is recession proof because consumers tend to see their homes as their primary asset and, therefore, protect its value.

The typical DIYer is a married male homeowner age 25 to 54 with a high school education or some college and an annual income of $20,000 to $40,000. However, the Home Improvement Research Institute suggests that there are additional ways to segment the market (see Exhibit 18-1).

HOME DEPOT

Home Depot helped stimulate the DIY market's rapid growth. Prior to Home Depot's founding in 1978, father-and-son lumber yards and a few specialty distributors who sold primarily to contractors and tradespeople dominated the hardware market. Home Depot opened the market to average consumers, allowing them to buy all the pieces for a home improvement project at one store.

Home Depot has become the world's largest home improvement retailer and one of the 20 largest retailers in the United States. As of 1997, it operates about 530 stores in the United States and 29 stores in Canada; and it has announced plans for its first international store in Santiago, Chile. The company plans to have 1,100 stores by 2000. Of the 724 stores operated by the 6 largest home improvement retailers in the top 50 U.S. markets, 390 were Home Depot Stores as compared with 96 for Builder's Square, 79 for Hechingers, 20 for Eagle, 78 for Lowe's, and 61 for HomeBase. Analysts estimate that Home Depot's 1997 sales would top $24 billion with an estimated net income of $1.2 billion (see Exhibit 18–2).

EXHIBIT 18.1 HOME IMPROVEMENT MARKET SEGMENTS

Hard-Core DIYer—15.9%. Will try anything without expert help. Saving money is important. Serves as source of information for others. Youngest group, mainly male. Gets advice from friends and relatives most often, but also from retailers. Tends to shop at only one store.

Frugal Hobbyist—15.6%. Shops for best price and watches ads. Seeks advice from magazines and books, especially home improvement magazines. Works in yard and on outside of home. 50/50 male/female. Lowest income group. Shops at different stores. Most price sensitive.

Type-A Gardner—16.9%. Wants the best yard. Convenience, not price important. Typically older male. Depends on retail store clerks. Most likely to buy from one store. Least price sensitive.

Help Me—18.1%. Takes little time or pleasure in home improvement projects. Most likely to let professional install. Installation service and retailer advice important. Typically older female. Likely to shop at different stores, but relatively less price sensitive.

Minimal Maintenance—14.7%. Does minimal home improvement. Takes no pride in home's appearance. Depends on friends and relatives for advice. Typically young male.

Style Trendsetter—19%. Likes to have unique decor, but gets little pleasure from DIY. Only interested in increasing home's value. Uses professional help and wants installation services. Depends on friends and relatives for advice. Lower dependence on retailers. Relatively price sensitive. Typically young female. Highest income group.

Source: Home Improvement Research Institute.

EXHIBIT 18.2 COMPARATIVE FINANCIAL AND OPERATING STATISTICS (FIGURES IN MILLIONS EXCEPT WHERE NOTED. FISCAL YEARS ENDING ON 1/31)			
Lowe's	**1997**	**1998**	**1999**
Net Sales	$8,600	$10,137	$12,245
Cost of Sales	$6,376	$7,447	$8,950
Operating Expense	$1,770	$2,131	$2,536
Net Earnings	$292	$357	$482
Total Assets	$4,434	$5,219	$6,345
Number of Stores (actual)	402	446	484
Total Square Footage	30	37	43
Number of Employees (actual)	53,492	58,504	65,706
Average Customer Purchase (actual)	$48.83	$49.09	$50.60
Home Depot			
Net Sales	$19,535	$24,156	$30,219
Cost of Sales	$14,101	$17,385	$21,614
Operating Expense	$3,908	$4,885	$5,944
Net Earnings	$938	$1,160	$1,614
Total Assets	$9,342	$11,229	$13,465
Number of Stores (actual)	512	624	761
Total Square Footage	54	66	81
Number of Employees (actual)	98,100	124,400	156,700
Average Customer Purchase (actual)	$42.09	$43.63	$45.05

The average Home Depot store has approximately 103,000 square feet of indoor selling space and an additional 20,000 to 28,000 square feet of outside garden center space, including houseplant enclosures. The typical store carries 40,000 to 50,000 SKUs (stock keeping units, i.e., individual items) and offers installation services for many products. The company has approximately 122,000 employees, whom it calls associates, and prides itself on the high level of customer service its associates offer. Analysts give Home Depot high marks for its operational execution.

Home Depot targets DIYers primarily, although home improvement contractors and other professionals are becoming increasingly important customers. In order to sustain its growth, Home Depot plans to target what it calls the PRO segments. By doing so, it can expand its defined market from about $140 billion (DIY and R&R) to about $360 billion as a result of including the property maintenance, heavy construction, building and general contracting, trade, and flooring sectors. In early 1997, Home Depot purchased Maintenance Warehouse/America Corporation, a direct-mail catalog company that targets repair and remodeling pros. It is also installing separate checkout areas for these professionals and adding special products. Analysts estimate that

professionals already account for about 30 percent of Home Depot's sales. The company is also reducing the number of SKUs it carries in order to focus on the best-selling items. Some analysts believe that Home Depot does not want to be seen as the "home solution" by offering a full range of goods and services to the homeowner. Rather, it wants to concentrate on home improvement products for both the homeowner and professional.

LOWE'S

In contrast to Home Depot, Lowe's has been in business since 1946 when the son of a dry-goods dealer founded the company in North Wilkesboro, North Carolina. The company grew by selling lumber, tools, and hardware to contractors in the rural South. In the 1980s, however, Lowe's began to cater to the retail consumer in an attempt to offset the ups and downs caused by swings in housing starts. The company added luxury housewares and fixed up its storefronts to attract women customers and to shift away from its contractor-oriented format. Chief Executive Officer Robert Tillman notes that men want to go into a store, get the item they want at a good price, and get out. Women, he notes, want a shopping experience and a welcoming atmosphere.

Lowe's shift in emphasis was reasonably successful, but its business really took off in 1989. Lowe's observed Home Depot's success with its "superstore" format and decided to try its own version, a 45,000-square-foot center with 2,000 more items than its smaller stores. Lowe's stores at that time ranged from 8,000 to 25,000 square feet. Sales skyrocketed, and Lowe's began gradually to increase the size of its new stores. By 1995, the smallest store Lowe's opened had 85,000 square feet; and its largest stores, "the big boxes," had 115,000 square feet and more than 40,000 SKUs.

Although Lowe's and Home Depot's product selections are similar, Lowe's sells washers and dryers, televisions, microwaves, refrigerators, stereos, and VCRs, whereas most Home Depot stores do not carry these items.

As it has developed bigger stores, Lowe's has also significantly lowered its prices and moved to an "everyday-low-price" strategy. Also, like Home Depot, Lowe's offers a low-price guarantee. A group of Prudential analysts priced the same basket of goods at a Lowe's and a Home Depot in Greensboro and found that Home Depot's total price was $2,006.54 versus Lowe's total price of $2,005.89. Many analysts attribute Lowe's success to its ability to lock up small, rural markets.

Through 1995, 60 percent of Lowe's new-store activity was in its existing markets. In 1996, however, the company changed its strategy and announced that about 80 percent of its expansion would be in new markets, especially in major cities such as Atlanta (Home Depot's headquarters) and Dallas. Lowe's intends to open 60 or more stores per year, increasing its total of 460 stores in late 1997 to 800 by the year 2001. Prudential Securities estimates that Lowe's 1997 sales would top $10 billion and produce net income of $351 million. Lowe's has about 60,200 employees.

Tillman notes that 50 percent of DIY sales take place in the top 25 urban cities, and Lowe's operates in only one of these cities. More importantly, much of its expansion will be in markets already served by Home Depot. By the end of 1997, about 119 of Home Depot's stores (19 percent) were competing directly with 106 of Lowe's stores (24 percent). Tillman speculates that by 2002, every U.S. market with 50,000 households will have both a Lowe's and a Home Depot. Analysts estimate that the United States will support about 2,000 "big box" stores; and by 2002 Lowe's and Home Depot combined should have that many.

Lowe's continues to see the DIY and contractor segments as its target markets, although contractor sales, including builders of new homes and contractors who perform repair and remodel jobs for homeowners, account for less than 20 percent of its sales, down from 35 percent in just five years. Lowe's operates 25 "contractor yards" to target that market.

Tillman indicates that Lowe's competitive strategy will capitalize on three societal trends. He notes that women have an increasing role in purchasing decisions, and many of them actually do the home improvement work. Yet, he adds, "Most of the industry's stores, staffing, advertising, and merchandising are targeted to and managed by men." Tillman also argues that baby boomers want less hassle, one-stop shopping, and someone they can trust to help with home improvement projects. Finally, he notes that Generation X consumers don't waste time shopping and are into convenience, trust, and technology.

Maybe so, but America's Research Group polled 800 consumers on the subject of large home-improvement centers. The company found that the chief complaints were long checkout lines, too big and too confusing stores, time wasted getting into and out of the stores and parking lots, failure to follow through on advertised items, and lack of qualified help.

BACK WITH JOANNE AND BUD

Bud turned left off Wendover Road. The huge Home Depot store loomed just a hundred yards to the right. Down the hill stood an equally large Lowe's.

"Well, what's your choice?" Bud asked Joanne.

"Let's try Lowe's. I mean, after all, if we don't like what we see, we'll just drive back to Home Depot."

Questions

1. Who are Lowe's and Home Depot's competitors and what strategies are those competitors employing?
2. Which of Porter's and Treacy and Wiersema's competitive strategies are Lowe's and Home Depot following?
3. What competitive position does Home Depot occupy in the DIY market? What position does Lowe's occupy?
4. What is Lowe's central marketing problem?
5. What marketing and competitive strategy recommendations would you make to Lowe's?

Sources: Nicole Harris, "Home Depot: Beyond Do-It-Yourselfers," *Business Week,* June 30, 1997; James M. Cory, "Mass Retail or Class Retail," *Home Improvement Market,* July, 1997, p. 10; Ken Clark, "Survival of the Biggest: Lowe's CEO: Giants Rule the Roost in Home Improvement Retailing," *HFN The Weekly Newspaper for the Home,* August 18, 1997, p. 1; W. Hood, "Lowe's Companies—Company Report," Prudential Securities, August 20, 1997; A. Rubinson, "Home Depot—Company Report," Paine Webber, Inc., August 25, 1997; Chris Roush, "Home Depot Is Top Home Improvement Retailer, But Lowe's Hopes to Gain," *Knight-Ridder/Tribune Business News,* August 26, 1997, p. 826B0953. Adapted from Lew G. Brown and Jerredith Shearin, "Lowe's Companies," published by the Bryan School of Business and Economics, University of North Carolina at Greensboro, June 1995.

CONCEPT CONNECTIONS

After studying this chapter, you should be able to
1. discuss how the international trade system, economic, political–legal, and cultural environments affect a company's international marketing decisions
2. describe three key approaches to entering international markets
3. explain how companies adapt their marketing mixes for international markets
4. identify the three major forms of international marketing organization

THE GLOBAL MARKETPLACE

What could be more American than basketball? The sport was invented in the United States, and each year tens of millions of excited fans crowd their local gyms or huddle around their television sets to cheer on their favorite rec league, high school, college, or pro teams. But basketball is rapidly becoming a worldwide craze. For example, a recent *New York Times* survey of more than 45,000 teenagers on five continents asked, "What are your favorite entertainment pursuits?" The answers: (1) watching television, (2) basketball.

No organization is doing more to promote worldwide basketball than the National Basketball Association (NBA). During the past decade, the NBA has become a truly global marketing enterprise. The 1999 NBA finals reached more than 600 million television viewers in 195 countries throughout the world, and worldwide sales of NBA-licensed basketballs, backboards, T-shirts, and other merchandise top $3 billion a year. The NBA is now a powerful worldwide brand. A *Fortune* article summarizes:

> Deployed by global sponsors Coca-Cola, Reebok, and McDonald's, well-paid [NBA superstars] hawk soda, sneakers, burgers, and basketball to legions of mostly young fans [worldwide]. That they are recognized from Santiago to Seoul says a lot about the soaring worldwide appeal of hoops—and about the marketing juggernaut known as the NBA. After watching their favorite stars swoop in and slam-dunk on their local TV stations, fans of the league now cheer the *mate* in Latin America, the *trofsla* in Iceland, and the *smash* in France. Care to guess the most popular basketball team in China? Why, it's the "Red Oxen" from Chicago, of course.

Basketball has even become a diplomatic tool. A few seasons back, the U.S. secretary of state, in an effort to preserve a fragile peace in Bosnia, requested that the NBA allow the broadcast of basketball games in the war-torn country. As a result, the NBA finals were aired in Bosnia for the first time ever. According to a State Department official, NBA broadcasts are "the most popular program there. The Bosnians are very big basketball buffs."

Like many other businesses, the NBA's primary motive for going global is growth. The league now sells out most of its games, and domestic licensing revenues have flattened in recent years. According to NBA Commissioner David Sterns, "There are just so many seats in an arena and so many hours of television programming, period.

The domestic business is becoming mature. That's why we're moving internationally." Compared with the NBA's overall yearly revenues of $2 billion, current international revenues are modest—estimated at a little more than $60 million from TV rights fees, sponsorships, and the league's share of licensing sales. But worldwide potential is huge, and the league is investing heavily to build its popularity and business abroad. For example, its international staff of 105 is nearly double the number of people who ran the entire league back in the early 1980s.

Thanks to skillful marketing, and to the growing worldwide popularity of basketball itself, the NBA's investment appears to be paying off. According to *Fortune,* the NBA enjoys huge natural advantages over football, baseball, and other rivals:

It's selling a sport, basketball, that's played nearly everywhere and easily understood. (Try explaining a nickel defense to a Swede.) Pro and amateur leagues have been thriving for years in Europe and Asia, and basketball has been an Olympic sport since 1936. The U.S. "Dream Team" in 1992 was a worldwide sensation, sparking even greater interest in pro basketball in the U.S. . . . By then the groundwork had been laid for the NBA's global growth. Two men deserve much of the credit: David Stern and Michael Jordan, with a big assist from Nike. [The NBA and Nike] turned Jordan into a worldwide celebrity, known not just for his gravity-defying skills but also for his winning personality and competitive zeal. . . . In China, which has its own professional basketball leagues, boys on the streets of Beijing and Shanghai [wore] Bulls gear because they wanted to be like Mike. . . . A 1997 survey of 28,000 teenagers in 45 countries by [a global ad agency] found that Jordan was the world's favorite athlete by far.

Broader forces also helped to promote the league's efforts to go global: the collapse of communism and the growth of market economies, the globalization of American consumer companies, and a revolution in worldwide television. Most recent is the explosion of the global Internet. The NBA's site (www.NBA.com) offers programming in several languages and draws 35 percent of its visitors from outside the United States.

However, beyond these natural forces, the NBA's success abroad results in large part from the league's strong marketing efforts. To exploit international opportunities

The NBA rolled out a marketing machine that's been fine-tuned for a decade in the United States. Television programming leads the way—not just broadcasts of games but an array of NBA-produced programs, mostly targeted at kids and teenagers, that promote the league and its players. Two weekly programs, a highlights show called *NBA Action* and a teen show called *NBA Jam* that features music, fashion, and player profiles, are produced solely for the international marketplace. . . . Once television has pried open a market, the NBA and its partners move in with an array of live events, attractions, and grassroots activities. [For example,] McDonald's and the NBA sponsor a program called 2Ball that teaches basic basketball skills to thousands of kids outside the U.S. Coca-Cola, meanwhile, targets basketball-crazed teenagers by putting NBA and team logos on Sprite soft drink cans sold in 30 countries. "We're using the NBA and their players to help sell Sprite, but at the same time it does a lot for the NBA," says [Coca-Cola's] director for worldwide sports.

The NBA has encountered a rash of recent problems—Michael Jordan's retirement and the end of the Chicago Bulls dynasty, negative publicity surrounding several high-profile players, and a prolonged player's strike that cut the 1998–1999 season in half. These and other events are presenting fresh challenges to the league's marketing prowess. In the post-Jordan era, the NBA faces the task of trying to extend one of pro sport's greatest growth spurts without the person most responsible for its past success. Still, the future looks bright. For example, the NBA emerged from the potentially disastrous player's strike nearly unscathed—overall attendance slipped only 2 percent and several teams actually saw large jumps in attendance. Although TV ratings for the NBA finals dipped in the year following Jordan's departure, the games still topped the Nielsen ratings.

Thus, most experts expect more slam dunks for the NBA as it continues to extend its international reach. One sustaining factor in the NBA's global appeal is the continuing presence of foreign-born players. Almost every team roster includes one: Toni Kukoc from Croatia, Luc Longley from Australia, Georghe Muresan from Romania, Arvydas Sabonis from Lithuania, or Detlef Shrempf from Germany. Such players attract large followings in their home countries. As *Fortune* concludes:

Imagine, then, the impact in China if a promising 18-year-old, 7-foot-1 center named Wong Zhizhi, who played for that country's . . .

Olympic team, develops into an NBA star. Basketball's popularity is already exploding in China, one of the very few nations where the NBA gives away its TV programming because [it] is determined to make inroads there. Nearly all of China's 250 million TV households get the *NBA Action* highlights show and a game of the week on Saturday mornings; this year China Central TV broadcast the NBA All-Star game live for the first time. Winning the loyalty of two billion Chinese won't be a *kou qui*—a slam-dunk—but Stern is, well, bullish. "The upside is tremendous," he says. Can Ping-Pong survive an NBA invasion? Stay tuned.[1]

In the past, U.S. companies paid little attention to international trade. If they could pick up some extra sales through exporting, that was fine. But the big market was at home, and it teemed with opportunities. The home market was also much safer. Managers did not need to learn other languages, deal with strange and changing currencies, face political and legal uncertainties, or adapt their products to different customer needs and expectations. Today, however, the situation is much different.

GLOBAL MARKETING IN THE TWENTY-FIRST CENTURY

The world is shrinking rapidly with the advent of faster communication, transportation, and financial flows. Products developed in one country—Gucci purses, Mont Blanc pens, McDonald's hamburgers, Japanese sushi, German BMWs—are finding enthusiastic acceptance in other countries. We would not be surprised to hear about a German businessperson wearing an Italian suit meeting an English friend at a Japanese restaurant who later returns home to drink Russian vodka and watch *Frazier* on TV.

International trade is booming. Since 1969, the number of multinational corporations in the world's 14 richest countries has more than tripled, from 7,000 to 24,000. Experts predict that by 2005, world exports of goods and services will reach 28 percent of world gross domestic product, up from only 9 percent 20 years ago. International trade now accounts for a quarter of the United States' GDP, and between 1996 and 2006, U.S. exports are expected to increase 51 percent.[2]

True, many companies have been carrying on international activities for decades. Coca-Cola, IBM, Kodak, Nestlé, Bayer, Sony, and other companies are familiar to most consumers around the world. But today global competition is intensifying. Foreign firms are expanding aggressively into new international markets, and home markets are no longer as rich in opportunity. Domestic companies that never thought about foreign competitors suddenly find these competitors in their own backyards. The firm that stays at home to play it safe not only might lose its chance to enter other markets but also risks losing its home market.

In the United States, names such as Sony, Toyota, Nestlé, Norelco, Mercedes, and Panasonic have become household words. Other products and services that appear to be American are in fact produced or owned by foreign companies: Bantam books, Baskin-Robbins ice cream, GE and RCA televisions, Firestone tires, Carnation milk, Pillsbury food products, Universal Studios, and Motel 6, to name just a few. Few U.S. industries are now safe from foreign competition.

Although some companies would like to stem the tide of foreign imports through protectionism, in the long run this would only raise the cost of living and protect inefficient domestic firms. The better way for companies to compete is to continuously improve their products at home and expand into foreign markets. Many U.S. companies have been successful at international marketing: IBM, Xerox, Corning, Coca-Cola, McDonald's, Gillette, Colgate, General Electric, Caterpillar, Ford, Kodak, 3M, Boeing, Motorola, and dozens of other American firms have made the world their market. But there are too few such firms. In fact, just 5 U.S. companies account for 12 percent of all exports; 1,000 manufacturers (out of 300,000) account for 60 percent.[3]

The longer companies delay taking steps toward internationalizing, the more they risk being shut out of growing markets in Western Europe, Eastern Europe, the Pacific Rim, and elsewhere. Domestic businesses that thought they were safe now find companies from neighboring countries invading their home markets. All companies will have to answer some basic questions: What market position should we try to establish in our country, in our economic region, and globally? Who will our

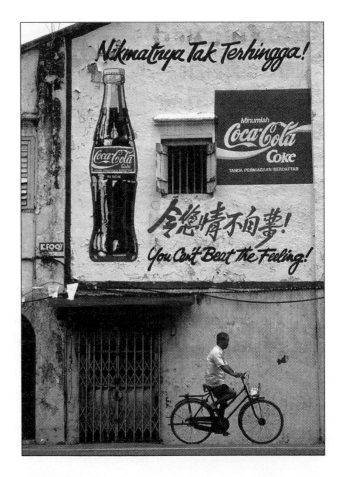

Many American companies have made the world their market.

global competitors be, and what are their strategies and resources? Where should we produce or source our products? What strategic alliances should we form with other firms around the world?

Ironically, although the need for companies to go abroad is greater today than in the past, so are the risks. Companies that go global confront several major problems. High debt, inflation, and unemployment in many countries have resulted in highly unstable governments and currencies, which limits trade and exposes U.S. firms to many risks. For example, in 1998 Russia created a global economic crisis when it devalued the ruble, effectively defaulting on its global debts. A more widespread Asian economic downturn had a far-reaching impact on Western firms with significant markets or investments there.

Governments are placing more regulations on foreign firms, such as requiring joint ownership with domestic partners, mandating the hiring of nationals, and limiting profits that can be taken from the country. Moreover, foreign governments often impose high tariffs or trade barriers in order to protect their own industries. Finally, corruption is an increasing problem—officials in several countries often award business not to the best bidder but to the highest briber.

Still, companies selling in global industries have no choice but to internationalize their operations. A *global industry* is one in which the competitive positions of firms in given local or national markets are affected by their global positions. A **global firm** is one that, by operating in more than one country, gains marketing, production, R&D, and financial advantages that are not available to purely domestic competitors. The global company sees the world as one market. It minimizes the importance of national boundaries and raises capital, obtains materials and components, and manufactures and markets its goods wherever it can do the best job. For example, Ford's "world truck" sports a cab made in Europe and a chassis built in North America. It is assembled in Brazil and imported to the United States for sale. Otis Elevator gets its elevators' door systems from France, small geared parts from Spain, electronics from Germany, and special motor drives from Japan. It uses the United States only for systems integration. Thus, global firms gain advantages by planning, operating, and coordinating their activities on a worldwide basis.

Because firms around the world are globalizing at a rapid rate, domestic firms in global industries must act quickly before the window closes. This does not mean that small and medium-size firms must operate in a dozen countries to succeed. These firms can practice global niching. In fact, companies marketing on the Internet may find themselves going global whether they intend it or not (see Marketing Highlight 19.1). But the world is becoming smaller, and every company operating in a global industry—whether large or small—must assess and establish its place in world markets.

As shown in Figure 19.1, a company faces six major decisions in international marketing. Each decision will be discussed in detail in this chapter.

Global firm
A firm that, by operating in more than one country, gains production, R&D, marketing, and financial advantages in its costs and reputation that are not available to purely domestic competitors.

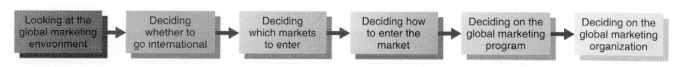

FIGURE 19.1   Major decisions in international marketing

WWW.THEWORLDISYOUROYSTER.COM

Just a few years ago, California-based Cardiac Science was itching to break into foreign markets. The company knew there was an overseas market for its defibrillators, heart monitors, and other medical devices and products, but it didn't know where to start. Yet today, fully 85 percent of Cardiac's revenue is international. Although much of that business was developed through conventional U.S. government export assistance channels, a growing number of Cardiac Science's overseas customers are simply finding the company's products by clicking on www.cardiac science.com.

Like Cardiac Science, more and more companies large and small are taking advantage of cyberspace's vanishing national boundaries.

Major marketers doing global e-commerce range from automakers (General Motors and Toyota) to computer makers (Dell and IBM) to direct-mail companies (L.L. Bean and Lands' End) to Internet super-stars like Amazon.com, which purchased three European companies to build its European book, video, toys, and consumer electronics sales.

For some companies, global cybermarketing has been a hit or miss affair. They put their Web site content in English for the American market, and if any international users stumble across and end up buying something, so much the better. Such orders can be gravy for U.S.-focused marketers. For example, Hyperspace Cowgirls, a three-year-old developer of children's software, has several

European deals in the works even though it does no overseas marketing. "We don't advertise overseas at all," says Susan Shaw, president of the company, whose Web address is www.hygirls.com. "People just find you."

Other marketers have made a more strategic decision to dive into the global marketspace. They're using the Web and online services to reach new customers outside their home countries, support existing customers who live abroad, source from international suppliers, and build global brand awareness. Many companies have adapted their Web sites to provide country-specific content and services to their best potential international markets, often in the local language. For example, in an attempt to increase brand awareness in individual European markets, Reebok has launched a multilingual European Web site—available in English, French, Italian, Spanish, Greek and Turkish. The site (www.europe. reebok.com) targets sports and fitness enthusiasts and includes local events in each market. Similarly, Dell Computer offers dozens of country-specific, local-language Web sites for markets ranging from France, Germany, China, and Japan to Belgium and Brunei.

For the most part, marketers have zeroed in on the countries or regions with the largest potential online populations. Europe and Japan are prime targets. Although European and Japanese online usage has lagged behind that of the United States, it's now catching up quickly. For example, online subscribers are

Many marketers are taking advantage of the Internet's global reach. For example, Dell computer offers dozens of different Web site choices tailored to the languages and situations of specific countries, such as China.

expected to grow from 7 percent of Europe's population in 1998 to 13 percent in 2001. The Japanese Internet user population is expected to double by the year 2001, with e-commerce jumping to $8.5 billion from only $1.7 billion today.

Despite encouraging e-commerce developments in Europe and Asia, Internet marketers sometimes overstate seemingly surefire global opportunities. The reality of the global Internet market depends on each country's economic, technical, cultural, political, and regional dynamics. Technological challenges abound. Because the backbone for the Internet originates in the United States, response times overseas can be dismal. Many countries remain technologically underdeveloped and have a low-income citizenry lacking PCs or even phone connections. Other countries have acceptable phone and PC penetrations, but high subscription and connection costs sharply restrict casual uses such as surfing on the Internet. For example, in Europe, net subscriptions typically run $75 a month, more than triple a U.S. rate that allows unlimited Internet access on free local lines. In the United Kingdom, connection rates can run over $3.50 per hour, with long-distance calling and data surcharges in rural areas running as high as $16 per hour.

In addition, the global marketer may run up against governmental or cultural restrictions. France, for instance, has laws against providing encrypted content. In Germany, a vendor can't accept payment via credit card until two weeks after an order has been sent. Also, it is against the law for credit card companies and direct-marketing firms to gather certain types of data on potential applicants—a precaution taken by the country to prevent the massive abuses of centralized information

experienced during the Nazi era. Such restrictions, sometimes combined with underdeveloped banking systems, have limited credit card and direct-mail usage in many countries. The issue of who pays taxes and duties on global e-commerce is murkier still. Subsequently, marketers outside the United States sometimes have to find alternative marketing and collection approaches.

Businesses need to realize that the Web does not offer complete solutions for transacting global business—and it probably never will. Most companies will always find it difficult to complete a big business-to-business deal via e-mail. The Internet will not surmount customs red tape or local regulations regarding import or export of certain goods. The Web can't guarantee that goods will arrive in perfect condition. Despite the barriers, however, global Internet enterprise is growing rapidly. In fact, 83 percent of managers surveyed recently by consulting firm KPMG Peat Marwick said that e-commerce will be a major export vehicle beyond the year 2000. For companies that wish to go global, the Internet and online services can represent an easy way to get started or to reinforce other efforts.

For larger companies, casting an international Web is a natural. For example, Hewlett-Packard uses a Web site to deal with its resellers Europe-wide, offering information in many languages. Nestlé's Web site links to company sites for Taiwan, Australia, Brazil, Chile, New Zealand, Switzerland, Spain, Germany, France, Japan, Sweden, Greece, and the United Kingdom. Texas Instruments' European Semiconductor group uses a "TI & Me" site to sell and support its signal processors, logic devices, and other chips across the European continent.

But small companies can also market globally on the Web. For example, upscale retailer and cataloger The Sharper Image now gets a full 25 percent of its online business from overseas customers. Online music marketer CDNow, which stumbled onto global markets almost by accident, now actively develops it global business. For example, in 1995 the company began shipping U.S. titles to Japanese customers who had found its Web site. The site wasn't written in Japanese and CDNow had no physical presence in Japan. As the number of Japanese orders grew, however, the company made a serious move into Japan. It paired up with a Japanese music distributor in a deal that has allowed it to offer domestic Japanese titles and market itself locally with Japanese-language advertising, newsletters, and Internet-based chat groups. Japanese customers also now can pay for their purchases on the Web site with yen credit cards. The investment to go global is paying off. About 20 percent of CDNow's $100 million in revenue last year came from international sources, with Japan being its largest single foreign market.

Sources: Peter Krasilovsky, "A Whole New World," Marketing Tools supplement, *American Demographics,* May 1996, pp. 22–25; Richard N. Miller, "The Year Ahead," *Direct Marketing,* January 1997, pp. 42–44; Jack Gee, "Parlez-Vous Inter-Net?" *Industry Week,* April 21, 1997, pp. 78–79; Michelle V. Rafter, "Multilingual Sites Give Companies Access to Global Revenue Sources," *Chicago Tribune,* May 11, 1998, Business Section, p. 9; "Reebok Targets Its New Web Site at Euro Markets," *Marketing,* October 1, 1998, p. 16; Shannon Oberndorf, "Europe Jumps Online," *Catalog Age,* June 1999, p. 10; Bill Spindle, "E-Commerce (A Special Report)," *Wall Street Journal,* July 12, 1999, p. R22; and Erika Rasmusson, "E-Commerce Around the World," *Sales and Marketing Management,* February 2000, p. 94.

LOOKING AT THE GLOBAL MARKETING ENVIRONMENT

Before deciding whether to operate internationally, a company must thoroughly understand the international marketing environment. That environment has changed a great deal in the past two decades, creating both new opportunities and new problems. The world economy has globalized. World trade and investment have grown rapidly, with many attractive markets opening up in Western and Eastern Europe, China and the Pacific Rim, Russia, and elsewhere. There has been a growth of global brands in automobiles, food, clothing, electronics, and many other categories. The number of global companies has grown dramatically. The international financial system has become more complex and volatile, and U.S. companies face increasing trade barriers erected to protect domestic markets from outside competition.

The International Trade System

Tariff
A tax levied by a government against certain imported products. Tariffs are designed to raise revenue or to protect domestic firms.

Quota
A limit on the amount of goods that an importing country will accept in certain product categories.

Embargo
A ban on the import of a certain product.

Exchange controls
Government limits on the amount of foreign exchange with other countries and on the exchange rate against other currencies.

Nontariff trade barriers
Nonmonetary barriers to foreign products, such as biases against a foreign company's bids or product standards that go against a foreign company's product features.

The U.S. company looking abroad must start by understanding the international *trade system*. When selling to another country, the U.S. firm faces various trade restrictions. The most common is the **tariff,** which is a tax levied by a foreign government against certain imported products. The tariff may be designed either to raise revenue or to protect domestic firms. The exporter also may face a **quota,** which sets limits on the amount of goods the importing country will accept in certain product categories. The purpose of the quota is to conserve on foreign exchange and to protect local industry and employment. An **embargo,** or boycott, which totally bans some kinds of imports, is the strongest form of quota.

American firms may face **exchange controls** that limit the amount of foreign exchange and the exchange rate against other currencies. The company also may face **nontariff trade barriers,** such as biases against U.S. company bids or restrictive product standards or other rules that go against American product features:

> One of the cleverest ways the Japanese have found to keep foreign manufacturers out of their domestic market is to plead "uniqueness." Japanese skin is different, the government argues, so foreign cosmetics companies must test their products in Japan before selling there. The Japanese say their stomachs are small and have room for only the *mikan,* the local tangerine, so imports of U.S. oranges are limited. Now the Japanese have come up with what may be the flakiest argument yet: Their snow is different, so ski equipment should be too.[4]

At the same time, certain forces *help* trade between nations. Examples include the General Agreement on Tariffs and Trade and various regional free trade agreements.

The World Trade Organization and GATT

The General Agreement on Tariffs and Trade (GATT) is a 50-year-old treaty designed to promote world trade by reducing tariffs and other international trade barriers. Since the treaty's inception in 1948, member nations (currently numbering more than 120) have met in eight rounds of GATT negotiations to reassess trade barriers and set new rules for international trade. The first seven rounds of negotiations reduced the average worldwide tariffs on manufactured goods from 45 percent to just 5 percent.

The most recently completed GATT negotiations, dubbed the Uruguay Round, dragged on for seven long years before concluding in 1993. The benefits of the

Uruguay Round will be felt for many years as the accord promotes long-term global trade growth. It reduced the world's remaining merchandise tariffs by 30 percent, which could boost global merchandise trade by up to 10 percent, or $270 billion in current dollars, by the year 2002. The new agreement also extended GATT to cover trade in agriculture and a wide range of services, and it toughened international protection of copyrights, patents, trademarks, and other intellectual property.[5]

Beyond reducing trade barriers and setting international standards for trade, the Uruguay Round established the World Trade Organization (WTO) to enforce GATT rules. One of the WTO's first major tasks was to host negotiations on the General Agreement on Trade in Services, which deals with worldwide trade in banking, securities, and insurance services. In general, the WTO acts as an umbrella organization, overseeing GATT, the General Agreement on Trade in Services, and a similar agreement governing intellectual property. In addition, the WTO mediates global disputes and imposes trade sanctions, authorities that the previous GATT organization never possessed. A fresh round of WTO negotiations began in Seattle in late 1999.

Regional Free Trade Zones

Economic community

A group of nations organized to work toward common goals in the regulation of international trade.

Certain countries have formed *free trade zones* or **economic communities**— groups of nations organized to work toward common goals in the regulation of international trade. One such community is the *European Union (EU)*. Formed in 1957, the European Union—then called the Common Market—set out to create a single European market by reducing barriers to the free flow of products, services, finances, and labor among member countries and developing policies on trade with nonmember nations. Today, the European Union represents one of the world's single largest markets. Its 15 member countries contain more than 370 million consumers and account for 20 percent of the world's exports. During the next decade, as more European nations seek admission, the EU could contain as many as 450 million people in 28 countries.

European unification offers tremendous trade opportunities for U.S. and other non-European firms. However, it also poses threats. As a result of increased unification, European companies will grow bigger and more competitive. Perhaps an even bigger concern, however, is that lower barriers *inside* Europe will only create thicker *outside* walls. Some observers envision a "Fortress Europe" that heaps favors on firms from EU countries but hinders outsiders by imposing obstacles such as stiffer import quotas, local content requirements, and other nontariff barriers.

Progress toward European unification has been slow—many doubt that complete unification will ever be achieved. However, on January 1, 1999, 11 of the 15 member nations took a significant step toward unification by adopting the Euro as a common currency. These 11 nations represent 290 million people and a $6.5 trillion market. Currencies of the individual countries will be phased out gradually until January 1, 2002, when the Euro will become the only currency. Adoption of the Euro will decrease much of the currency risk associated with doing business in Europe, making member countries with previously weak currencies more attractive markets. In addition, by removing currency conversion hurdles, the switch will likely increase cross-border trade and highlight differences in pricing and marketing from country to country.[6]

Even with the adoption of the Euro as a standard currency, from a marketing viewpoint, creating an economic community will not create a homogenous market. As one international analyst suggests, "Even though you have fiscal harmonization, you can't go against 2,000 years of tradition."[7] With 14 different languages and distinctive national customs, it is unlikely that the EU will ever become the "United States of

Wal-Mart and other companies are expanding rapidly in Mexico and Canada to take advantage of the many opportunities presented by NAFTA. The trade agreement establishes a single market of 360 million people in Mexico, Canada, and the United States.

Europe." Although economic and political boundaries may fall, social and cultural differences will remain, and companies marketing in Europe will face a daunting mass of local rules. Still, even if only partly successful, European unification will make a more efficient and competitive Europe a global force with which to reckon.[8]

In North America, the United States and Canada phased out trade barriers in 1989. In January 1994, the *North American Free Trade Agreement (NAFTA)* established a free trade zone among the United States, Mexico, and Canada. The agreement created a single market of 360 million people who produce and consume $6.7 trillion worth of goods and services. As it is implemented over a 15-year period, NAFTA will eliminate all trade barriers and investment restrictions among the three countries. Prior to NAFTA, tariffs on American products entering Mexico averaged 13 percent, whereas U.S. tariffs on Mexican goods averaged 6 percent.

Thus far, the agreement has allowed trade between the countries to flourish. Each day the United States exchanges more than $1 billion in goods and services with Canada, its largest trading partner. Over the past four years, exports from the United States to Mexico have increased 116 percent. In 1998, Mexico passed Japan to become America's second largest trading partner.[9]

Other free trade areas have formed in Latin America and South America. For example, MERCOSUR now links six members, including full members Argentina, Brazil, Paraguay, and Uruguay and associate members Bolivia and Chile. With a population of more than 200 million and a combined economy of more than $1 trillion a year, these countries make up the largest trading bloc after NAFTA and the European Union. There is talk of a free trade agreement between the EU and MERCOSUR.[10]

Although the recent trend toward free trade zones has caused great excitement and new market opportunities, this trend also raises some concerns. For example, in the United States, unions fear that NAFTA will lead to the further exodus of manufacturing jobs to Mexico where wage rates are much lower. Environmentalists worry that companies that are unwilling to play by the strict rules of the U.S. Environmental Protection Agency will relocate in Mexico where pollution regulation has been lax.[11]

Each nation has unique features that must be understood. A nation's readiness for different products and services and its attractiveness as a market to foreign firms depend on its economic, political–legal, and cultural environments.

Economic Environment

The international marketer must study each country's economy. Two economic factors reflect the country's attractiveness as a market: the country's industrial structure and its income distribution.

The country's *industrial structure* shapes its product and service needs, income levels, and employment levels. The four types of industrial structures are as follows:

★ *Subsistence economies:* In a subsistence economy, the vast majority of people engage in simple agriculture. They consume most of their output and barter the rest for simple goods and services. They offer few market opportunities.

★ *Raw material exporting economies:* These economies are rich in one or more natural resources but poor in other ways. Much of their revenue comes from exporting these resources. Examples are Chile (tin and copper), Zaire (copper, cobalt, and coffee), and Saudi Arabia (oil). These countries are good markets for large equipment, tools and supplies, and trucks. If there are many foreign residents and a wealthy upper class, they are also a market for luxury goods.

★ *Industrializing economies:* In an industrializing economy, manufacturing accounts for 10 to 20 percent of the country's economy. Examples include Egypt, the Philippines, India, and Brazil. As manufacturing increases, the country needs more imports of raw textile materials, steel, and heavy machinery, and fewer imports of finished textiles, paper products, and automobiles. Industrialization typically creates a new rich class and a small but growing middle class, both demanding new types of imported goods.

★ *Industrial economies:* Industrial economies are major exporters of manufactured goods and investment funds. They trade goods among themselves and also export them to other types of economies for raw materials and semifinished goods. The varied manufacturing activities of these industrial nations and their large middle class make them rich markets for all sorts of goods.

The second economic factor is the country's *income distribution.* Countries with subsistence economies may consist mostly of households with very low family incomes. In contrast, industrialized nations may have low-, medium-, and high-income households. Still other countries may have households with only either very low or very high incomes. However, in many cases, poorer countries may have small but wealthy segments of upper-income consumers. Also, even in low-income and developing economies, people may find ways to buy products that are important to them.

> Philosophy professor Nina Gladziuk thinks carefully before shelling out her hard-earned zlotys for Poland's dazzling array of consumer goods. But spend she certainly does. Although she earns just $550 a month from two academic jobs, Gladziuk, 41, enjoys making purchases: They are changing her lifestyle after years of deprivation under communism. In the past year, she has furnished a new apartment in a popular neighborhood near Warsaw's Kabaty Forest, splurged on foreign-made beauty products, and spent a weekend in Paris before attending a seminar financed by her university. . . . Meet Central Europe's fast-rising consumer class. From white-collar workers like Gladziuk to factory workers in Budapest to hip young professionals in Prague, incomes

Developing economies: Ads like this one appearing in Hungarian magazines cater to the new class of buyers with dreams of the good life—and buying habits to match, who are eager to snap up everything from the high fashions to the latest cell phones.

are rising and confidence surging as a result of four years of economic growth. In the region's leading economies—the Czech Republic, Hungary, and Poland—the new class of buyers is growing not only in numbers but also in sophistication. . . . In Hungary, ad agency Young & Rubicam labels 11 percent of the country as "aspirers," with dreams of the good life and buying habits to match. Nearly one-third of all Czechs, Hungarians, and Poles—some 17 million people—are under 30 years old, eager to snap up everything from the latest fashions to compact disks.[12]

Thus, international marketers face many challenges in understanding how the economic environment will affect decisions about which global markets to enter and how.

Political–Legal Environment

Nations differ greatly in their political–legal environments. At least four political–legal factors should be considered in deciding whether to do business in a given country: attitudes toward international buying, government bureaucracy, political stability, and monetary regulations.

In their *attitudes toward international buying,* some nations are quite receptive to foreign firms and others are quite hostile. For example, India has bothered foreign businesses with import quotas, currency restrictions, and limits on the percentage of the management team that can be nonnationals. As a result, many U.S. companies left India. In contrast, neighboring Asian countries such as Singapore, Thailand, Malaysia, and the Philippines court foreign investors and shower them with incentives and favorable operating conditions.[13]

A second factor is *government bureaucracy*—the extent to which the host government runs an efficient system for helping foreign companies: efficient customs handling, good market information, and other factors that aid in doing business. A common shock to Americans is how quickly barriers to trade disappear in some countries if a suitable payment (bribe) is made to some official.

Political stability is another issue. Governments change hands, sometimes violently. Even without a change, a government may decide to respond to new popular feelings. The foreign company's property may be taken, its currency holdings may be blocked, or import quotas or new duties may be set. International marketers may find it profitable to do business in an unstable country, but the unstable situation will affect how they handle business and financial matters.

Finally, companies must also consider a country's *monetary regulations*. Sellers want to take their profits in a currency of value to them. Ideally, the buyer can pay in the seller's currency or in other world currencies. Short of this, sellers might accept a blocked currency—one whose removal from the country is restricted by the buyer's government—if they can buy other goods in that country that they need themselves or can sell elsewhere for a needed currency. Besides currency limits, a changing exchange rate also creates high risks for the seller.

Most international trade involves cash transactions. Yet many nations have too little hard currency to pay for their purchases from other countries. They may want to pay with other items instead of cash, which has led to a growing practice called **countertrade.** Countertrade may now account for more than one-half of all international trade. It takes several forms: *Barter* involves the direct exchange of goods or services, as when Australian ranchers swapped beef on the hoof for Indonesian goods including beer, palm oil, and cement. Another form is *compensation (or buyback)*, whereby the seller sells a plant, equipment, or technology to another country and agrees to take payment in the resulting products. Thus, Goodyear provided China with materials and training for a printing plant in exchange for finished labels. Another form is *counterpurchase,* in which the seller receives full payment in cash but agrees to spend some portion of the money in the other country within a stated time period. For example, Pepsi sells its cola syrup to Russia for rubles and agrees to buy Russian-made Stolichnaya vodka for sale in the United States.

Countertrade deals can be very complex. For example, a few years back, DaimlerChrysler agreed to sell 30 trucks to Romania in exchange for 150 Romanian jeeps, which it then sold to Ecuador for bananas, which were in turn sold to a German supermarket chain for German currency. Through this roundabout process, DaimlerChrysler finally obtained payment in German money. In another case, when Occidental Petroleum Company wanted to sell oil to Yugoslavia, it hired a trading firm, SGD International, to arrange a countertrade. SGD arranged for a New York City automobile dealer-distributor, Global Motors Inc., to import more than $400 million worth of Yugoslavian Yugo automobiles, paid for by Occidental oil. Global then paid Occidental in cash. SGD, however, was paid in Yugos, which it peddled piecemeal by trading them for everything from cash to Caribbean resort hotel rooms, which it in turn sold to tour packagers and travel agencies for cash.[14]

Countertrade
International trade involving the direct or indirect exchange of goods for other goods instead of cash.

Cultural Environment

Each country has its own folkways, norms, and taboos. The seller must examine the ways consumers in different countries think about and use certain products before planning a marketing program. There are often surprises. For example, the average French man uses almost twice as many cosmetics and beauty aids as his wife. The Germans and the French eat more packaged, branded spaghetti than do Italians. Italian children like to eat chocolate bars between slices of bread as a snack. Women in Tanzania will not give their children eggs for fear of making them bald or impotent.

Companies that ignore such differences can make some very expensive and embarrassing mistakes. Here's an example:

> McDonald's and Coca-Cola managed to offend the entire Muslim world by putting the Saudi Arabian flag on their packaging. The flag's design includes a passage from the Koran (the sacred text of Islam), and Muslims feel very strongly that their Holy Writ should never be wadded up and tossed in the garbage. Nike faced a similar situation in

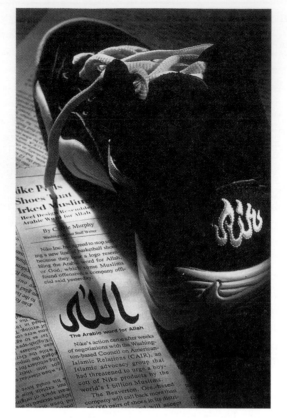

Overlooking cultural differences can result in embarrassing mistakes. When it learned that this stylized "Air" logo resembled "Allah" in Arabic script, Nike apologized and pulled the shoes from distribution.

Arab countries when Muslims objected to a stylized "Air" logo on its shoes that resembled "Allah" in Arabic script. Nike apologized for the mistake and pulled the shoes from distribution.[15]

Business norms and behavior also vary from country to country. American business executives need to be briefed on these factors before conducting business in another country. Here are some examples of different global business behavior:[16]

★ South Americans like to sit or stand very close to each other when they talk business—in fact, almost nose-to-nose. The American business executive tends to keep backing away as the South American moves closer. Both may end up being offended.

★ Fast and tough bargaining, which works well in other parts of the world, is often inappropriate in Japan and other Asian countries. Moreover, in face-to-face communications, Japanese business executives rarely say no. Thus, Americans tend to become impatient with having to spend time in polite conversation about the weather or other such topics before getting down to business. They also become frustrated when they don't know where they stand. However, when Americans come to the point quickly, Japanese business executives may find this behavior offensive.

★ In France, wholesalers don't want to promote a product. They ask their retailers what they want and deliver it. If an American company builds its strategy around the French wholesaler's cooperation in promotions, it is likely to fail.

★ When American executives exchange business cards, each usually gives the other's card a cursory glance and stuffs it in a pocket for later reference. In Japan,

Companies that understand cultural nuances can use them to advantage. L'Oréal's winning formula is to convey the allure of different cultures through its many products.

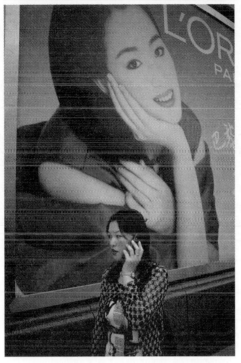

however, executives dutifully study each other's cards during a greeting, carefully noting company affiliation and rank. They hand their card to the most important person first.

By the same token, companies that understand cultural nuances can use them to advantage when positioning products internationally. For example, consider French cosmetics giant L'Oréal:

⭐ It's a sunny afternoon outside Parkson's department store in Shanghai, and a marketing battle is raging for the attention of Chinese women. Tall, pouty models in beige skirts and sheer tops pass out flyers promoting Revlon's new spring colors. But their effort is drowned out by L'Oréal's eye-catching show for its Maybelline brand. To a pulsing rhythm, two gangly models in shimmering lycra tops dance on a podium before a large backdrop depicting the New York City skyline. The music stops, and a makeup artist transforms a model's face while a Chinese saleswoman delivers the punch line. "This brand comes from America. It's very trendy," she shouts into her microphone. "If you want to be fashionable, just choose Maybelline." Few of the women in the crowd realize that the trendy "New York" Maybelline brand belongs to French cosmetics giant L'Oréal. . . . Blink an eye and L'Oréal has just sold 85 products around the world, from Redken hair care and Ralph Lauren perfumes to Helena Rubinstein cosmetics. In the battle for global beauty markets, L'Oréal has developed a winning formula: . . . conveying the allure of different cultures through its many products. Whether it's selling Italian elegance, New York street smarts, or French beauty through its brands, L'Oréal is reaching out to a vast range of people across incomes and cultures.[17]

Thus, understanding cultural traditions, preferences, and behaviors can help companies to avoid embarrassing mistakes and to take advantage of cross-cultural opportunities.

DECIDING WHETHER TO GO INTERNATIONAL

Not all companies need to venture into international markets to survive. For example, many companies are local businesses that need to market well only in the local marketplace. Operating domestically is easier and safer. Managers need not learn another country's language and laws, deal with volatile currencies, face political and legal uncertainties, or redesign their products to suit different customer needs and expectations. However, companies that operate in global industries, where their strategic positions in specific markets are affected strongly by their overall global positions, must compete on a worldwide basis if they are to succeed.

Any of several factors might draw a company into the international arena. Global competitors might attack the company's domestic market by offering better products or lower prices. The company might want to counterattack these competitors in their home markets to tie up their resources. Or the company might discover foreign markets that present higher profit opportunities than the domestic market does. The company's domestic market might be stagnant or shrinking, or the company might need an enlarged customer base in order to achieve economies of scale. The company might want to reduce its dependence on any one market so as to reduce its risk. Finally, the company's customers might be expanding abroad and require international servicing.

Before going abroad, the company must weigh several risks and answer many questions about its ability to operate globally. Can the company learn to understand the preferences and buyer behavior of consumers in other countries? Can it offer competitively attractive products? Will it be able to adapt to other countries' business cultures and deal effectively with foreign nationals? Do the company's managers have the necessary international experience? Has management considered the impact of regulations and the political environments of other countries?

Because of the risks and difficulties of entering international markets, most companies do not act until some situation or event thrusts them into the global arena. Someone—a domestic exporter, a foreign importer, a foreign government—may ask the company to sell abroad. Or the company may be saddled with overcapacity and must find additional markets for its goods.

DECIDING WHICH MARKETS TO ENTER

Before going abroad, the company should try to define its international *marketing objectives and policies*. It should decide what *volume* of foreign sales it wants. Most companies start small when they go abroad. Some plan to stay small, seeing international sales as a small part of their business. Other companies have bigger plans, seeing international business as equal to or even more important than their domestic business.

The company must also choose *how many* countries it wants to market in. Generally, it makes sense to operate in fewer countries with deeper commitment and penetration in each. The Bulova Watch Company decided to operate in many international markets and expanded into more than 100 countries. As a result, it spread itself too thin, made profits in only two countries, and lost around $40 million. In contrast, although consumer product company Amway is now breaking into markets at a furious pace, it is doing so only after decades of gradually building up its overseas presence. Known for its neighbor-to-neighbor direct-selling networks,

Amway expanded into Australia in 1971, a country far away but similar to the U.S. market. Then, in the 1980s, Amway expanded into 10 more countries, and the pace increased rapidly from then on. By 1994 Amway was firmly established in 60 countries, including Hungary, Poland, and the Czech Republic. Following its substantial success in Japan, China, and other Asian countries, the company entered India in 1998. Entering the new millennium, international proceeds account for over 70 percent of the company's overall sales.[18]

Next, the company needs to decide on the *types* of countries to enter. A country's attractiveness depends on the product, geographical factors, income and population, political climate, and other factors. The seller may prefer certain country groups or parts of the world. In recent years, many major new markets have emerged, offering both substantial opportunities and daunting challenges (see Marketing Highlight 19.2).

After listing possible international markets, the company must screen and rank each one. Consider the following example:

> Many mass marketers dream of selling to China's more than 1.2 billion people. For example, Colgate is waging a pitched battle in China, seeking control of the world's largest toothpaste market. Yet, this country of infrequent brushers offers great potential. Only 20 percent of China's rural dwellers brush daily, so Colgate and its competitors are aggressively pursuing promotional and educational programs, from massive ad campaigns to visits to local schools to sponsoring oral care research. Through such efforts, in this $350 million market dominated by local brands, Colgate has expanded its market share from 7 percent in 1995 to 24 percent today.[19]

Colgate's decision to enter the Chinese market seems fairly simple and straightforward: China is a huge market without established competition. Given the low rate of brushing, this already huge market can grow even larger. Yet we still can question whether market size *alone* is reason enough for selecting China. Colgate also must consider other factors: Will the Chinese government remain stable and supportive? Does China provide for the production and distribution technologies needed to produce and market Colgate's products profitably? Will Colgate be able to overcome cultural barriers and convince Chinese consumers to brush their teeth regularly? Can Colgate compete effectively with dozens of local competitors? Colgate's current success in China suggests that it could answer yes to all of these questions. Still, the company's future in China is filled with uncertainties.

Possible global markets should be ranked on several factors, including market size, market growth, cost of doing business, competitive advantage, and risk level. The goal is to determine the potential of each market, using indicators such as those shown in Table 19.1. Then the marketer must decide which markets offer the greatest long-run return on investment.

General Electric's appliance division sells more than 150 million appliances each year in 150 world markets under the Monogram, GE Profile, GE, Hotpoint, and RCA brand names. This experienced global marketer uses what it calls a "smart bomb" strategy for selecting global markets to enter. GE Appliances executives examine each potential country microscopically, measuring factors such as strength of local competitors, market growth potential, and availability of skilled labor. Then they target only markets in which they can earn more than 20 percent on their investment. The goal: "To generate the best returns possible on the smallest investment possible." Once targets are selected, GE Appliances zeros in with marketing smart bombs—products and programs tailored to yield the best performance in each market. As a result of this strategy, GE is trouncing competitors Whirlpool and Maytag in Asian markets.[20]

MARKETING HIGHLIGHT 19.2

EMERGING MARKETS: CHINA AND CENTRAL EUROPE

As communist and formerly communist countries reform their markets, and as the United States continues to dismantle its trade barriers, U.S. companies are eagerly anticipating the profits that await them. Here are "snapshots" of the opportunities and challenges that marketers face in two emerging markets: China and Central Europe.

China: 1.2 Billion Consumers

In Guangdong province, Chinese "yuppies" walk department store aisles to buy $95 Nike or Reebok sneakers or think nothing of spending $4 on a jar of Skippy peanut butter in the supermarket section. Although the average annual income amounts to only $360 per person, China's ever-growing pool of elite consumers still has plenty of spending money because of subsidized housing and health care and lots of savings under the mattress.

The prevalence of wide-screen televisions, fancy stereos, and home-karaoke machines in Shanghai apartments suggests that this new upper-middle class has more money than it admits to. . . . Among urban households, fewer than one in five households had a color television in 1985; today the average such home has more than one. Then, 7 percent had a refrigerator; now 73 percent do. Cameras are four times more common. Among richer urban households, more than half now have a VCR or video CD machine, a pager, air conditioner, and shower, and nearly a third of households also own a mobile phone.

In Shenzen, Guangdong's second-largest city, consumers have the highest disposable income in all of China—$3,900 annually. With purchasing power like this, a population of 1.2 billion, and the fastest-growing economy in the world, China is encouraging companies from around the planet to set up shop there. Instead of the communist propaganda of yore, modern Chinese billboards exclaim, "Give China a chance."

Yet for all the market potential, there are many hurdles to clear in establishing businesses in China and marketing to the Chinese. For one, China is not one market but many, and regional governments may discriminate against certain goods. Distribution channels are undeveloped, consisting of thousands of tiny mom-and-pop stores that can afford to stock only a few bottles or packages at a time. China's dismal infra-

Central Europe: In the Czech Republic, Poland, and Hungary, the oppression of 50 years of communist rule and hardship have given way to a capitalist economy rich with market potential.

structure can turn a rail shipment traveling from Guanzhou to Beijing into a month-long odyssey. Smart firms, such as Allied Signal and Kodak, try to jump these hurdles by partnering with Chinese government bodies—in some regions doing so is a must for establishing a business. Others acquire Chinese business partners who can help them penetrate distribution channels and hire experienced personnel.

A major concern to some U.S. businesses has been China's distressing human rights record. Levi-Strauss has turned its back on China's vast market for blue jeans because of such concerns. But other U.S. firms counter that industry can be part of the solution. "Supporting the business sector will result in economic and political freedoms for the Chinese people," says a 3M spokesperson.

Central Europe: Free to Buy

In the Czech Republic, Poland, and Hungary, the oppression of 50 years of communist rule and hardship has given way to a capitalist economy rich with market potential. In Central Europe, as in many developing economies, "after almost 10 years of transition, the disparity between the rich and the poor is beyond anyone's imagination," says a Western business executive. However, with a population of nearly 17 million, almost one-third of whom are under the age of 30, the region boasts a growing middle class with a can-buy attitude. A wide range of companies have entered the market, offering everything from compact disks and soft drinks to investment advice and

consumer loans, eager to show consumers that these products and services can improve and transform their lives.

Foreign investment currently accounts for a relatively small portion of Central Europe's economies. However, more and more Western companies are increasing their investments and the region's economy is expected to grow by 25 percent a year. There are risks, to be sure. The European Bank for Reconstruction and Development (EBRD) warns: "The potential for growth is large, but so is the possibility of being trapped by vested interests, monopolistic practices, and bureaucracy." In addition, high interest rates, a poorly functioning capital market, and political interference continue to discourage some investors. Despite the drawbacks of entering these relatively immature markets, companies trying to grab a piece of Central Europe's growing market potential will find themselves with plenty of company.

In these fast-developing markets, firms are investing heavily to get and hold customer attention. "It used to be as simple as putting your product out there and putting up a couple of billboards," says a Coca-Cola executive. Now, it takes big spending. Whereas companies have traditionally invested little on promotion in the region, last year they spent $2.3 billion on advertising—twice as much as they spent in 1995. Central Europe is awash in samples, sweepstakes, and other promotions as companies test new products and scramble to establish their brands. Distribution channels are also changing rapidly. In a region typically

dominated by mom-and-pop stores, shopping centers and hypermarkets are beginning to appear and multiply.

As more and more companies jostle for position in Central Europe, the region's painful transition to a market economy is paying off. The new consumer spending offers not just promising markets for foreign companies. It also offers Central European consumers a promise that someday they may match the prosperity of their neighbors to the west. The new consumption attitude is exemplified by Dusan Tefkal, 25, owner of a Prague brokerage. With an annual income of more than $80,000, he can spend freely on nice clothes, fine restaurants, and exotic vacations. Last spring, he took time off to ski in Austria and dive in the coral reefs off the coast of Belize. "When you want to escape, it's worth paying extra," he says. "It's worth making sure that everything is perfect." It's this kind of consumer thinking that makes Central Europe a perfectly attractive new market.

Sources: Quotes from David Woodruff, James Drake, Christopher Condon, and Peggy Smith, "Ready to Shop Until They Drop," *Business Week,* June 22, 1998, pp. 104, 108–113; and "Business: Not Quite a Billion," *The Economist,* January 2, 1999, p. 56. Also see Marlene Piturro, "Capitalist China?" *Brandweek,* May 16, 1994, pp. 22–27; Mark L. Clifford, "How You Can Win in China," *Business Week,* May 26, 1997, pp. 66–68; Louis Tong, "Consumerism Sweeps the Mainland," *Marketing Management,* Winter 1998, pp. 32–35; and Bruce Barnard, "Welcome a New Wave of Investment," *Europe,* July–August 1998, pp. 18–19.

TABLE 19.1 INDICATORS OF MARKET POTENTIAL	
1. Demographic Characteristics	**4. Technological Factors**
Size of population Rate of population growth Degree of urbanization Population density Age structure and composition of the population	Level of technological skills Existing production technology Existing consumption technology Education levels
2. Geographic Characteristics	**5. Sociocultural Factors**
Physical size of a country Topographical characteristics Climate conditions	Dominant values Lifestyle patterns Ethnic groups Linguistic fragmentation
3. Economic Factors	**6. National Goals and Plans**
GDP per capita Income distribution Rate of growth of GNP Ratio of investment to GNP	Industry priorities Infrastructure investment plans

Source: Susan P. Douglas, C. Samuel Craig, and Warren Keegan, "Approaches to Assessing International Marketing Opportunities for Small and Medium-Sized Businesses," *Columbia Journal of World Business,* Fall 1982, pp. 26–32. Copyright 1982, 1999. *Columbia Journal of World Business.* Reprint with permission. Also see Tamer S. Cavusil, "Measuring the Potential of Emerging Markets: An Indexing Approach," *Business Horizons,* January–February 1997, pp. 87–91.

DECIDING HOW TO ENTER THE MARKET

Once a company has decided to sell in a foreign country, it must determine the best mode of entry. Its choices are *exporting, joint venturing,* and *direct investment.* Figure 19.2 shows three market entry strategies, along with the options each one offers. As the figure shows, each succeeding strategy involves more commitment and risk, but also more control and potential profits.

Exporting

Exporting

Entering a foreign market by sending products and selling them through international marketing intermediaries (indirect exporting) or through the company's own department, branch, or sales representatives or agents (direct exporting).

The simplest way to enter a foreign market is through **exporting.** The company may passively export its surpluses from time to time, or it may make an active commitment to expand exports to a particular market. In either case, the company produces all its goods in its home country. It may or may not modify them for the export market. Exporting involves the least change in the company's product lines, organization, investments, or mission.

Companies typically start with *indirect exporting,* working through independent international marketing intermediaries. Indirect exporting involves less investment because the firm does not require an overseas sales force or set of contacts. It also involves less risk. International marketing intermediaries—domestic-based export merchants or agents, cooperative organizations, and export-management companies—bring know-how and services to the relationship, so the seller normally makes fewer mistakes.

FIGURE 19.2 Market entry strategies

Sellers may eventually move into *direct exporting*, whereby they handle their own exports. The investment and risk are somewhat greater in this strategy, but so is the potential return. A company can conduct direct exporting in several ways: It can set up a domestic export department that carries out export activities. It can set up an overseas sales branch that handles sales, distribution, and perhaps promotion. The sales branch gives the seller more presence and program control in the foreign market and often serves as a display center and customer service center. The company can also send home-based salespeople abroad at certain times in order to find business. Finally, the company can do its exporting either through foreign-based distributors who buy and own the goods or through foreign-based agents who sell the goods on behalf of the company.

Joint Venturing

Joint venturing
Entering foreign markets by joining with foreign companies to produce or market a product or service.

A second method of entering a foreign market is **joint venturing**—joining with foreign companies to produce or market products or services. Joint venturing differs from exporting in that the company joins with a host country partner to sell or market abroad. It differs from direct investment in that an association is formed with someone in the foreign country. There are four types of joint ventures: licensing, contract manufacturing, management contracting, and joint ownership.

Licensing

Licensing
A method of entering a foreign market in which the company enters into an agreement with a licensee in the foreign market, offering the right to use a manufacturing process, trademark, patent, trade secret, or other item of value for a fee or royalty.

Licensing is a simple way for a manufacturer to enter international marketing. The company enters into an agreement with a licensee in the foreign market. For a fee or royalty, the licensee buys the right to use the company's manufacturing process, trademark, patent, trade secret, or other item of value. The company thus gains entry into the market at little risk; the licensee gains production expertise or a well-known product or name without having to start from scratch.

Coca-Cola markets internationally by licensing bottlers around the world and supplying them with the syrup needed to produce the product. In Japan, Budweiser beer flows from Kirin breweries, Lady Borden ice cream is churned out at Meiji Milk Products dairies, and Marlboro cigarettes roll off production lines at Japan Tobacco, Inc. Tokyo Disneyland is owned and operated by Oriental Land Company under license from the Walt Disney Company. The 45-year license gives Disney licensing fees plus 10 percent of admissions and 5 percent of food and merchandise sales. And in an effort to bring online retail investing to people abroad, online brokerage E★Trade has to date launched E★Trade-branded Web sites in six countries outside the United States, initially forming licensing agreements and launching sites in Canada, Australia–New Zealand, France, and the Nordic region, whose Swedish site also serves residents of Denmark, Norway, Finland, and Iceland. In addition, E★Trade

*Licensing: Online brokerage E*Trade used licensing agreements to launch sites in Canada, Australia–New Zealand, France, and the Nordic region, whose Swedish site also serves residents of Denmark, Norway, Finland, and Iceland.*

established joint ventures and launched Web sites in both the United Kingdom and Japan. The Nordic licensee later became a wholly owned subsidiary of E*Trade.[21]

Licensing has potential disadvantages, however. The firm has less control over the licensee than it would over its own production facilities. Furthermore, if the licensee is very successful, the firm has given up these profits, and if and when the contract ends, it may find it has created a competitor.

Contract Manufacturing

Contract manufacturing
A joint venture in which a company contracts with manufacturers in a foreign market to produce its product or provide its service.

Another option is **contract manufacturing**—the company contracts with manufacturers in the foreign market to produce its product or provide its service. Sears used this method in opening up department stores in Mexico and Spain, where it found qualified local manufacturers to produce many of the products it sells. The drawbacks of contract manufacturing are decreased control over the manufacturing process and loss of potential profits on manufacturing. The benefits are the chance to start faster, with less risk, and the later opportunity either to form a partnership with or to buy out the local manufacturer.

Management Contracting

Management contracting
A joint venture in which the domestic firm supplies the management know-how to a foreign company that supplies the capital; the domestic firm exports management services rather than products.

Under **management contracting,** the domestic firm supplies management know-how to a foreign company that supplies the capital. The domestic firm exports management services rather than products. Hilton uses this arrangement in managing hotels around the world.

Management contracting is a low-risk method of getting into a foreign market, and it yields income from the beginning. The arrangement is even more attractive if the contracting firm has an option to buy some share in the managed company later on. The arrangement is not sensible, however, if the company can put its scarce management talent to better uses or if it can make greater profits by undertaking the whole venture. Management contracting also prevents the company from setting up its own operations for a period of time.

Joint Ownership

Joint ownership
A joint venture in which a company joins investors in a foreign market to create a local business in which the company shares joint ownership and control.

Joint ownership ventures consist of one company joining forces with foreign investors to create a local business in which they share joint ownership and control. A company may buy an interest in a local firm, or the two parties may form a new busi-

Joint ownership: KFC entered Japan through a joint ownership venture with Japanese conglomerate Mitsubishi.

ness venture. Joint ownership may be needed for economic or political reasons. The firm may lack the financial, physical, or managerial resources to undertake the venture alone. Or a foreign government may require joint ownership as a condition for entry.

KFC entered Japan through a joint ownership venture with Japanese conglomerate Mitsubishi. KFC sought a good way to enter the large but difficult Japanese fast food market. In turn, Mitsubishi, one of Japan's largest poultry producers, understood the Japanese culture and had money to invest. Together, they helped KFC succeed in the semiclosed Japanese market. Surprisingly, with Mitsubishi's guidance, KFC developed decidedly un-Japanese positioning for its Japanese restaurants:

> ★ While its initial reception in Japan was great, KFC still had a number of obstacles to overcome. The Japanese were uncomfortable with the idea of fast food and franchising. They saw fast food as artificial, made by mechanical means, and unhealthy. KFC Japan knew that it had to build trust in the KFC brand and flew to Kentucky to do it. There it filmed the most authentic version of Colonel Sanders's beginnings possible. To show the philosophy of KFC—the southern hospitality, old American tradition, and authentic home cooking—the agency first created the quintessential southern mother. With "My Old Kentucky Home" by Stephen Foster playing in the background, the commercial showed Colonel Sanders's mother making and feeding her grandchildren KFC chicken made with 11 secret spices. It conjured up scenes of good home cookin' from the deep American South, positioning KFC as wholesome, aristocratic food. In the end, the Japanese people could not get enough of this special American chicken made with 11 spices. The campaign was hugely successful, and in less than 8 years KFC expanded its presence from 400 locations to more than 1,000. Most Japanese now know "My Old Kentucky Home" by heart.[22]

Joint ownership has certain drawbacks. The partners may disagree over investment, marketing, or other policies. Whereas many U.S. firms like to reinvest earnings for growth, local firms often prefer to take out these earnings; and whereas U.S. firms emphasize the role of marketing, local investors may rely on selling.

Direct investment
Entering a foreign market by developing foreign-based assembly or manufacturing facilities.

Direct Investment

The biggest involvement in a foreign market comes through **direct investment**—the development of foreign-based assembly or manufacturing facilities. If a company has gained experience in exporting and if the foreign market is large enough, foreign production facilities offer many advantages. The firm may have lower costs in the form of cheaper labor or raw materials, foreign government investment incentives, and freight savings. The firm may improve its image in the host country because it creates jobs. Generally, a firm develops a deeper relationship with government, customers, local suppliers, and distributors, allowing it to adapt its products to the local market better. Finally, the firm keeps full control over the investment and therefore can develop manufacturing and marketing policies that serve its long-term international objectives.

The main disadvantage of direct investment is that the firm faces many risks, such as restricted or devalued currencies, falling markets, or government changes. In some cases, a firm has no choice but to accept these risks if it wants to operate in the host country.

DECIDING ON THE GLOBAL MARKETING PROGRAM

Standardized marketing mix
An international marketing strategy for using basically the same product, advertising, distribution channels, and other elements of the marketing mix in all the company's international markets.

Adapted marketing mix
An international marketing strategy for adjusting the marketing mix elements to each international target market, bearing more costs but hoping for a larger market share and return.

Companies that operate in one or more foreign markets must decide how much, if at all, to adapt their marketing mixes to local conditions. At one extreme are global companies that use a **standardized marketing mix,** selling largely the same products and using the same marketing approaches worldwide. At the other extreme is an **adapted marketing mix.** In this case, the producer adjusts the marketing mix elements to each target market, bearing more costs but hoping for a larger market share and return.

The question of whether to adapt or standardize the marketing mix has been much debated in recent years. The marketing concept holds that marketing programs will be more effective if tailored to the unique needs of each targeted customer group. If this concept applies within a country, it should apply even more in international markets. Consumers in different countries have widely varied cultural backgrounds, needs and wants, spending power, product preferences, and shopping patterns. Because these differences are hard to change, most marketers adapt their products, prices, channels, and promotions to fit consumer desires in each country.

However, some global marketers are bothered by what they see as too much adaptation, which raises costs and dilutes global brand power. As a result, many companies have created so-called world brands—more or less the same product sold the same way to all consumers worldwide. Marketers at these companies believe that advances in communication, transportation, and travel are turning the world into a common marketplace. These marketers claim that people around the world want basically the same products and lifestyles. Despite what consumers say they want, all consumers want good products at lower prices.

Such arguments ring true. The development of the Internet, the rapid spread of cable and satellite TV around the world, and the creation of telecommunications networks linking previously remote places have all made the world a smaller place. For instance, the disproportionately American programming beamed into homes in the developing world has sparked a convergence of consumer appetites, particularly among youth. One economist calls these emerging consumers the "global MTV generation." "They prefer Coke to tea, Nikes to sandals, Chicken McNuggets to rice, and credit cards to cash," he says.[23] Fashion trends spread almost instantly, propelled by TV and Internet chat groups. Around the world, news and comment on almost any topic or product is available at the click of a mouse or twist of a dial. The resulting convergence of needs and wants has created global markets for standardized products, particularly among the young middle class.

Proponents of global standardization claim that international marketers should adapt products and marketing programs only when local wants cannot be changed or avoided. Standardization results in lower production, distribution, marketing, and management costs, and thus lets the company offer consumers higher quality and more reliable products at lower prices. In fact, some companies have successfully marketed global products for example, Coca-Cola soft drinks, McDonald's hamburgers, Black & Decker tools, and Sony Walkmans.

However, even for these "global" brands, companies make some adaptations. Moreover, the assertion that global standardization will lead to lower costs and prices, causing more goods to be snapped up by price-sensitive consumers, is debatable. Consider these examples:[24]

★ Mattel Toys had sold its Barbie doll successfully in dozens of countries without modification. But in Japan, it did not sell well. Takara, Mattel's Japanese licensee, surveyed eighth-grade Japanese girls and their parents and found that they thought the doll's breasts were too big and that its legs were too long. Mattel, however, was reluctant to modify the doll because this would require additional production, packaging, and advertising costs. Finally, Takara won out and Mattel made a special Japanese Barbie. Within two years, Takara had sold over 2 million of the modified dolls.

★ Frito-Lay had successfully sold its Cheetos cheese snacks in dozens of countries with little modification, but the company was stymied when it came to China. How do you sell a cheese-based product in a country where cheese is not a dietary staple? Brand managers at Guangzhou Frito-Lay would not be deterred. After consumer tests of 600 different flavors, the company launched a cheeseless version of Cheetos in "Savory American Cream" flavor and teriyaki-tasting "Zesty Japanese Steak." The flexibility paid off; after six months the brand was selling out across China.

★ Even MTV, with its largely global programming, has retrenched along more local lines. Pummeled by dozens of local music channels in Europe, such as Germany's *Viva*, Holland's *The Music Factory*, and Scandinavia's *ZTV*, MTV Europe has had to drop its pan-European programming, which featured a large amount of American and British pop along with local European favorites. In its place, the division created regional channels broadcast by four separate MTV stations—MTV: U.K. & Ireland, MTV: Northern Europe, MTV: Central Europe, and MTV: Southern Europe. Each of the four channels shows programs tailored to music tastes of its local market, along with more traditional pan-European pop selections. Within each region, MTV further subdivides its programming. For example, within the United Kingdom, MTV offers sister stations M2 and VH-1, along with three new digital channels: MTV Extra, MTV Base, and VH-1 Classic. Says the head of MTV Europe, "We hope to offer every MTV fan something he or she will like to watch any time of the day."

In these cases, incremental revenues from adapting products far exceeded the incremental costs.

So which approach is best—global standardization or adaptation? Clearly, global standardization is not an all-or-nothing proposition but rather a matter of degree. Companies should look for more standardization to help keep down costs and prices and to build greater global brand power. But they must not replace long-run marketing thinking with short-run financial thinking. Although standardization saves money, marketers must make certain that they offer what consumers in each country want.[25]

Many possibilities exist between the extremes of standardization and complete adaptation. For example, although Whirlpool ovens, refrigerators, clothes washers, and other major appliances share the same interiors worldwide, their outer styling and features are designed to meet the preferences of consumers in different countries. Coca-Cola sells virtually the same Coke beverage worldwide, and it pulls advertisements for specific markets from a common pool of ads designed to have cross-cultural appeal. However, Coca-Cola is less sweet or less carbonated in certain countries. The company also sells a variety of other beverages created specifically for the tastebuds of local markets and modifies its distribution channels according to local conditions.

Similarly, McDonald's uses the same basic operating formula in its restaurants around the world but adapts its menu to local tastes. For example, it uses chili sauce instead of ketchup on its hamburgers in Mexico. In India, where cows are considered sacred, McDonald's serves chicken, fish, vegetable burgers, and the Maharaja Mac—two all-mutton patties, special sauce, lettuce, cheese, pickles, onions on a sesame-seed bun. In Vienna, its restaurants include "McCafes," which offer coffee blended to local tastes, and in Korea, it sells roast pork on a bun with a garlicky soy sauce.[26]

Some international marketers suggest that companies should "think globally but act locally." They advocate a "glocal" strategy in which the firm standardizes certain core marketing elements and localizes others.[27] The corporate level gives strategic direction; local units focus on the individual consumer differences. They conclude: global marketing, yes; global standardization, not necessarily.

Product

Five strategies allow for adapting product and promotion to a foreign market (see Figure 19.3).[28] We first discuss the three product strategies and then turn to the two promotion strategies.

Straight product extension
Marketing a product in a foreign market without any change.

Straight product extension means marketing a product in a foreign market without any change. Top management tells its marketing people: "Take the product as is and find customers for it." The first step, however, should be to find out whether foreign consumers use that product and what form they prefer.

Straight extension has been successful in some cases and disastrous in others. Kellogg cereals, Gillette razors, IBM computer services, Heineken beer, and Black & Decker tools are all sold successfully in about the same form around the world. But General Foods introduced its standard powdered Jell-O in the British market only to find that British consumers prefer a solid wafer or cake form. Likewise, Philips began to make a profit in Japan only after it reduced the size of its coffeemakers to fit into smaller Japanese kitchens and its shavers to fit smaller Japanese hands. Straight extension is tempting because it involves no additional product

FIGURE 19.3   Five international product and promotion strategies

development costs, manufacturing changes, or new promotion. But it can be costly in the long run if products fail to satisfy foreign consumers.

Product adaptation
Adapting a product to meet local conditions or wants in foreign markets.

Product adaptation involves changing the product to meet local conditions or wants. For example, Procter & Gamble's Vidal Sassoon shampoos contain a single fragrance worldwide but the amount of scent varies by country: less in Japan, where subtle scents are preferred, and more in Europe. General Foods blends different coffees for the British (who drink their coffee with milk), the French (who drink their coffee black), and Latin Americans (who prefer a chicory taste). In Japan, Mister Donut serves coffee in smaller and lighter cups that better fit the fingers of the average Japanese consumer; even the doughnuts are a little smaller. Gerber serves the Japanese baby food fare that might turn the stomachs of many Western consumers—local favorites include flounder and spinach stew, cod roe spaghetti, mugwort casserole, and sardines ground up in white radish sauce. In Brazil, Levi's developed its Femina jeans featuring curvaceous cuts that provide the ultratight fit traditionally favored by Brazilian women. Finnish cellular phone superstar Nokia customized its 6100 series phone for every major market. Developers built in rudimentary voice recognition for Asia where keyboards are a problem and raised the ring volume so the phone could be heard on crowded Asian streets.[29]

In some instances, products must also be adapted to local superstitions or spiritual beliefs. In Asia, the supernatural world often relates directly to sales. Hyatt Hotels' experience with the concept of *feng shui* is a good example:

> A practice widely followed in China, Hong Kong, and Singapore (and which has spread to Japan, Vietnam, and Korea), *feng shui* means "wind and water." Practitioners of *feng shui*, or geomancers, will recommend the most favorable conditions for any venture, particularly the placement of office buildings and the arrangement of desks, doors, and other items within. To have good *feng shui*, a building should face the water and be flanked by mountains. However, it should not block the view of the mountain spirits. The Hyatt Hotel in Singapore was designed without *feng shui* in mind, and as a result had to be redesigned to boost business. Originally the front desk was parallel to the doors and road, and this was thought to lead to wealth flowing out. Furthermore, the doors were facing northwest, which easily let undesirable spirits in. The geomancer recommended design alterations so that wealth could be retained and undesirable spirits kept out.[30]

Product invention
Creating new products or services for foreign markets.

Product invention consists of creating something new for the foreign market. This strategy can take two forms. It might mean reintroducing earlier product forms that happen to be well adapted to the needs of a given country. For example, the National Cash Register Company reintroduced its crank-operated cash register at half the price of a modern cash register and sold large numbers in Asia, Latin America, and Spain. Or a company might create a new product to meet a need in another country. For example, an enormous need exists for low-cost, high-protein foods in less developed countries. Companies such as Quaker Oats, Swift, Monsanto, and Archer Daniels Midland are researching the nutrition needs of these countries, creating new foods, and developing advertising campaigns to gain product trial and acceptance. Product invention can be costly but the payoffs are worthwhile.

Promotion

Companies can either adopt the same promotion strategy they used in the home market or change it for each local market. Consider advertising messages. Some global companies use a standardized advertising theme around the world. For

Standardized advertising: To help communicate its global reach, IBM Global Services uses a standardized advertising theme in dozens of countries around the world: "People Who Think. People Who Do. People Who Get It." These ads are from Canada and the United Kingdom.

example, to help communicate its global reach, IBM Global Services runs virtually identical "People Who Think. People Who Do. People Who Get It." ads in dozens of countries around the world. Of course, even in highly standardized promotion campaigns, some small changes might be required to adjust for language and minor cultural differences. For instance, when Heinz Pet Food introduced its 9 Lives cat food in Russia, it used its standardized advertising featuring Morris the Cat. It turns out, however, that Morris needed a makeover. Russian consumers prefer a fatter-looking spokeskitty (it's considered healthier), so Heinz put a beefier Morris on the package.[31]

Colors also are changed sometimes to avoid taboos in other countries. Purple is associated with death in most of Latin America; white is a mourning color in Japan; and green is associated with jungle sickness in Malaysia. Even names must be changed. In Sweden, Helene Curtis changed the name of its Every Night Shampoo to Every Day because Swedes usually wash their hair in the morning. Kellogg also had to rename Bran Buds cereal in Sweden, where the name roughly translates as "burned farmer." (See Marketing Highlight 19.3 for more on language blunders in international marketing.)

Communication adaptation
A global communication strategy of fully adapting advertising messages to local markets.

Other companies follow a strategy of **communication adaptation,** fully adapting their advertising messages to local markets. The Schwinn Bicycle Company might use a pleasure theme in the United States and a safety theme in Scandinavia. Kellogg ads in the United States promote the taste and nutrition of Kellogg's cereals versus competitors' brands. In France, where consumers drink little milk and eat little for breakfast, Kellogg's ads must convince consumers that cereals are a tasty and healthful

WATCH YOUR LANGUAGE!

Many global companies have had difficulty crossing the language barrier, with results ranging from mild embarrassment to outright failure. Seemingly innocuous brand names and advertising phrases can take on unintended or hidden meanings when translated into other languages. Careless translations can make a marketer look downright foolish to foreign consumers.

We've all run across examples when buying products from other countries. Here's one from a firm in Taiwan attempting to instruct children on how to install a ramp on a garage for toy cars: "Before you play with, fix waiting plate by yourself as per below diagram. But after you once fixed it, you can play with as is and no necessary to fix off again." Many U.S. firms are guilty of such atrocities when marketing abroad.

The classic language blunders involve standardized brand names that do not translate well. When Coca-Cola first marketed Coke in China in the 1920s, it developed a group of Chinese characters that, when pronounced, sounded like the product name. Unfortunately, the characters actually translated to mean "bite the wax tadpole." Now, the characters on Chinese Coke bottles translate as "happiness in the mouth."

Several U.S. carmakers have had similar problems when their brand names crashed into the language barrier. Chevy's Nova translated into Spanish as *no va*—"it doesn't go." GM changed the name to Caribe and sales increased. Ford introduced its Fiera truck only to discover that the name means "ugly old woman" in Spanish. Rolls-Royce avoided the name Silver Mist in German markets, where *mist* means "manure." Sunbeam, however, entered the German market with its Mist Stick hair curling iron. As should have been expected, the Germans had little use for a "manure wand." A similar fate awaited Colgate when it introduced a toothpaste in France called Cue, the name of a notorious porno magazine.

One well-intentioned firm sold its shampoo in Brazil under the name Evitol. It soon realized it was claiming to sell a "dandruff contraceptive." An American company reportedly had trouble marketing Pet milk in French-speaking areas. It seems that the word *pet* in French means, among other things, "to break wind." Hunt-Wesson introduced its Big John products in Quebec as Gros Jos before learning that it means "big breasts" in French. This gaffe had no apparent effect on sales. Interbrand of London, the firm that created household names such as Prozac and Acura, recently developed a brand-name "hall of shame" list, which contained these and other foreign brand names you're never likely to see inside the local A&P: Krapp toilet paper (Denmark), Crapsy Fruit cereal (France), Happy End toilet paper (Germany), Mukk yogurt (Italy), Zit lemonade (Germany), Poo curry powder (Argentina), and Pschitt lemonade (France).

Travelers often encounter well-intentioned advice from service firms that takes on meanings very different from those intended. The menu in one Swiss restaurant proudly stated: "Our wines leave you nothing to hope for." Signs in a Japanese hotel pronounced: "You are invited to take advantage of the chambermaid." At a laundry in Rome, it was: "Ladies, leave your clothes here and spend the afternoon having a good time." The brochure at a Tokyo car rental offered this sage advice: "When passenger of foot heave in sight, tootle the horn. Trumpet him melodiously at first, but if he still obstacles your passage, tootle him with vigor."

Advertising themes often lose—or gain—something in the translation. The Coors beer slogan "get loose with Coors" in Spanish came out as "get the runs with Coors." Coca-Cola's "Coke adds life" theme in Japanese translated into "Coke brings your ancestors back from the dead." In Chinese, the KFC slogan "finger-lickin' good" came out as "eat your fingers off." Frank Perdue's classic line, "It takes a tough man to make a tender chicken," took on added meaning in Spanish: "It takes a sexually stimulated man to make a chicken affectionate." Even when the language is the same, word usage may differ from country to country. Thus, the British ad line for Electrolux vacuum cleaners—"Nothing sucks like an Electrolux"—would capture few customers in the United States.

Sources: See David A. Ricks, "Products That Crashed into the Language Barrier," *Business and Society Review,* Spring 1983, pp. 46–50; David A. Ricks, "Perspectives: Translation Blunders in International Business," *Journal of Language for International Business* 7, no. 2, 1996, pp. 50–55; David W. Helin, "When Slogans Go Wrong," *American Demographics,* February 1992, p. 14; "But Will It Sell in Tulsa," *Newsweek,* March 17, 1997, p. 8; "What You Didn't Learn in Marketing 101," *Sales & Marketing Management,* May 1997, p. 20; Ken Friedenreich, "The Lingua Too France," *World Trade,* April 1998, p. 98; and Richard P. Carpenter, "What They Meant to Say Was . . ." *Boston Globe,* August 2, 1998, p. M6.

breakfast. In India, where many consumers eat heavy, fried breakfasts, Kellogg's advertising convinces buyers to switch to a lighter, more nutritious breakfast diet.

Media also need to be adapted internationally because media availability varies from country to country. TV advertising time is very limited in Europe, for instance, ranging from four hours a day in France to none in Scandinavian countries. Advertisers must buy time months in advance, and they have little control over airtimes. Magazines also vary in effectiveness. For example, magazines are a major medium in Italy and a minor one in Austria. Newspapers are national in the United Kingdom but are only local in Spain.

Price

Companies also face many problems in setting their international prices. For example, how might Black & Decker price its power tools globally? It could set a uniform price all around the world, but this amount would be too high a price in poor countries and not high enough in rich ones. It could charge what consumers in each country would bear, but this strategy ignores differences in the actual costs from country to country. Finally, the company could use a standard markup of its costs everywhere, but this approach might price Black & Decker out of the market in some countries where costs are high.

Regardless of how companies go about pricing their products, their foreign prices probably will be higher than their domestic prices. A Gucci handbag may sell for $60 in Italy and $240 in the United States. Why? Gucci faces a *price escalation* problem. It must add the cost of transportation, tariffs, importer margin, wholesaler margin, and retailer margin to its factory price. Depending on these added costs, the product may have to sell for two to five times as much in another country to make the same profit. For example, a pair of Levi's jeans that sells for $30 in the United States typically fetches $63 in Tokyo and $88 in Paris. A computer that sells for $1,000 in New York may cost £1,000 in the United Kingdom. A Chrysler automobile priced at $10,000 in the United States sells for more than $47,000 in South Korea.

Another problem involves setting a price for goods that a company ships to its foreign subsidiaries. If the company charges a foreign subsidiary too much, it may end up paying higher tariff duties even while paying lower income taxes in that country. If the company charges its subsidiary too little, it can be charged with *dumping*. Dumping occurs when a company either charges less than its costs or less than it charges in its home market. Thus, Harley-Davidson accused Honda and Kawasaki of dumping motorcycles on the U.S. market. The U.S. International Trade Commission agreed and responded with a special five-year tariff on Japanese heavy motorcycles, starting at 45 percent in 1983 and gradually dropping to 10 percent by 1988. Various governments are always watching for dumping abuses, and they often force companies to set the price charged by other competitors for the same or similar products.[32]

Recent economic and technological forces have had an impact on global pricing. For example, in the European Union, the transition by 11 countries to a single currency will certainly reduce the amount of price differentiation. In 1998, for instance, a bottle of Gatorade cost 3.5 European Currency Units (ECU) in Germany but only about 0.9 in Spain. Once consumers recognize price differentiation by country, companies will be forced to harmonize prices throughout the countries that have adopted the single currency. Companies and marketers that offer the most unique or necessary products or services will be least affected by such "price transparency." For instance, Mail Boxes, Etc., which has 350 stores in Europe, believes that customers who need to send faxes won't refuse to do so because it costs more in Paris than in Italy.[33]

The Internet will also make global price differences more obvious. When firms sell their wares over the Internet, customers can see how much products sell for in different countries. They might even be able to order a given product directly from the company location or dealer offering the lowest price. This will force companies toward more standardized international pricing.[34]

Distribution Channels

Whole-channel view

Designing international channels that take into account all the necessary links in distributing the seller's products to final buyers, including the seller's headquarters organization, channels among nations, and channels within nations.

The international company must take a **whole-channel view** of the problem of distributing products to final consumers. Figure 19.4 shows the three major links between the seller and the final buyer. The first link, the *seller's headquarters organization,* supervises the channels and is part of the channel itself. The second link, *channels between nations,* moves the products to the borders of the foreign nations. The third link, *channels within nations,* moves the products from their foreign entry point to the final consumers. Some U.S. manufacturers may think their job is done once the product leaves their hands, but they would do well to pay more attention to its handling within foreign countries.

Channels of distribution within countries vary greatly from nation to nation. First, there are the large differences in the *numbers and types of intermediaries* serving each foreign market. For example, a U.S. company marketing in China must operate through a frustrating maze of state-controlled wholesalers and retailers. Chinese distributors often carry competitors' products and frequently refuse to share even basic sales and marketing information with their suppliers. Hustling for sales is an alien concept to Chinese distributors, who are used to selling all they can obtain. Working with or getting around this system sometimes requires substantial time and investment.

When Coke first entered China, for example, customers bicycled up to bottling plants to get their soft drinks. Many shopkeepers still don't have enough electricity to run soft drink coolers. Now, Coca-Cola is setting up direct-distribution channels, investing heavily in refrigerators and trucks, and upgrading wiring so that more retailers can install coolers.[35] Moreover, it's always on the lookout for innovative distribution approaches:

> Stroll through any residential area in a Chinese city and sooner or later you'll encounter a senior citizen with a red arm band eyeing strangers suspiciously. These are the pensioners who staff the neighborhood committees, which act as street-level watchdogs for the ruling Communist Party. In Shanghai, however, some of these socialist guardians have been signed up by the ultimate symbol of American capitalism, Coca-Cola. As part of its strategy to get the product to the customer, Coke approached 14 neighborhood committees ... with a proposal. The head of Coke's Shanghai division outlines the deal: "We told them, 'You have some old people who aren't doing much. Why don't we stock our product in your office? Then you can sell it, earn some commission, and raise a bit of cash.' " Done. So ... how are the party snoops adapting to the market? Not badly, reports the manager. "We use the neighborhood committees as a sales force," he says. Sales aren't spectacular, but because the committees supervise housing projects with up to 200 families, they have proved to be useful vehicles for building brand awareness.[36]

FIGURE 19.4   Whole-channel concept for international marketing

A "neighbor committee" member sells Coke in Shanghai.

Another difference lies in the *size and character of retail units* abroad. Whereas large-scale retail chains dominate the U.S. scene, much retailing in other countries is done by many small, independent retailers. In India, millions of retailers operate tiny shops or sell in open markets. Their markups are high, but the actual price is lowered through haggling. Supermarkets could offer lower prices, but supermarkets are difficult to build and open because of many economic and cultural barriers. Incomes are low, and people prefer to shop daily for small amounts rather than weekly for large amounts. They also lack storage and refrigeration to keep food for several days. Packaging is not well developed because it would add too much to the cost. These factors have kept large-scale retailing from spreading rapidly in developing countries.

DECIDING ON THE GLOBAL MARKETING ORGANIZATION

Companies manage their international marketing activities in at least three different ways: Most companies first organize an export department, then create an international division, and finally become a global organization.

A firm normally gets into international marketing by simply shipping out its goods. If its international sales expand, the company organizes an *export department* with a sales manager and a few assistants. As sales increase, the export department can expand to include various marketing services so that it can actively go after business. If the firm moves into joint ventures or direct investment, the export department will no longer be adequate.

Many companies get involved in several international markets and ventures. A company may export to one country, license to another, have a joint ownership venture in a third, and own a subsidiary in a fourth. Sooner or later it will create an *international division* or subsidiary to handle all its international activity.

International divisions are organized in a variety of ways. The international division's corporate staff consists of marketing, manufacturing, research, finance, planning, and personnel specialists. They plan for and provide services to various operating units, which can be organized in one of three ways. They can be *geographical organizations,* with country managers who are responsible for salespeople, sales branches, distributors, and licensees in their respective countries. Or the operating units can be *world product groups,* each responsible for worldwide sales of different product groups. Finally, operating units can be *international subsidiaries,* each responsible for its own sales and profits.

Several firms have passed beyond the international division stage and become truly *global organizations.* They stop thinking of themselves as national marketers who sell abroad and start thinking of themselves as global marketers. The top corporate management and staff plan worldwide manufacturing facilities, marketing policies, financial flows, and logistical systems. The global operating units report directly to the chief executive or executive committee of the organization, not to the head of an international division. Executives are trained in worldwide operations, not just domestic *or* international. The company recruits management from many countries, buys components and supplies where they cost the least, and invests where the expected returns are greatest.

★ Proctor & Gamble recently took a big step in this direction by undertaking a global reorganization called Organization 2005. P&G is replacing its old geography-based organization with seven global business units organized by categories like baby care, beauty care, and fabric-and-home care. Each unit is located in a different country. The reorganization is intended to streamline product development processes and quickly bring innovative products to the global market. These units will develop and sell their products on a worldwide basis.[37]

Moving into the twenty-first century, major companies must become more global if they hope to compete. As foreign companies successfully invade their domestic markets, companies must move more aggressively into foreign markets. They will have to change from companies that treat their international operations as secondary, to companies that view the entire world as a single borderless market.[38]

REVIEW OF CONCEPT CONNECTIONS

In the past, U.S. companies paid little attention to international trade. If they could pick up some extra sales through exporting, that was fine. But the big market was at home, and it teemed with opportunities. Companies today can no longer afford to pay attention only to their domestic market, regardless of its size. Many industries are global industries, and firms that operate globally achieve lower costs and higher brand awareness. At the same time, *global marketing* is risky because of variable exchange rates, unstable governments, protectionist tariffs and trade barriers, and several other factors. Given the potential gains and risks of international marketing, companies need a systematic way to make their international marketing decisions.

1. Discuss how the international trade system, economic, political–legal, and cultural environments affect a company's international marketing decisions.

A company must understand the *global marketing environment,* especially the international trade system. It must assess each foreign market's *economic, political–legal,* and *cultural characteristics.* The company must then decide whether it wants to go abroad and consider the potential risks and benefits. It must decide on the volume of international sales it wants, how many countries it wants to market in, and which specific markets it wants to enter. This decision calls for weighing the probable rate of return on investment against the level of risk.

2. Describe three key approaches to entering international markets.

The company must decide how to enter each chosen market—whether through *exporting, joint venturing,* or *direct*

investment. Many companies start as exporters, move to joint ventures, and finally make a direct investment in foreign markets. In *exporting,* the company enters a foreign market by sending and selling products through international marketing intermediaries (indirect exporting) or the company's own department, branch, or sales representative or agents (direct exporting). When establishing a *joint venture,* a company enters foreign markets by joining with foreign companies to produce or market a product or service. In *licensing,* the company enters a foreign market by contracting with a licensee in the foreign market, offering the right to use a manufacturing process, trademark, patent, trade secret, or other item of value for a fee or royalty.

3. Explain how companies adapt their marketing mixes for international markets.

Companies must also decide how much their products, promotion, price, and channels should be adapted for each foreign market. At one extreme, global companies use a *standardized marketing mix* worldwide. Others use an *adapted marketing mix,* in which they adjust the marketing mix to each target market, bearing more costs but hoping for a larger market share and return.

4. Identify the three major forms of international marketing organization.

The company must develop an effective organization for international marketing. Most firms start with an *export department* and graduate to an *international division.* A few become *global organizations,* with worldwide marketing planned and managed by the top officers of the company. Global organizations view the entire world as a single, borderless market.

KEY TERMS

Adapted marketing mix
Communication adaptation
Contract manufacturing
Countertrade
Direct investment
Economic community
Embargo
Exchange controls

Exporting
Global firm
Joint ownership
Joint venturing
Licensing
Management contracting
Nontariff trade barriers
Product adaptation

Product invention
Quota
Standardized marketing mix
Straight product extension
Tariff
Whole-channel view

ISSUES FOR DISCUSSION

1. The world is shrinking rapidly with the advent of faster communication, transportation, and financial flows. The terms *global industry* and *global firm* are becoming more common. Define these terms and provide an example of each. Explain your examples.

2. When exporting goods to another country, a marketer may face various trade restrictions. Discuss the effects that each of these restrictions might have on an exporter's marketing mix: (a) tariffs, (b) quotas, and (c) embargoes.

3. What is a free trade zone? What have been the positive and negative benefits of NAFTA to each of its member nations? Why have U.S. trade unions been against NAFTA? If you were General Motors, how could you use NAFTA to build and market better vehicles?

4. A country's industrial structure shapes its product and service needs, income, levels, and employment levels. Discuss examples of countries exhibiting each of the four major types of industrial structures.

5. With all the problems facing companies that "go global," explain why so many companies are choosing to expand

internationally. What are the advantages of expanding beyond the domestic market?

6. Before going abroad, a company should try to define its international marketing objectives, policies, and modes of entry. Assume that you are a product manager for Nike. Outline a plan for expanding your operations and marketing efforts into Africa.

7. Once a company has decided to sell in a foreign country, it must determine the best mode of entry. Assume that you are the marketing manager for Mountain Dew and devise a plan for marketing your product in China. Pick a mode of entry, explain your marketing strategy, and comment on possible difficulties you might encounter.

8. Which type of international marketing organization would you suggest for the following companies: (a) eToys (www.etoys.com), (b) a European perfume manufacturer that plans to expand into the United States, and (c) DaimlerChrysler planning to sell its full line of products in the Middle East.

MARKETING APPLICATIONS

1. "Defend Our Forests—Clear-cut the WTO!" "WTO Breeds Greed." "WTO: Fix It or Nix It!" These statements were issued by protesters at the 1999 World Trade Organization talks in Seattle, Washington. The protests even led to riots, and the National Guard had to be called to restore order. Why all the mobilization against globalization? It used to be that free trade and globalization talks involved mostly discussions about tariffs and quotas. Now the two equate with culture, sovereignty, and power. Trade talks were once held in smoke-filled rooms by diplomats. Today, they are conducted via television and the World Wide Web. The Seattle protesters feel damaged by globalization. They argue globalization is about exploitation and environmental destruction. They feel that it will result in

the assimilation of people, markets, and cultures into a more generic whole. For more information, visit the Center for International Business Education and Research–Michigan State University (ciber.bus.msu.edu/busres.htm), the International Trade Association (www.ita.doc.gov), the *1998 World Fact Book,* a CIA publication (www.odic.gov/cia/publications/factbook/index.html), the World Bank (www.worldbank.org), and the World Trade Organization (www.wto.org).

a. What does the World Trade Organization attempt to do? Who are the member nations?

b. Why were so many protesters against globalization at the WTO's Seattle conference? How should the WTO proceed in the face of such protests?

c. Write a short position paper either defending or rejecting globalization.

d. What are the ramifications of China joining the World Trade Organization?

2. Nowhere is international competition more apparent than in the digital camera market. Overnight, the advent of digital cameras has changed the way many photographers view their equipment. Digital cameras offer opportunities for reproduction and Internet viewing unmatched by more traditional products. However, the market is also uncharted, chaotic, and increasingly crowded, with more than 20 manufacturers worldwide. The latest entrant is film giant Fuji (www.fujifilm.com). As the world's number-two producer, Fuji now plans to meet or beat Kodak (www.kodak.com), Sony (www.sony.com), Olympus (www.olympus.com), and Konica (www.konica.com) in digital camera products. Fuji introduced its first digital cameras in its own backyard—Japan, which is also a Sony stronghold. One factor motivating the move into digital cameras was its inability to erode Kodak's worldwide share of the film market. If the wave of the future turns out to be digital, Fuji plans to ride the wave's crest for as long as it can.

a. Analyze Fuji's strategy of entering the digital camera market. What challenges will Fuji most likely face? How might Fuji's traditional strengths in film aid its efforts in the new digital camera market?

b. What world markets should Fuji consider after Japan? Explain.

c. If you were the marketing manager of Fuji, what advertising strategy would you suggest for Fuji's new product venture? What distribution strategy?

d. What actions will Kodak, Olympus, Konica, and Sony probably take to counter Fuji's entry?

 INTERNET CONNECTIONS

"WORLD WIDE WEB" IS NOT A MISNOMER

U.S.-based Web sites often offer different services and products in different markets. One fertile market for U.S. firms is Europe. Visit www.yahoo.co.uk and compare the services offered there with their U.S. branch counterparts. Complete the following table.

Service	Offered by Yahoo! U.K. but not by Yahoo! U.S.	Offered by Yahoo! U.S. but not by Yahoo! U.K.

Now visit www.amazon.co.uk and complete a similar table.

Service	Offered by Amazon U.K. but not by Amazon U.S.	Offered by Amazon U.S. but not by Amazon U.K.

FOR DISCUSSION

1. What is the size of the U.S. Internet market vs. the U.K.? Visit Cyberatlas (cyberatlas.internet.com) or Nua (www.nua.ie) to answer this question.

2. What proportion of the U.S. population is online? The U.K. population?

3. How are the ads different on Yahoo!'s U.K. site?

4. What different search option is available on Yahoo!'s U.K. site?

5. Why do you think Amazon offers fewer services in the U.K. market?

6. Yahoo! provides free Internet access in the U.K. market. Why don't they do the same in the U.S. market? *Hint:* Research a company called FreeNet (www.freenet.com).

SAVVY SITES

- The International Trade Association (www.ita.doc.gov) is dedicated to assisting U.S. companies compete globally. The U.S. Department of Commerce maintains this site.
- The CIA World Factbook (www.odci.gov/cia/publications/factbook), maintained by the Central Intelligence Agency,

has economic and other information about most countries in the world.
- Another Department of Commerce site that provides lots of data about international business is STAT-USA (www.stat-usa.gov).

NOTES

1. Extracts and quotes from Marc Gunther, "They All Want to Be Like Mike," *Fortune*, July 21, 1997, pp. 51–53: © 1997 Time, Inc., all rights reserved; and Warren Cohen, "Slam-Dunk Diplomacy," *U.S. News & World Report*, June 8, 1998, p. 7. Also see Stefan Fatsis, "NBA Bravely Plans for Post-Jordan Era," *Wall Street Journal*, February 6, 1998, p. B1; "NBA Will Face Difficult Recovery from Lockout," *Greensboro News Record*, December 24, 1998, p. C2; Mark Hyman, "Another Ruined Season That Wasn't," *Business Week*, June 7, 1999, p. 40; David Bauder, "Mike Takes the Air out of NBA Ratings," *Raleigh News & Observer*, June 24, 1999, p. E7; "Worldwide TV Coverage of the 1999 NBA Finals," accessed online at www.nba.com, September 1999; and Daniel Roth, "The NBA's Next Shot," *Fortune*, February 21, 2000, pp. 207–215.

2. John Alden, "What in the World Drives UPS?" *International Business*, April 1998, pp. 6–7; Karen Pennar, "Two Steps Forward, One Step Back," *Business Week*, August 31, 1998, p. 116; and Michelle Wirth Fellman, "A New World for Marketers," *Marketing News*, May 10, 1999, p. 13.

3. See "Top 50 U.S. Industrial Exporters," *Fortune*, August 22, 1994, p. 132; Edmund Faltermayer, "Competitiveness: How U.S. Companies Stack Up Now," *Fortune*, April 18, 1994, pp. 52–64; and "The Fortune Global 5 Hundred," *Fortune*, August 2, 1999, p. F1.

4. "The Unique Japanese," *Fortune*, November 24, 1986, p. 8. For more on nontariff and other barriers, see Warren J. Keegan and Mark C. Green, *Principles of Global Marketing* (Upper Saddle River, NJ: Prentice Hall, 1997), pp. 200–203.

5. Douglas Harbrecht and Owen Ullmann, "Finally GATT May Fly," *Business Week*, December 29, 1993, pp. 36–37; and Ping Deng, "Impact of GATT Uruguay Round on Various Industries," *American Business Review*, June 1998, pp. 22–29. Also see Charles W. L. Hill, *International Business* (Chicago: Richard A. Irwin, 1997), pp. 165–68; "Special Article: World Trade: Fifty Years On," *The Economist*, May 16, 1998, pp. 21–23; and Helene Cooper, "The Millennium—Trade & Commerce: Trading Blocks," *Wall Street Journal*, January 11, 1999, p. R50.

6. Stanley Reed, "We Have Liftoff! The Strong Launch of the Euro Is Hailed Around the World," *Business Week*, January 18, 1999, pp. 34–37.

7. James Welsh, "Enter the Euro," *World Trade*, January 1999, pp. 34–38.

8. For more on the European Union, see "Around Europe in 40 Years," *The Economist*, May 31, 1997, p. S4; "European Union to Begin Expansion," *New York Times*, March 30, 1998, p. A5; Joan Warner, "Mix Us Culturally? It's Impossible," *Business Week*, April 27, 1998, p. 108; and Paul J. Deveney, "World Watch," *Wall Street Journal*, May 20, 1999, p. A12.

9. Aaron Robertson, "North America: Trade Brisk Despite Bumps in the Road," *World Trade*, May 1999, pp. 28–32; and Tom Foster, "The NAFTA Gateway," *Logistics Management and Distribution Report*, May 1999, pp. S10–S11.

10. Larry Rohter, "Latin America and Europe to Talk Trade," *New York Times*, June 26, 1999, p. 2.

11. For more reading, see Paul Magnusson, "NAFTA: Where's That Giant Sucking Sound?" *Business Week*, July 7, 1997, p. 45; David M. Gould, "Has NAFTA Changed North American Trade?" *Economic Review—Federal Reserve Bank of Dallas*, first quarter, 1998, pp. 12–23; Lori Wallach and Michelle Sforza, "NAFTA at 5," *The Nation*, January 25, 1999, p. 7.

12. David Woodruff, "Ready to Shop Until They Drop," *Business Week*, June 22, 1998, pp. 104–8.

13. Manjeet Kripalani, "As the Politicians Squabble, India Stagnates," *Business Week*, May 5, 1997, p. 58; and Amy Louise Kazmin, "Why New Delhi Is Picking on Pepsi," *Business Week*, May 18, 1998, p. 54.

14. For these and other examples, see Louis Kraar, "How to Sell to Cashless Buyers," *Fortune*, November 7, 1988, pp. 147–54; Nathaniel Gilbert, "The Case for Countertrade," *Across the Board*, May 1992, pp. 43–45; Kwanena Anyane-Ntow and Santhi C. Harvey, "A Countertrade Primer," *Management Accounting (USA)*, April 1995, p. 47; Darren McDermott and S. Karen Witcher, "Bartering Gains Currency," *Wall Street Journal*, April 6, 1998, p. A10; and Anne Millen Porter, "Global Economic Meltdown Boosts Barter Business," *Purchasing*, February 11, 1999, pp. 21–25.

15. Rebecca Piirto Heath, "Think Globally," *Marketing Tools*, October 1996, pp. 49–54; and "The Power of Writing," *National Geographic*, August 1999, p. 128–29.

16. For other examples, see Sak Onkvisit and John J. Shaw, *International Marketing: Analysis and Strategy* (Upper Saddle River, NJ: Prentice Hall, 1997), chap. 6, "Tips, Tricks and Pitfalls to Avoid When Doing Business in the Tough but Lucrative Korean Market," *Business America*, June 1997, p. 7; Dana May Casperson, "Minding Your Manners in Latin America," *Sales & Marketing Management*, March 1998, p. 96; Valerie Frazee, "Getting Started in Mexico," *Workforce*, January 1997, pp. 16–17; Teresa C. Morrison, Wayne A. Conaway, and Joseph J. Douress, *Dun & Bradstreet's Guide to Doing Business Around the World* (New York: Prentice Hall, 1997); and Philip Kotler, *Marketing Management: Analysis, Planning, Implementation, and Control*, 10th ed. (Upper Saddle River, NJ: Prentice Hall, 2000), chap. 7.

17. Gail Edmondson, "The Beauty of Global Branding," *Business Week*, June 28, 1999, pp. 70–75.

18. Charles A. Coulombe, "Global Expansion: The Unstoppable Crusade," *Success*, September 1994, pp. 18–20; "Amway Hopes to Set Up Sales Network in India," *Wall Street Journal*, February 17, 1998, p. B8; and Gerald S. Couzens, "Dick Devos," *Success*, November 1998, pp. 52–57.

19. See "Crest, Colgate Bare Teeth in Competition for China," *Advertising Age International*, November 1996, p. I3; Mark L. Clifford, "How You Can Win in China," *Business Week*, May 26,

1997, pp. 66–68; and Ben Davies, "The Biggest Market Retains Its Luster," *Asia Money,* January 1998, pp. 47–49.

20. Linda Grant, "GE's 'Smart Bomb' Strategy," *Fortune,* July 21, 1997, pp. 109–10; Richard J. Babyak, "GE Appliances: The Polar Approach," *Appliance Manufacturer,* February 1997, p. G22; and Joe Jancsurak, "Asia to Drive World Appliance Growth," *Appliance Manufacturer,* February 1999, pp. G3–G6.

21. Robert Neff, "In Japan, They're Goofy About Disney," *Business Week,* March 12, 1990, p. 64; and "In Brief: e-Trade Licensing Deal Gives It an Israeli Link," *American Banker,* May 11, 1998.

22. See Cynthia Kemper, "KFC Tradition Sold Japan on Chicken," *Denver Post,* June 7, 1998, p. J4.

23. Lawrence Donegan, "Heavy Job Rotation MTV Europe Sacks 80 Employees in the Name of 'Regionalisation,' " *The Guardian,* November 21, 1997, p. 19.

24. Karen Benezra, "Fritos 'Round the World," *Brandweek,* March 27, 1995, pp. 32, 35; Cyndee Miller, "Chasing Global Dream," *Marketing News,* December 2, 1996, pp. 1, 2; and Christian Lorenz, "MTV Europe Launches Channels," *Billboard,* February 27, 1999, p. 48.

25. See Theodore Levitt, "The Globalization of Markets," *Harvard Business Review,* May–June 1983, pp. 92–102; David M. Szymanski, Sundar G. Bharadwaj, and Rajan Varadarajan, "Standardization versus Adaptation of International Marketing Strategy: An Empirical Investigation," *Journal of Marketing,* October 1993, pp. 1–17, Ashish Banerjee, "Global Campaigns Don't Work; Multinationals Do," *Advertising Age,* April 18, 1994, p. 23; Miller, "Chasing Global Dream," pp. 1, 2; Jeryl Whitelock and Carole Pimblett, "The Standardization Debate in International Marketing," *Journal of Global Marketing,* 1997, p. 22; and David A. Aaker and Ericj Joachimsthaler, "The Lure of Global Branding," *Harvard Business Review,* November–December 1999, pp. 137–44.

26. See "In India, Beef-Free Mickie D," *Business Week,* April 7, 1995, p. 52; Jeff Walters, "Have Brand Will Travel," *Brandweek,* October 6, 1997, pp. 22–26; and David Barboza, "From Abroad, McDonald's Finds Value in Local Control," *New York Times,* February 12, 1999, p. 1.

27. See Martha M. Hamilton, "Going Global: A World of Difference," *Washington Post,* May 10, 1998, p. H1.

28. See Warren J. Keegan, *Global Marketing Management,* 4th ed. (Upper Saddle River, NJ: Prentice Hall, 1989), pp. 378–81; and Warren J. Keegan and Mark C. Green, *Principles of Global Marketing* (Upper Saddle River, NJ: Prentice Hall, 1997), pp. 294–98.

29. For these and other examples, see Andrew Kupfer, "How to Be a Global Manager," *Fortune,* March 14, 1988, pp. 52–58; Maria Shao, "For Levi's: A Flattering Fit Overseas," *Business Week,* November 5, 1990, 76–77; Joseph Weber, "Campbell: Now It's M-M-Global," *Business Week,* March 15, 1993, pp. 52–53; Zachary Schiller, "Make It Simple," *Business Week,* September 9, 1996, p. 102; Chester Dawson, "Gerber Feeding Booming Japanese Baby Food Market," *Durham Herald-Sun,* February 21, 1998, p. C10; and Jack Neff, "Test It in Paris, France, Launch It in Paris, Texas," *Advertising Age,* May 31, 1999, p. 28.

30. J. S. Perry Hobson, "*Feng Shui*: Its Impacts on the Asian Hospitality Industry," *International Journal of Contemporary Hospitality Management,* 6, no. 6, 1994, pp. 21–26; Bernd H. Schmitt and Yigang Pan, "In Asia, the Supernatural Means Sales," *New York Times,* February 19, 1995, pp. 3, 11; and Sally Taylor, "Tackling the Curse of Bad Feng Shui," *Publishers Weekly,* April 27, 1998, p. 24.

31. Erika Rasmusson, "Global Warning," *Sales & Marketing Management,* November 1998, p. 17; and Bradley Johnson, "IBM Talks Global Clout, in Foreign Languages," *Advertising Age,* June 7, 1999, p. 10.

32. See Michael Oneal, "Harley-Davidson: Ready to Hit the Road Again," *Business Week,* July 21, 1986, p. 70; and "EU Proposes Dumping Change," *East European Markets,* February 14, 1997, pp. 2–3.

33. Maricris G. Briones, "The Euro Starts Here," *Marketing News,* July 20, 1998, pp. 1, 39.

34. Ram Charan, "The Rules Have Changed," *Fortune,* March 16, 1998, pp. 159–62.

35. See Maria Shao, "Laying the Foundation for the Great Mall of China," *Business Week,* January 25, 1988, pp. 68–69; and Mark L. Clifford and Nicole Harris, "Coke Pours into China," *Business Week,* October 28, 1996, p. 73.

36. Richard Tomlinson, "The China Card," *Fortune,* May 25, 1998, p. 82; and Paul Mooney, "Deals on Wheels," *Far East Economic Review,* May 20, 1999, p. 53.

37. Peter Galuszka and Ellen Neuborne, "P&G's Hottest New Product: P&G," *Business Week,* October 5, 1998, p. 96.

38. See Kenichi Ohmae, "Managing in a Borderless World," *Harvard Business Review,* May–June 1989, pp. 152–61, William J. Holstein, "The Stateless Corporation," *Business Week,* May 14, 1990, pp. 98–105; and John A. Byrne and Kathleen Kerwin, "Borderless Management," *Business Week,* May 23, 1994, pp. 24–26.

COMPANY CASE

19

Wal-Mart: Piling 'Em High and Selling 'Em Cheap All Around the Globe!

The Internal Point of View: "Wal-Mart employees who do not think globally are working for the wrong company."—David Glass, chief executive, Wal-Mart

The External Point of View: "Wal-Mart must think and act as if it's a global company. Otherwise, it can't grow enough in the United States to maintain its stock price. It needs to be in South America. It needs to be in Asia. It needs to be in Europe."—George Rosenbaum, Leo J. Shapiro Associates

When a major retailer like Wal-Mart sets its mind and cash to global expansion, it's amazing what it can do. At the end of the 1980s, Wal-Mart was a mostly U.S. phenomenon;

by the end of the 1990s, it was a global presence, poised to become the world's dominant retailer. From a base of about 2,200 U.S. stores and sales of less than $85 billion in the early 1990s, Wal-Mart exploded to more than 3,600 stores worldwide, with sales at a staggering $137 billion and a net income of $4.4 billion. Not bad for a company that began its international expansion in 1993 with the purchase of 122 Woolco stores in Canada.

Spurred by NAFTA, Wal-Mart quickly moved into Mexico using joint ventures to end the decade with more than 400 Mexican stores. In Hong Kong, through a joint venture with Ek Chor Distribution System Co. Ltd., Wal-Mart established several Value Clubs, which became the first stepping stones to the mainland China, the most populous country in the world and a market with an emerging middle class. Because Ek Chor is actually owned by C. P. Pokphand of Bangkok, Wal-Mart also entered Thailand, and then Indonesia. In 1995, the retailing giant once again looked south, moving into South America with stores in Brazil, Argentina, and Chile.

Most of these countries appear to be good markets for Wal-Mart—each constitutes a heavily populated emerging market. Although not high in discretionary income, each of these markets exhibits growing income, giving people more money to shop while still retaining their price sensitivity. Wal-Mart's inventory of heavily discounted brand-name merchandise offers consumers in these markets the quality they desire at prices they can afford.

Initially, Wal-Mart's moves into emerging markets matched the expectations of industry analysts. Most experts predicted that Wal-Mart's next move would be into Eastern Europe, where the populace still sought discount prices rather than high-end goods. But in 1998 Wal-Mart confounded the experts by buying the 21-unit Wertkauf chain in Germany. In 1999, it purchased a second German retailer, the 74-unit Interspar hypermarkets chain. Within only one and a half years, Wal-Mart moved from having no presence in Germany to being the country's number-four retailer.

Why was this move into Germany so surprising? The Germany countryside is littered with the carcasses of other retailers, such as Toys "R" Us, which tried and failed to penetrate the market. Although Germany is the third-largest market in the world (behind the United States and Japan), it is an especially tough market. First, zoning laws, scarcity of land, and high real estate prices make it almost impossible to find affordable space for new supercenters or hypermarkets. Second, German retailing is dominated by a few large chains such as Metro, Rewe, and Edeka. As a result, the market is characterized by excessive price competition and extremely narrow margins—2 percent or less.

Third, Germany has very strong unions and German workers are among the most highly paid in the world. Wal-Mart will find it very difficult to make these workers gather early in the morning as they do in the United States to do the Wal-Mart cheer ("Give me a W! . . . *W.* Give me an A! . . . *A.*") Fourth, German laws governing retailing severely limit store hours. No retailers (except for bakeries and gas stations) are open on Sunday. And until recently, all stores closed at noon on Saturday (now, it's 4 P.M.) and stayed open late (until 8 P.M.) only one night a week—not an appealing policy for a company that keeps many of its U.S. stores open 24 hours a day.

Fifth, in attempting to apply the same low-price strategy in Europe as in the United States, Wal-Mart would run afoul of some manufacturers' marketing strategies. For example, many clothing brands that are positioned more as commodities in the United States and sold in many stores at discount prices (such as Levi's) are positioned as more high-end products in Europe. Thus, selling in Wal-Mart as a discount item would undercut such brands' positioning and damage international profits. Sixth, sales in Germany had been flat for the past four years and no increases were expected, given the country's high level of unemployment. Finally, consumers in Western Europe are considered to be more sophisticated and more demanding than United States consumers—not the kinds of buyers likely to be swayed by a greeter at the door who asks, "How are you today?" (or, rather, "Wie geht's?").

So, who was wrong here, Wal-Mart or the analysts? With so much seemingly going against it, how could Wal-Mart expect to be successful in Germany? What did it have to offer that established retailers didn't? The answer—service. In a country full of surly store clerks, sometimes described as having perfected "service with a snarl," customers might respond well to service with a *smile.* They might like to shop where their patronage is valued—where store clerks are trained when asked, "Who's number 1?" to respond, "The customer!" and where customers' purchases are bagged for them instead of by them.

In a country where it's difficult to get to the store because of its limited hours, Wal-Mart has pushed its store hours to the legal limit. It opens at 7 A.M. (the earliest allowed) despite the customary 8 A.M. or 9 A.M. opening times. Customers who work might appreciate the extra hour time to shop. Also, Wal-Mart helps shoppers reduce shopping time by using common U.S. practices, such as locating steak sauce or seasoning packets near the meats and salad dressings near the produce so that shoppers don't have to walk back and forth in the store to find complementary goods.

To make shopping more pleasant, Wal-Mart has begun to renovate its German stores, many of which were badly run-down. It has created wider aisles, refurbished fixtures, piled the goods higher, and renamed its stores Wal-Mart. Most importantly in a land of pfennig pinchers, Wal-Mart has introduced EDLP ("Every Day Low Prices"). *"Jeden Tag Tiefpriese"* signs throughout its stores proclaim drastically slashed prices on over 4,000 items. Wal-Mart's EDLP/JTT strategy has worked so well that other German retailers, who previously relied on specials and sales to reduce prices, have been forced to reduce their daily prices.

In a sense, low prices have pulled customers into Wal-Mart's German stores while other attributes, such as friendly clerks and wider aisles, have made shopping more pleasant. What allows Wal-Mart to out-discount the European discounters? The answer lies in its 101-terabyte computer system. Wal-Mart is the country's most sophisticated retailer in terms of using information systems. Every second, data from around the globe is transmitted via satellite to the Wal-Mart computer. Store managers can point handheld scanners at a product on their shelves and find out how much of the product the store has sold today at what price and profit contribution, what its inventory levels are (by color, size, and other characteristics), and whether more is on order. Analysts pore over thousands of pages of output to track sales everywhere. If a product is moving slowly in one store, it's shipped to another rather than being cleared through reduced prices. Very few goods sit in inventory for very long, which reduces costs. Orders and reorders are placed strictly on the basis of sales. Wal-Mart knows faster than any other retailer what's selling and what's not.

In addition, Wal-Mart's sophisticated distribution system backs up this information system. Wal-Mart has applied for and gotten several free-trade-zone distribution centers in Arizona and Georgia. Goods pour into these centers, where they are repackaged, marked, labeled, and reshipped. While goods remain in the zone, Wal-Mart pays no duty on them—duties are paid only when goods are shipped. Each zone saves Wal-Mart more than $500,000 annually. Such close attention to distribution costs saves Wal-Mart money and supports rapid shipment of goods.

Following its move into Germany, the analysts expected that Wal-Mart would expand next into France. However, the company confounded the experts once again by buying ASDA, the third-largest chain in the United Kingdom. Why? U.K. retailing has the highest margins in Europe—ranging from 5 to 7 percent. If Wal-Mart can survive on less than 2 percent in Germany, it can do very well with the higher margins in the United Kingdom.

Thus, Wal-Mart now poses a serious threat to European retailers. With the purchase of one more major European chain next year, Wal-Mart will become the biggest retailer in Euroland, irrevocably changing the face of European retailing. And it will have accomplished this feat in only four years.

How are European retailers retaliating? They have responded with a series of mergers. Wal-Mart's entry has spawned a series of mergers that can only result in a concentration of retailers worldwide. Carrefour and Promodes in France have merged to become the biggest retailer in five European countries—France, Spain, Belgium, Portugal, and Greece. Through their holdings in other firms, they will have significant shares of the Argentine, Brazilian, Taiwanese, and Indonesian markets. Metro, the largest retailer in Germany, bought the Allkauf chain and Kriegbaum-Unternemensgruppe in southwest Germany to consolidate its lead in Germany. Ahold, the major Dutch retailer, bought up several chains in Spain.

Questions

1. Describe Wal-Mart's global strategy? What tactics has it used to become a major global retailer?
2. Can Wal-Mart sustain its competitive advantage in global retailing?
3. Explain the importance of selling only brand-name merchandise to the Wal-Mart strategy.
4. Choosing markets to enter is of major importance in global expansion. If you were in charge of Wal-Mart, what European country would you enter next? Why? Would entering this country require adaptation of Wal-Mart's marketing strategy and tactics? If so, how?
5. If you were running Wal-Mart, what non-European country in the world would you enter next? Why? Would entering this country require adaptation of Wal-Mart's marketing? If so, how?

Sources: "A Foothold in Europe's Heartland," *Discount Store,* October 1999, p. 77; "Europe Seen as Tough, While Asia's a Natural on Wal-Mart's Globe," *WWD,* August 23, 1994, p. 1; "How Is Wal Mart Doing in Germany?" *Eurofood,* July 1, 1999, p. 11; "Wal Mart Doubles Its Size in Europe," *Eurofood,* December 17, 1998, p. 11; Stephen Armstrong, "Wal-Mart Goes Shopping in Europe," *The European,* March 2, 1998, p. 23; Carol Emert, "Wal-Mart Sets Up to Enter Europe, Central America," *WWD,* August 22, 1994, p. 8; Richard Halverson, "Wal-Mart 'Walks the Walk' of a Global Retailer; Eyes All Corners of the Globe," *Discount Store News,* December 5, 1994, p. 95; Samer Iskander, "Retailers Plan Biggest Store Chain in Europe," *The Financial Times,* August 30, 1999, p. 1; Tony Lisanti, "Europe's Abuzz over Wal-Mart," *Discount Store News,* May 3, 1999, p. 11; David Moin, "Wal-Mart to Enter Europe with Buy of German Chain," *WWD,* Dec. 19, 1997, p. 2; and Elliot Zwiebach, "Europe: In Wal-Mart's Wake," *Supermarket News,* September 20, 1999, p. 40.

After studying this chapter, you should be able to
1. identify the major social criticisms of marketing
2. define *consumerism* and *environmentalism* and explain how they affect marketing strategies
3. describe the principles of socially responsible marketing
4. explain the role of ethics in marketing

MARKETING AND SOCIETY: SOCIAL RESPONSIBILITY AND MARKETING ETHICS

When Ben Cohen and Jerry Greenfield first met in the seventh grade, they were, by their own admission, the "two slowest kids round the track." However, in 1978, after staring a life of mediocrity full in the face, the two friends decided to try something different. They took a $5 correspondence course on making ice cream, borrowed $12,000, and started their own scoop shop—Ben & Jerry's Handmade—in an abandoned gas station in Burlington, Vermont. The rest, as they say, is history. Two decades later, despite many growing pains, Ben & Jerry's has become the nation's number-two super-premium ice cream brand, with a 39 percent market share that trails only Häagen-Dazs's 43 percent share. Last year, Ben & Jerry's sold more than $209 million worth of ice cream and frozen yogurt products through supermarkets, convenience stores, and 150 Ben & Jerry's scoop shops around the country.

Why the strong appeal? For one thing, Ben & Jerry's is a master at creating innovative flavors such as Rainforest Crunch, Cherry Garcia, Chocolate Chip Cookie Dough, Phish Food, Chunky Monkey, and Chubby Hubby. Moreover, the company has taken on the appealing, laid-back personality of its founders. "If you passed [Ben and Jerry] in the street," notes one industry observer, "with their sloppy T-shirts and portly figures. . . , you'd probably think they were a couple of Grateful Dead roadies. [Under their leadership, Ben & Jerry's] markets its products with a combination of down-home hippie folksiness and 'right-on' credibility."

But behind the creative flavors and folksy image, Ben & Jerry's is a company that cares deeply about its social responsibilities. The company's mission statement challenges all employees, from top management to ice cream scoopers in each store, to include concern for individual and community welfare in their day-to-day decisions. It reads as follows:

Ben & Jerry's is dedicated to the creation and demonstration of a new corporate concept of *linked prosperity.* Our mission consists of three interrelated parts: *Product:* To make, distribute and sell the finest quality all natural ice cream and related products in a variety of innovative flavors made from Vermont dairy products. *Economic:* To

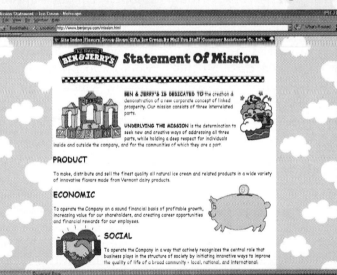

operate the company on a sound financial basis of profitable growth, increasing value for shareholders, and creating career opportunities and financial rewards for our employees. *Social:* To operate the company in a way that actively recognizes the central role that business plays in the structure of society by initiating innovative ways to improve the quality of life of the broad community—local, national, and international. Underlying the mission of Ben & Jerry's is the determination to seek new and creative ways of addressing all three parts, while holding a deep respect for the individuals, inside and outside the company, and for the communities of which they are a part.

The notion of linked prosperity—also called values-led business or caring capitalism—forms the heart and soul of the company. Ben & Jerry's aims to do well *while also* doing good.

Ben & Jerry's does more than just pay lip service to social and environmental concerns—the mission also translates into specific company policies and actions. For example, whereas the average U.S. corporation earmarks less than 2 percent of pretax profits to philanthropy, Ben & Jerry's has a set policy to donate a whopping 7.5 percent to a variety of social and environmental causes (last year that amounted to about $792,600). The funds are dispensed through the Ben & Jerry's Foundation, employee Community Action Teams, and corporate grants made by the company's Director of Social Mission Development. Each supports projects that exhibit "creative problem solving and hopefulness . . . relating to children and families, disadvantaged groups, and the environment."

The company routinely assesses the environmental and social impact of almost everything it does. For example, it buys only hormone-free milk and cream and uses only organic fruits and nuts. After two years of research, Ben & Jerry's last year switched to a new, environmentally friendly pint container they call the Eco-Pint. Its Rainforest Crunch ice cream contains Brazil nuts harvested by cooperative farms benefiting tribal peoples in the Amazon rain forests. Closer to home, Ben & Jerry's recently sponsored a concert in Burlington, Vermont, by rock band Phish to raise money to clean up Lake Champlain.

Ben & Jerry's also goes to great lengths to buy from minority and disadvantaged suppliers. For example, even though it raises ingredient prices a few cents a pint, Ben & Jerry's buys the brownies for its Chocolate Fudge Brownie ice cream from a nonprofit New York bakery that trains and employs disadvantaged workers. To use the brownies, it had to devise a new ice cream recipe and change its production process. Similarly, to support Vermont farmers and their causes, Ben & Jerry's buys its hormone-free milk and cream exclusively from Vermont dairies, an action which cost the company an extra $375,000 last year.

Ben & Jerry's obeys its social conscience in other ways as well. For example, it used to make a popular ice cream called Oreo Mint but discontinued the flavor because it didn't like doing business with tobacco merchant RJR, whose Nabisco unit at the time supplied the Oreos. The company changed recipes and started making a new flavor called Mint Chocolate Cookie. For their social responsibility and their involvement in community action programs, Ben and Jerry were awarded with the National Retail Federation's American Spirit Award for 1999.

Such caring capitalism has earned Ben & Jerry's a measure of respect and the loyal patronage of many consumers. However, there is a downside—having a double bottom line of values and profits is not easy. Such policies cost money, which some critics claim is "wasted on righteousness." In the words of one especially harsh critic, "Ben and Jerry want to use ice cream to solve the world's problems. They call it running a values-led business; I call it a mess. What makes it a mess are its conflicting objectives. Operating a business is tough enough. Once you add social goals to the demands of serving customers, making a profit, and returning value to shareholders, you tie yourself up in knots. [Ben and Jerry's] ideas are simplistic, and partly as a result their company has been hurt."

For sure, it's sometimes difficult to take good intentions to the bank. Over the years, the company has at times found it difficult to live up to the title of the founders' recent book *Ben & Jerry's Double Dip: Lead with Your Values and Make Money Too.* It's done fine with the values part but has produced less than stellar financial returns. Over the past several years, its once-meteoric sales growth has slowed, its profits have wavered, and its stock price has languished. Notes the critic: "As for dividends, to date they have been entirely spiritual."

However, such spiritual returns appear to satisfy Ben & Jerry's owners, still mostly small shareholders from Vermont rather than large institutions. Shareholder's meetings—which include a cabaret style production, a state-of-the-ice-cream address by the CEO, and plenty of free ice cream—are well attended. The general consensus among shareholders is that they're just happy to be a part of the company, regardless of the stock's performance. "According to Jerry, [shareholder meetings] are incredibly well attended by the locals in a carnival-type atmosphere," states an industry analyst. "The shareholders who do ask questions . . . ask the board why it isn't being more progressive and radical." They appear to agree with Alan Parker, Ben & Jerry's director of investor relations and social accounting, who says, "We . . . desire to be the kind of company that measures its success as much by its social contribution as by its financial success."[1]

Responsible marketers discover what consumers want and respond with the right products, priced to give good value to buyers and profit to the producer. The *marketing concept* is a philosophy of customer satisfaction and mutual gain. Its practice leads the economy by an invisible hand to satisfy the many and changing needs of millions of consumers.

Not all marketers follow the marketing concept, however. In fact, some companies use questionable marketing practices, and some marketing actions that seem innocent in themselves strongly affect the larger society. Consider the sale of cigarettes. On the face of it, companies should be free to sell cigarettes, and smokers should be free to buy them. But this transaction affects the public interest. First, the smoker is harming his or her health and may be shortening his or her own life. Second, smoking places a financial burden on the smoker's family and on society at large. Third, other people around the smoker may suffer discomfort and harm from secondhand smoke. Finally, marketing cigarettes to adults might also influence young people to begin smoking. Thus, the marketing of tobacco products has sparked substantial debate and negotiation in recent years.[2] This example shows that private transactions may involve larger questions of public policy.

This chapter examines the social effects of private marketing practices. We examine several questions: What are the most frequent social criticisms of marketing? What steps have private citizens taken to curb marketing ills? What steps have legislators and government agencies taken to curb marketing ills? What steps have enlightened companies taken to carry out socially responsible and ethical marketing? We examine how marketing affects and is affected by each of these issues.

SOCIAL CRITICISMS OF MARKETING

Marketing receives much criticism. Some of this criticism is justified; much is not. Social critics claim that certain marketing practices hurt individual consumers, society as a whole, and other business firms.

Marketing's Impact on Individual Consumers

Consumers have many concerns about how well the American marketing system serves their interests. Surveys usually show that consumers hold mixed or even slightly unfavorable attitudes toward marketing practices. Consumers, consumer advocates, government agencies, and other critics have accused marketing of harming consumers through high prices, deceptive practices, high-pressure selling, shoddy or unsafe products, planned obsolescence, and poor service to disadvantaged consumers.

High Prices

Many critics charge that the American marketing system causes prices to be higher than they would be under more "sensible" systems. They point to three factors—*high costs of distribution, high advertising and promotion costs,* and *excessive markups.*

High Costs of Distribution.   A long-standing charge is that greedy intermediaries mark up prices beyond the value of their services. Critics charge that there are too many intermediaries, that intermediaries are inefficient and poorly run, or that they provide unnecessary or duplicate services. As a result, distribution costs too much, and consumers pay for these excessive costs in the form of higher prices.

How do resellers answer these charges? They argue that intermediaries do work that would otherwise have to be done by manufacturers or consumers. Markups reflect services that consumers themselves want—more convenience, larger stores and assortment, longer store hours, return privileges, and others. Moreover, the costs of operating stores keep rising, forcing retailers to raise their prices. In fact, they argue, retail competition is so intense that margins are actually quite low. For example, after taxes, supermarket chains are typically left with barely 1 percent profit on their sales. If some resellers try to charge too much relative to the value they add, other resellers will step in with lower prices. Low-price stores such as Wal-Mart, Best Buy, and other discounters pressure their competitors to operate efficiently and keep their prices down.

High Advertising and Promotion Costs.   Modern marketing is also accused of pushing up prices to finance heavy advertising and sales promotion. For example, a dozen tablets of a heavily promoted brand of aspirin sell for the same price as 100 tablets of less promoted brands. Differentiated products—cosmetics, detergents, toiletries—include promotion and packaging costs that can amount to 40 percent or

A heavily promoted brand of antacid sells for much more than a virtually identical non-branded or store-branded product. Critics charge that promotion adds only psychological value to the product rather than functional value.

more of the manufacturer's price to the retailer. Critics charge that much of the packaging and promotion adds only psychological value to the product rather than functional value. Retailers use additional promotion—advertising, displays, and sweepstakes—that add several cents more to retail prices.

Marketers respond that consumers can usually buy functional versions of products at lower prices. However, they *want* and are willing to pay more for products that also provide psychological benefits—that make them feel wealthy, attractive, or special. Brand-name products may cost more, but branding gives buyers confidence. Heavy advertising adds to product costs but is needed to inform millions of potential buyers of the merits of a brand. If consumers want to know what is available on the market, they must expect manufacturers to spend large sums of money on advertising. Also, heavy advertising and promotion may be necessary for a firm to match competitors' efforts—the business would lose "share of mind" if it did not match competitive spending. At the same time, companies are cost-conscious about promotion and try to spend their money wisely.

Excessive Markups.   Critics also charge that some companies mark up goods excessively. They point to the drug industry, where a pill costing 5 cents to make may cost the consumer $2 to buy. They point to the pricing tactics of funeral homes that prey on the confused emotions of bereaved relatives and to the high charges for television repair and auto repair.

Marketers respond that most businesses try to deal fairly with consumers because they want repeat business. Most consumer abuses are unintentional. When shady marketers do take advantage of consumers, they should be reported to Better Business Bureaus and to state and federal agencies. Marketers also respond that consumers often don't understand the reason for high markups. For example, pharmaceutical markups must cover the costs of purchasing, promoting, and distributing existing medicines plus the high research and development costs of formulating and testing new medicines.

Deceptive Practices

Marketers are sometimes accused of deceptive practices that lead consumers to believe they will get more value than they actually do. Deceptive practices fall into three groups: deceptive pricing, promotion, and packaging. *Deceptive pricing* includes practices such as falsely advertising "factory" or "wholesale" prices or a large price reduction from a phony high retail list price. *Deceptive promotion* includes practices such as overstating the product's features or performance, luring the customer to the store for a bargain that is out of stock, or running rigged contests. *Deceptive packaging* includes exaggerating package contents through subtle design, not filling the package to the top, using misleading labeling, or describing size in misleading terms.

To be sure, questionable marketing practices do occur. For example, at one time or another, we've all gotten an envelope in the mail screaming something like "You have won $10,000,000!" In recent years, sweepstakes companies have come under the gun for their deceptive communication practices. In fact, many states have brought lawsuits against companies like American Family Publishers and Publishers Clearing House. The suits allege that the companies' promotional strategies entice people to buy thousands of dollars' worth of products hoping to better their odds of winning. The Wisconsin Attorney General asserts that "there are older consumers who send [sweepstakes companies] checks and money orders on a weekly basis with a note that says they were very upset that the prize patrol did not come."[3]

Deceptive practices have led to legislation and other consumer protection actions. For example, in 1938 Congress reacted to such blatant deceptions as Fleischmann's Yeast's claim to straighten crooked teeth by enacting the Wheeler-Lea Act giving the Federal Trade Commission (FTC) power to regulate "unfair or deceptive acts or practices." The FTC has published several guidelines listing deceptive practices. The toughest problem is defining what is "deceptive." For example, some years ago, Shell Oil advertised that Super Shell gasoline with platformate gave more mileage than did the same gasoline without platformate. Now this was true, but what Shell did not say is that almost *all* gasoline includes platformate. Its defense was that it had never claimed that platformate was found only in Shell gasoline. But even though the message was literally true, the FTC felt that the ad's *intent* was to deceive.

Marketers argue that most companies avoid deceptive practices because such practices harm their business in the long run. If consumers do not get what they expect, they will switch to more reliable products. In addition, consumers usually protect themselves from deception. Most consumers recognize a marketer's selling intent and are careful when they buy, sometimes to the point of not believing completely true product claims. One noted marketing thinker, Theodore Levitt, claims that some advertising puffery is bound to occur—and that it may even be desirable: "There is hardly a company that would not go down in ruin if it refused to provide fluff, because nobody will buy pure functionality. . . . Worse, it denies . . . man's honest needs and values. Without distortion, embellishment, and elaboration, life would be drab, dull, anguished, and at its existential worst."[4]

High-Pressure Selling

Salespeople are sometimes accused of high-pressure selling that persuades people to buy goods they had no thought of buying. It is often said that encyclopedias, insurance, real estate, cars, and jewelry are *sold,* not *bought.* Salespeople are trained to deliver smooth, canned talks to entice purchase. They sell hard because sales contests promise big prizes to those who sell the most.

Marketers know that buyers often can be talked into buying unwanted or unneeded things. Laws require door-to-door and telephone salespeople to announce that they are selling a product. Buyers also have a "three-day cooling-off period" in which they can cancel a contract after rethinking it. In addition, consumers can complain to Better Business Bureaus or to state consumer protection agencies when they feel that undue selling pressure has been applied. But in most cases, marketers have little to gain from high-pressure selling. Such tactics may work in the short run but will damage the marketer's long-run relationships with customers.

Shoddy or Unsafe Products

Another criticism is that products lack the quality they should have. One complaint is that many products are not made well and services not performed well. A second complaint is that many products deliver little benefit. For example, some consumers are surprised to learn that many of the "healthy" foods being marketed today, such as cholesterol-free salad dressings, low-fat frozen dinners, and high-fiber bran cereals, may have little nutritional value. In fact, they may even be harmful.

> [Despite] sincere efforts on the part of most marketers to provide healthier products, . . . many promises emblazoned on packages and used as ad slogans continue to confuse nutritionally uninformed consumers and . . . may actually be harmful to that group. . . . [Many consumers] incorrectly assume the product is "safe" and eat greater amounts

than are good for them. . . . For example, General Foods USA's new Entenmann's "low-cholesterol, low-calorie" cherry coffee cake . . . may confuse some consumers who shouldn't eat much of it. While each serving is only 90 calories, not everyone realizes that the suggested serving is tiny [one-thirteenth of the small cake]. Although eating half an Entenmann's cake may be better than eating half a dozen Dunkin' Donuts, . . . neither should be eaten in great amounts by people on restrictive diets.[5]

A third complaint concerns product safety. Product safety has been a problem for several reasons, including manufacturer indifference, increased production complexity, poorly trained labor, and poor quality control. For years, Consumers Union—the nonprofit testing and information organization that publishes *Consumer Reports*—has reported various hazards in tested products: electrical dangers in appliances, carbon monoxide poisoning from room heaters, injury risks from lawn mowers, and faulty automobile design, among many others. The organization's testing and other activities have helped consumers make better buying decisions and encouraged businesses to eliminate product flaws (see Marketing Highlight 20.1).

However, most manufacturers *want* to produce quality goods. The way a company deals with product quality and safety problems can damage or help its reputation. Companies selling poor-quality or unsafe products risk damaging conflicts with consumer groups and regulators. Moreover, unsafe products can result in product liability suits and large awards for damages. More fundamentally, consumers who are unhappy with a firm's products may avoid future purchases and talk other consumers into doing the same. Today's marketers know that customer-driven quality results in customer satisfaction, which in turn creates profitable customer relationships.

Planned Obsolescence

Critics also have charged that some producers follow a program of planned obsolescence, causing their products to become obsolete before they actually should need replacement. For example, critics charge that some producers continually change consumer concepts of acceptable styles to encourage more and earlier buying. An obvious example is constantly changing clothing fashions. Other producers are accused of holding back attractive functional features, then introducing them later to make older models obsolete. Critics claim that this occurs in the consumer electronics and computer industries. For example, Intel and Microsoft have been accused in recent years of holding back their next-generation computer chips or software until demand is exhausted for the current generation. Still other producers are accused of using materials and components that will break, wear, rust, or rot sooner than they should. One writer put it this way: "The marvels of modern technology include the development of a soda can which, when discarded, will last forever—and a . . . car, which, when properly cared for, will rust out in two or three years."[6]

Marketers respond that consumers *like* style changes; they get tired of the old goods and want a new look in fashion or a new design in cars. No one has to buy the new look, and if too few people like it, it will simply fail. Companies frequently withhold new features when they are not fully tested, when they add more cost to the product than consumers are willing to pay, and for other good reasons. But they do so at the risk that a competitor will introduce the new feature and steal the market. Moreover, companies often put in new materials to lower their costs and prices. They do not design their products to break down earlier, because they do not want to lose customers to other brands. Instead, they implement total quality programs to ensure that products will consistently meet or exceed customer expectations.

WHEN *CONSUMER REPORTS* TALKS, BUYERS LISTEN

For more than 60 years, *Consumer Reports* has given buyers the lowdown on everything from sports cars to luggage to lawn sprinklers. Published by Consumers Union, the nonprofit product-testing organization, the magazine's mission can be summed up by CU's motto: Test, Inform, Protect. With more than 5 million subscribers and several times that many borrowers, as dog-eared library copies will attest, *Consumer Reports* is

one of the nation's most-read magazines. It's also one of the most influential. In 1988, when its car testers rated Suzuki's topple-prone Samurai as "not acceptable"—meaning don't even take one as a gift—sales plunged 70 percent the following month. Last year, when it raved about Saucony's Jazz 3000 sneaker, sales doubled, leading to nationwide shortages.

Although nonreaders may view *Consumer Reports* as a deadly dull

shopper's guide to major household appliances, the magazine does a lot more than rate cars and refrigerators. In recent issues, it has looked at mutual funds, prostate surgery, home mortgages, retirement communities, and public health policies. In the 1930s, Consumers Union was one of the first organizations to urge a boycott of products imported from Nazi Germany, and it's been calling for nationalized health care since 1937.

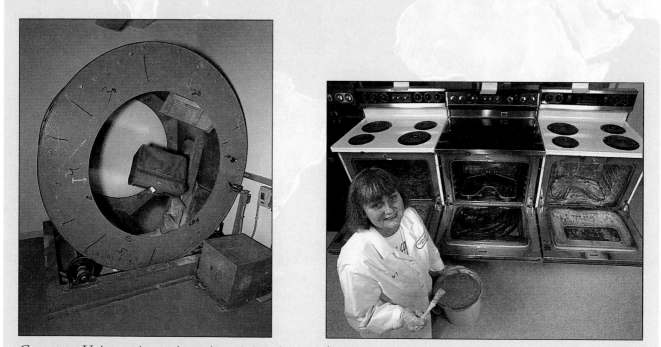

Consumers Union carries out its testing mission: Suitcases bang into one another inside the huge "mechanical gorilla," and a staffer coats the interiors of self-cleaning ovens with a crusty concoction called "monster mash."

Thus, much of so-called planned obsolescence is the working of the competitive and technological forces in a free society—forces that lead to ever-improving goods and services.[7]

Poor Service to Disadvantaged Consumers

Finally, the American marketing system has been accused of poorly serving disadvantaged consumers. For example, critics claim that the urban poor often have to shop in smaller stores that carry inferior goods and charge higher prices. A

In the 1950s, it warned the nation that fallout from nuclear tests was contaminating milk supplies. In the 1960s and 1970s, it prodded car makers to install seat belts, then air bags.

Yet the magazine is rarely harsh or loud. Instead, it's usually understated, and it can even be funny. The very first issue in 1936 noted that Lifebuoy soap was itself so smelly that it simply overwhelmed your B.O. with L.O. What reader didn't delight to find in a 1990 survey of soaps that the most expensive bar, Eau de Gucci at 31 cents per hand washing, wound up dead last in a blind test.

Consumer Reports readers clearly appreciate CU and its magazine. It is unlikely that any other magazine in the world could have raised $17 million toward a new building simply by asking readers for donations. To avoid even the appearance of bias, CU has a strict no-ads, no-freebies policy. It buys all of its product samples on the open market and anonymously.

A visit to CU's maze of labs confirms the thoroughness with which CU's testers carry out their mission. A chemist performs a cholesterol extraction test on a small white blob in a beaker, a ground-up piece of Turkey enchilada, you are told. Elsewhere you find the remains of a piston-driven machine called Fingers that added 1 + 1 on pocket calculators hundreds of thousands of times or until the calculators failed, whichever came first. You watch suitcases bang into one another inside a huge contraption—affectionately dubbed the "mechanical gorilla"— that looks like an eight-foot-wide clothes dryer.

Down the hall in the appliance department, a pair of "food soilers" will soon load 20 dishwashers with identical sets of dirty dishes. A sample dinner plate is marked off with scientific precision into eight wedge-shaped sections, each with something different caked to it— dried spaghetti, spinach, chipped beef, or something else equally difficult to clean. Next door, self-cleaning ovens are being tested, their interiors coated with a crusty substance—called "monster mash" by staffers—that suggests month-old chili sauce. The recipe includes tapioca, cheese, lard, grape jelly, tomato sauce, and cherry pie filling—mixed well and baked one hour at 425 degrees. If an oven's self-cleaning cycle doesn't render the resulting residue into harmless-looking ash, 5 million readers will be so informed.

Some of the tests that CU runs are standard tests, but many are not. Several years ago, in a triumph of low-tech creativity, CU's engineers stretched paper towels across embroidery hoops, moistened the center of each with exactly ten drops of water, then poured lead shot into the middle. The winner held seven pounds of shot; the loser, less than one. Who could argue with that? There is an obvious logic to such tests, and the results are plainly quantifiable.

From the start, Consumers Union has generated controversy. The second issue dismissed the Good Housekeeping Seal of Approval as nothing more than a fraudulent ploy by publisher William Randolph Hearst to reward loyal advertisers. *Good Housekeeping* responded by accusing CU of prolonging the Depression. To the business community, *Consumer Reports* was at first viewed as a clear threat to the American way of doing business. During its early years, more than 60 advertising-dependent publications, including the *New York Times, Newsweek,* and the *New Yorker,* refused to accept CU's subscription ads.

In 1939, in a move that would seem ludicrous today, Congress's new House UnAmerican Activities Committee (then known as the Dies Committee) branded CU a subversive organization. Through the years, many manufacturers have filed suit against CU, challenging findings unfavorable to their products. However, the controversy has more often helped than hurt subscriptions, and to this day Consumers Union has never lost or settled a libel suit.

Source: Adapted from Doug Stewart, "To Buy or Not to Buy, That Is the Question at *Consumer Reports,*" *Smithsonian,* September 1993, pp. 34–43. Also see Richard Siklos, "No Ads. No Links. Just Loyalty," *Business Week,* October 25, 1999, pp. 182–83. Additional information obtained from the Consumers Union Web site at www.consumersunion.org and the Consumer Reports Online site at www.consumerreports.org, January 2000.

Consumers Union study compared the food-shopping habits of low-income consumers and the prices they pay relative to middle-income consumers in the same city. The study found that the poor do pay more for inferior goods. The results suggested that the presence of large national chain stores in low income neighborhoods made a big difference in keeping prices down. However, the study also found evidence of "redlining," a type of economic discrimination in which major chain retailers avoid placing stores in disadvantaged neighborhoods. Similar redlining charges have been leveled at the home insurance, consumer lending, and banking industries.[8]

Clearly, better marketing systems must be built in low-income areas—one hope is to get large retailers to open outlets in low-income areas. Moreover, low-income people clearly need consumer protection. The FTC has taken action against merchants who advertise false values, sell old merchandise as new, or charge too much for credit. The commission is also trying to make it harder for merchants to win court judgments against low-income people who were wheedled into buying something.

Marketing's Impact on Society as a Whole

The American marketing system has been accused of adding to several "evils" in American society at large. Advertising has been a special target—so much so that the American Association of Advertising Agencies launched a campaign to defend advertising against what it felt to be common but untrue criticisms.

False Wants and Too Much Materialism

Critics have charged that the marketing system urges too much interest in material possessions. People are judged by what they *own* rather than by who they *are*. To be considered successful, people must own a large home, two cars, and the latest consumer electronics. This drive for wealth and possessions hit new highs in the 1980s, when phrases such as "greed is good" and "shop 'til you drop" seemed to characterize the times.

In the new millennium, even though many social scientists have noted a reaction against the opulence and waste of the previous decades and a return to more basic values and social commitment, our infatuation with material things continues.

The American Marketing Association runs ads to counter common advertising criticisms.

It's hard to escape the notion that what Americans really value is stuff. Since 1987, we've had more shopping malls than high schools. We average six hours a week shopping and only forty minutes playing with our children. Our rate of saving is 2 percent—only a quarter of what it was in the 1950s, when we earned less than half as much in real dollars. In each of the past three years, more U.S citizens have declared personal bankruptcy than have graduated from college. All this acquisition isn't making us happier; the number of Americans calling themselves "very happy" peaked in 1957.[9]

The critics do not view this interest in material things as a natural state of mind but rather as a matter of false wants created by marketing. Businesses hire Madison Avenue to stimulate people's desires for goods, and Madison Avenue uses the mass media to create materialistic models of the good life. People work harder to earn the necessary money. Their purchases increase the output of American industry, and industry in turn uses Madison Avenue to stimulate more desire for the industrial output. Thus, marketing is seen as creating false wants that benefit industry more than they benefit consumers.

These criticisms overstate the power of business to create needs, however. People have strong defenses against advertising and other marketing tools. Marketers are most effective when they appeal to existing wants rather than when they attempt to create new ones. Furthermore, people seek information when making important purchases and often do not rely on single sources. Even minor purchases that may be affected by advertising messages lead to repeat purchases only if the product performs as promised. Finally, the high failure rate of new products shows that companies are not able to control demand.

On a deeper level, our wants and values are influenced not only by marketers but also by family, peer groups, religion, ethnic background, and education. If Americans are highly materialistic, these values arose out of basic socialization processes that go much deeper than business and mass media could produce alone. Moreover, some social critics see materialism as a positive and rewarding force:

Too much materialism: Our infatuation with material things continues. It's hard to escape the notion that what Americans really value is stuff.

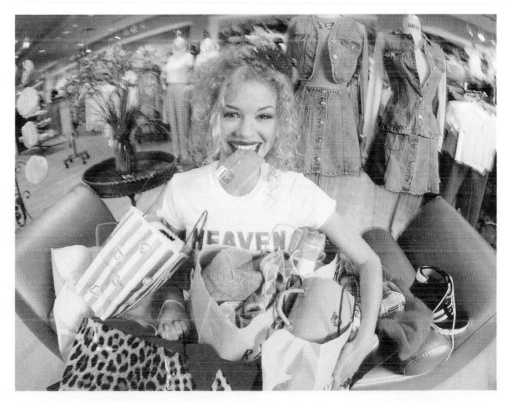

When we purchase an object, what we really buy is meaning. Commercialism is the water we swim in, the air we breathe, our sunlight and our shade.... Materialism is a vital source of meaning and happiness in the modern world.... We have not just asked to go this way, we have demanded. Now most of the world is lining up, pushing and shoving, eager to elbow into the mall. Getting and spending has become the most passionate, and often the most imaginative, endeavor of modern life. While this is dreary and depressing to some, as doubtless it should be, it is liberating and democratic to many more.[10]

Too Few Social Goods

Business has been accused of overselling private goods at the expense of public goods. As private goods increase, they require more public services that are usually not forthcoming. For example, an increase in automobile ownership (private good) requires more highways, traffic control, parking spaces, and police services (public goods). The overselling of private goods results in "social costs." For cars, the social costs include traffic congestion, air pollution, and deaths and injuries from car accidents.

A way must be found to restore a balance between private and public goods. One option is to make producers bear the full social costs of their operations. For example, the government could require automobile manufacturers to build cars with even more safety features and better pollution control systems. Automakers would then raise their prices to cover extra costs. If buyers found the price of some cars too high, however, the producers of these cars would disappear, and demand would move to those producers that could support the sum of the private and social costs.

A second option is to make consumers pay the social costs. For example, a number of highway authorities around the world are starting to charge "congestion tolls" in an effort to reduce traffic congestion:

> Already, in Southern California, drivers are being charged premiums to travel in underused car pool lanes; Singapore, Norway, and France are managing traffic with varying tolls; peak surcharges are being studied for roads around New York, San Francisco, Los Angeles, and other cities. [Economists] point out that traffic jams are caused when drivers are not charged the costs they impose on others, such as delays. The solution: Make 'em pay.[11]

Interestingly, in San Diego, regular drivers can use the HOV (high-occupancy vehicle) lanes, but they must pay a price based on traffic usage at the time. The toll ranges from 50 cents off-peak to $4.00 during rush hour.[12] More generally, if the costs of driving rise high enough, consumers will travel at nonpeak times or find alternative transportation modes.

Making consumers pay the social costs: On this private highway in California, consumers pay "congestion tolls" to drive in the unclogged fast lane.

Cultural Pollution

Critics charge the marketing system with creating *cultural pollution*. Our senses are being constantly assaulted by advertising. Commercials interrupt serious programs; pages of ads obscure printed matter; billboards mar beautiful scenery. These interruptions continually pollute people's minds with messages of materialism, sex, power, or status. Although most people do not find advertising overly annoying (some even think it is the best part of television programming), some critics call for sweeping changes.

Marketers answer the charges of "commercial noise" with these arguments: First, they hope that their ads reach primarily the target audience. But because of mass-communication channels, some ads are bound to reach people who have no interest in the product and are therefore bored or annoyed. People who buy magazines addressed to their interests—such as *Vogue* or *Fortune*—rarely complain about the ads because the magazines advertise products of interest. Second, ads make much of television and radio free to users and keep down the costs of magazines and newspapers. Many people think commercials are a small price to pay for these benefits. Finally, today's consumers have alternatives. For example, they can zip and zap TV commercials or avoid them altogether on many cable or satellite channels. Thus, advertisers are making their ads more entertaining and informative.

Too Much Political Power

Another criticism is that business wields too much political power. "Oil," "tobacco," "auto," and "pharmaceuticals" senators support an industry's interests against the public interest. Advertisers are accused of holding too much power over the mass media, limiting their freedom to report independently and objectively. One critic has asked: "How can [most magazines] afford to tell the truth about the scandalously low nutritional value of most packaged foods . . . when these magazines are being subsidized by such advertisers as General Foods, Kellogg's, Nabisco, and General Mills? . . . The answer is *they cannot and do not*."[13]

American industries do promote and protect their own interests. They have a right to representation in Congress and the mass media, although their influence can become too great. Fortunately, many powerful business interests once thought to be untouchable have been tamed in the public interest. For example, Standard Oil was broken up in 1911, and the meatpacking industry was disciplined in the early 1900s after exposures by Upton Sinclair. Ralph Nader caused legislation that forced the automobile industry to build more safety into its cars, and the Surgeon General's Report resulted in cigarette companies putting health warnings on their packages. More recently, giants such as AT&T, Microsoft, Intel, and R.J. Reynolds have felt the impact of regulators seeking to balance the interests of big business against those of the public. Moreover, because the media receive advertising revenues from many different advertisers, it is easier to resist the influence of one or a few of them. Too much business power tends to result in counterforces that check and offset these powerful interests.

Marketing's Impact on Other Businesses

Critics also charge that a company's marketing practices can harm other companies and reduce competition. Three problems are involved: acquisitions of competitors, marketing practices that create barriers to entry, and unfair competitive marketing practices.

Critics claim that firms are harmed and competition reduced when companies expand by acquiring competitors rather than by developing their own new products. The large number of acquisitions and rapid pace of industry consolidation over the past two decades have caused concern that vigorous young competitors will be absorbed and that competition will be reduced. In virtually every major industry—financial services, utilities, transportation, automobiles, telecommunications, health care, entertainment—the number of major competitors is shrinking.[14]

Acquisition is a complex subject. Acquisitions can sometimes be good for society. The acquiring company may gain economies of scale that lead to lower costs and lower prices. A well-managed company may take over a poorly managed company and improve its efficiency. An industry that was not very competitive might become more competitive after the acquisition. But acquisitions can also be harmful and, therefore, are closely regulated by the government.

Critics have also charged that marketing practices bar new companies from entering an industry. Large marketing companies can use patents and heavy promotion spending, and can tie up suppliers or dealers to keep out or drive out competitors. Those concerned with antitrust regulation recognize that some barriers are the natural result of the economic advantages of doing business on a large scale. Other barriers could be challenged by existing and new laws. For example, some critics have proposed a progressive tax on advertising spending to reduce the role of selling costs as a major barrier to entry.

Finally, some firms have in fact used unfair competitive marketing practices with the intention of hurting or destroying other firms. They may set their prices below costs, threaten to cut off business with suppliers, or discourage the buying of a competitor's products. Various laws work to prevent such predatory competition. It is difficult, however, to prove that the intent or action was really predatory. In recent years, Wal-Mart, American Airlines, Intel, and Microsoft have all been accused of various predatory practices. Take Microsoft, for example:

> [Last year,] Microsoft's $3.4 billion in net income accounted for 41 percent of the profits of the 10 largest publicly traded software companies. Its reach extends beyond the PC into everything from computerized toys and TV set-top boxes to selling cars and airline tickets over the Internet. In its zeal to become a leader not just in operating systems but on the Internet, the company bundled its Internet Explorer browser into its Windows software. This move sparked an antitrust suit by the government, much to the delight of Microsoft's rivals. After all, Web-browsing innovator Netscape has seen its market share plummet as it tries to sell what Microsoft gives away for free.[15]

Although competitors and the government charge that Microsoft's actions are predatory, the question is whether this is unfair competition or the healthy competition of a more efficient company against the less efficient.

CITIZEN AND PUBLIC ACTIONS TO REGULATE MARKETING

Because some people view business as the cause of many economic and social ills, grassroots movements have arisen from time to time to keep business in line. The two major movements have been *consumerism* and *environmentalism*.

Consumerism

American business firms have been the target of organized consumer movements on three occasions. The first consumer movement took place in the early 1900s. It was fueled by rising prices, Upton Sinclair's writings on conditions in the meat industry, and scandals in the drug industry. The second consumer movement, in the mid-1930s, was sparked by an upturn in consumer prices during the Great Depression and another drug scandal.

The third movement began in the 1960s. Consumers had become better educated, products had become more complex and potentially hazardous, and people were unhappy with American institutions. Ralph Nader appeared on the scene to force many issues, and other well-known writers accused big business of wasteful and unethical practices. President John F. Kennedy declared that consumers had the right to safety, to be informed, to choose, and to be heard. Congress investigated certain industries and proposed consumer-protection legislation. Since then, many consumer groups have been organized, and several consumer laws have been passed. The consumer movement has spread internationally and has become very strong in Europe.[16]

Consumerism
An organized movement of citizens and government agencies to improve the rights and power of buyers in relation to sellers.

But what is the consumer movement? **Consumerism** is an organized movement of citizens and government agencies to improve the rights and power of buyers in relation to sellers. Traditional *sellers' rights* include:

★ The right to introduce any product in any size and style, provided it is not hazardous to personal health or safety; or, if it is, to include proper warnings and controls.
★ The right to charge any price for the product, provided no discrimination exists among similar kinds of buyers.
★ The right to spend any amount to promote the product, provided it is not defined as unfair competition.
★ The right to use any product message, provided it is not misleading or dishonest in content or execution.
★ The right to use any buying incentive schemes, provided they are not unfair or misleading.

Traditional *buyers' rights* include:

★ The right not to buy a product that is offered for sale.
★ The right to expect the product to be safe.
★ The right to expect the product to perform as claimed.

Comparing these rights, many believe that the balance of power lies on the sellers' side. True, the buyer can refuse to buy. But critics feel that the buyer has too little information, education, and protection to make wise decisions when facing sophisticated sellers. Consumer advocates call for the following additional consumer rights:

★ The right to be well informed about important aspects of the product.
★ The right to be protected against questionable products and marketing practices.
★ The right to influence products and marketing practices in ways that will improve the "quality of life."

Each proposed right has led to more specific proposals by consumerists. The right to be informed includes the right to know the true interest on a loan (truth in lending), the true cost per unit of a brand (unit pricing), the ingredients in a product (ingredient labeling), the nutritional value of foods (nutritional labeling), product freshness (open dating), and the true benefits of a product (truth in advertising). Proposals related to consumer protection include strengthening consumer

Consumer desire for more information led to putting ingredients, nutrition, and dating information on product labels.

rights in cases of business fraud, requiring greater product safety, and giving more power to government agencies. Proposals relating to quality of life include controlling the ingredients that go into certain products (detergents) and packaging (soft drink containers), reducing the level of advertising "noise," and putting consumer representatives on company boards to protect consumer interests.

Consumers have not only the *right* but also the *responsibility* to protect themselves instead of leaving this function to someone else. Consumers who believe they got a bad deal have several remedies available, including contacting the company or the media; contacting federal, state, or local agencies; and going to small-claims courts.

Environmentalism

Environmentalism
An organized movement of concerned citizens, businesses, and government agencies to protect and improve people's living environment.

Whereas consumerists consider whether the marketing system is efficiently serving consumer wants, environmentalists are concerned with marketing's effects on the environment and with the costs of serving consumer needs and wants. **Environmentalism** is an organized movement of concerned citizens, businesses, and government agencies to protect and improve people's living environment. Environmentalists are not against marketing and consumption; they simply want people and organizations to operate with more care for the environment. The marketing system's goal, they assert, should not be to maximize consumption, consumer choice, or consumer satisfaction, but rather to maximize life quality. "Life quality" means not only the quantity and quality of consumer goods and services but also the quality of the environment. Environmentalists want environmental costs included in both producer and consumer decision making.

The first wave of modern environmentalism in the United States was driven by environmental groups and concerned consumers in the 1960s and 1970s. They were concerned with damage to the ecosystem caused by strip mining, forest depletion, acid rain, loss of the atmosphere's ozone layer, toxic wastes, and litter. They also were concerned with the loss of recreational areas and with the increase in health problems caused by bad air, polluted water, and chemically treated food.

The second environmentalism wave was driven by government, which passed laws and regulations during the 1970s and 1980s governing industrial practices impacting the environment. This wave hit some industries hard. Steel companies and utilities had to invest billions of dollars in pollution control equipment and costlier fuels. The auto industry had to introduce expensive emission controls in cars. The packaging industry had to find ways to reduce litter. These industries and others have often resented and resisted environmental regulations, especially when they have been imposed too rapidly to allow companies to make proper adjustments. Many of these companies claim they have had to absorb large costs that have made them less competitive.

Environmental sustainability

A management approach that involves developing strategies that both sustain the environment and produce profits for the company.

As we move into the twenty-first century, the first two environmentalism waves are merging into a third and stronger wave in which companies are accepting responsibility for doing no harm to the environment. They are shifting from protest to prevention, and from regulation to responsibility. More and more companies are adopting policies of **environmental sustainability**—developing strategies that both sustain the environment and produce profits for the company. According to one strategist, "The challenge is to develop a *sustainable global economy:* an economy that the planet is capable of supporting indefinitely. . . . [It's] an enormous challenge—and an enormous opportunity."[17]

Figure 20.1 shows a grid that companies can use to gauge their progress toward environmental sustainability. At the most basic level, a company can practice *pollution prevention.* This involves more than pollution control—cleaning up waste after it has been created. Pollution prevention means eliminating or minimizing waste before it is created. Companies emphasizing prevention have responded with "green marketing" programs—developing ecologically safer products, recyclable and biodegradable packaging, better pollution controls, and more energy-efficient operations (see Marketing Highlight 20.2). They are finding that they can be both green *and* competitive. Consider how the Dutch flower industry has responded to its environmental problems:

> Intense cultivation of flowers in small areas was contaminating the soil and groundwater with pesticides, herbicides, and fertilizers. Facing increasingly strict regulation, . . . the Dutch understood that the only effective way to address the problem would be to develop a closed-loop system. In advanced Dutch greenhouses, flowers now grow in water and rock wool, not in soil. This lowers the risk of infestation, reducing the need for fertilizers and pesticides, which are delivered in water that circulates and is reused. The . . . closed-loop system also reduces variation in growing conditions, thus improving product quality. Handling costs have gone down because the flowers are cultivated on specially designed platforms. . . . The net result is not only dramatically lower environmental impact but also lower costs, better product quality, and enhanced global competitiveness.[18]

FIGURE 20.1   The environmental sustainability grid

Source: Stuart L. Hart, "Beyond Greening: Strategies for a Sustainable World," *Harvard Business Review,* January–February 1997, p. 74. Copyright © 1997 by the President and Fellows of Harvard College; all rights reserved. Reprinted by permission of *Harvard Business Review.*

MARKETING HIGHLIGHT
20.2

THE NEW ENVIRONMENTALISM AND "GREEN MARKETING"

On Earth Day 1970, a newly emerging environmentalism movement made its first large-scale effort to educate people about the dangers of pollution. This was a tough task: At the time, most folks weren't all that interested in environmental problems. These days, however, environmentalism has broad public support. People hear and read daily about a growing list of environmental problems—global warming, acid rain, depletion of the ozone layer, air and water pollution, hazardous waste disposal, the buildup of solid wastes—and they are calling for solutions.

The new environmentalism has caused many consumers to rethink what products they buy and from whom. According to one recent study, nearly half of all Americans say they would change product brands to support environmental friendliness. "People are changing their brand loyalties based on things like a company's reputation for helping or harming the environment," comments an environmental researcher. For example, when the Massachusetts utility market recently was opened to competition, over 25 percent of customers chose to pay more by signing up with a utility employing "green" sources such as wind, geothermal, and solar power. Such consumer attitudes have sparked a major marketing thrust—*green marketing*—the movement by companies to develop and market environmentally responsible products. Committed green companies pursue not only environmental cleanup but also pollution prevention. True green work requires companies to practice the three Rs of waste management: reducing, reusing, and recycling waste.

McDonald's provides a good example of green marketing. It used to purchase Coca-Cola syrup in plastic bags encased in cardboard, but now the syrup is delivered as gasoline is, pumped directly from tank trucks into storage vats at restaurants. The change saved 68 million pounds of packaging a year. All napkins, bags, and tray liners in McDonald's restaurants are made from recycled paper, as are its carryout drink trays and even the stationery used at headquarters. For a company the size of McDonald's, even small changes can make a big difference. For example, just making its drinking straws 20 percent lighter saved the company 1 million pounds of waste per year. Beyond turning its own products green, McDonald's purchases recycled materials for building and remodeling its restaurants, and it challenges its suppliers to furnish and use recycled products.

Producers in a wide range of industries are responding to environmental concerns. For example, 3M runs a *Pollution Prevention Pays* program, which has led to substantial pollution and cost reduction. Xerox now remanufactures its copy machines and markets them as "proven workhorses" under names such as "Eco-series," "Renaissance," and "Green Line." Herman Miller, the large office-furniture manufacturer, set a trend in the furniture industry when it began using tropical woods from sustainably managed sources, altering even its classic furniture lines. But it went even further

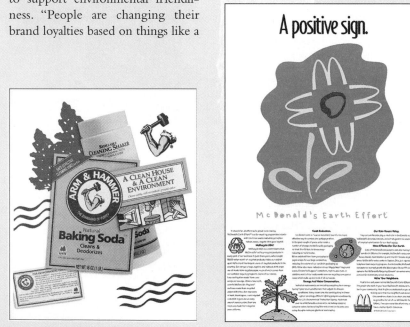

Corporate environmentalism: Enlightened companies are taking action not because someone is forcing them to, but because it is the right thing to do.

by reusing packaging, recapturing solvents used in staining, and burning fabric scraps and sawdust to generate energy for its manufacturing plant. These moves not only help the environment, they also save Herman Miller $750,000 per year on energy and landfill costs.

Service providers are going green, too. Studies indicate that 85 percent of travelers are willing to pay as much as 8 percent more to stay in an environmentally friendly hotel. Sheraton Hotels recently opened its first environmentally smart hotel in the United States. At a cost of $14 million, it built the Sheraton Rittenhouse Hotel in Philadelphia using only materials and fabrics that are produced without toxic bleaches or dyes. All of the hotel's furniture is made of wood harvested from managed forests and all of the carpets, draperies, paint, and wallpaper are free of toxic chemicals. The entire hotel is designated nonsmoking and a ventilation system ensures that fresh air is circulated into all rooms at all times. A six-story central atrium houses bamboo trees, which grow at a rate of one meter each day and produce oxygen at a rate 35 percent higher than most other plants. The walls of the atrium are fashioned from Wall Street Journal rejects and soybeans, while the floor is made from engineered bamboo.

Even retailers are jumping onto the green bandwagon. For example, Grow Biz International has developed a $100 million business selling used equipment through retail chains such as Play It Again, Once Upon a Child, Computer Renaissance, Music Go Round, and Disk Go Round. Wal-Mart is pressuring its 7,000 suppliers to provide it with more recycled products. In its stores, Wal-Mart runs videos to help educate customers, and the retailer has set up more than 900 recycling drop off bins in store parking lots around the nation. It's even opening "eco-friendly" stores. In these stores, the air-conditioning systems use non-ozone-depleting refrigerant, rainwater is collected from parking lots and rooftops for landscaping, skylights supplement fluorescent lighting adjusted by photo sensors, and the road sign is solar powered.

During the early phase of the new environmentalism, promoting environmentally improved products and actions ballooned into a big business. In fact, environmentalists and regulators became concerned that companies were going overboard with their use of terms like *recyclable, degradable, compostable,* and *environmentally responsible.* Perhaps of equal concern was that, as more and more marketers used green marketing claims, more and more consumers would view them as little more than gimmicks. In 1992, as a result of such concerns, the Federal Trade Commission issued a set of voluntary guidelines for green marketing terms to help guide marketers making environmental claims for their products. Revisions of the guidelines were finalized in 1998.

As we move into the twenty-first century, environmentalism appears to be moving into a more mature phase. Gone are the hastily prepared environmental pitches and products designed to capitalize on or exploit growing public concern. The new environmentalism is now going mainstream—broader, deeper, and more sophisticated. In the words of one analyst:

Dressing up ads with pictures of eagles and trees will no longer woo an environmentally sophisticated audience. People want to know that companies are incorporating environmental values into their manufacturing processes, products, packaging, and the very fabric of their corporate cultures. They . . . want to know that companies will not compromise the ability of future generations to enjoy the quality of life that we enjoy today. . . . As a result, we're seeing the marriage of performance benefits and environmental benefits . . . one reinforces the other.

In all, some companies have responded to consumer environmental concerns by doing only what is required to avert new regulations or to keep environmentalists quiet. Others have rushed to make money by catering to the public's mounting concern for the environment. But enlightened companies are taking action not because someone is forcing them to, or to reap short-run profits, but because it is the right thing to do. They believe that environmental farsightedness today will pay off tomorrow—for both the customer and the company.

Sources: Quotes from Robert Rehak, "Green Marketing Awash in Third Wave," *Advertising Age,* November 22, 1993, p. 22; and Lisa E. Phillips, "Green Attitude," *American Demographics,* April 1999, pp. 46–47. Also see Eric Wieffering, "Wal-Mart Turns Green in Kansas," *American Demographics,* December 1993, p. 23; Tibbett L. Speer, "Growing the Green Market," *American Demographics,* August 1997, pp. 45–49; "Way Beyond No-Smoking Floors," *Engineering News Record,* March 9, 1998, p. 30; "FTC Finalizes Green Marketing Guidelines," *Environmental Manager,* July 1998, p. 2; Christine Bittar, "Green Noise," *Brandweek,* February 22, 1999, pp. 28–36; Susan Bard Hall, "Allergies Trigger Need for Guestroom Amenities," *Hotel and Motel Management,* April 5, 1999, p. 69; and Michael Malley, "Turning Green Practices into Greenbacks," *Hotel and Motel Management,* May 17, 1999, p. 8.

At the next level, companies can practice *product stewardship*—minimizing not just pollution from production but all environmental impacts throughout the full product life cycle. Many companies are adopting *design for environment (DFE)* practices, which involve thinking ahead in the design stage to create products that are easier to recover, reuse, or recycle. DFE not only helps to sustain the environment, it can be highly profitable:

> Consider Xerox Corporation's Asset Recycle Management (ARM) program, which uses leased Xerox copiers as sources of high-quality, low-cost parts and components for new machines. A well-developed [process] for taking back leased copiers combined with a sophisticated remanufacturing process allows . . . components to be reconditioned, tested, and then reassembled into "new" machines. Xerox estimates that ARM savings in raw materials, labor, and waste disposal in 1995 alone were in the $300-million to $400-million range. . . . By redefining product-in-use as part of the company's asset base, Xerox has discovered a way to add value and lower costs. It can continually provide lease customers with the latest product upgrades, giving them state-of-the-art functionality with minimum environmental impact.[19]

At the third level of environmental sustainability, companies look to the future and plan for *new environmental technologies.* Many organizations that have made good headway in pollution prevention and product stewardship are still limited by existing technologies. To develop fully sustainable strategies, they will need to develop new technologies. Monsanto is doing this by shifting its agricultural technology base from bulk chemicals to biotechnology. By controlling plant growth and pest resistance through bioengineering rather than through the application of pesticides or fertilizers, Monsanto hopes to find an environmentally sustainable path to increased agricultural yields.[20]

Finally, companies can develop a *sustainability vision,* which serves as a guide to the future. It shows how the company's products and services, processes, and policies must evolve and what new technologies must be developed to get there. This vision of sustainability provides a framework for pollution control, product stewardship, and environmental technology.

Most companies today focus on the lower-left quadrant of the grid in Figure 20.1, investing most heavily in pollution prevention. Some forward-looking companies practice product stewardship and are developing new environmental technologies. Few companies have well-defined sustainability visions. However, emphasizing only one or a few cells in the environmental sustainability grid in Figure 20.1 can be shortsighted. For example, investing only in the bottom half of the grid puts a company in a good position today but leaves it vulnerable in the future. In contrast, a heavy emphasis on the top half suggests that a company has good environmental vision but lacks the skills needed to implement it. Thus, companies should work at developing all four dimensions of environmental sustainability.

Environmentalism creates some special challenges for global marketers. As international trade barriers come down and global markets expand, environmental issues are having an ever-greater impact on international trade. Countries in North America, Western Europe, and other developed regions are developing stringent environmental standards. In the United States, for example, more than two dozen major pieces of environmental legislation have been enacted since 1970, and recent events suggest that more regulation is on the way. A side accord to the North American Free Trade Agreement (NAFTA) set up a commission for resolving environmental matters. The European Union's Eco-Management and Audit Regulation provides guidelines for environmental self-regulation.[21]

However, environmental policies still vary widely from country to country, and uniform worldwide standards are not expected for many years. Although countries such as Denmark, Germany, Japan, and the United States have fully developed environmental policies and high public expectations, major countries such as China, India, Brazil, and Russia are in only the early stages of developing such policies. Moreover, environmental factors that motivate consumers in one country may have no impact on consumers in another. For example, PVC soft drink bottles cannot be used in Switzerland or Germany. However, they are preferred in France, which has an extensive recycling process for them. Thus, international companies are finding it difficult to develop standard environmental practices that work around the world. Instead, they are creating general policies and then translating these policies into tailored programs that meet local regulations and expectations.

Public Actions to Regulate Marketing

Citizen concerns about marketing practices will usually lead to public attention and legislative proposals. New bills will be debated—many will be defeated, others will be modified, and a few will become workable laws.

Many of the laws that affect marketing are listed in chapter 3. The task is to translate these laws into the language that marketing executives understand as they make decisions about competitive relations, products, price, promotion, and channels of distribution. Figure 20.2 illustrates the major legal issues facing marketing management.

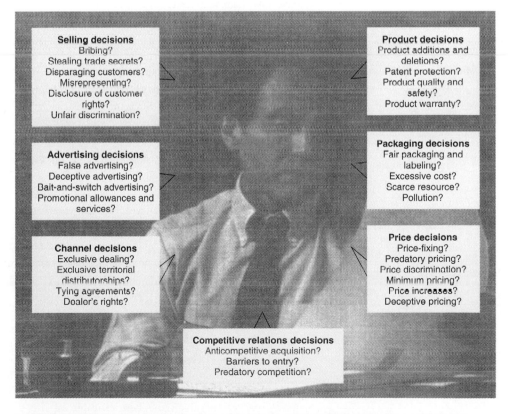

Selling decisions
Bribing?
Stealing trade secrets?
Disparaging customers?
Misrepresenting?
Disclosure of customer rights?
Unfair discrimination?

Advertising decisions
False advertising?
Deceptive advertising?
Bait-and-switch advertising?
Promotional allowances and services?

Channel decisions
Exclusive dealing?
Exclusive territorial distributorships?
Tying agreements?
Dealer's rights?

Product decisions
Product additions and deletions?
Patent protection?
Product quality and safety?
Product warranty?

Packaging decisions
Fair packaging and labeling?
Excessive cost?
Scarce resource?
Pollution?

Price decisions
Price-fixing?
Predatory pricing?
Price discrimination?
Minimum pricing?
Price increases?
Deceptive pricing?

Competitive relations decisions
Anticompetitive acquisition?
Barriers to entry?
Predatory competition?

FIGURE 20.2   Major marketing decision areas that may be called into question under the law

BUSINESS ACTIONS TOWARD SOCIALLY RESPONSIBLE MARKETING

At first, many companies opposed consumerism and environmentalism. They thought the criticisms were either unfair or unimportant. But by now, most companies have grown to accept the new consumer rights, at least in principle. They might oppose certain pieces of legislation as inappropriate ways to solve specific consumer problems, but they recognize the consumer's right to information and protection. Many of these companies have responded positively to consumerism and environmentalism in order to serve consumer needs better.

Enlightened Marketing

Enlightened marketing

A marketing philosophy holding that a company's marketing should support the best long-run performance of the marketing system.

Consumer-oriented marketing

A principle of enlightened marketing that holds that the company should view and organize its marketing activities from the consumer's point of view.

The philosophy of **enlightened marketing** holds that a company's marketing should support the best long-run performance of the marketing system. Enlightened marketing consists of five principles: *consumer-oriented marketing, innovative marketing, value marketing, sense-of-mission marketing,* and *societal marketing.*

Consumer-Oriented Marketing

Consumer-oriented marketing means that the company should view and organize its marketing activities from the consumer's point of view. It should work hard to sense, serve, and satisfy the needs of a defined group of customers. Consider the following example:

★ Barat College, a women's college in Lake Forest, Illinois, published a college catalog that openly spelled out Barat College's strong and weak points. Among the weak points it shared with applicants were the following: "An exceptionally talented student musician or mathematician . . . might be advised to look further for a college with top faculty and facilities in that field. . . . The full range of advanced specialized courses offered in a university will be absent. . . . The library collection is average for a small college, but low in comparison with other high-quality institutions."

"Telling it like it is" is intended to build confidence so that applicants really know what they will find at Barat College and to emphasize that Barat College will strive to improve its consumer value as rapidly as time and funds permit.

Innovative Marketing

Innovative marketing

A principle of enlightened marketing that requires that a company seek real product and marketing improvements.

The principle of **innovative marketing** requires that the company continuously seek real product and marketing improvements. The company that overlooks new and better ways to do things will eventually lose customers to another company that has found a better way. An excellent example of an innovative marketer is Colgate-Palmolive:

★ The American Marketing Association (AMA) recently named Colgate-Palmolive its new-product marketer of the year. Colgate took the honors by launching an abundance of innovative and highly successful new consumer products, including three AMA Edison "Best New Product" Award winners—Colgate Total toothpaste, the Colgate Wave toothbrush, and Softsoap Aquarium Series Liquid Soap. In all, more than a third of Colgate-Palmolive's current sales comes from products launched during the past five years. Perhaps the best example of the company's passion for continuous improvement is its recently introduced Total toothpaste. Marketing research showed shifts in consumer demographics and concerns—a growing population of aging, health-conscious, and better educated consumers. For these consumers, Colgate-Palmolive came up with Total, a breakout brand that provides a combination of benefits, including cavity prevention, tartar control, fresh breath, and long-lasting effects. The company also launched an innovative marketing program for the new product, which included advertising in health magazines targeting educated consumers who have high involvement in the health of their mouth and teeth. The new brand helped revitalize the mature toothpaste category. Consumers responded by making Colgate-Palmolive the toothpaste market leader for the first time since 1962, with a 32 percent share versus Procter & Gamble's 25 percent.[22]

Value Marketing

According to the principle of **value marketing,** the company should put most of its resources into value-building marketing investments. Many things marketers do—one-shot sales promotions, minor packaging changes, advertising puffery—may raise sales in the short run but add less *value* than would actual improvements in the product's quality, features, or convenience. Enlightened marketing calls for building long-run consumer loyalty by continually improving the value consumers receive from the firm's marketing offer.

Sense-of-Mission Marketing

Sense-of-mission marketing means that the company should define its mission in broad *social* terms rather than narrow *product* terms. When a company defines a social mission, employees feel better about their work and have a clearer sense of direction. For example, defined in narrow product terms, Ben & Jerry's mission might be "to sell ice cream and frozen yogurt." However, as discussed at the beginning of the chapter, the company states its mission more broadly as one of "linked prosperity," including product, economic, and social missions. Reshaping the basic task of selling consumer products into the larger mission of serving the interests of consumers, employees, and others in the company's various "communities" gives Ben & Jerry's a vital sense of purpose. Like Ben & Jerry's, many companies today are undertaking socially responsible actions or even building social responsibility into their underlying missions (see Marketing Highlight 20.3).

Societal Marketing

Following the principle of **societal marketing,** an enlightened company makes marketing decisions by considering consumers' wants and interests, the company's requirements, and society's long-run interests. The company is aware that neglecting consumer and societal long-run interests is a disservice to consumers and society. Alert companies view societal problems as opportunities.

A societally oriented marketer wants to design products that are not only pleasing but also beneficial. The difference is shown in Figure 20.3. Products can be classified according to their degree of immediate consumer satisfaction and long-run consumer benefit. **Deficient products,** such as bad-tasting and ineffective medicine, have neither immediate appeal nor long-run benefits. **Pleasing products** give high immediate satisfaction but may hurt consumers in the long run. An example is cigarettes. **Salutary products** have low appeal but benefit consumers in the long run; for instance, seat belts and air bags. **Desirable products** give both high immediate satisfaction and high long-run benefits—a tasty *and* nutritious breakfast food.

An example of a desirable product is Herman Miller's Avian office chair, which is not just attractive and functional but also environmentally responsible:

Value marketing
A principle of enlightened marketing that holds that a company should put most of its resources into value-building marketing investments.

Sense-of-mission marketing
A principle of enlightened marketing that holds that a company should define its mission in broad social terms rather than narrow product terms.

Societal marketing
A principle of enlightened marketing that holds that a company should make marketing decisions by considering consumers' wants, the company's requirements, consumers' long-run interests, and society's long-run interests.

Deficient products
Products that have neither immediate appeal nor long-run benefits.

Pleasing products
Products that give high immediate satisfaction but may hurt consumers in the long run.

Salutary products
Products that have low appeal but may benefit consumers in the long run.

Desirable products
Products that give both high immediate satisfaction and high long-run benefits.

MARKETING HIGHLIGHT
20.3

MISSION: SOCIAL RESPONSIBILITY

In a recent poll, 92 percent of consumers said they believe it's important for marketers to be good corporate citizens. More than three-quarters responded that they would switch brands and retailers when price and quality are equal for a product associated with a good cause. Companies have responded to this call for social responsibility with actions ranging from supporting worthwhile causes to writing social responsibility into the underlying mission statements.

Today, acts of good corporate citizenship abound. For example, American Express's Charge Against Hunger program—through which the company donates 3 cents from every transaction made during the traditional holiday season—has raised more than $20 million for hunger relief in the United States. Maxwell House, a division of Kraft Foods, recently created a partnership with Habitat for Humanity to build 100 homes in as many days, while working to raise awareness for the organization. Post Cereal celebrated its one hundredth anniversary in unique fashion by donating to Second Harvest—the nation's largest network of hunger-relief charities—enough cereal to feed more than 1 million people. In addition, Post partnered with grocery retailers to sponsor a 100-day food drive across the United States, supported by national and local ads to increase hunger awareness and to encourage consumer participation in the drive.

It seems that almost every company has a pet cause. Alarm company ADT gives away personal-security systems to battered women. Avon Products helps fund the fight against breast cancer. Dow donates employees' time and home construction materials to Habitat for Humanity. Coca-Cola sponsors local Boys and

The "Saturn Playgrounds" program: Backed by local Saturn retailers, Saturn retail team members and Saturn owners join with community members to build a community playground in a single day.

FIGURE 20.3   Societal classification of products

Girls Clubs, and Barnes & Noble promotes literacy.

In the chapter-opening example, we examined the socially responsible mission of Ben & Jerry's. Here are two more examples of companies working to better their communities:

Saturn. From its inception, Saturn Corporation has worked to distinguish itself as a unique car company. As its slogan states, Saturn is "A different kind of company. A different kind of car." The company claims to focus more on its employees, customers, and communities than on revenues and bottom lines. Saturn president and chairman Don Hudler notes that "a part of Saturn's business philosophy is to meet the needs of our neighbors." An example of this philosophy in action is Saturn Playgrounds, a company program for employee involvement and community betterment. The goal of the program is to provide young children in poor communities with a safe, fun environment during nonschool hours as an alternative to gangs, drugs, and crime. Backed by Saturn retail facility dollars, local Saturn employees and customers join with community members to build a community playground in a single day. So far, the Saturn Playgrounds project has built more than 100 playgrounds across the country. Joe Rypkowski, president of a local United Auto Workers union, commented that "the Saturn Playgrounds project is a perfect example of the partnership we've built at Saturn. Working together can bring powerful results, not just in our jobs, but in our communities."

The Body Shop. In 1976, Anita Roddick opened The Body Shop in Brighton, England, a tiny storefront selling beauty products out of specimen bottles. Now the company and its franchisees operate nearly 1,600 stores in 47 countries. Fundamental to this rapid growth, Roddick advocates including social responsibility alongside financial performance as a measure of company success. The Body Shop's mission is "to dedicate our business to the pursuit of social and environmental change." In keeping with that mission, the company manufactures and sells natural-ingredient-based cosmetics in simple and appealing recyclable packaging. All the products are formulated without any animal testing and supplies are often sourced from developing countries. Each franchise is required to participate in annual projects designed to better its community. In addition to these projects, The Body Shop is committed to continuous activism. For example, to promote AIDS awareness, the company has handed out condoms and pamphlets about safe sex at its over 290 U.S. stores. In addition, The Body Shop donates a certain percentage of profits each year to animal-rights groups, homeless shelters, Amnesty International, Save the Rain Forest, and other social causes. As The Body Shop grows, however, it appears to be moving from rebel to mainstream. As its markets are invaded by other retailers not shackled by The Body Shop's "principles before profits" mission, the retailer's sales growth and profits are flattening. Still, says Roddick, "Business innovation is no longer just about product [and profits]. It's about the very role of business itself."

Sources: Quotes from Anat Arkin, "Open Business Is Good for Business," *People Management,* January 1996, pp. 24–27; David Lennon, "Roddick Isn't Finished Yet," *Europe,* March 1997, pp. 39–40; "Saturn Dealers Build Six New Playgrounds in One Weekend," *PR Newswire,* June 4, 1997; and The Body Shop Web site, accessed online at www.bodyshop.com, January 2000. Also see Daniel Kadlec, "The New World of Giving," *Time,* May 5, 1997, pp. 62–64; Heather Salerno, "From Selling Cars to Building Playgrounds," *Washington Post,* June 9, 1997, p. F11; "Can Doing Good Be Good for Business?" *Fortune,* February 2, 1998, pp. 148G–148J; Ernest Beck, "Body Shop Founder Roddick Steps Aside as CEO," *Wall Street Journal,* May 13, 1998, p. B14; and Cathy Hartman and Caryn Beck-Dudley, "Marketing Strategies and the Search for Virtue: A Case Analysis of The Body Shop, International," *Journal of Business Ethics,* July 1999, pp. 249–63.

★ Herman Miller, one of the world's largest office furniture makers, has received numerous awards for environmentally responsible products and business practices. In 1994 the company formed an Earth Friendly Design Task Force responsible for infusing the company's design process with its environmental values. The task force carries out life cycle analyses on the company's products, including everything from how much of a product can be made from recycled materials to how much of the product itself can be recycled at the end of its useful life. For example, the company's Avian chair is designed for the lowest possible ecological impact and 100 percent recyclability. Herman Miller reduced material used in the chair by using gas-assist injection molding for the frame, which resulted in hollow frame members (like the bones of birds, hence the chair's name). The frame needs no paint nor other finish. All materials are recyclable. No ozone-depleting materials are used. The chair is shipped partially assembled, thus reducing the packaging and energy needed to ship it. Finally, a materials

Herman Miller's Earth Friendly Design Task Force infuses the company's design process with its environmental values. For example, the Avian chair is designed for the lowest possible ecological impact and 100 percent recyclability.

schematic is imbedded in the bottom of the seat to help recycle the chair at the end of its life. This is truly a desirable product—it's won awards for design and function *and* for environmental responsibility.[23]

Companies should try to turn all of their products into desirable products. The challenge posed by pleasing products is that they sell very well but may end up hurting the consumer. The product opportunity, therefore, is to add long-run benefits without reducing the product's pleasing qualities. For example, Sears developed a phosphate-free laundry detergent that was also very effective. The challenge posed by salutary products is to add some pleasing qualities so that they will become more desirable in the consumers' minds. For example, synthetic fats and fat substitutes, such as NutraSweet's Simplesse and Procter & Gamble's Olestra, have improved the appeal of more healthful low-calorie and low-fat foods.

Marketing Ethics

Conscientious marketers face many moral dilemmas. The best thing to do is often unclear. Because not all managers have fine moral sensitivity, companies need to develop *corporate marketing ethics policies*—broad guidelines that everyone in the organization must follow. These policies should cover distributor relations, advertising standards, customer service, pricing, product development, and general ethical standards.

The finest guidelines cannot resolve all the difficult ethical situations the marketer faces. Table 20.1 lists some difficult ethical situations marketers could face during their careers. If marketers choose immediate sales-producing actions in all these cases, their marketing behavior might well be described as immoral or even amoral. If they refuse to go along with *any* of the actions, they might be ineffective as marketing managers and unhappy because of the constant moral tension. Managers need a set of principles that will help them figure out the moral importance of each situation and decide how far they can go in good conscience.

But *what* principle should guide companies and marketing managers on issues of ethics and social responsibility? One philosophy is that such issues are decided by the free market and legal system. Under this principle, companies and their managers are not responsible for making moral judgments. Companies can in good conscience do whatever the system allows.

TABLE 20.1   SOME MORALLY DIFFICULT SITUATIONS IN MARKETING

1. You work for a cigarette company and up to now have not been convinced that cigarettes cause cancer. However, recent public policy debates now leave no doubt in your mind about the link between smoking and cancer. What would you do?

2. Your R&D department has changed one of your products slightly. It is not really "new and improved," but you know that putting this statement on the package and in advertising will increase sales. What would you do?

3. You have been asked to add a stripped-down model to your line that could be advertised to pull customers into the store. The product won't be very good, but salespeople will be able to switch buyers up to higher priced units. You are asked to give the green light for this stripped-down version. What would you do?

4. You are thinking of hiring a product manager who just left a competitor's company. She would be more than happy to tell you all the competitor's plans for the coming year. What would you do?

5. One of your top dealers in an important territory recently has had family troubles, and his sales have slipped. It looks like it will take him a while to straighten out his family trouble. Meanwhile you are losing many sales. Legally, you can terminate the dealer's franchise and replace him. What would you do?

6. You have a chance to win a big account that will mean a lot to you and your company. The purchasing agent hints that a "gift" would influence the decision. Your assistant recommends sending a fine color television set to the buyer's home. What would you do?

7. You have heard that a competitor has a new product feature that will make a big difference in sales. The competitor will demonstrate the feature in a private dealer meeting at the annual trade show. You can easily send a snooper to this meeting to learn about the new feature. What would you do?

8. You have to choose between three ad campaigns outlined by your agency. The first (a) is a soft-sell, honest information campaign. The second (b) uses sex-loaded emotional appeals and exaggerates the product's benefits. The third (c) involves a noisy, irritating commercial that is sure to gain audience attention. Pretests show that the campaigns are effective in the following order: c, b, and a. What would you do?

9. You are interviewing a capable female applicant for a job as salesperson. She is better qualified than the men just interviewed. Nevertheless, you know that some of your important customers prefer dealing with men, and you will lose some sales if you hire her. What would you do?

A second philosophy puts responsibility not in the system but in the hands of individual companies and managers. This more enlightened philosophy suggests that a company should have a "social conscience." Companies and managers should apply high standards of ethics and morality when making corporate decisions, regardless of "what the system allows." History provides an endless list of examples of company actions that were legal and allowed but were highly irresponsible. Consider the following example:

> ★ Prior to the Pure Food and Drug Act, the advertising for a diet pill promised that a person taking this pill could eat virtually anything at any time and still lose weight. Too good to be true? Actually the claim was quite true; the product lived up to its billing with frightening efficiency. It seems that the primary active ingredient in this "diet supplement" was tapeworm larvae. These larvae would develop in the intestinal tract and, of course, be well fed; the pill taker would in time, quite literally, starve to death.[24]

Each company and marketing manager must work out a philosophy of socially responsible and ethical behavior. Under the societal marketing concept, each manager must look beyond what is legal and allowed and develop standards based on personal integrity, corporate conscience, and long-run consumer welfare. A clear and responsible philosophy will help the marketing manager deal with the many knotty questions posed by marketing and other human activities.

As with environmentalism, the issue of ethics provides special challenges for international marketers. Business standards and practices vary a great deal from one country to the next. For example, whereas bribes and kickbacks are illegal for U.S. firms, they are standard business practice in many South American countries. The question arises as to whether a company must lower its ethical standards to compete effectively in countries with lower standards. In a recent study, two researchers posed this question to chief executives of large international companies and got a unanimous response: No.[25] For the sake of all of the company's stakeholders—customers, suppliers, employees, shareholders, and the public—it is important to make a commitment to a common set of shared standards worldwide.

For example, John Hancock Mutual Life Insurance Company operates successfully in Southeast Asia, an area that by Western standards has widespread questionable business and government practices. Despite warnings from locals that Hancock would have to bend its rules to succeed, Hancock Chairman Stephen Brown notes:

> We faced up to this issue early on when we started to deal with Southeast Asia. We told our people that we had the same ethical standards, same procedures, same policies in these countries that we have in the United States, and we do. . . . We just felt that things like payoffs were wrong—and if we had to do business that way, we'd rather not do business. Our employees would not feel good about having different levels of ethics. There may be countries where you have to do that kind of thing. We haven't found that country yet, and if we do, we won't do business there.[26]

Many industrial and professional associations have suggested codes of ethics, and many companies are now adopting their own codes. For example, the American Marketing Association, an international association of marketing managers and scholars, developed the code of ethics shown in Table 20.2. Companies are also developing programs to teach managers about important ethics issues and help them find the proper responses. They hold ethics workshops and seminars and set up ethics committees.

Further, more than 200 major U.S. companies have appointed high-level ethics officers to champion ethics issues and to help resolve ethics problems and concerns facing employees. For example, in 1991 Nynex created a new position of vice president of ethics, supported by a dozen full-time staff and a million-dollar budget. Since then, the new department has trained some 95,000 Nynex employees. Such training includes sending 22,000 managers to full-day workshops that include case studies on ethical actions in marketing, finance, and other business functions. One workshop deals with the use of improperly obtained competitive data, which managers are instructed is not permitted.[27]

Many companies have developed innovative ways to educate employees about ethics:

> Citicorp has developed an ethics board game, which teams of employees use to solve hypothetical quandaries. General Electric employees can tap into specially designed software on their personal computers to get answers to ethical questions. At Texas Instruments, employees are treated to a weekly column on ethics over an electronic news service. One popular feature: a kind of Dear Abby mailbag, answers provided by the company's ethics officer, . . . that deals with the troublesome issues employees face most often.[28]

Still, written codes and ethics programs do not ensure ethical behavior. Ethics and social responsibility require a total corporate commitment. They must be a component of the overall corporate culture. According to David R. Whitman, chairman of the board of Whirlpool Corporation, "In the final analysis, 'ethical

TABLE 20.2   AMERICAN MARKETING ASSOCIATION CODE OF ETHICS

Members of the American Marketing Association are committed to ethical, professional conduct. They have joined together in subscribing to this Code of Ethics embracing the following topics:

Responsibilities of the Marketer

Marketers must accept responsibility for the consequences of their activities and make every effort to ensure that their decisions, recommendations, and actions function to identify, serve, and satisfy all relevant publics: customers, organizations and society.

Marketers' Professional Conduct Must Be Guided By

1. The basic rule of professional ethics: not knowingly to do harm;
2. The adherence to all applicable laws and regulations;
3. The accurate representation of their education, training and experience; and
4. The active support, practice, and promotion of this Code of Ethics.

Honesty and Fairness

Marketers shall uphold and advance the integrity, honor, and dignity of the marketing profession by:
1. Being honest in serving consumers, clients, employees, suppliers, distributors, and the public;
2. Not knowingly participating in conflict of interest without prior notice to all parties involved; and
3. Establishing equitable fee schedules including the payment or receipt of usual, customary, and/or legal compensation for marketing exchanges.

Rights and Duties of Parties in the Marketing Exchange Process

Participants in the marketing exchange process should be able to expect that:
1. Products and services offered are safe and fit for their intended uses;
2. Communications about offered products and services are not deceptive;
3. All parties intend to discharge their obligations, financial and otherwise, in good faith; and
4. Appropriate internal methods exist for equitable adjustment and/or redress of grievances concerning purchases.

It Is Understood That the Above Would Include, but Is Not Limited to the Following Responsibilities of the Marketer: In the Area of Product Development and Management

- disclosure of all substantial risks associated with product or service usage;
- identification of any product component substitution that might materially change the product or impact on the buyer's purchase decision;
- identification of extra cost-added features.

In the Area of Promotions

- avoidance of false and misleading advertising;
- rejection of high-pressure manipulations, or misleading sales tactics;
- avoidance of sales promotions that use deception or manipulation.

Continued

TABLE 20.2   *(Continued)*

In the Area of Distribution

♦ not manipulating the availability of a product for purpose of exploitation;
♦ not using coercion in the marketing channel;
♦ not exerting undue influence over the reseller's choice to handle a product.

In the Area of Pricing

♦ not engaging in price fixing;
♦ not practicing predatory pricing;
♦ disclosing the full price associated with any purchase.

In the Area of Marketing Research

♦ prohibiting selling or fundraising under the guise of conducting research;
♦ maintaining research integrity by avoiding misrepresentation and omission of pertinent research data;
♦ treating outside clients and suppliers fairly.

Organizational Relationships

Marketers should be aware of how their behavior may influence or impact on the behavior of others in organizational relationships. They should not demand, encourage, or apply coercion to obtain unethical behavior in their relationships with others, such as employees, suppliers, or customers.

1. Apply confidentiality and anonymity in professional relationships with regard to privileged information;
2. Meet their obligations and responsibilities in contracts and mutual agreements in a timely manner;
3. Avoid taking the work of others, in whole, or in part, and representing this work as their own or directly benefiting from it without compensation or consent of the originator or owner;
4. Avoid manipulation to take advantage of situations to maximize personal welfare in a way that unfairly deprives or damages the organization of others.

Any AMA member found to be in violation of any provision of this Code of Ethics may have his or her Association membership suspended or revoked.

Source: Reprinted with permission from American Marketing Association Code of Ethics, published by the American Marketing Association.

---

behavior' must be an integral part of the organization, a way of life that is deeply ingrained in the collective corporate body. . . . In any business enterprise, ethical behavior must be a tradition, a way of conducting one's affairs that is passed from generation to generation of employees at all levels of the organization. It is the responsibility of management, starting at the very top, to both set the example by personal conduct and create an environment that not only encourages and rewards ethical behavior, but which also makes anything less totally unacceptable."[29]

The future holds many challenges and opportunities for marketing managers as they move into the new millennium. Technological advances in every area, from telecommunications, information technology, and the Internet to health care and entertainment, provide abundant marketing opportunities. However, forces in the socioeconomic, cultural, and natural environments increase the limits under which marketing can be carried out. Companies that are able to create new customer value in a socially responsible way will have a world to conquer.

REVIEW OF CONCEPT CONNECTIONS

In this chapter, we've closed with many important concepts involving marketing's sweeping impact on individual consumers, other businesses, and society as a whole. Responsible marketers discover what consumers want and respond with the right products, priced to give good value to buyers and profit to the producer. A marketing system should sense, serve, and satisfy consumer needs and improve the quality of consumers' lives. In working to meet consumer needs, marketers may take some actions that are not to everyone's liking or benefit. Marketing managers should be aware of the main *criticisms of marketing*.

1. Identify the major social criticisms of marketing.

Marketing's *impact on individual consumer welfare* has been criticized for its high prices, deceptive practices, high-pressure selling, shoddy or unsafe products, planned obsolescence, and poor service to disadvantaged consumers. Marketing's *impact on society* has been criticized for creating false wants and too much materialism, too few social goods, cultural pollution, and too much political power. Critics have also criticized marketing's *impact on other businesses* for harming competitors and reducing competition through acquisitions, practices that create barriers to entry, and unfair competitive marketing practices.

2. Define *consumerism* and *environmentalism* and explain how they affect marketing strategies.

Concerns about the marketing system have led to *citizen action movements*. *Consumerism* is an organized social movement intended to strengthen the rights and power of consumers relative to sellers. Alert marketers view it as an opportunity to serve consumers better by providing more consumer information, education, and protection. *Environmentalism* is an organized social movement seeking to minimize the harm done to the environment and quality of life by marketing practices. The first wave of modern environmentalism was driven by environmental groups and concerned consumers, whereas the second wave was driven by government, which passed laws and regulations governing industrial practices impacting the environment. Moving into the twenty-first century, the first two environmentalism waves are merging into a third and stronger wave in which companies are accepting responsibility for doing no environmental harm. Companies now are adopting policies of *environmental sustainability*—developing strategies that both sustain the environment and produce profits for the company.

3. Describe the principles of socially responsible marketing.

Many companies originally opposed these social movements and laws, but most of them now recognize a need for positive consumer information, education, and protection. Some companies have followed a policy of *enlightened marketing*, which holds that a company's marketing should support the best long-run performance of the marketing system. Enlightened marketing consists of five principles: *consumer-oriented marketing, innovative marketing, value marketing, sense-of-mission marketing,* and *societal marketing.*

4. Explain the role of ethics in marketing.

Increasingly, companies are responding to the need to provide company policies and guidelines to help their managers deal with questions of *marketing ethics*. Of course even the best guidelines cannot resolve all the difficult ethical decisions that individuals and firms must make. But there are some principles that marketers can choose among. One principle states that such issues should be decided by the free market and legal system. A second, and more enlightened principle, puts responsibility not in the system but in the hands of individual companies and managers. Each firm and marketing manager must work out a philosophy of socially responsible and ethical behavior. Under the societal marketing concept, managers must look beyond what is legal and allowable and develop standards based on personal integrity, corporate conscience, and long-term consumer welfare.

Because business standards and practices vary from country to country, the issue of ethics poses special challenges for international marketers. The growing consensus among today's marketers is that it is important to make a commitment to a common set of shared standards worldwide.

KEY TERMS

Consumerism	Enlightened marketing	Pleasing products
Consumer-oriented marketing	Environmentalism	Salutary products
Deficient products	Environmental sustainability	Sense-of-mission marketing
Desirable products	Innovative marketing	Societal marketing
		Value marketing

ISSUES FOR DISCUSSION

1. Marketing receives much criticism, some justified and much not. Which of the major criticism of marketing discussed in the chapter do you think are most justified? Which are least justified? Explain.

2. You have been invited to appear along with an economist on a panel assessing marketing practices in the soft-drink industry. You are surprised when the economist opens the discussion with a long list of criticisms (focusing especially on the unnecessarily high marketing costs and deceptive promotional practices). Abandoning your prepared comments, you set out to defend marketing in general and the beverage industry in particular. How would you respond to the economist's attack?

3. Comment on the state of consumers' rights on the Internet and in e-commerce. Design a "Bill of Rights" that would protect consumers while they shop for products and services on the Internet. Consider such issues as government regulation, ease and convenience of use, solicitation, privacy, and cost-efficient commerce.

4. Figure 20.1 shows a grid that companies can use to gauge their progress toward environmental sustainability. Where do most firms begin on this grid? Which cells are most difficult to achieve?

5. Which of the following firms, if any, practice the principle of enlightened marketing: (a) McDonald's, (b) Procter & Gamble, (c) General Motors, and (d) Johnson & Johnson?

6. Compare the principle of sense-of-mission marketing with the principle of societal marketing. How do these two concepts relate to the marketing concept and societal marketing concept presented in chapter 1?

7. Products can be classified according to their degree of immediate consumer satisfaction and long-run consumer benefit. Give an example of a product in each of the four cells of Figure 20.3 prepare a brief strategy statement for marketing each of the examples you give.

8. You are the marketing manager for small firm that makes kitchen appliances. While conducting field tests, you discover a design flaw in one of your most popular models that could potentially cause harm to a small number of consumers. However, a product recall would likely bankrupt your company, leaving all of the employees (including you) jobless. What would you do?

MARKETING APPLICATIONS

1. The "greening of America" has much more to do with lifestyles than forestry management. Adopting a "green" lifestyle means that consumers demand products and services that are environmentally responsible. As consumers turn greener, companies respond with environmentally responsible products and programs. McDonald's, Wal-Mart, Kmart, and Procter & Gamble are just a few of the companies that have now adopted a more "green" way of thinking and acting. (See the "Community" section of the McDonald's Web site [www.mcdonalds.com] and the Internet Green Marketplace Web site [www.envirolink.org] for more information.)

   a. Assume that you are a marketing manager for Crayola Crayons (www.crayola.com) and formulate a "green policy" that will make your product both competitive and environmentally responsible. As you formulate this policy, consider the product itself, packaging, distribution, promotion, and merchandising with distributors.

   b. Visit the McDonald's Web site. What is the company's specific "green policy"? Comment on the appropriateness of this policy.

   c. One organization that has been at the center of promoting an environmentally responsible "green policy"

   to corporations is Greenpeace (www.greenpeace.org). Do you find Greenpeace's proposals to be radical? Explain. How might Greenpeace react to the policies you devised for Crayola?

   d. Develop a set of rules that would guide organizations toward being environmentally responsible.

2. As a small child you were probably taught that "it is better to give than to receive." This advice is one of the cornerstones of philanthropy, including corporate philanthropy. Although it is sometimes hard to go from being a receiver to being a giver, Ted Turner and Bill Gates seem to have mastered the transition well. In the mid-1990s, Ted Turner pledged $1 billion (spread over 10 years) to the United Nations to help fight world hunger and other problems. Bill Gates's wife Melinda heads one of the world's largest philanthropies, with $17 billion at her disposal. This organization targets education and health programs for the poor. Other wealthy entrepreneurs and executives chosen different paths to charitable giving. Financial wizard Warren Buffett, worth an estimated $30 billion and the world's second-richest person behind Bill Gates, has chosen to keep his money working for him until his death. To date, the Buffett Foundation has received only a sliver of his wealth. For more information on charitable giving by business organi-

zations, see the National Charities Information Bureau (www.give.org) and the American Institute of Philanthropy (www.charitywatch.org).

a. Given the new environmentalism and social responsibility in America today, what should be an organization's view toward charitable giving? Explain.

b. What are the marketing ramifications of an organization's philanthropic activities?

c. Many corporations support worthy causes and contribute generously to their communities. Check out

the Web sites of one of the following or some other company and report on its philanthropic and socially responsible activities: Johnson & Johnson (www.jnj.com), Nike (www.nikebiz.com), Coca-Cola (www.cocacola. com), National Football League (www.nfl.com), Avon (www.avon.com), and Prudential Life Insurance (www.prudential.com).

d. How does philanthropy by corporations relate to the social criticisms of marketing?

 INTERNET CONNECTIONS

SPAMMING

Spamming refers to the bulk distribution of unsolicited, and often unwanted, e-mail messages. Because e-mail carries no postage cost, this form of direct marketing has grown rapidly in the past few years. Used properly, online direct marketing can inform consumers of products or updates of interest to them. When abused, spamming becomes at best an annoyance to Internet users and at worst patently offensive—for example, adult sites that spam to underage users. There are two ways

for consumers to stop spam. Technological solutions filter the spam either at the Internet service provider (ISP) level or right on the user's PC. Spam can also be controlled by industry self-regulation and government legislation. Marketers who want to build customer relationships and positive brand equity will only add customers to e-mail lists with their prior consent. Customers thus opt-in rather than having to opt-out of the list. Complete the following table—leave blank any items for which the organization does not offer a position.

Item	Direct Marketing Association www.the-dma.org	American Marketing Association www.ama.org	Federal Trade Commission www.ftc.gov
Support opt-in lists only			
Support requiring spammers to reveal their return address			
Support consumer's right to be removed from lists			
Provide tips on how to be removed from lists			

FOR DISCUSSION

1. Do these organizations promise to stop direct marketing entirely or just filter it for the items that you want?

2. If marketers were doing their job correctly would consumer filtering be necessary? Explain why or why not.

3. A particularly venal form of spamming disguises the sender's e-mail address so as to make it impossible to request removal from the list. Do you believe that this practice should be allowed?

4. Many e-mail programs now allow you to block mail coming from specific addresses. Is this an effective way to stop spamming?

5. Based on your understanding of spamming, write another item for the consumer's rights listed in this chapter. Then write an item for the marketers' rights list.

6. A service called BrightMail (www.brightmail.com) helps to remove spam at the ISP level. How does this service work?

SAVVY SITES

★ CAUCE, the Coalition Against Unsolicited Commercial E-mail (www.cauce.com), is a grass-roots organization that advocates legislation against spam.

★ Consumer Reports Online (www.consumerreports.org) offers tips about products as well as information about product recalls, product safety alerts, and other consumer issues.

★ Brian O'Connell (www.cs.ccsu.ctstateu.edu/~boconnel/ law_ethics.html), an attorney and computer scientist, maintains a great site with links to many e-commerce ethics and legal issues.

NOTES

1. Quotes and excerpts from Rhymer Rigby, "Tutti-Frutti Management," *Management Today,* February 1998, pp. 54–56; Alex Taylor III, "Yo, Ben! Yo, Jerry! It's Just Ice Cream," *Fortune,* April 28, 1997, p. 374; Frank Byrt, "Investors Get a Craving for Ben & Jerry's," *Wall Street Journal,* May 4, 1999; and "Ben & Jerry's Mission Statement," accessed online at www.benjerry.com/mission.html, January 2000. Also see Tom McInerney, "Double Trouble: Combining Business and Ethics," *Business Ethics Quarterly,* January 1998, pp. 187–89; Jennifer Karas, "Ben & Jerry's Co-Founders Honored for Commitment to Community Action," *Stores,* June 1999, p. 83; "Environmentally Conscious Carton," *Dairy Foods,* May 1999, p. 48; Andrew Serwer, "Ben & Jerry's Is Back: Ice Cream and a Hot Stock," *Fortune,* August 2, 1999, p. 267; and "Everything You Ever Wanted to Know About Ben & Jerry's," accessed online at www.benjerry.com/aboutbj.html, January 2000.

2. See John McCain and Robert Pitofsky, "Sorting Through Tobacco Dilemma," *Advertising Age,* March 16, 1998, p. 24; Kirk Davidson, "Up in Smoke: For Tobacco, There's No Turning Back," *Marketing News,* May 25, 1998, pp. 6, 21; and "A Victory for Tobacco's Victims," *New York Times,* July 1999, p. 14.

3. James Heckman, "Don't Shoot the Messenger: More and More Often, Marketing Is the Regulators' Target," *Marketing News,* May 24, 1999, pp. 1, 9.

4. Theodore Levitt, "The Morality (?) of Advertising," *Harvard Business Review,* July–August 1970, pp. 84–92. For counterpoints, see Heckman, "Don't Shoot the Messenger, 1999, pp. 1, 9.

5. Sandra Pesmen, "How Low Is Low? How Free Is Free?" *Advertising Age,* May 7, 1990, p. S10; and Karolyn Schuster, "The Dark Side of Nutrition," *Food Management,* June 1999, pp. 34–39.

6. Cliff Edwards, "Where Have All the Edsels Gone?" *Greensboro News Record,* May 24, 1999, p. B6.

7. For a thought-provoking short case involving planned obsolescence, see James A. Heely and Roy L. Nersesian, "The Case of Planned Obsolescence," *Management Accounting,* February 1994, p. 67. Also see Joel Dryfuss, "Planned Obsolescence Is Alive and Well," *Fortune,* February 15, 1999, p. 192.

8. See Judith Bell and Bonnie Maria Burlin, "In Urban Areas: Many More Still Pay More for Food," *Journal of Public Policy and Marketing,* Fall 1993, pp. 268–70; Alan R. Andreasen, "Revisiting the Disadvantages: Old Lesson and New Problems," *Journal of Public Policy and Marketing,* Fall 1993, pp. 270–75; Tony Attrino, "Nationwide Settles Redlining Suit in Ohio," *National Underwriter,* April 27, 1998, p. 4; Angelo B. Henderson, "First Chicago Unit Agrees to Lend $3 Billion in Detroit," *Wall Street Journal,* June 26, 1998; and Kathryn Graddy and Diana C. Robertson, "Fairness of Pricing Decisions," *Business Ethics Quarterly,* April 1999, pp. 225–43.

9. John De Graaf, "The Overspent American/Luxury Fever," *The Amicus Journal,* Summer 1999, pp. 41–43.

10. James Twitchell, "Two Cheers for Materialism," *The Wilson Quarterly,* Spring 1999, pp. 16–26; and Twitchell, *Lead Us into Temptation: The Triumph of American Materialism* (New York: Columbia University Press, 1999).

11. Kim Clark, "Real-World-O-Nomics: How to Make Traffic Jams a Thing of the Past," *Fortune,* March 31, 1997, p. 34.

12. Lee Hultgreen and Kim Kawada, "San Diego's Interstate 15 High-Occupancy/Toll Lane Facility Using Value Pricing," *ITE Journal,* June 1999, pp. 22–27.

13. From an advertisement for *Fact* magazine, which does not carry advertisements.

14. See Shawn Tully, "It's Time for Merger Mania II," *Fortune,* June 7, 1999, pp. 231–32.

15. Steve Hamm, "Microsoft's Future," *Business Week,* January 19, 1998, pp. 58–68; and Ronald. A. Cass, "Microsoft, Running Scared," *New York Times,* June 28, 1999, p. 17.

16. For more details, see Paul N. Bloom and Stephen A. Greyser, "The Maturing of Consumerism," *Harvard Business Review,* November–December 1981, pp. 130–39, Robert J. Samualson, "The Aging of Ralph Nader," *Newsweek,* December 16, 1985, p. 57; Douglas A. Harbrecht, "The Second Coming of Ralph Nader," *Business Week,* March 6, 1989, p. 28; George S. Day and David A. Aaker, "A Guide to Consumerism," *Marketing Management,* Spring 1997, pp. 44–48; and Benet Middleton, "Consumerism: A Pragmatic Ideology," *Consumer Policy Review,* November–December, 1998, pp. 213–17.

17. Stuart L. Hart, "Beyond Greening: Strategies for a Sustainable World," *Harvard Business Review,* January–February 1997, pp. 66–76. Also see Jacquelyn Ottman, "What Sustainability Means to Marketers," *Marketing News,* July 21, 1997, p. 4; and James L. Kolar, "Environmental Sustainability: Balancing Pollution Control with Economic Growth," *Environmental Quality Management,* Spring 1999, pp. 1–10.

18. Michael E. Porter and Claas van der Linde, "Green *and* Competitive: Ending the Stalemate," *Harvard Business Review,* September–October 1995, pp. 120–34.

19. Hart, "Beyond Greening," p. 72. For other examples, see Jacquelyn Ottman, "Environmental Winners Show Sustainable Strategies," *Marketing News,* April 27, 1998, p. 6.

20. Hart, "Beyond Greening," p. 73; Linda Grant, "Monsanto's Bet: There's Gold in Going Green," *Fortune,* April 14, 1997, pp. 116–18; and Carl Pope, "Billboards of the Garden Wall," *Sierra,* January–February 1999, pp. 12–13.

21. See John Audley, *Green Politics and Global Trade: NAFTA and the Future of Environmental Politics* (Georgetown University Press, 1997); Lars K. Hallstrom, "Industry Versus Ecology: Environment in the New Europe," *Futures,* February 1999, pp. 25–38; Joe McKinney, "NAFTA: Four Years down the Road," *Baylor Business Review,* Spring 1999, pp. 22–23; Andreas Diekmann and Axel Franzen, "The Wealth of Nations and Environmental Concern," *Environment and Behavior,* July 1999, pp. 540–49.

22. Michelle Wirth Fellman, "New Product Marketer of 1997," *Marketing News,* March 30, 1998, pp. E2, E12; and "Tooth Truths," *Discount Merchandiser,* June 1999, p. 52.

23. Information accessed online at www.HermanMiller.com/company/environment/conservation.html, January 2000.

24. Dan R. Dalton and Richard A. Cosier, "The Four Faces of Social Responsibility," *Business Horizons,* May–June 1982, pp. 19–27.

25. John F. Magee and P. Ranganath Nayak, "Leaders' Perspectives on Business Ethics," *Prizm,* Arthur D. Little, Inc., Cambridge, MA, first quarter, 1994, pp. 65–77. Also see Kumar C. Rallapalli, "A Paradigm for Development and Promulgation of a Global Code of Marketing Ethics," *Journal of Business Ethics,* January 1999, pp. 125–37.

26. Ibid., pp. 71–72. Also see Thomas Donaldson, "Values in Tension: Ethics away from Home," *Harvard Business Review,*

September–October 1996, pp. 48–62; and Patrick E. Murphy, "Character and Virtue Ethics in International Marketing: An Agenda for Managers, Researchers, and Educators," *Journal of Business Ethics,* January 1999, pp. 107–24.

27. Mark Hendricks, "Ethics in Action," *Management Review,* January 1995, pp. 53–55.

28. Kenneth Labich, "The New Crisis in Business Management," *Fortune,* April 20, 1992, pp. 167–76, p. 176.

29. From "Ethics as a Practical Matter," a message from David R. Whitman, chairman of the board of Whirlpool Corporation, as reprinted in Ricky E. Griffin and Ronald J. Ebert, *Business*

(Upper Saddle River, NJ: Prentice Hall, 1989), pp. 578–79. For more on marketing ethics, see Lynn Sharp Paine, "Managing for Organizational Integrity," *Harvard Business Review,* March–April 1994, pp. 106–17; Tom McInerney, "Double Trouble: Combining Business and Ethics," *Business Ethics Quarterly,* January 1998, pp. 187–89; John F. Gaski, "Does Marketing Ethics Really Have Anything to Say?" *Journal of Business Ethics,* February 1999, pp. 315–34; and Thomas W. Dunfee, N. Craig Smith, and William T. Ross, "Social Contracts and Marketing Ethics," *Journal of Marketing,* July 1999, pp. 14–32.

COMPANY CASE

20

Guns: Control Them, Ban Them, or Make Them Safe?

The fatal shooting of 12 students and a teacher at Columbine High School in Littleton, Colorado, shocked the nation and focused attention on issues of weapons and school safety, specifically on the issue of gun control. Outraged parents and concerned citizens asked; "How did those teenagers obtain the guns they used in their shooting spree? What can be done to prevent more high school shootings?" The following fall, schools across the United States installed safety precautions such as surveillance cameras, student ID programs, metal detectors, weapons checks by police and sheriff's deputies, and even the mandatory use of clear plastic book bags.

The "guns at schools" controversy is just the latest skirmish in a long standing war between supporters and opponents of gun control. On one side, the National Rifle Association (NRA), recreational users (hunters, target shooters, rifle sportsmen), and gun manufacturers claim that gun control violates citizens' constitutional rights to own weapons. Gun control, they maintain, would simply lead to a large black market for weapons. They promote the slogan: "When guns are outlawed, only outlaws will have guns." On the other side, an increasingly scared and angry population is demanding that something be done to control the sale of guns.

The major attack on the production and marketing of guns has been through the legal system. Over the years, a number of laws have been passed regulating gun production and sales. In 1968, in an effort to prevent the import of small, inexpensive, defect-prone handguns, legislators passed the Gun Control Act. This act required that imported guns meet certain safety, design, and quality tests not required of guns made in the United States. The 1994 Federal Crime Bill banned the manufacture of ammunition magazines that contain more than 10 rounds, except for police guns. (A magazine is the part that holds ammunition.) A new background-check law was enacted requiring background checks prior to the issuance of gun permits that would prevent guns from falling into the hands of criminals.

However, legal measures do not always have their intended effect. For example, the threatened passage of the background check legislation actually increased the sale of weapons, as individuals stocked up on guns in anticipation of the new restrictions. Limits on the size of magazines has had the curious effect of dramatically increasing the demand for used police guns, which still had bigger magazines.

To fully understand why legal restrictions don't always work, you need to examine the marketing of guns in the United States. A major segment of the gun-toting population is, of course, law enforcement officials. As gun manufacturers produce increasingly sophisticated and improved products, police departments nationwide need to provide officers with the latest and best weapons available. But when police departments purchase new guns, what happens to the old ones? Ideally, they would be destroyed. However, given the high costs of weaponry, many budget-constrained police departments end up trading in the old guns for new ones—a strategy encouraged by gun manufacturers to stimulate sales of new products and by wholesalers to get an inventory of big-magazine guns. The manufacturers then sell the used guns to gun wholesalers, who in turn sell them to dealers.

As a result, almost anyone can buy a former police weapon with one of those larger magazines. Indeed, some dealers market ex–police weapons heavily. In New Orleans, for example, one dealer advertised in the local paper: "Own a piece of New Orleans history. All are original duty weapons and are numbered and stamped N.O.P.D." As a purchase incentive, the guns came with two 15-round pre-ban clips. So much for keeping big magazine guns off the streets.

In fact, the gun used by neo-Nazi Buford O. Furrow Jr.—who wounded five people in an attack on a Jewish community center in suburban Los Angeles and then killed a U.S. postal worker of Filipino descent—was traced back to the Cosmopolis, Washington, police department. Further study found that at least 1,100 former police guns were among the 193,203 crime guns traced in 1998 by the Federal Bureau of Alcohol, Tobacco, and Firearms. This is not a very pleasing statistic.

Disgusted with the high costs to taxpayers of the law enforcement, medical, and legal expenses associated with gun crime, 28 cities have sued gun manufacturers over their failure to control the sale and distribution of their products. However, one of the cities suing is New Orleans, and incidents such as the flagrant ads by the New Orleans gun dealer and the Buford Furrow shooting have undermined these suits. When this was disclosed on the *Today Show*, the mayor of New Orleans tried to justify the gun trade-ins on the basis that the gun manufacturer, Glock, had agreed not to resell the weapons in Louisiana. However, transporting the guns out of state proved to do little more than make them another state's problem.

One other option is to force wholesalers and manufacturers to sell the police trade-ins and other used guns outside the United States. Most manufacturers, however, do not see this as a viable solution—the United States is the major international market. Given its size, affluence, and lack of tariff protection, the U.S. gun market is where most manufacturers expect to make the bulk of their sales. The international financial crisis of 1998 decimated gun sales around the globe, and 29 other countries have enacted much tougher gun control laws than those found in the United States. For example, Great Britain outlawed the sale of all handguns after an elementary school massacre in 1996.

In the 1960s, in an effort to give gun users maximum choice and the lowest prices, the NRA argued against import controls on guns. Firearms manufacturers found themselves in a bind—they could hardly argue for a limit on imports, because that might lead to more severe gun control measures in their own home market. The result was a bonanza for foreign companies such as Taurus of Brazil. In Taurus's home Brazilian market, gun control laws are so severe that the company has begun making motorcycle helmets, bulletproof vests, and auto parts. To get around U.S. gun laws limiting the import of guns with less than three-inch barrels, Taurus ships guns with five-inch barrels into the United States and then mills them down in a "gun-customizing" program—all perfectly legal. Faced with the specter of a total ban on handgun sales in Brazil, Taurus has built manufacturing facilities in the United States and has even attempted to sell its helmets here. But after paying $100,000 to the family of a young U.S. man who died in a motorcycle accident while wearing a Taurus helmet, Taurus has decided to stick to guns. As the company president says, "Product liability laws for helmets in the United States are just crazy."

Other options open to gun makers include the manufacture of safer guns. For example, Taurus has developed a gun with a safety lock. The lock sits on the back of a revolver's hammer and can be opened with a tiny key. The major advantage of this lock over others is that it can't be lost, broken, or pried off. To appeal to the female and more safety conscious markets, Smith & Wesson is developing a "smart gun" that uses microchip technology to prevent anyone other than an authorized owner to pull the trigger. However, the cost and reliability of such guns has been questioned. Savage Arms reduced the weight of its guns by using plastic parts and added devices

to reduce painful recoil, the "kick" in a gun that is being fired. This gun has been a hit with the senior market.

Making safer guns can be a dangerous strategy for manufacturers. In doing so, they are acknowledging that they really can do something to make their products safe. Antigun groups use this fact as crucial evidence in lawsuits indicating that gun manufacturers have been able to make safer product for years, but simply have failed to do so. According to Dennis Henigan, legal director for the Center to Prevent Handgun Violence, the Taurus lock "should have been made long ago and could have saved countless lives across the country." Others, such as Stephen Teret of The Johns Hopkins University Center for Gun Policy Research, argue that a small key and a lock aren't adequate protection—that perhaps the gun industry should do more.

At this point, gun manufacturers are between a rock and a hard place. Their sales are off by more than 20 percent. The proportion of men owning guns dropped from 52 percent in the 1980s to only 38 percent in 1998. Both hunting and target shooting are on the decline. Marketing efforts to expand gun sales appear to be having limited impact. For example, Smith & Wesson's efforts to target women with the LadySmith handgun failed, as did its marketing to teens through 4-H groups and the Junior Chamber of Commerce. Summer camps and schools have eliminated riflery courses due to public pressure. Declining sales, increasing lawsuits, prospects of tougher gun laws, and rising concerns over school shootings are all shooting down attempts by U.S. gun manufacturers to save their U.S. market.

Questions

1. In your opinion, how has marketing intensified the problems of selling and distributing guns?
2. What are the roles played by the various marketing intermediaries? How could each be controlled, if at all?
3. What are the pros and cons of the gun manufacturers' options discussed in the case: selling guns abroad, tougher gun control laws, or safer guns?
4. Take the part of Smith & Wesson and outline a marketing strategy for selling its products. Suggest a targeting and positioning strategy and a marketing mix that would support this strategy. Could the societal marketing concept be applied to the marketing of guns?
5. Take the part of the Center to Prevent Handgun Violence and outline a marketing strategy for accomplishing this organization's goals.

Sources: Paul Barret and Alexei Barrionuevo, "Guns: Handgun Makes Recoil as Industry Shakes Out," *Wall Street Journal,* September 20, 1999, pp. B1, B4; Peter Fritsch, "Brazil's Taurus Shows Why Gun Makers Are Grateful to the U.S.," *Wall Street Journal,* August 11, 1999, pp. A1, A8; Hunter T. George, "Police Debate What to Do with Old Guns," *Greensboro News and Record,* August 30, 1999, pp. A1, A6; Vanessa O'Connell, "Cities Suing Gun Firms Have a Weak Spot: They're Suppliers, Too," *Wall Street Journal,* August 16, 1999, pp. A1, A8; Vanessa O'Connell, "In the Market for Guns, The Customers Aren't Coming Back for More," *Wall Street Journal,* October 26, 1999, pp. A1, A10.

AOL: WORLD ONLINE?

AOL, ANYWHERE

America Online, Inc., is a $5 billion company that makes its money by selling dial-up Internet access services and advertising and by managing e-commerce activities for the 21 million members who connect to it via PCs. That's pretty impressive, especially when you consider that AOL is one of the few Internet companies that has actually made a profit.

One reason for AOL's success has been its narrow focus on average consumers and its determination to make using its service simple and clear. Other Internet service providers (ISPs) have offered complicated processes and provided little guidance for users. AOL, however, offers a single piece of software that integrates in one interface the viewing of content, e-mail, and instant messaging. Other ISPs offer these interfaces separately, often confusing users.

However, AOL's managers aren't satisfied. They have a vision that before long AOL will let you use your cell phone and AOL to send an instant message, your handheld pocket organizer and AOL to check your stock portfolio, your AOL TV to watch the news, and, of course, your PC to find that last-minute birthday present at Shop@AOL. Analysts call this "everywhere computing"—a vast array of companies offering many newly invented information devices that allow you to connect to the Internet. AOL calls its version AOL Anywhere. CEO Stephen Case admits, "We want to be as pervasive as the telephone or TV but even more valuable in people's lives."

BREAKING WINDOWS

Industry analysts predict that by 2002 companies will sell more than 55 million new information appliances a year, far outnumbering consumer PC sales. Although AOL is the dominant provider of PC-based Internet access, the company realizes that it must make the transition to information-appliance-based Internet access or risk being left behind.

AOL's major competitor is Microsoft, which it already battles in the Web portal business, dial-up access, and corporate software. Microsoft has a real advantage because of the dominance of its Windows operating system. Almost every time someone turns on a PC, they see Windows, no matter what other program they may eventually use. Moreover, Microsoft is using its massive cash hoard to make significant investments in interactive TV and cable, trying to establish its place as the access provider for cable TV set-top boxes.

However, because many analysts believe that many of the new information appliances will run on something other than Windows, AOL has a chance to catch up with Microsoft by becoming the brand that people see as they access the Web on these devices. Rather than having separate e-mail accounts and other functions for every device they own, AOL believes that people will want to use AOL's software and services for all their appliances.

AOL figures the first customers for the new services will be its existing customers, so there won't be much new revenue. The challenge will be getting new subscribers to sign up. However, the company admits that it doesn't know exactly how it will approach selling its new services. Still, AOL is plowing ahead with its investments. In 1999, it invested about $165 million on its Anywhere services. It has agreed to offer its instant messenger service through Motorola's smart phone and two-way pagers. It will put its e-mail service on 3Com's Palm Pilot organizers. Moreover, AOL announced it would work with Gateway to develop a small, inexpensive Web terminal that dials directly to AOL. It hopes to get Gateway and others to use its Internet browser, Netscape, in these devices, rather than Microsoft's Internet Explorer.

DOING DEALS

Because AOL collects membership fees and earns fees for sales completed over its service, as well as advertising fees, every member counts. So, in addition to developing new ways to serve customers, it needs to get more customers.

In December 1999, AOL and Wal-Mart announced an agreement for Wal-Mart to offer a co-branded Internet access service to its customers using AOL's Compuserve brand. Given that Internet users have been disproportionately higher-income households, the AOL-Wal-Mart service should open Internet access to more customers with lower incomes who often live in more rural areas that have lower Internet penetration.

AOL's move follows similar moves by Microsoft. Microsoft already has a co-branding alliance with RadioShack, the electronics retailer, and recently announced a deal with Best Buy, another consumer electronics retailer. Kmart and Yahoo! have also announced a *free* Internet access service.

FREE SURFING

The Kmart–Yahoo! service is just another challenge AOL faces, and not the first free one. NetZero, Inc., began offering free Internet access in 1999 and quickly gathered 1.7 million registered users. Other companies, like Freei

783

Networks, also offer free service, and some observers suggest that these free services threaten AOL's dominance. Others, however, argue that these free services will have the same costs to support their telecommunications networks but will not have AOL's $21.95 monthly subscription fee. They will have to amass enough users so advertisers will pay for advertising space on the free services' Web sites.

An investment analyst estimates that it costs AOL about $.40 per hour per user for telecommunications service. Because the average user is online about 27 hours per month, this means that AOL's total telecommunications costs per customer are about $10.80. In addition, AOL earns about $4.50 per month per user in advertising, e-commerce, and nonsubscription fee revenue. Subtracting the telecommunications costs from the fee revenue means that AOL would lose about $6.30 per customer per month if it were not for the subscription revenue. Moreover, that loss does not include the costs of marketing, customer support, and corporate overhead. Bob Pittman, AOL's president, also wonders if the free service providers will have enough network capacity to handle the traffic they might experience.

However, the free services argue that they can make their business model work. They believe that they can generate more advertising revenue because their users are willing to look at more ads given that they are getting service for free. The users must provide demographic information, and NetZero has a box that stays on the users' monitors whenever they are on the Internet, constantly providing targeted advertising messages. If the free services are successful, however, AOL would have to cut its prices. This would have a dramatic impact on its revenues. Already, AOL is responding by offering its Compuserve service as a "value brand" and charging $9.95 per month for 20 hours of access. In fact, this is the package that AOL will offer through Wal-Mart.

EUROPE ONLINE?

Although AOL is the world's largest Internet company, it has been slow to act like it outside of the United States. In 1999, it formed AOL Europe in a partnership with media conglomerate Bertelsmann AG. However, Deutsche Telekom AG's T-Online unit has out maneuvered AOL in Germany, gathering 3.4 million users. In fact, T-Online recruited 700,000 subscribers in 1999 alone—a total that matches AOL Europe's total subscriber base in Germany. For Europe as a whole, AOL has only 2.7 million subscribers.

In England, AOL Europe ran into another free service, Freeserve PLC. Although Freeserve offers free Internet access, consumers in England have to pay for local phone calls, whereas in the United States such calls are built into the monthly telephone service fee. This difference in how customers pay has confused AOL, which tried simply to carry over its U.S. flat-rate pricing scheme. AOL didn't pay much attention to Freeserve's arrival, and within months Freeserve had recruited 1 million users and taken over as the United Kingdom's top Internet service provider. Moreover, hundreds of UK retailers, sports clubs, and others jumped in with their own free Internet access plans. Freeserve and the other providers simply contract with a telecommunications company to provide the Internet access. When the user pays for the local call, Freeserve or the other providers actually receive a part of the fee, which is also enough to cover the cost of Internet access.

Europe has been a challenging market for many U.S. firms. Accustomed to first-mover advantages they gained in the United States, many firms like AOL have been sluggish in adapting to the European market. "Europe really seems to stretch the brains of the U.S. companies," one observer noted. Although Europe represents the second-largest Internet market, with 37.1 million users, that market is still in its infancy. In fact, Europe includes many customs and cultures that produce a fragmented market that's difficult to conquer. Many firms underestimate the difficulty of working in Europe. Moreover, good consumer or market information is often not available.

AOL Europe is responding to the competitive counterpunches, however. In Germany, it announced a plan whereby users will pay 9.90 Marks (about $5.39) per month for unlimited access to AOL and the Internet and pay only 3.9 pfennigs (2 cents) per minute for the local call. Although these rates are below T-Online's 8.00 Marks per month and 6.0 pfennigs per minute, they are more expensive for users who spend more than 20 hours online per month. AOL's slowness to offer the partial flat-rate plan was due in part to the complicated German regulatory environment.

In England, AOL also slashed its prices, cutting phone rates to 1 penny (1.6 cents), and began a national advertising campaign including full-page newspaper ads and movie and television commercials that attack Freeserve. It also began distributing millions of AOL disks, a direct-mail strategy that worked for it in the United States.

AOL plans to follow these moves with a plan to offer more affordable PCs in Europe, where home PCs are less common than in the United States, due perhaps to lower average incomes. AOL is also talking with PC manufacturers about offering rebates to customers who buy the PCs and subscribe to AOL, much as it has done in the United States with its Compuserve rebates that PC makers offer with their machines.

CHALLENGES, CHALLENGES

Being a global business means facing global challenges. AOL must battle cash-rich Microsoft in its U.S. market while it fends off free-service providers who seem to pop up everywhere. In addition, it must deal with many differences in cultures, customs, and legal systems as it moves to provide worldwide Internet access. Moreover, if it cuts prices in Europe to counter competition, will this open the way for price cuts in its vital U.S. market, endangering it revenue base?

Questions

1. How has AOL delivered customer value and satisfaction? Is customer retention important in its business?

2. Who are AOL's competitors, and what competitive strategies are they following?

3. Why has AOL not been as successful in Europe as it has been in the United States?

4. What social responsibility and ethical issues should AOL consider as it enters international markets?

5. What marketing recommendations would you make to AOL for its U.S. and European operations?

Sources: Richard Waters, "The Americas: Wal-Mart, AOL in Low-Cost Net Move," *The Financial Times,* December 17, 1999, p. 30; Walter S. Mossberg, "EarthLink Comes Close to AOL in Ease of Use but Needs to Do More," *Wall Street Journal,* December 9, 1999, p. B1; "There's No Escaping AOL," *Business Week,* December 6, 1999, p. 92; Christopher Cooper and Stephanie Gruner, "U.S. Internet Firms Must Hustle to Catch Up in Europe," *Wall Street Journal,* November 15, 1999, p. A25; Neal Boudette and Stephanie Gruner, "AOL Launches a Fresh Campaign in Europe," *Wall Street Journal,* October 1, 1999, p. A11; Laurie Freeman, "NetZero Hits Space Running: Mark Goldston Says He's Found His 'Life's Work'," *Advertising Age,* November 1, 1999, p. S36; Tim Jackson, "Wringing a Good Net Profit from Free Access," *The Financial Times,* September 28, 1999, p. 19; Nick Wingfield, "Free Web Services Challenge AOL's Dominance," *Wall Street Journal,* September 23, 1999, p. B8.

MEASURING AND FORECASTING DEMAND

When a company finds an attractive market, it must estimate that market's current size and future potential carefully. This appendix presents the principles and tools for measuring and forecasting market demand.

To develop effective targeting strategies, and to manage their marketing efforts effectively, companies must be good at both measuring *current* market demand and forecasting *future* demand. The company can lose a lot of profit by overestimating or underestimating the market. Overly optimistic estimates of current or future demand can result in costly overcapacity or excess inventories. Underestimating demand can mean missed sales and profit opportunities.

MEASURING CURRENT MARKET DEMAND

Marketers will want to estimate three different aspects of current market demand— *total market demand, area market demand,* and *actual sales and market shares.*

Estimating Total Market Demand

Total market demand

The total volume of a product or service that would be bought by a defined consumer group in a defined geographic area in a defined time period in a defined marketing environment under a defined level and mix of industry marketing effort.

The **total market demand** for a product or service is the total volume that would be bought by a defined consumer group in a defined geographic area in a defined time period in a defined marketing environment under a defined level and mix of industry marketing effort. Total market demand is not a fixed number but a function of the stated conditions. For example, next year's total market demand for ice cream in the United States will depend on how much the makers of Sealtest, Breyers, Häagen-Dazs, Ben & Jerry's, and other brands spend on marketing. It will also depend on many environmental factors, ranging from the level of consumer health concerns to the weather in key market areas. The demand for the premium ice cream brands will be affected by economic conditions.

Figure A1.1 shows the relationship between total market demand and various market conditions. The horizontal axis shows different possible levels of industry marketing expenditures in a given time period. The vertical axis shows the resulting demand level. The curve shows the estimated level of market demand at varying levels of industry marketing effort. Some minimum level of sales would take place without any marketing expenditures. Greater marketing expenditures would yield higher levels of demand, first at an increasing rate, and then at a decreasing rate. Marketing efforts above a certain level would not cause much more demand.

Market demand as a function of industry marketing expenditures

FIGURE A1.1   Market demand

Market potential
The upper limit of market demand.

Primary demand
The level of total demand for all brands of a given product or service—for example, the total demand for motorcycles.

Selective demand
The demand for a given brand of a product or service.

This upper limit of market demand is called **market potential.** The industry market forecast shows the expected level of market demand corresponding to the planned level of industry marketing effort in the given environment.[1]

Companies selling in mature markets often take **primary demand**—total demand for all brands of a given product or service—as given. They concentrate their marketing resources on building **selective demand**—demand for *their* brand of the product or service. For example, in the United States, where it faces a mature soft drink market, Coca-Cola directs most of its marketing energies toward building consumer preference for Coke, Diet Coke, Sprite, and its other brands. However, in countries such as China or Russia, which are characterized by huge but largely untapped market potential, Coca-Cola attempts to build the primary demand for soft drinks, as well as preference for its own brands.

Companies have developed various practical methods for estimating total market demand. We will illustrate two here. Suppose Warner Communications Company wants to estimate the total annual sales of recorded compact disks. A common way to estimate total market demand is as follows:

$$Q = n \times q \times p$$

where Q = total market demand
             n = number of buyers in the market
             q = quantity purchased by an average buyer per year
             p = price of an average unit

Thus, if there are 100 million buyers of compact disks each year, the average buyer buys 6 disks a year, and the average price is $14, then the total market demand for disks is $8.4 billion ($100,000,000 \times 6 \times \$14$).

A variation of this approach is the *chain ratio method.* This method involves multiplying a base number by a chain of adjusting percentages. For example, suppose that Sony wants to estimate demand for its new line of digital cameras, which store images on chips until they are downloaded into a personal computer. Once in the PC, photos can be resized, cropped, enhanced, grouped, and printed. Sony's digital cameras are priced higher than ordinary 35mm cameras. Thus, Sony first plans to target only serious amateur photographers who have home computers and enough money to afford the new cameras. Sony can make a U.S. demand estimate using a chain of calculations like the following:

Total number of U.S. households

× The percentage of U.S. households containing one or more serious amateur photographers

× The percentage of these households owning a personal computer

× The percentage of PC-owning households with enough discretionary income to buy Sony's new digital camera

This simple chain of calculations would provide only a rough estimate of potential demand. However, more detailed chains involving additional segments and other qualifying factors would yield more accurate and refined estimates.

Estimating Area Market Demand

Companies face the problem of selecting the best sales territories and allocating their marketing budget optimally among these territories. Therefore, they need to estimate the market potential of different cities, states, and countries. Two major methods are available: the *market buildup method,* which is used primarily by business goods firms; and the *market factor index method,* which is used primarily by consumer goods firms.

Market Buildup Method

Market buildup method

A forecasting method that calls for identifying all the potential buyers in each market and estimating their potential purchases.

The **market buildup method** calls for identifying all the potential buyers in each market and estimating their potential purchases. Suppose a manufacturer of mining instruments developed an instrument that can be used in the field to test the actual proportion of gold or silver in metal-bearing ores. By using it, miners would not waste their time digging deposits of ore containing too little gold or silver to be commercially profitable. The manufacturer wants to price the instrument at $1,000. It sees each mine as buying one or more instruments, depending on the mine's size. The company wants to determine the market potential for this instrument in each mining state. It would hire a salesperson to cover each state that has a market potential of over $300,000. The company wants to start by finding the market potential in Colorado.

To estimate the market potential in Colorado, the manufacturer can consult the North American Industrial Classification System (NAICS) developed by the U.S. Bureau of the Census.[2] The NAICS is the government's coding system that classifies industries, for purposes of data collection and reporting, according to the processes they use to produce goods and services. Each major industrial group is assigned to a two-digit code—mining bears the code number 21. Within mining are further breakdowns (the gold ore and silver ore mining category has the code number 21222). Finally, gold and silver ores are subdivided into further NAICS groups, with six-digit code numbers (gold is 212221 and silver is 212222).

Next the manufacturer can turn to the U.S. Census of Mining to determine the number of gold- and silver-mining operations in each state, their locations within the state, and the number of employees, annual sales, and net worth. Suppose that in consulting the census for Colorado, the company finds the data located in columns 1 and 2 of Table A1.1. It can then prepare the market potential estimate shown. Column 1 classifies mines into three groups based on the number of employees. Column 2 shows the number of mines in each group. Column 3 shows the potential number of instruments that mines in each size class might buy. Column 4 shows the unit market potential (column 2 times column 3). Finally, column 5 shows the dollar market potential, given that each instrument sells for

TABLE A1.1   MARKET BUILDUP METHOD USING NAICS: INSTRUMENT POTENTIAL IN COLORADO

NAICS	(1) Number of Employees	(2) Number of Mines	(3) Potential Number Instruments per Size Class	(4) Unite Market Potential	(5) Dollar Market Potential (at $1,000 Each)
212221 (gold ore mining)	Under 10	40	1	40	
	10 to 50	20	2	40	
	Over 50	10	3	30	
		70		110	$110,00
212222 (silver ore mining)	Under 10	80	1	80	
	10 to 50	50	2	100	
	Over 50	20	4	80	
		150		260	$260,000
					$370,000

$1,000. In this example, Colorado has a market potential of $370,000. Therefore, the mining instrument manufacturer would hire one salesperson for Colorado. In the same way, companies in other industries can use the market buildup method to estimate market potential in specific market areas.

Market Factor Index Method

Consumer goods companies also have to estimate area market potentials. Consider the following example: A manufacturer of men's dress shirts wishes to evaluate its sales performance relative to market potential in several major market areas, starting with Indianapolis. It estimates total national potential for dress shirts at about $2 billion per year. The company's current nationwide sales are $140 million, about a 7 percent share of the total potential market. Its sales in the Indianapolis metropolitan area are $1,100,000. It wants to know whether its share of the Indianapolis market is higher or lower than its national 7 percent market share. To find this out, the company first needs to calculate market potential in the Indianapolis area.

Market factor index method

A forecasting method that identifies market factors that correlate with market potential and combines them into a weighted index.

A common method for calculating area market potential is the **market factor index method,** which identifies market factors that correlate with market potential and combines them into a weighted index. An excellent example of this method is called the *buying power index,* which is published each year by *Sales & Marketing Management* magazine in its *Survey of Buying Power.*[3] This survey estimates the buying power, or "ability to buy," for each region, state, and metropolitan area of the nation. The buying power index is based on three factors: the area's share of the nation's *population, effective buying income,* and *retail sales.* The buying power index (BPI) for a specific area is given by

$$BPI = .2 \times \text{percentage of national population in the area}$$
$$+ .5 \times \text{the percentage of effective buying income in the area}$$
$$+ .3 \times \text{percentage of national retail sales in the area}$$

Using this index, the shirt manufacturer looks up the Indianapolis metropolitan area and finds that this market has .5596 percent of the nation's population, .5984 percent of the nation's effective buying income, and .6594 percent of the nation's retail sales. Thus, the buying power index for Indianapolis is

$$BPI = (.2 \times .5596) + (.5 \times .5984) + (.3 \times .6594) = .6089$$

That is, Indianapolis should account for .6089 percent of the nation's total potential demand for dress shirts. Because the total national potential is $2 billion each year, total potential in Indianapolis equals $2 billion $\times$ .006089 = $12,178,000. Thus, the company's sales in Indianapolis of $1,100,000 amount to a $1,100,000 $\div$ $12,178,000 = 9.03 percent share of area market potential. Comparing this with its 7 percent national share, the company appears to be doing better in Indianapolis than in other parts of the country.

Many companies compute additional area demand measures. Marketers now can refine state-by-state and city-by-city measures down to census tracts or zip codes. Census tracts are small areas about the size of a neighborhood, and zip code areas (designated by the U.S. Post Office) are larger areas, often the size of small towns. Information on population size, family income, and other characteristics is available for each type of unit. Marketers can use this data to estimate demand in neighborhoods or other smaller geographic units within large cities.

Estimating Actual Sales and Market Shares

Besides estimating total and area demand, a company will want to know the actual industry sales in its market. Thus, it must identify its competitors and estimate their sales.

Industry's trade associations often collect and publish total industry sales, although not individual company sales. In this way, each company can evaluate its performance against the industry as a whole. Suppose the company's sales are increasing at a rate of 5 percent a year and industry sales are increasing at 10 percent. This company actually is losing its relative standing in the industry.

Another way to estimate sales is to buy reports from marketing research firms that audit total sales and brand sales. For example, Nielsen Media Research audits retail sales in various product categories in supermarkets and drugstores and sells this information to interested companies. A company can obtain data on total product category sales as well as brand sales. It can compare its performance with that of the total industry or any particular competitor to see whether it is gaining or losing in its relative standing.[4]

 # FORECASTING FUTURE DEMAND

Forecasting
The art of estimating future demand by anticipating what buyers are likely to do under a given set of conditions.

Forecasting is the art of estimating future demand by anticipating what buyers are likely to do under a given set of future conditions. Very few products or services lend themselves to easy forecasting. Those that do generally involve a product with steady sales, or sales growth, in a stable competitive situation. But most markets do not have stable total and company demand, so good forecasting becomes a key factor in company success.

Companies commonly use a three-stage procedure to arrive at a sales forecast. First they make an *environmental forecast,* followed by an *industry forecast,* followed by a *company sales forecast.* The environmental forecast calls for projecting inflation, unemployment, interest rates, consumer spending and saving, business investment, government expenditures, net exports, and other environmental events important to the company. The result is a forecast of gross domestic product, which is used along with other indicators to forecast industry sales. Then the company prepares its sales forecast by assuming that it will win a certain share of industry sales.

TABLE A1.2 COMMON SALES FORECASTING TECHNIQUES	
BASED ON	**METHODS**
What people say	Surveys of buyers' intentions
	Composite sales force opinions
	Expert opinion
What people do	Test markets
What people have done	Post-sales analysis
	Leading indicators

Companies use several specific techniques to forecast their sales. Table A1.2 lists many of these techniques. All forecasts are built on one of three information bases: what people say, what people do, or what people have done. The first basis—*what people say*—involves surveying the opinions of buyers or those close to them, such as salespeople or outside experts. It includes three methods: surveys of buyer intentions, composites of sales force opinions, and expert opinion. Building a forecast on *what people do* involves putting the product into a test market to assess buyer response. The final basis—*what people have done*—involves analyzing records of past buying behavior or using post-sales analysis.

Survey of Buyers' Intentions

One way to forecast what buyers will do is to ask them directly. Surveys are especially valuable if the buyers have clearly formed intentions, will carry them out, and can describe them to interviewers. However, this is sometimes not the case, and marketers must be careful when using consumer survey data to make forecasts.

Several research organizations conduct periodic surveys of consumer buying intentions. These organizations ask questions such as the following:

Do you intend to buy an automobile within the next six months?

0	.1	.2	.3	.4	.5	.6	.7	.8	.9	1.0
No chance		Slight chance		Fair chance		Good chance		Strong chance		For certain

This is called a *purchase probability scale.* In addition, the various surveys ask about the consumer's present and future personal finances, and his or her expectations about the economy. The various bits of information are combined into a *consumer sentiment measure* (Survey Research Center of the University of Michigan) or a *consumer confidence measure* (Sindlinger and Company). Consumer durable-goods companies subscribe to these indexes to help them anticipate major shifts in consumer buying intentions so that they can adjust their production and marketing plans accordingly.

For *business buying,* various agencies carry out intention surveys about plant, equipment, and materials purchases. The two best-known surveys are conducted by the U.S. Department of Commerce and McGraw-Hill. Most of the estimates have been within 10 percent of the actual outcomes.

Composite of Sales Force Opinions

When buyer interviewing is impractical, the company may base its sales forecasts on information provided by the sales force. The company typically asks its salespeople to estimate sales by product for their individual territories. It then adds up the individual estimates to arrive at an overall sales forecast.

Few companies use their sales force's estimates without some adjustments. Salespeople are biased observers. They may be naturally pessimistic or optimistic, or they may go to one extreme or another because of recent sales setbacks or successes. Furthermore, they are often unaware of larger economic developments, and they do not always know how their company's marketing plans will affect future sales in their territories. They may understate demand so that the company will set a low sales quota. They may not take the time to prepare careful estimates or may not consider it worthwhile.

Assuming these biases can be countered, a number of benefits can be gained by involving the sales force in forecasting. Salespeople may have better insights into developing trends than any other group. After participating in the forecasting process, the salespeople may have greater confidence in their quotas and more incentive to achieve them. Also, such "grassroots" forecasting provides estimates broken down by product, territory, customer, and salesperson.

Expert Opinion

Companies can also obtain forecasts by turning to experts. Experts include dealers, distributors, suppliers, marketing consultants, and trade associations. Thus, auto companies survey their dealers periodically for their forecasts of short-term demand. Dealer estimates, however, are subject to the same strengths and weaknesses as sales force estimates.

Many companies buy economic and industry forecasts from well-known firms. These forecasting specialists are in a better position than the company to prepare economic forecasts because they have more data available and more forecasting expertise.

Occasionally companies will invite a special group of experts to prepare a forecast. The experts may be asked to exchange views and come up with a group estimate (group discussion method). Or they may be asked to supply their estimates individually, with the company analyst combining them into a single estimate. Finally, they may supply individual estimates and assumptions that are reviewed by a company analyst, revised, and followed by further rounds of estimation (called the Delphi method).

Experts can provide good insights on which to base forecasts, but they can also be wrong. For example, in 1943, IBM Chairman Thomas J. Watson predicted, "I think there's a world market for about five computers." A short time later, *Popular Mechanics* sagely observed that "Computers in the future may weigh no more than 1.5 tons." As recently as 1981, Bill Gates, a founder of Microsoft, proclaimed that "640K ought to be enough for anybody." In 1876, Western Union asserted, "This 'telephone' has too many shortcomings to be seriously considered as a means of communication. The device is inherently of no value to us." In 1946, Daryl F. Zanuck, head of 20th Century Fox, made this pronouncement: "TV won't be able to hold on to any market it captures after the first six months. People will soon get tired of staring at a plywood box every night."[5] Where possible, the company should back up experts' opinions with estimates obtained using other methods.

Test Marketing

Where buyers do not plan their purchases carefully or where experts are not available or reliable, the company may want to conduct a direct test market. A direct test market is especially useful in forecasting new-product sales or established-product sales in a new distribution channel or territory. Test marketing is discussed in chapter 9.

Past-Sales Analysis

Sales forecasts can be developed on the basis of past sales. *Time-series analysis* consists of breaking down past time series into four components (trend, cycle, seasonal, and erratic) and projecting these components into the future. *Exponential smoothing* consists of projecting the next period's sales by combining an average of past sales and the most recent sales, giving more weight to the latter. *Statistical demand analysis* consists of measuring the impact level of each of a set of causal factors (e.g., income, marketing expenditures, price) on the sales level. Finally, *econometric analysis* consists of building sets of equations that describe a system and proceeding to statistically fit the parameters.

Leading Indicators

Leading indicators
Time series that change in the same direction but in advance of company sales.

Many companies try to forecast their sales by finding one or more **leading indicators**—other time series that change in the same direction but in advance of company sales. For example, a plumbing supply company might find that its sales lag behind the housing starts index by about four months. The housing starts index would then be a useful leading indicator. The National Bureau of Economic Research has identified 12 of the best leading indicators, and their values are published monthly in the *Survey of Current Business* (see www.bea.doc.gov/bea/pubs.htm).

KEY TERMS

Forecasting	Market factor index method	Selective demand
Leading indicators	Market potential	Total market demand
Market buildup method	Primary demand	

NOTES

1. For further discussion, see Gary L. Lilien, Philip Kotler, and K. Sridhar Moorthy, *Marketing Models* (Upper Saddle River, NJ: Prentice Hall, 1992).
2. The NAICS system recently replaced the long-standing Standard Industrial Classification (SIC) system. It was developed by the United States, Canada, and Mexico to provide statistics that are comparable across the three countries. NAICS includes 350 new industries, and 20 (instead of the SIC's 10) broad sectors of the economy, changes reflecting how the economy has changed. Industries are identified by a 6-digit rather than a 4-digit code. The first information based on the new system was published in early 1999 in the new Economic Census data. For more information, see www.census.gov/epcd/www/naics.html.
3. For more on using this survey, see "The Power of the Survey," *1999 Survey of Buying Power, Sales & Marketing Management,* September 1999, pp. 6–7.
4. For a more comprehensive discussion of measuring market demand, see Philip Kotler, *Marketing Management: Analysis, Planning, Implementation, and Control,* 10th ed. (Upper Saddle River, NJ: Prentice Hall, 2000), pp. 119–28.
5. The Special Libraries Association, taken off the Internet, March 1997.

MARKETING ARITHMETIC

One aspect of marketing not discussed within the text is marketing arithmetic. The calculation of sales, costs, and certain ratios is important for many marketing decisions. This appendix describes three major areas of marketing arithmetic: the *operating statement, analytic ratios,* and *markups and markdowns.*

OPERATING STATEMENT

Balance sheet
A financial statement that shows assets, liabilities, and net worth of a company at a given time.

Operating statement (profit-and-loss statement, income statement)
A financial statement that shows company sales, cost of goods sold, and expenses during a given period of time.

The operating statement and the balance sheet are the two main financial statements used by companies. The **balance sheet** shows the assets, liabilities, and net worth of a company at a given time. The **operating statement** (also called **profit-and-loss statement** or **income statement**) is the more important of the two for marketing information. It shows company sales, cost of goods sold, and expenses during a specified time period. By comparing the operating statement from one time period to the next, the firm can spot favorable or unfavorable trends and take appropriate action.

Table A2.1 shows the 2000 operating statement for Dale Parsons Men's Wear, a specialty store in the Midwest. This statement is for a retailer; the operating statement for a manufacturer would be somewhat different. Specifically, the section on purchases within the "cost of goods sold" area would be replaced by "cost of goods manufactured."

The outline of the operating statement follows a logical series of steps to arrive at the firm's $25,000 net profit figure:

Net sales	$300,000
Cost of goods sold	−175,000
Gross margin	$125,000
Expenses	−100,000
Net profit	$ 25,000

Gross sales
The total amount that a company charges during a given period of time for merchandise.

The first part details the amount that Parsons received for the goods sold during the year. The sales figures consist of three items: *gross sales, returns and allowances,* and *net sales.* **Gross sales** is the total amount charged to customers during the year for merchandise purchased in Parsons's store. As expected, some customers returned

TABLE A2.1 OPERATING STATEMENT: DALE PARSONS MEN'S WEAR, YEAR ENDING DECEMBER 31, 2000			
Gross sales			$325,000
Less: Sales returns and allowances			25,000
Net sales			$300,000
Cost of goods sold			
Beginning inventory, January 1, at cost		$ 60,000	
Gross purchases	$165,000		
Less: Purchase discounts	15,000		
Net purchases	$150,000		
Plus: Freight-in	10,000		
Net cost of delivered purchases		$160,000	
Cost of goods available for sale		$220,000	
Less: Ending inventory, December 31, at cost		$ 45,000	
Cost of goods sold			$175,000
Gross margin			$125,000
Expenses			
Selling expenses			
Sales, salaries, and commissions	$ 40,000		
Advertising	5,000		
Delivery	5,000		
Total selling expenses		$ 50,000	
Administrative expenses			
Office salaries	$ 20,000		
Office supplies	5,000		
Miscellaneous (outside consultant)	5,000		
Total administrative expenses		$ 30,000	
General expenses			
Rent	$ 10,000		
Heat, light, telephone	5,000		
Miscellaneous (insurance, depreciation)	5,000		
Total general expenses		$ 20,000	
Total expenses			$100,000
Net profit			$ 25,000

merchandise because of damage or a change of mind. If the customer gets a full refund or full credit on another purchase, we call this a *return*. Or the customer may decide to keep the item if Parsons will reduce the price. This is called an *allowance*. By subtracting returns and allowances from gross sales, we arrive at net sales—what Parsons earned in revenue from a year of selling merchandise:

Gross sales	$325,000
Returns and allowances	–25,000
Net sales	$300,000

The second major part of the operating statement calculates the amount of sales revenue Dale Parsons retains after paying the costs of the merchandise. We start with the inventory in the store at the beginning of the year. During the year, Parsons bought $165,000 worth of suits, slacks, shirts, ties, jeans, and other goods. Suppliers gave the store discounts totaling $15,000, so that net purchases were $150,000. Because the store is located away from regular shipping routes, Parsons had to pay an additional $10,000 to get the products delivered, giving the firm a net cost of $160,000. Adding the beginning inventory, the cost of goods available for sale amounted to $220,000. The $45,000 ending inventory of clothes in the store on December 31 is then subtracted to come

Cost of goods sold
The net cost to the company of goods sold.

up with the $175,000 **cost of goods sold.** Here again we have followed a logical series of steps to figure out the cost of goods sold:

Amount Parsons started with (beginning inventory)	$ 60,000
Net amount purchased	+150,000
Any added costs to obtain these purchases	+ 10,000
Total cost of goods Parsons had available for sale during year	$220,000
Amount Parsons had left over (ending inventory)	− 45,000
Cost of goods actually sold	$175,000

Gross margin
The difference between net sales and cost of goods sold.

The difference between what Parsons paid for the merchandise ($175,000) and what he sold it for ($300,000) is called the **gross margin** ($125,000).

In order to show the profit Parsons "cleared" at the end of the year, we must subtract from the gross margin the *expenses* incurred while doing business. *Selling expenses* included two sales employees, local newspaper and radio advertising, and the cost of delivering merchandise to customers after alterations. Selling expenses totaled $50,000 for the year. *Administrative expenses* included the salary for an office manager, office supplies such as stationery and business cards, and miscellaneous expenses including an administrative audit conducted by an outside consultant. Administrative expenses totaled $30,000 in 2000. Finally, the general expenses of rent, utilities, insurance, and depreciation came to $20,000. Total expenses were therefore $100,000 for the year. By subtracting expenses ($100,000) from the gross margin ($125,000), we arrive at the net profit of $25,000 for Parsons during 2000.

 ANALYTIC RATIOS

Operating ratios
Ratios of selected operating statement items to net sales that allow marketers to compare the firm's performance in one year with that in previous years (or with industry standards and competitors in the same year).

The operating statement provides the figures needed to compute some crucial ratios. Typically these ratios are called **operating ratios**—the ratio of selected operating statement items to net sales. They let marketers compare the firm's performance in one year to that in previous years (or with industry standards and competitors in the same year). The most commonly used operating ratios are the *gross margin percentage,* the *net profit percentage,* the *operating expense percentage,* and the *returns and allowances percentage.*

Another useful ratio is the *stockturn rate* (also called *inventory turnover rate*). The stockturn rate is the number of times an inventory turns over or is sold during a

Ratio		Formula	Computation From Table A2.1
Gross margin percentage	=	$\dfrac{\text{gross margin}}{\text{net sales}}$	$= \dfrac{\$125,000}{\$300,000} = 42\%$
Net profit percentage	=	$\dfrac{\text{net profit}}{\text{net sales}}$	$= \dfrac{\$\ 25,000}{\$300,000} = 8\%$
Operating expense percentage	=	$\dfrac{\text{total expenses}}{\text{net sales}}$	$= \dfrac{\$100,000}{\$300,000} = 33\%$
Returns and allowances percentage	=	$\dfrac{\text{returns and allowances}}{\text{net sales}}$	$= \dfrac{\$\ 25,000}{\$300,000} = 8\%$

specified time period (often one year). It may be computed on a cost, selling price, or units basis. Thus the formula can be

$$\text{Stockturn rate} = \frac{\text{cost of goods sold}}{\text{average inventory at cost}}$$

or

$$\text{Stockturn rate} = \frac{\text{selling price of goods sold}}{\text{average selling price of inventory}}$$

or

$$\text{Stockturn rate} = \frac{\text{sales in units}}{\text{average inventory in units}}$$

We will use the first formula to calculate the stockturn rate for Dale Parsons Men's Wear:

$$\frac{\$175,000}{(\$60,000 + \$45,000)/2} = \frac{\$175,000}{\$52,500} = 3.3$$

That is, Parsons's inventory turned over 3.3 times in 2000. Normally, the higher the stockturn rate, the higher the management efficiency and company profitability.

Return on investment (ROI)

A common measure of managerial effectiveness—the ratio of net profit to investment.

Return on investment (ROI) is frequently used to measure managerial effectiveness. It uses figures from the firm's operating statement and balance sheet. A commonly used formula for computing ROI is

$$\text{ROI} = \frac{\text{net profit}}{\text{sales}} \times \frac{\text{sales}}{\text{investment}}$$

You may have two questions about this formula: Why use a two-step process when ROI could be computed simply as net profit divided by investment? and What exactly is "investment"?

To answer these questions, let's look at how each component of the formula can affect the ROI. Suppose Dale Parsons Men's Wear has a total investment of $150,000. Then ROI can be computed as follows:

$$\text{ROI} = \frac{\$25,000 \text{ (net profit)}}{\$300,000 \text{ (sales)}} \times \frac{\$300,000 \text{ (sales)}}{\$150,000 \text{ (investment)}}$$

$$8.3\% \times 2 = 16.6\%$$

Now suppose that Parsons had worked to increase his share of the market. He could have had the same ROI if his sales had doubled while dollar profit and investment stayed the same (accepting a lower profit ratio to get higher turnover and market share):

$$\text{ROI} = \frac{\$25,000 \text{ (net profit)}}{\$600,000 \text{ (sales)}} \times \frac{\$600,000 \text{ (sales)}}{\$150,000 \text{ (investment)}}$$

$$4.16\% \times 4 = 16.6\%$$

Parsons might have increased its ROI by increasing net profit through more cost cutting and more efficient marketing:

$$\text{ROI} = \frac{\$50,000 \text{ (net profit)}}{\$300,000 \text{ (sales)}} \times \frac{\$300,000 \text{ (sales)}}{\$150,000 \text{ (investment)}}$$

$$16.6\% \ \times \ 2 = 33.2\%$$

Another way to increase ROI is to find some way to get the same levels of sales and profits while decreasing investment (perhaps by cutting the size of Parsons's average inventory):

$$\text{ROI} = \frac{\$25,000 \text{ (net profit)}}{\$300,000 \text{ (sales)}} \times \frac{\$300,000 \text{ (sales)}}{\$75,000 \text{ (investment)}}$$

$$8.3\% \ \times \ 4 = 33.2\%$$

What is "investment" in the ROI formula? *Investment* is often defined as the total assets of the firm. But many analysts now use other measures of return to assess performance. These measures include *return on net assets (RONA), return on stockholders' equity (ROE)*, or *return on assets managed (ROAM)*. Because investment is measured at a point in time, we usually compute ROI as the average investment between two time periods (say, January 1 and December 31 of the same year). We can also compute ROI as an "internal rate of return" by using discounted cash flow analysis (see any finance textbook for more on this technique). The objective in using any of these measures is to determine how well the company has been using its resources. As inflation, competitive pressures, and cost of capital increase, such measures become increasingly important indicators of marketing and company performance.

MARKUPS AND MARKDOWNS

Markup
The percentage of the cost or price of a product added to cost in order to arrive at a selling price.

Markdown
A percentage reduction from the original selling price.

Retailers and wholesalers must understand the concepts of **markups** and **markdowns.** They must make a profit to stay in business, and the markup percentage affects profits. Markups and markdowns are expressed as percentages.

There are two different ways to compute markups—on *cost* or on selling *price:*

$$\text{Markup percentage on cost} = \frac{\text{dollar markup}}{\text{cost}}$$

$$\text{Markup percentage on selling price} = \frac{\text{dollar markup}}{\text{selling price}}$$

Dale Parsons must decide which formula to use. If Parsons bought shirts for $15 and wanted to mark them up $10, his markup percentage on cost would be $10/$15 = 67.7 percent. If Parsons based markup on selling price, the percentage would be $10/$25 = 40 percent. In figuring markup percentage, most retailers use the selling price rather than the cost.

Suppose Parsons knew his cost ($12) and desired markup on price (25 percent) for a man's tie and wanted to compute the selling price. The formula is

$$\text{Selling price} = \frac{\text{cost}}{1 - \text{markup}}$$

$$\text{Selling price} = \frac{\$12}{.75} = \$16$$

As a product moves through the channel of distribution, each channel member adds a markup before selling the product to the next member. This "markup chain" is shown for a suit purchased by a Parsons customer for $200:

		$ Amount	% of Selling Price
Manufacturer	Cost	$108	90%
	Markup	12	10
	Selling price	120	100
Wholesaler	Cost	120	80
	Markup	30	20
	Selling price	150	100
Retailer	Cost	150	75
	Markup	50	25
	Selling price	200	100

The retailer whose markup is 25 percent does not necessarily enjoy more profit than a manufacturer whose markup is 10 percent. Profit also depends on how many items with that profit margin can be sold (stockturn rate) and on operating efficiency (expenses).

Sometimes a retailer wants to convert markups based on selling price to markups based on cost, and vice versa. The formulas are

$$\text{Markup percentage on selling price} = \frac{\text{markup percentage on cost}}{100\% + \text{markup percentage on selling cost}}$$

$$\text{Markup percentage on cost} = \frac{\text{markup percentage on selling price}}{100\% - \text{markup percentage on selling price}}$$

Suppose Parsons found that his competitor was using a markup of 30 percent based on cost and wanted to know what this would be as a percentage of selling price. The calculation would be:

$$\frac{30\%}{100\% + 30\%} = \frac{30\%}{130\%} = 23\%$$

Because Parsons was using a 25 percent markup on the selling price for suits, he felt that his markup was suitable compared with that of the competitor.

Near the end of the summer Parsons still had an inventory of summer slacks in stock. Therefore, he decided to use a *markdown,* a reduction from the original selling price. Before the summer he had purchased 20 pairs at $10 each, and he had since sold 10 pairs at $20 each. He marked down the other pairs to $15 and sold 5 pairs. We compute his *markdown ratio* as follows:

$$\text{Markdown percentage} = \frac{\text{dollar markdown}}{\text{total net sales in dollars}}$$

The dollar markdown is $25 (5 pairs at $5 each) and total net sales are $275 (10 pairs at $20 + 5 pairs at $15). The ratio, then, is $25/$275 = 9 percent.

Larger retailers usually compute markdown ratios for each department rather than for individual items. The ratios provide a measure of relative marketing performance for each department and can be calculated and compared over time. Markdown ratios can also be used to compare the performance of different buyers and salespeople in a store's various departments.

KEY TERMS

Balance sheet
Cost of goods sold
Gross margin
Gross sales

Markdown
Markup
Operating ratios

Operating statement (or profit-and-
  loss statement or income
  statement)
Return on investment (ROI)

CAREERS IN MARKETING

Now that you have completed this course in marketing, you have a good idea of what the field entails. You may have decided you want to pursue a marketing career because it offers constant challenge, stimulating problems, the opportunity to work with people, and excellent advancement opportunities. But you still may not know which part of marketing best suits you—marketing is a very broad field offering a wide variety of career options. This appendix helps you discover what types of marketing jobs best match your special skills and interests, shows you how to conduct the kind of job search that will get you the position you want in the company of your choice, describes marketing career paths open to you, and suggests other information resources.

 ## MARKETING CAREERS TODAY

The field of marketing is booming in the twenty-first century, with nearly a third of all Americans now employed in marketing-related positions. Marketing salaries may vary by company, position, and region, and salary figures change constantly. In general, entry-level marketing salaries usually are only slightly below those for engineering and chemistry but are equal to or exceed starting salaries in economics, finance, accounting, general business, and the liberal arts. Moreover, if you succeed in an entry-level marketing position, it's likely that you will be promoted quickly to higher levels of responsibility and salary. In addition, because of the consumer and product knowledge you will gain in these jobs, marketing positions provide excellent training for the highest levels in an organization. A recent study by an executive recruiting firm found that more top executives come out of marketing than any other functional group.

Overall Marketing Facts and Trends

In conducting your job search, consider the following facts and trends that are changing the world of marketing.

Technology: Technology is changing the way marketers work. For example, price coding allows instantaneous retail inventorying. Software for marketing training, forecasting, and other functions is changing the ways we market. The

Internet is creating new jobs and new recruiting rules. For example, consider the explosive growth in new media marketing. Whereas advertising firms have traditionally recruited "generalists" in account management, "generalist" has now taken on a whole new meaning—advertising account executives must now have both broad and specialized knowledge.

Diversity: The number of women and minorities in marketing continues to rise. Traditionally, women were mainly in retailing. Now, women and minorities are rapidly moving into all industries. They also are rising rapidly into marketing management. For example, women now outnumber men by nearly two to one as advertising account executives. As marketing becomes more global, the need for diversity in marketing positions will continue to increase, opening new opportunities.

Global: Companies such as Coca Cola, McDonald's, MTV, and Procter & Gamble have become multinational, with offices and manufacturing operations in hundred of countries. Indeed, such companies often make more profit from sales outside the United States than from within. It's not just the big companies that are involved in international marketing. Organizations of all sizes have moved into the global arena. Many new marketing opportunities and careers will be directly linked to the expanding global marketplace. The globalization of business also means that you will need more cultural, language, and people skills in the marketing world of the twenty-first century.

Nonprofit organizations: Increasingly, colleges, arts organizations, libraries, hospitals, and other nonprofit organizations are recognizing the need for effectively marketing their "products" and services to their various publics. This awareness has led to new marketing positions—with these organizations hiring their own marketing directors and marketing vice presidents or using outside marketing specialists.

 # LOOKING FOR A JOB IN TODAY'S MARKETING WORLD

To choose and find the right job, you will need to apply the marketing skills you've learned in this course, especially marketing analysis and planning. Follow these nine steps for marketing yourself: (1) Conduct a self-assessment and seek career counseling; (2) examine job descriptions; (3) develop job search objectives; (4) explore the job market and assess opportunities; (5) develop search strategies; (6) prepare a resumé; (7) write a cover letter and assemble supporting documents; (8) interview for jobs; and (9) follow up.

Conduct a Self-Assessment and Seek Career Counseling

If you're having difficulty deciding what kind of marketing position is the best fit for you, start out by doing some self-testing or getting some career counseling. Self-assessments require that you honestly and thoroughly evaluate your interests, strengths, and weaknesses. What do you do well (your best and favorite skills) and not so well? What are your favorite interests? What are your career goals? What makes you stand out from other job seekers? The answers to such questions may suggest which marketing careers you should seek or avoid. For help in making an effective self-assessment, look at the following books in your local bookstore: Richard Bolles, *What Color Is Your Parachute?* (Berkeley, CA: Ten Speed Press, published annually) and Barbara Sher, *I Could Do Anything If I Only Knew What It Was: How to Discover What You Really Want and How to Get It* (New York: Bantam/Doubleday/Dell, 1995).

For help in finding a career counselor to guide you in making a career assessment, Richard Bolles, *What Color Is Your Parachute?* contains a useful state-by-state sampling. (Some counselors can help you in your actual job search, too.) You can also consult the career counseling, testing, and placement services at your college or university.

Career Counseling on the Internet
Today an increasing number of colleges, universities, and commercial career counselors offer career guidance on the Internet. In general, college and university sites are by far the best. But one useful commercial site you might look at is JobSmart (www.jobsmart.org/tools/resume/index.htm).

Examine Job Descriptions

After you have identified your skills, interests, and desires, you need to see which marketing positions are the best match for them. Two U.S. Labor Department publications in your local library, the *Occupation Outlook Handbook* and the *Dictionary of Occupational Titles,* describe the duties involved in various occupations, the specific training and education needed, the availability of jobs in each field, possibilities for advancement, and probable earnings.

Your initial career shopping list should be broad and flexible. Look for different ways to achieve your objectives. For example, if you want a career in marketing management, consider the public as well as the private sector, and regional as well as national firms. Be open initially to exploring many options, then focus on specific industries and jobs, listing your basic goals as a way to guide your choices. Your list might include "a job in a start-up company, near a big city, on the West Coast, doing new product planning, with a computer software firm."

Explore the Job Market and Assess Opportunities

At this stage, you need to look at the market and see what positions are actually available. You do not have to do this alone. Any of the following may assist you.

College Placement Centers
Your college placement center is an excellent place to start. Besides posting specific job openings, placement centers have the current edition of the *College Placement Annual,* which lists job openings in hundreds of companies seeking college graduates for entry-level positions, as well as openings for people with experience or advanced degrees. More and more, schools are also going on the Internet. For example, the Web site of the career center of Emory University in Atlanta, Georgia, has a list of career links (www.emory.edu/CAREER/main/Links.html).

In addition, find out everything you can about the companies that interest you by consulting business magazines, annual reports, business reference books, faculty, career counselors, and others. Try to analyze the industry's and the company's future growth and profit potential, advancement opportunities, salary levels, entry positions, travel time, and other factors of significance to you.

Job Fairs

College placement offices often work with corporate recruiters to organize on-campus job fairs. You might also use the Internet to check on upcoming career fairs in your region. For example, visit www.jobweb.org/search/cfairs.

Networking and the Yellow Pages

Networking, or asking for job leads from friends, family, people in your community, and career centers, is one of the best ways to find a marketing job. An estimated 33 percent of jobs are found through networking. The idea is to spread your net wide, contacting anybody and everybody.

The phone book's yellow pages are another effective way to job search. Check out employers in your field of interest in whatever region you want to work, then call and ask if they are hiring for the position of your choice.

Summer Jobs and Internships

In some parts of the country one in seven students gets a job where he or she interned. On the Internet, many sites have separate internship areas. For examples, look at Tripod (www.tripod.com/explore/jobs_career/) and the Monster Board (www.monster.com). If you know a company for which you wish to work, go to that company's corporate Web site, enter the personnel area, and check for internships. If there are none listed, try e-mailing the personnel department, asking if internships are offered.

The Internet

A constantly increasing number of sites on the Internet deal with job hunting. You can also use the Internet to make contacts with people who can help you gain information on companies and research companies that interest you. The Riley Guide offers a great introduction to what jobs are available (www.rileyguide.com). Other helpful sites are Employment Opportunities for People with Disabilities (www.disserv.stu.umn.edu/TC/Grants/COL/listing/disemp) and The Global Village: Resources for Minorities on the Internet (www.vjf.com/pub/docs/jobsearch. html), which contains information on opportunities for African Americans, Hispanic Americans, Asian Americans, and Native Americans.

Most companies have their own Web sites upon which they post job listings. This may be helpful if you have a specific and fairly limited number of companies that you are keeping your eye on for job opportunities. But if this is not the case, remember that to find out what interesting marketing jobs the companies themselves are posting, you may have to visit hundreds of corporate sites.

Develop Search Strategies

Once you've decided which companies you are interested in, you need to contact them. One of the best ways is through on-campus interviews. But not every company you are interested in will visit your school. In such instances, you can write (this includes e-mail) or phone the company directly or ask marketing professors or school alumni for contacts.

Prepare Resumés

A resumé is a concise yet comprehensive written summary of your qualifications, including your academic, personal, and professional achievements, that showcases why you are the best candidate for the job. Many organizations use resumés to decide which candidates to interview.

In preparing your resumé, remember that all information on it must be accurate and complete. Resumés typically begin with the applicant's full name, telephone and fax numbers, and traditional mail and e-mail addresses. A simple and direct statement of career objectives generally appears next, followed by work history and academic data (including awards and internships), and then by personal activities and experiences applicable to the job sought. The resumé usually ends with a list of references the employer may contact. If your work or internship experience is limited, nonexistent, or irrelevant, then it is a good idea to emphasize your academic and nonacademic achievements, showing skills related to those required for excellent job performance.

There are three types of resumés. *Chronological* resumés, which emphasize career growth, are organized in reverse chronological order, starting with your most recent job. They focus on job titles within organizations, describing the responsibilities required for each job. *Functional* resumés focus less on job titles and work history and more on assets and achievements. This format works best if your job history is scanty or discontinuous. *Mixed,* or *combined,* resumés take from each of the other two formats. First, the skills used for a specific job are listed, then the job title is stated. This format works best for applicants whose past jobs are in other fields or seemingly unrelated to the position.

Your local bookstore or library has many books that can assist you in developing your resumé. Two popular guides are Tom Jackson, with Ellen Jackson, *The New Perfect Resumé* (Garden City, NY: Anchor Press/Doubleday, revised, 1996); Yana Parker, *The Damn Good Resumé Guide* (Berkeley, CA: Ten Speed Press, 1996); and Arthur Rosenberg and David Hizer, *The Resumé Handbook* (Adams Media Corporation, 1996). Computer software programs such as *WinWay Resumé* provide hundreds of sample resumés and ready-to-use phrases while guiding you through the resumé preparation process.

Online Resumés

Today more and more job seekers are posting their resumés on the Internet. Preparing an electronic resumé is somewhat different from preparing a traditional resumé. For example, you need to know the relevant rules about scanning (including the font that your computer will be unable to scan the attractive fonts you used in your original resumé) and keywords. Moreover, if you decide to post your resumé in a public area like a Web site, then for security purposes you might not want to include your street or business address or the names of previous employers or references. (This information can be mailed later to employers after you have been contacted by them.) The following sites might assist you in writing your online resumé: JobSmart (jobsmart.org/tools/resume/index.htm) and ResumixResumeBuilder (www.resumix.com). In addition, placement centers usually assist you in developing a resumé. (Placement centers can also help with your cover letter and provide job interview workshops.)

After you have written your resumé, you need to post it. The following sites may be good locations to start: Monster.com (www.monster.com) and Yahoo! Resumé Services, a listing narrowed to business and economy companies (www.yahoo.com/Business_and_Economy /Companies/Employment/resume_services).

Resumé Tips
★ Communicate your worth to potential employers in a concrete manner, citing examples whenever possible.

★ Be concise and direct.

★ Use active verbs to show you are a doer.

★ Do not skimp on quality or use gimmicks. Spare no expense in presenting a professional resumé.

★ Have someone critique your work. A single typo can eliminate you from being considered.

★ Customize your resumé for specific employers. Emphasize your strengths as they pertain to your targeted job.

★ Keep your resumé compact, usually one page.

★ Format the text to be attractive, professional, and readable. Avoid too much "design" or gimmicky flourishes.

Write a Cover Letter and Assemble Supporting Documents

Cover Letter

You should include a cover letter informing the employer that a resumé is enclosed. But a cover letter does more than this. It also serves to summarize in one or two paragraphs the contents of the resumé and explains why you think you are the right person for the position. The goal is to persuade the employer to look at the more detailed resumé. A typical cover letter is organized as follows: (1) the name and position of the person you are contacting; (2) a statement identifying the position you are applying for, how you heard of the vacancy, and the reasons for your interest; (3) a summary of your qualifications for the job; (4) a description of what follow-ups you intend to make, such as phoning in two weeks to see if the resumé has been received; (5) an expression of gratitude for the opportunity of being a candidate for the job.

Letters of Recommendation and Other Supporting Documents

Letters of recommendation are written references by professors, former and current employers, and others that testify to your character, skills, and abilities. A good reference letter tells why you would be an excellent candidate for the position. In choosing someone to write a letter of recommendation, be confident that the person will give you a good reference. In addition, do not assume the person knows everything about you or the position you are seeking. Rather, provide the person with your resumé and other relevant data. As a courtesy, allow the reference writer at least a month to complete the letter and enclose a stamped, addressed envelope with your materials.

In the packet containing your resumé, cover letter, and letters of recommendation, you may also want to attach other relevant documents that support your candidacy, such as academic transcripts, graphics, portfolios, and samples of writing.

Interview for Jobs

As the old saying goes, "The resumé gets you the interview; the interview gets you the job." The job interview offers you an opportunity to gather more information about the organization, while at the same time allowing the organization to gather more information about you. You'll want to present your best self. The interview process consists of three parts: before the interview, the interview itself, and after the interview. If you successfully pass through these stages, you will be called back for the follow-up interview.

Before the Interview

In preparing for your interview, do the following:

1. Understand that interviewers have diverse styles, including the "chitchat," let's-get-to-know-each-other style; the interrogation style of question after question; and the tough-probing "why, why, why" style; among others. So be ready for anything.
2. With a friend, practice being interviewed and then ask for a critique. Or, videotape yourself in a practice interview so that you can critique your own performance. Your college placement service may also offer "mock" interviews to help you.
3. Prepare at least five good questions whose answers are not easily found in the company literature, such as, "What is the future direction of the firm?" "How does the firm differentiate itself from competitors?" "Do you have a new-media division?"
4. Anticipate possible interview questions, such as "Why do you want to work for this company?" or "Why should we hire you?" Prepare solid answers before the interview. Have a clear idea of why you are interested in joining the company and the industry to which it belongs.
5. Avoid back-to-back interviews—they can be exhausting and it is unpredictable how long they will last.
6. Dress conservatively and professionally. Be neat and clean.
7. Arrive 10 minutes early to collect your thoughts and review the major points you intend to cover. Check your name on the interview schedule, noting the name of the interviewer and the room number. Be courteous and polite to office staff.
8. Approach the interview enthusiastically. Let your personality shine through.

During the Interview

During the interview, do the following:

1. Shake hands firmly in greeting the interviewer. Introduce yourself, using the same form of address the interviewer uses. Focus on creating a good initial impression.
2. Keep your poise. Relax, smile when appropriate, be upbeat throughout.
3. Maintain eye contact, good posture, and speak distinctly. Don't clasp your hands or fiddle with jewelry, hair, or clothing. Sit comfortably in your chair. Do not smoke, even if asked.
4. Carry extra copies of your resumé with you. Bring samples of your academic or professional work along.
5. Have your story down pat. Present your selling points. Answer questions directly. Avoid one-word or too-wordy answers.
6. Let the interviewer take the initiative but don't be passive. Find an opportunity to direct the conversation to things about yourself that you want the interviewer to hear.
7. To end on a high note, make your most important point or ask your most pertinent question during the last part of the interview.
8. Don't hesitate to "close." You might say, "I'm very interested in the position, and I have enjoyed this interview."
9. Obtain the interviewer's business card or address and phone number so that you can follow up later.

A tip for acing the interview: Before you open your mouth, find out *what it's like* to be a brand manager, sales representative, market researcher, advertising account executive, or other position for which you're interviewing.

After the Interview

After the interview, do the following:

1. After leaving the interview, record the key points that arose. Be sure to note who is to follow up and when a decision can be expected.
2. Analyze the interview objectively, including the questions asked, the answers to them, your overall interview presentation, and the interviewer's responses to specific points.
3. Immediately send a thank-you letter, mentioning any additional items and your willingness to supply further information.
4. If you do not hear within the specified time, write or call the interviewer to determine your status.

Follow Up

If you are successful, you will be invited to visit the organization. The in-company interview will probably run from several hours to an entire day. The organization will examine your interest, maturity, enthusiasm, assertiveness, logic, and company and functional knowledge. You should ask questions about issues of importance to you. Find out about the working environment, job role, responsibilities, opportunity for advancement, current industrial issues, and the company's personality. The company wants to discover if you are the right person for the job, whereas you want to find out if it is the right job for you. The key is to determine if the right fit exists between you and the company.

MARKETING JOBS

This section describes some of the key marketing positions.

Advertising

Advertising is one of today's hottest fields in marketing. In fact, *Money* magazine lists a position in advertising as among the 50 best jobs in America.

Job Descriptions

Key advertising positions include copywriter, art director, production manager, account executive, and media planner–buyer. *Copywriters* write advertising copy and help find the concepts behind the written words and visual images of advertisements. *Art directors,* the other part of the creative team, help translate the copywriters' ideas into dramatic visuals called "layouts." Agency artists develop print layouts, package designs, television layouts (called "storyboards"), corporate logotypes, trademarks, and symbols. *Production managers* are responsible for physically creating ads, in-house or by contracting through outside production houses. *Account executives* serve as liaisons between clients and agencies. They coordinate the planning, creation, production, and implementation of an advertising campaign for the account. *Media planners* determine the best mix of television, radio, newspaper, magazine, and other media for the advertising campaign.

Skills Needed, Career Paths, and Typical Salaries

Work in advertising requires strong people skills in order to interact closely with an often difficult and demanding client base. In addition, advertising attracts people with high skills in planning, problem solving, creativity, communication, initiative, leadership, and presentation. Advertising involves working under high levels of stress and pressure created by unrelenting deadlines. Advertisers frequently have to work long hours to meet deadlines for a presentation. But work achievements are very apparent, with the results of creative strategies observed by thousands or even millions of people.

Because they are so sought after, positions in advertising sometimes require an MBA. But there are many jobs open for business, graphics arts, and liberal arts undergraduates. Advertising positions often serve as gateways to higher-level management. Moreover, with large advertising agencies opening offices all over the world, there is the possibility of eventually working on global campaigns.

Starting advertising salaries are relatively low compared to some other marketing jobs because of strong competition for entry-level advertising jobs. You may even want to consider working for free to break in. Compensation will increase quickly as you move into account executive or other management positions. For more facts and figures, see the Web pages of *Advertising Age,* a key ad industry publication (www.adage.com, click on the Job Bank button), and the American Association of Advertising Agencies (www.aaaa.org).

Brand and Product Management

Brand and product managers plan, direct, and control business and marketing efforts for their products. They are involved with research and development, packaging, manufacturing, sales and distribution, advertising, promotion, market research, and business analysis and forecasting.

Job Descriptions

A company's brand management team consists of people in several positions. The *brand manager* guides the development of marketing strategies for a specific brand. The *assistant brand manager* is responsible for certain strategic components of the brand. The *product manager* oversees several brands within a product line or product group. The *product category manager* directs multiple product lines in the product category. The *market analyst* researches the market and provides important strategic information to the project managers. The *project director* is responsible for collecting market information on a marketing or product project. The *research director* oversees the planning, gathering, and analyzing of all organizational research.

Skills Needed, Career Paths, and Typical Salaries

Brand and product management requires high problem-solving, analytical, presentation, communication, and leadership skills, as well as the ability to work well in a team. Product management requires long hours and involves the high pressure of running large projects. In consumer goods companies, the newcomer—who usually needs an MBA—joins a brand team as an assistant and learns the ropes by doing numerical analyses and watching senior brand people. This person eventually heads the team and later moves on to manage a larger brand, then several brands. Many industrial goods companies also have product managers. Product management is one of the best training grounds for future corporate officers. Product management also offers good opportunities to move into international marketing. Product managers command relatively high salaries. Because this job category encourages or requires a master's degree, starting pay tends to be higher than in other marketing categories such as advertising or retailing.

Sales, Sales Management

Sales and sales management opportunities exist in a wide range of profit and non-profit organizations and in product and service organizations, including financial, insurance, consulting, and government organizations.

Job Descriptions

Key jobs include consumer sales, industrial sales, national account manager, service support, sales trainers, sales management, and teleseller. *Consumer sales* involves selling consumer products and services through retailers. *Industrial sales* includes selling products and services to other businesses. *National account managers (NAM)* oversee a few very large accounts. *Service support* personnel support salespeople during and after the sale of a product. *Sales trainers* train new hires and provide refresher training for all sales personnel. *Sales management* includes a sequence of positions ranging from district manager to vice president of sales. The *teleseller* (not to be confused with the home consumer telemarketer) offers service and support to field salespeople.

Salespeople enjoy active professional lives, working outside the office and interacting with others. They manage their own time and activities. Competition for top jobs can be intense. Every sales job is different, but some positions involve extensive travel, long workdays, and working under pressure, which can negatively impact personal life. You can also expect to be transferred more than once between company headquarters and regional offices.

Skills Needed, Career Paths, and Typical Salaries

Selling is a people profession in which you will work with people every day, all day long. Besides people skills, sales professionals need sales and communication skills. Most sales positions also require high problem-solving, analytical, presentation, and leadership ability as well as creativity and initiative. Teamwork skills are increasingly important.

Career paths lead from salesperson to district, regional, and higher levels of sales management and, in many cases, to the top management of the firm. Today, most entry-level sales management positions require a college degree. Increasingly, people seeking selling jobs are acquiring sales experience in an internship capacity or from a part-time job before graduating. Although there is a high turnover rate (one in four people leave their jobs in a year), sales positions are great springboards to leadership positions, with more CEOs starting in sales than in any other entry-level position. Possibly this explains why competition for top sales jobs is intense.

Starting base salaries in sales may be moderate, but compensation is often supplemented by significant commission, bonus, or other incentive plans. In addition, many sales jobs include a company car or car allowance. Successful salespeople are among most companies' highest paid employees.

Other Marketing Jobs

Retailing

Retailing provides an early opportunity to assume marketing responsibilities. Key jobs include store manager, regional manager, buyer, department manager, and salesperson. *Store managers* direct the management and operation of an individual store. *Regional managers* manage groups of stores across several states and report performance to headquarters. *Buyers* select and buy the merchandise that the store carries.

The *department manager* acts as store manager of a department, such as clothing, but on the department level. The *salesperson* sells merchandise to retail customers. Retailing can involve relocation, but generally there is little travel, unless you are a buyer. Retailing requires high people and sales skills because retailers are constantly in contact with customers. Enthusiasm, willingness, and communication skills are very helpful for retailers, too.

Retailers work long hours, but their daily activities are often more structured than some types of marketing positions. Starting salaries in retailing tend to be low, but pay increases as you move into management or some retailing specialty job.

Marketing Research
Marketing researchers interact with managers to define problems and identify the information needed to resolve them. They design research projects, prepare questionnaires and samples, analyze data, prepare reports, and present their findings and recommendations to management. They must understand statistics, consumer behavior, psychology, and sociology. A master's degree helps. Career opportunities exist with manufacturers, retailers, some wholesalers, trade and industry associations, marketing research firms, advertising agencies, and governmental and private nonprofit agencies.

New-Product Planning
People interested in new-product planning can find opportunities in many types of organizations. They usually need a good background in marketing, marketing research, and sales forecasting; they need organizational skills to motivate and coordinate others; and they may need a technical background. Usually, these people work first in other marketing positions before joining the new-product department.

Marketing Logistics (Physical Distribution)
Marketing logistics, or physical distribution, is a large and dynamic field, with many career opportunities. Major transportation carriers, manufacturers, wholesalers, and retailers all employ logistics specialists. Increasingly, marketing teams include logistics specialists, and marketing managers' career paths include marketing logistics assignments. Coursework in quantitative methods, finance, accounting, and marketing will provide you with the necessary skills for entering the field.

Public Relations
Most organizations have a public relations staff to anticipate problems with various publics, handle complaints, deal with media, and build the corporate image. People interested in public relations should be able to speak and write clearly and persuasively, and they should have a background in journalism, communications, or the liberal arts. The challenges in this job are highly varied and very people oriented.

Nonprofit Services
The key jobs in nonprofits include marketing director, director of development, event coordinator, publication specialist, and intern–volunteers. The *marketing director* is in charge of all marketing activities for the organization. The *director of development* organizes, manages, and directs the fund-raising campaigns that keep a nonprofit in existence. An *event coordinator* directs all aspects of fund-raising events, from initial planning through implementation. The *publication specialist* oversees publications designed to promote awareness of the organization. Although typically an unpaid position the *intern–volunteer* performs various marketing functions, and this

work can be an important step to gaining a full-time position. The nonprofit sector is typically not for someone who is money driven. Rather, most nonprofits look for people with a strong sense of community spirit and the desire to help others. So starting pay is usually lower than in other marketing fields. However, the bigger the nonprofit, the better your chance of rapidly increasing your income when moving into upper management.

OTHER RESOURCES

Professional marketing associations and organizations are another source of information about careers. Marketers belong to many such societies. You may want to contact some of the following in your job search:

American Advertising Federation, 1101 Vermont Avenue, NW, Suite 500, Washington, DC 20005 (202) 898-0089 (www.aaf.org)

American Marketing Association, 250 South Wacker Drive, Suite 200, Chicago, IL 60606. (312) 648-0536 (www.ama.org)

Council of Sales Promotion Agencies, 750 Summer Street, Stamford, CT 06901. (203) 325-3911

Market Research Association, 2189 Silas Deane Highway, Suite 5, Rocky Hill, CT 06067. (860) 257-4008 (www.mra-net.org)

National Council of Salesmen's Organization, 389 Fifth Avenue, Room 1010, New York, NY 10016. (718) 835-4591

National Management Association, 2210 Arbor Boulevard, Dayton, OH 45439. (513) 294-0421

National Retail Federation, 701 Pennsylvania Avenue NW, Suite 710, Washington, DC 20004. (202) 783-7971 (www.nrf.com)

Product Development and Management Association, 401 North Michigan Avenue, Chicago, IL 60611. (312) 527-6644 (www.pdma.org)

Public Relations Society of America, 33 Irving Place, Third Floor, New York, NY 10003. (212) 995-2230. (www.prsa.org)

Sales and Marketing Executives International, Statler Office Tower, Number 977, Cleveland, OH 44115. (216) 771-6650. (www.smei.org)

Women Executives in Public Relations, P.O. Box 609, Westport, CT, 06881. (203) 226-4947

Women in Advertising and Marketing, 4200 Wisconsin Avenue NW, Suite 106-238, Washington, DC 20016. (301) 369-7400

GLOSSARY

Adapted marketing mix An international marketing strategy for adjusting the marketing mix elements to each international target market, bearing more costs but hoping for a larger market share and return.

Administered VMS A vertical marketing system that coordinates successive stages of production and distribution, not through common ownership or contractual ties but through the size and power of one of the parties.

Adoption process The mental process through which an individual passes from first hearing about an innovation to final adoption.

Advertising Any paid form of nonpersonal presentation and promotion of ideas, goods, or services by an identified sponsor.

Advertising agency A marketing services firm that assists companies in planning, preparing, implementing, and evaluating all or portions of their advertising programs.

Advertising objective A specific communication *task* to be accomplished with a specific *target* audience during a specific period of *time*.

Advertising specialty Useful article imprinted with an advertiser's name, given as a gift to consumers.

Affordable method Setting the promotion budget at the level management thinks the company can afford.

Age and life-cycle segmentation Dividing a market into different age and life-cycle groups.

Agent A wholesaler who represents buyers or sellers on a relatively permanent basis, performs only a few functions, and does not take title to goods.

Allowance Promotional money paid by manufacturers to retailers in return for an agreement to feature the manufacturer's products in some way.

Alternative evaluation The stage of the buyer decision process in which the consumer uses information to evaluate alternative brands in the choice set.

Attitude A person's consistently favorable or unfavorable evaluations, feelings, and tendencies toward an object or idea.

Baby boom The major increase in the annual birthrate following World War II and lasting until the early 1960s. The "baby boomers," now moving into middle age, are a prime target for marketers.

Balance sheet A financial statement that shows assets, liabilities, and net worth of a company at a given time.

Basing-point pricing A geographical pricing strategy in which the seller designates some city as a basing point and charges all customers the freight cost from that city to the customer location, regardless of the city from which the goods are actually shipped.

Behavioral segmentation Dividing a market into groups based on consumer knowledge, attitude, use, or response to a product.

Belief A descriptive thought that a person holds about something.

Benchmarking The process of comparing the company's products and processes to those of competitors or leading firms in other industries to find ways to improve quality and performance.

Benefit segmentation Dividing the market into groups according to the different benefits that consumers seek from the product.

Brand A name, term, sign, symbol, or design, or a combination of these intended to identify the goods or services of one seller or group of sellers and to differentiate them from those of competitors.

Brand equity The value of a brand, based on the extent to which it has high brand loyalty, name awareness, perceived quality, strong brand associations, and other assets such as patents, trademarks, and channel relationships.

Brand extension Using a successful brand name to launch a new or modified product in a new category.

Break-even pricing (target profit pricing) Setting price to break even on the costs of making and marketing a product; or setting price to make a target profit.

Broker A wholesaler who does not take title to goods and whose function is to bring buyers and sellers together and assist in negotiation.

Business analysis A review of the sales, costs, and profit projections for a new product to find out whether these factors satisfy the company's objectives.

Business buyer behavior The buying behavior of organizations that buy goods and services for use in the production of other products and services that are sold, rented, or supplied to others. It also includes buying of goods by retailers and wholesalers for the purpose of reselling or renting them.

Business buying process The decision-making process by which business buyers establish the need for purchased products and services and identify, evaluate, and choose among alternative brands and suppliers.

Business portfolio The collection of businesses and products that make up the company.

Buyer The person who makes an actual purchase.

Buyer-readiness stages The stages consumers normally pass through on their way to purchase, including awareness, knowledge, liking, preference, conviction, and purchase.

Buying center All the individuals and units that participate in the business buying decision process.

By-product pricing Setting a price for by-products in order to make the main product's price more competitive.

Captive-product pricing Setting a price for products that must be used along with a main product, such as blades for a razor and film for a camera.

Cash discount A price reduction to buyers who pay their bills promptly.

Cash refund offer (rebate) Offer to refund part of the purchase price of a product to consumers who send a "proof of purchase" to the manufacturer.

Catalog marketing Direct marketing through print, video, or electronic catalogs that are mailed to a select customers, made available in stores, or presented online.

Category killer Giant specialty store that carries a very deep assortment of a particular line and is staffed by knowledgeable employees.

Causal research Marketing research to test hypotheses about cause-and-effect relationships.

Chain stores Two or more outlets that are owned and controlled in common, have central buying and merchandising, and sell similar lines of merchandise.

Channel conflict Disagreement among marketing channel members on goals and roles—who should do what and for what rewards.

Channel level A layer of intermediaries that performs some work in bringing the product and its ownership closer to the final buyer.

Closing The step in the selling process in which the salesperson asks the customer for an order.

Co-branding The practice of using the established brand names of two different companies on the same product.

Cognitive dissonance Buyer discomfort caused by postpurchase conflict.

Commercial online services Services that offer online information and marketing services to subscribers who pay a monthly fee, such as America Online, CompuServe, and Prodigy.

Commercialization Introducing a new product into the market.

Communication adaptation A global communication strategy of fully adapting advertising messages to local markets.

Competition-based pricing Setting prices based on the prices that competitors charge for similar products

Competitive advantage An advantage over competitors gained by offering consumers greater value, either through lower prices or by providing more benefits that justify higher prices.

Competitive marketing strategies Strategies that strongly position the company against competitors and that give the company the strongest possible strategic advantage.

Competitive-parity method Setting the promotion budget to match competitors' outlays.

Competitor analysis The process of identifying key competitors; assessing their objectives, strategies, strengths and weaknesses, and reaction patterns; and selecting which competitors to attack or avoid.

Competitor-centered company A company whose moves are mainly based on competitors' actions and reactions; it spends most of its time tracking competitors' moves and market shares and trying to find strategies to counter them.

Complex buying behavior Consumer buying behavior in situations characterized by high consumer involvement in a purchase and significant perceived differences among brands.

Concentrated marketing A market-coverage strategy in which a firm goes after a large share of one or a few submarkets.

Concept testing Testing new-product concepts with a group of target consumers to find out if the concepts have strong consumer appeal.

Consumer buying behavior The buying behavior of final consumers—individuals and households who buy goods and services for personal consumption.

Consumer market All the individuals and households who buy or acquire goods and services for personal consumption.

Consumer-oriented marketing A principle of enlightened marketing that holds that the company should view and organize its marketing activities from the consumers' point of view.

Consumer product Product bought by final consumer for personal consumption.

Consumerism An organized movement of citizens and government agencies to improve the rights and power of buyers in relation to sellers.

Contests, sweepstakes, games Promotional events that give consumers the chance to win something—such as cash, trips, or goods—by luck or through extra effort.

Contract manufacturing A joint venture in which a company contracts with manufacturers in a foreign market to produce the product.

Contractual VMS A vertical marketing system in which independent firms at different levels of production and distribution join together through contracts to obtain more economies or sales impact than they could achieve alone.

Convenience product Consumer product that the customer usually buys frequently, immediately, and with a minimum of comparison and buying effort.

Convenience store A small store, located near a residential area, that is open long hours seven days a week and carries a limited line of high-turnover convenience goods.

Conventional distribution channel A channel consisting of one or more independent producers, wholesalers, and retailers, each a separate business seeking to maximize its own profits even at the expense of profits for the system as a whole.

Corporate VMS A vertical marketing system that combines successive stages of production and distribution under single ownership—channel leadership is established through common ownership.

Corporate Web site Web sites that seek to build customer goodwill and to supplement other sales channels rather than to sell the company's products directly.

Cost of goods sold The net cost to the company of goods sold.

Cost-plus pricing Adding a standard markup to the cost of the product.

Countertrade International trade involving the direct or indirect exchange of goods for other goods instead of cash. Forms include barter, compensation (buyback), and counterpurchase.

Coupon Certificate that gives buyers a saving when they purchase a specified product.

Cultural environment Institutions and other forces that affect society's basic values, perceptions, preferences, and behaviors.

Culture The set of basic values, perceptions, wants, and behaviors learned by a member of society from family and other important institutions.

Customer-centered company A company that focuses on customer developments in designing its marketing strategies and on delivering superior value to its target customers.

Customer database An organized collection of comprehensive data about individual customers or prospects, including geographic, demographic, psychographic, and behavioral data.

Customer delivered value The consumer's assessment of the product's overall capacity to satisfy his or her needs. The difference between total customer value and total customer cost of a marketing offer—"profit" to the customer.

Customer lifetime value The amount by which revenues from a given customer over time will exceed the company's costs of attracting, selling, and servicing that customer.

Customer sales force structure A sales force organization under which salespeople specialize in selling only to certain customers or industries.

Customer satisfaction The extent to which a product's perceived performance matches a buyer's expectations. If the product's performance falls short of expectations, the buyer is dissatisfied. If performance matches or exceeds expectations, the buyer is satisfied or delighted.

Customer value The difference between the values the customer gains from owning and using a product and the costs of obtaining the product.

Deciders People in the organization's buying center who have formal or informal power to select or approve the final suppliers.

Decline stage The product life-cycle stage in which a product's sales decline.

Deficient products Products that have neither immediate appeal nor long-run benefits.

Demand curve A curve that shows the number of units the market will buy in a given time period at different prices that might be charged.

Demands Human wants that are backed by buying power.

Demarketing Marketing to reduce demand temporarily or permanently; the aim is not to destroy demand but only to reduce or shift it.

Demographic segmentation Dividing the market into groups based on demographic variables such as age, gender, family size, family life cycle, income, occupation, education, religion, race, and nationality.

Demography The study of human populations in terms of size, density, location, age, gender, race, occupation, and other statistics.

Department store A retail organization that carries a wide variety of product lines—typically clothing, home furnishings, and household goods; each line is operated as a separate department managed by specialist buyers or merchandisers.

Derived demand Business demand that ultimately comes from (derives from) the demand for consumer goods.

Descriptive research Marketing research to better describe marketing problems, situations, or markets, such as the market potential for a product or the demographics and attitudes of consumers.

Desirable products Products that give both high immediate satisfaction and high long-run benefits.

Differentiated marketing A market-coverage strategy in which a firm decides to target several market segments and designs separate offers for each.

Direct investment Entering a foreign market by developing foreign-based assembly or manufacturing facilities.

Direct-mail marketing Direct marketing through single mailings that include letters, ads, samples, foldouts, and other "salespeople with wings" sent to prospects on mailing lists.

Direct marketing Direct communications with carefully targeted individual consumers to obtain an immediate response and cultivate lasting customer relationships.

Direct marketing channel A marketing channel that has no intermediary levels.

Direct-response television marketing Direct marketing via television, including direct-response television advertising or infomercials and home shopping channels.

Discount A straight reduction in price on purchases during a stated period of time.

Discount store A retail institution that sells standard merchandise at lower prices by accepting lower margins and selling higher volume.

Disintermediation The elimination of a layer of intermediaries from a marketing channel or the displacement of traditional resellers by radically new types of intermediaries.

Dissonance-reducing buying behavior Consumer buying behavior in situations characterized by high involvement but few perceived differences among brands.

Distribution center A large, highly automated warehouse designed to receive goods from various plants and suppliers, take orders, fill them efficiently, and deliver goods to customers as quickly as possible.

Distribution channel A set of interdependent organizations involved in the process of making a product or service available for use or consumption by the consumer or business user.

Diversification A strategy for company growth by starting up or acquiring businesses outside the company's current products and markets.

Echo boomers The generation born from 1977 to 1994, the children of the baby boomers now numbering 72 million.

Economic community A group of nations organized to work toward common goals in the regulation of international trade.

Economic environment Factors that affect consumer buying power and spending patterns.

Electronic commerce (e-commerce) The general term for a buying and selling process that is supported by electronic means.

Embargo A ban on the import of a certain product.

Engel's laws Differences noted over a century ago by Ernst Engel in how people shift their spending across food, housing, transportation, health care, and other goods and services categories as family income rises.

Enlightened marketing A marketing philosophy holding that a company's marketing should support the best long-run performance of the marketing system; its five principles include consumer-oriented marketing, innovative marketing, value marketing, sense-of-mission marketing, and societal marketing.

Environmental management perspective A management perspective in which the firm takes aggressive actions to affect the publics and forces in its marketing environment rather than simply watching and reacting to them.

Environmental sustainability A management approach that involves developing strategies that both sustain the environment and produce profits for the company.

Environmentalism An organized movement of concerned citizens, businesses, and government agencies to protect and improve people's living environment.

Exchange The act of obtaining a desired object from someone by offering something in return.

Exchange controls Government limits on the amount of foreign exchange with other countries and on the exchange rate against other currencies.

Exclusive distribution Giving a limited number of dealers the exclusive right to distribute the company's products in their territories.

Experience curve (learning curve) The drop in the average per-unit production cost that comes with accumulated production experience.

Experimental research The gathering of primary data by selecting matched groups of subjects, giving them different treatments, controlling unrelated factors, and checking for differences in group responses.

Exploratory research Marketing research to gather preliminary information that will help define problems and suggest hypotheses.

Factory outlet Off-price retailing operation that is owned and operated by a manufacturer and that normally carries the manufacturer's surplus, discontinued, or irregular goods.

Fads Fashions that enter quickly, are adopted with great zeal, peak early, and decline very fast.

Fashion A currently accepted or popular style in a given field.

Fixed costs Costs that do not vary with production or sales level.

FOB-origin pricing A geographical pricing strategy in which goods are placed free on board a carrier; the customer pays the freight from the factory to the destination.

Focus group interviewing Personal interviewing that involves inviting six to ten people to gather for a few hours with a trained interviewer to talk about a product, service, or organization. The interviewer "focuses" the group discussion on important issues.

Follow-up The last step in the selling process in which the salesperson follows up after the sale to ensure customer satisfaction and repeat business.

Forecasting The art of estimating future demand by anticipating what buyers are likely to do under a given set of conditions.

Franchise A contractual association between a manufacturer, wholesaler, or service organization (a franchiser) and independent businesspeople (franchisees) who buy the right to own and operate one or more units in the franchise system.

Franchise organization A contractual vertical marketing system in which a channel member, called a franchiser, links several stages in the production-distribution process.

Functional discount A price reduction offered by the seller to trade channel members who perform certain functions such as selling, storing, and recordkeeping.

Gatekeepers People in the organization's buying center who control the flow of information to others.

Gender segmentation Dividing a market into different groups based on sex.

General need description The stage in the business buying process in which the company describes the general characteristics and quantity of a needed item.

Geographic segmentation Dividing a market into different geographical units such as nations, states, regions, counties, cities, or neighborhoods.

Global firm A firm that, by operating in more than one country, gains marketing, production, R&D, and financial advantages in its costs and reputation that are not available to purely domestic competitors.

Government market Governmental units—federal, state, and local—that purchase or rent goods and services for carrying out the main functions of government.

Gross margin The difference between net sales and cost of goods sold.

Gross sales The total amount that a company charges during a given period of time for merchandise.

Group Two or more people who interact to accomplish individual or mutual goals.

Growth-share matrix A portfolio-planning method that evaluates a company's strategic business units in terms of their market growth rate and relative market share. SBUs are classified as stars, cash cows, question marks, or dogs.

Growth stage The product life-cycle stage in which a product's sales start climbing quickly.

Habitual buying behavior Consumer buying behavior in situations characterized by low consumer involvement and few significant perceived brand differences.

Handling objections The step in the selling process in which the salesperson seeks out, clarifies, and overcomes customer objections to buying.

Horizontal marketing system A channel arrangement in which two or more companies at one level join together to follow a new marketing opportunity.

Hybrid marketing channel Multichannel distribution system in which a single firm sets up two or more marketing channels to reach one or more customer segments.

Idea generation The systematic search for new-product ideas.

Idea screening Screening new-product ideas in order to spot good ideas and drop poor ones as soon as possible.

Income segmentation Dividing a market into different income groups.

Independent off-price retailer Off-price retailer that is either owned and run by entrepreneurs or is a division of larger retail corporation.

Indirect marketing channel Channel containing one or more intermediary levels.

Individual marketing Tailoring products and marketing programs to the needs and preferences of individual customers—also labeled *customized marketing, one-to-one marketing,* and *markets-of-one marketing.*

Industrial product Product bought by individuals and organizations for further processing or for use in conducting a business.

Influencers People in an organization's buying center who affect the buying decision; they often help define specifications and also provide information for evaluating alternatives.

Information search The stage of the buyer decision process in which the consumer is aroused to search for more information; the consumer may simply have heightened attention or may go into active information search.

Innovative marketing A principle of enlightened marketing that requires that a company seek real product and marketing improvements.

Inside sales force Inside salespeople who conduct business from their offices via telephone or visits from prospective buyers.

Institutional market Schools, hospitals, nursing homes, prisons, and other institutions that provide goods and services to people in their care.

Integrated direct marketing Direct marketing campaigns that use multiple vehicles and multiple stages to improve response rates and profits.

Integrated logistics management The logistics concept that emphasizes teamwork, both inside the company and among all the marketing channel organizations, to maximize the performance of the entire distribution system.

Integrated marketing communications (IMC) The concept under which a company carefully integrates and coordinates its many communications channels to deliver a clear, consistent, and compelling message about the organization and its products.

Intensive distribution Stocking the product in as many outlets as possible.

Interactive marketing Marketing by a service firm that recognizes that perceived service quality depends heavily on the quality of buyer–seller interaction.

Intermarket segmentation Forming segments of consumers who have similar needs and buying behavior even though they are located in different countries.

Intermodal transportation Combining two or more modes of transportation.

Internal databases Computerized collections of information obtained from data sources within the company.

Internal marketing Marketing by a service firm to train and effectively motivate its customer-contact employees and all the supporting service people to work as a team to provide customer satisfaction.

Internet The vast and burgeoning global web of computer networks with no central management or ownership.

Introduction stage The product life-cycle stage in which the new product is first distributed and made available for purchase.

Joint ownership A joint venture in which a company joins investors in a foreign market to create a local business in which the company shares joint ownership and control.

Joint venturing Entering foreign markets by joining with foreign companies to produce or market a product or service.

Leading indicators Time series that change in the same direction but in advance of company sales.

Learning Changes in an individual's behavior arising from experience.

Licensing A method of entering a foreign market in which the company enters into an agreement with a licensee in the foreign market, offering the right to use a manufacturing process, trademark, patent, trade secret, or other item of value for a fee or royalty.

Lifestyle A person's pattern of living as expressed in his or her activities, interests, and opinions.

Line extension Using a successful brand name to introduce additional items in a given product category under the same brand name, such as new flavors, forms, colors, added ingredients, or package sizes.

Local marketing Tailoring brands and promotions to the needs and wants of local customer groups—cities, neighborhoods, and even specific stores.

Macroenvironment The larger societal forces that affect the microenvironment—demographic, economic, natural, technological, political, and cultural forces.

Management contracting A joint venture in which the domestic firm supplies the management know-how to a foreign company that supplies the capital; the domestic firm exports management services rather than products.

Manufacturers' sales branches and offices Wholesaling by sellers or buyers themselves rather than through independent wholesalers.

Markdown A percentage reduction from the original selling price.

Market The set of all actual and potential buyers of a product or service.

Market buildup method A forecasting method that calls for identifying all the potential buyers in each market and estimating their potential purchases.

Market-centered company A company that pays balanced attention to both customers and competitors in designing its marketing strategies.

Market challenger A runner-up firm in an industry that is fighting hard to increase its market share.

Market development A strategy for company growth by identifying and developing new market segments for current company products.

Market factor index method A forecasting method that identifies market factors that correlate with market potential and combines them into a weighted index.

Market follower A runner-up firm in an industry that wants to hold its share without rocking the boat.

Market leader The firm in an industry with the largest market share; it usually leads other firms in price changes, new product introductions, distribution coverage, and promotion spending.

Market nicher A firm in an industry that serves small segments that other firms overlook or ignore.

Market penetration A strategy for company growth by increasing sales of current products to current market segments without changing the product.

Market-penetration pricing Setting a low price for a new product in order to attract a large number of buyers and a large market share.

Market positioning Arranging for a product to occupy a clear, distinctive, and desirable place relative to competing products in the minds of target consumers. Formulating competitive positioning for a product and a detailed marketing mix.

Market potential The upper limit of market demand.

Market segment A group of consumers who respond in a similar way to a given set of marketing efforts.

Market segmentation Dividing a market into distinct groups of buyers on the basis of needs, characteristics, or behaviors who might require separate products or marketing mixes.

Market-skimming pricing Setting a high price for a new product to skim maximum revenues layer by layer from the segments willing to pay the high price; the company makes fewer but more profitable sales.

Market targeting The process of evaluating each market segment's attractiveness and selecting one or more segments to enter.

Marketing A social and managerial process whereby individuals and groups obtain what they need and want through creating and exchanging products and value with others.

Marketing audit A comprehensive, systematic, independent, and periodic examination of a company's environment, objectives, strategies, and activities to determine problem areas and opportunities and to recommend a plan of action to improve the company's marketing performance.

Marketing communications mix (promotion mix) The specific mix of advertising, personal selling, sales promotion, public relations, and direct marketing a company uses to pursue its advertising and marketing objectives.

Marketing concept The marketing management philosophy that holds that achieving organizational goals depends on determining the needs and wants of target markets and delivering the desired satisfactions more effectively and efficiently than competitors do.

Marketing control The process of measuring and evaluating the results of marketing strategies and plans, and taking corrective action to ensure that marketing objectives are achieved.

Marketing environment The actors and forces outside marketing that affect marketing management's ability to develop and maintain successful transactions with its target customers.

Marketing implementation The process that turns marketing strategies and plans

into marketing actions in order to accomplish strategic marketing objectives.

Marketing information system (MIS) People, equipment, and procedures to gather, sort, analyze, evaluate, and distribute needed, timely, and accurate information to marketing decision makers.

Marketing intelligence Everyday information about developments in the marketing environment that helps managers prepare and adjust marketing plans.

Marketing intermediaries Firms that help the company to promote, sell, and distribute its goods to final buyers; they include resellers, physical distribution firms, marketing service agencies, and financial intermediaries.

Marketing management The analysis, planning, implementation, and control of programs designed to create, build, and maintain beneficial exchanges with target buyers for the purpose of achieving organizational objectives.

Marketing mix The set of controllable tactical marketing tools—product, price, place, and promotion—that the firm blends to produce the response it wants in the target market.

Marketing process The process of (1) analyzing marketing opportunities, (2) selecting target markets, (3) developing the marketing mix, and (4) managing the marketing effort.

Marketing research The systematic design, collection, analysis, and reporting of data relevant to a specific marketing situation facing an organization.

Marketing strategy The marketing logic whereby the business unit hopes to achieve its marketing objectives.

Marketing strategy development Designing an initial marketing strategy for a new product based on the product concept.

Marketing Web site Web sites designed to engage consumers in an interaction that will move them closer to a purchase or other marketing outcome.

Markup The percentage of the cost or price of a product added to cost in order to arrive at a selling price.

Maturity stage The stage in the product life cycle in which sales growth slows or levels off.

Merchant wholesaler Independently owned business that takes title to the merchandise it handles.

Microenvironment The forces close to the company that affect its ability to serve its customers—the company, suppliers, marketing channel firms, customer markets, competitors, and publics.

Micromarketing The practice of tailoring products and marketing programs to suit the tastes of specific individuals and locations—includes *local marketing* and *individual marketing.*

Mission statement A statement of the organization's purpose—what it wants to accomplish in the larger environment.

Modified rebuy A business buying situation in which the buyer wants to modify product specifications, prices, terms, or suppliers.

Motive (drive) A need that is sufficiently pressing to direct the person to seek satisfaction of the need.

Natural environment Natural resources that are needed as inputs by marketers or that are affected by marketing activities.

Need A state of felt deprivation.

Need recognition The first stage of the buyer decision process in which the consumer recognizes a problem or need.

New product A good, service, or idea that is perceived by some potential customers as new.

New-product development The development of original products, product improvements, product modifications, and new brands through the firm's own R&D efforts.

New task A business buying situation in which the buyer purchases a product or service for the first time.

Niche marketing Focusing on subsegments or niches with distinctive traits that may seek a special combination of benefits.

Nonpersonal communication channels Media that carry messages without personal contact or feedback, including major media, atmospheres, and events.

Nontariff trade barriers Nonmonetary barriers to foreign products, such as biases against a foreign company's bids, or product standards that go against a foreign company's product features.

Objective-and-task method Developing the promotion budget by (1) defining specific objectives, (2) determining the tasks that must be performed to achieve these objectives, and (3) estimating the costs of performing these tasks. The sum of these costs is the proposed promotion budget.

Observational research The gathering of primary data by observing relevant people, actions, and situations.

Occasion segmentation Dividing the market into groups according to occasions when buyers get the idea to buy, actually make their purchase, or use the purchased item.

Off-price retailer Retailer that buys at less-than-regular wholesale prices and sells at less than retail. Examples are factory outlets, independents, and warehouse clubs.

Online ads Ads that appear while subscribers are surfing online services or Web sites, including banners, pop-up windows, "tickers," and "roadblocks."

Online databases Computerized collections of information available from online commercial sources or via the Internet.

Online marketing Marketing conducted through interactive online computer systems, which link consumers with sellers electronically.

Online (Internet) marketing research Collecting primary data through Internet surveys and online focus groups.

Operating ratios Ratios of selected operating statement items to net sales that allow marketers to compare the firm's performance in one year with that in previous years (or with industry standards and competitors in the same year).

Operating statement (profit-and-loss statement, income statement) A financial statement that shows company sales, cost of goods sold, and expenses during a given period of time.

Opinion leader Person within a reference group who, because of special skills, knowledge, personality, or other characteristics, exerts influence on others.

Optional-product pricing The pricing of optional or accessory products along with a main product.

Order-routine specification The stage of the business buying process in which the buyer writes the final order with the chosen supplier(s), listing the technical specifications, quantity needed, expected time of delivery, return policies, and warranties.

Outside sales force Also known as *field sales force*. Outside salespeople who travel to call on customers.

Packaging The activities of designing and producing the container or wrapper for a product.

Patronage reward Cash or other award for the regular use of a certain company's products or services.

Percentage-of-sales method Setting the promotion budget at a certain percentage of current or forecasted sales or as a percentage of the unit sales price.

Perception The process by which people select, organize, and interpret information to form a meaningful picture of the world.

Performance review The stage of the business buying process in which the buyer rates its satisfaction with suppliers, deciding whether to continue, modify, or drop them.

Personal selling Personal presentation by the firm's sales force for the purpose of making sales and building customer relationships.

Personality A person's distinguishing psychological characteristics that lead to relatively consistent and lasting responses to his or her own environment.

Physical distribution (marketing logistics) The tasks involved in planning, implementing, and controlling the physical flow of materials, final goods, and related information from points of origin to points of consumption to meet customer requirements at a profit.

Pleasing products Products that give high immediate satisfaction but may hurt consumers in the long run.

Point-of-purchase (POP) promotion Display and demonstration that takes place at the point of purchase or sale.

Political environment Laws, government agencies, and pressure groups that influence and limit various organizations and individuals in a given society.

Portfolio analysis A tool by which management identifies and evaluates the various businesses that make up the company.

Postpurchase behavior The stage of the buyer decision process in which consumers take further action after purchase based on their satisfaction or dissatisfaction.

Preapproach The step in the selling process in which the salesperson learns as much as possible about a prospective customer before making a sales call.

Premium Good offered either free or at low cost as an incentive to buy a product.

Presentation The step in the selling process in which the salesperson tells the product "story" to the buyer, showing how the product will make or save money for the buyer.

Price The amount of money charged for a product or service, or the sum of the values that consumers exchange for the benefits of having or using the product or service.

Price elasticity A measure of the sensitivity of demand to changes in price.

Price pack (cents-off deal) Reduced price that is marked by the producer directly on the label or package.

Primary data Information collected for the specific purpose at hand.

Primary demand The level of total demand for all brands of a given product or service—for example, the total demand for motorcycles.

Private brand (or store brand) A brand created and owned by a reseller of a product or service.

Problem recognition The first stage of the business buying process in which someone in the company recognizes a problem or need that can be met by acquiring a good or a service.

Product Anything that can be offered to a market for attention, acquisition, use, or consumption that might satisfy a want or need. It includes physical objects, services, events, persons, places, organizations, and ideas.

Product adaptation Adapting a product to meet local conditions or wants in foreign markets.

Product bundle pricing Combining several products and offering the bundle at a reduced price.

Product concept The idea that consumers will favor products that offer the most quality, performance, and features and that the organization should therefore devote its energy to making continuous product improvements. A detailed version of the new-product idea stated in meaningful consumer terms.

Product development A strategy for company growth by offering modified or new products to current market segments. Developing the product concept into a physical product in order to ensure that the product idea can be turned into a workable product.

Product invention Creating new products or services for foreign markets.

Product life cycle (PLC) The course of a product's sales and profits over its lifetime. It involves five distinct stages: product development, introduction, growth, maturity, and decline.

Product line A group of products that are closely related because they function in a similar manner, are sold to the same customer groups, are marketed through the same types of outlets, or fall within given price ranges.

Product line pricing Setting the price steps between various products in a product line based on cost differences between the products, customer evaluations of different features, and competitors' prices.

Product–market expansion grid A portfolio-planning tool for identifying company growth opportunities through market penetration, market development, product development, or diversification.

Product mix (or product assortment) The set of all product lines and items that a particular seller offers for sale.

Product position The way the product is defined by consumers on important attributes—the place the product occupies in consumers' minds relative to competing products.

Product quality The ability of a product to perform its functions; it includes the product's overall durability, reliability, precision, ease of operation and repair, and other valued attributes.

Product sales force structure A sales force organization under which salespeople specialize in selling only a portion of the company's products or lines.

Product specification The stage of the business buying process in which the buying organization decides on and specifies the best technical product characteristics for a needed item.

Production concept The philosophy that consumers will favor products that are available and highly affordable and that management should therefore focus on improving production and distribution efficiency.

Promotional pricing Temporarily pricing products below the list price, and sometimes even below cost, to increase short-run sales.

Proposal solicitation The stage of the business buying process in which the buyer invites qualified suppliers to submit proposals.

Prospecting The step in the selling process in which the salesperson identifies qualified potential customers.

Psychographic segmentation Dividing a market into different groups based on social class, lifestyle, or personality characteristics.

Psychological pricing A pricing approach that considers the psychology of prices and not simply the economics; the price is used to say something about the product.

Public Any group that has an actual or potential interest in or impact on an organization's ability to achieve its objectives.

Public relations Building good relations with the company's various publics by obtaining favorable publicity, building up a good "corporate image," and handling or heading off unfavorable rumors, stories, and events. Major PR tools include press relations, product publicity, corporate communications, lobbying, and public service.

Pull strategy A promotion strategy that calls for spending a lot on advertising and consumer promotion to build up consumer demand. If the strategy is successful, consumers will ask their retailers for the product, the retailers will ask the wholesalers, and the wholesalers will ask the producers.

Purchase decision The stage of the buyer decision process in which the consumer actually buys the product.

Push strategy A promotion strategy that calls for using the sales force and trade promotion to push the product through channels. The producer promotes the product to wholesalers, the wholesalers promote to retailers, and the retailers promote to consumers.

Quality The totality of features and characteristics of a product or service that bear on its ability to satisfy stated or implied needs.

Quantity discount A price reduction to buyers who buy large volumes.

Quota A limit on the amount of goods that an importing country will accept in certain product categories; it is designed to conserve on foreign exchange and to protect local industry and employment.

Reference prices Prices that buyers carry in their minds and refer to when they look at a given product.

Relationship marketing The process of creating, maintaining, and enhancing strong, value-laden relationships with customers and other stakeholders.

Retailer Business whose sales come *primarily* from retailing.

Retailing All activities involved in selling goods or services directly to final consumers for their personal, nonbusiness use.

Return on investment (ROI) A common measure of managerial effectiveness—the ratio of net profit to investment.

Sales force management The analysis, planning, implementation, and control of sales force activities. It includes setting and designing sales force strategy; and recruiting, selecting, training, compensating, supervising, and evaluating the firm's salespeople.

Sales promotion Short-term incentives to encourage the purchase or sale of a product or service.

Sales quotas Standards set for salespeople, stating the amount they should sell and how sales should be divided among the company's products.

Salesperson An individual acting for a company by performing one or more of the following activities: prospecting, communicating, servicing, and information gathering.

Salutary products Products that have low appeal but may benefit consumers in the long run.

Sample A segment of the population selected for marketing research to represent the population as a whole; an offer of a trial amount of a product.

Seasonal discount A price reduction to buyers who purchase merchandise or services out of season.

Secondary data Information that already exists somewhere, having been collected for another purpose.

Segment marketing Isolating broad segments that make up a market and adapting the marketing to match the needs of one or more segments.

Segmented pricing Selling a product or service at two or more prices, where the difference in prices is not based on differences in costs.

Selective demand The demand for a given brand of a product or service.

Selective distribution The use of more than one, but fewer than all, of the intermediaries who are willing to carry the company's products.

Selling concept The idea that consumers will not buy enough of the organization's products unless the organization undertakes a large-scale selling and promotion effort.

Selling process The steps that the salesperson follows when selling, which include prospecting and qualifying, preapproach, approach, presentation and demonstration, handling objections, closing, and follow-up.

Sense-of-mission marketing A principle of enlightened marketing that holds that a company should define its mission in broad social terms rather than narrow product terms.

Sequential product development A new-product development approach in which one company department works to complete its stage of the process before passing the new product along to the next department and stage.

Service Any activity or benefit that one party can offer to another that is essentially intangible and does not result in the ownership of anything.

Service inseparability A major characteristic of services—they are produced and consumed at the same time and cannot be separated from their providers, whether the providers are people or machines.

Service intangibility A major characteristic of services—they cannot be seen, tasted, felt, heard, or smelled before they are bought.

Service perishability A major characteristic of services—they cannot be stored for later sale or use.

Service-profit chain The chain that links service firm profits with employee and customer satisfaction.

Service variability A major characteristic of services—their quality may vary greatly, depending on who provides them and when, where, and how.

Shopping center A group of retail businesses planned, developed, owned, and managed as a unit.

Shopping product Consumer good that the customer, in the process of selection and purchase, characteristically compares on such bases as suitability, quality, price, and style.

Simultaneous (or team-based) product development An approach to developing new products in which various company departments work closely together, overlapping the steps in the product development process to save time and increase effectiveness.

Single-source data systems Electronic monitoring systems that link consumers' exposure to television advertising and promotion (measured using television meters) with what they buy in stores (measured using store checkout scanners).

Slotting fees Payments demanded by retailers before they will accept new products and find "slots" for them on the shelves.

Social classes Relatively permanent and ordered divisions in a society whose members share similar values, interests, and behaviors.

Social marketing The design, implementation, and control of programs seeking to increase the acceptability of a social idea, cause, or practice among a target group.

Societal marketing A principle of enlightened marketing that holds that a company should make marketing decisions by considering consumers' wants, the company's requirements, consumers' long-run interests, and society's long-run interests.

Societal marketing concept The idea that the organization should determine the needs, wants, and interests of target markets and deliver the desired satisfactions more effectively and efficiently than do competitors in a way that maintains or improves the consumer's and society's well-being.

Specialty product Consumer product with unique characteristics or brand identification for which a significant group of buyers is willing to make a special purchase effort.

Specialty store A retail store that carries a narrow product line with a deep assortment within that line.

Standardized marketing mix An international marketing strategy for using basically the same product, advertising, distribution channels, and other elements of the marketing mix in all the company's international markets.

Straight product extension Marketing a product in a foreign market without any change.

Straight rebuy A business buying situation in which the buyer routinely reorders something without any modifications.

Strategic business unit (SBU) A unit of the company that has a separate mission and objectives and that can be planned independently from other company businesses. An SBU can be a company division, a product line within a division, or sometimes a single product or brand.

Strategic planning The process of developing and maintaining a strategic fit between the organization's goals and capabilities and its changing marketing opportunities. It involves defining a clear company mission, setting supporting objectives, designing a sound business portfolio, and coordinating functional strategies.

Style A basic and distinctive mode of expression.

Subculture A group of people with shared value systems based on common life experiences and situations.

Supermarket Large, low-cost, low-margin, high-volume, self-service store that carries a wide variety of food, laundry, and household products.

Superstore A store almost twice the size of a regular supermarket that carries a large assortment of routinely purchased food and nonfood items and offers services such as dry cleaning, post offices, photo finishing, check cashing, bill paying, lunch counters, car care, and pet care.

Supplier search The stage of the business buying process in which the buyer tries to find the best vendors.

Supplier selection The stage of the business buying process in which the buyer reviews proposals and selects a supplier or suppliers.

Survey research The gathering of primary data by asking people questions about their knowledge, attitudes, preferences, and buying behavior.

Systems buying Buying a packaged solution to a problem from a single seller, thus avoiding all the separate decisions involved in a complex buying situation.

Target costing Pricing that starts with an ideal selling price, then targets costs that will ensure that the price is met.

Target market A set of buyers sharing common needs or characteristics that the company decides to serve.

Tariff A tax levied by a government against certain imported products. Tariffs are designed to raise revenue or to protect domestic firms.

Team selling Using teams of people from sales, marketing, engineering, finance, technical support, and even upper management to service large, complex accounts.

Technological environment Forces that create new technologies, creating new product and market opportunities.

Telemarketing Using the telephone to sell directly to customers.

Territorial sales force structure A sales force organization that assigns each salesperson to an exclusive geographic territory in which that salesperson sells the company's full line.

Test marketing The stage of new-product development in which the product and marketing program are tested in more realistic market settings.

Third-party logistics provider An independent logistics provider that performs any or all of the functions required to get its clients' product to market.

Total costs The sum of the fixed and variable costs for any given level of production.

Total customer cost The total of all the monetary, time, energy, and psychic costs associated with a marketing offer.

Total market demand The total volume of a product or service that would be bought by a defined consumer group in a defined geographic area in a defined time period in a defined marketing environment under a defined level and mix of industry marketing effort.

Total quality management (TQM) Programs designed to constantly improve the quality of products, services, and marketing processes.

Transaction A trade of values between two parties.

Undifferentiated marketing A market-coverage strategy in which a firm decides to ignore market segment differences and go after the whole market with one offer.

Uniform-delivered pricing A geographical pricing strategy in which the company charges the same price plus freight to all customers, regardless of their location.

Unsought product Consumer product that the consumer either does not know about or knows about but does not normally think of buying.

Users Members of the organization who will use the product or service; users often initiate the buying proposal and help define product specifications.

Value analysis An approach to cost reduction in which components are studied carefully to determine if they can be redesigned, standardized, or made by less costly methods of production.

Value-based pricing Setting price based on buyers' perceptions of value rather than on the seller's cost.

Value chain A major tool for identifying ways to create more customer value.

Value-delivery network The network made up of the company, suppliers, distributors, and ultimately customers who "partner" with each other to improve the performance of the entire system.

Value marketing A principle of enlightened marketing that holds that a company should put most of its resources into value-building marketing investments.

Value pricing Offering just the right combination of quality and good service at a fair price.

Value proposition The full positioning of a brand—the full mix of benefits upon which it is positioned.

Variable costs Costs that vary directly with the level of production.

Variety-seeking buying behavior Consumer buying behavior in situations characterized by low consumer involvement but significant perceived brand differences.

Vertical marketing system (VMS) A distribution channel structure in which producers, wholesalers, and retailers act as a unified system. One channel member owns the others, has contracts with them, or has so much power that they all cooperate.

Want The form taken by a human need as shaped by culture and individual personality.

Warehouse club Off-price retailer that sells a limited selection of brand-name grocery items, appliances, clothing, and a hodgepodge of other goods at deep discounts to members who pay annual membership fees.

Webcasting The automatic downloading of customized information of interest to recipients' PCs, affording an attractive channel for delivering Internet advertising or other information content.

Wheel of retailing concept A concept of retailing that states that new types of retailers usually begin as low-margin, low-price, low-status operations but later evolve into higher-priced, higher-service operations, eventually becoming like the conventional retailers they replaced.

Whole-channel view Designing international channels that take into account all the necessary links in distributing the seller's products to final buyers, including the seller's headquarters organization, channels among nations, and channels within nations.

Wholesaler A firm engaged *primarily* in wholesaling activity.

Wholesaling All activities involved in selling goods and services to those buying for resale or business use.

Word-of-mouth influence Personal communication about a product between target buyers and neighbors, friends, family members, and associates.

Workload approach An approach to setting sales force size in which the company groups accounts into different size classes and then determines how many salespeople are needed to call on them the desired number of times.

World Wide Web (the Web) The user-friendly Internet access standard.

Zone pricing A geographical pricing strategy in which the company sets up two or more zones. All customers within a zone pay the same total price; the more distant the zone, the higher the price.

CREDITS

CHAPTER 12 429 Permission granted by Caterpillar Inc.; 437 (left, right) Courtesy of Do It Best Corporation; 439 Cereal Partners U.K.; 440 Courtesy of www.ibm.com; 445 Michael Rizza/Stock Boston; Dan Rubin/Medichrome/The Stock Shop, Inc.; 448 Charles Gupton/Stock Boston; 450 Courtesy of www.ge.com; 456 Courtesy of Roadway Express, Inc.; 458 Churchill & Klehr Photography; 462 Ryder Systems, Inc.

CHAPTER 13 471 Courtesy of Home Depot; 476 Bonnie Kamin/PhotoEdit; 477 © John Coletti/Stock Boston; 480 (left) Bill Horsman/Stock Boston; 480 (right) LearnRight Corporation; 483 Target; 484 (top) A. Ramey/PhotoEdit; 484 (bottom) © Katherine Lambert; 487 Antonio Ribeiro/Liaison Agency, Inc.; 490 Courtesy of www.peapod.com; 493 (top, bottom) Photos by B. Martin 1999, Courtesy Shopper Talk; 494 Michael Newman /PhotoEdit; 499 (left, right) Fleming Companies, Inc.; 500 Courtesy McKessonHBOC.

CHAPTER 14 509 William Cornett/Image Excellence Photography; 513 Hachette Filipacchi Magazines; 516 Jeff Jacobson, NJ; 521 Copyright Nissan 1989. Nissan, Infiniti, and the Nissan and Infiniti logos are registered trademarks of Nissan; 523 Courtesy of Volkswagen; 526 (left) Archive Photos; 526 (center) Chris Putman/AP/Wide World Photos; 526 (right) David Taylor/Allsport Photography (USA), Inc.; 530 Jon Feingersh/Stock Boston.

CHAPTER 15 541 Frank LaBua/Pearson Education/PH College; 545 McNeil Consumer Products, Inc.; 547 (left, right) Fross Zelnick Lehrman & Zissu, P.C. © 1985 V&S Vin & Sprit AB. Used by permission; 549 Harley-Davidson Motor Company; 550 Reprinted with permission of Outpost.com Marketing; 554 Michael J. Treola/AP/Wide World Photos; 567 The Image Works; 558 (left, right) © 1997 The Gillette Company; 562 Courtesy of www.pertplus.com; 564 © Jeff Scheid/Gamma-Liaison, Inc.; 566 Courtesy of www.ibm.com; 568 Cindy Lewis Photography/ © 1991 Cindy Lewis; 570 Courtesy of www.butterball.com.

CHAPTER 16 579 Courtesy of Lear Corporation; 581 (left) © John Henley/Stock Market; 581 (right) © Gabe Palmer/Stock Market; 585 © The Proctor & Gamble Company. Used by permission; 587 Courtesy of DuPont & Company; 588 Dan Bosler/Tony Stone Images; 592 John Coletti/Stock Boston; 597 Rob Nelson/Black Star; 598 American Express Incentive Services; 602 Walter Hodges/Tony Stone Images; 603 Courtesy of Advanced Sterilization Products, Irivne, CA.

CHAPTER 17 615 Darren Carroll/Liaison Agency, Inc.; 618 (left) Courtesy of www.lexus.com; 618 (right) Courtesy of www.ebay.com; 621 Mead-Johnson Nutritional; 626 (left, right) Ronald McDonald House Charities; 630 (left, right) Courtesy WFYI-TV; 633 Courtesy of www.archiemcphee.com; 634 Karen Leitza; 636 Courtesy of www.aol.com; 637 Courtesy of www.schwab.com; 640 Courtesy of www.candystand.com; 642 Courtesy of www.travelocity.com; 651 Courtesy of www.thedma.org.

CHAPTER 18 665 Layne Kennedy/Corbis; 668 Bob Sachs/Stew Leonard; 673 American Airlines; 674 Courtesy of www.tide.com; 678 Bank One Corp.; 683 Courtesy of Microsoft Corporation; 687 Trozzo Photography; 690 Courtesy of www.campbellsoup.com; 694 (left) Nathan Martin/AP/Wide World Photos; 694 (right) Melvin Calderon/Liaison Agency, Inc.; 696 Toni Raddler/Debra Bull/Hohner, Inc.

CHAPTER 19 707 Katsumi Kasahara/AP/Wide World Photos; 710 (left) Pablo Bartholomew/Liaison Agency, Inc.; 710 (right) Hugh Sitton/Tony Stone Images; 712 Courtesy of www.dell.com; 716 Wesley Bocxe/The Image Works; 718 Young & Rubicam, New York; 720 Cary S. Wolinsky/Trillium Studios; 721 F. Hoffmann/ The Image Works; 724 Joseph Polleross/Regina Maria Anzenberger; 728 Courtesy of www.etrade.com; 729 D. Bartruff/ The Image Works; 734 Courtesy of International Business Machines Corporation. Unauthorized use not permitted; 738 © Fritz Hoffman.

CHAPTER 20 747 Courtesy of www.benjerrys.com; 750 Churchill & Klehr Photography; 754 (left, right) Enrico Ferorelli; 756 (left, right) Courtesy of American Association of Advertising Agencies; 757 Tony Stone Images; 758 © California private Transportation Company; 762 Campbell Soup Company; 764 (left) Reprinted with permission of Church & Dwight Co., Inc.; 764 (right) Reprinted with permission of McDonald's Corporation; 770 Copyright 1998 GM Corp. Used with permission of GM Media Archives. All rights reserved; 772 Herman Miller, Inc.

SUBJECT INDEX

NAME/ORGANIZATION/ BRAND/COMPANY INDEX

READ THIS LICENSE CAREFULLY BEFORE OPENING THIS PACKAGE. BY OPENING THIS PACKAGE, YOU ARE AGREEING TO THE TERMS AND CONDITIONS OF THIS LICENSE. IF YOU DO NOT AGREE, DO NOT OPEN THE PACKAGE. PROMPTLY RETURN THE UNOPENED PACKAGE AND ALL ACCOMPANYING ITEMS TO THE PLACE YOU OBTAINED IT. *THESE TERMS APPLY TO ALL LICENSED SOFTWARE ON THE DISK EXCEPT THAT THE TERMS FOR USE OF ANY SHAREWARE OR FREEWARE ON THE DISKETTES ARE AS SET FORTH IN THE ELECTRONIC LICENSE LOCATED ON THE DISK:*

1. GRANT OF LICENSE and OWNERSHIP: The enclosed computer programs ("Software") are licensed, not sold, to you by Prentice-Hall, Inc. ("We" or the "Company") and in consideration of your purchase or adoption of the accompanying Company textbooks and/or other materials, and your agreement to these terms. We reserve any rights not granted to you. You own only the disk(s) but we and/or our licensors own the Software itself. This license allows you to use and display your copy of the Software on a single computer (i.e., with a single CPU) at a single location for *academic* use only, so long as you comply with the terms of this Agreement. You may make one copy for back up, or transfer your copy to another CPU, provided that the Software is usable on only one computer.

2. RESTRICTIONS: You may *not* transfer or distribute the Software or documentation to anyone else. Except for backup, you may *not* copy the documentation or the Software. You may *not* network the Software or otherwise use it on more than one computer or computer terminal at the same time. You may *not* reverse engineer, disassemble, decompile, modify, adapt, translate, or create derivative works based on the Software or the Documentation. You may be held legally responsible for any copying or copyright infringement which is caused by your failure to abide by the terms of these restrictions.

3. TERMINATION: This license is effective until terminated. This license will terminate automatically without notice from the Company if you fail to comply with any provisions or limitations of this license. Upon termination, you shall destroy the Documentation and all copies of the Software. All provisions of this Agreement as to limitation and disclaimer of warranties, limitation of liability, remedies or damages, and our ownership rights shall survive termination.

4. LIMITED WARRANTY AND DISCLAIMER OF WARRANTY: Company warrants that for a period of 60 days from the date you purchase this **SOFTWARE** (or purchase or adopt the accompanying textbook), the Software, when properly installed and used in accordance with the Documentation, will operate in substantial conformity with the description of the Software set forth in the Documentation, and that for a period of 30 days the disk(s) on which the Software is delivered shall be free from defects in materials and workmanship under normal use. The Company does *not* warrant that the Software will meet your requirements or that the operation of the Software will be uninterrupted or error-free. Your only remedy and the Company's only obligation under these limited warranties is, at the Company's option, return of the disk for a refund of any amounts paid for it by you or replacement of the disk. THIS LIMITED WARRANTY IS THE ONLY WARRANTY PROVIDED BY THE COMPANY AND ITS LICENSORS, AND THE COMPANY AND ITS LICENSORS DISCLAIM ALL OTHER WARRANTIES, EXPRESS OR IMPLIED, INCLUDING WITHOUT LIMITATION, THE IMPLIED WARRANTIES OF MERCHANTABILITY AND FITNESS FOR A PARTICULAR PURPOSE. THE COMPANY DOES NOT WARRANT, GUARANTEE OR MAKE ANY REPRESENTATION REGARDING THE ACCURACY, RELIABILITY, CURRENTNESS, USE, OR RESULTS OF USE, OF THE SOFTWARE.

5. LIMITATION OF REMEDIES AND DAMAGES: IN NO EVENT, SHALL THE COMPANY OR ITS EMPLOYEES, AGENTS, LICENSORS, OR CONTRACTORS BE LIABLE FOR ANY INCIDENTAL, INDIRECT, SPECIAL, OR CONSEQUENTIAL DAMAGES ARISING OUT OF OR IN CONNECTION WITH THIS LICENSE OR THE SOFTWARE, INCLUDING FOR LOSS OF USE, LOSS OF DATA, LOSS OF INCOME OR PROFIT, OR OTHER LOSSES, SUSTAINED AS A RESULT OF INJURY TO ANY PERSON, OR LOSS OF OR DAMAGE TO PROPERTY, OR CLAIMS OF THIRD PARTIES, EVEN IF THE COMPANY OR AN AUTHORIZED REPRESENTATIVE OF THE COMPANY HAS BEEN ADVISED OF THE POSSIBILITY OF SUCH DAMAGES. IN NO EVENT SHALL THE LIABILITY OF THE COMPANY FOR DAMAGES WITH RESPECT TO THE SOFTWARE EXCEED THE AMOUNTS ACTUALLY PAID BY YOU, IF ANY, FOR THE SOFTWARE OR THE ACCOMPANYING TEXTBOOK. BECAUSE SOME JURISDICTIONS DO NOT ALLOW THE LIMITATION OF LIABILITY IN CERTAIN CIRCUMSTANCES, THE ABOVE LIMITATIONS MAY NOT ALWAYS APPLY TO YOU.

6. GENERAL: THIS AGREEMENT SHALL BE CONSTRUED IN ACCORDANCE WITH THE LAWS OF THE UNITED STATES OF AMERICA AND THE STATE OF NEW YORK, APPLICABLE TO CONTRACTS MADE IN NEW YORK, AND SHALL BENEFIT THE COMPANY, ITS AFFILIATES AND ASSIGNEES. THIS AGREEMENT IS THE COMPLETE AND EXCLUSIVE STATEMENT OF THE AGREEMENT BETWEEN YOU AND THE COMPANY AND SUPERSEDES ALL PROPOSALS OR PRIOR AGREEMENTS, ORAL, OR WRITTEN, AND ANY OTHER COMMUNICATIONS BETWEEN YOU AND THE COMPANY OR ANY REPRESENTATIVE OF THE COMPANY RELATING TO THE SUBJECT MATTER OF THIS AGREEMENT. If you are a U.S. Government user, this Software is licensed with "restricted rights" as set forth in subparagraphs (a)-(d) of the Commercial Computer-Restricted Rights clause at FAR 52.227-19 or in subparagraphs (c)(1)(ii) of the Rights in Technical Data and Computer Software clause at DFARS 252.227-7013, and similar clauses, as applicable.

Should you have any questions concerning this agreement or if you wish to contact the Company for any reason, please contact in writing: Director of Media, Business Publishing, Prentice Hall, One Lake Street, Upper Saddle River, NJ 07458.